A CENTURY OF NEWS

from the Archives of the

Herald INTERNATIONAL Tribune

A CENTURY OF NEWS

from the Archives of the

International Herald Tribune

BRUCE SINGER

INTRODUCTION BY ART BUCHWALD

with 171 pages of illustrations

INTERNATIONAL HERALD TRIBUNE

THAMES AND HUDSON

Printed and bound in Spain by Artes Gráficas Toledo, S.A.
D.L.TO: 546-1987

CONTENTS

INTRODUCTION

The following pages encompass one hundred years of the *Paris Herald Tribune*.

Various managements, which have come and gone at the *Trib*, always argued about whether to call it *The Paris Herald Tribune* or *The European Edition of the Herald Tribune* or *The International Edition of the Herald Tribune*. I can go any way with the name although when I worked on the rue de Berri, everyone I knew called it *The Trib*, and let it go at that.

Despite stories to the contrary, I have not been on the *Paris Trib* for the entire one hundred years of its existence. My byline, in one form or another, has only appeared during thirty-eight of them. Fourteen years were spent at the *Herald Tribune*'s famed office building at 21 rue de Berri, the rest as a contributing columnist from Washington.

The Paris years were obviously the best in my career because I made no money and had a tremendous amount of fun. A great writer might call those days a moveable feast. But I like to think of it as just another job where one had to keep the three-star restaurants of France honest, and report back to the city room about what they were wearing at the sidewalk cafés of the Champs-Elysées.

Over the century many legends have grown up around the *Paris Trib*. All of them to my knowledge are true. Those of us who worked on the paper were a wild and woolly bunch—great lovers, outstanding reporters, and unforgiving editors with hearts of gold.

I was typical. Picture if you will, a shy, thin boy who left the University of Southern California to find his future in Paris—a city just coming alive again after World War II with wine, women, and more wine. Ladies strutted along the sidewalks in search of love for a price, and young Americans were searching for jobs. Taxi drivers tore through the streets searching for accidents. It was the best of times and the worst of times—but because I was in a hurry, it was the only time I had.

How did it all happen? I spent the best fourteen years of my life in Paris. Well, at least eleven when I was married were the best years of my life. The other three were miserable because I was a bachelor.

Everyone has a different version of how I got my job on the *Paris Trib*, so I would like to set the record straight.

I was working for *Variety* as a stringer in 1948 in Paris. I noticed that the *Herald Tribune* did not have a night-club columnist and was ignoring the show business scene. So I went to see Eric Hawkins, the managing editor, and volunteered to do a column.

Eric was a short, tough, crusty Englishman, and he said, "We don't need one, and if we did, we wouldn't ask you to write it. Get the hell out of here."

Some people would have taken this as a rejection.

But a few weeks later, I heard that Eric had gone on home leave, so I went back to the *Trib* and asked to see Geoffrey Parsons, the editor, and said to him, "Eric Hawkins and I have been talking about me doing a night-club column."

Geoff thought it was a good idea, so he hired me to do two columns a week, one on night-clubs and one reviewing films—for $25 a week. When Hawkins came back, he found me sitting at a desk, which irked him for a few days, but we soon became very good friends. He was one of the best editors I ever had.

Early in the game, in 1949, it dawned on me that visitors who came to Paris were far more interested in restaurants than they were in night-clubs. So, after four years in the Marine Corps and three years at the University of Southern California, and one year living in a dive called the Hotel des États-Unis, I appointed myself food and wine expert of the *Herald Tribune*.

When it came to writing about wine, I did what most people do—I faked it. But the job gave me an opportunity to eat two great meals a day on the *Trib*—I was making more in food than I was in salary.

I lived through many management and editorial convolutions on the *Herald Tribune*. It was, and I hope it will always be, a newspaper like no other in the world.

I would like to confess that one of my ways of spending time on the *Herald Tribune* was writing letters to the Mailbag, under fictitious names.

My favorite dealt with a campaign I started against a gift of carillons given to the American Cathedral in Paris. The people who ran the church were so pleased with them that thay rang them every hour of the day. This wouldn't have bothered me, except that I lived right across the street from the Cathedral on the rue de Boccador.

So I sat down at my typewriter and wrote a letter to the editor which read, "Dear Sir, My husband works on the Metro all night long and he can't get any sleep because the American Cathedral keeps ringing its bells. What right do Americans in Paris have to ring their bells in our city and keep French people awake?" I signed it, "Disgusted Parisian Housewife."

This provoked an onslaught of anti-American mail from French readers, all of whom sympathized with the poor French housewife.

Now Buel Weare, who was the publisher of the *Trib* at that time, also happened to be on the board of the American Cathedral, and he was catching hell from the members of the parish. One day he called one of the editors in and said, "Don't we have any letters *for* the bells?" The editor rushed into the city room and said, "Weare wants a letter *for* the bells."

"He's got it," I said. And I sat down and typed, "Dear Sir, I don't see why there is all this fuss about the American Cathedral bells. I can't hear them." And I signed it, "Giulio Ascerelli, Rome, Italy."

That was the last letter that appeared on the subject, but I am happy to report that the Cathedral stopped ringing their bells on the hour. I consider my crusade one of the greatest contributions I made to Franco-American relations.

My favorite subject to write about when I lived in Paris were tourists. I didn't have to make anything up because they provided me with a wealth of material.

Once when I was walking down the Champs-Elysées, an American with a camera stopped me and said, "Do—you—speak—English?"

"Yes," I said, "I'm an American."

"Good—," he said, "Where—is—the—Bois-de-Bologne?"

Another time I saw an American in his cups about to cross the street on the rue de Rivoli, and he turned to me and said, "Those dirty, no good, rotten French SOB's."

"What happened?" I asked him.

And he said, "Why should I tell you?"

But my favorite tourist story was about an elderly woman I started to chat with at Fouquets. She was country name-dropping and said, "I've been to Australia, Japan, Tahiti, Africa and Thailand."

"My goodness," I said, "You have traveled a lot."

"Yes," she said. "I have been so lucky. My husband died when I was very young."

And once when I was in Florence, an American lady tourist said to me, "I'm going to Rome next. Is the Pope worth seeing?"

I also had to deal with bored tourists. There was one, an American friend

Art Buchwald in his Paris days.

named Don McGuire, and we used to walk the streets of Paris together, while his wife went shopping. He was always looking for mischief. One day we were up at the Arc de Triomphe and he saw an American tourist trying to take a photo of the Arc. He went up to him and said in an authoritative voice with a French accent, "May I see your passport, please?"

The tourist immediately handed him his passport.

McGuire inspected it and then said, "Do you have permission to take a photograph of a French military installation?"

The tourist blubbered, "I didn't know the Arch of Triumph was a French military installation."

McGuire handed the tourist back his passport and said, "Well, *ask* the next time."

Tourists who came over always asked me if the French disliked Americans. I discovered when I first came to Paris that the French didn't like each other, so there was no reason why they should like Americans.

I also found out that the only way to deal with the French was to take the opposite side of whatever argument they were on. This was best illustrated once when my hot-water heater broke. I called a plumber and he asked what kind of hot-water heater it was. I said an electric one. He said, "Then call an electrician."

I called an electrician and he told me to call a plumber. I finally called a plumber and invited him over for an aperitif. As we were drinking it, I said, "Oh, by the way, would you be interested in seeing a broken hot-water heater?" He said that he would.

I gave him a ladder and he inspected it and said, "It's impossible to fix this hot-water heater. The valves are not made any more. These pipes are too old. Nobody could fix this hot-water heater."

"You're absolutely right," I said. "No one in this world could fix this hot-water heater."

The challenge was too much for him. "*I* could fix this hot-water heater."

I shook my head, "I'm sorry, Monsieur. But even you couldn't fix such a water heater."

He said, "I can fix any water heater."

And my wife screamed, "For God's sakes, let him try."

In half an hour we had a hot-water heater like new.

But the best example of the French inhumanity to the French, that I have witnessed personally, happened when I was at the Place de la Concorde and I saw a large Frenchman in an even larger Buick tap the bumper of a little Renault which was in front of him. The Renault owner jumped out of his car and started shouting at the owner of the Buick, questioning his parentage and crying about the damage to his little car. The Buick owner listened to the tirade, then got back in his car, put it in gear, and rammed the back of the Renault until it looked like an accordion. Then the Buick owner got out of his car and said, "Now you have something to scream about."

I don't plan to take you through a time warp of my days in Paris. But as far as I am concerned, the *Paris Trib* is the greatest newspaper in the world. I love it like no other. I guess I feel about it the way General MacArthur felt about West Point.

I learned my trade on the *Trib*, and I get misty-eyed every time I recall the magical days and nights I spent in that rickety building on the rue de Berri. The *Trib* has a soul and a legend which continues to this day.

To those who have worked on it, it's the place where we were born again.

Art Buchwald
March 1987

PREFACE

The story of any newspaper is primarily the story of its people—and the *International Herald Tribune* is no exception. From the outset in 1887, when it was founded in Paris by the larger-than-life character James Gordon Bennett, Jr., through a century of publishers right up to the present unusual combination of owners—Whitney Communications Corporation, the *New York Times* and the *Washington Post*—the *IHT* has known a unique collection of owners, managers, journalists, employees and readers.

Some of their names appear as bylines attached to articles reprinted in this book. Others are mentioned in the short texts that precede each chapter. But most of the people who have built the *IHT* during this century are not named in these pages. They include many hundreds of dedicated editors, reporters, printers, pressmen, proofreaders, photographers, copy-aides, researchers, managers, distributors, newsvendors, librarians, promoters, publicists, sales people, accountants, technicians, artists, clerks, secretaries, executives and workers of every sort, who, with humor, talent, energy, and care—occasionally in the face of mortal danger and often with a confidence unsupported by financial facts—helped to deliver the news. To all of them, we who work at the *IHT* today owe a tremendous debt.

James Gordon Bennett, Jr., founder of the *Paris Herald*, settled permanently in Paris in 1877, after his flamboyant lifestyle had closed almost every social door to him in his native New York. The son of a prominent newspaper proprietor, Bennett had inherited the famous *New York Herald* from his father a decade earlier and had worked to enhance its reputation as a serious and provocative newspaper with enormous popular appeal.

Born in 1841, Bennett had spent a good part of his childhood in Europe, particularly in Paris, where his Irish-born mother, unhappy in the harsh, knockabout world of nineteenth-century American newspaper politics, preferred to live. On his return to New York, as a rich, energetic, and original young man, Bennett quickly became known not only for his innovative management style but also for his lively and sometimes outrageous private life and his passion for sports. From an early age he was known as the "Commodore," having captained his own vessel to win the first transatlantic yacht race in 1866. He was a founder, and one of the youngest members, of the New York Yacht Club. He introduced polo to America, bringing an English team to the United States to demonstrate how the game was played. He was a founder of the elegant New York Coaching Club, hired Stanford White to design the Newport Casino, and took his exercise by cycling around the block of his Fifth Avenue home.

When Bennett moved to Paris in 1877, he brought with him a love of excitement, a craze for novelty, and a high temper that fit perfectly the European social climate of the day. He arrived as the Belle Epoque began with both a flair for living and the money to pay for it.

Bennett's father had taught him that a good newsman should be like an owl —alert throughout the night. The owl became Bennett's fetish: its image adorned his homes, offices, yachts, and cars; even his writing paper carried an engraving of an owl with the motto "La nuit porte conseil." Statues of more than a dozen giant owls perched on the roof of the *New York Herald* building in Manhattan, their illuminated eyes blinking rhythmically through the night. And legend has it that one evening, as Bennett stood meditating on the balcony

James Gordon Bennett, Jr., in an engraving from *Vanity Fair*, November 15, 1884.

of his house on the Champs-Elysées, the sound of an owl hooting reached him from the nearby Bois de Boulogne. He took this as a sign to move ahead with his latest project—the creation of a Paris edition of his newspaper.

Bennett's interest in new technology laid the groundwork for the paper. He was a partner in the newly created Bennett-Mackay Cable Company which facilitated the transmission of low-cost cables between Paris and New York. He saw that a European edition of the *Herald* could be produced in Paris by using material cabled from the New York paper and adding items that would be of interest to typical overseas Americans of the era—whom Bennett defined as people very much like himself. To his editors he declared, "I am the only reader of this paper."

The result was an extraordinary mix of important news, detailed accounts of the doings of royalty, the sporting life of the upper classes, and social gossip from every continent. War and politics shared the front page with reports of duels in the Bois de Boulogne and notes on the annual Paris dog show.

Bennett did not expect to make a profit on the European Edition and, until the very end of his life, he never did. Its circulation was prestigious (many copies went daily to the Court of the Czars), but actually numbered only 10,000 to 15,000 a day throughout its first thirty years. The project ate constantly into Bennett's fortune but it was a price he was happy to pay. Not until just before his death in 1918 did profits begin to accumulate, as the arrival of American soldiers pushed the paper's sales into the hundreds of thousands.

The headlines and stories presented here have not always been chosen because of their presumed importance to world history. Much of the material has found its way into this book because it is concerned with events which in some way changed the lives or thinking of those who came after, or entered a common mythology, remaining touchstones in the shared experience of the past century. Some stories are included simply because they make interesting reading.

Our special thanks go to all those whose experience in working for the paper, and whose love for it, led them to publish their recollections, including Al Laney, Eric Hawkins, Art Buchwald, and others, and to Charles Robertson, author of *The International Herald Tribune: The First 100 Years*. Our hope is that the present book manages to convey some of the enthusiasm and genuine excitement found in their accounts.

The story began on a Tuesday, the 4th of October, 1887, with a four-page newspaper printed in a small shop on the rue Coq Heron, in central Paris. The nameplate read, "The New York Herald, European Edition," but it quickly became known to Americans as the *Paris Herald*. To the French, it was simply "Le New York."

Bruce Singer

Bennett was a pioneer in cable communications and part owner of the Commercial Cable Company, which was located next to the *Paris Herald* Offices at 49 avenue de l'Opéra, and which provided most of the paper's international news coverage.

In 1898 Bennett introduced the first linotype machine to Europe, so revolutionizing newspaper production.

The *Paris Herald* moved in 1930 to a grand new building at 21 rue de Berri, formerly the site of the American Church in Paris.

1887-1899

Bennett took his new newspaper very seriously. As a teenager working under his father's guidance in New York, he had become an eager and experienced reporter. Now, in Paris, on at least some of those evenings when he did not feel the call to jump into his carriage and whip his horses to a frenzied trot through the Bois de Boulogne (sometimes shedding his clothing in the process), he would drop by the *Paris Herald* offices, directing the journalists and laying down the law about what was to go into his paper. "Names! Names! Names!—News! News! News!" was one of his favorite exhortations and he spared no expense in bringing both names and news to his readers. He was already famous for having sent the *New York Herald* reporter Henry M. Stanley to Africa to find the English missionary, Dr. David Livingstone. History's most famous greeting, "Dr. Livingstone, I presume," first appeared in Bennett's *Herald*.

He brought the same energy to the Paris paper, publishing the continent's first color comic strips, and following up every technological innovation that could possibly be of use. He introduced the first linotypes and the wire photo to Europe, and was the first to use the "horseless carriage" for newspaper delivery. Small trucks delivered the paper from the printing plant near Les Halles to the kiosks and train stations of Paris; later, a fleet of automobiles would rush it to resorts and other social centers.

Inevitably, Bennett's personal interests were reflected in the paper's coverage. A man who spent a great deal of his time aboard his luxurious steam yachts (communicating constantly with his newspapers by telegraph), Bennett included detailed information on yachts and yachtsmen as they made their way from New York or Newport to Kiel, Cowes, and around the Mediterranean. His paper mirrored the concerns and opinions of a clientele sure of its place in the universal order, and certain that civilization as they defined it and technology as they understood it would continue to be forces for human progress throughout the world.

Who were these *Paris Herald* readers? Many were Americans—not like the American tourists of today, but travelers and expatriates of a century ago, a class of people who made the long ocean crossing in the highest style, lived and traveled on the continent in the greatest comfort, ordered their custom-tailored wardrobes (London for men, Paris for women) and then made the rounds of major cities, spas, racetracks and ports where they were sure to meet other people much like themselves. For decades, newly arrived travelers in Paris were invited to register at the *Herald*'s business offices at 49 avenue de l'Opéra, so that their presence in town could be reported in the next day's edition.

Joining these American readers was a generous sprinkling of members of the English and continental aristocracy, who also featured in the *Herald*'s pages in various costumes and settings, in ballrooms, drawing rooms, gardens, restaurants and hotel lobbies. The numerous international marriages from within this set were given the fullest play, including details of trousseau and lists of wedding gifts. A man in whom the inclination to shock was well developed, Bennett did not ignore the peccadilloes of his contemporaries, and the antics of the demi-monde were also widely covered.

Among the most vivid elements of the *Paris Herald* were its advertisements, which record the tastes and fads of the society of the day. Business and advertising manager Alfred Jaurett kept a steady flow of advertising coming in from the likes of Thomas Cook, Louis Vuitton, the Duveen brothers, the Kodak camera (a new marvel), and the luxury hotels of Europe. The Sunday Fashion Supplement, alternating with the Art Supplement, facilitated the sales of special advertisements aimed more specifically at the *Herald*'s readership. Annual Christmas and Easter numbers, often with color pages, paint a detailed portrait of a way of life that even today has not lost its appeal.

No discussion of the Bennett years would be complete without mentioning the *Paris Herald*'s most frequent contributor, the forever anonymous letterwriter known as The Old Philadelphia Lady. She made her début on Christmas Day, 1899, with the following letter:

> To the Editor of the Herald:
>
> I am anxious to find out the way to figure the temperature from Centigrade to Fahrenheit and vice versa. In other words I want to know whenever I see the temperature designated on a Centigrade thermometer, how to find out what it would be on Fahrenheit's thermometer?
>
> Old Philadelphia Lady
> *December 24, 1899*

The origin of this letter is lost to us (it was probably invented by Bennett himself), but after this timid beginning, the same letter ran daily on page 2 of the *Paris Herald* for the next nineteen years. Only after the death of Bennett in 1918 was it finally stopped.

A letter that appears nearly 7,000 times does not pass unnoticed by readers, and through the years they contributed a wide assortment of responses aimed at getting the lady and her letter permanently retired. She was reported dead several times (as in "Old Philadelphia Lady reported to have died while turning Seville's summer temperature from Centigrade to Fahrenheit" and "Old Philadelphia Lady denies that she was killed on the Bridge of Avignon"). And in 1915 one gentleman was so enraged that the letter was wasting valuable paper in wartime that he offered to "wipe up the floor" with the editor of the *Herald* and anyone else from the staff "both at one and the same time." Few editorial positions taken by the paper drew such violent reactions, but the old lady continued to ask her plaintive question for nearly twenty years. And, in truth, most of her audience probably agreed with the reader who wrote in to report that he found the regularity of her appearances rather "cozy."

In the first section of this book, which covers the closing years of the nineteenth century, several figures appear who continue to be part of our common mythology—Jack the Ripper and Lizzie Borden haunt us still—and events are reported that proved seminal in the history of Europe and the United States. America continued its westward move and, with it, accelerated the spirit of adventure that still make both the Klondike Gold Rush and the Battle of Wounded Knee such fascinating and touching stories. The Dreyfus *affaire*, reported in detail from the *Herald*'s vantage point in Paris, revealed and reinforced the deep divisions in emerging Republican France. Britain, engaged in the Boer War, found itself indirectly opposed to its presumed ally, the new Imperial Germany, while it faced for the first time questions about the value of Empire. And by the end of the century, the United States had engaged in its first war abroad—against Spain—and, under the influence of Theodore Roosevelt and the banner of America's "manifest destiny," was forcing a re-evaluation of its place in the world. Interspersed with the *Herald*'s coverage of these major news events are the features, gossip, interviews, opinion and advertisements that make the archives of the paper a unique witness to the life and style of the period. Technology is here too, from flying machines to the latest inventions in photographic transmission, technology that would also change the way newspapers looked and the way the public would receive its news.

THE NEW YORK HERALD.

WHOLE NO. 18,670. EUROPEAN EDITION—PARIS, TUESDAY, OCTOBER 4, 1887. PARIS 10c., ELSEWHERE 15c.

AT FRIEDRICHSRUH.

Negotiations Between Signor Crispi and the Chancellor.

THE EASTERN QUESTION AGAIN.

[BY TELEGRAPH TO THE HERALD.]

FRIEDRICHSRUH, Oct. 3, 1887.—Signor Crispi, accompanied by his secretaries left here at eight o'clock this morning. Prince Bismark and count Herbert Bismark accompanied the Italian Premier to the railway station, walking with him to the door of the saloon carriage. Count de Launay, the Italian Ambassador, has returned to Berlin.

According to a special Berlin telegram, to-day's *Figaro*, the Bulgarian question was raised at the Friedrichsrul interview, and settled in a sense favorable to Russia. Prince Imeritinsky, and not General Ernrath, is said to be likely to go to Bulgaria Russian envoy.

Another special Viennese telegram states that a triple alliance was signed at the interview.

A PROJECTED RECONCILIATION OF THE VATICAN AND QUIRINAL.

[BY TELEGRAPH TO THE HERALD.]

ROME, October 3, 1887.

I am able to confirm the rumor that Signor Crispi's mysterious journey to Freidrichsruh is directly connected with an attempt to settle the Roman question. Bulgarian affairs may be touched on incidentally in the conferences of the Chancellor and the Italian Premier; but the main object of Prince Bismarck when he encouraged—if indeed he did not invite—Signor Crispi to undertake his journey was to prepare a reconciliation of the Pope and King Humbert, and so re-unite German Catholics and Protestants.

Prince Bismarck has, from politic reasons, long been manœuvering to obtain the advantages attaching to the position of a protector of the Papacy.

THAT VISIT TO BERLIN.

In a recent conversation with M. de Schloezer, he laid great stress on this point of his policy. On the occasion of Mgr. Galimberti's visit to Berlin last spring, the Chancellor took the opportunity of making it known to the Pontiff that he took a very real interest in the Roman question, and subsequently outlined his policy in a semi-official communication to the Vatican.

A few days ago King Humbert was officially, though secretly, informed that the Chancellor would be glad to confer with Signor Crispi on various matters of international importance, and letting it be understood that one of the these matters might be connected with the long-talked of reconciliation.

This is all that can be learnt with certainty with regard to the Friedrichsruh interview; but there is reason to believe that the basis of the reconciliation suggested was to be the cession to the Pope of all, or part, of Rome situate on the left bank of the Tiber.

WHAT HE USED TO SAY.

Some months since, in a conversation with Mgr. Galimberti at Vienna, I sounded that able diplomat as to the likelihood of such an arrangement being accepted by the Vatican. Speaking perhaps with the remembrance of the recent diplomatic successes of the Catholic Church in Germany strong in his mind, the Papal Nuncio remarked: "This would evidently not suffice for the dignity of the Holy See." I have no reason to think that the Pope is inclined to be more yielding now than last spring. At the same time Leo XIII would scarcely refuse to negotiate on the basis of the restoration of the "Leonine" City.

What ulterior interest Prince Bismarck may have in raising the Roman question at this particular moment remains to be seen; but it is, at least, probable that his chief aim is to ensure Germany's being able to show a united front to France in the possible event of foreign complications.

LONDON NOTES.

GOSSIP IN THE CITY AND IN POLITICAL AND SOCIAL CIRCLES.

[BY THE HERALD'S SPECIAL WIRE.]

LONDON, Oct. 4, 1887.

A strong article in *The Army and Navy Magazine* published to-day shows decidedly, if its facts and statistics are true, that the recent cession to Russia of frontier land by the Afghan Commission at the instigation of Sir West Ridgway, one of its members and now successor to Sir Redvers Buller at Dublin Castle, really gives the Russians the key to Herat and Candihar. This is because the ceded territory constitutes a camping ground for a Russian army of 150,000 men and with fertile supplies. The article bristles with startling facts as to the blunder.

THE PRESIDENT TRIP.

A VERY UNPLEASANT INCIDENT AT TERRA HAUTE.

[BY COMMERCIAL CABLE TO THE HERALD.]

NEW YORK, Oct. 3, 1887.

In Indianapolis Saturday, President Cleveland was escorted from the cars to the State House by a civic and military procession, where, in the presence of 5,000 people, he was welcomed by Governor Gray He then received the people in the State House Rotunda, and after lunching at the residence of Senator Macdonald, he left for Terre Haute.

WELCOMED EVERYWHERE.

At the latter city an address of welcome was made by Richard Thompson. The President made a brief address to the populace and took the train for Saint Louis, where he arrived after midnight. On his way to the station in Terre Haute a middle-aged enthusiast grasped the president's carriage from behind. The driver whipped up and tried to leave him, but in vain.

FORCE OF KIND WORDS.

The President's escort ordered the man away, but he energetically refused. Two or three of the mounted men tried to ride him down, but he cursed them savagely and refused to leave the side of the carriage.

Mrs. Cleveland turned to him and said: —"Please let go, sir"; and the fellow dropped off as if he had been shot, and slipped away in the darkness.

From Terre Haute to St. Louis the journey was made without incident.

The President and his suit will leave St. Louis for Chicago to-morrow evening.

ITINERARY OF THE REMAINDER OF HIS SOUTH-WESTERN TRIP.

TO-DAY AT ST. LOUIS.

Arrive at Chicago, Wednesday, Oct. 5, at 9 A. M.
Leave Chicago by Chicago and Northwesters Railroad. Thursday, Oct. 6, at 10 A. M.
Arrive at Milwaukie Thursday, Oct. 6, at 1 P. M.
Leave Milwaukie Friday, Oct. 7, at 10 A. M.
Arrive at Madison Friday, Oct. 7, at 1 P. M.
Leave Madison by Chicago, Milwaukee and St. Paul Railroad, Monday, Oct. 10, at 9 A. M.
Arrive at St. Paul Monday, Oct. 10 at 5½ P. M.
Leave St. Paul Tuesday, Oct. 11, at 12 noon.
Arrive at Minneapolis Tuesday Oct. 11, at 1 P. M.
Leave Minneapolis by Chicago, St. Paul, Minneapolis and Omaha Railroad Tuesday, Oct. 11, at 8 P. M.
Arrive at Omaha Wednesday, Oct. 12, at 11 A.M.
Leave Omaha, by Chicago, Burlington and Quincy Railroad, Wednesday, Oct. 12, at 12 noon.
Arrive at St. Joseph, Wednesday, Oct. 12, at 5¼ P.M.
Leave St. Joseph, Wednesday, Oct. 12, at 5¾ P.M.
Arrive at Kansas City, Wednesday, Oct. 12, at 8¾ P.M.
Leave Kansas City, by Kansas City, Fort Scott, and Gulf Railroad, Thursday, Oct. 13, at 11 P. M.
Arrive at Memphis Friday, Oct. 14, at 6 P. M.
Leave Memphis, by Louisville and Nashville Railroad, Saturday, Oct. 15, at 1 P. M.
Arrive at Nashville, Saturday, Oct. 15, at 11 P. M.
Leave Nashville by Nashville, Chattanooga and St. Louis and Western and Atlantic Railroad Monday, Oct. 17, at 11 a.m.
Arrive at Atlanta, Monday, Oct. 17 at 11 P.M.
Leave Atlanta Wednesday, Oct. 19, at 12 o'clock midnight.
Arrive at Montgomery Thursday, Oct. 30, at 8 A. M.
Leave Montgomery by Kennesaw and Western North Carolina routes Thursday, Oct. 20, at 1 P. M.
Reach Washington Saturday, Oct. 22, at 6 A. M.
No stops will be made, except at the points above mentoned.

A PARISH CONCERT.

AN ENJOYABLE EVENING AT THE AMERICAN CHURCH.

The sixth concert of the series to be given in the church rooms, 19 Avenue de l'Alma, under the direction of Mr. C. Lawrence Seker, took place last night before a fair and appreciative audience. The artists were Miss O'Rorke, Miss Hooper, Mr. F. Luckx (formerly of the Opera Comique), Mr. S. Magnus, Mr. Danvers, Mr. Ernest Wood, Mr. George MacMaster, Mr. J. Humphreys, Mr. Parkinson, Mr. Stephen P. Barter, Mr. G. Chaffer M. Fidèle Koenig and Mr. R. Meyrick Roberts. Miss O'Rorke sang "La Favorite" with feeling and power. Two scenes from the fifth act of "The Hunchback," interpreted by Miss Hooper and Mr. Danvers, formed a special feature of the entertainment. Miss Hooper was sweet and girlish in the part of Helen. Mr. Danvers was excellent as the lover, and his repeated appearances with Miss Hooper in private theatricals have been much appreciated by their audiences.

The choir boys "Wanderers Night Song," Mr. Luckx' air from Enlevement du Serail," and Mr. Magnus's "Fantasie Suedoise," were encored several times.

ANOTHER NAVY ACCIDENT.

FAULTY TACKLE CAUSING THE DEATH OF A STOKER.

A fatal accident occurred on Sunday on board her Majesty's ship Téméraire shortly after she had anchored at Spithead, on arrival from the Mediterranean station with relieved crews. While the steam pinnace was being hoisted out on the starboard bow, ready for lowering when required, a hook of the purchase suddenly gave way, with the result that the craft was precipitated into the water, sinking stern foremost. There was three men in the pinnace—a stoker named Finch, who was in the stoke hole getting ready the fires, and two able seamen who were adjusting the tackle. Perceiving the danger in time, the seamen jumped into the water, receiving some hurt in doing so, but Finch was unable to extricate himself from his positio, and it is believed that he received a heavy blow on the head from some of the falling tackle, which dashed out his brains. As she fell almost perpendicularly, the pinnace glanced against the protruding muzzle of a Nordenfelt gun, and the force of the contact occasioned some structural damage, several large splinters flying in all directions. Finch sank with the pinnace. As soon as the two seamen had been rescued a signal was made to the dockyard for a diver, who commenced his work as soon as possible. He discovered the pinnace bottom upwards, but no immediate efforts could be made to raise her, and Finch's body had not last night been recovered.

HUNGARY'S FINANCE SOUND.

[BY TELEGRAPH TO THE HERALD.]

Pesth, October rd, 1877.—With reference to statements regarding the deficit in last year's budget the *Pester Lloyd* to-day cites particulars to prove the groundlessness of these reports, and adds that the state of the finances of Hungary shows no change for the worse in the final accounts for 1886.

SPANISH INTERESTS IN MOROCCO.

MADRID, Oct. 3, 1887.—In consequence of the reports received here of the serious illness of the Sultan of Morocco, a military corps will leave Madrid to-day to reinforce the garrisons of the Spanish possessions in North Africa with the object of enabling Spain to be prepared to defend her interests in the event of the Sultan's death.

BUT BEANS ARE PLENTIFUL.

There is an onion blight throughout New England.

CAPEL COURT.

Heavy Gold Shipments From the Other Side.

AMERICAN RAILS DROP.

The Purchase of United States Bonds Threatens the Market.

[BY THE HERALD'S SPECIAL WIRE.]

LONDON, MONDAY, Oct. 3, 1887—6 P.M.

Eastward the star of Gold's empire took its way yesterday. Chili, on the steamer Galicia, sent £147,830; the West Indies, per Medway, sent £142,837; the Fulda and Aurania, from New York, landed £31,720; the Mondego, from the River Plate, brought about £10,000, and the Umbria sailed from New York with about £20,000 more. No bullion movements took place at the Bank. This state of facts opened tenders for a million and a half of Treasury bills. The average rate per cent. on the allotted amounts was on three months' bills £3 11s. 4d., and on six months' bills £3 10s. 11d. Call money has been in good demand at three and a half to four per cent., and discount rate for three months' bills was firm at three and seven eighths per cent. The stock markets were as quiet as Russian politics. In dealings such as there were both New York and London found Americans receding. Among home railways Metropolitan Consolidated fell ¼, South Eastern and Brighton deferred ¼, and Great Western, North Western and Midland ⅛; but Chatham Ordinary North British and North Eastern rose ⅛. Among American and Canadian railways St. Paul fell 1⅜, New York Central ¾, Lake Shore and Atlantic first mortgage ½, Erie and Louisville ⅜. and Central Pacific, Denver, Ohio and Mississipi, Ontario and Reading ¼. Mexican Railway First Preference and Ordinary receded ¾ and ditto Second preference ½.

Grand Trunk Stocks were steady, but Mexican Railway showed weakness. In the foreign market several of the International descriptions improved on Paris prices. Consols may be quoted as stationary at 101½ for money, and 101⅝ for account. There seems no longer room fo doubt that the full amount of Bonds which the United States Secretary of the Treasury is willing to buy will be sold to him. His purchases therefore will end on Saturday next; and the question is being eagerly asked: "What will happen then? Bond purchases, interest payment, and pension payments together will have transferred by that time about £5,000,000 sterling from the Treasury to the market; but on the other hand the collection of the taxes is taking into the Treasury over £100,000 a day, in the course of a few weeks when the accumulations in the Treasury will have counterbalanced the disbursements now going on; and unless something further is done the money market will be once more disturbed.

Following are the latest quotations:—

BRITISH AND INDIAN GOVERNMENTS AND BRITISH CORPORATION SECURITIES.	To-day.	Saturday.
Three per cent. Consols	101⅝	101½
Three per cent. Account	101⅝	101½
New and Reduced Three per cents.	100⅝	100½
2¾ per cents. (1905)	96	95½
2½ per cents. (1905)	92½	92¼
Egyptian, Three per cents., gtd	98¾	...
India, 4 per cents	...	100
India, 3½ per cents	101	100½
India, 3 per cents	89¼	88¾
COLONIAL GOVERNMENTS.		
Canada, 4 per cents. (1901-8)	108	108⅛
Canada (Reduced)	103	...
Canada, 3½ per cents	103½	102
Cape (1883)	102¼	102
Natal	101¼	100½
New South Wales, 4 per cents	112	111
New South Wales, 3½ per cents	98¼	96½
New Zealand, 4 per cents	98½	100
Queensland, 4 per cents	102½	102
South Australia, 4 per cents	103	102½
Victoria, 4 per cents., Jan., July	107½	106¼
Victoria, April, October	...	...
Western Australia	108	...
BRITISH RAILWAY STOCKS.		
Great Eastern	65⅝	65¾
Great Northern, ordinary	111½	110½
Great Northern, "A"	100	99
Great Western	136¼	136
London and Brighton, ordinary	135	133
London and Brighton, deferred	118	117½
London, Chatham and Dover, ord.	21⅝	21¼
Lon., Chat. and Dover 4½ p. c. pref.	97½	...
London and North-Western	161⅞	161¾
London and South-Western	128	126
Metropolitan	64¼	64½
District	35½	35
Midland	128	122⅝
South-Eastern, ordinary	...	126
South-Eastern, deferred	103	102⅝
FOREIGN RAILWAY SECURITIES.		
Mexican	41⅞	42¼
Mexican, 1st preference	114	114¼
Mexican, 2nd preference	72¼	72¼
MISCELLANEOUS SECURITIES.		
Imperial Ottoman Bank	9 11-16	..
Suez Canal shares	79	78½
Guinness, ordinary	280	278¼
Guinness, preference	140	137
S. Allsopp and Sons, ordinary	125	125

HIGH TREASON.

AN ANARCHIST PRISONER TRIED WITH CLOSED DOORS.

[BY TELEGRAPH TO THE HERALD.]

LEIPZIG, Oct. 3, 1887.—The case of the anarchist Christopher Neve, accused of high treason, came on for trial at nine o'clock this morning. A large force of police was in attendance to preserve order. The prisoner, who in his examination persisted in denying his identity with the anarchist Neve admitted it to-day. Herr Tessendorff demanded that the proceedings should be held with closed doors to which the court assented on the ground that the publicity of the proceedings might endanger public order.

WALL STREET.

Successful Bear Attack on St. Paul Stock.

JAY GOULD'S LATEST COUP.

Western Union Resists the Movement — Its Buoyancy Causes Suspicion.

[BY COMMERCIAL CABLE TO THE HERALD]

WALL STREET, NEW YORK, MONDAY, Oct. 3—6 P.M.

Mr. Addison Cammack and some of the other principal bear leaders took to selling St. Paul to-day and knocked down that stock 2½ per cent. The result was that the whole stock list took a tumble of about one per cent., and some stocks got down one per cent lower still. Western Union Telegraph, however, didn't drop. There is a suspicion in the street that its strange buoyancy was preserved in order that certain somebodies might get rid of their other stocks.

Money was easy, and there was no news to seriously affect values.

A NEW MONOPOLY.

The event of last week was that Gould and Huntington assumed control of the Pacific Mail Steamship Company. Mr. Hart relinguished the presidency to George Gould. The Pacific railroads therefore again own their only water competitor.

The following are the closing quotations of all active stocks to-day, compared with previous prices:—

	To-day.	Saturday.
Atch. Topeka and Santa Fe	..	..
Atlantic and Pacific	..	..
Canada Southern	53⅝	55¼
Canadian Pacific	51	52¼
Central Pacific	34	33¾
Ches. and Ohio	..	..
C. and O. 1s. pref	..	..
Chic. and N. W.	110½	112⅝
Chic. Burl. and Quincy	138	..
Chic. Mil. and St. Paul	75¼	78⅝
Chic. Mil. and St. Paul pref.	..	..
Chic. Rock. Is. and Pac.	..	..
Del., Lack. and W.	128⅝	129⅜
Den. and Rio Grande	25¼	25¼
Den. and Rio Grande pref.	..	..
Des Moins and Ft. D.	..	..
East Tenn. Va. and Ga.	..	..
East Tenn. Va. and Ga. 1st pref.	..	..
Fort Worth and Denver City	..	..
Kings and Pembroke	..	..
Lake Erie and Western	28¼	29⅜
Lake Erie and W. pref.	..	..
Lake Shore	93¼	94¼
Louis and Nashville	60¼	61⅜
Manhattan Elevated (cons.)	..	..
Michigan Central	86	87
Mil., Lake Shore and W.	..	..
Mil., Lake Shore and W. pref.	..	..
Minn. Saint Louis	..	..
Minn. and Saint Louis pref.	..	..
Missouri Pacific	..	..
Mo., Kansas and Texas	23¼	24⅜
Morris and Essex	..	..
Nashville C. and Saint Louis	..	..
New Jersey Central	..	..
New York Central	106¼	107½
New York and New England	..	..
New York Chi. and Saint Louis	..	..
New York Chi. and Saint Louis pref.	..	..
New York Lack. and Western	..	..
New York L. E. and W.	..	..
New York L. E. and W. pref.	..	..
New York Susq. and Western	..	..
New York Susq. and Western pref.	..	..
Norfolk and West pref.	..	42¼
Northern Pacific	23¼	24⅝
Northern Pacific pref.	49⅝	..
Ohio and Miss.	25	25¼
Ontario and West	16	..
Oregon Improvement Co.	..	..
Oregon R. and N.	..	..
Oregon and Transcontinental	25	22
Pacific Mail	40	..
Peoria Dec. and Evansville	25	..
Philadelphia and Reading	63	61
Philadelphia Natural Gas Co.	99	..
Richmond and West Point	29	..
Rich. and W. P. pref.	56	..
Rome, Watertown and Ogdensburg	85	..
St. Louis and San Francisco	37	37¼
St. Louis and San Francisco pref.	71	76¼
St. Paul and Duluth	73	...
St. Paul and Omaha	47	..
St. Paul and Omaha pref	110	..
St. Paul, Mil. and Manatoba	113	..
St. Louis, Arkansas and Texas	18	..
Tennessee, Coal and Ir'n	28	29
Texas Pacific	28	28
Union Pacific	55	53¼
Wabash, St. Louis and Pacific	18	18¼
Wabash St. Louis and Pacific pref.	33	32¾
West. Union Tel	78	78
PHILADELPHIA.		
Pennsylvania Railroad	55	..
MONEY AND BONDS.		
Call Money, U.S. Gov. Bds	5 p.c.	2 p.c.
Ditto, Other Securities	5 p.c.	2 p.c.
Exc. on Lon,. 60 days' sight	4.75¾	4.79½
Cable Transfers	4.84¼	4.84½
Exchange on Paris	5.27¼	5.27½
Exchange on Berlin	94¼	94¼
Four p. c. U.S. Funded Loan	124	124
Wheeling and L. E.	45	45

[NOTE.—The railways stocks left in blank in the above list will, after to-day, be quoted by cable from New York.]

PLACE DE LA BOURSE.

PARIS, Oct. 3, 1887.

Old 3%	82.30
Redeemable 3%	85.32
Old 4½ %	109.52
New 4½ %	—
Portuguese 3%	58.25
Italian 5%	98.75
Turkish 4%	13.90
Spanish Exterior	69.00
Austrian Gold 4%	92.75
Hungar Gold	82.00
Egyptian Unified	384.50
Egyptian Pref.	506.75
Russian 5% 1862	99.25
Russian 4% 1867	86.50
Russian 4% 1869	86.30
Russian 5% 1877	100.40
Belgian 4%	—
MISCELLANEOUS SHARES	
Ottoman Bank	495.00
Comtoir d'Escompte	1,025.00
Crédit Foncier	1,360.00
Crédit Lyonnais	571.25
Suez Canal	2,002.50
Panama Canal	363.75
Société Générale	456.50
Rio Tinto	213.12
Paris to N. Y., French cable	145.00
French Edison Light	—
Cie Transatlantique	—
Telephones	508.75

AFTER OFFICIAL HOURS.

French 4½%. 109fr. 52½c. French 3%.... 82fr. 30c.

COURSE OF EXCHANGE—PARIS.

NEGOTIATED AT SIGHT.

London,	25fr. 40c.	to	25fr. 41c.	less 4%
— Cheques,	25fr. 40c.	to	25fr. 41c.	
— Sovereigns,	25fr. 40c.			
— Banknotes,	25fr. 42c.			

ENGLISH SOCIETY.

There are still a good many yachts on the Cowes station. Among others, there are the Wildfire, Lieut.-General Baring; Lotus, Colonel Loyd; Oceana, Sir P. Shelley, Bart.; Aphrodite, Lord Porchester; Northumbria, Duke of Bedford; Ballerina, Mr. M. Guest: Caprice, Mr. P. Percival, and Modwena, Mr. J. Gretton.

The Empress Eugénie has derived great benefit from her stay in Scotland up to this, although she somewhat keenly feels the chill breezes that blow in the North. It may be easily imagined that, Spaniard as she is, the Empress scarcely likes the cold climate of the Highlands. The Queen and the Ex-Empress are much together. Her Majesty has some difficulty in inducing the Empress to drive out with her. Her Majesty is a lover of fresh air, and except for very heavy rain, will never allow her carriage to be closed, and the Empress knowing this, invariably tries to excuse herself from driving out with the Queen. The greatest friendship obtains between the Empress and Princess Beatrice. The Empress is never so happy as when in the nursery at Balmoral, petting the little Prince of Battenberg. The funeral ceremony at Farnborough will take place soon after the return of the Empress from Scotland. Everything is in readiness at the chapel which the Empress has caused to be built for the reception of the bodies of her husband and son.

Bath, the Queen City of the West, whose thermal waters are for the healing of nations (and individuals) is just beginning to fill again after its summer recess. The hotel-keepers and tradesmen say last winter was the best on record since "Beau" Nash's era or Bladud's royal bathings.

Mrs. Thompson—Lady Butler's mother —and almost as accomplished a painter in her line (miniatures) as her world-famous daughter, has just finished the composition of an oratorio, of which experts in music speak highly.

During the last fortnight London has been unusually full for September. It is generally supposed that this is the most unfashionable month, next to August, in the Metropolis; but certainly an exception must be made this year. A good many of the arrivals in town are doubtless owing to the cold weather, which has driven home some of the less hardy pleasure-seekers; and it must be remembered, too, that the season, though a brilliant one, ended early. Still, after all allowances are made under those heads, it is plain that Society does not intend to let autumnal London remain the desolate wilderness it was of yore.

AMERICAN NOTES.

It was reported in Wall-street yesterday that Jay Gould would sail for Europe about the middle of next month. It was said specifically that his yacht Atalanta would be sent over, and if it reached the other side safely Mr Gould would follow on an ocean steamship. The length of his trip varied in the street rumors from a few weeks to six months or a year.

The steamship Alesia, of the Fabre line, came up to Quarantine yesterday morning with the most startling bill of health that has been seen at this port for over twenty years. According to the ship's doctor's statement, six steerage passengers and two seamen had died of Asiatic cholera on the voyage from the Mediterranean, and four more passengers were down with the same fatal and infectious disease. Counting in the officers and crew, there were 609 persons aboard, all of whom were dangerously threatened with the plague. No time was lost in turning the steamer back to the Lower Bay and putting the passengers and crew under the strictest quarantine rules.

Some time ago Mrs. John Hostetter, of Perry County, Pa., gave birth to triplets, two boys and a girl. The parents decided to call them Grover, Cleveland and Frances, respectively. A letter was written to the President, to which he sent the following reply:—

EXECUTIVE MANSION, WASHINGTON, Sept. 19, 1887.

Mr. JOHN HOSTETTER:—

MY DEAR SIR:—Mr. Fry, of Newport, Penn., has informed me of the birth to you simultaneously of three children, two boys and a girl, and has also stated that you have selected Grover, Cleveland and Frances respectively for their names, in compliment to Mrs. Cleveland and myself. I have quite a number of namesakes, whose parents have been good enough to make manifest in this way their friendly feeing but it is exceptional that the opportunity is presented to show in such a marked degree, the confidence and regard your action implies. Thanking you for your courtesy, and expressing the hope that you may be permitted to see the children grow in years and strength, I am, very truly yours,

GROVER CLEVELAND.

Frederick H Cossitt, a well-known business man and heavily interested in real estate in New York, died yesterday morning, at his home, No. 183 Madison-ave. In his seventy-sixth year. He was of French descent, his ancestors being among the earliest settlers of Connecticut, going there as far back as 1720. Mr. Cossitt was born in Granby, Hartford County, Connecticut, on December 18, 1811.

Gen. James B. Ricketts, the sturdy commander of the famous Ricketts' Battery, died at his home, 1,829 G-street, Washington, yesterday afternoon at four o'clock. He had been ill for years, and at times his illness had taken alarming turns and threatened to terminate his existence. A gunshot wound through the lung, received at Winchester, gave him great trouble. Through exposure he contracted pneumonia several years ago, and it left him with a painful cough. His constitution was a strong one, and his recuperative powers astonished the physicians who from time to time saw him rally from assaults of disease that would have struck down most men not enfeebled as he was by wounds received in battle.

A CARGO OF CRIMINALS.

Five hundred convicts, says the *Figaro*, have just sailed from Toulon on the Orne, bound for Cayenne. Eighty-seven of them are "lifers," and of these nine had been sentenced to death. Among the convicts are a count, who had murdered his mother. Delmazure, the ghoul who desecrated the tombs of Montmartre cemetery; Leoni, who killed several soldiers; Sicard, the fratricide; and a great many other interesting criminals. As the convoy was being taken on board in chains, Sicard savagely assaulted one of the guard and made a desperate attempt to escape. He was not mastered til he had been threatened with a bullet in his head.

A HAPPY RELEASE.

SMYRNA, October 3rd, 1887.—The four Englishmen who were captured by brigands on the 26th ult., while shooting in the neighborhood of the town, were released last night, on payment of a ransom of £750.

NEW YORK LETTER.

Universal Interest Regarding the Political Campaign.

TRAVELLING IRISH ORATORS.

Very Little Hope of Another Race With the Thistle.

A HORRIBLE LONG ISLAND MURDER.

The Rev. Dr. Parker of the London Temple in Plymouth Church.

[BY COMMERCIAL CABLE TO THE HERALD.]

NEW YORK, Oct. 3, 1887.

The coming political campaign, from outset, has promised to be lively; but an element has now been added that will materially increase its interest. The Anarchists were kicked out of the Labor Convention by Mr. Henry George and Herr Shevitch. The leader of the expelled Anarchists, has challenged Henry George to a public debate. George has accepted, and if the liveliest kind of row is not the result politicians will be mistaken.

THE LABOR CONVENTION

The annual assembly of the Knights of Labor will be convened in Minneapolis to-morrow. Great interest centres in the election of a Master Workman. President Master Workman Powderly is too conservative to please the more advanced members. A strong opposition will attempt to oust him and elect a Master Workman more given to ordering strikes. The present outlook however strongly favors the success of Mr. Powderly and the conservative element.

GOING INTO BUSINESS

An effort will be made to get Knights of Labor to take some action regarding the Chicago anarchists now under sentence of murder, and also to induce the order as a body to carry on a co-operative establishment. The Knights are now doing that in Minnesota, where in one place alone they have accumulated a quarter million dollars' worth of property, and do a million dollars' worth of business yearly.

DAVITT AND EGAN.

Michael Davitt has reached Chicago, where he and Patrick Egan, the leader of the Irish sympathisers in this country and president of the National Land League of America were enthusiastically received.

TO TALK FOR IRELAND.

Sir Henry Grattan Esmond, or, as the afternoon papers will insist upon calling him, "Mr. Esmond," has turned up in New York with Mr. Arthur O'Connor. They are at the Hoffman House. They are both announced to plead for Ireland in Boston, Lowell, Jersey City, Philadelphia, Chicago, St. Louis and San Francisco, but they don't intend to give the English Government a chance of catching them up in Canada.

[illegible] ENOUGH

There is much talk at the New York Yacht Club over probable bringing over here by Mr. Sweet of a seventy foot water line cutter to win the America Cup, neat season. If this is done, a keel boat of the same size, will be built here by Burgess to beat her. The proposal of the Larchmont Yacht Club of New York to give a thousand dollar cup for the four big single stickers, the Mayflower, Puritan, Galatea, and Thistle, before the latter's return home has fallen through. The Thistle will not sail unless the Volunteer enters, which the Larchmont Club objects to, saying that it is "the same as presenting the Volunteer with a $1,000 cup, as the Volunteer evidently can't be beaten by the Thistle."

NOTABLE VISITORS.

Lord Herschell, with Lady Herschell, are in Philadelphia after a pleasant overland trip from San Francisco. They are accompanied by Mr. Charles Buller and Victor R. Williamson of London.

SWEENEY IN NEW YORK.

Peter B. Sweeney is in New York today, and insists that he is here only on personal business, and though many knowing ones hint that his advice will be quietly sought by the democratic politicians in connection with the coming campaign, Sweeney says he returns to Paris before the election.

THE MANITOBANS DOWNED.

Winnipeg's famous railroad to the United States boundary, according to a dispatch to the *New York Times*, has fizzled out at last, and the Canadian Pacific Railway has scored a great triumph over the people of Manitoba. Owing to a lack of funds, the constructor has thrown up his contract and given notice to stop work. There is very bitter feeling in Manitoba over the matter.

DANGEROUS COLLEGE FUN.

The faculties of the various American colleges have been taking active measures to stop "hazing." They have got a good text to-day to preach upon in the ruth in the case of Young Choate, son of Joseph H. Choate, the well known member of the New York Car, who lies dying it is feared

[CONTINUED ON THIRD PAGE.]

OCTOBER 1, 1888.

A FIEND AT WORK.

Two Brutal Murders in the East End of London.

WOMEN THE VICTIMS.

A Repetition of the Terrible Whitechapel Mutilations.

[BY THE HERALD'S SPECIAL WIRE.]

LONDON, September 30, 1888.

London is panic stricken. The metropolis woke with a shudder this morning, for once more the cry of murder rang through its streets. Not only one murder, but two murders. Not only murder, but murder and mutilation of that fiendish kind to which we have lately become familiar. Yes, undaunted by the fear of detection and the extra precautions of the police, there lurks among us one of the coolest and cleverest murderers that ever baffled the entire detective force. His work is apparently carried out under the very noses of the police. His victims are well nigh ripped to pieces, and yet the strange part is that the murderer leaves no trace or clue by which he can be followed. No wonder the ignorant people of Whitechapel and the East End of London look upon these deeds of blood as something supernatural. The women in the metropolis have become frightened of their own shadows and the men go about armed.

THE DOUBLE OUTRAGE.

Between one and two o'clock this morning two terrible murders were committed in the vicinity of Whitechapel. The victims were both women. The first was discovered in a yard in Berner street, St. George's, a distance of a third of a mile from where the recent Whitechapel murders were committed. The head of the victim was nearly severed from the body, but there was no attempt at mutilation. This, therefore, might be an ordinary case of murder.

MURDER AND MUTILATION.

But the second, and much more horrible, was evidently the handiwork of the slayer of Mrs. Chapman. It is supposed to have occurred at a quarter to two. The body was found by a constable on his beat, Mitre square, Houndsditch.

TUESDAY OCTOBER 2, 1888.

THE HORRIBLE LONDON MURDERS.

Reasons Why Warders of Asylums Should Act as Policemen to Trace the Bloodthirsty Wretches.

IS IT A HOMICIDAL MANIA?

[BY THE HERALD'S SPECIAL WIRE.]

LONDON, October 1, 1888.

It would be strange if a Ministry were to fall from power through murder. Yet if the country were to go to the hustings to-day the Conservative Government would be turned out neck and crop—not for their foreign policy, but on account of the Whitechapel murders. London is wild with rage and indignation. The people go to the fountain head, and ask in no measured tones, "Where is the Home Secretary at such a moment? Out with him. He allows the metropolis to ring with the cry of unavenged murder. He refuses even to offer a reward as demanded by the outraged inhabitants of Whitechapel."

UNRECOGNIZABLE.

There is a rumor that the woman murdered in Mitre square has been identified, and that she was known by the name of "May." This is not confirmed by the police, who state that no one has recognized her. And, indeed, the victim's face is so dreadfully mutilated that it is hopeless that she will be recognized except by her clothes or the pawn tickets she had. However, these latter were in a false name.

A HOMICIDAL MANIAC.

Sir James Risdon Bennett, M.D., F.R.S., in a long interview on the murders, says:—"My impression is that the miscreant is a homicidal maniac. He has a specific delusion, and that delusion is erotic. Of course we have at this moment very little evidence—indeed, in fact, I may say no evidence at all—as to the state of the man's mind, except so far as it is suggested by the character of the injuries which he has inflicted upon his victims. I repeat that my impression is that he is suffering under an erotic delusion, but it may be that he is a religious fanatic. It is possible that he is laboring under the delusion that he has a mandate from the Almighty to purge the world of unfortunates, and in the prosecution of his mad theory he has determined upon a crusade against the unfortunates of London, whom he seeks to mutilate.

IS HE A TEXAN?

THE NEW YORK SUPERINTENDENT OF POLICE AS TO THE IDENTITY OF THE MURDERER.

[BY THE HERALD'S SPECIAL WIRE.]

LONDON, October 2, 1888.—The *Daily News* this morning has a special from New York in which the following paragraphs occur:—New York, Monday. Not a great many months ago, a series of remarkably brutal murders of women occurred in Texas. The victims were chiefly negro women. The crimes were characterized by the same brutal methods as those of the Whitechapel murders. The theory has been suggested that the perpetrator of the latter may be the Texas criminal, who was never discovered. The *Atlanta Constitution*, a leading Southern newspaper, thus puts the argument:—"The mysterious crimes in Texas have ceased. They have just commenced in London. Is the man from Texas at the bottom of them all? If he is the monster or lunatic he may be expected to appear anywhere. The fact that he is no longer at work in Texas argues his presence somewhere else. The man who would kill a dozen women in Texas would not mind the inconvenience of a trip across the water, and once there he would not have any scruples about killing more women."

OCTOBER 3, 1888.

MURDER! MURDER!

One More Mutilated Body of a Woman Discovered in London.

[BY THE HERALD'S SPECIAL WIRE.]

LONDON, October 2, 1888.

And still the cry is "Murder!" 'Tis the bitter and horror stricken cry of our outraged citizens. As I write the streets resound with the strident voices of the newsboys crying:—"Another murder in Whitehall." Late this afternoon the mutilated body of a woman was found in Cannon row, on the Thames Embankment, near Westminster Bridge, at a spot where the National Opera House, which was never finished, was to have stood. The site, as is known, has been taken up for the new police buildings, and upon these workmen are now engaged excavating large vaults. It was in one of these that the discovery was made.

DISCOVERING THE TRUNK.

One of the workmen there discovered the trunk of a woman. The head, arms and legs were missing; in fact, nothing but the upper part of the trunk remains, the lower part having been removed, so that a portion of the bowels is protruding. The breasts, which were quite exposed, were tied round with two pieces of string, and the flesh appears quite firm, although it would seem that the body must have been dead for at least some days. The police were, of course, at once communicated with, and inquiries into the dreadful affair are being made, search being, of course, directed to the discovery of any other part of the remains.

MORE TRAGEDY.

How the trunk could have been carried to the place where it was found is not the least mysterious part of this horrible tragedy, which appears likely to be more connected with the recent discoveries of arms in Pimlico and Lambeth than with the East End horrors. The foreman and workmen seem tolerably certain that the trunk was not where it was found on Friday, and some assert that it could not have been there on Saturday as they must have seen it, lying, as it was, fully exposed on the ground at the bottom of the vault. It seems probable, therefore, that it must have been placed in that spot between the time the men left off work on Saturday and their beginning yesterday morning. Perhaps the worst feature of the present homicidal epidemic is its contagious effect. The papers teem with accounts of attempts at murders and assaults on women.

FRIDAY, OCTOBER 5, 1888.

LONDON'S FIEND.

The Police Still Baffled by the Whitechapel Murderer.

"JACK THE RIPPER."

His Phraseology Points to His Being An American.

[BY THE HERALD'S SPECIAL WIRE.]

LONDON, October 4, 1888.

The cauldron of murder still boils and bubbles. To-day the inquest was commenced upon the mutilated remains of the victim of Mitre court. The examination was held at the City Mortuary, Golden lane. The jury were sworn to inquire into "the death of Catherine Eddowes, alias Conway, alias Kelly," and thereafter proceeded to the Mortuary to view the body. The jury having returned after a lapse of a few minutes, Eliza Gold, a woman in humble circumstances, was the first witness called. She was the sister of the deceased, and wept bitterly whilst giving her evidence. She had not seen her sister for some months. Her evidence showed that the deceased had led a very immoral life.

TO FIND HER DAUGHTER.

John Kelly, who first identified the deceased as his paramour, was called. He had seen her alive for the last time on the Saturday the eve of the murder in Houndsditch. She parted with him on perfectly good terms, and said she was going to find her daughter Annie at Bermondsey. She said she would be back at four o'clock, but did not return. Afterwards he heard she had been taken into custody for drunkenness.

Police Constable Edward Watkin said that he had to cover the beat comprising Mitre square every twelve to fourteen minutes on the night in question. He had heard nothing nor seen anything to arouse suspicion until 1.44 A. M., when he found the body.

MEDICAL TESTIMONY.

Dr. Gordon Brown, surgeon to the City of London Police Force, testified to finding the deceased as already described in the HERALD. After detailing the mutilations the doctor was cross-examined by the Coroner.

"Can you tell us what was the cause of death?"

"The cause of death was hæmorrhage from the throat. Death was immediate."

"Were the other mutilations made before or after death?"

"After death."

"Does the nature of the wounds lead you to any conclusion as to the instrument that was used?"

"It must have been a sharp pointed knife, and, I should say, at least six inches long."

"Would you consider that the person who inflicted the wounds possessed anatomical skill?"

"A good deal of knowledge as to the position of the abdominal organs."

"Would the parts removed be of any use for professional purposes?"

"Not the slightest."

"Would such a knowledge be likely to be possessed by someone accustomed to cutting up animals?"

"Yes, sir."

"Have you been able to form any opinion as to whether the perpetrator of this act was disturbed?"

"I think he had sufficient time; but from certain marks he was probably hurried."

"How long would it take to inflict these wounds?"

"Five minutes. A skilled operator would take three and a half minutes to remove the womb. I can assign no reason for these parts being taken away. I feel sure that there was no struggle. The act was probably that of one person only. I can only account for no noise being heard by the fact that the throat must have been instantly severed, so that no noise could have been emitted. There would not be much blood on the person who inflicted the wounds. The wounds could not have been self-inflicted."

The inquest was then adjourned till Thursday next. To-day all kinds of reports of captures have been flying about, but no capture of any importance has really been made.

WHITECHAPEL'S MYSTERIOUS CRIME ILLUSTRATED.

Investigations of the Metropolitan Police and What the Chief Detectives of Paris and New York Think of their Efforts.

The situation in the Whitechapel district to-day did not differ much from that of preceding days since the murder. Excitement was less noticeable and one heard less discussion in the streets regarding the crime. People continued to go into Castle alley and to loiter about the scene of the crime, trying to satisfy their morbid curiosity by gazing at the spot where the body was found.

The way in which women of the class among whom the "Ripper" has found all his victims regard the matter is indicative of the depths of degradation to which they have descended. They are very indignant, very outspoken in their denunciation, and no one could be more ready than they are to lynch the murderer should he be discovered. Jack the Ripper is not hated more by the most moral and law abiding individual in London than he is by the habitually immoral and criminal persons of both sexes who "move in the same society" as have "Jack's" victims, and as "Jack" himself in all probability. Yet, abandoned women in the Whitechapel district do not appear to be in fear of the butcher. They go on soliciting just the same as they did before the horrible butcheries occurred.

TERRIBLE DEGRADATION.

Many of them have longed for death to relieve them of their miserable, degraded existence and joyless, hopeless life of wretchedness and suffering. They care little how soon their miseries end. "You will be the next victim," said a bar tender, jokingly, to one of those women last night, who was turning down her fifteenth or twentieth glass of liquor. "I don't care, if only I'm drunk," was her reply. Tone and manner indicated that she spoke her feelings.

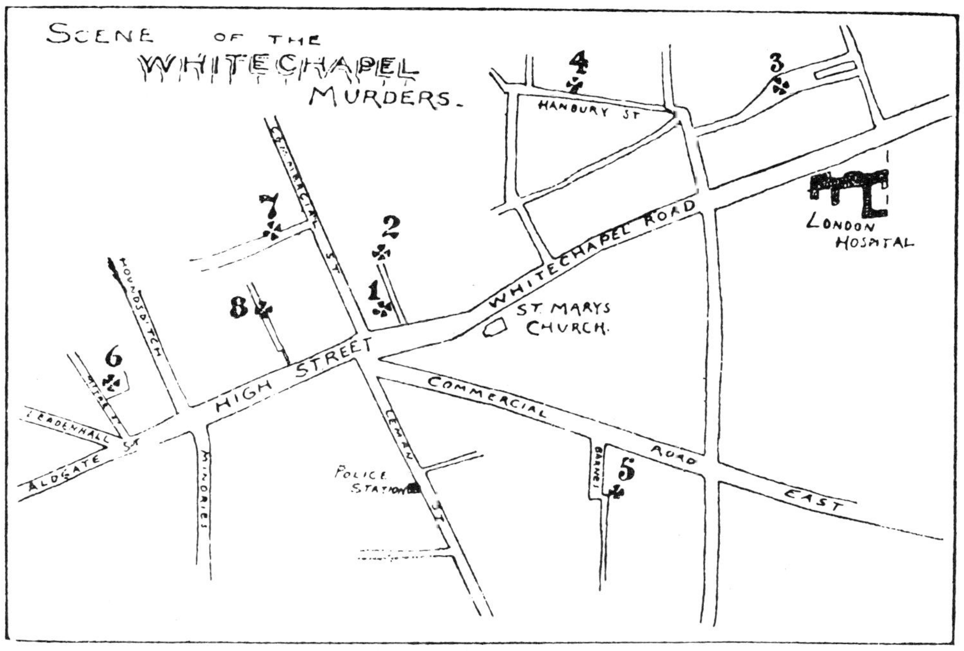

NAMES OF VICTIMS AND DATES OF THE CRIMES.

1. An unknown woman, Christmas week, 1887.
2. Martha Turner, found stabbed in 39 places on landing at George Yard buildings, Commercial street, Spitalfields, August 7, 1888.
3. Mrs. Mary Ann Nicholls, in Buck's row, August 31, 1888.
4. Mrs. Annie Chapman, Hanbury street, September 7, 1888.
5. Elizabeth Stride, Berner street, September 30 1888.
6. Catherine Eddowes, Mitre square, September 30, 1888.
7. Mary Jane Kelley, 26 Dorset street, Spitalfields.
8. Alice Mackenzie, July 17, 1889.

CASTLE ALLEY, FROM HIGH STREET ENTRANCE.

SENSATION IN NEW YORK.

INSPECTOR BYRNES AGAIN PASSES JUDGMENT ON THE LONDON POLICE.

[BY COMMERCIAL CABLE TO THE HERALD.]

NEW YORK, July 19.—Jack the Ripper is paramount again to-day in popular interest, and this last escapade of the eccentric London assassin is the talk of the town. The HERALD again led the fleet, so to speak, with its lengthy cabled addendum to the story of the murderer of Alice Mackenzie.

Inspector Byrnes, while apparently extremely fearful of saying anything that might be construed as a criticism of the Metropolitan police, thinks that a similar chain of tragedies would be almost impossible in New York. A lunatic, rather than a mere vulgar, bloodthirsty murderer, would give the police most trouble. The craft of insanity would prevent the ordinary and extraordinary methods of detection being successfully employed. The secret success of the famous New York detective lies in the fact of his having stood "pigeon" in every criminal gang. A thief may continue his depredations without molestation if he keeps within reasonable limits, so long as he can be relied on to secretly give away his brothers in crime who may be wanted. A lunatic would stand alone—*sans* confidants, *sans* friends.

ALICE MACKENZIE.

M. GORON ON THE MURDERS

PARIS AND LONDON DETECTIVES CONTRASTED TOGETHER WITH THEIR METHODS.

Out of the scorching noon sun into a building cool and vast as the Halls of Eblis, along mazy passages for guidance through which an Ariadne thread would be found of inestimable utility; past keen eyed men who scan you in such a way that it is to be hoped your conscience is an easy one, and past other men and women who do not seem to think of your conscience, but of less priceless and more material treasures easier of transference—such was the experience of a HERALD correspondent who went yesterday in search of M. Goron, the head of the Criminal Investigation Department of the Paris police, to ask him what he thought of Jack the Ripper and the series of crimes imputed to that slippery individual's daring hand.

ENOUGH TO DO AT HOME.

"You would like to know my opinion about the Whitechapel murders? I have none whatsoever. I have quite enough to do to look after my own affairs, without bothering myself with what goes on in my neighbors' preserves. At this very moment, the rue Bonaparte murder absorbs all my attention."

"But you must have some impression, M. Goron? This latest murder?"

"I have read ten lines in a newspaper about it. What impression could I obtain from that?"

Did M. Goron read English? He did, a little, and in a moment was reading the HERALD's telegraphic reports anent the murder of Alice Mackenzie in Castle alley.

"An interesting, a very interesting case!" was the view he took of it. "There have been seven or eight murders in the series, have there not? I don't see how the London police can sleep when they have not found their man. But I really can't say anything about the matter. I am not in a position to cast reflections upon the English police, but——" and the speaker went on to damn with faint praise.

MORNING SCENE IN CASTLE ALLEY.

LAMPOST NEAR WHICH BODY WAS FOUND.

SATURDAY, NOVEMBER 22, 1890.

THE THREATENING INDIAN OUTBREAK.

"Buffalo Bill's" Braves Expected to Play the Role of Peacemakers.

"HERALD'S" WEATHER SERVICE

The Land League Denounces Messrs. Dillon and O'Brien—General American News.

[BY COMMERCIAL CABLE TO THE HERALD.]

NEW YORK, Nov. 21.

The dread of an Indian outbreak still broods like a horrible nightmare over the country. Vague rumors of disturbances continue to come from the North-Western agencies, and the Government's assurance that the Indians are hemmed in by troops hardly suffices to allay public uneasiness. As a matter of fact, soldiers are massed around Standing Rock, Pine Ridge, and Rosebud Agencies, and at the first sign of trouble are prepared to mow the redskins down like corn.

General Crook, who is at Pine Ridge, fears the worst, and has, in consequence, sent all white women and children away from the Agency. At Standing Rock the troops have restored public confidence, and the alarmed settlers are gradually returning to their homes.

The Indians have never been the same since they signed the treaty last year opening up 11,000,000 acres to white settlers. They were worked up to a white heat at that time by the conflict between the rival chiefs, some opposing and some favoring it. Sitting Bull was bitterly denounced by Gall as a rascal and a traitor. One of the most dramatic scenes ever witnessed at Standing Rock was the sudden appearance of Gall in a secret council of the Indians, where he advised the Sioux not to sign away their lands, and even threatened to physically chastize Sitting Bull in the presence of his people.

GALL, THE CHIEF SOLDIER OF THE SIOUX NATION, URGING SITTING BULL, RUNNING ANTELOPE AND RAIN-IN-THE-FACE NOT TO SIGN AWAY THEIR LANDS.

MONDAY. FEBRUARY 9, 1891.

A GREAT FIGHT WITH THE REDSKINS.

Indian Treachery Causes a Bloody Encounter and Loss of Life.

CAPTAIN WALLACE KILLED.

Over Thirty Men of "Custer's Cavalry" Wounded, Many of them Severely.

TOMAHAWKS, KNIVES AND RIFLES.

Big Foot's Tribe Overpowered, Killed and Captured—Deadly Work by the Hotchkiss Guns.

[BY COMMERCIAL CABLE TO THE HERALD.]

NEW YORK, Dec. 30.

A great fight has taken place with the Indians at Wounded Creek, and there has been much loss of life. Big Foot, having declared that he was ill, surrendered with 150 of his braves to Major Whiteside and the Seventh Cavalry. Finding, however, that the remainder of the Indians were unwilling to give up their arms, the cavalry, which was five hundred strong, surrounded them and closed on them to within gun reach. Suddenly the braves, snatching their guns from beneath their blankets poured a concerted volley into the troops who were taken unawares.

A bloody fight ensued, and the Indians who were without guns used their knives and tomahawks. Captain Wallace, commanding the K troop of cavalry, was killed by a tomahawk blow. Four or five of the United States soldiers were killed and over forty were wounded, many of whom will die. Amongst the latter is Father Crafts, a priest. Recovering from the sudden and unexpected onslaught, the troops opened fire, and so deadly were the volleys that the braves were almost exterminated.

The news of the battle caused madness amongst the five thousand Indians who had surrendered at the Agency, and many of them broke away.

The special correspondent of the HERALD telegraphs this evening from Rapid City that all the troops along Cheyenne, including General Carr's, Colonel Offly's and Colonel Sanford's commands, were marching towards Pine Ridge this morning, and are rapidly nearing the scene of the trouble. The grass upon the Great Table and the fuel in the late camp of the hostiles has been burned, and this stronghold is now held by three companies of infantry. General Miles's headquarters will remain here for the present though he may leave to-morrow for the front on receipt of to-day's despatches.

General Miles said that this postpones the surrender looked for, and greatly complicates the situation.

WEDNESDAY. DECEMBER 31, 1890.

INDIAN CHIEFS IN WASHINGTON.

Sioux Warriors Have a Heap Big Talk with Secretary Noble.

[BY COMMERCIAL CABLE TO THE HERALD.]

NEW YORK, Feb. 8.

The Sioux Indian chiefs, who are in Washington, had a heap big talk yesterday with Secretary Noble at the Interior Department. American Horse Chief Hump, Hollow Horn and Bear aired their grievances of unfulfilled promises and pledges broken. They squatted down round the Secretary and expected immediate relief.

Medicine Man Bull, one of the veteran chiefs of the tribe, made an eloquent speech full of the picturesqueness of Indian oratory. He proclaimed himself a friend of the white man and said there was no blood on his hands. Very feelingly did the old man call the Secretary's attention to the fact that when the Indians shook their pockets there was nothing in them that would rattle.

Hollow Horn said he had some things he wanted to tell, but he thought it might shock the ladies present; still, if they did not mind, he would tell the story. Secretary Noble said he might reserve such matters until Monday.

The Secretary said he wanted the Indians to make up their minds to do the best they could to educate their children, and never to let their young men dream that they could ever get anything by force from the United States.

Then the Pow-Wow broke up. There were visible signs of dissatisfaction among the Indians. They felt that they had been blarneyed. Nothing definite had come out of the interview, and no assurances of more beef and flour had been received. In a general way they understood that their condition was to be investigated, but it had not been explained how much talk there was in the big promise.

"Ugh!" exclaimed Hollow Horn, as he filed out of the room.

TUESDAY. DECEMBER 30, 1890.

HOW SITTING BULL FELL.

Full Account of the Killing of the Famous Sioux Chief.

SHOT THROUGH THE HEAD.

Determined Attempt to Rescue Him from the Indian Police—A Sanguinary Battle.

[FROM THE "NEW YORK HERALD."]

FORT YATES, N. D., Dec. 18.

The HERALD correspondent, being with the cavalry at the front, is enabled to give some incidents of the death of Sitting Bull not heretofore sent out.

The plan was for Bull Head, first lieutenant of the Indian policemen, to march

SITTING BULL.

as close to Sitting Bull's camp as possible at night without being detected, and at the first break of day Bull Head and eight men were to go to Sitting Bull's tent and take him prisoner as quietly as possible. The other policemen were to remain concealed some distance away, ready to assist in case resistance was offered.

HOW SITTING BULL DIED.

He told the HERALD correspondent the story of the fight, which was to the following effect:—

The police carried out their instructions to the letter. When daylight appeared, forty-one policemen, with Bull Head commanding, were concealed in the brush, fifty feet from Sitting Bull's house. Bull Head, Shave Head and eight others quietly and unnoticed stepped into Sitting Bull's house and seized him in bed. He grabbed his revolver, the one given by Mrs. Weldon, the Brooklyn woman who has figured so prominently in Sitting Bull's affairs, but Red Tomahawk wrenched it from him. Bull Head tried to induce him to go with them quietly. This he promised to do and went out for his horses.

No sooner was he outside than he gave a yell that aroused the camp. Catch-the-Bear rushed to his relief almost instantly and fired at Bull Head, striking him in the leg above the knee. Bull Head then turned around quietly and took his revenge on Sitting Bull. The aim was steady and a bullet went crashing through the old chief's head. Red Tomahawk also turned and shot Sitting Bull through the body with the revolver he had just taken from him.

JUNE 21. 1893.

MISS BORDEN FOUND INNOCENT.

After a Short Deliberation the Jury Say that She Did Not Murder Her Parents.

STOLID UNDER DENUNCIATION.

The Arguments in Favor of Her Guilt Rested on a Weak Foundation.

[BY COMMERCIAL CABLE TO THE HERALD.]

NEW YORK, June 20.—The jury, in the case of Lizzie Borden, on trial at New Bedford, Mass., on the charge of murdering her father and stepmother at Fall River, returned a verdict of not guilty this afternoon, after deliberating one hour and twenty-five minutes.

Judge Dewey's charge to the jury was very favorable to the prisoner. There was great excitement in the court-room when the jury retired at 3.9 p.m. At 4 30 p.m. word reached the Court that they had agreed, and the lawyers who

MISS LIZZIE BORDEN.

had gone out to luncheon trooped back in a hurry, and the two Judges were sent for. Then came the verdict which was received with loud shouts.

When the Court adjourned last night District-Attorney Knowlton had not finished his address. He delivered a forceful and clear statement, better and more effective than that of the prisoner's counsel. He resumed his speech this morning.

Lizzie Borden listened to her counsel with eager and intense interest. She sat perfectly stolid and unmoved during Mr. Knowlton's scathing speech. The court-room was packed solid and the crowds filled the streets outside, awaiting the result.

THE FALL RIVER TRAGEDY.

Mr. Borden and his wife, who was Lizzie's stepmother, were found murdered in their house on the morning of August 2, 1892. In the house, which is in the heart of the city of Fall River, were two persons besides the victims at the time of the murder. They were the prisoner and the servant, Bridget Sullivan. The prisoner's uncle, John V. Morse, a guest of the family, had left the house some time before the murder occurred.

Mr. Borden was found dead in the sitting room and his wife in a bedroom upstairs. Their faces were so chopped and hacked, apparently with an axe, that they bore little resemblance to those of human beings.

The rooms in which the bodies were found were smeared and splashed with blood. With the exception of a spot the size of a pin's head no blood was found on the prisoner. The murder was not done for money, as there was nothing stolen from the house.

The argument in favor of Miss Borden's guilt was the rather weak one that the police could not see how anyone else could have done the bloody work. The motive attributed to her was that she hated her stepmother and wished to get her father's property, about $500,000.

YORK HERALD, PARIS, TUESDAY, APRIL 6, 189 .

NEW YORK HERALD

EUROPEAN EDITION.

SPECIAL EASTER NUMBER

APPEARS SUNDAY, APRIL 18.

ART AND LITERATURE.

Novelettes written expressly for the HERALD by seven of the principal novelists in Europe.

"RESURRECTION,"
By PAUL BOURGET,
Author of *Cosmopolis, Outre-Mer, Une Idylle Tragique.*

"LA PARABOLE DES VIERGES SAGES ET DES VIERGES FOLLES,"
By GABRIELE D'ANNUNZIO.
Author of *Trionfo della Morte*, and whose *Vergini delle Rocce* marks a new departure in modern literature.

"RRAN,"
By PAUL HERVIEU,
Author of *Le Petit Duc*, written for the HERALD'S Christmas Number in 1895.

"PAQUES, OU LA DÉLIVRANCE,"
By ANATOLE FRANCE,
The gentle ironist whose *Opinions de M. Jérôme Coignard* is already a classic.

"VACANCES DE PAQUES,"
By PIERRE LOTI,
The brilliant young author of *Mme. Chrysanthème, Matelot*, &c.

"LIZOTTE,"
By MARCEL PRÉVOST,
The authority on feminine psychology.

"UNE APPARITION,"
By CAMILLE FLAMMARION.
Astronomer and novelist, author of *Uranie, Stella*, &c.

Illustrated with original designs created by Boutet de Monvel, Calbet, Georges Jeanniot, Henry Tenré, Lafon, Tofani and Malher.

Colored Illustrations by some leading American artists. Notably — "THE SPIRIT OF THE CHIMES," Specially painted for the HERALD by LIART WALKER.

THE NEW YORK HERALD'S EASTER NUMBER can be obtained at Railroad Stations and leading Booksellers in France, Germany, Austria, Italy, &c., at Bookstalls and Libraries in London and Provinces at the regular price of the SUNDAY HERALD. Address all communications to NEW YORK HERALD, 49 avenue de l'Opéra, Paris.

LADIES' ATTIRE.

DRESSES. MADAME SPRENGEL, 20 rue Louis-le-Grand (Opéra). Late first hand and fitter at first houses in Paris. Stylish Dresses. Moderate Prices.

Madame BERTHON, MILLINER, has removed from 2 rue de la Paix, to 2 place Vendome.

MAISON HENRIETTE. DRESSES. MANTLES. TROUSSEAUX. *PARISIAN TOILETTES. LATEST NOVELTIES.* 95 RUE DES PETITS CHAMPS, 95. Few doors from rue de la Paix.

SUNDAY, APRIL 25, 1897.

AU BON MARCHÉ

Maison Aristide BOUCICAUT

PARIS | **PARIS**

Magasins de Nouveautés offering the most complete the richest and the most elegant choice of all classes of goods.

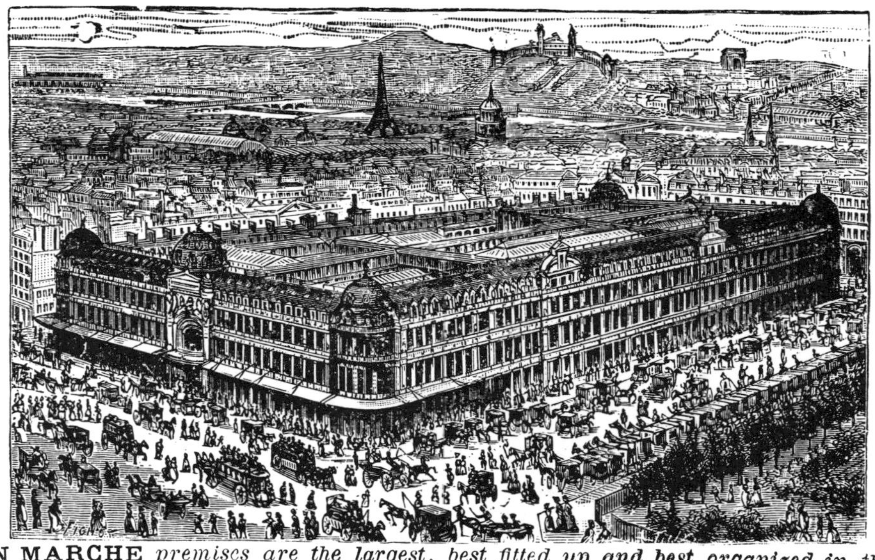

The system of selling everything at a small profit and of a thoroughly reliable quality is strictly maintained at the BON MARCHÉ

The BON MARCHE *premises are the largest, best fitted up and best organized in the World,* and form one of the most remarkable sights in PARIS.

INTERPRETERS FOR ALL LANGUAGES.

MANY FORMS OF FLYING MACHINES.

Outbreak of Invention in America Which May Rival the Bicycle Craze.

MANY PATENTS ALREADY FILED.

Some Have Succeeded Partially, but Most of Them Are in the "Model" Stage of Progress.

MR. FREYMANN'S ODD IDEA.

He Starts on a Bicycle, Others Adopt the Kite Principle, and Others the Balloon.

EXPLOSIVES AS A MOTIVE POWER

To judge from the newspapers that have recently arrived from the United States, the flying machine craze bids fair to soon eclipse the bicycle craze. Hundreds of

PROFESSOR OCTAVE CHANUTE'S FLYING MACHINE.

flying machines are being experimented with in all parts of the country.

At the Patent Office in Washington scarcely a day goes by which does not witness the filing of an application for letters patent upon some new aerial device. Their name is legion. All of them have attained some efficiency. Mr. Octave Chanute, ex-president of the American Society of Engineers, has, with his assistant, Mr. A. M. Herring, been actually fly-

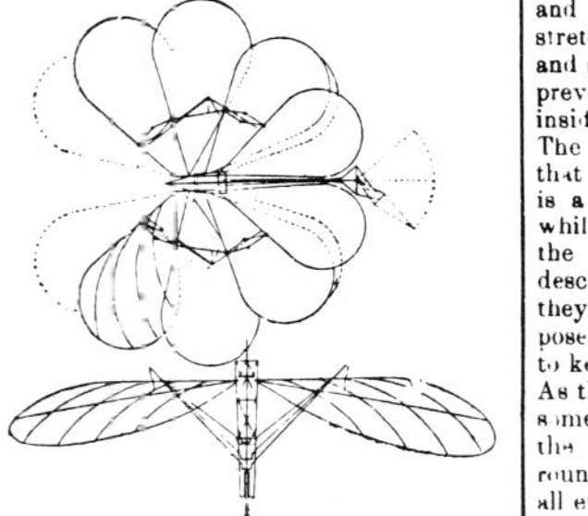

WING OF MR. FREYMANN'S MACHINE.

ing about the shores of Lake Michigan, near Dune Park in Indiana, in a flying machine which is described in the Sunday *Journal*. With the aid of the Herring regulator more than seventy-five successful flights were accomplished within a week, some of them three or four hundred feet in length, at an altitude of thirty feet.

A FLYING BICYCLE.

Mr. Oscar Freymann is the inventor of a brand-new flying machine which has several

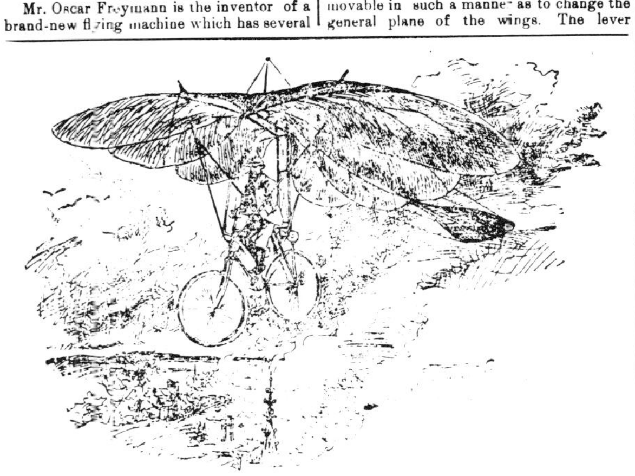

MR FREYMANN'S MACHINE.

novel features, and which, from his success in experimenting with a model, the *Sun* declares, bids fair to make a decided advance toward the solution of the problem of aerial navigation. A full-sized machine is now being constructed in New York city, under the inventor's supervision, and he expects that it will be finished and ready for trial in about two months.

Speaking broadly, Mr. Freymann's machine is a return to the principles upon which inventors have generally worked before Herr Otto Lilienthal of Berlin cut away from them two or three years ago, and contrived a machine by means of which he succeeded in flying, or rather in soaring, over considerable distances. The most vital defect of Lilienthal's aeroplane was the difficulty of accurately calculating the downward soar and the point at which the machine would reach the earth. Mr. Freymann's machine will be fitted with a lever, by means of which the tilt of the wings may be changed accurately and gradually as the emergency requires. Another novel feature of his machine is a bicycle arrangement, one of the functions of which is to assist in starting and alighting.

Mr. Freymann's plan is to start from the ordinary ground level. The bicycle is ridden along for a short distance, and when a certain degree of speed is attained the air pressure opens the wings and the machine begins to rise from the earth, the wing mechanism being worked also by the bicycle pedals. Thus Mr. Freymann's machine differs from Lilienthal's in being fitted for motive power, to be supplied by the legs. The hands are left free to manipulate two levers, one which regulates the tilt of the wings and another which operates a tail or rudder, fixed in a vertical plane behind.

Mr. Freymann is a Russian, about forty years old, and he has been studying the flying-machine problem for nearly fifteen years. He was born in Mitau, Livonia, and studied mechanical engineering in Germany. While at the University he studied the literature of the subject and went over carefully the plans of other inventors. He also examined many models of flying-machines and studied their defects. Soon after graduating he went to work as an engineer in the construction of railroads in Russia, and for twelve years he has been developing his idea of a flying-machine, subject to the interruptions caused by his professional duties.

The plans for Mr. Freymann's machine provide for eight wings, four on each side. They are to be concavo-convex, the form which nearly all recent inventors have agreed upon as essential. They come to a point where they join the body of the machine, and at the extremity are broad and rounded. They are to be of silk, stretched on a frame of light steel or willow, and stoutly braced on the convex side to prevent them from breaking or being turned inside out by the pressure of the air. The motion of the wings is based upon that of an eagle's. Mr. Freymann is a sportsman, and he studied this motion while stationed in Asia Minor. The tips of the wings, all of which work together, describe an ellipse. As they go forward they move upward slightly, at an angle supposed to give just enough sustaining power to keep the machine going ahead on a level. As the wings drop back they close together somewhat, and then they spread open to the full again as they rise on the next round. This is Mr Freymann's theory, at all events, and he says it will work out in practice.

The mechanism of the machine is comparatively simple, as may be seen by the accompanying plans. The wings are moved forward and upward and then downward and backward by means of steel rods connected with two wheels, which are revolved together by chains running from the pedals. The lever which is grasped by the right hand is connected by steel wires with the overhead structure, part of which is movable in such a manner as to change the general plane of the wings. The lever grasped by the left hand is connected in a similar manner with the rudder. The entire mechanism is under the control of these three things Gravitation and the wind are expected to do the rest.

The expense of building the trial machine will be about $600. In quantities they should be manufactured for $200 or $300 apiece, so that if the machine is successful, there is no reason why any well-regulated family should be without one.

WITH MOVABLE CYLINDERS.

One of the most startling of these inventions is that of Mr. James Sledon Cowdon, of Vienna, Fairfax County, Virginia. The claims which Mr. Cowdon makes for his invention are so astounding that, to most people, they will appear incredible, but he declares solemnly that he has actually solved the problem of aerial navigation, and that the only obstacle that now stands in his way is the necessity of conscripting capital with

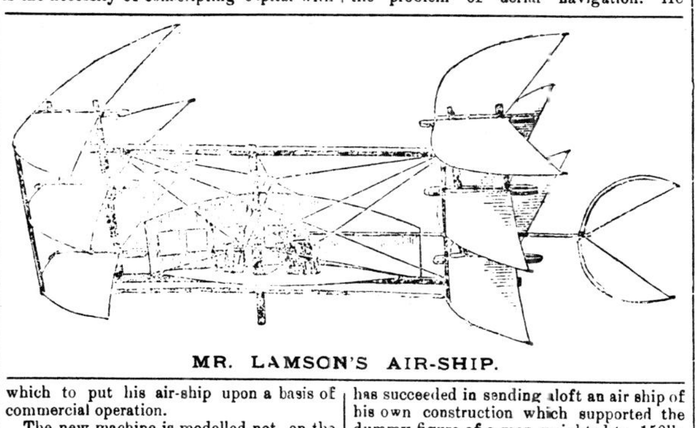

MR. LAMSON'S AIR-SHIP.

which to put his air-ship upon a basis of commercial operation.

The new machine is modelled not on the bird principle, but rather upon that of the fish in the water. While a bird cannot remain at rest in the air a fish can poise at perfect rest, can raise or lower himself by inflating or contracting his bladders. This is the idea upon which Mr. Cowdon bases his theories.

He has rejected also the old balloon motion. The balloon, he argues, is entirely at the mercy of the wind, and is compelled simply to drift with any current, thus being rendered practically useless for purposes of volitional transportation. But with his own machine Mr. Cowdon claims to be able to poise in the air at any distance from the ground, to rise and fall as softly as a feather would go to earth. He can with his apparatus, he declares, travel through the air at the rate of 100 miles an hour in the face of any current, and, what is more, the machine is always thoroughly under the control of the engineer.

The Cowdon machine consists of three cigar-shaped cylinders, two of which are placed on a level, and the third, which is midway between the two, is elevated several feet above them. These cylinders are filled with hydrogen or any similar gas, and when inflated will have a lifting power in proportion to their size. They are so shaped as to present the least possible resistance to the wind, and yet give a good surface for the expansion of the gas.

Just between each of the propellers and the engine are the two rudders which steer the affair in the face of the wind or enable the engineer to tack against it as may be desired. The motive power, Mr. Cowdon expects, will be steam. He is experimenting with a new engine which gives enormous force with very little expenditure of coal. Electricity could also be used, but as both steam and electricity can be secured from very small engines of great power, he will not decide this point until after several experiments.

Beneath the cylinders will hang the car containing the passengers. This car will be of wickerwork or some similar material, and will hold about twenty people. Sections can also be reserved for the conveyance of mail and express matter.

PROPELLED BY EXPLOSIONS.

A second machine, newly patented by Mr. Sumpter B. Battey, of New York, also lays strong claim to all the advantages of safety, speed and comfort for the voyage in the regions of the upper air. The cigar-shaped balloon that supports it is of thin sheet

MR. SUMPTER B. BATTEY'S AIR-SHIP.

Propelled by explosions of nitro-glycerine.

aluminium, and is non-collapsible, while the car carried beneath will accommodate a dozen passengers. It may be steered with perfect ease, and its upward and downward flight is controlled by means of wings, whose adjustment is altered at will by a lever.

But the most remarkable thing about this flying machine is the method of its propulsion. Its motive power is obtained by a series of explosions. At the rear end there is a sort of cup that opens rearward. Into this pellets of nitro-glycerine are dropped at the rate of six a minute. They drop out of a magazine tube, the action of which is controlled by clockwork. Each pellet in falling closes an electric circuit, and thus develops a spark which ignites and explodes it.

The aluminium balloon is exhausted of air before being filled with hydrogen. To prevent it from collapsing it is strengthened inside by a steel framework. The car, fastened beneath, has large windows.

BALLOON AND ROCKET.

One of the most remarkable of the recently invented airships is that designed by Mr. Carl Erickson, which is to be exhibited at the Mechanics' Fair, in San Francisco. It combines the silk balloon, filled with hydrogen gas: the cylinder, containing the motive mechanism, and the balancing wings. Electricity is the propelling force. The propeller, made of aluminium, regulates the speed. The car, which carries twelve passengers, in made of aluminium and prepared paper. Underneath it are regulators to control the upward and downward flight

Still another model is that of Dr. A. C. Smith, of San Francisco. It resembles in shape the body of a rocket, has a conical prow and at the stern a propelling screw, which is worked by electricity. Two wings, one on either side of the ship, and running its entire length, rise and fall from the top of the cylinder. The propelling screw will make 1,500 revolutions in a minute. The wings make from fifteen to twenty strokes a minute. The cylinder is 145ft. long, inclusive of the cone, and 39ft. in diameter. It contains 89,593 cubic feet of hydrogen. More than 16,000 square feet of aluminium are used. The engines are made of it. The pilot house is in the forward end, and from it three rudders at the rear are controlled. The inventor hopes to fly with this machine from San Francisco to New York in forty hours.

For twenty years Mr. Charles H. Lamson, of Portland, Me., has been studying the problem of aerial navigation. He has succeeded in sending aloft an air ship of his own construction which supported the dummy figure of a man weighted to 150lb.

The machine was elevated to a height of 600ft. A fifteen-mile breeze was blowing at the time A strong hempen rope was attached to the air-ship, and when the end of the rope was reached the air-ship tugged at it with such vigor as to snap it like a piece of twine. This accident tested the

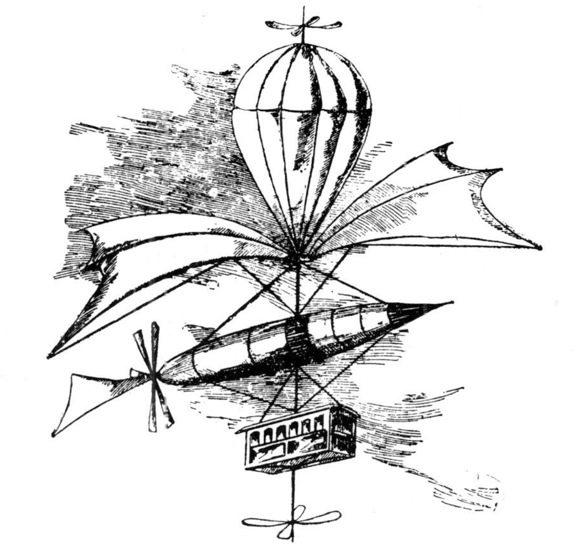

MR. CARL ERICKSON'S AIR-SHIP.

machine in another way, and the test was full of significance.

The framework of the Lamson air-ship is constructed of light, but tough spruce. The frame is braced and strengthened with the finest piano wire, which is tested more severely than the wire that forms the spokes in bicycles. Light cambric is stretched tightly over the frame.

The air-ship is 32ft. long. Each wing is 28ft. wide. Between the upper and lower surfaces of the sails there is a difference of 7ft. A light mast, 14ft long, pierces the framework which supports the sails. The carriage intended to hold a man swings from the centre of the machine. The lever by which the air-ship is controlled is attached to the framework. With it the front set of sails can be raised and lowered, and whichever way they point the ship will go.

Mr. Lamson says there is no limit to the possibilities of his air-ship. He thinks he can build one which, without difficulty, will carry 1,500 pounds up into the air, and float

DR. C. A. SMITH'S MODEL AIR-SHIP.

it there without a hitch of any kind. He is going to build such a ship to prove it. He predicts that within a short time men will sail through the air as an ordinary, everyday thing.

He Knew What He Was About.

"I understand you have got married, Jones."

"Yes, my friend, I've done it at last."

"By Jove, you've got courage to get married in these days when women are so extravagantly fond of dresses."

"Oh, I looked out for that. My wife don't wear much of anything."

"What?"

"No. I married a ballet girl."—Boston *Courier*.

DR. RICHET'S FLYING MACHINE.

A Huge Rocket-shaped Machine Twenty-four Mètres Long.

STEAM POWER TO BE USED.

A Small Engine Built with a Maximum of Force and a Minimum of Weight.

[FROM OUR SPECIAL CORRESPONDENT.]

TOULON, Oct. 2.—Of all the problems which have exercised the ingenuity of mankind during the last few years, none has aroused more general interest than the difficult one of aerial navigation. Not long ago Dr. Charles Abbott Smith, of San Francisco, seemed to be on the point of attaining success with the gigantic aeroplane which he had constructed, and undeterred by failure, is still seeking a solution. In France, too, many scientific men have turned their attention to this question, and foremost among them is Dr. Richet, who is pursuing his experiments on the shores of the Mediterranean, a few miles to the east of the port of Toulon.

A rapid drive through the country, charmingly pretty but looking rather sad under the gray autumn sky, brought me to Carqueiranne, where Dr. Richet's aerostatic park is situated, and where he lives in a neat little villa built in the English style. The savant receives as few visitors as possible, and it was with some difficulty that I persuaded the servant to take in my card, but I had not long to wait. He came out, smiling, the red ribbon of the Legion of Honor in the buttonhole of his brown suit and a Savoyard beret covering his iron-gray head, and asked courteously what he could do for me.

"No, not an interview," he cried, when I explained the object of my visit; "I detest interviews and have never given one. Besides, why should I tell you what I can explain just as well myself in the reviews to which I contribute, or at the meetings of the learned societies of which I am a member? The columns of several leading newspapers are open to me if I wish it, and I do not see why I should give the NEW YORK HERALD what I can publish just as well myself if I should have anything of interest to say. Besides, why all this fuss about my name?"

The doctor was not inexorable, however, and after a pause he added: "For the moment I can only tell you two things and give you a permission which no one has hitherto obtained.

"Firstly, let me tell you that the articles which have been published concerning my researches or schemes, though most kindly towards me, have not been distinguished by their accuracy. I have seen some that were most fantastic. Secondly, I have never spoken to anyone about my experiments, as I prefer to treat of them, when the time comes, in my papers or reviews."

"Could you not briefly give me the principal outlines?"

"No. But take this card and visit yourself the hall in which I conduct my experiments. You will tell what you have seen, your impressions, and I should much prefer that."

After thanking the doctor for his courtesy, and armed with the card which was to introduce me to the engineer in charge of the work, I went on to the promontory of the Penan battery, which overlooks the immense workshop in which Dr. Richet conducts his experiments. This workshop is surrounded on all sides by a high wooden fence, which effectually protects it from indiscreet curiosity.

From the main entrance, which is on the east, runs a strongly built wooden platform, which goes down to the sea and projects some thirty feet over the water. On it are four steel rails, one pair to carry the gigantic aeroplane down to its launching point, the other smaller, for experiments with the model.

In the workshop, which has an area of six hundred square mètres, a number of men were busily engaged, amid piles of cases and planks, in completing and adjusting portions of the great machine, the body of which is twenty-four mètres in length. In shape it resembles a huge rocket. The hinder part tapers and widens from top to bottom. The front is almost exactly in the form of a ship's ram, with the top flattened.

ALL OF WOOD AND STEEL.

Its width is 1m. 20cm., and in the centre are two large wings, which bring the total width to 23 mètres. The body is constructed entirely of thin pine planking, with bamboo ribs, which are strengthened by cross-pieces of steel wire. The wings, which can be opened and shut at will, are made of the same material. The two screws will be placed near the wings and not at the front or back.

It will be seen, therefore, that this machine, which is perhaps destined to solve the problem of aerial navigation, is not made, as has been said, of aluminium. The only materials used are light, strong wood, bamboo and steel. The body will be entirely covered with Chinese silk of the kind used for balloons.

All the pieces which make up the apparatus are as light as possible, and to obtain this lightness is one of the great difficulties with which Dr. Richet has had to contend.

Abandoning the system of electric propellers usually adopted, Dr. Richet has decided to use as the motive power of his machine steam, supplied by a little engine, which is not of a special character, but has been arranged, after careful study, to produce the maximum of power with a minimum of weight and volume. This engine is expected to work, at the first trials, for a period not exceeding ten minutes.

It is probable that the first serious experiments will not be made until some months have passed. The only trial of the model, made some time ago, was not altogether satisfactory, but the experiment enabled the doctor to perceive certain faults, which have been corrected in the large machine.

PRACTICAL AND PATRIOTIC.

TO THE EDITOR OF THE HERALD:—

No loyal American can fail to resent "U.S.A's" insult to his own flag (if indeed it be his own?) but at the same time we should recognise the justness of another portion of his letter.

Americans on the Continent are too prone to advertise their nationality, and in many instances this desire is accomplished by a liberal use of the American flag.

Whether it be on the scale adopted by the person in Paris who, on the occasion of the Tsar's visit, covered his housefront with huge flags, or in a lesser way, the effect is always displeasing to well-bred Americans. Why should Americans travel abroad with United States flags tied to their trunks, United States flag-pins in their cravats, United States flag "buttons" on their coat lapels, United States flags for pocket-handkerchiefs? (I have twice seen such handkerchiefs not only carried but *used* by their patriotic and practical possessors.)

Travelers from other nations are as loyal to their country and as proud of their native land as we are, but their love of fatherland is less ostentatiously displayed. Why should we indulge in patriotic exhibitions which are in questionable taste?

"Patriotism" so offensively displayed as to cause sneers among Europeans can scarcely be true patriotism when it really lowers our country in the eyes of onlooking foreigners.

I wish the HERALD would create as much agitation on this subject as it has already done on the tip question.

If all Americans traveling for the first time on the Continent were aware of the fact—a fact which must be known to all wide-traveled Americans—that it is the loudest class of Americans who are the loudest in their patriotism, they would, I am sure, avoid the error which is now so common.

God grant that some day "Old Glory" may be seen in every port of Europe and all the world, not in the shape of pocket-handkerchiefs, but flying over American vessels as it did in past days.

"FOR AMERICA."

Paris, October 16, 1896.

SUNDAY, DECEMBER 23, 18!4.

CAPTAIN DREYFUS CONDEMNED.

Reading of the Judgment by the President of the Court-Martial.

LIFELONG IMPRISONMENT

To Be Preceded by the Terrible Punishment of Military Degradation.

The trial of Captain Dreyfus, which has provided the entire Paris press with matter for comment during the past six weeks, was concluded yesterday. The prisoner, by the unanimous verdict of the Court, is sentenced to imprisonment for life in some fortified place and to military degradation.

At five minutes past seven o'clock yesterday morning the *Soleil* states that he passed along the rue Cherche-Midi, in civilian dress, pale and with bowed head. At one o'clock he appeared in uniform before the Council of War.

THE JUDGMENT.

At five minutes to seven a cry of "Present arms!" rang through the hall and Colonel Maurel and his colleagues entered and took their seats. Captain Dreyfus was not present, military custom requiring that an accused should be absent while sentence was pronounced on him.

Colonel Maurel, after a short silence shouted aloud the single word "Jugement." He then read as follows :—

"In the name of the French nation, and by unanimity of voices, *Monsieur* Dreyfus, Alfred, Captain of Artillery, stagiary of the army staff, guilty of having delivered to a Foreign Power or to its agents, documents of interest to the national defence, and of having thus practised machinations and kept up communications with the said foreign Power in order to encourage it to commit hostilities against France or to procure the said Power the means of doing so.

"Consequently sentenced him, also by unanimity of voices, to the penalty of transportation for life to some fortified place and to military degradation.

As soon as the words were pronounced a voice in the hall was heard to shout "Vive la patrie!"

FRIDAY, JANUARY 14, 1898.

M. ZOLA STIRS UP THE DREYFUS CASE.

The Famous Novelist's Letter to the President of the Republic Discussed in the Chamber.

PROSECUTION ANNOUNCED

Lieut.-Colonel Picquart Arrested and Imprisoned—Major Esterhazy Asks to Be Retired.

M. Emile Zola's letter to the President of the Republic, which was published in the *Aurore* yesterday morning, accusing General Billot, the Minister of War, with having in his possession the proofs of Dreyfus' innocence, created a great sensation in Paris. The matter came before the Chamber of Deputies at a quarter past five o'clock yesterday afternoon, and the Government announced that proceedings were going to be taken to put a stop to the campaign which was being waged against the army.

"J'ACCUSE! . . ."

M. Emile Zola's Letter to the President of the Republic.

The letter which M. Emile Zola publishes in the *Aurore* under the title of "J'accuse. . ." is addressed to the President of the Republic. He appeals to M. Félix Faure to intervene in favor of what he declares to be truth and justice.

M. Zola's contention is that the *deus ex machina* of the Dreyfus case is Colonel du Paty de Clam. This officer, he states, delights in romantic intrigues, anonymous letters, mysterious women who at night carry about with them crushing proofs. He it was who thought of dictating the *bordereau* to Dreyfus; who dreamed of studying him in a room, the walls, ceiling and floor of which were covered with mirrors; who wished to enter Captain Dreyfus' cell and cast upon the face of the sleeping man a flood of light from a dark lantern with the object of surprising his crime in the emotion of his sudden awakening. It was Colonel du Paty de Clam who arrested Dreyfus and placed him in secret, and who then went to the house of Mme. Dreyfus to tell her that if she spoke a word her husband was lost!

After laying particular emphasis on the worthlessness of the indictment, the writer comes to the Esterhazy case and says that the only honest man in the whole affair is Lieut.-Colonel Picquart, who is charged with having forged the card-telegram, which put the Ministry of War into a state of consternation, because the officials saw that there was a danger of the Dreyfus case being reopened.

M. Zola further contends that they could not hope that the second court-martial would undo the work of the first.

The writer then brings a series of charges against Colonel du Paty de Clam, General Mercier, General Billot, General de Boisdeffre, and General Gonze, General de Pellieux and Major Ravary; the three experts, Belhomme, Varinard and Couard; against the officials of the Ministry of War for having carried on an "abominable" press campaign, and against the first court-martial for having convicted a man on secret evidence.

M. Emile Zola concludes as follows :—

"By bringing these charges I am not ignorant that I bring myself under Articles 30 and 31 of the Press Law of July 29, 1881, which punishes for defamation. I am voluntarily running the risk.

"As to the men I accuse, I do not know them, I have never seen them, I have against them neither rancor nor hatred. To me they are only beings, spirits of social wrong-doing. And the act which I accomplish here is only a revolutionary means of hastening the outburst of truth and justice.

"I have only one passion, that for light, in the name of humanity which has suffered so much and which has a right to happiness. My passionate protest is but the cry of my soul. Let them dare then to bring me before the Assizes and hold the inquiry in the light of day!

"I wait."

JANUARY 16, 1898.

PARIS STUDENTS DENOUNCE M. ZOLA.

Fifteen Hundred Cross the River, Posing as Champions of the Army.

KISSING GAMBETTA'S STATUE

Some Fights with the Police—Noisy Demonstrations Before Newspaper Offices.

The students of the Latin Quarter continue to demonstrate against M. Zola, thus posing as the champions of the army. The effervescence yesterday was, however, more gay than annoying, though the Prefecture of Police had taken serious precautions—perhaps more serious than the circumstances necessitated.

About three hundred students formed a *monôme* yesterday morning before the Panthéon to "conspuer Zola," but this demonstration, says the *Figaro*, was dispersed without difficulty.

At the close of M. Beauregard's lecture the students came rushing from the lecture-room, crying: "Conspuez *l'Aurore!*" "A bas les traîtres!" One of them, leading the procession which had been formed, carried on the end of a pole a placard representing M. Emile Zola, and underneath which was written: "Zola à la potence."

The students, who numbered about one thousand five hundred, went to the Taverne du Panthéon, entering by one door, defiling and passing out by another. At the exit the police routed them.

Turning round, they next assembled on the place du Carrousel.

Some took the Pont-Royal, others the Pont du Carrousel and others the Pont des Arts. Assembled before Gambetta's statue, they uttered their usual war-whoops of "Conspuez Zola! Conspuez l'*Aurore!* A bas le syndicat!" Some students tried to climb up the base of the monument to kiss the statue.

SEPTEMBER 4. 1898.

DREYFUS CASE TO BE REVISED.

By a Majority of Its Members, the Cabinet Decides to Have It Reheard.

MINISTER OF WAR RESIGNS.

He Declares He Is Still Firmly Convinced that Captain Dreyfus Was a Traitor.

SUNDAY, SEPTEMBER 18, 1898.

MINISTERS DECIDE ON REVISION.

General Zurlinden and M. Tillaye the Only Dissentients in the Cabinet.

BOTH TENDER THEIR RESIGNATION.

General Chanoine Takes the Portfolio of Minister of War and M. Godin that of Public Works.

NO EXCITEMENT IN PARIS

Great Rush for Evening Papers on the Boulevards and the Subject Everywhere Discussed.

BOURSE FAVORABLY AFFECTED.

The decision of the Council of Ministers to enter on the preliminary stage of revising the Dreyfus case has caused an almost universal feeling of relief. The Brisson Ministry, about which all sorts of sinister predictions have been made, went quietly through the ordeal. M. Sarrien, Minister of Justice, explained his reasons, as a judicial authority, for deciding that there ought to be a revision, altogether apart from the question of the guilt or innocence of Captain Dreyfus, in order that the admitted illegality of his conviction might be repaired.

The Cabinet unhesitatingly adopted the views of the Minister of Justice, the only dissentents being General Zurlinden, Minister of War, and M. Tillaye, Minister of Public Works. Both Ministers sent in their resignation during the afternoon, but there were no signs of a Ministerial crisis. M. Brisson had already provided their successors, in the persons of General Chanoine and M. Godin, a Senator.

Thus everything will go on as usual and the case will at once be referred to the Revision Commission, composed of representatives of the Court of Cassation and the Ministry of Justice.

ALFRED DREYFUS.

MONDAY, AUGUST 7, 1899.

CAUSE CÉLÈBRE OF THE CENTURY.

Court-Martial of Captain Dreyfus Will Begin at Rennes This Morning.

THE CHARGE AGAINST HIM.

Accused of Having Communicated the Documents in the "Bordereau" to a Foreign Power.

THE ISSUE NARROWED DOWN.

Court of Cassation Declares that the "Bordereau" Was the Work of Major Esterhazy.

At seven o'clock this morning the greatest trial in the judicial annals of any country will begin. Captain Dreyfus, round whose name a conflict has raged for two long years, a conflict unexampled even in a country that has seen so many stirring political crises as France, will for the second time come up for judgment before his peers. It is now nearly five years (in 1894) since a report spread in the French press that an officer of the Great General Staff had been arrested for treason. A few days later it transpired that the accused man was Captain Alfred Dreyfus, a Jewish officer of the Second Bureau of the General Staff. In December he was brought before a court-martial, found guilty, sentenced to imprisonment for life in a fortress and public degradation before the troops of Paris. This painful ceremony was carried out on January 5, 1895. Captain Dreyfus was brought before the assembled troops, his epaulettes were torn from his shoulders, the facings and buttons from his uniform, his sword was snapped in two and flung at his feet, and General Darras publicly declared him unworthy to wear the French uniform. He was then led round the hollow square formed by the troops. At each corner he shouted, "I am innocent; vive la France!" A few days afterwards he was transported to the Ile de Ré, and thence to the Ile du Diable, off the coast of French Guiana.

The "Bordereau."

Some time afterwards the charge on which he had been condemned transpired. About the middle of the year 1894 a secret agent of the French Government brought to the Ministry of War a document alleged to have been found in the waste-paper basket of Colonel von Schwarzkoppen, the German military attaché. The document, which has since become historical under the name of the "bordereau," was pieced together, and found to be a list of confidential military documents, which its writer had forwarded to Colonel von Schwarzkoppen. An inquiry was held into the affair by Colonel Sandherr, Chief of the Intelligence Department of the General Staff. The writing was thought to have a resemblance to that of Captain Dreyfus. It was then submitted to experts in handwriting. Three declared it was his handwriting while two declared it was not.

The other evidence against him was chiefly circumstantial, and was in itself of little value. The only exception was the testimony of Colonel (then Major) Henry. "I have been informed by a diplomatist," he said, "that there is a traitor in the General Staff, and," he added, pointing to Captain Dreyfus, "there he sits." An officer on the court martial asked him to be more precise in his declaration, but he received the reply, "The 'képi' of an officer does not know what is in his head."

With the trial and condemnation of Captain Dreyfus the affair for two years' time seemed to have been settled for once and all. In 1897, however, M. Bernard Lazare, a well-known and much-respected writer on the French press, published a pamphlet in which for the first time he threw doubts on the guilt of the prisoner of the Ile du Diable.

M. Bernard Lazare in writing his pamphlet, was inspired only by a conviction of Captain Dreyfus' innocence, derived from communications with his family. He pointed out how out of the question it was that an officer with a private income of 35,000fr. a year and a brilliant future before him, should have betrayed his country for a few thousand francs, for which he had no possible need.

This pamphlet it was that started the avalanche. The reply was the famous article in the "Eclair," in which it was stated that Captain Dreyfus was condemned, not solely on the evidence before the court-martial, but that a secret "dossier" had been laid before the officers composing it after they had retired to consider their judgment. These documents, it was stated, were not shown either to Captain Dreyfus or his counsel.

These various discoveries produced a considerable sensation at the General Staff. Colonel du Paty de Clam, the officer who had been entrusted with the preliminary investigation into the charge against Captain Dreyfus, and Colonel Henry, the principal witness against him, thought it their duty to warn Major Esterhazy of the charges impending against him. Colonel Picquart, however, was in Tunis, M. Scheurer-Kestner was in pourparlers with General Billot, Minister of War, so that there seemed no immediate danger, when, all of a sudden, M. Mathieu Dreyfus formally denounced Major Esterhazy. This brought matters to a climax, and the military authorities were forced to take action. Major Esterhazy was called before a court-martial, and General de Pellieux was instructed with the preliminary investigation. It has since been proved by the inquiry of the Court of Cassation that while Major Esterhazy was being nominally prosecuted, he was being secretly protected and kept "au courant" by his supposed accusers. The result of the trial was his acquittal. The experts in handwriting swore that the "bordereau" was apparently in the handwriting of Major Esterhazy, but that this resemblance was due to the fact that it had been traced by the real criminal from the major's writing. The evidence was, of course, in flagrant contradiction with that of the experts in the Dreyfus court-martial.

On the Ile du Diable.

The "Matin" this morning publishes a copy of the official reports made to the Colonial Ministry on the treatment of Captain Dreyfus.

These confirm the facts stated by Professor Havet that Captain Dreyfus was placed in irons, that his hut was surrounded by a palisade, shuting out his view of the sea, and that there was a false alarm of a rescue which almost led to the prisoner being shot by one of his warders, who had orders to shoot him on any sign of an attempt to escape.

SCENE OF DREYFUS' FOUR-AND-A-HALF YEARS' IMPRISONMENT.

THE NEW YORK HERALD.

WHOLE NO: 23,039. EUROPEAN EDITION—PARIS, SUNDAY, SEPTEMBER 10, 1899—WITH SUPPLEMENT. PARIS & DEPARTMENTS, 25c.; LONDON, 2½d.

CAPTAIN DREYFUS FOUND GUILTY BY THE COURT-MARTIAL.

SENTENCE, TEN YEARS IN PRISON.

M. Marcel Prévost Says That a Deathly Stupor Greeted the Verdict of the Court.

FIVE FOR CONVICTION, TWO FOR ACQUITTAL.

Extenuating Circumstances Found Which Mitigate a Little the Old Sentence.

GOVERNMENT PRECAUTIONS.

A Great Display of Troops in Rennes and Elaborate Police Measures in Paris.

A NEW APPEAL TO BE TAKEN.

In Its Legal Aspect the Court of Cassation Is Alone Competent to Revise.

Captain Dreyfus was condemned yesterday afternoon by the court-martial at Rennes by a vote of five to two.

A majority of the Court found extenuating circumstances and he was sentenced to ten years' imprisonment.

Although there was great excitement, no serious disturbances are reported either in Paris or the provinces.

LIKE A DEATH KNELL.

Silence Greeted the Verdict, Which to M. Marcel Prevost Seemed Like a Sentence Against France.

[SPECIAL TO THE HERALD.]

RENNES, Samedi.—Dreyfus est condamné.

On lira les conditions nouvelles de la peine qu'il devra subir. Elles atténuent un peu la rigueur de l'ancien arrêt.

Mais.... il est condamné. Il va être dégradé de nouveau.

Une stupeur de mort a accuelli cette sentence.

Hélas! depuis quelques jours je ne la prévoyais que trop! Mais notre conscience se refusait à y croire.

Qu'on ne me demande pas de commentaires sur un tel événement. Mon cœur d'homme et de Français est trop douloureux. Il me semble que c'est mon pays qui vient d'entendre son arrêt.

MARCEL PREVOST.

TRANSLATION.

RENNES, Saturday.—Dreyfus is condemned.

The fresh conditions of the sentence he has to undergo will be found elsewhere. They slightly attenuate the rigor of the former sentence.

But.... he is condemned. He is going to be degraded afresh.

A deathly stupor was caused by this sentence.

Alas! for some days past I only too well foresaw it! But my conscience could not believe it.

No commentary must be expected from me on such an outcome. My heart as a man and a Frenchman is too sorrowful. It seems to me as if it were my country that had been passed in judgment.

MARCEL PREVOST.

Capitaine Beauvais *Commandant Merle* *Colonel Jouaust* *Capitaine Parfait* *Lieut.-colonel de Brongniart* *Commandant Bréon* *Commandant Profilet*

THE JUDGES OF THE COURT-MARTIAL.

[From the "Petit Bleu." Reproduction forbidden.]

BREAKING THE NEWS.

Me. Labori Bears the Bad Tidings—Dreyfus's First Thought Is for His Wife.

It was from the mouth of Me. Labori, who, says the "Figaro," was accompanied by his two secretaries, Mes. Hild and Monira, that Dreyfus learnt his second condemnation in the little room adjoining the audience hall. He was still—for the verdict was afterwards read to him in presence of the guard under arms—when Me. Labori approached him. Me. Demange, too much moved and exhausted by the great effort he had just made, had left this painful task to his colleague.

"You are condemned," murmured Me. Labori, clasping Dreyfus in his arms: "you are condemned to imprisonment, but you will not go back to the Ile du Diable."

Tearing himself from his counsel's embrace, and shaking hands with him and with his secretary, Dreyfus, who showed no signs of emotion, simply said:—

"Console my wife"

A few minutes later the Clerk of the Court read the verdict to him.

It is stated that Mme. Dreyfus received the news with resignation and courage.

After Me. Labori had broken the news to Dreyfus Me. Demange went to see him. Dreyfus embraced him and burst into tears. Me. Demange, who was much moved, withdrew almost immediately, and the interview was a very short one.

Me. Demange, Me. Labori, and Dr. Pozzi left Rennes for Paris last night.

READING THE SENTENCE.

Dreyfus Remains Calm, Upright and Soldierlike—Not the Least Sign of Emotion.

It was at five o'clock, says the "Figaro," that the fatal verdict was officially communicated to the condemned man. After the public had left the troops entered the "Salles des Fêtes," and Major Carrière ordered the clerk of the Court to read the sentence.

Captain Dreyfus listened to it upright, unmoved, soldier-like, "in the attitude," said an eye witness, "in which he would have heard his acquittal."

When the reading was over a captain of gendarmerie requested Dreyfus to follow him to prison.

"I was anxious," says the "Figaro's" correspondent, "to see him make for the last time this passage which he had made three hours before, with his heart full of hope. He left the Lycée with that calm which has never deserted him for five weeks. One would really have said that nothing had been changed in his life.

"As calm, as proud as on the previous day, he passed for the last time between the backs of the soldiers, and then climbed the little staircase which leads to his cell."

MADAME DREYFUS.

Displaying Great Courage—Scarcely Dared to Hope for an Acquittal.

M. Chincholle telegraphs as follows from Rennes to the "Figaro":—

I went to the house where Mme. Dreyfus is living, but, as will be well understood, I did not ask to see her.

I was received by one of her relatives, who told me of the courage which she was displaying.

I understood that if in the Dreyfus family wishes which were thought to be founded were entertained for an acquittal, it was scarcely hoped for.

They had coldly examined, for reasons foreign to justice, the possibility of the maintenance of the condemnation. Already they had made up their minds to remain at Rennes as long as the prisoner remained there. Of his innocence, of course, no one of them has the slightest doubt.

JUDGMENT OF THE COURT.

Text of the Decision, Finding Captain Dreyfus Guilty and Condemning Him to Ten Years' Imprisonment.

In the name of the French people:

This day, September 9, 1899, the Court Martial of the Tenth Region of Army Corps, sitting with closed doors:

The President put the following question:

"Dreyfus, Alfred, brevet-captain of the 14th Regiment of Artillery, stagiare at the General Staff, is he guilty of having in 1894, provoked machinations or entered into communication with a Foreign Power or its agents, to engage it to commit hostilities or undertake war against France, or to procure for it the means, by delivering to the said Power the notes and documents enumerated in the 'bordereau'?"

The votes having been collected separately, beginning with the lowest rank, and the youngest in each grade, the president giving his opinion last of all:

The Court declares:

On the question:

By a majority of five votes to two, the accused is guilty.

By a majority there are extenuating circumstances.

In consequence of which, and at the request of the Government Commissioner, the president put the question, and again took the votes in the order indicated above.

In consequence, the Court, by a majority of five votes against two, condemns the above named Alfred Dreyfus to the penalty of ten years' detention, by the application of Clauses 76 of the Penal Code, 7 of the Law of October 8, 1830, Clause 5 of the Constitution of November 4, 1848, of the Law of June, 1850, of Clause 20 of the Penal Code and of Clauses 189, 267 and 132 of the Code of Military Justice.

Fixes at the minimum the duration of confinement, in accordance with Clause 9 of the Law of July 22, 1867, modified by that of December 13, 1871.

Orders the Government Commissioner to have read immediately, in his presence, the present judgment to the condemned before the guard assembled under arms, and to inform him that the law grants him a delay of twenty-four hours to appeal for a revision.

WEDNESDAY. SEPTEMBER 20, 1899 -

DREYFUS NOW FREE.

His Pardon Decided on at Yesterday's Council of Ministers.

HAS ALREADY BEEN SIGNED.

Will Only Appear in the "Journal Officiel" To-morrow Owing to Formalities.

HIS APPEAL IS WITHDRAWN.

The President's Act Will Not Prevent Captain Dreyfus Demanding a Revision of His Trial.

The news yesterday connected with the case of Captain Dreyfus was calculated to cause both pleasure and mourning to the partisans of that officer.

At the Cabinet Council it was decided to pardon him, and almost simultaneously the news arrived in Paris of the death of M. Scheurer-Kestner, the ex-Vice-President of the Senate, who first threw the weight of his influence into the scale when the question of the unfortunate officer's guilt or innocence was raised.

Thus the very day the man for whom he fought such a gallant fight was pardoned, he passed away without having known the success which had crowned his efforts.

Probably Free Now.

The pardon of Captain Dreyfus was decided on at the Council of Ministers held yesterday, but it was agreed, says the "Figaro," that, on account of certain formalities which had to be accomplished, it should not be published in the "Journal Officiel" until to-morrow morning.

The "Figaro" adds, however, that it has already been signed, and that Captain Dreyfus will have left the prison by the time the paper reaches its readers.

The appeal to the Council of Revision signed by Captain Dreyfus the day of his condemnation by the Rennes court-martial, has now been withdrawn, as the President of the Republic could not exercise his right of pardon so long as the case was "in pendente lite."

The pardon of the President of the Republic will not, however, prevent Captain Dreyfus appealing to the Court of Cassation to have a revision of his second court-martial.

FRIDAY, JUNE 7. 1901.

HAPPENINGS OF THE DAY IN THE "VILLE LUMIÈRE."

Sensation Caused at the Law Courts by a Prisoner Who Is Tattooed with the Story of the Dreyfus Case.

Charged with battery and assault before the Eighth Correctional Chamber, Auguste Formain, an ex-coachman, aspires, nevertheless, to high distinction among prisoners. His body, says the "Matin," is a pictorial presentment of the Dreyfus case.

While serving with the Bataillon d'Afrique, Formain came across an expert in the art of tattooing, who was also doing penance under the African sun. To wile the weary hours away, he tatooed Formain with 21 scenes from the famous "affaire." The work lasted eighteen months, and is of remarkable merit. Black, blue, red and green are the colors used.

The arms are adorned with medallions. The Court-martial adorns the abdomen, and the degradation scene takes up the entire back.

FRIDAY, JULY 13, 1906.

Supreme Court Proclaims Captain Dreyfus Innocent.

It Declares that Conviction Was Wrongly Secured and that Nothing Subsists of Charges Made.

TRIAL BY COURT-MARTIAL THEREFORE UNNECESSARY.

As Result of This Decision M. Dreyfus Resumes His Original Position in French Army.

HIS PROMOTION IS PROPOSED.

Lieutenant-Colonel Picquart, Dismissed for Defending Revision, to Become Brigadier-General.

After a long investigation by its Criminal Chamber, and after examining the case for revision in its every detail, the Court of Cassation, "toutes chambres réunies"—the supreme judicial authority in France—yesterday declared that Captain Alfred Dreyfus was wrongly condemned and that he is innocent of the charges of treason brought against him.

SUNDAY, JULY 18, 1897.

GOLD MINING FEVER STARTS IN ALASKA.

Over a Million Dollars in Dust and Nuggets Brought Back by Lucky Miners.

SEATTLE HAS GONE MINING MAD.

Policemen Resigning, Carmen Leaving Work and Merchants Making Ready to Join the Rush.

BIGGER THAN CALIFORNIA.

Compared With the Klondike Fields the Camps of '49 Were Poverty Hollows.

[SPECIAL DESPATCH TO THE HERALD.]

(By Commercial Cable.)

SEATTLE, WASH., July 17.—The steamship Portland arrived here to-day from St. Michael, Alaska, bringing more than a million dollars in gold dust and nuggets, most of which was taken out of the ground during the last three months.

FORTUNATE MINERS.

Sixty-eight miners were aboard, and hardly a man has less than $7,000. Two or three have more than $100,000.

Prospectors say that the yield of gold dust and nuggets at the Klondike placer goldfields and vicinity during the year is approximately $5,000,000 and declare that the gold mines of California are poverty hollows compared with the Klondike camp.

MINING-MAD.

These reports make this city mining-mad. Policemen are resigning and every street carman has raised his stake and given notice to the company. Merchants are neglecting their business to discuss the new El Dorado.

All classes are represented in the feverish rush for the North.

THE GOLD FIELDS OF ALASKA.

One sometimes hears pretty big stories in Washington about the extent and richness of the placer gold deposits of the Yukon Valley, and it must be confessed that they agree fairly with one another. The latest contributor to the fund of information on this subject is C. H. Hamilton, who is the secretary and assistant manager of the North-American Transportation and Trading Company, which maintains a line of steamers between Seattle and the Yukon, and has trading posts at Fort Cudahy, British Columbia, and at St. Michael, Weare and Circle City, Alaska.

"We are a long way from civilization at Fort Cudahy," said Mr. Hamilton, "and it takes one of the company's steamers thirty-five days to make the trip from Seattle. The route is west on the Pacific to the Aleutian Islands, thence north through Behring Sea to the mouth of the Yukon, a distance of 3,000 miles, and then up that river 2,000 miles more, a total of 5,000 miles. I have been there for the last five years and have seen an enormous development of the gold fields. Last year $5,000,000 were taken out, and I think that the output this year will be nearly double that. There are now 3,000 men at work in the basin of the Yukon. It is all placer mining, and only a small fraction of the gold-bearing district has been touched. As soon as the country is opened up fully it will, in my opinion, go far ahead of the California boom in 1849. There is no room with us for anybody except miners, as the country is not fit for agriculture.

"There are no hard times in our region, although a dollar is never seen. Everything is purchased for cash, but gold dust is the circulating medium. A man comes to our stores and buys $5 worth of goods, tendering a bag of dust, from which we weigh out the amount due. An ounce goes for $17, because there is some admixture of dirt and lead which must be subtracted from the value of an ounce of the pure metal. The weather is quite cold for seven months—from 50deg. to 80deg. below zero—but we wear furs and there is little suffering. I have never seen any case of extreme privation during my five years' residence in that country. There is plenty to eat always, even if we are a trifle shy on luxuries. Wages are high, $10 per day being the standard for laborers."

WEDNESDAY, JULY 21, 1897.

RUSHING TO GOLD FIELDS OF THE YUKON.

Excitement of the Days of '49 in California Exceeded by the Present Fever.

(By Commercial Cable.)

NEW YORK, July 20.—Although the reports of the prospectors who have returned from the Yukon Valley may prove to be to some extent exaggerated, there is every reason to believe that the Klondike gold field will rival those of California and Australia.

THE KLONDIKE CAMP.

The Klondike stream is called the Reindeer River on the charts and empties into the Yukon at a point fifty miles above Big River. Bonanza Creek and El Dorado Creek are tributaries of the Klondike, and no doubt both are rich in gold fields. All are in British territory.

General W. W. Duffield, Superintendent of the Coast and Geodetic Survey, said in Washington yesterday: "I am convinced that the whole country along the 141st meridian is full of gold, and that the entire Klondike Creek, with the mines located along it, is within British territory."

It is thought likely that the Ottawa Government will send its officials to collect taxes at the passes, as goods are being brought free into British territory from the United States, this being due to the fact that traders from the United States are realizing that the route from Juneau to Klondike viâ the White Pass can be made in two weeks, as against three or four weeks by the American route viâ the Yukon River.

THE FEVER REACHES NEW YORK.

["STANDARD" CABLEGRAM.]

NEW YORK, July 20.—The Alaska gold fever has reached New York. An advertisement which has just appeared inviting men who can command a sum of $500 or upwards to join in an expedition which is being organized to the Klondike district in British Columbia has elicited no fewer than 2,000 replies from residents in and about this city. The qualification of $500 seems rather a heavy one, but it will be remembered that the region is very difficult of access, and involves a long sea journey from some western port.

AN INDIAN VILLAGE NEAR THE YUKON.

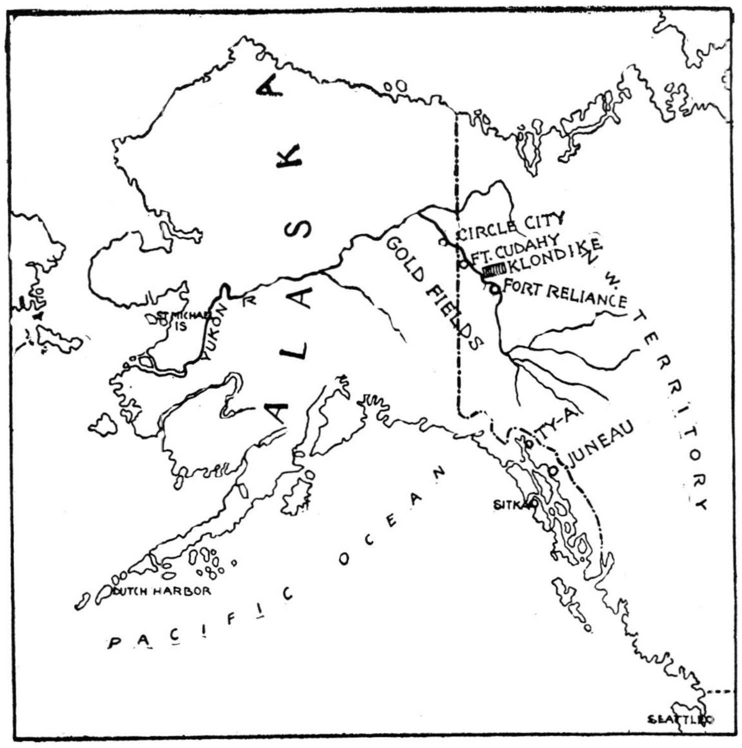

CHART OF THE NORTHERN GOLD FIELDS.

There Are Two Routes to Klondike—by Way of Juneau and the Chilkout, and from St. Michael's Up the Yukon River.

TUESDAY, AUGUST 31, 1897.

STARVATION AHEAD IN THE KLONDIKE.

First Authentic Report of the Situation from the "Herald" Correspondent.

CERTAIN TO BE A LACK OF FOOD.

["DAILY TELEGRAPH" SPECIAL DESPATCH.]

(By Commercial Cable.)

NEW YORK, Aug. 30.—The HERALD'S special correspondent who went to Klondike viâ the Yukon river, sends a long despatch from St. Michael's. He says:—

"Starvation stares the miners in the face during the coming winter, as little more food has been sent up the river by the transportation company this year than last, and there will be at least three or four times as many people to feed.

"Whisky forms a big item in the cargoes. Hundreds of barrels have been shipped in bond across the 141st parallel into the North-West Territory. The lowest estimates place the number of persons in the Yukon district on or about July 1 at from 3,000 to 3,500. Returning miners tell me that if it had been generally known in the mines that there was such a rush coming many would have arranged to leave, as they know what hunger and scurvy are along frozen creeks.

THE GOLD BROUGHT BACK.

"The Klondike bullion which was brought down on the ship's Excelsior and Portland in July, and which made such excitement, was from last winter's work. What is coming out now is the result of the summer diggings, but it is not expected that it will amount to more than $1,000,000.

This, the first authentic report from the Yukon, taken in connection with the state of affairs over the passes from Skaguay and Dyea, leaves little room for doubt that the winter at Klondike will be a most severe one for prospectors.

GOLD COMING DOWN THE YUKON.

Mr. McGillivray, of the "Herald's" Expedition, Sends More News of the Klondike Gold Fields.

[FROM OUR SPECIAL CORRESPONDENT.]

ON BOARD STEAMER HAMILTON, YUKON RIVER, OFF ANVIK, ALASKA, Aug. 23, viâ SEATTLE, WASH., Sept. 13.—That there will be privation, scurvy and sickness throughout the Yukon this winter no man going in doubts. The unholy greed for gold prevents even the most timid from turning back. Warnings now in the face of danger have no more effect than they did when heralded over the country before they started. This says much for the courage and self-reliance of the hardy men who may be going to their deaths, for they are not fools. It will be a struggle for existence, they know, but they are the men who believe in themselves.

At worst, they say, the blizzard-swept Chilkoot Pass will give them help, and even it they will go if need be. But there are not dogs, Indian guides or sleighs enough to take many out; the strong will refuse to go and the weak will leave their bodies to be buried to the requiem of the wolf's long howl on Alaska's snows.

TO TRADE UPON HUNGER.

A number of persons and syndicates had tried to buy up large quantities of supplies with a view to trading upon hunger during the winter. To these the companies refused to sell. None but those buying for themselves are allowed to purchase, and those only in small quantities. The older settlers, who are known to be buying for their own use, will not be allowed to buy more than six months' supplies. Not even the most favored can secure more than that.

The Palace, the principal restaurant in Dawson, is being closed, and the owners are going out for the winter because they cannot buy food to supply their customers. The wife of the owner of a rich mine in the Klondike, who is a passenger on this steamer, has just received a letter from her husband, telling her to go back, because he intends to leave for the winter for fear of starvation.

One good result of all this will probably be that many will go to the old camps, where mine owners have during the last year been vainly offering wages at $10 a day for men to work in mines that are good, but not as rich as those in the Klondike.

At Dawson tents are few; of log cabins there are not enough to cover any of those coming in. None can be bought or hired, and until they build themselves habitations hundreds will be without cover. Dawson is on swampy or moist, low ground, and the streets or roads are churned up by treading to a depth of a foot.

IMPOSSIBLE TO DRAIN THE GROUND.

Covered with a spongy moss, as it is, it is impossible to drain the ground. The water is bad and the dangers from malaria or typhoid fever are great. There has been a number of deaths from these causes of late.

However much concerned any of the returning miners may be when speaking of this winter's prospects of privations and hardships, as soon as they are asked about the mines they brighten up and tell you that the greatest mines ever discovered in the world are on the Yukon. The offer made by Henry Bratnober of $100,000 for a mine on El Dorado Creek has raised prices all around. It is known that he is the representative of the exploration company of London, which is backed by the Rothschilds.

While this offer was probably not made for that company, the effect was the same. The mine he tried to purchase is the one which I mentioned in a previous despatch as having been bought by T. C. Bell last fall for $85 and sold by him two months ago for $35,000. No. 26, above Discovery, was bought in January by the Densmore Syndicate for $35,000. In digging for a dam for turning the water of Bonanza Creek they took out enough to pay the purchase price.

MR. MAX W. NEWBERRY.

The HERALD'S *special artist in the Klondike*

ABOARD SHIP, BOUND FOR THE KLONDIKE.

[Sketched by the HERALD'S special artist.]

WOMEN GOING TO KLONDIKE.

Mrs. Gould's Band of "Widows and Bachelor Maidens" Who Are "En Route" to the Goldfields.

More than five thousand men and women have inspected the steamer City of Columbia and some of the adventurous passengers and queer outfits she is to carry around the Horn and up to the goldfields of Alaska before that region thaws out in the spring.

Mrs. Hannah S. Gould, a sprightly widow who, as she says, is going to convoy a band of "widows and bachelor maidens" to the Klondike, is on deck receiving visitors and assisting Captain Baker and Mr. Edward C. Machen in explaining the details of the proposed voyage of nearly twenty thousand miles.

The Columbia, which is to leave this port on December 1, will carry about four hundred passengers, nearly all from New York. There will be about sixty women in the band Mrs. Gould describes as made up of "widows and bachelor maidens."

Mrs. Gould had some rather awkward questions to answer, but she flinched at none of them. She has been engaged in several business enterprises, including railroading. Mrs. Gould, to begin with, says she is going to Dawson City to "grub stake" needy men and women in the interests of a syndicate, the members of which she declines to name.

"We're going to do good and make money," she said. "I'm a sort of chaperon and leader of the women. The arrangements are unexceptionable in point of comfort and the character of the passengers. It's an adventure, of course, but we shall go well prepared for the rigorous conditions obtaining there. In cold weather we shall wear fur garments, as the Indians do there, and in summer we'll have our corduroys and short skirts. Oh, yes; short skirts and heavy shoes; skirts heavier and shorter than those for bicycle wear.

"It is to be a record-breaking trip in some respects, for now, for the first time, first-class passengers are being booked for a trip covering 19,500 miles. They pay from $400 to $750 each, and the company lands them and their baggage in Dawson City, feeding and caring for them in the meantime."

Mr. Matchen says that great care was being exercised in order to keep the ship free of any objectionable element, and added that one party who offered $20,000 for a passage had been refused, as they were deemed unsuitable.

A CHAT WITH THE DIVINE SARAH.

Seen by a "Herald" Correspondent in London, She Declares Her Intentions of Playing Hamlet.

URGED TO DO SO BY H.R.H.

Delighted with Her Visit to England—Not Going to Berlin.

[FROM OUR SPECIAL CORRESPONDENT.]

LONDON, July 9.—"Madame, you, the great impersonator of the 'eternal feminine,' you intend to play Hamlet, not Ophelia?"

"Yes, indeed, the Prince of Wales wishes me to play Hamlet, or, rather, I ought to say His Royal Highness did me the honor to propose that I should do so, and I intend to carry out his wishes. Besides, you know in 'Lorenzaccio' I play a male character."

"May I ask, madame, how you are satisfied with your visit to London?"

"Satisfied! that is not the word. I am delighted. *D'abord, j'adore les Anglais!* In fact, I often have had violent quarrels with my friends in France in consequence. But, never mind, they are my sentiments, and I have never been afraid of sticking up for my opinions or my sympathies. Nothing could exceed the kindness with which I have been received here on all hands, from the Royal family downwards—by the Royal family in particular. Also the public has been in every way most kind and appreciative. When I leave London I am making my usual *tournée* in the provinces and then I return to *la belle France*, to *mon rocher* at Belle-Isle, off the coast of Brittany, where I shall take a rest."

MME. SARAH BERNHARDT.

Thus the start of our conversation in a charming apartment at the Savoy Hotel—overlooking the Thames. The great Sarah, looking her very best—and her very best is indeed majestic, ever virile and ever fascinating—reposed queenlike on a sofa, a book in hand. For the celebrated *tragédienne* is one of those to whom an hour unoccupied would mean an hour wasted.

A FALSE STORY.

"And how about that story, that you are thinking of appearing in Berlin?"

"No, that is false. Not that I do not appreciate the Germans. This would be ungrateful on my part. In America they always gave me an admirable reception. Besides, as a theatre-going public they are exquisite in their appreciation. But you see I am French, I am *chauvine*, and much as I should like to go to Germany as an *artiste*, if a false note were to get mixed up in my reception, if anything went wrong, I am passionate, I am extreme, *Française au bout des ongles*, I should hardly know myself and only remember that they once defeated us. My temperament, the romance of my country, would get the better of me, run away with me, for as a woman I love the *panaches*, the plumes of glory. . . . No, no, I must forego that journey. But that shall not make me unjust to the enemies of France. I can esteem them. I ever noted in America, that towns such as St. Louis, New Orleans, largely colonized by Frenchmen originally, were far from what they are to-day, until a certain leaven of German colonists came there. Yes, they are excellent people. I am not afraid of saying so; but after all I am French."

"Yes, but you have had it out with them long ago. You killed that poor German Ambassador, Baron Magnus, twenty years ago, when you greeted him with 'La France entière, M. l'ambassadeur.'" Sarah seemed touched at this little reminder of mine of her militant patriotism a generation ago, for she has *au fond* a kind heart, and exclaimed: "Et pourtant c'était un homme bien charmant!"

A LITTLE VISITOR.

At this moment a very pretty girl of about fifteen entered the room and came towards the sofa with every demonstration of delight and affection. Sarah's big collie dog jumped up to greet her. "But how you have grown; *comme tu as embellie, ma chère*." And it seemed to me as if there was more maternal love in Sarah's face, as she rose to kiss her young visitor, than many an average woman carries about in the whole of her body. "And what are you doing? Do you learn painting? Do you study music?" "Yes, music." "And what composer do you like best?" "Chopin." "Chopin, ah, *à la bonneheure j'aime ça*. That is the music for the young; Wagner—that is for later."

It was Mrs. Langtry's daughter.

"One more question, madame, if you please. I read in the HERALD that a certain Schumann has accused you of all sorts of ridiculous things."

"Yes, indeed, and I shall force him to contradict them. The very idea of my taking 33 per cent. of a charity performance. Not a sou did I accept. This fellow calls himself my *impresario* He was never anything more than my courier."

"The readers of the HERALD shall know this," I said, as I rushed out to the nearest telegraph office.

Sarah is, indeed, a big, a remarkable woman—a big personality. For she apparently fears nothing. Not even to speak what she holds to be the truth! What greater, rarer virtue can we hope to meet with in anybody nowadays!

TORRID HEAT IN AMERICA AND ENGLAND.

Over Two Hundred Deaths from Sunstroke in Chicago and Many in Other Cities.

PROSTRATIONS IN THE STREETS.

Fourteen Deaths in New York in Two Days and the Mercury Away Up in the Thirties.

HOT WEATHER IN ENGLAND.

Spectators of Athletic Games Suffer Greatly and One Death Recorded.

CITY MEN DOFF THEIR COATS.

[SPECIAL DESPATCH TO THE HERALD.]

(*By Commercial Cable.*)

NEW YORK, July 10.—The intense heat in this city continues, and there are no prospects of cooler weather to-morrow.

The HERALD's thermometer at 3 p.m. to-day registered 37.5deg. Cent.

Yesterday, there were eight deaths from heat in Greater New York up to noon, to-day, six; while prostrations in the streets were numerous.

There is a great rush to the seashore and near by mountain resorts. The business section of the city is practically deserted and also the residential portion.

The eastern portion of the United States is not the only section suffering under the throes of Old Sol. The Middle West and South are in simply scorching temperature, ranging from 16.5deg. Cent. in Denver to 36.5deg. Cent. in Nashville.

There have been many deaths in Western cities, Chicago heading the list with 216. Louisville had ten and Milwaukee four, while twenty-six smaller cities give a total of thirty-seven dead.

GREAT HEAT IN ENGLAND.

Spectators of Athletic Games Suffer and City Men Walking Coatless.

[BY THE HERALD'S SPECIAL WIRE.]

LONDON, July 11.—The heat in London and the home counties yesterday, especially in the afternoon, was intense.

Reports from all centres where Saturday's athletics were in progress state that the spectators in the open air suffered positive torture, and in London for the first time this year City men adopted a free and easy method of walking about with their coats over their arms.

From the country there are as yet no accounts of fatalities having occurred, but *Lloyd's Weekly* says that at the Harrow and Eton match there was a death which is partly attributable to heat. While the match was in progress, one of the waiters was seen to be taken apparently with a fainting attack.

Medical assistance was immediately rendered, but the unfortunate man expired in a few minutes, death being evidently due to syncope from heart disease, accelerated by excitement and heat. The police removed the body to the Marylebone Mortuary there to await an inquest.

PRINCE OF WALES'S HATS.

Leading London Hatters Say that the Reported Fluffy Bell Crown Is a Myth.

[BY THE HERALD'S SPECIAL WIRE.]

LONDON, July 11.—The statement sent out from London by a press agency to New York to the effect that the Prince of Wales has started a new type of hat based on the model of the fluffy beaver with the broad curled brim of many years ago, proves incorrect; at least representative hatters in London know nothing about it.

A HERALD correspondent called on Messrs. Lincoln, Bennett & Co., Piccadilly, and were received by a representative of that famous house who personally attends His Royal Highness for his "headgear."

"It is an extraordinary statement," said he, "the Prince does not limit his patronage to us absolutely, but we have a great deal to do in the matter. I have never heard of such a hat as that described, nor have I seen such a thing, nor seen or heard of any one who had seen or heard of it. We should be in a position to know or hear of such an innovation if it were true."

"Do you think if this hat were introduced it would be taken up?" I asked.

"I should be inclined to doubt," was the reply, "that it would be very much in favor. You see the making of such a sort of beaver is almost a lost art nowadays. Nothing of the kind has been known in London for forty years."

"Do you think it a joke?"

"Well, I don't care to say 'joke,' but it certainly is a great error."

Mr. A. J. White, of Jermyn-street, knew nothing of it. "It is not true," said he. "Why they have to get the beaver to begin with, and there are none. It's all twaddle."

Mr. Walter Barnard, of Jermyn-street, said: "I don't believe it, and certainly have heard nothing about it. If there was anything in it I should have heard of it. But go to Messrs. Lincoln and Bennett. If they don't know no one does."

AN IMPUDENT FRAUD.

According to the *Temps*, a Paris *restaurateur* has just been fined 50fr. by the First Court at the Palais de Justice for an impudent fraud on his customers.

Some of them having applied to him for hand-made cigarettes, declaring that they disliked those made at the Régie, he bought a stock of the particular brand known as "Grenade," stripped off the printed wrapper and put on a fine red label. He then offered them to his customers as contraband and they were perfectly satisfied with them.

On and after September 10, 1890,

THE POISSY AND RAMBOUILLET COACHES,

"COMET" AND "OLD ROCKET,"

Will run from the NEW YORK HERALD Office, 49 Avenue de l'Opéra, daily, Sundays excepted.

"THE COMET."

PARIS AND POISSY.

DOWN.		UP.	
Paris	a.m. 10.00	Poissy	2.00
Suresnes	10.35*	Andrésy	2.15*
Bougival	11.15*	Conflans bridge	2.30
St. Germain	11.40	Achères	2.55
Poissy	12.05*	St. Germain	3.20
		Bougival	3.45*
		Suresnes	4.25*
		Paris	5.00

Fares:—Single, to Poissy, 4fr.; return, 7fr. (Same price as the railway.) Parcels and game, low rates.
* Change horses.

"THE OLD ROCKET."

PARIS AND RAMBOUILLET

DOWN.		UP.	
Paris	9.30	Cernay la Ville	3.00
Versailles	10.38*	St. Remy	3.43
St. Remy	11.25*	Versailles	4.33
Cernay la Ville	12.18	Paris	5.45

Fares:—Single, 6fr.; return, 10fr. Parcels and game, low rates.
*Change horses.

PARIS-CHERBOURG-NEW YORK

IN SEVEN DAYS,

WITHOUT CHANNEL PASSAGE.

The enormous success attending the direct service of the HAMBURG-AMERICAN LINE from Paris to New York viâ Cherbourg, inaugurated last year, has induced the company to continue this service, which was appreciated to such an extent, especially by American travelers, that during the first four months more than 2,000 first-class passengers availed themselves of it.

This route, besides being the shortest—as it enables passengers leaving Paris on the Friday morning to reach New York early on the following Friday—saves all the discomforts of a Channel passage.

The Hamburg-American Line special train in connection with this service leaves the Gare Saint-Lazare at 8.25 a.m. every Friday for Cherbourg, and is provided with dining-cars and special accommodation.

For full particulars apply to

HAMBURG-AMERICAN LINE,
Passenger Department,
3 RUE SCRIBE,
PARIS.

HENRI PETIT,

5 BOULEVARD MALESHERBES
(Madeleine),
PARIS.

—o—

LADIES', GENTLEMEN'S
AND
CHILDREN'S TAILOR.

—o—

SPECIALTY FOR
SPORTING COSTUMES.

—o—

Highly recommended by high-class English and Americans.

COSTUME DE BICYCLETTE.

BICYCLE COSTUME COMBINATIONS, DIVIDED SKIRT AND TROUSERS.

BÉNÉDICTINE.

THE LIQUEUR
OF THE ABBEY OF FÉCAMP.

GENERAL VIEW OF THE BENEDICTINE DISTILLERY (SIDE FACING THE SEA).

BÉNÉDICTINE

OF THE
ABBEY OF FÉCAMP
(Seine-Inférieure).

AN EXQUISITE TONIC AND DIGESTIVE
THE BEST
OF ALL LIQUEURS

Always insist on having bottles the bottoms of which bear the rectangular label with the signature of the Director-General:

A. Legrand aîné

ALCOOL DE MENTHE

(MINT ALCOHOL)
AND
EAU DE MÉLISSE
OF THE
BENEDICTINES
OF THE
ABBEY OF FÉCAMP.

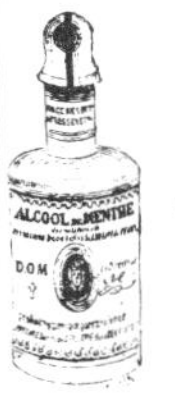

These most excellent Hygienic Products are to be found in all first-class establishments.

THE GREAT DISCOVERY OF THE CENTURY.

THE ELIXIR GODINEAU

Works a rapid cure in Lumbago, Kidney Complaints, diseases of the **Spinal Cord, Influenza,** Anæmia, and other kindred diseases. It rejuvenates and prolongs life. It is essentially a repairing element for worn-out constitutions, giving new blood and renewed strength. It contains no injurious substances, and may be taken without danger at all ages.

Price per bottle, 20fr. Apply to the Administration, 7 rue St. Lazare, Paris, for the pamphlet by Dr. Lafage, laureate of the Paris Academy of Medicine, which will be sent free on application.

CAFE-RESTAURANT DE LONDRES.

A LA MADELEINE, CORNER RUE DUPHOT, PARIS.
BREAKFAST, DINNER AND SUPPER. First-choice Wine and Table. CRU "CHARBONNIER," BORDEAUX.

DRESSES.

—:o:—

MAISON DESCHAMPS.
Mlle. E. SEGARD, SUCCESSOR.

Elegant Walking Dress . . . . from $36
Very pretty Silk Dress . . . . from $50

First floor. 5 RUE DE L'ÉCHELLE, Paris.

(Between the avenue de l'Opéra and the rue de Rivoli.)

SAMARITAINE.

RUE DU PONT NEUF,
PARIS.

Best and Cheapest DRY GOODS

TAILORING FOR LADIES, GENTLEMEN AND JUVENILES, READY-MADE AND TO ORDER.

INTERPRETERS IN ALL LANGUAGES.

THURSDAY, FEBRUARY 17, 1898.

DISASTER TO THE MAINE AND CREW.

Terrible Catastrophe Overtakes the United States Battleship in Havana Harbor.

MORE THAN 250 MEN LOST.

Explosion Under the Men's Quarters on Tuesday Night Followed by the Loss of the Vessel.

SANK BOW DOWN ON FIRE.

Many Men Drowned Before Help Could Reach Them—All But Two Officers Escape.

EXCITEMENT IN WASHINGTON.

Belief that the Accident Was Due to Spontaneous Combustion in the Coal Bunkers.

JINGOES TALK OF FOUL PLAY.

Messages of Sympathy Sent by the Madrid Cabinet and the Spanish Navy.

DESCRIPTION OF THE LOST VESSEL.

THE MAINE AND HER COMMANDER.

THE UNITED STATES BATTLE SHIP MAINE UNDER THE GUNS OF MORRO CASTLE

THE MAINE UNDER STEAM.

THE MAINE IN DRY DOCK.

HAVANA HARBOR.

The United States battleship Maine sank in Havana harbor at midnight, Tuesday, after an explosion which wrecked the forward part of the vessel, causing terrible loss of life among her crew.

There were more than four hundred men on board, of whom only 33, including all but two of the officers, are so far known to have escaped. Captain Sigsbee, the commander, is among the survivors. He was not on board at the time of the explosion.

Latest reports state that 253 lives were lost, including two officers.

President McKinley has ordered an inquiry to be made into the cause of the disaster, pending the result of which no action will be taken except in the direction of relief measures.

The explosion is said to have been due to spontaneous combustion in the coal bunkers around the forward magazine. Another supposition, for which there is no apparent foundation, attributes the disaster to outside causes.

TREACHERY SUGGESTED.

American Public Opinion Already Prejudges the Matter.

[BY THE HERALD'S SPECIAL WIRE.]

LONDON, Thursday.—A cablegram received by the *Globe* from New York says: "The astounding news received from Havana this morning of the blowing up of the United States battleship Maine may upset all the Administration's calculations as to peace with Spain. What details have reached Washington are suggestive of treachery, and, if any substantial facts are obtained pointing to the calamity being due to a Spaniard or Cuban, the outburst of fury throughout the States will compel the Executive to take immediate action.

"The explosion which wrecked the Maine could not, it is reasoned from all yet known, be due to internal neglect of the usual precautions. It occurred soon after every part of the vessel had been inspected for the night and at a time when watchfulness was least necessary.

"Consul-General Lee has telegraphed this morning advising that official and public opinion in the States should be suspended until something be learned of the cause of the catastrophe, but the terms of his message in themselves show that suspicions, which General Lee does not in the meantime care to put into words, are held by him. Already public opinion prejudges the affair and it will take direct evidence proving the catastrophe to have been undesigned to alter public suspicions."

APRIL 26, 1898.

WAR DECLARED BY CONGRESS ON SPAIN.

Declaration that It Exists and Has Existed Since and Including April 21.

PLAN OF CAMPAIGN DETAILED.

To Land Food Supplies in Cuba and Co-operate with the Insurgent Army Under Gen. Gomez.

TROOPS TO MOVE IN AUTUMN.

Capture of a Big Spanish Mail Steamer on the Way to Havana from Barcelona

FORMER CAPTURES RELEASED.

A Spanish Fleet Crossing the Atlantic and Two of the Ships Leave Hampton Roads.

NO ATTACK YET ON HAVANA.

[BY COMMERCIAL CABLE TO THE HERALD.]

NEW YORK, Monday.—In accordance with general expectation, Congress to-day formally declared war in the following form:—

"That war be, and the same is hereby declared to exist, and that war has existed since the 21st day of April, A.D. 1898, including the said day, between the United States of America and the Kingdom of Spain."

It was probably a sentimental idea on the part of the President that Congress should formally declare war, although international law is regarded here as defining with a sufficient degree of clearness that war exists, and is recognised as soon as the representatives of each Government receive their passports and diplomatic intercourse ceases.

WITH THE FLEET.

A Spanish Mail Steamer Captured, but the Warships Do Not Attack.

ON BOARD THE HERALD DESPATCH BOAT OFF HAVANA, Sunday, 10 a.m. — Since Thursday we have witnessed quite an exciting time here. The blockade of the port has been strictly maintained by the American squadron, and six Spanish vessels, three of them steamers and three sailing ships, have been captured. Two of these vessels were laden with coal, which will be very useful to the fleet.

The latest capture took place this morning, when the Spanish mail steamer Catalina, bound from Barcelona for Havana, was pursued and taken by the gunboat Machias. This particular Spanish vessel was sighted shortly after midnight, away to the westward, and was at once chased by the gunboats. She turned out to be rather too fast for a gunboat to be able to overtake her, but the flagship New York headed her off and fired a couple of shots across her bows, when she at once hove to and surrendered.

From the point at which our vessel is lying this morning we can see the Spanish ships moored under the protection of the shore batteries. but so far, none of these boats have ventured out within reach of the American warships. Last night a couple of alarms were given, but nothing came of them.

Since my last despatch to you was sent off, the captain and most of the crew of the despatch boat, on board of which I am a guest, refused to remain in Spanish waters, and took the vessel back to Key West. There we got a fresh crew and returned here yesterday. It is likely that the blockade may last for a couple of weeks or longer before any decisive action is taken.

FLEET TO ATTACK THE PHILIPPINES.

Asiatic Squadron Leaves Hong-Kong This Morning for a Descent on Manila.

SEVEN FINE WARSHIPS.

The Captain-General Expects to Be Able to Resist the Attack with Success.

[SPECIAL TO THE HERALD.]

HONG-KONG, Tuesday, 1 a.m. — Before this cablegram is in type Commodore Dewey's squadron of seven fine warships will have sailed from Mirs Bay to attack Manila.

The United States Consul at Manila, Mr. O. F. Williams, will arrive here early to-day and will be taken to Mirs Bay in a specially chartered steamer. The fleet will probably sail immediately and take Manila next Saturday.

MONDAY, AUGUST 8. 1898.

SPAIN ACCEPTS THE AMERICAN CONDITIONS OF PEACE.

She Insists, However, that She Has Only Yielded to Superior Force and that She Did Not Provoke the War Nor Desire It.

OFFERS TO APPOINT PHILIPPINE DELEGATES.

The Duke of Almodovar, Now Minister of Foreign Affairs, Senor Leon y Castillo and Senor Merry del Val Would Represent Spain on the Commission.

[SPECIAL TO THE HERALD.]

MADRID, Sunday.—After the Queen-Regent had consulted prominent political men, the Government met to approve the answer drawn up by Senor Sagasta and the Duke d'Almodovar, accepting the peace conditions proposed by President McKinley.

In this reply the Spanish Government reserves the utmost possible power of discussing details hereafter, in the hope of making better terms.

There is no Ministerial crisis.

LIEUTENANT-COLONEL ROOSEVELT IN HIS NEW UNIFORM.
[From a photograph taken for the HERALD.]

THE "NEW YORK HERALD" BUREAU IN HAVANA.

THURSDAY, AUGUST 18. 1898.

GENERAL MERRITT RECEIVES THE SURRENDER OF MANILA.

Preliminaries Arranged with General Jaudenes by Flag-Lieutenant Brumby—Solemn Hoisting of the Stars and Stripes—Outline of the Terms.

CAPITULATION OF THE PHILIPPINES.

Some Sharp Fighting Done by the Right Wing of the United States Forces —American Casualties Eight Killed and Forty Wounded —Spanish Losses Heavy.

[BY COMMERCIAL CABLE TO THE HERALD.]

NEW YORK, Wednesday.—The HERALD to-morrow prints the following despatch:—

HONG-KONG, Wednesday.—Manila surrendered, after a nominal defence, on August 13 and the American flag now flies over the capital of the Philippines without great expenditure of life.

One of the first who traversed the wall of the city, I have returned to tell the story.

On August 5 the Manila newspapers published a notification of General Augustin's supersession by the Segundo Cabo, Don Fermin Jaudenes Alvarez, and referred contemptuously to the Yankees.

THE CITY OCCUPIED.

Our troops quickly occupied the city on both sides of the Pasig, sleeping in the streets throughout the wet night. The conduct of the American troops was beyond praise and was simply admirable, they fraternizing good humoredly with Spaniards and natives. A group of regulars squatted in the Escolta, the principal business street, edifying the crowd with tuneful plantation ditties.

The ships engaged cruised freely for four hours at dead low water inside the three-fathom curve shown on the British Admiralty chart, although the Olympia was drawing twenty-four feet. As a matter of fact, Lieutenant Calkins, navigating lieutenant, during his stay here well surveyed the front of the city.

The Callao went within rifle range, covering the flank of the troops. Lieutenant Tappan's services are worthy of special mention. The Monterey had no chance of firing, but undoubtedly her presence and the boldness with which she was navigated within easy range of the city, greatly influenced the capitulation.

TYPES OF THE MOST SPEEDY VESSELS IN THE UNITED STATES NAVY.

MARCH 8, 1889.

BASEBALL IN PARIS.

President Carnot Approves of the American National Game. To-Day's Match at the Parc Aërostatique.

DESCRIPTION OF THE PLAYERS.

Chicago Versus All America.

BATTING ORDER.

CHICAGO.		ALL AMERICA.	
Ryan	centre field	Hanlon	centre field
Pettitt	right field	Ward	short stop
Sullivan	left field	Brown	right field
Anson	1st base	Carroll	1st base
Pfeffer	2nd base	Wood	3rd base
Williamson	short stop	Fogarty	left field
Burns	3rd base	Manning	2nd base
Tener	pitcher	Earle	catcher
Daly	catcher	Crane	pitcher

DIAGRAM OF A BALL GROUND.

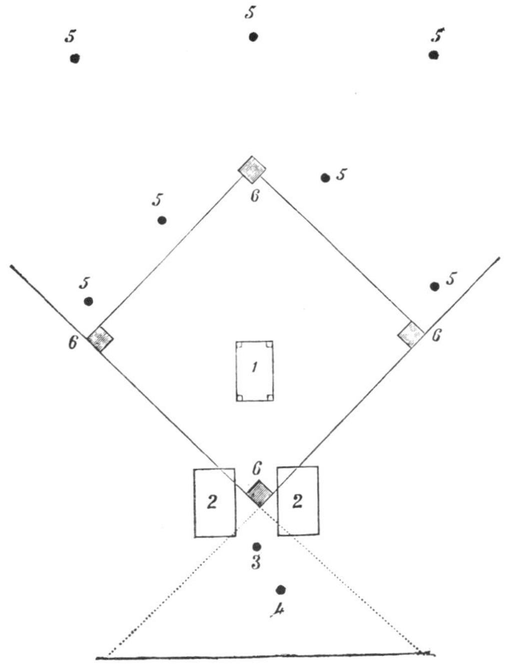

1.—Pitcher. 2.—Batsman. 3.—Catcher. 4.—Umpire. 5.—Basemen and Fielders. 6.—Bases.

This afternoon, weather permitting, Americans in Paris will be afforded an opportunity, of which, no doubt, all will gladly avail themselves. The two American baseball teams, which last Saturday night reached Paris upon their tour of the globe, and which embrace the pick of the professional baseball talent of America, are announced to appear this afternoon at two o'clock at the Parc Aërostatique, in a game which it is safe to say will fully demonstrate the beauties of the field sport over which Americans have been wildly enthusiatic for many years past. Some little difficulty has been experienced in securing grounds in Paris for the game. Lawns in the public parks were available, but enclosed grounds have seemed to be almost unobtainable, and arrangements for the Parc Aërostatique were perfected only a day or two ago. However, with favorable weather the game will take place this afternoon, as announced.

TUESDAY, MAY 27, 1890.

WORLD'S TENNIS CHAMPIONSHIP.

First Day's Play Between Messrs. Pettitt and Saunders.

AMERICA'S REPRESENTATIVE WORSTED

Characteristics of the Game—The Englishman's Strong Points—Sketches of the Contestants.

[BY THE HERALD'S SPECIAL WIRE.]

DUBLIN, May 26.

HEN Thomas Pettitt, the American champion, met Charles Saunders, the English premier player, for the tennis championship of the world, in the first round of play this afternoon, Sir Edward Cecil Guinness's beautiful marble court was thronged with a distinguished gathering.

Mr. Pettitt has received some rough treatment from the experts of the old school because of what they consider his unorthodox style of play. He hits so terrificly hard and yet so skilfully that he enrages those who believe that tennis should be played somewhat like scientific whist—that, roughly speaking, the ball should be landed where the opponent in the conventional game is awaiting it.

But in reply to cavilling about the force of his returns Pettitt remarks that he stands in a court simply to win a game according to the rules, and that if a chance to land a ball hot in the grille occurs he takes care to hit hard enough to keep a man from stopping it.

"But they say," said a HERALD correspondent to the American champion, "that you appear to forget that there is a floor in the court, and that your ferocious style is likely to abolish fine tennis?"

"Don't you believe it. They call it slogging. Fossil players expect one to do per rule, according to their reading only—to lob the ball in the spot they expect it. To send it in strong or in unexpected places is rank heresy. Indeed, some old ducks sixty years of age, as Barré when he tackled Tompkins, can play this antiquated tennis lively as the ancients danced a minuet."

NEVER KILLED AN ADVERSARY.

"Did you ever kill or maim an adversary?"

"No accident ever happened in my experience. To talk about danger from my style is all babble. They also decry my services as monotonous. Just you watch. If one sort is sufficient to puzzle 'em it is good enough for me every time, and if the style prove wearisome to the onlooker let the odium rest on the incapable who can't return. They acknowledge that Biboche was a crack in the matter of service. If I were twenty times more skilful than Biboche I should not as a rule try beyond the effective sort, which nonplusses an opponent and wins my match."

"What do you think of 'Le Bisquon,' the French champion?"

"Altogether too slow. In the game with him I had to give 30, a concession which should enable any man to win, assuming that he could hit the ball at all."

THURSDAY. OCTOBER 24. 1889.

NEW YORK, .659. BOSTON, .648.

How the Champions Won the League Pennant Again.

AN EXCITING FINISH TO A GOOD RACE.

Gotham Went Wild with Joy as the Tickers Told the Story of New York's Triumph.

[BY COMMERCIAL CABLE TO THE HERALD.]

NEW YORK, Oct. 23.

The third ball game for the Championship of the World was played here yesterday. Brooklyn beat New York by 8 to 7.

[FROM THE NEW YORK EDITION.]

After a memorable struggle, the like of which has not been seen since baseball

CONNOR. WHITNEY.

was invented, New York won the League pennant. It was a close shave. Ever since August the Boston nine had been practically even with the Giants. A more in-

WELCH. O'ROURKE.

tense contest of muscle, nerve and science can scarcely be conceived.

The pennant will float for another year on Manhattan Island. It was gloriously won from worthy antagonists.

In a few days the American Association will close its season. The victors—who will undoubtedly be the Brooklynites—must play with the New Yorkers for the Championship of the World. The Giants, under ordinary circumstances, can defeat any nine in the American Association with ease.

This has been a great year for the national game. Baseball has a status

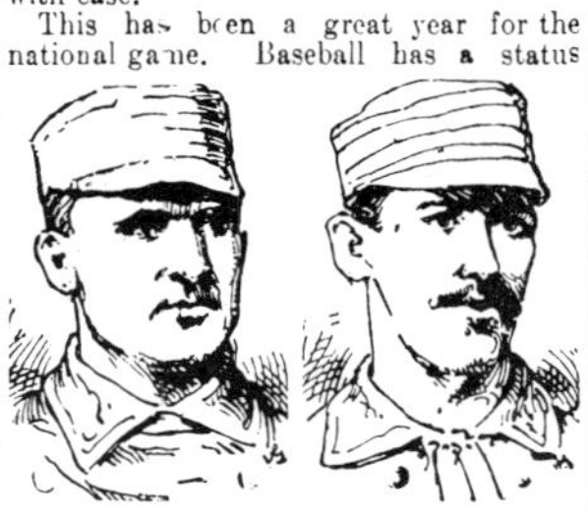

RICHARDSON. TIERNAN.

achieved by no other form of athletic sport. As played in the United States it is the squarest professional game in the world. Gamblers cannot control it and there is only one instance of fraud on record since the League was organized. In that case the four players involved were promptly expelled and they have been ostracized ever since. Americans may well feel proud of this game.

Considered from the standpoint of physical culture baseball surpasses all other pastimes. The only sport that is worthy of comparison is lacrosse, and that lacks the science and focus of baseball.

It is not too much to say that in America more people have turned out to

EWING. SLATTERY.

see the national game than have attended all other athletic exhibitions combined. A conservative estimate places the number of ball players in the United States at over three hundred thousand.

What all this out of door exercise has done for the public cannot be calculated except in a general way. It is certainly true that Americans are becoming noticeably more athletic than formerly. A race of strong limbed, big chested and iron nerved men is growing up. This will tell tremendously in the workshops and the armies of the future.

The results of this season show that professional baseball is on a sure financial basis. Many hundreds of thousands of dollars have been paid by the people for the pleasure of seeing the matches. The rivalry of cities, which is to some extent peculiar to America, has given an additional keenness to the battle for supremacy. Every year the interest in the championship grows deeper and wider.

But a storm cloud looms up. Goaded on by a few real and a multitude of imaginary grievances, the National Brotherhood of Ball Players are preparing for a fight with the managers and stockholders of the League and the Association. They aim to break away from their employers, hire grounds in the principal cities, organize co-operative associations and so take control of the entire system.

Our advice to the Brotherhood is to go slow. They are not business men. If they are hired by new capitalists they will be no better off than they are now. If they try co-operation they will fail. Such

WARD. KEEFE.

a plan would involve them in confusion and end in a wreck. Besides, the managers would organize new nines, and there would be a bitter competition. The goose that has laid the golden egg would be killed.

The chief grievance of the players is the classification system. Under this they are to some extent rated, and on these ratings their salaries are based.

The Brotherhood has the sympathy of the public. The managers will find it to their interest to abolish or satisfactorily

modify the classification system. Both sides should get together before it comes to open war.

SUNDAY, DECEMBER 16, 1894.

CURIOSITIES AT THE CYCLE SHOW.

From Michaux's First Pedal Machine Down to the Most Recent Inventions.

PETROLEUM BICYCLES.

The Latest Eiffel Tower—Novelties in "Steel Steeds" and their Accessories.

HORSELESS CARRIAGES.

The Salon du Cycle, or bicycle exhibition, at the Palais de l'Industrie has now been open for over a week, and still the public flock to see it. Last Sunday 15,000 persons passed through the turnstiles. What the number will be to-day is difficult to predict, for with the exception of the six hours' race at the Vélodrome d'Hiver there are no other important attractions for the sporting world.

That the exhibition is a success is undeniable, for although only the second held in France, it compares favorably with London's great shows, the Stanley and National, which are by many years its senior. The arrangements are capital, each exhibitor having ample space and the stands tastefully decorated, while after the eye is tired with the sight of the thousand and one machines, the ear is charmed with the strains of a capital band. Everybody seems, too, to be there. In fact, it is an indoors Champs-Elysées.

The HERALD having already devoted considerable space to the ordinary exhibits, it is its intention in the present article to point out some of the curiosities of the show, and its readers cannot do better on entering the building than turn immediately to the right and proceed to the top end of the hall, where they will not fail to run across the Retrospective Exhibition, which, to all lovers of cycling, is certainly one of the most interesting features of the show, containing as it does, not only a "Draisienne," or wooden bicycle which, in 1818, was ridden from Compiègne to Soissons, a distance of 40 kilomètres, but many machines made by Michaux, the inventor of the pedal, and virtually speaking, the first real cyclist, among these being a low bicycle built in 1868 for the Duke of Hamilton, the frame of which is steel, the wheels being made of wood with iron tyres and the pedals of brass. The illustration published is of this very machine mounted by the inventor's son Henry. How different the steel steed of the present day, with its ball bearings, pneumatics and toe clips! By the side of the Duke's bicycle is a racer's "Spider," constructed in 1878, and it is curious to note how little improvement had been made in the space of ten years. Other curiosities in this stand consist of a folding bicycle of 1867, a tricycle to carry five persons, Pierre Lallemant's machine of 1866 with wooden pedals, and the first Michaux machine (1868) on which iron rims were adopted for solid indiarubber tyres. Before leaving these antiquities I am reminded that at Michaux's stand (No. 41) in the French section may be seen side by side with the present-day models a bicycle presented by the firm to the Prince Imperial and ridden by him in 1867, also the first lady's machine ever constructed.

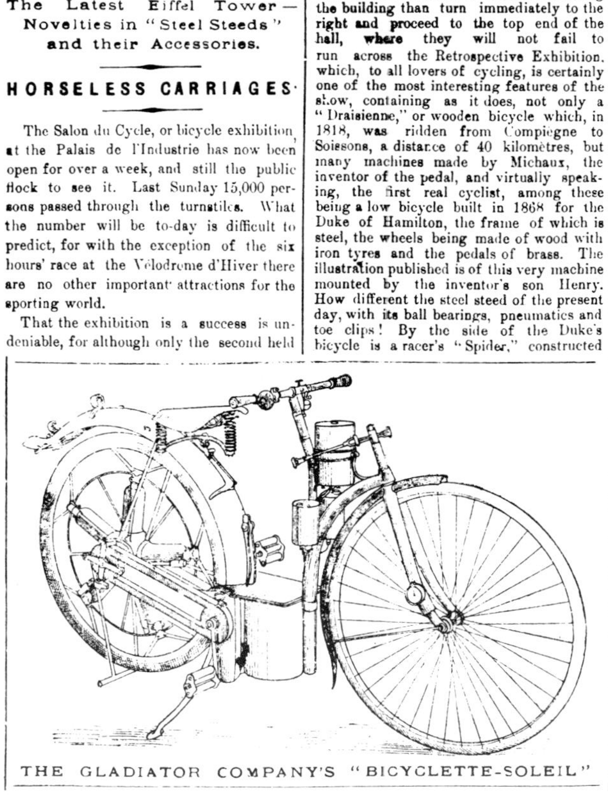

THE GLADIATOR COMPANY'S "BICYCLETTE-SOLEIL"

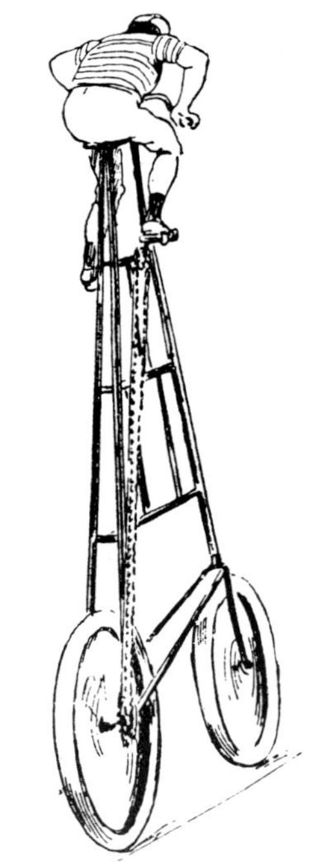

HUMBER'S EIFFEL TOWER.

THURSDAY, JULY 4, 1889.

HOW TO MAKE A RACQUET.

Formula for Tennis Players by Which They May Save Expense.

BE YOUR OWN CARPENTER.

Build Your Own Tools and Derive a Double Satisfaction.

[FROM THE NEW YORK HERALD.]

Every boy will admit that the pleasure of making his kite, with the possible exception of the tail part, is quite equal to the satisfaction derived in flying it, and I think those who are interested in the game of tennis, or lawn tennis as it is commonly termed, to distinguish it from court tennis, will agree with me that if they could make their own racquets their zest for this beautiful sport would be commensurately increased.

SELECTING MATERIALS.

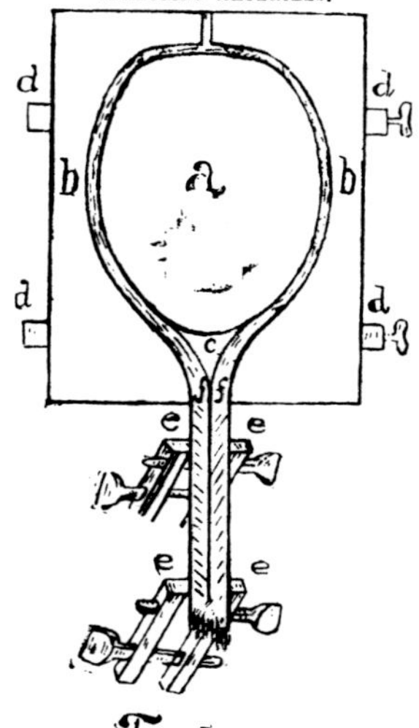

Fig I

a.—Inside form.
b.—Outside form.
c.—Throat.
d.—Jackscrews.
e.—Furniture screws.

It is indispensable to have a good racquet, else the game may not be fully enjoyed, and as that article is rather expensive, many who would otherwise be active players are simply lookers on.

Therefore I propose to add my quota to the popularity of the pastime by describing how, with a little patience and care, and the use of a few of the simplest joiner tools, any bright boy may provide himself with a racquet to compare favorably with the best in the market at but a trifle of expense.

The first thing to be done is to choose some ready made racquet, the shape of which hits the individual fancy, and from that draw an exact counterpart by tracing the inside (A, fig. I.), the outside (B, fig. I.) and the throat (C, fig. I.).

After the patterns have been made it is necessary to cut the middle piece (A) and the sides (B) from a straight grained, inch pine board. (Any other wood than pine would do as well, but pine is the cheapest.) These, of course, must correspond exactly with the patterns.

The throat (C, fig. I.) should be made out of a handsomely grained wood, such as curled maple or mahogany, one inch in thickness. If it be found too difficult to cut the throat out of so hard a wood with precision any turner will do it at a cost of not more than ten cents. As the throat is the most conspicuous part of the racquet it should be made of the prettiest grain to be obtained.

GLUEING.

Now, having accomplished the foregoing, it is in order to prepare five strips of white ash, well seasoned and straight grained, and six feet long, one inch wide and one-eighth of an inch in thickness.

The next thing is to heat the glue. While it is heating the strips should be placed near the fire, so that they may become thoroughly warmed. Then, if there is not a set of jackscrews handy (D, fig. I.), the nearest carpenter, for the sake of a smile and a polite bow, will lend his for the short time required.

When the glue has been heated it should be quickly spread on both sides of each of the strips already described, and this done, the strips should be taken together in the

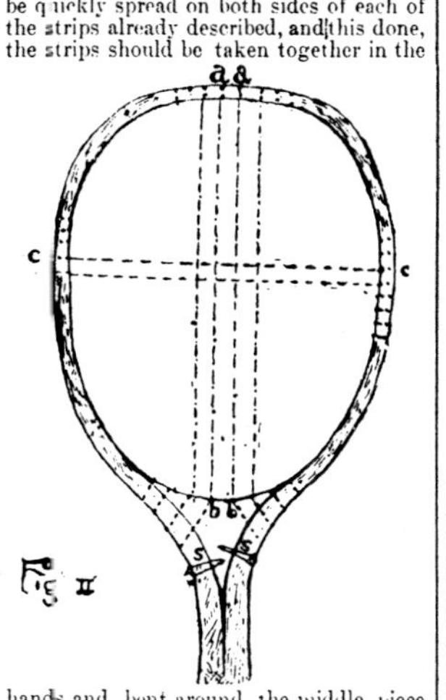

Fig II

hands and bent around the middle piece (A) of the model or form.

It must be borne in mind that no glue should be placed on the side of the strips nearest the form.

The side pieces (B) having been rapidly placed, the screws must be tightened, but not too quickly at first, and after having placed plenty of glue on the throat (C) the screws should be turned up to the maximum thread.

Two furniture screws having been adjusted to the handle (I E, fig. I.) it should be allowed to remain so for twenty-four hours, or at least until the glue is thoroughly dry.

In thus bending the racquet it should be observed strictly that everything is at hand, that the strips are thoroughly warmed, and that the glue does not set until everything is tightly adjusted.

THE WEIGHT.

When the glue is thoroughly dry the furniture screws (e e fig. I.) and the side pieces (b, fig. I.) should be taken off, leaving the middle (a, fig. I.) intact until two one-inch brass screws (s, fig. II.) have been inserted. The racquet is now ready for smoothing, which may be done with a plane and a piece of broken glass and some sandpaper. If any slight seams appear between the strips they may be filled with a mixture of glue and whitening and then made smooth. A well balanced racquet should be about twenty-seven inches long, but individual taste may be consulted. After the handle has been planed there should be glued on each side, from the lower point of the throat (f f, fig. I.), a strip of handsomely grained wood one quarter inch thick. Now the handle should be smoothed and rounded to suit the hand. Thus finished and ready for polishing and stringing, the racquet should weigh from 13½ to 14 ounces.

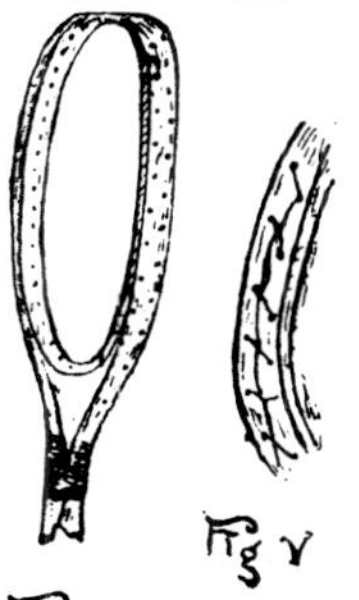

Fig V

Fig III

BORING HOLES.

In boring the holes for stringing the points (*a a* and *b b*, fig. II.) should be first located in a straight line from the handle and parallel with it. The distance between the points should be about half an inch. At right angles from (*a b*) the points (*c c*) should be located. At equal distance points for the remaining holes should be marked. The holes should be bored from the centre of the racquet on the inside to near the edge on the outside (*i e*, fig. III.). The direction of the throat holes is indicated in figure II. The whole racquet should now be rubbed thoroughly with linseed oil, and thus made ready for varnishing. The varnish is made by mixing one part white shellac with an equal part of alcohol. A light brush should be employed to put on three or four coats, with allowance of time for each coat to dry before putting on the next coat.

STRINGING.

In stringing, a few small wooden plugs should be whittled out of any hard wood, about an inch long and a little larger at one end than the size of the holes. The gut or string for racquets usually comes in two lengths.

One of the pieces should now be held to pass the end through one of the side holes (b, fig. IV.); then it should be drawn to within four inches of the end and fastened with one of the plugs. Then putting the gut through the opposite hole (c, fig. IV.) and drawing it tight another plug should be put in. Putting through the next pair of holes (x and d, fig. IV.), that should be plugged as before. Then the plug should be removed at c, fig. IV. In this manner the work should be continued across the racquet, fastening the first end (a, fig. IV.) as shown in fig. V. Care should be taken that the string goes through the throat holes in the direction as shown by the arrows in fig. IV. These vertical strings must not be drawn too tight, as the horizontal ones will tighten them sufficiently.

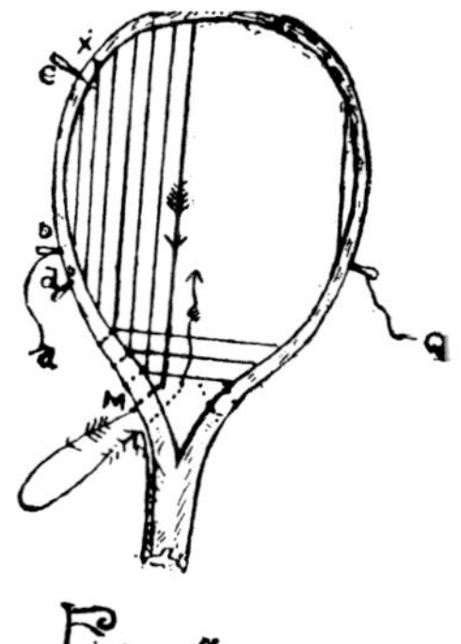

Fig IV.

Starting nearest the throat with the second length of gut, the stringing should proceed as before, passing the string alternately over and under the vertical strings, and fastening the last end of first string (g, fig. IV.) in the same manner as shown in fig. V. The remaining ends should be fastened by driving plugs securely and then cutting the ends off. Giving the strings a coat or two of varnish and tacking a narrow band of leather on the end of the handle, the racquet is complete. The gut will cost about 75 cents.

ADVANTAGES.

The advantages of this racquet over one made of a single piece of steamed wood are:—First, that it will not warp, as the latter are very apt to do: and secondly, not being steamed, the wood retains its natural elasticity and is not so apt to crack.

AMERICAN VISITORS.

The following Americans were registered at the Paris office of the New York Herald, 49 avenue de l'Opéra.

Allen, A., of New York.
Alvarez, Mr. and family, of New York; Hotel Brighton.
Ashmead, L. P., of Philadelphia; Londres.
Ballin, Julius, of New York; Grand Hotel.
Brown, Allen A., of Boston; Londres.
Brown, Joseph E. and Mrs., of Brooklyn, Hotel de Hollande.
Bodmau, O. C., of Chicago; Athénée.
Bristal, Dr. E. L. M, of New York City.
Cake, W. G., of Reading, Pa.; Hollande.
Clark, J. Fessenden, of San Francisco; Hotel Chatham.
Cotton, Francis and family, of Washington, D. C.; 3 rue Copernic.
Dodge, Mrs. W. Earl, of New York.
Creveling, H. C. and Mrs., of St. Louis; 29 boulevard des Capucines.
Caliga, T. W., of Boston; Etats Unis.
Crocker, C. F., of San Francisco; Grand.
Coleman, Evan J., of San Francisco; Grand.
Chopin, Mrs. Martha, of Cincinnati; Grand.
Cator, W. W., of Baltimore; Athénée.
Davison, J. C., of New York; Tamise.
Dodge, L. H., of New York; St. Pétersbourg.
Einstein, E. and Mrs., of New York; Hotel Vouillemont.
Ezeyza, Mrs. Fidel, of New York; Scribe.
Foster, J. H., of Boston; 19bis rue Clément Marot.
Foster, W. A., of Newport; 19bis rue Clément Marot.
Finck, Charles W., of Philadelphia; 5 rue de la Banque.
Fellheimer, August and Mrs., of New York; 35 rue Etienne Marcel.
Frank, George W., of San Francisco; 105 rue Lafayette.
Fisher, R. and Miss Miriam, of New York; Hotel du Rhin.
Flesch, David, of New York; Continental.
Guiterman, R., of New York; Grand Hotel.
Griscom, M., of Reading; Hollande.
Gardiner, Mrs. R, of New York.
Howes, E. T. and Mrs., of Portland, Oregon; 33 place de la Madeleine.
Hedstrom, A. Eric and Miss, of Buffalo, N. Y.; 69 avenue de l'Alma.
Hoffmann, A., of New York; Tamise.
Hopkins, H., of New York; Grand Hotel.
Hawthorne, Miss Grace, of London; Hotel Chatham.
Hunter, F. W. and Mrs., of New York; Hotel Continental.
Kahn, M., of New York; Continental.
Kimber, Arthur C., of New York; Hotel Rastadt.
Kohn, Mr. Aanou, of New York; Meurice.
Kelly, W. W., of London; Hotel Chatham.
Kennedy, A. M. and Mrs., of Washington, D. C.; 21 rue de l'Arcade.
Langan, John, of St. Louis; Grand Hotel.
Low, John G. and Mrs., of Chelsea, Mass.; 18bis rue Denfert-Rocherau.
Mayer, Oscar F. and Miss F., of New York; Hotel Continental.
Miller, Mrs. M. C., of Brooklyn; Burgundy.
Miller, Charles Dexter, of New York; Hotel Burgundy.
Macintosh, Grant, of Montreal, Canada; Hotel du Prince de Galles.
Milk, W. T. and Mrs., of Buffalo, N. Y.; Hotel Continental.
Macomb, Miss, of Denver; St. Augustin.
McAlpin, S., of New York; Hotel de Russie.
Platt, E. G., of Philadelphia; Central.
Richardson, Miss Francis, Harnelsville, N. Y.; 18bis rue Denfert-Rocherau.
Robinson, Miss Mary, of Harnelsville, N. Y.; 18bis rue Denfert-Rochereau.
Rogers, B. W. and family, of Denver, Col.; Hotel Chatham.
Smith, James O., of New York; Tamise.
Sweet, Mrs. Walter H. and Miss Marie, of Boston; 14 rue de la Tremoïlle.
Smith, Granger and Mrs., of Chicago; 14 rue de la Tremoïlle.
Sherman, Miss Josephine, of New York; Hotel Continental.
Schoninger, B. J. and Mrs., of New York; Hotel Bellevue.

TUESDAY. DECEMBER 2, 1890.

ROSY BEAUTIES ON THE ICE.

GALLANT CLUBMEN OUT IN FORCE.

How often in this troubled world
Of sorrow and of sin
Short-sighted man will buy his skates
Just as the thaw sets in!

Lay this teaching to your heart!

Why should anyone have gone to Versailles or Meudon yesterday, when there was such magnificent skating, both for the exclusive and for the *plebs sordida* in the Bois de Boulogne? Yet people were seen journeying, skates in hand, to the suburbs. As for ourselves, we followed the bulk of the crowd to the Bois de Boulogne.

The air was brisk and fresh as on Sunday; cabs whirled up and down the drives of the Bois, regardless of the ice underfoot; and the waiters of the cafés on our route peered through the windows, waiting for someone to venture in and swell the gains of their establishments. The horses of the Gardes de Paris, now stationed on the drives, showed tendencies to run away from pure exhilaration, and cavalry officers dashed gaily along the bridle paths towards the gates of the Cercle des Patineurs, lending color and brilliancy to the wintry scene.

THURSDAY, JUNE 8, 1893.

M. EMILE ZOLA ON BICYCLING.

France's Realistic Writer Declares Himself Benefited by Healthy Exercise.

A FACTOR IN FUTURE NOVELS.

The Bicycle Will Become a Household Necessity for Men, Women and Children.

A Herald Correspondent was yesterday lucky enough to have a very interesting conversation with M. Emile Zola, who both in theory and practice has become quite an enthusiastic apostle of bicycling.

When comfortably seated in M. Zola's sumptuous billiard-room in his artistic little hotel at Montmartre, I was asked most courteously by the author of *Nana*, about what particular subject I wished to question him.

"Why, about bicycling, M. Zola. How do you like it?"

M. Zola replied by throwing himself back in his chair and saying "Oh! Oh! Oh! Oh!"—each time more emphatically than before. "Why, I don't know much about it yet, I am merely a beginner. I can pedal along very fairly though, and the exercise does not seem to be any greater than walking. And then think of the distance you cover! In an hour or two hours' walk you cannot get very far, but in that time one can roll along easily on a bicycle from my house here to Médan, and think nothing of it."

FOR THE NERVES.

"How did you come to take up bicycling?"

"You see I am of a very nervous temperament, and have a great deal of sedentary work. I found my hands occasionally had a little nervous shake to them. All my friends said 'Vous devriez faire de la bicyclette.' I was dining one evening in company with Dr. Pozzi. He looked at me and said:—'Vous devriez faire de la bicyclette!' Wherever I turned the same words confronted me. I noticed the thousands of bicyclists spinning along the streets in Paris and near Médan. I took lessons, and in a few days I found that it suited me admirably. It clears my brain and blood, and I feel much better for it."

M. ÉMILE ZOLA.

"What are your impressions on bicycling in general?"

"I think the bicycle is destined to fill a most important rôle in our social condition. After a certain number of years the bicycle will become a necessary institution in every household—fathers, mothers, sons, daughters and children will take to it. Bicycling, in moderation, is to be warmly encouraged. It is, moreover, a great mental relaxation for those who are overworked, for there is always present the preoccupation of maintaining the balance—no matter how well one rides it is constantly in one's mind, although the rider may be so skilful as to be unconscious of it. It always exists, however, and it is this that prevents a bicyclist from pursuing too sedulously any train of serious thought or reasoning while working the pedals. And it is just here that the desired mental relaxation comes in."

A FACTOR IN ROMANCE.

"The bicycle has not yet become a factor in modern novels, as is the case with the horse or steam engine?"

"No, not yet; but the time will come most surely, for the future of bicycling is immense; and, as I said before, will become a household necessity for men, women and children."

"Do you believe in bicycling for women?"

"Certainly, if they like it—why not?"

"Some physicians have said that the constant trepidation of the saddle in bicycling will in the long run make people impotent—what do you say to that?"

"All nonsense! I never yet have heard a physician who has had any actual experience as a bicyclist say so. Moreover, there is no evidence that I know of to support any such theory. This may be classed with those wild assertions that were made when railways were introduced. People used to say gravely when the St. Germain railway was constructed that the wheels of the locomotive and carriages would simply turn round and round *en place*, and that the train would remain motionless!"

THE NEW YORK HERALD.

WHOLE NO: 21,681. EUROPEAN EDITION--PARIS, WEDNESDAY, JANUARY 1, 1896.—WITH NEW YEAR'S NUMBER. PARIS, 15c; DEPARTMENTS. 20c.

BRITISH INVADE THE TRANSVAAL.

Eight Hundred Men Under Dr. Jameson Enter Boer Territory.

ADVANCING ON JOHANNESBURG.

President Kruger Calls on His Countrymen to Defend the State.

BIRMINGHAM GUNSMITHS BUSY.

Thousands of Rifles Being Prepared for Shipment to the Transvaal.

LONDON PRESS ADVISES PRUDENCE.

Any Sudden Action Would Probably Precipitate a Financial Crisis.

GERMAN PUBLIC OPINION.

[BY THE HERALD'S SPECIAL WIRE.]

LONDON, Jan. 1.—The *Daily Chronicle* has received the following communication, which it gives with all reserve: "The National Press Agency has received from a commercial source the following information as to the present situation of affairs in the Transvaal. According to this authority, the trustworthiness of which there is no reason to doubt, Mr. Chamberlain's unexpected presence at the Colonial Office to-day (Tuesday) and his protracted interviews with Mr. J. B. Robinson and other gentlemen interested in the Transvaal is accounted for by the fact that Dr. Jameson, administrator of the British South Africa Company's territory, has led a body of 500 armed men across the Transvaal frontier with the object of aiding the Uitlander movement against the Transvaal Government.

The Colonial Secretary has ordered the immediate return of Dr. Jameson to British territory. The report of this serious development of affairs emanates in the first instance from Mr. Hoskins, vice-chairman of the National Union in Johannesburg, who has cabled the news to his business representatives in London, in explanation of his instructions that all shipments to his firm are to be summarily stopped."

In a conversation which a representative of the National Press Agency had yesterday with Mr. H. M. Stanley, that gentleman suggested the possibility of such action as is now reported on the part of the Chartered Company. Mr. Stanley spoke on the subject with such obvious restraint as to suggest a strong impression that his forecast was derived from actual knowledge of what was being contemplated.

Subscribers to the HERALD and purchasers of to-day's issue should see that they receive with it, without extra charge, the SPECIAL COLORED NEW YEAR'S SUPPLEMENT, consisting of twelve pages.

DECEMBER 30. 1899.

ENGLAND'S ENEMY IS TERRIBLE.

Mr. Churchill Says One Boer Soldier Is Worth Three British.

ADVISES REINFORCEMENTS.

Boers in Pretoria Hoped for Peace with Annexation of Kimberley and Natal.

GENERAL BULLER'S FORCES.

Enteric Fever at Ladysmith Adds to the Demoralization of Bombardment.

[BY THE HERALD'S SPECIAL WIRE.]

LONDON, Saturday.—In the absence of important news from the front, Mr. Winston Churchill's despatch, giving his views on the situation, with an insight acquired by several weeks' residence as a prisoner among the Boers, forms the principal topic of comment. The terms of peace which he says the Boers were prepared to grant, have, if such a thing is possible, strengthened the feeling that Great Britain must go on until the Boers are completely vanquished.

A Foe Not to Be Despised.

Mr. Churchill adds that on glancing at the situation one must be a fool not to recognize that England is fighting a formidable and terrible foe. One Boer on horseback, in a country to which he is accustomed, is worth from three to five English regulars.

The power of the Boer guns is such that frontal attacks would be repelled, and, on the other hand, the extraordinary mobility of the Boers protects their flanks. The only method of dealing with them would be to oppose to them either men possessing the same qualities, or, in default of that, to send enormous masses of troops.

An advance movement of an army of 80,000 men, covered by 150 guns, would be irresistible for the Boers, but columns of 15,000 men are only sufficient to suffer losses. There must be, besides, more irregular troops.

MONDAY. JANUARY 8. 1900.

BOER OR BRITON---LEADERS ON BOTH SIDES AND SCENE OF OPERATIONS.

PRESIDENT KRUGER.

LORD ROBERTS.

LORD KITCHENER.

BRITISH POSITION CRITICAL.

A Big Battle at Ladysmith and General Buller Can Give No Relief to the Town.

[BY THE HERALD'S SPECIAL WIRE.]

LONDON, Monday.—This morning's despatches from the seat of war show that the situation is more critical to the British arms than at any previous stage of the campaign. The Boers have at last attacked Ladysmith in force. While General White was able to repel the first assaults the last words received from the besieged town were: "Very hard pressed."

Gen. Buller, upon receipt of this news, moved General Clery's two brigades forward, only to find the Boers in force in their trenches at Colenso, showing that they are strong enough to attack Ladysmith and hold General Buller in check at the same time. Some fighting was begun by General Clery near Colenso Bridge on Saturday about five o'clock, since when no despatches have come through.

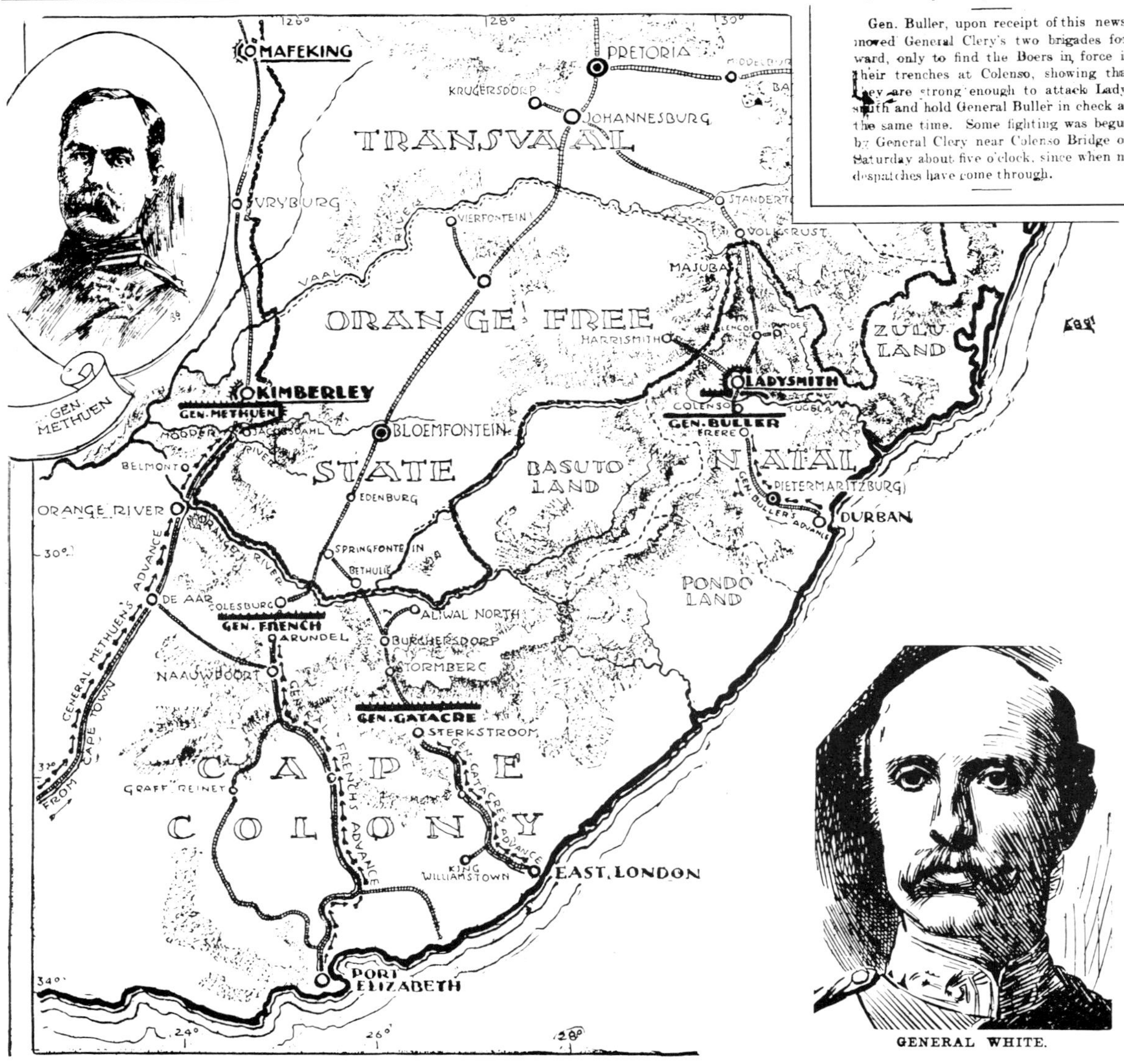

GENERAL WHITE.

SATURDAY, MAY 19, 1900.

MAFEKING'S LONG SIEGE OVER--- BOERS RETREAT--- BRITISH ENTER.

COLONEL BADEN-POWELL.
Who defended Mafeking for over Two Hundred Days.

Boer Laagers and Forts Severely Bombarded, and British Enter.

MAY ABANDON PRETORIA.

London Goes Wild with Joy on Reception of the News of Mafeking's Relief.

OCCUPATION OF NEWCASTLE.

Hoopstad Taken, Lindley Occupied and British Now Near Potchefstroom.

KROONSTAD, Thursday, May 17.—Preparations for the further advance proceed. I learn that most of the fighting on the Boer side now devolves upon foreigners. Both Transvaalers and Free Staters are shy.

It is thought unlikely that Pretoria will be defended. Certainly less than 5,000 Boers will support Mr. Kruger beyond Pretoria or go into the mountains.—Mr. Bennet Burleigh, in the "Daily Telegraph."

MR. KRUGER TO SURRENDER.

Belief that He Will Yield as Soon as Lord Roberts Crosses the Vaal.

KROONSTAD, Friday.—It is stated here on good authority that Mr Kruger intends to surrender as soon as Lord Roberts' army crosses the Vaal, in order to save the properties of the Transvaalers. The Free Staters are very bitter, realising that they have been made a catspaw. —Daily Mail.

THE NEWS IN LONDON.

In a Frenzy of Delight, Crowds Cheering Colonel Baden-Powell.

[BY THE HERALD'S SPECIAL WIRE.]

LONDON, Saturday.—At ten o'clock sharp last evening I happened to be at the Shaftesbury Theatre seeing the "American Beauty" when men rose in the gallery and cried out, "Mafeking has been relieved! This is official."

In a moment the whole house was on its feet. Mr. Arthur Weld, the musical director, seized the situation at once, and in a trice the orchestra was playing "God Save the Queen," the audience frantically applauding.

When Act 2 opened already the cheers of an excited and patriotic populace were heard from without. Within, a cheer arose as four Union Jacks suddenly appeared in the upper gallery, and yet more cheers when a red and white display sheet, bearing in heroic type, "Relief of Mafeking, official," was hung over the side, in view of the whole house. It was from the "Evening News."

The loud cheering outside made the people in the theatre very reckless. They rushed between the acts into the street, where most extraordinary sights were seen. All of a sudden the street seemed to have been turned into a forest of flags, the Union Jacks and the Stars and Stripes predominating.

WEDNESDAY, JUNE 6, 1900.

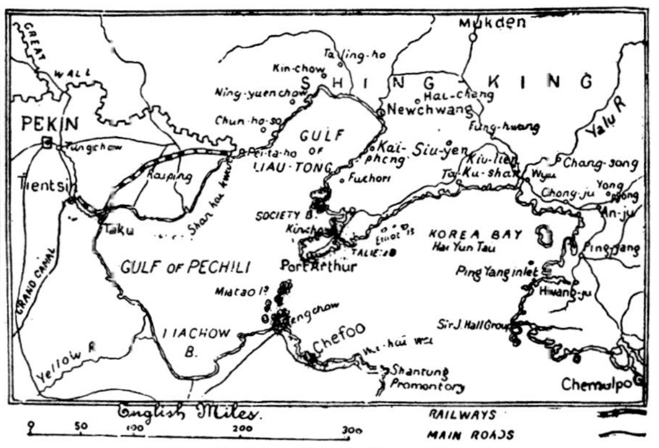

SCENE OF THE TROUBLES IN CHINA.
(Map showing Peking, Tientsin and Taku, the Gulf of Pechili, the Russian station at Port Arthur and the British at Wei-Hai-Wei.)

PRETORIA SURRENDERS TO LORD ROBERTS.

British Now in Possession of the Town, Which Was Not Defended; General Botha Asked for Terms, But Lord Roberts Would Grant No Conditions.

LONDON MAKES A WARM NIGHT OF IT.

Boers Capture a Whole Battalion of Imperial Yeomanry, Composed of Irishmen, Near Lindley—Lord Methuen Was Ordered to Their Rescue, but Arrived Too Late.

[BY THE HERALD'S SPECIAL WIRE.]

LONDON, Wednesday.—The following was issued at the War Office yesterday afternoon:—

From Lord Roberts to the Secretary of State for War.

PRETORIA, June 5, 11.40 a.m.—We are now in possession of Pretoria.

The official entry will be made this afternoon at two o'clock.

EX-PRESIDENT KRUGER.
Who, Conjointly with Mr. Steyn, Sent the Ultimatum Which Caused the War

WHOLE NO.: 24.021. EUROPEAN EDITION—PARIS, MONDAY. JUNE 2. 1902.—EIGHT PAGES. PARIS, 15c.; LONDON, 2d.; DEPARTMENTS, 20c.

BRITAIN'S WAR ENDED; THE BOERS FINALLY SURRENDER

GEN. KITCHENER TELEGRAPHS PEACE TERMS ARE CONCLUDED

Conflict That Has Lasted Three Years, Costing Great Britain Nearly £250,000,000 and the Flower of Her Army, Is Ended at Last.

TERMS SIGNED AT PRETORIA LATE ON SATURDAY NIGHT.

"Peace! Peace!" was the joyful cry of the British last night. The whole world takes up the cry to-day, on learning the news of the Boer surrender, which is detailed below.

London went mad with delight when Lord Kitchener's despatch conveying the news that the Boers had accepted the British terms was issued by the War Office.

Sunday observance could not prevail against the joy of the moment. Even the pulpit caught the contagion.

[BY THE HERALD'S SPECIAL WIRE.]

LONDON, Monday.—The war is over.

Lord Kitchener telegraphs as follows to the Secretary of State for War:—

PRETORIA, *May 31, 5.15 p.m.*

It is now settled that the Boer delegates will come here immediately, and also the High Commissioner from Johannesburg. It is possible that the document will be signed to-night. I have received from them a statement saying that they accept, and are prepared to sign.

Lord Kitchener further telegraphs to the Secretary of State for War as follows:—

PRETORIA, *May 31, 11.15 p.m.*

The document containing the terms of surrender was signed here this evening, at 10.30 o'clock, by all the Boer representatives, as well as by Lord Milner and myself.

These are the official despatches which announced the eagerly wished-for event.

Lord Kitchener's despatch, containing the joyful news as above, was given out by the War Office shortly before five o'clock, and was rapidly flashed all over the Kingdom.

A WAVE OF JOY.

The effect was marvellous. A feeling of suspense, and even doubt, suddenly gave place to a great wave of joy, and the entire nation plunged into a wild celebration.

It is believed that the issue trembled in the balance even so late as Friday, and the question whether a majority would be found to accept the British terms was doubtful almost to the very last.

It is not quite certain whether Mr. Balfour will be able to announce the conditions to-day, but they are understood to be thoroughly satisfactory to Lord Milner and to Lord Kitchener.

The Cabinet has been summoned to meet at half-past eleven o'clock this morning. The Ministers will then determine the form in which the announcement shall be made in Parliament by Mr. Balfour.

SIGNED LATE ON SATURDAY.

British Government Carries Every Vital Point.

PRETORIA, Sunday.—Peace was signed here late last night.

The acceptance of the British terms was voted unanimously by the Boer representatives at Vereeniging, and a document embodying them was subsequently signed by the specially accredited delegates, who came to Pretoria for that purpose. On the British side, Lord Kitchener and Lord Milner appended their signatures.

The result was certain after the surrender of the irreconcilable minority to the great majority.

I may add that the British Government absolutely rejected a proposal put forward earlier in the week by the Boer delegates at Pretoria, to the effect that the terms should be submitted for ratification to Mr. Kruger and the Boer representatives in Holland.

Hence, in the conclusion of peace, no notice whatever has been, or will be, taken of the Boers in Holland.

The terms will show that the British Government has carried its contentions on every vital point, while the minor concessions, particularly in regard to generous financial treatment, will greatly appeal to the Boers in general.

The value of Lord Kitchener's personality as a factor in the conclusion of peace can never be over-estimated. There is no doubt that the peace will be generally popular among the Boers.—Daily Mail.

ALL SHOUTING "PEACE."

Noisy, Jubilant Crowds in the Streets All Night.

[BY THE HERALD'S SPECIAL WIRE.]

LONDON, Monday.—All London was in the streets throughout the night. In fact at the time of wiring noisy, jubilant crowds are shouting "Peace!" and singing—not at all in unison—"God save the King!" and all the patriotic and popular songs they can think of, in a hilarious discordant medley to the accompaniment of squeaking trumpets.

Nobody seems to have any thought of going home before the usual breakfast hour, and this has been going on since quite early in the evening.

The scenes surpass even the wild enthusiasm of Mafeking night or the universal rejoicing of Ladysmith night. Almost everyone is waving a small Union Jack at the end of a cane or an umbrella.

It is remarkable where these flags came from. Before five o'clock not one was to be seen. In half an hour's time thousands were waving in the hands of the King's loyal subjects.

In the hotels there was an air of excitement, in marked contrast to the usual placidity of a London Sunday.

With the approach of evening the streets became more and more congested. Every omnibus had a top-load of shouting people, who were cheered vociferously by those walking in the street, while from hotels and office buildings large flags were flung to the wind.

When darkness fell many gas and electric light illuminations, which were in place for the coronation days, flashed out in beautiful designs.

AT BUCKINGHAM PALACE.

King Edward Hears the News in the Morning.

[BY THE HERALD'S SPECIAL WIRE.]

LONDON, Monday.—The King learned at midnight on Saturday, from Mr. Brodrick, the Secretary for War (who conveyed to him Lord Kitchener's first message), that the Boer representatives were on their way to Pretoria, and were prepared to sign the terms of surrender.

The definite announcement that their signatures, together with those of Lord Milner and Lord Kitchener, had been appended to the document which will restore peace to South Africa, was conveyed to His Majesty at Buckingham Palace early yesterday morning. Almost immediately afterwards the glad news was transmitted to the Prince and Princess of Wales.

LIEUTENANT-GENERAL LORD KITCHENER.
Who Telegraphed the News of the Boer Surrender.

LORD MILNER.
Who with Lord Kitchener Signed the Boer Surrender.

FIELD-MARSHAL LORD ROBERTS.
Whose Victory at Paardeberg Was the Turning Point in the War.

PICTURES FROM A THOUSAND MILES AWAY INSTANTANEOUSLY REPRODUCED.

H. H. KOHLSAAT
FROM CHICAGO TIMES HERALD.

"FATTY" BATES AND JOHN S. BRATTON
FROM THE BOSTON HERALD.

BALDWIN S. BREDELL

ARTHUR TAYLOR.
ARRESTED FOR COUNTERFEITING.

WILLIAM L. KENDIG
FROM PHILADELPHIA INQUIRER

STATE SEN. MAJOR
MISSOURI'S "LEXOW."
FROM ST. LOUIS REPUBLIC

WONDROUS WORK OF THE TELEDIAGRAPH.

Practical Efficiency of Mr. Hummell's Invention Demonstrated to the World by the "Herald."

Civilization was shoved ahead many notches by the NEW YORK HERALD and a new milestono planted when a picture of the first gun fired at Manila was recently telegraphed from New York to Chicago, St. Louis, Philadelphia and Boston simultaneously over a single wire by the HERALD.

And then, after this miracle, other pictures were flashed back by telegraph from those cities over the single circuit to New York.

It was no experiment, but the practical commencement of the HERALD's new business enterprise of telegraphing pictures, drawings, autographs and designs of all kinds by wire as if but ordinary telegraphic messages.

The machine had been tested and found to be in perfect order when the hour set for the long distance picture telegraphing feat had arrived.

The correspondents of the far away newspapers to receive the HERALD's lightning art service were on hand to observe the practical working of the new system.

The machines are a little larger than one of Edison's phonographs mounted on a cabinet stand.

THE PAPERS AND THE PICTURES.

The newspapers connected with the long distance circuit were: St. Louis "Republic," Houlder Hudgins, correspondent; Chicago "Times-Herald," Owen Oliver; Philadelphia "Inquirer," George S. Lenhart; Boston "Herald," L. T. Chapman. The preliminary adjustments of the machines had been made, and away went the picture of Dewey's Manila gun, over rivers, mountains and prairies, instantly, in the twinkle of a pretty girl's eye, into the busy, roaring newspaper offices half across the continent.

Word flashed back from Chicago and St. Louis, from Boston and Philadelphia that "the picture is coming; it is perfect."

In each of these distant offices an exact duplicate machine of the one in the HERALD office was receiving the sketch from the whispering wire.

HOW THE MACHINE WORKS.

It is a marvellous invention, but as simple as it is wonderful. Perhaps it may be instructive to many readers to go back to the beginning of transmitting ideas by telegraph.

Professor Morse's original device of ticking off dots and dashes is the foundation of the system. To get a continuous current of electricity, called a "circuit," two connected wires or other conductors are necessary.

A current sent over a Chicago wire from New York must return to its starting point or there is no circuit. It was early discovered that the earth is as good a conductor as any wire, and that by connecting the wire with the ground at Chicago and New York the current will complete the entire circuit.

As electricity travels round the globe sixteen times in a second, the interval between New York and Chicago is practically instantaneous. It is by suddenly breaking such a circuit by means of the ordinary telegraph key that the light and loud "ticks" are obtained.

If you strike a light, quick blow on the key in Chicago it is instantly repeated in New York.

After telegraphing by hand had been in practice for several years it was discovered that the "dots" and "dashes" indented in the slip of paper in Chicago could be reproduced by running the strip of paper under the key.

It is on this principle that the phonograph of to-day reproduces its records; the little invisible dots on the white cylinder when run under the bit of steel which originally made them will reproduce the song or speech at the other end of the wire.

HOW THE MIRACLE IS DONE.

This principle applied in telegraphing pictures works equally well. A drawing is made on a sheet of tinfoil wrapped around a cylinder in the machine similar to the waxed cylinder of a phonograph.

In Chicago there is a twin machine regulated to work in perfect harmony with the New York machine. In Chicago, instead of tinfoil, a sheet of carbon or manifold copying paper is placed between two blank sheets of paper. The New York current is turned on and the little needle or platinum point above the revolving cylinder in New York breaks the circuit when it touches the ink outlines of the picture.

The needle in the Chicago machine, which reproduces every pulsation made in New York, prints the same kind of record on the carbon paper because the steel point beats hard on the cylinder, and thus the picture in New York is faithfully copied by electricity in Chicago. The simplicity of the system is its wonder.

Yet experts have been years in perfecting a machine that would be of practical commercial value. Mr. Ernest A. Hummell, of St. Paul, is the inventor. He set up his first machine in the HERALD office in January, 1898, when a picture of Mayor Van Wyck was sent over a six-mile circuit without difficulty. Later pictures were sent to the HERALD from Camden, N.J., and Key West, Fla.

The success of the machine long ago passed beyond experiment.

The HERALD invention is of profound service to the world because it is practical and of commercial value. In all directions it opens new fields of usefulness. With it the picture of the escaping municipal robber can be sent to the police long before the fleeing boss reaches the next station. Hereafter it will be constantly employed by the HERALD in reproducing pictures from all parts of the country. A scene of a fire in Chicago, which takes place at ten o'clock at night, can be absolutely reproduced, line for line, in the HERALD office at eleven. Words have come by wire for fifty years and now the actual scenes come in the same way. The HERALD readers will greatly benefit by this invention.

THE TRANSMITTER.

REVOLUTION IN JOURNALISM.

The Memphis "Commercial Appeal" says of the recent tests by the HERALD:—

"In Thursday's issue of the NEW YORK HERALD appeared a picture of Harry F. Adams, the new Police Commissioner of Boston. There is nothing particularly exalted about the office of Police Commissioner, nor does the name of Harry F. Adams carry any especial significance with it for the American people, yet the publication of this picture in the leading paper of this country marks a new era in the newspaper business. Under the picture the HERALD prints the following inscription:—

"'Harry F. Adams.—The above picture, an excellent likeness of Boston's new Police Commissioner, was received by telegraph from Boston by the HERALD last evening.'

"This means nothing short of a revolution in the news publishing business. It means that the pen and the camera will conjointly report the news of the world. With such aid it can hardly be doubted that the news of the world will be much more accurately and vividly collected."

TYPEWRITING BY WIRE.

Another Invention by Means of Which Any One Who Can Spell Can Telegraph.

Mr. F. Hachmann, a young mechanical and electrical engineer, of Whitefish Bay, Wis., has recently invented and perfected a curious and exceedingly interesting machine, which, if it is able to accomplish all that he claims for it, will effect an improvement in telegraphy only less important than the art's invention.

The machine consists of a plain keyboard much the same as that on a typewriter, and having letters of a similar face. The letters are attached to the ends of flat bars of brass hanging on the end of a common pivot.

These bars are lying parallel and horizontally at the front of the machine. Underneath each letter is a thin, flat piece of platinum, attached only to one end. The other end hangs down suspended crosswise. Underneath the letters of the keyboard is a round brass cylinder about two inches in diameter; this cylinder has a lot of little brass pegs in it. Whenever a letter is pressed downward the little piece of platinum comes in contact with the peg on the cylinder as the cylinder revolves, and there is a click, the same as that made by the telegraph instrument.

To properly transmit messages it was necessary to devise the same speed at both the sending and receiving stations. For when the operator strikes the letter A, and the peg in the revolving cylinder makes the electrical connection, the connection at the other end of the wire must be made at the same time to strike the corresponding letter to insure accuracy. Here was a simple problem that had been solved when the clock was invented. By a series of gears Mr. Hachmann connected the revolving cylinder with a round bar, upon which a weight hangs suspended; this weight turns the bar, and thus the cylinder, the same as the weights of a clock, sets the wheels in motion.

HOW PICTURES ARE SENT BY WIRE.

A Simple Contrivance by Which Outline Drawings May Be Reproduced at Any Distance.

(Received by Telegraph from Chicago.)

DR. HENRY D. TIFFARD TESTIFYING BEFORE THE PURE FOOD COMMISSION.

THE MACHINE IN OPERATION.

THE TELEDIAGRAPH.

[From the Piqua (Ohio) "Call."]

This is the name of the new instrument that is made to copy and transmit photographs or any other pictures that may be sent. The first experiment made public was given out in the NEW YORK HERALD of April 23.

Photographs of Kohlsaat, of the Chicago "Times-Herald;" Bates and Bratton, of the Boston "Herald"; Senator Major of St. Louis; Kendig, of the Philadelphia "Inquirer," and a couple of prisoners for counterfeiting, were exchanged over a single wire running into the offices mentioned. When the wires were all ready and the word given to go ahead, in less than a second the pictures were delivered, as named above, just as perfect as they came from the photographer. We cannot describe the machinery by which it is done, but as perfectly as the phonograph copies and reproduces sounds, and by a variation of the same principle, pictures are copied and transmitted in perfection. As the telegraph delivers dots and dashes and copies them just as delivered; as the phonograph reproduces sounds and the chromograph colors, so the telediagraph sends and reproduces pictures of men, guns, ships, horses, houses or whatever may be pictured.

THE CHILLY BOSTON GIRL.

"Yes, the doctor told me he vaccinated the Boston girl last night. It was a funny affair."

"How so?"

"Why, when the doctor reached the house he found he had forgotten his lancet. But when he saw the girl he didn't despair. He just held the vaccine to her arm until it became an icicle and then he pricked her with the point!"—Cleveland Plain Dealer.

1900-1909

The twentieth century opened with two symbolic breaks with the immediate past, events that permitted the *Herald* to give full play to publisher James Gordon Bennett's fascination with technological progress and his concomitant belief in the forward march of the social order he knew.

The Universal Exposition of 1900 in Paris, built along the banks of the Seine from the Eiffel Tower to the Invalides, was an extraordinary spectacle of the best (and some of the worst) ideas produced in the closing years of the old century. After thousands of workmen had created elaborate gardens almost overnight and while dozens of national pavilions continued to be built, the *Herald* headlined the opening of this "French Love-Feast" on April 25, 1900. Competing for the attention of tens of thousands of visitors were a riverside reconstruction of "vieux Paris," a mammoth reflecting telescope, a "mareorama," and a celestial globe. The seemingly limitless outpourings of politicians, visiting royalty, scientists and journalists praising the inventiveness of the human race, its passion for progress, and the self-evident improvement in store for mankind were deeply felt, if perhaps dangerously naive.

Less than a year later, a second event completed this opening act of the new century—the death of Queen Victoria and the succession to the British throne of Edward VII. The queen and her son—two very different characters—are still seen as stereotypes of their times. The length of Victoria's reign—not to mention the moral strength of what we today would call her "image"—made her the dominant symbol of the nineteenth century. The new king, on the other hand, had a well-earned reputation as a playboy. Nevertheless, he took up his new role earnestly and gracefully, providing a reassuring sense of continuity amid the bravado and excitement of a new era.

The *Herald*'s columns in this period gave increasing space to the miracles of the age. "Nine Minutes to Encircle the Earth" ran the headline on July 6, 1903, reporting the success of Mackay's Commercial Cable Company in completing an around-the-world cable system. This step enabled the *Herald* to receive the latest news direct from points as far from its New York and Paris bases as the Philippines, California, and Asia—a precursor of the satellite technology that makes today's *IHT* possible.

Bennett, fascinated by all modes of transport from traditional four-in-hand coaching to the latest lunatic's flying machine, filled the *Herald* with drawings, photos and reports of every sort of airplane, and followed in detail the progress of the Wright brothers, Louis Bleriot, Santos-Dumont and their co-inventors, as well as the latest crazes in automobiling and ballooning. Naturally, given the wealth and mobility of the *Herald*'s readers, automobile makers were among the first major advertisers in the paper.

Bennett initiated several racing competitions—and donated their prizes—in the early years of the century and, though his own name never appeared in the *Herald*, the paper gave the competitions and their winners considerable coverage. The first trophy, offered by Bennett in 1900, was for an automobile race that was known in the *Herald* as the Coupe Internationale d'Automobile, but which everyone else called the Gordon Bennett Cup. In 1906, the race was broadened, came under the patronage of the Automobile Club de France, and has been known ever since as the Grand Prix de France.

Bennett also created a prize for ballooning (the Coupe Aéronautique) in 1906. The first race, of sixteen balloons, started from the Tuileries Gardens, and more than one million people turned out to watch from the bridges of the Seine, the Place de la Concorde and the surrounding neighborhoods. This competition has recently been revived as the Gordon Bennett Balloon Race, and it is once again an annual event.

Bennett added a cup for airplanes in 1909. The favorite in the first year's race was Louis Bleriot, who had just made the first flight across the English Channel, but he was bested by the American Glenn Curtiss.

The *Herald* continued to cover scientific novelties of all kinds ("Ice Deluge from South Pole," a 1901 prediction of the end of the world, is one of many examples), as well as to reflect the concerns and diversions of its very particular class of readers. Coronations, the threat posed to the *Herald*'s readers by jewel thieves, and the sensation caused by Buffalo Bill's Wild West troupe as it toured Europe competed in its pages with the San Francisco earthquake, Signor Marconi's latest wireless triumphs, and the sensational "crime passionel" murder of Stanford White, architect of many of the finest buildings in New York and Chicago, including Bennett's *New York Herald* headquarters on Herald Square.

As the first decade of the new century ended, the general wish for continuing stability and progress—the systematic advance of the "civilizing mission" of the European world—was being undermined by forces already clearly in place. Socialism and anarchism in their different ways were threatening the social and political fabric of Europe, while nationalistic movements across the continent were undermining the old imperial system and its flexible diplomatic arrangements. The new economic and military power of the United States would also serve to destabilize a Eurocentric world.

The 1900s have been variously identified as a time of great flowering in riches and style, as the final gasp of an old and decrepit order, and as a culminating moment in Western civilization when science was still believed to be uniquely a tool for good. Whatever the decade may seem to us with hindsight, for the readers of the *Herald* it was clearly a marvelous time to be alive.

The *Herald* was the first newspaper to be delivered by automobile. This 1904 photograph shows the red 80 h.p. Mercedes racer which sped copies to Trouville by 6:30 every morning.

THE NEW YORK HERALD.

WHOLE NO. 23,245. EUROPEAN EDITION—PARIS, SATURDAY, APRIL 14, 1900.—SIX PAGES. PARIS, 15c.; LONDON, 2d.; DEPARTMENTS, 20c.

FRENCH REPUBLIC'S THIRD EXHIBITION WILL OPEN TO-DAY

SUNDAY, APRIL 15, 1900.

A Few of the Principal Sights in the Great World's Fair Which is Opened to Visitors To-day.

The best birdseye view of the Paris Exposition, which is opened to the public to-day, would be obtained by an observer in a balloon over the Tuileries Garden. Nearest, on the place de la Concorde, is the grand entrance leading to the two Palaces of Art, which occupy the greater part of the Champs-Elysées side, and to the Alexander III. bridge, beyond which, on the left of the Seine, is the esplanade des Invalides, covered with numerous buildings extending as far as the Hotel des Invalides itself and the famous dome over Napoleon's Tomb.

The grand entrance on the place de la Concorde is not intended to be permanent, but merely serves to usher in, conveniently, the visitors who will flock to the Exposition. After passing under the spacious portal, surmounted by the statue of the City of Paris, a picture of which is given on another page, the visitors may enter the grounds by either of two arches, one looking towards the Seine, the other towards the Champs-Elysées. Each one has a span of over 66ft., and the ground plan of the portal covers an area of 29,500ft. There will be fifty-eight passages radiating from the entrance like the sticks of a fan, each one just wide enough for one person.

After viewing the Art Palaces and inspecting the Alexander III. bridge, of which the HERALD also reproduces a picture to-day, the visitor would naturally proceed along the right bank of the Seine towards the Trocadéro. On the right is the rue de Paris, where are grouped the features essentially characteristic of the City of Paris, such as the guignols, or Punch and Judy shows, the marionettes, the tableaux vivants, shadow pictures and other optical delusions. On the river bank there is an aquarium filled with strange creatures from all the waters of the earth.

Then there is a Palace of Dancing, where dances of all ages, from ancient Egypt to the present day, will be represented, linked together in a performance which will be given two or three times daily.

Beyond the Pont des Invalides, near the Alma bridge, is the Palais des Congrès et Economie Sociale, where the meetings of most of the great world's congresses will be held during the continuance of the Exposition. The building is 328ft. long, and has a wide corridor on the upper floor extending its whole length, with large windows looking out on the Seine.

Just beyond the place de l'Alma is the "Vieux Paris," a representation of mediæval Paris, with its crooked streets and old houses with the upper stories projecting over the lower, which is entered through an imitation of an ancient city gate. In all the buildings attendants in ancient costume will sell souvenirs of Paris and the Exposition, while there will be plenty of restaurants and cafés where modern food and drink will be served in ancient wares. Beyond this, on the river, is a mooring-ground for the exhibition of small yachts and sail boats.

After this, one comes to the Trocadéro Gardens, which are entirely occupied by the exhibits of the French colonies and protectorates. Algeria and the French African colonies are nearest the river, and above them are the buildings of Tonkin, Indo-China, New Caledonia, and the French Congo. Here also for purposes of geographical comparison have been placed the colonies of foreign nations. On the other side of the river is the building devoted to forestry, hunting, fishing and the gathering of fruit. Near by is the celestial globe, a gigantic sphere, 166ft. in diameter, representing the heavens covered with stars, to be viewed from the interior by spectators placed on a smaller globe, 40ft. in diameter, representing the earth.

Close at hand, too, is the Palace of Optics, where a gigantic telescope, the longest ever made, will throw pictures of the moon and heavenly bodies on a large screen in such a way that an audience of 2,000 people will be able to view them at once. It is 185ft. long, each of its two object-glasses being nearly 4ft. in diameter, and has a magnifying power of 6,000.

On the western side of the Champs de Mars will be the buildings devoted to education and instruction; literature, science and art; engineering and transportation and chemical industries. The practical demonstrations of transportation, trains of cars, automobiles, locomotives, fire engines and similar apparatus will be shown in the annex in the Bois de Vincennes, where space has been allotted as large as the whole of the Exposition grounds within the city.

At the end of the Champ de Mars will be the Palace of Electricity, and backed against it will be the Water Palace, with fountains and cascades irradiated by electric lights of different colors, forming a very pretty background to the scene as viewed from the banks of the Seine. The water is not entirely for ornamental purposes, as the power developed by the falling cascades will be utilized in furnishing electricity and illumination in the various buildings.

Along the Seine from the Champ de Mars to the Esplanade des Invalides are buildings devoted to the Merchant Marine, the Navy and Army and the Mexican building, behind which is one for the Press. From the Pont des Invalides to the Pont de l'Alma are the Foreign Government buildings, in the following order, counting from the former bridge: Italy, Turkey, the United States, Herzegovina, Bosnia, Hungary, England, Belgium, Norway, Germany, Spain, Monaco, Sweden, Greece and Servia. Those of other Governments are scattered about wherever they can find a lodging, some like the Transvaal, outside the Exhibition grounds, while Russia is given a conspicuous place on the Champs-Elysées.

PLACE DE LA CONCORDE ENTRANCE

LE VIEUX PARIS.

THE CELESTIAL GLOBE.

UNITED STATES GOVERNMENT BUILDING.

EXTERIOR VIEW OF THE MAREORAMA.

MAMMOTH REFLECTING TELESCOPE.

"THE CITY OF PARIS"—SYMBOLICAL FIGURE ON THE PORTE MONUMENTALE.

GIGANTIC MAP OF GREATER NEW YORK.

ICE DELUGE FROM SOUTH POLE MAY OVERWHELM THE RACE

SENSATIONAL THEORY OF A GEOLOGIST WHO TELLS US THE CATACLYSM MAY BE PRECIPITATED AT ANY MOMENT

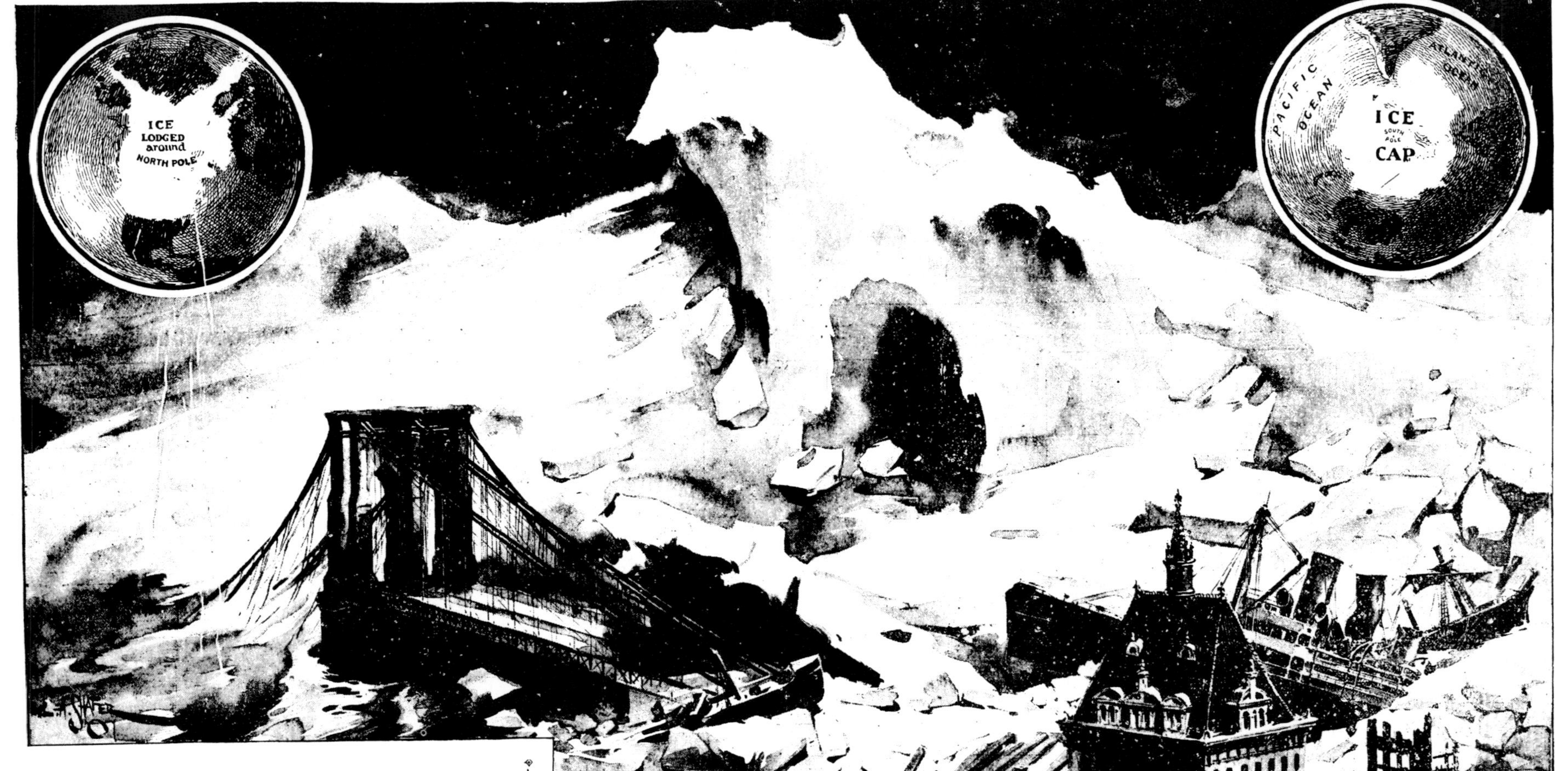

WHEN THE ICE DELUGE REACHES NEW YORK.

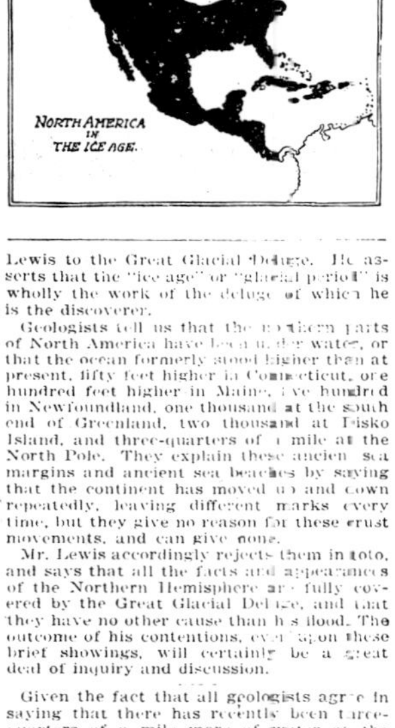

The Inevitable Disruption of the Fifty Million Cubic Miles of Ice Which Cap the South Pole, Says Leon Lewis, Will Result in a Wild Rush of the Fragments, with All the Waters Which Have Been Drawn Around It, for the North Pole via the Atlantic—Such Glacial Deluges Have Occurred Periodically in the Past, and, According to This Scientist, Another Is Now Due.

As if we were not in trouble enough before, here comes a scientist to tell us that the whole human race is liable to be destroyed at any moment by a universal glacial flood coming from the South Pole! And not only does he say these disagreeable things, but he invokes as proofs a host of remarkable and undoubted facts, which will surely "give us pause." The situation turns, it appears, upon alleged migrations and cataclysms of the ocean, which come again and again, ending in an awful catastrophe, which is now again due. Is our scientist right? Let the reader judge. These views are gathered from a startling work entitled "The Great Glacial Deluge and Its Impending Recurrence," by Leon Lewis, which is about to appear—if the great flood doesn't get here ahead of it.

THE GREAT ANTARCTIC ICE CAP AND ITS WORK.

"THE trouble begins," says Mr. Leon Lewis, "at the extreme southern end of our globe. The cold there is very excessive, as has been made plain by Mr. Borchgrevink and our other explorers. The snowfall there is almost continuous, Captain Ross tells us, it having snowed twenty-eight days out of the thirty he was cruising along the great ice wall presented by the edge of this so-called continent."

This account is confirmed by Commodore Wilkes, of the United States Exploring Expedition, from whose reports it is easy to figure that the total snowfall thereabouts amounts to fifty-seven miles in ten thousand years.

There are no rains or thaws at the South Pole, so that all the snow is converted into ice under pressure, and the whole mass thickens and widens constantly, despite the losses to which it is subjected by the breaking off of the immense tabular icebergs which have presented themselves to the notice of Lord Kelvin and all other navigators in those regions. The waters of the surrounding seas are below the freezing point, as was first noted by the famous circumnavigator Captain Cook, and hence there is a constant accretion from this source to the vast bulk resulting from the unwonted snowfall.

And now, what are the consequences of this state of things? Why, during many thousands of years the so-called "Antarctic Continent," or "ice cap," which is simply a huge mountain of ice, has been getting bigger and bigger, until it is now as large as North America, or one hundred and fifty times as large as the State of New York, and is estimated to possess a surface of eight million square miles. Dr. Croll ("Climate and Time") and H. B. Norton (Popular Science Monthly, October, 1879) speak of it as being twenty-eight hundred or three thousand miles in diameter.

It is more or less circular, and with its loose ice fills the whole space between Australia, Montevideo and the Cape of Good Hope, ranging northward from the pole through almost fifty degrees of latitude and upon the whole circuit of the earth. Its thickness at the edge may be put at two miles. At Robertson Bay, Balleny Island, for instance, Mr. Borchgrevink (Strand Magazine for October, 1900) found the ice wall twelve thousand feet high and so steep that there was no possibility of reaching the interior, which no man has ever seen or will see, and where there is neither animal nor vegetable life of any description.

From a thickness of two or three miles at its edges, the slope of this ice continent ascends gradually to the centre at the pole, where, it is estimated by Dr. Croll and many others, the ice is at least twelve miles thick, and is more likely fifteen or twenty. The total bulk of this great accumulation, therefore, cannot be less than fifty million cubic miles of ice.

And now a word as to what this great mass of ice has been doing.

During the whole period of its growth, say twenty-five thousand years, or ever since the latest of these recurrent floods, this vast ice continent has been drawing the ocean from the Northern Hemisphere across the Equator into the Southern. This movement, says Mr. Lewis, accounts for the present situation of affairs—the land in the Northern Hemisphere and the water in the Southern; the flooding of the Southern Hemisphere and the draining of the Northern.

This movement of the waters southward—their migration, as he calls it—has kept pace perfectly with the growth of the ice cap, and the consequence is that three-fifths of the waters of the globe have been drawn almost a mile to the southward of the earth's former centre of gravity, and are held in this precarious position by the gravitational "pull" of the ice continent—literally suspended almost a mile above our heads—in readiness to be let back upon our low lying lands at any moment.

II.

THE BREAKING UP OF THE ICE CAP A SURE THING.

As will be seen at a glance, our situation as residents of the Northern Hemisphere is not merely precarious—it is one of the most perilous that can ever menace us. **All there is between us and destruction,** says Mr. Lewis, **is the cohesion of those fifty million cubic miles of ice.** Just so long as the great ice cap at the South Pole remains whole, just so long will things remain as they now are, with the present distribution of land and sea. But the instant the ice cap is broken up, that instant we are lost.

The disruption of the ice cap will cause the "pull" of gravitation to be instantly transferred to the northern half of our globe, and the fragments of the ice cap, with all the waters which have been drawn around it, will enter immediately upon a wild rush for the North Pole via the Atlantic.

The present order of things, it thus appears, can be perpetuated only during the time the ice cap retains its cohesion. But how uncertain this time must be! As well count upon the perpetuation of an icicle hanging from your roof! The cohesion of the ice cap cannot possibly be prolonged beyond a certain point.

There is sure to come a time soon when the cohesion of this great ice mountain will be subjected to a strain it cannot possibly resist. No one can say how soon the event will take place, but it is just as sure to come in the near future, says Mr. Lewis, as that two and two make four.

III.

RUSH OF THE GREAT GLACIAL DELUGE NORTHWARD.

And when the ice cap breaks up, what then?

Why, the whole mass of water and ice thus gathered at the South Pole—the Great Glacial Deluge, as Mr. Lewis calls it—starts northward, centring upon the twentieth meridian of west longitude, which passes in mid-Atlantic. The bulk of the deluge, ice and water, exceeds a hundred million cubic miles. Imagine what a vacuum it makes in the region which has so long been its cradle! Into this vacuum, however, rushes the Indian Ocean from the east and the Pacific from the west, both being drawn tremendously into the cataclysm by its violence.

As our Croton water comes into New York upon a fall of one inch to the mile, it can readily be guessed how rapidly the Great Glacial Deluge will take its way northward, since the total fall in its case is not less than three-quarters of a mile. But why does it come up the Atlantic? Because the gravitational "pull" of the whole world has hold of it; because the line of disruption is midway between the Cape of Good Hope and Cape Horn, and for forty other reasons given by Mr. Lewis, but into which we need not enter.

In coming away from the South Pole the huge icebergs of the flood tear tremendous furrows in the floor of the ocean, and these furrows have been discovered by recent explorers, as is recorded in Appleton's Annual for 1899. The icebergs make a similar excavation between Montevideo and Tristan da Cunha, after they have been whirled against the southeast coast of South America by the diurnal rotation of the earth on its axis, and in one place they have left a hole eight miles deep.

Grinding along the coast of Brazil, the deluge crosses the Equator, reaching the coast of Africa at Cape Verde. Here it is subjected to such a "pull" from the Eastern Hemisphere that it hugs the coasts of Northwest Africa and Western Europe, overwhelming Great Britain, Jutland, the Netherlands, Southeastern Sweden, Finland and Northwestern Russia, and destroying all life and all the works of human hands throughout those regions.

IV.

THE HALF TURN OF THE DELUGE AROUND THE NORTH POLE.

Rushing into the Arctic Basin between Iceland and Norway, and so on between Greenland and Spitzbergen, the Great Glacial Deluge enters upon its wonderful half turn around the North Pole, which will be best comprehended from the map. Its icebergs, as much as they have been broken up during their wild flight northward, are still large enough to force the axial torrents of the flood to keep to their deeps and basins. They do this everywhere, and this is why the continental shelves of the Atlantic fall away everywhere from shallow depths to a thousand or more fathoms.

The channels followed in the Arctic Ocean are between two and four miles deep, as has been shown by Explorer Nansen and others. Keeping to its deep sea channels, therefore, but at the same time hugging the northern shores of Europe and Asia, the Great Glacial Deluge reaches the opposite side of the basin at the New Siberian Islands, where it begins piling up its ice and rising upon itself in a whirl which defies description. The Arctic Ocean, being substantially a closed sea here, with only the small opening of Behring Strait, which is soon choked by the ice, the waters and icebergs of the flood are forced to make a half turn upon themselves. While they are doing this the Arctic Basin becomes filled to overflowing.

The return of the deluge southward is made chiefly upon northwest and southeast lines. The presence of this flood has been known for two generations, or ever since the days of Dr. Edward Hitchcock, Dr. Charles T. Jackson, Sir James Hall and hundreds of other great scientists, but they have all been at a loss to explain this presence, for the reason that it never occurred to them—nor to anybody before Mr. Leon Lewis—to go to the South Pole for their cause, power and motion.

Off the Atlantic States, as also off Eastern Africa and Eastern Asia, as will be seen by the map, the deluge is converted into a great southwest drift, partly in consequence of the earth's rotation. These movements are succeeded by many others of a secondary character, especially during the melting of the ice sheet. It is enough to say that the whole Northern Hemisphere is buried beneath hundreds of fathoms of water and ice. Great Britain and the other countries of Northern Europe are covered by the deluge twice, both in coming northward and in returning, and this is why, says Mr. Lewis, Great Britain is merely a skeleton of what it was when it was joined—as Sir Charles Lyell, Reclus and others have shown—to Spain and Portugal on the south, the Continent on the east and Norway and Greenland northward.

V.

WHOLE FACE OF THE WORLD PROOF OF THIS DELUGE.

Turning now our attention to the face of the earth, remarks Mr. Lewis, we find it giving evidence everywhere that it has been worn and rent by furious floods. Sir Henry Howorth, in his "Glacial Nightmare," has placed this point beyond dispute. The habitable globe is covered everywhere by a vast washing and deposit known as the drift, which is indisputably, according to Mr. Lewis, the work of the great glacial deluge. We find also that the northern parts of Europe, North America and Asia have been covered repeatedly by nearly a mile of ice, and this is also ascribed by Mr. Lewis to the Great Glacial Deluge. He asserts that the "ice age" or "glacial period" is wholly the work of the deluge of which he is the discoverer.

Geologists tell us that the northern parts of North America have been under water, or that the ocean formerly stood higher than at present, fifty feet higher in Connecticut, one hundred feet higher in Maine, five hundred in Newfoundland, one thousand at the south end of Greenland, two thousand at Disko Island, and three-quarters of a mile at the North Pole. They explain these ancient sea margins and ancient sea beaches by saying that the continent has moved up and down repeatedly, leaving different marks every time, but they give no reason for these crust movements, and can give none.

Mr. Lewis accordingly rejects them in toto, and says that all the facts and appearances of the Northern Hemisphere are fully covered by the Great Glacial Deluge, and that they have no other cause than his flood. The outcome of his contentions, even upon these brief showings, will certainly be a great deal of inquiry and discussion.

Given the fact that all geologists agree in saying that there has recently been three-quarters of a mile more of water at the North Pole than now; given also another conceded fact, namely, that the ice and water now accumulated at the South Pole is amply sufficient to raise the level of the Arctic Ocean (as soon as the ice cap breaks up), to the above height—Mr. Lewis concludes that another recurrence of the Great Glacial Deluge is now due, and that any day or hour may bring us a cablegram from Montevideo or Buenos Ayres to tell us that it is on its way northward.

Home Made Aurora Borealis.

A FOREIGN scientist has recently made some wonderful experiments in electricity that will crown his name with honor. By plunging the negative wire of a powerful induction coil in a vessel of water and bringing the positive wire into contact with the surface of the water, or slightly below it, he has succeeded in creating the perfect aurora borealis, or northern lights, we have seen in the sky with such wonder and admiration.

The flickering streamers, now faint, now brilliant; the dark arc or half circle from which they flow—all the varied phenomena that have puzzled the mind of the observer are accurately repeated on a small scale.

M. Planté thinks that the aurora of our northern skies is produced by a flow of positive electricity through the upper regions of the air into planetary space, the fact that lightning and other similar phenomena are not frequent at the polar regions showing that the discharge is not toward the earth.

He believes that all the planets are charged with positive electricity, and that this flows out from the neighborhood of their magnetic poles. When it meets no resistance it goes off in obscure rays, but when it encounters masses of vapor then it becomes the glorious aurora.

These mysterious lights, waving and dancing in the northern sky, have always been a marvel and a puzzle to mankind, and any information that we can gain as to the cause of their coming and going is welcomed by old and young. This beautiful experiment proves that the aurora is but another form of the mysterious force that speaks to us through the telephone and telegraph, that heats our houses, cooks our food, gives us light in darkness and conveys us over land and sea.

Mamma—What's the matter, Kitty?

Four-Year-Old (with a snuffle)—I can't transpire through my nose.—Chicago Tribune.

Spontaneous Combustion of Trees.

SPONTANEOUS combustion is a mysterious thing at all times, but as long as it confines its attention to inanimate objects there is nothing very uncanny about it. But when trees become subject to it there is no telling where it will stop.

The banks of the River Cam, in Cambridgeshire, England, have recently exhibited an unusual number of such cases, and young growing willows have been the victims in nearly every case. Cambridge used to pride itself upon its beautiful willows, and it was therefore with sorrow that the people discovered one morning the charred remains of what had once been a really beautiful specimen of the willow tree.

The fate of the tree naturally attracted attention to the phenomenon, and thereafter but too much opportunity was afforded for the study of it. At one point in the river in particular the process was seen. Green trees covered with rich masses of foliage suddenly burst forth into conflagration and burned to their very cores. Fine willows in full vigor poured forth clouds of smoke from their half burned stems.

An examination of the charred remains of the trees revealed nothing in the way of explanation, but as the trees which met their fates were for the most part young there could hardly have been any putrescence or fermentation.

Just why the willows should meet such sudden ends is not apparent, but the peculiar formation of the tree, its pliant boughs and the drooping of its leaves and flower may have had something to do with it.

IN THE FAR WEST.

"How do you feel?" asked the leader of the mob, after the tar and feathers had been applied in liberal doses.

"Oh, I feel like a bird!" smiled the barnstormer, glancing at the feathers.

For such wit they allowed him to write home and tell the old folks he was leaving town by the all rail route.—Chicago News.

Curious Polyglot Newspapers.

THREE curious polyglot periodicals are now being published.

One is the China Times, which is regularly printed in seven languages. It is published in the capital of China, and the languages in which it appears are the English, French, German, Italian, Russian, Japanese and Chinese.

Another polyglot paper is the Austrian semi-monthly entitled Acta Comparationis Literarum Universarum. It has correspondents and subscribers all over the world, and the contributions of the former are invariably printed in the language of the countries from which they are sent. As a result it frequently happens that in one number of the paper there are articles in twenty-five or thirty languages.

The third polyglot paper is the "Pantolodion Magazine," which is published in St. Petersburg, and which contains critical essays regarding the new books published throughout the world. Each of these essays is printed in the language of the country where the new book of which the essay treats appeared. Thus a review of an American book is printed in English, a review of a French book is printed in French, and so on. One number of this periodical has contained articles in fifteen different languages, namely, German, French, English, Italian, Spanish, Dutch, Portuguese, Swedish, Danish, Hungarian, Roumanian, Russian, Servian, Bohemian and Polish

ABOUT TO MAKE A CHANGE.

"What is he going to do now?" breathlessly asked the agitated young woman, with her eyes on the daring aeronaut, who was clinging to his parachute.

"He is about to sever his connection with the balloon," replied her escort, "to accept a position a little lower down."—Chicago Tribune.

[From the NEW YORK HERALD.]

The Royal Procession from Buckingham Palace to Westminster Abbey.

Magnificent Horses, in Glittering Golden Harness and Gilded State Coaches, Will Convey the Sovereigns, Escorted by Household Cavalry and Officials of the Court.

KING WILL WEAR HIS CROWN ON THE WAY BACK FROM ABBEY TO PALACE.

Through Long Lanes of Dazzling Color, on Through the Multitudes Ranged on Lofty, Gaily Adorned Stands, the King and Queen Will Make Their Triumphal Progress.

LONDON DETERMINED TO ECLIPSE ALL RECORDS OF MUNICIPAL ADORNMENT.

PRINCES AND AMBASSADORS AT THE CORONATION.

LONDON, Saturday.

AT Buckingham Palace everything will be stirring early on Coronation morning. In the mews the horses will receive their final brushing, and the last touch be given to the glittering golden harness and gilded state coaches.

Life Guards in their gorgeous uniforms will be drawn up waiting for the hour of departure. The Earl Marshal's assistants will be dashing about, carrying the last orders. The Master of the Horse, the Duke of Portland, and his staff will be quite as busy with their part of the arrangements. The suites of the King and Queen Alexandra will be in attendance at an early hour.

The King and Queen Alexandra will leave Buckingham Palace at 10.30. The order of the procession will be as follows:—

An Officer of the Headquarters Staff.
Trumpeters.
Escort of Household Cavalry.
About eight dress carriages containing members of the English Royal Family,
including relatives of the King from various European Royal Houses.
THE PRINCE OF WALES,
with an escort of cavalry.
The Princess of Wales, Princess Victoria and Princess Charles of Denmark.
Household cavalry.
Four or five carriages containing members of the Household of the King and Queen.
Aides-de-Camp to the King.
Two Naval Aides-de-Camp.
The Headquarters Staff of the British Army, including the Commander-in-Chief.
Yeomen of the Guard in their ancient attire and carrying their halberds.
Escort of Indian and Colonial Cavalry.
A Sovereign's Escort of Household Cavalry.
The gilded State carriage containing
THE KING AND QUEEN.
Gold Stick, Silver Stick, and other State Officers.
A Sovereign's Escort of Cavalry.

On the journey to the Abbey by way of the Mall, Horse Guards and Whitehall, the King will not wear his crown, but after the actual ceremony His Majesty, for the first time as crowned monarch, will return along the more extended route—by way of Whitehall, Pall Mall, St. James' street, Piccadilly and Constitution Hill—crowned and robed.

WHAT THE CITY WILL LOOK LIKE BY NIGHT.

While the King and His Court Are Resting from Their Labors, the Crowds Will Be Enjoying the Illuminations.

LONDON, Saturday.—The night of Coronation day will be devoted to viewing the illuminations. The theatres will all be closed. So far, no big functions have been arranged for that night. All who were in the Abbey will be too tired to go out; besides, it will be impossible to get carriages through the crowd. The King, it is thought, will remain at Buckingham Palace, resting after the fatigue of the day.

Elaborate and magnificent as are the day decorations it is evident that London is expending more pains, and, naturally, more money upon the illuminations which will set the metropolis in a blaze at night. For some time past London has been in a state of semi-illumination every night, testing the lights, and from these it can be gathered what a brilliant display they will make.

Clubs, hotels and theatres have made most elaborate preparations and spent thousands upon thousands of pounds; but, judging from a tour through the streets, it would appear as if the banks and insurance offices are to make the most brilliant show of all.

Nothing can beat the grandeur of "The Old Lady of Threadneedle Street," as the Bank of England is called. The smoke-blackened walls have been transformed into a real fairy palace. They will be one blaze of red, white and green lights, and magnificent crystal electric-lit devices.

Over the roof, at the corner of Prince's and Threadneedle streets, and over the main entrance are huge representations of the Royal and the City arms in crystal studded with jewels. Along the cornices in double rows of red fairy lamps, while under the cornices run festoons of the same. Down the walls and across, in artistic designs, are still more lamps, while under the Corinthian capitals of the eight pillars will blaze immense circular wreaths of green crystals.

The Bank's Pre-eminence.

The Bank has done magnificently, and will quite outshine in brilliancy the Royal Exchange opposite, and even the Mansion House, which it also faces, elaborate as are the designs of illumination prepared by the members of the Stock Exchange and the Corporation of London.

But the Mansion House will be very pretty, too, with its crystal designs representing the City arms and the crests of other City companies, while the Exchange, with its long ropes of fairy lamps stretching from base to summit, across the eaves, and around the bas-relief at the top, will make a fine display.

With regard to the insurance offices, to which reference has already been made, King William street, which is the home, it may be said, of insurance companies, will be very brilliantly lit; but, so far as one can judge in advance, the Atlas Insurance Company building in Cheapside will be hard to beat.

If any fault can be found with it, the front is rather too crowded with fairy-lamps to be lit with tiny gas jets. It has for a centrepiece a very handsome device in colors, representing Atlas with the world on his shoulders, surrounded by an immense crystal wreath.

Along Fleet street and the Strand there will be hardly a window but will be picked out with fairy lamps. The newspaper offices, notably the "Daily Chronicle" building, in which are the London editorial offices of the HERALD, will be very handsomely lit up.

Thousands of tiny lamps, mostly of red and white, are already in position in most artistic fashion around the balconies and windows of the "Daily Chronicle" building and will make a very imposing show on the two nights the celebrations are to last.

In the Strand.

Coming into the Strand, a tremendous blaze of fiery designs will be seen on the fronts of the hotels and theatres. Messrs. Gatti will, it would seem, outshine all others, with perhaps the exception of the Gaiety and the Tivoli, in the elaborateness and splendor of their illuminations of the Adelphi and Vaudeville Theatres, for not only are there myriads of little colored lamps picking out the windows and ornamental masonry on the walls, but there are some beautiful devices, which will strike the spectator with admiration.

Turning into Holborn, one building which will attract a great deal of attention is the Birkbeck Bank. The method here is quite original, and different from anything to be seen elsewhere. The imposing new front of the building is covered most artistically with large ruby-colored globes about a foot in diameter, which will be lit by electricity.

In the centre is an immense crown composed of one hundred and fifty of these big lamps. Across the whole length of the building run the words, also composed of these red globes, in huge letters, "God Bless our King and Queen." Round the sides, down the walls, also hang immense ropes of these wonderful lamps, the grandeur of which, when lit, can hardly be imagined.

In Oxford-street, along Regent-street, along Piccadilly with its great mansions, in Pall Mall with its clubs, it would be difficult to select any particular building as being more magnificently illuminated than another. Electric light plays a great part in the elaborateness of the preparations for the great festival.

Take for instance, the Carlton Hotel and Her Majesty's Theatre, which is a part of that immense imposing block. Most ornate are the designs in crystal which sparkle on the walls, while festoons of tiny colored lights, the reflectors of which are shaped like four-leaved clovers of silver, are suspended all around the great block.

CORONATION GALA NIGHT AT COVENT GARDEN OPERA.

Performance of June 30 to Eclipse All Previous Records—Mme. Melba to Sing a Special "Patriotic Ode."

LONDON, Saturday.—During the last ten or fifteen years there have been several very brilliant gala nights at Covent Garden, but none will come up to the magnificence of the great performance in honor of the Coronation on June 30. At the time of writing I believe no announcement has been made as to what opera or selections from operas will be given, but it is quite likely that an act from "Romeo and Juliet," which is a great favorite of Queen Alexandra, will form part of the programme. The hour for commencement is nine o'clock, and when the curtain rises the whole of the Italian Opera chorus, with several of the best singers from the various choral societies of London, with Mme. Melba as the prima donna, will sing a "Patriotic Ode" specially composed for the occasion. There, of course, will be considerable enthusiasm over this composition, which, I am told, is very good and very spirited, and the music excellent. The whole entertainment is likely to last about two hours and a half.

On former occasions the beautiful crimson-hung Opera House has been decorated with roses and other sweet-smelling flowers, but it has been found that the perfume was too oppressive, and so, by a special command of the King, no real flowers will be used at all in the scheme of decoration. But one of the great florists in London has had made some exquisitely beautiful imitation roses which will be hung in sways and festoons along the front of the boxes and right up to the very top of the house.

As it is a state performance everybody will be in full court dress, though feathers and veils will not be worn by the ladies. But all men must appear either in uniform or ordinary Court dress, and this rule is to be rigidly adhered to. The great officers of state will wear their full uniforms, and Life Guards and, I rather fancy, Beefeaters will be stationed on the staircase and about the house.

Nearly the whole row of boxes on the grand tier in the centre of the house has been requisitioned by the King and converted into one for the Royal party, and at least half the stalls have been engaged for the various representatives and for the attachés of our foreign guests.

Those boxes that are not required by the King will be sold from prices varying from seventy to two hundred guineas. I hear bitter complaints from the box-holders of the present season, who think such charges excessive and ridiculous. Stalls too are to be sold for £25 and upwards and reserved seats in other portions of the house will be correspondingly high.

The King and Queen and their suite will drive to the Opera in state coaches with the Sovereign's escort of Life Guards and will be met in the lobby of the Opera House, not the usual Royal entrance, by the Lord Chamberlain and other great state officers, when the procession will be formed and Their Majesties conducted to their seats, with the Lord Chamberlain and his subordinates walking backwards the whole way.

THE KING'S STATE COACH.
In Which Their Majesties Will Drive to Westminster Abbey.

SOME IDEA OF PRICES PAID AT THE HOTELS.

Majority of Rooms in the Largest Hotels Already Taken, but No Enormous Increase Noticed Over Regular Charges.

LONDON, Saturday.—One question, which has had much to do with influencing people outside of London, and especially in America, in making up their minds about visiting the English capital during the Coronation, is naturally that of hotel accommodation. They have waited for the assurance that they would not have to pay fabulous prices for the privilege of being packed into hotel offices and dining rooms, or bath-rooms even for two or three days.

There is no question that the majority of rooms in the largest hotels are taken. I am informed at Claridge's, the Carlton and the Savoy that every room is engaged for the week. Most of the rooms at the Hotel Cecil are already taken, and though the hotel will accommodate 1,100 persons, the manager, Mr. Judah, told me he would have to put up a large number of cots to take care of the crowd of the three or four days.

Probably the Crown Prince Komatsu of Japan has the most expensive suite of rooms in London. He has magnificent quarters at Claridge's, for which he pays something like 65 guineas per day. From this the prices range down in different hotels to 6 to 8 shillings for regular patrons. The man who comes to London unknown may expect to pay a good sum for his room. If he is willing to go to the East End lodging houses, he may be taken in for about 4s. per night, provided he goes early.

In the suburbs it will be possible to get rooms for the same figure. In furnished-room houses, though, 10s. will be a more general figure. I went into a dingy little hotel near Waterloo Bridge the other day and inquired the price of rooms for Coronation Week. "Thirty shillings if you only stay one night," answered the clerk, consulting a paper. "If you will be here four or five nights, the price will be a guinea each." The usual tariff at this place is from half-a-crown to 3s. At a rather nice, quiet hotel, just off the Strand and near Covent Garden, I was offered a double room with board for two, for £3 per day, if I engaged to stay four or five days.

I have been around making inquiries as to rooms and charges during the coronation season. It is curious to notice the different views of different hotel proprietors on the subject of raising prices. Some declare they have no intention of so doing; others will not raise prices to their regular patrons; others make no secret of the fact that they intend to charge visitors a good advance. It must be remembered that prices during the season in London are always higher than in the winter, when there are few people about.

No Enormous Increase.

Consequently the increase in some cases over the regular prices will not be so enormous as might appear. Witness the following incident, which is better than argument: A gentleman was being shown through a certain hotel recently. "I want to show you this room and bath," said the hotel official accompanying him, opening a door on the third floor. "What is the rent?" enquired the other. "It is occupied at present by an American woman," answered the guide. "She pays thirty shillings per day." Then he showed the visitor a similar room and on the floor below, and named thirty-five as the price.

Claridge's Hotel in Brook street, I am told by the manager, will accommodate 250 persons with their servants. The Carlton will hold 280, the Hyde Park can take care of 250, the Savoy about 220, the Hotel Russell about 500, and the Hotel Cecil about 1,100. In these and the Gordon Hotels, the St. Ermin's, the Great Central and other of the larger and better known hotels something like 10,000 persons can be accommodated, and the smaller hotels, which are extremely numerous, will be able to handle from 25,000 to 30,000 persons. So that the majority of visitors, after all, will have to be cared for in boarding houses and furnished-room houses.

Of these last the number seems to be without limit in London, so that there need be no fear of anybody not being able to get a place, if he cares to pay the price. At Claridge's I was told that the price for two weeks about coronation week would be raised 100 per cent. At the Carlton I was told that the prices would not be advanced more than 50 per cent. At the Savoy and the Cecil prices will not be raised to regular patrons, while at the Russell I was told that from Monday to Saturday the prices would be considerably increased to patrons who had not been for some time resident at the hotel.

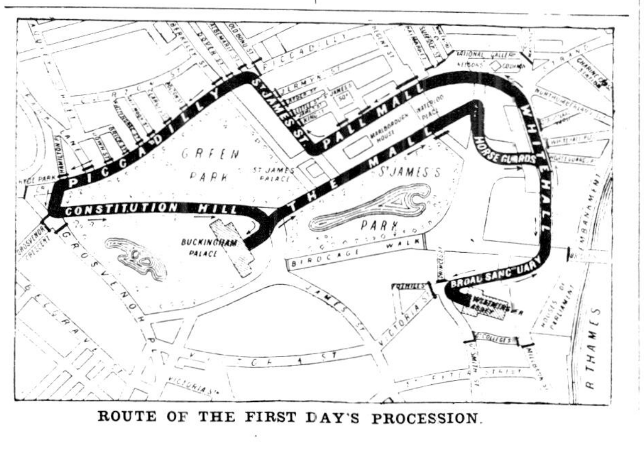

ROUTE OF THE FIRST DAY'S PROCESSION.

LONDON, Saturday.

NO PROPHET is needed to predict that the streets of London will hold, for the coronation, the most stupendous gathering ever known in the history of the Empire. People have been speculating on how the celebrations of the 26th and 2th will compare with those held in connection with the great Diamond Jubilee of the late Queen Victoria.

But there now remains not the least shade of a shadow of a doubt that the streets of London will present a far more magnificent show than even on that memorable occasion, great as it was. When the grand, flashing cavalcade emerges from Buckingham Palace on both days of the celebrations, it will be into long lanes of dazzling color well worthy of the supreme episode in the great sovereignty. On through the multitudes ranged on lofty, gaily-adorned stands the King and Queen will pass, amid the deafening cheers from thousands upon thousands of their loyal subjects

For weeks, nay, months past, London has been busy, working with feverish heat in its lavish preparations for these two great days. And now the uncouth wooden erections are putting on their dressings; red, white, and blue, the colors which make up the flag of the Empire, being chiefly used in the various schemes of decoration. In these colors the immense stands are being draped. On former occasions—and this was much noticed on the occasion of the Diamond Jubilee—there was little attempt at uniformity of decoration.

For the Coronation, public bodies have put their heads together so that, in striving to attain a higher standard of magnificence than has ever been witnessed in London before, there will be nothing incongruous to offend the eye, and that the colors of the decorations on buildings standing side by side will in all their dazzling magnificence blend together. In this the various corporations have taken the lead. Along the entire route of the two processions the decorations are most picturesque. At equal distances, about twenty feet apart, tower tall Venetian masts, but not the bald masts to which London has been accustomed in the past.

In the Mall.

Along the Mall, for instance, the masts, painted white, have three yards, like those of a sailing ship, finished off at the ends with gilt spear-heads. From the tops hang long pennons of different colors, from the yards hang little bannerettes, round the masts curl, snakewise, wreaths of myrtle and laurel leaves, garnished with crimson bows. Then from mast to mast hang festoons of the same. They present even already in their unfinished state a very brilliant sight.

The City of London proper has done even better. The masts along Fleet street, up Ludgate Hill and on to the Mansion House are most elaborate affairs. From the centre of each mast spread out in a semi-circle slender yards, four on each side, tipped with gilt spear-heads. Round these coil evergreens, with suspended flaglets and bannerettes.

Round these also are coiled evergreens garnished with artificial roses and rosettes of ribbons. Another new feature is that at the corners of the streets, and round the monuments which stand in the line of route, have been erected beautiful white and gold columns, instead of masts, which present a very imposing effect.

In the West End.

The West End clubs and hotels are, of course, making a very special effort in the adornment of their premises. Most of them have, where possible, erected stands for the accommodation of members and guests. To describe one is almost to describe the whole. As already said, the Union colors predominate, though some of the clubs have also introduced their own colors, using no little art and ingenuity in working them in so as to blend with the prevailing shades.

But the most striking feature, perhaps, of the whole scheme of decoration will be the triumphal arches which will be erected along the routes of the processions. One which stands at the end of Parliament Street is most imposing in appearance. It consists of a large central arch and two smaller ones in Gothic style, supported by slender red and white columns, the whole covered with cloth of gold and decorated with shields emblazoned with the arms of all the counties of the United Kingdom and Ireland.

On its summit an open balustrade of pinnacles supports the figures of St. George, St. Andrew, St. Patrick and St. David, grouped round the British lion. On both façades are the arms of the English counties. In the centre of both façades are also the Royal Arms with their supporters. The balustrade is decorated with flowering shrubs and plants, the whole effect being most dignified as well as artistic.

At Hyde Park Corner.

Another very fine arch is to be seen at Hyde Park Corner in Piccadilly, consisting of two sets of six columns on either side of the street, decorated with the Royal Arms and those of the chief colonies and of the Empire of India. These columns are linked together by wreaths of roses and surmounted by winged allegorical figures in gold playing musical instruments. An arch somewhat similar stands in Whitehall.

In the narrower thoroughfares, owing to past experience, triumphal arches have not been encouraged, but a very fine one, illustrative of the various City companies, is being built, and will be brought in pieces to Temple Bar the day before the coronation, and erected there, to be as quickly demolished the day after the procession through the City.

IS WOMAN TO BE TRUSTED AT THE AUTOMOBILE STEERING WHEEL?

(From the NEW YORK HERALD.)

TENDENCY in women to engage in the sports of men within the last ten years has resulted in the invasion of a strenuous field, where the element of danger is extreme. Nerves in women most highly tensioned have become stiffened. Matron and maid have developed courage and resolution. At the tennis courts, on the golf links, in the water, with the hounds across the fresh green fields and over fences and walls, at the wheel of fragile racing yachts, and lastly at the steering-wheel of the automobile, the American woman to-day even excels her English sister, who was the original exponent of outdoor sports for women.

Having mastered the difficulties of outdoor games, she now turns her attention to the high-speed automobiles. Now my lady has developed her nerve and courage through the encouragement of her brother until she is ready to play Mahout among the elephants of India or to take the tiller of an airship. She is ready, and of this there is no doubt, to don the goggles and coat of the "chauffeur" and annihilate space along country roads with the facility displayed by the men.

She is ready. But can she master these heavy machines of vast power, handle them in congested places and race them over the boulevards at that speed where an obstruction means instant application of the brakes and a cool hand at the guiding wheel?

"She will lose her nerve," comes the statement from the masculine cynic.

"We are just as quick and steady as the men," she says. "We bring our automobiles home, while the doughty fellows ofttimes hire a truck to drag their machine to the garage."

It is natural to believe that no woman has the strength and power of thought to serve in any great emergency. Driving a spirited horse in the Park requires the possession of one's full faculties. It is argued that high-power automobiles are infinitely easier to control than a mettlesome steed. Then, again, the automobile is supposed to possess more faults requiring attention in the operation of the machine with the simultaneous survey of the road ahead.

Be it as it may, more women are driving automobiles to-day than ever before, and the coming spring and summer months are expected to witness the spectacle of many women, young and old, behind the small wheels that steer the machines, and running them over a free road with the speed attained by Messrs. Vanderbilt, Brokaw, Astor, Keene, Collier and other residents of level-roaded Long Island.

A Pessimistic Expert.

There may come a disaster or two to emphasize the pointed statement of a man high in automobiling circles, who makes bold to declare:—

"Women have looped the loop and lived to gasp the details of the thrilling flight. Yet only a few weeks ago a plucky circus performer in attempting to complete the circle in an automobile was hurled to a horrifying death. Of course many men have been killed in their automobiles. I draw this picture not to show that women do not posses nerve, but I want to add that there are but few conspicuous cases. Now, you take one of our plucky society girls. She may not know the meaning of the word fear. In driving an automobile one must never relax the tension to which his nerves are strung in speeding along a course. The young woman sees a clear road ahead, and exhilarated by the speed is apt to forget that distance is traversed so quiskly in an automobile. Then the sharp curve in the road, a farmer's wagon directly before her, and no means by which she can avoid a collision.

"Look at the situation clearly and fairly. What is her first impulse? Why, to put her foot on the brake and cover her eyes and await the shock of impact. Now, a man's brain may not be more alert, but he has that power of becoming more cool and calculating in the face of danger, where a woman's nerve will be upset. He knows that there is a rail fence to his right through which he may possibly crash with safety and he takes the chance.

"No, decidedly no; a woman will never be as capable as a man in running an automobile of extreme speed with the same degree of nerve force as a man."

In spite of this emphatic statement, there are several women who have negotiated miles in exceedingly good time.

Mme. du Gast, one of the most expert drivers of automobiles in France, who took part in the Paris-Madrid race, where several lives were lost, is an example of a daring woman orerator. She has long been a conspicuous figure in the French capital and noted for her courage and skill.

Mrs. W. Jack Latta, of Goshen, Ind., who runs her automobile one hundred miles in five hours, is a noted figure in the Middle West, while Mrs. C. Arthur Benjamin, of Syracuse, whose mile on a track in 1m. 24 2-5sec. startled Central New York, illustrates the temerity of some women automobile drivers and the degree of skill they have developed

Woman can take a sewing machine to pieces, and why, then, can she not learn to master the intricate points in the machinery of an automobile? Women can repair minor breaks in machines on the road and they are becoming more proficient every day.

TUESDAY, MAY 27, 1902.

NEW YORK SAID TO BE ALMOST "AUTOMOBILE MAD."

But the Popularity of the Modern Sport Is Met by the Never-Failing Prejudice and Hostility of the Local Authorities, Frequent Conflicts Thus Resulting.

Automobiling is so popular a sport in New York that even the general public has been bitten by the mania. Seventy-five francs ($15) per hour are cheerfully paid for the hire of a machine. The price is pretty "steep," as the "Sun" observes, but it is not too steep for would-be automobilists, for the demand for machines is far greater than the supply.

In Constant Conflict.

Naturally enough, one consequence of the craze is that the "chauffeurs" and the local authorities are at daggers drawn. The same class of people who raised a howl against bicyclists some years ago are now up in arms against automobilists. The HERALD (American edition) recently opined that "speeding over the streets in Yonkers is likely to prove expensive sport. One well-known New York broker, C. V. B. Gunther, was fined $25 recently, the 'chauffeur' of J. F. Seligman was fined $25 yesterday, the "chauffeur" of Isidor Wormser is out on bail until Friday, and now Maurice Wormser is at liberty in the custody of his counsel."

It appears that thirteen New York bankers and brokers, headed by Mr. Jesse Seligman and the Wormser brothers, could not resist the temptation of trying their machines at top speed along Warburton avenue, "a level and unobstructed stretch of macadamized and asphalted pavement for two miles, with neither turns nor cross roads. The stretch has secured such a favorable reputation for fast time that the residents in the vicinity have made complaints to the police. The officers have been instructed to exercise great vigilance in prohibiting fast riding.

"Patrolman Henry Miller was at Phillips place and Warburton avenue in the afternoon, when three automobiles dashed into view, with great clouds of dust in their wake. They were going at a frightful clip. Miller took up a position in the roadway and waved his arms excitedly. No more attention was paid to him than if he were a wooden pole, and all three machines whizzed past him like the wind.

Automobilists, it must be admitted, are not accepting either fines or imprisonment without a protest. A prominent official of the Automobile Club of America recently remarked that, "although there had been undoubted violations of the law, yet also it was fast becoming a common practice to arrest any automobilist who gave his machine a few moments' 'free rein' in and about New York.

"Figger It Out!"

One member of the A.C.A. rather nonplussed the police when taken before the Morrisonia justices charged with excessive "speeding." This was Mr. Henry Winthrop. Asked what he had to say for himself he remarked that when summoned to stop he was going under eight miles an hour.

"How do you know?" asked the police justice.

"It took me five seconds to go from one telegraph pole to another," was the reply. "Now, as the telegraph poles are forty feet apart, you can calculate my speed for yourself."

The case was promptly adjourned—probably to give the law-giver time to make the calculations.

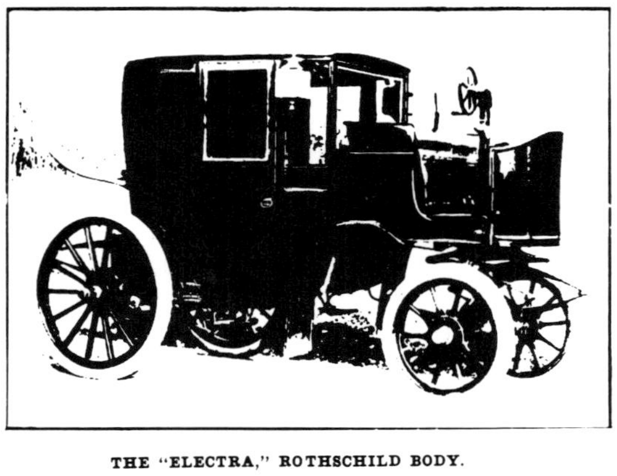

THE "ELECTRA," ROTHSCHILD BODY.

C.G.V., MULBACHER BODY

SECOND SECTION **THE NEW YORK HERALD.** PAGES 1 TO 4.

COMPLETE NUMBER 16 PAGES. EUROPEAN EDITION—PARIS, SUNDAY, SEPTEMBER 21, 1902.—WITH SUPPLEMENT. COMPLETE NUMBER 16 PAGES.

AUTOMOBILE COMPELLS A NEW ETIQUETTE

WHEN NO GUESTS ARE PRESENT THE CHAUFFEUR SITS BESIDE THE OWNER

(From the NEW YORK HERALD.)

MANY time-honored conventions of society have been overridden by the automobile. Speaking broadly, the amenities of life remain unchanged, whether one rides in an ox cart or an automobile, but the question of safety and convenience compels unexpected changes in their expression. If a horse be a vain thing for safety, then a racing automobile cannot be too indulgently humored. Beyond this question of necessity there is no court of appeal.

The new etiquette of the automobile is full of surprises. On coming to a standstill, the owner, or even the guests, help themselves in and out of the carriage with an amazing independence.

The owner, again, with apparent rudeness, crosses, in alighting, directly in front of the lady seated beside him. The new code of etiquette is followed in the most finely appointed automobiles by people of unquestioned taste. For the expert opinions embodied in the accompanying rules the HERALD is indebted to Mr. Proctor Smith, well known in automobile circles.

The New Code.

There is an excellent reason for every seeming breach of good manners. The new code is dictated by no less a master than common sense. It is merely because more is expected of the driver of a racing automobile in guiding his machine and protecting his guests that less is exacted of superficial manners. The use of the military salute on recognizing a lady in place of raising the hat, for example, has obviously the advantage of greater simplicity and safety. The innovation was first made in France, where such points of etiquette are universally observed.

It is obvious that the driver should be able to centre his entire consciousness, or nearly all, upon the guidance of his machine. Automobile caps, commonly worn, fit the head very closely, and can only be removed by a very determined jerk. To raise his hat, therefore, the driver would be obliged to take one hand from the steering wheel for several seconds and for so long to lose the control of his machine his right arm affords. Considering the rate at which most automobiles travel, it may be readily understood that much might happen during this second or so; even the safety of his guests might be imperilled. A military salute, on the other hand, is but the effort of an instant.

The distribution of the "chauffeur" and guests in an automobile is also a surprise to most people of conventional usage. It is considered correct form among the most careful people for the owner and "chauffeur" to sit side by side on the front seat of the machine at all times. The practice will appear somewhat surprising to those who have come to look upon the "chauffeur" as a sort of groom.

In Case of Accident.

In case of accident, it is, of course, important that both occupants of the machine should be within instant reach of the controlling gear.

Few of the best automobiles have any special provision for the "chauffeur." He is accommodated in the body of the machine like any guest, rather than removed to a footman's seat. If there be room in the tonneau, for instance, the "chauffeur" sits without embarrassment beside a guest, whether a lady or a gentleman. In case the automobile is carrying its full complement of passengers the "chauffeur" sits on the floor of the automobile or on the foot of the front seat, with his feet resting on the step. He should sit on the off side.

An adjustable seat is provided in many of the most expensive automobiles especially for this purpose. Though the practice may appear awkward, it is none the less logical, since it is at once comfortable and, in case of any accident, leaves the "chauffeur" in a position to render immediate assistance. The front seat is considered the post of honor, whether the vehicle be driven by the owner or by a "chauffeur."

On starting for a run, the owner, if he be the driver for the occasion, should be the last to take his seat. It is his place to see that his guests are all comfortable and that the door of the tonneau is securely fastened before taking his place at the wheel. When all is ready to start the driver passes to his seat from the off side of his automobile. Here is another innovation, compelled this time by the formation of the machine. In ordinary driving it would be a serious violation of convention to cross directly in front of the lady seated upon the front seat.

The reason for the innovation is that the machinery surrounding the driver's place makes it dificult for one to squeeze in between the guiding wheel and the seat. The passage way from the other direction is clear, and the driver is enabled to reach his seat more quickly and with less danger of disturbing the adjustment of the machinery. The front seats of the best machines are usually constructed with the idea of affording an ample passage way.

On leaving the machine the driver first adjusts all the machinery under his control, the work of several seconds, the guests remaining seated. The driver is the first to alight. By rigidly following this rule, the chance of accident, such as the unexpected bolting of the machine, is reduced to a minimum.

"Chauffeur" as Groom.

In the absence of the "chauffeur," the owner assists his guests to alight. When, on the other hand, no gentleman accompanies an automobile carrying ladies, the "chauffeur" acts as groom, standing at attention beside the step and giving what assistance is required. If the "chauffeur" be occupying a tonneau seat, whether the owner be driving or not, he must alight by the rear door, as the automobile slows down and pass around to the front to offer his assistance. In the case of a runaway or other accident, the "chauffeur" may climb over the front seat to reach the guiding machinery. He should also alight and hold the heads of frightened horses until the automobile has passed in safety.

At all times the "chauffeur" is expected to give the greater part of his attention to the machine itself, rather than to serving the owner or guests. Gentlemen occupying the automobile are expected to help themselves much more than in ordinary carriage driving. A gentleman occupying a seat in the tonneau, for instance, whether he be the owner or a guest, is expected to open the rear door without any assistance from the "chauffeur."

The question as to which side the driver should occupy is still an open one and is likely to remain so. The French and English machines are all constructed with the guiding machinery at the right of the automobile. In Europe, where all vehicles turn out to the right, this position, of course, gives the driver an advantage. He can control his machine more exactly and be a better judge of clearance. Many of the American machines are made with the guiding lever or wheel on the left, for the same reason. The relative advantages of both positions are much in dispute.

The guests of an automobile journey should be looked after exactly as guests on a coaching trip or a yachting cruise. In every emergency all expenses should be met by the owner.

COMPLETE NUMBER 12 PAGES. EUROPEAN EDITION—PARIS THURSDAY, DECEMBER 10, 1903. COMPLETE NUMBER 12 PAGES.

SALON D'AUTOMOBILE 1903

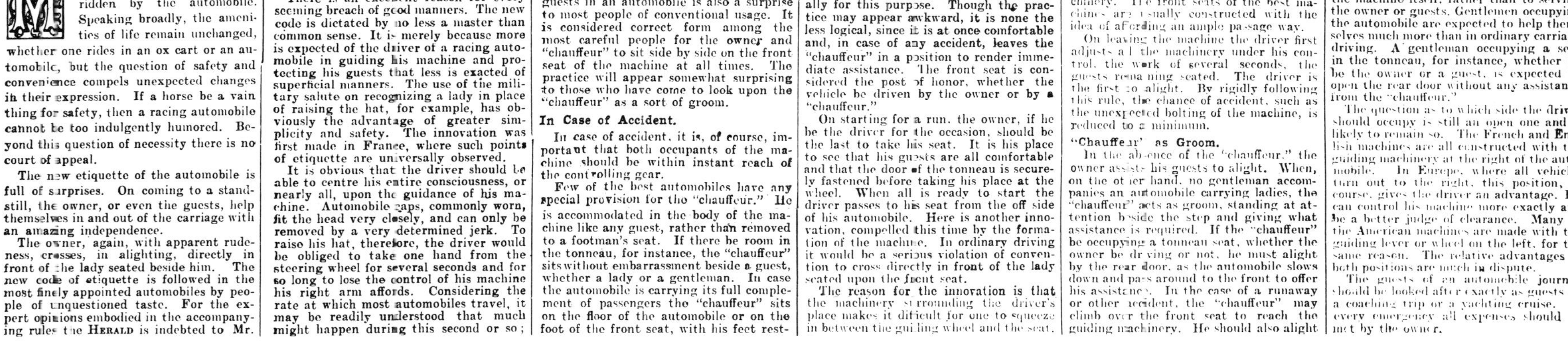

The Salon d'Automobile will open its doors to-day, and no sooner will the visitor have entered the Grand Palais, in the Champs-Elysées, than he will remark two characteristics which will constitute a marked difference between this exhibition and the ones which have preceded it. The great increase in the number of electric carriages and the great progress made in those possessing explosion motors.

No important advancement has been made in the electric motor itself, for it is difficult to modify the dynamo. It still remains what it has been, a motive organ of the first-class, noiseless and giving excellent power. Neither have the accumulators been greatly changed. Efforts have been made to lighten them and to make them more lasting, but the progress has been slow and the improvements but slight. Therefore, if there is a marked increase in the number of electric vehicles it is due to the fact that one has been forced to recognize, after a lengthened trial, that they are the carriages "par excellence" for city work, being fast, easy to handle and, above all comfortable.

Better than any other, the "châssis" of the electric carriage is capable of being stylishly and luxuriously upholstered, and broughams, landaulets, landaus without noise or odor are now coming into general use in Paris, New York and London, taking the husband to his office in the morning, the wife or daughters shopping or visiting in the afternoon, and the whole family to the theatre or receptions at night.

At a no far distant date they will probably possess lighter accumulators by which means they will be enabled to accomplish longer distances than at present, and they will then eclipse all other methods of locomotion.

On the other hand, petroleum carriages have shown a marked improvement in the progress accomplished up to the end of 1902, and to-day's Salon shows perfection rather than marked novelty. One does not find those radical modifications which in previous years caused certain models to go completely out of fashion, and upon this point constructors generally are to be congratulated. Convinced at the commencement of the year of having good motors, turning regularly, without the annoyance of valves (thanks to improved admission appliances), possessing reliable firing, etc., they have turned their attention to other parts of the "châssis," hitherto somewhat neglected, such as the springs, axles and wheels. The "châssis" are now almost universally made of Channel steel and are of greater length than in the past in order to place on them the handsome and comfortable bodies, with lateral entrances, for which such as Messrs. Rotschild, Muhlbacher, Labourdette and Kellner are famous.

The solid axles of the past, and even the hollow ones of a later date, have given place to those constructed in profiled steel which are lighter, stronger and more elastic. The springs, too, are being so arranged as to lower the body, and much greater attention is being paid to the manuufacture of the wheels, which, for the greater part, are of wood.

Thus, both in electric and explosion carriages, a great forward movement has been made, and the present Salon marks a new era in automobilism. It is thoroughly international, as the following visits to the principal stands will show.

Latter-Day Luxuries for Travellers "En Automobile."

NAPIER AUTO FITTED WITH TOOL CHESTS LUNCHEON OUTFIT MEDICAL APPLIANCES, TRUNKS FOR CLOTHES HATS ETC. TRUNKS UNDER SEATS.

LUNCHEON SERVICE WITH FOLDING TABLE

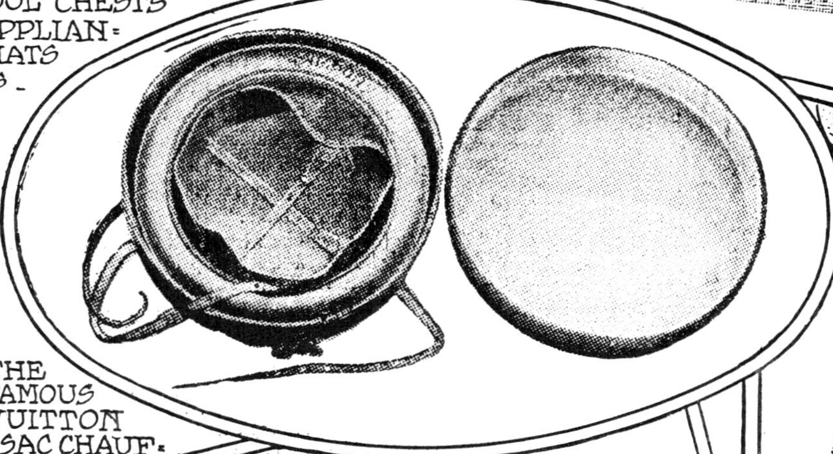

THE FAMOUS VUITTON "SAC CHAUFFEUR."

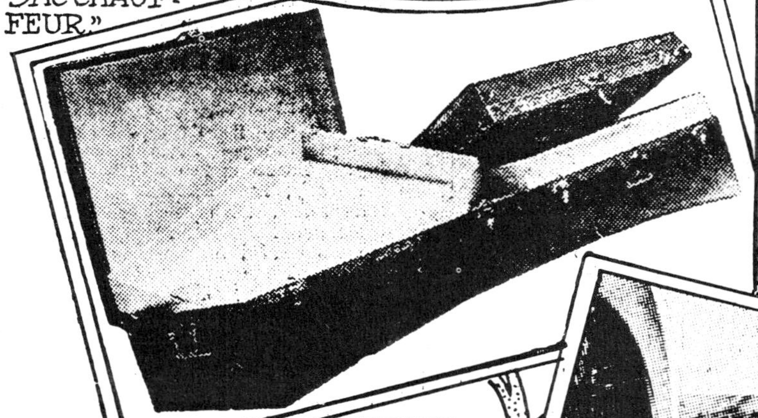

CARVED TRUNK FOR FITTING ON ROOF

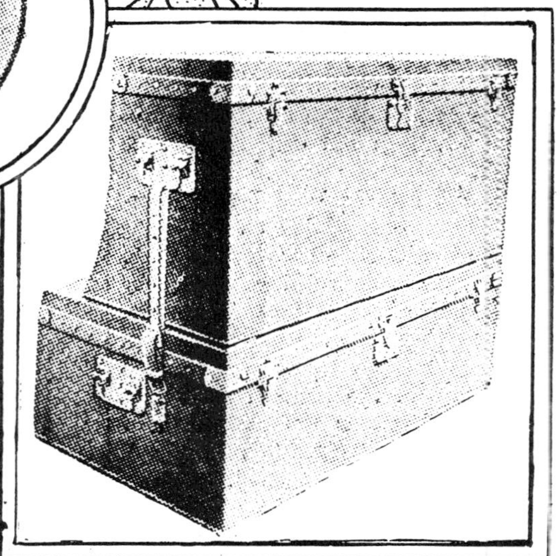

TRUNK SHAPED TO FIT COACHWORK.

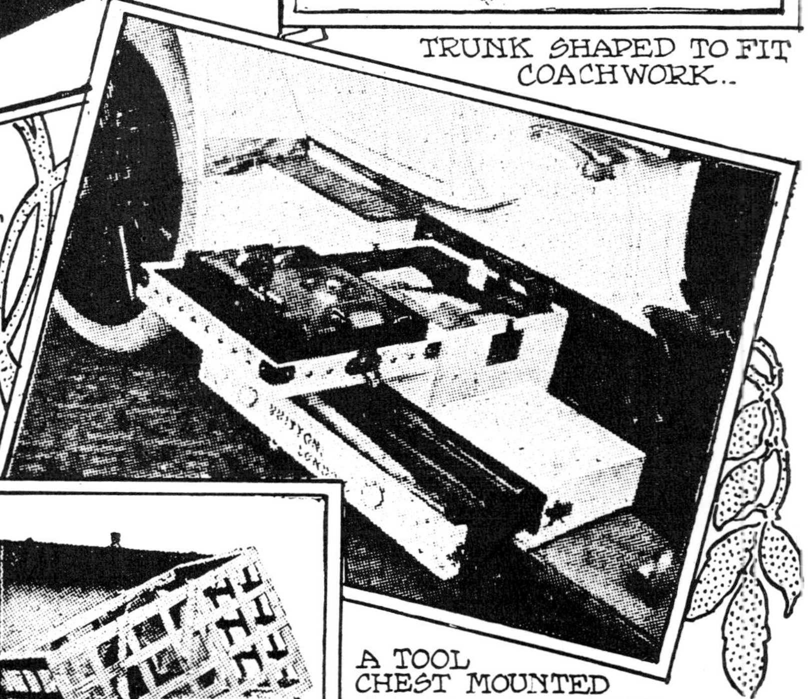

A TOOL CHEST MOUNTED ON THE FOOTBOARD.

LADIES HAT BOX, BY GOYARD AINÉ.

All the Comforts of a Modern Hotel Packed Away in These Convenient Boxes.

In the early days of automobiling, when a driver thought he had performed wonders if he succeeded in getting his motor to take him to Versailles and back without a couple of breakdowns, the idea of personal comfort when travelling by road was not very strongly developed. If a man took a few friends for a short tour, the order went round that as little luggage as possible was to be brought; and even ladies were compelled to limit themselves to a spare dress and a brush and a comb. This state of affairs continued for several years, but as by degrees the automobile became a more reliable form of locomotion, as body-work grew more and more luxurious and the closed type almost universally succeeded the open, so the ideas held by devotees of the new sport underwent a vast and sweeping change. To-day a party when touring can carry not only a sufficiency of dress, but a wealth of luxuries as well, so that country inns have been robbed of half their terrors, and unavoidable halts by the wayside turned into pleasant little picnics.

In fact, the revolution is complete. The horrible nightmare of dust, oil, filthy clothes and prevailing discomfort has been dispelled. A tour in a modernly equipped automobile may be considered one long course of undiluted pampering. Practically every comfort of a high-class hotel may be found stored away in the cunningly devised trunks and boxes for which hitherto unsuspected space has been found. Without disturbing the general lines of the vehicle, and, generally speaking, without destroying the balance, these receptacles have been ingeniously worked into position, and they have been constructed in such a manner that the all-pervading dust, with its unparalleled power for entering everywhere, fails to penetrate.

New Problems.

Two Paris firms have become particularly distinguished for the manner in which they have understood the growing needs of the automobile public, and set about solving the numerous problems presented. These are the maison Louis Vuitton and the maison E. GoyardAiné. M. Louis Vuitton, seen yesterday by a HERALD correspondent, said that the chief problem confronting the trunk constructor was the question of strength and weight. It was essential to produce goods which would resist vibration, shocks, knocking about and foul weather, and at the same time to construct them of material which had little weight. Further, it was essential to make these trunks and cases absolutely dustproof, a far more difficult thing than many people imagined. Moreover, the automobile public was always demanding novelties.

One of the most useful devices contrived by this house is the celebrated "sac chauffeur." This consists of a round box with lid of equal depth, lined with rubber. Tires are carried inside as well as ladies' hats, while at night the lid may be carried to the bedroom and utilized as a bath. This model has had an enormous success, and is seen in all parts of the world.

Table and All.

The latest Vuitton model of luncheon or dinner basket which may be placed against the back of the front seats is about the completest thing of its kind. The outfit comprises every table requisite, a coffee strainer and space for wine bottles and liqueurs. The forks and other metal fittings are in "metal blanc" silvered over. They are extremely light.

Automobilists are advised to drive with extraordinary care in the neighborhood of Survilliers (Seine-et-Oise). The police are keeping careful watch.

The panic caused by the Handcross auto-omnibus accident a month ago has not yet subsided in England. All the papers continue to discuss the merits and demerits of the auto-bus with extreme life and vigor.

BUFFALO BILL'S WILD WEST. | BUFFALO BILL'S WILD WEST | BUFFALO BILL'S WILD WEST. | BUFFALO BILL'S WILD WEST. | BUFFALO BILL'S WILD WEST. | BUFFALO BILL'S WILD WEST.

OPENING on the CHAMP DE MARS, SUNDAY, APRIL 2, for a FEW WEEKS ONLY.

Main Entrance, Avenue Rapp Transversale.

Two Performances Daily, at 2.30 and 8.30 p.m. RAIN OR SHINE. Doors Open at 1 and 7.

BUFFALO BILL'S WILD WEST

THE WORLD PRONOUNCES IT SUPREMELY ORIGINAL AND GREAT.

Brimful of Life, Action and Thrilling Interest; Crowded with Historical Fact and Correct Information; Presenting with Historical Accuracy the Exciting Sanguinary and Romantic Scenes of Pioneer Life on the Plains, in the Forest and at the Foot Hills during the Early Days of the Story of American Progress, in which will participate Redskin Braves, Western Frontiersmen, Scouts, Hunters and Cowboys in True Pictures of Border Life on the Western American Plains. Attack upon the Emigrant Train, Pony Express Riding, Famous Deadwood Stage "Hold-up," Burning of a Settler's Cabin.

Indian War Dances and Pastimes, Cowboy Fun, Lassoing Wild Horses, Riding Bucking Broncos, the Chase, Capture and Punishment of a Horse Thief.

BUFFALO BILL, THE MASTER EXPONENT

of Horseback Marksmanship, in his Wonderful Exhibition of Shooting while riding a Galloping Horse.

A HUNDRED NORTH AMERICAN INDIANS

from the Sioux, Ogallalla, Brule, Uncapappa, Cheyenne and Arapahoe Tribes. Genuine "Blanket Redmen," Chiefs, Warriors, Bucks, Squaws and Papooses in Indian Sports and War Dances.

AN INTERNATIONAL CONGRESS OF THE WORLD'S ROUGH RIDERS:

Great Cohorts of Daring and Dexterous Horsemen, Representative Native Equestrians of Every Clime, including Cossacks of the Caucasus, the Gaucho of Argentina, Vaqueros of Old Mexico, Rifflan and Bedouin Arabs from the Sahara, Cubans from the Antilles, Scouts, Cowboys, Indians from the American Prairies, Hungarian Czikos. Unquestionably the Equestrian Sensation of Modern Times.

Both Press and Public accord a Hearty Welcome to the World's Mounted Warriors.

AND

Congress of Rough Riders of the World.

Headed and Personally Introduced by

COL. W. F. CODY (BUFFALO BILL).

Now making positively its final tour of France. Will never return! See it now or never! Three special trains, 800 people, 500 horses.

The One Exhibition in all the World that has no Counterpart.

Exclusively Its Own Creation.

THE VETERAN CAVALRY OF MANY FLAGS

in Military Evolutions and Exercises.

A Corps from the United States Life Savers, exemplifying the Methods employed with the Breeches Buoy in Life Saving by the Guardians of Neptune's Stormy Coasts.

Imperial Japanese Troupe, in Ancient and Modern War Drill.

French Light Cavalry, Royal English Lancers, United States Cavalry and Artillery Veterans, the Devlin Zouaves, Expert Marksmen, Lasso and Bolas Throwers.

Magnificent, Magnetic and Truthful Reproduction of the Memorable Battle of Little Big Horn; the Awful Reality of Furious Conflict and Massacre in Savage Warfare presented with Perfect Historical Accuracy of Detail, introducing Eight Hundred

INDIAN CHIEFS,

Braves and Warriors, Soldiers, Scouts and Horses, with every Accessory of Arms, Accoutrements and Savage Decoration, whose Inconceivably Overpowering Apotheosis of Mortal Combat is the Illustrious Tableaux of Custer's Last Stand and Heroic Fall.

The World will Never See its Like Again! Everything Presented is Realism Itself. The Vast Arena Illuminated at Night by Special Electric Light Plants.

The Entire Grand Programme will positively be Presented Undivided and Uncurtailed.

ONE TICKET ADMITS TO ALL ADVERTISED ATTRACTIONS.

Price of Seats, 1fr. 50c.; 2fr. 50c., 3fr., 4fr. and 5fr. Box Seats, per Seat 5fr., 8fr. and 10fr. Children under 10 years admitted to the 2fr. 50c. Seats for 1fr. 50c., and to all Seats at 3fr. and over for Half Price.

Reserved Seat Tickets at the Bureaux.

GALIGNANI'S

Booksellers Stationers

CIRCULATING LIBRARY.

224 RUE DE RIVOLI, PARIS.
8 AVENUE MASSENA, NICE.

Newest Publications.

	Fr.C.
The Roe Deer: A Monograph by "Snaffle." Colored Illustrations. Edition limited to 100 copies	29.00
Three Generations of Fascinating Women. Lady Russell	45.00
The King in Exile. Eva Scott	20.00
Strategy Illustrated by British Campaigns. Captain Macquoid	14.50
The Women of America. E. McCracken	9.50
De Profundis. Oscar Wilde	7.00

Fiction.

The Marriage of William Ashe. Mrs. Humphry Ward	7.50
Amanda of the Mill. Marie Van Vorst	7.50
The Vicissitudes of Evangeline. Elinor Glyn	7.50
The Mirror of Kong-Ho. Ernest Bramah	7.50
The Gate of the Desert. John Oxenham	7.50
At Close Range. F. Hopkinson Smith	8.00

Latest English and American Books of Travel, Biography, Fiction, etc., always in stock.

LARGE SELECTION OF ENGLISH AND AMERICAN MAGAZINES AND PERIODICALS.

BRENTANO'S

Booksellers and Stationers,

37 Avenue de l'Opéra, PARIS.

General Literature.

	Fr.C.
Florence, painted by Colonel R. C. Goff, described by Mrs. Goff	29.00
A Belle of the Fifties, Memoirs of Mrs. Clay of Alabama. By Ada Sterling	15.00
The Heart of the Orient. By M. M. Shoemaker	15.00
Indians of the Painted Desert Region. By Geo. Wharton James	11.50
The Balkan Question. Edited by Luigi Villari	14.50
From a Holiday Journal. By Mrs. E. T. Cook	14.50

Fiction.

Fata Morgana. By André Castaigne	7.50
The Marriage of William Ashe. By Mrs. Humphry Ward	7.50
Amanda of the Mill. By Marie Van Vorst	7.50
The White Terror and the Red. By A. Cahan	8.00
A Lindsay's Love. By Charles Lowe	7.50
Shining Ferry. By "Q."	7.50
The Dryad. By Justin Huntly McCarthy	7.50
Fergy the Guide. By H. S. Canfield	8.50
The Clock and the Key. By Arthur H. Vesey	8.00
The Castle of the Shadows. By Mrs. C. N. Williamson	7.50
The Vicissitudes of Evangeline. By Elinor Glyn	7.50

BRENTANO'S CLEARANCE LIST of Popular Fiction Post Free on Application.

The latest American and English Books of Travel, Biography, Fiction, &c., always on hand.

The principal Magazines, Weeklies and American dailies received regularly.

Prompt attention given to all mail orders.

SWITZERLAND.

GENEVA. HOTEL BELLEVUE. Recently built, unexceptionally comf. Splend. sit. on the borders of the Lake. J. Sutterlin, pr.

GENEVA. HOTEL-PENSION BRISTOL. All modern comf. Lift. Bath. Elec. light. Central heating. Pension rates from 6fr. to 10fr.

GENEVA. HOTEL PENSION FLEISCHMANN, 1st cl. Gr. comf. Rd.Pt. de Plainpalais

SHOEMAKER. ONLY AMERICAN HOUSE IN SWITZERLAND. NICHOLLS, 5 rue des Alpes, GENEVA.

INTERLAKEN, HOTEL BEAU-SITE Near Station. Finest view.

LAUSANNE.—THE GRAND HOTEL. HOTELS BEAU-SITE and RICHE-MONT, Ltd. In the middle of a park of 20,000m. Modern comfort.

LUCERNE. SWITZERLAND. HOTEL D'ANGLETERRE (English Hotel). Best situation, facing the lake. 1st cl. Hotel. F. I. Steffen.

LUCERNE. Pension Splendide

MONTREUX-VEYTAUX. HOTEL BONIVARD

ST. LEGIER. SUR-VEVEY. HOTEL-PENSION DU ROC. Recently built. All mod. comf. Spl. sit. Vue du lac. F. Gartner

St. Moritz-Bad ENGADINE. **Neues Stahlbad Hotel** 400 BEDS. CHALYBEATE SPRING BATHS.

LE GRAND HOTEL DE VEVEY EUG. MICHEL, PROP. PARK of 50,000m. Two Tennis. BATHS IN LAKE

VEVEY HOTEL DES TROIS COURONNES (*Hôtel Monnet*)

VEVEY. William Cuénod and Co., Bankers, U.S.A Consul. Ad. Br. office, Clarens, Montreux

Grand Hotel Pierre à Voir. s.-Martigny, Valais, Suisse, alt. 1555m. 1ord. Ouvert 1er Juin. Climat sec. Vue grandiose. Vaste parc. Mélèzes. Excurs. voit. par Martigny.

WEGGIS. PENSION BUHLEGG, from 5 to 7fr. (Lake Lucerne). Magnificent view.

ITALY.

FLORENCE. VILLA TROLOPPE. First class. Hotel-pension. McNamee, prop

GÊNES. PENSION BRISTOL FIRST CLASS

GENOA GRAND HOTEL DE GÊNES First class. Full south. Gr. Restaurant.

LIDO-VENICE.—SEA BATHS SEASON—MARCH TO END OF OCTOBER. DAILY CONCERTS. FIRST CLASS ESTABLISHMENT **GRAND HOTEL DES BAINS.**

MENAGGIO. —GRAND HOTEL.

NAPLES. SAVOY HOTEL. PROMENADE CARACCIOLO. New and first class house, full southern asp. Splendid view of the whole gulf. ROSSANIGO, Prop.

ADVERTISEMENTS. | ADVERTISEMENTS. | ADVERTISEMENTS.

AU BON MARCHÉ

PARIS — Maison A. BOUCICAUT — PARIS

OVERCOAT, single breasted, latest style, silk lined throughout. 95 francs.	**SUIT,** single breasted coat, new cut, in tweed and blue or black cheviot, fine quality. 13 years. 39 francs. 2 fr. *for every extra year.*	**JUVENILE SUIT** for 3 to 6 years. In red or navy serge. Blouse with tucks in front and back, Eton collar and cream bengaline necktie, white leather belt. 3 years. . . 29 francs. 1 fr. *for every extra year.*	**SUIT,** single breasted coat, new colours. 75 francs.	**STYLISH SUIT,** for boys, in fancy cloth either grey or beige, or in blue diagonal cloth, blouse in striped woollen material. 6 years. . 32 francs. 1 fr. *for every extra year.*

PRIX: Pour Dames et Enfants . . . . . 8 francs
Pour Hommes et Jeunes Gens . . . 9 francs
Pour Athlètes . . . . 10 francs

ADVERTISEMENTS. | ADVERTISEMENTS.

AUTOMOBILISTS
CHAUFFEURS & TRAVELLERS GENERALLY
— Dr VALLE'S —
Antiseptic **EYE LOTION**
or "COLLYRE UNIVERSEL"
Strengthens the Eyes & prevents Inflamation; Soothes irritation caused by Dust or Currents of Air; Cures Bloodshot Eyes and the numerous inconveniences caused by Cold, or rapid travelling.
ROBERTS & Co Pharmaciens to the KING & QUEEN of ENGLAND
Paris Rue de la Paix. 5 | London 76. New Bond Street
4 oz bottles 3 frs; (franco Colis Postal-france - 4 frs)
7 bottles 18 frs; (franco Colis Postal-france - 19 frs)

WILLS'S CAPSTAN NAVY CUT TOBACCO.

En vente dans tous les Bureaux de Tabac, Paris et Province.
Vendu dans le Monde Entier.

THE NEW YORK HERALD.

ICE: 15 CENTIMES. EUROPEAN EDITION—PARIS. THURSDAY. APRIL 19, 1906.—EIGHT PAGES. NO. 25,441.

EARTHQUAKE DEVASTATES SAN FRANCISCO.

From One Thousand to Five Thousand Persons Are Reported Killed by Falling Buildings, Flames, or a Tidal Wave which Swept the Waterfront.

Fire which Sweeps Away Business Portion of California City Is Still Raging—Estimated Loss Is Already $75,000,000—Other Cities Suffer.

[BY COMMERCIAL CABLE TO THE HERALD.]

SAN FRANCISCO, Wednesday.—An earthquake disaster, the proportions of which are still unknown, befell San Francisco this morning, when, at about five o'clock, the city was shaken by tremendous convulsions.

The first slight tremors were enough to send the frightened populace into the streets half-clad, and then came a shock that toppled buildings over in the business district, hurled scores of brick tenements to the ground, and sank some streets from four to ten feet.

The waters from the bay rushed in like a tidal wave, snatching hapless victims as it receded, and then came fire, blazing up among the ruins in the lower part of the city, fed by leaking gas mains.

Hundreds of lives were lost in the collapse of buildings, in the inrushing waters or the spreading fires. Estimates of the loss are still conjectural, as in the disorganized state of affairs an accurate count is impossible. It is feared a thousand is not too large an estimate, and a more gloomy report is five thousand or even more.

Flames Are Spreading.

The flames got quickly beyond control, owing to a lack of water, and late this afternoon were still spreading, despite the efforts of firemen and police using dynamite to destroy the buildings. The latest despatch indicates that practically everything south of Market street, from Eighth street to the water front, and north of Market street from Sansoure to Broadway, will be destroyed. This includes the entire wholesale district, with the prominent downtown hotels, newspaper and telegraph offices, theatres, and many large office buildings.

The flames are spreading into the Hayes Valley residence district, and St. Ignace Cathedral is afire.

City Stupefied.

The city is stunned by the calamity, which came unheralded after a rarely beautiful day. Frightened visitors are hurrying to leave the city, which is now under the rule of the State military forces, with the Government troops ready to co-operate if needed.

The work of recovering the dead has barely begun, but it is reported four hundred bodies have already been found. It will probably be days before adequate forces are engaged, as railroad and telegraph communication is cut.

Other Cities Suffer.

The neighboring parts of California suffered with San Francisco. Oakland, Nevada City and Sacramento lost many buildings.

Several are reported killed at San José. An unconfirmed report says that the Leland Stanford University is demolished and one student killed.

The latest information from the Leland Stanford, Jr., University, is that all but one university building is damaged. The memorial chapel is ruined.

Five are killed at Oakland.

Thousands of homeless persons are camping in the parks.

Several vessels are reported sunk by the tidal wave that swept the water-front.

Eight Square Miles.

The area swept by flames up to five o'clock this afternoon is estimated at eight square miles. Many fine residences are destroyed between Market, Eighth and Folsome streets. The loss is already estimated at seventy-five million dollars.

THOUSANDS CRAZED BY FRIGHT THRONG STREETS OF THE DEVASTATED CITY.

Shock Came When Residents Were Sleeping—Earth's Convulsions Break Gas and Water Mains.

The first shock was felt at thirteen minutes after five o'clock this morning. It was very severe, lasting three minutes. All over the city persons inhabiting brick houses awoke to find walls collapsing, roofs falling in.

All who were uninjured rushed frantically into the streets in their night clothes. There they saw the surface of the streets bulge in waves under a succession of terrible pulsations, while all around buildings swayed back and forth with ominous creakings or fell with a terrific crash.

Panic Reigns Everywhere.

Residents in frame houses, principally outside the tenement districts, escaped harm, but the same panic possessed them. The tremors continued more than an hour. The streets were thronged with excited people, rushing hither and thither as if crazed. Fires started in a dozen places at once, spreading with great rapidity. As practically all the water mains were broken by the convulsions the firemen were helpless.

A brisk wind started, threatening the destruction of the entire business section.

Buildings Blown Up.

In desperation firemen, police and troops from the Government Reservation began blowing up the buildings with powder and dynamite in the hope of stopping the flames. The Militia was called out and the city put under martial law.

Another shock at a quarter-past eight accentuated the panic in the city, but caused little damage. With returning sanity the work of rescue began in disjointed fashion in the sections most damaged by the earthquake. The dead and injured were borne out from collapsed buildings while the police restrained frantic relatives. The Mechanics' pavilion was converted into a temporary hospital. Several hundred injured were treated by a corps of volunteer surgeons. The hospitals were overrun with victims. Out of town visitors at the hotels shared the general terror. Hundreds rushed after the first shock to telegraph stations to inform friends in the East of their safety, only to find that all but one postal telegraph wire were gone.

FRIDAY. APRIL 20, 1906.

FIRE COMPLETES DESTRUCTION OF STRICKEN SAN FRANCISCO.

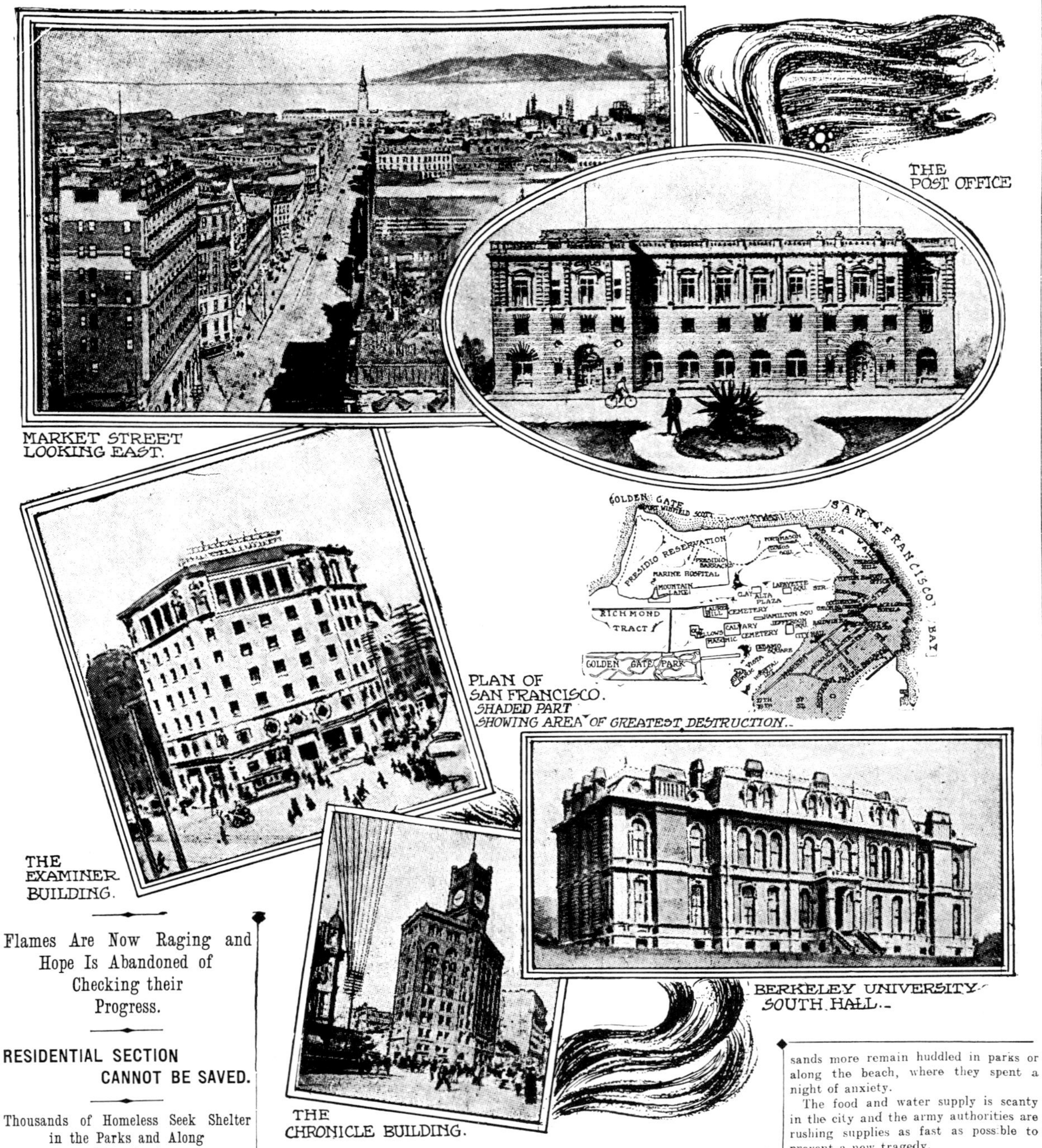

Flames Are Now Raging and Hope Is Abandoned of Checking their Progress.

RESIDENTIAL SECTION CANNOT BE SAVED.

Thousands of Homeless Seek Shelter in the Parks and Along Waterfront.

SITUATION IS DESPERATE.

From All Over America Contributions from Generous Cities Are Being Rushed to California.

[BY COMMERCIAL CABLE TO THE HERALD.]

NEW YORK, Thursday.—Surpassing in an appalling extent even the first wild reports, the San Francisco catastrophe grows with every hour.

The latest advices from California up to four o'clock this afternoon, Pacific time, indicated the destruction of practically the entire city by fire as almost inevitable.

In the absence of water nothing can stop the flames until they fail for want of material. The supply of explosives is reported as failing and the flames are raging unchecked.

The business district and the tenement quarter to the north and along the river front are laid waste and the fire is now eating its way rapidly into Nob Hill, the best residence section of the city.

Situation Terrible.

Brigadier-General Funston informs Washington that the situation could not be worse and 200,000 are homeless. Thousands of refugees have escaped from the city to places across the bay, but thousands more remain huddled in parks or along the beach, where they spent a night of anxiety.

The food and water supply is scanty in the city and the army authorities are rushing supplies as fast as possible to prevent a new tragedy.

Estimates Impossible.

In the still confused condition of affairs, estimates of the loss of life are almost guesswork. The known dead number 500 already, and hundreds more must be entombed in the tenement district over which the flames have swept.

One estimate this afternoon was from 2,000 to 3,000 dead, and the lower figure seems conservative.

Imprisoned and Burned.

Oakland hears of people being burned to death to-day in buildings from which they cannot escape.

Estimates of property loss are likewise conjectural, but $150,000,000 seems not an excessive figure, and the total is steadily rising as costly residences fall before the unquenchable fire.

Of the five structures of the departments that transacted the city's business only the scorched and dismantled fragments remain. Places of amusement, hotels, newspaper offices and most of the public buildings are virtually ash heaps.

Panic Subsides.

After the first panic the residents of the city have become calm in the face of an even greater disaster. A committee of safety supported by Federal troops and militia is holding the city in a firm grip. There is little disorder anywhere.

Sympathy for San Francisco is widespread. Movements have been started in every large city to raise large amounts of money. New York late this afternoon had almost $750,000 raised, and other cities are doing as well in proportion.

Congress appropriated a million dollars to-day with unheard-of speed. The Government Departments are giving aid in all possible ways.

Tents, rations and men are supplied by the army and navy.

The outpouring of money and supplies promises to be the most remarkable in American history.

New Disaster Feared.

Fears of a new disaster were roused this afternoon by reports of earthquakes at Los Angeles, 300 miles south of San Francisco, but later reports showed that apparently little damage was done.

Returns, slowly coming in from the valleys immediately north and south of San Francisco, point to a great loss of life, especially at Santa Rosa, whence only meagre details are obtainable. A most conservative estimate is 200 dead.

San José, Santa Clara, Monterey and Santa Cruz also had fatalities, but the number is still uncertain.

Cliff House Gone.

The famous Cliff House, at the western end of Golden Gate Park, it is reported, has been swept into the sea. It is understood that not a stick or stone remains to tell of the building which was occupied, but the number of patrons is not known. It is feared the loss of life at this place will be heavy. The Sutro baths are also reported destroyed. Apparently a tidal wave swept in after the earthquake and swallowed the hotel.

The Presidio Reservation, Richmond Hill and Golden Gate Park resembled this afternoon a vast picnic ground.

Tents with improvised coverings have been erected everywhere. Fireplaces are built in the streets and beds and mattresses are thrown down in convenient spots. Bakeries are already built within the reservation and the bread supply is still holding out.

The apparent impossibility of burying the dead, many of whom are still in the streets and ruins, is likely to cause the authorities to send the bodies out in boats for burial at sea.

Firemen are blowing up all the residences on the east side of Van Ness avenue between Golden Gate and Pacific avenues, a distance of a mile. Fairmont Hotel, in the same neighborhood and the Spreckels million-dollar mansion are reported on fire.

All traffic toward the city has been stopped by the military, who are sending the injured and dying to Oakland Hospitals as fast as possible.

Drinking water is being taken into the city on wagons.

The United States Mint is the only building in the burned district standing intact. The damage to it is small so far.

THOUSANDS OF HOMELESS PASS NIGHT OF TERROR IN THE DEVASTATED CITY.

Fire Battle Fought in Vain and Entire City Seems Doomed to Destruction.

[BY COMMERCIAL CABLE TO THE HERALD.]

SAN FRANCISCO, Thursday.—The day broke on the devastated city after a night of unspeakable horror. Through the hours of darkness flames flared, seeming to thousands of destitute, packed in parks and public squares in the western part of the city, like signal beacons of destruction.

The most substantial part of San Francisco had crumbled before the earthquake or withered under the fiery blast. Before nightfall one person in every four of the entire population was without a home, and the others awaited, in impotent expectation, the ruin of their domiciles.

Dynamite Resorted to.

Every now and then came the muffled sounds of dynamite explosions, like the booming of big guns at sea. All through the night firemen fought pluckily against nature's terrible odds to stay the destruction. Thousands of inhabitants had early abandoned hope from fear or weariness and had fled from the city panic-stricken. The refugees, chiefly women and children, carrying what few valuables they could snatch from the wreck and flames, crowded all the available tugs, ferryboats and launches, hurrying to the smaller cities along the bay. They had to force their way to the water front through the blackened streets choked with hot débris under a stifling pall of black smoke and flying cinders.

Police Are Powerless.

Government troops tried to turn the human tide back to the temporary security of the hills and parks west of the city, but two thousand soldiers with the police were powerless to handle scores of thousands of homeless ones.

Well-to-do residents of the Nob Hill district realized by night the destruction of their splendid houses was imminent. The roar of the flames from the business district, steadily growing louder, told the story of an unconquerable foe. Throughout the night they worked frantically to remove household effects, but it was impossible for many to get vehicles for transporting the goods. Pianos, costly bric-à-brac, trunks, paintings, beds and boxes were piled for miles along the streets, and are evidently doomed to fall a prey to the steadily advancing battle line of fire.

Widespread Desolation.

People from the district between Hayes Valley and Pacific street, including the beautiful Van Ness avenue section, took refuge in Golden Gate Park. Thousands of tents had been pitched there and in other parks, but these are inadequate to shelter the huge mob of mingled rich and poor that thronged for shelter.

2nd EDITION.

FIRE CHECKED.

[BY COMMERCIAL CABLE TO THE HERALD.]

NEW YORK, THURSDAY.—A LATE SAN FRANCISCO DESPATCH REPORTS THAT THE FIRE HAS BEEN CHECKED FOR THE PRESENT ON VAN NESS AVENUE, WHERE ARE THE CITY'S FINEST RESIDENCES. THE FIREMEN HAVE OBTAINED A SMALL SUPPLY OF WATER AND ARE NOW FIGHTING DESPERATELY TO EXTINGUISH THE FLAMES, AS IT SEEMS TO BE THE LAST CHANCE TO SAVE ANY PART OF THE CITY.

Photographs Just Received from San Francisco, Showing Extent of Ruin.

View at the Junction of Market & Larkin Streets, Showing Ruins of City Hall.

Nailing her Flag to the Mast *(From the New York Herald.)*

All that remains of Grace Church Stockton & California Streets

Grace Church before the Earthquake and Fire

Call Bldg. Mutual Savings Bank Bldg.

Kearny St. Looking Toward Market St. from Post St.

Panoramic View of San Francisco's Ruins, View Looking Down Market St. Toward the Mission

"ALL READY" THE RACE FOR THE COUPE INTERNATIONALE DES AÉRONAUTES.

LIEUT FRANK P LAHM (AMERICA)

M SANTOS-DUMONT (AMERICA)

COMTE CASTILLON DE SAINT VICTOR (FRANCE)

M JACQUES BALSAN. (FRANCE)

COMTE HENRY DE LA VAULX (FRANCE)

THE COUPE INTERNATIONALE DES AERONAUTES

MR FRANK H BUTLER (GREAT BRIT)

HON C S ROLLS (GREAT BRITAIN)

PROFESSOR HUNTINGTON (GREAT BRIT)

M VAN DEN DRIESCHE (BELGIUM)

SIGNOR ALF VONWILLER (ITALY)

The start of the race for the Coupe Internationale des Aéronautes takes place at four o'clock this afternoon in the Tuileries Gardens. Sixteen balloons, representing seven countries, will ascend and if the wind only happens to blow from the west, a long voyage lies before all of them. So much has already been written on this great aerial contest that there is not very much left to be said. A short recapitulation, however, at this, the starting-hour, may prove useful to those who intend to witness the proceedings.

About six months ago the Aéro-Club de France gratified the aeronautical world by the announcement that a cup, valued at 12,500fr., had been offered for competition by the donor of the Automobile Coupe Internationale, and that this cup was, moreover, backed up by a money prize of 12,500fr. The success of the proposed contest was immediate. It was felt on all hands that it would provide the long-needed publicity for the thorough popularization of the aerial sport, and the representatives of ballooning societies all over the world immediately commenced the necessary preparations. The streams of adhesions to the rules of the contest was long and steady, and in a short time France, Great Britain, America, Germany, Belgium, Spain and Italy sent their entries. Nowhere more than in England was the scheme welcomed, and the Aero Club of the United Kingdom, only recently founded, made great efforts in order to be worthily represented in the struggle.

The enthusiasm was general. During the last six months the press of the world has devoted more attention to the forthcoming race and to ballooning in general than to any other sport. Ballooning became almost at a bound the one sport in which it was fashionable to indulge. All over Europe and America there came about a notable change in the attitude of the public towards what had previously been considered a dangerous and foolhardy pastime. Such was the immediate effect of the offer.

Between now and next September there will be ample opportunity of seeing what the ultimate influence will be. It may not lead directly to the definite conquest of the air, but when flying machines and steerable balloons are as common as automobiles and the railway train remains as the only representative of the "poids lourd" category, it will be generally recognized that the Coupe Internationale des Aéronautes gave the needed impetus at the opportune moment.

The Tuileries Gardens are admirably suited for an aeronautical contest. Those people who cannot find room in the enclosure itself have the Champs-Elysées, the rue de Rivoli, the banks of the Seine and other points of vantage. For there is this notable difference between a balloon contest and every other form of sport, that in the former everyone can follow the entire proceedings. The committee of the Aéro-Club in charge of the proceedings to-day has made excellent arrangements.

All the pilots taking part in to-day's contest are well-known men. Some, of course, have had more experience than others, but not one can be described as a novice. The most celebrated team is that entered by France. Comte Henry de La Vaulx holds the world's record both for distance and endurance. He is a past-master in the science of aeronautics and is responsible for the growth of the movement perhaps more than any other living man.

The British team is composed of enthusiasts. In M. Santos-Dumont America has an experienced champion. All these men may be said to be on an equality so far as balloons are concerned.

The maximum capacity of 2,200 cubic mètres has been chosen by almost everyone, and thus the disproportion in capacity always seen in automobile races is absent.

At the start of a balloon race there is really only one danger—fire. Every imaginable precaution has been taken by the committee to guard against a disaster of this description. Strict orders against smoking have been issued, and the soldiers and police have full authority to execute them. The danger does not lie in actual smoking, but in the striking of matches.

The only other fear concerns the wind. Should it blow this afternoon as it has done throughout the week, the danger will be considerable. The wind has been bearing towards the English Channel. Of course, the cooler and less impulsive pilots, under such conditions, will descend on the shore, but there is a fear that among the sixteen pilots there may be some who, anxious to bear off the prize, will risk all and allow themselves to be blown out to sea, trusting to some passing vessel or change of wind to rescue them from their position.

Thus the success of to-day's proceedings depends upon the direction of the wind. At this period of the year the tendency of the wind is to blow towards the east or south-east, and that is the reason this date was chosen. The pilots have two objects in mind: One, the principal, to cover the greatest possible distance; the second is to remain in the air as long as possible. To-morrow morning or, at the latest, to-morrow evening news should be had of the first to descend. In one night, be it remembered, if the breeze holds fair, Austria or the southern part of Russia may be attained. By Tuesday, therefore, the result of the contest should be known.

AN ASCENSION IN THE JARDIN DES TUILERIES ALMOST READY FOR FLIGHT

[illegible] (SPAIN)

DON EMILIO HERRERA (SPAIN)

CAPTAIN KINDELAN Y DUANY (SPAIN)

BARON VON HEWALD (GERMANY)

HERR SCHERLE (GERMANY)

CAPT H VON ABERCRON (GERMANY)

MANY THOUSANDS ASSEMBLE TO WITNESS START OF GREAT BALLOONING CONTEST.

Enthusiastic Interest Marks the First Race for Coupe Internationale des Aéronautes.

SIXTEEN PILOTS SAIL AWAY IN A WESTERLY DIRECTION.

Wind Blows Them Out Towards the Shores of the Atlantic Ocean.

It is said that "art knows no frontiers." Neither do balloons. This was the one idea which must have been present in the minds of many thousands yesterday just before the start of the great race for the Coupe Internationale des Aéronautes—that purely sporting event which has been occupying the attention of the world for many weeks. The balloon knows no frontiers. It is swept wherever the wind blows and once well launched into space is beyond all human control from below. It knows neither "douanes" nor "octrois," and even such natural barriers as the Alps and the Pyrenees prove no obstacle. The balloon has but one enemy—the sea—and it was the fact that the wind bore towards the Atlantic yesterday that caused pilots to walk about with serious faces and augur ill for the coming night.

By three o'clock in the afternoon the place de la Concorde, the quais, the lower part of the Champs-Elysées and the Tuileries Gardens were black with spectators. Traffic was at a standstill. For the time-being aeronautics were triumphant and even the automobile was compelled to halt. It was not until the last balloon had left that circulation could be resumed.

In the Morning.

There are few finer spots for the start of a balloon contest than the Tuileries Gardens. The broad open space at the western end is ideal for the inflation of the gasbags, and the trees at the eastern end form a fitting screen and picturesque background. Yesterday morning all the balloons were in place, ready for inflation. Towards nine o'clock the gas was turned on and so perfect were the arrangements that by noon all the balloons were practically inflated. By three o'clock the crowd commenced to assemble. The conditions were exceedingly pleasant. The sun was as warm as in late summer, the wind, however annoying to the aeronauts, was distinctly agreeable to the spectators, and the gardens were in their prime. Last year, on the occasion of the annual contest of the Aéro-Club de France the conditions were far different. Heavy rain poured down in sheets, a violent gale blew towards the south-east, and even the most enthusiastic were dismayed.

The silence that marks the start of an aeronautical contest is charming. The only noise is the murmur of the crowd. There is no thundering din as at an automobile contest, no deafening exhausts, no dust. All is so calm and peaceful that even birds come circling round and perch on the competing aerostats. Yesterday this silence was more pronounced than ever. The wind was so light that it appeared to scarcely stir the leaves and each departure seemed more peaceful than that which preceded it.

Then and Now.

In the past thousands would assemble from time to time in the Champ de Mars or at the Crystal Palace, in England, to see some balloon soar heavenward with pigs and goats as passengers. Men and women would strain their necks to see a "professor" drop, clinging to a parachute, and they would cheer him to the echo when he reached the ground in safety. Yesterday there was none of this. It was sport pure and simple. Every competitor had but one object—to maintain the reputation of his club and to win, if possible, the trophy which would symbolize the feat. Even the crowd seemed to be aware of the change. There was none of that gaping curiosity which marked the early days of ballooning.

A walk round the enclosure before the start was very entertaining. It was a study in itself to mark the various types of aeronaut present—the stolid German, the sprightly Frenchman, the indifferent Spaniard and the cool Englishman. The difference in baskets was also well marked. Some were so small that two made a crowd within, others so spacious that it was possible to recline at full length on the floor. All were evidently strong and well stocked with provisions.

Cameras Busy.

M. Santos-Dumont had most of the photographic attention. The hero of the "heavier than air" theory looked perfectly at home, even with a gas-bag, though this was undoubtedly due to the novel equipment of horizontal propellers and a motor with which he provided his car. He was completing his device until a late hour on Saturday, and everything was ready. A preliminary spin of the motor towards half-past three o'clock showed that the propellers must have great influence on the ascensional force of the balloon. As a matter of fact, this equipment was about the only novelty presented. All the other balloons were of the usual shape and carried the usual ballast.

Towards four o'clock the stewards in charge of the proceedings, MM. Besançon, Rousseau, Mallet and Surcouf, ordered the first of the sixteen balloons to be placed in position by the side of the round pond. This was Signor Alfredo Vonwiller's balloon, the Elfe representing Italy. One by one the sand bags holding it to earth were removed and replaced by men. At eleven seconds past the hour the words "Lâchez tout!" were pronounced, and the Elfe began its voyage. Very slowly it mounted upwards and bore away towards the west. At a height of about 100 mètres the breeze smote it fair and square and carried it across the Seine towards Saint-Cloud. The band struck up the French national anthem and the crowd cheered. The race had begun.

Few Incidents.

One by one, at intervals of about five minutes, the other balloons were sent away. There were few incidents. The first was provoked by Comte de La Vaulx. The huge crowd raised a deafening shout as the French champion and holder of the world's long-distance record left the earth. And then a strange thing happened. The balloon rose very slowly, and, being caught by a contrary breeze, turned towards the Chamber of Deputies, passing over the Orangerie in the Tuileries. As it passed over the hot-house some cool current must have affected it, for it began to descend with astonishing rapidity and indeed came within a very few mètres of the ground. A bag or two of ballast had to be sacrificed in order to save the situation. The Walhalla, as the balloon is called, then rose to a moderate height, much inferior, however, to that of the two previous balloons, and thus continued its journey.

The second incident occurred in connection with M. Van den Driessche, who, in the Ojouki, represented Belgium. As the balloon left the ground it was noticed that the mouth, which is invariably opened before the start in order that any sudden expansion of gas may not produce an explosion, remained fastened. An attempt was made to catch the balloon, but the men were too late. Shouts were raised, and the attention of the aeronauts was thus drawn to the situation. The crowd had the satisfaction of seeing the refractory knot untied and the mouth liberated before the balloon disappeared.

M. Santos-Dumont.

M. Santos-Dumont's departure was not marked by any incident, but as it was novel it is worth noting. As soon as the balloon left the ground the horizontal propellers were set in motion in order to enable the balloon to clear the Orangerie. The crowd certainly had the impression that M. Santos-Dumont was really flying. Indeed, the spectacle of the two propellers whirling round at some feet from the car really produced this effect. So far as could be judged the device was a success.

M JAUBERT BEING CONSULTED ABOUT WEATHER CONDITIONS

COUPE INTERNATIONALE DES AERONAUTES WON BY MR. FRANK P. LAHM, OF AMERICA.

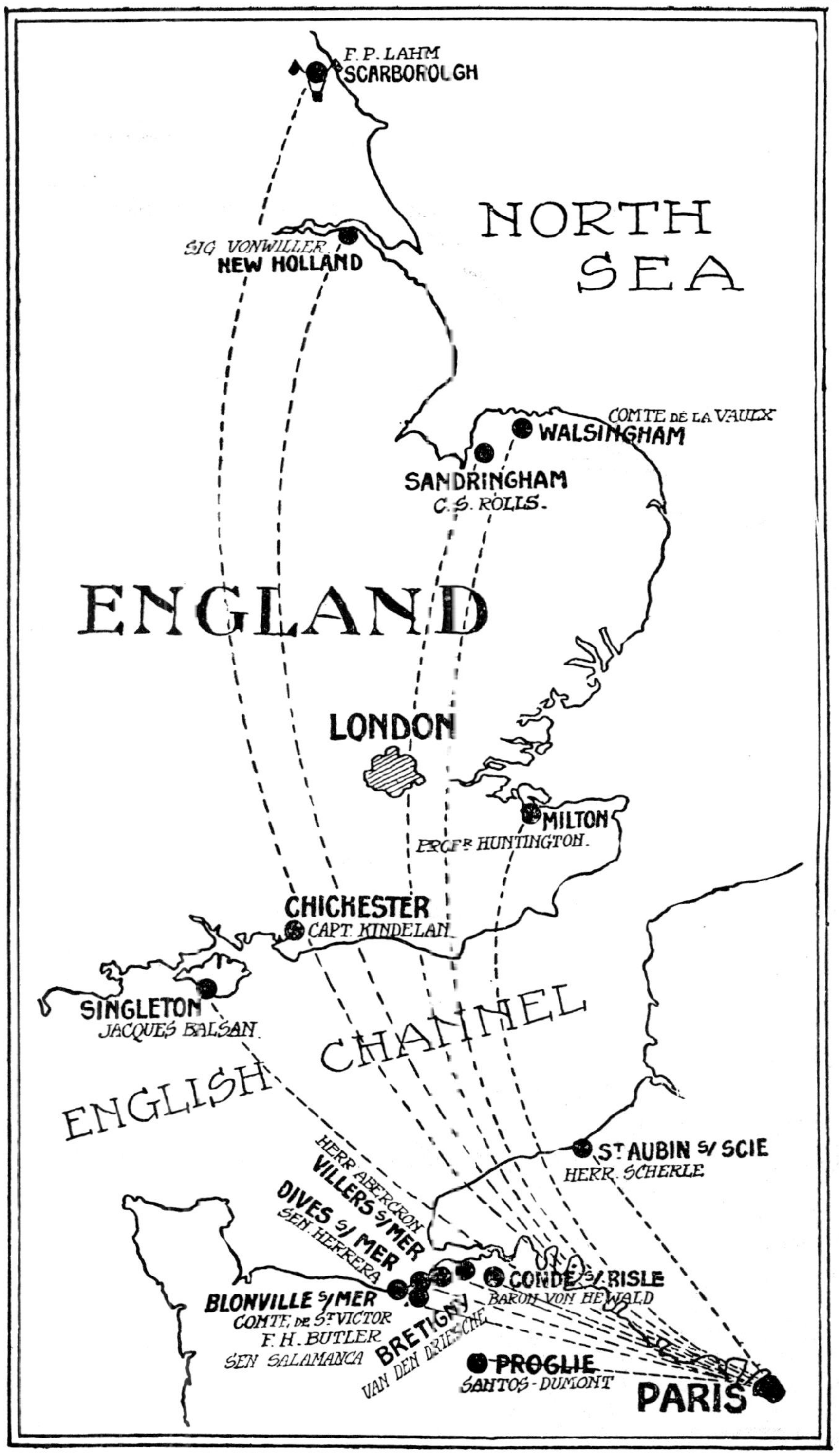

CHART OF AERONAUTS' LANDINGS.

Pilot of the United States, Accompanied by Major Hersey, Victor in Great Contest.

Signor Alfredo Vonwiller, Italian, Pilot of the Elfe, Second in the Classification.

COMTE DE LA VAULX THIRD.

Mr. Charles S. Rolls, Finally Heard From, Having Descended at Sandringham, in England.

America wins the Coupe Internationale des Aéronautes. Mr. Frank P. Lahm, lieutenant in the United States Army, son of Mr. Frank S. Lahm, one of the most enthusiastic of the Aéro Club members in France, has, by his remarkable voyage to Scarborough, beaten all other competitors and placed beyond all shadow of doubt the certainty of his victory. The only other man who came within measurable distance of defeating him was Signor Vonwiller, Italy's only representative, who, caught by practically the same air-current, succeeded in attaining New Holland, just in the neighborhood of Hull. The third is Comte Henry de La Vaulx, who descended at Wells, on the Wash, while the fourth place falls to Mr. C. S. Rolls, whose descent at Sandringham shows him to be a close competitor for third honors with the world's champion.

WEDNESDAY. JUNE 27, 1906.

MR. STANFORD WHITE INSTANTLY SLAIN ON ROOF GARDEN BY MR. HARRY KENDALL THAW.

Pittsburg Millionaire Declares He Shot Architect to Avenge Wife, a Former Artist's Model.

VICTIM, WATCHING PLAY, HAS SMALL WARNING.

Tragedy, Seen by Hundreds, Nearly Causes a Panic Among a Large Audience.

SLAYER'S NOTORIOUS CAREER.

Man He Killed Was Famous Throughout America as an Architect and Artist.

[BY COMMERCIAL CABLE TO THE HERALD.]

NEW YORK, Tuesday.—On the roof of the beautiful Madison Square garden, which he designed, Mr. Stanford White, a noted architect, prominent in society, was shot dead last evening during a theatrical performance by Mr. Harry K. Thaw, a member of a wealthy Pittsburg family and brother of the Countess of Yarmouth.

The crime was caused by intense jealousy and brooding over the alleged wronging of Mr. Thaw's wife by Mr. White years ago when she was Evelyn Nesbit, an artist's model.

Scores of theatregoers and attachés saw the tragedy, which was enacted so

MR. STANFORD WHITE.

quickly that it was several moments before they realized the terrible nature of the crime. The architect died instantly. The slayer, moving slowly towards the entrance, submitted quietly to detention, saying repeatedly to the police and reporters: "He deserved it," and declaring Mr. White had ruined his life.

The shocking deed involving men of such prominence in different aspects has profoundly stirred the city.

Defense of Insanity.

It is already evident that Mr. Thaw's relatives will use every effort to prove he is crazy and thus save him from the electric chair.

Mrs. William Thaw, his mother, sailed on Saturday on the Minneapolis to visit her daughter, the Countess of Yarmouth. Attempts are being made to reach her by wireless telegraphy before her arrival, in order to ensure her immediate return.

Harry Thaw

Friends of Mr. Thaw admit he is an inveterate user of drugs, especially of morphine. It is certain he had been drinking last evening before the shooting. His counsel will urge that his general mode of life and brooding over alleged wrongs to his wife made him irresponsible for his act.

Insinuations Denounced.

Friends of Mr. White indignantly deny that he was more than the friendly helper of Mrs. Thaw when she was trying to gain a place on the stage.

Mr. George W. Lederer, in an interview, denounced the insinuations against the architect.

Miss Masie Follette, a former stage chum of Mrs. Thaw, said: "I know the charge is false. Mr. White was always glad to assist young actresses. He did so out of kindness of heart."

MR. STANFORD WHITE ONE OF THE MOST NOTED OF AMERICAN ARCHITECTS.

Few architects in America were better known than Mr. Stanford White. Prominent socially, he occupied a position professionally that caused him to be consulted on nearly all of the important architectural and artistic projects undertaken by New York City, and he was often called in for advice on national enterprises.

His chief work from a popular standpoint will probably be accounted Madison Square Garden, the vast Moorish structure which is a unique feature of New York's architecture; but other works of his are not less important.

He designed the old Villard house, now the residence of Mr. Whitelaw Reid, the Century and Metropolitan Clubs and many of the most important of New York residences of the last quarter of a century.

He made the plans for the new University of Virginia, the beauty of which has occasioned wide comment.

Mr. White built many public monuments, but will be best remembered, perhaps, by the Washington Arch in Washington Park, New York, a marble arch much admired for its impressive, classic simplicity.

MR. THAW OFTEN BEFORE THE PUBLIC, FIGURING IN SENSATIONAL EPISODES.

For several years Mr. Harry Kendall Thaw has attracted public attention by various escapades. Of the estate left by his father, which was valued at $40,000,000, the son, Harry, was given $5,000,000, subject, however, to the control of his mother, who had the power, under the will, to reduce the young man's income which was normally $80,000 a year, to an annual allowance of $2,500.

Two Pictures of Mrs. Harry Thaw
NEE NESBIT

Miss Nesbit had gone from her home in Allegheny, Pa., which is just across the river from Pittsburg, to New York, and she leaped into quick notoriety as an artist's model. Her parents were obscure, and in Allegheny she had attracted no particular attention, but in the photographers' and artists' studios in New York, where she posed, she was hailed as a young girl of extraordinary beauty. Painters went into raptures over her and it was said that more portraits were made of her with camera and brush than of any other young woman in America.

Her stage career was limited to two engagements as a "show girl" in musical productions, and it was while so engaged that she met Mr. Harry K. Thaw.

The wedding in Pittsburg on April 4, 1905, in the Third Presbyterian Church, was marked by secrecy and haste.

An idea of the unconventionality of the wedding was gained by the fact that the bride wore to the church an opera cloak and a large picture hat, neither of which she removed while the ceremony was being performed. Afterwards there was a dinner party at Lyndhurst, the Thaw home at Pittsburg, which is one of the show places of the city.

JULY 10, 1906.

MRS. THAW'S STAGE FRIENDS TESTIFY.

AFFIDAVIT AGAIN FIGURES.

Former "Chums" of Mrs. Thaw Tell of an Old Rivalry for Miss Nesbit's Attentions.

[BY COMMERCIAL CABLE TO THE HERALD.]

NEW YORK, Monday. — This will be chorus girls' week in the Thaw-White tragedy if a large number of subpœnas issues by the District Attorney's office can be served. It is a current report that many young women of the stage have left the city to avoid what they regard as undesirable notoriety in connection with the case.

Miss Mazie Follette and Miss Edna McClure, former "chums" of Mrs. Thaw, have given testimony that is not favorable to the prisoner. Mr. Thaw threatened to kill Mr. White two years ago, says Miss Edna McClure in a statement to Assistant District Attorney Garvan. Miss Mazie Follette corroborates this, and goes farther, declaring that she heard Mr. Thaw say he would kill Mr. White if it took years to do it.

Their stories seem to indicate a bitter struggle between Mr. White and Mr. Thaw for Miss Nesbit's affections. Miss McClure and Miss Nesbit were in the "Wild Rose" company when the two men began pursuing Miss Nesbit with attentions. Every night there would be two cabs waiting for Miss Nesbit and every night two bunches of flowers arrived. Finally Miss Nesbit's mother took a dislike to Mr. Thaw, which caused him to be dropped.

Mr. White sent Miss Nesbit and her brother to school and, later, sent the chorus girl and her mother abroad. Mr. Thaw followed them, and again began to shower the girl with gifts. His attentions were so marked, Miss McClure said, that it was not long before Miss Nesbit, against the wishes of her mother, went with Mr. Thaw. They travelled through Europe, says Miss McClure, but Mr. Thaw's treatment was so brutal that the

District Attorney Nearing Real Motive in Thaw Case.

Damaging Affidavit Now Accepted as Having Most Important Bearing on Case.

NEW YORK, Wednesday.—As cabled to you, developments in the Thaw-White tragedy multiply daily and the newspapers continue, even at this long period after the shooting, to devote column after column to theories, analyses and all manner of reports, many of them undoubtedly manufactured.

The question of motive is the paramount one, and in this the affidavit in Evelyn Nesbit's threatened suit against Mr. Thaw as cabled you and which was first announced in the NEW YORK HERALD, plays a principal part. At first the existence of this affidavit was denied by Mr. Thaw and his lawyers, but there now seems little doubt that not only was such an affidavit made by the present Mrs. Thaw, but that a record of it is in existence.

This affidavit contained charges of a very damaging character against Mr. Thaw; and, as a result of it, he effected a monetary settlement with the girl. Shortly thereafter his infatuation for her led him to make her his wife. Mr. White knew of this affidavit. It is even said that he counselled her in bringing the suit and discussed her complaint.

Mr. Thaw has always cherished the deepest resentment against Mr. White's knowledge of the contents of the affidavit and his resentment had been constantly fanned by his wife. The NEW YORK HERALD published the substance of this affidavit and pointed out its bearing on the whole case for several days, and the District Attorney now considers that this is the most important contribution to the prosecution of Mr. Thaw. Sympathy for Mr. Thaw has lessened very materially and it is certain that he will have a hard trial.

It is the discovery of this selfish motive that has taken from the prisoner the sympathy of those who talk of an "unwritten law" and who accepted his statement on the night of the shooting to the effect that he had killed Mr. White because he had mistreated Evelyn Nesbit years before. All along this lapse of time has made the alleged motive appear decidedly insufficient, but now that it is shown that Mr. Thaw knew of Mr. White's acquaintance with the damaging affidavit the motive becomes a present and selfish one.

The affidavit was drawn up by the law firm of Messrs. Howe and Hummel, whom Evelyn Nesbit retained when she contemplated suit for breach of promise against Mr. Thaw. The affidavit, according to the District Attorney's office, was destroyed, but it is said that photographic copies of it exist and, according to reports that seem authentic, Mr. White was responsible for the preservation of the record. He had certain papers reproduced and placed under seal so that they are now available for the prosecution of the man who killed him. These documents furnish the apparent motive for the crime, as Mr. Thaw did not come into contact with Mr. White after they were drawn.

While Mr. Thaw's counsel are collecting evidence with a view to proving that he was insane at the time he killed Mr. White, Assistant District Attorney Francis P. Garvan continues to find new witnesses to swear Mr. Thaw frequently had threatened to kill the man who is supposed to have been his rival in the affections of Evelyn Nesbit before she became Mrs. Thaw.

The theory of the prosecution is that Mr. Thaw had no motive for the shooting except hatred and jealousy dating from the time Evelyn Nesbit consulted lawyers and made a sworn statement reflecting upon the man she soon afterward married.

Although the defence has adopted a policy of silence, Mr. Terence J. McManus, one of Mr. Thaw's lawyers, announced recently that if any document purporting to be an affidavit made by Mrs. Thaw was introduced, it would be proved a forgery.

"Then you expect to bring handwriting experts into the case?" was suggested.

"None will be necessary," returned Mr. McManus. "We can show that Mrs. Thaw never signed any paper and that whatever may have been prepared she was not cognizant of its contents and she did not subscribe to it."

Study of Mr. Harry K. Thaw and photographs of Mrs. Thaw taken when she was Miss Evelyn Nesbit, an artist's model.

---

girl returned home alone. She consulted Mr. White, it is said, and an affidavit was drawn. Mr. Thaw, on his arrival, began new advances and gave Miss Nesbit the most expensive presents. They went abroad again, but did not marry there, as reported. According to her friend, when they returned they went to Pittsburg and were married there. The original affidavit was destroyed, but a photographic copy exists, it is said.

When Mr. Thaw finally married the former show girl, Mr. White's attentions ceased, Miss McClure declares, but the old jealousy was intermittently fanned into flame, sometimes by Mrs. Thaw herself, according to those who were close to her.

Mr. Olcott visited Philadelphia yesterday, partly to establish the insanity of Miss Harriet Thaw, a cousin of Mr. Harry Thaw, and partly to engage Mr. George S. Graham, a noted criminal lawyer, to assist in the case. He succeeded in both quests. The insanity investigation will have value in helping the plea which the prisoner's counsel will apparently have to make to save Mr. Thaw from electrocution.

Pittsburg reports reach here that Mr. Thaw's counsel intend dropping the plea of emotional insanity and pleading plain insanity. Detectives are seeking evidence here to prove Mr. Thaw has been crazy for a long time, as the result of a life of degeneracy.

JULY 21, 1906.

ALIENISTS THINK MR. THAW INSANE.

Statement Made that Physicians so Reported to Counsel Whom Prisoner Dismissed.

PAPERS HELD TO BE COPIED.

Wife's Position Is Not Clear, but Mother Evidently Favors Lunacy Commission.

[BY COMMERCIAL CABLE TO THE HERALD.]

NEW YORK, Friday.—That Drs. Allan McLane Hamilton and Charles L. Dana, the alienists, hired by the Black, Olcott and Gruber law firm, reported Mr. Thaw as insane is the statement made to-day on apparently good authority.

It became known in court this afternoon that Mr. Olcott had not turned over all the papers in the case to Mr. Hartridge, whom Mr. Thaw picked as counsel, and would not do so until he had copied them. The papers withheld include all bearing on the insanity theory. This seems to confirm the current reports that Mr. Thaw's mother will ask for a lunacy commission, whether her son agrees or not.

The exact position of Mr. Thaw's wife in the matter is not clear. Morbid newspapers depict in words and pictures two women trying to pull Mr. Thaw in opposite directions, one towards the asylum, the other toward the electric chair. The mother and wife seem on cordial terms in public, but there are strong intimations that the elder woman blames her daughter-in-law entirely for the tragedy.

SATURDAY, NOVEMBER 17, 1906.

WRIGHT BROTHERS AND VIEWS OF THEIR APPARATUS.

One of the Wright Brothers in Flight in a Gliding Machine.

Wilbur Wright

Orville Wright

Crank shaft and Fly wheel of Wright Brothers' Flying machine motor.

Wright Brothers Still Maintain Their Claim.

American Aeronauts Again Assert that They Have Travelled More than 24 Miles in Continuous Flight—Speed of 38 Miles an Hour—Report Made to Aero Club of America—Details Given After Long Silence.

[BY COMMERCIAL CABLE TO THE HERALD.]

NEW YORK, Friday.—Renewed claim to having traversed in the air more than twenty-four miles in continuous flight, at a speed of thirty-eight miles an hour, is made by Messrs. Wilbur and Orville Wright, of Dayton, Ohio, in a report to the Aero Club of America.

This is the first time in a year that the Wright brothers have broken their silence, and the second time they have made public the results of their experiments.

Their absolute faith in aeroplanes is shown by this concluding statement: "Even in the existing state of the art, it is easy to design a practical and durable flyer that will carry operator and fuel for a flight of more than 500 miles at fifty miles an hour."

The report made to the Aero Club is on "the relations of the weight, speed and power of flyers," and it acquires special interest through the mystery the Wrights have thrown about their achievements. They have made no public demonstration except to a few residents of Dayton, who vouch for their success.

Power and Weight.

A notable portion of the report relates to the amount of power necessary to carry a given weight. They say: "The flyer of 1903 carried a four-cylinder gasolene motor, with 4-inch bore and 4-inch stroke, weighing a little more than two hundred pounds. The motor developed, at 1,200 revolutions to the minute, 16 horse-power for the first fifteen seconds, but after a minute or two the power did not exceed 14 horse-power.

"The flyer of 1904 was equipped with a motor similar to the first, but with an eighth of an inch larger bore. It developed, at 1,500 revolutions, 24 horse-power for fifteen seconds, but only 16 horse-power after a few minutes' run. It weighed, complete with water and full accessories, 240 pounds. The same engine, with a few modifications, was used in 1905, and the flights revealed a gain of three horse-power over that of 1904. Further improvements have been made during the last year, and our latest engines of 4-inch bore and 4-inch stroke produce about twenty-five horse-power continuously.

Comparisons.

"Comparisons of the flyers show other interesting facts. The flyer of 1903 weighed, complete with operator, 745 pounds. Its longest flight was 1min. 59 sec. at a speed of thirty miles an hour, using 12 horse-power. The 1904 flyer weighed about 900 pounds, including 70 pounds in iron bars. A speed of more than thirty-four miles an hour was maintained for three miles, with an expenditure of 17 horse-power.

"The flyer of 1905 weighed, with load, 925 pounds, and with an expenditure of 20 horse-power it travelled more than twenty-four miles at a speed of more than thirty-eight miles an hour.

"Thus sixty-two pounds per horse-power were carried in 1903 at a speed of thirty miles an hour, fifty-three pounds in 1904 at thirty-four miles an hour and forty-six pounds in 1905 at thirty-eight miles an hour, and thus the weight carried per horse-power is almost exactly in inverse ratio to the speed, as theory demands."

Another report to the Aero Club, interesting to all who pin their faith to the eventual supremacy of the "heavier-than-air" type of airships, is from Professor Todd, of Amherst College, who has been experimenting several years. He strongly favors the Aviator machine, declaring that balloons and "dirigible" cars are only passing stages on the way to the perfected type of aerial engine.

He presents interesting theories as to the design of a flying machine, asserting that the proper way to solve the problem is first to attempt the simpler problem of skimming the surface of still water. He would therefore investigate the physics of the hydroplane to an exhaustive degree. He would determine the relative efficiency of the various forms of screws and seek means of diminishing the skin friction of hydroplanes.

He adds finally: "If this question of water-skimming should prove incapable of trying out to a gratifying success it will be quite futile to push the experiment along the more difficult line of the practical aeroplane machine."

SUNDAY, DECEMBER 2, 1906.

M. Serge de Bolotoff Building Aeroplane.

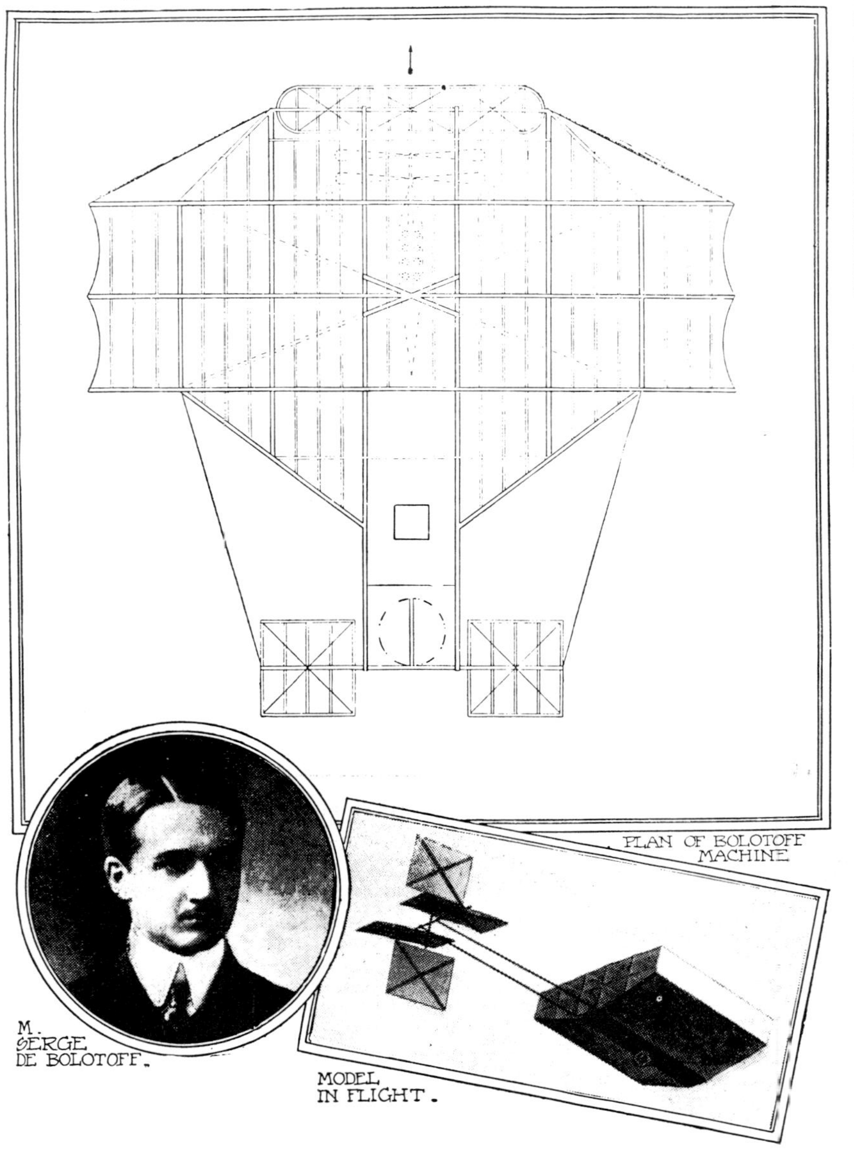

PLAN OF BOLOTOFF MACHINE

M. SERGE DE BOLOTOFF.

MODEL IN FLIGHT.

Furnished with Four Rudders, Two Propellers and a Hundred Horse-Power Motor.

M. Serge de Bolotoff, son of Princess Wiasemsky of Russia, after making a series of experiments at Vevey with various models, has now designed a new form of aeroplane, which he will very shortly commence to construct on a large scale. Seen in Paris yesterday by a HERALD correspondent, the inventor, who has already produced several interesting improvements in connection with automobile construction, such as the simplified change-speed lever described in the HERALD columns a few months ago, declared that he had studied aeronautical subjects for some years, and that his present design was the outcome of prolonged investigation. At the age of ten he had commenced experiments with kites, and it had always been his ambition to incorporate the knowledge gained in these undertakings in some really practical flying machine capable of transporting one or more people from point to point at a high rate of speed.

M. de Bolotoff, who is now only nineteen years of age, explained that his model had done exactly what he expected it to do from the calculations he had made. By means of a kite he had elevated the model several hundred mètres into the air, and by reason of a cord had allowed the model flying machine to become liberated. The result was that the machine descended slowly in vast circles towards the ground, and even when it was let loose in the air up-side-down, it immediately righted itself and came to earth in a correct manner. From this the inventor inferred that a real machine built on these lines would act precisely in the same manner, and would indeed have chances of being still more perfectly balanced by reason of the presence on board of some intelligent individual, who would have the various rudders and appliances of control within his grasp.

As may be seen from the design and photograph this machine is entirely of the aeroplane order. The main body is constructed in such a manner that it takes the form of a gigantic radiator on an automobile, though it is much more long than deep. At the rear four rudders are attached, two placed horizontally and two vertically. In front there is a movable plane for raising the apparatus from the ground once speed has been attained. The propellers, of which there are two, are placed in front, as it is the theory of the inventor that in this manner a much more powerful grip of the air is obtained. The propellers turn in opposite directions. The motor of 100 horse-power or thereabouts is placed in front of the driver, who occupies the position marked as a square between the motor and the tailpiece.

The building of this instrument will be commenced very shortly and by next spring should be in working order. When completed it is M. de Bolotoff's intention to compete for the various prizes offered, and then to present it as a gift to the Russian Government. During the last few days M. de Bolotoff has had several offers for his plans from private sources, but he has refused to sell. He wishes to carry out his own ideas and then, if they prove successful, to give his country the benefit of his skill.

The HERALD is the first paper to publish the plans, which in the opinion of every engineer to whom they have been submitted, have been found accurate.

THE GILLESPIE AEROPLANE.

ITALIAN BALLOON BEATS ALL RECORDS

Signor Usuelli and Signor Crespi Reach an Altitude of 8,800 Mètres.

KEPT ALIVE BY OXYGEN.

Temperature Falls to 34deg. Cent. Below Zero—Pulses Make 122 Beats a Minute.

[SPECIAL TO THE HERALD.]

MILAN, Monday.—Signor Usuelli and Signor Crespi, the two aeronauts who left the Exhibition grounds here yesterday morning in their balloon and landed in the afternoon at Aix-les-Bains, returned here to-day.

In the course of an interview on their aerial voyage, they stated that their ambition on leaving Milan was to cross the Alps, an enterprise often attempted, but hitherto without success. They took with them a number of tubes of oxygen and a considerable amount of water ballast.

An hour after their departure they reached a height of 4,900 mètres. The thermometer then marked 14deg. Cent. below freezing point. For some considerable time they floated over Lake Maggiore.

When they exceeded the height of five thousand mètres, they had recourse to the oxygen in order to combat the rarified air. Unfortunately the glass tube broke and they had to place their lips on the tube itself and absorb the gas direct from it.

As they were both very warmly clad, they did not feel the cold much. The wind kept carrying the balloon ever further towards the north, and they soon arrived near Mont Rosa, which the balloon almost touched in passing over the summit.

At two o'clock in the afternoon the balloon reached a height of 8,800 mètres and passed over the summit of Mont Blanc. The temperature was 34deg. Cent. below zero and their pulses were beating 122 to the minute.

Breathing was only rendered possible by the liberal use of oxygen, of which they had an abundant supply in reserve. The spectacle was sublime. Signor Usuelli was so deeply moved at its magnificence that he began to weep.

Beneath them they saw stretched out a limitless ocean of snow; the frozen lakes glittering in the sun were clearly visible. The water ballast froze into solid blocks and it became necessary to descend.

At a quarter to three the balloon sailed over the Isère department at an altitude of 5,350 mètres. The thermometer registered 30deg. below zero Cent.

M. SANTOS-DUMONT, WITH HIS "BIRD OF PREY," SOLVES THE PROBLEM OF AERIAL FLIGHT.

CROWD WAITING FOR START.

THE "BIRD OF PREY" DURING FLIGHT

M. CHAPIN, THE MÉCANICIEN.

LAST PREPARATIONS

His "Bird of Prey" Covers 210 Mètres in Twenty-One Seconds.

WINS TWO AERO CLUB PRIZES.

One Hundred Francs for Flying Sixty Mètres and Fifteen Hundred for One Hundred Mètres.

Those people who had been in any way sceptical with regard to previous experiments made by M. Santos-Dumont in that domain of aerostation known as "heavier than air" can no longer have the slightest grounds for their attitude after the marvellous and prolonged flight made by the dauntless Brazilian yesterday afternoon, just before dusk, on the field at Bagatelle ...

upon the ground, but he failed to obtain definite flight. By twelve o'clock it was decided to postpone further experiments until two o'clock, as one of the wheels required adjusting, after a slight shock

BRITISH AERO CLUB IN ITS NEW HOME.

It Takes Possession To-day of Its New Headquarters at 166 Piccadilly.

CENTRAL AND WELL SITUATED.

Club-house Will Form a Central Point for the Study and Discussion of Aeronautics.

[BY THE HERALD'S SPECIAL WIRE.]

LONDON, Tuesday.—The present winter will be a busy one among members of the Aero Club of Great Britain. What they lose in aeronautic practice they intend trying to make up for by a scientific study of the subject, so that a great deal of hard work will have been done towards solving aeronautical problems before next season opens.

With this object in view a new club-house has been leased at 166 Piccadilly and here, at various times during the coming months, the leading authorities will deliver lectures and some interesting and informing discussions are likely to be heard. The new premises, which will be taken possession of to-day, are centrally situated. They are about halfway along Piccadilly, face the south end of Bond Street and are within a few hundred yards of the Automobile Club, which will still continue to be the social headquarters of both automobilists and aeronauts.

The new club-house will be the special rendezvous of the balloon section of the members, as distinct from the automobile men, and it is hoped by thus endeavoring to specialize in the interest of this branch of sport, to place Great Britain on equal terms with both America and France. The new club-house will thus be more a meeting place among enthusiasts for the discussion and advancement of aeronautics than anything else.

Though the necessary arrangements are being made for providing luncheons and dinners whenever required, the great idea of the members is to have a place where aeronautics can be studied in all its branches, and they think their new premises will realize these hopes. At any rate, every endeavor will be made to make it the Mecca of aeronauts in Great Britain and Ireland, and a place where all foreigners interested in the sport will be heartily welcomed.

ATLANTIC FLEET FOR TANGIER.

[BY THE HERALD'S SPECIAL WIRE.]

LONDON, Tuesday.—The Atlantic fleet

THE NEW YORK HERALD.

PRICE: PARIS and FRANCE, 15 Centimes. ABROAD, 25 Centimes.

EUROPEAN EDITION—PARIS. MONDAY, JULY 26, 1909.—TEN PAGES.

NO. 26,635

CABLE AND OTHER NEWS.

King Leopold gives "Herald" correspondent his views regarding "Herald's" news bureau in Peking and commercial development of China. Page 3.

Tariff situation in Washington begins to excite ridicule. Page 3.

Count Witte goes to China on special mission for Tsar. Page 3.

British troops leave Crete—Other contingents depart to-day. Page 8.

PARIS EDITORIAL OPINION ON M. BLERIOT'S FLIGHT

An Epoch-Making Achievement in the History of Latter-Day Aeronautics.

M. Blériot's Achievement.

As was to be expected M. Blériot's brilliant achievement in crossing the Channel in his monoplane bulks largely in the editorial opinion of the Paris press this morning. The leading sentiment is one of pride that this marvellous performance should have been accomplished by a Frenchman. "This crossing of the Channel," says the "Petite République," "gives the impression of a definite conquest. It is the suppression of the Channel. It is the realization of a dream which has long been entertained. It gives to mankind, to ourselves, poor mortals who have not yet left the ground, a sensation of mastery over the air such as we have not yet felt. The legend of Icarus putting on wings to fly is no longer a myth. It suffices, in order to realize it, to have a little canvas a little iron and some petrol, to which one must add the genius of our engineers and the obstinate courage of our aviators, notably M. Blériot, whose falls were innumerable, but who never lost courage."

May Scale Mountains.

"The flying man," says M. Maxime Vuillaume in the "Aurore," "whom our fathers caricatured with so much irony, is no longer a myth. Yet a little patience and each of us can treat himself to his little tour in the clouds. Yesterday, without dithyrambics, is already inscribed in the annals of humanity. After M. Blériot's victory, the aeroplane is no longer a simply sporting machine, condemned to keep turning round the track of an aerodrome as did with so much brio the American aviator Wright. From the aerodrome the bird invented by Blériot launches itself resolutely into space. It flies above the plains, above the forests and rivers; he flies above the seas. Who knows how soon he will scale the mountains. He will raise us like Ganymede on the eagle of Jupiter to the summits."

The Channel Suppressed.

"I do not think," says M. Ernest Judet in the "Eclair," "that there could

WHILE DOVER AND CALAIS STILL SLEEP, M. BLÉRIOT FLIES ACROSS THE CHANNEL

BIRD'S EYE VIEW OF DOVER & DISTRICTS.

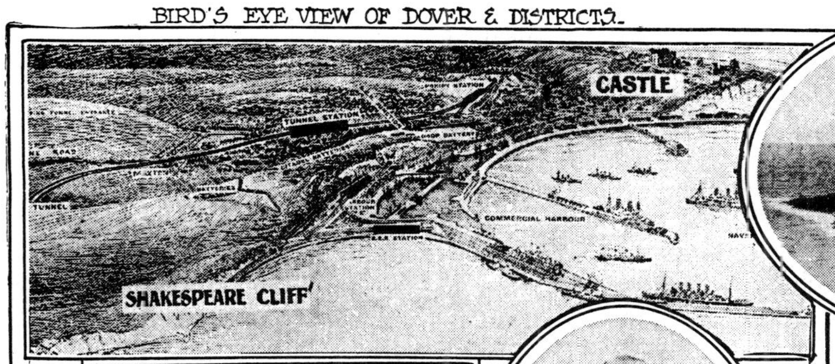

SHAKESPEARE CLIFF.

MAP SHOWING COURSE OF AEROPLANE.

ASPECT OF BLERIOT MONOPLANE.

M. BLERIOT IN AEROPLANE GARB.

IN VIEW OF DOVER CLIFFS.

VIEW OF DOVER, SHOWING CASTLE.

Successful Trial Trip Over, He Leaves Les Baraques and Steers His Aeroplane Out to Sea.

JOURNEY OCCUPIES 37 MINUTES

His Arrival in England Is Reported to the Authorities by Stolid English Policeman.

[SPECIAL TO THE HERALD.]

CALAIS, Sunday.—The English Channel has been crossed by aeroplane, and the "Daily Mail" prize of £1,000 has been won. The hero of the exploit is M. Louis Blériot, a man who was yesterday

ago at Issy. He walked with considerable difficulty, but when in the aeroplane declared that his injured foot did not in any way handicap him.

POLICE CONSTABLE REPORTS M. BLERIOT'S ARRIVAL.

Aviator Stops Only Few Hours in England.

[SPECIAL TO THE HERALD.]

to-morrow for further official celebrations and rejoicings.

FLIGHT WAS MAGNIFICENT, BUT LANDING DIFFICULT.

M. Blériot Tells the "Herald" of His Impressions.

[SPECIAL TO THE HERALD.]

DOVER, Sunday.—M. Louis Blériot was radiant when the HERALD's correspondent

died maps carefully, and had had the country described to me."

"Did your injured foot handicap you?"

"Not in the least; for the effort necessary to work the pedals was very slight, and after I landed I simply had to wait until an automobile arrived from Dover to take me down to the town."

MME. BLERIOT DESCRIBES TRIP ON BOARD DESTROYER.

Aeronaut Made Circle in Mid-Channel to Await Warship.

NEWS ON INSIDE PAGES.

Deerstalking prospects in Scotland are good. Page 7.

Roehampton beats Madrid in Junior Championship polo match at Ostend. Page 6.

Swimming race through Paris is won by M. Ooms, a Dutchman. Page 7.

Society notes from Thun, Homburg, Aix-les-Bains and Geneva. Page 7.

M. BLERIOT'S EXPLOIT ABSORBS LONDON PRESS

This Morning's Leader Writers Devote Their Attention to His Flight Across Channel.

[BY THE HERALD'S SPECIAL WIRE.]

LONDON, Monday.—The attention of editorial writers this morning is focussed on M. Blériot's flight across the Channel. The "Standard," while offering M. Blériot unstinted congratulations, submits that from the practical point of view his achievement leaves us pretty well where we have been hitherto in regard to aerial navigation. "Indeed," it proceeds, "it must still be said that aerial navigation in machines or vessels heavier than the air is an art in its infancy, and M. Blériot, much as we admire his pluck and dexterity, has not yet brought us near to a solution of the problem. The Channel steamer service is not yet threatened nor are we appreciably nearer the day when friends or enemies will fly to our shores."

What Does It Portend?

The "Daily Chronicle" asks: "What does M. Blériot's successful flight over the Channel portend? Given suitable weather, it is evidently not a difficult, although a risky, performance. The part which these aerial navigators will play in the wars of the future has yet to be determined, but it is clear that no nation can allow itself to be behindhand in aerial navigation. Before long airships and all kinds of flying machines will have to be regulated on an international basis, as they have no respect for frontiers or tariffs."

Shock to Englishmen.

The "Morning Post" considers that the news that at last the feat of flying the Channel has been accomplished will come to most Englishmen as a shock. It adds: "We are a cautious race, sceptical of all innovation, and not a few have at heart disbelieved the probability of success, at least for many years. But here it is; conjecture and theorising are at an end. This country not only can be, but has been reached, by mechanical flight. While fully and freely congratulating M. Blériot, it is impossible not to feel a touch of jealousy that this historic achievement has not fallen to the lot of an Englishman."

Wake Up, England!

The "Daily Graphic" thinks that if anything can wake England to the im-

TUESDAY, NOVEMBER 13, 1906.

AMERICA'S MOST REMARKABLE "SKYSCRAPER."

As told in a recent cable despatch, the Singer building, which will be the tallest building in America, towering far above the other New York "sky-scrapers," will be anchored to a concrete foundation by a steel bar extending to the top of the structure in order to prevent it toppling over in a high wind. This building, which represents the most daring attempt yet made in the construction of lofty buildings, is watched with great interest by architects as well as the public at large. The above illustration compares the Singer building which is in process of construction to some of the world's tallest structures.

SUNDAY. APRIL 22 1900.

MOVING STAIRWAY IN NEW YORK.

Inclined Elevators Proposed for the Elevated Roads, to Be Run by Electric Motors for the Convenience of Passengers, but they Will Have to Walk Down.

Excursions to the Universal Exhibition in St-Louis

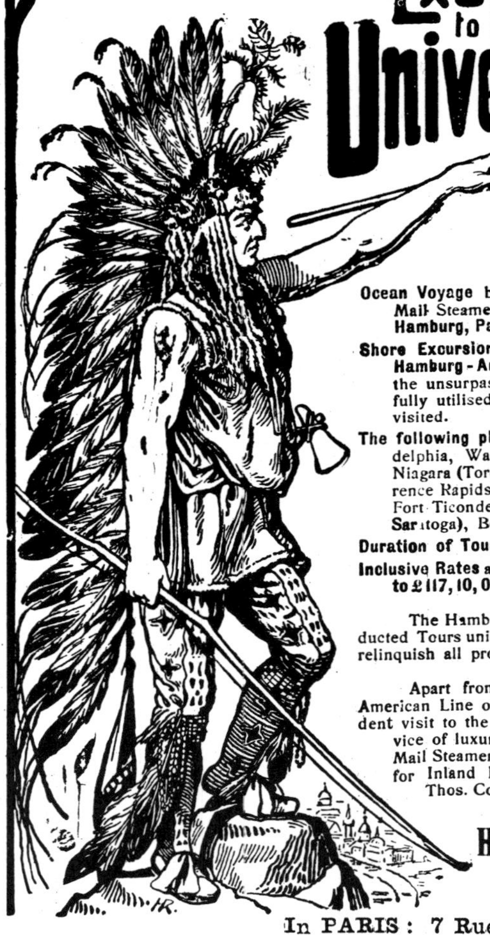

Ocean Voyage by the excellent Twin-Screw Express and Mail Steamers of the **Hamburg-American Line from Hamburg, Paris,** or **London.** Shortest Trip imaginable.

Shore Excursions under the entire management of the **Hamburg-American Line,** for the success of which the unsurpassed organisation of the Company will be fully utilised. Branch Offices in nearly every Town visited.

The following places will be visited: New York, Philadelphia, Washington, Pittsburg, St. Louis, Chicago, Niagara (Toronto, Kingston [Thousand Islands, St. Lawrence Rapids], Montreal, Plattsburgh [Lake Champlain, Fort Ticonderoga], Baldwin, [Lake George], Caldwell, Saratoga), Boston, Newport.

Duration of Tours from 38 to 45 Days.

Inclusive Rates according to Season and Steamer **£ 82, 10, 0 to £ 117, 10, 0,** including Hotels, Transportation, Fees, &c.

The Hamburg American Line offers with these conducted Tours unique advantages inasmuch as the Company relinquish all profits on the Shore Excursions.

Apart from the conducted Tours, the Hamburg-American Line offers unrivalled facilities for an independent visit to the World's Fair by its regular weekly service of luxuriously appointed Twin-Screw Express and Mail Steamers, in connection with which arrangements for Inland Excursions may be made with Messrs. Thos. Cook & Son, New York

For full particulars apply to the

Hamburg-American Line,

Abth. Personenverkehr, Hamburg,

and their Agents.

In PARIS: 7 Rue Scribe.

BOARD AND RESIDENCE.

A. CH.-ELYSÉES 4 Rue Boccador, corn. av. Montaigne. Mme. Beliot-Carol. Prof.

A.—TROCADERO. Fam. franç. rec. pens. dans conf. villa. Gd. jard., bain, rad. 10 rue Scheffer. Lec. de fr.

A.—TROCADERO.—SELECT FR. FAMILY offers comfortable home; moderate terms. Mmes. Delasalle, 100 rue de Longchamps. High refs.

CHAMPS-ELYSEES.—PENSION FRANCIS, 3 RUE Robert-Estienne (Marbeuf). Terms from 7fr. a day.

SWITZERLAND.

DO NOT!

Omit, if you pass through GENEVA, to pay a call at Dr. JAEGER'S ESTABLISHMENT there, PLACE LONGEMALLE, No. 1, where the REAL JAEGER UNDERWEAR and THE FAMOUS SWISS SILK UNDER-GARMENTS are sold at least 50 per cent. less than in the United States, and 25 per cent. cheaper than elsewhere in Europe. Write for the price list. The goods are forwarded free of charge to any place in Europe, marked with your initials.

THURSDAY, MAY 20, 1909.

Le Monde Artistique et Musical

ON APPLAUDIT, AU CHATELET, LES DÉBUTS DE L'OPÉRA RUSSE

La série d'opéras et de ballets russes a commencé hier soir au Châtelet. Une répétition générale, comme on en voit rarement, une brillante première font prévoir un succès certain. Ce succès est très mérité par les organisateurs, M. Serge Daghilew, qui assume tous les soucis de la partie artistique, et M. G. Astruc, chargé d'un agencement matériel fort réussi.

"Le Pavillon d'Armide."

Le spectacle commençait par "Le Pavillon d'Armide," ballet en trois actes dont M. Alexandre Benois composa le scenario, emprunt quelconque fait à la légende connue, brossa les décors et dessina les jolis costumes. La musique, qui n'a rien de saisissant, un peu banale et bruyante quelquefois, répond assez bien aux exigences chorégraphiques.

M. Tchérépnine, l'auteur, la conduit avec une vigoureuse conviction. Ce ballet est très bien dansé. Mlle. Karalli, Mmes. Karsavina, Baldina, Fédorova, Smirnova en ont été les protagonistes très applaudies. Les hommes, qui toujours dans les ballets en Russie, tiennent une place au moins aussi importante que les femmes, MM. Mordkine et M. Nijinsky surtout, sont d'une technique et d'une légèreté inusitées. Des entrées de bouffons et de sorcières montrent le degré exceptionnel de précision que peuvent atteindre les ensembles en Russie.

Danses polovtsiennes.

Avec des scènes et danses polovtsiennes du "Prince Igor," opéra de Borodine, a commencé vraiment l'attrait singulier et nouveau de cette soirée. Dans un décor de M. Anisfeld, gris-sombre, d'une apparence un peu confuse et poussiéreuse, la belle Kontchakowna a retrouvé le prince Wladimir. Ils se disent leur amour dans un duo auquel Mme. Petrenko et M. Smirnow, dont on connaît les jolies voix, ont donné une expression de tendresse infinie.

La musique de Borodine est profondément personnelle, aussi forte par l'inspiration que séduisante par l'originalité de ses rythmes. L'orchestre de l'Opéra de Moscou, que dirigeait M. Cooper, en a fidèlement traduit l'intensive beauté. Sur le théâtre et dans la coulisse, des chœurs accompagnant cette scène nous ont rappelé, par leur parfaite expression de vérité et de vie, les meilleurs moments de "Boris Godounow."

Des danses nationales et guerrières viennent s'y ajouter. C'est là que M. Fokine, maître de ballet à l'Opéra de Saint-Pétersbourg, a prouvé la conception unique qu'il a de son métier. Des groupes dansants de jeunes filles, d'esclaves, de jeunes garçons, d'archers polovtsiens surgissent de partout, se ruent, se fondent dans une prodigieuse mêlée de mouvement, d'attitudes sauvages, de combinaisons étranges qu'éclaire une demi-lumière habilement ménagée. Tout est en place dans ce chaos de jolies femmes, de guerriers alertes s'agitant avec furie, mais sans désordre, dans des costumes aux formes orientales et aux couleurs éclatantes.

"Le Pavillon d'Armide" et les Danses polovtsiennes de Borodine sont exécutés dans la Perfection.

Du grand Art.

De ces tableaux incessamment renouvelés résulte une impression de force, de grâce, de talent impossible à décrire. C'est véritablement de l'art, et du grand art. Il faudrait, pour rendre justice aux interprètes, reprendre la liste entière du programme. Tous sont également à louer, chacun ayant la conscience de sa personnalité et de son rôle.

"Le Festin."

"Le Festin" est une suite de danses composées par les principaux maîtres russes, Tchaikowsky, Glazounow, Moussergsky, Glinka. On ne peut imaginer rien de plus coloré, de plus élégant et de mieux rythmé que ces czardas, mazurka, pas hongrois et autres créations chorégraphiques.

MM. Fokine, Marius Pétipa, Gorsky, chef du ballet de Moscou, en ont réglé les détails, délicieusement dansés par cette troupe, dont il y aura encore beaucoup à dire pendant les jours de triomphe qui les attendent à Paris.

ADHEAUME DE CHEVIGNE.

L'Assistance est brillante.

La représentation de gala de la "saison russe" avait fait au Châtelet, hier soir, une chambrée d'un éclat exceptionnel.

Le grand-duc Paul de Russie occupait une grande loge de face avec la comtesse de Hohenfelsen, le marquis et la marquise de Ganay, et le vicomte et la vicomtesse René Vigier.

On notait dans la salle, dans les loges et baignoires, au balcon et à l'orchestre: le duc Georges de Leuchtenberg, l'ambassadeur de Russie, prince et princesse Murat, prince Louis Murat, prince et princesse Dominique Radziwill, comte et comtesse Nostitz, princesse Lobanoff, prince Cantacuzène, prince Troubetzkoy, le ministre de Norvège et la baronne de Wedel-Jarlsberg, princesse Edmond de Polignac, prince Galitzine, comte et comtesse Gérard de Ganay, marquis et marquise de Mun, princesse Lucien Murat, comte et comtesse Jean de Segonzac, M. et Mme. Jean de Reszké;

Le ministre de Serbie et Mme. Vesnitch, M. et Mme. Hersent, M. et Mme. F. Lebaudy, comte et comtesse Etienne de Beaumont, Mme. Gaston Legrand, vicomte et vicomtesse Eugène Melchior de Vogüé, comte et comtesse Joseph Potocki, Mme. et Mlle. Xantho, Mme. Conrad Jameson, Mme. Louis Stern, marquis et marquise de Chasseloup-Laubat, baronne de Langlade, Mme. Ferdinand Blumenthal, M. Léon Delafosse, comte et comtesse Stanislas de Castellane, M. Maurocordato, marquis Vitelleschi, vicomte de Gontaut-Biron, comte Bernard de Gontaut-Biron, comte de Jaucourt, M. Sands;

Prince Miguel de Bragance, duc et duchesse d'Uzès, marquise Paulucci, M. et Mme. de Mumm, marquis et marquise de Massa, comte et comtesse Arthur de Vogüé, comte et comtesse Gaston Chandon de Briailles, comte et comtesse Louis Cahen d'Anvers, comte et comtesse Sampieri, Mme. Michel Ephrussi, comte Bertrand de Durfort, comte Marcel de Germiny, M. Nicolopoulo, comte Henri de Vogüé, comte Louis de Talleyrand-Périgord, vicomte de Gouy d'Arsy, M. de Radwann, M. Alexis de Hitroff.

---

4 THE NEW YORK HERALD, PARIS, DIMANCHE 26 JUILLET, 1903.

FOR SALE. | FOR SALE. | FOR SALE. | FOR SALE.

PRINCELY ESTATE FOR SALE

Magnificent Freehold Property.

CHATEAU DE LA ROCHE DU ROI

AIX-LES-BAINS.

In a magnificent position, overlooking Aix, five minutes from the Etablissement Thermal and the Casinos, the Château de la Roche du Roi is situated on the boulevard of the same name, with a frontage of about 165 mètres and a façade of equal length on boulevard Marlioz. From the château stretches a terrace of some 150 mètres.

From the windows of the château one can perceive the celebrated Lac du Bourget. The interior of the château is constructed in the style of modern art; the staircase is in massive marble, the balusters in forged iron. Luxuriously furnished, and of recent construction, the château is ready for occupation. It is supplied with entirely new linen and crockery of unsurpassable elegance.

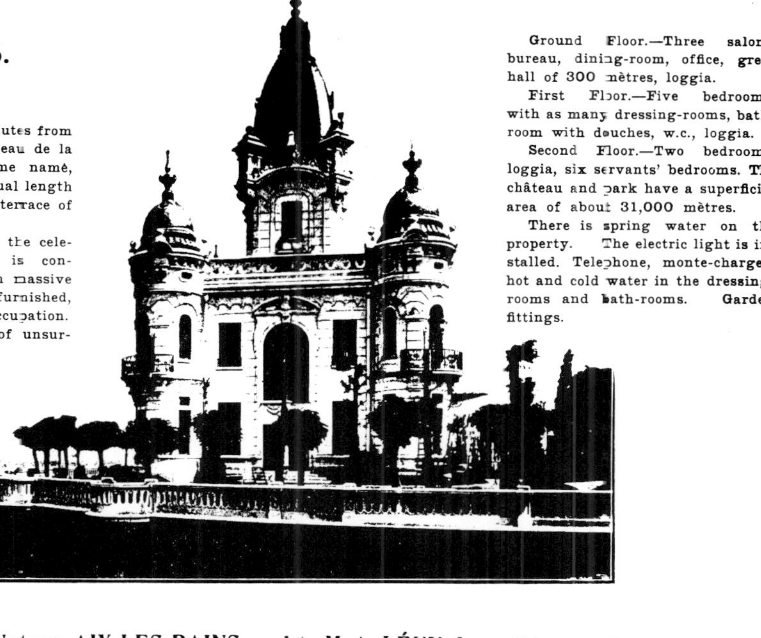

Ground Floor.—Three salons, bureau, dining-room, office, great hall of 300 mètres, loggia.

First Floor.—Five bedrooms, with as many dressing-rooms, bathroom with douches, w.c., loggia.

Second Floor.—Two bedrooms, loggia, six servants' bedrooms. The château and park have a superficial area of about 31,000 mètres.

There is spring water on the property. The electric light is installed. Telephone, monte-charges, hot and cold water in the dressing-rooms and bath-rooms. Garden fittings.

Apply on the premises to M. LECONTE, Notary, AIX-LES-BAINS, and to M. A. LÉVY, 9 rue Edouard Detaille, PARIS.

CHEMISTS, DOCTORS, ETC.

MRS. E. ADAIR,
5 RUE CAMBON, PARIS (Tel. 248.58)
90 NEW BOND STREET, LONDON,
52 WEST 35th STREET, NEW YORK.

Forehead Strap cures Deep Lines & Crow's Feet, 32fr.

Ganesh Chin Strap, 27fr., cures Double-Chins, Lost Contours. Stronger Strap, 32fr.

Patronized by Royalty, received by medical profession. The Ganesh Muscle Oil & treatment for tired-lined eyes, never draws the skin, braces muscles, which are the natural padding of skin, and frees the tissues. Diable Skin Tonic closes and cleanses the pores. Prices, 7fr., 10fr., 20fr., and 27fr. Ganesh Eastern Cream, the greatest skin food in the world. Price 5fr., 8fr., 14fr.

No goods are genuine preparations of Mrs. Adair's unless have the trade-mark "Ganesh" stamped upon them.

FIRST CLASS MEDICAL MASSEUSE (for obesity, wrinkles, etc.) Mme. Schalk, 342 rue Saint-Honoré.

GOUTTES DES COLONIES
CURE INSTANTLY
Cramps in the Stomach _ Indigèstion
Phie CHANDRON. 20, Rue Châteaudun, PARIS.

HYGIENIC MASSAGE, 42 rue de Trévise, 3rd floor, right.

MASSAGE medical, nervous and stomach complaints Mrs. Frank (R.C.S.), 2 rue Lavoisier.

MASSAGE médical. Electric epilation. Manicure. Mlle Servan, 19 bd. Capucines (op. Gd. Hotel).

MASSAGE médical suédois; nervous. Mme. Piernysse, 4 r. Robert-Estienne

MASSAGE. Nerves. Digestion. Electr. Miss Moore, 47 rue Washington, 2-7 daily. Tel. 556.34.

SOZODONT
BETTER THAN GOLD
for the teeth. It prevents decay. It hardens the gums and purifies the breath and mouth.
SAVES YOUR TEETH
1fr. 50c. Post Paid.
HALL & RUCKEL, 10 CHAUSSEE D'ANTIN, PARIS.
A postal card will bring you a free sample.

HOSPITAL TRAINED NURSES.

ENGLISH AND FRENCH HOSP. TR. NURSES. Miss MacClean, 190 bd. Haussmann. Tel. 556.34.

MISS JOAN MACKAY, DIPL. MASSEUSE, ELECtricienne, lessons, hair remov. Receives and visits patients. Great success in beautifying the face and improv. the bust. Assts. 47 av. Victor Hugo. Arc Triom.

INSTRUCTION.

BERLITZ SCHOOL OF LANGUAGES, PARIS.
27 avenue de l'Opéra—180 boulevard Saint-Germain.
49 av. des Champs-Elysées. 14 bd. Poissonnière.
BERLIN, 113 Leipzigerstr., New York, Madison square

ANGLO-SAXON SCHOOL FOR BOYS.
Thor. Anglo-French Educ. E. P. Denny, M.A. (Oxon.), lic.-ès-lettres (Paris). 55 BOULEVARD SUCHET.

DICTION, PRONONC., GENS DU M., étrangers, 24 place Dauphine. E. Duard, de l'Odéon, Off. I. P. Prépar. exam. Conservatoire.

PRIVATE TUITION CLASS., MATH., GERM. Rev. J. L. Bowley, M.A., 25 rue de Longchamps.

THREE FRANCS AN HOUR, French lessons by Mlle. Jourdain, 4 rue Troyon, Arc Triomphe. Speaks Eng. and Germ. Diction. Spec. for foreign. High refs.

GROCERIES.

H. CUVILLIER & FRÈRE
By special appointment to the Imperial Court of Russia and to the Royal Court of Greece.
Teas and Groceries. PARIS, 16 RUE DE LA PAIX.

1910-1919

The awful destruction that Europe was to know before the end of the decade was undreamed of in 1910. The pages of the *Herald* still reflected a world of royalties and riches, spas and grand tours, good manners, scientific innovations and progress.

The race to the South Pole between Amundsen and Scott was a perfect *Herald* story, fascinating a readership which saw it as an exciting adventure, a striking example of human progress, and the perfect occasion for a sporting wager. The sailing of the *Titanic*, the pre-eminent and presumably invulnerable transatlantic liner, was also triumphantly "Heralded" by Bennett, with passenger lists and detailed descriptions of the vessel. When, just days later, the ship foundered and sank, the shock to believers in progress and technology was evident in the *Herald*'s coverage. Many people whose names had long featured in the social and business pages of the *Herald* lost their lives. Bennett, on a rare trip to New York at the time, contacted a passenger he knew on the *Carpathia*, a ship going to the aid of the *Titanic*'s passengers, to wire full reports. As a result, the *Herald*—in both New York and Paris—carried the world's most complete accounts of the disaster. May Birkhead, the impromptu amateur reporter whom Bennett pressed into service to cover the story, later reigned for many years as the powerful society editor of the *Paris Herald*.

The sinking of the *Titanic* can be seen as the first tremor of the earthquake that was to hit the *Herald*'s stable world. In a very different way, that sense of stability was also shaken by the 1913 New York Armory Show, the first major exhibition in America of the more "extreme art" already current on the continent. The *Herald*'s reporter did his best to explain what he believed the painters intended ("The new school . . . tried to reproduce by means of color the mental impressions and feelings of the artist on beholding a certain object or scene"). But, alas, recognizing theory was easier than understanding practice. No one could be found who could explain what a Marcel Duchamp painting meant—"It looks like nothing quite as much as a pinwheel struck by a cyclone," read the report. Mystified by this canvas, called *The King and Queen Traversed by White and Blue Nudes*, by a Kandinsky entitled *Improvisations*, and by the paintings of Francis Picabia ("the spectator seeks in vain to find the least vestige of recognizable form in his productions"), the reporter obviously relaxed on reaching the more traditional rooms of the exhibition—reassured by paintings called *Before the Storm*, *Family Group*, and *Rain in the Rockies*.

More change was apparent as dances such as the Bunny Hug and the Turkey Trot reached the pages of the *Herald*. And Bennett himself succumbed to the winds of change when, after more than seventy years of frequently strenuous bachelorhood, he married in September 1914 his longtime companion, Maud Potter de Reuter (whose late husband had been the Baron de Reuter of another famous journalistic family). Bennett settled down to relative calm for the last years of his life. But his world was coming apart.

From the start of World War I, Bennett quickly recognized how important a role the *Herald* could play, both as a valuable source of information—given its unique geographical position—and as a compelling advocate of American intervention. As the Battle of the Marne took shape in September 1914, and, later, when the opposing armies settled into the muddy miles of trenches that latticed the north of France, the *Herald* was able to cover the Western Front with a rare thoroughness. Reporters set off to spend the day, or pass the night, on the banks of the Marne or in the trenches with the British and French forces, carrying back frontline reports to the newsroom the next day.

From early in the war, the back page was printed in French—an attempt to compensate for the lack of French papers in the capital (all but one had moved to Bordeaux with the government). Bennett soon became a vigorous proponent of US involvement, particularly after the sinking of the passenger ship *Lusitania* by the German navy in May 1915.

The loss of the *Lusitania* also marked the first day on the job at the *Herald* for a short-statured, but large-spirited Englishman who was to spend the next forty-five years in the editorial department. Hired by Bennett to augment his war-ravaged staff, Eric Hawkins would hold the post of managing editor from 1924 until his retirement in 1960.

The early days of the war brought great financial losses for the *Herald* as the mainstays of both its staff and its clientele disappeared. Luxury, travel and resort advertising evaporated, as did the American visitors to whom the advertisements had been targeted. It took all of Bennett's famous vigor and force to keep the Paris paper open, but he never hesitated, despite enormous pressures to stop. As the battle intensified he even encouraged his editors to join the military effort, continuing to pay their salaries to their wives. And to replace them, he abandoned entirely the role of absentee proprietor, rolling up his sleeves and, at the age of seventy-four, returning to the role of working editor and reporter—"Just doing some legwork," he would explain. Throughout the entire war, the *Herald* did not miss a single issue.

As the war continued, advertising slowly began to build again and, in 1917, sales of the paper shot up to levels never reached before or since. The American Army had arrived in France, and many tens of thousands of "doughboys" grabbed up the only newspaper they could read. For a brief period in 1918, circulation reached 350,000 copies daily.

The year 1917 also brought to Paris the *Herald*'s first serious competitor (though a variety of English language papers have come and gone in Paris throughout the *Herald*'s life). Colonel Robert McCormack, owner of the *Chicago Tribune*, fearing that the *Paris Herald*—obviously decadent after so many frivolous years in the Old World—would not make suitable reading for the fresh-faced American boys, created the European Edition of the *Chicago Tribune*. Ironically, it was the *Tribune* which over the next seventeen years would become the organ of the avant-garde Left Bank intellectuals, while the *Herald* swerved slightly away from Bennett's flamboyant heritage to serve the more traditional residents and visitors whose life, like the paper's, was centered on the city's Right Bank.

The competition between the two papers would eventually drive the *Tribune* from the field. But for the time being there was sufficient public for both papers. And for the *Herald*, suddenly and for the first time in its history, there were profits. Bennett, puzzled by the development, simply opened a bank account and left the money there.

On May 15, 1918, James Gordon Bennett, Jr., owner of the *New York Herald* and creator of its European Edition, died at his Riviera villa at Beaulieu. In reporting the passing of its celebrity publisher at the age of seventy-seven, the *Herald* mentioned his name in its own pages for the first time.

By the end of the year, the war had been won by the Allied Forces that Bennett had so strenuously supported. But Bennett was gone—and with him the world he had known. Even the daily letter from the Old Philadelphia Lady asking how to convert Fahrenheit to Centigrade had been removed from the *Herald*'s pages.

In the final year of the decade, the pages of the *Herald* foreshadowed the divisions and tensions of the postwar world. At great length, the paper reported the effort at Versailles to make a new Europe on the weak foundations of the old. Meanwhile, the paper was also living through another development which would have been unthinkable in Bennett's day, and which was in fact unreportable in the *Herald*: the first strike in the paper's history, which lasted for three weeks in November 1919.

WEDNESDAY. AUGUST 23, 1911.

Da Vinci's Famous Picture "La Gioconda" Stolen from Its Place in Louvre Museum

Missing Since Monday Morning, Alarm of Theft Was Only Given Yesterday.

Leonardo da Vinci's famous painting "La Gioconda," the pride of the Louvre museum, was yesterday found to have been stolen from its place in the Salon Carré of the museum.

The news caused a feeling bordering on consternation in Paris artistic circles. The fact that the picture had been removed from its accustomed place was noticed on Monday, but little attention was paid to the matter by the guardians, it being thought that it had been taken away temporarily for copying purposes. The Louvre museum is closed to the general public on Mondays, and only a few privileged persons, whose identity is known, are admitted. These include the conservators, the members of the Société des Amis du Louvre, a few copyists and photographers representing firms who reproduce the pictures and who profit by the closing of the museum to photograph the paintings without being disturbed by the general public.

At seven o'clock on Monday morning one of the guardians noticed that the "Gioconda" was in its accustomed place. At eight o'clock it was no longer there. It was thought at the time, however, that the painting had been removed to the office of one of the officials for some reason or another, or that photographers had taken it down and were photographing it in some quiet corner of the museum. Several painters turned up during the day to copy the picture, and were disappointed to find it missing, but they, too, were in no way surprised, expecting to find it back in its place on the morrow. One of the museum attendants even dusted the wall on which the picture had been hung in order that everything should be clean when it was returned.

Suspicions First Aroused.

Yesterday morning the museum was again thrown open to the public. The disappointed painters desirous of copying the picture, who had been compelled to go away the previous day, were surprised that it still had not returned. People began to ask where it was, and the guardians questioned one another. No one knew. It was then decided to try to find out what had been done with it. Calls were made on the various officials. No one had seen it.

The officials began to realize that the painting's prolonged absence called for some explanation. A general search was made, but without result, until finally the empty frame of the "Gioconda" was found in a small corridor leading to the lavatories reserved for the personnel.

Instantly the greatest excitement prevailed. The conservators were informed and a telegram was sent to M. Dujardin-Beaumetz, Under-Secretary of State for Fine Arts, who was absent from Paris. The Prefect of Police was notified, and M. Lescouvé, Public Prosecutor, proceeded to the museum to commence an inquiry.

No Trace of Framework.

Everyone who had been in the museum on Monday was questioned, but without result. It was doubted that the thief or thieves could have left the museum carrying the picture without being noticed. It measures 90cm. by 70cm. The idea that the canvas had been cut from its framework had to be abandoned, however, as no trace of the framework was to be found.

Among the possibilities that suggested themselves to the authorities was that the picture had been removed by some person or persons who desired to demonstrate that the museum was insufficiently guarded and that it would be returned to the Under-Secretary for Fine Arts with explanations. A HERALD correspondent was informed by M. Magny, in the absence of the Under-Secretary for Fine Arts, that he could merely confirm the news of the theft and that he had no news of what had become of the picture. "It is hardly possible to believe that it has been stolen," added M. Magny, "but it has gone!"

"LA JOCONDE" DU MUSÉE DU LOUVRE.

Frame Discovered in Small Corridor, But No Trace of Painting Is Found.

"'La Gioconda' of the Louvre does not correspond, in its present state at least, with the detailed description made by Vasari in his 'Lives of the Painters' of the original portrait of 'Mona Lisa,' the wife of Francesco del Giocondo, painted at Florence, about 1504 by Leonardo da Vinci.

"The Louvre shows but the ruin of a picture, blackened in some spots, faded in others. That poor 'Mona Lisa' has been so much repainted, besides, and submitted to so many 'processes of preservation,' in order to delay its final destruction, that it would be hard to swear to-day in which point of it the master put his brush. * * *

"What should we say if we know that there exists another portrait of 'La Gioconda' as old or rather older than the one at the Louvre, admirably painted like Leonardo's hand could do it only, perfectly preserved, and which corresponds exactly to Vasari's description?

"It can be seen at the Museum of the Prado. According to Madrazo, it is a copy, and as a copy it hangs now at the Prado, but, common-sense and Vasari have convinced me that it is the very original portrait of 'Mona Lisa,' painted by Master Leonardo da Vinci.

"Hung in the same room as Titian's portrait of Philip II., Raphael's admirable rendering of a young cardinal and other universally reputed masterworks of Paolo Veronese and Tintoretto, 'Mona Lisa' shines like a star, with the smile on her lips, the smile that inspired so many poets and so many painters. Her eyes are brilliant, crystal-like, her nostrils roseate and slender, and you can count the hairs in her eyebrows, eyelashes and locks, just like Vasari did. * * * Why call it a copy? * * * To give that name to the Prado's wonder is a rank injustice. * * *

"However this may be, while the 'Gioconda' at the Louvre, great as it might have been, is but the shadow of a once splendid work of art, the 'Mona Lisa' at the Prado is a reality and a marvel worthy of the name of Leonardo.

"THE SPANIARD."

SATURDAY. DECEMBER 13, 1913.

Leonardo da Vinci's Masterpiece, "La Gioconda," Stolen from Louvre Museum, Is Found in Florence

Picture Was Offered to Florentine Antiquarian, Who Promptly Communicated With the Police.

Authenticity of Painting Is Vouched for by Signor Poggi and Signor Corrado Ricci.

[SPECIAL TO THE HERALD.]

FLORENCE, Friday. — Leonardo da Vinci's masterpiece "La Gioconda," which was stolen from the Louvre Museum in Paris two years ago, has been discovered in Florence.

The picture was offered this morning to Signor Geri, an antiquarian in the via Borg' Ognisanti, by a man named Vincenzo Perugia, of Como. Signor Geri's suspicions were aroused, and he reported the matter to the police.

Signor Poggi, director of the Uffizi Gallery, and Signor Corrado Ricci declare the picture to be the original "Gioconda" stolen from the Louvre.

The picture has been in Perugia's possession since its theft.

I am authorized to make this statement by the Prefect of Florence and the police.

PAINTING WILL BE HANDED TO FRENCH AMBASSADOR.

Italian Government Promises Solemn Restitution of Masterpiece.

[SPECIAL TO THE HERALD.]

ROME, Friday.—News of the recovery of the "Gioconda" was received by Signor Credaro, Minister of Public Instruction, while the Chamber of Deputies was discussing the validity of the election of Signor Federzoni, Nationalist Deputy for Rome, which the Extreme Left, allied with the Radicals, was attempting to have annulled.

The sitting had just been suspended, as the debate had literally degenerated into a free fight, but the news of the discovery of the masterpiece restored calm, and the political fever suddenly gave way to general rejoicing. Signor Sonnino, leader of the Constitutionalist opposition, left his seat and walked over to Signor Credaro to congratulate him.

The Minister of Public Instruction informed me that the competence of Signor Corrado Ricci, who examined the painting, left no doubt of its authenticity. "It will be restored to M. Barrère, the French Ambassador," declared the Minister, "with the ceremonial that the restitution of so sacred a treasure demands."

TRAP WAS LAID TO CATCH PICTURE THIEF.

Perugia, However, Arrived Before Date Named.

(From the "Excelsior.")

FLORENCE, Friday.—The following are the latest details of the arrest of Perugia.

Signor Geri, the antiquary, in the first letter which he wrote to Perugia in reply to the latter's offer to sell the "Gioconda," requested Perugia to bring the picture with him to Italy. Perugia consented to do this on condition that he was guaranteed a reward of 500,000 francs. This condition was agreed to, and Perugia then announced that he would arrive in Florence on December 17.

It was therefore with no little surprise that Signor Geri received Perugia when he arrived unexpectedly on Tuesday last, saying: "I have come here with the picture. You absolutely must come and see it with me at my hotel."

Signor Geri replied that he would do so, but wished to be accompanied by a friend employed at the Uffizi Gallery, who would be better able to recognize the picture's authenticity.

Perugia agreed to this and said he would wait for them at his hotel at three o'clock.

At the hour named, therefore, Signor Geri and his "friend," no other than Signor Poggi, director of the Uffizi Gallery, called at the Hotel Tripoli and found Perugia awaiting them in his apartment. After locking the door with the utmost precaution Perugia went to his trunk and withdrew the masterpiece which has been sought throughout the world for the past two years.

Signor Poggi examined the painting minutely and was soon convinced of its authenticity. He therefore asked Perugia if he might take it with him to the Uffizi Gallery, there to examine it at his leisure.

Perugia raised no objection and Signor Poggi thereupon conveyed the "Gioconda" to the gallery, where a minute examination strengthened his conviction that the picture was genuine. Signor Poggi noticed two identification marks on the back of the canvas which he believed had been placed there by the Bureau des Arts de Versailles, and this in his opinion placed the authenticity of the picture beyond all doubt.

The police, who had been kept fully informed of all the negotiations, kept the man under constant observation until his arrest.

"To Avenge Napoleon's Thefts.

ROME, Friday.—It is stated that the man Perugia, who offered the "Gioconda" to the antiquarian Geri, is an Italian who had been living in Paris. When questioned after his arrest he declared that he stole the painting from the Louvre in order to avenge the thefts committed in Italy by Napoleon.

The picture has been seized and is now deposited at the Prefecture of Florence pending its transference to Rome.

The director of the Florence Museum states that he reserves his judgment as to the authenticity of the painting. All he will say is that if it is not the original "Gioconda," it is a very remarkable and very old copy.—Figaro.

Thief Left Paris Suddenly.

(From the "Matin.")

Vincenzo Perugia, who lived in a very modest room at 5 rue de l'Hôpital-Saint-Louis, in Paris, is by profession a house-painter. Close by him live his cousins Giovanni, Antonio and Giuseppe, the two latter married. Giovanni and Giuseppe Perugia left Paris a fortnight ago for Italy, while Vincenzo left quite unexpectedly on Wednesday, recalled by telegraph to his native country, as he told his concierge.

Giovanni Perugia stated last night that for the last few days Vincenzo had been talking of leaving Paris soon, and on Wednesday morning he requested Giovanni's wife to pack his bag. He was a bachelor and a steady and reliable workman, and after his day's work he would pass the evening with his relatives.

Signora Giuseppe Perugia stated that Antonio and her husband had left for Italy to settle an inheritance, and that she believed Vincenzo had gone there for the same purpose. She could not tell whether Vincenzo had been employed on repairs at the Louvre.

One of Vincenzo's friends declared that he was a good house-painter, but without any education and absolutely devoid of any knowledge of artistic matters.

He could not believe that he had stolen the "Gioconda," unless somebody had incited him to the theft, either for pecuniary benefit, or by working upon his patriotic feelings.

FRIDAY. MARCH 8, 1912.

SOUTH POLE REPORTED DISCOVERED, BUT RIVAL CLAIMS MAY BE MADE

CAPTAIN SCOTT.

THE TERRA NOVA.

THE BRITISH ANTARCTIC EXPEDITION

Doubt Exists as to Whether Captain Scott or Captain Amundsen Was Successful Explorer.

[BY THE HERALD'S SPECIAL WIRE.]

LONDON, Friday.—Has the South Pole been reached by either Captain Scott or Captain Amundsen or by both? It is curious that a situation should have arisen similar to the Peary-Cook controversy with regard to the North Pole in 1909. Yet telegrams received yesterday indicate that rival claimants are in the field for the honor of having vanquished the last stronghold of the mysterious Antarctic.

In a message despatched yesterday from Wellington, New Zealand, the "Standard's" correspondent says: "Amundsen has telegraphed the news that Captain Scott has reached the South Pole."

"Up to the time of going to press," says the "Standard" we have received no further details in regard to this message."

A Reuter's Wellington telegram, dated yesterday says: "A rumor, which, however, lacks confirmation, is current here that Captain Amundsen, who is at Hobart, states that Captain Scott has reached the Pole."

From Hobart, however, Reuter's correspondent telegraphs: "Captain Amundsen has returned here from the South Polar regions, but at present has not made any statement as to the success or failure of his expedition."

The first definite news of Captain Amundsen's claim to South Polar honors comes from Reuter's Christiania correspondent in the following message:—"The newspaper 'Social-Democraten' says that a private individual in Christiania has received a telegram from the Fram expedition stating that Amundsen had reached the South Pole. The informant of the journal asserts that the telegram is thoroughly trustworthy.

Another Christiania message, despatched at noon yesterday, stated that King Haakon had so far received no report from Captain Amundsen regarding his expedition to the South Pole.

Mrs. Scott Awaiting News.

Mrs. Scott, who is hourly expecting news from her husband, said yesterday: "I have had no word, and am, to tell the truth, sceptical as to the accuracy of the reports which have been published to-day."

Sir Ernest Shackleton views the possibility of success. He said: "I certainly hope that Captain Scott has reached the South Pole, and he has my heartiest congratulations. But, with the meagre facts now before me, there is very little that I can say. It is, of course, quite probable that Scott, having reached the Pole, sees no necessity to hurry home, and that he has stopped a little longer than he need have done to pick up his parties, and so accomplish a little more scientific exploration work.

"Amundsen, of course, is now going to the North Polar region. He declared that he was taking in the South Pole instead of going North in the first instance. There is nothing surprising in the news, except as to the way in which it came. I would have been very sorry had Scott not been successful on this occasion."

The Royal Geographical Society has received no news as to the results of Captain Amundsen's expedition to the South Pole. Indeed, some surprise is felt by the Society, states Reuter, at his return to civilisation at least two weeks before he was expected back.

Message Received in Christiania.

CHRISTIANIA, Thursday.—A telegram from Captain Amundsen has reached here, and is being published to-morrow by two papers having the sole right of publication. A full report of the expedition is expected shortly.—Daily Mirror.

CAPTAIN SCOTT PRAISED BY AMERICAN NEWSPAPERS.

Commander Peary Says He Always Had Faith He Would Win.

NEW YORK, Thursday.—Congratulatory comments appear in all the newspapers on the news of Captain Scott's success, and satisfaction is expressed that America has led the way to the ends of the earth.

Commander Peary says: "I sincerely hope that Captain Scott has succeeded. He deserves the fullest measure of success, and if he has won he has my heartiest congratulations. We always had faith that he would win, barring an entirely unexpected catastrophe.

"A month prior to Captain Scott's departure I talked with him in detail about his preparations, but I would not have it appear that what he has done was in any way due to the conferences I had with him. He would have succeeded in any event. He is a trained British naval officer, and there is no nonsense about him, and I am delighted he has found the South Pole."—Standard.

SATURDAY. MARCH 9, 1912.

CAPTAIN AMUNDSEN CONFIRMS REPORT THAT HE HAS DISCOVERED SOUTH POLE

Norwegian Sovereigns Consent to Use of Their Names for Newly-Discovered Territory.

[BY THE HERALD'S SPECIAL WIRE.]

LONDON, Saturday. — Captain Roald Amundsen, as intimated in yesterday's HERALD, announces that he has discovered the South Pole and that his object was attained between the 14th and 17th of December, 1911. But the most significant statement in connection with his reported discovery is contained in a despatch from Christiania, which says that King Haakon and Queen Maud have consented to the use of their names in maps of newly-discovered territory.

While none of the London newspapers questions the correctness of Captain Amundsen's statement that he has found the Pole, there is a disposition to reserve critical comment until the explorer has told his full story.

Some papers call attention to the peculiarity of the announcement that the Pole was attained between the 14th and 17th of December, and are anxious to have the mystery involved in this statement dispelled.

Others express the hope that Captain Scott has also found the Pole, and this hope was heartened to-day when Sir Ernest Shackleton, speaking at the Mansion House, in expressing his conviction that the Norwegian explorer had found the "big nail" of the South, said he believed that the British sailor had gained the goal also. In fact, there is an undercurrent of confidence here in Captain Scott, and until he has been heard from many newspapers and millions of Englishmen will cling to the belief that he reached the Pole first.

This hesitancy in hailing Captain Amundsen as the discoverer is due in a measure to the grim silence of the Norwegian sailor, who, according to despatches from Hobart, Tasmania, where the Fram is now anchored, peremptorily refuses to allow anyone to board the vessel and is the only member of the expedition who has lanced there. Although he declined to talk of his discovery, reports were circulated that during his dash to the Pole he and the members of his expedition endured hardships second only to those described by Dr. Cook and Admiral Peary upon their return from their quest of the North Pole.

CAPTAIN ROALD AMUNDSEN.

Captain Amundsen's Return.

A telegram received by the "Daily Express" from its Wellington (New Zealand) correspondent says: "After meeting Scott in the Bay of Whales on January 19, 1911 Amundsen camped with nine men at longitude 164 West, latitude 78. Amundsen's subsequent doings are not stated. Amundsen adds that he will submit charts and all information without delay. His plans are as follows. He proposes to sail to Buenos Aires next week, thence rounding Cape Horn for San Francisco, from there to go through the Behring Straits, and from there to drift with the ice across the Arctic, emerging between Greenland and Spitzbergen.

Captain Scott's New Zealand agent is of the opinion that Captain Scott must have changed his plans with a view to exploring and scientific work, thus possibly delaying the Terra Nova's return for some weeks.

Amundsen could have beaten Scott back to civilisation.—Morning Leader.

Sir Ernest Shackleton Believes Captain Scott's Expedition Also Has Been Successful.

Had Eighty Miles Start of Capt. Scott.

LONDON. — Captain Roald Amundsen started from the Bay of Whales, 400 miles south-east of McMurdo Sound, which was Captain Scott's starting point. Striking direct for the Pole, says the "Daily Mirror," he would have a shorter distance to cover than his English rival, his starting-point, at lat. 78deg. 40min., being eighty miles nearer to the Pole than McMurdo Sound.

But he may have diverged westward and followed Sir Ernest Shackleton's celebrated route up the Beardmore Glacier, which is also that to be taken by Captain Scott. If he took a direct route from the Bay of Whales his small party of eight men must have taken terrific risks in an utterly unknown route.

It was said, moreover, that the bold Norwegian explorer had the intention of trying to race for the Pole during the long Antarctic night. Captain Amundsen journeyed to the Bay of Whales on the Fram, the famous Arctic ship, in which Dr. Nansen sought the North Pole.

The circumstances of his expedition are somewhat extraordinary. For a long period he was busily engaged in preparations in Norway for a North Polar expedition on the Fram. He raised large sums in Norway, and also got a certain amount in this country, where, three years ago, he lectured before the Royal Geographical Society on his plans for a North Polar voyage.

He set out on the Fram, equipped apparently for work in Arctic regions, with the avowed intention of doubling Cape Horn and proceeding to Behring Strait. At Madeira, in October, 1909, he stopped, and suddenly came the announcement that he was proceeding thence not to the Arctic, but to the Antarctic.

Nothing more was heard of him in England for seventeen months. On February 4, last year, Lieutenant Pennell, on board the Terra Nova, reached the Bay of Whales, and to the overwhelming surprise of his party found that they were not alone in those desolate regions of ice. In the bay was the Fram, going into winter quarters with her eight men, 116 dogs and full equipment for a journey to the Pole.

CAPTAIN AMUNDSEN REMAINED AT POLE THREE DAYS, TO CONFIRM OBSERVATIONS

CAPTAIN AMUNDSEN IN FUR CLOTHING.

THE FRAM.

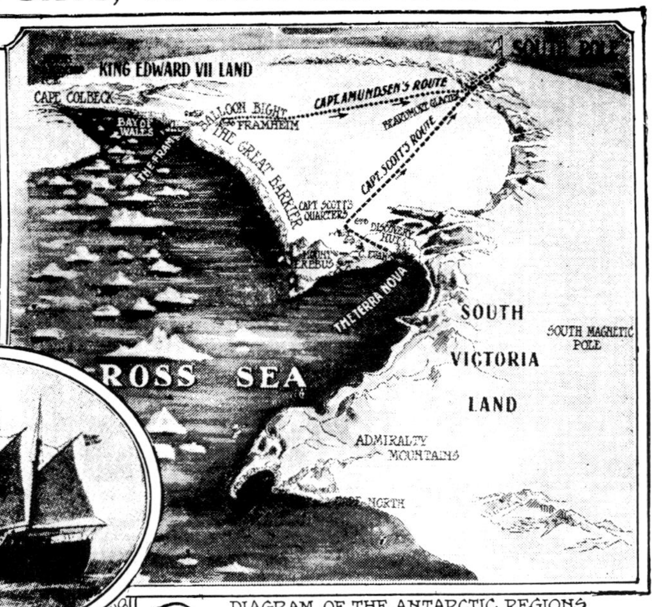

DIAGRAM OF THE ANTARCTIC REGIONS SHOWING CAPTAIN AMUNDSEN'S AND CAPTAIN SCOTT'S ITINERARIES.

Raised Flag of Norway on Icy Waste and Named It King Haakon's Plateau.

[BY THE HERALD'S SPECIAL WIRE.]

LONDON, Sunday.—The English press, while according Captain Amundsen due praise for his reported conquest of the South Pole, clings fondly to the belief that Captain Scott, the intrepid British explorer, hoisted the Union Jack at the southernmost end of the world before the Norwegian colors were raised on the icy waste by the Scandinavian sailor. So the question of the hour here is "Who reached the South Pole first—Captain Amundsen or Captain Scott?" England is backing Scott.

Captain Amundsen's story of his conquest of the Pole, published yesterday by the "Daily Chronicle," adds something valuable to the total of human knowledge contributed by Captain Scott and Sir Ernest Shackleton about the land, ice-covered seas and mountains of the Far South. In brief, in describing his arrival at the goal of his endeavor, Captain Amundsen tells of an icy waste about which he circled for three days, taking hourly observations to confirm the belief that he had indeed reached the South Pole. Then he recites how he raised the flag of Norway and the pennant of the Fram on this waste and called it King Haakon's Plateau.

Then Captain Amundsen's story, after detailing fatiguing marches over snow and ice-covered wastes, tells of exhausting climbs of ice-capped mountains, the establishment of ten dépôts at various stages of the journey, where seal meat and pemmican were cached, the loss of eighty of his 104 dogs and the sufferings from intense cold of himself and the four men who accompanied him in the final dash to the Pole.

The chief results of the expedition, according to his own contention, were the determination of the character and length of the Ross barrier, the discovery of the probable connection between Victoria Land and King Edward Land and their continuation in great mountains running for 850 kilomètres towards the south-east as far as 88deg. south, which, he says, probably continue across the Antarctic Continent.

Captain Amundsen declares also that the expedition to King Edward Land under Lieutenant F. Prestud achieved excellent results; that Captain Scott's discoveries were confirmed—this is a strong, positive note in the narrative—and that he is bringing a good geological collection from King Edward and South Victoria Lands. He describes his return from the Pole as a pleasure trip, and says that on January 16 the Japanese expedition arrived in the Bay of Whales, near his winter quarters, ending a long despatch from Hobart by announcing that all on the Fram, which, he declares, penetrated farther south than any other vessel, are well.

Await News of Captain Scott.

Newspapers and scientists here, though stirred by Captain Amundsen's story and lauding him for his achievement, are disposed to delay the ceremony of crowning him with laurel until Captain Scott is heard from and the question whether Norseman or Englishman first reached the pole is definitely and satisfactorily decided.

In commenting on Captain Amundsen's report of his journey to and his discovery of the Pole, Sir Ernest Shackleton, in "Lloyd's Weekly News," says: "Amundsen made his final dépôt in latitude 82 south, and it must be remembered that he had the advantage in latitude of starting 1 degree further south than Captain Scott. He appears to have passed the winter in comfort, though situated on the edge of the sea, where one would expect to have a heavy snowfall. But he records only two severe gales throughout the winter.

"The interesting scientific point is to be noted that at the edge of the Ross Sea the open water existed throughout the winter. A very low temperature was experienced in the early part of the spring, and Amundsen found that the start for the Pole would be eventually made on September 8. Amundsen found when he started on September 8 that the temperature was too low to enable him to make a protracted journey to the south and still keep his dogs efficient. We started our spring sledging journeys on the Nimrod expedition on August 12, nearly a month earlier than Amundsen, and we also found that in temperatures of 60deg. and 70deg. below zero Fahr. (—51deg. to —57deg. Cent.) we took so much out of ourselves because of the cold that it was not practical policy to continue.

"Amundsen returned, and eventually decided to start toward the end of October, and, instead of taking his whole party of eight men and all the dogs south, he took five men south and left three men to explore King Edward Land, discovered by Captain Scott in 1902, thus ensuring a certain amount of scientific and geographical work, quite apart from the important meteorological observations he carried out during the winter night.

Met Favorable Conditions.

"He seems to have had most favorable conditions on the barrier surface—smooth going, ample opportunity to use his skis and dogs in excellent condition. Though the temperatures were low they were able to march at a rate of over thirty kilomètres a day, and from this one must gather that the weather was fine and the surface good. After leaving the last dépôt made in latitude 82deg. south, Amundsen began to build snow cairns at each camping place, following out the same method that I used on our Southern journey from latitude 82deg. to 83deg. He reports fine going and a fair temperature and on the 9th he sighted Victoria Land.

"In latitude 83deg. south he established a dépôt, and on the 11th made what is one of the most important discoveries—that the Ross barrier terminated by the junction of the south-easterly range of mountains that we noted on our expedition with a range of mountains running south-westerly, evidently from King Edward VII. Land. Just here the cable is somewhat vague as regards the actual latitude and longitude.

"So far Amundsen's ground has been entirely new, and now that it might be expected he would proceed on the Beardmore Glacier, he does not do so but finds a new route of his own to reach the inland ice. Like we, who on our expedition saw great mountains, he also observes mountains rising from 2,000ft. to 10,000ft., and several others further south 15,000ft. in height. At a height of 4,500ft. they had to leave the side track they were going up, and came to what he describes as a mighty glacier, and he makes an interesting observation, which corroborates our own, that these great southern glaciers have but little movement now, and the crevasses are often snow-filled.

Four Day's Blizzard.

"At a height of 5,000 feet he again gets into trouble, but, in spite of this, reaches a height of 5,600 feet in record time. Amundsen's cable is somewhat obscure just here. He reached the inland plateau of ice at a height of 10,000 odd feet, killed some of his dogs, and kept eighteen for the final march. Then he was struck by that great bugbear of the Southern explorers, the blizzard, and for four days was held up by bad weather.

"In latitude 86deg. south he sees mountains stretching away to the south, with the weather clear, but still found his journey upwards. On December 3 he left the Devil's Glacier, and was about 9,100 feet above the sea. 'It is interesting to me to note that at latitude 86 deg. south our height above sea level was 8,500 feet.' Away to the south-east he still saw great peaks, some rising to a height of 15,000 feet, and in the misty weather he only caught glimpses of the mountains.

"At a height of 9,000 feet above the sea level Amundsen eventually reached the plateau proper, experiencing similar travelling conditions to those we experienced. He describes the march over these frozen wastes as being like walking over empty barrels, the hollow sound being due to the empty space beneath.

"On December 6 he notes, according to the hypsometer, a height of 10,750 feet in latitude 87.40, a similar height recorded by us in the same latitude before corrections were made to our hypsometric measurement. Amundsen now marched south in fine weather, a noon observation recording 88.16 south. Before him lay an absolutely flat plateau, with now and then a small 'sastrugi,' or wind-blown snow-heap, visible.

Beyond Former Human Footsteps.

"On December 8 our farthest south of 88.23 was passed, and Amundsen was beyond all former human footsteps in 88.25. Experiencing good weather still, he camps. He made his last dépôt, and then he notes that the plateau slowly dips towards the south. From now onward there are regular marches, and on December 14, in beautiful weather, but with a fairly low temperature, at three o'clock in the afternoon by dead reckoning, he thinks he has reached the Pole.

"Then comes the long-looked for moment when the Norwegian flag is hoisted and possession of the geographical South Pole is taken on behalf of Norway, and here I would like to point out that Amundsen, in taking possession and in planting the flag at the South Pole and naming the plateau after King Haakon VII. must, I presume, be unaware of the fact that we, on our expedition, named the same plateau after King Edward VII.

"Very carefully and methodically they proceeded to establish the position of the geographical Pole, marching south on the following day nine kilomètres (roughly six miles) in order to establish as far as humanly possible with the instruments they had the exact position. I note that they used a sextant and artificial horizon which for actual efficiency in very high latitudes is not as absolutely accurate as a theodolite. But I consider that if they located their position with no more possible error than two or three miles one way or the other by their marching round they have certainly left their footsteps on that point from which everything bears north."

Captain Amundsen Norway's Hero.

CHRISTIANIA, Saturday. — Captain Amundsen is the hero of the hour here. His telegram has aroused the greatest enthusiasm throughout Norway. All the towns are profusely beflagged.

The eminent meteorologist, M. Mohn, in an interview, insisted that the four days Amundsen stopped at the Pole or in the neighborhood were sufficient to enable him to make all the observations necessary to fix with scientific exactitude any disputed point, and to collect accurate data for the whole of the Polar regions. A national subscription has been started to cover the expenses of the expedition.—Lloyd's Weekly News

Congratulations to Explorer.

CHRISTIANIA, Saturday.—The Municipal Council, the University and a great number of associations have sent their congratulations to Captain Amundsen. King Haakon has received congratulatory telegrams from King George V. and the King of Denmark.—Reuter.

Four Other Expeditions in Antarctic.

[BY THE HERALD'S SPECIAL WIRE.]

LONDON, Sunday.—For the moment, the Antarctic has quite displaced the Arctic as a field of exploration, as Dr. W. S. Bruce points out in the current issue of "Nature." In addition to Scott and Amundsen, four other expeditions are carrying on researches in the South Polar regions, namely, the Australian, under Dr. Douglas Mawson; the German, under Lieutenant Dr. Filchner; the Japanese, under Lieutenant Shirase, and the Argentine expedition, which left for the South Orkneys to continue the meteorological and magnetical work initiated by the Scottish expedition at Scotia Bay in 1903 and continued by the Officina Meteorologica Argentina since 1904 at an annual cost of about £6,000.

STABS MAN WHO MURDERED HIS FATHER 15 YEARS AGO.

Terrible Drama Enacted in Corso Garibaldi, Naples—Dying Man Wounds Assailant.

[SPECIAL TO THE HERALD.]

NAPLES, Saturday.—A terrible drama was enacted in the Corso Garibaldi today, as the result of a long-standing feud.

A butcher, named Formicola, whose prison sentence of fifteen years for the murder of his benefactor, Signor Volpicelli, recently was completed, was stabbed in the Corso Garibaldi by the son of Signor Volpicelli. Although a child at the death of his father, he had sworn to avenge the crime. Formicola, although mortally wounded, fired upon his assailant with a revolver, wounding him seriously.

ARRESTED FOR THEFT.

[SPECIAL TO THE HERALD.]

NAPLES, Saturday.—The Naples police has arrested two Germans, Valentia Bremhorst and Emil Holle, who have been sought by the police in connection with the theft of 20,000 marks from a brewery company at Herne, Germany, in whose employment they were.

At the time of their arrest they still had nine thousand francs in their possession.

CAPTAIN SCOTT REACHES SOUTH POLE, BUT PERISHES ON THE RETURN JOURNEY

CAPT. SCOTT IN HIS POLAR KIT.

CAPTAIN R. F. SCOTT.

THE TERRA NOVA

DR. E. A. WILSON.

Four Companions Die With British Explorer Two Months After Attaining Their Goal.

Leader of Expedition Is Victim of Exposure and Want During Blizzard.

Captain Robert F. Scott and four of his companions have died in the Antarctic regions. Simultaneously with the report of their death comes the news that the British explorer had reached the goal for which he had striven—the South Pole.

The five explorers were struggling northward on the return journey when, one by one, they fell victims to exposure and want, or to diseases incident to the Polar climate.

CAPTAIN SCOTT AND FOUR COMRADES DIE IN BLIZZARD.

Returning Explorers Succumbed on or About March 29, 1912.

[BY THE HERALD'S SPECIAL WIRE.]

LONDON, Tuesday.—The tragic news reached London yesterday that Captain Robert Falcon Scott, R.N., C.V.O., the leader of the British Antarctic expedition, and four of his comrades, perished nearly a year ago. They reached the South Pole on January 18, 1912, but perished on the return journey. After reaching the Pole they struggled for some two months to get back to the "One Ton Dépôt" which they had established 150 miles north, but one by one they died on the way. Seaman Evans died from concussion on February 17. Captain Oates died from exposure on March 17, Captain Scott, Lieutenant Bowers, and Dr. Wilson died from exposure and want during a blizzard about March 29.

The news of the tragedy, the "Standard" says, comes from the Terra Nova, which arrived at Christchurch, New Zealand, yesterday, with the remainder of the ill-fated expedition, under the command of Lieutenant G. R. Evans. The following is the list of the dead: Captain R. F. Scott, in command of the expedition; Dr. E. A. Wilson, chief of scientific staff, zoologist and artist; Lieutenant H. R. Bowers, Royal Indian Marine Commissariat, officer of the southern party; Captain L. E. G. Oates, Inniskilling Dragoons, in charge of ponies and dogs; Seaman Edgar Evans, who had been a petty officer in the Royal Navy, and was in charge of the sledges.

A Touching Tribute.

A touching tribute to Captain Scott and his comrades was paid last night at a meeting of the Royal Geographical Society at Burlington Gardens. The chairman, Mr. Douglas Freshfield, said they met under the shadow of a great calamity, and he read a telegram of sympathy from Lord Curzon. He was not in a position to give any complete or consecutive account of the disaster.

Captain Scott intended to march from his base camp some 800 miles to the South Pole. Sixteen were to start, besides a leader, and at successive stages four were to be dropped, leaving the last four to go with Captain Scott to the final goal. They left in November, 1911. They did not return. They had not returned when the relief ship left the base camp, in February, 1912, but were reported as last heard of 150 miles from the Pole. The news that had come that day was as follows:—

On or about January 18, last year, the advance party, consisting of Captain Scott, Lieutenant Bowers, Dr. Wilson, Captain Oates (who had charge of the ponies) and Petty Officer Edgar Evans, reached the South Pole. They found there Amundsen's tent and records.

On the return journey, about eleven miles from the spot known as the "One Ton Dépôt," and on or about March 29—two months, therefore, after leaving the Pole—the party was caught in an overpowering blizzard. Scott, Bowers and Wilson died on the date given. Captain Oates succumbed some time later. Evans died of an accident. The word "concussion" is used.

No More Known Now.

"We know no more to-night," he proceeded. "To-morrow doubtless the sad story will be made clear. We shall learn how their comrades learned of the deaths of the pioneers and how their records were recovered, for it is evident, from the fact that we learn they found Amundsen's records, that their own must have been preserved.

"No Arctic or Antarctic party was, I believe, ever sent out better equipped or better fitted by the gallantry or experience of its members, from Captain Scott downwards, to meet with the ordinary perils of the Pole. All I can say to-night," he concluded, "is farewell to a band of heroes whose names will shine as examples of the endurance which is the highest form of courage, and noble evidence of the qualities of Englishmen."

Dr. W. Bruce, of the Oceanographical Laboratory, Edinburgh, who has achieved considerable distinction in Antarctic exploration, regards the reports of scurvy having broken out among the supporting party after they left Captain Scott as rather significant. They might indicate that Captain Scott's advance party was also afflicted with scurvy, and consequently would be weakened and unable to resist the severity of an Antarctic blizzard as a healthy party would have done.

Last Message to World.

Captain Scott's last message to the world was written on January 3, 1912, or just fifteen days before he reached the South Pole. He was then within 150 miles of his goal, and was completing his arrangements for the final dash southward. In briefly describing his arrangements, Captain Scott wrote:—

"We are now within 150 miles of the Pole. I am going forward with a party of five men. The advance party goes forward with a month's provisions, and the prospect of success seems good, provided that the weather holds and no unforeseen obstacles arise. The weather on the plateau has been good on the whole. The sun has never deserted us, but temperatures are low—now about —29deg. Cent. (—20deg. Fahr.), and the wind is pretty constant.

"However, we are excellently equipped for such conditions, and the wind undoubtedly improves the surface. So far all the arrangements have worked out most satisfactorily. It is more than probable that no further news will be received from us this year, as our return must necessarily be late."

Captain Scott was born at Outlands, Devonport, on June 6, 1868. He entered the British navy in 1882. He was torpedo lieutenant on the Majestic, the flagship of the Channel squadron, in 1898 and 1899, was made commander in 1900 and became captain four years later.

Captain Scott commanded the British Antarctic expedition of 1901-4. This expedition, aboard the Discovery, entered the South seas in December, 1901, and continued in a southerly direction till March 24, 1902, when the vessel was caught and held in the ice. Captain Scott, after establishing winter quarters near Mounts Erebus and Terror, led a party on sledges to 82deg. 17min. south, the most southerly point ever reached up to that time.

A relief expedition was equipped in 1902 on the Morning, which reached the Discovery in January, 1903. On this expedition, Captain Scott discovered King Edward VII. Land.

Captain Scott, on board his specially-constructed ship, the Terra Nova, left Port Chalmers, New Zealand, on November 29 1910, on his most recent tour of exploration. He had a picked crew and a full equipment of ponies and dogs.

The Terra Nova returned to Akaroa, New Zealand, on April 1, 1912, and announced Captain Scott's position when the vessel had left him. Until that time it was believed that the British officer might have beaten Capt in Amundsen to the Pole, but this news confirmed the previous report of the Norwegian's triumph.

Commander Evans, second in command under Captain Scott, after having returned home, left England on August 30 last year for New Zealand to resume command of the Terra Nova, and with her proceed to the Polar regions and find Captain Scott and his party. The Terra Nova left Christchurch, New Zealand, on December 14 last, intending to proceed to McMurdo Sound after clearing the ice pack.

Mrs. Scott Is Now at Sea.

NEW YORK, Monday.—Mrs. Scott is now on board the Aorangi, which is on the way from San Francisco to Auckland. The vessel's first point of call is Papeete, but there is no cable to that island, and the Aorangi will in fact not touch any point where there is a cable service until she reaches New Zealand. It is, therefore, improbable that Mrs. Scott will learn the sad news until her arrival there, although efforts are being made to reach the Aorangi by wireless telegraphy.—Reuter.

King George Expresses Grief.

[BY THE HERALD'S SPECIAL WIRE.]

LONDON, Tuesday.—In reply to a message from Lord Curzon, as president of the Royal Geographical Society, to the King, who is patron of the society, announcing the mournful news of the death of Captain Scott and his four companions, his Majesty telegraphed as follows: "I am deeply grieved to hear the very bad news which you give me of the loss of Captain Scott and four of his party, just when we were hoping shortly to welcome them home on their return from their great and arduous undertaking. I heartily sympathize with the Royal Geographical Society in the loss to science and discovery through the death of these gallant explorers. Please send to me any further particulars.—GEORGE, R. AND I."

Fellow Explorers' Sympathy.

NEW YORK, Monday.—American sympathy with England has been excited by the tragic loss of the Scott expedition, and is voiced to-day by the American press and public in tones of the deepest and most unmistakable sincerity.

Rear-Admiral Peary, on a bed of sickness at Washington, dictated an earnest message of admiration for Captain Scott and his brave companions, and a similar message comes from Wisconsin, where Captain Amundsen, the discoverer of the South Pole, just one month ahead of Scott, is now lecturing.

Sir Ernest Shackleton, when first seen to-day, could not bring himself to believe that his former commander, after all his mighty exertions, and after attaining the goal of his ambition, could have perished miserably in a blizzard. He preferred to await further details before expressing himself more fully.

The American press pays a splendid tribute to the valor of Captain Scott and his companions.—Daily Telegraph.

London Press Expresses Sorrow.

[BY THE HERALD'S SPECIAL WIRE.]

LONDON, Tuesday.—Profound sorrow at the disaster is expressed in this morning's press.

"Daily Telegraph."

"The nation mourns men who were of no ordinary clay, and the name and fame of Captain Robert Falcon Scott, dying in the prime of his manhood, is added to the country's imperishable roll of heroes."

"Morning Post."

"Lives so lost are not lives wasted. Lives wasted are lives passed in ingorious ease and safety, with enjoyment as the only consideration."

"Standard."

"Grief for these noble young lives, too early closed, will be mingled with pride in their energy, their daring and their skill. It has been a magnificent enterprise, and its scientific results must be invaluable."

"Daily Chronicle."

"It will be something to Mrs. Scott to know that the sympathetic thought of an Empire is with her in a dark hour of sorrow and trial—that England says: 'Well done!'"

ANNOUNCEMENTS. | ANNOUNCEMENTS.

AU **Printemps**

Rue du Havre - Boulev. Haussmann
(close to Saint-Lazare Station) **PARIS**

FIRST NOVELTIES
of the Season
Tea Rooms reserved for Ladies

CHATHAM. Telephone 302.24 132.95
RESTAURANT VOLNEY
16 Rue Volney, Paris.
AFTERNOON TEA. (Between Rue de la Paix and the Boulevards.) TZIGANES.

BIARRITZ HOTEL DU PALAIS
IMPERIAL AND ROYAL RESIDENCE
UNIQUE SITUATION, overlooking Ocean and the Grande Plage.
Large Private Garden, formerly the Imperial Park. - Up-to-date Arrangements.
General Manager: R. PATTARD, OF THE GRAND HOTEL, at MONTE CARLO.

CANNES GALLIA PALACE
Opened 1900.
40 PRIVATE BATHS
Garage for 30 Autos

THE PLAZA
NEW YORK
Fifth Avenue and Fifty-Ninth Street
The coolest Hotel in New York, overlooking Central Park. Convenient to theatres and shopping district.
Single Rooms, with bath . . . $4, $5 and $6 per day
Double Rooms, 2 beds, with bath, $6, $7 and $8 per day
Outdoor Terrace, Summer Garden with Russian String Orchestra
Passengers arriving from Europe will be met at wharf, if desired, by hotel porter and luggage wagon
Rooms may be reserved by Wireless
The Plaza-Copley, Boston, now under construction, opens May 1st, 1912, under same management as The Plaza, New York.
FRED STERRY — Managing Director

SITUATIONS WANTED—FEMALES.

Governesses.

A YOUNG ENGLISH LADY WISHES ENGAGEment to teach English conversation or read aloud, clear and correct pronounciation. B. N., 77 avenue Wagram.

A HIGHLY RECOMMENDED GERMAN GOVERness, excellent musician, 7 years' England, speaking French fluently, desires situation. Seiler, 22 rue Gustave Courbet.

ALLEMANDE, INSTITUTRICE DIPLOMEE, bonne musicienne, sachant à fond français, 6 ans Angleterre, cherche place; hautes références. Fräulein Chapin, 68 rue Saint-Didier.

ENGLISH LADY SEEKS MORNING ENGAGEment, pianist, conversation, teaching, walks; best Paris references. F. M. S., 77 avenue Wagram.

FRANCAISE, PARLANT ANGLAIS, DESIRE place pour enfants le matin; bonnes références. Gremillot, 19 rue Béranger.

GOUVERNANTE, ALLEMANDE, 45 ANS, 8 ET 6 ans même maison, bien recommandée, parle anglais, bonne couture et brodeuse, emballage, voyagerait, demande place femme de chambre. E. Mascher, Poste Restante, Rueil (Seine-et-Oise).

GOUVERNANTE, ALLEMANDE, DISTINGUEE, bonne instruction, désire occupation dans la journée; accompagnerait promenade; s'occuperait des enfants. P. N., Herald.

GOUVERNANTE (HANOVRE), PARLANT ALLEmand, plus pur français, sans accent, désire situation, enfants, dames; voyagerait. Lutz, 87 avenue Malakoff.

GOUVERNANTE, ALLEMANDE, 22 ANS, PARLE français, cherche place; libre de suite. A. S. 65, Bureau de Poste 35, rue Cambon.

INSTITUTRICE, ALLEMANDE, DIPLOMEE, 30 ans, Protestante, sachant anglais, très bien français, musique, cherche place à demeure; excellentes références Paris. L. M., 52bis boulevard Haussmann.

INSTITUTRICE, ALLEMANDE, DIPLOMEE, parlant français, bonne musicienne (Conservatoire), cherche occupation; bonnes références. Mlle. Benke, Herald.

JEUNE FILLE, 22 ANS, CONNAISSANT couture, service de table, désire place dans famille américaine; irait auprès des enfants; voyagerait. A. B., 25 rue Salneuve.

JEUNE FILLE ANGLAISE DEMANDE PLACE auprès d'enfants, tous les jours ou plusieurs fois par semaine. Ecrire ou s'adresser Grace Foster, Hotel Tronchet, rue Tronchet.

JEUNE DAME, PARISIENNE, PARFAITE EDUcation, a heures libres; littérature française, history, art, conversation. Mme. Langner, 6 rue Humblot, 15e.

JEUNE FILLE, ALLEMANDE, PARLANT PEU français, cherche place auprès d'enfants; bonnes références. N. Dix, 6 rue de Prony.

MRS. R—— HIGHLY RECOMMENDS HER French gouvernante, French (brevet), fluent German, good English; disengaged April 1. 38 Bayreutherstrasse, Berlin.

PROFESSEUR DIPLOME DES LANGUES ALLEmande, russe, anglaise, française, a des heures libres. Mlle. H. Pass, 22 rue de Naples.

YOUNG FRENCHWOMAN OF GOOD SOCIAL standing teaches French to foreigners. L. A. 170, Herald.

Companions.

DAME DU MONDE, HAUTES REFERENCES, désire situation dame de compagnie ou autre; arrangement si heures libres. De S., 22bis rue Pétrarque.

DAME, 25 ANS, BONNE EDUCATION, REFErences premier ordre, désire place dame de compagnie près personne seule, même souffrante; voyagerait. Mme. Franck, 16 rue Saint-Ferdinand.

DEMOISELLE, SERIEUSE, POUVANT DIRIGER intérieure, expérience, désire situation gouvernante ou dame de compagnie dans bonne famille; bonnes références. Ecrire Mlle. Berthe, 3 rue Vital.

DAME, VEUVE, DISTINGUEE, 30 ANS, REcherche situation auprès personnes étrangères. Querey, 6 quai Marché Neuf.

DEMOISELLE SERIEUSE DEMANDE PLACE près personne seule. Ecrire A. S., 13 rue d'Armaillé.

ENGLISH GIRL, AFTERNOONS FREE, WOULD take children or young ladies, make herself useful. J. N., 24 rue de Levis.

JEUNE FILLE, 23 ANS, SERIEUSE, BONNES références verbales, désire place avec dame étrangère, voyagerait et s'occuperait d'enfants, peut enseigner notions français. A. B., 27 rue d'Offémont.

JEUNE FEMME, SACHANT COUTURE, LINgerie, demande emploi après-midi, accompagnerait jeune fille, enfant. Mme. Ch. J., 140 rue Legendre.

JEUNE FILLE, 24 ANS, SERIEUSE, DEMANDE place chez dame ou personne seule; voyagerait. L. M., 18 rue des Dames.

LADY, POSSESSING SPECIAL FORMULA AND treatment for youth and beauty restoration, comprising electrical and other applications for removal of superfluous hair, etc., desires position as companion to well-to-do American lady (or other) of established social position; exceptional experience in the care of invalids, thorough knowledge of housekeeping and secretarial duties; English and Irish lace maker; has held similar position for many years with duke's daughter. Particulars X. Y. Z., Herald, Paris.

VISITORS TO OLYMPIADE.—REFINED Swedish person, linguist, traveller, practical, desires position now to travel with lady, family or party, in summer to Olympiade. Answer to "Serious," Poste Restante, Gothenbourg, Sweden.

YOUNG ENGLISH LADY, WELL EDUCATED, musical, fluent French, desires post as companion or governess; willing to travel. Miss E., Granville House, 73 Hornsey Rise, London.

Cooks.

BONNE CUISINIERE - PATISSIERE DEMANDE place ou extra; bonnes références. Ecrire Perthuis, 18 rue Vergniaud, Levallois.

BONNE CUISINIERE, 28 ANS, BONNES REFErences, demande place Paris. Reboux, 47 rue François Ier.

BONNE ET FINE CUISINIERE, 38 ANS, TRES recommandée, demande place. A. Besson, 115 rue de la Pompe.

BONNE CUISINIERE, FAISANT MENAGE, DEmande place, de préférence une ou deux personnes, 44 ans. J. L., 8 rue Paul-Bert.

BONNE CUISINIERE, CONNAISSANT pâtisserie, glaces, demande place; partirait à l'étranger. Ecrire A. P., 11 rue Franklin.

CUISINIERE, FAISANT DU MENAGE, demande place. F. Q., 112 rue Saint-Dominique.

SUISSESSE, PARLANT ANGLAIS, TRES BONNE cuisinière, glaces, pâtisserie, fait cuisine américaine, cherche place. Ecrire R. L., 54 rue de Longchamp.

TRES BONNE CUISINIERE, FAIT PATISSERIE, économe, propre, bonnes références, désire place. L. V., 13 rue d'Armaillé.

TRES BONNE CUISINIERE, 37 ANS, FAISANT glaces, pâtisserie, désire place sérieuse. M. L., 96bis rue Demours.

General Housework.

BELGE, 49 ANS, DEMANDE PLACE BONNE À tout faire; références. D., 33 rue de Palestro.

DEMOISELLE, 26 ANS, GENRE FEMME DE chambre, demande place bonne à tout faire; bonnes références. M. L., 25 rue d'Armaillé.

FEMME, 35 ANS, DEMANDE MENAGE, MATInée; bonnes références. L. Pautot, 9 passage Puebla.

Housekeepers.

A LADY SEEKS APPOINTMENT WHEREIN SHE could alleviate the responsibilities of household and domestic difficulties, secretarial work, etc., of her mistress, town, country or abroad. Write D. E. B., Willing's, 73 Knightsbridge, London.

DEMOISELLE, HAUTES REFERENCES, demande situation chez personne seule ou famille; dirigerait intérieur, soins; voyagerait. L. V., 31 rue Vaneau.

Ladies' Maids, Chambermaids, etc.

A FRENCH, TRUSTWORTHY LADY'S MAID, speaks English, Italian, experienced traveller, hairdresser, dressmaker; verbal references. Mlle. Marco, Hôtel Vendôme.

AN EXPERIENCED FRENCH MAID, SPEAKING several languages, hairdresser, seamstress, good packer, traveller; good references. A. M., 12 rue Saint-Roch.

AUTRICHIENNE, BONNE FAMILLE, DEMANDE place femme de chambre, pourrait accompagner grande demoiselle; bonnes références. A. U., 21 Villa Saïd.

AUTRICHIENNE, 25 ANS, DEMANDE PLACE femme de chambre, faisant lingerie, s'occuperait d'enfants; voyagerait; bonnes références. K. A., 89 rue de la Tour.

ALSACIENNE, CONNAIT BIEN SERVICE, COUture, un peu ménage, désire place femme de chambre; bonnes références. L. B., 25 rue Salneuve.

AS LADY'S MAID, GERMAN, SPEAKS ENGLISH, first-class recommendations; well experienced. A., 22 rue de l'Exposition.

BONNE FEMME DE CHAMBRE, FRANCAISE, 25 ans, parlant anglais, italien, connaissant coiffure, couture, emballage; voyagerait. S. C., 24 avenue Friedland

BONNE FEMME DE CHAMBRE, FRANCAISE, 35 ans, bonne éducation, couturière, lingère, habituée voyager, service de dame premier ordre; 4, 3 et 2 ans références. Henriette, 57 avenue Victor Hugo.

BONNE FEMME DE CHAMBRE, FAISANT COUture, coiffure, emballage, parlant anglais, italien, désire place. L. M., 45 rue Vauthier, Boulogne-sur-Seine.

BONNE FEMME DE CHAMBRE, FRANCAISE, parle anglais, connaissant service, couture, ménage, emballage; voyagerait; références. Henriette, 35 rue Jacob.

COUTURIERE, 30 ANS, CHERCHE PLACE femme de chambre; références maisons de couture; voyagerait. 19 avenue d'Eylau.

DEBUTANTE, 19 ANS, DESIRE PLACE FEMME de chambre ou seconde femme de chambre, s'occuperait enfants. Jeanne Saucet, 8 rue Puvis de Chavannes.

DEUX JEUNES FILLES, FEMMES DE chambre, 4 ans hôtel, très bonnes couturières, demandent place avec valet. A. M., 210ter, boulevard Pereire.

DEBUTANTE, PRESENTEE PAR PARENTS, couture, repassage, désire place deuxième femme de chambre ou enfants. Marie Dupré, 24 rue Brey.

ENGLISH PERSON SEEKS RE-ENGAGEMENT as maid or position of trust; good sewer, packer; used to travelling; Catholic; French and German. Address M. E. D., 157 boulevard Pereire.

FEMME DE CHAMBRE, CONNAISSANT couture, coiffure, emballage, parlant français, allemand, anglais; bonnes références. Fr. Gut, 1 rue Frédéric-Bastiat.

FRANCAISE, 25 ANS, REPRESENTANT BIEN, désire place femme de chambre ou gouvernante d'enfants, de préférence étranger; bonnes références. Rayral, 143 avenue Emile Zola.

FEMME DE CHAMBRE, 22 ANS, CONNAISSANT l'anglais, couture, désire place seconde. O. B., 25 rue Salneuve.

FEMME DE CHAMBRE, 30 ANS, DEMANDE place, connait très bien couture et voyages; bonnes références. A. P., 2 rue Brey.

FEMME DE CHAMBRE, 48 ANS, CONNAIT SERvice, couture, coupe, ferait cuisine chez personne seule, demande place. Mercerie, 37 rue Rennequin.

FEMME DE CHAMBRE, 29 ANS, PARLE italien, espagnol, désire place, Paris ou pour voyager; bonnes références. J. P., 21 rue Alexandre Dumas.

FEMME DE CHAMBRE, 26 ANS, CONNAISSANT couture, désire place avec valet de préférence. G. O., 22 avenue de la Grande Armée.

FEMME DE CHAMBRE, 30 ANS, CONNAISSANT service, désire place maison française ou étrangère; voyagerait. E. D., 1 rue Georges Bizet.

FEMME DE CHAMBRE, ESPAGNOLE, 28 ANS, désire place, étranger ou français; excellentes références. P. P., 43 rue Washington.

FEMME DE CHAMBRE, 28 ANS, SE PLACERAIT avec valet, couture et ménage. Ecrire S. D., 37 avenue de Saxe.

FEMME DE CHAMBRE, SERIEUSE, NE FAIsant pas neuf, entretien bien lingerie; s'occuperait enfants. T. D., 13 rue d'Armaillé.

FEMME DE CHAMBRE, 26 ANS, DESIRE place, Paris ou voyagerait; références premier ordre. Adresse C. D., 5 rue Daru.

FEMME DE CHAMBRE, REPRESENTANT bien, 25 ans, au courant du service, demande place pour voyager. Ecrire M. L., 95 avenue Victor-Hugo.

FEMME DE CHAMBRE, 22 ANS, SACHANT faire robes, demande place. J. D., 15 avenue du Trocadéro.

FEMME DE CHAMBRE, COUTURIERE, CONnaissant lingerie, repassage, service de table, désire place sérieuse. Ecrire M. D. C., 13 rue d'Armaillé.

FEMME DE CHAMBRE, 29 ANS, BIEN AU COUrant service, excellentes références, demande place stable. O. G., 20 avenue Friedland.

FEMME DE CHAMBRE ALSACIENNE, 27 ANS, sachant lingerie et couture; très bonnes références. J. K., 106 boulevard de Courcelles.

FEMME DE CHAMBRE, 32 ANS, BONNE COUturière, fait robes et lingerie; irait étranger; bonnes références. C. M., 44 boulevard Barbès.

THURSDAY, FEBRUARY 15, 1912.

"Turkey Trot" and "Bunny Hug" Dances Are Introduced to Palm Beach Society

Misses Adelaide Chatfield-Taylor, Dorothy Leslie and Lilla Gilbert Give First Performances.

(From the NEW YORK HERALD of February 5.)

PALM BEACH, Fla., Sunday.—The "turkey trot" and the "bunny hug" found their way into Palm Beach last night at the usual Saturday dance in the Hotel Royal Poinciana.

Miss Adelaide C. Chatfield-Taylor, of Chicago, and Miss Dorothy Leslie, who is passing the season here with her, presented Chicago's version of the "bunny hug" in response to requests from their friends. Their performance inspired Miss Lilla B. Gilbert, daughter of Mrs. H. Bramhall Gilbert, of New York, and Mr. Richard Forrest, of Lakewood, N.J., to an exposition of the "turkey trot." Both pairs held the floor at the same time. The usual dancing ceased for the moment, and all took opportunity to see the dancing novelties and decide for themselves as to their merits. None made any criticism, and Miss Chatfield-Taylor, Miss Leslie, Miss Gilbert and Mr. Forrest were loudly applauded. Many said they would try the new dances at the next opportunity.

THE TURKEY TROT AND THE GRIZZLY BEAR
BARRED FROM DANCE HALLS, BUT POPULAR IN SOCIETY —From "Life."

Colonel and Mrs. Samuel Goodman, of Philadelphia, entertained Mr. and Mrs. Mathew Rocke and Mr. John Rocke on board the power yacht Evelyn to-day and took them to the stationary house-boat for luncheon. Mr. and Mrs. Louis M. Stumer, of Chicago, and Mr. and Mrs. J. R. Benjamin, of New York, also had luncheon there. Mr. Charles Furthman, of New York, gave a dinner there to-night for several men.

Mr. Hamilton Perkins, of Boston, made a record catch this morning when he pulled in four sailfish, one measuring 7ft. 9in. long. It is said a like number of sailfish never had been caught by one person in one day in these waters before. Mr. Perkins will have the large specimen mounted.

Mr. and Mrs. Herbert Coppell, of New York, and Birchknoll House, Tenafly, N.J., and Mr. John Weeks, of New York, have been among visitors here.

Countess de Montsaulnin, Miss Helene Locke and Miss Jeanne Hassman, of Paris, and Mrs. M. E. Greene, of New York, arrived last night for a brief sojourn at the Royal Poinciana.

Among the callers at the usual Sunday afternoon reception of Mr. and Mrs. Charles I. Cragin at Rêve d'Eté were Mr. and Mrs. Norris W. Mundy, Mr. and Mrs. John S. Liggett, Mr. and Mrs. Alonzo M. Zabriskie, Mr. and Mrs. Delos O. Wickham, Mr. and Mrs. Frank Brewster and the Misses Lucia and Julia Temple.

Bridge whist has many followers at the Breakers. Mrs. T. B. Barry, Miss Katherine Barrol, Mr. S. P. Urner and Dr. John Blanchard are among them.

TUESDAY. APRIL 2, 1912.

Oxford, by Six Lengths, Wins University Boat Race; Time 22 Minutes 5 Seconds

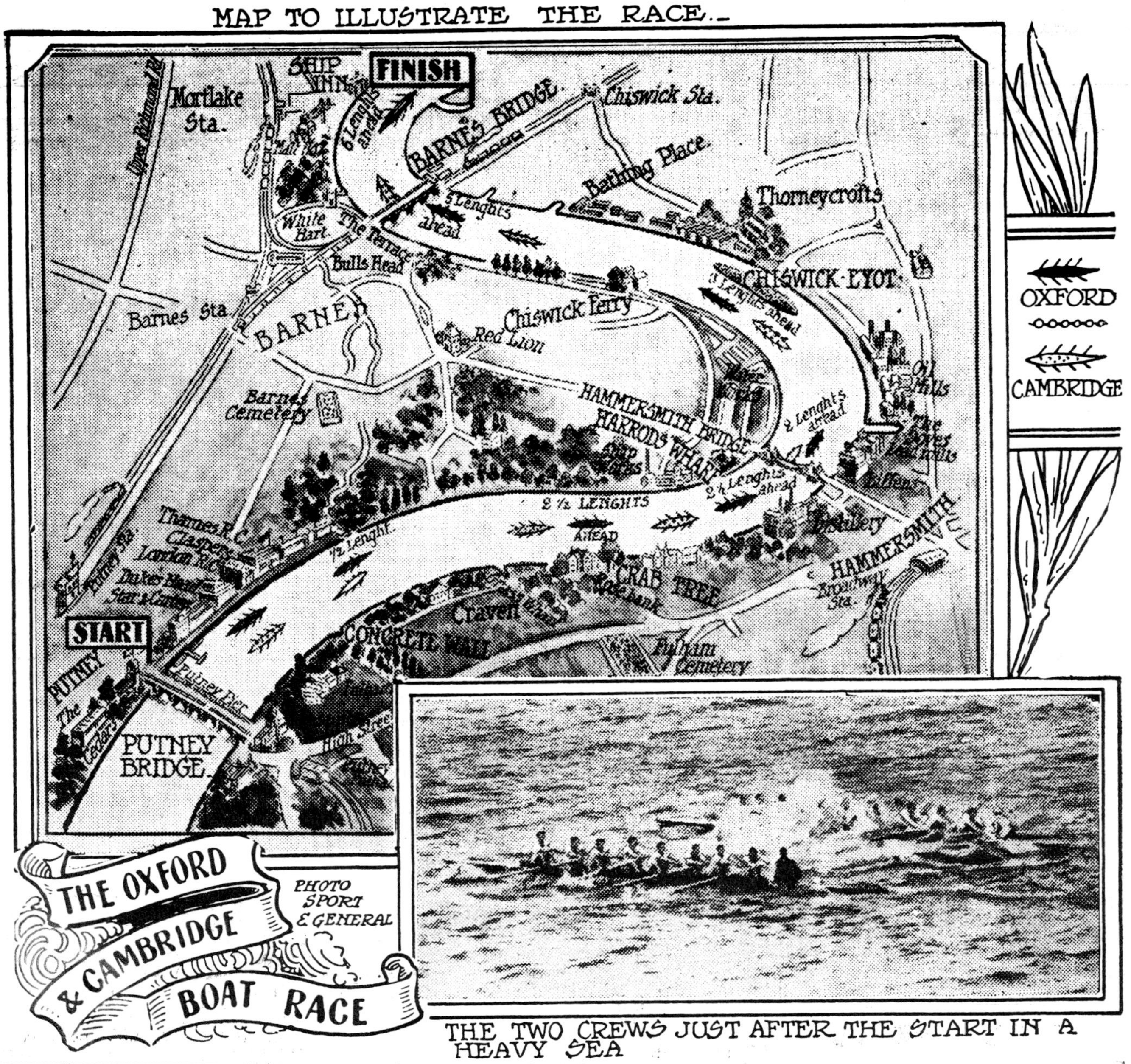

THE TWO CREWS JUST AFTER THE START IN A HEAVY SEA

Winners Master Cambridge Crew at Beverly Brook, and Thence Contest Is a Procession.

[BY THE HERALD'S SPECIAL WIRE.]

LONDON, Tuesday. — Oxford won the University boat race yesterday in good style by six lengths in 22min. 5sec., which time, considering the conditions that prevailed and the fact that the Dark Blues were never pressed after a mile of the course had been rowed, was an excellent performance. The winners had the measure of their lighter but very plucky rivals at Beverly Brook, and thence on it was a procession. The Cantabs spurted grandly time after time and succeeded in reducing the Oxonians' lead somewhat, but it was only on sufferance, for Bourne and his men easily regained their advantage, and, maintaining their fine form to the finish, were easy winners.

The rowing conditions were as bad as on Saturday, and the weather worse, for a strong northerly wind was blowing, and while the race was in progress the fickleness of April was exemplified, for in turn heavy rains, sunshine and a hailstorm were experienced.

Saturday's sensational happening added to the interest of the race, for the crowds lining the banks of the river were enormous, and the people gave voice to their enthusiasm all along the line.

The losers were all badly done up, but the Oxford men seemed little the worse for their exertions. The reception accorded the victors was of the most enthusiastic description, Bourne being specially singled out as the only University oarsman to stroke four consecutive winning crews from Putney to Mortlake.

Yesterday's contest was the sixty-ninth of the series, and Oxford has won thirty-eight and Cambridge thirty, one race, that of 1887, resulting in a dead-heat.

Carpentier Knocks Out Jim Sullivan in Second Round of Monte Carlo Fight.

JIM SULLIVAN

PHOTO T.NA

PHOTO ROL.

GEORGES CARPENTIER.

French Boxer Wins Big Purse and Title of Middleweight Champion of Europe.

MONTE CARLO, Thursday.—Georges Carpentier, of France, beat Jim Sullivan, middleweight champion of Great Britain, here this afternoon, and beat him badly by knocking him out with a blow on the point of the jaw in the second round. The thousands who witnessed the contest, among them many members of the aristocracy and experts in the noble art of self-defence, are proclaiming to-night that in Carpentier, the smooth-faced eighteen-year-old boy, who has proved himself to be a wonderful fighting machine, France has the coming pugilistic champion of the world.

The fight was to have been the event of the hour in Monte Carlo, but it proved to be a matter of only very few minutes. Carpentier looked like a mere boy as he stripped and smiled on the crowd round the ring. Sullivan looked older, harder and more phlegmatic. The two men were typical of the two nations. The crowd was fairly equally divided into French and English, with a scattering of Americans, and as the two names were announced, each nation cheered that of its own man, and the whole assembly roared encourgagement as the two men shook hands.

Both Start Cautiously.

"Seconds out!" said a voice, and the gong added its warning. There was a moment's dead silence. "Time!" and the two men circled cautiously round one another. Carpentier hit out first. Twice in quick succession he got home on Sullivan's immobile face. Sullivan tried hard to score, but his blows did not seem to have force behind them, and for some moments Carpentier's fists were all over his opponent's body with frequent "one, twos." When the gong sounded at the end of the first round the Englishman looked serious, the Frenchman triumphant. Carpentier went to his corner smiling. Sullivan looked punished.

The second round lasted little more than the time in which one could snap a watch. Carpentier's fists were a hailstorm, and Sullivan was nowhere. A crashing blow from Carpentier on the Englishman's jaw put the full-stop to the encounter. Sullivan fell like a tree under the axe, and the crowd bayed like bloodhounds.

"One, two, three," one could see the timekeeper's lips move, but the noise was so great that one heard not a word. His arm fell. It was all over. Sullivan had not risen. His seconds went to him, and Carpentier was rushed at by his manager and friends and carried off in triumph. The French boxer looked as pink and as smilingly happy as a girl who finds herself the belle of her first ball. Carpentier is a marvellous fighter.

Balloon Crashes Into Trees in Tuileries Gardens And Pilot and Passenger Fall With Basket to Ground

THE VICTIMS M. BLANCHET, AERONAUT AND M DUVAL, PASSENGER, JUST BEFORE THE START.

THE BALLOON "TOTO" AT THE MOMENT OF THE ACCIDENT

VIEWS OF THE TRAGIC BALLOON CONTEST

THE CAR AFTER THE ACCIDENT.

MME GOLDSCHMIDT & HER PASSENGER.

MLLE MARVINGT.

PHOTO MEURISSE — PHOTOS NYH.

Vast Crowd Sees Johnson Beat Moran on Points, Thus Retaining World's Heavyweight Boxing Championship

American Challenger Is Quite Outclassed, and Fails Even to Mark Champion.

Fight at Vélodrome d'Hiver, Paris, Results in Easy Victory for Negro.

The much-trumpeted fight between "Jack" Johnson, the negro pugilist, and Frank Moran, the American white, for the Championship of the World, took place last night at the Vélodrome d'Hiver and resulted in an easy victory on points for the holder of the title.

It was an easy win for Johnson, the difference in the class of the two men being only too evident from the very beginning of the match.

Although an immense crowd was present, the vast velodrome was by no means full, some of the galleries being practically empty. There was hardly a seat vacant, however, at the ringside.

The spectators included an unusually large proportion of women, including a large number of well-known Parisian actresses, whose bright dresses, bare shoulders and arms made splashes of color everywhere. The women, indeed, were not the least attentive and excited of all the people gathered there. Feminine exclamations and shouts of encouragement were heard at every instant during the fight. "Jack" Johnson's white wife was in the front row of the ring and, as usual, showered advice on her husband during the fight.

FRANK MORAN.

PHOTOS MEURISSE

JACK JOHNSON.

THE NEW YORK HERALD. PARIS. WEDNESDAY, APRIL 10, 1912.

The Titanic to Leave Southampton To-day on Her Maiden Trip Across the Atlantic

THE WHITE STAR LINER TITANIC. (PHOTO TOPICAL)

New White Star Liner Is Model of Comfort, Beauty and Attractiveness.

[FROM THE HERALD'S CORRESPONDENT.]

LONDON.—The White Star liner Titanic, which leaves Southampton and Cherbourg on her maiden voyage across the Atlantic to-day, is a sister ship to the Olympic, which she resembles in every respect except in a few details in accommodation and in the scheme of decoration. Her principal dimensions are: Length over all, 882ft. 6in.; breadth, 92ft. 6in.; height from bottom of keel to boat deck, 97ft. 4in.; height from bottom of keel to top of captain's house, 105ft. 6in.; distance from top of funnels to keel, 175ft. There are eleven steel decks.

In the immense dining-room 532 passengers can dine at once, but the room is so arranged that small parties may dine in semi-privacy in comfortable recessed bays. The room is decorated in a style peculiarly English—a style, in fact, which was evolved by the most eminent architects of Early Jacobean times. It differs from most of the great halls of that period chiefly in being painted white instead of the sombre oak which the sixteenth and seventeenth century builders would have used.

Old Halls Are Studied.

For details the splendid decorations of Hatfield, Haddon Hall and other contemporary great houses have been carefully studied, the coved and richly-moulded ceilings being particularly characteristic of the plasterer's art of that time. The furniture of oak is designed to harmonize with its surroundings and at the same time to avoid the austere disregard for comfort which seems to have been a feature of the furniture of those old days.

The restaurant is a magnificent room designed in the Louis XVI. period, and is panelled from floor to ceiling in beautifully marked French walnut of a delicate light fawn brown, the mouldings and ornaments being richly carved and gilded. In the centre of the large panels hang electric-light brackets, cast and finely chased in brass and gilt, and holding candle lamps. The room is lighted by large bow windows, which give a feeling of spaciousness. They are draped with plain fawn silk curtains, with flowered borders, and pelmets richly embroidered. The floor is covered with a rich pile Axminster carpet with a non-obtrusive design of the period in a delicate vieux-rose.

Dignity and simplicity are the characteristics of the reception-room, another spacious apartment decorated with white panelling in the Jacobean style, delicately carved in low relief. Some fine specimens of tapestry adorn the walls directly facing the staircase, having been specially woven for the Titanic on the looms at Aubusson.

Reservations for Women.

The reading and writing room, with its pure white walls and elegant furniture, has been furnished specially for women. Through the great bow window which almost fills one side of the room, one may look out past the deck, where fellow passengers are taking the air. In cold weather a cheerful fire burns in the English grate, and a thick velvety carpet covers the floor.

The great, wide, handsomely-decorated staircases are reminiscent of the days when Grinling Gibbons collaborated with his great contemporary Wren, and the veranda café is a delightful flowery arbor, over the green trellis of which grow climbing plants, fostering the illusion that one is still on land with a wide seascape beyond.

The first-class state-rooms are the last word in comfort so far as ship accommodation goes. Not even in the second-class is there a feeling of crampedness. All the rooms are designed to afford the maximum of fresh air.

Gymnasium and Games.

The passenger on the Titanic may keep himself fit by exercise in the gymnasium or by a game in the squash racquets court, proceed to the Turkish, electric or swimming baths and then finish with a two-mile stroll on the spacious decks.

But the pre-eminence of the Titanic is not to remain unchallenged. The new Hamburg - American liner Imperator, which is shortly to be launched, will have a gross tonnage of 50,000, a length over all of 900 feet and will accommodate 5,000 persons, with a promenade deck a quarter of a mile long. She will have an entertainment hall two stories high, holding 700 persons; a winter garden and a Ritz-Carlton restaurant.

Some of To-day's Passengers.

Among the passengers who will leave by the Titanic, which is commanded by Captain E. J. Smith, are: Mrs. E. D. Appleton, Major Archibald W. Butt, Mr. Norman C. Craig, M.P.; Mr. and Mrs. Washington Dodge, Mr. William C. Dulles, Colonel Archibald Gracie, Mr. Benjamin Guggenheim, Mr. and Mrs. Henry Harper, Mr. Henry B. Harris, the New York theatrical manager, and Mrs. Harris; Mr. and Mrs. Frederick M. Hoyt, Mr. Fletcher Fellowes, Mr. Washington Roebling, the Countess of Rothes, Mr. Adolphe Saalfeld, Mr. J. Clinch Smith, Mr. and Mrs. Frederick Spedden, Mr. and Mrs. Isidore Straus, Mr. and Mrs. Emil Taussig, Mr. and Mrs. J. B. Thayer, Mr. and Mrs. George Widener and Mrs. J. Stuart White.

EUROPEAN EDITION—PARIS.—TUESDAY, APRIL 16, 1912.

THE TITANIC, NEW WHITE STAR LINER, FOUNDERS OFF NEWFOUNDLAND; REPORTS ARE MOST CONTRADICTORY, BUT APPALLING LOSS OF LIFE IS FEARED

Additional Information Confirms Fear That Catastrophe Is Worst in Maritime History.

ONLY ONE VESSEL GIVES AID.

The Carpathia Alone, It Appears, Is Able to Take Passengers to Safety.

[BY COMMERCIAL CABLE TO THE HERALD.]

NEW YORK, Tuesday.—It was announced at the White Star Line office this evening that of the 2,358 persons aboard the Titanic, 868 were saved by the Carpathia. These survivors were picked up in thirty lifeboats, each of which, according to the regulations, would be manned by eight seamen and a petty officer. On this basis, 270 of the persons saved were of the crew, so that the number of surviving passengers is 598.

The names of 317 first and second-class passengers have already been cabled to the White Star Line office.

The Carpathia is expected to reach New York at eleven o'clock on Thursday night.

The property lost will amount to twelve million dollars, exclusive of the value of the Titanic, which is placed variously between ten and twelve millions.

Among the names added to the list of prominent persons who lost their lives are those of Mr. F. D. Millet, the artist, and the Rev. Dr. J. Stuart Holden, rector of St. Paul's, Portman square, London, W. It is believed that Messrs. George D. Widener, James Clinch Smith and Clarence Moore lost their lives.

Among persons of prominence whose names have not appeared on the list of survivors, and who are believed to have been lost, are: Colonel John Jacob Astor, Mr. W. T. Stead, Major Archibald Butt and Messrs. Isidor Strauss, Jacques Futrelle, H. B. Harris and Benjamin Guggenheim.

EUROPEAN EDITION—PARIS.—WEDNESDAY, APRIL 17, 1912.

GLOOM DEEPENS AS DETAILS OF THE TITANIC DISASTER COME; REPORTS AGREE THAT 868 OF 2,358 ON BOARD ARE RESCUED

THE CUNARD LINER CARPATHIA WHICH HAS SURVIVORS ON BOARD.

Latest despatches from New York and London indicate that 868 of the Titanic's passengers were saved. The number of persons on board is now given as 2,358.

None of the ships which hastened to the aid of the Titanic except the Carpathia has any of the survivors on board.

Below is a list of the survivors which the "Herald" received by special cable from New York.

THE NEW YORK HERALD.

PRICE: PARIS and FRANCE, 15 Centimes. ABROAD, 25 Centimes. EUROPEAN EDITION—PARIS.—FRIDAY, APRIL 19, 1912. NO: 27.633.

THE TITANIC SURVIVORS TELL THRILLING TALES

Rescued Passengers from the Sunken Liner. Describe Frenzied Scenes in Darkness on Decks in Moments Following Crash With Iceberg—Mr. Robert Daniel in Water for Hours.

[BY COMMERCIAL CABLE TO THE HERALD.]

NEW YORK, Thursday.—When the Carpathia, with the survivors of the Titanic disaster, reached port to-night, the passengers had thrilling tales to tell of the rescue of persons on the ill-fated liner. Many of the passengers jumped into the sea when the Titanic went down, while others clung in frenzy to cakes of ice until picked up. Others froze to death in the lifeboats.

TELLS OF FRENZIED SCENE AFTER CRASH AT NIGHT.

Men and Women Fight for Places in Boats.

[BY COMMERCIAL CABLE TO THE HERALD.]

NEW YORK, Thursday.—Mr. Robert Daniel, of Philadelphia, said: "I had just left the music-room and was in bed, when there came a terrific crash. The ship quivered, the lights went out and I rushed on deck. There seemed to be thousands fighting and shouting in the dark. Then the storage batteries worked and gave a little light.

"Captain Smith, on the bridge, shouted orders, and the crew obeyed as well as possible.

"Men and women fought, bit and scratched for places in the lifeboats, but Captain Smith seemed to restore order somewhat. The passengers went fore and aft, men praying and cursing, and women in evening dress and wearing diamonds fighting with others in night-dresses.

"Hundreds did not wait for the boats but jumped overboard. I grabbed something and went over to the side until I felt the Titanic sinking at the bows. The storage batteries then gave out and all was dark again.

"I leaped from the rail, struck the water and felt myself being drawn by suction. When I found a cake of ice I clung to it naked, and battled for five hours with the ice-cakes. I was then picked up by a boat.

"I did not see Mr. Ismay on the Carpathia. I am positive Captain Smith never would have permitted a man to enter one of those lifeboats."

Mr. Daniel heard nothing of any shooting, but a shot could not have been heard in the horrible grinding and noise following the crash.

"All the persons were rescued in the open sea. For hours we had nothing to eat, and the wind coming off the ice froze two persons in my boat to death," said Mr. Daniel. "All on the Titanic knew from the first that there was no hope. Two or three lifeboats filled with passengers were drawn under the steamer and lost.

"It was impossible to save any property. All the passengers were insane, and women, fearing death, collapsed. I believe some died where they lay."

Mr. Daniel carried a fainting woman from the Carpathia and gave her to her waiting father. Lifting his tattered hat, he exclaimed: "I did the best I could!" and fainted.

AS VEIL LIFTS OVER THE TITANIC TRAGEDY, SCENES OF HORROR UNSURPASSED IN MARITIME HISTORY ARE REVEALED

MRS. J. J. ASTOR TELLS HOW HUSBAND SAID GOOD-BYE.

Thought of Her Personal Comforts at Supreme Moment.

[BY COMMERCIAL CABLE TO THE HERALD.]

NEW YORK, Thursday. — Mrs. John Jacob Astor is suffering from her experiences, but is doing very well. Her husband kissed her and bade her good-bye and then gave her a flask of brandy, saying: "This will keep you up while you're in the boat."

After the boat was lowered she saw some men struggling in the water, and called out for the sailors to put back and take them aboard. "Row on!" was called out by other women, and the sailors, after hesitating, continued on their course.

Mr. and Mrs. Straus Die Together.

[BY COMMERCIAL CABLE TO THE HERALD.]

NEW YORK, Thursday. — Mrs. Isidor Straus was urged by her husband to go into one of the lifeboats, but refused to do so unless he would go also. Mr. Straus refused, so Mrs. Straus stood beside him, and they died together.

Six Women Save Their Pets.

[BY COMMERCIAL CABLE TO THE HERALD.]

NEW YORK, Thursday. — Five women saved their pet dogs. One American woman, coming from England to visit relatives here, saved a pet pig and deeply deplored the loss of her jewels.

MANY OF WOMEN AMONG SURVIVORS BECOME INSANE.

Boats Are in Open Sea Nearly Eight Hours.

NEW YORK, Thursday.—Mrs. Andrews, an elderly lady among the survivors, said that the crash occurred at 11.35 p.m. on Sunday. The women and children got off in the lifeboats at 12.45 a.m., she said. The Titanic sank at 2 a.m., and the Carpathia picked up the boats at 8.30 a.m.

"Many of the women have become insane," she added. "We did not know until daybreak whether we should be rescued. We were in the open boats for eight hours, and the suffering of all was indescribable."

STRAINS OF HYMN COULD JUST BE HEARD IN BOATS.

Craft Were Some Distance Away When Liner Sank.

NEW YORK, Thursday. — Among the survivors interviewed was Miss Bonnell, of Youngstown, O. She said the Titanic was ploughing through the icefields when the collision occurred. A large proportion of the passengers was asleep.

"The bottom of the bow drove into the iceberg," she continued, "and the lower plates were torn asunder. Large volumes of water rushed in with irresistible force, and the liner began to sink rapidly by the bow. The Titanic seemed to slide across the top of the berg. The passengers hurriedly seized their clothing and immediately the lifeboats were made ready.

"As the liner continued to sink into the trough of the sea, the passengers marched towards the stern. By that time most of the lifeboats were some distance away, and only a faint sound of the hymn "Nearer, my God to Thee!" could be heard.

"As we pulled away from the ship we noticed that she was hog-backed, showing that she was already breaking in two. She was not telescoped, the force of the impact being sustained on the keel more than on the bows.

"We were in the small boats for more than four hours before we were rescued by the Carpathia. There were icefields and icefloes all around us. They were constantly grinding and clashing together, and our boats were in danger of being crushed to pieces. The weather was extremely cold, and we suffered intensely. The men in the boats showed splendid heroism.

"There was no panic among the steerage or second-class passengers, though it is alleged there was a wild scramble among the first-class passengers, and I am informed shots were fired.

"We were well cared for on board the Carpathia, being shown every courtesy and kindness. The mental condition of all was good, considering the terrible ordeal, until the Carpathia reached New York Bay; then there were numerous cases of collapse and mental derangement."—Daily Express.

THERE WAS NO REAL PANIC, THOUGH A NUMBER JUMPED.

Miss May R. Birkhead Tells an Affecting Story.

[BY COMMERCIAL CABLE TO THE HERALD.]

NEW YORK, Friday morning.—Miss May R. Birkhead, a passenger on the Carpathia, tells an affecting story of the saving of survivors from rafts and boats, some of them so chilled that they had to be hauled up in bags. One man told her that he was in the smoking-room when the Titanic struck. He went on deck and found the boats being lowered.

Survivors from the Titanic Tell of the Circumstances of Their Escape and Rescue

New York, Friday.—The following account of the Titanic disaster is given by Mr. Lawrence Beesley, of London:—

"I had been in my berth about ten minutes when, at about a quarter-past ten, I felt a slight jar. Then, soon afterwards, there was a second shock, but it was not sufficiently great to cause any anxiety to anyone, however nervous they may have been. The engines, however, stopped immediately afterwards.

"A little later, hearing people going upstairs, I went out again, and found that everybody wanted to know why the engines had stopped. No doubt, many of them had been awakened from their sleep by the sudden stopping of the vibration, to which they had become accustomed during the four days we had been on board. Going up on the deck again I saw that there was an unmistakable list downwards from the stern to the bows, but knowing nothing of what had happened I concluded that some of the front compartments had filled and had weighed her down.

"Again I went down to my cabin, where I put on some warmer clothing. As I dressed I heard the order shouted: 'All the passengers on deck, with lifebelts on.'

Lifeboats Prepared.

"The ship was absolutely still, and, except for the gentle tilt downwards, which I do not think one person in ten would have noticed at the time, there was no visible sign of the approaching disaster. She lay just as if waiting for the order to go on again when some trifling matter had been adjusted. But, in a few minutes, we saw the covers being lifted from the boats and the crews allotted to them standing by and uncoiling the ropes which were to lower them. We then began to realize that it was a more serious matter than we had at first supposed.

"Presently, we heard the order, 'All men stand back from the boats. All ladies retire to the next deck below,' which was the smoking room, or B deck. The men all stood away and waited in absolute silence, some leaning against the end railings of the deck, others pacing slowly up and down. The boats were then swung out and lowered from A deck. When they were level with B deck where all the women were collected, the women got in quietly, with the exception of some who refused to leave their husbands.

Torn from Their Husbands.

"In some cases they were torn from their husbands and pushed into the boats, but in many instances they were allowed to remain, since there was no one to insist that they should go.

"Looking over the side, one saw the boats from aft already in the water slipping quietly away into the darkness.

"Presently the boats near me were lowered with much creaking, as the new ropes slipped through the pulleys and blocks down the ninety feet which separated them from the water.

"An officer in uniform came up as one boat went down and shouted out: 'When you're afloat, row round to the companion ladder and stand by with other boats for orders.'

"'Aye, aye, sir,' came up the reply, but I don't think any boat was able to obey the order, for, when they were afloat and had their oars at work, the condition of the rapidly settling liner was much more apparent. In common prudence the sailors saw that they could do nothing but row from the sinking ship and so save, at any rate, some lives. They, no doubt, anticipated that the suction from such an enormous vessel would be more than usually dangerous to the crowded boat, which was mostly filled with women.

MR. JOHN JACOB ASTOR.

CAPT. EDWARD J. SMITH

MR. ISIDOR STRAUS.

"Any More Ladies?"

"Presently word went round among us that men were to be put in boats on the starboard side. I was on the port side. Most of the men walked across the deck to see if this were true. I remained where I was, and shortly afterwards I heard the call, 'Any more ladies?' Looking over the side of the ship, I saw boat No. 13 swinging level with B deck. It was half full of women. Again the call was repeated, 'Any more ladies?' I saw none coming. Then one of the crew looked up and said, 'Any ladies on your deck, sir?' 'No,' I replied.

"'Then you'd better jump,' said he. I dropped and fell into the bottom of the boat as they cried: 'Lower away!'

"It was now one o'clock in the morning. The starlit night was beautiful, but as there was no moon, it was not very light. The sea was as calm as a pond. There was just a gentle heave as the boat dipped up and down in the swell. It was an ideal night, except for the bitter cold.

"In the distance the Titanic looked enormous. Her length and her great bulk were outlined in black against the starry sky. Every porthole and saloon was blazing with light. It was impossible to think that anything could be wrong with such a leviathan were it not for that ominous tilt downward in the bows, where the water was by now up to the lowest row of portholes.

Like the Death Rattle.

"At about two o'clock we observed her settling very rapidly, with the bows and the bridge completely under water. She slowly tilted straight on end, with the stern vertically upwards; as she did so the lights in the cabins and the saloons, which had not flickered for a moment since we left, died out, flashed once more, and then went out altogether. At the same time, the machinery roared down through the vessel with a groaning rattle that could have been heard for miles.

"It was the weirdest sound surely that could have been heard in the middle of the ocean. It was not yet quite the end. To our amazement, she remained in that upright position for a time which I estimate as five minutes. It was certainly for some minutes that we watched at least 150ft. of the Titanic towering up above the level of the sea, looming black against the sky. Then, with a quiet, slanting dive, she disappeared beneath the waters. Our eyes had looked for the last time on the gigantic vessel in which we set out from Southampton.

"Then there fell on our ears the most appalling noise that human being ever heard—the sound of hundreds of our fellow beings struggling in the icy waters, crying for help with a cry that we knew could not be answered. We longed to return to pick up some of those who were swimming, but this would have meant the swamping of our boat and the loss of all of us."—Reuter.

[BY THE HERALD'S SPECIAL WIRE.]

London, Saturday. — "The noblest death that man can die is when he dies for man," and it was thus that Colonel John Jacob Astor, Major Archibald W. Butt, Mr. Isidor Straus, Mr. Henry B. Harris, Mr. William T. Stead, Mr. Jacques Futrelle, once of the Herald's staff, and scores of other famous passengers of the ill-fated Titanic died.

Readers of the Herald will never forget the pathetically-beautiful story of the death in each other's arms of Mr. and Mrs. Straus, the woman, like Ruth of old, saying: "Your way is my way," and sinking with him into the deep as they stood on the deck of the liner. The passing of Colonel Astor, who, after tenderly kissing his young bride good-bye, gave a military salute and took his place by the side of Major Butt to await the inevitable, is an epic of heroism.

The friends and relatives of Mr. William T. Stead, a journalist of world-wide fame, and of Mr. Jacques Futrelle, who was hailed as "America's Conan Doyle," will mourn their death, but will glory in the way in which they went to it. But there was another hero, a modest American, who will be missed by hundreds of warm friends in London—Mr. Howard B. Case, the managing director of the Vacuum Oil Company, who lived at Coombe Grange, Ascot. He was forty-eight years old and came here twenty years ago from Rochester, N.Y.

News of Art and Artists in New York; Futurists' and Cubists' Exhibition Opens

Thousands of Persons Thoroughly Enjoy Display in the Sixty-Ninth Regiment Armory.

(From the NEW YORK HERALD of February 18.)

Nearly four thousand persons, the guests of the Association of American Painters and Sculptors, last night filled the Sixty-ninth Regiment Armory, Lexington avenue and Twenty-fifth street, at the formal opening of the International Exhibition of Modern Art.

This was because the examples of extreme art, the work of the cubists, the futurists and the post-impressionists, were located in that part of the building. So deeply packed was the crowd in front of the pictures that it was almost impossible to see them.

A reception committee, composed of the officers and the entire membership of the association, welcomed the guests. At the head of this committee were Mr. Walter B. Davies, the president; Mr. J. Mowbray-Clarke, the vice-president; Mr. Elmer I. MacRee, the treasurer, and Mr. Walt Kuhn, the secretary. Others in the receiving line were Messrs. George Bellows, D. Putnam Brinley, Leon Dabo, Guy Pene Du Bois, Robert Henri, Ernest Lawson, Jonas Lie, Jerome Myers, Bruce Porter and Allen Tucker.

All Schools Represented.

The exhibition was formally opened by Mr. John Quinn, one of the honorary members of the association, who described the objects of the exhibition and told of the manner in which the pictures and sculptures had been gathered. He paid a tribute to the work of Mr. Davies and Mr. Kuhn, who went to Europe on the mission which resulted in the display of all the examples of the new movement in art. A serious student of art may now see in New York City and study for the next month paintings which otherwise would require a trip to Europe and perhaps two or three years of study abroad.

NEW YORK STREET AS THE "FUTURISTS" SEE IT.

(From the NEW YORK HERALD.)

The crowd, as it inspected the work of the art extremists, made an interesting study. Amazement mixed with amusement was written on the faces of the bystanders. The comments most frequently heard were those of censure, but now and then an exponent of the new idea could be heard dilating on the "color music" that the artists are supposed to be presenting. It was with a different mood, however, that the throng beheld the hundreds of landscapes and figure subjects by American artists which constitute the greater part of the exhibition. Here earnest groups praised and criticized works that were comprehensible to the mind of the ordinary human being.

Every school and tendency in modern art is represented, but the abnormalities of the cubists, post-impressionists and futurists overshadow everything else in the exhibition.

"They are atrocious, the work of madmen," onebystander was heard to declare, "but I'm not going to say it out loud."

"Why not?"

"Because in another room down there is a collection of pictures by Delacroix, Corot, Manet, Degas and some others who when they first began to paint were called insane men who didn't know anything about art."

Work of the Modernists.

The new school does not seek to reproduce on canvas imitations of objects. Instead it tries to reproduce by means of color the mental impressions and feelings of the artist on beholding a certain object or scene. A portrait of a man may take the form of mere irregular-shaped patches of color which the artist believes conveys the attributes of the sitter to the beholder. Those who go in for poetry turn out compositions which they liken to music—color so arranged as to appeal to the eye and give a certain sensation to the spectator.

One of the most amusing as well as inexplicable of the compositions is M. Marcel Duchamp's "The King and the Queen Traversed by White and Blue Nudes." It looks like nothing quite as much as a pinwheel struck by a cyclone. Not a person could be found who could tell what the title meant or what the painting meant. One of the members of the Association of American Painters and Sculptors was asked.

"The artist never knew himself. He just felt that way," was the reply.

Some Wonderful Sculpture.

Then there is Signor Constantine Brancusi's "Portrait of Mlle. Pogany," a piece of sculpture that looks like an underdeveloped and deformed infant.

"I wish I knew Mlle. Pogany," said a lawyer who was in the crowd. "I'd like to handle her suit for damages on a contingent basis."

"Mozart-Kubelik" is the title of a painting by M. Georges Braque. Among a lot of confused lines and paint there can be indistinctly made out a few characters in music. The composition is supposed to be a portrait of Kubelik playing Mozart, or at any rate of Mozart dreaming that Kubelik is going to play his music.

A perfect gem in the way of a story picture is Wassily Kandinsky's "Improvisation." At least, that is the way it impressed one spectator yesterday, who was explaining it to a companion.

"It's plain enough to me," he said. "A young man and his sweetheart have gone for a walk in the fields. A ferocious red bull has come athwart their path. That is the bull's head in the corner. That bunch of lines on the other side, bound with a horizontal band, is the young woman, who, in her temerity, has thrown her arm about her escort's neck. That yellow smear in the centre with the divergent red lines represents danger, and that irregular-shaped mass near the top is two angels and represents what the couple think will happen to them if the bull carries out his threat."

"Isn't it marvellous?" cried his companion. "These pictures leave so much to the imagination."

One whole room is filled with the work of M. Odilon Redon, who is one of the new school who sometimes produces color harmonies whose message can be comprehended by the ordinary person. There are also several specimens of the work of M. Francis Picabia, who recently came to New York, and who is perhaps the furthest "advanced" of all his colleagues. He tries only to play "color music" and the spectator seeks in vain to find the least vestige of recognizable form in his productions.

Only six of the eighteen rooms are filled with examples of extreme art. Of the other twelve rooms some are devoted to modern European artists, whose work by the side of the extremists seems academic, but by far the greater number are given over to works by American artists of the present day.

There are Mr. D. Putnam Brinley's three paintings, "The Emerald Pool," "The Peony Garden" and "A Walled Garden," glad, colorful creations. Then there is Mr. Jonas Lie, who in "At the Aquarium" has gone to the deep sea for deep color. There also are several canvases by Mr. Childe Hassam, beautiful in color and vibrating with light; Mr. Frank A. Nankivell's rich "Apple Picking" and Mr. Karl Anderson's glorious golden "The Apple Pickers."

MR. HENRY C. FRICK PAYS $130,000 FOR A REMBRANDT.

Sale of Forty-two Paintings from Mr. Borden's Collection Produces $800,000, in New York.

New York, Friday.—A record price for America in one night's art auctions was made last night when forty-two paintings from the M. C. D. Borden collection fetched $800,000. The most valuable picture sold was Rembrandt's "Lucretia Stabbing Herself," which was bought for $130,000 by Messrs. Knoedler and Co., acting for Mr. H. C. Frick. This was the highest price ever paid for a Rembrandt in the United States.

Turner's "Regatta, Bearing to Windward" was sold for $105,000 to Mr. W. Seaman, an agent. "Children," by Romney, was bought by Messrs. Scott and Fowles, the dealers, for $100,000. Hoppner's portrait of Mrs. Arbuthnot went to the same dealers for $60,500. The representatives of the Agnew Galleries, London, paid $60,000 for Romney's "The Countess of Glencairn," and $13,250 for his "Lady Hamilton as the Madonna."

Mr. C. K. G. Billings, who had bid against Mr. Frick for Rembrandt's "Lucretia," bought "The Willow Tree," by John Crome, for $55,000. Mr. W. Seaman paid $45,000 for Frans Hals' portrait of the Rev. Caspar Sibelius, which measures only 10¼in. by 7¾in. The collection included many other masterpieces.—Daily Telegraph.

SALE OF MODERN PICTURES HELD IN CHRISTIE'S ROOMS.

Mr. Sampson Pays £2,100 for Painting by J. Israels—Water-Color by Fielding Fetches £525.

[BY THE HERALD'S SPECIAL WIRE.]

London, Saturday.—At the sale at Christie's yesterday of modern pictures of Continental and British schools which belonged to the late Sir Horatio D. Davies, of Torquay, and Mr. William Woodward, of Avenue road, London, £2,100 was paid by Mr. Sampson for "The Departure," by J. Israels, depicting a fisherman's wife and children watching a fishing boat putting out to sea; "Cattle in a Meadow," by E. Van Marcke, was bought by Mr. Cremetti for £588 and £525 was paid by Messrs. Gooden and Fox for a water-color by C. Fielding, of Loch Earn and Ben Voirlich, Perthshire.

"The Hay Cart," by Corot, was purchased for £315 by Mr. Cremette. Mr. King paid £294 for a water-color, "On the Witham, Lincolnshire," by P. De Wint, and Mr. Morton paid the same amount for J. M. Swan's 1897 Royal Academy picture, "Tigress and Cubs at a Torrent." Mr. Wallis gave £252 for a drawing by J. Maris of a meadow with cattle by a stream.

Among other works sold were "Ben Venue from Loch Achray," by C. Fielding, £241 10s. (Mr. Tooth); the transept of a cathedral, with figures, by J. Bosboom, £231 (Mr. Wallis); "Washing Day," by J. Israels, £220 10s. (Mr. Lefevre); "On the Dublin Mountains," by W. Orpen, £220 10s. (Mr. Neave), and a classical river scene by G. Barret, £220 10s. (Mr. Leighton).

NEWS OF ART, ARTISTS AND DEALERS IN AMERICA

Three Sculptors Are Busy Beautifying Mr. John D. Rockefeller's Estate at Pocantico Hills.

(From the NEW YORK HERALD of February 12.)

During the last year one sculptor has devoted nearly all his time and two others have executed commissions for beautifying the estate of Mr. John D. Rockefeller at Pocantico Hills, Tarrytown, N.Y., with works of art. They are in the form of fountains for the gardens and figures for a large grotto, which Mr. Rockefeller has had constructed in the side of the hill two hundred yards from the mansion, with which it is connected by a tunnel.

Mr. Emil Siebern is the sculptor who was commissioned by Mr. Rockefeller to carry out his scheme for the grotto, designed to be a cool and quaint retreat for warm summer days. Mr. Siebern's work consists of three life-sized fountain groups and eight colossal heads. The subjects are fauns and water nymphs, which are depicted in playful moods. The heads are more properly masks typifying characters in classical mythology, including Jupiter, Neptune, Vulcan and the other gods of the ancients, the aim being to carry out the idea of a subterranean trysting-place for these "old boys," as Mr. Siebern expressed it. Mr. W. W. Bosworth, architect, acted in collaboration with the sculptor in developing the idea.

Another charming piece of sculpture for Mr. Rockefeller's garden is a fountain set in the rocks, the work of Miss Janet Scudder. It depicts a boy blowing on pipes. The water, splashing over the boy, comes from a huge frog that sits on a rock in front of and below the figure.

Still another fountain is now being cast in bronze for Mr. Rockefeller after a model made by Mr. Rudolphe Evans, of Scarboro, N.Y. This will occupy a conspicuous place on the lawn. It is a standing figure of a young girl in the attitude of welcome. It will be placed at the end of a long walk, backed by a specially arranged landscape. The figure will stand in an archway, in front of which will be three basins.

Mr. Morgan's Old Masters.

(From the NEW YORK HERALD of February 12.)

The attendance at the Metropolitan Museum has increased so since the collection of Old Masters lent by Mr. J. Pierpont Morgan has been on exhibition that all records have been broken, with the exception of two days during the Hudson-Fulton exhibition, was the statement made yesterday by Dr. Edward Robinson, the director. On the four Sundays since the pictures were shown 45,600 persons have visited the museum, an average of more than 11,000 for each day. On one Sunday the attendance was 12,600. Only on two previous days, February 21 and 22, 1909, when more than 13,000 persons visited the museum, has the attendance exceeded that number. The average attendance during the weekdays has shown a proportionate increase.

THE NEW YORK HERALD

PRICE: PARIS and FRANCE, 15 Centimes. ABROAD, 25 Centimes. | EUROPEAN EDITION—PARIS.—MONDAY, JUNE 29, 1914. | NO 28,434.

ARCHDUKE FRANCIS FERDINAND AND HIS CONSORT, THE DUCHESS OF HOHENBERG, ARE ASSASSINATED WHILE DRIVING THROUGH STREETS OF SARAJEVO, BOSNIA

THE MURDERED COUPLE DRIVING TOGETHER

ARCHDUKE FRANCIS FERDINAND.

THE DUCHESS OF HOHENBERG.

THE ARCHDUKE AND HIS FAMILY.

THE TOWN HALL AT SARAJEVO

Student Fires at Them in Their Automobile, Inflicting Mortal Wounds.

BOMB HAD PREVIOUSLY BEEN THROWN AT THEM.

Imperial Couple Escaped from First Attempt Only to Fall Victims of Second.

Infernal Machine, Hurled by Compositor, Wounds Officers of Royal Suite.

UNDAUNTED, ARCHDUKE TAKES SECOND DRIVE.

With His Wife He Reappears in Streets and Falls by Assassin's Bullet.

Consternation was created throughout the Courts of Europe by the news, flashed across the wires yesterday afternoon, that Archduke Francis Ferdinand, heir to the thrones of Austria and Hungary, and the Duchess of Hohenberg, his morganatic wife, had been assassinated in the streets of Sarajevo, the capital of Bosnia.

Two separate attempts were made on the life of the Archduke and his wife. A bomb was thrown as they were driving to the town hall, but the Archduke caught the missile and threw it on to the road behind his automobile, where it exploded in front of another auto.

With magnificent courage, the Archduke, after ascertaining the result of the explosion, insisted on continuing on his journey to the town hall, where the official reception took place.

The ceremony at the town hall was marked by an extraordinary scene, the Archduke severely reproving the Burgomaster for the bomb-throwing in his town.

It was on the return from the town hall that the assassination took place. The Imperial automobile was passing through an open space at the corner of the Appel Quay when a student stepped out of the crowd and fired point-blank with an automatic pistol at the Archduke and his consort.

The first shot struck the Archduke in the head. The Duchess rose in the automobile to protect him, and received the assassin's second shot in the breast and fell forward across her husband's knees.

The Archduke made a feeble effort to clasp his wife in his arms, and they sank together to the floor of the automobile in a last embrace. They died almost simultaneously without regaining consciousness.

The assassin, a young Servian student, named Prinzip, was arrested.

ASSASSINATION WAS CLEARLY OUTCOME OF DEEP-LAID PLOT.

First Attempt on His Life Greatly Angered the Archduke.

VIENNA, Sunday.—Archduke Francis Ferdinand, heir to the Austro-Hungarian throne, and the Duchess of Hohenberg, his morganatic wife, were assassinated this morning while driving in an automobile through the streets of Sarajevo, the capital of Bosnia.

The aged Emperor, who went to Ischl, his summer seat, a few days ago, has been prostrated by the news, and it is feared that the shock may have grave consequences, for he is eighty-four, and has been in very weak health for some time past.

Vienna is a city of the dead to-night, for the murdered Archduke, in spite of his aloofness and his somewhat autocratic disposition, was very popular among the Austrophile section of the heterogeneous subjects of the empire.

That the assassinations were carefully thought out beforehand there can be no possible doubt. Two separate attempts were made on the lives of the Archduke and his consort.

A bomb was thrown at them as they were driving from the Archduke's headquarters with the army—he had been acting as commander-in-chief during the manœuvres of the last few days—to the Town Hall, where a civic reception had been arranged. The bomb struck the automobile, but was thrown off by the Archduke and rebounded on the road behind, where it exploded in front of another automobile containing four members of the suite.

Bomb Injures Several.

Colonel Merizzi, one of the Archduke's aides-de-camp, was struck in the neck by a splinter and badly injured. The other persons in the automobile were also hurt as well as several persons in the crowd.

Showed Magnificent Courage.

The Archduke behaved with magnificent courage. He ordered his chauffeur to stop the automobile, and, alighting, walked back among the crowd to see what had happened. After ascertaining the extent of the injuries of his aide-de-camp and giving peremptory orders to have him removed to hospital, he went back to his automobile, and, in spite of the entreaties of the members of his suite, declared his intention of proceeding to the Town Hall.

At the entrance, he was received by the Burgomaster and the members of the town council, and it was clear to all that he was then in a furious temper and bitterly resentful of what had happened.

The burgomaster stepped forward to read the address of welcome, but the Archduke could contain himself no longer. He waved the Burgomaster aside, and in fierce passionate tones cried: "Herr Burgermeister, we have come to Sarajevo on a friendly visit. We have been met by a bomb. It is outrageous."

A terrible silence followed the archduke's fierce indictment—fiercer in its tone and temper than in its actual wording.

Stumbles Through Address.

The Burgomaster fell back, but the archduke imperiously waved him forward with the command: "You may now speak." As soon as the Burgomaster recovered himself, he proceeded to stumble through the address in frightened tones and amid a dead, ominous silence.

The archduke, in stern tones, made a brief reply, and the crowd broke out into cheers.

The next half-hour was passed in the inspection of the Town Hall and in the presentation to the archduke of several Bosnian notabilities, but all the time he was obviously ill at ease and was sending messengers to ascertain the condition of his aide-de-camp and the other persons who were injured.

After half an hour he and the duchess who had also behaved with great coolness, left the Town Hall, the archduke announcing his intention of driving to the Garrison Hospital to see Colonel Merizzi.

The news of the attempt had spread rapidly through the town and a great crowd had gathered outside the town hall. They gave the archduke and his consort a splendid reception as they left.

Second Attempt Succeeds.

They had only left the Town Hall a few minutes when the second and successful attempt was made on their lives. The automobile was passing through the open space at the corner of the Appel Quay when a young man stepped out of the crowd and fired two shots from a Browning pistol point-blank at the archduke and the duchess.

The first shot lodged in the archduke's face. The duchess made a wild attempt to save him. She rose in the auto and threw herself in front of him with arms outstretched. She received the assassin's shot in the breast and fell forward across her husband's knees.

The archduke made a feeble effort to clasp her in his arms, and they fell together on the floor of the automobile in a last embrace.

Never Recover Consciousness.

The chauffeur dashed the auto to the Konak Palace and the archduke and duchess were tenderly lifted out. They died almost simultaneously, without ever showing a glimpse of consciousness.

The assassin is a young Servian student named Prinzip. He was seized by the spectators immediately after he fired the shots, and the gendarmes had the greatest difficulty in saving him from being lynched by the maddened crowd, but eventually they were able to take him to the prison, bleeding and almost fainting from his injuries.

Prinzip is stated to have studied in Belgrade, and some time ago conceived the idea of assassinating the archduke. He is said to have had a bomb prepared to-day, but hesitated to throw it when he saw the duchess was with her husband. A bomb was found near the scene of the tragedy.

Consternation in Vienna.

The news of the tragedy was circulated in Vienna this afternoon by special editions of the newspapers and created consternation everywhere. Numerous houses are this evening draped in black. All public fêtes have been stopped.

It is believed here that the assassination was carefully prepared by Servian conspirators, and a fresh outburst of indignation against Servia has already taken place.—Daily Express.

MEDICAL ASSISTANCE PROVES OF NO AVAIL.

Bodies Now Lie in State at Konak of Sarajevo.

SARAJEVO, Sunday.—After the firing of the two shots the automobile immediately proceeded to the Konak, where two doctors were in attendance without delay. Medical assistance was, however, of no avail. A priest was called in to recite the prayers for the dead. Both bodies will lie in state at the Konak for the present.

After the assassination the greatest excitement prevailed among the crowd, and many people wept. Large crowds assembled all day at the scenes of the two attempts, and the flags are flying at half-mast on all the buildings.

The following details of the first attempt are now available:—

The bomb was what is called a "bottle bomb." It was filled with nails and lead filings. The explosion was very violent, and the iron shutters of many of the shops in the vicinity were pierced by fragments of the bomb. About twenty persons were slightly injured, several women and children being among the number. In the course of the afternoon a considerable number of people reported slight injuries. An official of the local government received severe injuries in the legs from splinters of the bomb.

The assassin is a student named Gavrilo Prinzip. He is nineteen years of age and was born at Grabovo, in the district of Livno. He studied for some time in Belgrade.

On being interrogated Prinzip declared that he had intended for a long time to kill some eminent personage from nationalist motives. Prinzip denies having any accomplices.

The twenty-one-year-old compositor, Nedeljko Gabrinovic, whose attempt with a bomb failed, declared that he received the bomb from Anarchists in Belgrade, whose names he did not know. He, too, denies having any accomplices.

Gabrinovic behaved very cynically during the examination. After his attempt he sprang into the river Miljachka to evade the police, but several people from the crowd jumped after him and seized him.

The unexploded bomb which was found near the scene of the tragedy is thought to have been thrown away by a third assassin after he had seen the success of Prinzip's attack.—Reuter.

Eyewitness Describes Bomb-throwing.

(From the "Petit Parisien.")

VIENNA, Sunday.—An account of the first attempt on the life of the archduke was given by an eyewitness, a barber named Marossi. He said: "As the archduke's automobile approached, I saw a man on the quay near the bridge come up and throw something at the automobile. Another man, who stood near him, then went quickly away. I saw slight fumes escaping from the bomb as it was thrown. It rebounded from the archduke's automobile and fell into the one behind. At that instant a terrible explosion occurred.

"I then rushed after the second man I had noticed. But he saw me coming and jumped over the parapet of the Militza quay. I ran after him. A policeman, following me, wanted to fire at the man with his revolver. I called out: 'Don't fire! We must catch him alive!' We soon came up with the man and, with the aid of other policemen, easily arrested him."

After the first attempt, the Duchess of Hohenberg, who was overcome, did not want the archduke to go through the streets again in his automobile. General Potiorek, however, reassured her, saying, "All danger is over now. We shall only have demonstrations of sympathy. There is no need to fear anything."

MANY PEOPLE, IT SEEMS, ARE CONCERNED IN PLOT.

Servians Regarded Archduke as Their Great Opponent.

VIENNA, Sunday.—It appears that many persons were concerned in the plot against the archduke, who was regarded by the Servians as the greatest opponent of the Pan-Servian movement.

He was warned not to attend the manœuvres, but insisted on going. He wished, however, that his wife should not accompany him.

The latest reports state that the archduke was hit in the aorta. He attempted to sit up, but fell back. The Duchess of Hohenberg threw herself over him to cover him, but while so doing was hit by the second shot. Corps-Commander Potiorek, who was sitting opposite, escaped uninjured.

The Sarajevo police are reproached with neglecting necessary measures of precaution, but it is a fact that a large number of suspicious persons have been arrested in the course of the last few days.

The report that the assassins are Servians and that the bomb was manufactured at Belgrade will certainly increase the long-existing embitterment against the Servians here.

The news has caused an indescribable commotion of excitement and sorrow in Vienna and the provincial towns, where the news was published in special editions this afternoon. But, as the telegraph is either exclusively used for official messages or placed under the control of the authorities, no private reports of the details have so far been received here. Naturally concerts and theatrical performances were at once interrupted or countermanded.

Vienna is hung with black flags. Silent groups surround the sellers of the special editions, and the sheets are scanned with grave faces as the full horror and significance of the facts are borne in upon the readers.

The news of the death of their parents has not yet been communicated to the archduke's children, who are in Konopischt Castle.—Morning Post.

Would Not Modify Programme.

SARAJEVO, Sunday.—The Bosnian Government declares that after the first bomb attempt it wished to exclude the public from sharing in the further ceremonies connected with the visit of the archduke, but his Imperial Highness stated that he wished no change to be made in the programme.—Daily Chronicle.

Archduke's Last Speech.

(From the "Matin.")

SARAJEVO, Sunday.—This is the text of the last speech made by Archduke Francis Ferdinand in reply to the address of welcome read by the Burgomaster of Sarajevo:—

"It is with a quite particular satisfaction that I receive the expression of your fidelity and of your unshakable devotion to his Majesty, our very gracious Emperor and King.

"I am delighted, Mr. Burgomaster, with the ovations that have greeted me and my wife, all the more so as I see in them a mark of public thankfulness at the failure of the attempt"— (He referred to the first attempt.)

"I pray you to convey to the inhabitants of the beautiful capital of this province my most cordial greetings and the assurance of my lasting goodwill."

Bomb Said to Be from Belgrade.

VIENNA, Sunday.—Rumors are current that the bomb thrown by Gabrinovic had been sent to him from Belgrade.

It is noteworthy that the Archduke Francis Ferdinand was the only one of the archdukes who was popularly supposed to be in favor of the establishment of a great Croat kingdom having the same prerogatives as those possessed by Austria and Hungary.

In political circles hostile to the southern Slavs it is believed that he crime was not due to any sentiment of personal hostility to the archduke, but that it is the outcome of the serious anti-dynastic feeling which has for some time been growing in Bosnia.—Figaro.

EMPEROR BURSTS INTO TEARS ON HEARING NEWS.

Monarch to Return to Vienna Early This Morning.

VIENNA, Sunday.—When the news of the assassination was broken to the Emperor at Ischl, he burst into tears, and exclaimed: "Fearful! Fearful! No trial in the world will have been spared me!"

The Emperor immediately withdrew to his private apartments.

All Court and official ceremonies have been cancelled, and the theatres will be closed.

Duke Ernst August of Cumberland arrived by automobile at Ischl during the afternoon, and made a visit of condolence to the Emperor at five o'clock.

The Emperor will return to Vienna at six o'clock to-morrow morning.—Figaro.

BRITISH ROYAL FAMILY IS GREATLY SHOCKED BY NEWS.

State Ball at Buckingham Palace Is Postponed.

[BY THE HERALD'S SPECIAL WIRE.]

LONDON, Monday.—The King and Queen and other members of the Royal family were inexpressibly shocked by the news. The King has commanded that the Court shall go into mourning for one week for the late Archduke. The mourning is to date from yesterday, and the Court will go out of mourning next Sunday. The State ball arranged to take place this evening at Buckingham Palace has been postponed.

At Marlborough House the news came as an especial shock. Not only were the victims well-known there, but one of Queen Alexandra's guests at the present time is Queen Olga of Greece, whose husband, Queen Alexandra's brother, also died by the hand of an assassin at a comparatively recent date.

TRAGEDIES OF THE HOUSE OF HAPSBURG.

Emperor Francis Joseph has witnessed the following tragedies to members of his family:—

His brother, Archduke Ferdinand, who became Emperor of Mexico under the title of Maximilian I., shot at Queretaro on June 19, 1867;

His son, Archduke Rudolph, who was shot mysteriously on January 30, 1889, during a fête in his shooting box at Meyerling;

His wife, Empress Elizabeth, who was murdered at Geneva on September 10, 1898, by the anarchist Luccheni;

His nephew, Archduke Francis Ferdinand, and the latter's morganatic wife, who have been murdered at Sarajevo on June 28, 1914.

On page 2 will be found a biography of Archduke Francis Ferdinand and an article on the tragic history of the Hapsburg family, as well as despatches telling how the Kaiser received the news at Kiel and also the effect it produced at Carlsbad.

THE CALIFORNIA GOES ASHORE NEAR TORY ISLAND.

Bow of Anchor Liner Is Injured and Two Holds Are Full of Water.

[BY THE HERALD'S SPECIAL WIRE.]

LONDON, Monday.—A Lloyd's telegram from Malin Head wireless station, dated Sunday, 9.30 p.m., states that the Anchor liner California is ashore near Tory Island. An Exchange Telegraph Londonderry message says the California went ashore with such force that the lower part of her bow is badly stove in, and two forward holds are full of water. The California, New York for Glasgow, was signalled by wireless to be 343 miles west of Malin Head at 12.30 a.m. yesterday.

The "Daily Chronicle" correspondent in Londonderry telegraphs this morning: "The California grounded in an exceptionally heavy fog. It is reported that her bows are damaged and the forward hold is making water. Six destroyers steamed to her assistance from Lough Swilly and will reach her at dawn. The passengers and crew are safe.

"There was no panic when the accident occurred. The ship lies in rather a dangerous position, but if it be necessary to transfer the passengers to other boats it is believed that the operation will be speedily and safely effected, as the sea is fairly smooth and the wind light."

Other reports state that the California is stuck fast. She is in five fathoms of water forward and seven fathoms aft. Another liner is standing by. The Irish passengers are expected in Londonderry before noon to-day.

The California's Passengers.

[BY COMMERCIAL CABLE TO THE HERALD.]

NEW YORK, Sunday.—Among the California's passengers are: Mr. Lawrence Houghton, Mrs. William E. Bond, the Rev. B. D. Stevens, Mr. Andrew Baxter, Mr. O. A. Broomfield, Mr. John R. Clifford, Mr. Edwin Falk, Mrs. G. D. Ward Hunter, Mr. and Mrs. Francis O'Neill, Mr. Irving A. Sartorius, and Dr. William D. Husk.

GIFT FOR POLAR EXPEDITION.

[BY THE HERALD'S SPECIAL WIRE.]

LONDON, Monday.—Sir James Caird, the philanthropist and jute manufacturer, of Dundee, has given £24,000 to Sir Ernest Shackleton's Imperial Transantarctic Expedition.

New Heir-Apparent Is a Great Favorite of the Emperor

EMPEROR FRANCIS JOSEPH.

ARCHDUKE CHARLES FRANCIS JOSEPH & HIS CONSORT.

Archduke Charles Francis Joseph Was Brought Up Under Monarch's Guidance.

On his marriage, Archduke Francis Ferdinand abandoned all claims for his future children to the thrones of Austria and Hungary. With his untimely death, therefore, the heir-apparent is his nephew, Archduke Charles Francis Joseph, son of Archduke Otto Francis Joseph, who died in Vienna on November 1, 1906.

Archduke Charles Francis Joseph was born on August 17, 1887, and he married, on October 21, 1911, Princess Zita of Bourbon and Parma. He has one son, Archduke Francis Joseph Otto, who was born in November, 1912.

The new heir-apparent is a grand-nephew of Emperor Francis Joseph, and a great favorite with him. Tall and slim, he is a wonderful horseman, even in a country where everyone can ride bareback. A fearless shot and sportsman, he brings all who come in contact with him under his charm. His smile is engaging, his conversation lively and interesting, and his sharp intelligence quickly grasps the most abstruse facts.

Brought Up by Emperor.

He has been brought up altogether under the influence and direction of the Emperor, and celebrated his majority, on attaining his twentieth birthday, with his grand-uncle, at Ischl. He was the first scion of the House of Hapsburg to receive the early part of his education in one of the public grammar schools of Vienna, and in thus taking his place on the benches of these public institutions, beside the sons of petty tradesmen, artisans and laborers, he early came into intimate contact with the people over whom he is destined in the course of time to rule.

His secondary studies were carried on at the celebrated College of Schottenstift, which is directed by the Benedictines of Vienna. On leaving there the Emperor sent him to Prague. It is an old and delicate attention of the Hapsburgs in regard to Bohemia to send the archdukes there to begin their military studies.

His Military Career.

Archduke Charles Francis Joseph was appointed a lieutenant in the 7th Regiment of Dragoons of Lorraine and Bar,

His Marriage Three Years Ago to Bourbon Princess Caused Great Rejoicing in Austria.

which was garrisoned at Brandeis, on the Elbe. There, surrounded by distinguished officers and professors, he divided his life between military exercises and a deep study of political and social sciences. His masters praise his prodigious memory, which assimilates and retains everything with a surprising logic, and others who have had opportunities of observing him agree that they do not exaggerate.

Nearly three years ago he linked his fate to that of a princess, the direct descendant of French kings, gay, abrupt and slightly malicious. Princess Zita of Bourbon and Parma was born on May 9, 1892, and partly brought up in England. After studying with the Visitandines she was sent, as were all her sisters, to complete her education with the Benedictines of Solesmes, who are established at Ryde, in the Isle of Wight.

The marriage was marked by great rejoicing in Austria, and in a very short time the princess had become most popular with those over whom she will one day jointly reign.

THE NEW YORK HERALD

PRICE: PARIS and FRANCE, 25 Centimes. ABROAD, 35 Centimes.

EUROPEAN EDITION—PARIS.—SUNDAY. AUGUST 2. 1914.

NO 28,468.

GERMANY DECLARES WAR UPON RUSSIA; FRANCE ORDERS A GENERAL MOBILIZATION

NEWS ON PAGE 3.

Interstate Rate Commission grants 5 per cent. advance.

Americans in Paris and London "held up" by shipping changes.

Bank of England issues unprecedented number of bank notes.

BELGIUM HOPES TO AVOID CONFLICT

France and Germany Both Pledge Themselves to Respect Her Neutrality, for Time at Least.

(SPECIAL TO THE HERALD.)

BRUSSELS, Saturday. — News received here shows at once that peace must be despaired of and that Belgian territory is safe for the present moment, France having pledged herself to respect Belgian neutrality so long as other Powers do, and Germany has given the same pledge, while England will watch Belgium at a distance, only to interfere if her neutrality is threatened.

The money panic continues unabated.

GENERAL MOBILIZATION ORDERED IN SWITZERLAND.

Issue of Small Notes to Follow Federal Council's Decision.

BERNE, Saturday. — An immediate general mobilization of the Swiss Federal Army was ordered by the Federal Council this morning.

An extraordinary meeting of the Federal Chambers has been convoked by the Council for Monday next to consider the measures taken to maintain the safety, independance and neutrality of Switzerland, to nominate the commander-in-chief of the army, and to sanction the emission of five-franc bank notes.

All Post-Offices to Be Open To-day.

The French postal authorities have decided to leave the post offices open throughout France to-day.

The Paris postal employés spontaneously placed their services at the disposal of the authorities.

NEWS OF TO-DAY SUMMARIZED.

M. Albert Guilloux, the sculptor, has been made a Knight of the Legion of Honor.

A factory of soda-siphons in Paris was destroyed by fire in the early hours of yesterday morning.

The United States Treasury has been ordered to keep open to-day to issue new Bank currency.

Mr. Edmund James Payne, the Gaiety comedian, who died in July at the age of forty-nine, left estate of the gross value of £21,657.

The French Council of State has rejected the appeal of General Faurie against his being compulsorily placed on the retired list.

The departure of the Cunarder Saxonia, which was due to leave New York yesterday for the Mediterranean, has been cancelled.

Notification of Open Rupture Made to St. Petersburg Government at 7.30 Last Night.

GERMAN AMBASSADOR AND HIS STAFF LEAVE.

Mobilization Throughout Russian Empire Is Proceeding With Great Rapidity and Enthusiasm.

At an early hour this morning the news agencies circulated the following note:—

"We learn from an official source that Germany has declared war upon Russia."

War Declared at 7.30 p.m.

ST. PETERSBURG, Saturday.—The German Ambassador, in the name of his Government, handed to the Foreign Ministry a declaration of war at 7.30 this evening.

Ambassador Leaves St. Petersburg.

NEW YORK, Saturday.—An Associated Press telegram received here this evening says that the German Ambassador, on behalf of his Government, handed to the Russian Foreign Office a declaration of war, and the/staff of the German Embassy has left St. Petersburg.—Exchange Telegraph Company.

War Confirmed in London.

[BY THE HERALD'S SPECIAL WIRE.]

LONDON, Sunday.—The Russian Embassy has received information that Germany has declared war.

GENERAL MOBILIZATION PROCEEDING IN FRANCE.

Troops Began to Rejoin Corps at Midnight Last Night.

The French Government has ordered the general mobilization of the army and navy.

This action was instantly taken by the Cabinet when it learned in the course of the afternoon that a general mobilization was in progress in Germany.

Notice of the mobilization was contained in a Circular which was immediately posted on all public buildings in Paris and at every town hall and post-office throughout France.

The notice was as follows:—

MINISTRY OF WAR
Circular of Extreme Urgency
ORDER OF GENERAL MOBILIZATION
The First Day of the Mobilization is SUNDAY, AUGUST 2.

At the same time the Cabinet prepared a proclamation to the French nation inviting everyone to do his duty with calm and sangfroid.

The order for mobilization naturally created a great sensation, but it in no way came as a shock, for the French

FRENCH GOVERNMENT ISSUES PROCLAMATION TO THE NATION

The following proclamation was posted last night in Paris and the provinces:—

TO THE FRENCH NATION.

For some days past the situation in Europe has become considerably worse, despite the efforts of diplomacy.

The horizon has darkened. At the present moment most of the nations have mobilized their forces. Even the countries protected by neutrality have felt compelled to take this step as a matter of precaution.

Powers whose constitutional and military legislation does not resemble our own have, without issuing a decree of mobilization, commenced and continued preparations which are equivalent in reality to mobilization itself, and which are only the anticipated execution of it.

France, who has always affirmed her peaceful desires; who in these days of tragedy gave to Europe counsels of moderation and a living example of wisdom; who has multiplied her efforts to maintain the peace of the world, has prepared herself for every eventuality, and has taken, from the present moment, the first indispensable steps for the safeguard of her territory.

But our legislation does not permit us to render these preparations complete unless a decree of mobilization is issued.

Cognisant of its responsibility, feeling that it would neglect a sacred duty if it allowed matters to remain as they are, the Government has just issued the decree which the situation demands.

Mobilization is not war. In the present circumstances, it appears, on the contrary, as the best means of ensuring peace with honor.

Strong in its ardent desire to arrive at a peaceful solution of the crisis, the Government, sheltered by these necessary precautions, will continue its diplomatic efforts, and still hopes to succeed.

It counts on the sangfroid of this noble nation not to allow itself to give way to unjustifiable emotion. It counts on the patriotism of all Frenchmen, knowing that there is not one of them who is not ready to do his duty.

At this hour there are no parties. There is France eternal, France peaceful and resolute. The fatherland of right and justice is entirely united in calm, vigilance and dignity.

The President of the Republic,
RAYMOND POINCARE.

By the President of the Republic,
the Prime Minister,
Minister of Foreign Affairs,
RENE VIVIANI.
(The signatures of all the Ministers follow.)

of the Legion of Honor, formed a striking group seated tranquilly on their baggage at the end of one of the platforms, whence they were just about to leave for the extreme frontier.

Every now and then the ear-splitting whistle of a locomotive and the jolt and rattle of trucks and carriages rose above the steady hum of conversation and the bustle of movement. Outside the station the crowd was almost as dense and certainly more noisy than that on the platforms.

Soon after one o'clock there was a sudden hush which lasted for several minutes. The crowd had caught sight of a great airship, from beneath which fluttered the Tricolor. It swept magnificently above the station, its motor buzzing, its whirling propellers flashing in the sunlight, and gradually disappeared, travelling at a great speed eastward.

The silence was ended. The huge crowd shattered it with one heartfelt cry: "Vive la France!"

PARIS MUNICIPAL COUNCIL ISSUES APPEAL TO CITIZENS.

Everything Quite Ready for Revictualling of City.

The bureau of the Paris Municipal Council has prepared the following appeal to the population of Paris, which will be posted to-day:—

"At the moment when all Frenchmen must forget their differences and their quarrels to group themselves around the flag of the Fatherland an abominable outrage has been committed.

"This outrage arouses the legitimate indignation of all citizens without distinction of opinion or party. But everyone must contribute to his country, in the hour through which we are passing

appeared to have become reconciled to the inevitable.

The streets were thronged with people, who, as on previous days, eagerly bought up the latest editions of the papers. The crowds were, however, strangely quiet, and showed but little inclination to demonstrate their feelings.

The news that the French Government had issued orders for the mobilization of the army created no surprise; indeed it had been expected all day.

As on the preceding day, the Banque de France was besieged by those anxious to change their notes for currency. The issue of the new banknotes of five and twenty franc denominations did not seem to have had an appreciable effect in relieving the stringency, and all day long eager but orderly throngs were patiently waiting their turn to enter the building.

Not a few of the smaller shops were closed, their owners having already been recalled to their regiments.

All the principal railway termini were packed with foreigners returning home, the exodus continuing unabated all day.

About six o'clock a procession of a few hundred youths headed by tricolor flags paraded the boulevards cheering for war.

As a precautionary measure, a Viennese café on the boulevard Montmartre was closed, and was guarded by a posse of police.

GERMAN AMBASSADOR VISITS FRENCH PRIME MINISTER.

M. Viviani Justifies French Attitude to Baron von Schoen.

Baron von Schoen, the German Ambassador in Paris, called at the Ministry of Foreign Affairs yesterday after-

four o'clock this afternoon at the Café Américain, rue des Capucines, to discuss the formation of a corps of Slav volunteers for France.

BELGIANS AND DUTCHMEN TO VOLUNTEER FOR FRANCE.

They Decide to Raise Corps in Paris at Own Expense.

Belgian and Dutch citizens inhabiting Paris met yesterday morning and decided that, as they consider France as their adopted country, and as they have been living in France for several years, and have fulfilled their military duties in their respective countries, they will form a Belgian-Dutch corps of volunteers.

This corps will equip itself at its own cost and hold itself at the disposal of the commander-in-chief of the French army the moment hostilities break out.

French Bank Rate Raised.

The Bank of France yesterday raised its discount rate from 4½ to 6 per cent. and its rate for loans from 5½ to 7 per cent.

RUSSIA RESPONDS FIRMLY TO CALL TO THE COLORS.

Male Population Realizes General Mobilization Was Inevitable.

(From Harold Williams, "Lloyd's News" Special Correspondent.)

ST. PETERSBURG, Saturday.—All attention is now concentrated on the mobilization of troops. During the night bills were posted up in all parts of the city summoning the whole of the Reservists to the colors, and the population awoke to real startling news.

All the posters were printed in red. "Red!" cried the women, and there was

Reservists of French Army Start to Join Colors at Midnight When Notices Are Posted.

NATION RESPONDS WITH RESOLUTION AND CALM.

As One Man People Rise at Nation's Call of Liberty and Hasten to Regiments.

suspended. Many young men not liable to service are volunteering for the army. For once the Government has displayed remarkable tenacity of purpose and from all sides public opinion shows hardly a dissentient voice.

AUSTRIANS EVERYWHERE REPULSED BY SERVIANS.

Enemy Has Failed to Gain Footing on Servian Territory.

It is stated in well-informed circles in Paris that the despatches from Vienna announcing the occupation of Belgrade by the Austrians three days ago are inexact. Servian despatches which have arrived by roundabout route from Nish state that the Austrians continue to bombard the abandoned capital of Servia.

These despatches add that far from having occupied Belgrade, the Austrians have not yet succeeded in gaining a footing on Servian territory.

Every attempt they have made have failed, the Servian artillery driving them out of range after having sustained great loss.

The banks of the Save and the Danube are littered with Austrian corpses. —Figaro.

Montenegro to Support Servia.

(From Austin West, Special Correspondent of "Lloyd's Weekly News.")

MILAN, Saturday.—A special evening edition of "Il Secolo" makes an announcement from Bucarest that: "Montenegro intends to fight side by side with Servia. Prince Peter of Montenegro, who arrived in Bucarest yesterday, said in an interview:—

"'The union between the two countries will now undoubtedly be realized. I may say that before my departure from Cettinjo a project for a military and financial union was already agreed upon. Each country will retain her own King and her own sovereignty. The union already exists. In fact, all that is now necessary is the formal announcement to the world at large.'"

The same journal's special correspondent at Salonica states that the Græco-Bulgarian commission which is now sitting to settle the boundary dispute has abruptly terminated its sittings through inability to reach an agreement, and another war between the countries looms on the horizon.

Negotiations, however, are still proceeding between Athens and the Roumanian capital to devise means for preserving the Treaty of Bucarest. But the Greek Government, being hard pressed has ordered a general mobilization as a precautionary measure. All State ar-

KING GEORGE'S PEACE EFFORT.

King George V. telegraphs to Tsar of Russia and German Emperor in final desperate effort to save the cause of peace, but only reply is continuance of mobilizations. Page 3.

BRITAIN LOYAL TO HER PLEDGES

Her Attitude Will Not Be Affected by Announcement Italy Will Remain Neutral.

[BY THE HERALD'S SPECIAL WIRE.]

LONDON, Sunday. — London, particularly the districts in which foreigners reside, was seething with excitement last night. Special editions of the evening papers were bought wholesale. Several of the leading newspapers publish special war editions to-day, among them being the "Daily Telegraph," which makes the following announcement:—

"The policy of Great Britain will not be affected in any way by the announcement that Italy has decided to remain neutral on the ground, as she alleges, that no 'casus fœderis' has arisen for her intervention under the precise terms of the Triple Alliance.

"This merely proves how brittle an instrument the treaty is and Italy will have to settle later on with her own partners as to the justification for her action or inaction.

"The French Government has never, directly or indirectly, been led to believe that Great Britain was pledged to any particular method of discharging her obligations to France, although she will remain strictly loyal to the spirit and letter of the understanding.

"His Majesty's Government have not decided if they will interfere, or, if so, when they will interfere in the European war which has now broken out. They have always reserved to themselves the right of determining how we shall play our part in the Triple Entente.

"No particular course of action has been decided upon, although both at the Admiralty and the War Office various schemes of action have been worked out to the smallest detail, including the posting of officers commanding-in-chief, their staffs and their subordinates.

"The Cabinet will decide in the light of events what course England will pursue, but it may be taken for granted she will be absolutely loyal to her friends."

Sir Edward Grey, who was kept late at the Foreign Office yesterday evening, after seeing Mr. Asquith at 10 Downing street, went to Buckingham Palace and was received in audience by the King.

BRITAIN ASKS AMERICA TO TAKE OVER EMBASSIES.

France and Germany Make Similar Request to United States.

WASHINGTON, Saturday. — Germany, Great Britain and France have formally asked the United States to take charge of their Embassies "in case of emergency." American Ambassadors and Ministers abroad have been instructed to accept this trust.—Reuter.

Bankers and Chancellor Confer.

THE NEW YORK HERALD

PRICE: PARIS and FRANCE, 15 Centimes. ABROAD, 25 Centimes.

EUROPEAN EDITION—PARIS.—TUESDAY. AUGUST 4. 1914.

NO 28.470.

GERMANY OFFICIALLY DECLARES WAR UPON FRANCE; BRITISH FLEET PLEDGED TO PROTECT FRENCH COAST

FOR AMERICANS IN PARIS.

Full reports of the various meetings held yesterday in Paris to determine what steps shall be taken to help Americans stranded here will be found on page 2. The discussion of the measures likely to be adopted in London towards the same end is also dealt with.

NEWS OF TO-DAY SUMMARIZED

Meeting at Athens yesterday, the Greek Cabinet decided upon the neutrality of Greece.

The British Postmaster-General has taken over the control of all messages by wireless telegraphy.

General Joffre, the French Commander-in-Chief, left Paris for the frontier, says the "Matin," at 11.45 yesterday morning.

The London Gazette announces that King George has proclaimed a modified moratorium postponing the payment of bills of exchange.

The Compagnie Générale Transatlantique informs the HERALD that the Chicago will leave Havre for New York on Saturday, August 8.

In view of the present crisis, the cross-Channel passenger steamship service between Dieppe and Newhaven has now been entirely suspended.

Before the Government makes its announcement at to-day's session of the Chamber a declaration by the President of the Republic will be read.

As the result of the state of siege now prevailing in Paris, the Prefect of Police has ordered that all cafés and bars in the city are to close at 9 p.m.

By special desire of King George, the Cowes week and the regattas of the Royal Yacht Squadron and the Royal London Yacht Clubs have been abandoned.

After having consulted with the Under-Secretary of State for Fine Arts, the administrative council of the Théâtre-Français has decided to close the theatre until further notice.

The funeral of M. Jean Jaurès, the Socialist leader assassinated in Paris some days ago, will take place this morning, the procession starting from the residence of the deceased, 8 Villa de la Tour, Passy, at midday.

One of yesterday's picturesque incidents was a parade on the Grands Boulevards of a thousand or more employés of the Galeries Lafayette. Almost all of them were girls. They sang as they marched, and carried English and American flags, as well as the predominating French tricolor.

It is understood that the Theatre des Champs-Elysées, which was only recently built as a home for grand opera, will be offered to the French Government as a hospital. The theatre has 200 dressing rooms, supplied with hot and cold water, and can readily be made into an excellent hospital.

The North German Lloyd liner Kronprinzessin Cecilie, which left New York on July 28, will not run the gauntlet of the English Channel, says the HERALD's correspondent at Plymouth, telegraphing on Sunday, and will omit calling there and at Cherbourg. A report was current that the liner had been sighted off the north of Ireland that

Baron von Schœn Officially Notifies State of War Declared by His Government.

DECLARES AVIATORS INVADED GERMANY.

M. Viviani Immediately Afterwards Telegraphs to French Ambassador to Leave Berlin.

Germany officially declared war upon France at 5.45 yesterday evening.

The notification was made by Baron von Schœn, the German Ambassador to France, when he called at the Ministry of Foreign Affairs in Paris yesterday to ask for his passports.

Baron von Schœn declared that his Government had instructed him to inform the Government of the Republic that French aviators had flown over Belgium and that other French aviators had flown over Germany and dropped bombs as far as Nuremberg. He added that this constituted an act of aggression and violation of German territory.

M. Viviani listened in silence to Baron von Schœn's statement, and, when the German Ambassador had finished, replied that it was absolutely false that French aviators had flown over Belgium and Germany and had dropped bombs.

Immediately after this interview, M. Viviani telegraphed to M. Jules Cambon, French Ambassador in Berlin, instructing him to immediately ask for his passports and to make a report on France's protest against the violation of the neutrality of Luxemburg and the ultimatum sent to Belgium.

M. Cambon will leave Berlin to-day. —Matin.

Outstopped His Welcome.

Since acts of war were committed by German troops two days ago, the delay in the recall of the German Ambassador had appeared inexplicable to the great majority of French people, to whom Baron von Schœn appeared to be decidedly outstopping his welcome.

The Ambassador himself seemed conscious of this feeling, for not only did he take care to proceed to the Quai d'Orsay in as inconspicuous a manner as possible, but he also applied to the authorities to detail a policeman to accompany him in his automobile.

Baron von Schœn's departure from Paris last night was a solemn affair. The German Ambassador left the Embassy last after a vast collection of luggage had gone off in motor wagons and other vehicles. A few minutes before ten o'clock, wearing a soft felt hat and

Sir Edward Grey Declares British Fleet Will Act Immediately Any Such Move Is Made.

BELGIUM APPEALS FOR BRITISH PROTECTION.

London Government Will Be Forced to Act Energetically if Germans Menace Belgian Integrity.

[BY THE HERALD'S SPECIAL WIRE.]

LONDON, Tuesday.—Sir Edward Grey made this important announcement in the House of Commons yesterday:—

"On Sunday afternoon I gave the French Ambassador the following statement: 'I am authorised to give the assurance that if the German Fleet comes into the Channel or through the North Sea to undertake any hostile operations against the French coast or shipping, we will give France all the assistance in our power.'"

Never within memory of any living Englishman has Parliament held such important sessions as those of yesterday, when the entire United Kingdom hung on every word with breathless interest.

The sessions were called for the purpose of considering the financial situation and the unparalleled plight of international affairs. Sir Edward Grey's statement regarding the entire situation as it has been forced upon England since the delivery to Servia of the Austro-Hungarian ultimatum was one of the most remarkable speeches ever delivered in Parliament.

The very air of London was athrill with the importance of yesterday's action following the bewildering lightening-like changes of the last three days.

The great dominating fact of the situation and one that will apparently control it is the action of Germany in proceeding to violate the neutrality of Belgium which is protected by the treaty. To this neutrality France pledged herself the other day, while Germany had declined to make any disclosure of her intentions. The appeal made by Belgium to England to assist her and the bold rejection by the Belgian Cabinet of Germany's demands that she facilitate the passage of German troops into France have proven of tremendous importance. Belgium's bold defiance of the Kaiser has been one of the most splendid things in the preludes to the international war.

The view taken by England is that if the neutrality of Belgium goes, so goes her independence. Following Belgium will surely pass the neutrality of Holland and her independence, and after Holland, Denmark, directly opposite Great Britain.

Proceedings in the House of Commons have been patriotic and enthusi-

AMERICAN AMBULANCE OFFERED TO FRANCE

The proposed American Ambulance was organized yesterday afternoon, under the official patronage of the American Ambassador, Mr. Myron T. Herrick, and the auspices of the American Hospital of Paris.

At the request of the American Ambassador, Mr. Myron T. Herrick, a special meeting of the Board of Governors and of the Medical Board of the American Hospital of Paris was held yesterday afternoon. It was unanimously resolved that the Hospital would continue, as in the past, to take every means to care for all Americans needing its services.

It was also learned yesterday that the American Hospital authorities propose to equip and maintain at their expense, as a hospital for French soldiers, the Lycée Pasteur, if the French Government will turn it over to them for that purpose. The Lycée Pasteur is in Neuilly, not far from the American Hospital.

what we will do, she leaves her northern and western coasts unprotected and at the mercy of the German fleet coming down the Channel to do as it pleases in a war which is a war of life and death.

France Entitled to Support.

"Well," went on Sir Edward, "we felt strongly that France was entitled to know, and to know at once, whether or not in the event of an attack upon her unprotected northern and western coasts she could depend upon British support, and in that emergency and under these appalling circumstances, yesterday afternoon, I gave the French Ambassador the following statement: 'I am authorized to give an assurance that if the German fleet comes into the Channel or through the North Sea to undertake hostile operations against the French coasts, the British fleet will give all the protection in its power.'

"That assurance," explained Sir Edward, "was subject to the contingency that that action by the German fleet took place. It was not a declaration of war on our part.

"I understand that the German Government—I cannot state formally whether it is a fact—would be prepared, if we would pledge ourselves to neutrality, to agree that its fleet would not attack the northern and western coasts of France. (Some cries of "Hear! Hear!")

"I have only heard that," said Sir Edward, "shortly before I came to the House, but (with dramatic emphasis and rapping the table) it is far too narrow an engagement." (Loud and prolonged cheers.)

There was a more serious consideration, continued Sir Edward—the question of the neutrality of Belgium. When mobilization was beginning last week he telegraphed both to Paris and Berlin to say it was essential for the British Government to know whether the French and German Governments respectively were prepared to undertake an engagement to respect the neutrality of Belgium.

The French Government replied: "We are resolved to respect the neutrality of Belgium, and it will only be in the event of another Power violating it that France would be forced to act in her own defence."

the Opposition in any measures they found it necessary to take.

Mr. Ramsay Macdonald, leader of the Labor Party, said he thought that Sir Edward Grey was wrong, but if the Government confined the question to that of Belgian neutrality, the Labour Party would support it.

Mr. John Redmond followed with his dramatic statement that the Nationalist and Unionist volunteers were prepared to defend the coasts of Ireland.

The remainder of the Message had not been received at the time of going to press.

Britain Recalls Reservists.

NEW YORK, Sunday.—The British Consul-General has received instructions to call up all the reservists of the army and navy residing in the United States and to send them home as quickly as possible. —Matin.

TWO BRITISH STEAMERS SEIZED BY GERMANS.

Vessels Are Captured in the Kiel Canal.

[BY THE HERALD'S SPECIAL WIRE.]

LONDON, Monday.—A sensation was created last night by the report that Germany had seized two British-owned vessels in the Kiel Canal. The Wilson liner Castro, a vessel of 1,228 tons, bound from Dantzig to Hull, was captured by the Germans in the canal, and ordered to Hamburg. It is understood that the liner had no passengers on board. The capture of the vessel is confirmed at the Wilson Line offices in Hull, but no details are furnished.

It is further reported that the British steamer Saxon, which left King's Lynn on Thursday with a cargo of coal for Brunsbüttel, on the Kiel Canal, has been seized by the German naval authorities and taken into Cuxhaven.

AUSTRIANS EMBARRASSED BY MUTINY AND MINES.

Insubordinate Czechs Decimated, and Hungarian Regiment Annihilated.

(SPECIAL TO THE HERALD.)

ROME, Monday.—News has been re-

Germany, After Protésting of Her Good Intentions to Belgium, Allows Troops to Violate Frontier.

VIRTUAL ULTIMATUM SENT TO BRUSSELS.

Belgian Government, Rejects Preposterous Demand in Dignified but Firm Language.

(SPECIAL TO THE HERALD.)

BRUSSELS, Monday.—At 3.50 a.m. to-day German troops crossed the Belgian frontier at Vise, in the Province of Liège.

The German Minister has presented to the Belgian Government a Note asking whether Belgium is willing to negotiate conditions for the passage of the German army through the Belgian territory?

The Note adds that if a satisfactory reply has not been received by the German Government before seven o'clock this evening the troops will force their way through Belgium.

The King is holding a Council of Ministers, at which the reply to be made to the German Note is being discussed.

The inhabitants of Brussels, who are still asleep at this early hour, are as yet ignorant of this crossing of the frontier by a power whose Minister only yesterday issued a statement to the Brussels press declaring that his Government would never contemplate the violation of Belgian territory.

BELGIUM WILL NOT COMPLY WITH GERMANY'S ULTIMATUM.

Government Announces Country Will Energetically Defend Its Neutrality.

(SPECIAL TO THE HERALD.)

BRUSSELS, Monday.—The German ultimatum to Belgium explained the forward march of German troops by alleged preparations on the part of the French to invade Belgium along the line of Givet and Namur.

The reply of the Belgian Government was as follows: "We are very surprised at such a statement after the formal assurances we have received that France will respect our neutrality.

"Moreover, Belgium has too strong a sense of its duty, of its dignity and its interests, which it has made every effort to defend since 1830, to accede to the German demand.

"She refuses definitely to facilitate German operations and protests against all violation of her territory.

"Belgium is resolved energetically to defend her neutrality, which has been formally guaranteed by treaties, and notably by his Majesty, the King of Prussia."

The seat of the Belgian Government is to be transferred immediately to Antwerp. It is believed that the King will leave for the front.

FOR AMERICANS IN LONDON.

Various meetings were held yesterday both in London and Paris to decide what measures shall be taken to assist American citizens stranded owing to the outbreak of hostilities. Full reports will be found on page 2.

SWISS WILL FIGHT FOR NEUTRALITY

Compact Force of 100,000 Men Is Distributed Along Frontiers Likely to Be Threatened.

(SPECIAL TO THE HERALD.)

GENEVA, Monday.—The mobilization of the Swiss army is now practically complete, and the compact force of 100,000 men is distributed along the frontiers that are likely to be crossed or threatened, especially those on the German and French sides. The Swiss Confederation is resolved that the country's neutrality shall not be interfered with, and is prepared to resist any movement that might embroil the country in any way in the general European war.

In the matter of finance and food supply, the situation is already regarded with much less anxiety and excitement than in the first days of the war rumors. Gold and silver had disappeared from sight so quickly that there was almost no business transacted in the shops because the merchants could not or would not give change. The issue of 20-franc banknotes on Friday and of 5-franc notes to-day has eased the situation so much that silver is again in fairly general circulation.

As for food supplies, it is officially estimated that without importation Switzerland has enough food on hand or in sight for six months at least. Nevertheless, certain commodities, such as potatoes, have already advanced in price.

The hotels, or most of them, have undertaken to care for their visitors who may find themselves in money difficulties, but they have cut down their menus considerably and have warned visitors that the fare may become limited and inferior before the war is over. Nevertheless, many Americans are remaining in Switzerland, believing it to be the safest place for them in Europe. Opinions on the probable outcome of the war are naturally varied, but the general trend of opinion is that Germany has this time undertaken a contract somewhat too big for her.

FUND MAY BE CREATED TO HELP AMERICANS ABROAD.

[BY COMMERCIAL CABLE TO THE HERALD.]

NEW YORK, Monday.—The HERALD's Washington correspondent telegraphs that President Wilson and Mr. Bryan are organizing measures to assist Americans to return from Europe.

They have under consideration the idea of creating a fund which the Department of State would distribute among Americans needing help. It is proposed that relatives of the latter should deposit money with the Department, which then would issue orders for its payment to the persons concerned by

MAP TO ILLUSTRATE GREAT BATTLE IN BELGIUM AND OPERATIONS ON THE EASTERN FRONTIER

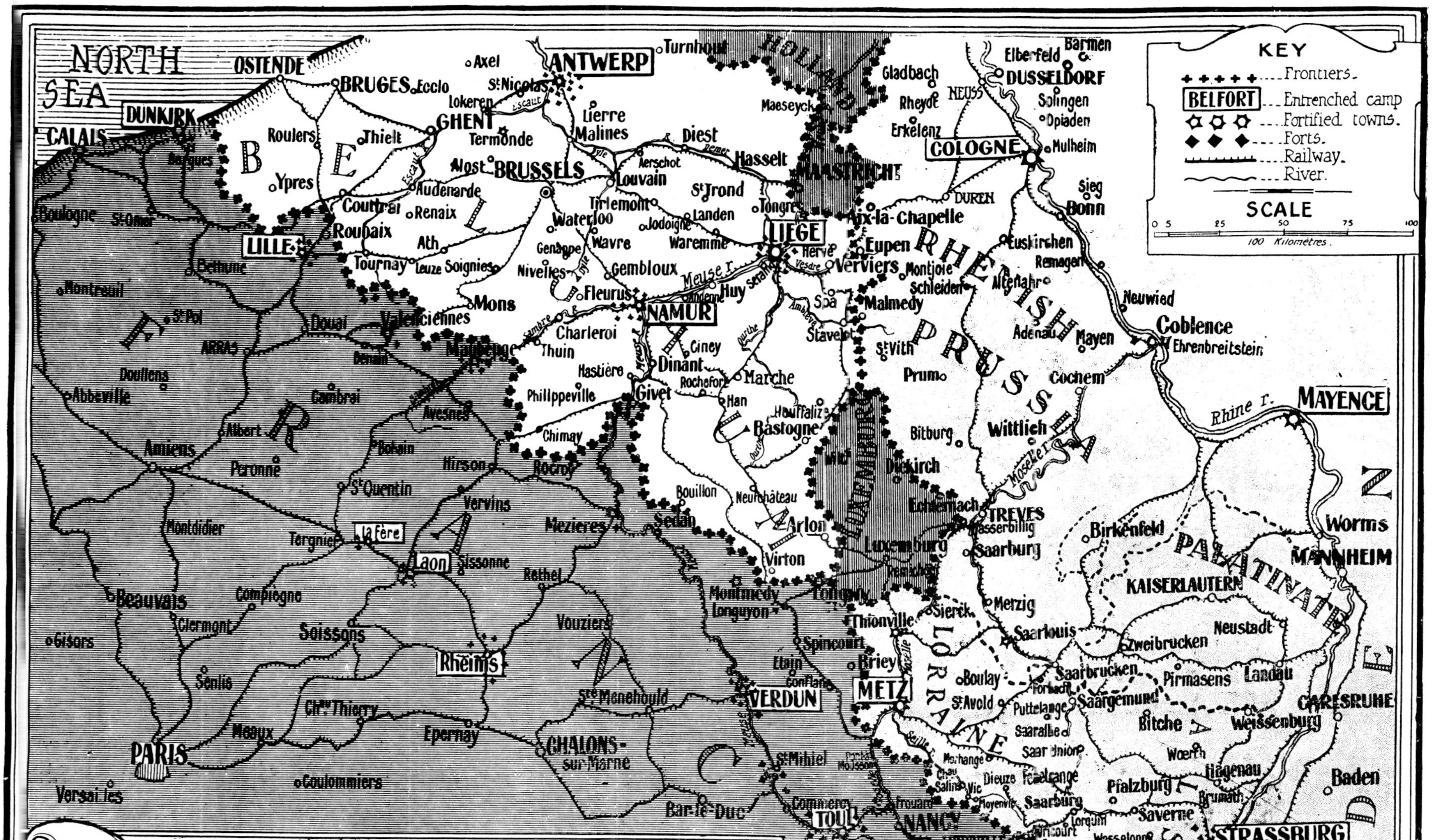

MAP TO ILLUSTRATE OPERATIONS ON RUSSO-GERMAN-RUSSO-AUSTRIAN AND AUSTRO-SERVIAN FRONTIERS

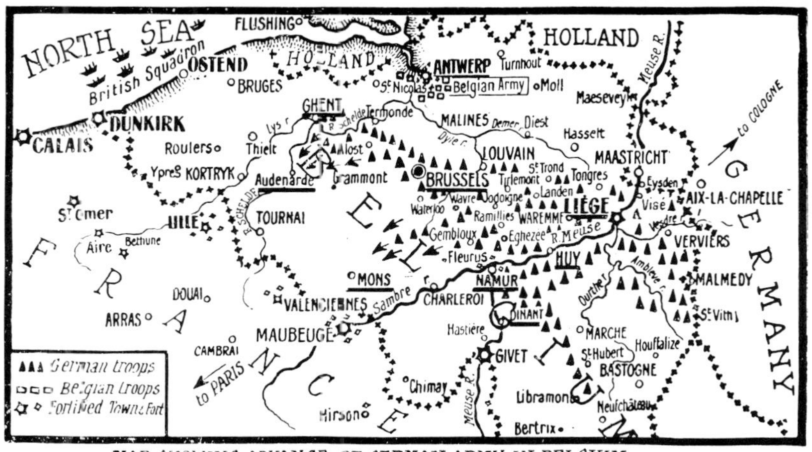

MAP SHOWING ADVANCE OF GERMAN ARMY IN BELGIUM.

MONDAY, JANUARY 11, 1915.

In the Trenches With Britain's First-Class Fighting Men

The DEPTH OF A COMMUNICATION TRENCH

Not All the Comforts of Home, but They Are Fine Places When the "Jack Johnsons" Are Working.

BRITISH SOLDIERS IN THE TRENCHES

LIFE IN A "DUG-OUT"

PHOTOS FROM THE SPHERE

"Eye-Witness" has described the remarkable trenches in which the allied forces have resisted every effort of the Germans to advance. In one of these trenches, which is in the nature of a "dug-out," officers are seen at dinner, in the shelter, which boasts of couches, bookshelves and other fittings. Behind another trench the reader can see British soldiers screened by a vegetable crop in front of their position, and the depth of the trenches is clearly shown by the figure of an English officer in one of them.

THURSDAY, OCTOBER 15, 1914.

Marked Differences Exist Between French and German Aeroplanes

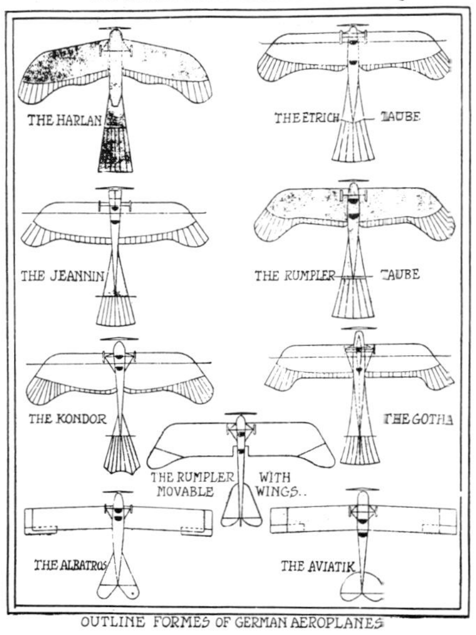

OUTLINE FORMES OF GERMAN AEROPLANES

War Office Issues Note to Enable Parisians to Distinguish Enemy's Biplanes and Monoplanes.

In view of the recent audacious flights above Paris of German bomb-dropping aeroplanes, the French War Office has issued an official note calling the attention of Parisians to characteristic differences between French and German machines, in order that the chances of their being confounded with one another may be reduced to a minimum. The note reads as follows:—

(1) All German machines, whether biplanes or monoplanes, are built with the body encased in canvas, and consequently all machines not so encased, and therefore, transparent, are not German.

(2) Regarded horizontally, all German biplanes are built in the form of a "V," that is to say, the extremities of the wings slope backwards towards the tail.

(3) All German monoplanes have the wing tips sloping backwards at a sharp angle.

(4) All German aeroplanes have the propellers in front of the wings.

"LES ALLIÉS"

LES CHIENS DE GUERRE

SATURDAY, FEBRUARY 27, 1915.

AN ENGLISH VIEW OF UNCLE SAM'S POSITION.

CAN HE STAY THERE?

THE NEW YORK HERALD

PRICE: Paris, Seine, Seine-et-Oise, 10c.; FRANCE, 15c. ABROAD, 25c. — EUROPEAN EDITION—PARIS, THURSDAY, JANUARY 21, 1915. — PRIX: Paris, Seine, Seine-et-Oise, 10c.; FRANCE, 15c. ETRANGER, 25c.

ZEPPELIN RAID AIMED AT THE LIVES OF GREAT BRITAIN'S KING AND QUEEN RESULTS IN MURDER FROM THE SKIES IN UNDEFENDED ENGLISH COAST TOWNS

A VIEW OF THE SMOKE FRONT AT YARMOUTH

THE WEST FRONT SANDRINGHAM HOUSE ONE OF KING GEORGE'S COUNTRY HOMES.

NIGHT FLIGHT OF A ZEPPELIN AIRSHIP

TWO BOMBS DROPPED CLOSE TO SANDRINGHAM

Fortunately King George, the Kaiser's Cousin, and Queen Mary Had Left Their Norfolk Home for London the Day Before.

(SPECIAL TO THE HERALD.)

LONDON, Wednesday.—The long-talked of Zeppelin air raid upon England is an accomplished fact. German airships, probably starting from Cuxhaven, came up over the North Sea to strike coward blows at undefended towns in East Anglia, in the dark of Tuesday night, on their way to bombard England's King and Queen, at Sandringham, their Norfolk country home.

The raiders dropped bombs at Yarmouth, Sheringham, King's Lynn, Beeston, Dersingham, Grimston and Snettisham, with the result that several persons were killed and several injured, women and children among the number.

Murder from the sky in Antwerp; murder from the seas in Scarborough and Hartlepool and other unfortified towns on the English East coast; murder, rapine and cruelty in Belgium and northern France; all are a fitting prelude to the wanton killing in East Anglia that has but added another item to the account which German "Kultur" has to settle with civilisation.

But the Kaiser's agents went farther than ever on Tuesday night when they attempted to assassinate the King of England, their master's cousin, and Queen Mary. Two bombs were dropped at Sandringham, but fortunately the King and Queen and other members of the Royal Family, who had been stopping at the Castle there, had returned to London some time before the Zeppelin arrived.

The first place to suffer from the raid was Yarmouth. A hostile airship flew over the town at 8.15 p.m., on Tuesday, and dropped several bombs, which killed two people, a man and a woman, and damaged many houses.

Another Zeppelin reached the coast at Sheringham at 8.35 and also dropped bombs.

The next attack was made, presumably by the same airship, upon the King's residence at Sandringham. Two bombs were dropped here, but fortunately neither struck the royal residence.

Proceeding to King's Lynn, the Zeppelin dropped several more bombs,

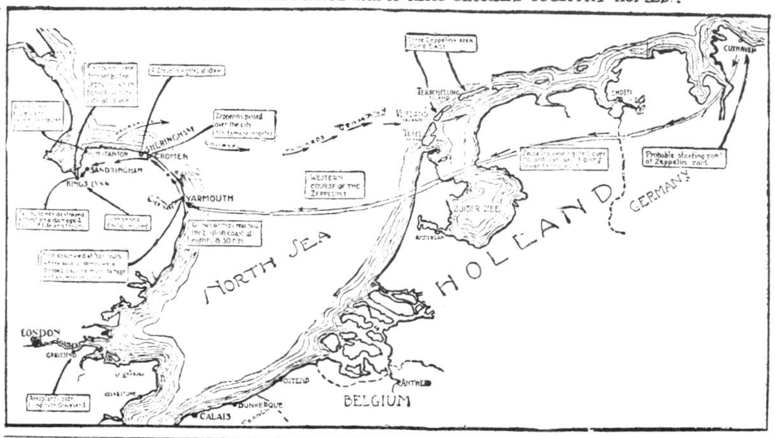

mediately took refuge there. Automobiles and trams were held up by sentries and ordered to put out their lights.

At ten o'clock came news that another air craft was expected, and at a quarter to twelve this news was confirmed, as an aeroplane passed over the town from inland. It did not drop any bombs, however.

A survey of the damaged property in Yarmouth to-day shows damage estimated at several thousand pounds. Many offices on the Fish Wharf were wrecked and the roof of one building was demolished.

Other bombs fell on the racecourse and the grand stand to-day presents the appearance of having been riddled by fragments of shell.

Another bomb fell on a row of cottages

> **"KEEP UNDER COVER!"**
>
> **What Not To Do.** — "People streamed out of their houses into the streets, the alarm being great." —Report of Yarmouth raid.
>
> **What You Should Do.**—"The civil population are warned to keep under cover, preferably in basements, upon hearing the sound of firing by guns or of explosives."—Scotland Yard order, issued December 28.

square with a wound in his chest. He was taken to hospital.

The town was in complete darkness, and it was difficult to ascertain definitely the total number of casualties. So far as is known they were limited to the three persons mentioned.

Fired Upon Air Craft.

Close by was stationed a sentry, who said that one bomb fell near him, but did no damage, and only struck the quay. He immediately fired on the air craft. All who were in the neighborhood at the time stated that they saw a high burst of flame and then heard a terrific report.

Premises occupied by Mr. J. E. Festell, a builder, in Lancaster road, suffered severely, and the roof was blown

NON-COMBATANTS KILLED AT KING'S LYNN AND YARMOUTH

Woman, a Boy, and a Baby Among the Known Victims of This Latest Application of the Kaiser's Doctrine of "Frightfulness."

that its fuse had become detached during its descent. The bomb which passed through the house was of a round shape and about three and a half to four inches in diameter.

Sheringham was in almost total darkness at the time of the attack. The Zeppelin and its bombs made a terrific noise and caused a great sensation.

Another bomb was dropped at Beeston, near Cromer, and this also failed to effect its sinister mission.

After dropping its bombs the Zeppelin made seaward, and people who had turned out in large numbers watched it disappear.

It is not definitely known what route was followed by the Zeppelin whose crew attempted to assassinate the King and Queen. At about half-past ten a bomb was dropped at Dersingham, a village about eight miles from King's Lynn and forming part of King George's West Norfolk estate.

Another bomb was dropped at Snettisham, a favorite resort of Queen Alexandra during her summer visits to Sandringham.

Missed Castle Twice.

Two bombs were then dropped at Sandringham, but both of them missed Sandringham House by a considerable distance.

An air-ship is also reported to have passed over Hunstanton and Cromer, though no bombs appear to have been dropped at either of these places.

The rumor that a Zeppelin was brought

NEW YORK HERALD, published under the heading, "Another Slaughter of the Innocents." The editorial commenting on the air raid, says:—

"Is it the madness of despair or just plain, everyday madness that prompted the Germans to select for attack peaceful undefended resorts on England's east coast? What can Germany hope to gain from these wanton attacks on undefended places and slaughter of the innocents? Certainly not the good opinion of the peoples of neutral nations, for these know that the rules of civilized warfare call for notice of bombardment even of places fortified and defended."

The following are extracts from editorials in the London evening papers:—

"Pall Mall Gazette."

The "Pall Mall Gazette" says: "The enemy despises not only the ordinary conventions of war, but also the instincts of humanity, which are evident even in the hearts of savages."

"Westminster Gazette."

The "Westminster Gazette" says: "There is no military purpose in this raid. It was undertaken to raise the spirits of the German people, which seem to need it, or to create a panic in our country."

"Evening Standard."

The "Evening Standard" says: "The raid of the Zeppelins on Yarmouth once more proves the absurdity of the claims made by their inventor regarding their efficacy. The only result will be an ex-

THE NEW YORK HERALD

PRICE: Paris, Seine, Seine-et-Oise, 10c.; FRANCE, 15c. ABROAD, 25c. — EUROPEAN EDITION—PARIS, SATURDAY, MAY 8, 1915. — PRIX: Paris, Seine, Seine-et-Oise, 10c.; FRANCE, 15c. ETRANGER, 25c.

THE LUSITANIA SUNK OFF THE IRISH COAST BY GERMAN PIRATES

Torpedoed 8 Miles from the Head of Kinsale by Submarine and All the Ships in Queenstown Harbor Raced to Rescue of Passengers.

MANY WELL-KNOWN AMERICANS WERE ON THE ILL-FATED VESSEL

Despite the Murderous Threats of the German Embassy in Washington, Mr. Alfred G. Vanderbilt and More than Two Hundred Others Refused to Cancel Passage.

FATE OF PASSENGERS IS UNKNOWN; NEW YORK REPORT SAYS ALL SAVED

(SPECIAL TO THE HERALD.)

LONDON, Saturday.—The giant Cunard liner Lusitania, with 1,978 souls on board, including hundreds of American citizens—scores of them famous on both sides of the Atlantic—was torpedoed and sunk by a German submarine off the Irish coast at 2.15 o'clock yesterday afternoon.

A despatch sent from Liverpool at 9.30 says that the Lusitania was sunk without warning. A number of boats with rescued passengers are now making for the coast.

As the Lusitania sank, her boats, which there had been no time to launch, swung from their davits and floated on the sea for a few moments after the ship's hull had disappeared.

The Lusitania remained afloat twenty minutes after she was torpedoed.

The first news of this latest and greatest outrage by the German pirates was given out by the Press Bureau at 5.28 yesterday afternoon, when the following statement was issued:—

"The Naval Censors have passed the statement that the Lusitania has been torpedoed. She went down at 2.35 p.m."

The Liverpool "Evening Express" is officially informed that the Cunarder was torpedoed and sunk eight miles south by west of the Old Head of Kinsale, on the south coast of Ireland, by a submarine.

The Lusitania had on board 290 saloon, 662 second class and 361 third class passengers, as well as a crew of 665 men.

Among the most prominent were: Mr. Alfred G. Vanderbilt, Mr. Charles Frohman, Sir Hugh Lane, Lady Mackworth, Miss Jessie Tait Smith, Mr. and Mrs. Montagu T. Grant, Lady Allan, Mr. and Mrs. Paul Compton, Mr. and Mrs. William S. Hodges, Dr. J. O. Orr, Major and Mrs. F. Warren Pearl, Commander J. Foster Stockhouse, Lady Marksworth and Dr. F. S. Pearson.

The Cunard Company was informed of the disaster to the Lusitania by the following wireless telegram:—

"Come quickly. Big list."

The Cunard Company during the afternoon published the following bul-

THE GIANT CUNARD LINER LUSITANIA TORPEDOED OFF THE OLD HEAD OF KINSALE IRELAND.

CAPTAIN DAVID DOW COMMANDER OF THE LUSITANIA

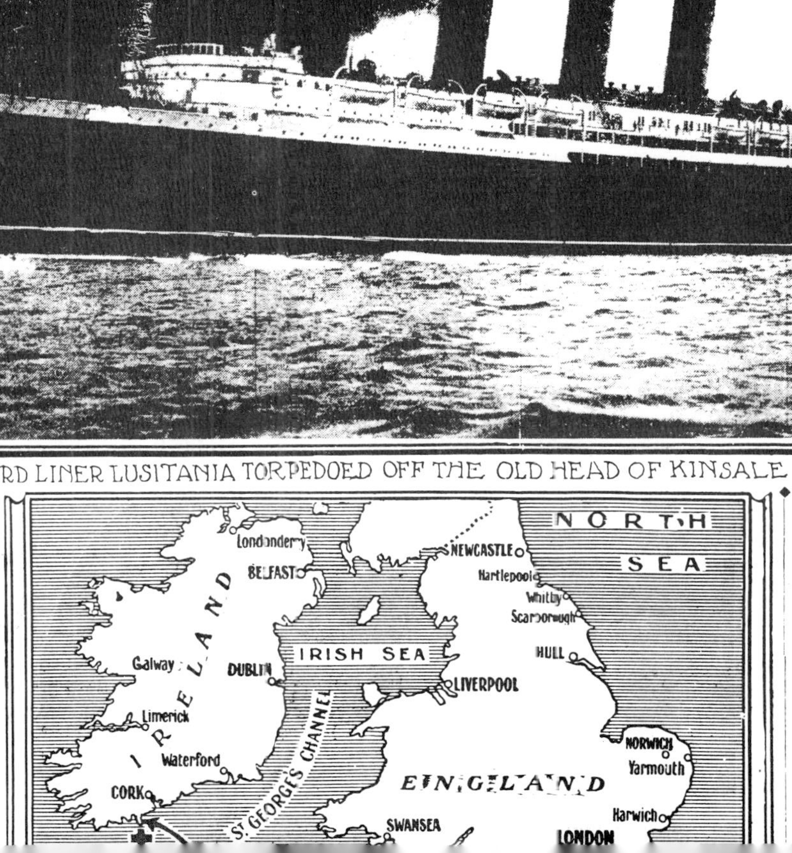

MR. ALFRED G. VANDERBILT

THE NEW YORK HERALD

PRICE: Paris, Seine, Seine-et-Oise, 10c.; FRANCE, 15c. ABROAD, 25c. — EUROPEAN EDITION—PARIS, MONDAY, MAY 24, 1915. — PRIX: Paris, Seine, Seine-et-Oise, 10c.; FRANCE, 15c. ETRANGER, 25c.

ITALY AT WAR! HOSTILITIES WITH AUSTRIA-HUNGARY HAVE COMMENCED

Barone Sonnino, Minister of Foreign Affairs, Hands Text of Declaration to Baron Macchio, Austro-Hungarian Ambassador, Together with Passport, Giving Him 24 Hours To Leave Country.

NOTIFICATION IN VIENNA DELAYED OWING TO CUT TELEGRAPH WIRES

In the Declaration of War, Italy Arraigns Austria for Duplicity During the Negotiations and Excoriates the Government of the Dual Monarchy for Its Oppression of Italians in the Stolen Territory.

(SPECIAL TO THE HERALD.)

ROME, Sunday.—HOSTILITIES BETWEEN ITALY AND AUSTRIA-HUNGARY HAVE BEGUN.

The text of the declaration of war was telegraphed yesterday to Duca d'Avarna, Italian Ambassador in Vienna, after the Cabinet Council.

As the telegraph wires to Vienna have been cut, however, Duca d'Avarna did not receive the telegram.

Therefore, Barone Sonnino, Italian Minister of Foreign Affairs, handed Baron Macchio, Austro-Hungarian Ambassador here, the text of the declaration at half-past three this afternoon, together with a passport, allowing him twenty-four hours to leave the country.

The Government's telegram eventually reached Duca d'Avarna in Vienna and he immediately communicated the text of the declaration to Baron de Burian, Austro-Hungarian Minister of Foreign Affairs.

King Victor Emmanuel Puts His Signature to Declaration of War

Ministerial Council Is Summoned to Confer on Austrian Note Received from Duca d'Avarna.

(SPECIAL TO THE HERALD.)

LONDON, Sunday.—Italy's preparations are complete.

The text of the declaration of war was **signed** by King Victor Emmanuel early this afternoon.

The Italian "Official Gazette" yesterday published, according to telegrams from Rome, a series of decrees relating:

1. To measures of an economical order tending to facilitate credit during the period of war;

2. To measures concerning the opening of closed correspondence transmitted through the post in order to verify whether it contains military news; the suspension of the parcels post service for the ordinary public.

The "Official Gazette" also publishes a series of measures concerning public safety, prohibiting particularly public meetings of all kinds and possible measures relating to recognized associations for the manufacture, introduction and sale of arms and explosive material; measures relating to the authorization for carrying firearms and to public entertainments, cafés, furnished rooms, etc.; a decree for the issue of postcards free of postage and envelopes with special stamps for correspondence destined for the army and navy.

Finally, there is a decree giving power to the Government to suspend, modify or limit telegraphic, telephonic and wireless services, inland or with foreign countries, as may be considered necessary.

General Conte Luigi Cadorna, head of the Italian General Staff; Signor Salandra and Barone Sonnino have also come to an agreement as to the organization of press services in war-time. The Minister of War, General Zuppelli, has decided that no special correspondents will be allowed to accompany the armies in the field. A Press Bureau will be installed and under control of the military authorities.

General Cadorna left Rome by the 9.5 express this evening for the front.

Contrary to what had been announced, a semi-official note states that the report that the Government would not permit the representatives of belligerent Powers at the Vatican to remain in Rome is devoid of foundation.

No communiqué was issued after the important Ministerial Council held yesterday morning, and all sorts of rumors were current during the day.

Yesterday was a busy day at the Consulta. Barone Sonnino, Minister of Foreign Affairs, went to the Palazzo Braschi in the morning, but he was back before eleven o'clock. While he was away, M. de Giers, the newly-appointed Russian Ambassador, was closeted with the Secretary of the Ministry.

A little before noon, Naby Bey, the Turkish Ambassador, came to see Barone Sonnino and remained with him for more than an hour.

Then came M. Barrère, the French Ambassador, who as he left again was cheered by the soldiers on duty in the courtyard. To their cries of "Long live France!" he replied "Long live the Italian army!"

The Spanish Ambassador was the next visitor at the Consulta.

Then, at half-past three o'clock an automobile drove up with Prince Bülow, who disappeared inside the Italian Foreign Office. He was immediately received by Barone Sonnino and remained with him until a quarter to four. As he left Prince Bülow seemed very excited and jumped hastily into his automobile.

Nearly an hour later, at twenty minutes to five, another automobile brought Baron Macchio. When he in his turn left he also appeared anxious, and the rumor immediately spread that the two Ambassadors had been handed their passports.

All Italy is delirious with joy at the prospect of going to war and voluntary enlistments increase in number every day.

Every prince of the House of Savoy will be in the fighting line.

The "Popolo Romano" publishes a list of Roman noblemen who will take part in the war either as volunteers or as regulars.

Among the names are those of the Mayor of Rome, Principe Colonna, and his three sons; another Principe Colonna and his two sons Duca Sforza and his son, Principe di Piombino and his son, Principe Aldobrandini, the brothers Principi Lancellotti, Principe Alfieri, the two Principi Caffarelli, Principe Potenziani, the four Principi Ruspoli, the two Principi Caetani di Sermoneta, the three brothers Principi Rospigliosi and Principe Cenot. There are also the names of countless dukes, marquises, counts and barons. The list in fact contains the names of all the liberal and clerical aristocracy.

Signor Eduardo Scarfoglio, editor of the "Mattino," and his three sons have enlisted as volunteers in the army. Of all Italian newspapers the "Mattino" was until recently the strongest advocate of neutrality and it is now the warmest upholder of the interventionist policy.

Duca d'Aosta, cousin-german of the King and elder brother of the Duke of the Abruzzi, who is to take over the command of the Italian fleet, and Duchessa d'Aosta, who is herself an experienced nurse, have placed their Palazzo Cisterna in Turin at the disposal of the Red Cross to be converted into a hospital.

The Holy See has put at the disposal of the military authorities four huge seminaries, and the Vatican hospital of Santa Maria has been offered fully equipped to the Italian Red Cross.

Princess Nathalie of Montenegro, sister-in-law of the Queen of Italy, has volunteered as a nurse in the Italian Red Cross.

Both Prince Bülow and Baron Macchio have informed the Consulta of their requirements in regard to the special trains which will take them out of Italy.

The Austro-Hungarian Consul-General left Rome this evening.

Austria Replies.

This morning Barone Sonnino received a report from Duca d'Avarna in Vienna of the Austrian Note. The Note arrived late owing to the direct telegraph wires being cut.

A Ministerial Council was instantly summoned to discuss the contents of the Note.

Baron de Burian, Austro-Hungarian Minister for Foreign Affairs, has handed to Duca d'Avarna, Italian Ambassador in Vienna, says an Amsterdam despatch, a Note in reply to the communication announcing the annulment by Italy of the Triple Alliance.

The Austro-Hungarian Government, says the Note, is painfully impressed by the step taken by the Italian Government to end the Alliance, which was for so many years a guarantee of peace and of the interests of both countries.

The Note reminds Italy of the preliminary history of the war and of the history of the negotiations between Austria and Italy. During these negotiations Austria was always prepared to come to an agreement with Italy, and offered concessions so great that they were only justified by the wish of the Austrian Government to maintain the Alliance.

Austrian goodwill and readiness to placate were beyond any doubt, declares the Note, and the statement by the Italian Government that there was no hope of reaching an understanding was in no sense justified. But an agreement was only possible if both parties honorably wished to come to an understanding.

The Austro-Hungarian Government, therefore, refuses to accept the statement of the Italian Government that the latter claims a free hand to denounce the treaty. Such action would conflict with the obligation agreed to in the treaty of December 5, 1912, to continue the Alliance until July, 1920. Austria refuses all responsibility for the arbitrary breach of these obligations.

Despite the protestations contained in this Note, despatches from Rome show that Austria is prepared for war.

The bridge at Caffaro has been mined and two Austrian guns are now directed at this important point.

Great masses of German and Austro-Hungarian troops, too, are reported to be concentrated in the Adige Valley.

AUSTRIANS DESTROY BRIDGES AND RAILWAYS AT FRONTIER.

40,000 Fresh Troops Are Reported in the Trentino.

VERONA, Sunday.—It is reported from Peri that, even on this frontier, all communications have been interrupted. The Austrian authorities have ordered that the rails on the railway between Vosine and Borghetto be pulled up.

A bridge has been destroyed by dynamite. Another very important bridge over the high road has been destroyed

NEWS OF THE DAY IN BRIEF FORM.

During the last raid of the Allies' aviators above Bruges ten German soldiers were killed and a great number wounded.

General Chomer, formerly a member of the French Upper War Council, died at Versailles yesterday. He was born at Metz in 1849.

The death roll of the Carlisle railway disaster is reported to be 170. A story of the wreck, the main details of which were published in the HERALD yesterday, will be found on page 3 this morning.

According to a Note issued by the Ministry of War, the French military authorities have been informed that special trains and other means of conveyance were to be organized to carry travellers to the battlefields in the neighborhood of Paris. These excursions, on account of the inconvenience they would cause, will not be permitted.

Peking advices to Tokio say that the United States Government has warned China to see to it that the treaty with Japan does not affect the rights of Americans in China.

Three bombs were thrown at noon yesterday by a German aeroplane at Château-Thierry. The first two caused slight material damage; the third, according to the "Figaro," killed a factory workman, who leaves five children.

Brigandage is rife in the region of Ispahan, Persia. The Teheran mail has been pillaged. A carriage in which the Governor-General of Teheran, M. Paquet, the Controller of Finances, and his son were travelling was riddled with bullets, but the travellers escaped unhurt. Gendarmes have placed machine-guns in the streets of Ispahan.

MAP OF ITALO-AUSTRIAN FRONTIER SHOWING MOUNTAIN PASSES AND PRINCIPAL BORDER TOWNS.

KING OF ITALY AND HIS STAFF

Italian Government Explains Its Reasons for Entering Into War

BRITISH SMASHING THE TURKS BY SEA AND ON THE LAND

Repulse Two Divisions Under Liman von Sanders Pasha and Sink Two Torpedo Boats and Transports.

The following communiqué was issued by the French Press Bureau last night, concerning the operations in the Dardanelles:—

"Two Turkish divisions, personally commanded by General Liman von Sanders, made a furious attack against the British troops near Kala Tepe.

"The enemy was completely repulsed and suffered very heavy losses.

"At the same time our Allies gained another success on sea, where one of their submarines sunk two torpedo boats and two transports, one of which was carrying troops.

"In the southern region of the Peninsula our troops are separated from the Turkish trenches by only a few mètres. They have made considerable progress despite the very solid organization of the enemy."

BOMBARDMENT OF NARROWS CONTINUES SUCCESSFULLY.

Allies' Efforts Mostly Directed Against Forts on European Side.

(SPECIAL TO THE HERALD.)

LONDON, Sunday.—The bombardment of the Dardanelles was continued throughout Friday. The principal effort of the Allies is being made against the forts on the European side. The operations are said to be progressing successfully.

Athens advices state that mutiny has broken out in one of the regiments of the Smyrna garrison. A large number of officers and soldiers took refuge on the Allied warships cruising before the town. In order to prevent the rest of the regiment from following, the Turkish authorities have sunk all the small sailing ships and all rowboats in the ports of Vurla and Gulbakshe.

FIGHTING IN THE CAUCASUS.

(SPECIAL TO THE HERALD.)

LONDON, Sunday.—The Army of the Caucasus reports that in the direction of the coast the fusilade continues.

In the direction of Van a fight is going on between Russian troops and the Turkish troops in the region of the Shussag Pass and Hukub.

From the evidence of Russian soldiers who have escaped the Germans' clutches, it appears the Germans are throwing the Russian wounded into the San.

Fever Follows Operation Upon

ALLIES WINNING THE BIG BATTLE OF THE NORTH

French and British Troops Are Gaining Ground and Inflicting Heavy Losses on Enemy.

In all the region north of Arras, following the signal repulse of the enemy on Saturday night, a great battle is being fought, and the official communiqué states that the fighting is being marked by extreme violence at certain points. The tide of victory is flowing with the Allies. The French are inflicting terrible punishment on the enemy north-east of the Chapel of Notre-Dame de Lorette, and the toll of German dead on the battle front to the north of Neuville-Saint-Vaast is very heavy.

The British continue to advance east of Festubert, and they, too, are avenging the Lusitania and poison gas outrages to the full.

FRENCH OFFICIAL COMMUNIQUES.

SUNDAY, 15 o'clock (3 p.m.).

During last night the enemy made several counter-attacks between the sea and Arras. He was everywhere repulsed and suffered extremely heavy losses.

The first of these attacks occurred north of Ypres, to the east of the Yser Canal. It failed.

Two others had the elevated plain of Lorette as objective. Starting from the north-east and south-east, the enemy failed to reach our lines.

Two others were made against our positions of Neuville-Saint-Vaast—in the village, in the cemetery and further to the south, in the region known as "The Labyrinth." At one point only the enemy set foot for a moment in one of our advanced trenches, but he was driven out, and left numerous prisoners in our hands.

In Argonne, the enemy exploded several mines near our positions, and endeavored, with strong forces, to occupy the excavations. Our infantry drove them back to their starting points, inflicting enormous losses upon them with a hail of bombs and grenades. The check of the enemy was complete.

SUNDAY, 23 o'clock (11 p.m.).

In all the region to the north of Arras, following checks experienced by the Germans in the course of last night, combats have continued, at certain points with extreme violence.

The British army has made progress to the east of Festubert.

SUNDAY, AUGUST 29, 1915.

Paris Living Up to Its Classic Reputation as Centre Of Artistic Creation for Fashion in Women's Dresses

HIS LETTER. DRESSES CREATED BY DOEUILLET, BEER, MARTIAL ET ARMAND, BEER, CHÉRUIT.

IT'S STILL RAINING. TAILOR-MADE DRESSES BY PAQUIN, LANVIN, DOEUILLET, COAT BY PAQUIN

THE BOUQUET. DESIGNED FOR LA GAZETTE DU BON TON

Embroidered Muslins, Organdies and Tulles, Used with Great Simplicity, Recall Models of 1840.

Fashions have made their appearance this season as in former years and despite the anxiety and difficulties caused by the war. Was it not always thus? During the Revolution and up to the time of the Restoration, during the whole period of the great wars of the Republic and the Empire, Paris continued to create fashions, as is shown by the numerous prints which are still used as typical by certain present-day publications.

Even during the gigantic struggle in which the great nations of Europe are engaged, Paris has lived up to its reputation. It has shown, as is its wont, that it is and will always remain the creator of styles and the arbiter of the world's fashion. It has succeeded once again, thanks to the genius and the fruitful, untiring efforts of Paris dressmakers.

But the fashions of yesterday, that is to say of last spring, the whims of which still linger about us in the drawings of Valentine Gross reprinted above, have called forth the following very apt remarks from "La Princesse de Clèves" in the "Gazette du Bon-Ton," from which these drawings are taken:

"It is our pleasure to welcome all the revivals in dress. Stamped with an evident moderation and harmonizing thus with our dearest conceptions, the fashions of 1915 are like a garden abounding with flowers, but flowers of charming simplicity. For embroidered muslins, organdies and tulles adopt a simplicity in form that frequently recalls 1840. Sometimes, too, we find the puffs and transparencies dear to the fashionable frequenters of the Tuileries although, fortunately, without their exaggerations, but adapted to present-day life. It is in the details rather than in the ensemble that the rapprochement should be realized."

Puffs and Transparencies Dear to the Fashionable Frequenters of the Tuileries of Old.

Further on she adds: "Wherever I look I find, even in war time, the elegance that is so deep-rooted in the heart of Paris, and whence is derived the dress, not only of the Parisienne, but also of women abroad, whose inclinations it divines and guides while making allowance for the customs and climate of the country they live in.

"Vicomte de Launay once said that fashions were like national costumes: 'They have their full grace only in their own country; to be shown to their fullest advantage they need the ideas and climate of the country in which they are created.'

"To this I would reply that the fashion of France alone is the costume of all nations."

Monster Aerial Battleship Building at Buffalo, N.Y.

New Dreadnought of the Air Destined to Fight Submarines and Zeppelins.

(From the NEW YORK HERALD of December 9.)

BUFFALO, N.Y., Wednesday. — The "aeroplane battleship," so long regarded as an engineering impossibility, is here. In embryo at present, it is true, yet still it is here in Buffalo; many of its parts are already finished and ready to go to the assemblers, many more are coming in daily, and within a very few months a flying monster will emerge from the Curtiss factory to astonish the world.

For this dreadnought of the skies is to be approximately six times the size of the America.

It is less than two years ago—the summer of 1914—that news of the America spread through the land, and into Hammondsport, N.Y., itself a sleepy little town of 1,500 set among the vineyards on the shores of Lake Keuka, came a throng of more than thirty thousand visitors, drawn by the desire to see for themselves that which many believed could exist only in the imagination of another Jules Verne—an aeroplane built to fly across the Atlantic. From all corners of the globe they came, eager to behold the marvel, to scatter again to say to wondering neighbors, "I saw." And many engineers of aerodynamics exclaimed: "This is the ultimate in size of the heavier than air flying machine."

Yet Mr. Curtiss has now undertaken, and is actually building, a flying boat of six times the weight, of five times the wing area and more than five times the motor power of the America. And not a man connected with the Curtiss industry has a shadow of a doubt that this great bird will take wing on its first trial.

The details are as yet guarded carefully as a state secret, and, though some of these may never be known except to the designers and the actual crew, the dimensions and data herewith are substantially correct. The better to appreciate what this monster really will be, the following tabulation of its weight is given:—

	Pounds.
Weight of hull and planes	8,000
Weight of seven motors	4,000
Weight of crew of eight men	1,200
Weight of 700 gallons of gasolene	4,750
Weight of sixty gallons of oil	500
Weight of useful load (ammunition, etc)	3,000
Total	21,450

A matter of more than ten tons to be supported by thin air. And the specifications will read about as follows:—

Number of wings	3
Span of wings, feet	133
Chord of Wings, feet	10
Length over all, feet	68
Rudder area, square feet	54
Elevators' area, square feet	96
Fixed tail area, vertical, square feet	46
Fixed tail area, horizontal, square feet	126
Capacity, passengers	8 or more
Capacity, gasolene, gallons	700
Capacity, oil, gallons	60
Capacity, useful load, pounds	*3,000

*By translating the useful load capacity into passengers, the number of men carried may be increased to thirty.

The power plant will consist of seven motors, six of the V2 Curtiss type of 160 horse-power each and one Curtiss 40 horse-power.

As the gasolene consumption an hour will be about twenty-eight gallons for each pair of motors, or eighty-four gallons total, the extreme flying range with the above scheduled distribution of weights will be about nine hours. At a speed of seventy-five miles an hour this is a cruising range of 675 miles. This could be increased considerably by application of some of the useful load into a greater fuel capacity.

To start these huge motors (it takes three men pulling a rope attached to the starting crank to start a single V2), an auxiliary motor of about 40 horse-power will be installed amidships and—something else new from the Curtiss mind—this motor will also drive a water propeller set at the rear below the air rudder, to be used in starting the huge craft in motion and for manœuvring upon the water at low speeds. A separate water rudder will be added, of course.

AERIAL MONSTER NOW BEING BUILT FOR WAR PURPOSES BY GLENN CURTISS

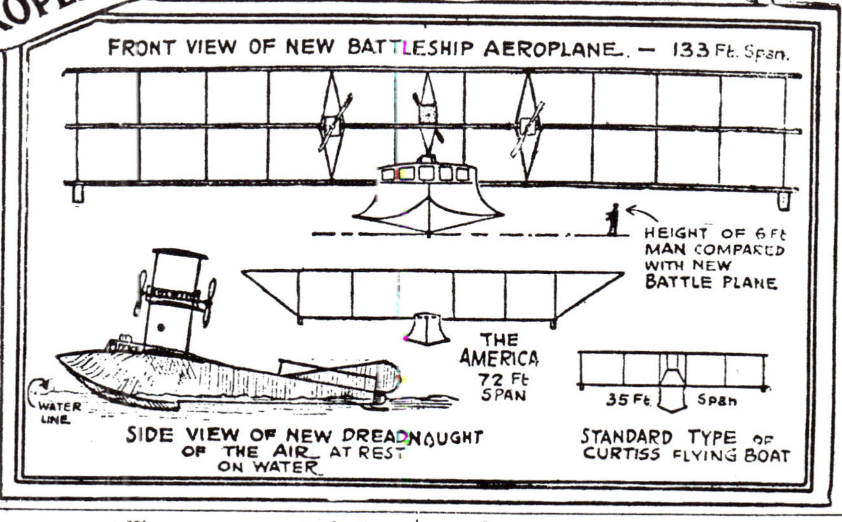

LA CRISE DES MUNITIONS RÉSOLUE EN ANGLETERRE

VUE PRISE DANS L'UNE DES 715 GRANDES FABRIQUES PLACÉES SOUS LE CONTRÔLE DU GOUVERNEMENT ANGLAIS

(D'APRÈS THE SPHERE)

TIEPOLO FRESCO RUINED BY BOMBS FROM AEROPLANES

Austrian Aviators Thrice Attack Venice in Twenty-Four Hours, Wounding Three.

(SPECIAL TO THE HERALD.)

VENICE, Monday.—There was a raid upon Venice last night by enemy aeroplanes, which, with its intervals, lasted two hours and a half. The bombs thrown struck the Scalzi Church, the fine monumental construction on the Canalazzo. The splendid ceiling, with Giambattista Tiepolo's magnificent fresco, "Il Transporto della Santa Casa," a valuable painting by the master, was completely destroyed.

Other bombs fell in the Piazzetta di San Marco, near the Palazzo Zecca, which was built by Sansovino. Several of the bombs fell in the basin.

The enemy, irritated by his failure on the front in the Alps, is making attacks upon the wonderful City of the Lagunes, which receives the attack with admirable serenity.

NIGHT RAID OF ZEPPELINS OVER PARIS COST NO LIVES AND DID LITTLE DAMAGE

Four Dirigibles Attempted to Reach City, Two Being Turned Back—Bombs Dropped at Levallois, Neuilly, Courbevoie, La Garenne, Colombes, Saint-Germain, and Batignolles Arrondissement of Paris, But Less Than a Dozen Persons Were Wounded.

Count Zeppelin has achieved the height of his ambition! After raiding Antwerp, the east coast of England, and Calais, his dirigibles have at last paid a nocturnal visit to Paris, the Mecca of the world and the seat of one of the Governments at war with the Kaiser. But instead of leaving the indelible marks of their coming, instead of dealing death to hundreds and sowing devastation far and wide, instead of blowing up historic monuments and leaving the inhabitants cowed and trembling, they have merely wounded nearly a dozen men, destroyed a factory and damaged a few houses. And the citizens of Paris and their wives are as unmoved as they were by the Tauben in September. Many people slept through the raid and yesterday morning visited the spots where bombs had fallen, impelled by mere curiosity. The great Zeppelin raid on the City of Light has failed!

The French Press Bureau summarizes the effects of the raid in the following laconic statement:—

"Yesterday morning, between a quarter past one and three o'clock, four Zeppelins approached Paris, coming from the direction of Compiègne and travelling down the valley of the Oise.

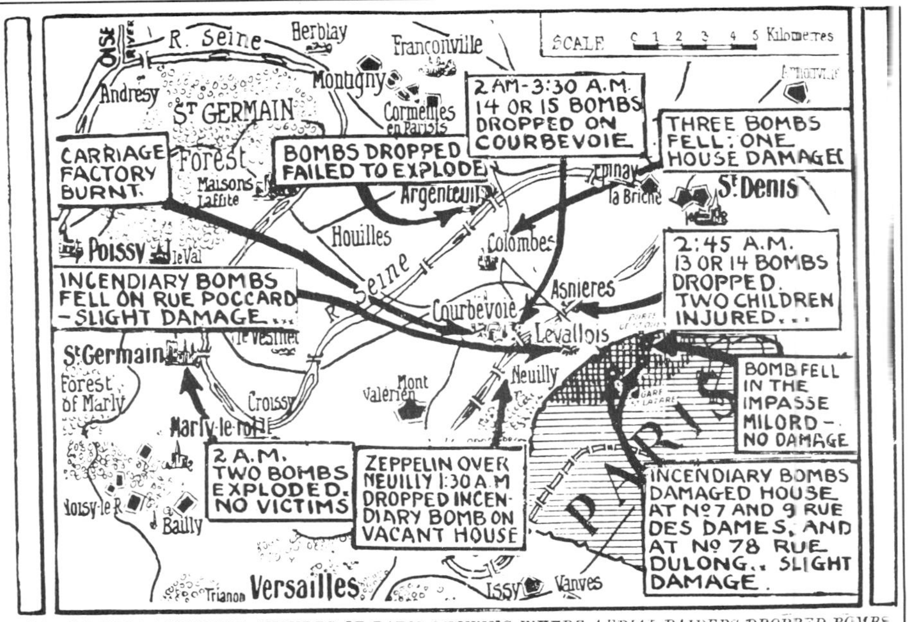

MAP OF NORTH-WESTERN SUBURBS OF PARIS SHOWING WHERE AERIAL RAIDERS DROPPED BOMBS. SHADED PORTION SHOWS QUARTERS TRAVERSED BY ZEPPELINS.

"Two of them were compelled to turn back before reaching Paris, one at Ecouen and the other at Mantes.

"The two others, attacked by the defence artillery, passed over only the north-western quarters of the Paris district and over the adjoining suburbs. They withdrew after dropping a dozen bombs, several of which did not burst.

"The material damage is not important. Seven or eight persons have been wounded, only one seriously.

"The different posts of defence against dirigibles opened fire on the Zeppelins, which were constantly illuminated by searchlights. One Zeppelin appears to have been struck.

"The aeroplane squadrons took part in the action, but the mist hindered their chase.

"Altogether the Zeppelin raid on Paris has failed completely and has shown how well the means of defence worked.

"The Parisian population was, as usual, perfectly calm.

"During their return journey the Zeppelins dropped twelve incendiary or explosive bombs on Compiègne, but only did material damage of no importance.

"Three other bombs fell on Ribécourt and Dreslincourt, north of Compiègne, without result."

Mr. Henry James Espouses Allies' Cause by Becoming an Englishman

Novelist Assumes Nationality of Country in Which He Has Lived for Forty Years.

(FROM THE HERALD'S CORRESPONDENT.)

LONDON, Wednesday.—The "Times" this morning says:—

"We are able to announce that Mr. Henry James was granted papers of naturalization on Monday and took the oath of allegiance as a British subject. All lovers of literature in this country will welcome the decision of this writer of genius, whose works are an abiding possession of all English-speaking peoples, and they will welcome it all the more on account of the reasons which Mr. James gives in his petition for naturalization, namely:—

"'Because of his having lived and worked in England for the best part of forty years; because of his attachment to the country and his sympathy with it and its people; because of the long friendships and associations and interests he has formed here—these last including the acquisition of some property; all of which things have brought to a head his desire to throw his moral weight and personal allegiance, for whatever they may be worth, into the scale of the contending nation's present and future fortune.'

"Mr. Henry James' friends have long known how intense were his sympathies with the cause of the Allies. It may be recalled that last December he wrote a delightful little appreciation of the work at the front of the American Volunteer Motor Ambulance Corps, formed of old Harvard, Yale and Princeton graduates. He also wrote a noble prefatory address and translated a contribution by M. Maurice Barrès for 'The Book of France,' published last week."

MR. HENRY JAMES.

According to the New York "Times," Mr. James has abandoned American nationality because he is dissatisfied with the course of action taken by the United States Government with regard to German atrocities.

Mr. Henry James, says the "Daily Telegraph," was born in New York in April, 1843, but, although he was brought up in the United States, his writings have always been regarded as rather more English than American, and, perhaps, more cosmopolitan than either. He has written novels of English and American life, based on his experience of both hemispheres. His artistic inspiration is derived mainly from French sources, and England has been his permanent home for many years.

In Italy he has been a frequent sojourner. His art, like that of J. M. Whistler, another American, who lived and worked in England, is far from expressing the characteristic ideals of the country that gave him birth. In their subtlety, delicacy of technique their aloofness from obvious and traditional forms of art, the writer and the painter have much besides nationality in common. In this Mr. Henry James differs from his brother, William James, the leader of the philosophical movement known as Pragmatism, who always showed a preference for his native country.

Among the best known works of Mr. Henry James, which include writings both of fiction and criticism in abundance, are "The American"—published in 1877, and regarded by many as his best novel; "Poor Richard," "The Bostonians" and "The Tragic Muse."

His two most recent books are "A Small Boy and Others," a volume of autobiography, and "Notes on Novelists," a critical work dealing with Mr. H. G. Wells and Mr. Arnold Bennett and their disciples.

CE QUE DOIT RÉALISER UN BON MASQUE PROTECTEUR DES GAZ ASPHYXIANTS

N'oublions pas que le Chlore s'insinue facilement entre la Peau du Visage et le Masque, s'il est de petites Dimensions.

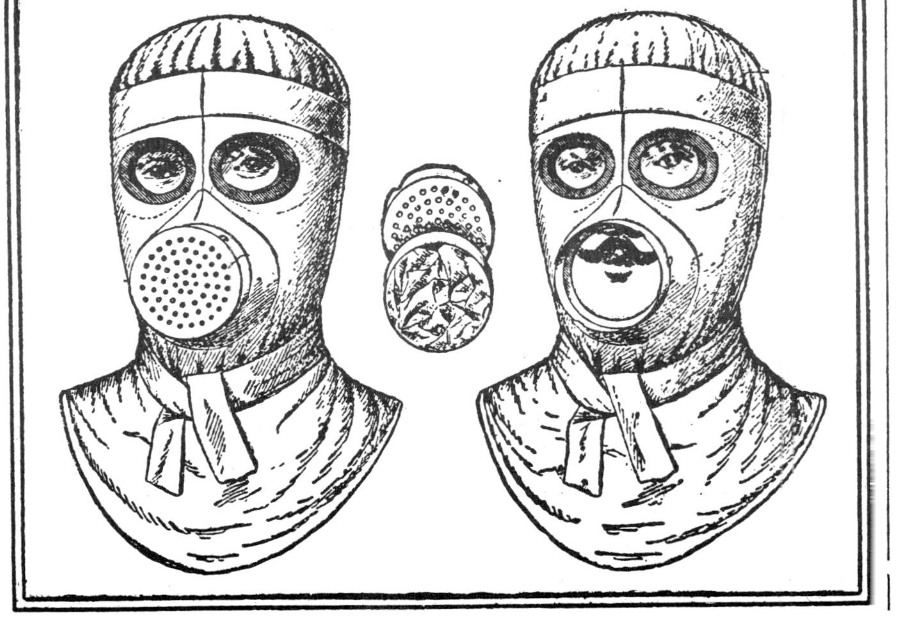

M. Santos-Dumont Makes His First Flight Over American Waters in American Aerial Boat

M. SANTOS-DUMONT MAKES A FLIGHT IN A CURTISS AERIAL BOAT.

Curtiss Machine, Piloted by Frank Burnside, Takes Pioneer of Aviation For Trip Over Long Island.

From the NEW YORK HERALD of October 13.)

LONG BEACH, L.I., Tuesday.—Rear-Admiral Robert E. Peary's first experience in aviation to-day was to find himself seated in a Curtiss flying-boat 1,200 feet above the marshy shore of Long Island near Long Beach, with the motor suddenly "gone dead" from a defective magneto. Fortunately the machine was under the control of Frank H. Burnside, a pilot of several years' experience. So cleverly did he bring the disabled aircraft around in a graceful spiral, coming head-on into the wind so that he volplaned safely into the mouth of a broad inlet, that the explorer knew nothing of the accident until he was told when on the water's surface that the flying-boat would have to be towed ashore.

Through the courtesy of Mr. Truman W. Post, owner of the flying-boat, flights were arranged for Mr. Peary and Mr. Santos-Dumont, the pioneer of aeronautics in Europe, who never before had made a flight in this country. With them were a party of friends from the Aero Club of America and Mrs. William H. Bliss, who made the first flight with Mr. Burnside.

The next passenger was Mr. Santos-Dumont. He protested against donning a life-preserver and appeared anxious to explore the flying-boat from wing-tip to wing-tip and from stern to stern. He was prevailed upon to sit down and permit the pilot to attend to the steering-gear and the manifold intricacies of the Curtiss 100 horse-power driving engine.

Mr. Santos-Dumont was the first man to make a public flight and the first man to pilot a dirigible balloon, but he never had made a flight over American soil or in an American aeroplane.

Motor Stops in Mid-Air When Rear-Admiral Peary Is the Passenger, But Explorer Never Perceives Mishap.

The flight was made out beyond the foam-flecked shore. Along the horizon to the southward could be discerned the ghostlike shape of war vessels, probably the cruisers of the British squadron which is maintaining a close watch on New York's harbor to interrupt German merchantmen.

Back through the haze came the flying-boat, and with a neat volplane to the inlet's surface the aircraft shaped her course shoreward.

The next passenger was Mr. Peary.

1812 CAMPAIGNS IN RUSSIA 1915

History Repeating Itself.

On September 14, 1812, Napoleon entered Moscow. War had been declared in May and the "Grande Armée" had crossed the Niemen on June 24. Thus, less than four months had sufficed to place Napoleon in possession of Russia's ancient capital and to make him apparently master of Russia's destinies.

To-day, September 12, 1915, another invader is on Russian soil. War has raged since August, 1914. In that interval, the Austro-German coalition, utilizing the crafty preparation of forty years, has hurled against Russia forces that in numbers completely dwarf Napoleon's "Grande Armée," and that, in artillery and supply equipment, have no equal in history.

How, then, does the balance stand? How do the achievements of this military machine in thirteen months of war, compare with the achievements of the "Grande Armée" in less than four months? One hundred and three years ago, after a campaign of only eleven weeks, Napoleon held the heart of Russia. With their vastly superior resources the Germans expected to have Russia at their mercy in less time. But what are the facts? To-day, after thirteen months of fighting, after six months of loudly heralded successes, after herculean efforts and at a cost in lives that will stagger Germany when Germany learns the truth, the Austro-Germans hold a little strip of territory that measures not more than 250 miles at its widest part and rather less than 70 miles at its narrowest. The nearest points of the Austro-German front, from the Gulf of Riga to Bukovina, are about 300 miles, as the crow flies, from Petrograd, 700 miles from Moscow, 200 miles from Kieff. And between the invaders and each of these possible objective-points there are formidable topographical difficulties—numerous rivers, extensive marshes, great forests—and, in addition, the unbroken Russian army, steadily increasing in numbers, rapidly improving in equipment.

Comparison of these facts shows that there is no ground for uneasiness in the Russian retreat. There is only ground for regret that it should be necessary. In 1812, the Russians retired still further toward the interior, and more rapidly; yet Napoleon was defeated.

But, cry the pessimistic wiseacres enrolled by the "Daily Mail," "the comparison of 1812 with 1915 is a stupid delusion."

Is it? The analogy is, on the contrary, startling in its completeness. Who can read Ségur's "Campagne de Russie" and not be struck by the resemblance between the slow, methodical and aggressive withdrawal of the Russians in 1812, and their slow, methodical and aggressive withdrawal in 1915? Ostrovna, the capture of Vitepsk and Smolensk, the Valentina engagement, the glorious but costly battle of Moskova have one point, a vital point, of similarity with the Austro-German victories in 1915: it is their hollowness as regards results. After each triumph the Russians escaped, and the victors were compelled to follow the vanquished. They had taken the wolf by the ears and dared not let go. After one battle, another battle; but the essential result, the crushing of the enemy, was never achieved. The Russians withdrew

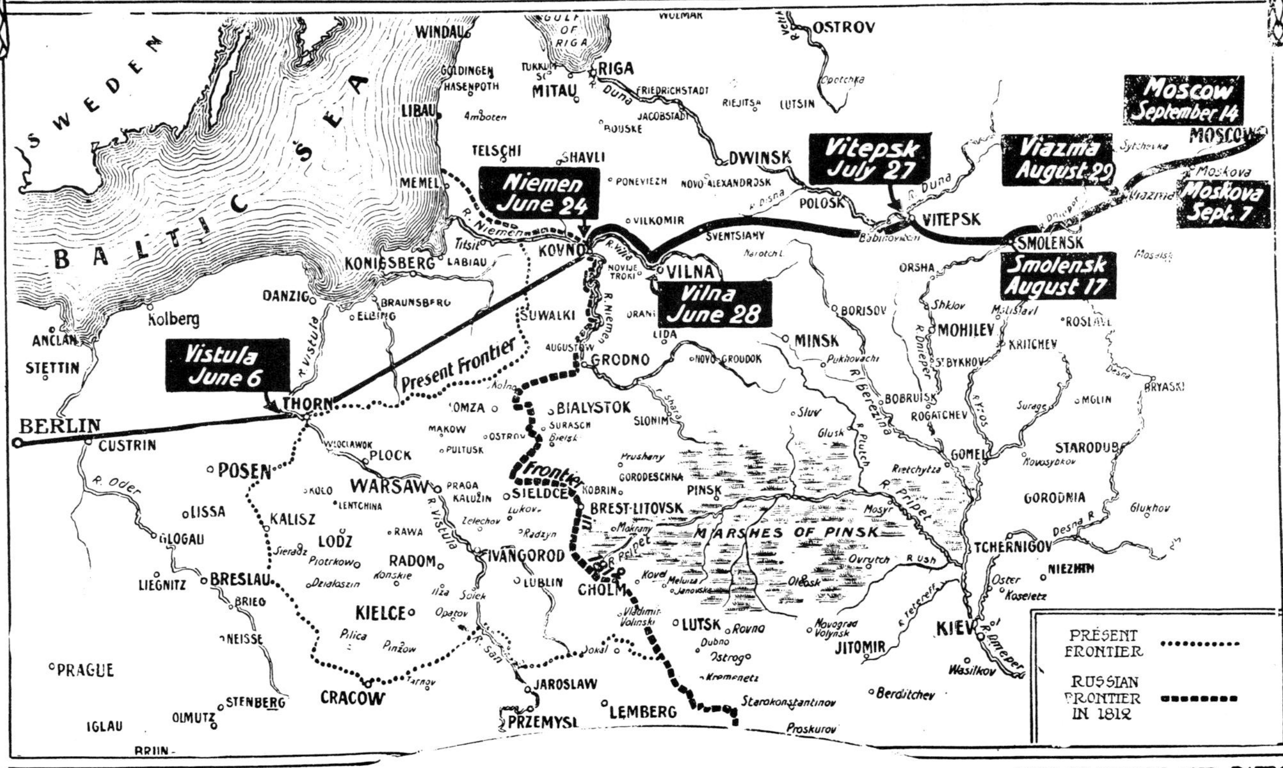

MAP SHOWING THE ADVANCE OF NAPOLEON'S "GRANDE ARMÉE" IN THREE MONTHS.

LINE OF MARCH AND DATES OF PRINCIPAL MILITARY EVENTS

1812—1915.

in 1812, as they are withdrawing in 1915, striking deadly blows on every occasion and leaving a desert behind. Read the letter written by an Austrian officer and published in the Viennese press. "The retreat is a masterpiece of systematic and terrifying devastation; it resembles the retreat of 1812." Then read Ségur's wistful comments on his leader's victories: "Victories almost fruitless; the smoke enveloping us seemed our sole achievement and a too faithful symbol."

But, urge the inconvertible pessimists, conditions nowadays are so different. The Germans can advance without anxiety; no supply difficulties exist for them; they have at their service railways and countless automobiles. Napoleon had neither.

The conclusion should be the Germans will advance more quickly. But what are the facts? The Germans, with infinite toil, have not accomplished in thirteen months a third of that which Napoleon accomplished in three months. The Emperor entered Kovno on June 24, sent out Oudinot toward Ianoff, and, with Davoust, Murat's cavalry and the Guard, left for Vilna, which he entered on June 28. The Germans are still struggling painfully toward Vilna, though Kovno fell into their hands on August 18. The Germans have failed to do in four weeks what Napoleon did in four days.

The fact is, the analogy between 1812 and 1915, instead of being a "stupid delusion," is incontestable. And study of it is instructive and should reassure the pessimists. For, in military genius, Hindenburg, Mackensen and the Kaiser together do not come up to Napoleon's ankle. Yet in 1812 "retreating" Russians defeated Napoleon.

TUESDAY, NOVEMBER 30, 1915.

YES! FROM "JUDGE" NO!

SUNDAY, FEBRUARY 13, 1916.

Ballet Russe Takes American Theatregoers by Storm; Only Stone-hearts Unmoved by Mr. Walter's New Drama

Mme. Xenia Maklezowa Is Première Danseuse in M. Serge de Diaghileff's Company.

(From the NEW YORK HERALD.)

January, 1916, was not only productive of a number of new plays in New York, but also signalized the first appearance in America of M. Serge de Diaghileff's widely-heralded Ballet Russe—a riot of color—at the Century Theatre. It literally took the city by storm.

The chief novelty was the opening number, "L'Oiseau de Feu," a fantastic tale set to ultra-modern music, in which Mme. Xenia Maklezowa, the première danseuse, was the bird of the title-rôle. Other artists in the cast were Mmes. Valentine Kachouba, Lobow, Tchernichowa and Folres.

THE NEW YORK HERALD

PRICE: Paris and France, 15c.; Abroad, 25c. — EUROPEAN EDITION—PARIS, FRIDAY, MARCH 10, 1916. — Prix: Paris et France, 15c.; Etranger, 25c.

News Summary

News Told in Brief

Italian Monarch to Inspect Front.

The King of Italy has left Rome, on his way to the Italian front.

Tsar Ferdinand to Visit Hungary.

Tsar Ferdinand of Bulgaria, after visiting Emperor Francis Joseph at Schönbrunn, has left Vienna for Hungary.

To Visit Allied Capitals.

The Crown Prince of Servia and M. Pashich will leave Corfu shortly for Paris and London. They will probably visit Rome also.

Germans Hurrying from Portugal.

Germans residing in Portugal are leaving that country in large numbers, their Consul having advised them to lose no time in getting away.

Present Tea to French Army.

The Brazilian Government, following the example of that of the State of Parana, has sent 10,000 kilos of South American tea to the French army.

Deferred Cable Service Resumed.

The Commercial Cable Company announces that its service of deferred cablegrams at reduced rates between France and America has been resumed.

Italy Requisitions Wheat.

Owing to the scarcity of cereals in certain provinces, the Italian Government has issued orders for the requisitioning of all the stocks of wheat in the kingdom.

Fire Ravages Koritza.

A great fire, of which the cause is so far unascertained, has destroyed the barracks of the Greek garrison at Koritza, the prisons and one of the quarters of the town.

Chinese Rebels Attack Warship.

According to a Hong-Kong newspaper, the rebels early on Tuesday morning attacked the cruiser Chao-Hao and the Whampoa forts, below Canton. They were easily repulsed.

Fresh Rioting in Berlin.

News has been received at The Hague that fresh disorders have occurred in Berlin and that only a few days ago the crowd threw stones at the windows of the Chancellor's residence.

New Taxes to Yield 100,000,000fr.

It is anticipated that the new taxes decided upon by the Hellenic Government will produce 100,000,000fr. The profits derived from merchant shipping will be taxed 50 per cent., the taxes to be retrospective from the beginning of the war.

"Derby" Men in Paris Meet To-night.

Men attested in Paris under Lord Derby's scheme are reminded that a meeting to discuss their position will be held at the Café de la Terrasse, Salle Dehouve, 74-76 avenue de la Grande-Armée, at eight o'clock sharp this evening. The meeting is strictly confined to "Derby" recruits, who must show their attestation paper and permis de séjour to gain admittance.

Professor Nielsen Dead.

The death is announced at Christiania, at the age of seventy-three, of the Norwegian historian, Professor Yngvar Nielsen. He was a friend of King Oscar II., and during that monarch's reign he played a remarkable rôle in the policy of the Union, writing a number of books on the subject. His work on Norway has become a classic, and it has been translated into English.

Servian Youths at Fontainebleau.

Fifty Servian youths, aged from fifteen to twenty, who fled from Belgrade before the Austrian cavalry, are now installed at the Fontainebleau college. During the retreat, says the "Figaro," they found the mutilated body of one of their comrades lying in the wayside. The older youths are awaiting the call to return to Salonica and fight to regain their country from the hands of the invader.

BERLIN SEVERS DIPLOMATIC RELATIONS WITH LISBON.

GENEVA, Thursday.—The following official despatch, issued by the Wolff Agency, was received here at seven o'clock to-day:—

"Berlin, Thursday.

"The German Minister in Lisbon has been notified that he must to-day ask the Portuguese Government for his passports and at the same time he must present a detailed declaration. Simultaneously the Portuguese Minister in Berlin will be given his passports.

"This measure was foreseen, as Portugal had not furnished Germany with the explanations demanded relative to the requisition of interned German merchant ships.

"The German Minister will probably proceed to Spain, where the crews of the ships that have been requisitioned have already gone, for it will be impossible for him to return to Germany without running the risk of being captured by an Allied warship."—Figaro.

GEN. VILLA RAIDS AMERICAN TOWN, KILLING MANY

500 Mexicans Dash Across Border and Attack Columbus, N.M., Remaining 90 Minutes Before American Troopers Drive Them Out, Shooting Several.

(BY COMMERCIAL CABLE TO THE HERALD.)

NEW YORK, Thursday.—At the head of 500 troopers, General "Pancho" Villa, bandit leader of the Mexican rebels, dashed across the New Mexican border at daybreak this morning and raided the town of Columbus, sixty miles west of El Paso, Texas.

The Mexican raiders swept through the deserted streets of the little town, emptying revolvers and carbines through windows and doors of the houses and firing volleys at every person who made an appearance to see the nature of the disturbance.

Dismounting, the Mexicans forced their way into several saloons, then, crazed by drink and excitement, several of them set fire to houses and shot at every inmate who sought to leave the burning buildings.

Meantime, from the station of the El Paso and South-Western Railway, just outside the town, a call for help had been flashed by telegraph. In less than an hour and a half a troop of United States regulars was approaching the scene. The advanced guard were dismounted cavalrymen in automobiles. The sound of the machines alarmed the rioting Mexicans, who mounted their horses and rode southward to the border.

The regulars fired at the bandit-rebels, who spread out, however, and dispersed. Half a dozen of the Mexicans were shot down. The automobiles were unable to follow across the border, there being no roads. When a troop of mounted cavalrymen arrived, they started at once in pursuit.

It is reported, but not confirmed, that five United States soldiers were killed or wounded.

Columbus is in Cuna County, New Mexico, within a mile of the border. Federal authorities believed that General Villa was far in the interior of Mexico, as he has not shown himself since the hold-up and murder of Americans on a Mexican railway train several months ago.

This is the first recorded attack made by organized Mexicans on American soil since the raids by "cattle rustlers" made near Brownsville and Corpus Christi, Texas, a year ago.

Silent on New Note, Mr. Wilson Awaits Overt German Act

Washington Believes "Note-Writing" Is Over and Slain American Will Mean Drastic Course.

(BY COMMERCIAL CABLE TO THE HERALD.)

WASHINGTON, Thursday.—No reply has been made to Germany on the old proposition, put forth again yesterday by Count Henry Bernstorff, offering to "trade" respect for American lives on the high seas in exchange for an easement of the British blockade.

It is believed in the capital that the President, well satisfied with his recently adopted policy of "standing pat," will refrain from answering this modified Memorandum, as he refused to accept its prototype offered shortly after the sinking of the Lusitania.

Diplomatic circles are unanimous in their belief that there will be no more Note-writing to Germany, but that immediate and drastic action will follow the slaying of another citizen of the United States by a submarine of any member of the Triple Alliance.

GEN. AYLMER ADVANCES; IS SEVEN MILES FROM KUT.

(SPECIAL TO THE HERALD.)

LONDON, Thursday.—The Press Bureau to-day issued the following report concerning operations in Mesopotamia:—

General Aylmer advanced on Monday along the right bank of the Tigris and reached Es-Simm, a position situated seven miles from Kut-el-Amara.

General Aylmer on Wednesday attacked the position without succeeding in dislodging the enemy, on whom he inflicted heavy losses. The enemy has fortified the position, but shows no activity.

The British losses are small.

General Smuts Presses Forward.

(SPECIAL TO THE HERALD.)

LONDON, Thursday.—The Press Bureau to-day issued the following report of operations in East Africa:—

The troops commanded by General Smuts have advanced against the German troops in the region of Kilimandjaro.

General Smuts on Tuesday occupied fords of the Lumi, with insignificant losses.

Several German counter-attacks were repulsed with success.

LORD RONALD SUTHERLAND-GOWER DIES AT AGE OF 71.

(SPECIAL TO THE HERALD.)

LONDON, Thursday. — Lord Ronald Sutherland-Gower died at his residence at Tunbridge Wells this evening at the age of seventy-one.

SPANISH ELECTIONS ON APRIL 5.

The elections for the Spanish Chamber of Deputies have been fixed for April 5 next.

Map Illustrating French Official Communiqués of Thursday

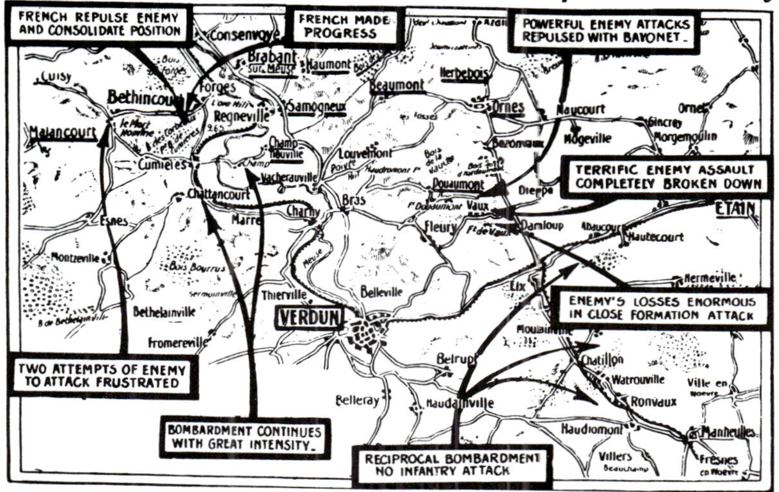

MR. ROOSEVELT BREAKS SILENCE ON CANDIDACY

Says the American People Would Make a Mistake to Nominate Him Unless They Feel a Devotion to Ideals.

WASHINGTON, Thursday. — Colonel Theodore Roosevelt's first public intimation as to his possible candidacy for nomination for the Presidency has been cabled from Trinidad, where he is on a vacation. He stated that he does not wish to enter the race as a preliminary candidate, but he might accept the nomination in the event of a crisis in the United States.

"The country would make a mistake in nominating me," he said, "unless it feels not only devotion to ideals, but confidence in my purpose measurably to realize those ideals in action."

He said further: " hypocrisy and infamy. I am disgusted with its unmanly failure to do its duty in an international crisis, and its abandonment of national honor."—Reuter.

Again Marks Drop In Wall Street To Record Depth

Further Slumps Startle Market—No Definite Reason Accepted for the Further Decline.

(BY COMMERCIAL CABLE TO THE HERALD.)

NEW YORK, Thursday. — Further slumps in marks startled Wall Street today, the exchange on the standard coin of Germany, after opening at 72¼, dropping to 72⅛ at noon. This is exactly one-fourth of a point lower than the low record established yesterday, when they sank to 72⅜. It was on January 7 last that the exchange dropped to the former low figure of 72¼.

German bankers in this city issued statements to-day denying reports current that the weakness was caused by wholesale "dumping" by Berlin interests on this market. These banking houses asserted that the business from Berlin was no heavier than usual and that there was no unloading of German holdings at this time.

To-day's favorable French communiqué was not regarded as cause for the weakness in marks, since they dropped yesterday and the day previously, in the face of admissions of having retired at certain points in the great Verdun battle.

Kronen are quoted to-day at 12.52 and francs at 5.90½.

Avalanches Freed By Enemy's Bombs

Austrians in Mountainous Regions Seek to Profit by Continuance of Bad Weather.

General Cadorna yesterday issued the following communiqué from Italian Headquarters:—

The bad weather persists in the mountainous regions, and the enemy is seeking to profit by it.

Thus, during yesterday, in the Lagaznof zone (Upper Travenanzes valley), he caused a fall of avalanches upon our positions by means of high-explosive grenades, but without causing any damage.

Despite the bad atmospheric conditions of the season and the ruses resorted to by the enemy, our troops are unshakable, and their actions are full of audacity.

During the past few days our troops succeeded thus in extending our line of occupation in a much disputed zone between the first and second valleys of Tofana and in making some progress in the Middle Isonzo valley and the Zagora sector.

BRITISH SHIP TORPEDOED OFF BOULOGNE PIER

Five of Crew Perish When Anchored Steamship Is Blown Up by Submarine—Was Waiting Tide to Enter Harbor.

The small British steamer Hermatrice—formerly a German ship—was torpedoed without warning at one o'clock on Wednesday morning while anchored about a kilomètre of the pier of Boulogne-sur-Mer. Five of the crew perished. The remainder—about thirty-five men—succeeded in getting away in boats.

The explosion was terrific, shaking windows and shutters in Boulogne and rousing the inhabitants, who rushed to the cellars or into the streets, believing the town was being bombarded from the air. The detonation was heard a considerable distance inland.

The Hermatrice, says a Boulogne telegram to the "Figaro," had crossed from England during the day and was waiting for the tide to enter the harbor. The fact that the sea was perfectly calm does not admit the belief that first prevailed that the vessel had been blown up by a floating mine.

The steamer sank horizontally, and the upper deck, the funnel and the masts are visible from the shore, where a large crowd is gathered.

The sunken vessel was about 140 mètres in length and was a prize taken by the British, by whom she was renamed, soon after the outbreak of the war.

Kurds Butchered 40,000 Armenians Within Erzerum

When Stronghold's Fall Was Inevitable, Entire Armenian Population Was Put to the Sword.

(SPECIAL TO THE HERALD.)

LONDON, Thursday.—Information has been received here from Petrograd that the population of Erzerum before the fall of the fortress included 40,000 Armenians, of whom the Russians on their entry found but sixteen living.

A Turkish inhabitant of Erzerum, whose word may be relied on, has declared that several days before the taking of the said fortress all the Armenians were driven from the town by the gendarmes in a westerly direction, where the Kurds, who were lying in wait, assassinated them.

Huns Admit Loss of 2,684,215 Men

German Official Lists Acknowledge Minimum Obviously Inferior to Actual Casualties Sustained.

According to the German official casualty lists issued up to February 29 last there has been a total German loss since the war began of 2,684,215 officers and men. This total is made up of: Killed, 667,833; wounded, 1,658,547; missing, 357,835.

In view of the fact that the official casualty lists necessarily refer to losses sustained considerably before the date of publication it may be assumed, says the "Temps," that the total of 2,684,215 only represents losses in the German army and navy up to the end of January, 1916. In any case, none of the Verdun casualties are included in the total.

Moreover the German figures can only be regarded as an officially admitted minimum and there are strong reasons to believe that the totals given are very considerably inferior to the real losses.

TURKEY AWAITS VERDUN BATTLE TO MAKE PEACE

Constantinople Government Already Has Ordered that the Dardanelles Be Stripped of Mines, Is Report Received from Athens.

LONDON, Thursday.—At a meeting of the new Ottoman committee, held just before the attempt on Enver Pasha, the Grand Vizier declared that peace must be made immediately with the Entente Powers. This information is telegraphed by the Athens correspondent of the "Daily Chronicle."

The Ministers agreed that before coming to a definite decision they would await the result of the offensive against Verdun.

The Government nevertheless has decided on the necessity of ordering the local authorities to withdraw the mines in the Dardanelles.—Reuter.

Talaat Bey Sues Russia.

NEW YORK, Thursday.—Despatches received here from a reliable source assert that Talaat Bey has made representations on behalf of the Ottoman Government for a separate peace with Russia.

Germany, for diplomatic reasons, in connection with her relations with neutral Powers, will issue a denial of these reports.

Precise information coming from a trustworthy quarter has reached Washington. It shows that the object of the war between Turkey and Russia no longer exists, and that the Ottoman Government is desirous of ending hostilities.

This it not the first time that proposals for a separate peace with Russia have come from Turkey. These latest representations are not likely to be more successful than the first, Russia having signed the Allies' pact not to conclude a separate peace.

The Washington correspondent of the New York "Times" telegraphs that it is known that Turkey is unable to resist the Russian forces, which are fired with extraordinary enthusiasm by the victories of Erzerum and Bitlis.—Journal.

RUSSIANS STORM TRENCH, BAYONETING DEFENDERS.

The following communiqué was issued in Petrograd yesterday:—

Western Front.

An important German contingent which attempted to cross the Dvina near Schloss Kockenhusen, east of Friedrichstadt, was driven back by our fire.

North-west of Jacobstadt the German artillery has bombarded our cantonments. The enemy's heavy artillery has fired upon the small town of Lievenhov and the regions of the Tsargrad and Nietzgal stations.

Near Illukst our scouts have destroyed an enemy post and taken some prisoners.

North-west of Olyka station our scouts stormed an enemy trench in full daylight, bayoneting some of the defenders and taking the remainder prisoner.

In the region of the Upper Ikva our fire dispersed an important enemy contingent which was attempting to approach our trenches.

In Galicia, in the region of Cebrov, north-west of Tarnopol, the enemy made a night attack under cover of squalls of artillery fire. He was repulsed by our rifle fire and we made some prisoners.

Caucasus.

In the region of the littoral our troops have driven the Turks beyond the river Kalapotamos.

Way Open from Erzerum to Sea.

PETROGRAD, Thursday.—The military critics consider that the occupation of Rizah places the Russians in possession of the shortest route from Erzerum to the sea.

The Turks continue to flee in the direction of Trebizond.—Figaro.

Russophile Persian Premier.

TEHERAN, Thursday.—Prince Firman has resigned. Prince Sipah-Salar, a partisan of the Russians, succeeds him as Premier and Minister of the Interior.—Figaro.

GERMANS REEL BACK FROM DEATH-DEALING LINES ABOUT VERDUN

French Shatter Series of Desperate Attacks at Béthincourt and From Douaumont to Vaux—Bois des Corbeaux Swept Almost Clear of Enemy, Whose Enormous Losses Do Not Gain Him Single Yard's Advance.

There is good reason to believe that the climax of the great Verdun battle has been reached and that the colossal German effort to win this stronghold has definitely failed.

According to the latest French communiqués, the Crown Prince's troops were repulsed at every point yesterday with losses which are officially described as "enormous," while Verdun's defenders, growing stronger as the attackers weaken, consolidated their advance in the Bois des Corbeaux and drove the Germans from fresh positions, so that the wood is almost entirely in their hands and L'Oie Hill is again secure.

It is not too much to say that the fighting yesterday was disastrous for the Germans. Huge masses of men were flung with the most reckless fury upon the French positions both west and east of the Meuse, but in every instance the attacks were met with a tornado of artillery and rifle fire, before which they broke and recoiled.

Germans Falsely Claimed Vaux.

The German onslaught was particularly violent from Douaumont as far as Vaux, which latter village the Germans officially claim to have taken. This claim is a calculated and deliberate lie of great significance. The village of Vaux remains in French possession after a magnificent defence that never yielded a foot.

That the Germans make a claim which is so impossible of substantiating is evidence that the high command is desperately anxious to find something to satisfy the anxiety of the home population.

It is a military axiom that any successful offensive gains in speed and force with its own momentum, but the offensive of the Crown Prince, far from accelerating, has been first checked and now stopped by a resistance that is becoming more and more stubborn and by troops that are already capable of hitting back with the utmost vigor.

German Press Admits Anxiety.

These facts cannot be altogether concealed from the German public, though a realization of them may be postponed by false communiqués. But the anxiety exists and the "Vossische Zeitung" has given it very open expression. In a recent issue this journal says: "The German armies cannot always triumph and we should never have thought that our Headquarters Staff would have undertaken a great operation without adequate preparation. It is evident, however, that an operation which falters after the first attack, like that at Verdun, was very badly prepared."

What is "evident" to the "Vossische Zeitung" must soon become apparent to the German people and the disillusionment will be the more bitter because of the widely proclaimed boast that Verdun would be occupied by the Germans not later than February 29. Germany was expecting the Kaiser to make a triumphal entry into the fortress by March 1, and it is now the 10th, with the War Lord back in his capital, and his exasperated heir flinging away fresh masses of German troops—masses that melt away before the French guns and the French bayonets that ring Verdun about with death.

"Beware the Ides of March."

When the Germans decided to make their huge attempt in this theatre their aim was probably as much political as strategic. They sought to strike a deadly blow at the military prestige of France. In failing to do what they set out to do they have damaged their own military prestige to an extent that it is not yet possible to estimate. Neutral peoples have been watching the struggle of the Titans with absorbed interest, and it is significant that in all the neutral countries the mark has fallen steadily.

Germany is in such a position that she cannot give up the struggle. Not to succeed means failure almost as decisive as a defeat. Therefore, it is to be supposed that many more thousands of the Kaiser's troops will be driven to slaughter before the effort is finally abandoned. The Verdun battle still rages, but there are signs that it is burning itself out. It is time for some prophet in the "Vaderland" to warn the Kaiser, as another and a greater Cæsar was warned many centuries ago: "Beware the Ides of March."

FRENCH OFFICIAL COMMUNIQUES

THURSDAY, 3 p.m.

In Argonne our artillery has continued the shelling of the enemy's communication roads, notably in eastern Argonne and in the Montfaucon-Nantillois region.

West of the Meuse the enemy endeavored several times during the night to repair his yesterday's failures. Two attempted attacks, preceded by intense artillery preparation, on the village of Béthincourt, were stopped by our curtain fire, which prevented the Germans from debouching. IN THE BOIS DES CORBEAUX THE RENEWED EFFORTS OF THE ENEMY FAILED TO DISLODGE US FROM THE LARGE SPACE OF GROUND WHICH WE HAD RECONQUERED AND WHICH WE ARE CONSOLIDATING.

East of the Meuse the desperate struggle continued late last evening, and during the night in the region comprised between Douaumont and the village of Vaux. The Germans directed several attacks with powerful effectives on our positions. Despite the intensity of the artillery fire and the violence of the assaults, the enemy could not break our line and was promptly repulsed. SEVERAL ELEMENTS OF THE GERMAN INFANTRY WHICH HAD MOMENTARILY PENETRATED THE VILLAGE OF VAUX WERE IMMEDIATELY DRIVEN OUT BY A COUNTER-ATTACK WITH THE BAYONET.

In Voivre there has been a reciprocal and intermittent bombardment without any infantry action.

In Lorraine a surprise attack to the west of the Bois Le Prêtre enabled us to make twenty prisoners.

THURSDAY, 11 P.M.

In Belgium, our artillery has displayed activity against the enemy positions south of Lombaertzyde.

In Champagne, we have effectively bombarded the enemy's defensive organizations west of Navarin, east of the Butte du Mesnil and in the region of Massiges.

WEST OF THE MEUSE, OUR TROOPS CONTINUED TO MAKE PROGRESS DURING THE DAY IN THE BOIS DES CORBEAUX, WHICH IS NOW ALMOST ENTIRELY IN OUR HANDS.

East of the Meuse, the Germans have directed several attacks upon our front, from Douaumont as far as Vaux.

At the entrance to the village of Douaumont, an attack was shattered by our infantry and artillery fire. FURIOUS ASSAULTS UPON THE VILLAGE OF VAUX WERE ALSO REPULSED WITH GREAT LOSSES FOR THE ENEMY.

Finally, the Germans hurled a number of attacks in massed formation against our trenches bordering the foot of the hillock which rises above the fort of Vaux. ALL THESE ATTACKS WERE FLUNG BACK, THE ENEMY SUFFERING ENORMOUS LOSSES OWING TO OUR CURTAIN FIRE.

The activity of the artillery, both west and east of the Meuse, has been very violent on both sides.

In Upper Alsace, after a struggle with grenades, we carried an enemy trench element in the region of Entre-Largues, east of Seppois.

GUNS ACTIVE IN BELGIUM.

(BELGIAN COMMUNIQUE.)

Thursday.

There have been reciprocal artillery actions, particularly in the region of Dixmude and more to the north.

SIR ROGER CASEMENT CAPTURED AS HUNS TRY TO LAND IN IRELAND

Auxiliary Cruiser and Submarine Sent to Bottom by British After Discovery of Collapsible Boat, Laden With Arms and Ammunition, Beached in Tralee Bay—Knight Is Picked Up With Survivors of Sunken Warships.

(SPECIAL TO THE HERALD.)

LONDON, Monday.—The Admiralty today issued the following statement:—

"Between midday on Thursday and nine o'clock Friday morning, a vessel disguised as a neutral merchantman, but in reality a German auxiliary warship, acting in concert with a German submarine, attempted to land arms and ammunition in Ireland.

"The vessel was sunk and a certain number of prisoners was taken.

"Among these prisoners was Sir Roger Casement."

Boat Beached in Tralee Bay.

Although the exact point where the attempted landing was made is not announced officially, it is believed to be at a spot in Tralee Bay, on the south-western coast of Ireland.

On Sunday the report was received here of the arrest of three Dublin men at Currahane Strand, on Tralee Bay.

Their arrest followed the finding by coast guards of a small collapsible boat, containing arms and ammunition, which was discovered beached on the sands which extend for miles along the North Kerry coast and are flanked by high ranges of sand. This part of the coast is not navigable except to small boats, and few persons live in the region. There are no towns in the district.

The strand was watched following the discovery of the collapsible boat, which had been left by its occupants, who had evidently proceeded inland to some point to notify fellow-conspirators.

The trio of alleged plotters were seized as they stopped their automobile at the point where the collapsible boat touched the shore. They were charged with having gone to the spot to take off the arms and ammunition when they were landed.

Collapsible from Submarine.

It is believed that this collapsible boat was one sent ashore by a reconnoitring party from the German submarine, all of which craft carry boats of such type. The submersible and the auxiliary cruiser were forced to stand too far out, because of shoal water, to witness the seizure of the small boat.

Following the discovery of the small boat, it is reported, the Admiralty was notified.

It signalled by wireless to British warships patrolling the south-west Irish coast of the presence of the suspected ships. That these vessels engaged the enemy successfully is conveyed in the official statement.

It is not known if the men who put ashore in the collapsible boat were captured. It is believed, from the context of the Admiralty announcement, however, that Sir Roger Casement was among survivors picked up from the auxiliary cruiser after she had been sunk by British gunfire.

Sir Roger Casement, created a Knight in 1911, made a Companion of St. Michael and St. George in 1905, was Consul-General to Rio de Janeiro from 1909 to 1913.

He was born on September 1, 1864, and was British Consul at Lourenço Marques in 1895. He was British Consul for the Portuguese Possessions in West Africa south of the Gulf of Guinea, Consul in the Gaboon and Consul to the Congo Free State from 1898 to 1905. He was British Consul at Santos in 1906 and was appointed Consul-General to Haiti and Santo Domingo in 1907, but did not proceed to his post. He was British Consul at Para in 1908 and 1909. He reported for the British Government on Putumayo atrocities in 1912. He was retired on a pension in 1913.

Noted for Seditious Utterances.

It was shortly after this that Sir Roger Casement became notorious through his seditious utterances with regard to England.

On the outbreak of war he was received with open arms by the Kaiser and his advisers, who seem to have readily accepted his boasts that he could foment trouble in Ireland.

The suggestion that the Irish prisoners of war in Germany would willingly accept service in an Irish legion to be formed to fight the English, is supposed to have emanated from Sir Roger Casement.

Interned Irish Scorn Offers.

Tempting offers were made to the Irish soldiers interned in Germany, but they refused to become traitors. Irish non-commissioned officers were accorded special accommodation and food with the object of subverting their loyalty. They, however, addressed a spirited letter to the Kaiser stating that they desired no privileges and assuring him of their steadfast loyalty to King George.

Nothing had been heard of Sir Roger Casement lately, and it was understood that he had lost favor with the German military authorities.

RUSH MORE TROOPS AS DUBLIN IS PLACED UNDER MARTIAL LAW

Messrs. Asquith and Birrell Reassure Commons—Troops On Way from England and Belfast — Rebel Headquarters Captured by Soldiers.

(SPECIAL TO THE HERALD.)

LONDON, Wednesday.—Mr. Augustine Birrell, Chief Secretary for Ireland, and Mr. Henry Herbert Asquith, the Prime Minister, were targets for a volley of questions concerning the Sinn Feiners' revolt in Dublin from members of the House of Commons to-day.

Replying to demands for a statement on the situation, Mr. Birrell and Mr. Asquith made the important statements that martial law has been proclaimed in both the city and county of Dublin and that reinforcements of troops have been sent from Belfast and from England.

They said drastic action would be taken to suppress the insurgents and that elaborate preparations were under way to insure the arrest of all rebels and sympathizers implicated in the outbreak.

Liberty Hall, the rebel headquarters, and St. Stephen's Green are now occupied by the Government troops, Mr. Birrell asserted.

Eleven Rebels Killed in Riots.

He also said that eleven rioters were killed in the action with the troops.

Mr. Birrell stamped as untrue reports that Vice-Regal Lodge had been seized by the rebels, and said that, outside of the capital, Dublin County is tranquil.

The rebel association, which is believed indentical with the Sinn Feiners organization, has been officially proclaimed illegal.

Mr. Asquith said that as far as he knew the rebels were not in possession of any machine-guns, and added that at Drogheda armed Nationalists volunteers turned out to assist the Government. This announcement was received in the House of Commons with loud cheers.

Announcing that the censorship on news from Ireland will be removed in the very near future, Mr. Birrell stated that he would start for Dublin to-night.

In the House of Lords Lord Lansdowne read a message from the general officer in command of troops in Ireland, stating that a complete cordon of soldiers had been drawn around the centre of the city of Dublin.

Captured Ship Blew Herself Up.

Further information concerning the attempted landing by German warships of arms and ammunition on the Irish coast, when Sir Roger Casement was captured, was also divulged in the House of Lords.

A German auxiliary cruiser, disguised as a Dutch trader, was used to transport the arms and ammunition. This vessel blew herself up after being captured by British warships.

Casement and two other persons, whose names have not been made public, landed in a collapsible boat from a German submarine which accompanied the auxiliary cruiser. Then he was seized with his associates.

Lord Lansdowne admitted that the situation presented considerable danger if it were not grappled with effectively, but he stated his belief that the rebellious movement was predestined to complete and immediate failure.

Lord Midleton said the Lord-Lieutenant of Ireland went to Belfast on Easter Monday, and that a large number of officers had been allowed to attend a race meeting in the neighborhood of Dublin on the same day.

Several of these officers were seized by the rebels as they were attempting to return to duty.

Where the Principal Fighting Occurred in Streets of Dublin

ST. STEPHEN'S GREEN PARK. POST OFFICE IN SACKVILLE STREET.

MAY 4. 1916.

Maison Chanel's Embroidered Jerseys Capture the Fancy of Parisiennes

"Model of the Week" Is Likely to Prove a Leader for the Demi-Saison.

The dress of the hour that is a marked success in Paris is the Chanel embroidered jersey costume, which the HERALD reproduces to-day as the "model of the week," the latest creation of the Maison Gabrielle Chanel, 21 rue Cambon.

The first metal embroidered model in jersey was shown in the Chanel shop some three or four weeks ago, but only within the last ten days have these costumes sprung up like mushrooms over-night, in the streets.

The well-dressed Parisiennes have taken hold of them by the dozens, and they are proving the rage.

The model above is a dark green soft wool jersey. The coat which is made to be worn is a "middie" blouse or "jumper," extends a little below the hip. A band of embroidery in gold thread at the hip line is just above the hem.

The opening down the front and cuffs are outlined by the same gold embroidery and a belt of jersey or gold cloth ties loosely around the waist. The skirt is a simple pleated or umbrella design. The same model in navy blue, embroidered in gold, is equally effective and smart, as is the gray silk jersey embroidered in silver.

Mlle. Chanel herself wears a chic navy blue jersey done in a lighter shade of pastel blue chenille embroidery, which is unusual.

A MODEL OF THE WEEK BY MAISON GABRIELLE CHANEL

TUESDAY MAY 2. 1916.

ALL REBEL FORCES IN DUBLIN SURRENDER

British Officially State That Outbreak Has Been Quelled—1,000 Have Been Made Prisoners, 400 on Saturday Night and Sunday Morning—James Connolly, Leader, Reported Killed, Now Named As Captive With Pearse.

(SPECIAL TO THE HERALD.)

LONDON, Monday.—After a week of fighting, which has resulted in the loss of many lives and the total destruction of several important buildings and enormous damage to many others, the attempt to establish the Irish Republic has ended ignominiously by the surrender of all rebel leaders in Dublin. To-night the city is officially reported to be quite safe and elsewhere the situation is well in hand, according to the report of General Sir John Maxwell.

Official Press Bureau Report.

The Press Bureau this evening issued the following:—

The Field-Marshal Commanding-in-Chief Home Forces reports:—

The General Officer Commanding-in-Chief Irish Forces reports that all the groups of rebels in Dublin have surrendered.

More than 1,000 prisoners have been taken. Of these 489 have been sent to England for incarceration.

In the county of Enniscorthy, the rebels asked that only their leaders be taken as prisoners and that the rank and file of insurgents be permitted to go free.

This proposal was refused.

At six o'clock this morning, the rebels announced their unconditional surrender. All were placed under military guard.

Quiet prevails in Wicklow, Arklow, Dunlavin, Bagenalstown, Wexford, New Ross and the Counties of Cork, Clare, Limerick, Kerry and the whole of Ulster.

James Connolly and H. Pearse, the ringleaders of the revolt, surrendered on Saturday under dramatic circumstances, and signed an appeal to their followers to lay down their arms. Connolly had previously been reported as killed.

The self-appointed "president of the Irish Republic' and members of his Government had been shelled out of the Post Office, which had been their headquarters, and had sought terms of surrender under a flag of truce. The only terms granted were unconditional surrender.

The wording of the two proclamations issued by the leaders of the republic offer a pathetic contrast. The first, given out last Monday, announced the establishment of the new "Government," while the other acknowledged the complete failure of the movement.

AUGUST 4. 1916.

ROGER CASEMENT HANGED.

(SPECIAL TO THE HERALD.)

LONDON, Thursday.—Roger Casement, sentenced to death for high treason, was hanged at nine o'clock this morning in Pentonville Prison.

A small crowd had gathered outside the prison, and some cheers were sent up as the toll of the prison bell announced that Casement had paid the penalty. The crowd then dispersed quietly.

During his last days Casement showed no sign of discouragement. He ate and slept well and conversed light-heartedly with his warders, to one of whom he is said to have admitted that he had been a traitor to his country and deserved the sentence passed on him.

THURSDAY, NOVEMBER 30. 1916.

Why Not "Madame Speaker," When Addressing Chair in Next Congress?

There Is a Good Chance for Miss Jeannette Rankin Who Is a Reputed Orator.

(SPECIAL TO THE HERALD.)

WASHINGTON, D.C., Wednesday.—"Mme. Speaker!"

Why should not this be the method of addressing the chair in the new House of Representatives?

Four men and one woman will hold the balance of power in that body, according to the present indications. This probably means there will be one of the most spectacular fights over the Speakership in the history of the country.

As a compromise why not elect Miss —beg pardon — Representative-elect Jeannette Rankin, of Missoula, Mont., as the next Speaker? This suggestion has been made here by one of the members of the Republican party.

"The old landmarks have been swept away," he remarked. "The women evidently are responsible for the unexpected shift in the political complexion of many Western States. Neither of the old parties is likely to have enough members in the House to insure control. They will have to begin coaxing Representative W. O. Martin, of Louisiana, and T. D. Schall, of Minnesota, progressives; Representative Meyer London, of New York, Socialist, and Representative Alvan T. Fuller, of Massachusetts, Independent.

"Miss Rankin was elected as a Republican, but who knows what a woman in Congress will do? There are no precedents. If neither side can elect its candidate, it will be a gracious thing to compromise on Miss Rankin; it would typify the new order of things in this country."

THURSDAY. APRIL 27. 1916

UNCLE OSTRICH.

(From the "Evening Telegram.")

TUESDAY. SEPTEMBER 26. 1916.

COMBLES ENCIRCLED AS RESULT OF HUGE VICTORY ON SOMME

Great Concerted Attack by Franco-British Troops Carries Powerfully Organized Villages of Morval, Lesbœufs and Rancourt and Completes Investment of Important Town, Which Is Now Definitely Doomed.

Yesterday was a black day for the German armies on the Somme front and one of the most glorious in the history of the Allied offensive. The Franco-British forces north of the river scored a series of magnificent successes which, besides advancing their lines a considerable depth along an extended front, resulted in the capture of the three villages of Rancourt, Morval and Lesbœufs, and completed the investment of the town of Combles.

The concerted attack by the two armies was the carrying out of an extensive scheme of operations which had been prepared to the last detail to ensure unqualified success, and the results even surpassed expectations. The stupendous bombardment of the German positions within the last few days proved so effective that the infantry accomplished their work with comparatively slight losses, while the enemy paid an enormous toll in men in addition to losing a number of his most powerful strongholds on the western front.

Line of Allies' Attack.

The line of the French attack, which was launched about midday, extended eastwards from Combles to Rancourt and then southwards as far as the river, a front of roughly twelve kilomètres. The British attacking front was along the 9½ kilomètre salient between Martinpuich and Combles.

Despite the formidable network of German defences, built up during long occupation and fortified in every conceivable manner, the Allied troops made a clean sweep along practically the whole of the line of battle, and carried all their objectives. "Tommies" and "poilus" attacked with incomparable dash and courage in a mighty onslaught, which paralyzed the enemy's energies. The shock was irresistible, and the German line swayed, crumpled and fell back before the avalanche. At places the enemy made a determined stand, but elsewhere where he had no solid support to cling to he broke and scattered at the first impact.

Combles' Last Outposts Fall.

The villages of Morval, Lesbœufs and Rancourt, the only remaining German outposts of Combles were all engulfed by the waves of Allied troops, the first two falling to the British and Rancourt to the French. These three villages were veritable fortresses, strengthened specially to form a line of support for the German troops in Combles. By their capture the Allies have effectively barred the enemy's exit from this town, which is now strongly surrounded and is definitely doomed.

General Haig's troops, beside capturing Morval and Lesbœufs, wrested from the enemy a stretch of territory nine and a half kilomètres long and more than 1,600 mètres deep, including several lines of trenches.

Importance of French Gains.

The ground captured by the French is equally important. North-east of Combles they pushed forward their lines to the southern borders of Frégicourt and took all the ground between this point and Rancourt, including this village and Hill 148 which dominates it. The French front in this region now forms a solid barrier to the east of Combles, while the British lines further north complete the circle.

East of the Béthune road the French troops pushed forward their lines over the greater part of the front from south of Rancourt to the Somme, the advance being about a kilomètre over about two kilomètres of this front. The high ground north-east of Bouchavesnes was conquered as well as Hill 130, about a kilomètre south-east of the village. Between this point and the river several strong enemy trench systems were captured.

SUNDAY. AUGUST 13. 1916.

PUSHING BACK THE LINE.

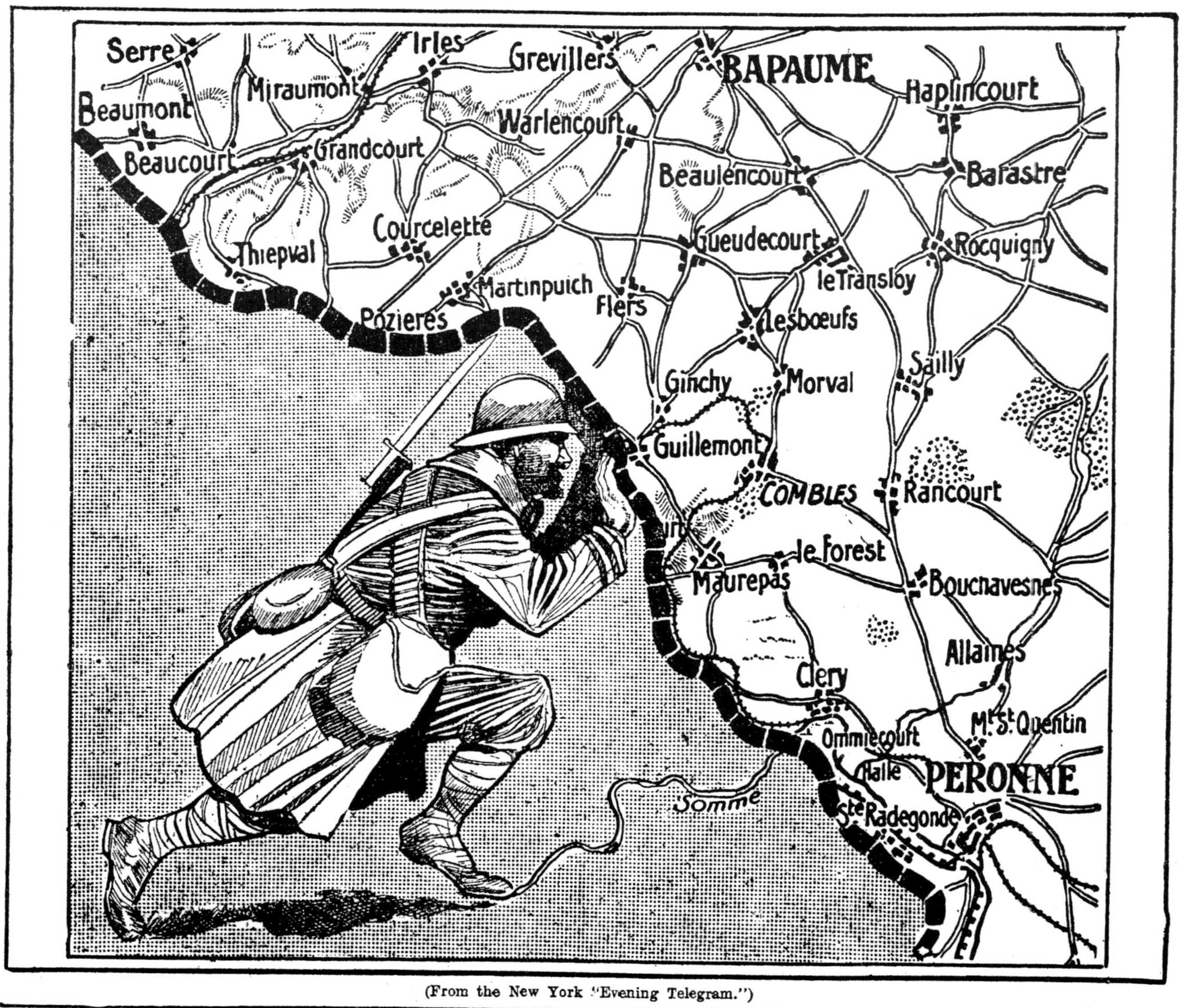

(From the New York "Evening Telegram.")

THE NEW YORK HERALD

PRICE: Paris and France, 15c.; Abroad, 25c. EUROPEAN EDITION—PARIS. SATURDAY. MARCH 17, 1917. Prix: Paris et France. 15c.; Etranger, 25c.

THE TSAR OF RUSSIA ABDICATES

Duma, Army and People Revolt Against Pro-German Influence and Food Crisis; Tsar's Brother as Regent; Battles in Street; Three Days' Bloodshed; Ministers in Prison.

THE NEW GOVERNMENT.

Prime Minister and Minister of the Interior	PRINCE LVOV
Minister of National Defence	M. GUCHKOV
Minister of Justice	M. KERENSKY
Minister of Finance	M. TERESHCHENKO
Minister of Foreign Affairs	M. MILIUKOV
Minister of Agriculture and Food	M. SHINGAREV
Minister of Commerce	M. KONOVALOV
Minister of Ways of Communication	M. NEKRASOV
Procurator of the Holy Synod	M. LVOV
Imperial Controller	M. GODNEV

The abdication of the Tsar has come as a climax to the state of revolution which has existed in Petrograd for some days past. This was the dramatic news announced in the House of Commons on Thursday afternoon by Mr. Bonar Law, and learned by the public in Paris yesterday. The statement made by the British Chancellor of the Exchequer was contained in a telegram from Sir George Buchanan, his Majesty's Ambassador in Petrograd.

Following his original statement on Thursday, Mr. Bonar Law yesterday announced in Parliament that he had received a second despatch from Sir George Buchanan, in which he regretted the categoric declaration made in his first telegram, and added that the statement that the Tsar had abdicated was not absolutely definite.

Despite the British Ambassador's partial retraction, the prevailing opinion everywhere is that while the official news of the Tsar's abdication has not yet been made known it is nevertheless an accomplished fact.

The news contained in numerous despatches from Petrograd, now released after several days' almost complete isolation of the Russian capital, shows that the Cabinet has been overthrown, and that a Provisional Government established by the Duma has chosen Grand Duke Michael Alexandrovich, brother of the Emperor, as Regent during the minority of the Cesarevich.

TSAR FAILS TO MEET DEMAND.

The Duma, backed by the army, has carried out an astonishing and epoch-making coup d'état. With the Petrograd garrison in command of the city, under parliamentary orders, M. Rodzianko, President of the Duma, demanded of the Tsar a new Government. Failing to receive satisfaction, he placed himself at the head of a Provisional Government of twelve members.

This new Ministry immediately assumed control and adopted drastic measures to completely overthrow the old régime. Many of the late Ministers were seized and are now in prison.

The causes of the revolution are now more or less clearly defined, and show that the condition of affairs throughout the Tsar's dominions recently made the change inevitable.

Pro-German influences in high places were deliberately impeding military operations and striving to detach Russia from the Entente. Popular exasperation at this betrayal of Russia's cause came to a head in the latter part of last week, and for three days Petrograd was the scene of fierce fighting.

DISCONTENT WITH PRO-GERMANS.

STORY OF REVOLUTION RELATED IN DESPATCHES FROM RUSSIAN CAPITAL

Scores of People Killed Before Duma Assumes Control—Rioters Acclaim Allied Ambassadors.

(SPECIAL TO THE HERALD.)

LONDON, Friday.—The story of the revolution is told graphically by the Petrograd correspondent of the "Times" in the following despatches sent off between Monday and Wednesday mornings:—

MONDAY, 11.45 A.M.—The events of Friday were multiplied manifold yesterday. Scores of people were killed and wounded in various parts of the Nevsky Prospect during the afternoon. The fine weather brought everybody out of doors, and as the bridges and approaches to the great thoroughfare were left open, crowds of all ages and conditions made their way to the Nevsky, till the miles separating the Admiralty from the Nicholas Station were black with people. [...] the Ministry of the Interior and the Office of the Commandant of the City. Early in the day the prisons were captured and all who were detained in them were set free.

M. Shtcheglovitov, the reactionary president of the Upper House, refused to convoke that Assembly after the Ukase of prorogation. He was arrested by order of the Committee and imprisoned in the Tauris Palace.

According to the latest news from the Duma, the Socialist members seceded from the Committee, finding its demands too moderate. This may impair the usefulness of the Committee as a rallying point, whereas order could be evolved from the present chaos.

The Council of Ministers decided last night to resign and so advised the Emperor, who is said to have replied that he was sending General Alexeiev, the Chief of the General Staff, as dictator.

Convicts Set Fire to Law Courts.

The liberated convicts set fire to the Law Court, but the building was saved [...] ist leaders signified their entire concurrence and withdrew their resignations from the committee, decided to form a provisional Government. A final vote was deferred in consequence of an invitation telephoned to M. Rodzianko to attend a meeting of the Council of Ministers at the Marie Palace.

Duma's Decisive Step.

M. Rodzianko proceeded thither, safely traversing the entire city under a guard of the Duma troops in armored automobiles. He found all the Ministers assembled and also Grand Duke Michael, brother of the Tsar. M. Rodzianko informed them that the Duma, acting in accordance with the nation, had decided to constitute a provisional Government, as they saw no other way of re-establishing order in the capital, of saving the country from anarchy and of enabling Russia to continue the war to a victorious finish.

The majority, if not all, of the Ministers appeared to be willing to surrender and seemed disposed to agree to the [...] yesterday was the sacking of the residence of Count Fredericksz, which adjoins the Telegraph Office. It was thought at first that the Telegraph Office was in danger, but as I telegraphed last night, the Preobrajensky Guards saved it. They could not save Count Fredericksz' house. Meanwhile harrowing scenes occurred. The aged wife of the Minister of the Imperial Court was carried out from the burning residence in a fainting condition. Her daughter, a hunchback, rushed out carrying a favorite dog. The animal was killed and the cripple girl ill-treated by the drunken mob. Both ladies were eventually removed to a place of safety. Count Fredericksz himself is in attendance on the Emperor.

The Social-Democratic party has issued a proclamation of a most seditious character, which was spread broadcast throughout the city. They are mere doctrinaires, but their power for mischief is enormous at a time like the present. The Provisional Committee has, appreciating the dangers ahead, pur-

Members of the Russian Royal House Who Figure in the Establishment of the New Government — M. Rodzianko, Head of Provisional Government.

Nicholas II., Tsar of Russia, has had a tempestuous reign. He was born at Petrograd on May 6, 1868. In 1894 he married Princess Alix of Hesse-Darmstadt, by whom he has had five children, four girls and a boy, Alexis, who was born in 1904.

The Tsar's entire life has been punctuated by the assassination of his relatives and his officials. In 1882 his grandfather, Alexander II., fell.

The year 1905 was one of especial terror. On New Year's Day the Tsar attended the age-old ceremony of "Blessing the Neva." The saluting guns of the fortress of Peter and Paul fired a volley of case-shot in mistake for blank cartridge, and the Tsar and his suite narrowly escaped death.

The end of 1904 and the opening months of 1905 were a period conspicuous even in the terrible annals of Russia. On June 24 of the first-named year 60,000 strikers, most of them armed, sustained a pitched battle with the soldiery in the streets of Lodz.

The Tsar took no considerable part in the development of the war. At one moment he stood out conspicuously when he assumed the command of the army in the place of Grand Duke Nicholas, but the effect was greater among civilians than among soldiers.

The New Tsar.

The health of Prince Alexis, the lad who now, as it appears, is to succeed to the Russian throne under a Regency, has always been a source of great anxiety to his parents.

In 1912 the story was circulated that he had been injured while at play in the palace gardens, but there were rumors of a Nihilist attempt on his life. Four years later he had sufficiently recovered to be able to accompany his father to the Field Headquarters.

He has been described as a bright, high-spirited boy, "a militarist of the most ardent type." He never tires, it is said, of hearing stories of the legendary heroes of Russia.

Grand Duke Michael's Career.

Grand Duke Michael Alexandrovich is the younger brother of the Tsar Nicholas, and was born in Petrograd on November 22, 1878. Until the birth of the Cesarevich Alexis he was heir-presumptive to the Russian throne. He has

THE NEW YORK HERALD

PRICE: Paris and France, 15c.; Abroad, 25c. EUROPEAN EDITION—PARIS. WEDNESDAY, SEPTEMBER 12, 1917. Prix: Paris et France. 15c.; Etranger, 25c.

Latest American News

News Summary

NEWS BULLETINS POSTED.

Telegrams received after the hour of going to press and throughout the day are posted on the HERALD'S bulletin boards at 49 avenue de l'Opéra and 38 rue du Louvre.

DAILY HINT FROM GERMANY

Another "Scrap of Paper."

"German aviators have bombarded army ambulances in Flanders and at Verdun."
—Official communiqués.

"The only exemption from bombardment recognized by international law, through the medium of the Geneva Convention, concerns hospitals and convalescent establishments."

("Usages of War on Land," issued by the German General Staff for the guidance of German officers.)

News Told in Brief.

Von Bernstorff in New Post.

Count von Bernstorff has arrived at Constantinople.

China at War with Austria.

Reuter's Agency learns that China has declared war on Austria-Hungary.

Nice Dailies Dearer To-morrow.

Beginning to-morrow, the Nice daily newspapers will increase their price to 10 centimes per copy.

Fatal Case of Anthrax at Pau.

Two men at Pau contracted anthrax while skinning beasts. One man is dead and the other is dying.

Bavarian General Killed.

General Wenninger, commanding a division of infantry in the Bavarian army, has died of wounds.

To Resume Amsterdam Service.

Service between London, Hull and Amsterdam will soon be resumed by the Holland Navigation Line.

Destructive Fire at Pantin.

Serious damage was caused yesterday morning by a fire in a tarpaulin factory at Pantin. Paris firemen extinguished

PRESIDENT WILSON TO DEAL LENIENTLY WITH STOCKHOLM

Believes Embargo Best Method of Reprisal Against Violations of Neutrality.

"SPURLOS VERSENKT" IS "SCRAP OF PAPER" RIVAL.

The phrase "spurlos versenkt," used in the Swedish "diplomatic" correspondence between the Argentine capital and Berlin, seems to be adding zest to the work of the American army and navy preparations. It is expected the phrase will soon rank with a "scrap of paper" as emblematic of the German mind and methods. Americans have little sympathy with the policy of "spurlos versenkt," and they are asking to-day how many instances have occurred in which peaceful cargo ships have been sunk "without any trace."

NEW YORK, Tuesday.—President Wilson refuses to take stringent measures against Sweden following the revelations made by Mr. Lansing. He considers that the embargo is the most effective means agianst violations of neutrality.—Matin.

May Shut Off on Code.

A report from Washington to the London "Times" states that President Wilson, in his trip on board the Mayflower to see Colonel House at Gloucester, Mass., took up the question of the recent exposure of German intrigues in the Argentine Republic.

The first act of the United States, in conjunction with the Allies, will probably be to refuse to authorize the exchange of telegrams in code between the Swedish diplomatists and the Ministry of Foreign Affairs. Until that question is settled, commercial relations will be suspended automatically by the embargo on American goods to Sweden.

SWEDEN HASN'T RECEIVED REPORT, SO CANNOT MOVE.

LONDON, Tuesday.—Newspapers publish a despatch from Copenhagen giving the text of the Swedish response to the Washington Luxburg exposé as follows:

"The Swedish Minister of Foreign Affairs has received no report on the subject of the transmission of the telegrams mentioned in the declarations of the United States Government, and therefore the Swedish Government can take no attitude on the questions raised. * * * The Minister of the United States in Stockholm in certain cases has asked and obtained the authority to transmit letters

CIVIL WAR BREAKS OUT IN RUSSIA AS KORNILOV ARMY MARCHES ON PETROGRAD TO ASSUME POWER

Members of Provisional Government Resign to Give M. Kerensky Liberty in Dealing with a Situation Most Dangerous Since the Revolution.

Russia is in the throes of civil war and is laboring in a crisis more grave than any that has occurred since the revolution.

General Kornilov, the dismissed Commander-in-Chief, is marching on Petrograd, and the members of the Provisional Government have resigned office in order to leave M. Kerensky full liberty of action to deal with the extremely dangerous situation.

A Havas message from Petrograd, dated yesterday, says that little hope is entertained of a pacific solution of the conflict. The Ministers themselves make no effort to disguise the fact that the situation is extremely critical, and consider it impossible to avoid a collision between the rival factions.

The new situation is presented in the following official communiqué from Petrograd, which shows that the Provisional Government is supported by the Council of Workmen's and Soldiers' delegates and the Committee of the Peasants' Delegates:—

Would Depose Government.

To the army at the front, to the naval committees and to the army generally:

General Kornilov, having put himself at the head of the military counter-revolutionary conspiracy, has moved troops toward Petrograd. His purpose is the deposition of the Provisional Government and the seizure of its powers. The troops directed to Petrograd have been deceived into believing that they are sent to crush a conspiracy of the Maximalists which is non-existent.

The Government has dismissed General Kornilov from his duties. The Central Committees have declared him to be a traitor and an enemy of his Fatherland.

The problem of the Army Committees is to maintain the Provisional Government, to frustrate the criminal designs of General Kornilov and to apply all measures to prevent his conspiracy from reflecting itself disastrously in the stability of the front. We request you:—

1. Not to carry out any orders of General Kornilov and of those traitors who have adhered themselves to him.

2. Quickly and punctually to carry out all demands of the Central Committees, and the commands of the Provisional Government, and of all men who are true to it in command in the forces.

3. To explain to all soldiers, especially among wavering detachments, the true meaning of General Kornilov's plot.

4. To take all measures of precaution

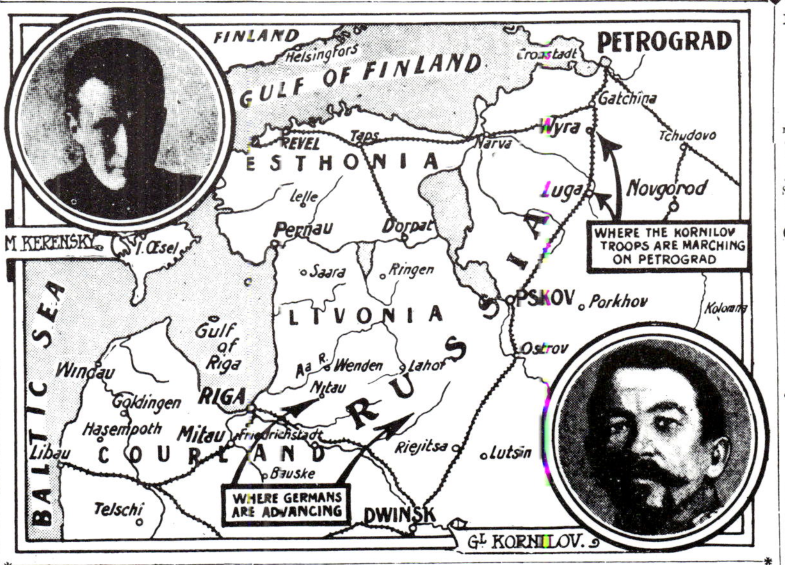

The Russian troops now marching on Petrograd to support General Kornilov's bid for military dictatorship are reported at Luga and Wyra (Viritza), shown on the above map. The former place is a small town on the river of the same name, and is situated at a distance of a little more than sixty-six miles south-west of Petrograd. The railway station of Wyra (Viritza) at which place Kornilov's Cossack division known as the "Savages" is reported, is on the line from Rybinsk to Petrograd. It lies at a distance of about thirty-six miles from the capital. The German army of Prince Leopold of Bavaria, advancing on Petrograd from Riga is just about the same distance from Luga as Luga is from Petrograd.

Klembovsky, appointed provisional generalissimo by M. Kerensky, has not yet assumed command owing to the impossibility of his reaching General Headquarters.

General Vassilkovsky, Military Governor of Petrograd, has resigned. He is succeeded by M. Savinkov, chief of staff at the Ministry of War.

General Kornilov has placed under arrest M. Filonenko, the Commissioner of the Provisional Government at General Headquarters, while M. Kerensky has ordered the arrest of Vladimir Lvov, the Octobrist member of the Duma and former Procurator of the Holy Synod, who transmitted General Kornilov's summons to the Premier to resign office. Eighty other persons also have been arrested by the Government. Other arrests, including that of M. Pourischevich, the notorious reactionary of the Tsarist regime, are expected.

Full Support for Premier.

M. Kerensky is occupying himself with the reconstitution of the Cabinet. Various combinations are discussed, among others being a partial reconstitution of the Ministry with the creation of a special National Council, recalling in cer- [...] events, and the editions of the newspapers are exhausted as soon as they are on sale in the streets.

Appeal to Baltic Fleet to Prepare For the Enemy

PETROGRAD, Tuesday.—On the occasion of the removal of General Kornilov from the chief command, the commander of the Baltic fleet, Admiral Razozov, in an order of the day, invites the fleet to watch for the enemy, to avoid disunion and to submit to the orders of the Provisional Government.—Havas.

General Kornilov Has a Brilliant Military Record

[...] pages in the history of the conquest of Galicia and of the retreat. He sacrificed himself to save the left wing south of Tarnow. Wounded, he fought with a small rearguard till all had fallen. His captivity and escape from an Austrian prison and his triumphal return to Russia last year brought him immense popularity. At the beginning of April he became commander of the forces in Petrograd, but, unable to endure the systematic misrule of the committees, he asked to return to the front. His capture of Halicz and Kalusz signalized him as a leader of men.

Of middle height, spare and erect, he is hardy and untiring, like his Cossack ancestors. His features are rugged and swarthy, his eyes small and piercing and his manner calm and collected.

It is six weeks since General Kornilov succeeded General Brusilov as Commander-in-Chief, after holding for twelve days the command on the Russian south-western front, to which, in recognition of his brilliant work as commander of the army that recaptured Halicz and Kalusz last summer, he had been promoted.

Before accepting the chief command General Kornilov stipulated that there was to be no interference with his fight-

New Commander-in-Chief Unable to Leave Capital to Take Up Duties —Baltic Fleet Will Be Loyal to Its Present Chief.

[...] nity of the town of Radon, an attack on the Russo-Roumanian positions was repulsed, and in the region east of Kimpolung the Russo-Roumanian troops captured the heights near the village of Striptura. North-west of Slonica, the Austrians were repulsed.

GRAND DUKE NICHOLAS' DISAPPEARANCE REPORTED.

COPENHAGEN, Tuesday.—The Helsingfors correspondent of the "Politiken" reports that in Petrograd there are persistent rumors that Grand Duke Nicholas has disappeared from his estate in the Caucasus. — Exchange Telegraph Company.

Japan Promises Russia All Help

NEW YORK, Tuesday—Viscount Ishii, chief of the Japanese Mission in the United States, has informed Mr. Lansing that Japan's full resources will be utilized in as great a measure as possible for the intensive production of military supplies for Russia.

In Washington it is considered that Tokio's decision is the outcome of the many proofs which the Japanese Mission has received that the United States is decided to play a preponderant rôle in the European war and of the impression produced by the enormous military preparations which have been accomplished to bring the war to a rapid and victorious conclusion. Japan's attitude has created keen satisfaction in political circles here. Her promise to place unconditionally her full resources at the disposition of Russia will stop the machinations of the demagogues on both sides of the Pacific.—Matin.

Along the Italian Front, Artillery Action Is General

ROME, Tuesday. — Artillery actions were the principal feature yesterday along the entire front. West of the lake of Garda, however, the enemy, after an intense artillery preparation, attacked our advanced posts between the Concei valley and the lake of Ledro. He succeeded in entering one of them, but was immediately driven out.

Detachments of the enemy's assault troops, supported by waves of infantry, who were marching against our positions of the extreme right wing at the mouths of the Timavo, were stopped and put to flight by our barrage fire. They suf-

THE NEW YORK HERALD

PRICE: Paris and France, 15c.; Abroad, 25c. EUROPEAN EDITION—PARIS, SATURDAY, APRIL 7, 1917. Prix: Paris et France, 15c.; Etranger, 25c.

News Summary

PAGE TWO—
Montreux season opens.
Personal intelligence.
"La Folle Nuit" at the Edouard VII.
Letters to the Editor.

PAGE THREE—
French win ground north-west of Rheims.
British and Russian communiqués.
M. Kerensky calls on deposed Tsar.
British casualties.

PAGE FOUR—
L'Amérique est en guerre.
Nicolas II est à Tsarskoie-Selo.
Paris Society.
Les premières représentations.

NEWS BULLETINS POSTED.

Telegrams received after the hour of going to press and throughout the day are posted on the HERALD'S bulletin boards at 49 avenue de l'Opéra and 38 rue du Louvre.

News Told in Brief.

Scarcity of Coins in Nice.

To remedy the situation caused at Nice by the lack of coinage, the local syndical chamber of tradesmen and shopkeepers has decided to issue cash coupons.

Derbyshire Novelist Dead.

The death is announced of Mr. Murray Gilchrist, the Derbyshire novelist, from pneumonia, at his home, Cartledge Hall, Holmsfield, Derbyshire. He was 49 years of age.

More Belgian Deportations.

News was received recently from Berlin to the effect that the German Emperor had ordered the deportations of Belgians to cease. There is, however, no change in the situation, says the Havas Agency, for on March 24 600 or 700 men were deported to Aix-la-Chapelle, and the following day were sent to Duisberg, where they were stoned by children, and women spat in their faces.

Entente Rugby Game.

To-morrow's Rugby game on the municipal ground at Vincennes will be of particular interest because, as already announced, a team of New Zealand soldiers (all internationals) and a French combination of soldier-internationals will be in opposition. The public will be admitted free, except to the grand stand and the inner enclosures. Play begins at 3 o'clock.

Up the Loire to Orleans.

The waters of the Loire are expected

PRESIDENT WILSON SIGNS WAR MOTION

House, Following the Senate's Lead, Approves Resolution by 373 Votes to 50, and President's Signature Ratifies America's Entry into Conflict Beside the Allies—German Ships Are Seized—Huge War Credits Will Be Granted.

(BY COMMERCIAL CABLE TO THE HERALD.)

WASHINGTON, Friday.—At three o'clock this afternoon, President Wilson signed the resolution declaring that a state of war exists between the United States and Germany, which was voted at three o'clock this morning by the House of Representatives, by 373 votes to 50, with 8 abstentions and 4 absentees. The United States is, therefore, formally aligned with the Entente Powers in the fight against Prussianism. A determined, and if need warrants, ruthless war will henceforth be waged until an unequivocal triumph for humanity is an accomplished fact.

Accordingly, the State Department is already despatching notifications to this effect to all neutral Governments, imposing upon them the necessity of proclaiming their neutrality in the new conflict.

Vice-President Thomas Marshall signed the measure shortly after noon. Already active steps have been taken.

Although fifty members of Congress voted against the war resolution, it is a significant fact that each declared his intention of unwaveringly supporting the Administration in conducting the war once the resolution had been passed.

The actual roll-call on the resolution proceeded without confusion and with calmness, befitting the gravity of the occasion. Practically the only demonstration came when Miss Jeannette Rankin said, tearfully:—

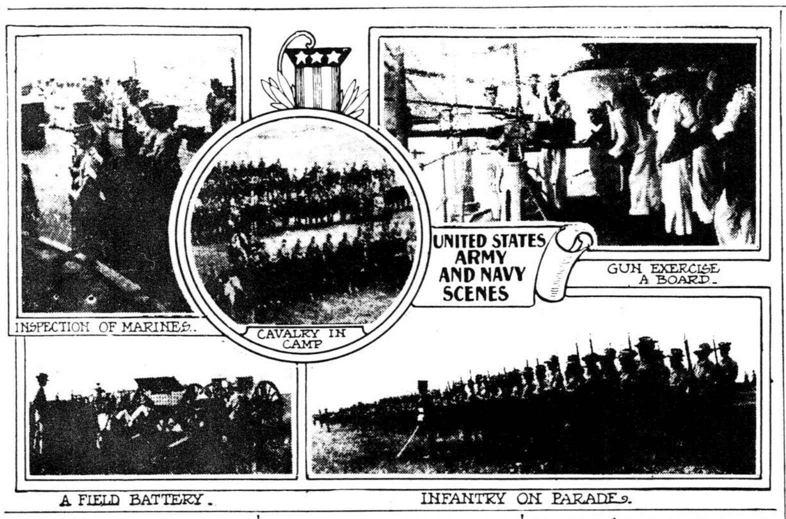

million men in two successive batches of 500,000 men each.

It should be remarked moreover that more than 32,000 companies or trusts have offered their factories and workshops to the Government for the duration of the war. Among these companies are the greatest industrial establishments in the world, such as the Bethlehem Steel Company, the United States Steel Company, the Fore River Shipbuilding Company and the United States Rubber Company.

The Mexican Petroleum Company has placed several million gallons of petroleum at the disposal of the army and navy.

A department of scientific studies has been created and is already working at the Navy Department. Mr. Thomas Edison is giving every assistance to this department.—Matin.

Villistas Moving On Texas Border?

Forces Officered by German Reservists Are Marching Toward Rio Grande, Is Report.

(BY COMMERCIAL CABLE TO THE HERALD.)

WASHINGTON, Friday. — Unusual activity of Pancho Villa's forces is reported from El Paso and San Antonio. Rumors are current that the troops are marching toward Rio Grande officered by German reservists.

Reports from Government agents show that more than 1,000 Germans have

zilian Minister in Paris, relative to the sinking of the Brazilian cargo-boat Parana. He immediately called the Ministers together in order to discuss this incident, the gravity of which is plainly recognized.

The public is not yet informed of the circumstances surrounding the torpedoing, but as soon as the complete details are given out it is expected that they will arouse a great wave of popular wrath against Germany.—Information.

PRESS OF PERU AND CHILE CLAMORS TO JOIN ALLIES.

(BY COMMERCIAL CABLE TO THE HERALD.)

NEW YORK, Friday.—Despatches from the NEW YORK HERALD'S correspondents in Lima, Peru, and Santiago de Chile report that the newspapers of both these cities are up in arms against Germany and demand that their respective Gov-

Signor D'Annunzio Extols America in Prose Masterpiece

Soldier-Bard Salutes President Wilson as "The Knight of Humanity" and Compares Stars of the Republic's Banner to the Pleiades Lighting the Seas "Dishonored by Assassins and Thieves."

The genius of Signor Gabriele D'Annunzio, the greatest living Latin poet, the soldier-bard of the present world-war, who has been wounded, decorated and promoted for his services to the nation, could not fail to respond to America's noble adhesion to the cause of Humanity, says an Associated Press message from Rome.

Signor D'Annunzio has sent the American people, through this agency, the following address, which is acclaimed in its original version as one of the greatest prose masterpieces of modern Italian literature:—

"Venice, April 6, 1917.

"To-day the soul of Italy is in the Capital of Washington, which has become a beacon light like unto the Roman Rock. A garland wreathes the bust dedicated to the hero whom free men call by the glorious name of 'The Knight of Humanity.'

"This garland is as pure as the lilac branch offered by the poet on the bier of Lincoln. It is as sacred as the ever-lowering bough 'with heartshaped leaves of rich green.'

"It seems as though in this April of passion and tempest there re-echoes the cry of that April, dense with joy and

SIGNOR GABRIELE D'ANNUNZIO

burg, on the soil sanctified by the blood of the combatants. All the States of the North, the South, the East and the West heard them in heroic night. Here only shines the Constellation of Spring——.

"I tell you that this nation under God, shall have a new birth of Freedom. "GABRIELE D'ANNUNZIO."

Germany's Press

THE NEW YORK HERALD

PRICE: Paris and France, 15c.; Abroad, 25c. EUROPEAN EDITION—PARIS, THURSDAY, APRIL 19, 1917. Prix: Paris et France, 15c.; Etranger, 25c.

News Summary

PAGE TWO—
Geneva hotel keeps up tradition.
Franco-American trade boom coming.
New York and London financial reports.
Personal intelligence.

PAGE THREE—
Russian Socialists disavow M. Lenine.
Court and society news from London.
Casualties among British officers.
Mr. Walter Raphael sued by daughter-in-law.

PAGE FOUR—
Nouveaux succès de l'offensive française.
Les grèves de Berlin.
Paris Society.
Bourses de Londres et de Paris.

NEWS BULLETINS POSTED.

Telegrams received after the hour of going to press and throughout the day are posted on the HERALD'S bulletin boards at 49 avenue de l'Opéra and 38 rue du Louvre.

News Told in Brief.

Another Grandchild for the Kaiser.

The Duchess of Brunswick, daughter of the German Emperor, has given birth to a daughter.

Greek Cabinet Crisis Imminent?

An Athens despatch states that the resignation of the Lambros Cabinet is considered to be imminent.

Auxiliaries of the 1918 Class.

The recruits of the 1918 class declared fit for the auxiliary service will be incorporated on May 4 next.

German Avions Over Switzerland.

German aviators again flew over the Swiss frontier yesterday morning. Swiss border posts fired upon them.

Germany's "Forlorn Hopefuls."

The German military authorities have ordered the examination of conscripts of the 1919 class to begin to-morrow.

New Governor of Belgium.

The Governor-General of Belgium, Von Bissing, who had already been laid low by illness, is again in failing health and has been replaced by General von Zwehl.

Accident in French Mine.

About forty miners employed in pit No. 9 of the Nœux mines, at Barlin, near Hazebrouck (Nord), were severely injured on Monday by an explosion of fire-damp.

Toulon Arsenal Blast: Nine Killed.

Nine men were killed and seven were more or less seriously injured on Tuesday by an explosion in Toulon arsenal. Rear-Admiral Habert has been instructed to report on the explosion.

Marks But Not Money.

According to the "Kölnische Volkszeitung," the subscriptions to the sixth German war loan will total 12,000,000,000 marks. The amount of fresh money in this total is not mentioned.

Southern France's Gift to Verdun.

At yesterday's sitting of the Conseil-Général of the Department of the Bouches-du-Rhône, held at Marseilles, it was decided that the grant of 250,000fr. already voted by the assembly for the city of Verdun, should be devoted to the rebuilding of its schools.

Gas Restrictions Continue.

The Prefect of Police has extended until further notice the dispositions of the ordinances of December 18 and 21 last concerning the consumption of gas and electricity in Paris and the Department of the Seine. The regulations were originally applicable only until April 15.

DECREE RESTRICTING SALE OF PETROL NOW SIGNED.

Ten Litres of Combustible Is Limit of Day's Supply Except in Specified Cases.

A decree regulating the consumption

U BOAT LAUNCHES TORPEDO AT AMERICAN DESTROYER OFF NEW YORK, JUST MISSING

Actual Hostilities Open When the U.S.S. Smith Is Attacked by German Submarine in Small Hours of Tuesday Morning About 100 Miles South of Sandy Hook, Projectile Crossing Her Bow Barely Thirty Yards Away.

(BY COMMERCIAL CABLE TO THE HERALD.)

WASHINGTON, Wednesday.—Hostilities between America and Germany opened in real earnest yesterday morning, when a German submarine, 100 miles south of New York, attempted to sink the United States destroyer Smith (Lieutenant R. T. Merrill, 2nd, commanding) by launching a torpedo, which missed her by only thirty yards. The following is the statement issued yesterday at the Navy Department by Mr. Josephus Daniels, Secretary of the Navy.—

"It has been reported to the naval wireless stations at Boston and New York, that, at 3.30 a.m. to-day (Tuesday, April 17), an enemy submarine was sighted by the United States warship Smith, running apparently submerged. The submarine fired a torpedo at the Smith and missed her by thirty yards. The wake of the torpedo was plainly seen crossing the Smith's bows. The submarine then disappeared before the Smith could engage her."

Attack Occurs in Shipping Lanes.

This, the first official act of war, occurred somewhere within a radius of 100 miles from Sandy Hook, N.J. The naval censor allows the sending of an unconfirmed unofficial report which says that the scene of the action took place about thirty-eight miles south of Sandy Hook.

The Navy Department is awaiting further details. It is known that the Smith sent a wireless "flash" to the light cruiser Chester, which is acting as temporary flagship of the First Naval District, worded as follows: "Apparently sighted enemy submarine."

The Charlestown navy yard, which was the first to be informed of the attack, has notified the State Department that the attack constitutes the recognition by Germany of the existence of a state of war with the United States.

"Barred Zone" in American Waters.

During the past week the Government learned in a roundabout manner that Germany was about to proclaim that the territorial waters of the ports of Boston, New York, Charleston, Savannah, the Delaware and Virginia capes and, in fact, all the ports on the Atlantic seaboard form a new "barred zone."

In official circles this action by Germany is believed to be highly probable. The Germans apparently are resorting to their old tactics, seeking to terrorize neutrals in order that they will steer clear of all American Atlantic ports.

New York and Philadelphia report that the stock markets to-day were not unduly affected.

Stimulates Naval Recruiting.

The news of the attack was generally known throughout the national capital by midday. It roused everyone here, except Administration officials, to a high pitch of excitement. Its first effects were to give a decided impetus to recruiting for the navy, just as the Zeppelin raids on England acted as a stimu-

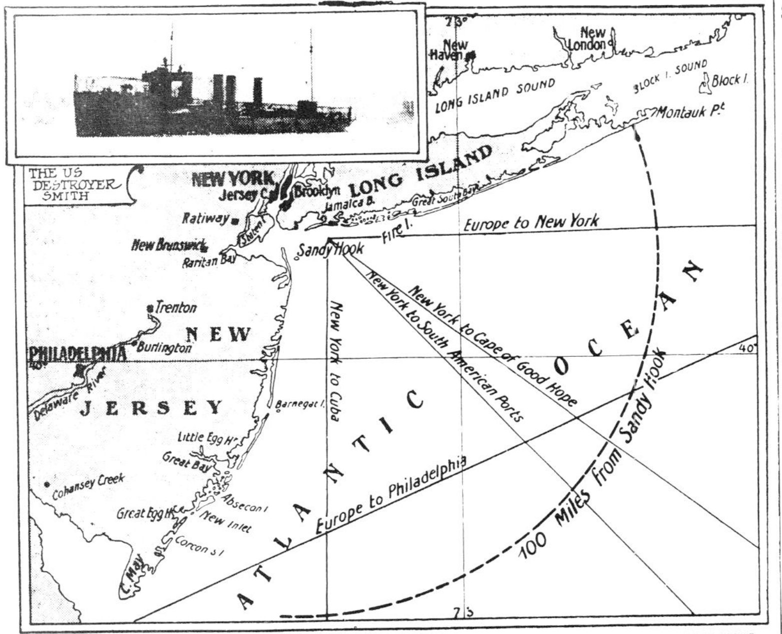

CHART SHOWING AREA WITHIN WHICH THE UNITED STATES DESTROYER SMITH WAS ATTACKED. SHIPPING ROUTES TO AND FROM NEW YORK AND PHILADELPHIA ARE ALSO INDICATED.

Senate Solidly Votes the "Old Glory War Loan"

Even Rabid Pacifists Support $7,000,000,000 Bill Slightly Altered from House Measure.

WASHINGTON, Wednesday.—The Senate yesterday unanimously voted the $7,000,000,000 war revenue bill, popularly known as the "Old Glory loan." Slight changes in the wording of the resolution as passed by the House of Representatives were made, necessitating a conference between both branches of Congress. After these have been held, the approved text will be presented to President Wilson for his signature.

During the purely formal debates that preceded the vote, Senator William S. Kenyon, Republican of Iowa, said that he hoped that the vote would be unanimous and that France would never be asked to pay back the money loaned her.

Senator W. K. Vardaman, Democrat of Mississippi, and Senator William F. Kirby, Democrat of Arkansas, both of whom had voted against the armed neutrality and state-of-war resolutions, and who hitherto have been classed as the most rabid of pacifists, cast their votes in the affirmative.

The Kaiser and the German people, said one Senator, have proclaimed to

United States Officials Perceive Clouds in Mexico

Carranza Government Reported Hostile to Washington and in League With Germany.

(BY COMMERCIAL CABLE TO THE HERALD.)

NEW YORK, Wednesday.—A special despatch from El Paso, Tex., to the HERALD this morning says that the Government officials at El Paso are expecting a serious turn of affairs in Mexico following reports received from agents in the larger Mexican cities. The attitude of President Carranza toward the Government is not conducive to the continuance of good relations with the United States.

Mexico is lending her moral support to Germany and is accepting financial support from German bankers and business men.

The majority of the members of the Cabinet of the "de facto" Government are hostile to the United States and are staunch supporters of Germany.

Four Reasons to Expect Trouble.

Reports forwarded to Washington give four reasons to expect trouble: firstly, that fifteen thousand Carranza soldiers are leaving the Southern States and are being mobilized in Chihuahua; secondly, that disorders occurred in the Mexican Congress over the discussion of Carranza's plea for Mexico to remain neutral, his suggestions being re-

America's Entry Hailed by Both British Houses

Parliament Expresses Appreciation of Uncle Sam's Championship of Freedom's Cause.

(SPECIAL TO THE HERALD.)

LONDON, Wednesday.—The House of Commons this afternoon passed by acclamation a resolution welcoming the entry of America into the war.

The resolution, which was in the following terms, was proposed by Mr. Bonar Law, in the absence of the Prime Minister, who has been called to an important conference on the Continent:—

"That this House desires to express to the Government and people of the United States of America their profound appreciation of the action of that Government in joining the Allied Powers and thus defending the high cause of freedom and the rights of humanity against the gravest menace by which they have ever been imperilled."

Mr. Bonar Law said that the people of the British Empire and their Allies rejoiced at the adhesion of the new Ally, as the greatest event which had marked the decisive moment of the war.

"The hour of change approaches," he continued, "and the end of the long period of sadness and anguish which desolates the world is less distant. We

HUGE GAINS CROWN FRENCH ONSLAUGHT

Seven Powerfully Fortified Villages Are Carried by Victorious Troops—More Than 3,000 Prisoners Taken With Many Guns and Enormous Quantities of Material—British Still Advance.

France's mighty offensive is assuming the proportions of a great strategic and tactical victory.

The military results of three days' action comprise the capture of the whole of the German front line over an extent of sixty kilomètres, the acquisition of a number of important villages, 17,000 prisoners and seventy-five guns.

Yesterday all three armies operating along the front between Soissons and Aubérive scored magnificent successes. On the left wing Nanteuil-la-Fosse, Vailly, Chavonne, Chivy, Ostel and Braye-en-Laonnais were stormed. On the centre formidable enemy defences in the Ville-aux-Bois sector were carried, while on the right wing the last elements of the network of fortifications on the Moronvilliers massif were won.

Yesterday's results surpassed those of either Monday or Tuesday. From this, it may be deduced that operations are developing satisfactorily, and confidence in the future is supreme.

GERMAN JOURNAL PREDICTS FRESH STRATEGIC RETREAT.

BALE, Wednesday.—Two significant admissions in connection with the war on the western front are made by the "Vossische Zeitung" and the Schwabische Tagwacht," respectively.

"Vossische Zeitung."

"Hindenburg is going to make a new strategic retreat in the sector to the north of Arras. This removal of our lines will cause us to abandon a few of our positions in order to bring our line to a point further in the rear and more suitable for defence."

"Schwabische Tagwacht."

The "Schwabische Tagwacht" says: "We have no longer any need to hide the truth. We shall never be able to vanquish and it is useless that the people be deceived any longer."

"Deutsche Tageszeitung."

Count Reventlow in the "Deutsche Tageszeitung," deplores the opposition of the democrats to territorial expansion, and pays a somewhat doubtful compliment to the Emperor by saying: "The German victory and the German monarchy depend one upon the other. Without a German victory the monarchy will cease to exist."

FRENCH OFFICIAL COMMUNIQUES

WEDNESDAY, 2 p.m.

In the region to the south of Saint-Quentin the night was marked by very great activity of both artilleries. There were also numerous encounters between patrolling parties to the south of the Oise, in the sector to the east of the Lower Coucy forest.

North-east of Soissons a surprise attack on the enemy's lines to the north of Laffaux enabled us to bring in about twenty prisoners.

Between Soissons and Aubérive our troops, during the night, effected at divers points of the front detail operations which brought us considerable advantages. To the west, an action, brilliantly carried out, enabled us to seize the village of Chavonne and to

occupants were killed or taken prisoners. Our line has been completely restored.

Between Soissons and Aubérive we vigorously continued our action at various points despite persistent bad weather.

On the western part of the front of attack the operations were crowned with the most brilliant success. North of Chavonne our troops captured the village of Ostel and drove the enemy a kilomètre northward.

Braye-en-Laonnois was also conquered as well as all the ground eastward as far as the outskirts of Courtecon. Under the vigorous pressure of our infantry and the deadly action of our guns the enemy retired in disorder, abandoning an important quantity of material and leaving his food stores in our hands.

One of our regiments alone took three hundred prisoners belonging to seven different regiments. We captured nineteen guns including five howitzers.

South of Laffaux our troops, covered on the south by divisional cavalry succeeded in rushing the enemy and capturing Nanteuil-la-Fosse.

Finally, on the southern bank of the Aisne, an attack vigorously carried out gave us the bridgehead organised by the enemy between Condé and Vailly as well as the whole of this latter locality.

In the Ville-aux-Bois Forest an important unit surrounded by our troops was forced to lay down its arms. Thirteen hundred prisoners and one hundred and eighty machine-guns used for the defence of a wood were thus captured.

About 4.30 p.m. the Germans, two divisions strong, launched a very violent counter-attack on our positions between Juvincourt and the Aisne. Our curtain and machine-gun fire broke up the attack and inflicted heavy losses on the enemy who was unable to reach our lines at any point.

East of Courcy, the Russian brigade completed its successes by capturing a fortified work and taking prisoners.

During the operations, in the whole of this region, we captured twenty-four heavy and field guns. Three 150mm. guns intact, with a thousand shells for each gun, have been turned by our artillerymen against the enemy.

In Champagne we have reduced several isolated points of resistance and captured some enemy supporting points. Twenty guns, including eight heavy, and five hundred more prisoners fell into our hands.

The number of valid prisoners brought to the rear since the beginning of the battle now exceeds seventeen thousand. Seventy-five guns have so far been counted.

BRITISH OFFICIAL COMMUNIQUES

WEDNESDAY, 11.15 a.m.

A fresh advance was effected during the night to the south-east and to the

THE NEW YORK HERALD

PRICE: Paris and France, 15c.; Abroad, 25c. — EUROPEAN EDITION—PARIS, THURSDAY, JUNE 14, 1917. — Prix: Paris et France, 15c.; Etranger, 25c.

News Summary

NEWS BULLETINS POSTED.

Telegrams received after the hour of going to press and throughout the day are posted on the HERALD'S bulletin boards at 49 avenue de l'Opéra and 38 rue du Louvre.

News Told in Brief.

Thunderstorms in the Provinces.

Numerous thunderstorms have occurred in Burgundy and Morvan. Several persons are reported to have been killed in Bresse and Auxunois.

Montenegrin King at Vichy.

The King of Montenegro is expected soon at Vichy, where he will undergo treatment, as he did last year.

French Officer Drowned.

Lieutenant Doé, a French officer living at the Château des Cours, near Troyes (Aube), was drowned while boating on the Seine near that town yesterday.

M. Viviani to Report.

It is said that M. René Viviani, Keeper of the Seals, will make an official declaration at the opening of the Chamber today on the results of his voyage to the United States and the co-operation of America in the war.

Fire Epidemic in Germany.

According to Reuter's agency, an epidemic of fires would appear to be raging in Germany and Austria. Seventeen farms and 47 houses have been destroyed at Klietz and, among many conflagrations, three which broke out at Budapest were due to malevolence.

Senate and the Stockholm Conference.

The resolution voted unanimously in the French Senate on June 6, regarding the Stockholm conference, was telegraphed yesterday by the Premier to the French Ambassador in Petrograd, with instructions that it be transmitted to the Russian Government as a sequel to previous communications on the same subject.

Woman Wins Croix de Guerre.

Mme. Liouville, wife of Dr. Jacques Liouville and daughter-in-law of Mme Waldeck-Rousseau, has been awarded the Croix de Guerre and mentioned in despatches as follows: "Since March, 1915, has assisted in perilous evacuation work under heavy fire. On May 10, 11 and 12, 1917, assured the safety of many wounded civilians during the bombardment of a village."

Seek Traitor or Spy for Leakage of Naval Secrets

(BY COMMERCIAL CABLE TO THE HERALD.)

WASHINGTON, Wednesday.—During the investigation into the recent naval accidents before the Senate Committee on Naval Affairs, Mr. Josephus Daniels, Secretary of the Navy, last night charged that a spy or traitor has access to the files of the Navy Department.

This statement caused the committee to go into secret session. Mr. Daniels made his declaration following the reading of a letter sent to Senator Joseph S. Frelinghuysen, Republican, of New Jersey, which quoted data which had been supposed to be of the most secret nature.

The identity of the sender of the letter is not known. The Federal Secret Service dragnet is endeavoring to locate him.

Giants Maul Cubs; Reds Whip Robins

(BY COMMERCIAL CABLE TO THE HERALD.)

NEW YORK, Tuesday (*delayed in transmission*).—Although all the games scheduled to be played yesterday in the American League were postponed on account of the rain, the National League clubs were all able to hold their contests, fine weather prevailing in the west, where the eastern teams are now engaging their diamond rivals.

The New York Giants took some of the starch out of "Fred" Mitchell's Chicago Cubs by handing them a severe 8 to 2 lacing. Father Knickerbocker's boys and the Boston Braves were the only easterners to turn back their foes, the Dodgers and Phillies succumbing to the superior prowess of their wild and woolly opponents.

"Matty's" Cincinnati nine just managed to nose out "Robbie's" Brooklyn Dodgers in an extra inning game by 3 runs to 2. Poor base-running cost the Robins the pastime. St. Louis took Philadelphia into camp in another hot encounter by 5 runs to 4, while the final tally in the Pittsburg-Boston dispute was: Braves 2, Pirates 0.

LIFE EMPTY IF PRUSSIANS WIN, DECLARES MR. GERARD

(BY COMMERCIAL CABLE TO THE HERALD.)

NEW YORK, Wednesday.—Mr. James W. Gerard, former American Ambassador in Berlin, addressing a dinner of the Presbyterian Social Union at the Hotel Astor yesterday evening, said: "If you want to send missionaries abroad you ought to send them to Germany. Liberty and honor are without value if we allow Prussian military autocracy to succeed in this war."

PARIS WILDLY WELCOMES GENERAL PERSHING AND FIRST AMERICAN FIGHTING UNIT IN HISTORIC DEMONSTRATION

Hundreds of Thousands Greet Soldiers of the Sister Democracy in a Tremendous and Spontaneous Outburst of Sympathy.

Democracy greeted democracy yesterday when Major-General John J. Pershing arrived in Paris with the first American contingent ever to land on European soil on a belligerent mission.

Democracy was the keynote of the day. Paris greeted Pershing as New York greeted Joffre, with all the formalities, but behind them a genuine sympathy and a subtle understanding that leaped the barriers of language.

The reception of the leaders of the United States army can best be described as the sort that brought tears to American eyes. It was from the heart.

The crowds cheered themselves hoarse. They blocked the passage of the procession at a dozen points; they wrung the hands of soldiers and officers; they showered flowers upon them. The reception not only astonished the American soldiers and officers, it deeply moved them.

America will never forget this great spontaneous outpouring of Paris' millions; nor will the members of the first American contingent, which has come to France to shed its blood that democracy may live.

Great Crowd Awaits Train.

As early as 4.30 yesterday afternoon the streets around the Gare du Nord were packed and police lines were established. The station itself was filled with a great crowd. The first-class waiting-room had been converted into a "salon de réception." Tapestry curtains of red velvet, trimmed with gold braid and twenty feet high, adorned the entrance to the mirrored reception room, which was carpeted with costly rugs.

At 5 p.m. two companies of agents de police cleared the crowd from part of the platform of the station and corraled it a hundred feet away from the corridor down which General Pershing was to pass. Squads of sweepers polished the cement platform until it was spotless.

One noticed among the crowd two American girls, ambulance drivers, one

As Marshal Joffre and General Pershing came down the platform the crowd in the station and several hundred urchins on the tops of wagons in the train shed cheered wildly. The crowd

GENERAL PERSHING.

BY COURTESY OF THE "PETIT PARISIEN."

CROWD IN THE PLACE DE LA CONCORDE CHEERING GENERAL PERSHING ON THE BALCONY OF THE CRILLON.

GENERAL PERSHING ARRIVING AT BOULOGNE.

MAJOR ROBERT BACON.

GENERAL PERSHING'S GREETINGS TO FRANCE.

'We Have Come to Fight, Whatever May Befall," Says American Commander as Marshal Joffre Welcomes Him to France.

which was translated by Lieutenant Jacques Cartier.

"You are the first to come to France," he said, "of that American army which we have so eagerly awaited, but you are not the first to fight in our ranks. Some of the most valiant among you have already proved themselves our equals, in particular among our aviators, and if America was not yet at our side, her heart was with us all the time.

"I am happy this evening to salute you in the name of the Paris garrison and in that of the whole French army, which is happy to welcome you as the last, but not the least dear to us, and as brothers. I bid you welcome with all my heart."

American Embassy Dinner.

Shortly before eight o'clock General Pershing and staff left for the American Embassy, where they had dinner with Mr Sharp, Marshal Joffre, MM. Ribot, Painlevé, Viviani, Chambrun, French Cabinet members and their wives, the members of the American Embassy staff and prominent members of the American colony in Paris identified with relief work.

Boulogne Starts France's Welcome

The sun shone brilliantly from a serenely blue sky as General Pershing set foot on French soil at Boulogne yesterday morning.

The cross-channel steamer Invicta, transporting the general and his staff and a large contingent of British troops, steamed into the Chanzy basin at Boulogne at 9.40 amid the acclamations of crowds of French and British soldiers and civilians on shore.

The vessel was escorted from England by numerous destroyers, hydro-aeroplanes and dirigibles.

Military bands struck up the "Star Spangled Banner" and the "Marseillaise" as the ship berthed, and General Pershing was seen on deck saluting sur-

41 KILLED IN NEW LONDON AIR RAID BY HUNS

Fleet of Fifteen Aeroplanes Drops Bombs Also on County of Essex.

(SPECIAL TO THE HERALD.)

LONDON, Thursday.—A fleet of fifteen German aeroplanes executed a fresh raid on London and the county of Essex this morning, dropping a large number of bombs which in the London region alone killed 41 people and injured 121. These totals are stated to be incomplete and are likely to be swelled when reports from outlying districts come to hand.

Details given in official reports and by Mr. Bonar Law in the House of Commons show that the hostile craft passed over the Essex coast about 10.30 this morning travelling in the direction of London. They separated en route and a number of them arrived over the eastern suburbs about 11 o'clock.

One bomb fell on a school, killing 10 children and injuring 50 others, while another hit a train as it arrived in a railway station, 7 passengers being killed and 17 injured.

A number of buildings were wrecked, and fires broke out here and there.

The raid on London and suburbs lasted about a quarter of an hour. Immediately the enemy was signalled on the coast a large flotilla of British aeroplanes took the air and endeavored to drive off the hostile machines. The special batteries of anti-aircraft guns on the coast also engaged the raiders and the air defences of the capital also entered into play.

A number of air duels were fought, and it is reported that at least one of the enemy was brought down. The inhabitants of the East End of London witnessed a thrilling aerial battle between two machines and saw the enemy turn tail and make off toward the coast hotly pursued by the British craft.

During the raid the sound of the exploding bombs and the violent cannonade which greeted the raiders could be heard over a considerable radius. After dropping their bombs, those of the enemy who had managed to penetrate as far as the eastern districts of the metropolis made off in a north-easterly direction.

...ounced refer to ...ly details received ...cted by the raid ...persons were in...ped on the coast ...nd and along the ...on King George ...of the East End ...attack.

...Sink ...ore Ships

...made last night of ...ssian submarines. ...p Sequana, 5,357 ...bottom on June 8, ...0 persons on board ...ed American tank ...,710 tons, was the ...wenty of her crew

...llapse ...ncourt ...Eighteen

...enault factories at ...e Seine, collapsed ...sterday morning, ...ve been recovered ...some 68 people are

...the first reports of ...Paris were greatly ...aster occurred in ...about 150 yards ...heavy machinery ...cture of automo...

...s of danger were ...ordered the 800 ...building to leave, ...d to do calmly. A ...its, however, re...es and effects, and ...owed by others. ...ing collapsed and ...sexes were buried ...ccident created a ...orkshops and the ...streets crying for ...firemen arrived ...d and injured were ...as possible

SUNDAY, JULY 1, 1917

ARRIVAL OF AMERICAN TROOPS IN FRANCE

BEFORE DISEMBARKATION.

TWO OF THE TRANSPORTS

PHOTOS BARRIERE

MAJOR-GENERAL SIBERT.

EN ROUTE FOR CAMP.

UNDER THE FLAG — GERMAN PRISONERS AT WORK

HAPPY TO BE FRANCE

THE NEW YORK HERALD

PRICE: Paris and France, 15c.; Abroad, 25c. — EUROPEAN EDITION—PARIS, WEDNESDAY, AUGUST 1, 1917. — Prix: Paris et France, 15c.; Etranger, 25c

Latest American News

News Summary

NEWS BULLETINS POSTED.

Telegrams received after the hour of going to press and throughout the day are posted on the HERALD'S bulletin boards at 49 avenue de l'Opéra and 38 rue du Louvre.

DAILY HINT FROM GERMANY

PRUSSIA'S PRINCIPLES.

"In politics, sentiment is foolishness, humanitarianism, stupidity. Profits should be shared only with one's countrymen. Justice and injustice are ideas that exist only among individuals."

(From "Greater Germany," by Otto Richard Tannenberg.)

News Told in Brief.

Mr. Churchill Wins Election.

Mr. Winston Churchill has been elected to the House of Commons by 7,302 votes against 2,036 for Mr. Scrymgeour, the temperance candidate opposing him.

Suspects Arrested in New York.

Two individuals representing themselves as members of the British Royal Flying Corps were recently arrested as suspects in New York. They claimed to be on a secret mission and were going from Canada to Florida.

Germans' "Soft Cash."

The "Reichsanzeiger," German Imperial "official journal," published a decree recently providing for the demonetization of silver and nickel coins. Everything is to be done to hasten the return from circulation of this money.

A Pound for Pound of Butter.

The "Daily Express" correspondent in New York says: Information which has reached Washington shows that the majority of Hungarians are living on vegetables, of which the supplies are limited, while only the rich can purchase meat. Déjeuners cannot be bought at restaurants in Austria for less than 21s. a person, while three pounds of meat costs a similar amount. Olive oil is 42s. a quart, butter 20s. a pound and chickens 42s. each.

Storm Havoc in France.

Violent storms are reported from the Departments of the Alpes-Maritimes, Aube, Seine-et-Marne and Seine-Inférieure. Cereals, fruit, vegetables and vines were destroyed in the region of Nice. Provins, in the Seine-et-Marne, presents the spectacle of a bombarded town, roofs having been stripped off, the streets being littered with débris and shopfronts blown in. Six communes in that region were devastated by the storm, which caused damage estimated at more than 10,000,000fr.

M. Pierre Baudin Dead.

M. Pierre Baudin, Senator for the Ain Department and ex-French Minister, has just died, in his fifty-fourth year. He was a nephew of Alphonse Baudin, who was killed in December, 1851, at the barricade in the Faubourg Saint-Antoine. M. Pierre Baudin was Minister of Public Works in the Waldeck-Rousseau Cabinet, in 1899, and Minister of Marine during M. Barthou's term of office as Premier, in 1913. He succeeded M. Alfred Mézières as president of the Paris Association of Journalists.

FRENCH STEAMER FOUNDERS OFF ADEN, FOUR DROWNED.

(SPECIAL TO THE HERALD.)

ADEN, Monday *(delayed in transmission)*.—The French steamer Tadjoura foundered, yesterday at noon, capsizing in moderate weather, when 25 miles off Aden.

Two engineers and two Arabs were drowned. The remainder of those on board were saved, after they had been in the water for several hours, by an Aden steamer.

The Tadjoura was a steamer of 518 tons displacement, owned by the Compagnie de l'Afrique Orientale, of Marseilles and Djibouti. She was built at Port de Bouc in 1911.

MISS JULIA MEYER TO WED ITALIAN DIPLOMATIST.

(BY COMMERCIAL CABLE TO THE HERALD.)
HERALD OFFICE,
NEW YORK,
July 31, 1917

Mr. George von L. Meyer, formerly Secretary of the Navy, and Mrs. Meyer, now living at Boston, announce the engagement of their daughter Julia to Signor Giuseppe Brambilla, Councillor of the Italian Embassy. Signor Brambilla is one of the most popular figures in Washington diplomatic circles. The romance started when Miss Meyer's father was Ambassador to Italy.

LOGAN.

PRESIDENT SCORES AS CONFEREES KILL FOOD TRIUMVIRATE

They Grant Him Free Hand to Name Single Administrator Without Senate's Confirmation.

(BY COMMERCIAL CABLE TO THE HERALD.)
HERALD BUREAU,
WASHINGTON, D.C.,
July 31, 1917.

President Wilson won a victory over the Senatorial recalcitrants when the food control bill conferees of the Senate and the House of Representatives decided, at a late hour last night, by a vote of 11 to 3, to eliminate the triumvirate provision from the measure, leaving it to the President to name a single Food Administrator, without the necessity of the latter's appointment being confirmed by the Senate.

J. K. OHL.

Censor Head in Emphatic Denial

(BY COMMERCIAL CABLE TO THE HERALD.)
HERALD BUREAU,
WASHINGTON, D.C.
July 31, 1917.

Rumors that Mr. George Creel will resign his position as Chairman of the Committee on Public Information, as a result of the criticism of the censorship, are emphatically denied by Mr. Creel.

J. K. OHL.

Exercise Keeps President Fit

(BY COMMERCIAL CABLE TO THE HERALD.)
HERALD BUREAU,
WASHINGTON, D.C.
July 31, 1917.

Despite the war burdens, President Wilson is in the best physical condition since he took office, it is thought, as the result of his not permitting his war duties to interfere with his exercise. His mornings are devoted to golf, riding and motoring, and his afternoons and evenings to state business.

J. K. OHL.

Harrison G. Otis Dies in the West

(BY COMMERCIAL CABLE TO THE HERALD.)
HERALD OFFICE,
NEW YORK,
July 31, 1917.

General Harrison Grey Otis, proprietor of the Los Angeles "Times," died yesterday after a sudden attack of heart disease at the home of his son-in-law, Mr. Harry Chandler, in Los Angeles. Although in poor health recently General Otis had not missed a day at his desk in the "Times" office for several weeks.

KILBON.

COMMISSIONS IN MARINES TO BE GIVEN TO NON-COMS.

(BY COMMERCIAL CABLE TO THE HERALD.)
HERALD BUREAU,
WASHINGTON, D.C.,
July 31, 1917.

Major-General George Barnett, commandant of the Marine Corps, announces that officers' vacancies during the war will be filled by meritorious non-commissioned officers who demonstrate their ability by distinguishing themselves in active service. This follows the announcement that sixty-five such non-commissioned officers will receive commissions.

J. K. OHL.

GOVERNMENT STOPS SPEECH BY SENATOR LA FOLLETTE.

(BY COMMERCIAL CABLE TO THE HERALD.)
HERALD BUREAU,
WASHINGTON, D.C.,
July 31, 1917.

Senator Robert M. La Follette has been silenced for a day by the Government. When the Department of Justice asked the police to withhold permission for a meeting at Pittsburg protesting against the draft at which he was billed as the principal speaker, the meeting was called off. It had been sponsored by the Socialists. Another meeting was held outside the city limits, but Senator La Follette did not appear.

KILBON.

M. Tardieu on France's War Work

NEW YORK, Tuesday.—The achievements of France since 1914 were the subject of a speech delivered to-day by M. André Tardieu, the French Commissioner, at a luncheon given by Mr. Robert Lansing, Secretary of State, for the purpose of introducing M. Tardieu to the superior officers of the New York National Guard.

M. Tardieu spoke of the enormous increase realized by France of effectives and material, and emphasized the development of the output of shells and guns of all calibres. Major-General O'Ryan, replying to M. Tardieu, spoke of the enthusiasm with which the soldiers of America were looking forward to joining the French army on the battlefield.—Havas.

FRENCH AND BRITISH TROOPS BREAK DEEPLY INTO ENEMY'S LINES IN GREAT YPRES DRIVE

Allied Forces, Opening Up Formidable Flanders Offensive on 15-Mile Front, Advance on Whole Battle-Line, Storming Series of Village Fortresses and Taking 3,500 Prisoners So Far Counted.

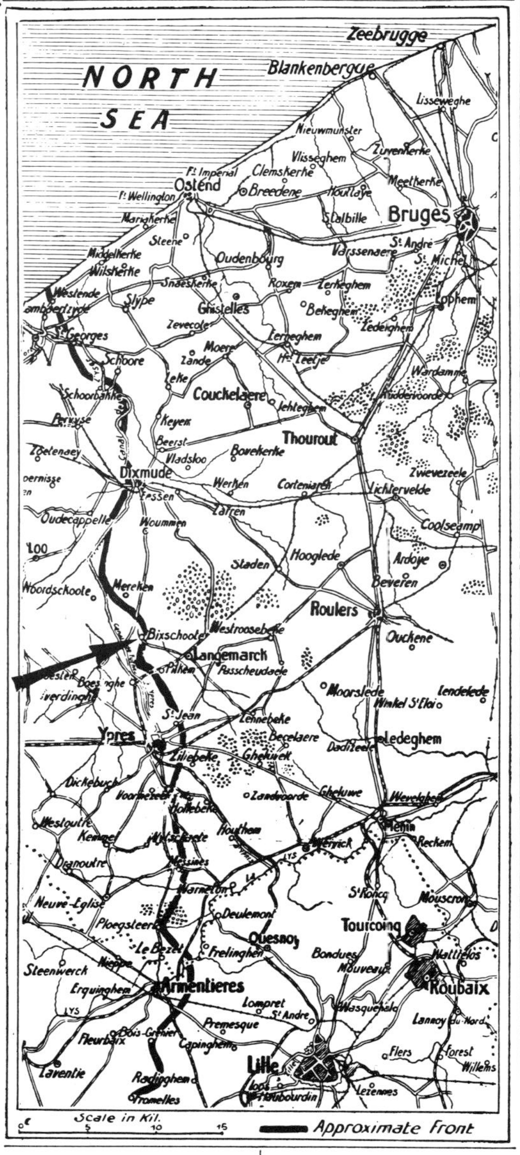

With their way prepared by a protracted bombardment of unparalleled intensity, the British and French troops swarmed "over the top" at daybreak yesterday in Flanders, and began what will probably prove the greatest battle of the war.

Attacking on a front of fifteen miles in the Ypres region, between the Lys and the Yser, the Allied troops won a magnificent victory, advancing deeply in the German lines along the whole battlefront, despite fierce resistance.

A great series of formidable positions was stormed, including many village fortresses and the powerfully-organized Sanctuary Wood, while the crossings of the river Stebeck were also captured.

Three thousand five hundred was the first count of prisoners given in last night's British communiqué, but in all probability the exact total is considerably in excess of this figure.

Successes from Outset.

The onslaught was marked by important successes from the outset, Steenstraete and Basse-Ville, the two extreme points of the front of attack, being carried by the French and British troops, respectively.

The French troops, operating on the left flank, gained their objectives with extraordinary rapidity and then pushed on, breaking down the efforts of the Germans to hold them, and captured the village of Bixschoote, together with all the defensive organizations covering the locality on the south-east and west.

Meanwhile, on the centre and right of the front of attack, the British tide was also engulfing important positions, the villages of Frezenberg, Verlorenhoek, Saint-Julien, Pilckem, Hooge, Westhoek and Hollebeke being stormed after heavy fighting.

Operations Began Monday.

General Anthoine, who won great distinction in the Verdun and the recent Champagne battles and who is in command of the French troops taking part in the Flanders drive, began his operations during Monday night with a preliminary movement in which, under heavy fire, his men crossed the Yser. When they started to the attack at daybreak, they found the first German line positions completely wrecked by the storm of shells which has been sweeping them and the line had been abandoned. Protected by a curtain of intense shellfire, they pushed ahead as rapidly as the barrage could be advanced.

Meanwhile, on their right, the British forces, commanded by General Plumer and General Gough, were meeting with a more stubborn resistance, which delayed their advance while the French were pushing ahead. But, cutting a way through, they shattered every obstacle and, having gained all objectives, were soon in line again with the French. Sir Douglas Haig reported in last night's communiqué that heavy fighting was still in progress in the Westhoek region, on the Ypres-Menin road.

It is clear, according to French military writers, that the battle thus begun, and which is likely to last for weeks, will be waged in accordance with a plan of campaign providing for an advance by small stages.

FRENCH OFFICIAL COMMUNIQUES

Tuesday, 2 p.m.

An attack launched by us at 8.15 last night, on a front of 1,500 mètres, south of the Royère (west of the Epine de Chevregny), was completely successful. We attained all our objectives and smashed the German counter-attack, during which we took 167 prisoners, including two officers, and about 15 sub-officers belonging to three different regiments.

The artillery struggle, followed by infantry actions, has continued very keen in the Cerny-Hurtebise sector.

In Champagne and north-west of Prosnes, the enemy, after a violent bombardment, carried out a raid which collapsed under a vigorous reply from our artillery and infantry fire.

Reciprocal artillery activity on both banks of the Meuse.

TUESDAY, 11 p.m.

After having effected during the night the passage of the Yser Canal our troops attacked this morning at four o'clock in conjunction on their right with the British armies.

The formidable artillery preparation had completely levelled the German organizations to the ground and caused heavy losses to the defenders. At the end of the morning our troops had captured the enemy's two positions and in their ardor had spontaneously passed beyond the objective which had been assigned to them.

They advanced on the Lizerne-Dixmude road and captured the village of Bixschoote and the Kortekerrt cabaret. Our losses were extremely slight. We captured an important quantity of material and took prisoners who have not yet been counted. The battlefield is covered with German dead, which fact indicates the importance of the losses sustained by the enemy.

On the Aisne front the artillery struggle has been particularly violent. Information so far received on the operation carried out south of La Royère emphasizes the very fine attitude of our troops.

On the whole front of the attacks, the objectives having been passed we were able to clear out the enemy trenches which we found filled with German dead. The number of prisoners taken so far exceeds 210. Our losses were small.

About 11 o'clock in the morning the enemy attempted to attack our trenches west of the Epine de Chevregny, but was repulsed.

After an intense bombardment of our lines from Cerny to Hurtebise, the enemy, three regiments strong, attacked our positions east of Cerny on a front of about 1,500 mètres, but our immediate counter-attacks repulsed him and enabled us to progress on the whole front.

The day was comparatively quiet on both sides of the Meuse.

BRITISH OFFICIAL COMMUNIQUE.

TUESDAY, 9.45 p.m.

The operations of the Allied troops which began this morning in the region of Ypres continued with success during the day, despite bad weather.

We penetrated the enemy's positions and advanced our line on a front of more than fifteen miles between La Basse-Ville on the Lys and Steenstraete on the Yser. Both these localities are now in the hands of the Allied troops.

On the extreme left the French troops, closely co-operating with the British forces and covering their left flank, captured the village of Steenstraete and rapidly penetrated the German defensive organizations to a depth of two miles. Their objectives for the day having been early attained they pushed their attacks further with the greatest bravery, capturing Bixschoote and the German positions south-east and west of that locality on a front of about two and a half miles, including the Kortekeert Cabaret. A counter-attack was repulsed in the afternoon.

At the centre and to the left of the centre of our front of attack, British divisions penetrated the enemy's positions to a depth of two miles. They captured the passages of the river Stebeck, which constituted their last objective.

In the course of their attack, our troops carried powerful defensive organizations and stormed the villages of Verlorenhoek, Frezenberg, Saint-Julien and Pilckem, and a large number of strongly defended farms and woods and fortified localities.

Farther south, on the right of our centre of attack, our troops, after attaining the whole of their first objective, including the village of Hoove and the Sanctuary Wood, opened up a way forward, despite the desperate resistance of the enemy, across the difficult region bordering the Ypres-Menin road and captured the village of Westhoek.

In the region where a violent struggle lasted all the morning and is still in progress, we penetrated the enemy's defensive organizations to a depth of a mile. Numerous and powerful counter-attacks were repulsed.

On the extreme right, south of the Zillebeke-Zandvoordt road, all our objectives were attained at the outset of the attack and we captured the villages of Basse-Ville and Hollebeke.

The enemy, who sustained heavy losses, left prisoners in our hands, the number of whom, so far as known, reaches 3,500, but it is not yet possible to give the exact figures of our captures.

VIOLENT RAINSTORM IN LONDON

(SPECIAL TO THE HERALD.)

LONDON, Tuesday.—A rainstorm of an almost tropical character, accompanied by high winds, swept over the metropolitan area and the surrounding districts to-day. The rain fell in torrents. The low-lying districts of the Thames Valley are inundated.

M. RIBOT FLAYS MICHAELIS FOR BASE MANŒUVRE

German Chancellor's Imputation that France Covets Annexations Evokes Crushing Exposure of His Anxiety to Save Potsdam War Gang.

The German Chancellor's brazen attempt to unburden the Kaiser and his Prussian coterie of war-makers of responsibility for the world conflict by imputing greed of territorial annexations to the French Government was unmasked by M. Ribot, French Premier, in a crushing speech delivered yesterday in the Chamber.

Text of Premier's Speech.

"The German Chancellor has publicly asked the French Government to declare if, during the secret session of June 1, the Chamber of Deputies was not informed of a secret treaty concluded on the eve of the Russian revolution, by which the Tsar undertook to support our pretensions with regard to German territory on the left bank of the Rhine.

"There are grave inexactitudes and veritable falsehoods in the Chancellor's version, notably as regards the rôle which he attributes to the President of the Republic of having given orders to sign a treaty over the head of M. Briand. The Chamber and the Senate know what happened. M. Doumergue, after his conversations with the Tsar, asked for and obtained from M. Briand the authorization to put on record the Tsar's promise to support our claim to Alsace-Lorraine, which was torn from us by violence, and to leave us free to seek guarantees against a new aggression, not by annexing to France the territories on the left bank of the Rhine, but in forming these territories, if necessary, into an autonomous State, which would protect us as well as Belgium against an invasion from across the Rhine. We never dreamt of doing what Bismarck did in 1871. We have therefore the right to oppose a denial to the allegation of the Chancellor, who evidently has knowledge of the letters exchanged with Petrograd in February, 1917, and has allowed himself to falsify their sense, as his most illustrious predecessor did with the Ems despatch.

"The day the Russian Government consents to publish these letters we shall make no objection.

Issues Evaded by Chancellor.

"But the Chancellor was careful to say nothing about my declaration of March 24, when I repudiated, in France's name, all policy of conquest and annexation by force. He has purposely forgotten the language I used on May 22 in the Chamber of Deputies, when I said that we were ready to enter into conversations with Russia regarding the war's objects, and that if the German people, whose right to live and to pacific development we do not contest, realized that we desire a peace founded on the rights of peoples the conclusion of peace would be singularly facilitated by this fact.

"Finally, the Chancellor passed over in silence the resolution unanimously voted after the secret session of June 1-5 last.

"To say now that we desire annexations is a manœuvre which is too clumsy to deceive anyone.

"What does the Chancellor want? He is endeavoring to dissimulate the difficulty he experiences in defining the war objects of Germany and the conditions on which she will make peace. Above all, he is endeavoring to detract attention from the terrible responsibility which rests on the consciences of the German Emperor and his counsellors. It was on the day following the publication of the decision come to on July 5, 1914, in a council held at Potsdam, at which all the consequences of the ultimatum which was to be sent to Serbia were envisaged, that the Chancellor attempted this diversion. With such responsibilities, it is impudence to ask for a statement of our intentions."

Germany Must Be Made "Free Or Powerless"

LONDON, Tuesday.—"Until Germany is either made powerless or is made free, I do not believe the peace of Europe can be regarded as secure."

Mr. Balfour made this unequivocal statement in the House of Commons last night, in the course of a memorable speech—his first speech in the House as Foreign Secretary on the general war situation—which formed a complete reply to the German Chancellor's latest talk of "plans of conquest." He made this further declaration:—

"If we are to reform the map of Europe, if the result is that the map of Europe will be more stable than any peace congress has yet left behind, can anyone doubt that one of the arrangements of territory that must take place is the restoration to France of that territory of which she was violently robbed forty years ago?"—Daily Express.

RUSSIANS MAKE HEROIC EFFORTS TO REORGANIZE

M. Kerensky Has Hard Task in Choosing New Cabinet—Miliukov Party Wants M. Chernov, Minister of Agriculture, Ousted.

(SPECIAL TELEGRAM TO THE HERALD.)

PETROGRAD, Friday *(delayed in transmission)*.—According to the latest information, Lenin escaped on a Cronstadt ship dressed in a sailor's uniform, thus ending a noble chapter of gigantic conspiracy, provocation and bloodshed.

M. Kerensky, the Premier, has not decided upon the personnel of the new Cabinet, but undoubtedly representatives of the Constitutional Democratic party will accept posts. M. Nabokov, M. Kokoshkin, M. Astrov and M. Tretyakov, famous representatives of the Miliukov party, are among those who are being urged to take portfolios. They insist upon the retirement of the Minister of Agriculture, M. Chernov, whose project to solve the agrarian problem they regard as most dangerous. The Premier may sacrifice M. Chernov for the sake of unity.

I have talked with M. Nicholas Tchaikovsky, the famous revolutionist, widely known in America. He said: "I always maintained that social revolution during war is madness. War, to be successful, needs a strong, well-organized state, while social revolution needs demoralization, economic and financial disorganization and intense class struggle.

"We have two gigantic problems before us, war and revolution. Each is enough to test the country's powers, but the Russian people having endured and suffered long will survive both. I have faith in the endurance and power of Russia. People did not know at first how to use liberty after all revolutions. Russia has passed through the same process. We are making heroic efforts to reorganize the army and eliminating the dangerous elements. The Leninists are quite crushed now. They overreached themselves and the extremists met with the Black Hundreds."

Discussing the formation of the new Cabinet, M. Tchaikovsky declared that M. Kerensky is confronted with extraordinary difficulty. The Constitutional Democrats definitely oppose the Minister of Agriculture, M. Chernov, and his retirement might stir up a hornet's nest, for his agrarian promises are most popular with the peasantry.

HERMAN BERNSTEIN.

MATA HARI, DANCER AND GERMAN AGENT, PAYS THE PENALTY

Dangerous Spy Is Shot at Vincennes for Communicating Information to the Enemy.

Mata Hari, the dancer of Dutch nationality, was executed at Vincennes yesterday morning for espionage and communicating with the enemy.

Mata Hari, whose real name was Marguerite Gertrude Zelbe, was about forty years of age, and was a most dangerous

Mme MATA HARI

spy. She was unanimously condemned to death by a court-martial in Paris on July 24 last. She had an intimate knowledge of several European capitals, particularly of Paris. She was arrested on February 13, 1917, in the course of her second visit to the French capital since the beginning of hostilities. Documents which had come into the possession of the authorities clearly demonstrated her guilt and the importance of the intelligence which she had furnished to the enemy.

Activities in Berlin.

At the time of the declaration of war Mata Hari was frequenting political, military and police circles in Berlin. She was enrolled under a number in the German espionage service, and had communicated directly, outside French territory, with high enemy personalities, notorious espionage chiefs, and had received from Germany on several occasions since May, 1916, important sums as remuneration for the information supplied by her. In the presence of the material proofs furnished to the court-martial she was forced to recognize the facts.

Since the Court of Cassation rejected her appeal Mata Hari's only hope was in the clemency of the President; and that hope vanished a little after five o'clock yesterday morning, when her cell at Saint-Lazare Prison was entered by the director of the establishment, her advocate, Me. Clunet; Pastor Arboux and Captain Bouchardon. She realized the situation at once.

Soon afterwards, wearing a dark costume, with a large felt hat and a cloak, she entered an automobile, accompanied by Pastor Arboux and her advocate, to whom she handed two long letters. An hour and a half later she was shot by a platoon at Vincennes. She was courageous up to the end and refused to have her eyes bandaged.

A Centre of Espionage.

The "Matin" says: "Mata Hari was not simply a spy, but a centre of espionage. She centralized the information, which was carried to a great number of agents, the greater part of whom have also been unmasked, and it was transmitted to Berlin by mysterious ways. Later, when the secret history of German espionage in France during the war can be related, the figure of the Hindu dancer will appear as one of the most odious and her punishment as one of the most just."

THE HOHENZOLLERN HOBBY-HORSE.

1:- The Hohenzollern Hobby-horse
Is rocking to and fro;
It has rocked all over Europe,
Spreading famine, fire and woe.
It has raised a crop of devilry
From seeds of hatred sown,
But its domineering rider
From his seat will soon be thrown.

Chorus:—
Rock-a-bye, rock-a-bye, rock-a-bye Bill;
Riding so grandly, you're due for a spill.
A wooden kimono your pieces will fill
When the hobby-horse throws you, my Rock-a-bye Bill.

2:- The Hohenzollern Hobby-horse
Is Rocking on the bud
Of Germania's young manhood,
And it's reeking in the blood
Of mothers' sons a-plenty;
When its rider gets a fall,
We will brew the juice of Freedom
From his wormwood and his gall.

Chorus:—
Rock-a-bye, rock-a-bye, rock-a-bye Bill;
Soon on the coals of remorse may you grill.
The hounds of Old Nick would their lean bellies fill
As they bark for a bite of you, Rock-a-bye Bill.

3:- The Hohenzollern Hobby-horse
Has seared the souls of men.
It has seemed to rock to victory
Through the mists of now and then;
But the rockers' screws are loosening
And we're looking to "the day"
When the hobby and its rider
To the scrap heap find their way.

Chorus:—
Rock-a-bye, rock-a-bye, rock-a-bye Bill;
Now that we've started, we'll go with a will
To the trenches in France and we'll be there to fill
The grave of your hobby-horse, Rock-a-bye Bill.

George Willard Bonte.

(From the NEW YORK HERALD.)

THE NEW YORK HERALD

PRICE: Paris and France, 15c.; Abroad, 25c. | EUROPEAN EDITION—PARIS, WEDNESDAY, MAY 15, 1918. | PRICE: Paris and France, 15c.; Abroad, 25c.

JAMES GORDON BENNETT IS DEAD

Proprietor and Director of the "New York Herald" Passes Away at Age of Seventy-seven at Beaulieu Residence, Heart Failure Following Broncho-Pneumonia.

(SPECIAL TELEGRAM TO THE HERALD.)

NICE, Tuesday.—James Gordon Bennett, owner and director of the NEW YORK HERALD, of New York and Paris, and the "Evening Telegram," of New York, died this morning at his Beaulieu residence, Villa Namouna, of heart failure. For several months he had been ailing, never having completely recovered from a severe cold caught in Paris in November last.

He came South with his wife in the beginning of December. The change at first seemed beneficial, but toward the end of the year he caught another chill which developed into broncho-pneumonia. His situation rapidly became critical, necessitating the calling from Paris of his friend and physician, Professor Albert Robin.

Again Mr. Bennett's marvellously robust constitution triumphed, and he passed the crisis safely and seemed on the high road to complete recovery, when about three weeks ago he had a relapse. Symptoms of uræmia made their appearance. Under these repeated blows and the prolonged strain, the heart gave way.

Every remedial measure known to science was resorted to, but without avail, by his medical attendant, Dr. Albert Coste, with Professor Hayem, eminent heart specialist from Paris; Dr. Hérard de Bessé, of Beaulieu, and Dr. Rolla Rouse, of Monte Carlo, in consultation.

While the gravity of the case was manifest, it was hoped the fatal issue might be averted, or at any rate still long deferred, but on Friday last, Mr. Bennett's birthday, a distinct change for the worst took place. His strength declined steadily, though his immense vitality enabled him to offer protracted resistance, which buoyed up the hopes of those around him, but nothing now gave relief.

On Saturday evening Mr. Bennett became unconscious and remained so practically to the end. His breathing gradually became fainter and fainter, and this morning, at fifteen minutes after five o'clock, he slipped from life into eternity.

At his side solely was Mrs. Bennett, his widow.

Mr. Bennett had just entered his seventy-eighth year, as he was born on May 10, 1841.

Until the last two days he retained all his mental vigor, displaying an unflagging interest in the news of the day and regulating personally details of the editorial and business direction of his three journals, following with penetrating attention all of the developments of the war, discussing with keen insight the fluctuations of the battle now raging and exulting patriotically over the magnitude of America's participation in the war and every reported action of the American forces—"our men," as he always called them with affectionate pride.

Besides his widow, the surviving relatives of Mr. Bennett include a sister, Mrs. Isaac Bell; a nephew, Isaac Bell, Jr., and two nieces, Comtesse Paul d'Aramon and Mrs. Ricardo. Of his two stepsons, one, Baron Oliver de Reuter, is on the Riviera with his mother, and the other, Second Lieutenant de Reuter, is with his regiment, the Grenadier Guards, in France.

OFFERS CONDOLENCES ON BEHALF OF GOVERNMENT.

(SPECIAL TO THE HERALD.)

BEAULIEU-SUR-MER, Tuesday.—News of the death of Mr. Bennett spread rapidly and created a painful sensation along the Riviera. Messages of sympathy were received from every quarter. Among the earliest callers were M. Armand Bernard, Prefect of the Alpes-Maritimes, who expressed condolences on behalf of the French Government; Mr. and Mrs. Edward Tuck, Mr. and Mrs. Ralph Curtis, Mr. Dulany Hunter, American Consul at Nice, and Mr. Robinson Riley, American Vice-Consul.

Mr. Bennett's Many Enterprises

Mr. James Gordon Bennett was born in New York on May 10, 1841, and was educated abroad by private tutors, returning to New York in 1866. Six years later, upon his father's death, he assumed the direction of the NEW YORK HERALD of which he remained in active control up to the time of his death, mostly by cable while residing in France or travelling in all parts of the world, besides also personally directing the Paris edition of the HERALD.

One of Mr. Bennett's greatest newspaper exploits was the sending of Henry M. Stanley to find Livingstone, an enterprise in which the "Daily Telegraph" participated. Several reports had been received that Livingstone had been murdered by negroes, and Mr. Bennett decided to allay the public uneasiness. Starting from Zanzibar Stanley met with much opposition from native chiefs, but on November 10, 1871, he discovered Livingstone at Ujiji, near Unyanyembe. Livingstone had arrived there in very bad condition, having been robbed and deserted by his attendants. Stanley remained with him until March 14, 1872, and brought away his diary and other documents. Livingstone, in letters to Mr. Bennett, gave the situation of the Nile springs, described his explorations and told of the horrors of the slave trade in Eastern Africa.

Later Mr. Bennett and the "Daily Telegraph" supported Stanley's expedition, in which he surveyed Lake Victoria Nyanza and Lake Tanganyika and crossed Africa from east to west. Mr. Bennett attended a banquet given to Stanley by the French Geographical Society in Paris in January, 1878.

The Jeanette Expedition.

The subject of Arctic exploration had long fascinated Mr. Bennett, and in 1879 he fitted and manned at his own expense the yacht Jeanette with a view, as he explained to Congress, "to prosecute and, if possible, bring to a successful issue the Polar explorations which have so long occupied the attention of the scientific world." The expedition left on July 8, 1879, under the command of Captain De Long, but it met with disaster, the Jeanette being crushed by ice on June 23, 1881.

Two boats, with a portion of the crew, were received by Russians at the mouth of the Lena in the following December, but one boat was lost, with Captain Long and others of the crew, whose bodies were found near the mouth of the Lena on March 23, 1882. They were conveyed to Philadelphia and buried there in February, 1884.

One of the most beneficent works Mr. Bennett took in hand was the organization, through the HERALD, of a fund for the relief of the victims of the terrible famine in Ireland in 1879-80. In an appeal issued by the HERALD to the people of America in February, 1880, it stated: "Over 300 people are starving. 'For God's sake give us food or money' is their piteous cry." The HERALD headed the fund with a gift of $100,000, and it speedily grew to about $350,000.

Food, clothing and other necessaries were transported to Ireland in a special relief ship, and distributed through the HERALD's relief committee in almost every nook and corner of the island. Thousands and thousands of families were daily and weekly saved from starvation. Public bodies all over the country expressed their gratitude to the HERALD for its timely help.

The Submarine Cable.

Mr. Bennett played an important part in the development of submarine cabling. With Mr. John W. Mackay, he established the Commercial Cable Company. They signed a contract with Messrs. Siemens Brothers in September, 1883, for two transatlantic cables, which were opened to the public the following year. The HERALD, in announcing the signing of the contract, said: "This cable enterprise will be an essentially American one. These cables will be owned entirely by Americans, and this will be the only American company owning cables under the seas between England and America."

When twenty-four years of age, in 1866, Mr. Bennett won the great transatlantic yacht race with his yacht the Henrietta, from Sandy Hook to the Isle of Wight. In the following year he was elected vice-commodore of the New York Yacht Club and after accepting challenges of the owners of the English yacht Cambria and the Sappho, he took part, in 1870, in the second ocean race, from Queenstown to New York in his yacht the Dauntless. In the following year he was elected commodore of the New York Yacht Club.

Mr. Bennett remained a fervent yachtsman throughout his life, passing much of his time at sea, his yachts being the Namouna and later the Lysistrata. A great lover of dogs, Mr. Bennett was honorary president of the Pekingese Club of America, and he gave a trophy for competition in London to encourage the breeding of this species.

Encouragement of Sport.

The encouragement given by Mr. Bennett to automobilism, aviation and sports generally is told of by M. Georges Prade in this morning's "Journal." M. Prade says:—

"Mr. James Gordon Bennett created the most celebrated sporting events the world has known. There were innumerable Gordon Bennett cups and all were destined brilliantly to justify their founder's enterprise.

"Two of these cups stand out preminently from the others, however: the Automobile Cup and the Gordon Bennett Aviation Trophy. The latter was first won at Rheims by the American aviator Glenn Curtiss, defeating Blériot; then in America by the Englishman Grahame-White, on a Blériot machine; in 1911 by C. T. Weymann, on a Nieuport machine in England; in 1912 by Jules Védrines, and finally, in 1913, by the Frenchman Prévost, who was the first to exceed 200 kilomètres in the hour. Two years later the engineer M. Bechereau, who constructed Prévost's machine, constructed the famous Spad on which the victories of Guynemer and Fonck have been won.

"For James Gordon Bennett had seen clearly ahead. He knew that it was sport that created the intense energy which in peace time wins races and in war time wins battles."

Mr. Bennett married in September, 1914, Baroness George De Reuter, daughter of the late Mr. John Potter, of Philadelphia.

JAMES GORDON BENNETT.

FRENCH PRESS LAMENTS LOSS OF A FRIEND

All of the Paris newspapers, in commenting on the death of Mr. Bennett, pay tribute to him as a friend of France. Below are given extracts from the editorials:—

M. BERARDI, IN "EXCELSIOR."

M. Gaston Berardi, in the "Excelsior," says: "Mr. Bennett was more than a great journalist; he was one of the most striking and original figures of his time. It may be said that no one ever had any direct influence over him. All his numerous ventures in modern journalism whereby he sought to make the press more than a mere organ of opinion originated in his own mind. His papers were controlled and directed personally and effectively by him alone each day from wherever he might be, often in a remote corner of the earth.

"His foresight was remarkable. In his journalistic field of action Napoleon's words could apply to him: 'I live always one year in advance.'

"All Paris knew his tall, slim figure. Of all his characteristics, that which stood out most prominently, especially at this time of universal upheaval, was his fervent friendship for France, which never failed and which strengthened in our hours of trial.

"Mr. Bennett took up our cause from the very beginning and pleaded ardently in America. His faith in justice and in the triumph of the Allied cause was immense. In face of the menaces of powerful pro-German organizations he persisted untiringly and with noble calmness in his advocacy of America's entry into the war, saying: 'Not only is it America's duty, but her obvious interest, and I speak both as an American and as a friend of France. If America stands out of such a conflict, she will be after the war merely a great Switzerland.'

"And one of the greatest, perhaps the most glorious, days of his life was April 6, 1917. He dies before President Wilson's great action has produced its effect. France will remember the support he gave to her cause and which, perhaps, advanced the day on which General Pershing pronounced those words over the tomb of the great Frenchman: 'Lafayette, we are here.'"

"PETIT PARISIEN."

"The news of the death of Mr. James Gordon Bennett will be received with sincere emotion in France. Here this great American journalist was considered as one of us. He was an old friend and defender of our country, his expressive face impregnated with will was familiar to all in the world of politics and art.

"Wherever he went he was preceded by his renown as a man of action. In him we saw, above all, the journalist who placed the NEW YORK HERALD at the service of France, publishing in its columns the works of our best writers and our greatest artists.

"During this terrible world-struggle, Mr. Bennett made himself in America one of the best and one of the most eloquent pioneers of the Entente. He had before the war made every effort possible for the United States and France to understand each other. We can guess with what dash he pursued his task that the union between the two peoples be completed and cemented by blood spilled in common for the most noble of causes.

"It is a duty for us to recognize solemnly his unfailing confidence in our triumph. Mr. Gordon Bennett died too soon to see this realized."

"JOURNAL."

"Among the members of the American colony who are practically permanent residents in France, Mr. Bennett was in the very front rank.

"He was the son of the celebrated founder of the NEW YORK HERALD, the amazing forerunner of the press of to-day, which showed the immense part the newspapers could play in the life of the world. Mr. Bennett inherited his father's fondness for vast and daring enterprises.

"Mr. Bennett in America was a power whose decisions weighed heavily in the political balance. He spoke little, and even in his great age his ideas were transformed immediately into action."

"MATIN."

"Mr. Bennett, by his influence on the Continent, was one of the most powerful workers for Franco-American amity. His activity in the past as well as during the present war has rendered eminent service to the Entente, and his name must be associated with those clear-sighted men across the Atlantic who have brought America and all her forces to our aid."

"TEMPS."

"Mr. James Gordon Bennett, who was for many years a thorough Parisian, was one of the most remarkable figures in American journalism and he was very popular on both sides of the Atlantic.

"Carefully prepared by his father, the first James Gordon Bennett, founder of the NEW YORK HERALD, to ensure the continuation of that powerful newspaper's brilliant career, Mr. Bennett founded an edition in Paris, which he directed personally.

"Since the outbreak of the war this American, imbued with French ideas, furthered the cause of the Allies in the great organ of opinion which he owned and he had his share of influence in the final decision of the American nation to enter the world struggle."

"LIBERTE."

"With Mr. James Gordon Bennett disappears a thorough Parisian, for the director of the great American journal, the NEW YORK HERALD, resided during the greater part of the year in Paris, where he had numerous associations. Under his intelligent direction the NEW YORK HERALD has never ceased to be prosperous. Like his father, he was a man of daring initiative. To him was due the establishment of the first submarine cable between America and France, by which the HERALD was first to receive the news of Europe."

"INTRANSIGEANT."

"Mr. James Gordon Bennett will be sincerely regretted by French society, among which he had so many friends. Living in France for many years past, following with interest the politics and sports of our country, he divided his time between his Paris residence, his handsome villa at Beaulieu and his yacht.

"He directed his papers by brief orders, telegraphed often, when on yachting cruises, from all parts of the world. He was one of the greatest workers for Franco-American amity, and later on for the Franco-American alliance. He placed his powerful organs at the service of this noble cause. In him we lose a great friend."

"DEBATS."

"Mr. Bennett adopted the principle of allowing no financial consideration to stand in the way of giving the best and latest news to the world. He resided almost permanently in our country and was a striking figure among Parisians."

L'HEURE.

"Gordon Bennett! What an original figure and what memories! Never again shall we see the Napoleonic director of the NEW YORK HERALD, the inventor of the 'grand reportage,' the man who sent Stanley in search of Livingstone.... It is a great pity, in all sincerity. And what a friend of France! What sound judgment! His Paris edition of the HERALD was always a little chef-d'œuvre of elegance.... Our grateful recollection will remain attached to that great figure of the press who contrived to be—oh! miracle—a journalist at the same time."

"A CLEAR-SIGHTED PROPHET AND A LEADER OF MEN."

NICE, Tuesday.—Commenting upon the death of Mr James Gordon Bennett, the "Eclaireur de Nice" says:—

"Mr. Bennett did not wait for this war to show himself an ardent Francophile. It may be said that his personal influence was great in the decision of America to declare war on Germany. He showed himself in this way, as he had done on many other occasions, to be a clear-sighted prophet and a leader of men.

"What France and her Allies owe to Mr. Bennett is not known to-day, but history will tell it and our children will not forget it.

"Mr. Bennett loved the Mediterranean coast. He was an old resident of Beaulieu, where he returned from his long cruises on his marvellous yachts, the Namouna and the Lysistrata, for of all the sports which he loved intensely yachting was his favorite. He was an eminent seaman and a matchless captain."—Havas.

Work for Franco-American Relations Praised by M. Pierre Veber in "Figaro"—"All He Has Done for France Will Be Remembered With Gratitude."

M. Pierre Veber, writing in the "Figaro" this morning, says:—

"The Frenchman is not forgetful. The news that Mr. Gordon Bennett was seriously ill caused a stir in Paris, where all that this great American had done for France before and since the war was remembered with gratitude. Mr. Bennett was in many ways more Parisian than American, though an ardent patriot. He had two homes, Paris and New York, which he had the joy of uniting in a single affection.

"Mr. Gordon Bennett was the son of a Scotch schoolmaster. His mother was Irish. The Great Bennett, as his son called him, emigrated to New York, became a printer and founded the NEW YORK HERALD, which newspaper is as celebrated in the annals of our profession as is Théophraste Renaudot's 'Gazette.' I have seen the first copy of it framed and hung on the wall of the office of the Great Master in the Herald Square building. In this modest one-story palace, which seems to defy the surrounding skyscrapers, French thought found a refuge while the pro-German press was abusing us. The King of Paris, as he was called in America, never deserted his friends, the French. We know what he did for France before the war.

"Mr. Gordon Bennett was educated at the College of Versailles, where he had as friends the great Frenchmen of our day, and such was his affection for the noble town that he desired to have his summer residence there. One day as he was strolling he came upon an old, abandoned barn. It was the old rendezvous of Louis XIV. and Mme. de Maintenon. What had not been remarked by the conservator did not escape Mr. Bennett's notice, and it was here that he built his charming country home.

"As a young man Mr. Bennett was the first to attempt to cross the Atlantic on a small sailing yacht, the Dauntless. Five were on board when the Dauntless started, but only three reached the other side.

"He was endowed with extraordinary foresight. He foresaw the Chinese revolution, sending out a correspondent a year before the upheaval in the Far East. He was an adversary of the Panama Canal, but he proposed to the Government of the time to devote French financial resources to the realization of the Canal des Deux Mers project, offering even to provide the initial facilities. He was not listened to; nor was he listened to seven years later, when he took up the Channel tunnel idea.

"Mr. Bennett had profound confidence in the French during the war. In the dark days of September, 1914, he remained in Paris, predicting that the Germans would never reach the capital. With all his heart, all his strength and all his resources he prepared the Franco-American alliance. His campaign in America before America entered the war cost nearly four millions. Pro-German organizations boycotted the 'French' newspaper, as they called the NEW YORK HERALD, while supplying funds to the Germanophile sheets.

"He who showered gifts on a multitude of unfortunate people, who sacrificed a part of his fortune to support our cause, has never taken anything in exchange. He has refused all ribbons and all honors.

"I have known Mr. Bennett for nearly twenty years and have always felt respect, affection and sincere admiration for this master of action. He founded the Paris HERALD not as a commercial enterprise, but to create a bond between France and America. He said at one time: 'If the Paris HERALD's circulation reaches 13,000 I shall be satisfied.' This prince of journalism saw the HERALD at its beginning exceed 20,000 and, disappointed, he used the profits to improve his journal. The HERALD was the pioneer of modern journalism.

"Loving France ardently, Mr. Bennett wanted her to be the home of sports. When the bicycle made its appearance he founded a prize for cycle races. He founded a cup to encourage the development of the automobile and he was the first to encourage aviation. Before that he had established a mail-coach service to favor the art of driving.

"So ardent was his enthusiasm in encouraging scientific discoveries that though part proprietor of the Mackay Bennett cable, he developed a campaign in favor of wireless telegraphy."

THE NEW YORK HERALD

PRICE: Paris and France, 20c.; Abroad, 30c. EUROPEAN EDITION—PARIS. MONDAY, SEPTEMBER 30, 1918. PRIX: Paris et France, 20c.; Etranger, 30c.

BIG ADVANCES MADE ON ALL FRONTS: AMERICANS ATTACK HINDENBURG LINE; DIXMUDE AND MESSINES RIDGE FALL IN GREAT ANGLO-BELGIAN ONSLAUGHT

BRITISH IN CAMBRAI; CAPTURE OF WHOLE TOWN IS IMMINENT

Scheldt Canal Is Forced in British-American Drive—Belgians Three Miles from Roulers.

Magnificent news of victory continues to flow in from every active front from Belgium to Palestine.

In the north, King Albert's forces, with General Plumer's British army co-operating, have won a series of brilliant successes, smashing up the German front north of Ypres and advancing several miles to within a short distance from Roulers. Taking Dixmude, the Belgians have advanced nearly five miles to the east and captured Zarren. Among other localities captured are Terrest, Stadenberg and Poelcappelle and the famous Passchendaele Ridge is being turned in brilliantly executed operations.

More to the south General Plumer's army has re-won the formidable Messines-Wytschaete ridge and taken seve-

United States Army, attacked the Hindenburg line on a front of 6,000 yards, at a point where the Scheldt Canal passes under a tunnel. With great dash the American troops advanced to the assault of these defences, and on the right seized Bellicourt and Nauroy. On the left hard fighting continues in the neighborhood of Bony.

On the centre of our attack English troops took Villers-Guislain.

New Zealand troops cleared the Welsh Ridge and after having broken an enemy counter-attack they pursued their advance and seized La Vacquerie and the spur which runs from Bonay to Masnières.

During this time the 62nd Division, having assured the passages of the Scheldt Canal, continued its advance. After having given combat in the western outskirts of Masnières and Les Rues Vertes, it carried these two villages, as well as the defensive system protecting Rumilly, and reached the western borders of this locality. On the left the 2nd Division crossed the canal near Noyelles and advanced more than a mile and a half, reaching the heights situated west of the canal. The 63rd Naval

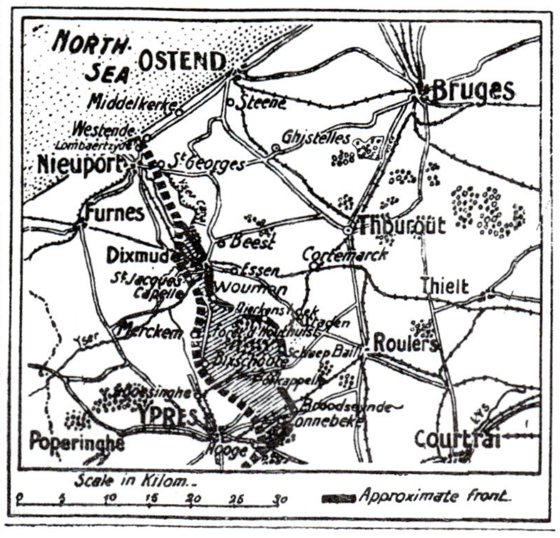

AMEXES AT GRIPS WITH THE ENEMY IN WEST ARGONNE

In Face of Most Bitter and Stubborn Opposition, They Continue Their Progress.

(SPECIAL TELEGRAM TO THE HERALD.)
By DON MARTIN.
WITH THE AMERICAN ARMIES, Sunday.

In the operations between Verdun and the western edge of the Argonne, the Americans are engaged in what may develop into the stiffest brush the American troops have yet had with the Germans.

The Germans have for two days been hurrying reinforcements to check the advance of the Americans, but have failed to do more than lessen its speed. On Saturday, in face of most bitter and stubborn opposition, the American boys continued their progress.

ALLIED COMMANDER RECEIVES BULGARIAN PEACE DELEGATES

Mission from Sofia Reaches Salonica to Confer with General Franchet d'Esperey.

The French Ministry of Foreign Affairs issued the following Note yesterday evening:—

"The Bulgarian 'parlementaires,' M. Liaptcheff, Minister of Finance; General Lukoff, commanding the second army, and M. Radeff, former Minister, arrived on Saturday evening at Salonica in order to negotiate conditions for an armistice.

"General Franchet d'Esperey receives them to-day (Sunday)."

The Note also defines the present situation as follows:—

"As contradictory and, on certain points, inexact reports on Bulgarian affairs are circulating on different sides or have been published in France, it appears necessary to make clear the following facts:—

"No diplomatic negotiation is going on

cesses. Our troops, driving the enemy before them, are now on the Platckhavitza, near Tzarevo-Selo, Sveti-Nikola and north of Veles.

Great fires are seen in the environs of Skoplie (Uskub).

According to an approximate estimate, the Serbian army alone has captured about 160 guns so far, without counting trench guns.

Enemy Swept from Jordan Passages: 50,000 Prisoners

LONDON, Sunday.—The following communiqué from Palestine has been issued by the War Office:—

During Friday the enemy offered some resistance in the region to the north of Lake Tiberias, occupying the upper Jordan passages at Jisr and Er Rente, athwart the roads toward Mezerib and

THE NEW YORK HERALD

PRICE: Paris and France, 20c.; Abroad, 30c. EUROPEAN EDITION—PARIS. SATURDAY, NOVEMBER 2, 1918. PRIX: Paris et France, 20c.; Etranger, 30c.

GREAT ALLIED DRIVE RESUMED FROM COAST TO VERDUN; REVOLUTION SPREADS IN AUSTRIA; TISZA ASSASSINATED

ALLIED FORCES SMASH FOE IN TREMENDOUS GENERAL BATTLE

British, French and Americans Inflict Crushing Defeat on Germans—Ten-Mile Advance Is Made by Franco-Americans in Flanders—Fall of Ghent Imminent

While Germany is asking for armistice terms, the general offensive has been resumed on the Western front in France. In Flanders, south of Valenciennes, in the "Hunding Stellung" between Saint-Quentin-le-Petit and Herpy, east of the Aisne, in the Vouziers region and in the American sector, important progress was made yesterday by the Allies. Everywhere the German resistance was broken, and the new positions attained will lead to a further advance that will soon compel the enemy to withdraw once more from his present line.

The attack in Flanders began on Thursday morning. The results so far achieved are capital. While the Belgians kept the enemy busy along the

which were strongly held and stubbornly defended.

To the east of Attigny, we captured Ailly-aux-Oies. Further south our troop crossed the Aisne and stormed Semuy and Voncq. Pushing vigorously eastward they drove back the enemy more than three kilometres in this locality and penetrated far into the Bois de Voncq.

The battle was equally violent on the heights east of Vouziers. We have gained a foothold on the Alleux Plateau north-east of Terron, and reached the western outskirts of the Bois de Voudy as well as the brook east of Chestres.

On our right, our troops have gone beyond Falaise and won the heights south-west of Primat.

So far, the reports show that the prisoners taken number several hundreds; many cannon, including four batteries of 105's, have been captured.

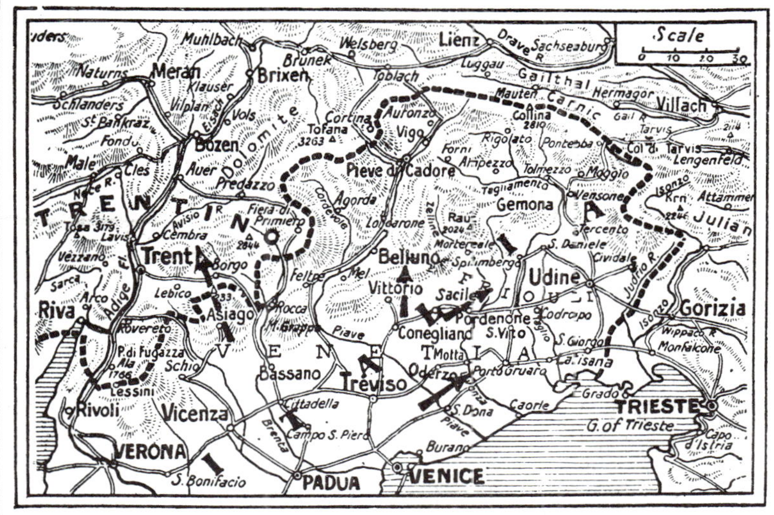

SHOWS MAIN DIRECTIONS OF DRIVE IN ITALY.

REPORTS OF REVOLT FROM ALL PARTS OF THE DUAL MONARCHY

Former Hungarian Premier, Germany's Tool, One of Principal Authors of the War, Is Murdered in Great Upheaval Against Habsburg Régime.

The revolution in Austria-Hungary is spreading rapidly. From all parts of the collapsing Dual Monarchy come reports of revolt.

Count Tisza, former Premier of Hungary, the tool of Germany, one of the principal authors of the great war, has been assassinated.

Many of the reports from Austria are vague and conflicting, but there is no doubt that the world will soon have details of a tremendous upheaval, which will end the Habsburg régime. There is as yet no confirmation of the report that Emperor Charles is in flight.

Tisza Killed in

Austria reminds us that our situation is incredibly serious."—Havas.

WILL THE KAISER ABDICATE? AND WHEN?

BALE, Friday.—The Berlin and German press is animatedly discussing the question: Will the Kaiser Abdicate? And When? The Socialist papers report that the War Cabinet yesterday discussed the Constitutional reforms in Germany and their consequences for "certain highly-placed personalities."

The "Vorwärts," after reviewing the Kaiser's activity in the last ten years, asks: "What will he do? WHEN WILL HE DO WHAT EVERYONE IS AWAITING?"

The "Strasburg Post" says there is no longer any reason to hide the fact that the abdication of the Kaiser is being considered by the War Cabinet, but no de-

THE NEW YORK HERALD

PRICE: Paris and France, 20c.; Abroad, 30c. EUROPEAN EDITION—PARIS. TUESDAY, NOVEMBER 12, 1918. PRIX: Paris et France, 20c.; Etranger, 30c.

THE WAR IS WON!

(OFFICIAL.) *The Armistice was signed on Monday Morning at 5.40. Hostilities were suspended at 11 o'clock.*

Armistice Conditions Place Strangle-hold on Germany, Calling for Immediate Evacuation of All Invaded Territory and of Alsace-Lorraine; Allies' Occupation of Both Banks of Rhine, with Garrisons at Mainz, Coblentz and Cologne; Surrender of 5,000 Guns, 25,000 Machine-Guns, 1,700 Aeroplanes, 26 Big Warships, 50 Destroyers, All Submarines; Free Passage Through Cattegat; Repatriation of All Prisoners, without Reciprocity.

INHABITANTS OF PARIS! VICTORY!

As soon as the news of the signing of the armistice was known in official circles yesterday morning, the Paris Municipal Council sent out, to be posted all over the city, a stirring appeal to the population to celebrate the greatest victory ever won. How Paris responded to the appeal is told in a special article elsewhere. The poster read as follows:—

"Inhabitants of Paris!

"Victory! Triumphant victory! On all fronts the defeated enemy has laid down his arms. Blood will now cease to flow.

"Let Paris throw off the noble reserve for which it has been admired by the whole world.

"Let us give free course to our joy and enthusiasm, and hold back our tears.

"To show our infinite gratitude to our magnificent soldiers and their incomparable leaders, let us decorate all our houses with the French colors and those of our dear Allies.

"Our dead may rest in peace. The sublime sacrifice they have made of their lives to the future of the race and the salvation of France will not be in vain.

"For them, as for us, 'the day of glory has arrived!'

"Vive la Republique!
"Vive la France immortelle!
"For the Municipal Council,

DEPUTIES ACCLAIM PREMIER AT [illegible] CHAMBER SESSION

M. Clemenceau's Reading of Armistice Terms and Speech Stir All to Enthusiasm.

The Chamber of Deputies yesterday afternoon was the scene of a manifestation which can never be forgotten. The reading of the conditions of the armistice by M. Clemenceau raised the enthusiasm of Deputies and visitors to the highest pitch, and a touching tribute

The men who have led the Allied Armies to victory: The great chief, Marshal Foch, surrounded by the King of the Belgians (bottom, left), Field-Marshal Sir Douglas Haig (top, left), General John J. Pershing (top, right) and General Diaz (bottom right).

Pealing of Church Bells and Boom of Cannon Announce to Parisians Signature of Armistice and Victorious End of War—News Fires Capital With Frenzied Joy—Seething Multitudes Swarm Through Streets and Boulevards, Singing "Marseillaise" and Acclaiming Triumph of Allied Arms.

The armistice is signed! Germany has capitulated! The war is won! A thousand church bells clanged out the news in joyous peals at eleven o'clock yesterday morning, while 1,200 guns told in thundering tones of the victorious end of the war. People who happened to be in the central quarters of the city had already heard of the news. As early as nine o'clock huge white bands on the front of newspaper offices announced that the armistice was signed, provoking scenes of wild excitement. But to the majority of Parisians the glorious tidings came later, with the first boom of cannon and the sudden pealing of the bells. Ah! There can be no doubt now! Windows opened everywhere, and people listened to the wonderful music a few second in ecstasy before rushing down into the streets to mingle their joy with that of their fellow-citizens. Soon the streets were avenues of color: flags were waving from every apartment in the city, and the physiognomy of Paris was transformed as though by a magic wand.

ing. The Hôtel de Ville was rapidly covered with the Allied colors, and the banks and other establishments as well as private buildings in every quarter of the city were by now ablaze with bunting.

M. Clemenceau, the Grand Old Man of France, received the congratulations of the whole Cabinet during the morning, all the Ministers and Secretaries of State calling at the Ministry of War for the purpose. Five or six hundred students also marched to the Ministry and gathered in the court yard to acclaim the Premier who has so magnificently fulfilled his promise "to make war" till the attainment of victory.

Dense Crowds Everywhere.

As the day wore on the crowds grew denser and denser on the Boulevards, the place de la Concorde, in the Champs-Elysées and outside the Chamber of Deputies.

Improvised speakers climbed on to the German guns on the place de la Concorde and harangued the multitude on the armistice terms and on the anticipated conditions of peace. The Boule-

THE NEW YORK HERALD

PRICE: Paris and France, 20c.; Abroad, 30c. — EUROPEAN EDITION—PARIS, SATURDAY, DECEMBER 14, 1918. — PRIX: Paris et France, 20c.; Etranger, 30c.

PRESIDENT WILSON ARRIVES IN FRANCE

WHERE AND WHEN TO SEE PRESIDENT IN PARIS TO-DAY

He Will Arrive at Bois de Boulogne Station at 10 o'clock This Morning.

The President and Mrs. Woodrow Wilson will reach Paris at 10 a.m. to-day. They will be welcomed at the avenue du Bois de Boulogne station by the President of the French Republic and Mme. Raymond Poincare, with M. Georges Clemenceau, the Premier; the president of the Senate, the president of the Chamber of Deputies, the Ministers of Justice, of Finance and of Labor, the Prefect of Police and a host of other prominent personages.

M. and Mme. Poincaré will accompany the President and Mrs. Wilson to the marvellous Murat mansion in the rue de Monceau.

Line of Route.

The route will be:—

Avenue du Bois-de-Boulogne, place de l'Etoile, avenue des Champs-Elysées, avenue Nicolas II., pont Alexandre III., quai d'Orsay, pont de la Concorde, place de la Concorde, rue Royale, place de la Madeleine, boulevard Malesherbes, boulevard Haussmann, avenue de Messine, rue de Monceau.

The Presidential procession will be formed as follows: In the first carriage will be President Wilson with President Poincaré. In the second carriage will be Mrs. Woodrow Wilson, Mme. Raymond Poincaré, Mme. Jusserand and Miss Margaret Wilson. The third carriage will convey Mr. William G. Sharp, the American Ambassador to France; M. Georges Clemenceau, General Duparge and General Mordacq.

Mr. Robert Lansing, M. Stephen Pichon, M. Saincere and General Léorat will be in the fourth carriage; General Bliss, Mr. Henry White and Colonel Bonel in the fifth; General Pershing, M. Jusserand and Captain de Blanpré in the sixth; Admiral Benson, M. André Tardieu and Colonel de Boigne in the seventh; Admiral Grayson, General Harts and Colonel Lobez in the eighth.

Déjeuner at the Elysée.

At 12.30 M. and Mme. Poincaré will give an official déjeuner party at the Palais de l'Elysée in honor of the illustrious visitors.

Magnificent Fleet of Allied Warships Escorts the George Washington Into Brest—Strikingly Impressive Scenes—Cheered by Mile of Khaki-clad Soldiers and Enthusiastic Populace.

"Outlaw" is the Term Used by Chief Executive in Reference to Germany—Peace He Hopes for is One "Conforming to the Ideal of France and the United States."

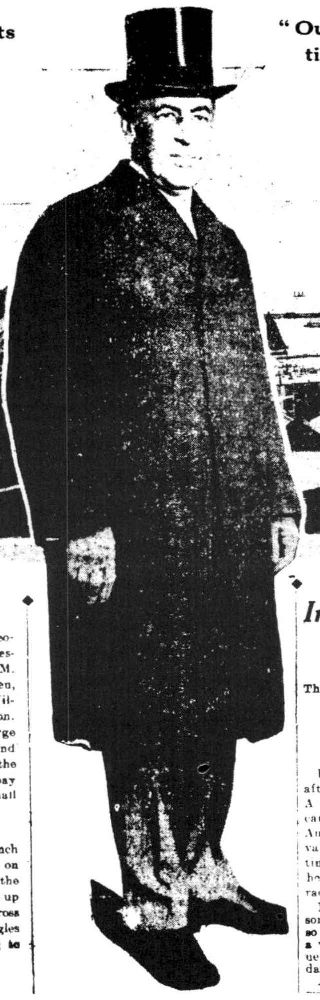

"GOULET DE BREST." — *PORT DU COMMERCE, BREST.*

(SPECIAL TELEGRAM TO THE HERALD.)

BREST, Friday.—The boom of the shore batteries at 1 o'clock told the people of Brest that the George Washington had anchored in the harbor. The President's ship had been sighted two hours before. It was half-past one when M. Pichon, Minister of Foreign Affairs; Leygues, Minister of Marine, and Tardieu, High Commissioner for America, with General Pershing and Miss Margaret Wilson debarked on a little despatch boat to go out to the George Washington. When at 3 o'clock President Wilson and his party left the side of the George Washington, the sun was struggling to shine through the thick rainclouds and although the effort was not a success it resulted in a distinct brightening of the dull skies and a delicate violet tinted the wall of battleships encircling the bay and glinted on hovering aeroplanes. President Wilson came ashore in the small gunboat Pas-de-Calais.

COMES ASHORE SMILING BRIGHTLY.

As the vessel came alongside the quay, the band of a regiment of French Marines played "The Star-Spangled Banner." The President was standing on the deck with Mrs. Wilson, his head bared. Then from another band burst the martial strains of the "Marseillaise." Immediately the President's face lit up with one of his famous smiles and he was still smiling when he stepped across the gangway after Mrs. Wilson and trod the soil of France, while the bugles sounded the salute. All the ships' guns were now firing salvoes of greeting to the first American President to visit France.

MRS. WILSON KISSES LITTLE GIRL.

Impressive Ceremonies Mark France's Reception of American Executive

The Republic Represented by Ministers, Senators, Deputies and Military and Naval Personages.

BREST, Friday.—President Wilson this afternoon set foot on the soil of France. A moment of profound historic significance as that in which the head of the American Republic confirms by his arrival in Europe the fact that the two continents are forever rejoined and must henceforth form but a single human race in the Old as in the New World.

Never has any predecessor of Mr. Wilson, while in office, crossed the Atlantic, so that the saying of Gœthe applies in a way to this unprecedented event: "A new order of things dates from this day."

At an early hour this morning Brest ...

... for us. He carries the nation's flag.—Havas.

THIRD AMERICAN ARMY WENT ACROSS RHINE YESTERDAY

Coblentz Bridgehead Is Occupied as Troops March Forward Across Thirty-Kilomètre Zone

(AMERICAN OFFICIAL.)

Friday, 9 p.m.

The Third American Army crossed the Rhine to-day and occupied the Coblentz bridgehead.

FRENCH COMMUNIQUE.

Friday, 11 p.m.

The troops of the Tenth Army continued their forward march after having occupied Kreuznach. On December ... they had gone beyond the line Bretzenheim, Sprendlingen, Eichloch, Biebelsheim, Gau, Odernheim.

BRITISH COMMUNIQUE.

Friday evening.

Our advanced troops yesterday crossed the Rhine and began the occupation of the Cologne bridgehead. This evening they had reached the general line ..., Kassel, Siegburg, Odenthal, Opladen.

MEDAL FOR ALLIED TROOPS

LONDON, Friday.—The "Daily Chronicle" understands that an international medal for Allied troops who have fought in the field will shortly be struck. A metal bar will be worn for each year of service.—Havas.

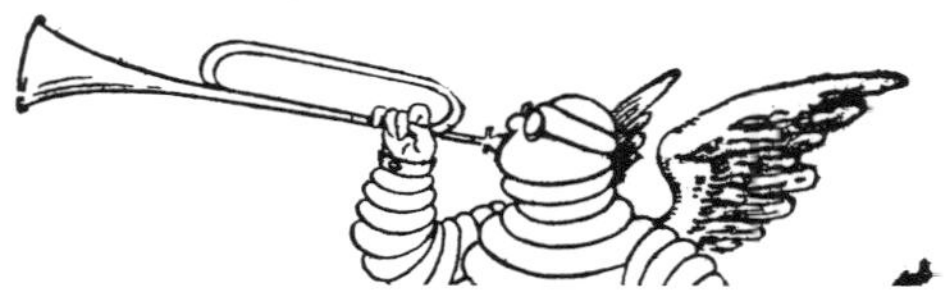

THE NEW YORK HERALD

DISTRIBUTED BY AMERICAN Y.M.C.A. — DISTRIBUTED BY AMERICAN Y.M.C.A.

PRICE: Paris, France and Belgium: 20c.; Abroad, 30c. — EUROPEAN EDITION—PARIS, SUNDAY, JUNE 29, 1919. — PRIX: Paris, France et Belgique: 20c. Etranger, 30c.

WORLD PEACE PACT SIGNED AT VERSAILLES

German Plenipotentiaries Sign Treaty Which Seals the Doom of Their Imperialism.

By WADE CHANCE.

It was a rare privilege to witness yesterday's ceremony, when the predatory Hun appeared in person to admit temporary interruption in his conquest of Europe, and attach his dishonored signature to a presumptive undertaking that his recent invasion of France, the twentieth in number in recorded history, would be his last. It was the fourth full session of the Peace Conference, and the largest, the long Hall of Mirrors being filled with an audience tense with expectancy when Clemenceau arose, to make his brief announcement and stated that the German delegates would now be invited to enter and sign the documents prepared. The great war gods which had led in the great assault on humanity were strangely missing, and the five little men, whom a strange cycle of fate had thrown into this bewildering assemblage, must have wondered to see the mighty leaders of the world come to meet them. After signing the four documents, they retired to their seats, their duties finished.

Following the Germans, first came the American delegates, Wilson, Lansing, House, White and Bliss, who did not directly cross the room, but walked around all the table space, passing by the correspondents, who occupied one end of the hall, seated on upholstered benches, with a view of the gardens through great windows, where thousands more were gathered. Then followed the British Delegation, Lloyd George, Bonar Law, Balfour, Milner and Barnes. Then came France's representatives, headed by Clemenceau, the one great outstanding figure of the Conference of unquestioned single-minded purpose and patriotism, striving only for France's security and a sound peace. After that the nations followed rapidly, and the assembly began to break up and move about. Mr. Wilson went over to talk to General Bliss, and all the chief delegates were called upon to sign their names for a multitude of autograph hunters, including many of the delegates themselves.

Notable Procession.

It was a notable procession which moved back and forth from the table holding the Treaties, and I noticed especially Bikiniz, providing the one single note of color in a very drab assemblage of frock coats, with scarcely a uniform; Hughes, of Australia, the little giant who never compromised nor varied his denunciation of the enemy and claims for a sound peace; Smuts, Botha, Massey, Tardieu, Pichon, all the well-known figures of the caste of this world drama, which had run so long. The signing was completed in the short space of forty-five minutes, Clemenceau announced the proceedings ...

SIGNING THE TREATY IN THE GALERIE DES GLACES.

CROWDS CHEERING CLEMENCEAU, WILSON AND LLOYD G...

... tions—ruined France, Belgium and Poland. France has shown a sorry lack of faith in the hypothetical guarantee of the architects—the League which is to direct future building operations from the frigid, but correctly neutral, atmosphere of Geneva.

France accepted the Treaty only after the promise of guarantees from America and England for immediate assistance in case of attack. Thus Clemenceau retains, after all, his old reliable balance of power, still in fashion, since it was this balance, this alliance, which saved Europe, for it functioned from the first day of hostilities, and not after three years of watchful waiting and obscure thinking.

No search of the German delegates was made to-day to discover secret orders to scuttle the Treaty and the fledgeling League of Nations, in true Scapa Flow style.

Since Germany has specifically announced, by word and deed, that she has no intention of carrying out the terms of this Treaty, to-day's ceremony can have but one meaning: It binds, in the eyes of the world—not the Hun, but the Allies—and for its fulfilment the world looks not to perjured Germany, but to them.

VERSAILLES CROWD SURGES ROUND THE "BIG THREE."

The signing of the German Treaty, which for months was heralded as "the greatest dramatic event in history," in reality turned out to be a ...

Treaty is a Great Charter For New Order,

He Issues Statement Indicating Benefits To Be Derived Under Pact.

The benefits which may be derived from the Peace Treaty were pointed out yesterday by President Wilson in a message addressed: "To my fellow-countrymen." The following is the text of the message:—

... subjected to the domination and exploitation of a stronger nation, but shall be put under the friendly direction and afforded the helpful assistance of governments which undertake to be responsible to the opinion of mankind in the execution of their task by accepting the direction of the League of Nations.

"It recognizes the inalienable rights of nationality; the rights of minorities, and the sanctity of religious belief and practice. It lays the basis for ...

... again, I leave ... regret, my ... people and ... firmed, my ... privilege of a ... men, conscious ... fectionate fri... foundly grate... tality and for countless kindnesses which have made me feel welcome and at home. I take the liberty of bidding France God-speed as well as good-bye, and of expressing once more my abid- ...

... They left the Palace immediately after all the delegates had signed.

Among the most interested spectators were fifteen German newspaper men, dressed in black, and of solemn ...

Chinese Representatives Decline to Sign Because of the Clauses Relative to Shantung.

... room, apparently anxious to taste of their newly-restored privileges in a country which until a few minutes before had been an enemy.

The fact that the American Delega- ... the Allied and ... sign the Treaty ... America, for ... Clemenceau to ... o insisted that ... ould sign first, ... it thought M. ... his honor.

... read among the ... nese Delegation ... to sign and did ... resentative, offi- ... e ceremony re- ... delegates. The ... while sympathe- ... ne, was the one ... front which the ... Powers have ... throughout the ... a surprise, and ... did not decide ... sterday ... ed by General ... elsewhere, also ... and many took ... eral could have ... until later with ...

... mony seemed to ... Big Powers had ... the spectators ... to the crowds ... or watched the ... m the big glass ... smen occupied ... aphing souvenir ... they exchanged ... President Wilson ... laughed and ... George and the ... decidedly in- ... unimpressive. ... ates after M. ... ed the ceremony ... the "most signi- ... history of the ... Delegates left ... down the road ... mile was lined ... ands of cheering ... dren.

... e was coincident ... ary of the assas- ... Franz Ferdinand ...

... Supreme Council ... nce was handed ... erday, in which ... that the block- ... ically lifted so ... ified the Treaty.

... *signature of the* ...

1920–1929

The decade began momentously for the *Herald*, when on January 16, 1920, the front page announced that the *New York Herald* and its European Edition had been bought from the Bennett estate by Frank A. Munsey, owner of the *New York Sun*. Munsey named as editor and general manager Laurence Hills, the *Sun*'s correspondent at the Versailles Peace Conference. Hills would stay at the helm of the Paris paper until the Germans occupied Paris two decades later.

The look of the *Paris Herald* changed too. It became more sober, with fewer photos and fewer illustrated sections. Color sections and color advertisements, which had been a regular part of the paper since as early as the 1890s, disappeared for sixty years, not to reappear until 1979.

Munsey remained in control just long enough to appropriate the handsome balances which had almost inadvertently accumulated in the paper's bank accounts in 1918 and 1919. Then, after several years in which the *Herald* lost money (in New York as well as in Paris), Munsey sold the *Herald* properties in 1924 to one of New York's most distinguished newspaper families. Elizabeth Reid, along with her son and her daughter-in-law, were the owners of the *New York Tribune*, which had been founded by Horace Greeley in 1841.

Elizabeth Reid was an extraordinary personality who had made a successful social passage from her early days in frontier California through New York and eventually to the upper reaches of London society. She had taken over the *Tribune* in 1913, on the death of her husband, Whitelaw Reid, who had been its editor for almost forty years. By 1924 she was joined by her son Ogden, who acted as editor, and his wife, the former Helen Rogers of Appleton, Wisconsin, who would later succeed her mother-in-law as the company's driving force.

Immediately after the Reid takeover, the two New York papers merged to form the *New York Herald-Tribune*. The Paris-based European Edition did not yet take the hyphenated name, but carried instead the complicated title, "The New York Herald, European Edition of the New York Herald-Tribune."

Editorially, the *Paris Herald* was now addressed to the needs and interests of a more heterogeneous group of tourists, travelers, American residents and other English-speaking Europeans. A regular "Sporting Gossip" column by Sparrow Robertson became one of its most noted features—the term "sporting" stretched to include not only the capital's playing fields and boxing rings, but its bars and nightclubs as well. Already in his late sixties when he began his twenty-year career with the *Herald*, Robertson was as thoroughly original an American as ever set foot in France, with his eccentric, fractured writing style, his omnipresent fedora and his inveterate greeting, "My old pal!"

As the twenties progressed, the *Herald*'s economic fortunes picked up sharply again. Circulation doubled from the historic norm of 15,000 to nearly 30,000 copies. This was partly due to the fact that prohibition and the economic boom in America brought a new style of American visitor to Europe. Masses of tourists and residents arrived who were drawn less exclusively from America's social aristocracy than had previously been the case. The *Herald*'s audience was also swollen by a lively group of expatriate intellectuals who came to savour the Old World's greater sophistication, and to establish closer ties to literature and art than they felt were possible in an America judged increasingly consumerist and puritanical. The days of the luxurious swing through Europe were now largely part of a prewar past, as students, middle-class travelers, struggling writers, entertainers and corporate managers dominated the passenger lists of the transatlantic liners.

The *Herald* of this era was resolutely conservative in its outlook, becoming the newspaper of record for the growing community of Americans based in Paris, reporting on the activities of their clubs, churches, library, hospital, and of course, of the American Legion Post—a community which by this time numbered about 20,000.

Cable news from New York, and especially from Wall Street, was more important now than ever, but reporting such news required a particular talent. The cables, naturally reduced to a mere handful of words, had to be fleshed out into stories of several hundred words. This led occasionally to an excess of imagination when, on a slow news day, a ten-word cable would have to be stretched to fill a couple of front-page columns.

Under the ownership of the Reids, with additions to the staff of such colorful but capable characters as Al Laney, Ralph Barnes, Elliott Paul and Vincent Bugeja, and under the genial supervision of Eric Hawkins, morale was high and a feeling of community among those who put out the paper became a strong element in its success.

By the end of the 1920s, the *Herald* could draw upon a sizable combination of news sources—Havas, Associated Press, and United Press, as well as the *New York Herald-Tribune* cables and its local Paris reporters—and was clearly a better and more thorough journal than ever before. Advertising categories appeared that reflected material changes of the postwar decade (films, inexpensive automobiles, commercial airlines). Prewar celebrities, such as Bernhardt, Duse and Melba, were replaced by the new era's famous names: Josephine Baker, Gloria Swanson, Al Jolson, Maurice Chevalier, Isadora Duncan.

The sense of looking at a distant world, quite unlike our own, that the modern reader often feels when leafing through very old newspapers largely disappears when we reach the pages of the 1920s. As the first postwar decade begins, recognizable elements of the twentieth century clamor for our attention on virtually every *Herald* page: from women in government to the rise of fascism, from general strikes to the emerging motion picture industry. Events, movements, faces that still seem current at the close of the century abound in these pages, their images clear and strong thanks to the newly improved wire photo.

Perhaps the biggest story of the decade for the *Herald* (and surely one of the biggest of the century) was the marvel of the Spirit of St. Louis and the quiet, captivating Charles Lindbergh. Following his rapturous welcome at Le Bourget Airport, Lucky Lindy took refuge in the American Embassy—where he was tracked down by a novice and enterprising *Herald* reporter named Ralph Barnes. Barnes's interview was the first to be published with the world's newest superhero, and Barnes himself went on to become one of the best-known and best-loved of all the *Herald*'s correspondents.

For all but the first two of its first forty-three years, the *Herald*'s newsroom was located in central Paris, on the rue du Louvre, its spacious windows overlooking the teeming, all-night marketplace of Les Halles, its walls an ever denser tangle of graffiti (including journalists' do's and don'ts dating back to Bennett's early whims and prejudices), its ceiling an intricate web of exposed wiring leading to the bare light bulbs that dangled above the copydesks. But the relative prosperity which came to the *Herald* in the late 1920s was to change all that. Laurence Hills decided to sink the paper's profits into the construction of an ambitious new building, located on a site formerly occupied by the American Church on the rue de Berri, just off the Champs-Elysées.

In early October 1929, the *Herald* announced that construction had begun on the new H-shaped edifice that would finally house under one roof all of the *Herald*'s editorial and business offices, as well as its typesetting and printing facilities. The ceremony of the laying of the cornerstone was covered at length in the paper, and a new era of expansion and prosperity for the *Herald* was predicted. But the timing could not have been worse. Events in Wall Street just three weeks later would have much more negative and far-reaching effects than the editors of the *Herald* could ever have imagined, as the 1920s ended with a crash.

THE NEW YORK HERALD

PRICE: Paris and France, 25c.; Abroad, 35c. EUROPEAN EDITION—PARIS. SUNDAY, MARCH 21, 1920. PRIX: Paris et France, 25c.; Etranger, 35c.

Communists In Ruhr Area Capture Leading Centres; Proclaim Soviet Republic

Workers Take Essen in Fight Costing 300 Lives — National Government Alarmed as Four Other Towns Are Seized.

SENDING OF TROOPS MEANS FRESH PERILS FOR BERLIN

Authorities Face Alternative of Exposing Capital to Riot Terror or Permitting the Spartacist Wave to Spread Unchecked.

(SPECIAL TO THE HERALD.)

STUTTGART, Saturday. — President Ebert and Herr Noske are admittedly perturbed at the situation in the Ruhr area, which is getting beyond the control of the authorities. The latest official news is that the fighting is severe in several towns, principally in the Elberfeld district, where there are numerous killed and wounded. Communication with that district ceased this morning.

A telephonic message from Berlin states that Herr Noske has been authorised to despatch two brigades of the Reichswehr to proceed to the Ruhr district. The troops are willing to go, but crowds in the streets menaced them and prevented their departure. The Government must decide quickly whether to send troops, thereby leaving Berlin open to the rioters with no military protection, or to leave the Ruhr district in the hands of the workers, who are filled with the communistic spirit.

Fighting was continuing in Saxony, especially in Dresden and Chemnitz, at noon to-day.

SPARTACIST ARMY HOLDS MANY TOWNS IN RUHR AREA

Despatches received in Paris yesterday from South Germany show that the situation is very threatening in the Ruhr district. The Spartacists after sharp fighting have captured Essen. The total killed on both sides is 300. It is said that the Soviet Republic has been proclaimed and that the Spartacist army has been increased to 100,000 men. It is equipped with 3in. guns and armored cars.

Mulheim, Oberhausen, Elberfeld and Kattwig have also fallen into the hands of the Spartacists. The Government troops were outnumbered and forced to withdraw. Some of them took refuge in the British zone and were disarmed. A Note issued by the Allied mission says that 1,000 Reichswehr men and a general entered the territory and were disarmed and placed under British military supervision. The Reichswehr troops on attacking the town of Remscheidt were overwhelmed by the Communists and forced to retreat.

Düsseldorf fell into the hands of the Spartacists on Friday night, the Government troops evacuating the town without fighting. Belgian troops on the right bank of the Rhine retired to the left bank without interference. Precautionary measures have been taken to guard the Rhine bridges against eventual Spartacist attacks. The occupation of Duisburg by the Spartacists is expected.

The Communists and independent workers have also taken possession of Barmen, Bochum, Glucksburg and Kreimshalle after severe fighting. They are led by Captain von Gober and an officer named Pewer, who was formerly attached to German Headquarters.

Some 7,000 Belgian troops have been sent to the manœuvre ground at Elsenborn, nominally for firing drill. But this step is evidently a measure of precaution against the communist disorders in Westphalia. Several other international detachments are being moved towards the danger area.

LEIPZIG STILL FIGHTING; BOMBS DROPPED ON TOWN

According to despatches received in Paris from Germany, fighting has ceased at Kiel, where Admiral Evers has been appointed Governor and the troops disarmed. One report says that the dead number 1,000. At Leipzig, the workers have refused to submit to the military authorities, and fighting continues. A military aeroplane dropped bombs on the Johannisplatz, and another machine was shot down by the workmen. Conflicts between the workers and the Reichswehr have occurred at Halle.

NO PERMIT GIVEN TO GERMAN TROOPS FOR RUHR DISTRICT

BRUSSELS, Saturday.—According to a despatch from a German source, the Allied Governments are said to have authorised the Bauer Government to send Reichswehr troops into the Occupation Zone, on account of the agitation which prevails in the Ruhr district.

This news is entirely false. The Allies have received a request of this nature from the Berlin Government, but they have not replied. If, therefore, the German troops have entered the zone which extends fifty kilomètres to the east of the Rhine, the Treaty of Versailles has been violated. —Havas

LORD MAYOR OF CORK KILLED BY MASKED MEN AT HIS HOME

CORK, Saturday.—The Lord Mayor of Cork was murdered at his home about one o'clock this morning by a band of masked men who forced their way into the house.

They made their escape in an automobile.

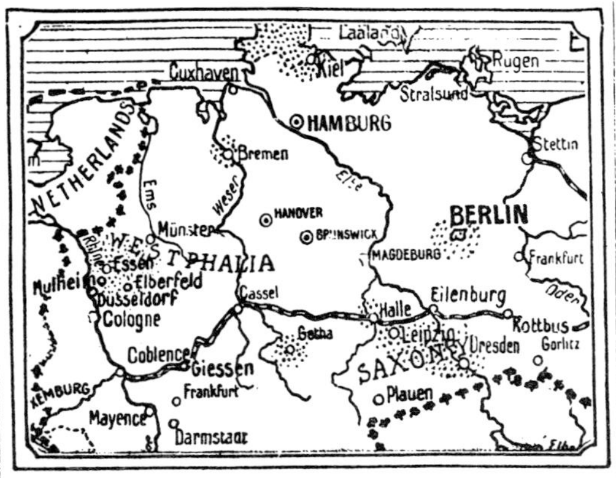

MAP SHOWING DISTRICTS HELD BY COMMUNISTS.

BERLIN AFRAID BALTIC TROOPS MAY COME BACK

Sensational Rumors Among Surging Crowds in Streets—Situation in City Still Unsettled.

(SPECIAL TO THE HERALD.)

STUTTGART, Friday. — Negotiations are still being carried on between the Berlin Trade Union League and the Government, but without much hope of success. Labor demands the retirement of the national Prussian Government, the disarmament of the Reichswehr and permission for the army of workers to form a home guard. Herr Heime is conducting the pourparlers for the Government.

It is reported that several members of the Cabinet left Stuttgart by aeroplane, but on the way called at Weimar and decided to remain there when they learned of the unsettled situation in Berlin.

The Trade Union League represents also the Free Employés' League and the League of German Officials. While the Independent Socialists are taking no active leadership, they have given the trade unionists the promise of their full support in the demands. The renewal of the general strike on the Prussian railways has led to an intensifying of public anxiety, but the NEW YORK HERALD learns from Berlin that the food directors there are in possession of 20,000 tons of oatmeal and dried vegetables, besides 6,000 tons of fats, which are stored in the city's warehouses and which can be distributed if the strikers agree that this is sufficient to tide the capital over for as long a time as four weeks.

In Berlin there are still surging crowds in the streets and occasional shots are to be heard. After the police had used hand-grenades before the Hotel Adlon this morning the hotel visitors gathered on the second floor and talked in groups, while in a darkened foyer downstairs the manager and his clerks were engaged in a heated discussion as to how to behave if the crowd entered the building again. Nearby, a charwoman, with rag and pail, was mopping up from the marble floor the blood of the wounded who had been carried in after the grenade-throwing.

Baltic Troop Rumors.

All sorts of rumors are circulating among the crowds. On the one hand it is said that the Baltic troops have already returned to Berlin and are encamped in the Zoological Gardens, and on the other that these troops are still waiting for the development of a Soviet régime in order to march into the city again and suppress it. An effort is being made to issue the Independent Socialist organ "Freiheit" again.

The most significant feature of the situation is the complete collapse of all political leadership among the workers. The Independent Socialists are distrustful of one another and are making no effort to assert themselves. The Communists also are without any outstanding men, while the International Socialists, who are led by Huysmanns, have given up the attempt to unite the Socialist wings as hopeless, and lay the blame at the door of the Independents. Labor is now expressing itself wholly through its economic organisations, which have come forward and imposed rigid demands.

It is too early to prophesy what is likely to develop. There is no reason to fear the general establishment of a Communist government, nor to interpret the fighting against the Noske guard in numerous industrial circles as having bolshevist objectives. The so-called Soviets of several cities are not Soviets in any sense except that of taking over the municipal functions by the workers. So far no demands, attacking property, have been voiced. The trade union leaders are not Communists, nor are the great majority of Germany's Labor men. But there are heavy scores to be settled with Noske and his colleagues, as well as with the military, which Labor feels can be more safely carried out if done now.

The army's exit from Berlin will remain one of the blackest episodes in German history, and is already being spoken of to-day as having been a surprising revelation and as having symbolised the end of the long tradition of militarism.

LABOR CONFLICT STILL DOMINATES BERLIN SITUATION

One Report Has Strike Settled, Others Say Negotiations Are Broken Off.

According to despatches received in Paris, the chaotic condition of affairs in Berlin continues to be a source of grave anxiety to the representatives of the Ebert Government. The general strike, which is maintained as a protest against the military usurpation, is said from a London source to have been settled, the Government having made numerous concessions to the workers. Other reports state that negotiations have been broken off.

The labor demands include among others: the disarming of the Baltic troops and the punishment of their leaders; the formation of guards composed of workmen; trade-union representatives to be comprised in the new government; the nationalisation of the coal and potash mines.

In their visit to the Vice-Chancellor yesterday, the Allied Chargés d'Affaires renewed their assurances that the Allies have had no relations with the usurpers, but have considered the Constitutional Government as the only one to which they are accredited. They expressed the hope that the crisis would be rapidly overcome, so that Germany might resume her task of reconstruction. Lord Kilmarnoch presented the Supreme Council's Note, which states that the Allies will supply no food or raw material to a monarchist or soviet Germany. Credits and supplies can be furnished only to a democratic Germany which respects the Constitution.

In Berlin Governmental circles it is hoped that if concessions were made to the workers, they might prevent the Independent Socialists from throwing in their lot with the Communists. The Independents have all along adopted a hostile attitude to the Ebert Government, and it is doubtful whether they will accept any portfolios in the new Cabinet, as they would then be practically muzzled.

Troops in Readiness.

Great agitation still prevails in Berlin and the troops are held in readiness to act. The streets are in darkness, as the gas supply is still cut off. Water can be obtained only at intervals. Barbed wire has been placed at the principal street crossings. No troops are seen, except a few patrols. The Spartacists are plundering shops in the north of the city, stopping vehicles and turning out the occupants, but apparently there is now no fear of a Spartacist rising on a large scale.

The Spartacists posted pickets in many places to prevent strikers from returning to work. At one time they occupied five railroad stations on the east of the City and Reichswehr troops, with armored cars, were sent to disperse them. Apparently their object was to prevent the return of Ebert's Government.

Trampled to Death.

An eye-witness of the fighting in Berlin says that near the town hall of the Schœneberg district he saw the bodies of fifteen officers of the Baltic troops, who had been trampled to death by the crowd. Three other officers were killed yesterday near the Brandenburger Tor by the Sicherheitswehr. Train traffic has again stopped and no newspapers are being published.

FIVE THOUSAND BRIDES FROM EUROPE REACH U.S.

(BY SPECIAL CABLE TO THE HERALD.)

HOBOKEN, Saturday.—The commanding general of the port of embarkation has reported that 3,709 members of the Army, Navy and Marine Corps returned to the United States with foreign brides. He explained that this is an incomplete list and estimates that fully 5,000 men were married overseas.

Of those returned of which the port office has record there are 2,295 French brides, 1,101 British, 79 Belgian, 41 Italian, and 31 German.

IRISH FEALTY IS FORESWORN TO BE CITIZEN

Chicago Judge Requires Embryo American to Renounce His Allegiance to Ireland as Well as to Great Britain.

(BY SPECIAL CABLE TO THE HERALD.)

CHICAGO, Saturday.—The Irish "Republic" was officially recognised today by Judge Marcus Kavanaugh, when he compelled Mr. Patrick King, seeking American citizenship, to forswear allegiance to the De Valera government. King had readily renounced fealty to the British Government, and then was called back by the judge to make complete renunciation by forswearing citizenship in the Irish republic.

King hesitated for a few moments, but finally complied.

DE VALERA SATISFIED WITH SENATE ACTION

NEW YORK, Saturday. — Mr. de Valera, "President of the Irish Republic," has cabled to Mr. Arthur Griffiths, acting president, in Dublin, that the United States Senate having adopted a Treaty reservation regarding Ireland, he considered his mission here ended. He proposes that a Te Deum be chanted throughout Ireland.

UNITED STATES OBJECTS TO TREATY INTERPRETATION

WASHINGTON, Saturday.—The United States Government has raised objections to the decision of the Reparation Commission which sets forth that the Peace Treaty permits the sale of certain German property in neutral countries if such sale be necessary for the initial payment of the indemnity due by Germany.

The State Department announces that it is preparing other protests declaring that the interpretation of the Reparation Commission does not conform with what had been officially decided between Germany and the Allied Powers.

With regard to a report that Great Britain has requested that the Reparation Commission should take over German properties and all rights of German citizens in electrical enterprises in South America and transfer them to Great Britain as part payment of the indemnity, Mr. Frank L. Polk, Acting Secretary of State, in a letter just published, says that he has no information thereon. It is understood, however, that the Government's representative on the commission has provisionally adopted a construction of Article 235, which would empower the commission to demand payment of Germany's initial instalments of the indemnity in any commodities—gold, ships or other—which the commission desired. Under such power it would be possible to request the sale of securities controlled by German corporations in South America.

PROPOSES TO TAX BIG WAR PROFITS TO RAISE BONUS

(BY SPECIAL CABLE TO THE HERALD.)

WASHINGTON, Saturday.—Representative Rainey, of Illinois, has introduced a bill in the House proposing a 50 per cent. tax on all war profits above $20,000 annually made by any individual, as a means of providing the revenue necessary to grant bonuses to men who served during the war. This levy would apply to the years from 1915 to 1919 inclusive and, it is estimated, would yield $5,000,000,000.

The author of the bill suggested also that the bonus should take the form of an honor certificate with coupons attached, each worth $40. There would be a coupon for each month's service and the Government would start redemption in September, taking up one coupon each month until all had been paid, with a limit of September, 1925, at which time all must have been redeemed.

APPROVAL IS GIVEN TO COLBY NOMINATION

WASHINGTON, Saturday. — The Foreign Relations Committee of the Senate has recommended the approval of the nomination of Mr. Bainbridge Colby as Secretary of State.

It is expected that the Senate will act on the nomination within a few days.

POLICE COMMISSIONER HELD BY GRAND JURY

(BY SPECIAL CABLE TO THE HERALD.)

NEW YORK, Saturday.—The Grand Jury has indicted Mr. Augustus D. Porter, Third Deputy Police Commissioner, on a charge of neglect of his official duties under the Penal Code. The jury acted after listening to the testimony of two policemen, who testified that they found Mr. Porter in a disorderly house when they raided it.

Mr. Porter is reported to have told the policemen: "Forget about it; I'll protect you."

MAJOR HYATT IS NAMED AS ATTACHE IN LONDON

(BY SPECIAL CABLE TO THE HERALD.)

WASHINGTON, Saturday. — Major Robert F. Hyatt, Field Artillery, has been named as assistant military attaché at the Court of St. James's. Major Hyatt served in France with the Chemical Warfare Service of the United States Army.

Treaty Is Rejected By Democrat Votes: Sent Back to Wilson

Ratification Lacks Seven of Necessary Vote, Democrats Dividing Equally—Knox Offers Resolution for Separate Peace.

WASHINGTON, Saturday. — The long-drawn-out fight over the Treaty of Versailles came to an end last night with the defeat of the ratification resolution. Senator Lodge immediately offered a resolution, which was adopted, calling for the return of the Treaty to the President with notification of the refusal of the Senate to ratify it. The Treaty was returned to the President this morning.

The vote was: for ratification, 49; against ratification, 35. Those voting for ratification included 28 Republicans and 21 Democrats, while the vote against it was made up of 23 Democrats and 12 Republicans. Last November, only seven Democrats voted with the Republicans for ratification with the Lodge reservations. The vote for ratification last evening lacked only seven votes of the 56 which would have given it the necessary two-thirds of those present. There were twelve absentees or Senators not voting.

Senator Knox, of Pennsylvania, Republican, after the failure of the ratification resolution to secure the necessary vote, offered a resolution to the effect that the United States shall conclude a separate peace with Germany.

TREATY FIGHT IN BRIEF.

Oct. 24, 1918.—President Wilson appeals to country to return Democratic majority.
Nov. 5, 1918.—Election results: Republicans, 49 votes; Democrats, 47.
June 6, 1919.—Senate demands full text of Treaty.
June 10, 1919.—Senator Knox introduces resolution warning Peace Conference that Senate will not ratify Treaty incorporating League of Nations.
June 28, 1919.—Treaty signed at Versailles.
July 10, 1919.—Treaty laid before Senate.
August 23, 1919.—Committee adopts Shantung reservation.
August 29, 1919.—Reservation on British Empire votes adopted.
Sept. 4, 1919.—Senate Committee reports resolution ratifying Treaty with reservations.
Oct. 16, 1919.—Shantung reservation defeated.
Oct. 17, 1919.—Reservation withdrawing from commissions defeated.
Oct. 22, 1919.—New set of reservations adopted by Senate.
Oct. 29, 1919.—Amendment on British votes defeated.
Nov. 19, 1919.—Mr. Lodge submits Treaty for ratification with 14 reservations. Motion rejected by 55 votes to 39. Motion to ratify unconditionally also defeated by 53 votes to 38. Senate adjourned sine die.
Jan., 1920.—Senate again takes up Treaty.
March 19, 1920.—Senate fails to ratify by seven votes.

VERSAILLES TREATY MAY NOW BECOME CAMPAIGN ISSUE

The failure of the Versailles Treaty for the second time to secure the necessary two-thirds vote of those present and voting, as required by the American Constitution, leaves the Treaty technically in the exact position in which it was left at the end of the last session of the Congress. It is still before that body and can be called up at any time by a member, and, if the necessary approval is secured, can be referred again to the Foreign Relations Committee for further deliberation. On the other hand, the President has it still within his power, the Treaty having failed of ratification twice, to withdraw the Treaty and submit it afresh either with or without changes, as a result of further negotiations. This belongs to him as the Executive empowered to negotiate treaties, which, however, to be valid must have the approval of the Senate.

It appears to be doubtful, considering the position of the two parties in America, whether either course will be followed. Whether for the good or ill of the world, the Treaty now seems to have become an issue in the campaign for the Presidency. That would seem to postpone its future consideration for many months, for the Congress to be elected in the coming autumn does not take office until March 4 next, and only then if called into extraordinary session by the new President.

Wilson Was Adamant.

President Wilson has adhered to the position he took in the letter he addressed to the Jackson Day dinner of the Democrats, namely, that rather than see his work at the Peace Conference changed, except by reservations that would be purely interpretive, he would prefer to have the people at the polls pass upon the whole question at issue. This likewise has been the demand of the so-called irreconcilables, the faction led by Senators Borah, McCormick and Brandegee. But, on the other hand, the position which the larger group of Republicans led by Senator Lodge will take will be that they wanted to ratify the Treaty with certain amendments intended to protect America and comporting with its Constitution, and that the President through his instructions to his followers in the Senate refused to accept it in this form.

The question before the people thus becomes—the Treaty unchanged or the Treaty with the Republican reservations, described by the Republican majority as "Americanising" it. This is likely to be the transcendent issue in the campaign.

On this issue on the Democratic side, Mr. William G. McAdoo, the President's son-in-law, has, as a prospective candidate, already announced, quite naturally, his intention to adhere to the President's position. Attorney-General A. Mitchell Palmer, whose hat is also in the Democratic ring, on the contrary, has shown that he would accept the Treaty with some reservations. It is for the Democratic Convention in San Francisco to decide which it shall name, without overlooking the possibility of Mr. Herbert Hoover, whose position regarding the Treaty, while undefined of late, seems, from a letter just published, to be nearer that of the Republicans than of Mr. Wilson. The extremist candidate on the Republican side is Senator Hiram Johnson, who would have none of the Versailles Treaty in any form. General Leonard Wood, Senator Harding and ex-Representative Lowden have all taken the position of the Lodge Republicans in the Senate. It is for the Republican Convention in Chicago to decide which of those shall be its standard-bearer in the coming fray. That twenty-one Democrats should have voted for the Treaty with the Lodge reservations, as compared with only seven last November, would seem to indicate a weakening of the President's cause in the last few months. It is also interesting to note that the Treaty failed of ratification this time by only seven votes.

MARLBOROUGH DIVORCE SUIT STIRS LONDON

Years Back, Rumors of Probably Similar Proceedings Led King Edward to Intervene on Account of Duchess' Honored Position.

(BY TELEPHONE.)

LONDON, Saturday. — Seldom has there been a bigger sensation in British society circles than the Marlborough divorce suit. Though it had been rumored for some twelve years that the couple was unhappy, the details were carefully suppressed at the desire of the Royal family, with whom the duchess, since the days of Queen Victoria, has been a warm favorite.

The suit which is to be tried on Monday may not lead to a divorce. The British law demands that a woman prove both desertion and unfaithfulness. Monday's suit is aimed to prove desertion. The duke's name is not coupled with any third party. He served as a King's Messenger during the war.

Coming to Paris.

The duchess is remaining in London for a few days, but will fly to Paris next week to meet her mother.

The Duchess of Marlborough has been prominently identified with British municipal politics for many years. As a member of the London County Council she has been active in providing for women's and children's welfare, health and facilities, such as public bakeries, laundries, baths and clinics in the East End slums.

When rumors were current that a suit was imminent, the late King Edward, it is reported, intervened and declared it impossible for persons as prominent as the Marlboroughs were at Court to be allowed to scandalise the country with a divorce. After that the duke lived at Blenheim, where he was engaged in politics and entertained the most [illegible] Ulster Covenanters. He also indulged in scientific farming.

THE NEW YORK HERALD

PRICE: Paris and France. 30c.; Abroad. 40c. — EUROPEAN EDITION—PARIS. SATURDAY, MARCH 5, 1921. — PRIX: Paris et France, 30c.; Etranger, 40c.

"BACK TO NORMALCY," HARDING'S KEYNOTE

Simplicity Marks Ceremonies in which New President Is Sworn into Office by Kissing Same Bible Used In Inauguration of Washington.—Ideal Weather Brings Out Huge Crowds.— Mr. Wilson Witnesses Oath.

(By Special Cable to the Herald.)

WASHINGTON, Friday.—Mr. Warren G. Harding to-day became the twenty-ninth President of the United States of America.

Ideal cloudless and not too chilly weather graced the simplest inauguration ceremonies in modern Washington's history. Standing at the Capitol entrance before a sea of humanity, President Harding with upraised hand repeated the oath administered by Chief Justice of the Supreme Court Edward D. White, and then kissed the same Bible which Washington had used in his first inaugural, opened to a passage selected by the President which reads:—

"What does the Lord require of thee but to do justice and love mercy and walk humbly with thy God."

Crowds Throng Street.

The solemn hush of the throngs that blackened the streets in front of the Capitol turned to pandemonium when the ceremony was finished and the President began his inaugural address.

Declaring his belief in the God-given destiny of the American Republic, the President reaffirmed his pre-inauguration promises that he would call an international conference to organise a court of justice, that he would strive to promote an understanding of government purely as an expression of popular will, and that he would do all in his power to support the high idealism which he declared had always been the inspiration of the politics of the United States.

The brief inaugural programme began at ten o'clock, when the congressional delegation passed through the crowds lining the avenue to the New Willard Hotel, where formal calls were paid on Mr. Harding and Mr. Coolidge.

Calls at White House.

Mr. Harding and his party then drove to the White House with the Congressional committee, where felicitations were exchanged with ex-President Wilson and his family. Mr. Wilson appeared in the best of spirits and showed no signs of the strain of the ceremonies.

The party then proceeded to the Capitol building. In the first automobile were Mr. Harding, Mr. Wilson, Senator Knox, "Uncle Joe" Cannon; in the second automobile were Mrs. Harding and Mrs. Wilson, Senator Nelson and Representative Rucker. In the third were Mr. Thomas Marshall, Mrs. Coolidge, Senator Overman; in the fourth, Mr. Coolidge and Mrs. Marshall. The double, surrounded by a cavalry escort, was heartily cheered as it passed through the crowds. Mr. Harding and Mr. Wilson were in earnest conversation during the procession although they were repeatedly compelled to take off their hats to acknowledge the cheers of the masses in Pennsylvania avenue.

Marked by Simplicity.

There was no music until the party reached the Peace Monument at the foot of the Capitol grounds, where a band was stationed. They went immediately to the President's office to await the Senate ceremonies.

President Harding entered the Senate chamber for the joint session to hear Mr. Calvin Coolidge take the oath of office as Vice-President. Foreign diplomats in uniform also attended the Senate ceremonies.

After prayer by the chaplain, Mr. Coolidge took his place beside Mr. Thomas Marshall, his predecessor. There was deep silence throughout the chamber. Then both men raised their right hands, and Mr. Marshall recited the Vice-President's oath, and Mr. Coolidge repeated it after him.

At the termination of this ceremony and while the new Senators were being sworn in the remainder of the party moved out to the east portico of the Capitol, where guests took their places and Mr. Harding's inaugural ceremonies began. Sounding-boards and amplifiers carried Mr. Harding's voice as he took the oath and made his address to the outer bounds of the crowd.

Mr. Wilson, on the advice of his physicians, did not stay for the inaugural address, but went to the White House immediately. After the oath the band played the National Anthem, while the crowd stood with bared heads and then Mr. Harding began speaking.

Text of Message.

The following is the text of President Harding's inaugural address:—

MY COUNTRYMEN:—

When one surveys the world about him after the great storm, noting the marks of destruction, and yet rejoicing in the ruggedness of the things which withstood it, if he is an American he breathes the clarified atmosphere with a strange mingling of regret and new hope.

We have seen a world-passion spend its fury, but we contemplate our Republic unshaken and hold our civilisation secure.

Liberty—Liberty within the law—and civilisation are inseparable and, though both were threatened, we find them now secure, and there comes to Americans the profound assurance that our representative government is the highest expression and surest guaranty of both.

Standing in this presence, mindful of the solemnity of this occasion, feeling the emotions which no one may know until he senses the great weight of responsibility for himself, I must utter my belief in the divine inspiration of the Founding Fathers. Surely there must have been God's intent in the making of this New World Republic. Ours is an organic law which had but one ambiguity, and we saw that effaced in a baptism of sacrifice and blood, with union maintained, the nation supreme and its concord inspiring. We have seen the world rivet its hopeful gaze on the great truths on which the founders wrought. We have seen civil, human and religious liberty verified and glorified. In the beginning the Old World scoffed at our experiment; to-day our foundations of political and social belief stand unshaken, a precious inheritance to ourselves, an inspiring example of freedom and civilisation to all mankind. Let us express renewed and strengthened devotion, in grateful reverence for the immortal beginning, and utter our confidence in the supreme fulfilment.

Progress Proves Wisdom.

The recorded progress of our Republic, materially and spiritually, in itself proves the wisdom of the inherited policy of non-involvement in Old-World affairs. Confident of our ability to work out our own destiny, and jealously guarding our right to do so, we seek no part in directing the destinies of the Old World. We do not mean to be entangled. We will accept no responsibility except as our own conscience and judgment, in each instance, may determine.

Our eyes never will be blind to a developing menace, our ears never deaf to the call of civilisation. We recognise the new order in the world, with the closer contacts which progress has wrought. We sense the call of the human heart for fellowship, fraternity and co-operation. We crave friendship and harbor no hate. But America, our America, the America builded on the foundation laid by the inspired Fathers, can be a party to no permanent military alliance. It can enter into no political commitments, nor assume any economic obligations which will subject our decisions to any other than our own authority.

I am sure our own people will not misunderstand nor will the world misconstrue. We have no thought to impede the paths to closer relationship. We wish to promote understanding. We want to do our part in making offensive warfare so hateful that governments and peoples who resort to it must prove the righteousness of their cause or stand as outlaws before the bar of civilisation.

Association for Counsel.

We are ready to associate ourselves with the nations of the world, great and small, for conference, for counsel, to seek the expressed views of world opinion, to recommend a way to approximate disarmament and relieve the crushing burdens of military and naval establishments. We elect to participate in suggesting plans for mediation, conciliation and arbitration, and would gladly join in that expressed conscience of progress which seeks to clarify and write the laws of international relationship, and establish a world court for the disposition of such justifiable questions as nations are agreed to submit thereto. In expressing aspirations, in seeking practical plans, in translating humanity's new concept of righteousness and justice and its hatred of war into recommended action, we are ready most heartily to unite, but every commitment must be made in the exercise of our national sovereignty.

Since freedom impelled, and independence inspired, and nationality exalted, a world super-government is contrary to everything we cherish and can have no sanction by our Republic. This is not selfishness, it is sanctity. It is not aloofness, it is security. It is not suspicion of others, it is patriotic adherence to the things which made us what we are.

To-day, better than ever before, we know the aspirations of human mankind and share them. We have come to a new realisation of our place in the world, and a new appraisal of our nation by the world. The unselfishness of the United States is a thing proven, our devotion to peace for ourselves and for the world is well established, our concern for preserved civilisation has had its impassioned and heroic expression. There was no American failure to resist the attempted reversion of civilisation, there will be no failure to-day or to-morrow.

Rests on Popular Will.

The success of our popular government rests wholly upon the correct interpretation of the deliberate, intelligent, dependable popular will of America. In a deliberate questioning of a suggested change of national policy, where internationality was to supersede nationality, we turned to a referendum, to the American people. There was ample discussion, and there is a public mandate in manifest understanding. America is ready to encourage, eager to initiate, anxious to participate in any seemly programme likely to lessen the probability of war and to promote that brotherhood of mankind which must be God's highest conception of human relationship.

Because we cherish ideals of justice and peace, because we appraise international comity and helpful relationship no less highly than any people of the world, we aspire to a high place in the moral leadership of civilisation, and we hold a maintained America, the proven Republic, the unshaken temple of representative democracy, to be not only an inspiration and example, but the highest agency of strengthening good-will and promoting accord on both Continents. Mankind needs a worldwide benediction of understanding. It is needed among individuals, among peoples, among governments, and it will inaugurate an era of good-feeling to mark the birth of a new order.

In such understanding men will strive confidently for the promotion of their better relationships and nations will promote the commitments so essential to peace.

Trade Ties Bind Closely.

We must understand that ties of trade bind nations in closest intimacy and none may receive except as he gives. We have not strengthened ours in accordance with our resources or our genius, notably on our own Continent, where a galaxy of Republics reflects the glory of New World democracy, but in the new order of finance and trade we mean to promote enlarged activities and seek expanded confidence. Perhaps we can make no more helpful contribution by example than to prove a republic's capacity to emerge from the wreckage of war. While the war has embittered travail, it did not leave us devastated lands nor desolate cities; it left no gaping wounds, no breast with hate, but it did involve us in a delirium of expenditure, in expanded currency and credits, in unbalanced industry, in unspeakable waste and disturbed relationships. While it uncovered our portion of hateful selfishness at home, it also revealed the heart of America as sound and fearless, and beating in confidence unfailing.

Amid it all we have riveted the gaze of all civilisation to the unselfishness and the righteousness of our representative institutions, where our freedom never has made offensive warfare, never has sought territorial aggrandisement through force, never has turned to the arbitrament of arms until reason has been exhausted. When the governments of the earth shall have established a freedom like our own, and shall have sanctioned peace as we have practised it, I believe the last word of international warfare will have been written.

PRESIDENT HARDING.

Our supreme task is the resumption of our onward normal way—reconstruction, readjustment, restoration, all these must follow. I would like to have them if it will tighten the spirit and add to the resolution with which we take up the task. Let me pray for our Nation that we shall give no people just ice to make war upon us. We hold no national prejudices. We entertain no spirit of revenge. We do not hate. We do not covet. We dream of no conquest, nor boast of armed powers.

If, despite this attitude, war is forced upon us, I earnestly hope a way may be found which will unify our individual and collective strength and consecrate all America, materially and spiritually, body and soul, to national defence. I can vision the ideal Republic where every man and woman is called under the flag for assignment to duty, for whatever service, military or civil, the individual is best fitted; where we may call to universal service every plant, agency or facility, all in sublime sacrifice for country. And not one penny of war profit shall inure to the benefit of private individual, corporation or combination, but all above the normal shall flow into the defence chest of the Nation. There is something inherently wrong, something out of accord with the ideals of representative democracy when one portion of our citizenship turns its activities to private gain amid defensive war, while another is fighting, sacrificing or dying for national preservation.

Unity of Spirit and Purpose.

Of such universal service will come a new unity of spirit and purpose, a new confidence and consecration, which would make our defence impregnable, our triumph assured. Then we should have little or no disorganisation of our economic systems, no staggering war debts, no swollen fortunes to flout the sacrifice of our soldiers, no excuse for sedition, no pitiable slackerism, no outrage of treason. Envy and jealousy would have no soil for their menacing development, and revolution would be without the passion which engenders it.

A regret for the mistakes of yesterday must not, however, blind us to the tasks of to-day. War never left such an aftermath. There has been staggering loss of life and measureless wastage of materials. Nations are still groping for the return to stable ways. Discouragement confronts us like all the war-torn nations, and these obligations must be provided for. No civilisation can survive repudiation. We can reduce abnormal expenditures, and we will. We can strike at war taxation, and we must. We must face the grim necessity, with full knowledge that the task is to be solved, and we must proceed with a full realisation that no statute by man can repeal the inexorable laws of nature.

Our most dangerous tendency is to expect too much of government, and at the same time do for it too little. We contemplate the immediate task of putting our public household in order. We need a rigid and yet sane economic policy, with fiscal justice, attended by individual prudence and thrift, which are so essential at this trying hour and reassuring for the future.

Reflection of War's Reaction.

The business world reflects the disturbance of war's reaction. Herein flows the life-blood of material existence. The economic mechanism is intricate and its parts interdependent. It has suffered the shocks and jars incident to abnormal demands, credit inflations and price upheavals. The normal balances have been impaired, the channels of distribution have been clogged, the relations of labor and management have been strained. It must seek readjustment with care and courage.

Our people must give and take. Prices must reflect the receding fever of war activities. Perhaps we never shall know the old levels of wage again. Because war invariably readjusts, compensation and the necessaries of life will show their inseparable relationship, but we must strive for normalcy to reach stability. All the penalties will not be light, nor evenly distributed.

There is no way of making them so. There is no instant step from disorder to order. We must face a condition of grim reality, charge off our losses and start afresh. It is the oldest lesson of civilisation. I would like Government to do all it can to mitigate them. In understanding, in mutuality of interest, in concern for the common good, our tasks will be solved. No altered system will work a miracle. Any wild experiment will only add to the confusion. Our best assurance lies in efficient administration of our proven system.

From Destruction to Production.

The forward course of the business cycle is unmistakable. Peoples are turning from destruction to production. Industry has sensed the changed order and our own people are turned to resume their normal, onward way. The call is for productive America to go on.

I know that Congress and the Administration will favor every wise Government policy to aid the resumption and encourage continued progress.

I speak for administrative efficiency, for lightened tax burdens, for sound commercial practices, for adequate credit facilities, for sympathetic concern for all agricultural problems, for the omission of unnecessary interference of Government with business, for an end to Government experiments in business, and for more efficient business in Government administration. With all of this must attend a mindfulness of the human side of all activities, so that social, industrial and economic justice will be squared with the purposes of a righteous people.

With the nation-wide induction of womanhood into our political life, we may count upon her intuitions, her refinements, her intelligence and her influence to exalt the social order. We count upon her exercise of the full privileges and the performance of the duties of citizenship to speed the attainment of the highest state.

Prayer for Industrial Peace.

I wish for an America no less alert in guarding against dangers from within than it is watchful against enemies from without.

Our fundamental law recognises no class, no group, no section. There must be none in legislation or administration. The supreme inspiration is the common weal. Humanity hungers for international peace, and we crave it with all mankind. My most reverent prayer for America is for industrial peace, with its rewards, widely and generally distributed, amid the inspirations of equal opportunity. No one justly may deny the equality of opportunity which made us what we are. Due concern for making all citizens fit for participation will give added strength of citizenship and magnify our achievement. If revolution insists upon overturning established order, let other peoples make the tragic experiment—there is no place for it in America.

When world war threatened civilisation, we pledged our resources and our lives to its preservation, and when revolution threatens we unfurl the flag of law and order and renew our consecration. Ours is a constitutional freedom, where the popular will is the law supreme and minorities are sacredly protected. Our revisions, reformations and evolutions reflect a deliberate judgment and an orderly progress. We mean to cure ourselves, but never destroy or permit destruction by force. I had rather submit our industrial controversies to the conference table in advance than to a settlement table after conflict and suffering. The earth is thirsting for the cup of goodwill. Understanding is its fountain source.

I would like to acclaim an era of good feeling amid dependable prosperity and all the blessings which attend.

Protection of Industries.

It has been proved again and again that we cannot, while throwing our markets open to the world, maintain American standards of living and opportunity and hold our industrial eminence in such unequal competition. There is an alluring fallacy in the theory of banished barriers of trade, but to preserve American standards requires our higher production costs to be reflected in our tariffs on imports. To-day, as never before, when peoples are seeking trade restoration and expansion, we must adjust our tariff to the new order. We seek participation in the world's exchanges because therein lies our way to widened influence and to the triumphs of peace. We know full well we cannot sell where we do not buy, and we cannot sell successfully where we do not carry.

Opportunity is calling not alone for restoration, but for a new era in production, transportation and trade. We shall answer it best by meeting the demand of a surpassing home market, by promoting self-reliance in production, and by bidding enterprise, genius and efficiency to carry our cargoes in American bottoms to the marts of the world.

We would not have an America living within and for herself alone, but we would have her self-reliant, independent and ever nobler, stronger and richer. Believing in our higher standards, reared through constitutional liberty and maintained opportunity, we invite the world to the same height. But pride in things wrought is no reflex of a completed task.

Common welfare is the goal of our national endeavor.

Wealth is not inimical to welfare. It ought to be its friendliest agency. There never can be equality of rewards or possessions so long as the human plane contains varied talents and differing degrees of industry and thrift, but ours ought to be a country free from great blotches of distressed poverty. We ought to find a way to guard against the perils and penalties of unemployment.

We want an America of homes, illumined with hope and happiness, where mothers, freed from the necessity for long hours of toil beyond their own doors, may preside, as befits, the hearthstone of American citizenship. We want the cradle of American childhood rocked under conditions so wholesome and so hopeful that no blight may touch it in its development. And we want to provide that no selfish interest, no material necessity, no lack of opportunity shall prevent the gaining of that education so essential to best citizenship.

There is no short cut to the making of these ideals into glad realities. The world has witnessed, again and again, the futility and the mischief of ill-considered remedies for social and economic disorders.

But we are mindful to-day as never before of the friction of modern industrialism, and we must learn its causes and reduce its evil consequences by sober and tested methods. Where genius has made for great possibilities, justice and happiness must be reflected in a greater common welfare.

Service, the Supreme Commitment.

Service is the supreme commitment of life. I would rejoice to acclaim the era of the Golden Rule and crown it with the autocracy of service. I pledge an Administration wherein all the agencies of government are called to serve, and ever promote an understanding of government purely as an expression of the popular will.

One cannot stand in this presence and be unmindful of the tremendous responsibility. The world upheaval has added heavily to our tasks. But with the realisation comes the surge of high resolve, and there is reassurance in belief in the God-given destiny of our Republic. If I felt that there is to be a sole responsibility in the Executive for the America of to-morrow, I should shrink from the burden.

But here are a hundred millions, with common concern and shared responsibility answerable to God and Country. The Republic summons them to their duty, and I invite co-operation.

I accept my part with single-mindedness of purpose and humility of spirit, and implore the favor and guidance of God in his heaven.

With these I am unafraid, and confidently face the future.

I have taken the solemn oath of office on that passage of Holy Writ wherein it is asked: "What doth the Lord require of thee but to do justly and to love mercy and to walk humbly with thy God?"

This I plight to God and Country.

President Harding Asks Confirmation of Cabinet

For First Time Since Washington Chief Executive Appears at Executive Session of Senate — Confirmations Are Voted Quickly

(By Special Cable to the Herald.)

WASHINGTON, Friday.—For the first time since the days of President Washington, a President attended an executive session of the Senate when Mr. Harding, as soon as his inauguration was completed, went before such a session to-day and personally presented his Cabinet nominations. The old rule provided that the President should be seated at the Vice-President's right. This was done and then President Harding arose and said he was mindful of the relations between the President and Congress, but he wished to submit a list of his Cabinet appointments. He said all the nominees had his full approval and he hoped they would likewise be acceptable to the Senate.

No Opposition Made.

Then he read the names in the prescribed order, beginning with the Secretary of State. When he had completed the reading he bowed and left the Chamber. Senator Fall resigned his seat immediately and Senator Lodge announced that it was customary to confirm Cabinet appointments by the Senate without reference to committees and moved that this be done, after Senator Fall had stood a lot of badinage about being out of a job.

Senator Fall was unanimously confirmed, and then the other names were taken up in order. Each nomination had been previously subject to a poll of the particular committee under which it came, and as each was read the committee reported favorably and confirmation was effected immediately.

The expected opposition by Senator Reed to the nomination of Mr. Herbert C. Hoover did not develop, and the entire session lasted only fifteen minutes.

The following is a brief outline of the lives and political careers of the Cabinet members:—

MR. CHARLES EVAN HUGHES, Secretary of States.—Distinguished jurist, born in 1862, educated at Brown, Colgate, Harvard and Yale. Practised law in New York and was special lecturer on law at New York Law School. Twice Governor of New York and appointed Justice of the Supreme Court. Ran for President on Republican ticket in 1916 against ex-President Wilson.

MR. ANDREW W. MELLON, Secretary of the Treasury.—Pittsburg banker, born in 1852 at Pittsburg. Educated at Pittsburg University. Associated with Henry C. Frick in development of coal, coke and iron enterprises. Director of several banks and iron and coal companies in Pittsburg. Was trustee of Carnegie Institute and founded town of Donora, Pa., where he founded great steel mills.

MR. JOHN W. WEEKS, Secretary of War.—Banker, member of House of Representatives and of Senate, candidate for Republican nomination for President in 1916. Born in New Hampshire in 1860. Graduate of United States Naval Academy and served some time in navy as midshipman. Served ten years in Massachusetts Naval Brigade and in the Volunteer Navy during the Spanish-American war.

MR. HARRY K. DAUGHERTY, Attorney-General.—Pennsylvania lawyer, born in Pennsylvania in 1868. Admitted to the bar in 1865, and served in the Spanish-American war. Appointed assistant attorney for defence of claims before the Spanish Treaty Claims Commission. Has served as arbitrator in several industrial controversies and was Deputy Attorney-General of Pennsylvania.

MR. W. H. HAYS, Postmaster-General.—Indiana lawyer, born in 1879. Has practised law in Indiana continuously and has been active in politics since the age of twenty-one. Chairman of the Republican National Committee since 1918.

MR. EDWIN DENBY, Secretary of the Navy.—Former Congressman and lawyer, born in Indiana in 1870. Spent some time in China, where father was United States Minister. Served in Customs service in Orient. Gunner's mate in Spanish-American war and sergeant in Marine Corps during European war. Is on reserve as major in Marine Corps. Active in Michigan State politics, and served in Congress from Michigan from 1905 to 1911.

MR. A. B. FALL, Secretary of the Interior.—United States Senator, born in Kentucky in 1861. Taught school and practised law, 1889-904. Has been miner, cattle rancher and farmer. Served as member of New Mexico Legislature, and was member of State Supreme Court. Served in Spanish-American war as captain. Elected Senator from New Mexico in 1912.

MR. HENRY C. WALLACE, Secretary of Agriculture.—Editor and publisher of farm papers, born in 1866. Educated in Iowa State College. Has been farmer and breeder of livestock. Interested in many farmers' and agricultural associations in Iowa, and chairman of State Executive Committee of Iowa.

MR. HERBERT C. HOOVER, Secretary of Commerce.—California mining engineer, born in 1874. Degrees from several American and European universities. Was active in mine development in Western States and in China. Commissioner for Relief in Belgium from 1915-1918. "Food Dictator" for United States during war. Commander of Legion of Honor, and has score of other honors for services in Europe during war. Author of several treatises on mining.

MR. JAMES COX DAVIS, Secretary of Labor.—Iowa lawyer, born in 1857. Taught school and practised law in Iowa most of life. Solicitor for Chicago and Northwestern Railroad Company. Has been delegate to National Convention and chairman of Iowa State Republican Convention.

HIGHLIGHTS OF HARDING ADDRESS

The recorded progress of Our Republic proves the wisdom of keeping out of Old World Affairs.

America can enter no political commitments which will limit her own authority.

We are ready to associate ourselves with the nations of the world for conference, for counsel to recommend a way for disarmament.

Our Supreme task is the resumption of our onward normal way.

I speak for administrative efficiency, lightened tax burdens, sound commercial practises, concern for agricultural problems.

American standards require our higher production costs to be reflected in our tariffs on imports.

NAVY SUPPLY BILL KILLED IN SENATE

Prohibition Puts Damper on Rollicking Closing Hours of Former Congresses.

(By Special Cable to the Herald.)

WASHINGTON, Friday.—Twelve supply Bills were passed during the closing hours of Congress, cleaning up the slate for the new Administration except the Naval Appropriation Bill, which died through filibustering. The rollicking horseplay of pre-prohibition days was entirely absent and the air was unusually serious throughout the capital.

Veto Kills Some.

President Wilson announced the death of the Immigration Restriction and the Army Bills through a pocket veto, but he signed the other supply Bills. The Emergency Tariff Bill which was vetoed by the President, failed to obtain the necessary votes when it was reintroduced in the House, and so is another piece of dead legislation.

PRESIDENT WILSON IS VERY FEEBLE

(By Special Cable to the Herald.)

WASHINGTON, Friday.—President Wilson performed his last official duties at the Capitol this morning and his appearance was a shock to many who had not seen him for many months. His face is drawn and pale and his hair is completely white. He is thin almost to the point of emaciation, and his enfeebled condition brought tears to the eyes of many watchers.

It took him ten minutes to walk from the entrance of the Capitol to the President's room. He walked with the support of Secretary Tumulty, and Dr. Grayson was in constant attendance.

SEES HARDING AS FRIEND OF FRANCE

LONDON, Friday.—M. Aristide Briand, the French Premeir, paid a warm tribute to ex-President Wilson to-day and said he was sure that President Harding would be just as sure a friend of France.

"France will be forever thankful to the United States," declared M. Briand, "for having so powerfully contributed to the victory of Right and Justice throughout the world. And the name of the eminent statesman who took the responsibility for the intervention of the United States is inseparable from the victory and will remain graven in the hearts of Frenchmen.

"We are familiar with the generous idealism which animates American politics and which has always inspired those who have been called to the highest post in the gift of the American people. I know that President Harding will be for France, the Sister Republic of the United States, a

LONDON CONSIDERS BREAK WITH BERLIN IS STILL UNLIKELY

Behind the Scenes Pressure Is Brought to Bear on Germans to Accept Paris Figure.

(By Special Leased Wire.)

LONDON, Friday.—The Conference is marking time while waiting for the German answer, but behind the scenes, as usual, private dickerings are going on, which point more clearly than yesterday to the improbability of a rupture. The French, it is believed, would not be extremely disappointed to see the negotiations broken off, believing that the Germans' mood will not be changed and that German evasions will continue on many points of the Treaty, until they are given a salutary lesson. They are not maintaining even informal contact with the Germans. But the British are working tooth and nail to avoid a break and are bringing all possible pressure privately to bear on the Germans to come back with what would be a basis for new negotiations, insisting that they must, however, accept the Paris figures.

Hopeful Indications.

These moves gave every indication to-day of being successful, unless the situation in Berlin interferes. It is regarded as unlikely that the Germans will answer before the time limit. Consequently, M. Briand made plans to-day to pass the week-end at Hythe as the guest of Sir Philip Sassoon. This caused speculation here, as the tentative plans had been for M. Briand to spend the week-end at Chequers. That Mr. Lloyd George may possibly be in a better position to continue to put pressure upon the Germans without his French guest was suggested when these plans were made known to-day.

With the situation in Berlin still confused, all surveys of the situation to-day included as a computing factor President Harding's speech. Regarding this, the first reaction is one of disappointment. Uncertain just what effect their ultimatum may have on the future of Europe and anxious above all things to know what co-operation, if any, they are to have from America, Allied diplomats read the speech eagerly to-day for a possible cue, which they confessed they were unable to find.

"Disappointingly Vague."

The disappointment is keener in French circles than in British. "Disappointingly vague" was the comment of the French diplomatists, but the British frankly said they understood President Harding's position and expected little more at this time. French disappointment is due to fear of the Germans taking advantage of its vagueness to continue to place on it an unwarranted construction for their own purposes.

What the Allies were hoping for was an expression from President Harding on America's relations towards Germany, in order to adjust their own, and some intimation as to whether in withdrawing from active participation, the United States also withdrew moral support of their present efforts to get reparation from Germany. There is also a complaint that the vague reference to the repudiation of debts has not made clear the American attitude on inter-Allied indebtedness, which is a factor in the reparation problem.

It was learned to-night that, failing to find any guidance in the speech, the Allies will open through their Ambassadors informal conversations with Washington immediately on these points, the two most important questions being: Do President Harding and Secretary of State Charles E. Hughes view with any sympathy the position the Allies have taken here and do they intend to order American troops from the Rhine?

SPEAKER SUSPENDS REICHSTAG SITTING

SUNDAY, OCTOBER 8, 1922.

DAUGHERTY RULING FORBIDS LIQUOR IN AMERICAN SHIPS

Intoxicants Banned Even on High Seas, with Restrictions on Foreign Vessels.

SUPREME COURT DECISIONS CITED TO SUPPORT OPINION

Shipping Men See Death-blow to American Merchant Marine If Sustained.

(By Special Cable to the Herald.)

NEW YORK, Saturday.—Liquor must not be carried in any American vessel, merchant or private, in any part of the world, and no foreign vessels may bring liquor either as cargo or in sealed bars within the three-mile limit of the United States. This is the ruling announced to-day by Attorney-General Daughtery and approved by President Harding, the latter sending notices to the Treasury Department and the United States Shipping Board demanding its enforcement, though it is not applicable to foreign ships now en route here or so far loaded as to give them insufficient time to make the required change.

MILLION IN LIQUOR FOUND BEHIND WALL

(By Special Cable to the Herald.)

NEW YORK, Saturday.—After tearing down a false wall and breaking into the cellars of the Standard Carpet Company, Government agents found whiskey, champagne and liquors worth nearly $1,000,000, including some obtained from Government warehouses with withdrawal permits alleged to have been faked.

Following the seizure the dry sleuths declared that they had carried their work through despite the fact that a bribe of $150,000 had been offered them.

MONDAY, OCTOBER 9, 1922.

PRESS FLAYS LIQUOR RULE, BUT EUROPE NOT WORRIED

In Stinging Editorial, "Herald" Calls Daugherty Ruling Affront to World.

CIVILISED WORLD'S RESPECT IMPERILLED BY NEW DECISION

Reprisals Expected and Passengers Already Cancelling Bookings on American Liners.

(By Special Cable to the Herald.)

NEW YORK, Sunday.—Under the caption, "Flouting International Usage," The NEW YORK HERALD in an editorial to-day strongly attacks Attorney-General Daugherty's ruling on prohibition and declares that banning liquor in American ships is logical, but banning it in foreign ships is "more than logical, it is dangerous. This country," the editorial continues, "in announcing to all other countries that no ship, whatever flag it flies, will be permitted within the three-mile limit if it carries intoxicating beverages, is doing something which would be ridiculous if it were not so rash.

"When we make vessels dry, all we lose is money. But when we attempt to overthrow the maritime usage of the civilised world, we lose more than money—we lose the respect and friendship of the nations we harass. This country is sensitive to its rights on the sea, and once went to war because another nation seized and searched its vessels. It has been jealous of its territorial rights and has insisted on them.

"If other nations could afford to laugh, there would be something to laugh at The spectacle of the United States, with its failure to enforce the Eighteenth Amendment, its miserable scandal of bootlegging bribery, attempting to purify the cargoes of ships of other nations is ludicrous indeed...."

French Line Head Amazed, but Says Ships Will Not Abandon New York.

LIQUOR WILL BE RETAINED, BUT WITHOUT BREAKING LAW

Americans in Paris Say No Court Will Sustain Attorney-General's Ruling.

If Attorney-General Daugherty's drastic interpretation of the National Prohibition Act, in which he ruled against liquor in American ships anywhere and in foreign ships within the three-mile limit, is to have the full force of law, the French Line will continue to operate between Havre and New York and will conform with American demands. However, until the question is closely studied and reports are received from the company's American agents, the Compagnie Générale Translantique will continue its policy of supplying its ships with the usual quantity of liquors, to be sealed up when the three-mile limit is reached.

Surprise in Paris.

The news of the surprising ruling was eagerly read in Paris hotels and bars yesterday, Americans generally refusing to treat the decision seriously and maintaining that the Supreme Court would certainly upset the Attorney-General's edict.

New York's Loss.

"In the event of diversion of liners, however, it would be a serious loss for the port of New York, not only from the labor standpoint but for the fact that New York's statistics, which are a vital factor in maintaining the city's prestige, would show a material falling off."

Though the general tone of comment on the decision is serious, bar-room humor in Paris has found a new and most promising subject for the wits, the sallies being mostly of an ironical nature. One facetious seafarer caustically suggested that the American law should go a step further and insist that no passenger be allowed to land unless he can present a certificate proving that he had attended regularly all chapel services on board ship during the crossing. Most Americans, however, discount the personal effects of the ruling, explaining that the law cannot prevent the West-bound traveller from having his cabin well stocked with his favorite drinks and mathematically calculated to yield one last toast to the Statue of Liberty just before crossing the three-mile limit.

OCTOBER 12, 1922.

PROHIBITION SPOILS CENTENARIAN'S JOY

(By Special Cable to the Herald.)

NEW YORK, Wednesday.—Mrs. Frances Levapesto, celebrating her 101st birthday at her home in Staten Island to-day, says that the lack of wine is the greatest hardship of old age. She was born in Brest, of French parents, and came to the United States in 1862, living happily, she avows, until the Volstead Act deprived her of her daily wine, "because Americans do not know how to drink."

OCTOBER 20, 1922.

VOLSTEAD ACT TO STAY

Harding Says Eighteenth Amendment Is Permanent.

(By Special Cable to the Herald.)

WASHINGTON, Thursday.—In a message to the Allied Christian Societies, in convention here, President Harding declared that he believes the country will always keep the Eighteenth Amendment.

The President gave a hint of his opinion in the current liquor tangle when he said the law follows the flag in every respect.

OCTOBER 14, 1922.

DIRGES PLAYED AS "DRY" SHIP DOCKS

(By Special Cable to the Herald.)

NEW YORK, Friday.—To the United American liner Resolute fell the somewhat doubtful honor of being the first "dry" ship to arrive in this port following the application of Attorney-General Daugherty's ruling. As this liner, in from Cherbourg and Hamburg, yesterday came up the river to her berth the ship's band played "Sahara," "How Dry I Am" and funeral dirges and the passengers stood with bared and bowed heads. The bar was closed in mid-ocean after the receipt of orders from Washington by wireless on Tuesday night. Passengers seeking an eye-opener on Wednesday morning were given a disagreeable surprise when a notice on the door of the bar gave out the information that the ship was henceforth "dry."

SATURDAY, JANUARY 2, 1926.

Valiant 'Dry' Squad Beaten As Broadway Drinks to 1926

(By Special Cable to The Herald.)

NEW YORK, Friday. — Riding on the crest of an enormous wave of alcohol which completely inundated Broadway and the adjacent thoroughfares of the White Light district, New Yorkers indulged last night in the wildest, noisiest and most extravagant New Year's Eve celebration since the war, completely indifferent to the fact that somewhere along the turbulent sea of liquor a frail Prohibition craft was being buffeted about as its brave little band of enforcement agents strove valiantly, but hopelessly, to make New York dry. They had set out from Prohibition headquarters at 10 o'clock with final instructions to come back with their shields or on them, and at 2 this morning they gave up the ship, returning the shields by messenger boy, in silent token of defeat.

No Tears Shed.

And among the tens of thousands who pressed up and down Broadway between Thirty-fourth street and Columbus Circle, tooting horns, throwing paper streamers, pushing and treading on each other's feet, never a tear was shed for the sad fate of this Lost Battalion.

Market Gets Credit.

Never was so much money spent in a New Year's Eve celebration, Broadway's wiseacres attributing the orgy of spending to the extended bull market which has given everybody connected with Wall Street ample funds for amusement.

Prohibition, the cause of great excitement during the celebration of four years ago, has apparently come to be regarded as a joke, and Broadway last night saw in it nothing about which to get excited. Only seventeen persons were arraigned in Night Court, and of these only five for intoxication and one for firing a revolver from an automobile.

SUNDAY, FEBRUARY 18, 1923.

Mummy of Pharaoh Found In Splendid Gold Shrine

Two Caskets in Rich, Immense Catafalque, in Second of Which, When Opened, Will Probably Be Found Remains of the King.

LUXOR Upper Egypt, Saturday.—Experts were at work early to-day amid the new marvels which the unsealing of the funeral chamber of the Pharaoh Tutank-Hamen yesterday brought to light. The tomb was opened at eight o'clock, and Mr. Howard Carter, with Professor Alan Gardiner, Professor Breasted and Mr. Lythgoe, of the New York Metropolitan Art Museum, and Mr. Winlock, head of the American excavation mission, with Mrs. Lythgoe and Mrs. Winlock, went in.

Two trays containing seals were brought out this morning. It is intended to enlarge the gap into the tomb, the narrowness of which has baffled the efforts of stouter members of the party, particularly one or two Egyptian notables, to wriggle through, in order to have everything in order for the visit of the Queen of the Belgians and Lord Allenby.

Magnificent Shrine.

The greatest interest has been created by the discovery of the sarcophagus of Tutank-Hamen in an immense imposing canopy or shrine of wood covered with gold instead of pink granite as is generally expected. A similar shrine was erected by the heretic Akhnaton for Queen Tiy, with a door in front, as in this case. Queen Tiy's canopy has been hitherto the only one known, but this form of sarcophagus was apparently favored by rulers of this era, the 18th Dynasty.

The immense catafalque-like mass bulking hugely in the narrow chamber produced an ineffaceable impression on the fortunate few who, grouped behind Mr. Carter, watched the hole he was making wider in the sealed door. At first, as the electric beam fell on the high shrine, watchers thought it was painted blue or green, so brilliantly did the blue glazed lozange pattern running round it shine in the light.

Second Chamber Filled.

It was then seen, as the gap increased, that the great shrine was a mass of rich gilding, while suddenly on the right a stray beam from the torch carried by Mr. Carter piercing the gloom enabled the explorers to realise the great fact that beyond this funeral chamber, practically wholly filled by this noble shrine, another chamber lies crowded with an treasures of incalculable interest to Egyptologists.

The shrine contains two caskets, the second with frontal doors like the first, within which is a richly painted mummy-case. Here, it is confidently reckoned, will be found lying the anointed clay of Tutank-Hamen, wrapped from head to foot in sheets of thin gold, with crossed hands, one shut and the other open, symbol of Upper and Lower Egypt, over which he held sway.

Open Mummy-Case Later.

As every stage of the proceedings has had to be photographed and recorded, the opening of the shrine will be a long task and therefore there is little chance of the mummy-case being opened for some time yet.

FEBRUARY 19, 1923.

PHARAOH'S TOMB REVEALS SPLENDOR

Royalty and Notabilities at Official Opening Dazzled by Magnificence of Tutankh-Hamen's Shrine.

QUEEN OF BELGIANS ADMIRES MANY WONDERFUL TREASURES

Opening of Gilded Shrine Brings to Light Number of King's Beautiful Jewels.

LUXOR (Upper Egypt), Sunday. — Pharaoh Tutank-Hamen, after the lapse of more than three thousand years, to-day once again held Court and Royalties and notabilities galore paid homage to the vestiges of his earthly splendor. The Queen of the Belgians and Prince Leopold of Belgium, Lord Allenby and Lady Allenby, diplomatic representatives of the United States, France and other countries, as well as members of the Egyptian Government and noted Egyptologists, were among the spectators present at the official opening of the tomb to-day, when further wonderful treasures came to light, although the actual investigation of the mummy case is deferred to a later date.

Dazzled by Magnificence.

All who were privileged to view the scene expressed themselves dazzled with the magnificence of the mortuary chamber. The chamber was lit to-day by electricity, which showed up clearly the brilliance of the huge sarcophagus with its blue glaze ornamentation and gold casing. It is not quite in the middle of the chamber so that on one side there is a space of only four inches and on the other side ten inches. On the ground are model boats and paddles to enable the King's soul to be ferried betwixt Death and Life.

The first visitor was the Dowager Sultana of Egypt. Then Lord and Lady Allenby arrived and waited at the entrance to the Royal tomb to receive the Queen of the Belgians and Prince Leopold. These distinguished visitors immediately entered the tomb, accompanied by Lord Carnarvon, Lady Evelyn Herbert, Mr. Howard Carter and M. Cappart, director of the Brussels Museum.

Most of these visitors entered the mortuary chamber, but the very narrow space between the wall and the side of the sarcophagus made it necessary for them to edge along sideways and the difficulty of this progress was amply testified when Lord Allenby's stalwart and shirt-sleeved figure emerged and he began shaking off the dust.

Three trayloads of jagged fragments of masonry bearing the royal seals have been carried out of the tomb and deposited along with two baskets full of remnants in the workshops near by.

Inside the tomb a small platform with barriers was erected for the convenience of visitors at the official opening to-day. Four cases, or shrines, one inside the other, have been discovered within the inner chamber. There is a door leading into the outer-casing of the gilded shrine which is ornamented with an ancient Egyptian lock, from which a key is suspended by a cord and sealed with Tutank-Hamen's seal.

Beautiful Jewels.

This door, when opened, brought to light a number of the King's jewels of the most beautiful description, including turquoises and green scarabs. The most remarkable scarab bore the King's name. There were also found triple-calixed alabaster cups, the central calix bearing the King's name. The finds further include many amulets, besides a number of magnificent statues, one being that of the vulture-headed god Horus.

The second case of the shrine, which also bears the King's name, is covered with a piece of finely-worked material encrusted with gold half-moons. Experts express the opinion that when the third case is opened it will probably be found to contain a richer collection of jewels than any yet discovered.

The mummy of the King will be in the fourth case. The outermost case has a concave lid overlaid with gold encrusted with enamel and inlaid with semi-precious stones. Above the head of the mummy at one end of the case there is a figure of Isis with outstretched wings. At the other end is a figure of the goddess Nephtys.

"Guardians of the Dead."

On either side of the case are representations of the four "Guardians of the Dead," and in between them are some religious inscriptions. It is anticipated that the work of removing the treasures will occupy the efforts of the explorers until next winter.

FEBRUARY 20, 1923.

EGYPTIAN MOTIF THRILLS GOTHAM

(By Special Cable to the Herald.)

NEW YORK, Monday. — The Egyptian motif is to be in everything during the coming months. Costume designers, jewellers and even hairdressers are crowding the Egyptian sections of the museums to get points from the ancients on their own art. This is all because of the discoveries from the Valley of the Tombs of the Kings, of which nearly everyone is talking, not alone in the clubs and society, but in the street cars and the cafeterias.

WEDNESDAY, JULY 22, 1925.

Scopes Fined $100 After Farmers Find Him Guilty

Jury Takes Only Seven Minutes to Return Expected Verdict—Bryan-Darrow Repartee Principal Show of Last Day of Famous Trial.

(By Special Cable to the Herald.)

DAYTON, Tenn., Tuesday.—Professor John Thomas Scopes, aged twenty-four, to-day was found guilty of teaching Darwinism in the local high school, in violation of a Tennessee statute, by a farmer jury that took seven minutes to put an end to the case that grew from drug-store gossip to world discussion. The jury, figuring for the third time in the historic proceedings as a supernumerary, filed listlessly from the courtroom after Judge Raulston, in matter-of-fact tones, had charged it to find Professor Scopes guilty if it had been proven that he taught man had evolved from a lower order of animal, with the admonition that religious truths did not enter into the case. Most of the seven minutes were consumed by the twelve men in filing in and out of the jury-room.

Gets $100 Fine.

The internationally famous case had a most commonplace dénouement. When the jury foreman, with rustic dignity, answered "guilty," Judge Raulston dryly imposed a $100 fine, the minimum allowed under the statute. Scopes, his distinguished legal battery, the prosecution, newspaper men and Dayton had anticipated the verdict.

Past Trial Statements.

But evolution was not downed by such judicial routine. Mr. William Jennings Bryan, volunteer Fundamentalist prosecutor, and Mr. Clarence Darrow addressed eager crowds after they had filed out of the courthouse which for some reason did not crack to-day because, as somebody suggested, of the unsensational nature of the verdict.

Judge Raulston praised the defence as great men with a passion for their idea of truth.

Bryan on Stand.

The feature of the last day was the examination of Mr. Bryan by Mr. Darrow. Answering a question regarding his beliefs Mr. Bryan said he considered everything in the Bible was true, that the flood occurred about the year 2,500 B.C., and wiped out all living things except those in the Ark.

Darrow: "Don't you know that there are any number of civilisations that have been traced back 5,000 years before that date?"

Bryan: "I am not willing to give up my belief in the Bible in deference to the views of others who make that estimate."

Joshua and the Sun.

Bryan further said that he believed that Joshua made the sun stand still.

Darrow: "Don't you know that for Joshua to have made the sun stand still it would have been necessary to have lengthened the day?"

Bryan: "I don't know about that, but I do know that with my puny hand I can defy the great law of gravitation and prevent this glass of water from falling to the ground. I certainly would not hesitate to believe that the Almighty God could stop the sun and the earth in their courses."

The witness said he did not know the population of Egypt 3,500 years ago and was not interested in the matter. He was never sufficiently interested to inquire into the old civilisations and never had studied Chinese civilisation and never read much about religion outside the Bible.

He said that he believed that until Babel the world had but a single language.

Bryan was loudly cheered during and after his testimony. Taking advantage of a break in the cheering Darrow sarcastically remarked once: "They are cheering you who insult every man of science, who does not agree with your fool religion."

"I am simply trying to protect the World of God against the greatest agnostic in the world," replied Mr. Bryan.

Lady Astor's Triumphant Accession to Parliament Stirs Women to Begin Great Electoral Campaign

MRS. LLOYD GEORGE. LADY ASTOR. THE COUNTESS OF LIMERICK

Movement Aims at Finding Funds for at Least One Hundred Feminine Candidates.

(SPECIAL CORRESPONDENCE.)

LONDON, Saturday.—A widespread and earnest campaign to extend the sphere of women in English politics has been begun during the Parliamentary recess as the result of Lady Astor's triumphant accession to the hitherto masculine House of Commons. This movement has two principal objects: the first, to get as many women as possible to stand in the next general election for seats in Parliament; the other, to fill as many important Government positions as possible with prominent and efficient members of the same sex.

The backers of this movement do not hide their hope that at least a hundred women will step forth as candidates in the next Parliamentary election, an event which is still in the dim future, due to the reticence of the existing administration and the uncertainty as to the life of the Lloyd George-Bonar Law coalition. The leaders in this new phase of the feminist movement confidently express the belief that the next few years will see women in such important positions as that of Home Secretary, as well as in the under-secretaryships of the more important Ministries.

Women's Ambitions Spurred.

The entry of Lady Astor into the Commons has not only had the natural effect of arousing political ambition among women, but it has, according to the sponsors of the new movement, been a tremendous encouragement in the collection of funds with which to wage the women's fight for public advancement.

A few days ago the enterprise of this new political element was attested in a letter written to the "Times," in which it was proposed that the officials of the Government and the people should ask themselves whether the time had not arrived for placing women in all the Ministries as assistant and under secretaries. Appended to the letter were the names of a half-dozen leaders in the new movement. This request was represented to be the very minimum of what the Government should grant, and it was declared that, as a matter of fact, the more important of the women's organisations in London thought the demand too modest.

Premier's Wife on Platform.

One of the women taking a leading part in this campaign is the wife of the Prime Minister, Mrs. David Lloyd George, who on earlier occasions has plainly shown her views on women in public life. She was one of the campaigners for Lady Astor, and she has been seen and heard on other political platforms.

Mrs. Lloyd George is to speak on February 12 at a big meeting of women in London on the topic of the need for more of their sex in Parliament. This meeting is being arranged by the National Council of Women and the National Union of Societies for Equal Citizenship and will mark the first big move in the campaign for a full ticket of women in the next general election.

There have been all manner of tentative announcements concerning prominent women who might make the Parliamentary race but in nearly every instance the proposal of offer has been declined. The Duchess of Marlborough was talked of, but she denied any such aspirations. Lady Lee of Fareham was another, but she declined. It was believed on all sides that Lady Beaverbrook, whose husband, the owner of the "Daily Express," served in the Lower House as Sir Max Aitken, would make the race, but she withdrew. The Countess of Limerick has been suggested, and thus far she has issued no denial. The same is true as to the Countess of Warwick. However as the sponsors of the feminine Parliamentary campaign say, there is ample time and still more ample material.

Regarding some of the Government offices which the women think should be allotted to them, Miss Florence Underwood, of the Women's Freedom League, has spoken very plainly.

"First of all," she said in an interview, "I would like to see a woman Home Secretary. Why? Because, among other reasons, we should have intelligent prison reform. Then, why should we not have a woman Minister of Health? There are plenty of skilled doctors and organisers among women."

THE NEW YORK HERALD, PARIS, FRIDAY, OCTOBER 4, 1929 — 9

It is this very post of Health Minister that is constantly being suggested as a place for Lady Astor.

"The Minister of Education," Miss Underwood said, "is a position for which a woman would be eminently fitted. A good 67 per cent. of the teachers in this country are women. The care of children is essentially a competent woman's business. A woman Minister of Education would tend to make education in England less commercial. The general idea underlying education at present is to make the country more commercially progressive. The influence of a woman at the head of the Ministry of Education would be to show that there is something higher than commerce—real education.

"I believe women as a rule take a wider view of education than most men. Then, too, women most certainly should have been consulted on the housing problem. I believe that if women had been given hold there would be more houses in England today.

"Although we have got the vote," she concluded, "we live in a man-controlled state. It is true that women do hold positions in Government departments, but they are subordinate positions. The time will come when women will have equal chances with men, and this will come when we have more women in Parliament. We want a hundred serious women candidates, and this may happen at the next general election. The desire to see women holding high positions in the State is not caused by the wish for feminine supremacy. It is simply the outcome of the belief that the modern woman could fill certain positions better than men do now. Anyhow, when the time comes, and women get those responsible posts, they will not hold them unless they are fitted to do so."

It would seem as if the American peeress, as first member of the British House of Commons, had really started something.

SUNDAY, OCTOBER 29, 1922.

Fascisti Defy Government And Begin March on Rome

Committee of Action Formed at Milan, which Has Become the Facist Headquarters—General Mobilisation Ordered and Martial Law Decreed.

The Fascisti and the constitutional forces are now face to face in a moral and possibly physical trial of strength, according to the rare despatches percolating through from Italy. Milan has become the Fascist headquarters and Rome continues to be the centre of resistance, which the Facta Government, after tendering its resignation, has been hurriedly organising in the hope of averting a coup d'Etat. One of the measures adopted by the Cabinet yesterday was the proclamation of martial law throughout Italy; but it is understood the King refused to sign the decree, so that the measure was not enforced.

Proclamation Issued.

The Ministers, who are sitting in permanent session at the Ministry of the Interior, closely guarded, yesterday issued the following proclamation to the nation: "Seditious manifestations are being held in various provinces of Italy, co-ordinated and directed against the normal functioning of the powers of the State, and of a character to throw the country into the gravest disorder. So long as it was possible the Government tried all means of reconciliation in the hope of restoring concord and of assuring a peaceful solution of the crisis.

"Faced by attempts at insurrection the Government which has just resigned feels it its duty to preserve public order by all means and at whatever cost, and this duty it will accomplish wholly for the security of citizens and of free constitutional institutions. In the meantime let all citizens keep calm and have confidence in the measures of safety which have been adopted." The document is signed by all the Ministers of the Facta Cabinet.

Demonstrations in Rome.

The Cabinet was in constant touch all day yesterday with the Prefects of the various provinces, especially those of the North, issuing orders to garrisons and the regional police forces of Carabinieri and Royal Guards with a view to preventing disturbances. No serious conflicts were reported anywhere except at Cremona, where a clash occurred with the Fascist squadrons. In Rome all was quiet yesterday and the city bore its normal aspect, but for the stoppage of the street cars and the continuous patriotic demonstrations of the Fascisti and the Nationalists before the Royal Palace and in the streets.

FASCISTI LEADER

SIGNOR MUSSOLINI

MUSSOLINI SHAPES ITALY'S DESTINIES

Signor Benito Mussolini, chief of the Fascisti, who in a few days has virtually made himself dictator of Italy, is still on the right side of forty, having been born in 1883, the son of an unlettered blacksmith in a village of Romagna. Becoming a teacher in a Milan college, he developed into an ardent Socialist. Always of a combative spirit and ready to fight duels on any occasion, he manifested his patriotism in January, 1915, by demanding Italy's entry into the war. He fought as a volunteer and was seriously wounded. Joining the Fascisti since the war, he has proved an energetic leader, organising "Black Shirt" forces to repress agitation by Socialist extremists and Communists and issuing ultimatums to put down strikes. Quite recently, he told an interviewer that Italy is not a mere museum for tourists and that the Fascisti have had enough of the glory of antiquity, of the Forum and the Colosseum, and are looking to a greater future for Italy.

Europe Watching Fascist Successes As Danger to Peace of Continent

French Anxious Lest Mussolini's Aim of Greater Italy May Inspire Hot-head Reactionaries.

The Chancelleries of all Europe are anxiously watching developments in Italy and wondering how far the unforeseen success of Signor Mussolini, leader of the Fascisti, may upset political calculations or even fan into dangerous flame smouldering Nationalist passions from the North Sea to the Mediterranean. Italy's spontaneous response to Mussolini's picturesque appeal for a Greater Italy is generally recognised as a grandiose exaltation, growing out of Italy's being hailed as a great victor in the war on an equal footing with mightier nations.

However, between the French policy of keeping hands off what is considered Italy's interior policies and letting the new extra-Parliamentary leader endanger European peace by setting a bad example to hot-headed Nationalists in other countries, there is a wide difference, and none of the other countries yet know how to approach the situation. Two fears are frankly expressed in Paris: First, of the effect Mussolini's success will have on Italy's general foreign policy; and second, of the repercussion a Fascist victory may have elsewhere by tempting reactionaries to employ Italian methods even in France.

MONDAY, OCTOBER 30, 1922.

FASCIST CHIEF DICTATOR OF ITALY; CALLED BY KING TO FORM CABINET

"Black Shirt" Army, in Swift Mobilisation, Assumes Control of Country, Entering Rome Unopposed by Regular Troops and Cheering Monarch at the Quirinal.

Signor Mussolini and his "Black Shirts" are now masters of Rome and most of Italy. The King, acknowledging his mastery of the situation, yesterday afternoon asked Mussolini to form a Cabinet. It is expected that his Cabinet will be composed chiefly of Fascisti, although there are only forty Fascist Deputies in the Italian Chamber. Italy will thus have an unrepresentative Government, at least until the new elections are held and the people express their verdict on this remarkable movement, which has seized the reins of Government in less than three days and for the moment given its chief the power of a Garibaldi.

First the King and then much of the Army went over to him. Having failed to secure Mussolini's support for a Cabinet to be formed by any of the constitutional leaders, such as Facta, Giolitti and Salandra, while the mobilised Fascist Army was marching on Rome, the King yesterday formally asked the "Black Shirt" leader to take over the Government. Mussolini had refused to sanction any Cabinet not definitely Fascist, though Salandra had promised four places to his followers. This proved the last attempt to secure a Government which, though including Fascisti, would still be constitutional in that it would represent the Italian Chamber.

The coup d'Etat seems to have been accomplished with little bloodshed so far, despite the resistance ordered by the Facta Government on Saturday morning, this resistance being quickly brought to an end by the King himself when, at two o'clock in the afternoon, he cancelled the decree proclaiming martial law. At that time a great part of Italy had already been placed under martial law, but reports were reaching Rome that the northern towns were rapidly capitulating to the forces of the Fascisti, who, outnumbering the garrisons which were really in sympathy with the movement, quickly gained possession.

SUNDAY. FEBRUARY 25, 1923.

Fountain of Youth Is Discovered, But Secret Is Jealously Guarded

M. Knap, Paris Chemist, Will Give Discovery to World When It Deserves It.

The Fountain of Youth has shifted from a mythical spring in Florida to an office at 22 rue Taitbout, Paris. But there, hidden behind dusty retorts and moulding skeletons, M. Georgia Knap, the discoverer, refuses to reveal his secret or to permit the world to drink of the waters of perpetual youth.

M. Knap, disciple and boyhood friend of M. Coué, doctor, inventor and master of eighty professions, claims to have mastered the secret of life. M. Knap proves his statements. He shows you his hands—one withered and wrinkled and the other young and active. "Through all my experiments," he says, "I have faithfully let my left hand get just as aged as it wished, while I have been watching over the rejuvenation of the remainder of my body."

As a reporter of THE NEW YORK HERALD entered M. Knap's office M. Coué was leaving. M. Coué refused to be interviewed, but suggested that M. Knap had a good story. As a matter of fact, M. Knap has a good story—M. Knap's story is almost too good to be true.

Secret Guarded.

"I won't tell you what it is, my secret," said M. Knap. "But you can see the results for yourself. I have discovered a way of keeping myself young. I am sixty years old and I am younger than you at thirty. My secret is a mixture of auto-suggestion, modes of living, diet and exercise, all made potent by the Elixir of Life which I have discovered. When the world gets ready for the discovery I shall give it out free. It doesn't make any difference whether it takes twenty years or fifty, for I will still be alive."

As far as appearances go, M. Knap is actually about thirty-five or forty, though his papers show that he is sixty. He walks up and down his research room while he talks, fingers skeletons that hang on the walls, plays with the X-ray outfit, and volubly tells his interviewer that the world is missing something good in not being ready for his great discovery.

"The best way to judge the real age of a human," said M. Knap, "is to X-ray his stomach and see how far it is distended. My stomach is like it was when I was twenty years old. I could fix anybody's stomach in four days if I wanted to do it. But the world is not yet ready for such a thing, and I don't want to start until I can carry the process through. I have had many patients in here to see me, and to each one I give a little part of my treatment, and each one gets younger. If I really started to work in earnest, we would all live—oh, a long time."

Coué Interested.

M. Coué and M. Knap are on the best of terms as old friends, and, according to M. Knap, M. Coué thinks the Fountain of Youth idea is quite a scheme.

"Auto-suggestion has not yet been touched," said M. Knap yesterday. "I know men who have died through auto-suggestion. And I also know that by auto-suggestion alone I could make lots of men live who otherwise are going to die shortly. But my secret is the real Fountain of Youth, and I have to guard it carefully until I decide that everyone is good enough to live."

FRIDAY, FEBRUARY 19, 1926.

Luxury of Labor Saving Devices Attract Many to American "Home"

THE DINING-ROOM OF THE AMERICAN MODEL HOME.

Probably no exhibit held in Paris in recent years has aroused such genuine interest among French visitors as the American Home, now being shown at the Grand Palais as a feature of the Exposition of Household Arts. Thousands pass through its cozy, modern-fitted rooms every day, and, as the Exposition is to close Sunday evening, it is expected that the next three days will provide a record-breaking attendance.

Elderly matrons, school-girls, young brides, and even French housemaids join in the daily throng that marvels at the simplicity of the American Home, and the ease it offers to the housewife in her daily tasks. While much skepticism is expressed concerning the likelihood of France ever adopting the 1775 style of architecture which prevails in the American Home, few are ever heard to criticize the furniture, household appliances, and the general arrangement of the rooms.

The handiness of the parlor on the main floor, with its inviting sofas, offering a new lesson in the use of cushions, and soft lighting, immediately captures the visitors, while the soft lighting, and tactful use of small tables in contrast to the wide fireplace, is invariably commended. Then, across the main hall way, with its winding stairway, is found the dining-room, small, but adequate for a family of six. Here again the colonial style of furniture has been observed, with such pleasing success that orders have already been placed for several articles.

Bedrooms Attractive.

It is the bedrooms that particularly impress the majority of visitors, if for no other reason than their contrast with all French traditions. Four-poster beds, chaises-longues, comfortable arm-chairs, and handy tables for favorite bed-time books. "How neat and clean it all is," whispered one woman visitor. "I'm going to put chintz curtains in our room to-morrow." But it is with frank awe that the majority of visitors peer into the bathrooms, one for each room, with marble fixtures, bathtubs, and even a shower-bath encased in a glass cage.

And a private bathroom for the maid, not differing the slightest from the one her mistress uses a floor below! But the servant-girls visiting the room looked long and wistfully at the comfort that contrasts so strikingly with their little cubby-holes under some mansard roof, and wondered how long it would take to save enough to pay their fare to the land of such promise.

Ice for Cocktails.

The women visitors usually linger longest over the labor-saving devices in the modern kitchen. First, an auto-

FOR SALE

NEAR PARIS, IN FONTAINEBLEAU FOREST

Former Residence of Mr. Singer

Very beautiful 30.000-Mètre Park, Very Luxurious Estate (Large Salon, Dining-Room, Billiard Room, Winter Garden, Living Room, 8 Masters Rooms with Clothes Closet, 8 Baths, and 4 Servants'-Rooms, All Supplied with the Latest Comforts. In the Park, Pretty Dutch Building, Very Beautiful, Championship Tennis Court with Pavilion, Magnificent Lakes and Ponds.

In the Court of Honor, Two One-Story Cottages of the same style as the House. Very large Outhouses, Garage for 20 Cars and Lodgings for chauffeurs.

IMMEDIATE POSSESSION

Price Asked: 150.000 Dollars

Great Facilities for Payment.

APPLY TO THE AGENCIES OR TO

Mr. LACOSTE, Proprietor

35 Rue du Rocher PARIS

Sole Agents U.S.A.: FRANKLIN SIMON & Co., 414 Fifth Avenue, New York

matic dish-washer, which will turn the greasiest platter onto a tray, clean and dry in about three minutes. Then, the kitchen cabinet, containing all the pots and pans, the sugars and spices, and the hundred and one little articles that a good housewife likes to keep close at hand. A washing machine such as France has never seen before, with a special machine for drying clothes, and an automatic ironer, ready to handle anything from a handkerchief to a bed-sheet without tiring the house-keeper in the least. To say nothing of an electric refrigerator, ready to serve little chunks of ice for cocktails, if needed, and the gas range that can handle half a dozen different dishes at the same time. And to further bewilder the housewife, a gas boiler that furnishes the heating of the ten rooms of the American Home, and an odorless incinerator, ready to be installed in the backyard, or even in the basement. "It seems too good to be true," was the comment of an old lady whose worn hands testified to years of hard work with broom and wash-tub.

The only regrettable feature of the exhibit is that the American firms which furnished the American Home are not as capably represented as they might be. Visitors yesterday, when they asked the cost of various articles, were scornfully told that the price in dollars was "too high for French pocketbooks," while, instead of explaining the operation of various appliances, some of the attendants preferred to jest at the expense of the visitors.

THE NEW YORK HERALD succeeded in drawing a statement that to duplicate the American Home complete would cost "more than $100,000," but how much more would not be revealed. Of this sum, about $9,000 would represent the building. The Home will be presented during the latter part of next week to one of four French organizations—the Legion of Honor Society, the Bienvenue Française, the General Confederation of French Athletic Societies or the Society of Household Organizations. Not an article will be removed from the Home as it now stands, and it will probably be re-erected somewhere in Paris to be visited by housewives and school classes during many months.

An extra three francs is being charged to view the exhibit at the Grand Palais, but it was explained yesterday that this fee is used to cover the cost of transport from Havre, the American donors having paid all costs as far as that port.

PETITES ANNONCES
(CLASSIFIED ADVERTISEMENTS)

SITUATIONS WANTED—WOMEN
(6fr. a line).

COMPANIONS.

ENGLISH LADY, GOOD FAMILY, seeks resident work "au pair" south of France, in best American family only, expert housekeeping in large households, secretary, chaperon, knowing French and customs thoroughly, age 39. Roxton, Herald.

YOUNG FRENCH GIRL, SPEAKING English, would accompany American ladies, Paris. Kilp, 42 rue Sainte-Anne.

DAME SUISSE, FAMILLE DISTINGUEE, demande situation auprès de jeunes filles, habitude voyages, langues. Sassot, Herald.

DEMOISELLE, PLUSIEURS LANGUES, désire place femme de chambre pour voyager avec dame, bonnes références. S.B., Herald.

DEMOISELLE FRANCAISE CHERCHE situation dame compagnie ou gouvernante pour enfants. S'adresser: Mlle. Thimonier, 10 avenue Montaigne.

REFINED YOUNG WOMAN, FLUENT French and English, some Spanish and German, desires post companion, secretary, etc. Please write to G.G., Herald.

PETITES ANNONCES
(CLASSIFIED ADVERTISEMENTS)

SITUATIONS WANTED—MEN
(6fr. a line).

CHAUFFEURS.

CHAUFFEUR, TRES EXPERIMENTE, 34 ans, sérieux, bonnes références, demande place stable Paris et voyagerait. Perrier, 13 rue Gît-le-Cœur, Paris, 6e.

BON CHAUFFEUR-MECANICIEN, TRES bonnes références, sérieux, sobre, habitué fortes voitures, libre de suite. André Fouchet, 83 avenue d'Italie, Paris, 13e.

EXCELLENT CHAUFFEUR, SUISSE, 4 langues, références 1er. ordre. Job, 88 rue Commerce, 15e.

CHAUFFEUR-MECHANIC, BEST REFERENCES English, speaks French, all cars, age 36, 6ft. Frank, Herald.

COMMERCIAL.

SECRETAIRE, DACTYLO FRANÇAIS, désire place chez particulier. H.T., Herald.

ENGLISHMAN, 30, GENTLEMAN, SEVEN years India, now offers himself as secretary-companion, or other position of trust. Capable, cheerful, healthy, sportsman, literary, musical, savoir faire. Highest credentials. Box No. 1336, Dorland Advertising Ltd., 14 Regent street, London, S.W.I.

TODAY'S WEATHER FORECAST
Cold, fine or cloudy and foggy.
Wind E, very light.
Temperature yesterday: Max. 5 (41 Fahr.), min. 1 (34 Fahr.).
Channel crossings: Moderate.

THE NEW YORK HERALD
EUROPEAN EDITION

EXCHANGE RATES
Dollar in Paris - - - 22fr. 8 cent.
Dollar in London - - - 4s. 8 1/4d.
Dollar in Berlin - - - 4,200 billions
Dollar in Rome - - - 23 lire 8 cent.
Pound in Paris - - - 94fr. 35 cent.

PRICE: Paris and France, 30c.; Abroad, 45 Centimes (French).
PARIS, SUNDAY. JANUARY 27. 1924
PRIX: Paris et France, 30c.; Etranger, 45 Centimes (Français).

COOLIDGE MAY CANCEL LEASES

Grand Jury Inquiry Into Oil Scandal May Also Be Started Next Week.

DOHENY OFFERS LAND

Wahlberg Says Sinclair Checks Were Given to Trainer, Not to Fall's Foreman.

(By Special Cable to the Herald.)

WASHINGTON, Saturday.—With a view to cancelling the navy oil leases, President Coolidge to-day asked the Department of the Interior to advise him as to the wisdom of the policy under which Mr. Harry Sinclair, representing the Sinclair oil interests, and Mr. E. L. Doheny, the California oil magnate, got the leases from former Secretary of the Interior Albert B. Fall, and whether the interests of the United States were protected.

Criminal Action Likely.

The President is expected to announce next week plans for annulling the leases and, it is understood, that the Department of Justice will present to a special grand jury evidence for indictments on the charge of fraud. The President, however, feels that to take definite action before the testimony of Mr. Fall on Monday would be to appear to be prejudging the case without hearing the principal participant.

The Senate committee investigation of the navy reserve leases continued to-day, and Mr. Doheny presented a statement of his willingness to cancel the lease of 37,000 acres of oil land in California, provided his company, the Pan-American Petroleum and Transport Company, is reimbursed for its outlay of about $3,500,000 for a storage plant and other improvements at Pearl Harbor, Hawaii, which it undertook to complete for the navy in return for the oil land lease.

Note Is Presented.

Mr. G. T. Standford, counsel for Mr. Harry Sinclair, offered as evidence former Senator Fall's twelve-month note for $25,000, which Colonel Zevely testified yesterday had been given following Mr. Fall's return from his trip to Russia last year, which was made with $100,000 loaned him by Mr. Sinclair, it has been testified.

Mr. Archibald Roosevelt, who told the Senate Committee some days ago that he had resigned as vice-president of the Sinclair Oil Company because he suspected that Mr. Fall had been loaned or given money in return for the Teapot Dome oil lease, was again on the stand to-day and repeated his conversation with Mr. G. D. Whalberg, secretary of Mr. Sinclair. He insisted that Mr. Wahlberg had said that he had cancelled checks for $68,000 given to Mr. Fall's ranch foreman by Mr. Sinclair. He said that Mr. Wahlberg had confirmed this statement to him by telephone and then called back and retracted it.

The Sinclair Checks.

Wahlberg then being called to the stand testified that he had resigned from the service of Mr. Sinclair and offered a new explanation of the checks, which several days ago he said had been a misunderstanding of Mr. Roosevelt of his statement about some cows which had been given to Mr. Fall. He said to-day that the checks were given to Mr. Sam Hildreth, Mr. Sinclair's racing trainer, for salary and split purses, and never to Mr. Fall's ranch manager.

VON HOOGSTRAETENS LEAVE FOR EUROPE

(By Special Cable to the Herald.)

NEW YORK, Saturday.—Count Ludwig Salm von Hoogstraeten, former Austrian cavalry officer, motion-picture actor and sportsman, who won the heart and hand of Miss Millicent Rogers, daughter of Mr. and Mrs. H. H. Rogers, of this city, and an heiress to the Standard Oil millions of the late H. H. Rogers, sailed to-day in the Veendam with his bride for a six-month honeymoon abroad.

The count, whose marriage on January 10 to Miss Rogers at the City Hall without previous announcement caused a social sensation, again stated before sailing that they were reconciled with Colonel and Mrs. Rogers. They have spent their time since their marriage partly at the Ritz-Carlton in the apartment of the countess' parents, whom they also visited at Tuxedo Park.

The sensation which was caused by the marriage and reports that the count was engaged to marry Mrs. Montgomery Coffin some months ago, as well as various other gossip which has found its way to the Press since, has continued to attract much attention to the couple.

It is expected that they will go to St. Moritz soon after their arrival abroad and will also visit the South of France.

Mrs. Coffin and her friend, Mme. Traini, also a friend of the count and countess, sailed some days ago in the Paris for France.

THIRTY-SEVEN DIE IN MINE EXPLOSION

(By Special Cable to the Herald.)

WEST FRANKFORT, Ill., Saturday.—Thirty-seven miners were killed by a blast of fire-damp in the workings of the Crerar Coal Company here late yesterday, but 350 others escaped the blast and the subsequent fire in the lower workings. Mr. Herbert McCullough, manager of the mine, is dead.

The entombed victims telephoned to the surface that all was well after the blast. The bodies of the miners killed were burned so they were unrecognisable when brought to the surface.

Canadian Railway Men To Listen in to Chief

(By Special Cable to the Herald.)

NEW YORK, Saturday.—Addressing the Bond Club of New York, Sir Henry Thornton, president and chairman of the Canadian National Railways, announced that a plan has been prepared for the sale of radio apparatus at cost price to employes of the 22,000-mile system of the National Railways. This plan is intended to enable the chairman to address the employes at least once a week.

COOLIDGE FOR MELLON PLAN AS IT STANDS

Republican Congressmen Believe Increase in Surtax Is Expedient.

(By Special Cable to the Herald.)

WASHINGTON, Saturday.— G.O.P. leaders in Congress are disposed to consider increasing the surtaxes in the Mellon Tax Bill as expedient, but President Coolidge is represented as believing the Mellon plan will be adopted, without compromise when deliberate study reveals the superiority of this plan to the alternate proposals.

The G.O.P. steering committee met to-day to consider the chances of the passage as introduced of the Bill, which takes off $103,000,000 in indirect taxes. The Ways and Means Committee, in considering the measure, would repeal entirely the tax levies on candy, telegrams, telephones and theatre admissions up to fifty cents.

BRITISH KNIGHT TO WED AMERICAN

(By Special Cable to the Herald.)

NEW YORK, Saturday.—Sir Charles Higham, the well-known British advertising man, announced here before sailing in the Aquitania his engagement to marry Miss Eloise Rowe, a Buffalo society girl, in London next May.

Miss Rowe has been in London for the past three years.

Sir Charles was knighted for war service.

FINE ARTS COMMITTEE URGED TO ABOLISH ELECTRIC SIGNS

(By Special Leased Wire.)

LONDON, Saturday. The newly-formed Committee of Fine Arts is being urged to make its first objective the extinction of the electric signs, wherewith the West End of London was lately enlivened in emulation of New York's White Way.

Mr. George Moore, the writer and connoisseur, declares that the twinkling signs "would offend the taste of negroes. Nothing invented by savages could be more absurd." Several important British concerns recently voluntarily scrapped countryside signs as eyesores.

EXPERTS STUDY GERMAN RAILWAYS

A separate budget for Germany, which will include payments to the reparation account from the German railroads and other State resources, is now being studied by the first Committee of Experts, headed by General Dawes. Two sessions, with the railroad authorities, Sir William Acworth and M. A. Leverve, in attendance, have been directed towards this idea. In conversations of the friendliest character, the Committee of Experts has continued the study of German railroad statistics, and it will probably hear the two invited experts on Monday before leaving for Berlin, although Sir William Acworth and M. A. Leverve will both go to Berlin at the end of next week to confront German railroad experts with statistics and plans for overcoming the present deficit.

The present investigation, a reporter of The New York Herald is assured, includes the Ruhr railroad receipts as part of Germany's budget resources. The experts are now agreed that there can be no disjoining of any portion of the income of the Reich, if a solution applicable to the whole of Germany is to be found, although it is possible to allocate a certain portion of the receipts, such as those from the Ruhr, for the reparation account only.

It was decided yesterday not to accept German figures as entirely reliable during the fortnight's discussion in Berlin. Accordingly the experts will be accompanied by several French, British and Belgian expert accountants, who will delve into the German records with a view to seeing whether their conclusions coincide with the opinions hitherto expressed by the Committee of Guarantees of the Reparation Commission.

FIGURES OF WAR BUDGETS COMPARED IN FRENCH PAPER

To refute charges that France is a profoundly militarist country, the "Petit Parisien" publishes comparative figures for the Army and Navy Budget estimates of the United States, Great Britain and France for 1923-24.

According to these figures, the United States appropriates for the Army, Navy and Aviation a total of $708,970,654, equivalent to 3,544,853,270 gold francs, or 15,689,520,573 paper francs with the dollar at 22.13. Great Britain provides under the same heads £128,500,000, equivalent to 3,212,500,000 gold francs, or 11,877,030,000 paper francs with the pound at 93.58. France is to expend under the same heads 4,595,002,335 paper francs, that is, eleven billions of paper francs less than the United States and 7,282 million paper francs less than Great Britain.

Mr. MacDonald First Strap-Hanging Premier

Head of Labor Ministry Comes to Work in Subway with 9 o'Clock Crowds and Entire Cabinet Is Breaking Union Rules Regarding Working Hours.

(By Special Leased Wire.)

LONDON, Saturday.—Mr. Ramsay MacDonald can certainly lay claim to being Great Britain's first "strap-hanging" Premier. Since he succeeded Mr. Baldwin he has come in as usual each day on the Underground from Hampstead, as he has done for years past. Owing to his habit of showing up at the Foreign Office soon after breakfast, he has made some of his trips in crowded trains as a strap-hanger unknown to those who packed the car with him.

The Premier and his Ministers did an almost unforgivable thing to-day by working throughout Saturday, something alien to the minds of most Government employés. At the close of the day, he intimated that he expected to show up at his office to-morrow, Sunday, for a time. What many of the so-called "limpets" fear is that the Labor Government, by working more than union hours, will make it possible in the interests of economy to cut down the still large army of Government office-holders.

Mr. J. H. Thomas and several other Cabinet Ministers intimated to-day that the usual week-end habit, which has prevailed in official quarters except in periods of the greatest emergency, is for the time being in abeyance, because there is too much to do just now.

Mr. Baldwin bade farewell to No. 10 Downing Street to-day. Some of the servants were weeping as the former Premier and his wife drove off. By Tuesday, it is expected that Mr. MacDonald will move in, bringing with him many of his favorite books.

Mr. MacDonald and five of his Ministers have resigned from the Executive Committee of the Labor and Socialist International. At Labor party headquarters, it was said that their acceptance of office automatically ended their membership, for members of the Government are barred from holding office on the Executive Committee of the International.

While members of the Labor Government do not want secret service men to follow them about to afford protection from cranks, Scotland Yard is not taking any chances and is maintaining bodyguards, especially for the Premier, who is said to have already received threats from persons believed to have unbalanced minds. It is difficult to look after the Premier, because he insists on using the Underground trains.

GEDDES LEAVES AS AMBASSADOR

British Envoy Guest at Notable Dinner in New York Before Sailing.

(By Special Cable to the Herald.)

NEW YORK, Saturday.—Sir Auckland Geddes, the retiring British Ambassador to the United States, sailed for England to-day in the Aquitania. Just before sailing he told newspapermen that the provision in the new rum treaty between the United States and England providing for search within an hour's sailing of the American coast would not be any cause of confusion. "Customs officers in boarding a boat can determine the speed in proximity to the coast by examining the engines," he said.

The retiring Ambassador was the guest last night at a dinner given in his honor by the English-Speaking Union here, at which hundreds of guests were present. Sir Auckland, in his remarks, predicted a continuance of Anglo-American friendship, and Sir Robert Horne, former Chancellor of the Exchequer, spoke in a similar strain. The retiring Ambassador was greeted by a special guard of honor composed of British Army veterans, and was loudly cheered as he entered the banquet hall of the Hotel Astor.

Geddes Congratulated.

Secretary of State Hughes, who was unable to be present at the dinner, telegraphed a message which stated that Sir Auckland Geddes "has not only discharged the duties of his mission with an eminent ability and fidelity to the interests of his country, but with an unfailing manifestation of friendship towards our people. We are therefore glad to believe he has faithfully interpreted the sentiments of his country, and we most gladly reciprocate them."

Mr. John W. Davis, former American Ambassador to the Court of St. James', who presided at the dinner, read the following cablegram from Lord Balfour, president of the English-Speaking Union of the British Empire: "The English-Speaking Union of the British Empire desires to add its tribute to that which its sister society is giving to Ambassador Geddes on his retirement from the British Ambassadorship. During his term of office many important questions have been discussed and settled by our respective Governments, and his fellow-countrymen regard with gratitude the part Sir Auckland has played in maintaining the friendliest relations between the two countries."

LENIN'S FUNERAL TO-DAY

Ceremony Postponed to Complete Arrangements.

BERLIN, Saturday.—The funeral of Lenin has been postponed till to-morrow. A provisional wooden mausoleum is being constructed in the Red Square close to the wall of the Kremlin, and there the embalmed body will lie for some time in a coffin with a glass lid to enable thousands of people to take a farewell glance at their leader. A guard composed of the older members of the Communist party is keeping watch over the coffin.

DARING HOLD-UP PLACE VENDOME

Three Bandits Enter Jewelry Store at Noon and Shoot Two Clerks.

The centre of Paris' fashionable shopping district was the scene of an unusually daring daylight hold up and shooting yesterday when three men entered the jewelry shop of M. S. A. Ostertag, 16 place Vendôme, at 1.12 p.m. and shot down two clerks who were the only occupants of the place over the noon hour. The screams of the concierge frightened the robbers away before they had touched any of the gems, estimated at three million francs, in the windows and showcase. One of the victims, M. Lembourg, died in the evening.

An American, Mr. William Courtemanche, of Portland, Ore., employed in the office of the Cadillac Tours next door to the jeweller's shop, and alone in the office at the time, heard the shots and rushed into the street in time to see the three men escaping across the great square in the direction of the rue de Castiglione. He gave chase for some distance until they dodged out of sight, and he then called a passing policeman. He was able to describe the fugitives as small and well dressed, in clothes of French cut, but they held their coat collars over their faces to escape recognition. Up to last night they had not been caught.

Shot Twice.

According to the story told to the police by the two wounded men, the three robbers entered the shop and pounced upon M. Alfred Saulnier, aged 63, an employé of the store, as he was brushing his hair before a mirror on the point of going out to lunch. As he grappled with his assailants they drew revolvers and shot him twice in the head. M. Sylvain Lembourg, who was in an inner room shaving, rushed to the assistance of the other, and was struck down at the door of the room by two shots in the stomach and back. He was able, however, to drag himself through a back door to the concierge's loge. At this point the criminals took flight without stopping to bag any of the valuables in the shop.

Excited crowds gathered in the place Vendôme all through the afternoon, gazing at the blood stains on the floor and walls which were visible through the show window.

DUELL MAY MARRY NOTED FILM STAR

(By Special Cable to the Herald.)

NEW YORK, Saturday.—Coincident with the announcement from Paris that Mrs. Charles Holland Duell, the former Miss Lillian Tucker and prominent actress, had obtained a divorce, comes the statement by friends of Mr. Duell that he will wed Miss Lillian Gish, the film star.

The Duell wedding at Meadowbrook, Pa., in October, 1921, was one of the society events of the season. Mr. Duell is a cousin of Mr. Elihu Root, a graduate of Yale in the class of 1911, and served as a lieutenant in the navy during the war.

America Wins Opening Event Of Chamonix Olympic Sports

By "SPARROW" ROBERTSON

(Special to the Herald.)

CHAMONIX, Saturday.—The first day of the Olympic winter sports opened up in a blaze of glory, the United States, with Charlie Jewtraw, of Lake Placid, winning the opening event of the meet, the 500 mètres, and the great Finnish skater, Glas Thunberg, winning the 5,000 and furnishing thrills for the big attendance that turned out for the morning and afternoon sessions. At the end of the day the point score placed Finland ahead of its nearest competitor, Norway, 4 points.

The morning session opened up the 500-mètre event. The first heat had Joe Moore, of New York, and Erik Blomgren (Sweden). At the fall of the flag Moore went from the mark like a ball out of a cannon and at half the distance he held his opponent safe with a lead of about five yards. Entering the homestretch, Moore led by eight yards and when he crossed the line, winning the first Olympic skating race ever given, he was ten yards to the good. His time was 45 3/5sec.

Eight heats went along before that time was bettered by Vallenius, of Finland, who did 45sec. flat; then O. Olsen,

(Continued on Page Eight, 2nd Column)

AMERICA FIRM AGAINST RUSSIA

Great Britain's Action Will Have Little Bearing on United States Policy.

ATTITUDE UNCHANGED

Senator Borah Finds British Recognition Pointing Way to New Spiritual Régime.

(By Special Cable to the Herald.)

WASHINGTON, Saturday.— Great Britain's resumption of full diplomatic relations with Russia will, in the opinion of President Coolidge, have less bearing on the attitude of the United States towards Russia than the investigation of the question of Soviet recognition which the Senate Foreign Relations Committee is now conducting. It is pointed out that nothing has occurred to change the attitude of the Administration, as stated in the President's Message to Congress in December.

Borah Statement.

Senator Borah (Rep.), of Idaho, in a statement to-day says that he presumes that for all practical purposes "we may regard the British recognition of Russia as a fact. It is a statesmanlike and courageous thing to do, and it marks a distinct break with the bitterness, hatred and intolerance of war times and points to a new moral and spiritual régime."

QUANTITY OF MORPHINE FOUND IN ITALIAN BOAT

(By Special Cable to the Herald.)

NEW YORK, Saturday. — More than $150,000 worth of morphine was found secreted behind the panels in the cabin of the chief electrician of the Italian liner Colombo by Customs agents here. The drug was seized, and Salvatore Scodalato, the electrician, was arrested.

STRIKE COMMITTEE PLANS SETTLEMENT

(By Special Leased Wire.)

LONDON, Saturday.—Mr. Tom Shaw, Minister of Labor, to-day received proposals formulated by the strike committee of the Trade Union Council, which he was requested to forward to the railway managers in the hope that they may become the basis for re-opening negotiations for the settlement of the railway strike.

If the proposals are accepted by the managers, another ballot will be taken by the strikers' union. Meanwhile the country is facing an indefinite continuation of the railway tie-up, which is dislocating trade and industry at a cost variously estimated at from five to eight million dollars daily.

SENATOR DUPUY ENTERTAINS AMERICAN COMMITTEEMEN

Senator and Mme. Paul Dupuy gave a luncheon yesterday in Paris in honor of General Dawes and Mr. Owen Young, the American members of the Committee of Experts. The guests included: M. Doumergue, President of the Senate; Marshal Foch, MM. Ratier, Bienvenu-Martin, Jénouvrier, René-Renoult, Vice-Presidents of the Senate; MM. de Selves and Millies-Lacroix, presidents of the Foreign Affairs and Finance committees of the Senate, and M. Robineau, Governor of the Banque de France.

Referring to the departure of the Committee of Experts for Berlin to-morrow, Senator Dupuy expressed gratification over the fact that his American guests had been able to witness in Paris the unprecedented financial effort that France is making and looked forward to its favorable effect upon Franco-American friendship.

The guests of honor replied that they had been happy to find good-will and high competence among their colleagues and were persuaded of the good results to be expected from the labors of the committee.

PRIVATE LONDON HEARING OF AMERICAN'S OPERETTA

LONDON, Saturday.—A musical comedy, "Chiquita," written by Mr. Wilfred Eyre, formerly connected with the American Consulate here, was given a try-out to-day as a private theatrical at the home of his sister, Lady Campden. While some of the book and all of the lyrics and music were composed by Mr. Eyre, the play is largely a family affair, as another sister, Miss Edith Eyre, collaborated in writing the story and Viscount Campden had a rôle.

Mr. Eyre, who is now employed in the financial district, said to-day that he wrote the piece in his spare moments. The scenes are laid in California and Spain. The title in Spanish means "little girl." If the play proves successful before private audiences Mr. Eyre expects to give performances as charity benefits later. Mr. Eyre, who is the son of Mr. Edward Eyre, of New York, has been living in England since 1905.

ITALIANS ASKED TO JUDGE FASCISM AT NEW ELECTIONS

ROME, Saturday. — The Royal decree dissolving the Chamber and fixing the holding of general elections on April 6 is accompanied by a report which explains that the purport of the new electoral law is to prevent the political manœuvring of minority parties and to ensure that that party shall be returned to power which enjoys the confidence of the most notable portion of the nation.

The report recalls the main achievements of the Fascist party during the time it has been in power, and states that at the coming elections the nation must pass judgment on the work accomplished and the Fascist program.

Pastor Announces Plan For Church Skyscraper

(By Special Cable to the Herald.)

NEW YORK, Saturday.—Dr. John Roach Straton, pastor of Calvary Baptist Church, announces that plans are complete to demolish the present church and to build a 20-story church building on its site with the upper stories devoted to a Christian hotel. The proposed hotel, he says, would be "where solid men and women could rest in peaceful fellowship without the attention of scarlet women and lounge lizards."

PLOT ON FRANC, SAYS PREMIER IN CHAMBER

M. Poincaré Exposes International Campaign in Asking Dictatorial Powers.

Representatives of both wings of the French Chamber of Deputies yesterday criticised or attacked the French Government's plan of defending the franc by economies and additional taxation, to be carried into effect under special powers, of financial dictatorship, but M. Poincaré defended the scheme and declined to recede in any way from the position he has already taken up that the matter involves urgency and cannot be dealt with through the ordinary machinery of government.

As an illustration of the special character of the menace to be met by France, the Prime Minister cited a circular issued by a German bank in the United States inviting all holders of francs throughout the world to sell in order to put an end to the occupation of the Ruhr. There was no denying the existence of a regular campaign against the franc. "Sell francs and Poincaré will fall," was the cry of the conspirators, he said.

News from Washington and other centres showed the Premier that the mere announcement of the measures asked for by the French Government had disturbed the parties which were waging the campaign and had delighted the friends of France.

Appeals to Countrymen.

M. Poincaré appealed to his countrymen not to play into the hands of the foreign holders of francs who are throwing them on the market for political purposes.

"To-day," he said, "the Government asks you to balance otherwise than by loans the expenditure required for our sufferers from war havoc and our war cripples and widows. These measures do not imply any abandonment of our rights: we renounce none of our just claims and we retain hold on our pledges. The first of these measures will be the effecting of economies in our various administrations. The Government has, in this respect, sought inspiration in the report of M. Louis Marin." Each of these phrases was punctuated by general applause, indicating that a large section of the House was with the Government.

Anticipating objections against expeditive carrying into effect of these measures by decree instead of waiting months or years till special Bills could be enacted, M. Poincaré explained that the ratification of the Chamber would be required, and the Conseil d'Etat would be consulted regarding the legality of each Ministerial enactment. He pledged himself to pursue relentlessly all frauds against the Treasury, either in connection with relief advances or assessment of taxes.

Cannot Be Passive.

France, insisted M. Poincaré, could not remain passive while a campaign was being waged against her national independence. He was very keen for co-operation, of which the present work of experts afforded a fresh proof, but "our alliances must not become a servitude; we must be treated as equals."

Concluding with a reference to the new treaty with Czecho-Slovakia and other international associations of France, the Premier declared that France counted on her Parliament to form an invincible bulwark around her Government in order to repulse the attack now being waged against the franc, and would save her national currency.

The debate was adjourned until Monday.

FRANCE AND CZECHS SIGN MILITARY PACT

M. Poincaré and Dr. Benes on Friday signed "a Treaty of Alliance and Friendship between Czecho-Slovakia and France," which is to be ratified at the earliest moment by the respective Legislatures and communicated to the League of Nations. Besides providing for arbitration in any possible disputes between the two Republics, the treaty is specifically aimed at safeguarding the established peace of Europe by maintaining the peace treaties signed by them and consulting together for the adoption of necessary measures of self-defence.

Any attempt to restore the Hohenzollerns or the Habsburgs will be regarded by the contracting Powers as a direct menace to their security and call forth joint measures on their part.

It is expressly stated in the new treaty that its provisions do not run counter to the Franco-Polish alliance or to the Little Entente, which links up Czecho-Slovakia with Serbia and Rumania, or to the recent agreement concluded by Czecho-Slovakia with Italy.

From the foregoing summary it is apparent that the new treaty is, indeed, complementary to the arrangements already binding together certain Powers of Central and Southern Europe and that France thereby comes into more or less direct contact with these Powers.

There are no secret clauses to the new treaty, it is authoritatively declared.

REED TOSSES HAT INTO RING

Missouri "Firebrand's" Candidacy Announced by Campaign Manager.

FOURTH DEMOCRAT

Senator Was One of Few Democrats Who Opposed Versailles Treaty and League of Nations.

(By Special Cable to the Herald.)

WASHINGTON, Saturday. — The battered old war bonnet of Senator James A. Reed, the Missouri "rebel," was tossed into the already crowded Democratic Presidential ring to-day, when his candidacy for the party's nomination was announced by his campaign manager, Mr. E. D. Glenn, at St. Louis.

Four Candidates Out.

That brings the Democratic list up to four, with former Secretary of the Treasury William Gibbs McAdoo leading the field, trailed by Senator Oscar Underwood and former Ambassador John W. Davis, but Eastern Democrats feel that the real candidate has not yet entered the competition and look for the party's standard-bearer to be found in either New York or New Jersey, with the Governors' mansions as the probable place.

Senator Reed came into national prominence when he was named to the Senate in 1911, and his aggressive attitude, particularly on questions of international relations, has earned for him the sobriquet of "rebel" and "Missouri firebrand." Twice since that time Senator Reed has been returned by the Missouri voters, and each time with increased majorities.

Hostile to Wilson.

He is hostile to the Wilson faction of the party and particularly anxious to do battle with the former President's son-in-law, Mr. McAdoo. The Missourian was one of the few Democrats who stood with the Republican "irreconcilables" against the ratification of the Versailles treaty and the League of Nations and is hostile to participation in the League Court or in European affairs.

OBREGON TROOPS JOIN HUERTA'STS

NEW YORK, Saturday.—From Mexico comes news that 1,500 recruits drilled for President Obregón's army have changed their minds on the question of allegiance and, after receiving their arms, enlisted with Huerta.

A private car belonging to Obregon is reported to be held in readiness at San Louis Potosi, with a locomotive, which is ordered to keep steam up night and day.

DANCED WITH KING EDWARD

Pensioned Attendant, Once Prominent in Society, Reinstated.

NEW YORK.—Mrs. Florence M. Foye, aged seventy-three, who has for many years been an attendant at Brooklyn Park, after being pensioned on account of her age, has appealed to be reinstated in order to be able to meet her living expenses.

Mrs. Foye claims that her father, Edward Darby, was at one time prominent figure in the City of London, and that as a girl she danced with the then Prince of Wales, later King Edward VII.

She studied art in Vienna and Paris and came to the United States in 1875 with a fortune of $195,000, which, she states, her husband spent. Her pension has amounted to about $25 per month, and the park commissioners have passed a resolution favoring her reinstatement.

LENGLEN WINS OUT LENGTHY ENCOUNTER

(Special to the Herald.)

CANNES, Saturday.—Miss Elizabeth Ryan and C. F. Aeschliman gave Mlle. Suzanne Lenglen and Colonel Mayes their hardest battle of the season in the final round of the Gallia Club tennis tournament this afternoon, the Swiss-American combination losing out after the third set had gone to 28 games.

Mlle. Lenglen and Mayes found the opposition hard in the opening set, but were favored by luck and won out 6—4. The American woman played a splendid volleying game in the second set and was largely responsible for the defeat of Lenglen-Mayes, 6—1. The third set was run out to 15—13 before Ryan-Aeschliman were defeated.

Mlle. Lenglen and Miss Ryan won the women's doubles with comparative ease, defeating Mrs. Covell and Mrs. Barron, 6—3, 6—4. Crawford and Aslangul beat Mayes and Lamb for the men's doubles title, 9—7, 3—6, 6—3, 6—3.

"PULLING BISHOP'S LEG" BRINGS CURATE TROUBLE

LONDON, Friday. — A pla[illegible] curate, who "pulled the leg" of the Bishop of Sodor and Man by sending him a telegram purporting to have been filed by ex-Premier Baldwin and causing the bishop to postpone action with regard to the Church Bill in the Legislative Assembly and to make a fruitless trip to Liverpool, was fined £10 and 25 guineas costs to-day.

He is the Rev. Walter Kaisan, curate of St. Matthew's Church, Douglas. The telegram he sent to the bishop read: "Meet me Adelphi three to-morrow—most important—Baldwin." The defendant said he did it as a joke to divert the attention of a lady friend from seasickness. The stipendiary told the curate that he thought his explanation made his joke a very unpleasant one. That a clergyman should so conduct a wicked thing shocked him.

OCTOBER 25, 1922.

BOSTON'S MAYOR BARS ISADORA

(By Special Cable to the Herald.)

BOSTON, Tuesday. — Following Isadora Duncan's demonstrations on Saturday and Sunday nights at Symphony Hall, when she waved a red scarf at the close of her dance program and announced that she was just as Red herself, Mayor Curley has ordered that the dancer will not be permitted to appear again on any stage in Boston.

The famous dancer proved the truth of her assertion that she would not let herself be tamed by making an attack on Boston and Bostonians before leaving the city.

"Bostonians," she declared, "are afraid of the truth. They want to satisfy their baseness without admitting it. A suggestively clothed body delights them. They have a Puritanical instinct for veiled lust. All Puritanical vulgarity centres in Boston."

FEBRUARY 16, 1923.

ISADORA DUNCAN AND POET SPOUSE IN NEW TROUBLE

Gentle Russian Genially Inebriated, Smashes Hotel Apartment and Is Locked Up.

A further episode in Isadora Duncan's Russian romance was staged early yesterday morning at the Hotel Crillon in Paris, when the gentle poet-husband, Serge Essenin, in a fury wrecked the apartment which the couple occupied, and made such threats that policemen were called in, and Essenin spent the night in the lock-up at the Mairie of the Eighth Arrondissement. Isadora escaped without physical injury, although most of her toilet articles were used as missiles by the poet.

May End Romance.

Isadora Duncan insisted to the last that she could manage her husband, but the hotel management was not willing to take any chances. The dancer is quoted as having said after he left: "This must be the end of it all."

Serge Essenin and his wife dined quietly at the hotel on Wednesday evening and retired to their apartment before ten o'clock. At eleven, Essenin left. What he did in the next few hours is a mystery, but he returned very genially inebriated. The night porter helped him along the hall and into the elevator and deposited him at the family door.

Considerable Wreckage.

Fifteen minutes later the trouble started. A terrific noise was heard, and it seemed as if a squad of waiters had dropped all the bottles and glasses in the hotel. It turned out to be only Essenin smashing everything in sight. An eye-witness—or more correctly an ear-witness—gives the following account: "I heard a sudden crashing of glass and remarked to a friend upon passing through the hall that the waiter must be 'some peach of a waiter' to drop that tray of bottles and glasses. When the noise continued, I thought that another war had suddenly been declared. Upon the arrival of four policemen I discovered that Essenin was the war. He had smashed windows, chairs, tables, mirrors and every other object that came his way, and yelled in Russian and German. Finally he was dragged out bodily by four policemen."

Isadora's New Dance.

Isadora stepped round the room in very spry fashion, according to witnesses, but although she used all her arguments in Russian and German, they made no impression. Essenin was out for blood.

Isadora was ordered to leave the hotel before 11 o'clock yesterday morning. It is understood that she is now at Versailles. It is understood also that the authorities have intimated to Essenin that he must leave the country.

Such was a result of making the trip from America in a "dry" boat, that from his arrival in Paris Essenin proceeded to make up for lost time. It seems there was also a prelude to the Hotel Crillon incident. One of the passengers in the George Washington who crossed with Isadora Duncan and her husband, told a reporter of THE NEW YORK HERALD yesterday that they remained in their cabin throughout the trip, but when once they landed in Cherbourg, Essenin's pent-up thirst was apparently let loose, and he was carried more than once to his compartment in the train.

SEPTEMBER 15, 1927.

Isadora Duncan Killed as Auto Runs over Body

Shawl Catches in Wheel, Throwing Noted Dancer Under Machine.

(By United Press)

NICE, Wednesday.—Isadora Duncan, world famous dancer, was killed here this afternoon when she was thrown from the running board of a motor car which she was trying out before purchasing. The accident happened on the Promenade des Anglais, directly in front of her studio.

Mme. Duncan was about to step into the car, and her chauffeur had already started the motor. As she placed her foot upon the running board a flowing Spanish shawl which she wore caught in one of the wheels. She was thrown violently to the ground, one of the rear wheels passing over her body. Death was almost instantaneous.

SUNDAY, OCTOBER 22, 1922.

Drinkers Find Millennium on American Liner

(By Special Leased Wire.)

LONDON, Saturday. — The President Polk, of the United States Lines, arrived in Plymouth to-day absolutely dry. She had been instructed to leave the United States dry, and dry she became before leaving port.

The American liner Minnekhada had a more interesting story to tell on her arrival. It is reported that she had been instructed by wireless to go dry, and the officials obeyed instructions up to a point and then decided, instead of dumping the stores overboard, to supply everyone —for nothing. So, for the rest of the voyage, the passengers and crew had all their drinks free of charge. All the stores were not exhausted when the liner arrived at Plymouth, but with the maintenance of a free bar until her arrival in Hamburg, it is hoped that the Minnekhada will be absolutely dry when she reaches Germany.

TUESDAY, MAY 4, 1926.

GENERAL STRIKE ON AS 4,000,000 QUIT WORK PARALYZING BRITISH INDUSTRIES

Eleventh Hour Attempt to Avert Walk-out Fails—Newspapers and Factories Close—Government Moves to Insure Food Supplies—Warrant Out for Saklatvala.

(By Telephone from Herald Bureau.)

LONDON, Tuesday, 1 a.m.—On the stroke of midnight began the first general strike in British history. At the moment of telephoning, four million British trades unionists are under orders to cease their usual occupation. To what extent the strike order, called by the General Council of the Trades Unions Congress, has been obeyed will not be known until late this morning, when the roll is called at the hours the workers of the country usually start their daily routine. However, the fact that midnight—zero hour, in the parlance of the day—was allowed to pass without any peace negotiations progressing automatically put the general strike order into effect, and early reports indicated that the response thereto would be widespread.

Anthems Sung as Strike Begins.

At seven minutes past eleven last night Parliament adjourned. Within a couple of minutes Mr. A. J. "Emperor" Cook, who has risen to Labor's front ranks during the past few days, ran along the corridors of the House of Commons to the lobby where the miners' leaders and executives, to use their own phrase, "had been cooling their heels" for a couple of hours.

"It is pretty well all broken down," was the laconic phrase in which Mr. Cook announced the failure of his final consultation with the Government and then passed out of the Palace of Westminster.

In ones and twos, the miners' leaders drifted away to Eccleston square, where the General Council of the Trades Union Congress and the miners' executives held a joint meeting. This finally broke up at midnight without any settlement being reached and without any statement being issued.

At the Houses of Parliament, Messrs. J. H. Thomas, Pugh and other Trades Union leaders remained in communication with Premier Baldwin—obviously trying to minimize the effect of the general stoppage, which was now inevitable.

Outside, a crowd numbering several thousands waited despite the fact that the precincts of Parliament were deserted. As Big Ben tolled midnight, and the strike officially began, one section of the crowd struck up "The Red Flag," which was then sung through. Then someone started "God Save the King," and the whole assembly uncovered and sang the national anthem. There was no suggestion of any sort of disorder, and after finishing the national anthem, the sightseers broke into a rush for the last street cars and buses that may run in Britain for an indefinite time.

Bicycles in Demand.

Railroads to-night were planning to maintain skeleton services, but facilities on communters lines will in any case be cut to the bone. As a result there has been a rush all day long to buy or hire bicycles, while beds to provide shakedowns for office staffs are in brisk demand.

Reassuring statements on the maintainance of supplies of food, gas and electricity were issued formally during the course of the day. Food supplies throughout the nation seem to be normal, but the Government this evening broadcast an appeal to the public to assist in a fair distribution by refraining from stocking up in excess of ordinary requirements.

A similar appeal was issued for conservation of petrol supplies, but the response to this is rather doubtful in view of the fact that if normal transportation ceases to function to-morrow, all sorts of automobiles of mature vintage are bound to reappear on the roads for the first time in years.

MONDAY, MAY 10, 1926.

POLICE BATTLE STRIKERS, ARREST SCORES; 100 HURT IN HULL AND GLASGOW CLASHES

British Government's Show of Force in London Embitters Unionists—Tension Growing—Good Convoy System Now in Operation.

(By Special Leased Wire.)

LONDON, Sunday.—The British general strike to-day took a more warlike aspect. While in London the change in appearance was manifested only in a show of military force by the Government, in the provinces several violent clashes were reported. Police, so far, have been able to put down the outbreaks, but not without real battles, and many arrests have been made.

The most serious disturbances were reported from Hull and Glasgow. In these two cities nearly 100 persons have been injured in the clashes during the week-end, and scores have been arrested. The Government's show of force in London in sending troops, armored cars and large bodies of special police to guard trains of lorries carrying food from docks and warehouses has futher embittered the strikers, who declare that the Government is attempting to force them into an attitude of resisting the law and creating disorder.

Verbal barrages have been hurled from both sides, and each side seems to be trying to foist the responsibility for possible trouble on the other. Although in London and many other sections there have been no further hostilities than battles of words, there is a growing tenseness and an increasing bitterness.

Serious disturbances were reported from Glasgow, where a party of youths went on a window-smashing rampage. Several police patrols had to be summoned to end the rioting. Thirty-five were arrested, but many others of the rioters scattered and fled. Another outbreak there occurred when several public houses in the Anderston district were looted. Police were compelled to make a baton charge and arrested a couple of dozen men. The total of arrests since the beginning of the strike was thus brought to eighty.

Forty Injured at Hull.

At Hull, forty-one persons were injured in disorderly scenes. In one instance rowdies attempted to resist a police baton charge with pit props from the dock side. They were beaten in a hand-to-hand battle and many arrests were made. The windows of many large business houses were shattered by stone-throwers, and in a few cases the stores were looted of valuable goods.

At Newcastle the first police baton charge since the strike began was made last night. Trouble between union and non-union sympathizers broke out in the market place and threatened to reach serious proportions, but the police in large numbers charged the crowds and soon were able to clear the streets.

There was no sign of disturbance at Liverpool. No trains were running, but they will be resumed to-morrow. Street car service is being operated by volunteers. Despite the strike of the dockers, twenty-three vessels were unloaded to-day, and two were loaded with volunteer labor.

Appeal to Galleries.

One week after the rupture of negotiations between the Government and the Trades Union Congress and on the sixth day of the operation of the general strike, the Government and the strike committee to-day both appeared more anxious to put over an appeal to the galleries than to go on with the job of waging civil war, which the watching world seems more anxious to see staged than either party to the dispute does.

London assumed a warlike appearance this morning, however, with troops, special constables and police guarding the transportation of food supplies from the docks to the distributing station at Hyde Park. But the illusion that civil war might at last have broken out was shattered by an announcement from strike headquarters that all workers had been instructed to keep away from the dock area, and the strikers' organiation registered pained surprise at the display of military force in view of the fact that interference with food supplies was furthest from the thoughts of the strikers at the present stage of the conflict.

Strikers Beat Police, But Only at Football

PLYMOUTH, Sunday. — "The strikers have won. The police were beaten hollow." This was the cry which passed from mouth to mouth here last night, throwing the town in consternation and putting the authorities on the alert. But neither military nor naval aid was found to be necessary when it was learned that the strikers had engaged the local police in a friendly football match and had beaten them by 2 goals to 1 to the delight of thousands of spectators who found the match an excellent way of spending a Saturday afternoon during a general strike.

Ruth, Gehrig, Huggins Have Different Theories for Increase in Homerun Hitting

BABE DECLARES IT'S BECAUSE BATTERS ARE NOW "SWINGIN' FROM THE HIPS"

Changes in Pitching Rules Limit Hurlers, Lou Holds.

"LIVELY BALL"—HUG

"Ruth Is the Hardest Hitter We Have Ever Had," Yankee Pilot Declares.

By W. B. HANNA.

NEW YORK.—The expert opinion of three eminent authorities, two of them foremost exemplars, about home runs, a subject dear to the heart of the fan and the slugger has been sought. The experts were Babe Ruth, Lou Gehrig and Miller Huggins, who presides for the time being over the destinies of the two sluggers. They were asked why there are more home runs than ever before.

Ruth's reply was typical. It was blunt and meagre in words. That is Ruth's way. His vocabulary, unassisted by the amanuensis, is a long way short of the standard glossary, and he likes to get it over with. Still he says a good deal in his terse way, just as he puts a good deal into his swing. He said:—

"I always used to hit the old ball as far as the new one, and they're hittin' this one farther because they're all swingin' from their hips."

A lucid explanation, but not enough. The better made ball now on the market, better in materials used and more uniform and livelier, is a factor in harder and longer hitting that cannot be dismissed. Undoubtedly it is partly accountable for the home run increase, but it is not wholly accountable. "Swingin' from the hips" has something to do with it.

Mr. Ruth, however, didn't explore sufficiently into the ways and wherefores. He didn't touch upon other causes of import. He was not disposed to search and analyze, as was Huggins.

'It's Pitching,' Says Gehrig.

"It's the pitching for one thing. I don't go back to the days of the dead ball, and all I know about the hitting is with the lively ball, so please don't get me as posing as an authority; but we do know that the days of the shine ball, the sailer, the fingernail ball and what not are gone. They made the ball do things that pitchers aren't allowed to do now.

"Babe tells me that when he pitched umpires used to come on the field wtih not more than four balls for the pitchers' use. Now they bring on two dozen and a new ball is thrown in if the cover on the other is the least scratched or marred. Naturally that keeps better balls in the game to hit, and the fresher they are the better shape they're in and the farther they will go."

"Lively Ball," Declares Hug.

Miller Huggins said, "Lively ball, more good balls in use and increased opportunities make the increase in home runs. It is not natural development to my way of thinking, unless that is part of increased opportunities. Men were as strong years ago and had as much to follow through and wrist action. We heard all about 'wrist' twenty-five years ago. Joe Kelley, for one, had all of that stuff."

"What creates the increased opportunities you speak of?"

"Changes in playing due to the lively ball. The lively ball means more runs, and more runs mean more times at bat. There isn't as much bunting or as much sacrificing as there used to be, and, consequently, there are more opportunities to hit the ball out. Further, they hit at two and none and three and one nowadays where they didn't use to do it at all, and that means more chances accepted.

"Ruth is the hardest hitter we've ever had. I think there is no question of that, and as a left-hander Gehrig is even more wicked than Elmer Flick, one of the hardest of the old left-handers, or than Sam Crawford, and when we recall that Frank Baker hit fifteen home runs one season and what a hard hitter he was it is wonderful to realize how far that home run hitting has been surpassed."

THE HOMERUN TWINS

Babe Ruth (left) and Lou Gehrig are providing the chief excitement of the American League race this season in their struggle for slugging honors. For the moment Columbia Lou is leading with thirty-eight circuit clouts, with the Bambino two behind.

SPORTING GOSSIP

By Sparrow Robertson

THE writer was talking with a recent arrival from the States the other night who in his younger days frequented the Fourth and Sixth Wards of New York when seeking a little quiet amusement. One remembrance we had was a bare-knuckle fight, held in the rear of a saloon on Franklin street, right near the Tombs prison. At that time 'Big Tim" Sullivan was leader of his district, and in addition ran a saloon directly opposite the wrong-doers residential place. Tim, who was not as strong as he became afterwards, attended the scrap along with some friends. The ring was pitched back of a board and glass partition. There was only one way to get to the street from the place, as we all realized later on.

—oo—

About fifty persons were present and before the fifth round had come to an end there was a great commotion when the board and glass partition was battered down by a bunch of cops under Inspector Alec Williams. The fighters and seconds were arrested, and the on-lookers were chased into the street through two lines of policemen who certainly knew how to wallop with their big night sticks. We both recalled many men who afterward became very strong politically, some of whom are now holding high offices in New York State, who on the night referred to were chased out and given the air assisted by the cops' night sticks just as others were. The recent arrival, like many other old-timers, considers such a happening was in the "good old days" as far as New York City is concerned.

—oo—

The main attraction at Cap Gris Nez this season appears to be the Zitenfeld twins, the two American girls who recently swam from Albany to New York. Both are amateurs and have registration cards from the Amateur Athletic Union certifying to it. The twins will probably make their attempt to swim the Channel before the end of this month. There are about one dozen others, male and female, who are training at the Cape, for an attempt at a crossing to be made during the next six weeks.

—oo—

If the New York Yankees win the pennant this year there is a great chance of the team making a trip to Europe along with another team selected from the National League clubs. If it should come to pass that the Yankees make the trip, Babe Ruth will surely be with them. The American game is certainly beginning to take good hold in Europe and another visit of two teams giving exhibitions here of the real stuff would do wonders to give an extra impetus to the sound establishment of the game on this side.

—oo—

Track and field sanctions issued by the American Amateur Athletic Union for the coming fall and winter season throughout the States outnumber greatly those ever before applied for in the history of the United States, which is attributed to the near approach of the Olympic Games. At all of the games promoted in the States from now on and up until the try-outs next year, a certain percentage of the profits made in each set will be turned over to the American Olympic Fund, to go toward the financing of the Amsterdam trip of next year.

—oo—

They are already discussing in the States as to which coach will be named as chief for the American Olympic track and field team next year. They would have to look a long way to find a more capable man than Lawson Robertson, who was head of the Paris Olympic team. Lawson, who is head coach to the University of Pennsylvania, is one very level-headed fellow who knows the athletic game from beginning to end, and is also a coach who can get all possible out of an athlete by his just handling.

—oo—

The United States had altogether too many sub-coaches at the Paris Games. Some of them did not appear to know they were alive, and were more a hindrance than a help. There were trainers for sprinters, trainers for middle-distance, long-distance, and all the different brands of fields events. Pull, evidently, went a long way to get a free trip to Europe under the disguise as a trainer for the 1924 Olympic team.

—oo—

The Western States will be in the field next year to have their trainers well represented at Amsterdam. The Middle and Far Western States from present indications will furnish the bulk of the 1928 team, and it will be right for the Western States to look for and expect proper recognition on the list of trainer appointments.

ALLISON, TEXAS U., IS RANKED AT NO. 1 IN COLLEGE TENNIS

NEW YORK.—Wilmer L. Allison, of the University of Texas, intercollegiate singles tennis champion, has been named No. 1 in the 1927 intercollegiate ranking, the U.S.L.T.A. has announced. John Van Ryn, of Princeton, is No. 2, and Ben Gorchakoff, of Occidental College, No. 3.

In doubles the Princeton team, Van Ryn, and Kenneth Appeal, is named at No. 1, with Gorchakoff and N. Craig, of Occidental, No. 2, and Allison and E. O. Mather, of the University of Texas, No. 3.

Eight colleges and universities are represented in the singles ranking, and seven in the doubles. Stanford University leads, with three places in the singles, and Princeton in the doubles, with two. The ranking was prepared by Charles N. Beard, chairman of the Intercollegiate Tennis Committee.

The complete rankings:

SINGLES.

1—Wilmer L. Allison, University of Texas.
2—John Van Ryn, Princeton University.
3—B. Gorchakoff, Occidental College.
4—J. F. W. Whitbeck, Harvard University.
5—A. Herrington, Stanford University.
6—C. B. Marsh, Jr., Williams College.
7—L. Ogden, Stanford University.
8—R. McElvenny, Stanford University.
9—M. Partridge, Dartmouth College.
10—M. Hofkin, University of Pennsylvania.

DOUBLES.

1—J. Van Ryn and Kenneth Appel, Princeton.
2—B. Gorchakoff and N. Craig, Occidental.
3—Wilmer Allison and E. O. Mather, Texas University.
4—R. McElvenny and A. Herrington, Stanford.
5—W. B. Evans and S. E. Ewing, Jr., Princeton.
6—J. F. W. Whitbeck and L. H. Gordon, Harvard.
6—C. B. Marsh, Jr., and H. F. Wolf, Williams.
8—T. Clines and W. Clines, St. Xavier College.

DEMASIUS CAPTURES THREE KULM TITLES

(Special to the Herald.)

SAMADEN, Sunday. — Treble honors fell to Demasius in the finals of the Engadine championship in the Kulm tennis tournament, which concluded here today. He won the men's singles title by default and shared in two doubles titles. With Fräulein Eisenmanger, of Vienna, he captured the mixed doubles finals, defeating Heinrich Kleinschroth and Mrs. Fuller, an American, 6-1, 6-2. With the Italian, Balbi, he took the men's doubles title, beating Count Salm and Kleinschroth, who defaulted in the singles.

Fräulein Eisenmanger won the women's singles title when she beat Signorita Miclavez, 6-2, 6-2.

Members of the Harvard-Yale tennis team which has been playing in England and on the Continent will enter the Palace tournament, which opens at St. Moritz tomorrow.

HARVARD-YALE LOSE

(Special to the Herald.)

LEGHORN, Sunday. — Italian tennis stars defeated the combined Harvard and Yale tennis team by five matches to four. The Americans captured both doubles matches yesterday, J. H. Whitbeck and L. H. Gordon, Harvard, defeating the Ricordi brothers, 6-4, 6-4, and T. B. McGlinn and W. M. C. Reed, Yale, defeating Amici and Pistra, 6-3, 6-3. In singles Gaslini beat Whitbeck, 0-6, 7-5, 6-2, and Bonzi beat Hill, 6-1, 6-3.

KING OFFERS CUP.

(By United Press.)

SYDNEY, Sunday.—King George intends to present a cup valued at $500, to be competed for annually, for horse-racing in each State, Lord Stonehaven, Governor-General, announced here today on behalf of his Majesty.

Ogden Mills' Lost Friend Wins Prix de la Touques at Deauville

THE WEEK'S CALENDAR.

Today: Deauville. Fri.: Pont l'Evêque.
Tuesday: Caen. Saturday: Deauville.
Wednesday: Caen. Sunday: Deauville.
Thursday: Deauville.

(Special to the Herald)

DEAUVILLE, Sunday.—The race meeting was completely spoiled by the wretched weather. Horses ran hoof high in mud, and, although a couple of favorites were successful, it may safely be said that future running will upset, in many cases this afternoon's placing.

Just before the main event, the Prix Jacques Le Marois, the first of the Deauville classics, the sun burst through the clouds, and the eleven runners went to post in favorable conditions. Queen Iseult was the most heavily supported, with the de Rothschild pair, Tradelinan and Vitamine next in demand. The "Queen" could not get through the heavy going, and Vitamine, with Guy Garner up won easily by two lengths and a half, form Henry Count's Pédant, with the winner's stable companion a fair third. The stake to the winner, trained by W. Barker, amounted to 112,300 fr.

Mr. Sol K. Joel's colors are often successful at this meeting. His Peacemaker, a 6 to 1 chance, with E. Gardner up, proved a clever first in the Prix des Chenettes. The rider was in reality the winner, for Brûlante II appeared to have the verdict safe, when Gardner came up with a rush and got home by three-quarters of a length.

In Lost Friend, Mr. Ogden Mills has a good two-year-old, and a rare mud colt, for he easily landed the odds of 7 to 4, for his backers by beating Abd el Krim by three good lengths, with Nancucha, a neck behind. A son of the Grand Prix winner Comrade, he gives promise of making as good name for himself as did his sire.

Mr. J. D. Cohn had a little compensation for the defeat of Queen Iseult, in the final handicap, his Marshal French defeating Mr. A. K. Macomber's High Flyer by half a length.

Horses in black-face type denote THE NEW YORK HERALD selections.

PRIX DES BERGERIES
Claiming plate, two-year-olds, 10,000fr., 1,000m.

Nelson (M. Toussaint), E. Heliopoulos, won; Prenez Moi (C. H. Semblat), R. Levylier, second; **Rhum Row** (J. Peckett), James Hennessy, third. Also ran: Nosegay (fourth), Chauve Souris, Dame de Trèfle and Etna. A length and a half; three-quarters of a length.

10fr. bets: w., 78fr. 50c.; p., 31fr., 20fr. 50c.
5fr. bets: w., 83fr. 50c.; p., 36fr., 16fr. 50c.

PRIX DES CHENETTES
Three-year-olds and upwards, 15,000fr., 2,000m.

Peacemaker (E. Gardner), Sol Joel, won; Brûlante II. (F. Garcia), A. J. Le Héron, second; Tramontaine (G. Vatard), Em. Marchand, third. Also ran: Forêt Auvray, Clovis, Le Paillon, Hésione and Magnum III. Three-quarters of a length; a neck.

10fr. bets: w., 70fr.; p., 31fr., 49fr. 50c., 56fr.
5fr. bets: w., 43fr. 50c.; p., 17fr. 50c., 25fr., 24fr. 50c.

PRIX JACQUES LE MAROIS
Three-year-olds, 100,000fr., 1,600m.

Vitamine (G. Garner), Baron E. de Rothschild, won; Pédant (F. Keogh), H. Count, second; Tradelinan (C. Bouillon), Baron E. de Rothschild, third. Also ran: Caulet Flori (fourth), Gerbert, Songe, Enéas, Mordicus, Quincampoix, Queen Iseult and Farnèse. Two lengths and half; two lengths.

10fr. bets: w., 49fr.; p., 36fr., 26fr., 30fr.
5fr. bets: w., 29fr. 50c.; p., 19fr., 20fr., 17fr. 50c.

PRIX DE LA TOUQUES
Two-year-olds, 25,000fr., 1,200m.

Lost Friend (A. Esling), Ogden Mills, won; Abd el Krim (C. H. Semblat), Em. Marchand, second; **Nancucha** (D. Torterolo), S. J. Unzue, third. Also ran: Sari Signy, Bien Joué and Petit Poucet. Three lengths; a neck.

10fr. bets: w., 27fr. 50c.; p., 16fr., 27fr.
5fr. bets: w., 13fr.; p., 8fr., 11fr.

PRIX DE LONRAY
Handicap, 15,000fr., 2,400m.

Marshal French (A. Sharpe), J. D. Cohn, won; Highflyer (M. Brethès), A. K. Macomber, second; Leilah (A. Esling), G. Wattinne, third. Also ran: Beaumarchais and Gabrielle. Half a length; three-quarters of a length.

10fr. bets: w., 20fr. 50c.; p., 15fr., 15fr.
5fr. bets: w., 13fr.; p., 7fr. 50c., 10fr.

HOLIDAY CARD AT DEAUVILLE TRACK LISTS GOOD FIELDS

PRIX DE DOZOLE: Ithaque, Asalto.
PRIX DU QUESNAY: Mary Legend, Remembrance.
PRIX FLORIAN DE KERGOLAY: Bois Josselyn, Sou du Franc.
PRIX DE LA VALLEE: Massabielle, Bachelier.
PRIX DE SAINT PIERRE AZIF: Polly Flinders, Cornelius.

(Special to the Herald)

DEAUVILLE, Sunday.—The Prix Florian de Kergolay (60,000fr., 3,000 mètres), for three-year-olds and upwards, is the feature of a good card which has been provided for tomorrow's holiday meeting.

It will probably attract eight runners, of which Bois Josselyn is unquestionably the class horse. Second to Cerulea in the Prix des Maréchaux, he has been among the placed runners in all his races. In La Coupe he defeated not only Fils du Ciel, but Bouda, the subsequent winner of the Prix de l'Espérance.

The four-year-olds have to concede 14 pounds on the present occasion to their juniors, the best of which are Sou du Franc, winner of the Prix Henry Ridgway over Château Palmer and Loubier; the aforesaid Bouda, Fenimore Cooper, the hero of the Prix Noailles, in which he defeated Carmélite and Royal Academy, and Bahr el Gazal, who has shown marked improvement of late and who is on his distance. Accalmie and Ibéria are good fillies, but they will doubtless find the 3,000 mètres too far. Choice falls on Bois Josselyn to win with Sou du Franc for a place.

The other races are all open, and it does not look like being a good outing for backers of favorites.

Horses in black-face type are THE NEW YORK HERALD selections.

PRIX DE DOZULE.
Claiming plate, three-year-olds and upwards, 10,000fr., 2,000m.

Loup Berger (G. Wildenstein), 62k. ... R. Brethès
Asalto (Sol Joel), 62k. ... Gardner
Sans Galettte (A. Schwob), 60½k. ... Chancelier
Nadar II. (Mme. G. Delas), 59k. ... Semblat
Saint Bonet (Ogden Mills), 56k. ... Esling
Josselin (J. Wittouck), 54½k. ... Allemand
Yola II. (G. L. Redmond), 51½k. ... Lee
Barhilde (A. Espirt), 51½k. ... Marsh
Ithaque (M. D. Cohn), 51½k. ... Pantall

PRIX DU QUESNAY.
Two-year-olds, 15,000fr., 1,000m.

Xandar (M. Boussac) ... Sibbritt
Chef d'Œuvre (Mme. Fockenberghe) ... Chancelier
Denain (J. Fribourg) ... R. Brethès
Bravida (J. Hennessy) ... Jennings
Isengrin (J. Hollier-Larousse) ... Bottequin
Mourad (L. Mantacheff) ... J. Winkfield
Le Landy (P. Wertheimer) ... Bontemps
Isolde (Comte G. de Chavagnac) ... Garner
Mary Legend (Lady Mortimer Davis) ... Keogh
Remembrance (Lord Derby) ... Esling
Septante (Vicomte du Pontavice) ... Garcia
Ortie Pourpré (J. Wittouck) ... Allemand

PRIX FLORIAN DE KERGOLAY.
Three-year-olds and upwards, 60,000fr., 3,000m.

Fils du Ciel (A. Pellerin), 62k. ... Esling
Mont Bernina (Baron E. de Rothschild), 62k. ... Bouillon
Bois Josselyn (J. Wittouck), 62k. ... Allemand
Sou du Franc (Princesse de Faucigny), 55k. ... Keogh
Fenimore Cooper (Marques de Llano), 55k. ... Chancelier
Bahr el Cazal (R. B. Strassburger), 55k. ... Vatard
Chicardeau (H. Ternynck), 55k. ... Garcia
Bouda (H. Ternynck), 55k. ... Sharpe

PRIX DE LA VALLEE D'AUGE.
Two-year-olds, 25,000fr., 1,000m.

Puccini (S. Guthmann) ... Torterolo
Massabielle (R. Meyer) ... Jennings
Gratis (A. Pellerin) ... Esling
Goldilocks (M. Goudchaux) ... Esling
Ofelita (Vicomte du Pontavice) ... Garcia
Hobby (J. E. Widener) ... Gardner
Galopin X. (Mme. H. Polak) ... Bartholomew
La Moqueuse (M. Boussac) ... Sibbritt
Mourad (L. Mantacheff) ... J. Winkfield
Bachelier (Comte de Rivaud) ... Chancelier
Astir (G. Wildenstein) ... R. Brethès
Ortie Pourpré (J. Wittouck) ... Allemand

PRIX DE SAINT PIERRE AZIF
Handicap, 15,000fr., 1,600m.

Galloper King (L. de P. Machado), 62k. ... Hervé
Scamandre (S. Guthmann), 60k. ... Torterolo
Loup Berger (G. Wildenstein), 59½k. ... R. Brethès
Sans Souci IV. (A. Monnier), 59k. ... Esling
Oudry (Marques de Llano), 57k. ... Chancelier
Polly Flinders (E. Esmond), 54½k. ... Garner
Bobsleigh (Baron E. de Rothschild), 54k. ... Bouillon
Défi (L. Olry-Rœderer), 53k. ... Allemand
Royal Flush (L. Olry-Rœderer), 52½k. ... Allemand
Bertina (A. Schwob), 52½k. ... Semblat
Cornélius (R. Sibilat), 50½k. ... Luquet
Deena Slee (M. Boussac), 48k. ... Duffy
Nicephore Phocas (S. W. Beer), 47k. ... Garcia
Lemberg Beauty (A. K. Macomber), 47k. ... M. Brethès
Roya (P. Wertheimer), 47k. ... Deforge
Corfiote (J. Wittouck), 47k. ... Vatard
Lais VI. (J. Fould), 45k. ... Béguiristain
Gamin de Paris (J. Hollier-Larousse), 45k. ... Dairé

Doubtful starter: La Moldava.

ENGLISH RACING PROGRAM OPENS AT WOLVERHAMPTON

LONDON, Sunday. — The English racing week opens at Wolverhampton tomorrow. Public form has received so many shocks in the past week that it comes almost as a relief to find a card like the Wolverhampton program when there are no pointers supplied by backers of form.

Selections for Wolverhampton.

KINGSWINFORD HANDICAP: Repaid or Barrie Boy.
STANTON PLATE: Orenza or Palefroi.
DUNSTALL PLATE: Golden Araby or John Silver.
STAFFORDSHIRE HANDICAP: Rath Duth or Paintbox.
SUMMER HANDICAP: Chase Me Charley or Wings of the Morning.
NETHERTON STAKES: Roselake or Lanson.

The SPORTLIGHT by Grantland Rice

Oldtimers and New.

Mr. Bernard Gimbel, Mr. William Muldoon, and other students of boxing have rendered the opinion that modern-day boxers and fighters are many points above the oldtimers.

They base this claim largely upon the fact that nearly every record that can be measured or timed has been improved upon year after year. The sprinters are faster, the jumpers jump farther and higher, the long-distance runners are far better, and the same goes for other competitions. They figure that there are now ten competitors under fine trainers against one competitor twenty or thirty years ago. Their claim sounds reasonable enough. Yet in the case of boxing it doesn't work out quite to the extent that one would think, wherein there is proof to offer.

Corbett and Tunney.

It must be admitted that Gene Tunney is now the class of the heavy-weight boxers. He made Dempsey look like a second-rate beginner at Philadelphia. He has outboxed every opponent in sight and certainly used better boxing judgment than Jack Sharkey did.

If there is one field in pugilism where any notable advance has been made, it should be in the art or science of boxing. But some time ago I got Gene Tunney and Jim Corbett to box two rounds for a Sportlight motion picture. Corbett was then sixty years old; Tunney, twenty-eight. Corbett had won his title thirty-three years before and had lost it twenty-eight years before the picture in question was made. Yet for two rounds Gene never saw as many gloves in his life—not even in the first fight with Harry Greb. Corbett was like a shadow, in and out, under and over, feinting, jabbing, blocking, swaying and ducking, harder to hit than a ghost.

Corbett at the age of sixty looked to be a better boxer than any man in the game today—and that goes from the heavy-weights down to the fly-weights. No one could ever persuade any one who had ever seen Jim Corbett box that any one in the ring today is in his class. Dempsey lacks his skill and speed. Tunney lacks his speed of hand, foot and eye. Sharkey isn't close to him. Neither is Jack Delaney as a boxer.

A Few Things to Remember.

Many of the broken records are due to modern improvements. Wefers and Duffy were timed in 9 3/5 over tracks that were not as fast as the cinder tracks of today. Golf balls and baseballs are made out of far better material and are more expertly made than the old supply of ammunition, making homerun hitting simpler and it adds to low scoring possibilities at golf.

It may be that time puts on a haze of greatness that was never quite there. The new record marks that can be measured are not so much better in other sports. John Paul Jones, of Cornell, and Norman Taber, of Brown, ran the mile, between 4.12 and 4.13 on outdoor tracks. How many mile runners are there today who can beat 4.13 outdoors? Nurmi did, but most of the winning mile marks today are around 4.20. A 4.20 miler today won't lose many races.

AMERICANS BEAT ALL-BRITISH, 10-9, BY LATE RALLIES

(By Special Leased Wire.)

LONDON, Sunday.—Hitting hard in the closing innings, the All-Americans beat the All-British nine, 10 to 9, in the final game of the London baseball season at Stamford Bridge today. The game was scheduled for seven innings to permit the playing of a double header but a two-run rally in the seventh tied the score with the Americans winning out in the second extra inning.

In the second half of the double header, the Chipping Nortons, 1926 British Isles champions, defended their title against St. Joseph's College, defeating the Southerners 8 to 6. The St. Joe's, who recently beat the All-Americans, although playing good ball, could not hold the Oxfordshire nine, which has been playing the American game for several years.

In the game between the London teams the British nine got a flying start when they bunched hits for six runs in the first two innings. The Americans got one run in the opening session. In the third, however, they connected solidity to shove across four counters. The fourth and fifth innings were scoreless. Both teams counted once in the sixth.

With the game scheduled to end in the seventh and the British two runs in the lead, Gildersleeve, crack American centrefielder, started a rally with a ripping double to left. An infield error put another American on the path, and then Steve Newell slammed out another double to left centre, and two runs came across to tie the score. Each team scored in the eighth, but in the ninth, the Americans drove over the winning run.

Ernie Stanton, who was sent to the mound in the fourth after the British had scored seven runs, struck out a half dozen Englishmen at the most critical moments, combining sharp breaking curves with vaudeville psychology and tricks.

Arlie Latham, Major league veteran, who umpired, got a warm razzing from both sides on every close play.

GLENNA COLLETT HAS AUTO CASE NOLLED

NORWALK, Conn.—Miss Glenna Collett, twice women's national golf champion, who was arrested here for reckless driving July 22, as she was speeding to Fairfield to participate in the annual gold golf ball tournament of the Fairfield Court. Miss Collett went from the courtroom to the Shore Haven Country Club, where she played in a foursome that had been arranged by friends after they learned that she would be in the city. Miss Collett had posted a $50 cash bond to assure her appearance in court.

In the course of explanation of the case Albert Ranney, of New York, took responsibility for Miss Collett's fast driving on the assertion that he was acting as pacemaker. He was charged with violation of rules of the road and fined $10 and costs.

WEEK'S PLAYING FAILS TO CHANGE AVERAGES

(By Special Cable to the Herald.)

NEW YORK, Sunday.—Four of the leading batters in the National League and one in the American did their share of playing during the past week and yet did not gain or lose a point in their batting averages, according to the major league statistics issued here today.

Paul Waner this week and last had an average of .386. His two teammates, Joe Harris and Hank Barnhardt stood fast at .377 and at .366, respectively. Waner went to bat twenty times and made eight hits but did not change his average. Harris in five times at bat got two hits, and Bernhardt got four hits in eleven trips to the plate. Hafey, the Card outfielder, also put in a fruitless week, getting one hit in three times at bat to hold his average at .341.

Fothergill, the Tiger slugger, cracked out five hits in his fourteen trips to the plate but his figure still stood at .352.

The leading batters in both leagues follow:—

NATIONAL LEAGUE

	AB	H	Pc.
P. Waner, Pittsburgh	440	170	.386
Harris, Pittsburgh	257	97	.377
Barnhardt, Pittsburgh	224	82	.366
Frisch, St. Louis	432	153	.354
Harper, New York	337	118	.350
Hornsby, New York	403	138	.343
Stephenson, Chicago	400	137	.343
Hafey, St. Louis	185	63	.341
L. Waner, Pittsburgh	423	142	.336
Hendrick, Brooklyn	317	106	.334

AMERICAN LEAGUE

	AB	H	Pc.
Simmons, Philadelphia	351	138	.393
Gehrig, New York	421	162	.385
Schang, St. Louis	184	68	.370
Heilmann, Detroit	323	119	.368
Speaker, Washington	384	140	.365
Ruth, New York	380	137	.361
Fothergill, Detroit	389	137	.352
Combs, New York	458	160	.349
Meusel, New York	352	122	.347
E. Miller, St. Louis	324	112	.346

The five leading pitchers in the two major leagues follow:—

NATIONAL LEAGUE

	W	L	Pc.
Benton, New York	10	3	.769
Meadows, Pittsburgh	14	5	.737
Haines, St. Louis	17	7	.708
Root, Chicago	21	9	.700
Hill, Pittsburgh	16	7	.696

AMERICAN LEAGUE

	W	L	Pc.
Hoyt, New York	16	4	.800
Reuther, New York	12	4	.750
Miller, Cleveland	8	3	.727
Lisenbee, Washington	12	5	.706
Lyons, Chicago	18	8	.692

Results of Saturday's Games.

NATIONAL LEAGUE

	R.	H.	E.		R.	H.	E.
Philadelph.	7	14	1	Chicago	2	6	1
Boston	0	5	2	Cincinnati	1	9	1
(1st game)				(10 innings)			
Boston	4	12	1	Pittsburgh	6	13	2
Philadelph.	3	8	0	St. Louis	2	8	2
(2nd game)							
New York	5	8	0				
Brooklyn	1	7	0				

AMERICAN LEAGUE

	R.	H.	E.		R.	H.	E.
Philadelph.	6	11	0	Detroit	8	17	0
Boston	2	14	0	St. Louis	7	12	1
Cleveland	1	8	0	New York	6	7	2
Chicago	0	4	3	Washington	3	8	1
				(10 innings)			

5.30 A.M. EDITION

TODAY'S WEATHER FORECAST
Warm, very cloudy.
Wind NW, moderate.
Temperature yesterday: Max. 21
70 Fahr.), min. 8 (46 Fahr.).
Channel crossings: Rather rough.

THE NEW YORK HERALD

EUROPEAN EDITION OF THE NEW YORK HERALD TRIBUNE

EXCHANGE RATES (CABLES)
Dollar in Paris - - - 25fr. 54 /2c.
Dollar in London - - - - 4s. 2d.
Dollar in Berlin (gold mk) 4m 21pf
Dollar in Rome - - - - 20 lire 01c.
Pound in Paris - - - 124fr. 02c.

40th YEAR. No. 14,476. Business Office and Information Bureau: 49 AVENUE DE L'OPERA. Tel.: Gutenberg 04-28 and 28-15. PARIS, SATURDAY, MAY 21, 1927. Editorial Office: 38 RUE DU LOUVRE. Tel.: Gutenberg 03-18 and 03-19. PRICE: Paris and France, 30c.

LINDBERGH NOW SPEEDING ALONE TOWARD PARIS

Daring 25 Year-Old Aviator Due at Le Bourget Tonight; Great Paris Reception Ready

BULLETIN.

(By United Press.)

ST. JOHN'S, Newfoundland, Friday. — Lindbergh thrilled this city tonight at 8.45 p.m. (12.45 a.m., Paris time), with a daring feat by passing through the narrow St. John's gap, 200 feet wide, flying far below the summit of its rocky walls. As he passed through he rose again, taking a course towards the open sea about East by North and increased his speed. Crowds in the streets and in the windows witnessed the plane as it slowed down and dipped low in a spectacular flight over the city. As he headed out to sea Lindbergh had put 1,200 miles, one third of his daring flight, behind him.

(By Special Cable to the Herald)

NEW YORK, Friday.—Alone, without navigating instruments other than an ordinary magnetic compass to guide him, Captain Charles A. Lindbergh, daring young American flier, is somewhere over the Atlantic tonight, winging his way eastward under a bright moon towards Paris, as far as was known at a late hour tonight. Undaunted by the death of four American fliers and the unknown fate of two heroic French airmen in efforts to span the 3,600 miles between the two cities, this twenty-five-year-old, fair-haired youth, embarked on the great adventure from Roosevelt Field this morning at 7.51 a.m. (12.51 p.m., Paris time).

To Gain Speed.

As his load lightens with the fair weather ahead, it is expected he will be able to speed the plane up to nearly 135 miles an hour, which, naval observers estimate, will bring him in sight of the French coast at about dusk. All United States Naval vessels have been notified of his departure and of his proposed route by Admiral Eberle, chief of Naval Operations, and Captain Fried, of the United States liner President Roosevelt, wirelessed he was altering the vessel's course to the Northward to bring it in line with the flier's route.

Flight Stirs Broadway.

Enthusiasm swept the Long Island flying fields and Broadway tonight as the reports showed that this ecentric easy-mannered youth—Lindbergh—was boring his way toward his goal after starting the thirty-six-hour grind alone with only two hours sleep.

This morning some alarm was felt for his safety, following reports that a plane passed near Brockton, Mass., with a sputtering engine. Others said the motor seemed to be functioning perfectly and a seaplane was sent up, but failed to report the flier.

Hopes soared again however when further reports showed he was gradually putting hours and miles behind and the crowds before newspaper bulletin boards stood their ground, cheering each new report until the news was flashed that he was headed across the vast stretch of sea.

This morning as she soared northward after a difficult take off five planes, including that of Commander Byrd escorted him across Long Island and the Sound leaving him as he turned east across Rhode Island. Arthur Capteron, Curtiss pilot, who was one of the fliers in the escort, said that Lindbergh's plane had developed phenomenal speed considering the load, bettering one hundred miles an hour.

DARE-DEVIL FLIER

Charles A. Lindbergh

PERFECT WEATHER

With perfect weather cutting a clear lane across the sea and his plane travelling at more than a hundred miles an hour when last sighted over land, his chances for success seemed bright to experienced airmen here tonight. According to the United States Naval Hydrographic Office, after studying weather charts and the flier's estimated speed, he should reach Paris (Le Bourget) Saturday night at 9.30 p.m. (French summer time) if all goes well.

GOES 100 MILES AN HOUR

At 4 o'clock this afternoon (9 p.m. Paris time) the plucky airman left the North American Continent and headed across more than 1,800 miles of sea. At that hour he had put approximately 800 miles behind him in slightly fewer than eight hours, averaging nearly 100 miles an hour despite his heavy load.

He was sighted at Main à Dieu, Nova Scotia, heading eastward toward Ireland, which he expects to reach sometime tomorrow afternoon.

Blue Skies and Calm Seas Forecast for Flier's Path

The promise of a vast area of fine weather and favorable winds stretching from Ireland to the Bermudas and reaching its highest perfection in mid-ocean, should buoy up the hopes of the well-wishers of Captain Charles A. Lindbergh, the Mid-Western viking, in his daring, single-handed attempt to conquer the Atlantic by air.

Nature's contribution toward the success of Captain Lindbergh's flight in the promise of good weather directly in the path that he will probably take, was announced last night by officials of the Office National Météorologique. The prevision covers both sides of the Atlantic.

A wireless message received from the Olympic last night stated that the liner was at forty-eight degrees north latitude and twenty-seven degrees west longitude with a slight northwest wind blowing and an overcast sky, though visibility remained good.

Reports from the British Air Ministry covering weather conditions over the Atlantic in the vicinity of England indicated fresh westerly winds, partly cloudy, and the possibility of some rain, with visibility generally good and the temperature moderate.

Cabled weather reports from Washington, D.C., last night, indicate that the weather conditions over Captain Lindbergh's route are as nearly perfect as possible. Off the Newfoundland coast, however, there was a blanket of fog last night, acording to reports from Cape Race and ice patrol vessels.

No Radio Equipment On Lindbergh's Plane

(By Special Cable to the Herald)

NEW YORK, Friday.—Like Captains Nungesser and Coli, Lindbergh, once he leaves land behind and is over the open sea, is cut off from communication with the world, as he is not carrying a radio sonding or receiving set. Despite efforts to get the pilot to install the equipment he steadily refused, even when it was pointed out that it might be the means of saving his life if he was forced down. His only means of communication in case of emergency are flares. The radio equipment was sacrificed for weight and to make room for extra fuel.

Route Across the Atlantic of Charles A. Lindbergh, the "Lone Flier"

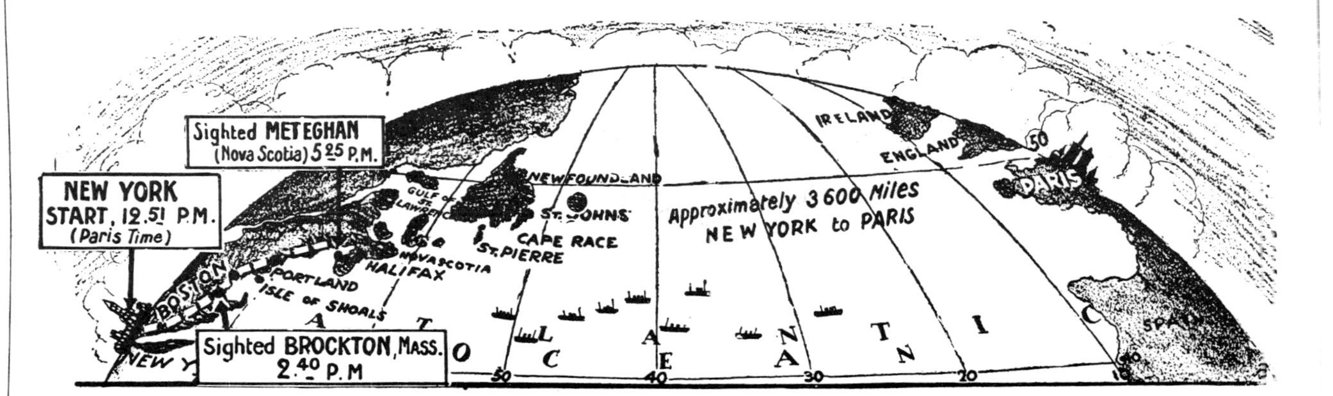

The large dot east of Newfoundland on the map indicates the calculated position of Charles A. Lindbergh and his Ryan monoplane at two o'clock, Paris time, this morning. He was last sighted at St. Johns, on the east coast of Newfoundland, at 12.45, Paris time. This point is nearly 1,200 miles out from Roosevelt Field, L.I., the starting point. Lindbergh made the distance, approximately one-third of the total from New York to Paris, in almost exactly twelve hours, maintaining an average speed of about 100 miles per hour. The dot shows the point Lindbergh should have reached at the time indicated, provided he continued on the same course at the same speed. He is now out over the open sea without chance of again sighting land, unless driven off his course.

CHEERING THRONG OF 50,000 STORMS PLANE TO EMBRACE LINDBERGH; POLICE BATTLE CROWDS TO ESCORT IDOLIZED AVIATOR TO PAVILION

American Lands Tired and Smiling, After 33 Hours and 30 Minutes in Air

Completes 6,200-Mile Trip from California to Paris and Wins $25,000 Orteig Prize — Machine Makes Perfect Landing at Le Bourget Field.

Pessimism at Start.

Every seasoned pilot before his hop continued to point out why he could never make the flight. He was flying alone, a superhuman task of endurance to sit at the controls in one position for more than thirty-three hours. No man could stand it, they said.

He was depending on a simple magnetic compass to guide him over the sea and to the coast of France which he must cross after dark. Navigators declared it was impossible to maintain a course and pick up Paris by day, let alone by night, and his attempt was considered as doomed to fail.

Yet, last night here he was in Paris. He had steadily kept a true course across the 1,900 miles of sea, picked up Plymouth and Cherbourg and descended upon Paris at night and within fifty-two minutes of his scheduled time. Not only was his feat one of daring and brilliant achievement but of skill that left experienced airmen stunned.

6,200-Mile Trip.

Besides his phenomenal feat his plane has probably the greatest performance to its credit on record. Just ten days ago, on May 11, Lindbergh was in San Diego, Cal., 2,600 miles from New York. Last night he had put more than 6,200 miles behind in fewer than two weeks without changing his motor.

His boyishness and his spectacular performances loomed strong in the minds of the thousands that waited his arrival and there was a note of skepticism in the crowd, though every voice echoed his success. Late in the afternoon and early in the evening when unconfirmed reports began to come pessimism increased as thought of the false reports of the two heroic French airmen flashed through the minds of the spectators. Only meagre reports reached the field and they were varying and conflicting.

Hamburg American Club Extends Felicitations

SHORTLY after the arrival of Lindbergh at Le Bourget last night The New York Herald received a telephone call from Mr. James T. Scott, of the American Trade Commission in Berlin, extending the congratulations of the American Club of Hamburg and the officers of the United States destroyers, Case and Isherwood, now in port. Mr. Scott said that the Club and officers from the ships were meeting at a special dinner to celebrate the feat of the daredevil flier in successfully crossing the Atlantic.

Flood Lights Put On.

As the sun sank, a brilliant ball of fire behind the trees and buildings to the West, light began to flicker on the field, outlining the buildings and the landing runways from the air. As darkness shrouded the field, the flood lights flashed across the broad expanse occasionally and workmen stood by the powerful searchlights ready to pick the flier out of the sky.

The thousands began to crowd forward, as the hour for his arrival was drawing near. Rockets and lights shot into the air periodically to light the field and to guide the flier and the surging thousands sensed that he was nearing his goal. Fashionably dressed women edged alongside of a simply clad mother and child for a point of vantage, while others not fortunate enough to be inside the flying field hung tensely on the high fence that kept them outside.

Thousands Rush Plane.

When the daring flier swung over the field out of a starry sky the thousands behind the iron-grilled enclosure lost all semblance of control and smashed the barriers, trampling policemen, officials, and spectators. Across the field they swept, like an angry wave, brushing all resistance aside. Here and there soldiers swung the butts of their rifles in an effort to stem the tide which tore everything aside.

Clothes were torn, hats were lost, and women were bruised as they stumbled to their knees across the field to catch a glimpse of the youthful airman. It was a mad mob that fought its way breathlessly across the expanse of green to hold out the hand of France to the United States in a sportsman's greeting. No one cared—the one desire was to get close enough to shout a greeting or a "bravo" in his ear.

FRIDAY IN NEW YORK, SATURDAY IN PARIS!

This photograph of the craft Charles A. Lindbergh landed on Le Bourget field last night was taken from another plane during preliminary tests in San Diego before the intrepid pilot started from the Pacific coast for Paris.

NIGHT WAS ONLY REAL DANGER, SAYS YOUNG AVIATOR DESCRIBING FLIGHT; NEVER GOT MORE THAN 200 MILES OFF COURSE; HIGH HONORS FOR HIS MACHINE

Flew Over Ireland Three Miles From Point He Selected In N.Y. Does Not Think It All 'Luck'

The only real danger I had was at night. In the daytime I knew where I was going, but in the evening and at night it was largely a matter of guessing. However, my instruments were so good that I never could get more than 200 miles off my course, and that was easy to correct. And I had enough extra gasoline to take care of the number of such deviations.

All in all, the trip over the Atlantic, especially the latter half, was much better than I expected. The laymen have made a great deal of the fact that I sailed without a navigator and without the ordinary stock navigation instruments. But my real director was my earth-induction compass. I also had a magnetic compass, but it was the induction compass which guided me so faithfully that I hit the Irish Coast only three miles from the theoric point I might have hit it had I had a navigator. I replaced the navigator's weight by the induction compass. This compass behaved so admirably that I am entirely ashamed to hear anyone talk about my luck.

Maybe I am lucky, but all the same I knew at every moment where I was going. The inductor compass is based on the principle of the relation between the earth's magnetic field and the magnetic field generated at the compass. When the course had been set so that the needle registered zero on the compass, any deviation would cause the needle to swing away from zero in the direction of the error. By flying the plane with the needle at an equal distance on the other side of zero for about the same time the error had been committed, the ship was back on her course again. This inductor compass was so accurate that I really needed no other guide.

Fairly early in the afternoon I saw a fleet of fishing boats. On some of them I could see no one. But on one of them I saw some men, and I flew down, almost touching the craft, and yelled at them, asking if I was on the right road to Ireland. They just stared. Maybe they did not hear me. Maybe I did not hear them. Or maybe they thought I was just a crazy fool.

An hour later I saw land. I have forgotten just what time it was. It must have been shortly before four o'clock. It was rocky land and all my study told me it was Ireland. And it was Ireland. I slowed down and flew low, low enough to study the land and be sure of where I was; and, believe me, it was a beautiful sight. It was the most wonderful-looking piece of natural scenery I ever beheld. After I made up my mind it was Ireland, the right place for me to strike, rather than Spain or some other country, the rest was child's play. I had the course all marked out carefully from approximately the place where I hit the coast, and you know it is quite easy to fly over strange territory if you have good maps and your course prepared.

THE HERO ACKNOWLEDGES CHEERS OF PARIS CROWDS

When Charles Lindbergh appeared on the balcony of the American Embassy before the thousands of demonstrative men and women in the street yesterday afternoon, Ambassador Herrick brought out a large French flag, and he and the flier unfurled it before the enthusiastic crowd. "Le drapeau américain" shouted men and women down below, as they had done on the previous night on the boulevards. The Ambassador and the aviator then unfurled the Stars and Stripes, and cheers went up with redoubled force for Lindbergh and America.

THE NEW YORK HERALD, PARIS, MONDAY, OCTOBER 21, 1929

Wall Street Market Suffers Heavy Losses in Bear Drive

Confidence in Stock Values Has Undergone Severe Test

Lack of Rallying Power and Failure of Brokers' Loans to Decline with Declining Prices Blamed for Losses to Many Shareholders.

(By Special Cable to The Herald.)

NEW YORK, Sunday.—Confidence in stock values and indirectly in the strength of business position has undergone a severe test during the past week.

After recovering about half of the September and early October decline, the market again weakened and gave up the bulk of the preceding week's recovery. Yesterday, under a severe bear drive, things went further to make a picture of a week about as gloomy as has been seen for several years.

Lack of rallying power and failure of brokers' loans to decline with declining prices has done much to create bearish sentiment and to bring prices to levels really serious for many holders of shares. Those who have suffered losses are in a naturally pessimistic frame of mind, while others less directly interested feel the need of reassurance over the business situation.

Wall Street has so long been regarded as the barometer of business that declines of the last six weeks have naturally caused foreboding.

FRIDAY, OCTOBER 25, 1929

12,894,600 Shares Turned Over In Record Wall Street Session; Banks Aid Last Minute Recovery

New Records Are Set In Wall Street Market

(By Special Cable to The Herald.)

NEW YORK, Thursday. — Some new records set in today's wild session of selling were:—

"Big-board" sales were 12,894,600 shares, as compared with 8,239,600 on March 26 last, the previous record day.

Curb sales totalled 6,337,400 as compared with Monday's high mark of 3,715,400 shares.

Cities Service set a new record for single issue sales with a total of 1,150,000 shares.

Sales for the first half hour were 1,676,300, exceeding yesterday's volume record of 26,000 shares in fifty minutes, and the biggest previous first half hour sales of 13,438 on September 9, following the increase in the rediscount rate.

Today's session also set a new high mark for breadth of trading with 950 issues as against 920 on October 21, last.

Nation's Financiers Meet at Morgan's and Reassure Public After Momentous Unloading of Stocks; Vast Throng on Hand; Curb in Record.

BULLETIN.

(By United Press.)

NEW YORK, Thursday. — Soon after the noonday break some market observers estimated the total paper losses at about $5,000,000,000. Much of this, however, must have been recouped by the rally which followed the support given to the market by the banks in the final hour.

(By Special Cable to The Herald.)

NEW YORK, Thursday.—Near-panic seized stock traders today in the wildest session Wall Street has ever seen. A new record was set in the volume of trading, which was so great as to make trading facilities quite inadequate, but the day ended with prices well on the way to recovery.

It is hard to say how far the collapse would have gone if banking support had not been given to the market. When market values began falling five to ten points between sales, representatives of the country's biggest banking interests met at the Morgan Company's offices and announced that conditions were sound and that prices of many stocks had fallen to unwarranted levels.

Their findings served to check what threatened to become a full-sized panic.

Sales on the Stock Exchange set a new high record of 12,894,600 shares as compared to the previous high record of March 26, of this year, when sales totalled just more than 8,000,000 for the day.

Americans in Paris Throng Boards As Big Stock Break Stirs Flutter

Market traders of the Paris financial community found that a 13,000,000-share day in New York was an occasion which could bring high tension and excitement much after the New York manner. Paris brokerage houses were crowded with persons anxious to see the opening after the sharp sell-off at the close on Wednesday, and the customers' men were kept busy answering insistent telephone calls and trying to reassure traders in the office.

As news of the great volume of stocks that had been turned over in New York and of the midday break began to buzz around in Paris, a still higher pitch of interest began to manifest itself, and late last night board rooms seemed to have become the rendezvous of the entire American colony of Paris. Many persons were unable to get calls through to brokers' offices, and telephoned banks and investment houses, seeking verification of the reports they had heard. The financial department of the Paris edition of The New York Herald Tribune was pressed into service to answer inquiries ranging from the market prices of various issues to an opinion on the soundness of the business of the United States.

An amusing incident that could almost be termed ironical occurred in the customers' room of the brokerage department of the Banque de Saint-Phalle. The smoke-filled room was crowded with worried and harassed customers, watching every move of the boys, who were rushing around trying to keep up with the constant flow of cabled quotations.

A flash was relayed from the floor by the New York office, which read:—

"Last minute prices will be blasted from the floor."

Prices had gone to the bottom, and the people were still further dazed by the suddenness of this extraordinary announcement. The hubbub of excitement that was waxing more apprehensive was interrupted by a boy rushing up with another cable that had come blazing across the ocean. Quickly the "blasted" was wiped out and the correction "flashed" put in its place, which brought laughs from everybody.

TODAY'S WEATHER FORECAST
Cold, unsettled.
Temperature yesterday: Max. 12 (54 Fahr.), min. 4 (39 Fahr.).
Wind: Moderate, W.
Channel crossings: Moderate.

TODAY'S ISSUE CONSISTS OF 14 PAGES

THE NEW YORK HERALD

EUROPEAN EDITION OF THE NEW YORK HERALD TRIBUNE

EXCHANGE RATES (CABLES)
Dollar in Paris - - - 25fr. 37 1/2c.
Dollar in London - - - - - - 4s. 2d.
Dollar in Berlin - - - - - 4m. 18pf.
Dollar in Rome - - 19 lire 08 1/2c.
Pound in Paris - - - 123fr. 82 1/2c.

43rd YEAR. No. 15.369. Editorial Offices: RUE DU LOUVRE. Tel.: Gutenberg 03-18 and 03-19. * PARIS, WEDNESDAY, OCTOBER 30, 1929 Business Office and Information Bureau: 49 AVENUE DE L'OPERA. Tel.: Gutenberg 01-23 and 25-15. PRICE: In France, One Franc.

Coast Guards Rescue 43 from Ship Sunk by Lake Michigan Storm

One of Worst Blows in History Probably Has Taken Thirty-five Lives in Disaster to the Wisconsin, Including Captain and First Mate.

(By United Press.)

KENOSHA, Wis., Tuesday.—Scenes of heroism were witnessed today when, despite tremendous waves, Coast Guardsmen got alongside the Goodrich liner Wisconsin as she was sinking in a storm in Lake Michigan, and took off 43 of the 78 passengers and crew on board. One lifeboat containing 15 persons from the vessel is reported to have capsized and the fate of 20 others is unknown.

Survivors declare that Captain Douglas Morrison, First Mate Edward Halvordson and Quartermaster William Stranheim, last seen on the starboard deck, went down with the ship.

The Wisconsin sent out a wireless appeal for help in the early hours of the morning, stating that the vessel was in immediate danger and her fire holds were flooded.

Coast Guardsmen immediately put out from here in the tug Butterfield, but at first were unable to go near enough to rescue any of those aboard the liner, owing to the high seas, and no more wireless messages were received from the vessel after 6 a.m.

After two hours' battle with the waves the rescuers finally were able to get a line to the ship. There were only three passengers on board, who were taken off by means of a breeches buoy. Captain Morrison's body was recovered by the rescuers, who picked up all but three of the other officers who stuck to the vessel till she sank.

Many of the survivors were near death from exposure when saved from the Wisconsin.

There were no women aboard. The cabin maid missed the boat when she left Chicago Monday night for Milwaukee.

The Wisconsin, a steamer of 1,900 tons displacement, is a veteran of the lake fleet. During the war she was pressed into commission as a hospital ship. Few other steamers ventured out of their ports today into the storm, one of the worst in the history of Lake Michigan.

THEODORE E. BURTON DIES IN WASHINGTON AFTER LONG ILLNESS

Ohio's Grand Old Man of Politics Was Nearly 78.

(By United Press.)

WASHINGTON, Tuesday. — Senator Theodore E. Burton, "Ohio's grand old man of politics," is dead at his home here. He would have been 78 had he lived until December 20.

Death was not a surprise to his friends, among the closest of whom is President Hoover, since the Senator had been in ill-health for more than a year, and a month ago he suffered a severe attack of influenza against which his fading strength could not compete.

The Senator was not married.

Born in Jefferson, O., Mr. Burton entered Congress in 1889 as a Representative and served twelve terms, 1889 to 189[illegible] and from 1895 to 1909 when he resigned to enter the Senate, where he served until [illegible] the House a[illegible] the last [illegible] support o[illegible] or the Pr[illegible] nomination [illegible] elected [illegible]

He was a [illegible] parliamentary [illegible] its meetings [illegible] va. The H[illegible] Berne and [illegible] in many [illegible] 192[illegible] as [illegible] Debt Comm[illegible] and 1927 as [illegible] delegation [illegible] Control of [illegible] He was [illegible] books, among [illegible] The Life o[illegible] Constitution [illegible] features."

HOOVER [illegible] AT[illegible]

(By Spec[illegible]

WASHING[illegible] Hoover will [illegible] services wh[illegible] Senate Cha[illegible] ator Theo[illegible] no died he[illegible] able ne[illegible] also became[illegible] The Sena[illegible] arrow [illegible] and ar[illegible] to its decea[illegible] minutes ses[illegible] an adjou[illegible] mittee of [illegible] the bod[illegible] by. It is sever[illegible] owing. Th[illegible] posed City[illegible] ms of Ch[illegible]

Tipless Taxicabs Will Appear in England Jan. 1

Machines Economizing with Air-cooled Motor Also to Be Used in Edinburgh.

(From the Herald and Herald Tribune Bureau)

LONDON, Tuesday.—An experiment in no-tip taxicabs for London was announced today.

A fleet of 50 new machines will be put on the streets soon after the first of the year. They will be painted light blue, and drivers will wear uniforms of the same shade.

The new taxicab company claims that an air-cooled motor will permit sufficiently low operating costs to eliminate tips.

The announcement is greeted with skepticism by London newspapers, and it is conceded that there will be greater chances of success in another city where the experiment will be tried simultaneously—Edinburgh.

Plane Lost Two Days With 5 Arrives Safely After Storm

Western Air Express Craft Arrives Safely at Albuquerque Following Forced Landing as Fleet of Machines Scour West and Nation Waxes Anxious.

(By Special Cable to The Herald.)

ALBUQUERQUE, N.M., Tuesday.—After two days of nation-wide anxiety reminiscent of that felt a month ago in a similar incident which turned out to be disastrous, the big tri-motored Fokker Western Air Express plane which disappeared in a snowstorm in Arizona yesterday morning en route from California to Kansas City landed safely tonight at this city.

The plane, which had five persons aboard, two as passengers, was forced down at Trechado, N.M., late yesterday and spent the night there, continuing on to Albuquerque today. All on board were well and the pilot reported no untoward incident.

Announcement of the big plane's safe arrival sent a flutter of cheer throughout the region and brought to an end a widespread search undertaken by a fleet of planes by both the Western Air Express and the Trans-Continental Air Transport Company, sent out from Los Angeles and Albuquerque.

The searching craft scoured the area around Mount Taylor, Ariz., where on September 7 the big Fokker plane of the Trans-Continental firm crashed with a loss of eight lives.

The craft had aboard as passengers Dr. A. W. Ward, a San Francisco dentist and Mr. W. E. Merz, of Mount Vernon, N.Y., and the others, members of the crew, were J. A Dole, of Los Angeles; A. A. Barrie, of Burbank, Cal., and R. L. Briten, also of Los Angeles. It took off from Alhambra, Cal., the California base, flying to Kingman, Ariz., where it left at 7.25 a.m. for Albuquerque. It should have reached here at 11.15, but last was seen soaring over Navajo, Ariz.

GRUNDY PROTESTS STATE INEQUALITY IN TARIFF FIXING

Areas Not Interested as Well Represented as Those That Are.

(By Special Cable to The Herald.)

WASHINGTON, Tuesday.—Joseph R. Grundy, representative of the American Tariff League in Washington and president of the Pennsylvania Manufacturers' Association, resumed the stand at today's lobby hearing, and told the Senate investigating committee that the "tragedy" of tariff legislation resulted from the unequal representation of the States most vitally interested in it.

He complained that the States contributing negligible amounts in Federal taxes "and with no chips in the game" had as much vote in fixing tariff rates as the States which contributed many times as much money.

He rated Georgia, Nebraska, Louisiana, Oklahoma, Kansas, and South Carolina as backward States, and defended the election expenditures in his own State because of its large population.

Grundy admitted conferring with Chester Gray, of the Farm Bureau Federation over farm rates, but denied that he had conferred with Mathew Woll, of the American Federation of Labor, or that he had formed an alliance with the latter for protective legislation. He will be called again tomorrow.

Further discussion in the Senate on the part Senator Hiram Bingham is

FRANCE'S APPROVAL OF LEO J. KEENA AS U.S. CONSUL ASKED

Proposed Envoy to Paris Officially Named to Quai d'Orsay.

Request for the recognition of Leo John Keena as American Consul-General in Paris was made yesterday to the French Government, it was announced by the Embassy here. Mr.

BRIAND MAY BE ASKED TO HEAD NEW MINISTRY

Daladier Declines to Make Another Attempt Today, After Conflicting Reports of Renouncing the Task.

TO SEE DOUMERGUE THIS MORNING

Socialist National Council Refuses Support of Projected Cabinet by a Vote of 1590 to 1451.

BULLETIN.

It is believed that, following M. Daladier's failure, M. Briand will be called upon to form the new Cabinet. He will ask M. Daladier's Socialist-Radical party for its support. The request is not expected to be immediately affirmative.

At the end of the first week of the French political crisis the solution seems to be as far off as it was the first day. At 9 o'clock this morning M. Edouard Daladier, Socialist-Radical leader, will go to the Elysée to inform the President of the Republic that he renounces the mission entrusted to him to form a Cabinet.

This decision was announced by M. Daladier himself at his father-in-law's home in the avenue des Champs-Elysées, at 1 o'clock this morning to a group of bewildered newspaper men, who had been informed from sure sources at 7.30 p.m. that the Socialist-Radical leader had abandoned his task, and shortly before midnight that this was all a mistake: that he would have the list of Cabinet Ministers ready early this afternoon at the latest.

Never in the history of French Cabinet-making, fantastic as that operation has ofteen been, has such confusion reigned in the shifting and reshifting of party and group declarations and line-ups.

Extra editions of the evening newspapers were published last night with big headlines announcing that M. Da-

(Continued on Page Four.)

LABOR OPPONENTS BEGIN ATTACK AS PARLIAMENT OPENS

Unemployment Hit Upon by Foes While Foreign Affairs Are Ignored.

(From the Herald and Herald Tribune Bureau)

LONDON, Tuesday.—From the moment the autumn session of Parliament opened today the hammering of the Opposition began in Commons. Opportunists chose unemployment and related problems as a possible weak spot in the Labor Party's armor, and every phase of Britain's domestic ills, from jobs for the unemployed to miners' working hours, were brought up during a spirited first day's sitting.

Mr. Philip Snowden the Chancellor of the Exchequer, who acted as Prime Minister in the absence of Mr. MacDonald, promised an early report on most of them.

Meanwhile, the Labor Government's record in foreign affairs, where developments have been more spectacular, was momentarily neglected. Even the Prime Minister's recent visit to Washington and the forthcoming five-Power [illegible]sing no- [illegible] ent House [illegible] nemploy- [illegible] H. Tho- [illegible] present [illegible] the in- [illegible] eal, is to [illegible] ifficulties, [illegible] of most [illegible] re levelled [illegible] all with [illegible] an op- [illegible] xt week. [illegible] xplained, [illegible] honorable [illegible] rec)

[illegible]S [illegible] DEATH

[illegible] Informed [illegible] her husband [illegible] theatre [illegible] aulting a [illegible] ife, Mrs. [illegible] and is [illegible] She was [illegible] killing a [illegible] motor- [illegible] m and is [illegible]'s prison

[illegible]S FOR [illegible] PLANE

[illegible] earch for [illegible] of seven [illegible] ail plane [illegible] inued by [illegible] Besides [illegible] pher, and [illegible] will be [illegible] eral ser- [illegible] buried in

SATURDAY, NOVEMBER 2, 1929

Wall Street at the Height of Last Week's Crash

An unusual photograph showing the crowds before the Stock Exchange in New York at the height of the scramble in which thousands of fortunes (many simply on paper) were wiped out within a few minutes. The throngs on the left, having no means of admittance to the trading room, are simply waiting for relayed news that occasionally trickled across the street.

16,419,000 Shares Turned Over And Billions in Values Lost As Market Breaks Third Time

All Records Fall and Optimism Engendered by Bankers' Report Collapses; First Failure Comes; Exchanges All Over Nation Hit; Slight Recovery at End.

(By Special Cable to The Herald.)

NEW YORK, Tuesday.—In a day replete with bankers' meetings, conferences of Stock Exchange officials, meetings of brokers and publication of opinions from high and low in the world of finance, business and all else, stock prices broke to new low levels in a volume of trading far in excess of anything hitherto seen.

In five hours' trading, 16,419,000 shares changed hands, in comparison with 12,894,600 which made the previous record day last Thursday. Sales on the Curb market added another 7,096,300 shares to the day's total.

Today came the first failure of the present reaction. It was insignificant compared with the failures during the panics of the past, but it was seized upon by a hysterical public as an occasion for fresh worry. The failure was that of the firm of John J. Bell and Company, members of the Curb Exchange, whose officials announced its suspension through inability to meet its engagements. Its obligations, it was said, were small.

Today's transaction broke all records, even those established in Thursday's collapse. The first three and a half hours saw 12,652,000 shares change hands, or within 250,000 of the record for a full five-hour session, established during Thursday's debacle.

Total sales for the day were 16,419,000 shares.

The new drive today set at naught all optimistic feeling engendered last night by the report that the banking group which acted to prevent a complete panic on Thursday would again take action to help in bolstering prices. It had been explained that the function of this pool was not to save any of the day's profits, but to prevent the decline from getting out of hand.

Today, however, huge blocks of shares were thrown on the market at the opening and prices were quickly hammered down from these lower openings.

Violence Brings Relief.

The very violence of today's liquidation brought some relief by mid-afternoon. Under the combined influence of buying by the banking consortium, investment trusts and strong interests, the market steadied appreciably.

Such rallying as occurred, however, seemed to be based on internal conditions rather than on external support. While price declines were continuous from the opening until mid-afternoon, trading was handled with less confusion than on some recent days and bids were available at all times.

All sorts of rumors were again in circulation among traders. It was said that huge bull operators had been forced to the wall and that some of the more newly-formed investment trusts were being forced to unload. Both these rumors were occasioned by the fact that shares were offered in huge blocks and prices again crumbled as rapidly as on any previous day since the crash started.

Weak Rallies Made.

It was about noon before the effect of buying by those still possessing ample credit began to stem the tide and start half-hearted rallies. These made no great headway, but it was a relief to those watching prices on the news tickers to find stocks headed upward, if only a little way and grudgingly.

From serious and important sources came statements declaring that the bottom was reached this morning, and that an upturn was certain. From the State Superintendent of Insurance, Albert Conway, came the advice to insurance companies to buy common stocks, as the present prices made them an excellent investment. Several investment trusts with large resources announced themselves buyers of shares.

The Comptroller of New York City announced that "owing to the most demoralized condition of the Stock Exchange ever seen," bankers had suggested that it would be a "patriotic action" to postpone for a time the offering of $60,000,000 of the city's corporate shares scheduled to be made

(Continued on Page Three.)

For full market reports see Pages 10, 11 and 12.

12 Principal Declines On N. Y. Stock Exchange

	High for Year.	Yesterday's Closing.	Difference.
Gen. Motors.	91 3/4	40	51 3/4
Radio Corp.	114 3/4	38 1/2	76 1/4
Ana. Copper	174 7/8	85	89 7/8
Allegh. Corp.	56 1/2	20 5/8	35 7/8
Com. Solv., n.	63	20 5/8	35 7/8
Inter. Nickel	72 3/4	30	42 3/4
U.S. Steel...	261 3/4	174	87 3/4
Mtgy. Ward.	156 7/8	53 3/4	103 1/8
Unit. Corp...	75 1/2	25 3/4	49 3/4
Chrysler C.	135	35	100
Gen. Elect.	403	222	181
I. T. & T...	119 1/4	61	88 1/4

FUNDAMENTALIST DIES

DR. JOHN ROACH STRATON

DR. STRATON DIES OF HEART DISEASE IN SANATORIUM

Fiery N.Y. Fundamentalist Noted for Battle on Vice.

(By United Press.)

NEW YORK, Tuesday.—The Reverend John Roach Straton, famous Fundamentalist pastor of Calvary Baptist Church here, died today at Clifton Springs, N.Y., according to an announcement issued from the minister's local residence here. Death was due to heart disease.

For years, the stormy petrel of the Baptist Church of America, Dr. Straton made himself famous as the self-styled "enemy of Satan" and as a vigorous, colorful and militant crusader against vice, liquor, cabarets, atheism, evolution and Alfred E. Smith, whom, during the last Presidential campaign, he termed the "deadliest foe in America today of the forces of moral progress and true political wisdom."

Platform Debater.

He debated on platforms from one end of the country to the other with opponents of his doctrines—a tall white-haired, leather-lunged man with an expansive smile, which in no wise meant lenity for those who thought counter to his ideals.

After Dr. Straton made his charges against former Governor Smith, the latter roused himself and challenged the pastor to meet him in debate on the subject in Calvary Baptist Church, just as the Presidential campaign was gaining momentum last fall. Dr. Straton stated he was willing to meet Mr.

(Continued on Page Four.)

James Ricalton, Traveller, Is Dead

(By Special Cable to The Herald.)

NEW YORK, Tuesday. — James Ricalton, writer, war correspondent, globe-trotter and photographer, died in his home in Waddington, N.Y., today. He had wandered in every country in the world and his collection of photographs numbered more than 100,000. It was Mr. Ricalton who combed jungles of the Orient in 1888 for specimens of bamboo, which might serve as filament in Thomas A. Edison's new-fangled incandescent lamp.

TE DEUM CELEBRATED ON QUEEN'S BIRTHDAY

BUCHAREST, Tuesday. — A Te Deum was sung in honor of Queen Marie's fifty-fourth birthday in Bucharest Cathedral today. A Cabinet deputation visited the Queen in Balczyk and extended the Government's congratulations.

STOCK EXCHANGE DECIDES AGAINST ACTING IN CRASH

Lamont Announces After Parley That Bankers Do Not 'Unload.'

(By Special Cable to The Herald.)

NEW YORK, Tuesday.—The Governor's Committee of the Stock Exchange, after considering the situation at some length today, late tonight issued the following statement:

"The committee carefully considered the present situation, but failed to find that any action was necessary, consequently adjourning until the regular meeting tomorrow."

Following the Governors' meeting, Mr. Thomas W. Lamont, in a statement to the Press, reiterated that the bankers are co-operating to stabilize the market as a group, but that no effort was being made to stop the decline abortively. He added that individual bankers were not "unloading" themselves, as has been hinted.

WALL ST. COLLAPSE SENDS PRICES DOWN ON EXCHANGES HERE

European Industrials Suffer by Liquidation of U.S. Holdings.

The collapse of the Wall Street stock market had a depressing influence on the leading European stock exchanges yesterday. This was felt in varying degrees and for various reasons, the most seriously affected being Amsterdam. On all European bourses American stocks followed closely the Wall Street trend, while Anglo-American and Canadian stocks quoted in Capel Court were big losers on the day.

On the Paris and Berlin bourses the leading French and German industrials were marked down appreciably, owing to heavy liquidation by American holders. For some time American capital has been increasingly engaged in European industrial investment, but

(Continued on Page Three.)

FALL FROM ROOF KILLS CIGAR HEAD

(By Special Cable to The Herald.)

NEW YORK, Tuesday. — Anthony Snyder, president of the Union Cigar Company and Webster E. Eisenlohr, the stock of which latter concern fell from its year's high of 113 3/8 to 4 at yesterday's closing, plunged five stories to his death from the roof of a Lexington avenue apartment building to that of an adjoining theatre today.

Snyder, who was 60 years old and unmarried, is said to have lost his balance while repairing a radio aerial.

45th Metropolitan Opera Season Begins with Customary Brilliance

(By Special Cable to The Herald.)

NEW YORK, Tuesday.—The forty-fifth regular season of the Metropolitan Opera and the twenty-second under the management of Giulio Gatti-Casazza opened brilliantly last night with Lucrezia Bori in the title rôle of "Manon Lescaut," supported by Giuseppe De Luca and Beniamino Gigli.

Ever since the establishment of grand opera in New York its first subscription night has been looked upon as a forerunner of the fashionable season.

The audience which gathered at the Metropolitan last night was quite up to expectation, a brilliant company filling the double row of boxes and orchestra seats, and no vacancies appearing anywhere.

All reserve seats were sold out days in advance. The line for the family circle began at 4.30 yesterday afternoon and finally at 7.45 the first 400 waiting music lovers were admitted. The others were turned away.

Among the boxholders and their guests were: Mr. Robert Goelet, who had as his guests Mrs. R. T. Wilson, Mr. Ogden Goelet, Miss Marian M. Wilson and Justice and Mrs. Norman S. Dike; Brigadier-General and Mrs Cornelius Vanderbilt, whose guests

(Continued on Page Three.)

PARIS AMUSEMENTS

CINEMAS. CINEMAS.

GAUMONT-LOEW-METRO THEATRES

CINEMA MADELEINE

Ventilated by Carrier Engineering system

buster keaton in spite marriage

METRO-GOLDWYN-MAYER
TITLES IN FRENCH AND ENGLISH
2.45 "THE REVELLERS" and Fox Movietone News 9 p.m.

GAUMONT PALACE

GAUMONT-FRANCO-FILM MANAGEMENT

MAURICE CHEVALIER

IN HIS FIRST TALKIE FILM

LA CHANSON DE PARIS

MATINEE EVERY WEEKDAY AT 2.45.
Next Sunday, two different matinees: at 2 and at 4.45)
Every Evening at 8.45.
Seats can be reserved for any evening and for the 2 Sunday matinees

---

TODAY at the CINE
Max Linder-Pathé
First Grand Guignol Cinematographic Show

GARDIENS DE PHARE

Scenario by J. FEYDER
Staged by Jean GREMILLON

AUBERT PALACE

24 boulevard des Italiens 24

AL JOLSON

In a Talking Film (Vitaphone)

"THE JAZZ SINGER"

ENGLISH & FRENCH SUB-TITLES.

CLICHY-PALACE

49 avenue de Clichy 49
THE ONLY ENGLISH TALKIE IN PARIS
VITAPHONE

WEARY RIVER

with
Richard BARTHELMESS
and Betty COMPSON
Continuous from 2 to 7. Evening 8.45.

STUDIO DES AGRICULTEURS

8 rue d'Athènes. Tel.: Louvre 49-49.
ONLY PICTURES OF HIGH ARTISTIC VALUE. CONSULT THE DAILY CINEMA COLUMN FOR OUR PROGRAMS.

FIRST CONCERT
SERGE

KOUSSEVITZKY

Tomorrow, May 21, at 1.30 o'clock, at the THEATRE DES
Champs-Élysées

Paramount

Eric von Stroheim

see hear
The Wedding march
Paramount's Master-Sound film
Doors open at 11 a.m.
The best show in town

Coming soon
Metro Goldwyn Mayer

THE BROADWAY MELODY

CINEMA MADELEINE

ANNOUNCEMENTS. ANNOUNCEMENTS. ANNOUNCEMENTS.

THE NORTH AFRICAN MOTOR TOURS

Organised by the French Line
(Compagnie Générale Transatlantique)
Link Up
ALGERIA - TUNISIA - MOROCCO and the DESERT
(French)

Now is the Ideal Season to Visit NORTH AFRICA
The land of Romance and Magic Dreams with its striking contrasts and perpetual sunshine. —
"It Is Summer There"

THEIR INCLUSIVE TICKET carries you through this wonderful country under ideal conditions, after a SHORT STEAMER CROSSING.

UP-TO-DATE MOTOR-CAR SERVICES by Luxurious Renault Cars with "Pullman" seats, or torpedo, or Limousine Cars, on excellent roads.

UP-TO-DATE HOTELS: 31 "Transatlantique" Hotels with modern conveniences.

CROSSING THE DESERT between Touggourt and Tozeur by special Renault cars with six-Twin wheels.

There are no unforeseen expenses "en route"—every detail is arranged before departure by the same organisation. Specially organised Baggage Service.

ONLY THE NORTH AFRICAN MOTOR TOUR "ALL INCLUSIVE TICKET" of the Cie. Gle. Transatlantique gives you the assurance that you will find your rooms awaiting you on your a[illegible] the Transatlantique Hotels even during the height of the season.

For information, write to the Sté. [illegible] VOYAGES et HOTELS NORD-AFRICAINS, 6bis r. Auber, or call at the new Arab Salon at the

French Line

COMPAGNIE GÉNÉRALE TRANSATLANTIQUE
RUE AUBER (First Floor) PARIS.

LONDON S.W.1: 22, Pall Mall. [illegible]: 125, Via del Tritone. BIARRITZ: 17 Place de la Mairie. NICE: 12, Avenue de Verdun.
NEW YORK: 19, State Street. [illegible]: 29, rue Adolphe-Max. STRASBOURG: 19, r. de la Nuée-Bleue
or COMPAGNIE FRANÇAISE [illegible], 30 boulevard des Capucines, PARIS, or COMPAGNIE INTERNATIONALE DES WAGONS-LITS

It Is This Evening

AT

FLORIDA

20 RUE DE CLICHY
DURING THE GREAT REOPENING GALA
THAT

MAURICE CHEVALIER

WILL SING FOR THE LAST TIME
— BEFORE HIS DEPARTURE —
FOR THE BENEFIT
of the AMIS DE PONT-AUX-DAMES
(Founded by O. Dufrenne)
and of the Home for Former Stage Folk at Ris-Orangis.
RESERVE YOUR TABLE: GUT. 23-38.

THE ONLY NIGHT CLUB IN THE WORLD WITH ICED AIR

SHEHERAZADE

EVERY NIGHT
2000 CUBIC METRES OF ICED AIR
3 rue de Liége. Tel.: Gutenberg 16-72.

EXCLUSIVE SHOWING

MADELEINE CINEMA

Direction
GAUMONT-LOEW-METRO

STARTING TO-MORROW, MATINEE
BIG DOUBLE PROGRAM

GLORIA SWANSON

IN

"STAGE STRUCK"

And Big Added Feature

"GRASS"

The story of a forgotten race!
Titles in French and English
MATINEE: Continuous 2 to 7.45
EVENING, 8.45 (all seats reserved without extra charge). Louvre 36-78.

EXCLUSIVE SHOWING

GAUMONT PALACE

Direction
GAUMONT-LOEW-METRO

ENTIRE CHANGE of PROGRAM TO-MORROW

MARION DAVIES

in the Metro-Goldwyn Film

"Janice Meredith"

.......Big Vaudeville Acts.......
Fosse and his 50 Music Masters
Arthur Flagel at the Wonder Organ
2.30 — TWO SHOWS DAILY — 8.30

1930-1940

The move by the *Paris Herald* into its new headquarters late in 1930 coincided with an important innovation in its distribution system: the paper would now be delivered regularly by air to ten cities in England, Germany, Holland, Austria and France. But this advance was offset by the damaging effects of the economic climate.

The Great Depression was to reshape the life of the *Herald* in the 1930s, cutting steadily into the size and affluence of both its audience and its advertising base. Salaries, never very generous, were now even less adequate, and staff turnover increased.

But if the *Paris Herald* was crippled by the Depression, the rival *Chicago Tribune*'s Paris Edition was destroyed. In 1934, the *Herald*'s singular position was consolidated when its owners bought out the competition for the sum of $50,000. For a brief period in 1935 the resulting newspaper carried the logo "The New York Herald with the Chicago Tribune," before finally taking on the name it was to bear for thirty years, "The New York Herald Tribune, European Edition."

With the new name came another addition to the nameplate which is still in place more than fifty years later, the drawing known as "the dingbat"—first introduced to the front page of Horace Greeley's *New York Tribune* on its 25th anniversary in 1866. Dominated by a clock whose hands are mysteriously set at 6:12 (some think that was the time of Greeley's birth), it shows both the past and the future stretching away at each side of the clockface, symbolizing the newspaper's mission to capture history on the run.

One veteran journalist who would claim, even four decades later, to be the paper's oldest alumnus because of his earlier service on the *Chicago Tribune* was Waverley Root, who would write off and on for the *Herald Tribune* on subjects as varied as the history of food and the European political scene until his death in 1981. Young journalists such as Eric Sevareid and William Shirer, come to witness at close hand the agitation that would soon again turn Europe upsidedown, crossed paths on the *Herald Tribune* staff.

The news in this fourth decade of the century reflected the political and economic turbulence caused by the confrontation of the old systems with new, or newly clothed, philosophies. A related development which mounted in intensity as the decade neared its end was the growing plight of refugees. Nazis, fascists, communists, socialists, republicans and royalists battled their way across the front pages of the 1930s, and these struggles were sometimes reflected in the corridors of the *Herald Tribune* itself. For example, the paper's editorial stand against fascism was not easily arrived at, despite the vigorous anti-fascist position of its New York parent. Increasingly dependent on advertising from Germany and Italy, the paper under Laurence Hills adopted an editorial position in which criticism of those governments was distinctly muted; occasional words of understanding were even known to creep in. But at the same time, Ralph Barnes and other strongly anti-fascist journalists filled the news pages with detailed coverage of the events in Spain, Germany, Italy, Ethiopia and Eastern Europe.

In 1939, Hills, now in ill health, sharply changed his views on the dangers of fascism and in front-page editorials recanted his earlier positions. Back in New York, the Reids, who had largely let the paper go its own way, were persuaded to take more direct control of Paris editorial policy, a control that was to tighten further when they reopened the European edition after the Allied liberation of Paris in 1944.

One of the most dramatic indicators that the thirties would be no repeat of the twenties was the abdication in 1936 of Edward VIII of England, formerly the Prince of Wales. The fox-trotting, trend-setting bachelor of the first postwar decade had become a sad-eyed middle-aged man by the time he gave up his throne after less than a year to marry a twice-divorced American. But the public wanted strength and tradition, rather than romance, in these menacing times, so the Duke and Duchess of Windsor moved off center stage, trailed by a gaggle of society reporters.

There were still heroes, however, among them Amelia Earhart, the first woman to fly the Atlantic. Her disappearance in the South Pacific on an attempted flight around the world gripped public attention in the summer of 1937.

From spring 1938, when Hitler declared Austria to be part of Germany, to the arrival of the German armies in Paris in June 1940, the news columns of the *Paris Herald* reflect an increasing dismay. The opening days of World War I had been faced with a certain detachment, born of the expectation that reason would reassert itself and that the struggle would be short. But "We'll be home by Christmas," the catchphrase of the soldiers of September 1914, had turned out to be a sad and fatal joke. Now, twenty years after the end of that war, such hopes were not even entertained.

It was a period when keeping one's sense of humor could be difficult. Nine-year-old movie star Shirley Temple sued writer Graham Greene in 1939 for what the judge in the case characterized as "a gross outrage." It appears that Mr. Greene, in reviewing the latest Temple movie *Wee Willie Winkie*, expressed doubts as to whether the star was still as young as advertised and mentioned also that the manner of her acting left him unconvinced of her entire sexual innocence. Miss Temple won a $10,000 judgment (turned over to charity, of course).

Many shadows darkened the end of the decade, but one event pointed to a more hopeful future: the New York World's Fair of 1939. Erected over a tidal swamp, its declared purpose was Building the World of Tomorrow—a peaceful world, where technological ingenuity would once again be in the service of beneficent progress.

But the events of Munich, the occupation of Madrid by Franco's armies, and the Soviet-German non-aggression pact of 1939 brought only a greater sense of menace.

On Sunday, June 9, 1940, a massive exodus from Paris began as German armies poured into France and moved on the capital. Mindful of Bennett's stirring decision in 1914 to keep the paper in place, the *Herald Tribune* again held on, continuing to publish with whatever resources it could muster even after other papers had left. But its owner Ogden Reid also knew that objectivity and independence would be impossible under Nazi occupation and when that occupation became inevitable, the decision was made to close. The last issue—a single sheet published on June 12, 1940—carried the front-page headline, "Great Battle for Paris Reaches Crucial Stage." The back of the sheet displayed a few advertisements; the rest was blank. There had been no time to set the page—and perhaps there really was nothing more to say.

On June 14 the Germans occupied Paris. The European Edition fell silent for 4½ years.

SUNDAY, NOVEMBER 30, 1930

READY FOR OCCUPANCY

"H" construction. Maximum of light and air. EVERY window faces "outside"

"AMERICAN" SERVICE Night and day elevators. Ownership management.

EUROPE'S MOST MODERN OFFICES

THE NEW YORK HERALD Building

21, Rue de Berri, Paris
(just off the Champs-Elysées)

Still for lease - a limited amount of desirable office space on upper floors

5 th Floor - Front Half of Floor 1,230 square feet
(For sub-lease by The H.K. McCann Corporation)

5 th Floor	- Rear.	1,675 square feet
6 th Floor	- Rear.	753 square feet
7 th Floor	- Front.	210 square feet
» »	Rear.	895 square feet

Penthouse - Overlooking Paris. 432 square feet

A chance to locate your business or profession at the heart of American activities in Europe. The first four floors will house the Paris Edition of The New York Herald. Other tenants include The H. K. McCann Corporation, a leading American advertising agency, The National Automobile Chamber of Commerce, and Harold L. Smith, representing The Motion Picture Producers and Distributors of America, Inc. Write, or apply on the premises to The Business Manager, The New York Herald, 21, rue de Berri, Paris, 8e - Telephone Elysées 12-88 or Elysées 03-57.

H.P. Job. 14

THE NEW YORK HERALD

IS EUROPE'S COMPLETE AMERICAN NEWSPAPER

■

BECAUSE IT HAS

United Press Service
Special Correspondents
Walter Lippmann
American Stock Prices
Continental Markets
Commodity Prices
Local News
Culbertson on Bridge
Society News
Latin Quarter Notes
Cinema and Theatre Reviews
Views on Fashions
Art Criticism
'Sparrow Robertson
'Mr. and Mrs.' Cartoons
Resort News
Readers' 'Mailbag'
Cartoons by Webster
London Social Notes
Gourmet's Food Hints
Cartoons by "Ding"

■

THE NEW YORK HERALD

Has by far the largest sale of any American newspaper published in Europe

FINAL EDITION: 11 A.M.

TODAY'S WEATHER REPORT
Milder, cloudy, some rain.
Temperature yesterday: Max. 10 (50 Fahr.), min. 2 (36 Fahr.).
Wind: SE., light.
Channel crossings: Slight.

THE NEW YORK HERALD

EUROPEAN EDITION OF THE NEW YORK HERALD TRIBUNE

EXCHANGE RATES (CABLES)
Dollar in Paris - - - - 25fr. 48c.
Dollar in London - - - - 6s. 01/2d.
Dollar in Berlin - - - 4m. 21 1/4pf.
Dollar in Rome - - - - 19 lire 55c.
Pound in Paris - - - - - 84fr. 19c.

46th YEAR. No. 16,475. Business and Editorial Offices: 21 RUE DE BERRI Tel.: Elysées 12-87, 12-88, 12-90, 26-65, 03-37. *** PARIS, WEDNESDAY, NOVEMBER 9, 1932 Branch Office and Information Bureau: 49 AVENUE DE L'OPERA Tel.: Gutenberg 04-... PRICE: In France, One Franc.

Roosevelt Sweeps Nation in Record Election; Democrats Rout G.O.P. in Forty-four States

Win Congress; Moses, Smoot, Watson, Bingham Fall

Other Titans Ousted; 77 Seats in House, 18 in Senate Gained

Watson, Jones and Glenn Heavy Losers in Election; M'Adoo Winner; Wagner Is Re-elected in New York.

MRS. CARAWAY WINS; FIRST WOMAN ELECTED

Democrats Are Leading in 19 Congressional Districts; More Senate Seats Seen.

(By United Press)

WASHINGTON, Wednesday.—The crushing defeat administered to Republicans by the Democrats in yesterday's congressional elections, assures President-Elect Roosevelt a substantial working majority in both the House and Senate of the 73rd Congress, which comes into power on next March 4.

At 3 a.m. the Democrats were definitely conceded 77 seats in the new House and the Republicans 24. The Democrats were leading in 19 congressional contests and the Republicans in nine.

With Senator James E. Watson, Republican floor leader, definitely eliminated from the race in Indiana and with Senator George Moses, one of the pillars of Republican strength, defeated in New Hampshire, the Democrats had captured 18 Senate seats with returns still incomplete from 11 states at an early hour this morning

Smoot Defeated.

Another Republican upset came in Utah, where Senator Reed Smoot, chairman of the Senate finance committee, conceded defeat early this morning. Senator Hiram Bingham, of Connecticut, also lost to his wet opponent, Augustine Lonergan.

In Washington, Senator Wesley Jones, chairman of the Senate appropriations committee and author of the famous "five and ten" act, imposing severe penalties for infraction of prohibition laws, lost his seat to Homer T. Bone, Democrat.

Senator Otis F. Glenn was beaten in the Democratic landslide in Illinois.

The odds favor Democrats in close senatorial contests in Colorado, Idaho, Kansas, Nevada and Oregon, but Senator James L. Davis is running ahead in Pennsylvania and Senator Gerald P. Nye in North Dakota.

In California William Gibbs McAdoo, Democratic nominee, who served as secretary of the treasury in President Wilson's cabinet, won his contest with Tallant Tubbs, San Francisco anti-prohibitionist, who defeated Senator Shortridge, incumbent, in the Republican primaries.

Senator Watson went down to defeat in the Democratic landslide which swept Indiana yesterday and his opponent, Frederick Van Nuys, was pushed into the Senate seat he has held for the last decade.

Senator Watson, a high protectionist, was elected to the House of Representatives in 1894, and since that time, with few interruptions, has served either in the House or Senate.

Moses Also Loses.

He has had a large voice in Republican national councils for more than a quarter of a century and his defeat is taken as indicative of a public drift away from the old leaders.

One of the worst defeats suffered by the Republicans was in New Hampshire, where Senator George Moses, coiner of the phrase "Sons of Wild Jackasses," with which he characterized insurgent legislators, lost his seat to Fred H. Brown.

One of the few Republican senatorial victories was won by Frederick Steiwer in Oregon. In Colorado Alva B. Adams, Democrat, won the long term and Walter Walker, Democrat, the short term election

In addition to taking control of the Senate for the short term session, the Democrats are also expected to muster a substantial majority in the short term beginning in December through victories in contests for unexpired terms.

In Connecticut, a hitherto Republican stronghold, Augustine Lonergan, Democratic nominee, was leading Senator Bingham, staunch administration supporter, who has held his seat in

(Continued on Page 2, Col. 4.)

Hoover Congratulates Governor in Telegram

(By United Press.)

PALO ALTO, Tuesday. — Shortly after conceding Governor Roosevelt's election tonight, Herbert Hoover sent the President-elect the following telegram:—

"I congratulate you on the opportunity that comes to you to be of service to the country and I wish you a most successful administration. In the common purpose of us all, I shall dedicate myself to every possible effort."

Afterwards the President went to the seclusion of a room on the upper floor of his home.

VOTE 'TIDAL WAVE' FOR CHANGE, SAYS HERALD TRIBUNE

(By Special Cable to The Herald.)

NEW YORK, Wednesday. — Under the caption "A Tidal Wave" the New York Herald Tribune in an editorial this morning says:—

"What swept the country yesterday was no ordinary ebb and flow of partisanship. Here was a tidal wave of popular emotion demanding a change. Beneath its flood familiar landmarks of party lines vanished.

"Matters which normally decide elections, the merits of candidates, debates of policies and allegiance to party were forgotten in a very real sense.

"The country yesterday experienced the final upheaval from the World war. What is recorded as a blind protest against the forces of destruction defies analysis. There is no simple remedy for it save time.

"Our judgment is that yesterday's verdict was a gross injustice to an able President and this history will not be slow to uphold.

"But none can remonstrate with a cataclysm. Plainly the Republican case was hopeless from the start. The depression was the major cause of the result yet we think prohibition must be ranked as a contributing cause with some of the dryest spots in the Union going to Roosevelt.

"The folly of placing any reliance in the dry vote cannot be missed. The truth is that in respect to this vital issue President Hoover lagged months behind the sentiment of the nation.

"A difficult four months lie ahead. The more co-operation between parties

(Continued on Page 2, Col. 4.)

ONE KILLED IN JAIL BREAK

(By United Press.)

CUCUTA, Colombia, Tuesday.—A policeman was killed today when a group of prisoners in the local jail staged a break. Two guards were gravely wounded and one of the prisoners was seriously injured when he closed a door to prevent his companions from escaping.

LIPPMANN CALLS VICTOR A 'MESSIAH'

(By Wireless to The Herald.)

NEW YORK, Tuesday.—In a nationwide broadcast tonight, Walter Lippmann, political commentator of the New York Herald Tribune, expressed great satisfaction in the victory of the Democratic party.

He said Governor Roosevelt was fortunate indeed and was the bringer of a new solution for the problems the country faced. He also called him a political Messiah, speaking of the nationwide significance today of the change of parties.

Mr. Lippmann said that all nations had been engrossed in a commercial war, and that all had been living in fear of a military war.

Hoover's friends tonight, he asserted, are more numerous than the number of voters who went to the polls for him. For 12 weeks, said Mr. Lippmann, the President had fought for his administration and the people, he warned, should not interpret the verdict as a complete denial of Mr. Hoover and his policy.

LEHMAN VICTOR; O'BRIEN POLLS BIG CITY VOTE

Gubernatorial Candidate Is Conceded the Election; Tammany's Mayor Choice Beats Even Walker Mark.

M'KEE'S SUPPORTERS COME OUT IN FORCE

Hillquit, Socialist, Piles Up 230,918 Votes in Surprise; N.Y. Has Biggest Election.

(By United Press.)

NEW YORK, Wednesday.—With Colonel William (Wild Bill) Donovan, Republican, conceding the gubernatorial victory to Lieutenant-Governor Herbert H. Lehman and Surrogate Judge John P. O'Brien placed in City Hall here by Tammany with a total of 1,055,786 votes against Republican Lewis H. Pounds' 439,032, New York is sleeping off the biggest election in memory.

Donovan conceded the victory late yesterday when upstate returns showed Lehman was leading him by about 76,000 to 40,000.

A citywide testimonial to Acting-Mayor Joseph V. McKee and coincidentally a stinging rebuke to Tammany Hall was recorded in the municipal balloting.

Beats Walker Poll.

The staggering majority rolled up by O'Brien mocks the election in 1929 of "Jimmy" Walker, who polled 865,522 against the 367,675 of Fiorello La Guardia.

The present total votes cast, as far as is known, are 1,791,428. Powerful and irresistible as the Tammany machine is, returns still rolling in show the citywide extent of indignation over the manner McKee was shelved.

The pencilled votes for the unnominated official so far total 65,692 and only one-third of the precincts have been counted.

Another surprise was the indicated growth of Socialism in municipal politics. Morris Hillquit polled 230,918 votes whereas Norman Thomas, mayoralty candidate in 1929, drew only 175,697. Unemployment is considered responsible for the growing adherence to liberal doctrines.

Total Vote Record.

The total vote in 1929 was 1,408,894, or 316,842 less that the number so far recorded today. Since 2,300,000 were registered this year it is believed the last election figure will be further dwarfed.

It is estimated that 20 per cent of the voters wrote in the name of McKee as a protest against his being shelved in favor of Judge O'Brien.

The automatic voting machines used here are equipped with a slide under which is a slip of blank paper for the names of persons not included among the regular nominees. The delay and

(Continued on Page 5, Col. 6.)

Death Blow Is Struck to Prohibition Law; Greatest Triumph in Democratic History Assures Governor of 472 Electoral Votes

Thirty-Second President

FRANKLIN DELANO ROOSEVELT

Wet Deluge Floods Oases Of Prohibition in Upsets

(By Special Cable to The Herald.)

NEW YORK, Tuesday.—The dryest spots in the Volsteadian sahara have gone dripping wet!

The manner in which Rooseveltian sentiment crashed through Republican strongholds, according to observers, shows a veritable tidal wave of anti-prohibition opinion.

Wet propositions won in Michigan, Colorado, Wyoming and New Jersey, while the trend indicates distinct humidity in Arizona, California, Louisiana, North Dakota, Oregon and Washington, although the outcome will not be definitely known until tomorrow.

Dry leaders tonight are stunned by returns, giving such bulwarks of their cause as Indiana, Nebraska, Montana and Iowa to Governor Roosevelt, the vote indicating full support of the Democratic plank for uncompromising modification of the prohibition laws.

Wet circles are gleeful.. This is not only a Democratic landslide, they say, but a Democratic downpour of light wines and beer.

In the Solid South, tolerance of prohibition has been gradually turning into resentment. Now, with nearly a dozen hide-bound Republican states voting Democratic, wet prophets foresee the repeal of the 18th amendment being effected with a rapidity exceeding their fondest dreams.

In the district of Representative John Q. Tilson, Connecticut, wets are hailing the outcome of the national mandate to repeal the dry law. They feel tonight there is an excellent chance of legal beer in the next session of Congress.

Not only has the nation endorsed a wet president, but it has returned a largely Democratic Congress with a platform which, observers say, admits of nothing but the immediate initiation of legislation legalizing beverages of considerable alcoholic content.

It will undoubtedly be argued that the repeal of prohibition is an economic necessity, extending even into the foreign policy.

The Electoral Vote
As Given by New York Herald Tribune

FOR ROOSEVELT

Alabama	11	Nebraska	7
Arizona	3	Nevada	3
Arkansas	9	New Jersey	16
California	22	New Mexico	3
Colorado	6	New York	47
Florida	7	North Carolina	13
Georgia	12	North Dakota	4
Idaho	4	Ohio	26
Illinois	29	Oklahoma	11
Indiana	14	Oregon	5
Iowa	11	Rhode Island	4
Kansas	9	South Carolina	8
Kentucky	11	South Dakota	4
Louisiana	10	Tennessee	11
Maryland	8	Texas	23
Massachusetts	17	Utah	4
Michigan	19	Virginia	11
Minnesota	11	Washington	8
Mississippi	9	West Virginia	8
Missouri	15	Wisconsin	12
Montana	4	Wyoming	3
TOTAL			472

FOR HOOVER

Delaware	3	New Hampshire	4
Connecticut	8	Pennsylvania	36
Maine	5	Vermont	3
TOTAL			59

SOCIALIST POLL NEARS MILLION

(By Special Cable to The Herald.)

NEW YORK, Tuesday. — Socialist sentiment in favor of Norman Thomas, third candidate for the presidency of the United States, promised to roll up a total of nearly 800.000, according to latest returns at hand tonight

A count of 153.811 votes, with only one-fifth of the full returns received, indicates the figure approximating a million. This will represent the greatest poll ever obtained by a Socialist candidate for the highest office in the land

Thomas was candidate for mayor of New York in 1929. In that race he received 175.000 votes. In 1928, as presidential candidate, he amassed 267.000, on complete returns.

Party Rides Into Full Control of Government, Dealing Republicans Unprecedented Defeat; Hoover Sure of Only 23 Ballots; Poll 10,162,000 to 7,060,000

(By Special Cable to The Herald)

NEW YORK, Wednesday.—In the greatest political upheaval that has ever shaken the nation, Franklin Delano Roosevelt, of Hyde Park, N.Y., has been swept into the presidency of the United States by an electoral college landslide unprecedented in the country's history.

The terrific onslaught of emotional discontent not only dealt the Republican party the most humiliating defeat it has ever suffered, but erased from political life some of the most prominent senators in the country and gave the Democratic party undisputed power of both the House and Senate with a wet majority that sounds the death knell of prohibition.

At 5 o'clock this morning (10.00 a.m. Paris time), Governor Roosevelt appeared certain of 472 electoral votes, a majority never achieved by any candidate since the days of Washington, while President Hoover, who four years ago had the confidence of the country in a then record vote, was sure of but 23.

EVEN PENNSYLVANIA WAVERS

Even Pennsylvania, the great bulwark of the Republican party, in late returns, was cracking under the Democratic attack, and the outcome is now in doubt. Should President Hoover finally succeed in carrying the state, his electoral total will reach 59.

While the electoral college defeat of the President is terrific, the popular vote plurality of President-Elect Roosevelt will not reach such triumphal proportions. The United Press tabulation of the vote at this hour gives Roosevelt 10,162,980 and President Hoover 7,060,755.

Roosevelt carried New York by more than 650,000 and plundered the Republican strongholds of Illinois by 220,000, by 200,000 in Indiana, 100,000 in Massachusetts, 150,000 in Nebraska, and 100,000 in Minnesota.

He also carried President Hoover's adopted state of California by two to one and his native state of Iowa by a narrower margin, but he failed to win his home town of Hyde Park. President Hoover carried Palo Alto, his present home, and West Branch, Ia., his birthplace.

At 9.30 p.m., Pacific Coast time, the President, after being pictured as being bitterly disappointed at the trend of the early returns, conceded Governor Roosevelt's election and sent him a telegram of congratulations. He later retired to the seclusion of a room on the upper floor and declined to mingle with his neighbors gathered to hear the returns.

Governor Roosevelt left his headquarters at the Hotel Biltmore for his Hyde Park home at 1.30 a.m., but declined to make any formal statement to the staff, whom he thanked, however, for their loyal support.

"The returns are still incomplete, hence I am not making any formal statement now," he said. "If the victory is as great as the returns indicate I hope the next four years all of us will do what we can to help the country return to prosperity."

The Democratic landslide also drove deep into dry territory with the indication that the 73rd Congress will be preponderantly wet. Propositions either to repeal state prohibition laws or amend them carried in Michigan, Colorado, Wyoming and New Jersey, while the trend indicated they would also carry in Arizona, California, Louisiana, North Dakota, Oregon and Washington.

G.O.P. Pillars Crushed.

The deep-seated resentment against the administration that carried Roosevelt into the White House laid low such outstanding and veteran Republican senators as George H. Moses, of New Hampshire; James E. Watson, of Indiana; Reed Smoot, of Utah; Wesley Jones, of Washington, and Otis Glenn, of Illinois.

The collapse of the Republican party after 12 years in office also swept out of office many prominent members of the House as well as voting into office a host of Democratic governors. Only a few Republican governors and senators were able successfully to withstand the Democratic onslaught.

The defeat suffered by the President is only equalled by the 1912 election, when the late President Roosevelt, running as a progressive, split the Republican ranks, and gave the election

SMITH HEADS LIST OF CABINET TIMBER

(By United Press.)

NEW YORK, Tuesday.—With Governor Roosevelt's election assured at an early hour tonight, speculation turned to the makeup of his cabinet, with the names of Alfred E. Smith, John W. Davis, former ambassador to England; Owen D. Young, Newton D. Baker, Wilson's secretary of war, and James A. Farley, Democratic national chairman, all prominent among the possibilities.

It is possible that for the first time in history a woman may enter the cabinet, as Governor Roosevelt is understood to favor Miss Frances Perkins, present industrial commissioner of New York, for secretary of labor.

John W. Davis is prominently mentioned for secretary of state, but Norman Davis who virtually has been President Hoover's ambassador in Europe on disarmament and economic affairs although a staunch Democrat, is also considered as a possibility.

Others mentioned are: Frank Polk, Bernard Baruch, New York banker; John Cohen, publisher of the Atlanta "Journal," and Senator George W. Norris.

$1,000,000 ART LOST IN LONG ISLAND FIRE

(By Special Cable to The Herald.)

NEW YORK, Wednesday.—Fire early this morning destroyed Martin Hall, 42-room Georgian mansion of Preston P. Satterwhite at King's Point, L.I., causing damage of more than $1.000.000.

A precious collection of Italian furniture, paintings, tapestries and a pipe organ were destroyed. Only a shell of the building remains.

TUESDAY, JANUARY 31, 1933

Hitler Named Reich Chancellor; Papen, Hugenberg Join Cabinet; Daladier Forming Ministry Here

Premier's Bid Turned Down By Socialists

Declaring that he had decided to form a cabinet without the Socialists, Edouard Daladier, the French premier-designate, at 1 o'clock this morning announced. the following list of ministers:—

Premier and War	**Edouard Daladier**
Finance	**Georges Bonnet**
Budget	**Lucien Lamoureux**
Interior	**Camille Chautemps**
Foreign Affairs	**Joseph Paul-Boncour**
Marine	**Georges Leygues**
Colonies	**Albert Sarraut**
Education	**Anatole de Monzie**
Agriculture	**Henri Queuille**
Posts and Telegraphs	**Laurent-Eynac**
Pensions	**Hippolyte Ducos**
Commerce	**Louis Serre**
Public Works	**Joseph Paganon**
Under-secretary for the Presidency of the Council	**Raymond Patenôtre**

The new cabinet, M. Daladier declared, would be completed before noon today, and the ministers would present themselves before President Lebrun this afternoon.

The government would accept the budgetary program approved by the finance committee, M. Daladier said, but would not necessarily adhere to the Socialists' financial program.

The cabinet which is now being formed, the premier-designate further stated, will "face the immediate necessities of the situation, which calls for rapid financial restoration."

Socialist Refusal.

Earlier in the evening the Socialists refused to participate in the ministry.

It was even reported that the Socialists had refused parliamentary support such as they gave to the two previous governments of Edouard Herriot and Joseph Paul-Boncour. Although this report was not confirmed, it was generally believed that the position taken by the Socialists made it impossible for M. Daladier to form a ministry during the night, if at all.

ADOLF HITLER

Nazi Chief Reaches Highest Pinnacle of Power When Hindenburg Appoints One-time Private to Be Premier

REPUBLICANS HAUNTED BY FEAR OF DICTATOR

Coalition Still in Minority with Fate in Reichstag Depending on Catholics.

(From The Herald and Herald Tribune Bureau)

BERLIN, Monday. — Adolf Hitler, an obscure corporal in the German army in the World war, achieved the most glittering triumph in his life today, when President von Hindenburg, commander-in-chief of the Central European armies in the great conflict, finally bowed to the inevitable and appointed his defeated rival for the presidency chancellor of the Reich.

The leader and founder of the National-Socialist movement, who only a year ago was a "man without a country" and publicly threatened by the Berlin chief of police with being "whipped out of Prussia like a dog," now heads a "Harzburg coalition cabinet," consisting of his own party and the Hugenberg Nationalists.

Republicans Apprehensive.

This coalition, though representing considerably more than a third of the Reichstag, is, still, a minority government. But the cabinet hopes to win the "toleration" of Heinrich Brüning's Catholic Centre party.

Only 44 years old, Hitler, with the exception of Joseph Wirth, is the youngest man ever to become German chancellor. German Republicans faced with consternation today the fact that the man they most dread has at last attained the highest office in the state, excepting the presidency, and that his cabinet includes the most dangerous foes of the Weimar Constitution and parliamentary democracy, with such figures as Alfred Hugenberg, the powerful newspaper magnate and outstanding protagonist of government by dictatorship; former Chancellor Franz von Papen, who drove a Republican ministry from power in Prussia; Wilhelm Frick, who introduced anti-Young Plan prayers into the schools of Thuringia, as minister in that state, and Franz Seldte, the one-armed head of the Steel Helmets' organization of royalist and militarist former soldiers.

The new cabinet is composed as follows:—

Adolf Hitler, chancellor.

Franz von Papen, vice-chancellor and federal commissioner for Prussia.

Baron Konstantin von Neurath, foreign minister.

Wilhelm Frick, minister of the interior.

General Werner von Blomberg, Reichswehr minister.

Count Lutz Schwerin von Krosigk, finance minister.

Alfred Hugenberg, minister of commerce and agriculture.

Franz Seldte, minister of labor.

Baron Paul von Eltz-Ruebenach, posts and communications.

Guenther Gereke, federal commissioner for employment.

Reichstag President Hermann Goering, minister without portfolio and federal commissioner for aviation.

WEDNESDAY, DECEMBER 13, 1933

1st All-Nazi Reichstag Opens, Does Its Work, Adjourns in 10 Minutes

(From the Herald and Herald Tribune bureau.)

BERLIN, Tuesday.—The first all-Nazi Reichstag required a scant ten minutes here today to organize itself and complete its business in what is probably the shortest opening session of a parliament on record. General Hermann Goering, who selected for this occasion the uniform of an officer of the Nazi stormtroopers, presided over the sitting, which was held in the disused Kroll Opera House. Like an old-fashioned drill sergeant he put through the agenda with ruthless military proficiency, and then adjourned the house *sine die*.

All speeches were dispensed with. The tedious reading of the rollcall that normally consumed hours, was omitted, and all the officers of the Reichstag were elected in a block by a rising vote of the 660 deputies, constituting the largest German Reichstag.

Even the singing of the "Horst Vessel" song, the Nazi anthem, was dropped and the only sign of a demonstration was a triple "victory cheer" for Germany that Goering, acting as the cheer leader, called for as a wind-up to the inaugural session of this most curious of all modern parliaments.

The fact that all the deputies appeared in uniform gave a military aspect to the Nazi parliament. The brown uniform of Nazi stormtroopers dominated, but there was a sprinkling of the blue uniforms of the S.S. men —the Nazi prætorian guard—and some green uniforms of the Steel Helmets.

Vice-Chancellor Franz von Papen, sitting in civilian dress in the front row, appeared as out of place as a man in clothes at a nudist colony. So many cabinet ministers sat as deputies that the ministerial benches were occupied principally by the chief permanent officials of various departments.

From the crowded diplomatic gallery, Fulvio Suvich, the Italian foreign secretary, viewed the colorful scene with an interest doubtless reflecting that imitation is the sincerest form of flattery.

To judge by this Hitler Reichstag, Germany has set the clock back so far that the 19th century may be said not to have existed as far as it is concerned. Not a Democrat, not a Liberal, neither Socialist, Republican nor Fascist sits in the Reich's present chamber, which apparently was only called into being to form an appropriate background for important declarations on foreign policy that Nazi leaders may want to deliver to the world from time to time.

No Women Members Seated.

And for the first time since the war, no German woman sits in the Reichstag—a clear intimation that in the Third Reich, woman's place is in the home.

Send Champagne to U.S.? But Non! She Is Dry! Say Paris Mail Clerks

Americans who attempted to send packages of Christmas champagne, cognac or wine to friends back home yesterday met with disappointment. French authorities have not yet recognized the fact that prohibition has been repealed.

Inquiries at the American consulate revealed that the United States customs authorities will accept packages of less than $100 value, provided invoices, obtainable through the consul-general, are sent to the consignees.

However, though American customs officials will admit gift packages, the difficulty on this side lies in convincing the "colis postaux" authorities that the "régime sec" is finished. When Americans attempted to send packages of liquor yesterday, notably at the office in the rue de Rennes, the clerks considered it a huge joke.

"What!" they said, incredulously, "you're trying to send champagne and cognac to America?—Don't you know that country is dry?"—And they laughed heartily.

When told that prohibition had been repealed, the chief clerk said with complete skepticism:—

"Yes, we've heard something about that, but frankly, it is just a lot of talk. America is dry. You're wasting your time trying to send liquor to that country."

The Americans insisted, and finally demanded to see the "chef de bureau." He waved his hands and shrugged his shoulders.

"It may be true," he said, when the Americans told him that America has repealed prohibition. "But I've never been officially notified, and as far as we are concerned, America is still dry."

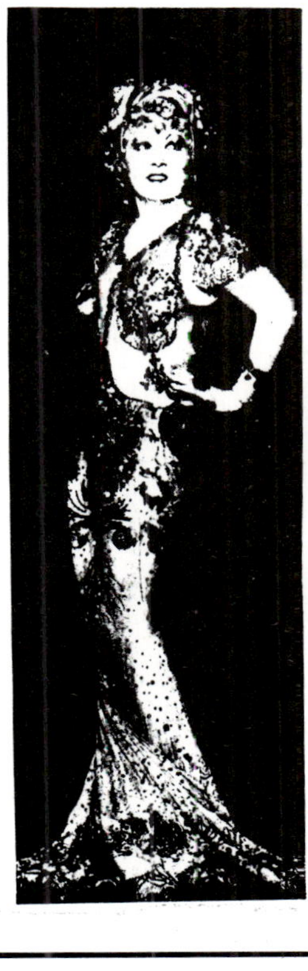

INTRODUCING SUZANNE KAAREN, former New York high-school girl, who has been signed by Fox Films and is being hailed as a screen "find" of much promise.
N.Y. Herald photo.

MAE WEST, who created such a sensation as the enchanting "Lady Lou," has had an even greater success in "I'm no Angel," shortly to be released in Paris.

TODAY'S WEATHER REPORT
Warmer, fine to cloudy.
Temperature yesterday: Max. 26 (78 Fahr.), min. 13 (55 Fahr.).
Wind: NW., Light.
Channel crossings: Moderate.

THE NEW YORK HERALD

EUROPEAN EDITION OF THE NEW YORK HERALD TRIBUNE

EXCHANGE RATES (CABLES)
Dollar in Paris - - - 15fr. 16 1/2c.
Dollar in London - - - 3s. 11 1/2d.
Dollar in Berlin - - - 2m. 51 1/2pf.
Dollar in Rome - - - - 11 lire 69c.
Pound in Paris - - - 76fr. 42 1/2c.

47th YEAR. No. 17,098. Business and Editorial Offices: 21 RUE DE BERRI. Tel: Elysees 12-87, 12-88, 12-90, 35-65, 03-87 PARIS, THURSDAY, JULY 26, 1934 Branch Office and Information Bureau, 49 AVENUE DE L'OPERA. Tel: Opera 67-49 PRICE: In France, One Franc.

Dollfuss Slain by Nazi Raiders in Own Office; Schuschingg Takes Reins; Civil War Feared

DROUGHT TOLL NEARING 800; RELIEF RUSHED BY GOVERNMENT

Deaths in Parched Areas Mount at Ten Per Hour as Record Heat Grips Two-Thirds of U.S.; Thousands of Acres Now Desert-Like.

TOPEKA RESIDENTS DANCE IN DOWNPOUR

Government Gives Relief Fund of $20,000,000 to 16 States; Drillers Bore Feverishly for Water.

BULLETIN

(By Special Cable to The Herald.)

KANSAS CITY, Wednesday.—A thundershower with a brief downpour of rain at Topeka late this afternoon set adults and children dancing in the streets in bathing suits. Scattered showers in Missouri, Nebraska, Kansas and Oklahoma merely added to the humidity, with temperatures rising quickly after the showers.

(By Special Cable to The Herald.)

CHICAGO, Wednesday.—The death toll in the parched drought areas wheer cattle are dying by the thousands and where water shortage is becoming acute, was estimated today be mounting at the rate of 10 an hour and is approaching 800 as tempeartures at or above records of many years continued to hold nearly two-thirds of the country in the grip of the most disastrous drought the nation has ever known.

In the section lying between Wyoming and New Mexico eastward to the Alleghenies, hundreds of thousands of fertile acres are fast becoming desert-like, with the entire area tindery dry presenting a fire hazard. Frantic efforts are being made to drill wells in hopes of finding water to relieve the needs of millions of people, as well as to water live stock which are being shot by the thousands.

$19,976,535 Relief Advanced.

Federal agencies tonight, besieged with requests for relief, reported that 400,000 families, including 1,600,000 persons are already receiving emergency drought relief. An additional $19,976,535 was advanced to sixteen states today, most of it for relief purposes. In many instances, government agencies have advanced funds to sink deep wells in hopes of finding water and to lay pipe lines to tap sources hitherto untouched.

Showers are predicted in some secthions, but long rains are needed to rejuvenate streams, which have been reduced to mere trickles. Ponds and wells have been dried up in thousands of sections.

Chicago and the surrounding area had some relief today as cooling breezes swept down from Canada to lower the blistering temperature of 105 yesterday, a record high for thitry-four years.

Suffering is probably greatest in Kansas, where the temperature has exceeded 100 for more than thirty days and stood above 90 for fifty-one days. Yesterday and today at Topeka the thermometer touched 110. The water situation in the state is desperate.

Well-Drillers Hasten.

Well-drillers, reinforced from crews from oil fields, were rushed into Kansas and Oklahoma last night and worked by the flare of floodlights driving wells to a depth of 200 feet in quest of subterranean streams. Geological parties, hurriedly mobilized by the

(Continued on Page 3, Col. 4.)

WALL STREET

	High	Low
U.S. Steel	36 1/2	35 1/8
General Motors	28 7/8	27 3/4
N.Y. Central	23 1/8	21 3/8
Montgom. Ward	25 3/8	23 3/4

Market trend stronger. Trading active. Sales totaled 1,350,000 shares. Movements were irregular in the forenoon. Stocks rallied at noon. The recovery was maintained to the close. Gains ranged from fractions to more than a point. Full market reports: Pages 6 and 7.

America Beats Australia in Davis Cup Play

By AL LANEY

LONDON, Wednesday.—The Davis Cup team of the United States, overcoming a nearly impossible handicap of its own making, earned the right to challenge England for the trophy next Saturday by defeating Australia, 3-2, in the inter-zone final at Wimbledon today.

The Americans won the two remaining singles matches, one of them an abbreviated contest that will nevertheless be long remembered as a Davis Cup classic, the other just an ordinary tennis match.

Sidney Wood, continuing against Jack Crawford with a two sets to love lead, an advantage gained before rain interrupted play yesterday, won in a fifth set by 6-3, 9-7, 4-6, 4-6, 6-2, and Frank Shields defeated Vivian McGrath with ease in straight sets, 6-4, 6-2, 6-4.

Wood had been beaten by McGrath and Shields by Crawford on Saturday, giving Australia what appeared to be a winning lead of two matches to love with only three left to play. On Monday George Lott and Lester Stoefen put America back into the running by winning the doubles match from Crawford and Adrian Quist, and Shields today scored the deciding point after Wood had brought the score level at two matches for each side.

Wood saved the day for his country; to Shields fell the honor of scoring the victory. Each redeemed his poor showing on the opening day. Shields' task today turned out to be by far the easier one. It was an erratic slap-dash giant who came into court to play the all-important fifth and deciding match. Immediately he revealed his intention of hitting everything that

(Continued on Page 8, Col. 1.)

COTY DEATH AT 61 DUE TO PNEUMONIA

Famed Perfumer-Publisher Succumbs at His Château.

François Coty, famed as perfumer, politician and publisher, died at his château at Louveciennes, near Paris, last night at 8.32 o'clock, from double pneumonia, following a short illness. He was 61.

M. Coty's illness only became known a few days ago. His condition rapidly became worse and it was announced Monday that his state was critical. Yesterday afternoon he began to sink. Mgr. Chapal was called to administer the last sacraments. Shortly afterward, M. Coty lapsed into a coma and died at 8.32. His family was at his bedside. Arrangements for the funeral have not yet been completed.

Claimed Bonaparte Kinship.

François Coty, whose real name was Spoturno, and who was born in Ajaccio, Corsica, in 1873, claimed that his family was related to that of Napoleon Bonaparte. Like the "Little Corporal," he was a man of small stature.

His extraordinary and picturesque career as perfumer, politician, journalist and millionaire, began some thirty years ago as an exporter of essences from the flower fields of Grasse on the Riviera, which he first peddled to the barbers of Paris in a small way.

But, like most Corsicans, he was endowed with immense energy and lively imagination and, in a business way, with at least something of Napoleon's genius. Coty brought new ideas to the perfume business, particularly the idea of selling his luxury products in luxury settings. It did not seem right to him that attar of roses, which cost $100 or more a pound, and jasmine oil, which was worth from $700 to $800 a pound should be sold in undignified containers, so he engaged famous ceramists and other artists to provide his products with bottles and boxes. Powder boxes which were works of art; perfumes and make-up for every mood and every dress were the next steps and his business grew amazingly.

Within a few years Coty was selling perfumes to the world in such quantities that he could, despite their extra expense, compete with or undersell most of his competitors. He revolutionized the business.

He developed vast flower plantations in France and Italy and built a model factory at Suresnes, while opening up branches and factories in many other countries. His firm in America became one of the greatest, due to his plan for

(Continued on Page 2, Col. 3.)

U.S. DENIES TOKIO REPORT

(By United Press.)

WASHINGTON, Wednesday.—White House officials disclaim all knowledge of a United States-British agreement to eliminate political questions from the forthcoming naval conference as reported in Tokio despatches. It was stated authoritatively that the question has so far not arisen.

AUSTRIAN NAZIS MOBILIZING ON REICH FRONTIER

Exiles' Barracks Hum with Activity at Munich with City Believing Invasion of Homeland May Be Near.

(Special to The Herald.)

MUNICH, Wednesday.—Rumors of an intended putsch of the Austrian Foreign Legion are current here. Intense activities in the Austrian section of the Nazi party for the last four days have aroused considerable suspicion among foreign diplomatic representatives here.

Reports that 3,000 Austrian Nazis are now under arms waiting to march into Austria from various points along the Austrian and Bavarian frontier cannot be confirmed, although there is convincing evidence that these reports are not without foundation.

Austrians Get Arms.

From a personal investigation the correspondent of The New York Herald finds that several thousand Austrian Nazis residing in Munich have received word to stand by for orders. All barracks are now guarded by Austrians wearing steel helmets and carrying rifles. The barracks in Franziskanerstrasse, with a capacity of a thousand men, was full of military preparedness today. Five other barracks in the center of the town were equally ready for mobilization.

People living in the neighborhood of the barracks reported that army trucks loaded with military equipment have been stationed in the yards ready to move. Outside the cmfw shr cmfwyb there are other signs that the Austrian Nazis are preparing for action.

Since the beginning of this week army lorries filled with Austrian stormtroopers in steel helmets and carrying army rifles frequently have been seen stealing through the streets of Munich.

Inhabitants along the road leading

(Continued on Page 3, Col. 3.)

HOME TOWN FILES BY DILLINGER'S BIER

(By United Press.)

MOORESVILLE, Ind., Wednesday.—The body of John Dillinger was brought home today to this town where he was born 32 years ago and from which he embarked a few years ago on the career of robbery and murder that ended in Chicago Sunday night when he was shot and killed by Federal agents.

Throughout the day townspeople filed through the local undertaking parlor to view the remains of the man whom they once knew as a Quaker farmer's son, but who finished by becoming the most notorious outlaw in the United States.

The body was brought to Mooresville by the gangster's 70-year-old father, John Dillinger, who rode on the driver's seat with the chauffeur of the hearse during the 210-mile trip from Chicago, where the bullet-riddled body was handed over to the father in a wicker basket late yesterday afternoon.

The hearse on leaving Chicago, where it was already an object of curiosity, soon was heading a procession of motorcars, many of which followed it all the way to Mooresville. The procession presented a weird appearance as it filed through Indianapolis late last night. Traffic was blocked for some time before police could clear the way. Despite the late-

(Continued on Page 3, Col. 1.)

Mutineers Seize Radio Station, Chancellery In Daring Sortie and Capture Three Ministers

Slain by Nazi Raiders

CHANCELLOR ENGELBERT DOLLFUSS

Martial Law with Death Penalty Proclaimed; Sporadic Fighting Is Reported from Capital; Fey, Wounded by Rebels, Begs Besiegers Not to Attack Office Where Captives Are Held; Chancellor Is Shot Trying to Escape.

(Special to The Herald.)

VIENNA, Wednesday.—Engelbert Dollfuss, Austria's 42-year-old Chancellor, was shot and killed by a band of Nazis this afternoon who, disguised as Federal troops, invaded the historic Chancellery in the Ballhausplatz and held it for several hours until dislodged tonight by government troops.

His place as head of the badly shaken government has been taken by Dr. Karl Schuschnigg, Minister of Education, who was personally designated by Dollfuss in his dying breath to succeed him.

Government Believed in Control.

But so shattering have been today's events, that though the government maintains that it is in absolute control of the capital and that the provinces are quiet, civil war once more threatens to grip the country, with the Socialists, still bitter at the loss of their 300 dead and thousands wounded in the February uprising, joining the Nazis in an attempt to install Hitlerism in Austria, an accomplishment which, if successful, might in the opinion of diplomatic circles here bring another European war.

The attempted "coup d'état" which cost the life of the diminutive Chancellor, who has fought against the constantly increasing Nazi forces for more than a year in a desperate effort to maintain Austria's independence, must have been carefully planned.

Squads of Nazis dressed in the uniform of the Heimwehr occupied the Chancellery and the radio broadcasting station just off the Kaertnerstrasse, the capital's main thoroughfare simultaneously at 1 p.m. today.

While a Nazi was announcing through the radio that Dollfuss had resigned and was replaced by Dr. Rintelen, Austrian Minister to Rome, the Nazi detachment at the Chancellery were making prisoners of Dollfuss, Major Fey, who put down the February Socialist revolt, and Herr Karwinsky, Minister of State, at the point of their guns.

Shot by Invading Nazis.

When the intruders entered the conference-room, Dollfuss attempted to get away into the next room and was shot and mortally wounded from behind. Fey and the State Secretary were arrested and both were held as hostages by the invaders who immediately began to search all offices. All officials were told to clear out and assemble in the second courtyard of the building.

Dollfus lay wounded for several hours on a sofa in the cabinet-room and expired shortly before dark. A priest who had been called and was allowed by the Nazis to enter arrived too late to administer the last sacraments. Fey was only slightly wounded.

Dollfuss had been scheduled to go to Italy today as a guest of Premier Mussolini.

The new chancellor, Dr. Schuschnigg, and Major Fey both broadcast tonight over a national hook-up, the former giving a moving account of how the dying chancellor handed over his office to him and begged him to look after his family—his wife and children—now staying with Mussolini at Riccione.

Orders have been issued tonight that all places of amusement in the city are to be closed until further notice as a mark of respect to the dead chancellor.

In spite of the recapture of the chancellery and the broadcasting station, the degree of control which the government is exercising is still not definitely known.

The chief of police has proclaimed martial law and has ordained the death penalty for incitement to rebellion. All cafés and shops must be closed by 8 p.m., and congregating on the street is forbidden.

Despite this, sporadic fighting was reported going on in various parts of the city. The extent to which the army can rely upon its armed forces is uncertain. The army in particular is believed to contain many Nazi sympathizers.

Communications between Vienna and the outside world were cut off for several hours during the afternoon, but restored tonight. There have been several outbreaks in the provinces, but the government claims to have the upper hand.

Details of Chancellery Raid.

At 1 p.m., while one detachment of Nazis was occupying the Federal broadcasting office and after killing a director and overpowering the others, and announcing that Dollfuss had resigned, another band, in the disguise of Federal troops, drove up in five trucks before the Chancellery—the famous Ballhaus Platz where Metternich reigned and took possession.

The guards on duty thought they were reinforcements arriving to protect the Chancellor because of the wave of ill-feeling which had swept the city after yesterday's execution of Josef Gerl, a Socialist turned Nazi.

The Nazis swarmed through the inner court and up to the Cabinet room, where Chancellor Dollfuss was conferring with Major Fey, his trusted minister who put down the Socialist uprising February 12, and Herr Karwinsky, his newly-appointed Minister of State.

Vice-Chancellor Schuschnigg, Minister of Education, and Major-General Zehnen, Minister of Defense, already had left the Chancellery and gone to the War Office at the other end of the inner city.

The Nazis rushed into the Cabinet room and held Chancellor Dollfuss and his two ministers up at the point of their guns. It is not yet clear exactly what happened then. It is reliably reported

(Continued on Page 3, Col. 2.)

Dollfuss Confides Family To Successor in Last Gasp

(By United Press.)

BERLIN, Wednesday.—In a radio speech from Vienna, Vice-Chancellor Schuschnigg announced with tears in his voice how he found Chancellor Dollfuss lying gravely wounded on a sofa and how Dollfuss asked him to take care of his wife and children after he was dead. Shortly after he informed his listeners that Dollfuss had succumbed to his injuries.

Chancellor Dollfuss, while asking Schuschnigg to take care of his family, also surrendered the office of Chancellor to the government. Schuschnigg further related how President Miklas earlier gave him the power to deal in a crisis as he saw fit, but did not commission him to reshuffle the Cabinet.

Upon receiving this commission, Schuschnigg immediately issued an ultimatum to the 140 men to surrender within 15 minutes, assuring them free exit to any country they wished. Schuschnigg, upon delivering the ultimatum to the besiegers, contacted the German Minister and asked for admission of the mutineers to Germany. Later reports say that the mutineers with their arms had been conducted to the German frontier and sent to Germany. This information was not from the radio, but from a reliable source

Continuing his radio speech, Schuschnigg said that the mutineers had occupied the radio station and the Chancellery dressed in uniforms of the Heimwehr and that the band was led by an alleged major, who was a Nazi stormtroop leader. They forced the radio broadcaster to make his statement about the resignation of the government.

A number of clashes occurred simultaneously in the provinces, but it is now claimed that the government is in control everywhere.

Schuschnigg announced that all theaters and cinemas will be closed in Vienna as a sign of national mourning

(Continued on Page 3, Col. 7.)

TROOPS NOT MOVING SAYS WORRIED ROME

(From the Herald and Herald Tribune bureau.)

ROME, Wednesday.—A situation filled with serious potentialities for all Europe is recognized by the Italian government as having been precipitated by the attempted coup d'état at Vienna.

In view of the strong stand taken by Premier Mussolini in support of Austrian independence and the Dollfuss government, the threat to upset that government has inevitably raised for the public, although it is not directly admitted by officials, the question of possible active intervention on the part of this country.

According to a statement tonight, the reports that are being circulated in other capitals about the movement of Italian troops toward the Austrian border are without foundation.

However, in the situation as pictured at Rome, the threat which extends the importance of the Vienna events far beyond the borders of Austria lies in the as yet unknown attitude of two governments—Germany and Yugoslavia—which might take more than a passing interest in seeing a Nazi government established in Austria.

Any serious gesture on the part of other powers obviously would leave Italy with small choice. The peculiarly intimate connection of the Italian government with the Dollfuss régime is reflected in the fact that the family of the Austrian Chancellor is now visiting Premier Mussolini and his wife on the Adriatic that Dollfuss is expected here within a few days, and that Prince von Starhemberg at the moment is at Venice.

Although sensational reports from other capitals might picture Italy as preparing to act precipitately alone in the defense of the Dollfuss government, in informed circles here it is the opinion that the action of this country

Reid Hall Director Named Knight in Legion of Honor

In recognition of her outstanding work in France, and its contribution to the friendly relations of this country and the United States, a knighthood in the Legion of Honor has been conferred upon Miss Dorothy Leet, director of Reid Hall, the American University Women's Center of Paris.

The nomination, recommended by the Ministry of Foreign Affairs, will delight Miss Leet's countless friends in France and America, and the innumerable students who have enjoyed her companionship and care during their residence at Reid Hall.

Miss Leet first came to Paris in 1924 to take charge of the Reid Hall Club for college women and American students. Largely through her efforts, the organization has grown into an international intellectual center and become a meeting place for scholars and professors as well as a charming residence for American women in Paris.

Founded by the late Mrs. Whitelaw Reid, during the time her husband was minister to France, the club was first a hostel for American girl art students, and this formed the basis of the present university women's club known as Reid Hall. The site of the clubhouse itself has an interesting history, it having at one time been a hunting box on the estate of the Duc de Chevreuse.

After serving as a hospital during the war, the club became Reid Hall in 1922. About 10,000 Americans have enjoyed the comforts of the club during its 12 years of existence. Miss Leet has done her utmost during that time to give the students housed there an idea of French social life and cultural movements. Her aim has been not only to give them a home but also to expand the activities of the club and to offer opportunities for American university women to have wider contacts with women of other nations.

French women lawyers, doctors and architects now have their headquarters at Reid Hall and hold monthly meetings and teas there. Scholarships are

(Continued on Page [illegible], Col. [illegible])

EXCHANGE RATES (CABLES)
Dollar in Paris - - - - - 15fr. 18c.
Dollar in London - - - - - 4s. 1d.
Dollar in Rome - - - - - 12 lire 23c.
Dollar in Berlin - - - 2m. 48 3/4pf.
Pound in Paris - - - - - 74fr. 43c.

NEW YORK
Herald Tribune

SAILINGS to NEW YORK
Washington - - - - - Oct. 10
Pres. Roosevelt- - - - Oct. 17
Manhattan- - - - - - - Oct. 24
Pres. Harding- - - - - Oct. 31
UNITED STATES LINES

48th YEAR. No. 17,532. EUROPEAN EDITION PARIS, THURSDAY, OCTOBER 3, 1935 THE NEW YORK HERALD (ESTABLISHED IN EUROPE 1887) PRICE: In France, One Franc.

Invasion Starts as Duce Demands 'Justice'

CREDITORS END CASE AGAINST NEIDECKERS

Defense Counsel Requests Dismissal of Petition in Bankruptcy, But Referee in N.Y. Reserves Decision.

HOLDS BANKER NEVER RESIDED IN FRANCE

Attorney Declares French Action Illegal Because No Notice Given Paris Firm.

(By Special Wireless.)

NEW YORK, Oct. 2. — The French Consulate General and petitioning creditors in their move to determine whether B. Coles Neidecker, founder and head of the closed Travelers Bank of Paris, and his brothers, George and Aubrey Neidecker, are subject to the United States bankruptcy laws, completed their case today before Referee Ehrhorn.

Milton Kupfer, attorney for the Neidecker brothers, immediately moved for dismissal of the petition on the ground that Herbert Stern, counsel for the creditors, failed to prove his case. Referee Ehrhorn reserved decision.

The only witness called this afternoon was George Neidecker, who gave his address as 829 Park Avenue and who disclaimed any connection with the Travelers Bank since about 1924. He said he had had no business connections for the last two years.

George Neidecker testified on Stern's examination that he had been sup-

Army Transport Barely Escapes Big U.S. Guns

(By United Press.)

FAR ROCKAWAY, N.Y., Oct. 2. — The Army transport Republic was almost fired on today by two 16-inch guns from Fort Tilden when it entered the danger zone after the order to fire had been given in a test of coast defense artillery in the New York area. The order was countermanded in time to prevent two two-ton projectiles from being fired at the transport.

A half hour later the big guns fired at a moving target at a distance of fifteen miles. They scored three direct hits out of a dozen shots at a floating canvas target the size of a battleship. The projectiles weighed 2,200 pounds each and traveled at an estimated velocity of 2,750 feet a second. They took 40 seconds to reach the target.

The shots cost approximately $3,000 apiece. It was the first time that the guns had been fired in eleven years. The roar could be heard ten miles. The extreme range of the big guns is a possible thirty miles, with an average life of 200 to 250 shots. The ammunition shed is 200 yards from the gun, and the crew of twenty-six officers and men was allowed ninety seconds to reload.

There are two 16-inch guns also at Boston. However, they never have been fired because of the nearby residential district; the detonation would break all windows.

Will Rogers's Insurance Man Held in Fraud

(By United Press.)

NEW YORK, Oct. 2.—John J. Kemp, insurance broker to many stage and film celebrities, some of whom trusted

Mussolini, in Tears, Asks British and French Support; Negus Notifies League Italians Have Crossed Frontier; England, Resigned to War, Ponders Economic Sanctions

Cabinet and King Take All Preliminary Steps Toward Momentous Decision in View of Mussolini's Word.

FRANCE HOLDS BALANCE IN FATEFUL SITUATION

Defense Ministers, Financial and Military Advisers Are Consulted by Premier.

By JOSEPH DRISCOLL
(From the Herald Tribune Bureau.)

LONDON, Oct. 2.—Resigned to the inevitability of war in Abyssinia, the British Cabinet and the British King today gave solemn thought to the possibility that the Italo-Ethiopian conflict might under certain circumstances flame out across the Mediterranean and start another great "war to end all war."

This feeling of intense gravity was strengthened tonight as London received reports of Mussolini's warning that if the League of Nations powers made war on him he would make war on them. Nevertheless, the decision of the British government is supposed close at hand.

Second Step Unknown

The first step in that policy envi-

Protest Forwarded to Geneva Council, Member States; Ethiopian Mobilization Today; Rome Uninformed.

REPORT IN EGYPT OF ALLIANCE MOVE

Madrid Rumor of British Request for Use of Ports Brings President Back.

The Emperor of Abyssinia telegraphed the League of Nations yesterday, announcing and protesting that Italian troops had crossed the Ethiopian frontier near Mount Mussa Ali, on the French Somaliland border.

Although the report was immediately denied from Rome, on account of the fact that the frontier has never been demarcated at this point, together with the almost simultaneous announcement from the Italian capital of the civil mobilization of 10,000,000 Fascists, the news stirred the capitals of the world into the belief that the long-expected Italo-Ethiopian conflict had begun.

Later Addis Ababa dispatches tended

Point of Italian Invasion

Arrow points to area where troops are reported to have entered Abyssinia. The section has an undefined boundary.

U.S. To Avoid Foreign Wars,

Twenty Million Black Shirts Answer Mobilization Test As Duce, Back to Wall, Appeals Against Sanctions.

'WAR WILL BE MET WITH WAR,' HE SAYS

Premier Warns Foes, Says 'No One Should Delude Himself He Can Beat Us.'

By JOHN T. WHITAKER
(From the Herald Tribune Bureau.)

ROME, Oct. 2.—Mobilizing his black-shirted millions, Premier Mussolini stood today on the balcony of the Palazzo Venezia in Rome and claimed a place in the sun for Italy as his loyal Fascist followers of every city village and hamlet roared the country's solidarity from Sicily to the Alps.

Asking the Italian people to rise to its feet and lift a cry "which will reach our soldiers ready to fight in East Africa," Mussolini pleaded with the British and the French to give the Italians who fought with them against Germany "not sanctions but justice."

EXCHANGE RATES (CABLES)
Dollar in Paris - - - 15fr. 18 3/4c.
Dollar in London - - - - - 4s. 1d.
Dollar in Rome - - - - 12 lire 31c.
Dollar in Berlin - - - - - 2m. 49pf.
Pound in Paris - - - - - 74fr. 41c.

NEW YORK
Herald Tribune

SAILINGS to NEW YORK
Washington - - - - - Oct. 10
Pres. Roosevelt- - - - Oct. 17
Manhattan- - - - - - - Oct. 24
Pres. Harding- - - - - Oct. 31
UNITED STATES LINES

49th YEAR. No. 17,533. EUROPEAN EDITION PARIS, FRIDAY, OCTOBER 4, 1935 THE NEW YORK HERALD (ESTABLISHED IN EUROPE 1887) PRICE: In France, One Franc.

3 Ethiopian Towns Bombed As War Starts; Hundreds Killed, Negus Protests to League

Laval Conveys Answer To Eden on Support; London Not Satisfied

French Cabinet Takes Grave Decisions Today After Statesmen's Conference; 300 Peace Meetings Called; Sanctions Opposition Rises

With public opinion throughout France hardening against any involvement of France in a conflict arising out of the Ethiopian dispute, Premier Laval yesterday discussed with Anthony Eden the nature and extent of sanctions against Italy, which the Council of the League may have to consider at its meeting tomorrow, and the French tti-

London Remarkably Calm; Press Is Very Reticent; Bid for Spanish Aid Reported; City Holds Italian Finance Weak.

By JOSEPH DRISCOLL

LONDON, Oct. 3. — Now that the Italo-Abyssinian conflict has passed overnight from an international debate into a grim war, Britain intends — through the League of Nations, of course — to bring all possible economic pressure against Italy, in the hope of ending hostilities as soon as possible.

Gives Signal for War

BENITO MUSSOLINI

Adowa, Adigrat, Agame Bombed As Mussolini's Airplanes Follow Troops Across Frontier at Dawn

Mussolini Cabled Order to Advance Few Minutes Before Addressing Fascist Mobilization Wednesday.

120,000 TROOPS USED IN FIRST OFFENSIVE

Italians March to Wipe Out Ignominy of 39-Year-Old Defeat by Abyssinians.

By JOHN T. WHITAKER

ROME, Oct. 3. — Carrying the Roman Eagle of Fascism toward Adowa, the Italian armies of

Unconfirmed Report Sets 1st Day's Fatalities At 1,700; Rome Denies Emperor's Charge of Bombing Hospital, Killing Women, Children; Air Attack on Addis Ababa Expected Today

War began in Ethiopia yesterday with the advance of Italian troops on two fronts.

Adowa, scene of Italy's defeat 39 years ago, when 14,000 Italians fell before the spears and guns of Ethiopian warriors, was bombed by Italian warplanes. Mussolini's Air Force also rained bombs on the nearby towns of Adigrat and Agame.

Hundreds of people, including women and children, were killed, according to Addis Ababa dispatches. Rome dismissed the charge as "an old and much-abused expedient."

Messages which poured out of the Ethiopian capital all yesterday and last night, told of the Italian advance.

49th YEAR. No. 17,804. EUROPEAN EDITION PARIS, WEDNESDAY, JULY 1, 1936 THE NEW YORK HERALD (ESTABLISHED IN EUROPE 1887) PRICE: In France, One Franc.

Negus Assails Italy and League in Assembly

Asks 'What Reply Can I Take Back?'

Terrific Philippic Made in Amharic Language Denounces Italians for Way Warfare was Carried On.

The Negus delivered a scathing attack against Italy and the League before the Assembly at Geneva yesterday, in a last effort to keep his empire on the map.

History Will Remember Judgment, Says Negus.

By JOHN ELLIOTT.
(Special to Herald Tribune.)

GENEVA, June 30. — Despite the organized attempt by a group of Italian journalists to prevent the Negus from having a hearing Haile Selassie delivered a terrific philippic against Italy and the League of Nations alike in his speech before the opening meeting of the extraordinary session of the Assembly here this afternoon.

Addressing delegates of fifty-one nations in his native Amharic language the fallen emperor denounced Italy for her methods and the League for its pusillanimity in failing to redeem its promises to save his country from aggression.

People Await Answer.

Telling statesmen that "God and history will remember your judgment," Haile Selassie called on the League not to create a fatal precedent of bowing to force by accepting Italy's *fait accompli* in Ethiopia and concluded his moving oration with the words: "Representatives of the world, I have come to Geneva to fulfill the most painful duty a chief of state can be called upon to discharge. What answer will I have to bring back to my people?"

The emperor did not mince his words in condemning the way in which the League has supported the efforts of his country to resist Italian aggression and the conscience of many delegates must have cringed at his unsparing words. He reminded the League of Nations that he had taken up the gage of battle with Mussolini relying on promises of support made by the League of Nations. "Despite the inferiority of my arms and the complete absence of aviation, of artillery, of munitions and of hospital service my confidence in the League of Nations was absolute.

The Negus reminded the League that it had confidently said that this was not merely a conflict between Italy and Ethiopia but a conflict of the Italian government with the League of Nations. Consequently Haile Selassie said he had confidently refused favorable offers made him by Italy.

'America Is Beautiful, All of It'

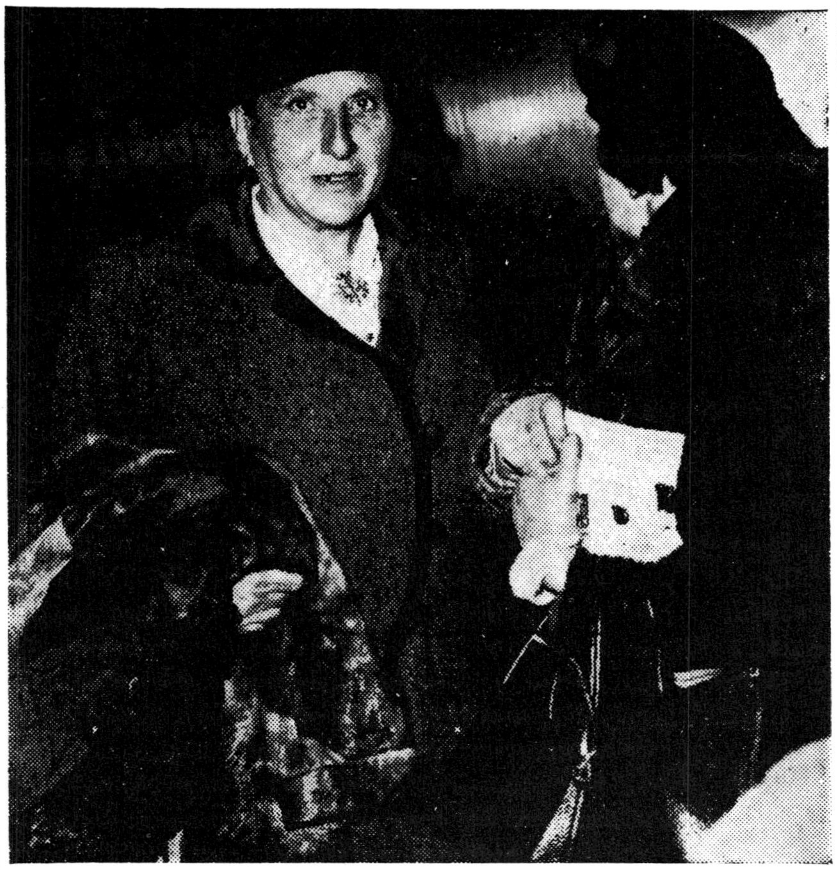

Gertrude Stein faces the camera at the Gare St.-Lazare on arriving from the Champlain, but Alice B. Toklas is too busy looking after luggage. —N.Y. Herald photo.

500 of Champlain's 600 Passengers Come to Paris

The swing of tourists back to France continued yesterday with a deluge descending on the country after crossing from America on the French liner Champlain and debarking at Havre. Of nearly 600 passengers, including Gertrude Stein, returning in triumph from her American lecture tour, and John Van Druten, one of the best of England's young playwrights, 500 came directly to Paris on last night's boat-train.

Miss Stein appeared on the Gare St.-Lazare platform wearing exactly the same brown tweed suit and velvet hunter's hat that graced her square figure when she departed last fall for her first trip to the United States in many years. While Alice B. Toklas, her companion and secretary, bounced around nervously as usual worrying about Miss Stein's baggage, Miss Stein herself stood calmly in a whirl of trucks, porters and tourists giving orders in inadequate French and said that she was homesick for America already.

"It's wonderful," she said, her small eyes staring with childlike intentness. "America is beautiful, all of it. I never knew that before. Everything is beautiful, the country and the city." Asked if America had been any different twenty years ago, she replied in the negative. "I mean," she amended, "the difference in the country and the difference in me doesn't tell the whole story. A person changes and a country does too. It's hard to tell which has changed the most. It's like a bachelor that goes along fine for twenty-five years and then decides to get married. That's the way I've been, I mean, about America."

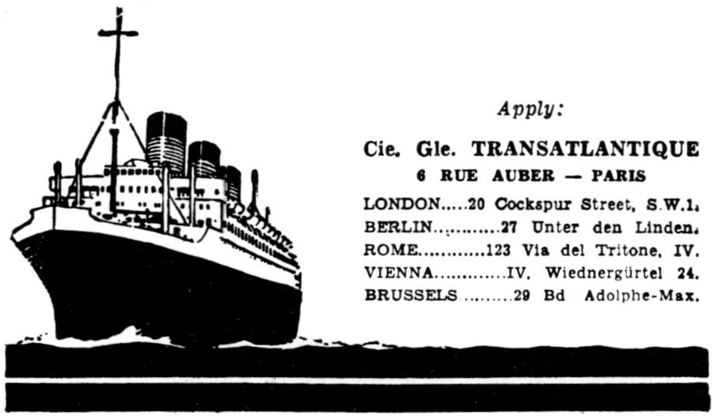

SUNDAY, JULY 19, 1936

Spanish Army Seizes Morocco; Revolution Spreads Into Spain

General Strike Called by Government to Halt Insurgents; Telephones, Telegraphs Cut Off; Monarchists Blamed for Outbreak.

BULLETIN

MADRID, July 19 (Sunday).—The Socialist and Labor leaders today proclaimed a general strike in all localities in Spain and Morocco where the insurgent garrisons have decreed martial law.

(Compiled from News Agency Reports.)

The Spanish army in Morocco rose in revolt late Friday night and by yesterday morning it was in control of the whole of Spanish Morocco.

Fierce fighting broke out between the insurgents and the civil element of the Spanish population, causing heavy loss of life. Arab natives are not taking part in the movement, it was reported.

Late last night rebel troops were said to have landed in southern Spanish ports to carry the revolt into Spain.

Telephone, Telegraph Communications With World Suspended.

As soon as the Madrid government received the first news of the uprising, all telephonic and telegraphic communication with the outside world was cut off and a strict censorship was established.

Reports of disorders in various Spanish cities and rumors of an impending military coup d'Etat in Madrid and Barcelona trickled across various points of the French frontier.

Meanwhile, a radio battle of contradictory news went on all day between the Ceuta station, which is in the hands of the rebels, and the government station near Madrid.

MONDAY, AUGUST 3, 1936

Owens Sets World Record for 100 Meters at Berlin

AS 5,000 MARCHED AT OPENING OF OLYMPIC GAMES

Above, the Olympic Stadium where 110,000 persons watched the review of the athletes of 50 nations. Left, a rank of the U.S. team, with Nate O'Connor, color bearer.—A.P. photo.

TUESDAY, AUGUST 4, 1936

U.S. Runners Shine at Berlin; Owens Equals Record for 100

By J. P. ABRAMSON

(From the Herald Tribune Bureau.)

BERLIN, Aug. 3.—Jesse Owens, the fastest human, on his record all-conquering and unconquered this year, outran the world's fleetest sprinters today to win the Olympic 100-meter crown in the world-record-equalling time of 10.3 seconds before another full house of 110,000 sports enthusiasts in the Reichsportsfeld stadium. The Ohio youth, a moving picture of grace and rhythm in sepia, thus retained for America and the Negro race the Olympic title won by Eddie Tolan four years ago in identical time.

WEDNESDAY, AUGUST 5, 1936

Franco Launches Drive on Madrid From South as Reds Win in North; Britain Accepts Neutrality Plan

London Agrees 'In Principle' to French Proposal of Keeping Hands Off Fighting; Admits Sale of Planes

EXTENSION OF TALKS TO BERLIN SUGGESTED

Italy Believed Favoring Conversations with Russia, But Does Not Send Reply

By JOSEPH DRISCOLL

(From the Herald Tribune Bureau.)

LONDON, August 4.—The British government agreed "in principle" tonight to the note which France addressed to Britain and Italy appealing for "the rapid adoption and rigid observance of an agreed arrangement for non-intervention in Spain." Italy has not answered yet.

Britain's decision means the government will not help either side in the Spanish revolution and will not permit the private export of arms. However, it does not bind her as to the export of civil airplanes and it is reported unofficially that many British planes already have been sold to the Spaniards and delivered in Spain, where they could easily be converted into war craft.

Soviet Workers Asked To Aid Madrid Reds

(By Special Dispatch.)

MOSCOW, Aug. 4. — Soviet workers today poured thousands of rubles into the Trade Union office in response to appeals to aid the finances of the Spanish government in the civil war. M. Shvernik, the Trade Union chief, predicted that each of his 18,000,000 members would make some sort of contribution. He asked yesterday that workers contribute one half of one per cent of their monthly wages to bolster the Spanish Communists' resistance. If this request is complied with, at last $7,000,000 would be collected. The need of haste in making offerings has been stressed by authorities, who are watching closely the developments in Spain and possibilities of international complications.

Southern Leader Reported Pouring 1,000 Men Daily Into Spain from Africa; Insurgents Take Ronda

GOVERNMENT CLAIMS VICTORY OVER MOLA

200 Loyalists Killed in Fight at Ciudad Real; German Warship Stops at Ceuta

Heavy fighting continued on several fronts in Spain yesterday.

Both sides claimed successes in the North, but none was of major importance.

In the South, General Francisco Franco launched his drive toward Madrid by defeating a government force near Ciudad Real. Gibraltar announced that the insurgents had captured Ronda.

Franco was said to be pouring a thousand men a day into Spain from Morocco in preparation for extensive movements.

The danger of international complications remained acute. Great Britain replied to the French neutrality note, accepting the suggestions in principle. It was revealed in London, however, that heavy purchases of British civil planes were being made by Spaniards. With Premier Benito Mussolini away from the capital, the Italian reply to the French note has not been forwarded.

Rome and London were said to be desirous that the neutrality conversations be extended to Germany and Russia, and Paris was said to be willing to comply. The French government admitted that three transport planes sent to Spain to bring out refugees had been seized.

U. S. Runners Take 4 Finals; Owens Sets Broad Jump Mark

By J. P. ABRAMSON

(From the Herald Tribune Bureau.)

BERLIN, Aug. 4.—Led by their talented and thus far invincible Negro, America's standard bearers asserted their mastery over the world with the crushing victory of their track and field powers on this third day of the rain and windswept Olympics.

They swept all three men's finals—broad jump, 800-meter run and 400-meter hurdles—smashing Olympic records in the jump as well as the 200-meter sprint trials, while 110,000 individuals rose again and again to the strains of "The Star-Spangled Banner."

It was a red-letter day in American Olympic history. Owens, indomitable and tireless, fought an all-day battle to win his second Olympic crown in two successive days, overcoming the great challenge of the German Long in his last two leaps, both over 26 feet, the last creating an Olympic mark of 26 feet 5 3/8 inches that has been surpassed by no other human except Owens himself.

FOREIGN EXCHANGE RATES
Dollar in Paris - - - - 21fr. 44 1 4c.
Dollar in London - - - - - 4s. 1d.
Dollar in Rome - - - - - - - 19 lire
Dollar in Berlin - - - - - 2m. 43pf.
Pound in Paris - - - - - 105fr. 15c

NEW YORK
Herald Tribune

SAILINGS to NEW YORK
Manhattan - - - - - - - Dec. 15
Pres. Roosevelt - - - Dec. 23
Washington - - - - - - Dec. 30
Pres. Harding - - - - - Jan. 7
UNITED STATES LINES
10 R. Auber, Paris. — 7 Haymarket, London.

50th YEAR. No. 17.960 EUROPEAN EDITION PARIS, FRIDAY, DECEMBER 4, 1936 THE NEW YORK HERALD (ESTABLISHED IN EUROPE 1887) PRICE: In France. One Franc.

Abdication of King Edward Held Inevitable

Marriage Opposed; Mrs. Simpson Is Ill

(By Special Dispatch)

LONDON, Dec. 3. — In a comment headed "Church and Crown" "The Church Times," in its edition published today, says that the King's proposed marriage would be a fatal blow to the prestige of the British monarchy.

"It is with profound sorrow and dismay that the country learned this week of the King's intention to marry an American woman who has divorced two husbands," the paper said.

"It has been suggested that the King might marry Mrs. Simpson as the Duke of Cornwall and that Parliament might pass an act of exclusion barring any issue of the marriage from the throne. This would not affect in the least the position of the Church. If the King marries Mrs. Simpson relations between the Church and the State must be fundamentally affected."

Mrs. Ernest Simpson has been far from well for several weeks, it was learned today. She is suffering from indigestion of a nervous type and her physicians believe it is directly due to worry and the nervous strain to which circumstances have submitted her.

She has been living quietly in her new home in Cumberland Terrace, off Regent's Park, only occasionally leaving on shopping expeditions or for visits to her hairdressers. She recently attended a performance of "Ariadne in Naxo" at Covent Garden with Lady Diana Cooper, wife of the Minister of War, and other friends.

Announcement of Move Expected Monday; Reported Ruler May Leave England Then

By FRANK R. KELLEY
(By Special Dispatch)

LONDON, Dec. 3.—The abdication of King Edward VIII because of his romance with Mrs. Wallis Warfield Simpson, of Baltimore, is "practically inevitable" and is expected to be announced in the House of Commons on Monday, the New York Herald Tribune was informed tonight on the highest authority.

The King's uncompromising refusal to bow to the wishes of his Ministers and end his association with Mrs. Simpson is understood to have been made clear to Prime Minister Stanley Baldwin in an interview with the King at Buckingham Palace late tonight.

The King and Mr. Baldwin talked for an hour. At eleven o'clock the Prime Minister rushed to Downing Street and conferred with Dominions officials to tell them of the King's decision.

After seeing Mr. Baldwin the King went immediately to Marlborough House for a forty-minute interview with Queen Mary.

The Duke of York, as next in line for the throne, will automatically become King when the decision is made known Monday. Unforeseen developments meanwhile, it was stated, might occasion an earlier announcement of the King's abdication after less than a year on the throne.

ROYAL ROMANCE HEROINE SEEN THROUGH CAMERA

Mrs. Simpson Noted as Popular Débutante and Charming Hostess

LACK OF WEALTH OFFSET BY SOCIAL STANDING AS GIRL

Ancestry Goes Back to First Virginia Legislators and Norman Knight

(By United Press)

BALTIMORE, Dec. 3. — The early life of Mrs. Wallis Warfield Simpson, although lacking in luxury, was that of a socially popular American girl, and even today, persons here who have known the noted hostess in London assert she has not become Anglicized to any noticeable extent. She is forty years of age, two years younger than King Edward VIII and, like the Monarch, looks less than her age. There were no children born of her two marriages.

Mrs. Simpson was christened Bessie Wallis Warfield, but the Bessie disappeared during the days of her first coming-out parties in Baltimore.

After two years of social life in Baltimore, Annapolis, Washington and Philadelphia, Mrs. Simpson met her first husband, Lieutenant Earl Winfield Spencer jr., now a commander aboard the aircraft-carrier Ranger. Spencer was then an aviator. The couple were married in Baltimore November 18, 1916, and their first year of married life was spent mostly at naval stations in Florida and California.

In 1927, Mrs. Simpson established legal residence in Warrenton, Va., and sued for divorce against Spencer, charging desertion. The divorce was granted in December, 1927.

Mrs. Simpson met her second husband, Ernest Aldrich Simpson, of New York, official of a ship-chartering firm, Harvard graduate, and former officer of the crack Coldstream Guards, in 1928. They were married in England July 28, 1928, and at a hearing of her divorce suit against her husband in Ipswich, England, October 27 last, Mrs. Simpson testified that they lived happily "until 1934."

PRESS INTRODUCES MRS. W. SIMPSON TO BRITISH PUBLIC

By JACK BEALL
(From the Herald Tribune Bureau)

LONDON, Dec. 3.—From a city in which the name of Mrs. Wallis Simpson was taboo in the press and unknown to the masses, London has overnight become sibilant with the name of King Edward's intended bride. She is undoubtedly the most discussed woman in the world at this moment, and more vigorously here than anywhere else, although they have a long way to go to catch up on many spots of the globe. And the press is fairly revelling in its new-found freedom of using Mrs. Simpson's name.

Unknown at Noon

Whereas at noon one could actually walk along the Strand or in Piccadilly and hear the people ask in startled voices as they viewed the placards: "Who is this Mrs. Simpson?" by 6 o'clock there was no one left who did not know. A singular development in practically all the afternoon papers was the "good press" she got. It would seem that editors and owners, either favoring the King's side or taking out insurance against all eventualities, had conspired to "sell" her to the public. Some were positively flowery.

There are some papers which make a special point of the story that Mrs. Simpson's mother took paying guests into her Baltimore home and that she, as a girl, was known as "Bessie" and affected a monocle, hung by "a thick satin ribbon around her neck." All the papers show that their editors and writers have assiduously read American weeklies and newspapers, which have featured Mrs. Simpson's background.

SATURDAY, DECEMBER 5, 1936

KING, MRS. SIMPSON MET IN 1926 AT COURT CEREMONY

LONDON, Dec. 3. — King Edward VIII first met Mrs. Wallis Warfield Simpson when she was presented with other Americans at the English Court in 1926 but their friendship did not start until 1928, when both were in Biarritz, according to members of the circle in which Mrs. Simpson moves here.

Not until May 27 last did Mrs. Simpson's name appear in official announcements. Then her name was given among the guests at the private Derby Day dinner given by the King at St. James's Palace. Mr. Simpson also attended, with members of nobility. From May until October, Mrs. Simpson was mentioned often in official lists, including those of the King's Mediterranean yachting vacation in August and the Balmoral house party of September 23-30.

During the shore excursions of the royal yachting cruise, Mrs. Simpson rode with King Edward in his automobile, as he received the plaudits of Greek and Turkish crowds.

Mrs. Simpson is reputed to have influenced King Edward in his consideration of internal policies, such as housing and unemployment. On the other hand, she is not devoted to night clubs, drinks sparingly, and is careful in money matters, according to friends.

Top left: Mrs. Simpson shopping recently in London. Top right: King Edward, then Prince of Wales, walking with Mrs. Simpson in Vienna in February last year. Right inset: Mrs. Simpson as débutante. Center: Mrs. Simpson photographed at Warrenton, Va., in 1927. Left inset: a recent portrait of Mrs. Simpson. Below: a recent portrait of the King.

THE KING AND MRS. SIMPSON IN SUMMER VACATION MOODS

A motorboat scene at the right shows the King and his American friend in a Dalmatian bay in August. At the left are the couple, with friends in the background, at Salzburg, Austria, after the Dalmatian vacation. The latest photograph of Mrs. Simpson is in the inset.
—(New York Herald Tribune photos.)

FOREIGN EXCHANGE RATES
Dollar in Paris - - - 21fr. 45 3/4c.
Dollar in London - - - - - 4s. 1d.
Dollar in Rome - - - - - - 19 lire
Dollar in Berlin - - - - - 2m. 49pf.
Pound in Paris - - - - - 105fr. 15c.

NEW YORK
Herald Tribune

SAILINGS to NEW YORK
Manhattan - - - - - - - Dec. 15
Washington - - - - - - - Dec. 30
Pres. Harding - - - - - - Jan. 7
Manhattan - - - - - - - Jan. 16
UNITED STATES LINES
10 R. Auber, Paris. — 7 Haymarket, London

50th YEAR No. 17.967 EUROPEAN EDITION PARIS, FRIDAY, DECEMBER 11, 1936 THE NEW YORK HERALD (ESTABLISHED IN EUROPE 1887) PRICE: In France, One Franc.

King Abdicates in Favor of Duke of York

George VI to Be Proclaimed Tomorrow After Speedy Formality

U.S., ARGENTINE AGREE TO LIMIT ANTI-WAR PACT

Scope Confined to Western Hemisphere, Thus Permitting Supply of Raw Material to Europe in War

BRAZIL PLAYS ROLE IN BRINGING ACCORD

Only Cloud on Conference Horizon Now Is Chaco, Dispute Still Unsettled

(By United Press)

BUENOS AIRES, Dec. 10.—The first big problem to confront the Inter-American Peace Conference in session here was solved today when the Argentine and the United States reached an agreement that the proposed anti-war pact now under discussion shall be limited to the Western Hemisphere. This accord has removed the first threat to the success of the conference.

Secretary of State Cordell Hull stated in connection with the accord that "the only interpretation of the proposed pact is that its scope shall be continental, and not world-wide." In this sense the Hull-Saavedra Lamas accord has now been incorporated in the draft convention which the delegates here are considering at present.

Only New World Involved

In a further statement Secretary Hull said that "the American republics would only be called upon under the proposal to consult through the suggested permanent committee when the peace or safety of one or more nations of this hemisphere was involved." This declaration is interpreted here as designed to calm the fears of European states that supplies of cotton, oil and copper might be cut off from them in case they went to war.

Statesmen who participated in the conferences for the ironing out of the differences between Argentina and the United States consider that the new machinery for consultation which has been agreed on will prove to be one of the most important contributions of recent years to the cause of world peace. They believ... machinery migh... we... Europe and elsewher...

Brazil's Rôle

Brazil's important ... Argentina and the U... ter is being praised ... ference quarters. T... ation has, in the m... that all the republic... be asked to explain ... not having ratified ... existing pacts to in... two Americas.

At today's meetin... for the organiza... proval was given t... sented by the Unit... ratification of exis... ments, including an... made to the Monte... the creation of a p... son of conciliation... no agreement was, ... to measures cov... behalf of peace ... ras. The attitude ... toward the League ... be, at present. ... make any steps to ... with this body feasi...

The only cloud ... horizon today was ... Chaco war. The d... Paraguay and Boli... being settled, desp... statements that have ... delegates to the con...

The W...

Predictions ...

Cold overcast, se... light easterly win... yesterday: Max. 2 (... 28 Fahr.).

The cold weather will continue in the Paris area today. The sky will be overcast again, and there may be a little snow or sleet. Winds will remain light, but will shift to east. There will be a slight sea in the Channel.

The weather was cold and dull throughout northern and central Europe yesterday. In Paris the maximum temperature was 36 in Paris 34 and in Berlin 33. In the London area and some parts of northern France there were ground fog or mists.

In New York the weather was rainy and mild, with the temperature rising to 51.

Text of Abdication Statement Read by Baldwin in Commons

The following is King Edward's statement of abdication, which was read to the House of Commons yesterday by Prime Minister Stanley Baldwin:—

After long and anxious consideration I have determined to renounce the throne to which I succeeded on the death of my father, and I am now communicating this, my final and irrevocable decision. Realizing as I do the gravity of this step, I can only hope that I shall have the understanding of my peoples in the decision I have taken and the reasons which have led me to take it. I will not enter now into my private feeling, but I will beg that it should be remembered that the burden which constantly rests upon the shoulders of the Sovereign is so heavy that it can only be borne in circumstances different from those in which I now find myself.

I conceive that I am not overlooking the duty that rests upon me to place in the forefront the public interest when I declare that I am conscious that I can no longer discharge the heavy task with efficiency or with satisfaction to myself. I have accordingly, this morning, executed an instrument of abdication in the terms following:

I, Edward VIII of Great Britain, Ireland and the British Dominions Beyond the Seas, King, Emperor of India, do hereby declare my irrevocable determination to renounce the throne for myself and for my descendants and my desire that effect should be given to this instrument of abdication immediately.

In token whereof I have hereunto set my hand this 10th day of December, 1936, in the presence of the witnesses whose signatures are inscribed.

Signed: EDWARD, R.I.

My execution of this instrument has been witnessed by my three brothers, their Royal Highnesses the Duke of York, the Duke of Gloucester and the Duke of Kent.

I deeply appreciate the spirit which has actuated the appeal which has been made to me to take a different decision, and I have, before reaching my final determination, most fully pondered over it. But my mind is made up. Moreover, further delay cannot but be most injurious to the peoples whom I have tried to serve as Prince of Wales and as King, and whose future happiness and prosperity are the constant wish of my heart. I take my leave of them in the confident hope that the course which I have thought it right to follow is that which is best for the stability of the throne and Empire and the happiness of my people.

I am deeply sensible of the consideration which they have always extended to me, both before and after my accession to the throne, and which I know they will extend in full measure to my successor. I am most anxious that there should be no delay of any kind in giving effect to the instrument which I have executed and that all necessary steps should be taken to secure that my lawful successor, my brother, H.R.H. the Duke of York, shall ascend to the throne.

Signed: EDWARD, R.I.

All Titles To Be Relinquished by Tonight; 'Mr. Windsor' Broadcast to Empire at 10 p.m.

New King and Emperor

The Duke of York who will be proclaimed King George VI on Saturday

'We Talked in Friendship,' Says Baldwin in Statement

(By Special Dispatch)

LONDON, Dec 10.—Prime Minister ... that during this last week I have had but little time in which to compose a speech for delivery today, and so I ...

Former Ruler Expected To Leave England Immediately after Radio Talk, Possibly Forever; Will Probably Get Dukedom

By FRANK R. KELLEY
(By Special Dispatch)

LONDON, Dec. 10.—King Edward VIII renounced his throne today because the vast empire over which he had ruled for only ten months refused to let him take Mrs. Wallis Warfield Simpson, of Baltimore, as his Queen.

The King announced his "irrevocable decision" to abdicate and named his eldest brother the Duke of York, as his successor in a dramatic message which was read to both Houses of Parliament this afternoon.

A bill was immediately introduced giving effect to the King's unprecedented action and barring him and his children from the throne. It will be rushed through both Houses and Edward will cease to be King and relinquish all his titles when he signs it tomorrow evening.

As plain "Mr. Windsor," the King will make a world-wide radio broadcast at 10 o'clock tomorrow night. Immediately he finishes he will leave the country—perhaps for ever.

New Ruler Will Be 41 Monday

As the King lifts his pen from the final papers of abdication, Albert, Frederick, Arthur, George, Duke of York, who will be 41 years old on Monday, will reign in his stead as George VI, a title which he has chosen in preference to Albert I, because of Queen Victoria's expressed wish that no future King should rule under the name of her Prince Consort.

The new Sovereign will be proclaimed throughout London and the Empire Saturday morning, following a second meeting of the Privy Council at St. James's Palace. One of his first acts will be to confer a high peerage, probably a dukedom, on his brother.

The King's action stunned the nation and Empire which had been hopeful to the last minute that he would stay on the throne. Hushed thousands massed outside Parliament as his message was being read. Crowds poured into the streets and headed for Buckingham Palace, the Duke of York's home and other central places to stand in silence.

There was little or no cheering.

Downcast Crowd Stand Before Palace

Edward VIII, who was on his way toward becoming the most popular King in England's history, had "walked out." It was as though he had died. Saddened throngs gathered in front of the ...ed in seclusion at Fort Belvedere, his ...gdale, where, this morning, with the ...loucester as witnesses, he signed the ...d then completed preparations for his

...ry into the World War, and hardly ... stirring, tense scenes in the House ... this afternoon when King Edward's ... read by the Speaker, the bewigged ...rime Minister Baldwin followed it up ...tion and defense of his own leading ...ngs which resulted in departure from ...Edward VIII and the substitution of ...k, who cannot hope to equal Edward's ... but who will be an effective, sober ... this critical era of world affairs.

...ons was so overcrowded that it ...to Parliament Square. Long queues ... and peers formed a queue to gain ... Mrs. Baldwin squeezed herself into ...r's chair.

...ous Laughter

...son, robbed of her usual seat, elected ... the diplomatic section were Robert ... Ambassador to the Court of St. ... France, Belgium, Turkey, Argentina, ...rway, Austria, Switzerland, Estonia, ...hoslovakia.

...verflowing and the public and other ... women were present. Eager to dis...s, members roared with laughter over ...mmunist, Willie Gallacher. Laughter ...rom all sides as the man of the hour, ...3:35 p.m.

...o a respectful murmur of expectation ... bar of the House. In great stillness, ...choked voice, announced, "A message ... signed by His Majesty's own hand." ... morning coat with a dark blue hand...reast pocket. He advanced slowly to... three times and handed the King's ... resumed his seat.

...ow craned to watch the proceedings. ...as Captain Fitzroy began the memor...anxious consideration. . . . " His voice ... he read the sheets which the King

... of the Speaker, the King announced ...ng and anxious consideration" he had ...able decision" to renounce the throne, ...Without going into his private feelings ...ld Simpson, the King reminded listen...len is so heavy it can be borne only in ...m those in which I now find myself."

(Continued on Page 2, Col. 1)

... Saturday wou... Edward would ... cumstances. Th... divorce nisi, g... October, does ... until April, a... anything whic... chance of fulfil...

Airports, ...

However, the ... guard outside ... chances on a ... slipping throug... lines. All airp... are being wat... that last night ... conditions. Ar... leaves Genoa ... Villefranche ... Janeiro, an u... treat for the ... under surveilla...

PARIS, SATURDAY, DECEMBER 12, 1936

ENGLAND'S THRONE NOW HAS TEN-YEAR-OLD HEIRESS

Princess Elizabeth, whose parents will be the new King and Queen of England, is shown at the left above with her small sister, Princess Margaret Rose. In the center above the little princess is shown as she drove to her home in Piccadilly a few days ago. On the right is a photograph taken shortly before she was bridesmaid at the wedding of the Duke of Kent and Princess Marina. Below, she is shown with her sister and parents on her arrival at a tournament last May. At the extreme right the camera caught the little princess unawares.—(New York Herald Tribune photos.)

King's Farewell to Empire

Introduced only by the words, "Prince Edward speaking from Windsor Castle," the former King addressed the British Empire by radio as follows:—

"At long last I am able to say a few words of my own. I have never wanted to withhold anything. Now it is at last possible for me to speak. A few hours ago I discharged my last duty as King and Emperor, and now that I have been succeeded by my brother, the Duke of York, my first words must be to declare my allegiance to him. This I do with all my heart.

"You all know the reasons which have compelled me to renounce the Throne, but I want you to understand that in making up my mind I did not forget the country nor the Empire, which as Prince of Wales and lately as King, I have for twenty-five years tried to serve. But you must believe me when I tell you that I find it impossible to carry the heavy burden of responsibility and to discharge my duties as King as I would wish to do without the help and support of the woman I love. I want you to know that the decision I have made has been mine and mine alone. This was a thing I had to judge entirely for myself. The only other person concerned tried up to the last to persuade me to take a different decision.

"I have made this, the most serious decision of my life, only upon the single thought of what would in the end be better for all of us. This decision has been made less difficult for me by the sure knowledge that my brother, with long training in the public affairs of this country, and with his fine qualities, will be able to take my place forthwith without interruption or injury to the life and progress of the Empire. And he has one great blessing enjoyed by so many of you and not bestowed on me, a happy home with his wife and children. In these hard days I have been comforted by her Majesty, my mother, and by my family. The Ministers of the Crown and in particular Mr. Baldwin, the Prime Minister, have always treated me with thought and consideration. There has never been any constitutional difference between me and them and between me and Parliament.

"Reared in the constitutional tradition created by my father, I should never have allowed any such issue to arise. Ever since I was Prince of Wales, and later on when I occupied the Throne, I have been treated with the greatest kindness by all classes of people wherever I have been or journeyed throughout the Empire. For that I am very grateful.

"I now quit altogether public affairs and I lay down my burden. It may be some time before I return to my native land, but I shall always follow the fortunes of the British race and Empire with profound interest and if at any time in the future I can be of service to his Majesty in a private station I shall not fail.

"And now we all have a new King. I wish to him and to you, his people, happiness and prosperity with all my heart. God bless you all! God save the King!"

SATURDAY, JULY 3, 1937

Earhart, Short of Fuel, Feared Down in Pacific

'Fuel for 30 Minutes,' She Radioes After Fog Makes Her Miss Goal

Honolulu Cutters Set Out on Long Journey Toward Howland Island to Seek Airwoman, Hours Overdue

APPROACHING ISLAND BEFORE GAS DWINDLED

Trouble Indicated One Hour After Flash Plane Was 100 Miles from Howland

BULLETIN
(3 a.m. Paris Time)

HONOLULU, July 2.—Two coast Guard cutters are racing to the area where Amelia Earhart and her navigator, Fred Noonan, were thought to be down in the Pacific Ocean six hours after the plane was due at Howland Island. United States Navy officials here are holding sea planes ready to be pressed into the search for the missing aviatrix. Experts said the plane could not remain afloat more than two hours. A rubber raft was included in the equipment, and it is thought Miss Earhart and Noonan must be afloat somewhere northwest of the island.

Down at Sea

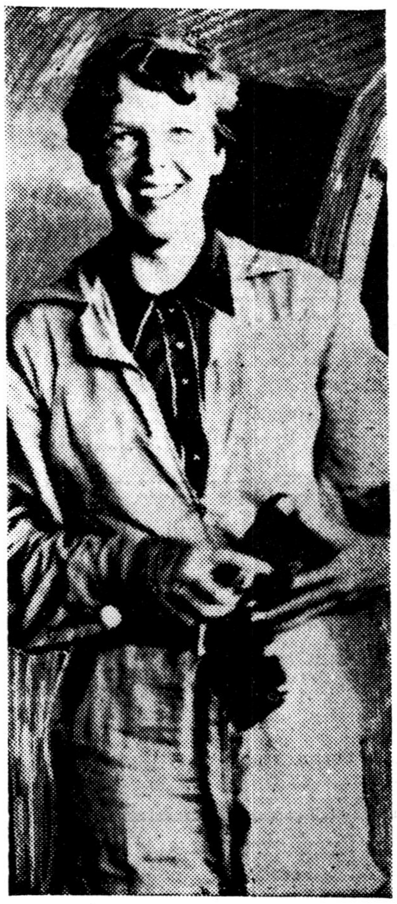

AMELIA EARHART

TWO-WAY TEST HOPS ON OCEAN AIR LINE SCHEDULED MONDAY

(Special to Herald Tribune)

NEW YORK, July 2.—The first test flight of trans-Atlantic commercial planes will start Monday, when a Pan American clipper and an Imperial Airways flying boat will take off at the same time to make the crossing in both directions simultaneously. They should pass in mid-ocean.

The American ship will leave Port Washington tomorrow to fly to Botwood, Newfoundland, where it will stay until Monday. This first lap is a distance of 1,075 miles. From Botwood, it will put out over the Atlantic for the mouth of the River Shannon, slightly more than 2,000 miles away. Then, following the river, it will continue to Southampton, which is 330 miles more. The westward route will be over the same course.

Juan Trippe, president of Pan American Airways, today said the main purpose of the test flights was to establish a regular schedule. He emphasized the commercial flights would differ from all previous trans-Atlantic flights in that they would be made on a regular schedule regardless of atmospheric conditions.

The clipper is driven by four motors of 1,000 horsepower each. The crew is composed of seven men under the orders of Pilot Harold Gray. Starting at 5:30 p.m. (G. M. T.), Monday, the American plane should land in Southampton early Tuesday morning.

JOHN T. UNDERWOOD DIES; BUILT FIRST VISIBLE TYPEWRITER

(By Special Cable)

NEW YORK, July 2.—John T. Underwood, inventor of the first practical visible typewriter and manufacturer of millions of the machines which bear his name, died this morning at his summer home on Cape Cod, Mass. He was eighty years old.

He was born in London, where his father, John Underwood, was a pupil of the great Michael Faraday, English chemist and physicist, and in turn became a chemical inventor, specializing in copyable inks.

Though the history of the typewriter dated back to the crude, and not strictly typewriting, device of Henry Mills (1714) and Sholes and Glidden had turned over their modern invention to the Remington Arms Company for manufacture in 1875, Mr. Underwood's conception of the machine on which copy could be read as it was written took many prizes and resulted in the founding, first, of the Underwood Typewriter Company in 1910 and then in the Underwood-Elliott-Fisher Company in 1927.

It is ranked today as the world's largest producer of typewriters and supplies and also leads in the production of flat-surface writing and accounting machines. One of the latest inventions of the company is all adding machine designed to facilitate the collection and recording of sales taxes.

Mr. Underwood retired from chairmanship of the company recently.

SUNDAY, JULY 4, 1937

Storms Force Back Earhart Rescue Planes

Putnam, Waiting to Greet Wife, Collapses; Freak Snow, Electrical Storms Rage in Howland Area

BATTLESHIP COLORADO ORDERED TO SEARCH

Technical Adviser Thinks Radio Signals Indicate Plane Reached an Island

(By Special Wireless)

SAN FRANCISCO, July 3. — A freak snow and electrical storm in mid-Pacific late this afternoon blocked the search for Amelia Earhart and her navigator, Fred J. Noonan, who were forced down in the Pacific near tiny Howland Island yesterday, and added to fears for their safety.

Navy planes, which were speeding to Howland Island to search for the missing flyers, were forced to turn back to their base at Pearl Harbor, Hawaii, after battling for two hours with snow, sleet and electrical disturbances. The destroyers Talbot and Dent and two aircraft tenders are stationed along the route of the Navy plane in case it too is forced down.

George Palmer Putnam, Miss Earhart's husband, who had come to San Francisco to greet his wife on her return from her round-the-world flight, is suffering from a nervous breakdown and is in the hands of a doctor.

For hours during the night and early this morning, faint SOS calls were received by various radio stations, but none revealed the position of the flyers. Operators said the calls were made by a woman. Late this afternoon, weak signals, including a man's voice imploring help, were heard in San Francisco.

EARHART, CHEMIST AND SOCIOLOGIST, WAS FLYER AT 19

The glamour of her flying achievements was such that few persons knew Amelia Earhart Putnam was wealthy in her own name, a linguist and a brilliant student with outstanding research work in experimental and calculative chemistry to her credit.

This tall, slim woman with a shock of unruly hair and a boyish smile burst casually into national prominence in June, 1928, as "only a passenger" on the trans-Atlantic flight of Wilmer Stultz and Louis Gordon. At that time she was an obscure social worker in Boston, and only a few intimate friends knew she had been flying since she was nineteen years old and held the seventeenth international license ever issued. But her daring caught the popular imagination, and, when the flight from Trepassey Bay, Newfoundland, to Burryport, Ireland, was made in 20 hours 49 minutes, she was held up as the "heroine."

Prepares for Flight

She vowed she would some day fly the Atlantic alone, and, from then on, she occupied herself less with her sociological work — giving extension courses in English to New England factory workers—and went into training for the flight. She had written a book about her trans-Atlantic trip, and became a friend of the publisher, George Palmer Putnam, and his wife. Later, Mrs. Putnam divorced her husband, and Miss Earhart and the publisher were married, February 7, 1931.

On May 28, 1932, Miss Earhart flew to Harbour Grace, and hopped off from there for Europe, landing near Londonderry, Ireland, 14 hours and 56 minutes later—the fastest trans-Atlantic flying time then on record.

Ice formed on the wings of her plane during this flight, for 500 miles she battled against storms, her altimeter broke and flames from the exhaust threatened to set the plane afire. Nevertheless, she kept on and her safe landing made her the first person to have flown the Atlantic twice.

Foreign Exchange Rates
Dollar in Paris............ 31fr. 50c.
Dollar in London.................. 4s.
Dollar in Rome................ 19 lire
Dollar in Berlin...... 2m. 48 7/8pf.
Dollar in Brussels.......... 29fr. 67c.
Pound in Paris........... 157fr. 70c.

NEW YORK
Herald Tribune

SAILINGS to NEW YORK
Pres. Roosevelt Mar. 17 Apr. 14
Washington .... Mar. 24 Apr. 21
Pres. Harding.. Mar. 31 Apr. 28
Manhattan ...... Apr. 7 May 5
UNITED STATES LINES
10 R. Auber, Paris. — 7 Haymarket, London

51st Year No. 18,423 European Edition PARIS, SUNDAY, MARCH 13, 1938 THE NEW YORK HERALD ESTABLISHED IN EUROPE 1887 In France, 1fr. 25c.

Hitler at Linz Proclaims Austria Part of Germany As Reich Army Sweeps Through Country to Brenner

Blum's Plan For National Government Abandoned

Premier-Designate Opens Consultations With Left Parties for Formation Of Popular Front Group

Right, Center Balk Pleas for Unity

Completion of Cabinet by Late Today Is Forecast With Socialists, Radicals But Without Communists

M. Léon Blum's attempt to form a National Union government, including representatives of all parties, collapsed last night, as the Right and Center groups refused their participation.

All, with the exception of the small Popular Democratic group, objected to the inclusion of the Communists, on which M. Blum insisted.

Faced with this refusal, the Premier-

(Continued on Page 3, Col. 4.)

The Weather

Predictions for Today:

Milder, sunny, fine. Light north-easterly winds. Temperature yesterday. Max. 15 (59 Fahr.); min. 1 (34 Fahr.).

The Paris region will again have pleasant weather today. It will be sunny and slightly milder than yesterday. Winds will be light and north-easterly, with some stronger gusts. The sea in the English Channel will be light.

It was mild and sunny in Paris yesterday. London weather was fair. The maximum temperature in the two cities was respectively 59 and 54. It was bright in Berlin, where the temperature at noon was 43.

New York had a fair day, and the noon temperature was 39.

Nicholas Bukharin Hits Back At Prosecutor Vishinsky with Slashing Protest Over Charges

BULLETIN

By United Press

MOSCOW, March 12.—The Special Soviet Court handed down death sentences for all but three of the twenty-one on trial here for treason.

Among the defendants who will be executed are: Henry Yagoda, former G. P. U. head; Alexei Rykov, former President of the Council of People's Commissars; Nicholas Bukharin, former editor of "Izvestia"; A. P. Rosenholtz, former Trade Commissar, and N. N. Krestinsky, former Vice-Commissar for Foreign Affairs.

Those sentenced to prison were: Dr. D. R. Pletnev, heart specialist, twenty-five years; K. G. Rakovsky, former Ambassador to France, twenty years, and S. A. Bessanov, former Counselor of the Soviet Embassy in Berlin, fifteen years.

By Joseph Barnes

MOSCOW, March 12.—Nicholas Bukharin, former editor of the official "Izvestia," struck back tonight at Prosecutor Vishinsky in the most slashing protest ever heard at a major Soviet treason trial.

A few hours before the Supreme Court's Military Collegium retired to consider the verdicts against the twenty-one prisoners, Bukharin in his final words to the court protested against the prosecutor's tactics and repeated his personal innocence of many of the charges against him. He recognized his guilt and assumed responsibility for conspirators' actions of which he had never even heard.

"I have committed enough crimes to deserve shooting ten times," he said.

But he insisted that Vishinsky had ... group of men many of whom never saw each other before," he said. "The logic of the struggle led us to take certain acts and decisions for which we must assume full responsibility. But this is something different from what Vishinsky accuses us of."

Bukharin's final words required more than an hour near the end of a long series of abject, cringing self-denunciations from the other prisoners. Most of them pleaded for mercy, but outdid Vishinsky himself in bitter denunciation of their crimes.

All Ask for Mercy

By Havas Agency

MOSCOW, March 12. — The verdict for the twenty-one prisoners in the Moscow treason trial is expected to be

Nazis Turn Down Paris, London Note

Protest Against Invasion Held 'Inadmissible' as German Bayonets Control Key Points in Austria

By Ralph Barnes

From the Herald Tribune Bureau

BERLIN, March 13. — With Reich German bayonets controlling Austria this morning, the German government has bluntly rejected the strongly-worded French and British protests against invasion as if they were two equally worthless scraps of paper.

It would be difficult to overestimate the symbolic importance of the fact that when the diplomatic representatives of the two "great European democracies," one of which in the present crisis is without a government, called at the Foreign Office, they were received by a functionary of second rank, in the absence of any one higher up, who described the protest as "inadmissible." That is what Herr Hitler in his new hour of triumph thinks of the chancelleries in London and Paris.

When German soldiers wearing a uniform similar to that in which their fathers left the trenches in 1918, set foot on Austrian soil at 5 30 yesterday ... official time announced ... Goebbels, the mask was ... new version of Prussian ... Maddened by the heroic ... Kurt von Schuschnigg to ... Chancellor Adolf Hitler ... Bismarck's "iron," there ... use the whole phrase ... iron" since the steel- ... ttalions goose-stepping ... ustrian villages are meet- ... rally with no resistance. ... up to yesterday, Herr ... rebuilding of Germany, ... fficial acts involving the ... powers or military force ... Reich frontiers. The ... ers marched into the ... violation of the "dic- ... but that was Reich ter-

...M. From Sea ...00,000 in Drive

'Show World Germans' Unity,' Fuehrer's Call in First Speech; To Make Vienna Entry Today

German Soldiers Cross Frontier Before Dawn, Reach Brenner At 1 p.m., Fraternize With Italian Border Guards, Vienna Is Entered by Evening; 15,000, Planes, Tanks in Country; Paris and London Protest and Map Action for Future

CHANCELLOR ADOLF HITLER yesterday proclaimed Austria to be part of Greater Germany and the country was virtually annexed as Nazi troops swept through and occupied all important points. Austria is to be given a status that will make it a kind of dominion of the Reich.

Crossing the border south of Munich in the middle of the afternoon, the Führer arrived in the evening at Linz, where he addressed an excited crowd. He passed the night at an unrevealed village and is expected to arrive today in Vienna. He was hailed triumphantly. Throughout Austria the wildest enthusiasm greeted the arrival of German troops.

German soldiers crossed the Austrian frontier at 5:30 a.m., according to an official announcement from Berlin. By 1 o'clock, the first truckloads reached the famous Brenner Pass. A mixed mobilized division of Austrians and Germans were in Vienna by 8 p.m., while others goose-stepped through cheering Austrian crowds in the country's principal cities.

Field Marshal Hermann Goering was left in charge of the government in Berlin, starting reports that Hitler's right-hand man might become Chancellor of Germany, with the Führer as head of all Germans in the "Greater Reich," and Dr. Arthur Seyss-Inquart as head of Austria.

Schuschnigg Is Held Prisoner

Former Chancellor Kurt von Schuschnigg was held prisoner yesterday in his villa in the grounds of Belvedere Castle, while Dr. Arthur Seyss-Inquart went to join Chancellor Hitler at Linz. Black Shirts surrounded the villa. Former Burgomaster Richard Schmitz of Vienna was also a prisoner, his place being taken by Fritz Lahr, former Heimwehr strong-arm man.

Socialists, members of the Fatherland Front and other anti-Nazis fled hurriedly to the Swiss, Czechoslovak and Hungarian borders, but many failed to escape from the country before the Nazis closed down the borders. Throughout the country, former officials were placed in protective custody. Last night, marching men and women with Nazi emblems kept order in Vienna. Their orders came from Heinrich Himmler, Gestapo chief, and Rudolf Hess, Deputy Führer.

Chancellor Hitler left Berlin by plane at 8 o'clock in the morning and arrived in Munich at 10. He went by automobile to his birthplace, Braunau, and laid a wreath on the grave of his parents. He reached the suburbs of Linz about 6:10 p.m. and proceeded slowly through the dense throngs of heiling Austrians and Nazi troops to the town hall.

England and France Plan Action

Faced with a *fait accompli* in Austria, the governments of Great Britain and France made identical formal protests in Berlin, but are expected to bend most of their energies to formulating a strong joint Central European policy for the future. In both countries, officials now feel that forceful measures alone can have any effect on Chancellor Hitler, and that interference in Czechoslovakia will be strenuously opposed.

Britain has abandoned all thought of negotiating with Germany over colonies, but intends to redouble efforts to reach an agreement with Mussolini, which may mean dissolution of the Rome-Berlin axis. It is felt that, with German soldiers on the Brenner, Italy will be more ready to strengthen its ties with its World War allies.

France, in the person of Charles Corbin, Ambassador in London, informed the British government that if Czechoslovakia were attacked, it would take drastic action. Lord Halifax, Foreign Secretary, is said to have replied encouragingly. A Cabinet meeting tomorrow will decide whether England and France are to make an open military alliance to back their words.

The inevitability of French intervention in the event of an attempted coup by Hitler in Czechoslovakia was reiterated in official circles in Paris. French politicians were convinced that Britain is now sufficiently impressed with the scope of Hitler's plans to join in military action in case of another Central European crisis.

Germany to Respect Brenner Frontier

Official Italy appeared unalarmed by the arrival of German troops on its border. Hitler sent Mussolini an assurance that the Reich would respect the Brenner frontier forever. The attitude of the Italian government, radically changed from that of two days ago, now is that Schuschnigg's plebiscite was ill-advised, and that Austria was in need of Nazification.

Cordell Hull, Secretary of State, reiterated the intention of the United States to keep clear of the problem of Central Europe. The feeling in Washington was that Germany's aggressiveness was a sign of the weakness of England and France, but that the democracies would stand firm against any further encroachments by Hitler.

The Führer's official proclamation on the Austrian crisis was read over the radio by Dr. Josef Goebbels, Minister of Propaganda, at noon, while German airplanes were wheeling in the sky over Vienna.

Fuehrer Proclaims 'True Plebiscite'

By Walter B. Kerr

Herald Tribune Staff Correspondent

VIENNA, March 12.—Führer Adolf Hitler came to Austria tonight on the heels of 15,000 German soldiers and before a delirious crowd in the Hauptplatz of Linz proclaimed that Austria was a part of Germany,

The speech was broadcast to millions of Germans in Austria, Germany and other countries gathered around loud speakers in the streets, shops and public halls. The German Chancellor said:—

"Fellow countrymen and countrywomen, thank you for your words of welcome. Above all, thank you who have come here to witness the fact that it is not just the desire of a few persons to create this big Reich of the German nation, but that it is the will of the German people themselves.

"This evening, I would like to have some of our international know-

Hull Says U.S. To Keep Hands Off in Austria

American Defense Program Believed Given Strong Impetus by Developments

By United Press

WASHINGTON, March 12.—After conversations today with the German Ambassador and the French and British envoys, Secretary Cordell Hull reiterated the determination of the United States to maintain a hands-off policy on the Austrian situation.

Washington has not expressed its views to Berlin and has no intention ... German ... ined that ... tria were ... g's "breach ... ws of the multiple attitude ... United ... y, tremen- ... d military ... npanied by ... ilitary and ... ch $2,000,- ... gement to ... lidarity of ... to their ... fourthly, ... there is ... curity sys- ... J.P.).—Ap- ... t move in ... animously ... today, all ... nt on the ... Schusch- ... "Times," ... gain, and ... nt is the ... ry sense, ... The edi- ... an inevit- ... ks: "Will ... oral, now ... of Czecho- ... oil fields ... ine?" It ... to wish ... e as large

...t Gets ...ld Gay

... 12.—Mrs. ... ained an ... rce today ... e worker.

The heiress, who was married in October, sued her mother in 1936, alleging that she had been tricked into undergoing sterilization on the pretext that it was an operation for appendicitis. The action was dropped when the plaintiff refused to give evidence against her mother.

She accused Mr. Gay of drinking heavily and said that constant quarrels caused him to lose his love for her. She described how he struck her, knocking her down on New Year's Eve.

"He criticized me for extravagance even though I paid all the bills," she told the court.

... in the most solemn thing,— ... see in this action any- ... legitimate defense, and ... man of character in my ... accomplish in the same ... itical moment for Italy, ... ed the firmness of my ... Do not doubt that for ... thing will be changed. ... er may be the con- ... coming events, I have ... se German frontier on ... rance, and now I trace

(...ed on Page 2, Col. 2.)

MONDAY, MARCH 14, 1938

Scenes of the Sudden Nazi Occupation of Austria

Upper, two photos show the street crowds welcoming German Army troops as the divisions entered Austria and Vienna. Bottom photo shows Herr Hitler making his proclamation at Linz from balcony overlooking central plaza. —(Associated Press photo.)

German Fuehrer Enters Land of His Birth

The Nazi dictator shown after stepping from his automobile on to Austrian soil to take over control of the government. With him is the head of the Reich Army, General Keitel. —(Associated Press photo.)

Foreign Exchange Rates
Dollar in Paris .... 36fr. 85c.
Dollar in London .... 4s. 1 3 1d.
Dollar in Rome .... 19 lire
Dollar in Berlin .... 2m. 49 3/8pf.
Dollar in Brussels .... 29fr. 59c.
Pound in Paris .... 178fr. 70c.

NEW YORK Herald Tribune

SAILINGS to NEW YORK
Pres. Harding. Oct. 13 Nov. 10
Manhattan .... Oct. 20 Nov. 17
Pres. Roosevelt Oct. 27 Nov. 24
Washington .... Nov. 3 Dec. 1
UNITED STATES LINES
10 R. Auber, Paris — 1 Haymarket, London

51st Year. No. 18,624 | European Edition | PARIS, SATURDAY, OCTOBER 1, 1938 | THE NEW YORK HERALD (ESTABLISHED IN EUROPE 1887) | In France, 1 fr. 25c.

Czechs Accept Munich Decision With Resignation; 'Peace Heroes' Get Triumphal Welcome on Return As Europe Relaxes, Forecasts General Settlement

U. S. Envoys Are Praised By Roosevelt

Their Efforts in Crisis Are Called Fine Teamwork Crowned With Success; Hull and Welles Lauded

Press Sees Europe In 'Breathing Spell'

Stock Exchange Responds To News From Munich With Huge Buying Wave

By United Press

WASHINGTON, Sept. 30.—With the war crisis in Europe apparently past, President Roosevelt today prepared to leave for his Hyde Park, N.Y., home Sunday night. At the same time, the Department of State relaxed its pressure on Americans in Europe to come home.

The capital was speculating on whether the new four-power pact of Munich would bring a permanent peace to Europe, including Spain, or would merely postpone an inevitable war by making the Fascist states so powerful that they could march roughshod over the rest of the Continent.

President Roosevelt stressed the service on behalf of peace performed by Secretary of State Cordell Hull, Under-Secretary of State Sumner Welles and other diplomatic officials in the various capitals. He declared it was a fine example of team play and co-operation which met with great success.

Calls Crisis Real

The President called the recent tension a real crisis, compared with many so-called crises. He said he sent the Czech note, asking United States arbitration if the Munich conference failed, to the State Department for answering. The President seems relaxed and gratified at the conclusion of weeks of strain.

Secretary Cordell Hull, in a guarded statement on the Munich agreement, declared, "as to immediate peace results, it is unnecessary to say that they afford a universal sense of relief.

Should Redouble Efforts

"I am not undertaking to pass comment upon the merits or the differences to which the four-power pact related. It is hoped, in any event, that the forces which stand for the principles governing peaceful and orderly international relations under proper application should not relax but redouble efforts to maintain the principles under law resting upon a sound economic foundation."

In New York, the Stock Exchange experienced an immense buying wave after the disappearance of the war clouds. Afternoon newspapers' bannerlines announcing the signing of the Anglo-German accord overshadowed the actual settlement on Czechoslovakia.

Breathing Spell Seen

The New York "World-Telegram," in an editorial captioned: "Peace — or Truce?" said:

"Civilization has apparently been given a breathing spell. . . Hitler indicated that he intends to push on to the Black Sea, the Baltic and into the Ukraine."

The paper urges immediate "liquidation of the vexatious, war-causing problems" in Europe to prevent recurrence of the crisis.

The New York "Post" had a huge front-page bannerline saying: "Britain, Reich Pledge Never to Fight Again." It editorially declares the price of peace is costly. However, "because we have the Atlantic between us and the terror, we dare not in decency denounce the peace of Munich."

The New York "Journal" front-page headline was almost identical with that of the "Post," except that it was larger.

Queen Has Laryngitis

LONDON, Sept. 30 (Special).—Queen Mary is suffering from an attack of laryngitis and will be unable to lay the foundation stone of the children's ward at West Herts Hospital at Hampstead tomorrow, it was announced yesterday. She last appeared in public in the gallery of the House of Commons Thursday to hear Prime Minister Neville Chamberlain's address.

The Weather

Predictions for Today:

Mild, generally fair. Moderate southwesterly winds. Temperature yesterday: 20 (68 Fahr.); min. 10 (50 Fahr.).

It will continue mild in the Paris region today, and will be generally fair. Winds will be moderate and southwesterly. The sea in the English Channel will be slight.

It was mild and partly cloudy in Paris yesterday. The maximum temperature was 68. In London, there was rain and a maximum temperature of 66. Berlin weather continued bright, and the temperature was 69 at noon.

There was rain in New York, where the noon temperature was 64.

Army Theories Hit By Mosely On Retirement

Declares U.S. Wastes Huge Sums on Untried Ideas; Woodring Raps General As 'Flagrantly Disloyal'

By Special Wireless

ATLANTA, Ga., Sept. 30. — A few minutes after leaving the Army's active list on reaching retirement age, Major General George V. H. Mosely, in a statement, decried the "unfortunate attitude of some of our government officials," but lauded the Army as "the one stable element in the unstable and shifting domestic scene."

Angered at this attack on the government by an officer drawing a government pension, Secretary of War Harry Woodring in Washington immediately branded General Mosely's statement as "flagrantly disloyal" and an exhibition of "pique and bad taste."

'Faces Decay From Within.'

General Mosely declared:—

"In addition to the lack of an outstanding leadership, the government has recently suffered from an indigestible mass of untried theories, on which we have lavished the greatest peacetime appropriation in the nation's history. . . . The United States is facing the danger of decay from within."

Secretary Woodring, after the "flagrantly disloyal" remark, said of General Mosely:—

Declares Mosely Disappointed

"He has celebrated his retirement by assailing the government, and inferentially its commander in chief, because he was disappointed in his ambition to become the chief of staff of the American armies.

"I have an idea his brother officers will be as much astonished as dismayed by this exhibition of pique and bad taste. As a general run, they are citizens who have always accepted the theory that an officer's loyalty to his chief does not cease when he has retired."

Arab Terrorists Prepare To Organize Own Cavalry

8 British Killed, 36 Wounded In September

JERUSALEM, Sept. 30. — British casualties during the month of September throughout Palestine, according to the Palestine "Post," were eight soldiers and policemen killed and thirty-six wounded.

There were 359 other persons killed, including 146 terrorists, and 174 wounded.

Wholesale stealing of horses, mules and even polo ponies, from police stations and private owners in Palestine is being carried on by Arabs, who are said to be forming their own cavalry units.

In one day seventeen police horses were stolen while proceeding between Majdal and Gaza, and ten riding horses were taken from a livery stable and equestrian school on the outskirts of Tel Aviv.

It is believed that the terrorists have over 300 horses, mules and ponies in their possession.

Wall Street

	High	Low	Close
U.S. Steel	59 1/4	58 3/8	59
Gen. Motors	48	47 1/4	47 1/2
Int. Tel. & T.	9 7/8	9 1/8	9 3/4
N.Y. Central	17 1/2	17	17 1/8

Market trend higher. Trading active. Volume 1,900,000 shares. Leaders gained fractions to five points. Heavy buying brought sharp advances at the outset. Nearly 800,000 shares changed hands in first hour. Stocks were bought in large blocks. The ticker was clogged. Some initial quotations were delayed twenty-five minutes. Motors were strong on increased output. International issues were favored. Gains included: Chrysler 2 3/4, General Motors 1 5/8, U.S. Steel 2 1/8, Union Pacific 4, Case 5, Allied Chemical 5 1/2, Eastman Kodak 6 1/4 and Johns-Manville 3. Full market reports: Page 5.

Chamberlain Acknowledges Cheers of Crowd Before Buckingham Palace

Premier Chamberlain smiles and waves in response to plaudits of the crowd as he appears on the balcony of Buckingham Palace with his wife, King George VI and Queen Elizabeth. The King, at the right, smiles his appreciation of the Prime Minister's efforts on behalf of world peace. —A.P. Radio photo.

Mussolini Given Great Welcome On Return Home

'Peace With Justice Won,' Says Taciturn 'Mediator' While Britons Wave Flag

By James M. Minifie

From the Herald Tribune Bureau

ROME, Sept. 30.—Premier Mussolini, accompanied by Count Galeazzo Ciano, his Foreign Minister, returned from Munich to Rome this evening amid the tumultuous enthusiasm of his people who regard him as the savior of world peace. At the height of his glory at home and esteemed as never before abroad, he was strangely taciturn and spoke only three sentences from the historic balcony of the Palazzo Venezia.

He was welcomed with spontaneous demonstrations of delight and affection surpassing anything that this city has seen since the war. As his car rolled slowly along the main streets from the station to the Palazzo Venezia, with Il Duce standing alone in the back, vast throngs broke through the police cordons and surged after him.

Axis Forged Year Ago

It was a year to the day, to the hour even, of his return from his first visit to Germany when the Rome-Berlin axis was forged.

Today's welcome was in strong contrast with the elaborate preparations which had been made a year ago, with triumphal arches and the streets strewn with laurel leaves, with cannon booming and rockets flashing. This afternoon, a few flag poles used during Hitler's visit were hastily erected near the station and flags hung from the houses along the route. They were Italian flags only, with the exception of the Piazza Venezia, where the strange spectacle was seen of a British flag the first time for many years. It was the Red Ensign of the British Mercantile Marine, waved vigorously by a group of Scotch and Irish Catholics on pilgrimage who had stationed themselves hard by the main door of the Duce's palace. There were no German or French flags.

Il Duce's car, escorted by two motorcycle police and followed by cars with Count Ciano and members of the Cabinet, reached the Palazzo Venezia at 6:15 o'clock. Ten thousand people massed in the square applauded frenziedly, not with the staccato regimented cry of "Duce, Duce," but by clapping their hands and shouting. Many women wept.

Five minutes later, Il Duce stepped out on the balcony and looked down at his people, a mosaic of upturned faces and waving arms. Not till then

(Continued on Page 3, Col. 2)

Britain, Germany Pledge Peace

Special to Herald Tribune

MUNICH, Sept. 30.—The mutual desire of Germany and Britain never to go to war with each other again, as well as the determination of the two countries to assure peace by removing the causes of difficulty in Europe and to adopt the method of consultation in dealing with Anglo-German problems was announced by Prime Minister Neville Chamberlain this afternoon after a private conversation of an hour and a half with Chancellor Adolf Hitler.

Mr. Chamberlain made the following statement to the British press:

"I have always had in mind that if we could find a peaceful solution of the Czech problem it would pave the way to a general appeasement of Europe.

"This morning I talked with the Fuehrer. We both signed the following declaration:

"We, the German Führer and Chancellor, and the British Prime Minister, have had a further meeting today and are agreed in recognizing that the question of Anglo-German relations is of the first importance for the two countries and for Europe.

"We regard the agreement signed last night and the Anglo-German Naval Agreement as symbolic of the desire of our peoples never to go to war with one another again.

"We are resolved that the method of consultation shall be the method adopted to deal with any other question that may concern our two countries, and we are determined to continue our efforts to remove possible sources of difference and thus to contribute to the assurance of peace in Europe."

Mr. Chamberlain would not say whether the question of colonies was discussed with Herr Hitler. He merely said that he had had a general discussion, which was of a very friendly nature. It would be followed by further personal meetings, if need arose.

Thousands Hail 'Peace Premier' Thousands Cheer

'I Believe It Is Peace for Our Time,' Chamberlain Tells Downing St. Crowd

From the Herald Tribune Bureau

LONDON, Sept. 30.—Prime Minister Neville Chamberlain returned to London from Munich this evening bringing with him what he described as "peace with honor" and hundreds of thousands of peace-loving hero-worshiping Britishers turned out to give him a grateful welcome home in stirring street scenes the like of which have not been equalled in London since Armistice Day 1918.

Mr. Chamberlain came back from a bloodless two-day war fought out over tea and beer and sandwiches by the "Big Four," who have taken over direction of European affairs from the League of Nations—Adolf Hitler, Benito Mussolini, Edouard Daladier and Chamberlain himself. Germany won the diplomatic war in that it is marching into Bohemia tomorrow to dispossess the Czechs, but all Europe and the world were victors to the extent that there has been averted at the eleventh hour a repetition of the World War of 1914-1918 in which over eight million were killed.

'Peace With Honor'

Standing on the balcony of his home at 10 Downing Street tonight Mr. Chamberlain told the cheering thousands below him:—

"My good friends, this is the second time in our history that there has come back from Germany to Downing Street peace with honor.

"I believe it is peace for our time.

Early this morning, Mr. Chamberlain and the rest of the "Big Four" had signed a peace treaty which authorized Herr Hitler to take over the Sudeten land areas by gradual stages, beginning tomorrow. Not satisfied with this alone, Mr. Chamberlain and Herr Hitler got together again after breakfast and signed an Anglo-German pact of friendship, whereby the two nations resolve never to go to war against each other and to settle all disputes by consultation and negotiation.

Another Conference Foreseen

No one need be surprised if Mr. Chamberlain follows this up by arranging another conference in the near future, at which Britain would attempt to appease Germany's hunger for a colonial empire by offering her an

(Continued on Page 3, Col. 1)

Poles Threaten Action Unless Prague Yields

Warsaw Demands Immediate Withdrawal From Teschen Area in Virtual Ultimatum

By United Press

WARSAW, Sept. 30.—While the rest of Europe was rejoicing over the prospects of a long period of peace as the result of the Munich agreement, an ominous warning came from the Warsaw Foreign Office today that Poland would "resort to measures which may have far-reaching consequences," if Prague does not agree to the immediate cession of the disputed Teschen district.

The statement was issued after a long meeting held under the chairmanship of President Ignatz Moscicki. It said:

Demands Immediate Settlement

"Poland is determined to settle the conflict with Czechoslovakia independently. The Czech answer to the Polish note, which has been expected for three days, will be handed over in Warsaw tonight. It will be examined immediately. Should the Czech answer contain no agreement to the immediate cession of the disputed territory, the Polish government in the course of the evening will resort to measures which may have most far-reaching consequences. The responsibility will be Prague's."

The Polish government is reported to be annoyed at not having been invited to Munich.

Today's note to Czechoslovakia, which is said to insist on the early evacuation of the Teschen district by Czech troops, is the third Warsaw has sent Prague in the last week.

1925 Treaty Denounced

In the first note the Poles denounced the 1925 minority treaty with Czechoslovakia. The Czechs replied that they accepted the note as a basis of discussion. The second note stated that Warsaw appreciated the good will of the Czech government, but demanded the evacuation of Teschen before negotiations began. When no answer was received to this today, the Polish government sent the third note.

Meanwhile, the radio and press campaign against Czechoslovakia increased in violence.

EUROPEAN EDITION PRICES IN FOREIGN COUNTRIES
England, 4d.; Germany and Austria, 25pf.; Italy, L. 1.50; Belgium, Belg. Fr. 1.75; Czechoslovakia, Kc. 2.50; Switzerland, 35 cent.

Fannie Brice Sues Billy Rose, New York Producer, for Divorce

Comedian, of 'My Man' Fame, Charges Mental Cruelty And Desertion in Action

By Special Wireless

LOS ANGELES, Sept. 30. — Fannie Brice, the comedienne who made the world cry with her song, "My Man," today sued Billy Rose, diminutive New York show producer for divorce on the grounds of mental cruelty and desertion.

She asked no alimony.

Last spring, she announced she would file the suit—but not because Billy was reported last year to be more interested in Eleanor Holm Jarrett.

Train, on Champagne

Mrs. Jarrett, shapely swimming star, broke into the headlines two years ago when the American Olympic Committee disagreed with her claim that she could sip champagne en route to Berlin and still be fit to take on the world's best swimmers.

Bill Rose, whose size belies his huge ideas when it comes to extravaganzas like "Jumbo" or "Casa Manana," promptly hired Mrs. Jarrett to star with Johnny Weissmuller in his water show at the Cleveland Exposition.

Later, Mrs. Jarrett was divorced from her orchestra-leader husband, Arthur Jarrett. Fannie Brice, in Hollywood, remarked of the reported romance between Eleanor and Billy:—

"That doesn't sound like the Billy Rose I know."

Stuck by Nicky Arnstein

Fannie Brice's "My Man" song swept the country after her second husband, Nicky Arnstein, went to jail for his part in a $5,000,000 bond theft and Fannie stood by him—sheltering him from police for a time and waiting for him until he served his sentence. They lived together after his release until Nicky assertedly became involved with another woman, when Fannie divorced him.

Czech Army Starts Sudetenland Evacuation German Troops Move in This Afternoon New Anglo-German, Franco-German and Mediterranean Accords Reported Likely

BULLETIN

By Special Dispatch

LONDON, Sept. 30. — It is understood that Benito Mussolini has invited Prime Minister Chamberlain to visit him as the guest of Italy in Rome. Following the meeting of Parliament Monday Mr. Chamberlain expected to make arrangements for a holiday cruise in the Mediterranean aboard a yacht. On the cruise he is to meet Signor Mussolini and continue discussions with him on Anglo-Italian relations, particularly the situation in Spain.

Accepted by Czechoslovakia at noon yesterday, the decisions of the Munich conference went into effect after midnight when Czechoslovak troops began to evacuate the first zone in southern Bohemia.

At 2 o'clock this afternoon German troops will march into the evacuated district.

Czechoslovakia's acceptance was formally notified to Premiers Daladier and Chamberlain at Munich after a Cabinet meeting in Prague held in the morning.

General Sirovy Breaks News to Czechs

The news of acceptance was announced to the Czechoslovak people by General Sirovy, the Premier, in a radio speech at 5 p.m.

The decisions reached at Munich were published in Prague after this speech.

The people's first reaction was one of amazement and indignation, but later in the evening calm and resignation set in, and consolation was sought in the statement by General Sirovy that hereafter the Czechs and the Slovaks will live happily among themselves.

'Peace Heroes' Returns Triumphal

The homecoming of Mr. Chamberlain, Premiers Daladier and Mussolini was made the occasion of delirious scenes of joy, such as have not been witnessed in Europe since Armistice Day, twenty years ago.

Mr. Chamberlain who appeared by the side of King George on the balcony of Buckingham Palace last night, told the crowds that he had repeated Disraeli's feat sixty years ago in bringing from Germany "peace with honor." "Peace for our time," he added, borrowing a phrase used by another British Premier, Stanley Baldwin.

Flowers Thrown to Premier Daladier

M. Daladier's progress through Paris, after landing at Le Bourget, was triumphal. Flowers were thrown at his car, women wept with joy, and the strains of the "Marseillaise" filled the courtyard of the War Ministry for more than ten minutes.

Premier Mussolini was welcomed in the Tyrol by children bearing flowers, and in Florence by King Victor Emmanuel. Rome accorded him a spontaneous and vociferous welcome, but the Duce was taciturn, and he disappointed hundreds of thousands in the Piazza Venezia when his response to the cheering multitudes turned out to be a fifteen-second speech.

Turning Point of History Seen

Comments on the Munich conference were almost unanimous that the historic meeting marks a turning point in European history.

It was hailed as the beginning of an era of real peace and the end of the international system built up with the peace treaties as a foundation.

Before leaving Munich, Mr. Chamberlain had another long talk with Mr. Hitler, and then made the momentous announcement that Great Britain and Germany will in future strive to settle all issues among themselves without war.

A similar Franco-German understanding is understood to be under way with the active interest of Marshal Goering.

Prague Gloomy, Stores Masks

By Havas Agency

PRAGUE, Sept. 30. — After a first movement of amazement and indignation, Prague tonight appeared calm and resigned to the amputation of Czechoslovakia, which the government earlier in the day accepted while protesting before the whole world that it had neither been consulted nor asked to participate in the formulation of the Munich decisions.

Although various and contradictory reports were in circulation all day, regarding the deliberations and decisions of the Munich Conference, it was not until 5 o'clock this afternoon that the Czechoslovak people learned of the sacrifice imposed upon it in the interests of European peace. The announcement was made over the radio by the Premier, General Jan Sirovy, who read the terms of the government's acceptance which was sent to Premier Chamberlain and Premier Daladier at Munich in the morning.

Evacuation Order Issued

Tonight, an official communique announced that in accordance with the arrangements agreed to by the four powers in Munich, the evacuation of the first zone in southern Bohemia will begin after midnight.

All through the day, huge crowds assembled outside the newspaper offices, but the censorship withheld publication of the Munich plan until General Sirovy spoke on the radio.

His address was listened to in silence, but when it was over a wave of wrath swept over the city. "It was not for this that we put a general at the head of the government," many shouted across the streets. Foreign veterans, who had fought with General Sirovy

(Continued on Page 3, Col. 4)

Berlin Sees Long Peace

By Ralph Barnes

From the Herald Tribune Bureau

BERLIN, Oct. 1.—German mechanized troops are scheduled to cross the frontier into Czechoslovakia at 2 p.m. today. Through this "invasion" Chancellor Adolf Hitler, without precipitating a European war, and under the "Big Four" agreement signed at Munich twenty-four-hours ago, will keep his "promise to the German people" to begin on October 1 the "liberation" of the Sudeten Germans and the "conquest" of their territory to the glory of Greater Germany.

On the eve yesterday of the day when the wheels of the Teuton advance guard are scheduled to rumble on to Czechoslovak soil the new "Iron Chancellor" and Neville Chamberlain signed at Munich a joint declaration in which they express "the desire of our two peoples never again to go to war against each other."

Franco-German Accord Seen

Reports are current that soon a similar Franco-German declaration will be signed.

These declarations, it is said, will be the first steps in a new western European settlement in which the statesmen who, in the twelfth hour "prevented a European conflagration" will play the leading roles. Besides Chancellor Hitler and Premier Chamberlain they are Premier Mussolini and Premier Daladier.

Other Questions Ahead

Two issues to be given precedence in the projected European settlement are, it is understood, the Spanish civil war and the colonial claims of Germany. Other questions which are expected to

(Continued on Page 3, Col. 5)

:: LIFE IN BERLIN ::

Shirley Temple Given $10,000 In London Suit Libel Settlement

Magazine Also to Pay Movie Company, English Branch $7,500, All to Go to Charity; Article, Not Read In Court, Roundly Condemned by Bench

By Special Dispatch

LONDON, March 22.—Shirley Temple, the child movie star, was awarded $10,000 today in settlement of a libel suit against the defunct "Night and Day" magazine, a humorous English publication.

Lord Hewart, Chief Justice, in approving of the terms of the out-of-court settlement, said that the libel was a "gross outrage." Sir Patrick Hastings, K.C., counsel for the movie moppet, said that he would "not even read" the libelous article.

The action arose from an article in "Night and Day," written by Graham Greene, one of the defendants, last fall. The article was a criticism of one of the latest Shirley Temple movies, "Wee Willie Winkie," based on the Rudyard Kipling story of India.

In addition to the child star, Twentieth Century-Fox brought suit against the magazine, the author of the article and the publishing firm of Chatto and Windus. The defendants agreed to pay Shirley Temple $10,000, the movie company $5,000 and its English subsidiary, $2,500.

In announcing the settlement, Sir Patrick told the court "that it was one of the most horrible libels that one can imagine about a child nine years of age.

"Obviously I shall not read it—it is better that I should not—but a glance at the statement of claim, where a poster is set out, is sufficient to show what the nature of the libel is against this child.

"This beastly publication was written but it is right to say that every respectable news distributor in London refused to be parties to its sale." he declared.

Had the libel, he added, appeared in an American paper about an English child there was no doubt that American courts would have taken the same action as today's.

He added that probably the child

(Continued on Page 3, Col. 6)

Shirley Temple

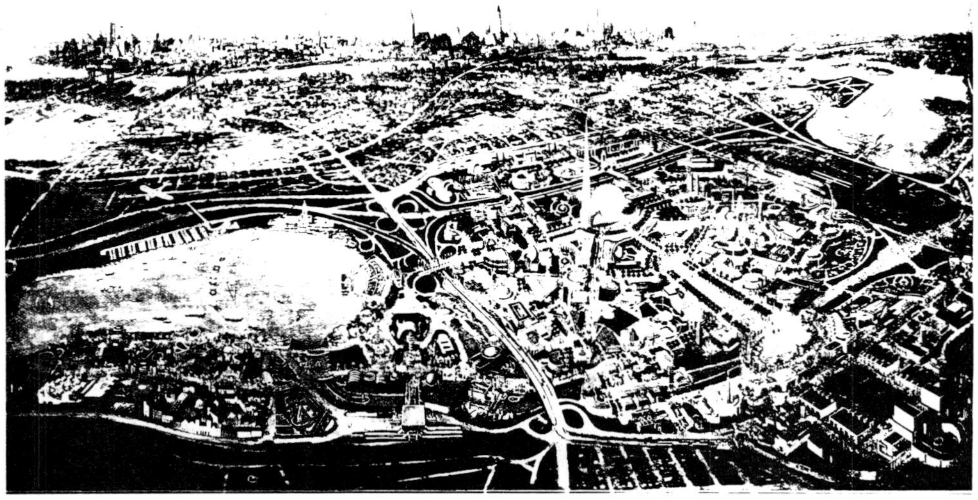

General view of Exposition Grounds. — Vue d'ensemble de l'Exposition.

N.Y. World's Fair, Greatest Ever Held, A Pre-View of Tomorrow's Civilization

CONCEIVED and carried out on a gigantic scale, the $155,000,000 New York World's Fair 1939 is not only the world event of this year. For years to come its influence on civilization, its impetus to international trade and good will, are destined to be felt with increasing force.

No other exposition has been dedicated to the praiseworthy task of "Building the World of Tomorrow." No other exposition can rival it in scope of mankind's activities, in participation by industry, business, states of the Union and foreign nations, in sheer physical enormity. Independent surveys forecast that at least 60,000,000 admissions will be paid during the six-month period, that $100,000,000 will be spent at the Fair, $1,000,000,000 in the New York area, and that business activity in the United States will benefit by a $10,000,000,000 fillip attributable to the Fair.

Covers 1,216 1/2 Acres

Occupying a tract of 1,216 1/2 acres, the New York World's Fair has been zoned into four major divisions: Main Exhibit Area, Court of States, Foreign Zone, and Amusement Area. Other sections include parking lots for 43,000 cars, a boat basin on Flushing Bay for crafts up to 12-foot draft, and picnic areas.

The heart of the entire exposition is the Perisphere and Trylon, the one a gleaming sphere 200 feet in diameter, the other a 700-foot triangular spire.

Past, Future Depicted

All that mankind has accomplished and all that can be foreseen now which he is likely to accomplish, unfold in the exhibit area, covering hundreds of acres.

In the Medical and Health exhibit is a model of a human eye so large that it permits several visitors to enter at the same time. The lens, or pupil, of the eye looks upon a busy avenue of the Fair. The scene is projected upon an artificial retina within the model. By the manipulation of levers, visitors view the lively scene as it appears to a nearsighted or far-sighted person, and to one of normal vision.

Travel in Rocket

The logical goal toward which transportation is advancing is portrayed by one of the exposition's focal exhibits. Movement, sound and light combine to bring about a remarkable simulation of a rocket flight, including the arrival of travelers at the rocketport, their entry into the cabin-projectile, the loading of this into the rocket-gun and the explosion sending the "ship" hurtling toward Mars or whatever destination is indicated on the tickets of passengers.

One of the most familiar household adjuncts is the medicine cabinet. Picture one twenty feet high and fifteen feet wide, with a door-mirror large enough to reflect 3,000 faces at one time. Then watch the cabinet transformed into a theater with puppet actors fourteen feet tall dramatizing the well-known cupboard as the family's first line of defense against disease and infection.

Perhaps no major section of the exposition better illustrates this tendency toward co-operation than the Foreign Zone. Never in history have three score foreign lands assembled in one restricted area to make a peaceful display of each country's contribution to civilization.

Travelers, real and potential, find the Foreign Zone a realization of that hitherto imaginary goal, "Around the World in 80 Minutes." It becomes a fact at the Fair. People, scenes and products from countries representing 90 per cent of the inhabited portions of the globe can be glimpsed within that brief period of time.

Every exposition must have its lighter side, and the New York World's Fair offers 280 acres of diversion and entertainment.

Thrills will be plenty, whether on the rides or such innovations as the 250-foot parachute tower. Youngsters have a Funland all their own in the Children's World.

Constitution Mall, the central esplanade, leads from the Theme Center to the Lagoon of Nations. This lagoon, 700 feet long and 400 feet wide, is a formalized development of the river that existed before a large tidal gate was installed to hold back the waters of Long Island Sound. It is the stage for nightly spectacles in which fountains, flame, sound and light combine to produce effects that could only be equalled in nature by piling Vesuvius on top of Niagara. At the climax of the display, which lasts half an hour all valves are closed instantaneously leaving 50 tons of water in the air to crash down in a tremendous finale.

Such is the New York World's Fair 1939. It has risen over a tidal swamp and, true to its purpose of Building the World of Tomorrow, it will leave a magnificent park to replace an eye sore. It is elaborate beyond compare yet it appeals to everyone. Visited by royalty, rulers and eminent statesmen it nevertheless is everyman's exposition and looks toward everyman's future.

Fair Visitors Can Hold Cost At Any Level

Comfortable Living in N.Y. Within Reach of Every Purse; Prices to Be Held Down Despite Exposition

IT IS remarkable how little—and how much—a visitor may spend in New York. Probably no city in the world presents a greater variety of ways for spending money. And yet no city is more hospitable and eager to co-operate with the visitor who must live inexpensively.

As in any great city eager to extend hospitality to everyone, the visitor usually gets what he pays for, but the important thing is for him to make up his mind how he wants to live, and how much he wants it to cost hm

Sky's the Limit

If he wants the luxury and social distinction of the largest suite in one of the city's most famous hotels, he must be willing to pay the customary $25 to $50 daily. If he wants more modest, he may pay $10 to $15 daily, and so on down the scale to the small, quiet hotels just off Times Square, or in the upper part of Manhattan where rooms are available for as low as $2 daily, or $10 weekly.

Eat at Any Price

Restaurant prices vary, of course, just as hotel prices do, but it is safe to set the minimum from $5 daily in the more expensive eating places to as low as $1 daily, if one wants to eat in the automatic, or cafeteria-type eating places. Three or four well-known restaurant chains operate in New York, and will also operate at the Fair. Fifty cents for breakfast, seventy-five cents for lunch, and $1.25 for dinner, plus 10 per cent tips, will guarantee a healthful and adequate fare.

Careful management can bring down the costs of incidentals to a minimum. Subway travel anywhere in New York costs only 5 cents; from New York to the Fair itself, the fare will be ten cents, to compensate the city partially for the cost of constructing a whole new railroad bed to the Fair. Subway service will be much cheaper and faster too, than taxi-cabs or buses. Entrance to the Fair will be 75 cents, and while many of the concessions and amusements will charge nominal fees, many will also be free.

Cheap and Expensive Fun

New York theaters and amusements have no intention of increasing their prices this summer. Musical shows command the highest prices, from $1.10 to $4.40 a ticket, while non-musical shows and motion pictures range from ten cents to $3.30. An evening in the city's night-clubs and cabarets may be had for as little as the price of a drink or two, as in many of the Greenwich Village cabarets, to the luxurious revues, which may have a "couvert" of $2 or $3. It is safe to say that an evening in the more luxurious night spot will cost the single visitor at least $10

The cost of living in American resort cities may be slightly higher than in New York, but in the other large cities, such as Chicago, Boston and Philadelphia, the costs will be about the same, with perhaps a slightly lower scale for hotels and restaurants.

World's Fair Views

A section of the roundhouse of the Railway Building

Above: The Hall of Fashion will contain exhibits representing the latest styles.

■■

Below: Casino of Nations, with retractable roof and 110-foot bar where 1,500 diners are served, waiters taking orders in twelve languages.

Two huge 80-foot prows flank the Maritime Building. In the left foreground is a novel lighting standard.

■■

The Trylon and Perisphere, theme center of the Exposition, with the Consumer Building in the foreground and fronting on the $60,000,000 Constitution Mall. The circular shadow cast by the Trylon on the Perisphere is visible for an hour early each morning.

Gleaming towers flank the entrance of the Hall of Communications, devoted to the history of communications.

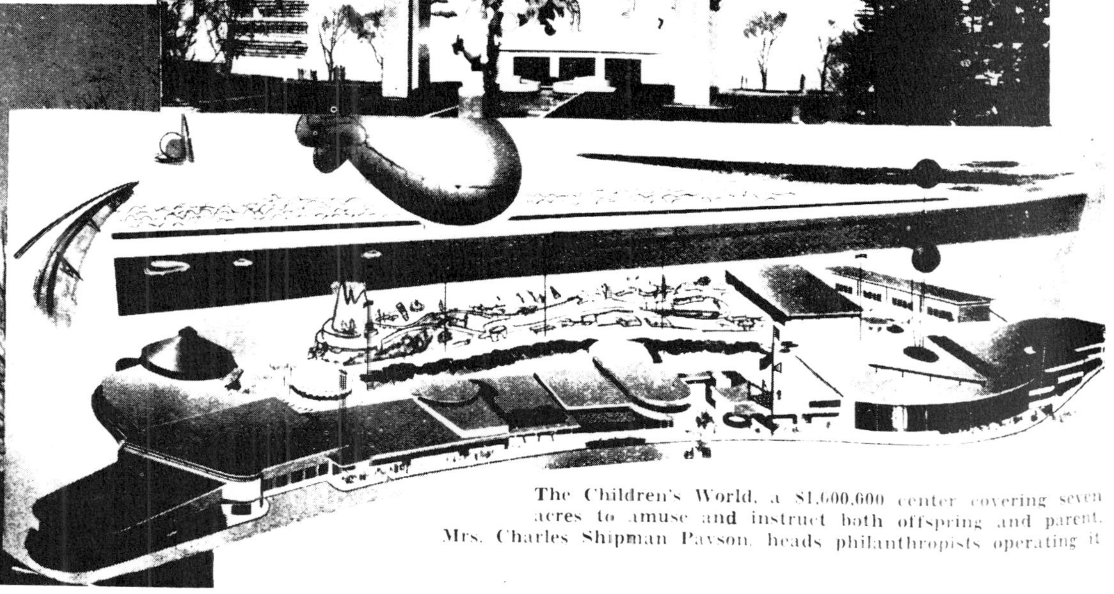

The Children's World, a $1,600,600 center covering seven acres to amuse and instruct both offspring and parent. Mrs. Charles Shipman Payson, heads philanthropists operating it

A general view of Rockefeller Center at night, with the Maison Française at the left of its base.
Vue générale du Centre Rockefeller à New York. On aperçoit la Maison Française au bas, à gauche.

Millions Visit Rockefeller Center, Citadel of America's Work, Play

Hanging Gardens, Largest Music Hall in World, Home Of Nation-Wide Radio Network Are Only Small Part of Attractions in Nation's Show Place

THE tourist who "does" London never fails to list Westminster Abbey as the number one visual necessity. When in Paris, it's Napoleon's Tomb, but in America, Rockefeller Center is first on the list.

More than 125,000 persons visit this great American shopping and business center daily, where in addition to seeing radio broadcasts and television programs presented from the world's largest broadcasting studio, they see more than ninety major works of art, the world's loftiest supper clubs, permanent and temporary exhibitions, the largest theater in the world with its famous Rockettes, the world's fastest elevators traveling at the rate of 1,400 feet per minute, and a series of lovely gardens flourishing high above the streets of Manhattan on the roofs of the Rockefeller Center buildings.

Starting with the Observation Roof atop the seventieth floor of the R.C.A. Building and going down, the varied attractions which may be seen in the Center include the Rainbow Room and the Rainbow Grill on the sixty-fifth floor, where nightly the sophisticated folks of Manhattan assemble; the Gardens of the Nations, on the eleventh floor, where high above the busy streets of Manhattan and framed by New York's mighty skyline are grown rare plants from such distant lands as South Africa, India and Tibet, and are reproduced in full size replicas of the gardens of many nations.

On the ground floor of the building is the Museum of Science and Industry, where are gathered for the visitor to see and operate, many famous discoveries, inventions and developments of the scientific world.

At the foot of the R.C.A. Building, adjoining the world-famous Prometheus Fountain, is the Promenade Café which in winter is turned into New York's only artificial outdoor skating pond and is constructed of more than two miles of pipe lying beneath the surface of the ice.

The Radio City Music Hall, which seats 6,200 persons and is the world's largest theater, and the Center Theater, housing the world's largest chandelier —this fixture, 25 feet in diameter, weighs six tons and is so large that a special ventilating system had to be designed to carry off the intense heat of its 400 floor lights—occupy separate buildings on the western portion of the development.

The National Broadcasting Company's studios cover some 400,000 square feet of space and occupy about six floors of the R.C.A. Building. Within this space is housed the world's largest broadcasting studio, which is seventy-eight feet by one hundred and thirty-two feet, and three stories high. This studio will accommodate a four-hundred-piece orchestra. All of the studios are supplied with conditioned air from an air-conditioning plant which washes the air, humidifies or dehumidifies it, according to conditions, and circulates it through the studios at a rate of 2,000,000 cubic feet an hour.

Situated on the northwest side of the center and occupying almost two entire floors of the 41-story International Building is Pedac, the House of Homes, and a hundred displays of home equipment. These houses are complete with the latest in home furnishings. The exhibition is the first clearing house in America for home-owners

Reasons for 'Oh's,' Ah's' Among Fair's Attractions

The New York World's Fair 1939 will be liberaly sprinkled with touches of the bizarre and here are a few of them:—

A parachute tower, 250 feet high, from which patrons may "bail out" and be sure of landing safely.

The world's most costly wheat field in full growth, with eventual harvesting of the crop and conversion of it, after milling, into bread.

A $5,000,000 display of precious gems and, as a separate exhibit, the largest opal in the world.

"Steve Brodie" jumping six times a day from a reproduction of the Brooklyn Bridge.

A "Rocket Gun" which will shoot passengers to the "moon"; also a separate flight to "Venus."

An oil well operated by bona fide drillers.

Puppets fourteen feet tall dramatizing the family medicine cabinet as man's first defense against disease.

Orchids by the thousands every three days from Venezuela.

Man-made lightning—10,000,000 volts of it—in a spectacular discharge.

A floor made of cotton.

A trumpeter sounding the Polish "heynal" from a tower every noon to commemorate the slain bugler who warned Cracow against the approach of Genghis Khan 700 years ago.

A waterfall cascading from the roof of a high building.

Fireworks set to music; also a singing fountain.

A city entirely populated by midgets.

Foreign Exchange Rates
Dollar in Paris .... 37fr. 75c.
Dollar in London .... 4s. 3 1/4d.
Dollar in Rome .... 19 lire
Dollar in Berlin .... 2m. 49 1/4pf.
Dollar in Brussels .... 29fr. 43c.
Pound in Paris .... 176fr. 71c.

2 a.m. EDITION

NEW YORK
Herald Tribune

SAILINGS to NEW YORK
Washington .... Aug. 24 Sept. 21
Pres. Roosevelt Aug. 31 Sept. 28
Manhattan ...... Sept. 7 Oct. 5
Pres. Harding .. Sept. 14 Oct. 12
UNITED STATES LINES
10 R. Auber, Paris.—7 Haymarket, London

52nd Year. No. 18,949 — European Edition — PARIS, TUESDAY, AUGUST 22, 1939 — THE NEW YORK HERALD (ESTABLISHED IN EUROPE 1887) — In France: 1 fr. 25c.

Soviet-German Non-Aggression Pact Announced in Brief Berlin Broadcast; Ribbentrop Flies to Moscow Tomorrow

Reich Foreign Minister to 'Conclude Negotiations' Already 'Agreed to' Says Unexplained Statement

Soviet Chargé Leaves On Half-Hour Notice

Russian Circles in Berlin Uninformed on Sudden Move, Nazis Surprised

By Joseph Barnes
From the Herald Tribune Bureau

BERLIN, Aug. 21.— Germans dropped a diplomatic bombshell into the current European crisis tonight with a short and unadorned announcement that Foreign Minister Joachim von Ribbentrop would leave for Moscow by airplane on Wednesday "to conclude negotiations" for a non-aggression treaty between Germany and the Soviet Union.

The announcement further stated that the two governments "had agreed to conclude a non-aggression pact with each other."

No further details have been made public here and it is clear that the move is as complete a surprise for all but possibly a half-dozen Germans as it is for the rest of the world.

Announced by Radio

First news of this development was broadcast over the German radio at 11 o'clock tonight when a musical broadcast was interrupted for "a special message." This manner of making it known and its repetitions at intervals later tonight were eloquent testimony to the serious view of the present crisis taken now by Germans and to their relief at the prospect of at least partially blocking the "encirclement front" being formed against them.

Whether this move will really block collective action against German aggression was anybody's guess here tonight. For what it is worth it is a fact that many Germans, who have been hinting during recent weeks at a possible improvement of German-Soviet relations, have also expressed privately their skepticism of any real alliance being formed and their belief that Moscow's policy is still based primarily on suspicion of English sincerity and on the desire to reinsure Soviet Socialism against war on as many fronts as possible.

Whatever new strength this non-aggression pact may bring to Germany, observers were convinced here tonight that Hitler has never yet had to pay such a heavy price in former Nazi principles. The Nazi régime, which featured itself as Europe's bulwark against Bolshevism and which was given by Hitler himself the sacred mission of expansion to the east at the expense of Russia, has apparently decided that this price had to be paid.

Soviet Press Unaware

George Astakhov, Soviet Chargé d'Affaires in Berlin, left tonight for Moscow at what was apparently a half-hour's notice.

Soviet newspaper circles in Berlin were uninformed about the move until it was announced here, but they privately repeated earlier Soviet assurances that Stalin's policy against aggression in Europe has not changed.

They insisted that any renewal of the old non-aggression treaty with Germany is likely to be in terms which will leave Russia's hands free—as the usual wording of non-aggression pacts would do—to oppose Germany with arms if Hitler commits an act of aggression against a third nation.

Germans who are best informed about the Soviet Union make no bones about admitting this, even tonight. They are convinced that the Soviet desire for peace without a second Munich is still the strongest determinant of Russian policy and that tonight's move indicates even stronger Russian skepticism of the Anglo-French bickering, which has been going on in Moscow.

Hitler Reported Absorbed in Russia

Among the strange stories of Hitler's personal life which filter through to foreign reporters in Berlin, many in recent weeks have concerned his new interest in Russia. It is reported that he has had several dozen Soviet books translated for his personal use in the last few weeks.

One of these stories claims that Hitler saw a picture of Stalin in one of these books. He is said to have covered Stalin's Asiatic-looking mustache with his finger and said: "Without the mustache it is the face of an intelligent man."

Foreign reaction to today's development, which is likely to predict that hobgoblin of English Tories—a German-Soviet alliance—has already been strongly discounted here.

While George Dimitrov, who told Goering to his face what Communists think of Nazis at the Reichstag trial, is still in Stalin's close entourage, Germans will suspect any Soviet overtures. Besides showing Germany's diplomatic weakness, any Soviet move toward Berlin reminds too many Germans of the old Communist trick of "embracing my enemy in order the better to choke him."

Parliament May Be Summoned By British Ministers Today

Chamberlain After Long Talk With Halifax Following Return From Interrupted Vacation Decides to Call Full Cabinet Meeting Today on Danzig Crisis

By Frank Kelley
From the Herald Tribune Bureau

LONDON, Aug. 21.—After a day of consultations at 10 Downing Street with Foreign Secretary Viscount Halifax and other advisers, while crowds lined the sidewalks outside, Prime Minister Neville Chamberlain decided this evening that the deepening crisis in Europe was serious enough to require a full-fledged meeting of the British Cabinet tomorrow in place of the informal "meeting of Ministers" originally planned.

Accordingly, the summons went out to all Ministers to "report." The only absentee is expected to be Lord Maugham, the Lord Chancellor, who is in Canada. All the Defense Ministers will attend, including War Minister Leslie Hore-Belisha, who stopped off in Paris on his way back from Cannes today to confer with Premier Edouard Daladier. Many observers thought Mr. Chamberlain's move foreshadowed major decisions by the government which would require the sanction of the full Cabinet.

Parliament May Be Called

Reports persisted, although without official confirmation, that the government might adopt important additional measures of military preparedness, issue a blunt warning to Chancellor Adolf Hitler that a "putsch" in Danzig means war, and perhaps recall Parliament in special session.

In its news bulletins tonight, which also were transmitted in German, the British Broadcasting Corporation, which is virtually under government control, appended to Berlin reports that influential Germans did not believe that Britain would fight for Danzig or Poland a statement that Britain's position and its determination to honor its pledges to Warsaw already have been made clear beyond doubt.

The European situation, as the British government views it, was described in a luncheon speech today by Leslie Burgin, Minister of Supply, who said it was "a sort of twilight when peace certainly has ended and war has not yet begun."

Hope Seen in Belgian Talk

One development today that appeared to offer hopes for the British was the invitation which King Leopold of the Belgians issued to Holland, Denmark, Norway, Sweden, Finland and Luxemburg to send representatives to a seven-power conference of small nations in Brussels Wednesday. It was reported that the conference would issue a "joint peace appeal" to the great powers.

Officials in London said they had no formal confirmation of King Leopold's action and refused to comment beyond saying that they regarded his attempt "with sympathetic interest."

Less reassuring to Whitehall were reports in Lord Beaverbrook's two newspapers, the "Daily Express" and the "Evening Standard," that Germany, using little known agents as a "front," had quietly bought up in London during the last few weeks large stocks of such essential war commodities as copper, nickel, rubber, tin and lead. With

(Continued on Page 3, Col. 5)

Calls Peace Conference

King Leopold of the Belgians

7 Oslo Powers To Hold 'Peace' Meeting Today

Small States Summoned By Leopold to Consider Way to Preserve Neutrality

By United Press

BRUSSELS, Aug. 21.—King Leopold of the Belgians today called a "peace conference" of the seven nations which are signatories of the Oslo Pact to consider practical methods of safeguarding the neutrality of these states should Europe be plunged into war. The conference will meet here tomorrow morning.

Though the conference will examine questions of common interest and make a "tour of the horizon" of the European political situation with a view to a joint peace plea to the big powers, it also will examine the delicate problems inherent in military flights over neutral countries in time of war.

Political Import Secondary

Spokesmen here tonight declared that too much political importance was being attached to the conference abroad, which, it was insisted, will probably yield only small results.

It is believed the conference powers, including: Belgium, Holland, Luxemburg, Denmark, Norway, Sweden and Finland, will address a last appeal to the "humanitarian sentiments" of Germany and Italy and possibly, also, France and Britain, to favor the maintenance of peace.

It is emphasized, however, that any initiative for mediation in the Danzig dispute should not for the present be considered as coming from King Leopold.

Four Foreign Ministers Coming

The Foreign Ministers of Norway, Sweden, Denmark and Holland have already accepted invitations. Luxemburg will be represented by its Minister in Brussels, taking the place of the Luxemburg Foreign Minister, at present touring the United States with Prince Felix.

Premier Pierlot of Belgium, who holds the portfolio of Foreign Minister, will open the conference at 10 a.m. tomorrow in the Foreign Ministry.

Nazi Atrocity Propaganda Reaches Old Landmarks

Next Step, Playing of Military Marches, Awaited

From the Herald Tribune Bureau

BERLIN, Aug. 21.—On the timetable of political crises, which many Germans know by heart after the last two years, a significant point was passed tonight when the German official news agency reported that an expectant German mother had been roughly handled in Koenigshuette, in Poland. In the Sudeterland crisis last September and in the Czech crisis last March, exactly the same stories—with different names and places—were published each time close to the peak of the German press campaign.

A second familiar landmark in this campaign was featured here today in another tale of a five-month-old German baby being beaten by Poles. Many Germans in Berlin make grim jokes about this well-established pattern and add that they will not be really worried until the German radio begins to play military marches between broadcasts. This has not started yet this time.

EUROPEAN EDITION PRICES IN FOREIGN COUNTRIES
England 4d.; Germany and Austria, 25pf.; Italy, L. 1.50; Belgium, Belg. Fr. 1.75; Czecho-Slovakia, Kc. 2.50; Switzerland, 35 cent.

Federal Grand Jury Indicts Five More In Louisiana Fraud

Illegal Use of Mails Cited In Charges on Refunding Of Debt by Levee Board Involving $496,000 Fee

Suicide of Witness Blow to Government

State's Oil 'Czar' Shoots Self; Said Was Forced To Break 'Hot Oil' Law

By Special Wireless

NEW ORLEANS, Aug. 21.—The late Huey Long's political machine again suffered smashing blows today when a Federal Grand Jury here indicted Abram L. Shushan, powerful ally of the "Kingfish" and president of the New Orleans Levee Board, and Robert Newman, socialite member of the well-known Southern investment firm of Newman, Harris and Company, on charges of using the mails to defraud.

Norvin Trent Harris, a junior partner in the same firm, and two others were also named in the indictment.

The grand jury charged that the five men named had used the mails to defraud in the Levee Board's huge debt refunding operations in which the defendants allegedly shared a $496,000 fee.

Key Witness Kills Self

Despite today's indictments, Federal investigators were seriously hampered in the probe of Louisiana political corruption by the suicide last night of Dr. J. A. Shaw, key government witness and titular "czar" of the state's oil industry. A revolver was found near Shaw's body. He failed to regain consciousness.

At his home his family revealed that he had been extremely nervous in the last few days. He had testified last week that "higher-ups" had forced him to sign the order allowing increased production in violation of the Connally "hot oil" act prohibiting interstate shipments of illegally-produced oil.

Shaw had been expected to be the chief prosecution witness against former Governor Richard W. Leche, Seymour Weiss, New Orleans and New York hotel man, and Freeman W. Burford, Texas oil millionaire, recently named in "hot oil" indictments.

Trial Begins September 5

Weiss, together with Dr. James Monroe Smith, former president of Louisiana State University, Monte Hart, prominent contractor, Louis C. Lesage, suspended assistant to the president of the Standard Oil Company of Louisiana, and J. Emory Adams, Mrs. J. M. Smith's nephew, will go on trial September 5 to answer charges of mail fraud.

All will be specifically charged with using the mails in selling Louisiana State University $75,000 worth of furnishings it received when $575,000 was paid for the Bienville Hotel, "lock, stock, and barrel."

The Louisiana scandal was precipitated by the disappearance of Dr. Smith on June 25, a few weeks after Grand Jury investigations into the complicated political heritage left by the slain "Kingfish." The day after the university president's flight the then Governor Richard W Leche resigned and Earl K. Long, brother of Huey, was quickly invested as Governor.

Educator's Affairs Bared

Several days later Dr. Smith surrendered with his wife in Ontario. They were flown back to Louisiana in a university plane and Dr. Smith was lodged in Baton Rouge jail.

An official report released at Baton Rouge recently showed that the educator's holdings included the following:

1. Life insurance policies totaling $2?7,000.
2. Many shares of stock in fifteen companies.
3. 601 unexecuted university bonds of $1,000 each.
4. Numerous liquor warehouse receipts.

Dr. Smith's financial operations crashed when he plunged in the wheat futures market to the extent of 2,000,000 bushels. The disclosure led to further investigations by Federal, state, and parish authorities. Dr. Smith is charged with embezzling university funds to finance his wheat speculations and has been indicted or charged on forty-one counts since his surrender.

Morgenthau Off for Stockholm

HELSINGFORS, Aug. 21 (U. P.)—Secretary of the Treasury Henry Morgenthau jr. visited the Finnish Parliament, the Olympic Stadium and the Municipal Allotment Gardens—a co-operative organization of farmers—and the workers dwelling which he desired to see. He was later a guest at a luncheon given in his honor by Mr. Risto Ryti, Governor of the Bank of Finland. Mr. Morgenthau, together with his family, left by airplane for Stockholm this afternoon.

Bruno Walter's Daughter Slain; Husband Suicide

Double Tragedy at Zurich Revealed When Toscanini Substitutes in Concert

Special to Herald Tribune

ZURICH, Aug. 21.—Mrs. Marguerite Walter-Neppach, thirty-three-year-old daughter of Bruno Walter, orchestra conductor, was shot and killed by two revolver bullets in the head fired by her husband, M Neppach, forty-seven, who immediately committed suicide with the same weapon, lodging two bullets in his heart, it was revealed here today.

The shooting occurred Friday night in a Nuschalar Strasse pension but became known only today through an announcement that Arturo Toscanini would replace Dr. Walter at the conductor's desk for the Mahler-Mozart concert scheduled at Lucerne tonight. Dr. Walter, born German, was naturalized as a French citizen last September and recently decorated with the Legion of Honor.

Walter Dashes to Scene

He was at work in his study at Lucerne Friday when a telephone call informed him that his daughter had been shot and killed during her sleep. He rushed from Lucerne to Zurich in a taxi. The double tragedy had been discovered by a chambermaid some time after the shooting.

Neppach was an Aryan of Bavarian origin.

His wife recently had filed suit for divorce, and, police learned, had refused to reconsider her decision despite the entreaties of her husband. This situation was believed to have been the cause of the shooting.

Neppach Fled Anschluss

The couple were married in Vienna five years ago. Neppach, a war veteran and architect, sought refuge with his father-in-law at Lugano soon after the Anschluss. He tried his hand at directing films but more recently had sought to establish himself in Switzerland as an architect.

His marriage to Miss Walter was his second. His first wife, Nelly Bamberger, of Frankfort, was a German tennis champion well known in France. She committed suicide in 1933 when, under the measures taken against Jews in the Reich, she was forbidden to represent German colors in international tennis matches.

The delay which caused news of the tragedy to come out only today was believed due to Dr. Walter's hope that he would be able to go through with the concert tonight with the public not knowing of his grief. He is sixty-three years old.

Atlantic Clipper Arrives Bringing 24 Passengers

Hunt Master Delayed by Storm Misses Meet

LONDON, Aug. 21.—Pan American Airways' flying boat Atlantic Clipper arrived at Southampton Water twenty-four hours late this afternoon, after having been delayed by storms over New Brunswick.

The delay prevented Harvey Ladew, Long Island and Maryland huntsman, from joining the first meet of the Devon and Somerset stag hounds. He is master of the Elkridge Harford pack of Maryland, and had planned to ride Friday with his own club and Monday morning with the Devon and Somerset pack.

Among passengers aboard were: Webb Miller, general European manager of the United Press; Mrs. Edward Carry, widow of the president of the Pullman Car Company; Mr. and Mrs. Lorenz Iverson, Mr. and Mrs. Edward McLean, of New York; C. L. Moore, Frank Reece, Waldo Tucker, F. C. R. Speyer, Vivien Kellems, Dr. and Mrs. Otto Fisher, Ernst Stinnes, Jane Alden, Mrs. Phyllis Pengra, Dana Clark, George Herron, Mr. and Mrs. Thomas Dewre, William Pawley, E. Carleton Grandberry and Mr. Lister.

The Weather

Predictions for Today:

Showers, bright spells, possible storms, cooler. Light northwesterly to westerly winds. Temperature yesterday: Max. 23 (73 Fahr.); min. 16 (61 Fahr.).

The French Weather Bureau predicts cooler, cloudy and less stormy weather today in the Paris region. Winds will be light and northeasterly to westerly. The sea in the English Channel will be slight.

It was sultry in Paris yesterday, with thundershowers. The highest temperature was 73. It was sultry in London, and there were thunderstorms. The maximum temperature was 78. There was sunshine in Berlin, and a noon temperature of 85.

New York weather was fair and the temperature was 91 at noon.

China Flood, Still Rising, Engulfs City

Toll of Deaths Estimated In Thousands as Tientsin Concessions Go Under

Special to Herald Tribune

TIENTSIN, Aug. 21.—Thousands of persons are believed to have perished in Tientsin and the surrouding country as the waters of the Haiho River continued today to pour over the greater portion of the city.

Officials estimated that the inundation was one of the worst in the history of North China. Most of the casualties are believed to be in villages along the Haiho, near the city.

The only spots above water are a small section of the French Concession, most of the Italian Concession, the international bridge and the railway station.

Sacks of earth in the French Concession finally gave way this morning before the fury of the yellow waters.

Water Six Feet Deep

The collapse of the makeshift barrier allowed the flood to rush over the French area and through the British Concession. Victoria Street, principal thoroughfare of the British Concession, is under six feet of water.

The flood level reaches the second story of houses in some quarters.

The crest of the flood is not expected until tomorrow.

Telephone service is disrupted. Drinking water is not obtainable in the British Concession, which is also deprived of lighting.

All sampans were requisitioned by the police for rescue work. Others among the population who refuse to remain marooned can only get about on makeshift rafts.

The economic situation and the blockade are expected to make the situation in the foreign concessions particularly difficult after the floods have subsided.

Japanese Maintain Blockade

Despite the perilous position of the entire population, Japanese military authorities have not given up efforts to control traffic and have posted soldiers waist-deep in water to inspect all craft in the flooded streets.

The right-of-way of the Peiping-Tientsin-Mukden Railway is seriously threatened.

Only one street in the Japanese Concession is dry. Most of the Nipponese have been concentrated in two schools.

Four fires have broken out in the Chinese city.

Authorities estimated that the flood may last three months. Japanese authorities thought that with the cooperation of the Chinese they could drain the city in six weeks.

Tree Limb Kills Passenger Riding Atop 5th Ave. Bus

Driver Races Through Traffic To Hospital With Victim

By Special Wireless

NEW YORK, Aug. 21.—A tree limb today fell on to the top of a Fifth Avenue bus, killing one passenger instantly and seriously injuring another, in one of the queerest freak accidents of the year.

Frank Goesch, forty-seven, was sitting on the upper deck, riding south along Fifth Avenue when the huge branch hit him. It was twenty feet long and eight inches in diameter. The accident occurred between Ninety-third and Ninety-fourth Streets.

When he heard the crash, the bus driver turned around and raced through traffic to the Mount Sinai Hospital but Goesch was already dead.

Bus, Fire Truck Hit; 29 Hurt

PHILADELPHIA, Aug. 21 (Havas).—Twenty-nine persons including five firemen, were injured here today when a crowded bus and a fire engine collided.

Undue Influence In U.S. Colleges Laid to German

University Head Charges Consul With Propaganda Before Dies Committee

By Special Wireless

WASHINGTON, Aug. 21.—The Dies Committee investigating un-American activities today heard President John N. Sherman, of the University of Tampa, testify that the German Consul in New Orleans, Baron Edgar von Spiegel, had tried to influence faculty members on the Tampa campus and Tulane University through gifts of German books.

President Sherman said that Baron von Spiegel had first demanded that a professor of German at the University of Tampa and a foe of the Nazi régime should prove "adequate." The German Consul reportedly told President Sherman that he would eventually "regret" having Jewish students and trustees at the university.

Tulane Head Quoted

The Tampa educator said that the president of Tulane University had told him he did not like the way Baron von Spiegel "snuggled up" to his faculty, and expressed dislike of the Consul's activities on the Tulane campus.

Dr. Sherman also declared he believed that Baron von Spiegel directed attacks against Professor Otto Kraus, a German instructor and a native of Vienna, and said that anonymous persons had insinuated that Professor Kraus did not know correct German.

Von Spiegel Denies Charges

Late today Baron von Spiegel in New Orleans angrily denied Dr. Sherman's accusations and said that many colleges and universities had accepted his offer of books.

The Dies Committee, which is believed to have ended its investigations into left wing activities in the United States, is now engaged in probing right wing organizations, notably the German-American Bund and the Knights of the White Camelia, as well as evidences of foreign propaganda in the United States.

Roosevelt in Halifax for Mail

NEW YORK, Aug. 21 (Havas).—President Roosevelt, on a vacation cruise in Canadian waters aboard the Tuscaloosa, returned to Halifax, Nova Scotia, today to claim his mail. A Navy plane, which had planned to drop the Presidential pouch on the Tuscaloosa's deck, was delayed by fog

Farley Is Mum on World Affairs; He Says Stamps Are His Business

Postmaster General Says Trip Is Purely Vacation; Guest Today of Daladier, Tomorrow of M. Bonnet

By George Polk

"My business is selling stamps," said James A. Farley, Postmaster General of the United States, upon his arrival in Paris yesterday. "I came to Europe for a vacation and rest, and since I'm here unofficially I haven't any comment on the international situation."

Mr. Farley and his two daughters, Elizabeth and Ann, were met at the Gare de Lyon on their arrival aboard the Rome express by William C. Bullitt, United States Ambassador to France, and officials of the French Postal Department. Although Mr. Farley declined to make any statement on affairs in Europe, he posed with his daughters for the large group of photographers who were awaiting their arrival.

The Postmaster General and his daughters have been touring in Europe. "We have had a most interesting trip," he said. "I have made official calls only in Poland and at the Vatican. We were in Germany for three days, but, except for a call by postal executives in Hamburg, I met no one connected with the German government."

When questioned during a press interview at the American Embassy regarding his observations in Poland, Mr. Farley said that the Poles are determined to fight for their freedom and independence. Replying to a query concerning the thirty-day truce proposed by Representative Hamilton Fish, New York Republican, at the Interparliamentary Union meeting in Oslo, Mr. Farley said laughingly:—

"It is rather amusing to me that Mr. Fish seems so excited over his plan. He is part of that group in Congress

(Continued on Page 3, Col. 3)

Wall Street

	High	Low	Close
U.S. Steel.....	44 3/4	43 3/8	44 1/4
Chrysler........	77 5/8	75 3/4	76 1/2
U.S. Rubber...	38 3/8	36 7/8	37 3/4
N.Y. Central.	13	12 1/2	12 3/4

Market trend lower. War talk brought sharp setback. Trading moderately active. Selling was heavy in the forenoon. Volume 650,000 shares. Leaders lost one to more than two points. Earlier losses up to four points were reduced in a later rally. Calling of the Belgian conference checked the decline. Speculative issues suffered most. Steels and motors led the decline. U.S. Steel lost 1 1/4 and Bethlehem 2 3/8. Chrysler dropped 2 1/2 and General Motors 1 3/4. Douglas Aircraft was 2 1/2 down. Full market reports: Pages 6 and 7.

Campaign for Third Term Mistake, Declares Wheeler

Montana Senator Sees Victory If Roosevelt Out

By United Press

LOS ANGELES, Aug. 21.—Senator Burton K. Wheeler (D., Mont.) said here today that if President Roosevelt is nominated for a third term in 1940 and is defeated it will mean "repudiation by the Democrats of President Roosevelt himself and everything he advocates."

Senator Wheeler expressed doubt that President Roosevelt would run again, however, and said it would be a "mistake" if he does. "If the President becomes a candidate," Senator Wheeler added, "the most outstanding issue of the campaign would be the third term."

He termed the chances of success for the Democratic party excellent unless the party becomes divided.

West Wants Third Term

ATLANTA, Aug. 21 (U.P.).—Western voters are demanding that President Roosevelt seek a third term, unless a candidate in sympathy with his policies can be found, L. W. Roberts, secretary of the Democratic National Committee, declared here today. "Sentiment is strong west of the Mississippi River for a third term," he said.

W. G. Sharp Jr. Killed by Car

TAUNTON, Mass., Aug. 21 (Wireless).—William G. Sharp jr., thirty-eight-year-old artist and son of the late American Ambassador to France, was killed by a hit-and-run driver here today.

Italian Royalty Hinted Ill

BERNE, Aug. 21 (Havas).—A famous Zurich surgeon flew to Rome this afternoon to perform an operation on a member of the Italian royal family, the Swiss Telegraph Agency reported tonight.

Foreign Exchange Rates
Dollar in Paris .... 41fr. 85c.
Dollar in London.....4s. 8 1/2d.
Dollar in Rome.......... 19 lire
Dollar in Brussels.......... 29fr.
Pound in Paris.......175fr. 60c.

NEW YORK
Herald Tribune

2 a.m. EDITION

SAILINGS to NEW YORK
President Harding .. Sept. 9
Washington .... Sept. 9
UNITED STATES LINES
10 R. Auber, Paris. — 7 Haymarket, London

52nd Year. No. 18.960 | European Edition | PARIS, SATURDAY, SEPTEMBER 2, 1939 | THE NEW YORK HERALD (ESTABLISHED IN EUROPE 1887) | In France: 1 fr. 25c.

German Army Invades Poland Along Four Fronts; France, Great Britain Order General Mobilization

Ban City Air Raids, Plea by Roosevelt

President Wires 5 Powers Urging Bombers Refrain From Ruthless Slaughter By Attacks on Open Towns

Governments Asked For Immediate Reply

Roosevelt Told at 1 a.m.; 'Hopes' U.S. Can Stay Out; Hugh Wilson Quits Post

By Havas Agency

WASHINGTON, Sept. 1.—Informed telephonically by United States Ambassadors in Warsaw and Paris of the German invasion of Poland and the aerial bombing of four Polish towns, President Roosevelt cabled an appeal to the British, French, Italian, German and Polish governments to refrain from bombing civilian populations in open towns.

The text of the President's latest plea to European governments follows:

"The cruel aerial bombardments of civilian populations in open towns in the course of recent conflicts, resulting in the maiming and killing of thousands of defenseless women and children, have wrung the hearts of all civilized men and women and have profoundly shocked humanity's conscience.

Asks for Immediate Reply

"If this form of barbarism is resorted to during the tragic conflagration which now confronts the world, hundreds of thousands of innocent human

French Cabinet Acts to Honor Pledge to Poles

Parliament Will Meet Today To Consider Hostilities Between Reich, Poland

By John Elliott

For the third time within a century, those ancient foes, France and Germany, are likely to be at war today. Reacting immediately to Hitler's annexation of Danzig and the Reichswehr's invasion of Polish territory, the French government yesterday moved swiftly and energetically to carry out its pledge to come to the aid of Poland if that country were the victim of unprovoked Nazi aggression.

The French Cabinet met at the Elysée Palace under the chairmanship of President Albert Lebrun at the very moment that Hitler was addressing the Reichstag, and decided on the following measures:—

1. It decreed a general mobilization of the French army, navy and air forces in France and in the French Empire;

2. It proclaimed martial law throughout France;

3. It convoked the French Parliament for today.

Stop War, Berlin Told

It will presumably be the duty of the French Parliament to declare that a state of war exists between Germany and Poland unless the German government gives satisfaction to the French démarche that was made in Berlin last

British Tell Reich to Call Back Troops

Virtual Ultimatum Served on Berlin; Commons Hear Premier Assail Hitler; Credit, Men Mobilized

By Havas Agency

LONDON, Sept. 1.—With the entire man power of the country mobilized or about to be mobilized and most of the war-time measures already in effect, Great Britain today made ready to fulfill its obligations to Poland to the last remnant of its vast resources.

Although the word "ultimatum" has not yet figured in official pronouncements, Premier Neville Chamberlain left no doubt about Britain's attitude in a declaration to Parliament this afternoon, in which he said that Sir Nevile Henderson, the Ambassador in Berlin, had been instructed to warn the German government that "if no satisfactory assurances were given pledging the cessation of all aggressive action and the withdrawal of German troops from Poland, the British government would unhesitatingly carry out its obligations."

No Time Limit Mentioned

The Prime Minister added that if the reply from Berlin was unfavorable, the British Ambassador would demand his passport.

Meanwhile, all arrangements have been made for the immediate formation of a War Cabinet, which will include Winston Churchill, Anthony Eden and the leaders of the opposition, Arthur Greenwood for Labor and Sir Archibald Sinclair for the Liberals.

After hearing Mr. Chamberlain the House of Commons voted £500,000,000 credit for "the defense of the realm,

Air Raids at Dawn Herald Nazi Attacks; Warsaw Bombed; Poles Resisting Stiffly

Strategic Points of Fighting in Poland

Moscicki Calls on All Poland To Fight for 'Holy, Just Cause'

Series of Air Raids, Informs Polish Capital Residents Of Start of Hostilities; Berlin Informed Thursday Of Poland's Willingness to Negotiate

German Fleet Bombards Port of Gdynia: Reichswehr Column Enters From Free City of Danzig; Poles Down 7 Planes In Early Raids, Shell German Town

War broke out in Europe yesterday at about dawn.

Nazi German troops invaded Poland—Warsaw sources said on four fronts—and, last night, with bombing planes and tanks were striving to break down the resistance of Marshal Smigly Rydz's armies.

As Warsaw invoked its pact with France and Britain, both nations prepared to carry out their pledge by decreeing general mobilization and warning Hitler the promise to Poland would be fulfilled if he did not halt hostilities and order his men back to the Reich.

The diplomatic démarches amounted to virtual ultimatums.

Fuehrer Informs Reichstag of Start of Invasion

Führer Chancellor Hitler, in a thunderous speech to the Nazi Reichstag, assembled in the Kroll Opera House, Berlin, announced hostilities, reiterated he had no designs on France and said he could settle Poland without Mussolini's aid.

At Rome, the Council of Ministers decided not to intervene with its armed forces in behalf of Hitler, but approved "precautionary" military steps.

French mobilization affected all arms of the service throughout France and the colonies. The Council of Ministers, meeting at the Elysée Palace, under President Albert Lebrun, also proclaimed martial law throughout France and summoned Parliament to meet today for action dependent on Berlin's action to the diplomatic warning.

Britain and France replied favorably to an appeal of President Roosevelt to spare civilian populations the horrors of air attacks provided their own non-combatants were not wantonly bombed.

Foreign Exchange Rates
Dollar in Paris ...... 41fr. 85c.
Dollar in London ...... 4s. 9d.
Dollar in Rome ...... 19 lire
Dollar in Brussels ... 29fr. 15c.
Pound in Paris ...... 175fr. 60c.

NEW YORK
Herald Tribune

3 a.m. EDITION

SAILINGS to NEW YORK
Frequent Sailings
UNITED STATES LINES
10 R. Auber, Paris. — 7 Haymarket, London

52nd Year. No. 18.962 | European Edition | PARIS, MONDAY, SEPTEMBER 4, 1939 | THE NEW YORK HERALD (ESTABLISHED IN EUROPE 1887) | In France: 1 fr. 25c.

Great Britain and France Declare War on Germany When Hitler Refuses to Call Off Attack on Poland

Nation Told By Roosevelt 'I Hate War'

By Special Wireless

WASHINGTON, Sept. 3.—President Roosevelt speaking over the radio tonight to "the whole of America" said that "as long as it remains within my power to prevent it, there will be no black-out of peace in the United States."

The President said it was impossible to predict what the future holds in store, but that nevertheless "this nation will remain a neutral nation."

He added, however, that he could not "ask every American to remain neutral in thought as well.

"Even a neutral," he said, "has a right to take account of facts. Even a neutral cannot be asked to close his mind or conscience. I have said not once, but many times that I have seen war and that I hate war. I say that again and again."

The President said a proclamation of American neutrality was being prepared at the moment and that even had there been no neutrality act this would have been done in accordance with international law and American policy.

President Roosevelt said that another proclamation will follow as required by the existing neutrality law, but he did not disclose when either proclamation will be issued.

The President added that he trusted that "in the days to come our neutrality can be made a true neutrality."

He declared that it was of the utmost importance that Americans with the best information in the world "think things through."

Calls on Press, Radio for Truth

The President emphasized the importance of the press and radio using the utmost caution to discriminate between actual and verified fact and mere rumor.

"When peace is broken anywhere the peace of all countries is in danger . . . passionately though we may desire detachment we are forced to realize that every word that comes through the air, every ship that sails the sea, every battle that is fought does affect the American future. Let no man or woman purposely or falsely talk of

1,500 Set as Toll In Nazi Air Raids On Polish Centers

(From Havas Agency Dispatches)

As Britain and France entered into a state of war with Germany yesterday, aerial bombardments by German planes continued in scores of Polish towns and cities.

According to the Polish Embassy in Paris, the number of victims of the air raids of Friday and Saturday was about 1,500, including a large number of women and children.

The city of Czestowa, known as the Polish Lourdes, because of its miraculous Virgin, was in flames as a result of intense bombardment.

Nazi Planes Over Warsaw

Between 8 and 9 a.m. yesterday, German planes constantly flew over Warsaw at such a height that they were invisible.

These planes bombarded the outlying districts of Praga and Okecie in an attempt to destroy railroad bridges and a motor factory. From the capital six large fires could be seen, as the sound of explosions mingled with the ringing of church bells.

Four civilians are known to have been killed and ten seriously wounded in this morning's raid.

In two air attacks Saturday, thirty persons were killed, fifty-eight wounded, and five buildings demolished in Ludblin.

The population of Warsaw followed with interest successive reports of the desperate fighting at Danzig, where the Polish garrison at Westerplatte is still holding out against repeated attacks by German troops and heavy shelling by the German vest-pocket battleship Schleswig-Holstein.

Polish Plane Fights Twelve

Thousands watched a thrilling battle between twelve German light bombers and a single plane piloted by Sub-Lieutenant Palusinki of the Polish aviation. Coming unexpectedly on the German planes, Palusinki flew above them, managed to shoot down one, and, when he was wounded and his machine was hit, volplaned 10,000 feet to a safe landing.

The Polish Pat Agency reported

Britain Enters Conflict at 11 a.m., France at 5 p.m.; Fleet Blockades Reich; U.S. Studies Arms Em[illegible]go

Text of King George's Speech

By United Press

LONDON, Sept. 3.—King George VI tonight broadcast the following message to the British Empire at 6 o'clock:—

This grave hour is perhaps the most fateful in our history. I would send to every household of my peoples both at home and overseas this message, spoken with the same depth of feeling to each one of you as if I were able to cross your threshold and speak to you myself.

For the second time within the lives of most of us we are at war. Over and over again we have tried to find a peaceful way out of the differences between ourselves and those who are now our enemies. But it has been in vain. We have been forced into this conflict. For we are called with our Allies to meet the challenge of the principle, which if it should prevail, would be fatal to civilization and order in the world.

It is the principle which permits a state in pursuit of selfish power to disregard its treaties and its solemn pledges; which sanctions the use of force or threats of force against the sovereignty and independence of other states. Such a principle stripped of all disguise, is surely the mere primitive doctrine that might is right, and if this principle were established throughout the world, the freedom of our own country and the whole British commonwealth of nations would be in danger.

Far more than this—the peoples of the world would be kept in bondage of fear and all hopes of settled peace, security, of justice and liberty among nations would be ended.

This is the ultimate issue which confronts us. For the sake of all we ourselves hold dear and the world's order and peace, it is unthinkable that we should refuse to meet the challenge.

It is for this high purpose that I now call my people at home and my peoples across the seas who will make our cause their own. I ask them to stand calm and firm and united during this time of trial. The task will be hard. There may be dark days ahead and war can no longer be confined to the battlefield. But we can only do right as we see right. We reverently commit our cause to God. If one and all we keep resolute and faithful to it, ready for whatever service or sacrifice it may demand, then with God's help we shall prevail.

May He bless us and keep us all.

Fighting Speech Made to Nation By Chamberlain

'We Defend the Right, Right Will Prevail in This Fight,' Premier Says in Broadcast

By Havas Agency

LONDON, Sept. 3.—Premier Neville Chamberlain's broadcast this morning, at 11.15 o'clock announcing a state of war with Germany, follows:—

I am speaking to you from the Cabinet meeting room at 10 Downing Street.

This morning the English Ambassador handed to the German government an official note declaring that unless we were informed by it before 11 o'clock that it was prepared to withdraw its troops immediately from Poland a state of war would exist between the two countries.

I must tell you now that no promise has been received and that in consequence this country is at war with Germany.

Did Everything Possible for Peace

You can imagine what a cruel blow it is for me to note that my long fight for peace has failed. Nevertheless, I do not believe that I could have done anything more or acted otherwise with more success.

Until the last minute it would have been entirely possible to elaborate a pacific and honorable settlement between Germany and Poland but Hitler did not want one.

He was evidently resolved to attack Poland, arrive what might, and, although he now declares that he had made reasonable proposals which were rejected by the Poles, his declarations do not conform with the truth.

These proposals were never revealed to the Poles nor to us and

Australia, New Zealand Join [illegible]ties, Canada Pledges Its Support [illegible]ain; Nazis Reject French Ultimatum[illegible]ore London's: Japanese Promise Neutrality

A quarter of a century after the outbreak of the World War, France and Britain again went to war with Germany yesterday.

Britain was in a state of war at 11 a.m., while France entered the war at 5 p.m.

The immediate cause was the failure of Chancellor Adolf Hitler to reply to the ultimatum sent him by the two countries demanding that he withdraw his troops from Poland.

Prime Minister Neville Chamberlain announced a state of war with Germany in a broadcast at 11:15 a.m.

Daladier Announces War to French People

France's declaration of war was announced to the French people in a radio broadcast last night by Premier Daladier.

"This morning," Mr. Chamberlain said, "the English Ambassador at Berlin handed the German government an official note declaring that unless we were informed by it before 11 o'clock that it was prepared to withdraw its troops immediately from Poland, a state of war would exist between the two countries.

"I must tell you now that no promise has been received and that in consequence this country is at war with Germany."

Hitler Renews Encirclement Complaint

Premier Daladier told his countrymen that he and the British government had made a final appeal to the Reich to cease hostilities, and "Germany's response was a refusal."

In Berlin, Chancellor Hitler exhorted the Germans to resist the "new British policy of encirclement," launched just when "the peaceful revision of the Treaty of Versailles seemed about to succeed."

The formation of a British War Cabinet, in which Winston Churchill will be First Lord of the Admiralty and Anthony Eden Secretary of State for Dominions, was announced in London.

President Roosevelt called a Cabinet meeting for today. He

Foreign Exchange Rates
Dollar in Paris .. 44fr. 85c.
Dollar in London 4s. 9d.
Dollar in Rome 19 lire
Dollar in Brussels 29fr. 15c.
Pound in Paris . 175fr. 60c.

NEW YORK **Herald Tribune**

2 a.m. EDITION

SAILINGS to NEW YORK
Frequent Sailings
UNITED STATES LINES
10 R. Auber, Paris — 7 Haymarket, London

52nd Year. No. 18,963 European Edition PARIS, TUESDAY, SEPTEMBER 5, 1939 THE NEW YORK HERALD ESTABLISHED IN EUROPE 1887 In France: 1 fr. 25c.

Guns Roar Again on West Front As Fighting Starts; British Fleets Are Reported 'Active On All Seas'

U.S. Awaits Neutrality Declaration

President, Special Cabinet Meeting Draft Statement; Pan-American Meeting May Write Western Pact

McAdoo Is Convinced U.S. Will Be Involved

More Ships for Americans Abroad; Green Demands Strict Neutrality for U.S.

By United Press

WASHINGTON, Sept. 4.—News of the sinking of the Athenia profoundly shocked the nation this morning, and is expected to be a leading factor in the debates when Congress discusses neutrality.

Following the sudden realization that the lives of American citizens were involved by the European struggle, commentators generally agreed that the clash across the Atlantic will have an immense effect on the United States.

Roosevelt Prepares Proclamation

President Roosevelt will issue a neutrality proclamation by 6 p.m. tomorrow at the latest according to a White House spokesman. Plans in connection with this were studied at a special Cabinet meeting this afternoon.

In his broadcast last night, President Roosevelt implied that it would be impossible for the United States to

2,331 Landed At New York By Queen Mary

Big British Liner Made Swift Trip Under Convoy With $45,000,000 Gold and J. P. Morgan Aboard

By Special Wireless

NEW YORK, Sept. 4.—The Queen Mary arrived today in New York with 2,331 passengers who found safe haven after crossing the Atlantic under wartime conditions involving a double shift of convoying British warships.

During the swift trip the windows and portholes were blackened and the lights dimmed. The British cruisers Berwick and York convoyed the giant liner during the last 900 miles. They relieved two other cruisers of which the names were not mentioned.

Officials of the Cunard White Star Line confirmed the Queen Mary would remain at New York until further notice.

The large number of passengers necessitated placing cots in the libraries, gymnasium, drawing-room, tea-dance-room, travel room and general rooms. The passengers were forbidden to smoke on deck.

J. Pierpont Morgan arrived on the liner. He turned over his suite of staterooms to others and took a small cabin. Declining to comment on reports that he would become an agent of the British government and on the fact that the Queen Mary brought over $45,000,000 of gold bullion, he expressed pleasure over the upswing in security prices.

The question of bringing Americans in the war zone to this country was discussed at the White House between President Roosevelt, Secretary of State Cordell Hull, Assistant Secretary of Navy Charles Edison, and Admiral

First War Communiques Issued, Meager in Details; Nazis Use Gas Bombs in Furious Polish Fighting

First Air Raid For London and North Lasts Hour

Alert Signal Is Sounded At 2:30 a.m., End 4:12; No Details Made Public

By Havas Agency

LONDON, Sept. 4.—London was subjected to its first air raid in the early hours of the morning.

All details of the damage done were withheld, but the raid was over a large area and is believed to have lasted at least an hour.

The following official communiqué was issued by the British government:—

"Sirens warned of an air raid at the beginning of the morning over an extensive area comprising London, part of the Midlands and Northern counties.

"The first signal was given about 2:30 a.m. and the signal announcing the definitive end of the alarm at 4:12 a.m.

"No details can be given."

Planes Came From Two Directions

According to a Havas dispatch, it is believed raiding planes came from two directions. This agency said the population calmly descended to air-raid shelters to wait until the attack was over.

Hundreds of marriages were celebrat-

Poles Open Counter Attack

Arrow pointing into East Prussia shows rallying point of Marshal Smigly-Rydz's forces.

Germans Torpedo and Sink Ship With 300 Americans Aboard

R.A.F. Raids Reich and Scatters Leaflets; Details Withheld of First Air Raid on England; Blockade of Germany in Full Force; Polish 'Lourdes' in Ruins, Falls

Guns roared yesterday on the western front.

A Nazi imitation of Von Tirpitz's submarine frightfulness (schrecklichkeit) was held responsible for the sinking of the 13,500-ton British liner Athenia, carrying 1,400 passengers, of whom about 300 were Americans, off the northwest coast of Scotland.

In the furious fighting in Poland, the Germans were reported to have employed asphyxiating and mustard gas, together with an unknown chemical.

The possibility of the United States sending Navy units to convoy American merchantmen repatriating nationals in the war zone was discussed by President Roosevelt, Secretary of State Cordell Hull, Assistant Secretary of Navy Charles Edison and Admiral Harold R. Stark, Chief of Naval Operations.

Two brief communiqués told the story of French military activity.

The first said: "Operations have begun involving all the land, naval and aerial forces."

The second explained: "Contacts have been progressively made on the front. The French naval forces have proceeded to the posts which have been assigned to them. Aerial forces are making the necessary reconnaissances."

Planes Drop Leaflets in Germany

Royal Air Force planes made an uneventful round trip into Germany during which they scattered more than 6,000,000 leaf-

Foreign Exchange Rates
Dollar in Paris 43fr. 30c.
Dollar in London 4s. 10 3/4d.
Dollar in Rome 19 lire
Dollar in Brussels 29fr.
Pound in Paris 175fr.

NEW YORK **Herald Tribune**

2 a.m. EDITION

SAILINGS to NEW YORK
Frequent Sailings
UNITED STATES LINES
10 R. Auber, Paris — 7 Haymarket, London

52nd Year. No. 18,964 European Edition PARIS, WEDNESDAY, SEPTEMBER 6, 1939 THE NEW YORK HERALD ESTABLISHED IN EUROPE 1887 In France: 1 fr. 25c.

Paris Has First Air Raid Alarm on 3rd Day of War; Heavy Fighting in Poland, As West Front Livens Up

Neutrality Proclaimed By President

Roosevelt, Hull Sign Paper Paving Way for Embargo on Arms to Belligerents Under Existing U.S. Law

BULLETIN

WASHINGTON, Sept. 5 (Wireless).—President Roosevelt this evening signed a proclamation invoking an arms embargo against belligerents under the Neutrality Act.

By Havas Agency

WASHINGTON, Sept. 5.—President Roosevelt signed a proclamation declaring the United States neutral in the European conflict according to international law shortly after 2 p.m. New York time today. Secretary of State Cordell Hull affixed his signature immediately afterward.

At a midday conference with Secretary Hull, the President put the final touches on the neutrality and arms embargo proclamation. The latter, in conformity with the present neutrality Act, is expected to be signed at about 6:30 p.m. (New York time).

The neutrality proclamation was made in a 4,000-word document containing seventeen articles defined by the United States laws on neutrality passed in 1909 and 1917. Details include the prohibition of the recruiting of Americans for service in armed forces of the belligerents, delivery of armed vessels to belligerents, and the formation of armed units destined for service with a belligerent.

Restrictions on Vessels

Belligerent vessels are also prohibited from replenishing their munitions in American ports and are limited to a definite period of call in American waters.

In the face of the war in Europe, Secretary Hull today introduced new restrictions on Americans traveling to Europe. All Americans possessing pass-

War Communiqués From French Army

COMMUNIQUE No. 3

September 5, morning: Movements are being carried out normally by land, naval and air forces.

COMMUNIQUE No. 4

September 5, evening: Our troops are everywhere in contact at the opening of our frontier between the Rhine and the Moselle. It is appropriate to recall that on the Rhine permanent fortifications are on either bank.

French Director Of Information Explains Duties

Jean Giraudoux Reassures Public, Promises All News Compatible With Safety

Jean Giraudoux, General Commissioner for Information, made the following announcement over the radio last night:

Frenchmen, Frenchwomen—General Commissioner for Information speaking. In the days and weeks to come, it will be his business to keep you informed of the phases of the struggle in which France is now engaged. This work, evidently, will not be easy.

Whatever may be your anxiety to have the news or his desire to keep you informed, he will only be able to give you information on strategic events which does not risk serving as warning or an indication to the enemy.

In this period of preparation, during which, I can assure you, nothing has transpired on our frontiers, it is quite natural that he can give you no details about concentration of the armies or on

Berlin Is Raided Without Loss by 30 Polish Planes; R.A.F. Bombers Damage Ships in Reich Naval Bases

R.A.F. Bombers Raid Nazi Naval Bases, Hit Ships

Another British Ship Is Sunk, One Life Is Lost; British Cabinet Completed

By Havas Agency

LONDON, Sept. 5.—News of the sinking of another British ship, presumably by a German submarine, on the heels of the sinking of the Athenia, and of the daring raid of R.A.F. bombers on German naval bases further stirred the British public today. Meanwhile, the government and the public moved swiftly to put the war machinery of the country into full operation.

The raid on the German naval bases took place last night and, according to the Ministry of Information, "was effected with success on ships of the German fleet at Wilhelmshafen and Brunsbuttel, at the entrance of the Kiel Canal.

Details of Raid on German Fleet

"Several bombs of large caliber hit a warship in the roads of Schilling, off Wilhelmshafen, causing much damage.

"At Brunsbuttel, the attack centered on a warship anchored near the pier and also caused important damage.

"During the operations, which were effected under unfavorable atmospheric conditions, our aviation was attacked by the enemy aviation and by the anti-aircraft guns and suffered several losses."

Cabinet Is Completed

The British War Cabinet, announced on Sunday, was completed as follows:

Secretary of State for the Colonies: Malcolm MacDonald.

Iron and Concrete Walls Along West Front

Survivors of Athenia Landed, Bringing Details of Sub Attack

Aerial Activity Features Day's Operations; Blast Reported at Nazi Zeppelin Plant; Union of South Africa Breaks With Germany; Spain Declares Its Neutrality

While hostilities flared on the Maginot and Siegfried lines and in Poland, both Nazi Germans and the British and Poles intensified their aerial attacks on the second day after the declarations of war on Germany by France and Great Britain.

Parisians left their beds yesterday at 3:50 a.m. for a sojourn in air-raid shelters that lasted officially for three hours, although some dwellers ventured into the streets before the "all clear" signal was sounded.

A communiqué said the warning was due to the appearance of German planes over the frontier on a reconnaissance

Parisians were informed, however, that every time enemy aircraft is detected at the frontier, the city's sirens will rouse them.

British War Planes Bomb German Fleet

R.A.F. bombers achieved the most spectacular feat of the day by bombing units of the German fleet at Wilhelmshafen and Brunsbuttel, at the entrance of the Kiel Canal.

The horse was mightier than steel in the Poles' rally in southern Poland, according to a Warsaw communiqué which stated that several brigades of the crack Polish cavalry had disrupted the advance of tanks and armored cars and captured several of them with their occupants.

The gist of French communiqués was that the operations of all France's forces are being carried out normally, which indicated that the fighting along the Maginot Line is a prelude to a more important effort and is probably confined to artillery fire and reconnaissance raids.

Official Exchange Rates
Dollar in Paris.. 43.70 to 43.90
Dollar in London.. 4s. 11 1/2d.
Dollar in Rome ... 19 lire 80c.
Dollar in Brussels... 30fr. 15c.
Pound in Paris 176.50 to 176.75

NEW YORK Herald Tribune — 2 a.m. EDITION

53rd Year. No. 19,212 — European Edition — PARIS, SATURDAY, MAY 11, 1940 — THE NEW YORK HERALD (ESTABLISHED IN EUROPE 1887) — In France, 1 fr. 25c.

Reich Invades Low Countries, Luxemburg

Chamberlain Is Replaced By Churchill

71-Year-Old Premier Bows to Public's Will After Laborites Refuse To Accept His Leadership

Special to The Herald Tribune

LONDON, May 10.—As a new and critical phase of the war was opened today with the German invasion of Belgium and Holland, 71-year-old Neville Chamberlain bowed to the will of an aroused British public and surrendered the Premiership to the First Lord of the Admiralty, dynamic Winston Churchill.

The announcement that Mr. Chamberlain would go, considered a foregone conclusion with the disclosure this afternoon that Labor leaders would only accept Cabinet posts under a new Premier, was issued shortly after 8 o'clock tonight from 10 Downing Street.

"The Right Hon. Neville Chamberlain, M.P., resigned the office of Prime Minister and First Lord of the Treasury this evening, and the Right Hon. Winston Churchill, M.P., accepted His Majesty's invitation to fill the position," the statement read.

"The Prime Minister desires that all Ministers should remain at their posts and discharge their functions with full freedom and responsibility while the necessary arrangements for the formation of a new administration are made."

In what is generally considered here the most dramatic speech of his career, Mr. Chamberlain this evening broke the news to the British public that he was handing over the office he had held for almost three years.

Chamberlain's Farewell Talk

"I handed my resignation to His Majesty, who kindly accepted it, and His Majesty has entrusted to Mr Winston Churchill the task of forming a new administration on a national basis.

"In this task I have no doubt he will be successful. For that purpose

Hitler's Latest Victims

It is useless to blind one's self to the deadly dramatic import of yesterday's developments. The "guerre totale" has commenced. Poland and Norway now appear as but a prelude to it. France and Great Britain are facing a new menace and a more terrible form of warfare. It is a time for courage and resolution.

Gone are the promises made by Germany to the small neutral countries, Belgium, Holland and Luxemburg; the solemn assurances given them that their neutrality and their independence would be respected, their cities and countrysides saved from cruel bombardment.

As we have pointed out before, neutrality no longer exists as a status under international law and it is idle for any nation not yet actually involved to pretend that it does. Good faith on the side of the Germans long ago ceased to exist. The old adage that "necessity knows no law" has been adopted by Germany in place of the formerly accepted principles of international law and as an excuse for violating its promises. That necessity, as Hitler and his leaders seem to see it, is above all to beat Great Britain, to wrest from the British what they fatuously believe is a sort of world domination and to regain Germany's former colonies.

In the last few days it was evident that the rattlesnake was coiling and about to strike again. Nothing can possibly justify Germany's latest invasion. The excuse offered is more hollow than even in the case of Norway. France and Great Britain have both scrupulously observed the independence and neutrality of Holland, Belgium and Luxemburg, yet the temptation to forestall this German move has been great. No doubt the results in Norway encouraged the Germans to strike as quickly as possible. The political situation in Great Britain also seems to have played into their hands.

The United States has now before it another example of the contempt Germany holds for any real neutrality and its disrespect for its own promises. The United States is confronted with grave decisions. Protests and diplomatic notes have already proved to be useless. And in this war, as in no previous war, quick action has become a factor of incredible importance.

L. H.

U.S. to Stay Out, Roosevelt Says After Long Defense Conference

First Informed by Cudahy, President, After Most of Night at Desk, Freezes Low Countries' Credits, Calls Advisers, Ends Day by World Broadcast

By Special Wireless

WASHINGTON, May 10.—After a long conference at the White House with

Allies Answer 3 Countries' Call for Aid; Terrific Air, Land Battles Over All Area

Germans Bomb French Cities; Civilian Dead

Casualties at Nancy; Lyons, Colmar, Luxeuil, Pontoise 'Strafed' in Early Raids; National Union Formed

By John Elliott

The news that French troops had crossed the frontier between 7 and 8 o'clock yesterday morning in immediate response to the call for aid from Holland, Belgium and Luxemburg, the latest victims of Nazi aggression, was broadcast to the French nation last evening by Premier Paul Reynaud.

But even before the French troops were advancing beyond the borders of their own country for the first time since their brief incursion into the Saar in September, French cities were being bombed for the first time in this war by German airplanes, serving a grim warning to all Frenchmen that the war was now on in earnest.

Nancy, Lille, Colmar, Luxeuil and Lyons were the chief cities "strafed" by the Germans yesterday morning. In most of these places the Germans were apparently aiming for the airfields with a view to preventing Allied planes from coming to the help of the Low Countries. The heaviest casualties appear to have occured in Nancy. Some soldiers were killed at Lyons. Paris had a two-hour alert beginning at five o'clock. No bombs were dropped on the French capital, but Pontoise, twenty miles to the northwest, was hit.

National Union Announced

With the French Army going forth to give battle to the ancient foe beyond the Rhine, the French Premier was also able to announce to his countrymen last evening that in her hour of need France had found a government of national union representing all the

French Communiqués

Communiqué No. 499

May 10 (Morning).—In the early hours of May 10 German troops began to invade Holland, Belgium and Luxemburg. During the night, the French armies had been warned to stand by. The governments concerned have appealed to the Allied governments.

Moreover, the enemy carried out aerial bombardments in the north and east of France. Several enemy airplanes, the number of which is not yet known, have been brought down by anti-aircraft guns as well as by our fighters.

Communiqué No. 500

May 10 (Evening).—The attack by the German troops on Holland, Belgium and Luxemburg was preceded in the early hours of May 10 by an aerial attack on a large scale.

Apart from attacks by bombardments, numerous enemy detachments were landed by airplanes or by parachutes at various points in Belgium and Holland. In Holland, notably, these detachments tried to take airfields by surprise. On the whole, they were successfully counter-attacked by the local troops.

The enemy's aerial attack, begun in the latter part of the night on French territory, was continued during the day. Some material damage of small importance was done by this bombing.

Our fighters and anti-aircraft guns came into action against these expeditions and inflicted heavy losses on the German aviation. Forty-four enemy airplanes were brought down on French territory.

The Dutch, Belgian and Luxemburg governments having appealed to the Allies this morning, Franco-British troops at once responded to the appeal and advanced on the

Amsterdam, Brussels, Antwerp and Other Open Cities Are Fiercely Air Bombed; Scores of Nazi Planes Downed; Belgians Halt Invaders, Reported Near Aachen

Germany invaded without warning Holland, Belgium and Luxemburg at dawn yesterday morning.

In response to appeals for help from the three countries, the Allies immediately moved into Belgium, where, according to a Paris military spokesman, the most gigantic battle of all time may be imminent.

Neville Chamberlain announced his resignation as Prime Minister in a farewell address by radio last night. He will be succeeded by Winston Churchill, First Lord of the Admiralty.

The former Prime Minister appealed to all Englishmen to support his successor. Speaking of Hitler, he said: "We must fight until this savage beast who has sprung from his lair at us is finally overthrown."

Cities Bombed, Parachute Troops Land

The triple invasion by Germany was accompanied by intensive bombings of Amsterdam, Brussels, Antwerp and all the main airports of Holland and Belgium. Hundreds of parachute troops were dropped in the invaded countries by heavy transport planes.

While the new aggression was being staged, German bombers for the first time carried out a series of attacks on French cities, including Pontoise, near Paris, Nancy, Lyons, Lille, Colmar and other points. Nancy was raided three times.

Raids on French towns resulted in a number of civilian deaths. Anti-aircraft firing was heard in Paris itself, which had its second-longest air-raid alarm.

Seventy German planes were shot down during attacks on Dutch airports. Forty-four others were brought down in France. Four German armored trains were wrecked in Holland.

Battles Rage in Invaded Countries

Heavy fighting was reported last night in all three invaded countries. Hitler is directing operations personally from a secret

Official Exchange Rates
Dollar in Paris.. 43.70 to 43.90
Dollar in London.. 4s. 11 1/2d.
Dollar in Rome..... 19 lire 80c.
Pound in Paris 176.50 to 176.75

NEW YORK Herald Tribune — 2 a.m. EDITION

53rd Year. No. 19,235 — European Edition — PARIS, MONDAY, JUNE 3, 1940 — THE NEW YORK HERALD (ESTABLISHED IN EUROPE 1887) — In France: 1 fr. 25c.

Axis Peace Drive Soon Is Forecast

Ultimatum by Duce May Mark Joint Move When Battle in Flanders Ends

By Havas Agency

WASHINGTON, June 2.— Well-informed circles in Washington believe that a German-Italian peace offensive, threatening that Italy will enter the war if its terms are not accepted, will be launched at the conclusion of the present battle in Flanders, the Associated Press political correspondent, Andrue Berding, wrote today.

The writer declared that officials have no precise information, but that their conclusions are based on information from reliable sources.

It is believed that the peace proposal will be made in the name of both Germany and Italy and that Mussolini will outline the general terms for a peace conference to fix the details. It is obvious that Il Duce will make territorial demands on France and Britain, Mr. Berding stated.

"Some observers in Washington believe that the Italian preparation and belligerent gestures of the last few days are part of a build-up for an early peace offensive, with the purpose of heightening the effect of an ultimatum announcing its entrance into the war in case the Allies do not accept the peace terms," the article said.

"These observers do not believe that Mussolini is merely bluffing. They think that if he sends an ultimatum he will have to go through with it."

It was recalled that similar rumors have been heard here before, but that none of them has as yet materialized Most circles believe the Allies have clearly shown they will not countenance any such maneuver, and that it may be only another German propaganda device to stir up trouble in the public mind.

N.Y. Paper Warns Duce

NEW YORK, June 2 (Havas). — Any action of Mussolini against the Allies would be considered by the American government as a deliberate threat to democracy and the free institutions of the Western Hemisphere, Ludwell Denny wrote today in the New York "World Telegram," commenting on President Roosevelt's message to Congress Friday.

"When Mr. Roosevelt stressed the 'possible consequences of events' and the 'possibility that not only one or two continents, but all the continents, will be drawn into a world war,' he referred to Mussolini and the Italian people,' the article said.

"Official circles believe that Mussolini is deluding himself, not only about the attitude of the United States government, but also about that of all the American people. He does not yet understand with what rapidity American public opinion would turn against him if he attacked the Allies.

"The opinion prevails that such an act by Mussolini would provoke even

Pius XII Pleads for Civilians, People in Occupied Territories

Pontiff Invokes God's Pity in Depicting Sad Vision Of Europe as War Grows in Fury

By Havas Agency

VATICAN CITY, June 2. — Pope Pius XII today appealed to the belligerent powers to respect the laws of humanity, pathetically implored neutrals to stay out and voiced his earnest hope for the return of a peace which will be just, honorable and lasting.

The Pope was addressing the College of Cardinals, members of which had assembled to express their best wishes on the occasion of the feast of St. Eugene, his patron saint.

"With the end of the ninth month of the war," the Pope said, "the conflict has become more impetuous and exterminating on bloody battlefields and on the sea. . . and is extending to peoples in no wise involved in the original hostilities."

After recalling his unavailing efforts to help preserve peace the Pope added: "If we turn our eyes on Europe today and contemplate the territories which by Divine vocation are truly the land of the faith and of Christian civilization and consider the vast destruction, the ruins and cruel suffering which constantly accumulate and spread in flourishing regions and estimate the sad economic, social, religious and moral results and repercussions extending beyond the oceans. . . a profoundly sad vision weighs our spirit and causes us to raise our eyes to heaven to invoke the immense pity of God on His unhappy sons, divided by ideas and opposing interests. . . .

"Is there not a clear demonstration of this in the fact that regions and populations which more than all others were attached to peace have been drawn into the storm of the war? . . .

"If we insist anew and conjure the hostile parties to recall always duties to humanity . . . we accomplish no partisan work, but a duty which is dictated to us by truth and love. . .

"We cannot forbear on this occasion to express our sadness in seeing the treatment inflicted on non-combatants in more than one region, treatment which is far from conforming to the rights of humanity. . . concern for the well-being of populations in occupied territory is a duty in the exercise of public power. Justice demands that occupied territories be treated in the same way as a nation's own territory and people."

Pepper Confers With President On Aid to Allies

By Havas Agency

WASHINGTON, June 2.—After conferring with President Roosevelt here today, Senator Claude Pepper (D., Fla.), author of a bill which would authorize the sale to the Allies of airplanes now being used by the United States Army and Navy, said the President should be given the power to allow the sale of planes and material not needed immediately in America.

"If the American people authorize the President, in whom they can have confidence, to sell to the Allies airplanes and material without which we can get along, I believe that the situation would change completely in Europe."

Ships for South America

WASHINGTON, June 2 (Havas).—A final vote will be cast in the House within two weeks on the bill providing for the co-operation of United States shipyards and arsenals in building warships and making arms for South American nations, Representative Sol Bloom (D., N.Y.) predicted here today.

The original measure was approved by the House a year ago, but was passed in the Senate only a week ago, with an amendment stipulating that the building aid must not interfere with the progress of America's national defense program. The amendment is now being considered by the House.

Paper Drops Isolationism

PHILADELPHIA, June 2 (Havas).—The isolationist Philadelphia "Record"

South America Seen Menaced By 5th Column

By United Press

NEW YORK, June 2.—Under a seven-column headline, the New York "Times" said today, "United States Studying Nazi Threat in South America."

The "Times" Washington correspondent wrote that a statement by General George Marshall, Army Chief of Staff, regarding the possibility of "dangerous developments in this hemisphere," has caused considerable excitement in Congressional circles and served to strengthen persistent reports that American soldiers may be sent to South America to aid several nations handle their Fifth Column problems.

It has formally been denied, said the "Times," that a maximum of 25,000 men might be requested to guard ports and harbors "of such countries as Brazil and Uruguay."

Another "Times" headline stated, "War Alarm Grows in South America," with subheads, "Nations Speed Arms Programs as Rumors of Peril Fray Nerves of the Public—Nazis Admit Invasion Aim—But Stress Plan to Bore from Within Pending Victory of Reich in Europe."

The headlines were over an article from Montevideo in which the correspondent stressed that, although a majority of the alarmist rumors are undoubtedly false, the public is perturbed.

U.S. Seeks Cape Verde Islands

WASHINGTON, June 2 (U.P.).—The United States will ask Portugal for use of the Cape Verde Islands as a naval or air base, the unofficial "Army and

Allied Artillery Guards Last Approach To Dunkirk as Evacuation Nears Close

Troops Crowd Dunkirk Area Awaiting Boats

around Dunkirk yesterday

the evacuation of Allied troops to England continued at a normal pace.

Troops were in entrenched positions in a twelve-mile arc around the port. Warships bombarded the Germans beyond the arc. The invaders bent every effort with planes and artillery to halt the evacuation and destroy the troops not yet embarked.

As fast as the retreating regiments returned to within the protective arc they were sent to camp to insure their own protection and general well-being until called to embark. The wounded received special attention, being given cover

Badly Wounded Men Left

Hundreds of other wounded men had to be left behind in villages that are now being engulfed by the pursuing German armies. Doctors and nurses often volunteered to remain behind with them.

Thousands of French, Belgian and British soldiers milled around looking for food and cigarettes. Occasional trucks came with supplies. Planes from England dropped food by parachute.

Dunkirk itself was a large target with scores of fires burning in the city. Some of the city's normal population of 80,000 was living in cellars and in the deep-arched crypt of the monastery.

Night Gives Only Respite

Praising the co-operation of Allied air, naval and artillery protection, a British officer broadcast over the B.B.C.:

"We had one thing in our favor. The German is a great soldier but night operations have never been his strong point. When the British were retreating from Mons in 1914, he more than once heard the welcome sound of his cookhouse bugles at sundown and knew he was safe a while."

A naval expert on the B.B.C. explained that a particular difficulty in embarking troops was that shoals and sand banks off Flanders run miles into the sea and are now unmarked by navigation buoys and lighthouses. No warship much larger than a destroyer can work there, he said, and any accident would block the harbor. He described the feat of a British destroyer, attacked by dive bombers, which re-

Official Communiqués

Communiqué No. 545

JUNE 2 (Morning).—In the Dunkirk region our troops, resisting with admirable vigor the unceasing attacks of the enemy, have kept every German effort in check, and the evacuation continued actively during yesterday and last night, despite air bombing and artillery fire.

On the Somme, the enemy attempted some raids with no result.

On the remainder of the front, artillery activity at various points.

Communiqué No. 546

JUNE 2 (Evening).—Ever since the order was given them to fall back on Dunkirk, the French and British troops, engaged on three fronts, from Saint-Omer to the outskirts of Arras, to Valenciennes and to Courtrai, where they connected with the Belgian Army, have compelled the enemy, who expected their surrender, to give battle without interruption under the hardest and most violent conditions.

Firstly, they occupied the line of La Bassée Canal and the Scarpe River, after that the Lys, then the zone marked by Gravelines, Cassel, Ypres and Nieuport; lastly, the entrenched camp itself, partly protected by inundations. During each one of these movements they maneuvered in good order, under the fire of artillery, aviation and tanks, unceasingly keeping the enemy in check by numerous and effective counter-attacks.

This retreat, accomplished by troops harassed on every side with no rest for twenty days and suddenly left exposed on their left flank by the capitulation of King Leopold, will remain as an example of heroic tenacity in the history of the French and British Armies.

Thanks to the valor and relentless energy of the northern troops, the territorial successes obtained by the enemy have been set off by immense losses of human lives and material. The German strength has been severely tried and, our armies, whose morale is higher than ever, are ready to face further battle.

The greater part of the troops retiring to the coast have already been embarked at Dunkirk, the defenses of which are still holding out.

France may be proud of the officers and men of the heroic Army of the North.

During June 2, on the Somme front, on the Aisne front, and in the east, activity has been limited to artillery firing and to some firing of automatic weapons in the region of Rethel.

During the night of June 1-2, our

Greater Part of Troops Escapes Capture; Last Thousands Seek Shelter Nazi Bombers Again Raid Rhône Valley

Under German pounding the evacuation at Dunkirk yesterday drew toward its close; siege guns opened fire against the great fortresses of the Maginot Line, and German bombers soared over the Rhône Valley and east of Marseilles.

Remnants of the retreating Flanders Army

The last of General Prioux's division was fighting a rearguard action. The state of these units and the fate of General Prioux was not clear.

The British planted naval guns at either end of the arc. One hundred Allied warships and 200 assorted craft—transports, yachts, trawlers and even paddlewheel excursion boats—were subjected to bombs and shells. But they continued the ferry service to England.

Four-fifths of the British Expeditionary Force and tens of thousands of French have been evacuated from Dunkirk to England, British War Secretary Anthony Eden stated in a broadcast to the United States.

French fortresses west of the Moselle and east and west of the Vosges were subjected to 220mm. projectiles fired from twelve or more miles away. The Germans used the same type of guns on Liége and Namur forts. The French said that this time the distance was too great for effectiveness.

Rhône Raids Made in Three Waves

Air raids over the Rhone and the Southeast behind the Riviera were made in three waves between 7:10 and 9:45 a.m. Defense batteries reportedly downed twelve of them. The Swiss sent one crashing, their third since Saturday.

They saw in these raids a political gesture to Mussolini regarding the support he could expect if he joined Germany.

The French gave no details of their own reprisals on Germany beyond the bare mention of successful raids on the Ruhr industrial basin.

A total of 149 German planes was downed Friday and Saturday in the Dunkirk region, the French stated. They also claimed the destruction of forty-four tanks.

Other operations are stagnating and entering a period of regrouping of forces on both sides, a French War Ministry spokesman stated.

Premier Paul Reynaud, Vice-Premier Henri-Philippe Pétain and Armament Minister Raoul Dautry yesterday visited the Somme front.

German Pressure on Port Diminishes

Behind an almost complete ring of rising waters and with massed artillery filling the only dry breach, General Georges-Maurice Blanchard yesterday kept control of the last twelve miles of roads around Dunkirk as the Germans closed the steel wall around the pocket by means of fifteen fresh divisions.

Official Exchange Rates
Dollar in Paris.. 43.70 to 43.90
Dollar in London.. 4s. 11 1/2d.
Dollar in Rome..... 19 lire 80c.
Pound in Paris 176.50 to 176.75

NEW YORK Herald Tribune

2 a.m. EDITION

53rd Year. No. 19,244 | European Edition | PARIS, WEDNESDAY, JUNE 12, 1940 | THE NEW YORK HERALD (ESTABLISHED IN EUROPE 1887) | In France: 1 fr. 25c.

Roosevelt Pledges Allies Utmost Aid

Fullest Resources to Be Harnessed for Defense, Aid Opponents of Force; Duce Scored for 'Dagger in Back of Neighbor'

By Special Wireless

CHARLOTTESVILLE, Va., June 11. — "The United States, with all its strength and with all its unity, will hereafter pursue two obvious and simultaneous courses: it will extend to the opponents of force the fullest material resources of this nation and it will harness and speed up these resources in order that we ourselves in the Americas may have equipment and training equal to the task of any emergency and every defense," declared President Roosevelt yesterday in an address to the graduating class of the University of Virginia here. The speech was broadcast throughout the world in seven languages. His youngest son was a graduate of the law school.

Departing from the prepared form of his speech outlining American policies and doctrine in the present emergency, Mr. Roosevelt reviewed efforts over the course of months to keep the war from spreading, particularly by offering his good offices to Italy.

"Unfortunately," the President added, after outlining his efforts to assure Italy that its aspirations would be considered and it would be assurred an equal place at the conference table after the war "unfortunately, to the regret of all of us and to the regret of humanity the chief of the Italian government was unwilling to accept the procedure suggested and he has made no counter-proposals."

"On this tenth day of June, 1940, the hand that held the dagger has struck into the back of its neighbor," the President said. "On this tenth day of June, 1940, in this university founded by the great American teacher of democracy we send forth our prayers and our hopes to those beyond the seas who are maintaining with magnificent valor their battle for freedom."

The President's speech follows in full:—

Speaks to All Classes

My friends of the University of Virginia:—

I notice by the program that I am asked to address the class of 1940. I avail myself of that privilege, but also take this very happy occasion to speak to many other classes, classes that have graduated beyond the years, classes that are still in the period of studying, classes not alone in the schools of learning of the nation, but classes that have come up to the great schools of experience.

In other words, the cross-section, just as you who graduated today are a cross-section, and the older generations have questions to ask the world. Most of the time they ask simple but nevertheless difficult questions. Questions of what to do, of opportunities to find, ambitions to satisfy. Ever now and again in the history of the Republic a different kind of question presents itself. A question that asks, not about the future of an individual, or even of the generation, but about the future of the country, the future of the American people.

Former Questionings

There was such a time at the beginning of our history. At the beginning of our history as a nation young people asked themselves what lay ahead, not for themselves, but for the new United States.

There was such a time again in the seemingly endless years of the war between the States. Young men of both sides of the line asked themselves not what trades or professions they would like to enter, what lives they would make, but what would be the trend of the conquest they had known.

There is such a time again today. Again today, the young men and young women of America ask themselves with earnstness and a deep concern this same question: What is to become of the country we know? Now they ask it with even greater anxiety than before. They ask not only what the future holds for this Republic, but what the future holds for all peoples of all nations that have been living under Democratic forms of government.

Under the free institutions of a free people it is understandable to all of us, I think, that they should ask this question. For there are those who are telling them that the ideal of individual liberty, the ideal of free franchise, the ideal of peace and justice is a decadent ideal. They read the word and hear the boast of those who say that a belligerent force—force directed by self-chosen leaders is the new and vigorous system which will overrun the earth. We have seen the tendency of this philosophy, of course, in nation after nation where free institutions and individual liberties were once maintained.

The Ultimate Result

It is natural and understandable that the younger generation should first ask itself what the extension of the philosophy throughout the years would lead to ultimately.

We see today, for example, in stark reality some of the consequences of what we call machine age. Where control of machines has been retained in the hands of mankind, on the whole untold benefits have accrued to mankind. But mankind was then master and the machine was the servant. But this new system of force, the mastery of the machine, is not always now in the hands of mankind. It is in the conrtol of infinitely small groups of individuals who rule without a single one of the checks of the democratic sanctions that we have known. The machine in the hands of the irresponsible conqueror has become the master. Mankind is not only the servant, it is the victim too. Such mastery abandons with deliberate contempt all of the moral values to which even this young country for more than 300 years has been accustomed and dedicated.

The new philosophy grows from month to month and could have no possible conception of the laws of life or the way of thought of a nation whose origins go back for nearly a thousand years. Neither descendents of our pioneers, nor those who have come hither in later years can be indifferent to the destruction of freedom in their ancestral lands across the sea.

The danger to our institutions may come slowly, or it may come with a rush and a shock as it has come to the people of the United States in the past few months. The conception of danger, danger in a world-wide area has come to us clearly and overwhelmingly. We perceive the peril in this world-wide arena that may become so narrow that only Americans will retain the ancient phase.

Some still hold to the now somewhat obvious illusion that we of the United States can safely permit the United States to become a lone island. A lone usland in a world dominated by the philosophy of force. Such an island may be the dream of those who still talk and vote as isolationists. Such an island represents to me and to the overwhelming majority of Americans today a helpless nightmare. A helpless nightmare of people without freedom. Yes, a nightmare of a people lost in prison, handcuffed, hungry and fed through the bars from day to day by the contemptuous, unpitying masters of other continents.

It is natural also that we should ask ourselves how we can prevent the building of that prison and the placing of ourselves in the midst of it. Let us not hesitate, all of us, to proclaim certain truths overwhelmingly. We as a nation and this applies to all the other American nations. We are convinced that military and naval victory for the gods of force and hate would endanger the institutions of democracy in the western world and that equally therefore the whole of our sympathies lie with those nations that are giving their life blood in combat against those forces.

The Italian Coup

The people and the government of the United States have seen with utmost regret and with grave disquietness that the chief of the Italian government has decided to engage in the hostitlities now raging in Europe. More than three months ago the chief of the Italian government sent me word that because of the determination of Italy to limit so far as might be possible the spread of the conflict so that more than millions of people in the region of the Mediterranean might be enabled to escape the suffering and the devastation of war. I informed the chief of the Italian government that this desire on the part of Italy to prevent the war from spreading met with full sympathy and response on the part of the government and people of the United States and I expressed the earnest hope of this government and of this people that this policy on the part of Italy might be continued.

Extension of War Area

I made it clear that in the opinion of the government of the United States any extension of hostilities in the region of the Mediterranean might result in a still greater enlargment of the scene of the conflict, a conflict in the Near East and in Africa, and that if this came to pass no one could foretell how greater the theater of the war eventually might become.

Again, on a subsequent occasion, not so long ago, recognizing that certain aspirations of Italy might form the basis of discussions betwen the powers most specifically concerned I offered in a mesage addresed to the chief of the Italian government to sent to the governments of France and of Great Britain such specific indications of the desires of Italy to obtain readjustments with regard to its position as the chief of the Italian government might desire to transmit through me.

While making it clear that the government of the United States in such an event could not and would not assume responsibility for the nature of the proposals submitted, not for agreements which might thereafter be reached and proposed that it Italy would refrain from entering the war I would be willing to ask assurances from the the other powers concerned that they would faithfully execute any agreement so reached and that Italy's voice in any future peace conference would have the same authority as if Italy had actually taken part in the war as a belligerent.

Offers Are Rejected

Unfortunately, to the regret of all of us and to the regret of humanity the chief of the Italian government was unwilling to accept the procedure suggested and he has made no counter-proposals.

This government directed its efforts to doing what it could toward the work of preserving peace in the Mediterranean area and it likewise expressed its willingness to endeavor to co-operate with the government of Italy when the appropriate occasion arose for the creation of a more stable world order through the reduction of armaments and through the construction of a more liberal international economic system which would assure to all powers equality of opportunity in the world's markets and in the securing of raw materials on equal terms.

I have likewise, of course, felt it necessary in my communications to Signor Mussolini to express the concern of the government of the United States because of the fact that any extension of the war in the region of the Mediterranean would inevitably result in great prejudice to the ways of life and government and to the trade and commerce of all the American republics. But the government of Italy has now chosen to preserve what it terms its freedom of action and to fulfill what it states are its promises to Germany. In so doing it has manifested disregard for the rights and security of other nations: disregard for the lives of the peoples of those nations which are directly threatened by the spread of this war and has evidenced its unwillingness to find the means through pacific negotiation for the satisfaction of what it believes are its legitimate aspirations.

"On this tenth day of June, 1940, the hand that held the dagger has struck into the back of its neighbor. On this tenth day of June, 1940, in this university founded by the first great American teacher of democracy we send forth our prayers and our hopes to those beyond the seas who are maintaining with magnificent valor their battle for freedom.

In our unity, in our American unity, we will pursue two obvious and simultaneous courses. We will extend to the opponents of force the material resources of this nation. And at the same time we will harness and speed up the use of these resources in order that we ourselves in the Americas may have equipment and training equal to the task of any emergency and every defense.

Future of Nation at Stake

All roads leading up to the accomplishment of these objectives must be kept clear of obstructions. We will not slow down nor détour. Signs and signals call for speed, full speed ahead. Yes, it is right to say that each new generation should ask questions. But recent months the principle question has been somewhat simplified. Once more the future of the nation—the future of the American people, is at stake.

We need not and we will not in any way abandon our continuing effort to make democracy work within our borders. Yes, we still insist on the need for vast improvements in our own social and economic life. But that is a component part of national defense itself. The program unfolds swiftly and into that program will fit the responsibility and the opportunity of every man and woman in the land to preserve our heritage in days of peril. I call for effort, courage, sacrifice, devotion, the love of freedom, all of these are possible and the love of freedom is still fixed in the nation today.

Washington Stopped by Submarine

Unknown Craft Said to Have Menaced Refugee Ship; Near Panic Caused

WASHINGTON, June 11. — Already stirred to its depth by Italy's entrance into the war and President Roosevelt's great speech yesterday the nation was further shocked tonight when the news was flashed across the country by wire and radio that an unidentified submarine had hailed and thrreatened to sink the liner Washington with over 1,500 American refugees from Europe off the coast of Portugal.

The Washington left Bordeaux late Saturday and was believed to have reached Lisbon tonight after its exciting adventure.

Details were lacking early this evening but the first reports stated that a ten-minute near-panic was created aboard the crowded ship when the submarine appeared and flashed signals to the ship.

The excited passengers rushed toward the lifeboats demanding that they be let down. However, it seems that after the reply the underwater craft disappeared.

The Washington is sailing fully lighted, without escort and with the American flag conspicuously painted on its side. After its Lisbon call it will call at Galway.

Defense Speed-Up

WASHINGTON, June 11.—Spurred by President Roosevelt's speech yesterday Congress went full speed ahead today with its defense and preparedness program.

The Senate voted 67 to 18 a resolution authorizing the trading in of surplus army equipment of all kinds to be sent to the Allies.

Two armament bills made rapid speed in House Committees. One provides for twenty-two new warships, 10,000 planes and the training of 16,000 pilots.

Senate bills, one calling for the expenditure of over $1,800,000,000 for planes and warships, the other the $1,-760,000,000 supplementary defense bill providing for an increase of 175,000 in Army effectives, moved ahead in Committee as did the $1,000,000,000 tax bill.

A record number of telegrams deluged the White House congratulating the President on his speech.

Hull Statement on Italy

WASHINGTON, June 11.—The entry of Italy into the war "will prove a great disappointment to people everywhere and a great human tragedy," Secretary of State Cordel Hull declared today at his press conference.

In reply to an inquiry as to when a proclamation bringing Italy under the Neutrality Act might be expected, Mr. Hull said that "something like a day" would probably be required to establish facts on Italy's position and take the necessary steps for application of the act.

The possibility of keeping open American shipping routes to Spain and Portugal under the new conditions Mr. Hull declined to discuss "without careful examination and the President's recommendation."

Mr. Hull also revealed that a number of Americans in Italy had insisted on remaining despite the conflict, and that he did not believe the State Department had a complete count of Americans still in Italy. He estimated the number of American ships in the new danger zone as eighteen on Saturday. It was later confirmed that two passenger vessels and fourteen cargo ships are in the Mediterranean, and two other freighters in the Black Sea.

In answer to another querry Mr. Hull said that American ships in the Mediterranean would be instructed to return directly to the United States, in accordance with past practice.

He told reporters he had no information concerning the capacity in which Ambassador William C. Bullitt had reportedly attended a French Cabinet meeting. He admitted that he knew nothing new in connection with the reported embargo on machine tools which had been discussed at his conference last week.

Eight-Year-Old Killed by Bomb

WASHINGTON, June 11.—The State Department announced today that an eight-year-old American child named Alfred Paul Ritter was killed during a bombing attack at Kliengestein, Germany, on June 4. The message, sent by Samuel W. Honaker, American Consul-General in Stuttgart, stated that the boy had been living with his grandparents in Germany.

Italian Bombers Take War to Asia, Africa; Great Battle for Paris at Crucial Stage

Flight from Paris Nears End As Black Smoke Shroud Lifts

Some French Troops Arrive in Wake of Exodus; Few Planes Over City, No Air Raid Alarms During Day

By Walter B. Kerr

The great mass flight of the people of Paris to the south of France was almost ended by sundown yesterday.

All last night and all morning and afternoon, men, women and children piled out of town by train, bus, truck, automobile, bicycle, baby carriage and on foot. They took with them what they could, everything from a loaf of bread and a bottle of wine for the evening meal to matresses, chairs, clothing, bird cages, dogs and cats.

And almost as the last of them were leaving, soldiers began arriving.

But the more obvious story in Paris yesterday was the flight to the south. Literally hundreds of thousands of people left the city and its suburbs. I do not suppose there will be more than a few hundred thousand still here by dawn today.

Those who left last night and this morning left while the entire valley of the Seine within many miles of here was covered with black cloud of smoke. This smoke seemed to come from burning gasoline or oil stores west and north of the city. And it brought with it a black dust that was in everyone's mouth and nose when he got up from bed.

At nine o'clock yesterday morning from the Rond Point on the Champs Elysées it was so smokey that you could not see the Obelisk on the Place de la Concorde nor the Arc de Triomphe at the Place de l'Etoile, both short distances away.

Smoke Lifted at Noon

The smoke began to pass away about eleven o'clock and before noon it had been cleared away by a fairly strong wind and the sun shone and it was hot for the rest of the day.

But even then in the smokey morning hours thousands were fleeing southwards across the bridges of the Seine. Thousands were riding and thousands were walking. They pushed carts and wheelbarrows. I talked with one man of about forty who was wheeling his sick daughter away. He did not know where he was going but he wanted to get away. His wife had died six weeks ago and two sons were with the army. One man staying behind was a blind veteran from the last war. He was playing an accordian at the Porte Maillot. In his coat lapel were ribbons of the Croix de Guerre and Legion of Honor.

oflCwqz shrdl shrd lshrdl hrdl hrdluf

Some men and women had so much baggage with them they had to pusth their bicycles. Two men, in order to escape with a trunk-load of stuff, placed it on the cross bars of their wheels and pushed along.

Long Lines of Farmers

They came in long straggling parades, farmers from the country, taking away their families and things on those old-fashioned French hayricks, drawn by three horses in single file. These ricks went along in groups of ten, twenty, and thirty. The parades entered the city from every road on the right bank of the river and crossed the bridges toward the south.

All day there was a steady stream across the bridge running from the Place de la Concorde to the Chamber of Deputies.

Where they are going and what they expect to find when they get there are unanswered questions. They cannot possibly be enough food in the southwest to feed them all, a even for more than a few months. And the cars going out, although their gas tanks are full and there are full contains in the back seat, cannot be driven all the way. Some place tonight there must be the greatest traffic jam in history.

These people are taking with them things they could never use and the stuff is weighing them down. I have seen old men and women carrying baggage that would tire a strong man after a while.

The number of push carts is as astonishing as it is tragic, but you cannot push a cart all the the way to Bordeaux or wherever it is they are going.

I don't know what they will do for doctors and nurses on the way. Perhaps first-said stations have been organized in every village. I hope so or the suffering will be unbearable.

May Have Been Bombed

Nor do we know here whether these people who have gone have been bombed on the roads. There was no enemy plane ever Paris yesterday and only one this evening up until seven-thirty o'clock. And anti-aircraft guns blazed away at him.

No matter what happens the French will protect their city against planes as long as possible.

It is easy to be repetitious in tailing of the refugees. They have gone in such numbers and for so many hours that the detail is quickly forgotten, and only an impression that families are running remains fixed in your mind.

I have seen two women driving a donkey cart, one woman leading four dogs on leashes and carrying a suitcase in each hand. I have seen hundred of cars broken down and abandoned while the family continued on foot, leaving behind on the road half of their belongings.

Last night Paris was abnormally quiet. At six o'clock there was no one standing around the tomb of the Unknown Soldier where the eternal flame still burns was guarded by three policemen. I counted only twelve cars on all the Champs-Elysées.

Almost every office has closed. Hundred of cafés and restaurants have been shut tight. Fouquet's went out of business yesterday afternoon. Hotels are closing fast, the Plaza Athénée today and the Crillon tonight or tomorrow. Small bistrots have shut down.

But some cafés and restaurants are still open, a few on the main boulevards and quite a few in the side streets. But Paris will be only a shadow city if it falls into German hands.

The American Embassy issued certificates to American property owners, certifying that the property was American. The Stars and Stripes were hung from many windows, even from the Belgian Embassy and its annex, for the United States is looking after Belgian affairs here.

Of the normal sights yesterday, I saw men still digging air-raid shelters in the small parks in front of the Petit Palais and the Grand Palais. And a gardener was watering the lawn behind the Elysee Palace which until he left the city was the residence of the President of the Republic Albert Lebrun.

It has been announced that Premier Paul Reynaud has gone to General Headquarters.

Official Communiqués

Communiqué No. 564

June 11 (Evening). — The combat attained greatest violence along the entire front. It is evident that the enemy is attempting to force a decision. He redoubled his efforts on the Seine between Rouen and Vernon. Covering himself by thick artificial clouds he attempted to throw a series of poonton bridges o nthe river to permit tanks to reach the south bank. Our troops counter-attacked without respite in an attempt to contain him. East of the Oise River, enemy divisions were engaged on the Ourcq River from Ferté-Milon to Fère-en-Tardenois and renewed their assaults with the aid of numerous tanks. They only found in front of them our rear-guard since the bulk of our divisions had received orders to carry their resistance south of the Marne. Farther east, the enemy had massed heavy tanks to intervene between the valleys of the Vesle and Agre to attempt to over run Rheims by the east and by the southeast. Pressure on this region was extremely violent.

In the Champagne sector, the enemy during the night established new positions south of Ay.

Fighting re-started at dawn along the whole course of the Rethondes River, crossings of which were very dearly contested. Our troops executed several counter-attacks south of Ay and inflicted serious losses on the enemy. Between Aisne and the Meuse all enemy assaults were repulsed.

Several squadrons of our planes bombed the airfields of Neustadt, Frankfort and the blast furnaces at Wolthingen. A formation of naval sea planes bombed and partially set afire the Heinkel factories in the vicinity of Rostock.

Newsmen Say Road Travel South Is 'Slow But Sure'

The New York Herald Tribune talked by telephone late last night with several American newspaper correspondents who left Paris with the government.

They said that traffic on the roads was slow but sure and that most persons were arriving. Two men who left Paris at 1 a.m. yesterday reached their destination by 9 p.m., while several others who started out Monday afternoon arrived several hours later.

Franklin Roosevelt Jones Has Little Brother Now

SALEM, N.J. (U.P.).—Franklin D. Roosevelt Jones, whose christening after the President and a popular song caused national comment a year ago, has a new brother.

Mr. and Mrs. Franklin Jones, the parents, were impressed by the absence of boys in the Cantor family and named their twelfth child Eddie Cantor Jones.

Rip Van Winkle Tug on Skids

BUFFALO, N.Y. (U.P.).—The [illegible]-year-old Tug International, Rip Van Winkle of Niagara River boats, will slumber here no longer. It will be sold "down the river" for whatever it will bring.

Englishman Father at 80

GORLESTON, England (U.P.).—Captain David St. Clair Donaldson, father of a six-week-old baby, in his eightieth year is believed to be the oldest [illegible] with the youngest family in Great Britain.

Malta Air Attack Heralds Fascist Entry; French Hold Desperate German Thrusts; Move to Declare Paris an 'Open City'

The war spread yesterday from Arctic Norway almost to the Equator in Africa as Mussolini's Fascist legions joined Hitler's feldgrau troops driving for a decision in the battle for Paris.

An air raid on Malta heralded Italy's entry into the war. Later in the day Malta was bombed several times, as was Aden. A drive for Jibuti was started. Italy lost a number of planes and ships in the first day. King Victor Emmanuel was reported in the field with his troops on the French border, but there was little news of fighting there.

World interest still centered, however, on the great battle for Paris now in its crucial stage. Fighting seemed to reach its highest stage of violence since the drive started just one week ago. Millions of Germans, backed by the most formidable assembly of planes and tanks in history, were hurled against the French along the entire 185-mile front from the Channel near Dieppe to the Maginot line.

Germans Throw Smoke Screen Over Battle

General Weygand also threw in reserves to halt the Nazi hordes daily getting a little nearer to Paris.

As both sides attacked and counter-attacked the battle line swayed to and fro.

The Germans used a new trick for this war when they sought under cover of a smoke cloud to throw a series of poonton bridges over the Seine between Rouen and Vernon. The French counter-attacked without respite to hold them.

New tanks were thrown in by the Germans in a vain attempt to break the French lines south of the Ourcq. The French rear-guard held, while the main forces established strong positions south of the Marne. Intense fighting with little change extended beyond the Champagne region right into the Argonne.

Allied Air forces took a heavy toll of the enemy by bombing concentrations and communications while airfields and military objectives in Germany were also attacked.

Cabinet Is 'Somewhere in France'

The French government which left Paris Monday evening is now set up "somewhere in France." However, most of the Ministries remain open. Premier Paul Reynaud went to the front.

The exodus of the Parisian population reached a new height. All the French newspapers, a few of which got out Paris editions yesterday, are now located in the provinces. The Paris Bourse was closed for the first time since the war started but is reopening in a provincial city. Many banks and innumerable shops and other establishments were closed.

The Military Governor of Paris and the Prefect of Police rule city will the army. Conferences held by the authorities yesterday may, it was reported, shortly lead the announcement that Paris is now "an open city" with no military objectives warranting air raids due to the transfer of vital industries, the transfer of the Ministries and other changes.

Italy Opens War With Raid on Malta

LONDON, June 11.—Italy started war on Britain early this morning by an air raid on Malta. Britain retaliated by raids on Libya and Italian East Africa. The British Fleet won the first round at sea by seizing or causing the scuttling of twenty-seven Italian ships in various parts of the world. The biggest prize was the 10,000-ton motorship Remo, the crew of which was brought into a Scottish port.

Other raids on Malta during the day caused little damage and few casualties the B.B.C. announced tonight. One of the ten enemy planes participating was brought down

British targets in Libya and in East Africa were principally airfields. Considerable damage was done and a number of planes destroyed on the ground. The attacking planes apparently caught the enemy by surprise. Most of them got away before the ground guns got into action. Three of the British planes failed to return after the long desert flights.

Other Countries in War

There was little news here today of Italian land attacks but it is believed that the first French objectives will be Corsica and Tunisia.

The Italian Cabinet held its first war meeting, decreeing the requisitioning of industries, fixing prices and imposing new taxes. The communiqué issued afterwards gave no information on fighting, but warned the public that results will not be obtained without grave sacrifices.

A decree bringing Albania into the war beside Italy was published at Tirana.

Australia, New Zealand, South Africa and India followed the Canadian example last night by declaring a state of war with Italy.

The Admiralty has given notice that numerous areas in the Mediterranean adjacent to Italy or Italian possessions are dangerous because they have been mined.

Attlee Stigmatizes Duce

Lord Privy Seal Clement R. Attlee in a statement in Commons on behalf of Prime Minister Winston Churchill likened Italy to a jackal. He expressed sympathy for the Italian people who, he said, will soon like the Reich feel the full effects of the sea blockade and who were the victims of the "overwhelming ambition and blood lust of their leader. "The attack on France, at this moment, he described as the "most wanton in history."

"Mussolini," he added, "was making a great mistake by stabbing France in the back and would be deceived in his hope of finding the British Empire easy picking. The two dictators had united to destroy democracy."

Major Attlee thanked President Roosevelt for his "vitally inspiring" speech and concluded that the Italian aggression had struck no dismay in British hearts" but only increased their determination for they know that they are not fighting for themselves alone but for a greater cause. He expressed sympathy for the Pope.

Military experts in London estimated that Italy has available from seventy to eighty divisions and admitted that the Italian navy, under German tutelage, might make a better showing than it did in the last war. Little fear is felt here for Tunisia, defended by fortifications and a strong army. Egypt is protected by 300 miles of desert but may be drawn in, it was thought by a new aggression.

NEW YORK
Herald Tribune
EUROPEAN EDITION

Published by The New York Herald Co.
OGDEN REID,
President
LAURENCE HILLS,
Editor and General Manager
European Edition founded in 1887. Offices: HERALD BUILDING, 21 Rue de Berri, Paris. Tel.: Elysées 12-87, 03-67. Long distance: Inter-Elysées 112. Telegrams: Herald Paris 46. Chèques Postaux No. 380-13 Paris.

NEW YORK, 230 West 41st Street. LONDON: Bush House, Aldwych, W.C. ROME: 54 Via della Mercede. MILAN: Palazzo della Borsa.

Terms to Subscribers (Daily and Sunday):

		1 mo.	3 mos.	6 mos.	1 yr.
France	Francs	35	95	180	350
Italy	Lire	40	120	225	420
Foreign (except Italy)		55	165	320	600

Paris, Wednesday, June 12, 1940

PARIS—NEW YORK HERALD
Printing Establishment, 21 Rue de Berri, Paris
MAURICE GAZENGEL, Gérant.

1944–1949

In late August 1944, more than two months after landing on the Normandy coast, the Allied armies reached Paris. US forces in Europe were served by the military newspaper *Stars and Stripes*, and the *Herald Tribune* plant in Paris seemed the perfect place from which to publish it. During the occupation, the rue de Berri building had been used by a French government agency, but it had escaped requisition by the Germans. The paper's building manager, the formidable Mademoiselle Renée Brazier, jealously guarded the owners' interests for 4½ years and, though some archives were burned by the wartime occupants to help heat the building, many of the files and most of the equipment remained intact.

Laurence Hills had died in Paris in the early months of the occupation. So, at the age of eighty-six, had Sparrow Robertson, whose last months were spent in a valiant but pathetic attempt to stop history in its tracks by continuing his nightclub rounds each evening and returning to the dark and deserted rue de Berri offices to write his column and place it dutifully on Eric Hawkins's empty desk.

The linotypes and presses were as they had been left in 1940 and, with the help of Hawkins (who had narrowly escaped to the South of France in June of 1940 and to England in 1941), *Stars and Stripes* began printing at the rue de Berri soon after the liberation. Meanwhile, the *Herald Tribune*'s owners decided to move quickly to get the European Edition on the stands. Advertising manager Bill Robinson was sent over from New York and he enlisted the support of General Eisenhower for the revival effort. London bureau chief Geoffrey Parsons, Jr., was named editor and, on December 22, 1944, in the middle of the Battle of the Bulge, the first issue rolled off the presses. Hawkins resumed his duties as managing editor, with Les Midgeley in charge of the newsroom.

The new paper was more serious and more international than its predecessor, and a much more faithful counterpart of its increasingly distinguished parent. Many famous bylines from the New York paper now appeared even more frequently in its pages. But the editors knew that small things could also be important and the first civilian transport plane to land in Paris since 1940 carried a special cargo of fifty crossword puzzles for use in the European Edition.

Nineteen forty-five was a remarkable year. Accounts of Allied victories in Europe and the Pacific shared the first months' pages with reports of shortages of food and fuel—exacerbated by the bitter winter of 1945/46 in which Europe experienced its harshest weather for decades.

The financial health of the European Edition was closely linked to the reconstruction of Europe. As civilian production gradually recovered, hotels reopened, and life slowly returned to normal, advertisers started trickling back. But, most important to the paper was the rapid reconstruction of civilian transportation systems. At the end of the war the European railway network was severely disrupted and its rehabilitation was an urgent priority not only for the transport of food and fuel, but also for the revival of international communications.

By 1947 the European Edition could boast that it carried more international news than any American newspaper except its own parent in New York (and, of course, the *New York Times*)—and twice as much as the London *Times* or *Le Monde*. Although the war was over, its aftermath dominated the news. Independence movements heralded the end of European colonial empires in Africa and Asia. India became the world's largest democracy. By the end of the decade, new power struggles surfaced, both inside and outside the newly organized United Nations. When East and West came face-to-face in Berlin it was no longer as allied conquerors of Nazism but as bitter ideological foes. The Berlin airlift set the tone for the ensuing cold war. The creation of the State of Israel introduced a new element into perennial struggles in the Middle East. Communism emerged as the victor in China, and became an increasingly serious political force in Europe.

The European Edition's "back of the book"—the inside pages dedicated to features and arts and sports—was now graced by an even richer array of bylines, including a homegrown newcomer named Art Buchwald, who talked his way into a job in the Paris newsroom in 1949. Beginning as a movie and restaurant critic (it was said that he took on the restaurant job because it meant regular meals), Buchwald soon achieved his distinctive voice—that of the innocent American abroad in a bewildering world. Although he moved his base of operations from Paris to Washington in 1962, his internationally syndicated column is still hugely popular with readers nearly forty years after it began. Buchwald describes his years in Paris as "the best years of my life" and the old *Herald Tribune* as "the only newspaper I ever really loved."

Another key figure in the paper's history also started at the rue de Berri in 1949: production manager André Bing, who helped to spur a complete reorganization of the paper's business and financial arrangements. A former leader of the French Resistance, Bing was to become a central force in the period of expansion and innovation that lay ahead.

Price: 5 Francs

Subscription Rates Listed on Page Two

NEW YORK Herald Tribune

EUROPEAN EDITION

57th Year—No. 19.245

PARIS, FRIDAY, DECEMBER 22, 1944

THE NEW YORK HERALD (ESTABLISHED IN EUROPE 1887)

Nazi Spearhead Now 30 Miles from Old Front; U.S. Troops Slow Tide, Reoccupy Stavelot; Flanks Contained, Echternach Holding Out

Yanks Slug Foe in Final Leyte Battle

Japanese Defense Line Falls, Back of Enemy Resistance Is Broken

Outcome Decided In 2 Months' Fight

1,541 Enemy Dead After Battle to Keep U.S. Out of Philippines

By the Associated Press

GENERAL MACARTHUR'S HEADQUARTERS, PHILIPPINES, Dec. 21.—Two months after the landing of General Douglas MacArthur at Leyte, organized Japanese resistance on the island has collapsed, it was officially announced today. Only mopping up and the pursuit of stragglers remain to be done.

The long-drawn battle drew rapidly to its close with the complete destruction in the last few days of the Yamashita line, the once powerful Japanese defense position in the Ormoc corridor. American troops are now cleaning up the shattered line of fortifications and the surrounding hills which are infested with guerrillas. In the course of these operations another 1,541 dead Japanese were counted. The booty includes six months' food supplies.

Considerable aerial activity was reported from other sectors of the Pacific. Allied heavy bombers attacked enemy targets on Borneo Island, the Celebes, the Moluccas, and the New Guinea and Solomon Islands area, destroying or damaging several grounded planes and enemy vessels, including one 400-foot tanker and two big freighters.

The American Air Corps personnel at the Leyte air base has been so busy fighting the Japanese that it has only just discovered that its airstrip is the busiest in the Pacific theater—possibly in any theater.

Lieutenant Colonel James Pettus, acting commander of the Leyte airdrome, estimated that until recently the strip averaged between six and seven hundred daylight takeoffs daily. It hit a record when 894 takeoffs and landings were made during daylight hours, or one in every 45 seconds.

Treasury Denies It Plans Release of French Funds

No Change in Rules for Use Of Frozen $7,400,000,000

WASHINGTON, Dec. 21 (U.P.).—Denying a New York newspaper report that complete release of French funds in the United States was imminent, the Treasury Department said tonight there had been no change in its previously broadened licensing plan for the use of frozen French funds, estimated at $7,400,000,000.

The Treasury said President Roosevelt had ordered no such action and none was expected.

French officials told the United Press that plans were being considered by the French and Allied governments to assure France a definite supply of much needed imports in the next few months.

They said Jean Monet, on a special mission from the French government, had arrived to arrange an end to the present unsatisfactory day-to-day basis for imports

Nazi Drive Stops Food Relief in French Areas

Allies Need Ship Space to Meet New Threat

WASHINGTON, Dec. 21 (AP).—One result of the German offensive in western Europe is that the food relief supplies which the Allies promised liberated countries are not being delivered, Allied supply officials said today.

While it was believed that the war in Europe would be over early in December, several ships were diverted from the Pacific to carry supplies to Europe, but now, these officials said, it was necessary to use every available shipping space in the Atlantic to meet the new threat on the Rhine.

Share Your Copy of The Herald Tribune

Newsprint is strictly rationed. This newspaper is printed on four pages only by cutting in half its potential circulation as a two-page paper. Under existing conditions, there cannot be enough copies to meet every demand. You can ease the shortage by sharing your copy with another reader.

European Edition Reappears In Freed Capital of France

New York Herald Tribune, Last Paper to Print In Paris As Germans Approached, Resumes Publication After Four and a Half Years

The European edition of the New York Herald Tribune resumed publication in Paris today after a lapse of four and a half years.

The last issue was published on June 12, 1940, two days before the Germans entered Paris. By then, the Parisian press had already moved out of Paris, and the New York Herald Tribune was the last free newspaper to be printed in the French capital before the entry of the Germans.

The United States was not then at war with Germany. By trimming its freedom to suit the dictates of the invaders, the European edition doubtless could have continued to publish for a period even after the German occupation. Nevertheless, Mr. Ogden Reid, president and publisher of both the New York and European editions of the newspaper, promptly ordered the paper to cease publication. He was convinced, as he stated in his cable to Paris at the time, that it was impossible for a free newspaper—free by either American or French standards—to exist in German-occupied Paris.

The last issue published before the Germans marched in was No. 19,244. Today, the European edition resumes with No. 19,245. The paper, having been launched first on October 4, 1887, as a venture by James Gordon Bennett then owner of the New York Herald, was in 1940, in its fifty-third year. Today, after a hiatus of more than four years, it is in its fifty-seventh.

The newspaper resumes publication today, nearly four months after the liberation of Paris through the generous co-operation of the French authorities. Since early September, its modern printing plant in the Herald Tribune building at 21 rue de Berri has been turned over to the American Army for the publication of its official troop newspaper, "The Stars and Stripes." From today on the Army daily and the New York Herald Tribune will publish side by side in the same plant.

The paper, the ink, and most of the other supplies necessary to the publication of a paper in Paris will come from the French authorities through the co-operation of the French Ministry of Information and the French Federation of the National Press. Although the bulk of the present circulation, restricted because of the shortage of newsprint supply in France, will be for general public consumption in the Paris area, a substantial fraction of the daily output will be turned over to the United States Army for

(Continued on page 4, col. 6)

Eden Discloses Peace Overture In Greek Crisis

British Foreign Minister Tells of Government Hopes for Early Action

By Ned Russell

LONDON, Dec. 21.—Anthony Eden, the Secretary for Foreign Affairs, indicated in the House of Commons today that the British [illegible] new suggestions for ending the civil war there, and he expressed the hope that peace could be restored soon throughout Greece.

Mr. Eden's suggestion that there are grounds for new optimism over the Greek situation was made during another stormy session in the House of Commons, which was followed by a brief debate in the House of Lords, where Viscount Cranborne, Dominions Secretary, defended King George II of Greece, now in London, against attempts to "blacken his character."

Both the Secretary for Foreign Affairs and Mr. Attlee, Deputy Prime Minister, who spoke for Mr. Churchill, were subjected to a con-

(Continued on page 2, col. 1)

King of Greece Seeks English Country Home

Reported Willing to Pay a 'Five-Figure' Price

From Herald Tribune Bureau

LONDON, Dec. 21. — King George II of Greece is planning to buy a country home in England and it is understood that he has almost decided to pay a "five-figure" price for a mansion of one of Britain's most famous art authorities, "The News-Chronicle" reported today.

The Greek monarch, who is apparently one of the major obstacles to British efforts to securing a peaceful settlement of the civil war in his country, has been looking around the English countryside for a permanent home for two months, the newspaper said.

King George is believed to have a large personal fortune. The last financial budget published by the Greek Government in Cairo, February 1944, showed that his annual emoluments paid from the Greek Treasury amount to £53,210.

De Gaulle Calls For Alliance With England

General Pays Tribute to British Ally in Speech To Assembly in Paris

By Sonia Tomara

Having concluded an alliance with Soviet Russia, General Charles de Gaulle turned towards the west yesterday when he spoke in the Consultative Assembly and stated that France needed also an alliance with Great Britain. He reminded the assembly that France could have no real security without the United States and that collective peace would be organized after consultation of all the parties concerned.

In their respective reports to the assembly on their recent trip to Moscow and their conversations with Russian statesmen both General de Gaulle and Georges Bidault, his Minister of Foreign Affairs, went obviously out of their way to allay any possible fears that they might have thrown France into arms of Communist Russia. Their speeches indicated that they wanted to maintain France in perfect balance between west and east and hoped to lead the victorious allies to a new second post-war system of collective security.

Overture to Britain

De Gaulle made a frank overture to Britain when he said "France, in whose soil lie buried a million of Britain's sons who went to war at the same moment as the nation which found, on British soil, help and refuge when our territory was overrun, who saw her liberation coming largely from old England, who fully measures the primary role of Britain and her Dominions in all theaters of the war—that France cannot conceive of any organization for world security not based on an alliance between Paris and London."

The general spoke at the end of the assembly debate on the Moscow treaty. Needless to say, the treaty was enthusiastically approved by the members. It will be ratified tomorrow by the Council of Ministers.

M. Bidault, who opened the debate, explained that the Moscow alliance, intended to muzzle Germany, was merely the beginning of

(Continued on page 2, col. 5)

Eisenhower and Caffery Note Return of European Edition

In a letter to the European Edition of the New York Herald Tribune, Jefferson Caffery, American Ambassador to France, said yesterday that the reappearance of the newspaper "is a milestone not only in journalism but in Franco-American relations."

General Dwight D. Eisenhower, Supreme Commander-in-Chief of the Allied Expeditionary Force, took advantage of the resumption of publication by the Herald Tribune to express appreciation for the help that the paper had given the Army newspaper "The Stars and Stripes."

In his letter to the editor of the paper, Ambassador Caffery said "From its foundation by James Gordon Bennett and afterwards for more than half a century, this newspaper has played an important role in European journalism as well as in the trans-Atlantic relations of our day.

"It was rightly praised for continuing to publish during the years of 1914 to 1918, and again rightly praised for having ceased publishing promptly when the German hordes rolled over France. Now, in the last phase of the European struggle, the newspaper faces a new era full of hope. I am sure it will continue to be a medium of American information and opinion for all the peoples of Europe.

"I can wish you nothing better than this: that the next 50 years in the life of the newspaper may be as splendid as its first half century."

General Eisenhower wrote: "I have just learned that the Paris edition of the New York Herald Tribune is to resume publication.

"This seems an appropriate time for me to express to you my deep appreciation of your generosity in making your printing facilities available for use by 'The Stars and Stripes.' Speaking for the American soldiers of this theater of war, I thank you very much."

Red Army Driving On Budapest

Soviet Troops 12 Miles From Hungarian City; New Slovakia Drive

LONDON, Dec. 21 (AP).—Marshal Tolbukhin was striking strongly from the south today in an offensive aimed at strangling Budapest and opening the road to Vienna.

The German radio reported that his 3d Ukrainian army—conquerors of Sofia and liberators of Belgrade—had hurled more than 100,000 men in two attacks along a 40-mile front between Lake Balaton and the Danube river.

As long ribbons of silver bombers filled the skies, the Red Army forces reached for vital German supply lines feeding the Hungarian capital and drove hard against Szekes-Fehrvar, a German bastion 41 miles southwest of Budapest.

While this new operation was roaring through its opening phases, Marshal Malinovsky's 2d Ukrainian army, fighting 150 miles northeast, smashed against the outer fortifications of Kassa (Kosice) in eastern Slovakia.

The German Transocean News report that the Russians were repeatedly penetrating German lines south and northeast of Kassa.

When Tolbukhin lit the fire of his latest offensive, his troops were only 12 miles south of Budapest on the west and seven miles south of Szekes-Fehrvar, northern anchor of the main German lines, and shield to all vital lifelines that run northwest from the besieged Hungarian capital.

The Soviet right wing may be planning to drive north behind Budapest, severing the road and railway which feed the garrison, and then link-up with Malinovsky's forces somewhere above the capital.

The left wing then would concentrate on Szekes-Fehrvar and then strike toward Vienna, cutting Budapest communications farther to the northeast.

Marshal Tolbukhin's troops already have made some local penetrations, the German radio admitted. The assault was supported closely by large forces of fighter-bombers, the Germans said.

Allies Drive Japs From Five Burmese Villages

Chinese Troops Slay 200; Indians Move on Coast

By the United Press

LONDON, Dec. 21.—Operations on the Burma front today included the occupation of Wuntho and Nankan, fifteen miles apart, on the Myitkyina-Mandalay railway by troops of the 4th Corps of the 14th Army. In the northern combat area command troops of the 30th Chinese Division yesterday captured three villages near the Bhamo-Namhkam road, killing 200 Japanese and taking equipment and ammunition.

Indian troops have now advanced half the distance from Maungdaw to Foul Point on the 15th Indian Corps front in the coastal strip.

One air unit destroyed a railyard and damaged tracks at the Pyinmana junction on the Rangoon-Mandalay line. Other aircraft bombed a headquarters area serving the Japanese who are retreating from the Chindwin, and a village on the Irawaddy south of the railway.

Sec. Stettinius May Visit London on 'Big-3' Meet

Report Follows Eden's Call For Meeting of Secretaries

WASHINGTON, Dec. 21 (A.P.).—Possibility that Secretary of State Edward R. Stettinius jr. might go to London for a preliminary "Big Three" meeting is seen here as a result of British Foreign Secretary Anthony Eden's call for the re-establishment of "a quarterly meeting of the foreign secretaries of the great powers."

Whether Mr. Stettinius will travel to London before the "Big Three" meet depends on President Roosevelt, well-informed sources here said today. So far, no decision has been taken, they said.

The reorganization of the State Department with new under-secretaries and assistant secretaries is expected to take much of the detailed tasks off Mr. Stettinius.

Court Upholds Jap Ouster

WASHINGTON, Dec. 18 (Delayed).—The Supreme Court of the United States declared today it justified the United States Army's order which excluded all Japanese from the west coast area.

An American 105 Howitzer Prepares to Speak

With a light blanket of snow helping their camouflage, artillerymen of the American Seventh Army prepare their piece for action somewhere along the Western Front.

Stimson Sees Drive Speeding War to an End

Expresses Full Confidence In Strategy and Ability Of the Allied Command

WASHINGTON, Dec. 21 (AP).—Henry L. Stimson, Secretary of War, asserted today that if the gigantic German counter-offensive failed it undoubtedly would shorten the war.

The Germans' ability to launch the offensive was a significant development in the war, Stimson said, as he acknowledged that the Nazis had penetrated Allied territory distances of from 5 to 20 miles. Allied counter-measures are under way, he added.

In his weekly news review of the war, Secretary Stimson said the Germans chose for their attack a sector "which was loosely held by both sides. It was terrain which had not offered the Allies much incentive for exploitation."

Expressing "utmost confidence" in the strategy and aggressive fighting attitude of the Allied command, Stimson said the Nazis did not stand to lose a great deal from the offensive and had a chance to make some gains before they must account for "the misery they have inflicted on the world."

Acknowledging the Nazis had been able to build up their forces despite severe losses, Stimson pointed out that the American Armies had been reinforced steadily and that the movement of supplies to support them had been enlarged greatly.

Stimson warned the Germans that they must be prepared to meet a steadily increasing winter aerial onslaught as well as a Russian winter offensive.

The Secretary expressed belief that the Germans gambled some elite divisions rather than wait an inevitable end on the defensive.

Roosevelt Gives D-Day Prayer As Xmas Gift

White House Aides Get Scroll Copies of Invocation

WASHINGTON, Dec. 21.—President Roosevelt's Christmas gift to the employees of the White House today was a scroll of his D-Day prayer for victory over "the unholy forces of our enemy."

More than 300 guards, servants and secretaries received their presents early so that the President's family could pass Yuletide quietly with his daughter, Mrs. John Boettiger, and a few of his grandchildren. His four sons, who are in uniform, will be absent.

The President will read Dickens "Christmas Carol" on Sunday night, and community tree exercises will be held Sunday afternoon. The President will broadcast worldwide a Christmas message on Sunday.

Britain Seeks Steel Panels

NEW YORK, Dec. 21.—"The Iron Age" reports that the British are inquiring in the United States for many thousands of pre-fabricated steel panels to be used in construction for emergency housing.

Prospect of Nazis' Return Spreads Alarm in Belgium

People Fear Vengeance for Joyous Welcome To Allied Liberators; News Blackout Heightens Their Uneasiness

By Russell Hill

BRUSSELS, Dec. 21.—Brussels today is strangely reminiscent of Cairo during the end of June and the beginning of July 1942, when Field Marshal Erwin Rommel was rapidly advancing across the desert on Alexandria.

Many Belgians are alarmed at the prospect of the Nazi approach—with far less cause for worry, it must be admitted, than the residents of Cairo had when they took off for Jerusalem, Assouan, Khartoum and Capetown.

The news blackout on military operations in the battle area east of the Meuse doubtless contributes to some feeling of uneasiness. For the people, not being told where the Germans are, naturally imagine they have come further than is actually the case.

Better founded are the fears expressed by the Belgians for friends and relatives who live on what is being generally referred to as "the wrong side" of the Meuse. The plight of these people is in reality one of the most tragic elements of the whole situation. For after having been liberated and having openly expressed their pro-Allied feelings they now face a second occupation by the Nazis, with memories of the first one still fresh in their minds.

The Canadian Army newspaper "Maple Leaf" wrote today: "Belgians who knew the terror of occupation are reported to be getting worried in some places. Confidently they had never thought of the possibilities of a German return. Allied soldiers are stopped on the streets everywhere and asked 'Will the Germans come back?'"

The article concluded cryptically: "American soldiers, playing the defense for the first time, are doing magnificently. But they're steadily charging to the forward line and their plays are gaining in effect as they get organized."

U.S. Production Hit By New Nazi Offensive

Official Says Civilian Output Now Frozen Indefinitely

From Herald Tribune Bureau

WASHINGTON, Dec. 21.—Samuel W. Anderson, vice-chairman of the War Production Board, said today that the German offensive confronts the United States with war production problems of a new and critical character.

The freezing of civilian output at present levels is likely to be prolonged indefinitely, he said. In order to assure sufficient brass for the 1945 arms output, he gave the brass mills priority in the labor demand, and he is arranging to have brass strip produced in Canada. Copper-coated steel, instead of brass, will be used in the manufacture of ammunition for small arms, Mr. Anderson said.

Indianapolis Gets Archbishop

INDIANAPOLIS, Dec. 21. — The Most Rev. Joseph E. Ritter was installed as the first Archbishop of Indianapolis in the Cathedral of St. Peter and Paul by the Most Rev. Amleto Giovanni Cicognani, Apostolic Delegate from the Vatican. The ceremony took place in the presence of five archbishops and twelve bishops.

First Task of Bridge Blowers Foxes Germans, Halts Panzers

STAVELOT, Belgium, Dec. 21 (A.P.).—The Belgians, or whatever they called themselves in those days built it in 1770. The Germans crossed it three days ago in their grand offensive and last night 15 brave and scared American combat engineers blew it up.

"It" was the 60-foot brick and stone bridge spanning the boisterous Lambleve River—a span needed badly by the Germans if they were to keep their armoured columns rolling through the American lines.

This was the first bridge ever destroyed by Capt. James Rice and his men and this is the way the 29-year-old former Richmond, Calif., oil refinery employee did it.

"We had never had to destroy a bridge before because we never knew before what it meant to be on the defensive," said Rice, whose expenditure of 1,000 pounds of dynamite was one of many factors in halting the Nazi forward thrust. "We usually have to repair bridges blown by the Jerries."

Rice assembled his men just before dark, loaded them on a truck and drove them to the last corner before the bridge. They parked there until Nazi observers in the hills beyond the river could no longer see the bridge.

"When it was completely dark we carried the half ton of explosive in 50-pound boxes three blocks down the street," Rice added. "There was a lot of glass and debris in the street. To keep the Nazis from hearing the noise we made, we had our artillery throw smoke shells into the town twice a minute for 15 minutes. The smoke also gave us further cover.

"By the time the last shell landed we had the dynamite in place. When we set off the fuse, we ran like hell. After running a block into some building to get out of the way of the flying debris, we saw the bridge blow up like a Roman candle.

"Stores near the bridge crumbled into the street and made a perfect road block. We also had made a 20-foot gap in the bridge. No Jerry tank can broadjump that far. As soon as the bridge blew up, the Nazis woke up and for 20 minutes they plastered the whole area with tank and machine-gun fire."

Paris Radio Warns Nazis In British and U.S. Uniforms in Rear Areas

Weather Still Bad But Planes Go Up

Fighting Most Fluid in Area Around Malmedy

By John O'Reilly

SUPREME HEADQUARTERS, Allied Expeditionary Force.—The advances of enemy troops engaged in the German counter-offensive were continuing and up to noon Tuesday the greatest German advance was the spearhead which had driven to Habiemont thirty miles in a direct line from where the thrust started near Honsfeld on the German-Belgian frontier. In accordance with the new ruling at Supreme Headquarters all news of the offensive issued today dealt with happenings forty-eight hours earlier.

Today's publishable reports indicated that the German offensive was being contained on its flanks near Monschau and around Echternach. This meant that the area of the German effort and where the fighting is still fluid is along a front of approximately fifty miles reaching between these two points. The Americans had slowed the tide of the advance at some points and had recaptured Stavelot.

Enemy in Rear Areas

While the great battle was in progress Allied military authorities issued a warning to the French population that groups of Germans in British and American uniforms and in possession of identification papers had filtered through the lines and were being found in rear areas. The warning was broadcast over the French radio. Police were on the lookout for suspicious persons.

Flying weather continued bad all along the front, but the 9th American Air Force did manage to send out a hundred fighter-bombers to hunt around as best they could for targets. A force of Lancasters also was sent over from England. The main target of the day was Trier, but the weather was so bad that nothing like the full weight of the air forces could be brought into play to help stop the German advance.

Thunderbolts of the 9th Air Force bombed Trier and having dropped their bombs went to join the force of Lancasters which they escorted to the same target. The attacks were made in poor visibility and results were not observed. Thunderbolts also hit Speicher, twenty miles east of Trier, where they think they hit an oil dump, and a road junction at Hermeskeil, twenty miles east of Trier. But the Germans continued to get the breaks as far as the weather was concerned.

Echternach Holds Out

The ground situation as of noon Tuesday was that in the southern part of the area of the offensive, fighting continues around Echternach, where the town is holding out as well as several small villages south and southeast of Echternach. The force which previously advanced to Consdorf made further gains to the west. Consdorf is thirteen miles northeast of the city of Luxembourg.

The drive which started at Vianden on the Luxembourg frontier had penetrated to a point just east of Wiltz, which is thirteen miles west of Vianden. Another force, moving parallel to this one and six miles to the north, reached the vicinity of Clerf, which is five miles west of the frontier and seven miles northeast of Wiltz.

Pincers Slowed Down

The pincer movement, which had been directed toward St. Vith, was making little progress at the time of the report and had been slowed down temporarily. St. Vith was still in American hands.

It also was disclosed that additional paratroops were dropped Monday night a few miles southwest of Habiemont. It was not disclosed whether the German force which had pushed forward to Habiemont by Tuesday had joined with these airborne troops.

Stavelot was recaptured by the Americans and there was fighting going on around Malmedy. It was in this area that the fighting was most fluid.

It also was reported that enemy troops had been captured wearing American and British uniforms and that they were using American army vehicles marked with the white or yellow five-pointed star. This was in accordance with the warning issued over the radio to the French population. The warning said:

"The French population is advised by the Allied military authorities that groups of Germans completely equipped in American and British

(Continued on page 2, col. 6)

'Big-3' Agree to Strip Germany Of All Its War-Making Powers; Plan New Blows to Hasten Peace

The 'Big-Three' Statement

The text of the joint statement issued by Marshal Stalin, Prime Minister Churchill, and President Roosevelt at the conclusion of their eight-day conference in the Crimea follows:

We have considered and determined military plans of the three Allied powers for the final defeat of the common enemy. The military staffs of the three Allied powers have met in daily meetings throughout the conference. These meetings have been most satisfactory from every point of view and have resulted in closer co-ordination of the military effort of the three Allies than ever before.

The fullest information has been interchanged. Timing, scope and co-ordination of new and even more powerful blows to be launched by our armies and air forces into the heart of Germany from east, west, north and south have been fully agreed upon and planned in detail. Our combined military plans will be made known only as we execute them, but we believe that the very close working partnership among the three staffs attained at this conference will result in shortening the war.

Meetings of the three staffs will be continued in the future whenever the need arises. Nazi Germany is doomed. The German people will only make the cost of their defeat heavier to themselves by attempting to continue hopeless resistance.

We have agreed on common policies and plans for enforcing unconditional surrender terms, which we shall impose together on Nazi Germany after German armed resistance has been finally crushed. These terms will not be made known until the final defeat of Germany is accomplished. Under agreed plans, the forces of the three powers will each occupy a separate zone of Germany. Co-ordinated administration and control has been provided for under the plan through a central control commission consisting of the supreme commanders of the three powers, with headquarters in Berlin.

Three Generals Confer in Bastogne Street

Keystone

General Dwight D. Eisenhower (center) talks with General Omar N. Bradley (left) and General George S. Patton jr. (right) among the ruins of Bastogne, which was the beginning of the end of the German bulge in the Ardennes.

Allied Meetings, Held at Yalta, in Crimea, Are In Full Accord on Aims

Justice Promised To War Criminals

France to Share in Zone System to Occupy Reich

By the United Press

LONDON, Feb. 12.—President Roosevelt, Prime Minister Churchill and Premier Josef Stalin met at Yalta, in the Crimea, for their second momentous conference of the war, it was officially announced today, and laid down severe terms for Germany to insure she never again endangers the world peace. The Chiefs of State of the United States, Great Britain and Russia were accompanied by their Foreign Secretaries, chiefs of staff and other advisers.

The communique said the "fullest information has been interchanged. The timing, scope and co-ordination of new and even more powerful blows to be launched by our armies and air forces into the heart of Germany from the east, west, north and south have been fully agreed upon and planned in detail. Our combined military plans will be made known only as we execute them, but we believe that the very close working partnership among the three staffs attending at this conference will result in shortening the war.

"The meetings of the three staffs will be continued in the future when the need arises. Nazi Germany is doomed. The German people will only make the cost of their defeat heavier to themselves by attempting to continue the hopeless resistance."

Results of Conference

The conferees agreed upon unconditional surrender terms and their enforcement, but the terms will not be revealed until the defeat of Germany is accomplished. The results of the Big Three conference may be set down as follows:

1. Disarm and disband all German forces.
2. Break up for all time the German General Staff, that has repeatedly contrived the resurgence of German militarism.
3. Remove or destroy all German military equipment.
4. Eliminate or control all German industry that could be used for military production.
5. Bring all war criminals to justice and swift punishment and exact reparations in kind for the destruction wrought by the Germans.
6. Wipe out the Nazi party laws, organizations and institutions.
7. Remove all Nazi and militarist influences from public offices and from the cultural and economic life of the German people.
8. Take in effect such other measures in Germany as may be necessary to the future peace and safety of the world.

Zones To Be Occupied

Each of the "Big Three" powers will occupy separate zones of Germany with a co-ordinated administration through a central control commission of the "Big Three" supreme commanders in Berlin, the communique stated. France has been invited to take one zone of occupation.

The communique stated flatly that the reparations commission will sit in Moscow.

"It is not our purpose to destroy the people of Germany but only when Nazism and militarism are exterminated will there be hope for a decent life for Germans and a place for them in the comity of nations," the communique said.

A United Nations conference was called by the "Big Three" for San Francisco, Calif., in April to prepare a charter for an international peace organization along the lines of the Dumbarton Oaks agreement. France and China will be consulted and invited to participate.

The leaders of the three nations pledged jointly to assist any European or liberated state or former Axis satellite to establish conditions of peace and to carry out emergency measures for the relief of distressed peoples. Also they agreed to form interim governmental authorities and to facilitate the holding of elections if necessary.

THURSDAY, FEBRUARY 15, 1945

'Big-Three' Leaders at Yalta Conference

Keystone

In this picture, taken at the close of the Yalta Conference, standing immediately behind Prime Minister Churchill, President Roosevelt and Marshal Stalin are: Foreign Secretary Anthony Eden; Secretary of State Edward R. Stettinius, Jr.; Foreign Minister V. M. Molotov, and Averell Harriman, United States Ambassador in Moscow.

TEMPORARY PRICE: 3 Francs

NEW YORK Herald Tribune

EUROPEAN EDITION

58th Year—No. 19,296

PARIS, TUESDAY, FEBRUARY 20, 1945

THE NEW YORK HERALD (ESTABLISHED IN EUROPE 1887)

Marines Land on Iwo Jima, Form Beachhead; Troops Seize Artillery Sites on Corregidor; Canadian Army Clears Two-Thirds of Goch

Churchill And Eden Back Home

Report on Yalta Results And Reveal They Held Conferences in Cairo

French Situation Cause of Concern

Foreign Secretary May Make Paris Visit Soon

By Ned Russell

From the Herald Tribune Bureau

LONDON, Feb. 19.—Prime Minister Churchill and Foreign Secretary Eden returned to London tonight from the Crimea conference and subsequent meetings on their way home, and together they reported to an informal meeting of the War Cabinet on the results of their eight-day "Big Three" meeting at Yalta.

Simultaneously with their arrival in England by air, it was announced that both Mr. Churchill and Mr. Eden had spent three days together in Cairo enjoying a rest in the sunshine, and conferring presumably on all current problems of the Middle East. The Prime Minister will issue a statement tomorrow describing the Cairo talks, it was learned.

The House of Commons is scheduled to hold a two-day debate on the Crimea conference as soon as possible.

Concerned Over France

It was understood tonight that both the Prime Minister and Mr. Eden are deeply concerned over the latest developments in the French situation, arising from General Charles de Gaulle's reported refusal to meet President Roosevelt in North Africa to discuss the Yalta decisions. It was even reported in some diplomatic quarters that Mr. Eden may go to Paris shortly to try to smooth the ruffled tempers, now more evident than ever, in the French government.

It is strongly felt in London that in view of the sensitiveness of French officials, especially General de Gaulle, concerning the so-called "snub" of France by the three major powers, one of the higher participants in the Crimea talks should discuss the whole matter personally with General de Gaulle as soon as possible.

French Wary on Parley

By Sonia Tomara

Georges Bidault, French Foreign Minister, explained to the Foreign Affairs Committee of the Consultative Assembly yesterday why France was reluctant to accept whole-heartedly the agreement signed by the "Big Three" at Yalta, and why he asked Washington, London and Moscow for further information concerning the statement published after the Crimean conference.

It is understood the Minister told the committee that while his government was anxious to co-operate in creating some real system of collective security, it would, nevertheless, pursue without flinching its policy of obtaining control of the German Rhine. He said also that France would not participate in the San Francisco conference unless its government were given satisfactory information about its aims and its agenda. His point of view was approved by the committee.

The main fear entertained by the French government is that the "Big Three" want to establish a kind of control not only over Europe, but also over the colonies and mandates of the smaller European powers. Although France has not yet the material means of playing the role of one of the world's greatest powers, she feels that she is entitled to this role by her previous position, by the part she has played and is still playing in the war and also by her geographical situation in Europe.

Meanwhile, news of General Charles de Gaulle's refusal to meet President Roosevelt outside of France (reported exclusively in Sunday's European edition of the New York Herald Tribune) has not been published in the French press and French diplomats were reluctant to comment on it yesterday. It was felt, however, that Frenchmen who know about their leader's refusal back him up. They think he was not treated right when he was not invited to the Yalta parley and when he was asked to meet the President fleetingly on the latter's way home without any preparation for such a meeting.

No French Reply Yet

WASHINGTON, Feb. 19 (A.P.).—Acting Secretary of State Joseph C. Grew reported today that France has not yet replied to the "Big Three's" invitation to join in sponsoring the compromise provision on voting procedure in the Dumbarton Oaks plan. Mr. Grew had no comment to offer on reports that General de Gaulle had declined to meet the President outside France.

Drivers' Strike in Bronx Halts Produce Delivery

Special to the European Edition

NEW YORK, Feb. 19.—A strike of 400 drivers and porters at the Bronx Terminal Market this morning halted deliveries of fresh produce to retailers and wholesalers in the Bronx.

The Teamsters Union called the walkout in protest of the failure of dealers to sign a new contract on wages and hours.

Byrnes to Close Night Clubs and Bars at Midnight

Entertainment Curfew Is Ordered Primarily for Saving of Coal

From the Herald Tribune Bureau

WASHINGTON, Feb. 19.—James F. Byrnes, War Mobilization Director, asked all places of entertainment in the United States to close by midnight daily, beginning on February 26. The War Manpower Commission will back up the action by denying employment ceilings to any violators.

Mr. Byrnes said the purpose is "primarily to save coal consumed in heating and providing electricity." Mr. Byrnes added: "But it will also be helpful in the field of transportation, manpower and other ways."

Places of entertainment were defined as night clubs, saloons, bars, arenas, theaters, dance halls, roadhouses and "other similar enterprises, whether public or private, excluding restaurants engaged exclusively in serving food."

Closing at midnight would mean patrons must leave in time to permit a full closing at that hour. The statement said that, in addition to the W.M.C. action, "the War Production Board, Office of Defense Transportation and the Office of Price Administration are being requested to use their powers to the full extent consistent with the law to assist."

Mr. Byrnes said previous conservation measures "do not appear to suffice in view of coal shortage. I am advised by the W.P.B. that industrial coal stocks on hand are inadequate. Unfavorable weather conditions and possible spring floods render the coal situation even more serious than a few weeks ago. Closing of places of entertainment at midnight should impose no real hardship and I am convinced our people at home will gladly comply with this request in view of the fact that in the period just ahead of us those in the armed services will be making greater sacrifices than ever before."

Stimson Cites Peril in Delay On Labor Draft

Says 'Deadly Shortages' Loom at Moment When Utmost Power Is Needed

From the Herald Tribune Bureau

WASHINGTON, Feb. 19.—Administration pressure for enactment of the May-Bailey modified national service bill increased last night as Henry L. Stimson, Secretary of War, warned the nation that because of the failure of Congress thus far to pass a labor-draft law, "deadly shortages" of manpower and materials are looming "at a moment when every ounce of our power should be thrown into combat."

Making one of his rare radio talks, Secretary Stimson declared that the nation is "in danger of delay — unnecessary delay — which may cause thousands of unnecessary casualties." At this moment, he said, "our armed forces are at the very peak of combat, and the time of the conclusion of the war hangs in the balance."

Secretary Stimson noted that the bill has been pending in the Senate Military Affairs Committee for nearly three weeks. Addressing himself to the relatives of American fighting men, he said:

"I say to you, as a pledge of my official duty, that passage of this measure by the Senate is needed by the Army and Navy to satisfy critical shortages in our essential civilian plants and to help fill the places of young vigorous workers who may then be sent as replacements for battle-weary troops."

Senator Joseph C. O'Mahoney, Democrat, of Wyoming, a member of the Military Committee, said Secretary Stimson gave "an utterly unbalanced" picture. He added that "it would be a pity" if soldiers and their families got the impression that "management and labor have let them down . . . I like to think that we alone of all nations in the world have done this job in a free system by the voluntary acts of our people."

Lag Shown In Supplies To France

Leaders Here Surprised At American Shipping 'Achievement' Report

By Russell Hill

The delicate topic of Allied supplies to France for the rehabilitation of the national economy has been raised again by an official release from Communications Zone headquarters, stating that more than 400,000 tons of supplies were imported into France by the United States Army up to January 31.

While the release claims that "there probably has been no parallel in previous history that can compare with this achievement," high French sources feel that this is a gross exaggeration and is moreover ill-timed, because the statement was made just when deliveries promised under the Monnet agreement were falling behind schedule.

Of twenty-six ships that were due to arrive in French ports during the first three months of the year, only eight docked in the first half of the period—six in January and two, so far, in February.

Brigadier General C. P. Stearns, G. 5 Communications Zone, was quoted as saying in reference to the supply and reconstruction program for France: "Through the rehabilitation program, France is rapidly being placed on an operational basis. We have seen that great nation, after having survived the vicissitudes of the enemy occupation, take its old place in the battleline and in the world. All this has been accomplished in a few short months."

French Take Opposite View

All qualified observers would doubtless agree that this is taking rather a rosy view of the picture. Competent French sources say almost exactly the opposite, namely, that unless the badly needed raw materials and essential equipment are rushed to France immediately the collapse of the national economy within three months must be faced.

The best way to judge the value of the imports brought into France to date would be to compare the official figure of 400,000 tons, which covers about five months, with France's pre-war imports. In 1936 those imports totaled 48,000,000 tons, which means that we have been supplying France at the rate of two per cent of the country's normal requirements.

Of the total mentioned above, 40,000,000 tons represented raw materials and more than six million were food products. The breakdown of the figure for imports since the liberation shows that 200,000 tons of food were brought in during the period. At the time when six million tons of imports were required to help feed the French population, the agriculture of the country was functioning normally. French economists estimate that the present agricultural yield is no more than 50 per cent of what it was before the war.

Want Raw Materials

Despite the difficult food situation, the French authorities are asking for raw materials and such things as railway trucks and machine parts in preference to food, because they want to get the national economy on its feet again.

Coal is one badly needed item of which France has always had to import considerable quantities. Yet in the month of December, three times as much coal was turned over to the Allied armies by the French as was brought into the country from abroad, according to French figures.

It is felt in France that statements suggesting that imports to France are rehabilitating the country are out of place, since these imports represent only a small fraction of the most urgent needs and France's whole economic life is endangered by the lack of essential imports.

Pope Suffers Relapse

VATICAN CITY, Feb. 19 (U.P.).—Pope Pius XII is suffering from a relapse with increased fever, resulting from his insistence on continuing to work while recovering from a slight attack of influenza, it was reported today. His condition is not causing undue alarm, it was stated.

British Submit Plan to Arabs For a Middle-East Federation

By the United Press

CAIRO, Feb. 19.—A British government proposal for an all-round settlement of Middle East problems by the creation of an Arab Federation, under joint British and American recognition, has been submitted to the leading Arab heads of state at present in Egypt, it was learned from reliable sources today.

The proposal was reported to have been submitted to King Farouk of Egypt, King Ibn Saud of Saudi Arabia and the President of Syria, who are here in connection with the Pan-Arab conference which opened on Saturday. Seven Arab states of the Middle East—Egypt, Saudi Arabia, Irak, Transjordan, Syria, Lebanon and Yemen—are represented at the conference by their respective Foreign Ministers. They met, primarily, to draw the statutes of an Arab League of Nations, which the Arabs hoped would result in the Middle East's 60,000,000 Arabs working in close co-operation and presenting a united front.

The British proposal, which is said to have received the strongest American endorsement, contains two other important points, it was reported: 1. That Irak, Syria, Transjordan and the Palestine Arab districts of Nablus and Djenin be linked up to form one Arab state under the rule of Emir Abdullah, King of Transjordan; 2. That the remainder of Palestine—the Jewish part—be joined up with Lebanon to form a Jewish-Christian state, which would be free if it wished to join the general Arab Federation.

The proposal that Irak, Syria, Transjordan and Arab Palestine link up into one kingdom is a compromise on the Greater Syria scheme for the union of Irak, Syria, Lebanon, Palestine and Transjordan under one ruler, which Ibn Saud, guardian of the Moslem holy cities of Mecca and Medina, refused to accept, and which at one time threatened the constitution of an Arab Federation.

Saudi Arabia has been urging the complete independence of Syria and Lebanon under the protection of the Pan-Arab League as an alternative to the inclusion of the two Levant states within a larger kingdom. Side by side with the British proposal the Pan-Arab conference today had before it a memorandum from the government of Saudi Arabia emphasizing the independence of Syria and Lebanon and urging the future Pan-Arab League to take joint action if the sovereignty of any Arab country is threatened.

Crerar's Troops Drive Germans from Most of Battered Highway Hub

American 3d Army Expands Its Front

Overruns Seven More Towns Inside Germany

By Austin Bealmear

Associated Press Correspondent

SUPREME HEADQUARTERS, Allied Expeditionary Force.—General H. D. G. Crerar's fighting Scots cleared a major portion of the bomb-battered Siegfried bastion of Goch, keystone city on the northern German flank, yesterday as the American 3d Army expanded its assault front to fifty-five miles and overran seven more towns inside the Reich.

Routing the Germans out of the rubble of Goch with tanks and bayonets, Scottish troops of the Canadian 1st Army cleared all of the city north of the Niers River, and at least half of that portion south of the river, leaving less than one third of the ruined highway center in enemy hands.

Four of the five Allied air forces in this theater joined in western front battles, flying nearly 3,000 sorties after the weather cleared slightly around midday with American and British heavy bombers supporting the Canadian Army drive in the absence of grounded British tactical air units.

More than 1,100 8th American Air Force Fortresses and Liberators hammered a dozen industrial and transport targets in and around the Ruhr, including the rail centers of Munster, Osnabruck, Rheine and Siegen on lines leading to the flaming northern battlefront while Royal Air Force Lancasters pounded the Rhine city of Wesel, fifteen miles ahead of General Crerar's troops, for the sixth time since February 1.

Germans Bombard Town

No sooner had the Scots seized the northern half of Goch than the Germans began pouring artillery and mortar fire into the town.

Meanwhile, other Canadian Army troops to the northeast were threatening to outflank Calcar, the road hub which the Germans are fighting savagely to hold, now that they have lost Goch. They slashed across the Goch-Calcar highway at a new place only two miles southwest of Calcar as other forces northwest of Calcar beat off counter-attacks south of Moyland.

Although Goch itself was virtually cleared less than twenty-four hours after its entry from two directions, the Germans immediately to the north of the town were still holding out against Welsh troops in a factory and railroad area on the highway from Cleve.

At the close of the twelfth day of General Crerar's offensive, his advanced elements were seventeen miles beyond their jump-off line and the prisoner bag had soared past the 9,000 mark. The flooded Maas and Rhine Rivers forming the boundary of the attack, have dropped considerably in the past twenty-four hours.

The American 3d Army, already through the Siegfried Line in breaches measuring nine and seven miles, extended its operations to the southward yesterday when the 94th Division jumped off in a new attack on the divisional front southwest of Saarburg.

Attack Wins Ground

The attack eastward from Sinzig gained up to a mile to a point near Muzingen against resistance that was light at first but stiffened later. In the first few hours, doughboys captured 207 prisoners and fourteen Siegfried pillboxes.

In the Echternach bridgehead farther north, the 80th Division cleared Nusbaum, Freilingerhohe, Kewernig and Niedersgegen in a mile advance, while the 5th Division hurled back two counter-attacks and the 76th Division cleaned out a few more pillboxes. The 90th Division also gained a mile in the area southwest of Prum, clearing Niederuttfeld, Oberuttfeld and Masthorn.

The Roer River, along which three armies are spread, continued to drop slowly but the current was as fast as fifteen miles an hour in some places. The water behind the big Schwammenauel dam dropped eight and-a-half feet in twenty-four hours to noon yesterday, making a total drop of eighty feet since the Germans opened the sluice gates and destroyed the controls.

There is still enough water behind the 180-foot-high dam to take several days in getting out at the present rate. The river several miles upstream from the reservoir system also dropped a few inches, indicating that the effect of the thaw feeding the river now is dwindling.

Three Labor Groups Vie To Break Wage Ceiling

WASHINGTON, Feb. 19 (U.P.).—Labor's drive to break through the steel wage ceiling, limiting increases to 15 per cent above the January, 1941, level, has developed into a bitter contest among the American Federation of Labor, the Committee of Industrial Organizations and the United Mine Workers.

The C.I.O. drive has won some Congressional support and it is there it hopes to enlarge its campaign. The A.F.L. intends to renew its drive through the White House when President Roosevelt returns from the Big Three conference.

Keystone

AMERICAN GUNFIRE POUNDS SIEGFRIED LINE DEFENSES.—An American field artillery unit near the town of Winterspelt, Germany, in action against Germany's strongholds on the west front.

Russians Press Attack to Weld Fronts in Reich

Reach Out for Guben and Cottbus to Consolidate Offensive Toward Berlin

By the Associated Press

LONDON, Feb. 19.—The Red Army reached today for Guben and Cottbus, both of them just beyond fifty miles southeast of Berlin, in operations to weld the fronts of Marshals Ivan S. Koniev and Gregory K. Zhukov.

The Germans gave away the fact that the Russians once had their hands on Guben, with a Trans-ocean broadcast that the important communications town on the Neisse was recaptured. The agency did not state whether Marshal Koniev's or Marshal Zhukov's troops had succeeded in penetrating Guben.

Attack Aimed at Cottbus

The right wing of Marshal Koniev's 1st Ukrainian Army, however, is making a determined effort to break through to Cottbus from the area above Sorau. Lying on the Spree, Cottbus is another strategic communications point.

Both bastions are needed to give the Red Army control of the roads and railways in the Oder bend and to consolidate its position on the German southern flank for the impending battle for Berlin.

The enemy is reported from Moscow to be throwing big Luftwaffe formations against the Russians in an effort to keep the "side door" to the capital closed. Soviet troops, massing beyond the Oder, are taking jumping-off places for what might develop into the most decisive assault of the war in the East. Berlin reported that the atmosphere was one of "acute tension" along Marshal Zhukov's front directly to the east.

Neuenberg Is Captured

In its march on Danzig, the Red Army today seized Neuenberg, the German bastion forty-seven miles to the south of the former free city. Marshal Konstantin K. Rokossovsky's tanks advanced ten miles north of Grudziadz along the Vistula in twenty-four hours to reach Neuenberg.

Gross Kommarsk and Unterberg, south of Neuenberg, were also captured, and operations have begun for the annihilation of the enemy garrison in Grudziadz, which was surrounded yesterday.

The Red Army's separate war behind the front—that of encircled German garrisons—continued at white hot pitch as Marshal Koniev's middle army edged closer to Breslau, the surrounded capital of Silesia. The first units to push into the city encountered unusually stiff fire.

Cooper, Sarnoff, Zanuck Receive Willkie Awards

Special to the European Edition

NEW YORK, Feb. 19.—At the first "One World" dinner, held last night at the Hotel Astor on the birthday of the late Wendell Willkie, awards were made to three members of the communications field who have furthered the ideals of international unity. They are Kent Cooper, executive director of the Associated Press; Brigadier General David Sarnoff, president of Radio Corporation of America, and Darryl F. Zanuck, film producer. The American Nobel Center was sponsor of the awards.

Mr. Cooper was cited for his work on behalf of the promotion of "the free and untrammeled flow of news between the nations"; General Sarnoff for his recognition of the radio as a cultural and educational agency, and Mr. Zanuck for producing pictures which "have helped focus the attention of the nation and the world on grave social and economic problems."

MacArthur and Halsey a Team

WASHINGTON, Feb. 19 (U.P.).—Admiral William F. Halsey, asked whether there was any "danger" of General Douglas MacArthur's fleet getting to Tokio before his, today answered, "No, we go there together." This is the latest clew to Washington's number one mystery: who will command the coming grand assault against Japan and lead the victory march in Tokio?

Halsey Demands Full Surrender From Japanese

Declares It Will Be 'Crime' If Enemy Is Allowed to Qualify Capitulation

By Bert Andrews

From the Herald Tribune Bureau

WASHINGTON, Feb. 19.—Admiral William F. Halsey jr., who hates the Japanese so bitterly that the mildest names he can find for them are rats, monkeys and stupid beasts, sprinkled those names throughout thirty-eight minutes of memorable conversation today as he warned that America will be committing "the greatest crime in the history of our country" if it fails to exact "absolute and unconditional surrender of Japan."

The sixty-two-year-old commander of the 3d Fleet has just come home after shellacking the Japanese from Okinawa to the coast of Indo-China and separating them from 7,315 planes, ninety warships and 2,000,000 tons of merchant and transport vessels. He displayed his picturesque vocabulary in a manner that left lesser experts humble in front of the man who could outswear them without using a single cussword.

On up-to-the-minute topics Admiral Halsey predicted complete success for the American invaders of Iwo Jima. He hoped that the battle there would not be as tough as it was at Tarawa. He doubted that the "ex-Japanese navy" would come out and fight, explaining "we will have to go in and dig them out. They have very little left to fight with and what they have is not in good shape."

Writing on the Wall

He pounded home his "unconditional surrender" theme when he was reminded of the recent Japanese broadcast which suggested they might soon be shopping around for a negotiated peace.

"I think the handwriting is pretty thoroughly on the wall," Admiral Halsey said. "I am one of the few people who from the very beginning thought the Japs would break eventually. Their industrialists undoubtedly see that their empire is rapidly getting in the position where it is going to absolutely crumble, and a dollar means as much to them as it does to the industrialists in any other part of the world.

"When the industrialists get the upper hand of those beasts from the army who control the government, they will take over and they will begin to put out very attractive peace feelers.

"To my mind that is the most dangerous period America will face until the peace is actually declared."

Oumansky Ashes in Moscow

MOSCOW, Feb. 19 (U.P.).—An urn containing the ashes of the late Constantin E. Oumansky, Soviet Ambassador to Mexico who was killed in a plane crash in January, arrived here last night. A state funeral will take place in the capital.

Troops Seize Artillery Sites On Corregidor

Foe Being Cleared from Tunnel Entrenchments, MacArthur Announces

By the Associated Press

MANILA, Feb. 20 (Tuesday).—The American forces swarming over rocky Corregidor were mopping up the Japanese in the rear of their defense batteries while other United States forces reduced enemy remnants on Bataan and in the Manila battle area. General Douglas MacArthur announced the capture of Fort William McKinley, at the southern outskirts of Manila, by airborne troops. The towns of Hagonoy and Tacig on the northwest shore of Lagunard Bay, south east of Manila, also were taken.

American paratroopers and doughboys on Corregidor have captured important artillery positions and are clearing the Japanese from their tunnel entrenchments, General Douglas MacArthur announced today.

The communique said that Malinta Hill, an excellent artillery site, has been seized, and that a landslide caused by bombardment blocked the east entrance of the extensive tunnel on "the rock."

Seventh Fleet units are shelling the Cavite shoreline south of Corregidor, to clear the Manila Bay entrance of enemy guns.

In the bloody capital, the Americans captured the Philippine General Hospital, and freed 7,000 patients, internees and civilians. The hospital was a prime enemy strongpoint, with big guns mounted on the upper floors. Among the patients were 100 Americans.

"Systematic destruction" of the trapped garrison is proceeding, General MacArthur said.

48,000 Nazi Prisoners Put to Work in France

A total of 48,000 German war prisoners, captured by the French Army, have been put to work in France and 60,000 more, captured by American troops, will be placed at the disposal of the French authorities, it was said in Paris yesterday. Of those already working, 27,000 are employed by the French Army doing road repairs and cleaning up debris, and 21,000 have been sent to civilian jobs in public works.

The American military authorities have agreed to transfer to the French a first total of 30,000 Germans and add to it later two lots, of 20,000 and 10,000. Prisoners of war working for the French are given the same rations as French soldiers.

As prisoners of the Americans, they get cigarettes and, if available, can buy American rations of chocolate, chewing gum, soap and fruit juice. This has made the French very angry. Thousands of letters from French prisoners, now in Germany, arrive in France daily, telling of indescribable hunger in the prisoner camps.

General Cherniakovsky Killed; A Russian Field Leader at 37

By the Associated Press

LONDON, Feb. 19.—Soviet jubilation over the phenomenal and sustained progress of the winter offensive was clouded over today with the news of the death of General Ivan Danilovich Cherniakovsky of wounds received yesterday on the East Prussian battlefield, where his 3rd White Russian Army yesterday captured seven places south of Koenigsberg in the battle of annihilation against twenty German divisions surrounded and cut off from all land contact with the rest of the Reich.

At thirty-seven, General Cherniakovsky was the youngest Soviet army group commander and one of Russia's outstanding strategists. Plans for a hero's funeral have been made for the conqueror of East Prussia and the liberator of Lithuania, to be held in Vilna, capital of the Lithuanian Soviet Republic.

Death Saddens People

MOSCOW, Feb. 19.—The death of General Cherniakovsky, son of a railway worker, deeply saddened the Russian people and brought grief to many Soviet youths who hero-worshipped the young Jewish officer, who rose to the high post of commander of an army, first to enter German territory.

He made a fine impression on Marshal Stalin and Marshal Zhukov for the way in which he carried out the orders of the High Command, and was said to be slated for early promotion to marshal.

Most of his traveling at the front was in a jeep, and he often took the wheel if the driver had had a hard day.

Two American Divisions Storm Ashore on Island 750 Miles from Tokio

Beachhead Force Placed at 30,000

Landing Accomplished By Armada of 800 Ships

By the United Press

ADMIRAL NIMITZ'S HEADQUARTERS, Guam, Feb. 20 (Tuesday).—The 5th Corps Marines who streamed ashore on Iwo Jima yesterday have reached the largest airfield on the Island and are driving at a swift pace against the stiff Japanese resistance, Admiral Chester W. Nimitz announced this morning.

By William F. Tyree

United Press War Correspondent Representing the Combined American Press

IN A PLANE OVER IWO JIMA ISLAND, Feb. 19.—Two veteran divisions of American marines have stormed ashore, and after two hours of bitter fighting have established a beachhead 5,000 yards wide and 500 yards deep on the tiny pear-shaped island of Iwo Jima, 750 miles south of Tokio and only twenty-eight miles from the Japanese mainland island of Kyushu.

Below us the island resembles a fat pork chop sizzling on a skillet smoking under one of the heaviest bombardments of the entire Pacific war.

Twice, as we have swung in past the smoldering volcanic crater of Mount Suribachi at the island's southern tip, the Japanese anti-aircraft fire has reached out toward us with heavy bursts. One American fighter has crashed in flames. There is not a single Jap plane in the sky.

Hundreds of Small Craft Seen

As we first approached the island we could see hundreds of small craft streaming through the water toward the beach, unleashing thousands of rockets as they went. Forty-five minutes later, waves of heavier landing craft followed. Now columns of dust and smoke-screen much of the island's eight square-mile plot of ground.

By now perhaps 30,000 American troops have landed on the south-eastern coast and pushed north and inland to the rim of the Suribachi Yama airfield.

Whirling in below us are swarms of planes from the many aircraft carriers forming part of the invading armada of 800 ships. They are strafing and bombing every Japanese and every installation they can find. Suribachi's 546-foot high crater quivers and steams from a succession of hits along her ridge.

Battleships Pour Tons of Steel

In the calm waters offshore, the big rifles of the battleships New York, Texas, Nevada, Arkansas, Idaho and Tennessee are pouring tons of steel and explosives into the island from their great gun platforms. It is systematic murder and destruction.

None of our surface fleet has been disturbed by enemy action, although the water is literally alive with Buffalo tanks and landing craft either carrying troops ashore or going back for more supplies for the beach. The giant American armada spreads out to the horizon for scores of miles on every side. There can be no mistake. The Americans have arrived on this doorstep to Tokio to stay.

But overlooking the beaches I can see many formidable enemy pillboxes along the shoreline, as well as the rusty hulls of several Japanese ships put out of action earlier in pre-invasion raids. Resistance is increasing already in several sectors, and all indications are it will be the toughest kind of fight. High American officers have predicted it will take a week at best of bitter battle to complete the job. There will be a lot of blood spilled before this fight is won.

Tokio Raid Toll

By the Associated Press

ADMIRAL NIMITZ'S HEADQUARTERS, Guam, Feb. 19.—Americans destroyed 509 Japanese planes, and sank thirteen and damaged twenty-two Japanese vessels, in a "decisive" victory in the mighty 1,500-plane raid over the Tokio-Yokohama area on Friday and Saturday, Admiral Chester W. Nimitz announced today.

Admiral Nimitz said that forty-nine American planes were lost in the two-day attack on the Japanese mainland, and thirty to forty American flyers were lost. "None of our ships suffered damage from enemy action," he said.

Tokio Pounded Again

WASHINGTON, Feb. 19.—Still reeling from the two-day carrier-plane assault, Tokio was again pounded today by a big fleet of Super-Fortresses while other B29s hit installations at Kuala Lumpur, Malay, it was revealed here today.

Twentieth Air Force headquarters reported that upwards of 150 Super-Fortresses from the Marianas plastered industrial plants at the enemy's capital. "Good results" were reported from the strike of about sixty India-based B29s against the railyards and repair shops at Kuala. This first strike of B29s at Kuala aimed at communications lines between Indo-China and Burma.

TEMPORARY PRICE:
3 Francs

NEW YORK
Herald Tribune

EUROPEAN EDITION

58th Year—No. 19,362

PARIS, TUESDAY, MAY 8, 1945

THE NEW YORK HERALD (ESTABLISHED IN EUROPE 1887)

VICTORY

Eyewitness Tells Of Berlin Ruins

Nothing Left, Says Correspondent, Except Mountains of Debris And a Few Shell-Riddled Walls

The following story by a New York Herald Tribune war correspondent was written after a visit to Berlin as a guest of the Red Army.

By Seymour Freidin

BERLIN, Thursday, May 3 (Delayed).—Atop the rubble that remains of the most bomb-leveled city in the world the red banner of Soviet Russia snapped triumphantly this afternoon as exultant Russian soldiers swept into the hedgerows of the Tiergarten, opposite the Reichstag, and silenced the last of the Nazi defenders.

A chilling rain, fanned by a northeast wind slanted across the smoking vestiges of the dead capital, converting the crater-pocked streets into huge pools of brackish water, while Red Army men advanced into the park congratulating each other and promising extermination for the fanatical S.S. troops making their last stand for Führer Adolf Hitler.

The steady downpour provided the remaining mournful note for the passing of Berlin. This once-great capital, whose decisions frightened the world a few years ago, is a charred, twisted, unrecognizable graveyard.

Nothing is left in Berlin. There are no homes, no shops, no transportation, no government buildings. Only a few walls, and even these riddled with shell-fire, is the heritage bequeathed by the Nazis to the people of Berlin.

Joins Reds at Brandenburg Gate

Beside historic Brandenburg Gate—the German symbol of military glory now blocked by concrete, its chariot of victory drawn by four horses twisted beyond recognition with three red flags entwined about the driver—this correspondent joined a wave of the Russian mopping-up party driving into the last enemy pocket.

Once a magnificent zoological park covered with heroic statues and monuments to men who played leading roles in German history, the Tiergarten had become a shell-shredded no man's-land with paths and lawns chewed up by fire and trees interlaced with toppled statuary.

Crawling behind an upright statue of Moltke, because the Russians don't wear helmets and mine might be mistaken for a German, I removed the tin hat and watched the Russians overrun the dug-in enemy positions. With speed, efficiency and terrific fire-power born of long battle-experience, the Russians rooted out the defenders in jig time and it was 3:08 p.m. according to my watch, when the resisting Germans ceased firing.

Extirpation of final enemy resistance, however, merely tolled off Berlin officially as a German entity. Berlin can now be regarded only as a geographical location heaped with mountainous mounds of debris. The air power with which Hitler threatened to destroy all opposition boomeranged with a vengeance on Berlin, and Russian artillery finished off what was left standing in the German capital.

Few Civilians Left in Metropolis

Moreover, this late metropolis, which once teemed with a population of 4,000,000, has been virtually deserted by civilians. Apparently those who were unable to flee the ghost city have remained hidden in cellars.

Those who emerged from shelters were bent over picks and shovels under guard. They were engaged in clearing main thoroughfares of the cascades of debris. They were dazed and fear-ridden. Their arms and legs moved like limbs of puppets without direction, spasmodically and unco-ordinated.

As the civilians picked at the rubble they had a first-hand opportunity to view for themselves the problem of reconstruction which confronts Germany in the future. Round-the-clock air bombing has reduced all the buildings to powdered brick and teetering walls, very little of which can be salvaged. Only a perimeter of homes in the outskirts is habitable.

From such famed streets as Unter den Linden, once proudly described by Berliners as the most beautiful avenue in the world, the Wilhelmstrasse, the Friedrichstrasse and the Wallstrasse to those as relatively unimportant as Bergstrasse, the chaos is mute testimony to the efficacy of the Allied air assaults. Much of the wreckage ... opportun...

Reich's ...

Victory Crowd Cheers in Flag-Draped Times Square

A. P. Radiophoto

The Great White Way—looking south from Times Square to 42d Street—celebrates V-E Day minus one. Thousands deserted offices, plants, and homes to mill about in tears or laughter—or dazed unbelief that half the battle was over.

SHAEF Silence Fails to Halt Paris Bedlam

Soldiers on Leave from Front That Was Join Civilian Merrymakers

By Carl Levin

All Paris went wild last night, as Parisians and soldiers of the Allied nations decided that they could wait no longer for official confirmation that peace has returned to Europe. As far as they were concerned, a day-long outpouring of radio announcements such as they had not heard since this Continent was plunged into war five years and eight months ago, blaring headlines in Paris papers which could wait no longer to announce that Germany has surrendered and an accumulation of other evidence was sufficient to signal the advent of the greatest day in the history of Europe.

Only the clinching formal announcement from the heads of state of the Allied powers was missing but it didn't matter. Without anything but circumstantial evidence and an intuition born of living under the cloud of war for almost six years, every one here was satisfied of the truth of what they had been hearing and reading "unofficially" all through the afternoon and evening.

A.P. Sent Out Report

Supreme Headquarters, all but enveloped in the swelling tide of enthusiasm which by last night had reached fever pitch, and embarrassed by the premature distribution by the Associated Press of a report that Germany surrendered unconditionally to the Western Allies and Russia at 2:41 o'clock yesterday ...dents ...A.E.F. ...fficial ... that ...4)

New York's Emotional Binge Leaves Hangover for Today

For 5 Hours 5 Boroughs Celebrate Victory With Bottles, Flags, Ticker-tape, Jigs; Taper Off as Officials Keep Silent

By John G. Rogers
Special to the European Edition

NEW YORK, May 7—Whether victory in Europe was official or unofficial, New York at long last let itself go today after forty-one months of war and staged a five-borough, five-hour show of delirious celebration over news of Germany's surrender.

With shouting and paper-throwing, with horn-tooting and dancing, with banners and bottles, the city's millions swarmed in the streets from mid-morning to mid-afternoon in ebullient revelry that defied restraint.

Touched off almost simultaneously by morning radio reports from Europe and impelled onward by contagion and big black headlines in afternoon newspapers, the spirit of carnival happiness persisted unabated until after 3 p.m. Then it began to die down, when admonitions from Mayor LaGuardia and news from Washington and London indicated that tomorrow, not today, would stand in history as the day of official ending for the most destructive conflict of all time.

Feeling like a sprinter who had been duped into jumping the gun, the city slipped back into its normal Monday routine. Whitewings began to sweep up thousands of tons of needed paper that was wasted out of windows. Whether the city would revive in time to go all out again on a real celebration tomorrow was anybody's guess.

Even at the height of today's celebration, contortions of joy were not the universal expression. Thousands went immediately to houses of worship for prayer. Many looked on with distaste at such antics as street corner jitterbugging, sidewalk bottle-waving and Hitler burlesques enacted by wags.

Sobering Reminder

Sight of a slender young corporal with his left leg off at the knee, picking his way on crutches through packed Times Square at the peak of the civilian shouting, was a sobering reminder that there was still a war on, that several millions of Americans may be required to defeat Japan.

Men who knew this best did not take much part in the exaltation of extroverts. Private Ed Suchu, of Cleveland, back from Europe told a reporter "I have no reaction. I've been fighting."

Corporal Martin Sweeny, of Chicago, a marine who won his ribbons in the Pacific, stared stonily at the Times Square revelry. "I guess it's all right," he said, "if they feel like it. They don't know what it's all about, though."

Today's celebration could not compare in size or intensity with the twenty-four-hour emotional binge New York put on on Nov. 11, 1918, and there were good reasons for it.

This time the end of Germany had been a foregone conclusion for so long that the edge was taken off the final climax, and this time the casualties have been so high that many had no heart for celebrating.

Truman to Aid Philippines

WASHINGTON, May 7 (A.P.)—President Truman indorsed today the late President Roosevelt's Philippine independence policy and named a committee of nine to accompany Senator Millard Tydings, Democrat, of Maryland, on a special mission to Manila to examine conditions there and report to him.

Eisenhower May Be Kept Here

From the Herald Tribune Bureau

WASHINGTON, May 7.—General Dwight D. Eisenhower is not expected to be able to move to the Pacific as swiftly as some of his troops, if at all. He faces a task of great importance in ordering directly the occupation of that part of Germany to be controlled by the United States 15th Army under command of General Leonard T. Gerow, with whom he has already had several conferences.

Also to be considered is the fact that it will take the Supreme Commander as long as six months to move the bulk of his American armies to the Pacific or toward mustering-out centers. Other loose ends of the occupation problem, such as prisoners and re-assignment of Army personnel, will claim General Eisenhower's attention.

Finally, there is the question of General MacArthur, who was specifically chosen by the Combined Chiefs of Staff on April 5 to command all the Army forces against the Japanese. It is agreed that the presence of General Eisenhower in the Pacific would present difficulties.

...pects Occupation ...o Last for Years

...ys ...au

...condi- ...many, ...3 p.m. ...Chur- ...ounce- ...oscow, ...ritory ...Allied ...s and ... on do ...opean ...s and ...aphic ... settle ... Ger- ...et be- ... par- ... con- ... deter- ... peace ...ations ...pt to ...before ... Axis ...rmany ...by an ... and ...mmis- ...r the ...n na- ... never ... Eu-

rope, has been long in train and which should be ready for its responsibilities at an early hour.

Occupational zones for remnants of the Third Reich were fixed long ago. The Red Army, in accordance with agreement, will extend itself over the greater part of Germany. Its zone reaches from the Polish frontier in the east and west to the Elbe River, but Berlin is contained within this great sweep of the Nazi domain that was to stand for one thousand years and now is to be the seat of the Allied Control Commission.

British armies will occupy the north and northwest of Germany, including the great ports of Hamburg and Bremen. The United States forces will be responsible for the south and southwest and the French will move in the Rhineland zone, in which France has a more vital interest than any other Allied power.

While the peace conference and the final settlement of the German frontiers is accepted as being a matter for a decision no less than two years hence, it is expected that interim adjustments may be made. The extension of Poland's frontiers to the Oder and the inclusion of East Prussia in the reconstructed Poland is a clear part of the Allied plan to make Poland strong and independent.

20,000 Freed at Buchenwald Honor 51,000 Slain by Nazis

By Marguerite Higgins

WEIMAR, Germany, April 20.—Twenty thousand liberated prisoners at the Buchenwald concentration camp shuffled slowly up the hill to their meeting grounds at dusk tonight to join in a memorial service for the 51,000 of their comrades murdered there by the Nazis.

The solemn train of men, most of whom still wore their gray-striped outfits and on whom the mark of suffering and hunger lay deep, marched forward to the same mournful tune that the prison band used to play for them each morning when they were sent to work in the aircraft factories and each evening when they gathered for roll call.

It was played at their own request to evoke the grim memory of the past so that it might never be forgotten now that the future is at hand.

The healing hand of freedom was already evident in the men, who, in contrast with the broken people of a week ago, stood with pride and confidence under the flags of their homelands to hear their representatives speak with admirable brevity of the past and with resoluteness of the fight against Fascism to which they were all re-pledged. Their flags were a testament of the uprooted and the persecuted. Side by side were those of Germany (for the anti-Nazi political prisoners) Russia, Holland, France, Belgium, Denmark, Norway, Poland, Hungary, Romania, Yugoslavia, Italy and Czechoslovakia.

On the platform was draped a great American flag. Behind it was a plastic wall on which hung a wreath and where was inscribed "Buchenwald Concentration Camp 51,000."

The prepared text at the memorial service, which was organized by the international committee running the camp and approved by the American camp commandant, Major Lorenz Schmuhl, of Michigan City, Indiana, was given in five languages.

It said in part: "We anti-Fascists of Buchenwald are assembled here to honor the 51,000 of our dead comrades—51,000 shot, hanged, trampled down, slain, choked, starved, drowned, poisoned, tortured. The thought that kept us alive as we saw with helpless rage our comrades fall was that "the day of vengeance will come." We thank the Allied armies, the American, the English, the Soviet and all the armies of the free world who bring us all freedom and peace. We honor the great friend of the anti-Fascists of all countries, one of the leaders and pioneers of the battle for a new democratic and peaceful world: Franklin D. Roosevelt."

At the end the prisoners in unison took a solemn oath not to give up the fight "until the last guilty has been judged by the tribunal of all nations and the absolute destruction of Nazism has been achieved."

Following this, Major Schmuhl, on the part of the United States Army, thanked the prisoners for their tribute to President Roosevelt and assured them: "The American armies have come to Europe to eradicate the Nazis and to create a world of peace and of wellbeing for all."

There was then a minute of mourning and taps. Then, in silence, they filed away. Leading the procession were the thirty youngest prisoners—children, ranging from two and a half years to ten years of age. All of the children, most of whom were Jewish, had been hidden in the camp barracks by the prisoners to save them either from death or transportation to an even worse camp.

Back they proceeded to the barracks, which once housed 50,000 political prisoners and which all hope to be leaving soon for home and a free life.

Nazi Surrender Unconditional

By Leslie Midgley

The German Army announced yesterday that it had surrendered unconditionally, laying down its arms in defeat after five years and eight months of bitter warfare raging over Europe.

While no official announcement of the surrender came from Supreme Headquarters, Allied Expeditionary Force, the British Ministry of Information announced that today will be celebrated as Victory in Europe Day and that Prime Minister Churchill will make a broadcast statement at 3 p.m. Agence France-Presse announced officially last night that General de Gaulle, President Truman and Premier Stalin will make statements at the same hour and it is believed that the De Gaulle message "will be the official announcement of the victory." The White House confirmed last night that the President will speak at 9 a.m., Eastern War Time.

The capitulation was admitted at 2:30 p.m. yesterday in a broadcast by Germany's new Foreign Minister, Count Schwerin von Krosigk, who proclaimed to the German people that they had "succumbed to the overwhelming might of your enemies." The Fuehrer, Karl Doenitz, has ordered all troops to lay down their arms, he said, speaking over the Flensburg, Denmark, radio.

Proclaims Collapse

Count Schwerin von Krosigk.

Victory celebrations were in full swing yesterday in London and New York, and Parisians marched shouting and singing last night down the Champs-Elysées as rockets broke over the Arc de Triomphe.

The news reached America in a dispatch from Rheims by the Associated Press, signed by Edward Kennedy, chief of the Paris bureau. It stated that the surrender was signed at 2:41 a.m. yesterday in the schoolhouse where General Dwight D. Eisenhower has his headquarters. It was to take effect at 11:01 a.m. today. Extra editions of American newspapers immediately proclaimed the news and radio stations broadcast the report.

As a result, all transmission facilities of the Associated Press in Europe were suspended yesterday afternoon by the Army Public Relations Division, which claimed that the news should have been held for official release.

Even in the face of official silence last night, there was no doubt anywhere that the struggle was over.

Radio reports from Prague last night conflicted, some stating that fighting was continuing under a German commander who refused to recognize the surrender, others claiming that the capitulation was complete in Czechoslovakia.

President Truman said in Washington that he had agreed with the London and Moscow governments to make no announcement on surrender of enemy forces "until simultaneous announcements can be made by the three governments."

News of the surrender was broadcast at 7:30 a.m. by B.B.C. on its Danish program. The American Broadcasting Station in Europe, which is operated by the Office of War Information, also reported the capitulation.

At 9:30 last night, King George VI sent a

(Continued on page 3, Col. 2)

Daniels Protests A.P. Suspension

Special to the European Edition

RALEIGH, N.C., May 7.—Josephus Daniels, publisher of "The News and Observer" and Secretary of the Navy in the first world war, sent a telegram to President Truman today protesting the suspension of the Associated Press in Europe for sending a story on the surrender to America. His wire follows:

"I have just seen the report that the Associated Press facilities have been suspended in Paris. In 1918 when the United Press sent a cable from Brest, I was asked to recommend action against Roy Howard. I declined, saying that any good newspaperman would have been justified in what Howard did. I can see no justification for suspending the Associated Press."

Ezra Pound Captured

ROME, May 7 (A.P.).—Ezra Pound, American writer who turned Fascist propagandist, has been captured in northern Italy, according to word received here from 5th Army headquarters.

Canada Suspends Draft

OTTAWA, May 7 (U.P.).—The Canadian Labor Minister, Humphrey Mitchell, announced today that call-ups for military services will be suspended on and after tomorrow.

Price: 5 Francs
Subscription Rates Listed on Page Two

NEW YORK Herald Tribune

EUROPEAN EDITION

58th Year—No. 19,405 PARIS, WEDNESDAY, JUNE 27, 1945

THE NEW YORK HERALD ESTABLISHED IN EUROPE 1887

United Nations Adopt World Charter

B29s Bomb 10 Japanese War Plants

Four Industrial Areas On Honshu Blasted by 450 to 500 Super-Forts

Aircraft and Parts Factories Attacked

Osaka Army Arsenal One Of Targets of Raiders

BULLETIN

WASHINGTON, June 26 (A.P.).—A medium force of Super-Forts launched a new attack on industrial targets on the Japanese main island of Honshu, the 20th Air Force announced. The attack was made by the 21st Bomber Command shortly after midnight [June 27, Japanese time]. The target was Yokkaichi, near Nagoya, which was blasted only fourteen hours after an attack by about 500 B29s on ten Honshu war plants.

By Homer Bigart
Special to The European Edition

GUAM, June 26.—In the war's heaviest raid on Japan's aircraft industry, between 450 and 500 B29s attacked ten aircraft and parts factories in four industrial areas on Honshu shortly before noon today. They were escorted by fighters from Iwo Jima.

With the exception of the April 25 strike against eleven Kyushu factories, this was the greatest number of targets struck in one day by Super-Fortresses. Six of the factories raided today were contributing directly to Japanese aircraft production, and all of the targets had suffered damage in previous strikes.

War Factories Bombed

The targets included Chigusa factory, Atsuta factory, Nippon Vehicle Company, Sumitomo Dualumin mill and Aichi aircraft works in Nagoya; Mitsubishi aircraft company [Kagamigahara plant] and Kawasaki factory at Gifu, twenty miles north of Nagoya; Suomotomo light metals company [Osaka plant] and Osaka army arsenal at Osaka and Kawasaki aircraft company at Akashi, ten miles west of Kobe.

The Chigusa and Atsuta factories in Nagoya both had suffered 34 per cent damage in total roof area from previous raids. The Chigusa works, lying in the northeast part of the city, were damaged June 4, and the Atsuta plant, in the south central part of the city in a fairly well built-up industrial area, was damaged in three or four incendiary raids on Nagoya.

The adjacent factory of the Nippon Vehicle Company was 30 per cent destroyed in incendiary attacks on May 14 and 17. Once Japan's second largest producers of boilers and steam and electric cars, the company now produces munitions.

Near-by Sumitomo mill is a large new plant producing dural sheets and other aircraft parts. It had suffered slightly more than 32 per cent damage by high explosives and incendiaries.

Aircraft Works Raided

On the extreme southwest ridge of Nagoya is the Aichi aircraft works, which produce navy Judy dive-bombers. It was 20 per cent destroyed in previous raids. The Kamamighara plant of Mitsubishi had escaped damage in the June 22 attack. It is used exclusively for aircraft assembly.

Super-Forts had better luck that day with the near-by Kawasaki aircraft plant, destroying or damaging 35 per cent of the facilities. This plant assembles Tonys and the twin-engine Lily.

In Osaka, the Sumitomo light metal industries company is one of the largest producers of propellers for the Japanese combat aircraft. It had escaped noticeable damage in recent incendiary strikes. The Osaka army arsenal, largest in Japan, suffered damage to the extent of 200,000 square feet of the roof area in the first incendiary strike on Osaka on March 13, and four more buildings were destroyed in a daylight attack of June 15. However, that represented only minor damage to the sprawling establishment, which is Osaka's most prominent landmark.

Two previous raids had been directed at the Akashi plant of the Kawasaki Aircraft Company. The first strike in January put the plant temporarily out of business. About 25 per cent additional damage was inflicted June 22.

A 'Boy at the Dike' In a Modern Setting

Special to The European Edition

KANSAS CITY, June 26—Lieutenant Commander Wayne A. Parker, engineer officer on the U.S.S. Ringgold, told today how he backed into a hole below the waterline when the vessel was ripped by Japanese shore batteries.

"The jagged hole was mighty uncomfortable," he said. "And it cost me five minutes of anxiety and a new pair of trousers."

But the human plug saved the ship and won a Navy Cross.

Crowley Says Reich Policing Must Be Lasting

Asserts Germany Still Has Her Industrial Strength, Despite Allied Bombing

From the Herald Tribune Bureau

WASHINGTON, June 26.—Leo T. Crowley, Foreign Economic Administrator, testifying today before Senator Harley M. Kilgore's subcommittee of the Military Affairs Committee on German social and political conditions, said:

"Peace of the world requires considerable organized governmental attention to the course of industrial and economic development and operations in Germany. This will be true at least until generations of peace from German aggression have demonstrated that it is no longer necessary to keep open the watchful eye and maintain the necessary surveillance and control.

"Allied bombing did not reduce most German plants to utter ruin," he pointed out. "Germany has the better part of her economic and industrial strength today, even though she could not marshal it immediately for a third world war. It is there to build."

Mr. Crowley recommended that complete disarmament take precedence over all other problems, applying it to all German industry. He said that policing must be "lasting in character" and must not "expire into feeble and impractical ineffectiveness in 1956 or 1976."

He asked that the plan for Germany be made "simple and understandable to the common people of the world" to be understood as a "measure of security and not a device for punishment."

Montgomery Declares America Saved Britain

WIESBADEN, June 26 (A.P.).—Field Marshal Sir Bernard L. Montgomery told a group of American officers and enlisted men today that Britain was finished in 1941 and could not have survived without American aid.

"We were finished, and you came along and gave us a helping hand," Marshal Montgomery declared at a ceremony in which 100 Americans received the Distinguished Service Order and other military medals and the Military Cross from his hands.

Marshal Montgomery declared that American entry into the war "was the only thing that saved Britain." "But after that victory for us was certain," he added: "It is a tremendous debt that we can never repay."

Fahy Gets Reich Post

From the Herald Tribune Bureau

WASHINGTON, June 26.—Solicitor-General Charles Fahy was named today to be director of the legal division of the United States Group Control Council for Germany. General Dwight D. Eisenhower selected him, with President Truman's approval. Joseph Warren Madden, of the United States Court of Claims, and Herman Phleger, a San Francisco attorney, will accompany him to Berlin as advisors.

Federal Pay Rise Proposed

From the Herald Tribune Bureau

WASHINGTON, June 26.—A bill increasing the pay of 1,200,000 Federal employees by an average of 15.9 per cent was sent to the White House today. The bill's maximum cost was estimated at $780,000,000 yearly.

Seized Gold Seen Put to Reich's Use

France Unable to Learn Details of Hoard Seized By American 3d Army

By Geoffrey Parsons Jr.

Gold captured in Germany, so far as the French government can discover from British and American authorities, is to be used during the coming winter to pay for feeding and rebuilding Germany, regardless of whether or not the gold was stolen from the Allied governments.

All efforts of the Belgian and French governments to check the identity of the gold discovered by the American 3d Army at Frankfurt have been bluntly discouraged, despite United Nations declarations of January 5, 1943, and February 22, 1944, in which it was specifically stated that the transfer of gold from one occupied country to another by the Nazis would never be recognized.

The gold question, hitherto unreported, is one of the major factors in the rapidly deteriorating relations between Britain and America on the one hand and their major ally in Western Europe, France, on the other. French authorities say they have been unable to get a civil answer or any answer whatsoever from the British and American governments for nearly two weeks on the gold subject.

"We don't mind being appealed to on our sentiment, our honor or our sympathy," said one member of General Charles de Gaulle's Cabinet, "but we certainly don't react favorably to force. We are as human as any other country and though we are more than willing to respond to appeals to our generosity, we must resist every attempt to apply force to us as a means of persuasion."

Spilled the Goods

The French would have never discovered the whereabouts of the Belgian gold if the 1st French Army had not had the great good luck to capture Herr Puhl, vice-president of the Reichsbank directorship. Puhl, according to French Treasury authorities, spilled the goods about what happened to the gold which the Germans stole from the Bank of France much to the embarrassment, it appears, of Allied authorities, who up to then had been content to receive stolen property.

The story begins at the end of 1939. At that time the National Bank of Belgium deposited with the Bank of France about 200 tons of gold worth about $200,000,000 or 10,000,000,000 francs.

The Germans forced the Bank of France to send the gold to Berlin, where it was melted down, largely because the Reichsbank had had its fingers burned by some gold it had accepted from the Russian government at face value.

The Belgian government quite naturally complained bitterly and legally to the Bank of France for having let its gold be transferred to Germany. The provisional French government repaid to the Belgian government the gold owing it with the understanding that if the gold were ever discovered in Germany France should get it back.

The French are particularly irritated because they have reimbursed the Belgian government for the gold the Germans stole from France. Vice-president Puhl said more than a quarter of the total Belgian holdings was secreted in the Thuringia salt mines captured near Frankfurt by the American 3d Army. All efforts by the French and Belgian governments to inspect the gold seizures, however, have been unsuccessful.

"Apparently, if we are not big shots we can't see anything," said one important French government official. "After all, we get a little irritated if we can't even get an answer to our requests to see what's going on up there in Frankfurt."

High Winds Sweep New York

NEW YORK, June 26.—High winds swept the Atlantic coast today as a tropical storm moved seaward from the Virginia coast. New York was hit by rain and a thirty-mile wind.

4-Power Conference Agrees On Early War-Criminal Trials

By Richards Vidmer

LONDON, June 26.—American, British, Soviet and French representatives at the four-power War Crimes Conference agreed today on the urgency of completing preliminary work as soon as possible, and bringing war criminals to an early trial.

Discussing the methods of procedure and organization, the delegates expressed hope that completed plans could be placed before the "Big Three" in Berlin next month and that the trials would take place in August, in keeping with Justice Robert H. Jackson's target date of "the late summer."

The American plan of a military tribunal is the only one which has been advanced and Justice Jackson is confident that it will be adopted. British approval of the plan has been indicated unofficially, but neither the Russians nor the French have expressed their views. However, no alternative schemes have been suggested, either in Paris or Moscow.

Whereas Justice Jackson has President Truman's full authority to reach any agreement he deems fit, a delay may be necessitated in reaching final agreements because the representatives of other nations, specifically Russia, are not likely to have the same authority.

The objectives of the current conference are to create a tribunal, to outline offenses over which it would have jurisdiction and to establish procedure.

The task of drawing indictments of Nazi arch criminals will involve actual trainloads of evidence which has been accumulated by the United Nations War Crimes Commission, the Russian State Commission and other investigating bodies, and probably will take a minimum of one month in itself.

China Wants Hongkong From British After War

By the Associated Press

WASHINGTON, June 26.—China wants Hongkong back from the British after the war, Representative Mike Mansfield, Democrat, of Montana, told the House today.

Asking for the "end of imperialism" in China, Mr. Mansfield, who made a trip to that country as an emissary of President Roosevelt last year, said that he was confident that the Chinese were not interested in aggrandizement.

"I do know they are very desirous of getting back all China proper, including the French lease of Kwangchow-Wan, Macao held by Portugal, and the British crown colony of Hongkong-Kowloon," Mr. Mansfield said.

Ban on Aggression Is Voted, Human Rights Guaranteed

United Nations' New World Charter Provides for Collective Peace Measures and Solution of Social, Economic and Cultural Problems

By the Associated Press

SAN FRANCISCO, June 26.—The essential functions of the new world charter—a document 10,000 words long and nine weeks in the making by delegates of fifty nations—may be summarized as follows:

It will enable the United Nations to take collective measures for the prevention and removal of threats to peace and for the suppression of acts of aggression or other breaches of the peace, and to bring about by peaceful means the settlement of international situations which might lead to a breach of the peace.

It will achieve international co-operation in solving problems of an economic, social, cultural or humanitarian character, and in encouraging respect for human rights and fundamental freedoms without distinction as to sex, language or religion.

All members shall settle their international disputes by peaceful means and shall refrain from the threat or use of force against the territorial integrity or political independence of any state. Members must aid the United Nations organization to enforce provisions of the charter, and cannot assist any state against which the United Nations is taking preventive or enforcement action. However, the United Nations cannot intervene in matters essential within the domestic jurisdiction of any state.

Membership in the United Nations is open to all peace-loving states, but members may be suspended or expelled by the General Assembly upon the recommendation of the Security Council. The General Assembly consists of all members of the United Nations, while Soviet Russia, France, China, the United Kingdom and the United States have permanent seats on the Security Council and six non-permanent members are to be elected for terms of two years each.

The Security Council, to enforce its own decision, may call upon the United Nations members to take action short of armed intervention, such as disrupting communications or severing diplomatic relations. If such action is inadequate, the Council can utilize land, sea and air forces. Members of the United Nations must make available to the Council armed forces and other facilities.

Regional pacts may be made by the members provided they are consistent with the principles of the United Nations.

The International Court of Justice shall be the principal judicial organ of the United Nations, and members may ask the Security Council to enforce its verdicts.

The World Charter

Special to The European Edition

SAN FRANCISCO, June 26.—Following is the complete text of the Charter of the United Nations.

We, the peoples of the United Nations, determined to save succeeding generations from the scourge of war, which twice in our lifetime has brought untold sorrow to mankind, and

To reaffirm faith in fundamental human rights, in the dignity and worth of the human person, in the equal rights of men and women and of nations large and small, and

To establish conditions under which justice and respect for the obligations arising from treaties and other sources of international law can be maintained, and

To promote social progress and better standards of life in larger freedom, and for these ends

To practice tolerance and live together in peace with one another as good neighbors, and

To unite our strength to maintain international peace and security, and

To insure, by the acceptance of principles and the institution of methods, that armed force shall not be used, save in the common interest, and

To employ international machinery for the promotion of the economic and social advancement of all peoples, have resolved to combine our efforts to accomplish these aims.

Accordingly, our respective governments, through representatives assembled in the city of San Francisco, who have exhibited their full powers found to be in good and due form, have agreed to the present charter of the United Nations and do hereby establish an international organization to be known as the United Nations.

Chapter I
Purposes and Principles
Article 1

The purposes of the United Nations are:

1. To maintain international peace and security, and to that end: to take effective collective measures for the prevention and removal of threats to the peace and for the suppression of acts of aggression or other breaches of the peace, and to bring about by peaceful means and in conformity with the principles of justice and international law, adjustment or settlement of international disputes or situations which might lead to a breach of the peace;

2. To develop friendly relations among nations based on respect for the principle of equal rights and self-determination of peoples, and to take other appropriate measures to strengthen universal peace;

3. To achieve international co-operation in solving international problems of an economic, social, cultural, or humanitarian character, and in promoting and encouraging respect for human rights and for fundamental freedoms for all, without distinction as to race, sex, language, or religion; and

4. To be a center for harmonizing the actions of nations in the attainment of these common ends.

Article 2

The organization and its members, in pursuit of the purposes stated in Article one, shall act in accordance with the following principles.

1. The organization is based on the principle of the sovereign equality of all its members.

2. All members, in order to ensure to all of them the rights and benefits resulting from membership, shall fulfill in good faith the obligations assumed by them in accordance with the present charter.

3. All members shall settle their international disputes by peaceful means in such a manner that international peace and security, and justice, are not endangered.

4. All members shall refrain in their international relations from the threat or use of force against the territorial integrity or political independence of any state, or in any other manner inconsistent with the purposes of the United Nations.

5. All members shall give the United Nations every assistance in any action it takes in accordance with the present charter, and shall refrain from giving assistance to any state against which the United Nations is taking preventive or enforcement action.

6. The organization shall ensure that states which are not members of the United Nations act in accordance with these principles so far as may be necessary for the maintenance of international peace and security.

7. Nothing contained in the present charter shall authorize the United Nations to intervene in matters which are essentially within the domestic jurisdiction of any state or shall require the members to submit such matters to settlement under the present charter; but this principle shall not prejudice the application of enforcement measures under chapter seven.

Chapter II
Membership
Article 3

The original members of the United Nations shall be the states which, having participated in the United Nations Conference on International Organization at San Francisco, or having previously signed the declaration by United Nations of January 1, 1942, sign the present charter and ratify it in accordance with Article 110.

Article 4

1. Membership in the United Nations is open to all other peace-loving states which accept the obligation contained in the present charter and, in the judgment of the organization, are able and willing to carry out these obligations.

2. The admission of any such state to membership in the United Nations will be effected by a decision of the General Assembly upon the recommendation of the Security Council.

Article 5

A member of the United Nations against which preventive or enforcement action has been taken by the Security Council may be suspended from the exercise of the rights and privileges of membership by the General Assembly upon the recommendation of the Security Council. The exercise of these rights and privileges may be restored by the Security Council.

Article 6

A member of the United Nations which has persistently violated the principles contained in the present charter may be expelled from the organization by the General Assembly upon the recommendation of the Security Council.

Chapter III
Organs
Article 7

1. There are established as the principal organs of the United Nations: a General Assembly, a Security Council, an Economic and Social Council, a Trusteeship Council, an International Court of Justice and a Secretariat.

2. Such subsidiary organs as may be found necessary may be established in accordance with the present charter.

Article 8

The United Nations shall place no restriction on the eligibility of

(Continued on page 2, col. 4)

Closes Conference

President Truman

Truman Text Sees Basis for A Better World

President Says Charter Signed by United Nations Is a Solid Structure

Special to The European Edition

SAN FRANCISCO, June 26.—*Following is the text of the address delivered here today by President Harry S. Truman at the final session of the United Nations Conference on International Organization:*

Mr. Chairman and delegates to the United Nations Conference on International Organization:

I deeply regret that the press of circumstances when this conference opened made it impossible for me to be here to greet you in person. I have asked for the privilege of coming today, to express on behalf of the people of the United States our thanks for what you have done here, and to wish you godspeed on your journeys home.

Somewhere in this broad country, every one of you can find some of our citizens who are sons and daughters, or descendants in some degree, of your own native land. All our people are glad and proud that this historic meeting and its accomplishments have taken place in our country. And that includes the millions of loyal and patriotic Americans who stem from the countries not represented at this conference.

We are grateful to you for coming. We hope you have enjoyed your stay and that you will come again. You assembled in San Francisco nine weeks ago with the high hope and confidence of peace-loving people the world over.

Confidence Justified

Their confidence in you has been justified. Their hope for your success has been fulfilled.

The charter of the United Nations which you have just signed is a solid structure upon which we can build a better world. History will honor you for it. Between the victory in Europe and the final victory in Japan, in this most destructive of all wars, you have won a victory against war itself.

It was the hope of such a charter that helped sustain the courage of stricken peoples through the darkest days of the war. For it is a declaration of great faith by the nations of the earth—faith that war is not inevitable, faith that peace can be maintained.

If we had had this charter a few years ago—and above all, the will to use it—millions now dead would be alive. If we should falter in the future in our will

(Continued on page 4, col. 2)

President Hails Parley's Success

Truman Tells Closing Session of San Francisco Conference It Has Laid Foundation for Lasting Peace

Special to The European Edition

SAN FRANCISCO, June 26.—The charter of the United Nations, a document written in conference here by the representatives of fifty nations to outline their hopes and plans for a future world of peace and security, was formally signed today.

President Harry S. Truman witnessed the signing by delegates of the United States, and addressed the closing session of the conference, praising it for creating "a great instrument for peace and security and human progress in the world."

"But now the world must use it" he said, "otherwise, we shall betray all those who have died in order that we might meet here in freedom and safety to create it."

The delegates, who voted their final approval of the charter at a plenary session late last night, began affixing their signatures at noon. The first was Wellington Koo, of China, who put on his signature with a Chinese writing brush. Sitting in a blue chair before the oval table, Mr. Koo said, "This is a great day for all. In the name of the Chinese Republic I sign this document. Twice within our lifetime war has swept the world. I am glad to be the first to sign because we were the first to be attacked by these forces of evil."

The Russian delegation followed the Chinese and the Earl of Halifax was next, for Great Britain. The other nations followed, concluding with the United States at 3:15 p.m. The delegates awaited their turns in gilded chairs. Flags of all nations flanked the table.

In Washington, leaders of the Senate said that President Truman will personally deliver the charter to the Senate Monday and hopes are high that it will meet with approval, in contrast to the failure of the League of Nations proposal. Present plans are for two weeks of hearings and possibly another two weeks of floor debate before a vote on ratification. Senator Arthur Vandenberg, Republican member of the American delegation, announced today that he will use all his influence to obtain its approval.

Plan Against War

Throughout President Truman's address ran the theme that the charter of the new world league is only an instrument, a machine built from the universal desire that never again shall the world be engulfed in war. It is not perfect, he said, and there must be a will among nations to use it well. But like the American Constitution, he said, it can be improved and developed.

"The charter you have just signed," he told the delegates gathered in the Opera House, where they have labored for the last nine weeks, "is a solid structure upon which we can build a better world.... Between victory in Europe and final victory in Japan in this most destructive of all wars you have won a victory against war itself.

"If we had had this charter a few years ago," Mr. Truman said, "and above all the will to use it, millions now dead would be alive. If we should falter in the future in our will to use it, millions now living will surely die."

Formation of the charter, President Truman said, "was proof that nations, like men, can state their differences, can face them and then can find common ground on which to stand. That is the essence of democracy; that is the essence of keeping the peace in the future. By your agreement, the way was shown toward future agreement in the years to come."

He warned against force by the greater powers, saying, "We all have to recognize—no matter how great our strength—that we must deny ourselves the license to do always as we please."

Powers Responsible

Out of the war, he said, have come powerful military nations, but they have no right to dominate the world. "It is rather" he said, "the duty of these powerful nations to assume the responsibility for peace. That is why we have here resolved that power and strength shall be used not to wage war, but to keep the world at peace and free from the fear of war.

"By their own example the strong nations of the world should lead the way to international justice. That principle of justice is the foundation stone of this charter. That principle is the guiding spirit by which it must be carried out—not by word alone but by continued concrete acts of good will."

The charter not only provides a framework for political co-operation but is a basis for the solution of trade and economic problems, President Truman said, adding that freedom from want was an economic matter and one of the basic freedoms toward which the conference was aiming.

The signing of the charter, he said, has given reality to the ideal of Woodrow Wilson and is a movement toward "the goal for which that gallant leader in this second world struggle worked and fought and gave his life—Franklin D. Roosevelt."

Edward R. Stettinius, jr., Secretary of State, affixing his signature to the charter as chairman of the United States delegation, said, "We are all aware that this is an historic occasion. The charter for world peace has been completed. But this is not the end—it is only the beginning. The great task lies before us. With faith in our cause and good will in our heart we will complete this task. I am confident that with God's help we will reach our goal."

Text of Charter Printed in Full

The European edition of the New York Herald Tribune and the London "Times" are the only newspapers in Europe which today are printing the full text of the United Nations charter, as far as could be ascertained last night.

Delegates Met Their Mandate, Stettinius Says

Special to The European Edition

SAN FRANCISCO, June 26.—Secretary of State Edward R. Stettinius jr., chairman of the United States delegation to the United Nations Conference, told the final session today that "the San Francisco conference has fulfilled its mandate" in producing a charter embodying "our hope for a good and lasting peace.

"Two months ago the delegates here assembled met for the first time," Mr. Stettinius said. "We came from many parts of the earth, across continents and oceans. But we came here first of all as representatives of humanity and as the bearers of a common mandate—to draw up a charter of a world organization for peace . . .

"The San Francisco conference has fulfilled its mandate," he went on. "The charter of a permanent United Nations has been written. Today we meet together for the last day of this conference. Tomorrow we shall separate and return home, each to his own country. But in this charter we will carry to our government and to our people an identical message of purpose and an identical instrument for the fulfillment of that purpose.

"In this charter, born of suffering and war, now rests our hope for good and lasting peace.

Delegates of the fifty nations made public yesterday the text of a resolution praising the work of Mr. Stettinius as conference president. The resolution, adopted Saturday by acclamation, expressed:

"Our profound appreciation for his able guidance of the work of our committee and, as the president charged with the responsibility for conducting the business of the conference, for his wise and steadfast leadership of the conference."

London Press Greets Charter, Declares Unity Is Necessary

By Don Cook
From the Herald Tribune Bureau

LONDON, June 27 (Wednesday).—The United Nations charter was welcomed editorially in London today with warm satisfaction tempered nevertheless with the warning that "only if all the powers are joined together in strength, faith and good will can collective security become a reality."

With election campaign news vying with the San Francisco proceedings for space in Britain's newspapers, which average only four pages, the only paper able to carry the full text of the charter was "The Times" of London. All papers, however, summarized the high spots of the document as well as the principal speeches which brought the conference to a close.

"The Daily Mail" declared the signing to be "an outstanding event in human history," adding, however, that the charter "is an imperfect instrument as it was bound to be in an imperfect world." It hailed the document as "more realistic than its predecessors" and declared that its success depends upon the will of the signatory nations to make it succeed.

"The Times" hailed the charter as evidence of the United Nations' "unshaken determination to work together and to make by process of give and take those mutual concessions which are the conditions of all co-operation."

"The Daily Telegraph" placed special emphasis on the new charter's improvements over the Covenant of the old League of Nations. "It is fully recognized," the newspaper said, "that the charter, as drafted at San Francisco, is the result of many compromises. . . There is plenty of encouragement for the hope that the charter will serve its purpose more adequately than the Covenant did."

Price: 5 Francs

Subscription Rates Listed on Page Two

NEW YORK Herald Tribune

EUROPEAN EDITION

58th Year—No. 19,441 • • PARIS, WEDNESDAY, AUG. 8, 1945 THE NEW YORK HERALD (ESTABLISHED IN EUROPE 1887)

City Reported Erased by Atom Bomb; Shock Felt by Plane Ten Miles Away

British Pact Revealed at Petain Trial

Chevalier Says England Eased Blockade After Pledge on French Fleet

Germany Never Heard of Accord

Pretense of Bad Relations Shielded Its Existence

By Marguerite Higgins

The full story of a secret British agreement with Vichy France in which the blockade was relaxed in return for a promise that France would not turn over her fleet or colonies to the Germans was told yesterday for the first time at the fourteenth session of the treason trial of Marshal Henri-Philippe Pétain.

The accord, which was kept so quiet that the Germans never discovered its existence, was described during the testimony of the man who acted as intermediary in its negotiation —Jacques Chevalier, seventy-three-year-old former Minister of Education under the Vichy regime.

The British proposed the accord, Chevalier said. And a key point of the British proposal was the insistence that existence of the secret agreement be camouflaged by keeping up between France and England a "pretense of misunderstanding." Thus, he said, the British government actually encouraged Marshal Pétain, then the ruler of Vichy France, to play a double game. The double game argument is expected to form the greatest part of Defense Lawyer Fernand Payen's attempt to absolve the

B29s Spatter Enemy Arsenal In 800-Ton 'Nuisance' Raid

125 Super-Forts Score Good Results in Daylight Assault on Ammunition Plant Near Nagoya With Plain, Old Pre-Atom Vintage Bombs

BULLETIN

Special to The European Edition

MANILA, Aug. 7.—General Douglas MacArthur announced today that more than 300 Far East Air Force bombers and fighter-bombers raided Kagoshima and Niyakonojo on southern Kyushu on Monday.

He added that Japanese planes "harmlessly raided our Okinawa positions before dawn" Monday. One enemy plane was destroyed, another probably downed.

It also was disclosed by the Navy that Admiral William F. Halsey's 3d Fleet is still in waters off Japan, but has been inactive for a week to avoid a threatening typhoon.

By Mac R. Johnson

Special to The European Edition

GUAM, Aug. 7.—Toyokawa naval arsenal, principal producer of naval ammunition in Japan, was attacked at noon today by approximately 125 Marianas-based Super-Forts. About 800 tons of high explosives were dropped on the installation, on the narrow coastal plain northeast of Atsumi Bay and about thirty-seven miles southeast of Nagoya Castle.

General Carl A. Spaatz said that the bombers were escorted by Iwo-based Mustangs in the first daylight strike in several days. The B29s found the weather clear and were able to bomb visually, scoring "good to excellent" results. Flak and fighters were described as "nil to meager."

[The Associated Press, reporting that the Japanese radio was maintaining a tight-lipped silence on the use of the atomic bomb at Hiroshima, noted that it was significant that the Osaka radio announced the cancellation of various trains in the Hiroshima prefecture. General Spaatz's headquarters announced that all Hiroshima eyewitness stories would pass through the War Department at Washington before being released.]

Toyokawa arsenal is rated one of the ten major arsenals of its type in Japan. It produces machine-guns, aircraft cannon, ack-ack guns, ammunition, and also is reported to be the production center for Diesel engines and landing craft frames.

A final report on the Super-Fort mission on the night of Aug. 5 shows that 572 B29s struck primary targets, while twenty-eight dropped mines and nine bombed targets of opportunity. The crew on the one bomber that failed to return was rescued.

Dwarfs 580-Plane Raid

By the Associated Press

SAN FRANCISCO Aug. 7.—The unleashing of the awesome atomic bomb on Hiroshima dwarfed all other activity of the Pacific war—even the raid by 580 Super-Forts Sunday night which devastated four more Japanese cities.

About 100 Mustangs which swept the Tokio area on Sunday returned there in equal strength today, 20th Air Force headquarters reported. They hit nine airfields, railway yards, shipping and other targets. They destroyed or damaged twenty grounded planes.

General Douglas MacArthur reported that 400 of his Far East Air Force bombers and fighters made their biggest fire raid Sunday, blasting the port of Tarumi on southern Kyushu. They left the city enveloped in smoke and flame.

Admiral Chester W. Nimitz, Pacific Fleet commander, in the shortest fleet communique of the war, reported Marine air raids on the Palaus, southwest of Guam.

Tokio Rose Receives U.S. Navy Citation

By the Associated Press

WASHINGTON, Aug. 7.—Tokio Rose, the seductive-voiced Japanese girl propagandist, won a citation today from the United States Navy for "meritorious service, contributing greatly to the morale of the United States' troops in the Pacific."

As a further tribute to her ability to "bring laughter and entertainment" to Americans, the Navy gave her permission to broadcast "soon" a description of Admiral Halsey riding the Japanese Emperor's white horse through the streets of Tokio.

Dutch Training Fighting Army 200,000 Strong

Will Help in War on Japan And Participate in the Occupation of Germany

By the Associated Press

LONDON, Aug. 7.—A fighting Dutch Army 200,000 strong is being organized and trained to carry on the war against Japan and help in the occupation of Germany, informed London sources said today.

About 100,000 of the Dutch soldiers will learn military tactics in Great Britain, while an additional 50,000 will train for occupation work. Administration personnel will number 20,000.

The remaining 30,000 were expected to train in Australia, but latest reports indicate that it may be some time before they are ready and that British troops will carry the burden of clearing the Japanese out of the Dutch Crown colonies in the opening phase of the campaign.

Some difficulty may be experienced in training troops in Australia, the London source said,

Atom Bomb A Columbia Brainchild

Rock-Hewn Vault Under College Campus Scene Of Successful Research

Nazi Experiments Led World for Time

All Nations Were in Race For Same Goal by 1941

By Robert S. Bird

From the Herald Tribune Bureau

NEW YORK, Aug. 7.—The atomic bomb, which has opened for mankind a fateful door to a new era, was born under the campus of Columbia University in rock-hewn vaults at the corner of 120th Street and Broadway.

There in January, 1939, Dr. John R. Dunning, assistant professor in the Physics Department, and Dr. Enrico Fermi, Nobel Prize winner of Italy, who had recently joined the Columbia staff, successfully performed an experiment, perhaps the most momentous in all history.

In their deep cavern laboratory, they split the uranium atom and unlocked the basis energy of the universe. Unknown to them, this experiment had been performed in Berlin two weeks before, but the Dunning experiment paved the way for the development in this country of the complex processes that resulted in the bomb.

Top Military Project

Within a year and a half, the tremendous significance of their experiment has engaged the attention of the highest military minds of the nation and the experiment

13-Pound Source of Energy Could Wreck All Manhattan

Area Five Times That of Central Park Would Be Destroyed, So That Nothing Would Remain But Crater, Perhaps Hundreds of Feet Deep

By John J. O'Neill

Herald Tribune Science Editor

NEW YORK, Aug. 7.—A new chemical element, Pluto, was created by science to produce a super atomic energy source. The new element never existed in nature. It was created entirely by artificial processes and was found to have explosive properties even greater than those of uranium-235, which was the original source through which tremendous amounts of atomic energy were released from matter—three million times as much as is released in equal weights of TNT. That is the nature of the energy unleashed against Japan.

Pluto is the heaviest element in existence. It has atomic weight of 239, one unit heavier than uranium-238. It is created by shooting a neutron, a sub-atomic particle of matter, into uranium-238.

Pluto and uranium provide a double atomic energy source. Either can be used alone or both can be used together.

The bomb launched against Japan, as announced by President Truman, has more power than 20,000 tons of TNT. This would be equal to forty million pounds of TNT. Since one pound of uranium yields approximately three million times as much energy as a pound of TNT, this statement gives the information that the atomic energy bomb contained approximately thirteen pounds of uranium-235, or of the new element Pluto.

The energy released by one pound of uranium—sixty-two trillion 500 billion foot pounds—would be sufficient to raise the Empire State Building twenty miles high. It is sufficient to raise a square mile of midtown Manhattan buildings to the height of 600 feet.

The energy released by a thirteen-pound source of atomic energy in the bomb would therefore be sufficient to wreck completely an area the size of Manhattan. An area of ten square miles, more than five times the size of Central Park, would be utterly destroyed so that nothing would remain but a crater perhaps hundreds of feet

in the bomb were usefully applied for destructive purposes—if the

Terrific Nippon Blast Blows Down Wall St.

By the Associated Press

NEW YORK, Aug. 7.—Wall Street interpreted the atomic bomb development today as meaning a quicker end to the Japanese war than was expected, and stock market prices dropped as much as three points.

Heavy war-rated stocks, such as rails, aircrafts, steels and utilities, showed the widest decline, with lesser falls in metals, rubbers, oil and motors.

In London, the news of the bomb had a different effect. Optimism over prospects for shortening of the war was reflected in appreciable gains, especially in some groups subjected to selling pressure in the wake of British election results. Japanese bonds advanced 1/4 to 3/4 of a point.

Japan to Get New Allied Ultimatum

Will Be Warned to Quit War or Be Destroyed By Awesome Weapon

Cannot Be Slighted, Is Tokio's Verdict

Tokio Is Called Probable Next Target for Erasure

Special to The European Edition

GUAM, Aug. 7. — The atomic bomb dropped Monday on Japan by the United States Army Air Forces struck squarely in the center of Hiroshima. The concussion brought an exclamation of "Oh, my God" from a Flying Fortress crew ten miles away.

Colonel Paul W. Tibbets jr., of Miami, who piloted the Fortress, and Captain William S. Parsons, U.S.N., of Santa Fe, an ordnance expert, described the resulting explosions as "tremendous and awe-inspiring." Neither could estimate the damage, but both said it "must have been extensive."

There is reason to believe that the Japanese city no longer exists.

Shock Felt Ten Miles Away

Captain Parsons said: "It was 9:15 when we dropped our bomb and we turned the plane broadside to get the best view. Then we made as much distance from the ball of fire as we could. We were at least ten miles away and there was a visual impact, even though every man wore colored glasses for protection.

"We had braced ourselves for shock when the bomb was gone and Tibbets said, 'close flak' and it was just like that—a close burst of

Price: 5 Francs

Subscription Rates Listed on Page Two

NEW YORK Herald Tribune

EUROPEAN EDITION

58th Year—No. 19,447 • • PARIS, WEDNESDAY, AUG. 15, 1945 THE NEW YORK HERALD (ESTABLISHED IN EUROPE 1887)

Tokio Surrenders Unconditionally; Allies Accept, Halt Their Offensives; MacArthur Made Supreme in Japan

Petain Guilty, Mercy Urged

BULLETIN

Marshal Henri-Philippe Pétain, 89-year-old former Vichy Chief of State, was sentenced to death at 4 o'clock this morning. He was found guilty of high treason by a jury of twenty-four who reached their verdict after seven hours' deliberation. But it was recommended that the death sentence be not carried out because of the defendant's advanced age.

By Marguerite Higgins

The treason trial of Marshal Henri Philippe Pétain went to the jury at nine o'clock last night after the 89-year-old former ruler of Vichy France had made a dramatic last-minute plea, in which he declared: "In my life already long and on the threshold of death my only ambition was to serve France."

With the prosecution asking death before a firing squad, Marshal Pétain was expected to learn his fate probably some time between midnight and 4 a.m. this morning. The jury had to base its verdict on two main charges: "Traffic with the enemy and suppression of

Supreme Commander of Occupation

General Douglas MacArthur.

Reds Gain 93 Miles in Big Finale

Sensational Push Brings Capture of an Important Manchurian Rail Center

Two Armies Drive Closer to Harbin

Enemy Force May Have Jumped Surrender Gun

By the United Press

MOSCOW, Aug. 14.—As the war against Japan came to an end tonight, the Red Army announced that the final day's operations has resulted in sweeping advances in Manchuria and on Sakhalin Island.

[The Associated Press reported from London that Russian Far Eastern troops had made a sensational advance of ninety-three miles in Manchuria to capture an important rail center.]

On the sixth day of war between Russia and Japan there was still no indication that Japan's vaunted Kwantung Army was standing to fight a major engagement.

Quit Before Note

To some observers it appeared that long before Japan had handed the Swiss government a reply to Allied surrender demands, Nippon's field commanders had ceased all active operations.

In the main Russian drives on Harbin, a primary objective in Manchuria, Marshal Rodion Y. Malinovsky's Trans-Baikal Army captured a town 175 miles west of the key city. From the east,

Truman Announces Potsdam Terms Met

From the Herald Tribune Bureau

WASHINGTON, Aug. 14.—Japan has surrendered.

President Truman announced at 7 o'clock tonight that history's most destructive war has ended with the unconditional surrender of the Asiatic enemy. Allied armies and navies have ceased their offensives.

At the same time—midnight in London and 1 a.m. Wednesday in Paris—the news was broadcast in London and Moscow.

The President said the capitulation was under the terms of the ultimatum conveyed to Japan on July 26, during the tri-power conference at Berlin.

Hit eight days ago by the first of the terrible new atomic bombs and two days later by a Russian declaration of war, Japan revealed last Friday that she would ac-

U.S. Works Out Control Plan To Rule Japan

Occupation Policy to Be Along Same Lines as Those Now Applied in Germany

By John C. Metcalfe

From the Herald Tribune Bureau

WASHINGTON, Aug. 14.—The United States government is nearing the completion of its plan for political and economic treatment of defeated Japan, it was learned today in diplomatic circles, and will propose to Russia, Britain and China for their approval a control program strikingly similar to that which is being applied to Germany.

At the same time it has formally been agreed among the Big Four that matters pertaining to the preparation of a peace treaty with Japan—which is not to be effected until the Allies are prepared to withdraw all controls and which may be several years distant—will be turned over to the Council of Foreign Ministers established at the Berlin conference.

Specific authority to deal with the Pacific peace settlement was set forth in the Potsdam communique, diplomats said, pointing to the opening section dealing with the

Horns Toot, Kisses Are Free As U.S. Blows Off Victory Lid

150,000 Celebrators Move Ankle Deep in Paper In Times Square; San Francisco Cuts Loose,

De Gaulle Forms New Cabinet; 20 Nazi Leaders Plead 'Not Guilty'

Hitler Aids Show Spirit In Denials

Ribbentrop Plans to Call U.S. Diplomat and Top Britons in His Defense

Goering's Attempt At Speech Halted

Hess Simply Says 'Nein'; Fritz Saukel Defiant

By Russell Hill

Special to the European Edition

NUREMBERG, Nov. 21.—The twenty leaders of Adolf Hitler's Third Reich who are on trial for their lives in Nuremberg, the city of the National Socialist party congresses, showed spirit and fight today in their emphatic and in some instances defiant pleas of "not guilty."

The five minutes during which they were allowed to speak out to the world for the first time since the collapse of the Nazi state were filled with suppressed drama. The defendants wanted to say more than the tribunal would let them, and they packed all sorts of meaning into the few words that were permitted to them.

Hermann Goering, once Germany's No. 2 Nazi, was the first to step to the microphone which had been placed before the defendants' box. He spoke out forcefully, and instead of answering simply "guilty" or "not guilty," he tried to make a speech, beginning, "Before I answer the question of the High Court whether or not I am guilty. . ."

Goering Is Shut Off

He was interrupted by the president of the tribunal, British Lord Chief Justice Sir Geoffrey Lawrence, who said sharply, "I informed the court that the defendants were not entitled to make a statement. You must plead guilty or not guilty."

In an injured tone, as though he had been deprived of a sacred right, Goering said, "I declare myself in the sense of the indictment not guilty."

He was followed by Rudolf Hess, who is believed to be suffering from hysterical amnesia and has sat through the proceedings to date with a childlike look on his face. He stepped quickly to the microphone, said, "Nein," and sat down as quickly.

The president said judiciously, "That will be entered as a plea of not guilty," provoking laughter in the courtroom.

Former Foreign Minister Joachim von Ribbentrop, in a harsh tone of voice, repeated Goering's formula, "I declare myself in the sense of the indictment not guilty," stressing the "not."

May Call U.S. Diplomat

Ribbentrop has taken great interest in preparing his defense, and it was learned that he will ask to call an American diplomat and several leading figures in British public life as witnesses in his defense. One source said the list would include Lord Beaverbrook, the right-wing publisher of the "Daily Express," which advocated appeasement of Germany in the pre-war period.

Nazi War Leaders Brought to Justice Before the International War Crimes Court at Nuremberg

Keystone and New York Times.

Above: The defendants surrounded by MP guards listen to the indictment. Front row, from left to right: Goering, Hess, Von Ribbentrop, Keitel, Rosenberg, Frank, Frick, Streicher, Funk and Schacht (partly hidden behind MP on extreme right). Back row, left to right: Doenitz, Raeder, Schirach, Sauckel, Jodl, Von Papen, Seyss-Inquart, Speer, Von Neurath and Fritsch (partly hidden behind Schacht). Below: The judges' bench with the four Allied flags indicating the nationality of the judges; from left to right, Russian, British, American and French.

Eva's Diary Shows How Hitler Gave Her Lots of 'Kopfweh'

By Carl Levin

Special to the European Edition

FRANKFURT, Nov. 21. — The Military Intelligence Division of USFET disclosed today that the only part of Eva Braun's diary which has been found covers the period from February 6, 1935, to May 28 of the same year—a period in which Hitler's mistress might well have been referred to as "poor little Eva."

The last notation, and the most dramatic note in the entire diary, after Eva had pined away for three months as what she termed "the mistress of Germany's and the world's greatest man" without even once getting to speak to him, was an entry written in desperation. "I have decided on thirty-five pills, so as to make it dead certain this time," she wrote. "If he would at least have some one call up for him."

Just how poor little Eva got past that rough spot in history is left untold. But she does relate in the diary that the Reich's Chancellor had already selected her as his favorite early in 1935, when she had just reached her twenty-third year. Thereafter, from her entries, she apparently had her ups and downs and at one period she was doing so poorly financially that she wrote: "I'm getting on everybody's nerves because I want to sell everything, from my clothes down to my camera and even theater tickets."

She felt philosophical at this period, though, and bravely added the notation: "Oh well, things will improve. After all, my debts are not that big."

The thing that really got her, though, was when, during the period of waning attention from Hitler, she heard from Frau Hoffmann, wife of Hitler's photographer, for whom Eva had worked, that Der Fuehrer had found a substitute for her named "Die Walkuere." Her name, Eva wrote with characteristic feminity, "is Die Walkuere and she looks it, including her legs."

France Gets Three Party Coalition

Compromise Is Found To Settle Communist Demand for Key Post

De Gaulle Is Head Of Defense Agency

Leading members of the new De Gaulle government: On left, from top to bottom, Vincent Auriol (Socialist), Minister of State; Charles Tillon (Communist), Minister of Armed Forces; Tanguy-Prigent (Socialist), Minister of Agriculture and Food. Center: Maurice Thorez (Communist leader), Minister of State; Rene Pleven (Socialist-Resistance), Minister of Finance. Right: Louis Jacquinot (URD), Minister of State; Jacques Soustelle (Socialist-Resistance), Minister of Colonies; Adrien Tixier (Socialist), Minister of the Interior.

SATURDAY, AUGUST 16, 1947

India Now Free Nation, New Regime Issues Plea For Hindu-Moslem Ties

Mountbatten Takes Oath As Governor General Amid Royal Splendor

Princes Are Absent From Ceremonies

'Interim Period' Slated To End Next March 31

By the Associated Press

NEW DELHI, Aug. 15.—With royal pomp and oriental splendor Viscount Louis Mountbatten took oath today as Governor General on this first day of official existence for the new Dominion of India.

In the famous Durbar hall of Government House, which until today was the Viceregal palace, Viscount Mountbatten stood before the new Chief Justice of India and kissed the Bible to seal his oath.

Members of this first people's government of free India, led by Prime Minister Jawarharlal Nehru, occupied seats which heretofore would have been held for major princes of the realm. The princes were conspicuously absent today.

Mountbatten to Resign

Within minutes of entering, Viscount Mountbatten announced in a prepared-text speech to members of the Constituent Assembly that he would ask to be relieved as Governor General on March 31, 1948, at the end of what he called the "interim period" or completion of the details for the division of the subcontinent into Hindu India and Moslem Pakistan.

The newly constituted Cabinet issued an appeal tonight for cessation of Hindu and Moslem violence in both India and Pakistan as the first official act of the government headed by Prime Minister Nehru.

"Whatever differences we may have must be resolved by peaceful and democratic methods," the Cabinet statement said. "We would venture to extend this appeal to those who live now in Pakistan. We are a free people today. Let us act then as free men and women."

Lord Mountbatten, who had so much to do with the agreements which led to the negotiated freedom through Dominion status, told how he came to India with June, 1948, as the objective date for freedom and many in England contending that would be too early to get the job done.

"However, I had not been more than a week in India before I realized that this date of June, 1948, was too late rather than too early; communal tension and rioting had assumed proportions of which I had had no conception when I left England.

Gives Thanks to Leaders

"By open diplomacy with the leaders, the freedom date was advanced to today and the success of the plan is chiefly attributable to them—these statesmen placed me in their debt for ever by their sympathetic understanding of my position."

SATURDAY, JANUARY 31, 1948

Gandhi Is Assassinated by Hindu

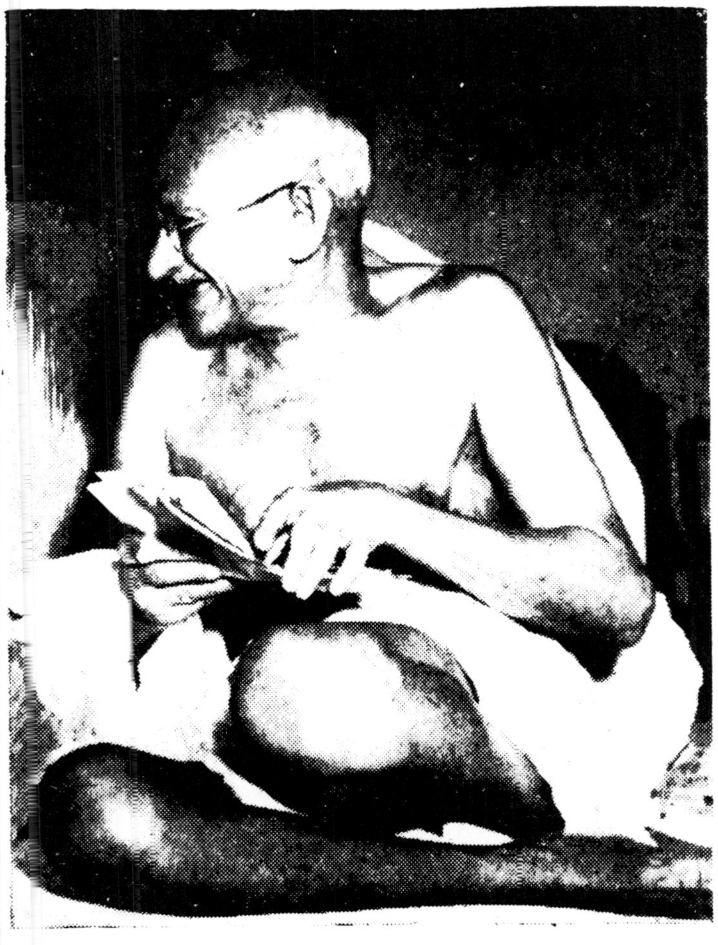

Mohandas K. Gandhi

Leader Shot On His Way To Prayers

Felled by Three Bullets While Walking Among Throng in Delhi Garden

Murderer Mauled By Furious Crowd

His Victim Dies Without Gaining Consciousness

By Margaret Parton

Special to the European Edition

NEW DELHI, Jan. 30.—Mohandas K. Gandhi, spiritual leader of the Indian people, was shot this evening by a Hindu fanatic and died within half an hour.

The assassin, who gave his name as Nathuram, fired three times at Gandhi as the Mahatma was walking through the garden of Birla House at 5:10 p.m. on his way to address the daily prayer meeting. Gandhi was carried back into the house unconscious and died at 5:40 without regaining consciousness.

Nathuram, who attempted to shoot himself before capture, was seized by the crowd which had gathered to attend the prayer meeting and was severely mauled before being handed over to the police. In order to forestall further mob violence he was immediately taken to a near-by jail where he announced he would explain the motives for his act in court but that he was "not at all sorry."

Walks Up Garden Path

According to eyewitness reports, Gandhi emerged from Birla House where he has been living for several months, shortly after 5 o'clock this evening, and, leaning on the shoulders of his two grand-nieces, walked slowly up the garden path and mounted the steps leading to the terrace where the prayer meeting was being held. He was barefooted as usual, and wore his customary white loin cloth and soft shawl.

As he reached the top of the steps the crowd parted to let him pass. Then, from the crowd, a young man stepped forward and raised his folded hands in the customary Hindu gesture of greeting. Gandhi smiled at him and said, according to some reports: "You are late tonight."

As Gandhi spoke, the young man whipped a small revolver from under his coat and fired three times, hitting the Mahatma in the stomach and chest. He then tried to turn the revolver on himself, but was disarmed by a young Indian Air force sergeant standing near by.

Lifts Hands to Audience

Gandhi, meanwhile, collapsed slowly to the ground. As his hands slipped from the shoulders of his grand-nieces he lifted them, folded in a gesture of prayer, toward his stunned audience of Indian devotees.

While the crowd milled about the assassin, Gandhi was carried into Birla House and laid upon a simple pallet in the bare room where he lived and worked. Despite feverish efforts by doctors to save his life, he died there while his closest disciples read prayers from the Gitas.

News of Gandhi's assassination spread quickly throughout New Delhi, and within a few minutes of the attack a huge crowd of whispering Indians began to collect in the darkened street outside Birla Gardens. Within an hour they had broken through the police lines and surrounded the two-story mansion, peeping through the windows and attempting to enter. By 7 o'clock 2,000 men and a few weeping women were moving about outside the small room where Gandhi lay.

Funeral Plans Announced

Shortly after 7 p.m., Prime Minister Jawaharlal Nehru, who for many years has been Gandhi's closest associate, attempted to quiet the crowd. Climbing to the top of the white picket gate, he told the people of Gandhi's death and announced that the funeral would be held at noon tomorrow following a formal procession through the city. He was so deeply moved by the death, however, that his further words were unintelligible and he ended in tears and a state bordering on collapse.

Among the government clerks, laborers and others who stood in the gathering darkness outside Birla House the mood was a somber one. There seemed to be little anger, but only a sense of stunned loss.

"This is the end of the world," said one shabbily dressed young man. "Everything is in chaos and Gandhi was our only hope. Now that hope is gone."

Communal Riots Rock Bombay After News of Gandhi's Death

15 Killed, 50 Injured in Wave of Stabbings; Mobs Form in All Parts of the City; Stone-Throwing, Shop-Looting Flares

By the United Press

BOMBAY, Jan. 30.—Fifteen persons were killed and fifty injured from stabbings today which followed news of Mohandas K. Gandhi's assassination.

The news, which was broadcast throughout Bombay fifteen minutes after Gandhi's shooting, touched off a wave of communal rioting. Mobs formed in all parts of the city as police rushed to the rioting areas and troops stood by.

Bombay's police commissioner announced at 11 p.m. that "the situation is under control but we will have to keep a close watch tomorrow."

At first, the Bombay populace was stunned by the news but communal passions soon swelled into full-bloom riots, which Gandhi had devoted his life to prevent.

Scenes of stone-throwing, shop-looting and stabbings, which have become tragically common in this city in the last year, were repeated.

Britain Mourns Gandhi, Fears Riots in India

Attlee, Churchill Join in Expressions of Shock at Death of Free-India Chief

By Ned Russell

From the Herald Tribune Bureau

LONDON, Jan. 30.—The assassination of Mohandas K. Gandhi, who devoted his life to the cause of freeing India from British rule, was mourned tonight by British leaders of every political group. The government hinted at fears that his death may set off a new wave of violence in India.

Expressions of deep grief and horror came from all sections of London, from Prime Minister Clement Attlee and former Prime Minister Winston Churchill to little people who had marveled for years at the power of the frail, colorful little leader of millions of Indians to sway the destiny of his country and the world.

British Fear New Riots

Shortly after the news of Gandhi's assassination at New Delhi was confirmed here, a statement was issued from 10 Downing Street, official residence of Mr. Attlee, expressing the "profound shock" felt by the Labor government.

SATURDAY, MAY 15, 1948

Jewish Palestine State Is Recognized by U.S.; Jerusalem Battle Starts

Bagpipes Skirl, Snipers Duel As Britain's Mandate Ends

Cunningham Leaves in Bullet-Proof Car Without Farewell From Either Side; Red Cross Flag Replaces Union Jack on King David Hotel

By Kenneth Bilby

By Wireless to the European Edition

JERUSALEM, May 14.—Great Britain surrendered its mandate over Palestine at midnight today in the midst of carnage and violence which testified to the failure of a thirty-year mission.

As dawn broke over embattled Jerusalem today, the Union Jack was lowered for the last time from the King David Hotel, center of the Palestine government for ten years. While bagpipes skirled and while Jewish and Arab snipers dueled intently, the British standard was replaced by the Red Cross flag, lone symbol of neutrality in a city at war.

The ceremony was repeated soon afterward at Government House, where Sir Alan Gordon Cunningham, High Commissioner of Palestine, left his residence without farewell from either Arab or Jew. A guard of honor from the First Battalion, Highland Light Infantry, greeted the High Commissioner as he stepped into his bullet-proof Daimler for a final journey through Jerusalem.

Troops guarded the route to Kalandia Airport, north of the city, where Sir Alan boarded a Royal Air Force transport for Haifa and a waiting British cruiser. The plane's departure was the signal for lowering of the Union Jack above Government House, and for hoisting of the Red Cross banner.

By nightfall every British government official and most of the British troops had left the Holy City. A convoy of the British 2d Brigade, which had garrisoned Jerusalem, left through sunlit streets this morning with tanks and armored cars on the alert, and with Jews and Arabs watching impassively.

Government Called De Facto Authority

White House Secretary Says U.S. Still Desires A Truce in Palestine

Proclamation yesterday of a new State of Israel in Palestine had been followed early this morning by these developments:

In WASHINGTON, President Truman announced de facto recognition of the new regime by the United States government.

In NEW YORK, United Nations officials expressed surprise at President Truman's move. The special United Nations Assembly defeated the American proposal to establish a trusteeship type regime for Jerusalem.

In LONDON, officials said any recognition would be withheld "for the time being."

In CAIRO, Prime Minister Nokrashy Pasha said that Egyptian armed forces had been ordered to enter Palestine to "restore security and order."

By the Associated Press

WASHINGTON, May 14.—President Truman formally proclaimed United States recognition of the new Jewish state today.

The President, acting after the proclaiming of the Jewish state, announced:

"This government has been informed that the Jewish state has been proclaimed in Palestine and recognition has been requested by the provisional government thereof."

Mr. Truman added: "The United States recognizes the provisional government as the de facto authority of the new State of Israel."

In a separate White House statement the President's press secretary, Charles Ross, also announced:

"The desire of the United States to obtain a truce in Palestine will be in no way lessened by the proclamation of the Jewish state.

"We hope that the new Jewish state will join with the Security Council Truce Commission in redoubled efforts to bring an end to the fighting, which has been throughout the United Nations' consideration of Palestine a principal objective of this government."

A leading spokesman of the Jewish Agency in the United Nations, when informed of American recognition of the war state, said:

"This is what we have been praying for—marvelous."

THURSDAY, MAY 20, 1948

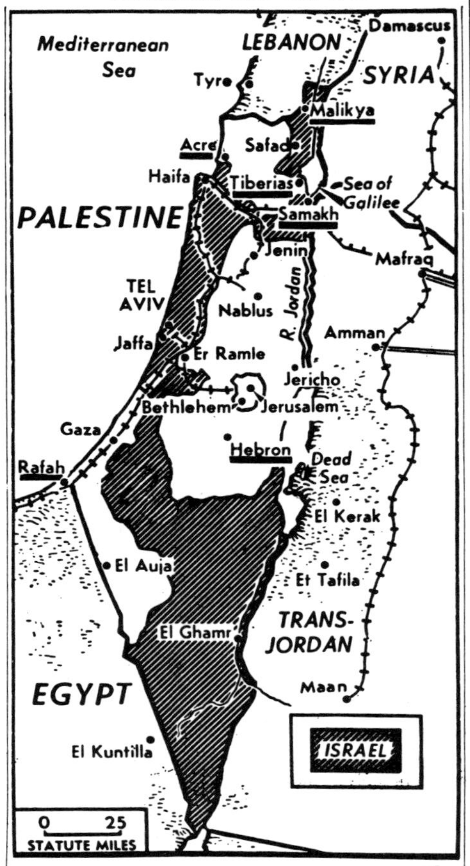

A.P.

Map indicates scenes of Arab-Jewish fighting reported since the State of Israel was proclaimed. Acre has surrendered to the Jews.

SATURDAY, MAY 29, 1948

Jews Surrender in Old City; Two Rabbis Negotiate Terms For 1,500 Ringed by Legion

Bevin and Douglas Discuss Palestine

British Offer to Recall Officers From Legion Seen Narrowing Gap

By Jack Tait

From the Herald Tribune Bureau

LONDON, May 28.—Foreign Secretary Ernest Bevin and Lewis W. Douglas, American Ambassador to the Court of St. James's, conferred unexpectedly tonight on the Palestine situation.

Mr. Bevin, it is understood, initiated the meeting. In the meetings of the last week between the Foreign Secretary and Mr. Douglas, the American Ambassador has impressed upon Mr. Bevin the development of anti-British feeling in the United States as a result of Britain's policy toward Palestine.

Government sources were confident tonight that the latest British offer to withdraw British officers from the Arab Legion and to review treaty commitments with the Arab states had narrowed the gap of misunderstanding between the two countries.

British Officers Recalled

[The British Foreign Office announced yesterday that orders have been sent to Amman calling on twenty-one British officers loaned to the Arab Legion to withdraw from Palestine, the Associated Press said. A spokesman emphasized in an interview that these men are to leave Palestine and not the Arab Legion.]

The Foreign Office tonight denied two reports published today. The first was that Britain was actively considering a maritime blockade of Palestine, and the second was that Mr. Bevin had conceived and urged a new plan for the partition of Palestine.

Meanwhile, it was announced tonight that the Archbishop of Canterbury, Dr. Geoffrey F. Fisher, with the support of the clergy and bishops of the Province of Canterbury, has sent the following cable to Trygve Lie, Secretary General of the United Nations:

'Offense and Scandal'

"With the support of bishops and clergy of the Province of Canterbury, I urgently represent that all parties shall combine to establish a temporary truce in Palestine or at least in Jerusalem, that the distress and shame of fighting in the Holy City, which is an offense and scandal to religious conscience of Christians, Moslems and Jews, may be ended."

Garrison Runs Out Of Food, Munitions

Non-Combatants Will Be Given to Red Cross; Internment for Fighters

By the Associated Press

JERUSALEM, May 28.—The Jewish quarter of the Old City of Jerusalem surrendered today to the Transjordan Arab Legion. The surrender was negotiated by the Legion area commander after the arrival at the Arab lines of two rabbis carrying white flags.

Under the surrender terms women and children—estimated to number 300—and old men will be turned over to the International Red Cross. Younger men will be placed in a concentration camp "outside Palestine."

Jewish negotiators said their people numbered between 1,500 and 1,600. Of this number, the leaders said, many were dead or wounded. Four Jews, they said, died of an "unidentified disease."

The Jewish negotiators said they were completely without food and short of ammunition after the eleven-day pounding by Arab League guns.

Cordon Rings Area

The conditions were accepted by the Old City Jewish mukhtar (mayor) and two Haganah officers who were brought inside the Arab lines under a white flag. Legion guards and armored cars immediately began throwing a tight cordon around the battered Jewish occupied area.

All Old City residents and irregular fighters were ordered to remain in their homes while Legion troops began gathering up the surrendered arms and preparing to evacuate the prisoners.

The Arab Legion's assault on the three remaining buildings in Jewish hands was halted at 9:30 a.m. after the two old rabbis appeared at a Legion forward post, bearing white flags and asking to surrender in the name of their people.

The truce appeal followed a night of heavy firing during which the Old City's remaining synagogue was destroyed and an attempt by Jews outside the walls to relieve the besieged city failed.

A Jewish attack from the Mount of Olives toward the Legion's Jericho Road route to the walled city was beaten back at Bethany.

[The Jewish Army announced at Tel Aviv yesterday that its forces had captured the Arab villages of Beit Jiz and Beit Sassin, in the battle of Latrun, key to the Jerusalem road. Haganah and the Arab Legion are locked in combat, with thousands on both sides.

[Other details of the battle around the Latrun monastery of monks pledged to silence were tightly guarded under military security. Information reaching Tel Aviv from Jerusalem, however, indicated that the battle had reached an intensity which might be the decisive fight for Palestine. The Arab Legion was reported to have drawn troops out of Jerusalem and pushed them down through Bab el Wad Gorge in an attempt to stem the Jewish attack.]

The capture of the great Hurva Synagogue confined the Jewish community and the fighters to three large stone blocks of apartments of three floors each, one below the earth's surface.

Final Warning

During the night Legion loudspeakers broadcast a "final warning" to the Old City Jews to "surrender or expect no mercy."

At the morning surrender overtures the Legion area commander demanded the surrender of all men as prisoners of war and proposed that women and children remain in their homes under Legion protection.

The two rabbis were permitted to return to confer with the besieged Jews. At 10 a.m. they reentered the Arab lines with the Jewish mukhtar, Nordecai Weingarien. Haganah senior officer Saul Tawil, Haganah officer David Eisen and Mr. Weingarten's daughter, Judith.

The agreement concluded, the Jews returned to their people with Legion troops and medical personnel to care for the sick and wounded.

France Asks UN to Demand Halt to Fighting in Jerusalem

Proposal Provides Forceful Measures If Arabs And Jews Reject Appeal; U.S. and Russia Again Urge Order to End Hostilities

By the Associated Press

LAKE SUCCESS, N. Y., May 28.—France proposed today that the United Nations tell the Arabs and Jews to stop fighting in Jerusalem by noon tomorrow. The proposal provides that the Security Council shall consider forceful measures if the appeal is rejected.

Alexandre Parodi interrupted the general debate on Palestine to present the plan, saying delegates must consider the Holy City immediately to meet the serious situation in Jerusalem.

The Council adjourned until Saturday without reaching a vote.

The Council received a telegram from the Truce Commission in Jerusalem saying the Holy Sepulchre was in imminent peril from Arab bombardment.

The commission said in another telegram that the Jewish military commander of Jerusalem had informed the commission the Jews would take reprisals on the holy places if the Arabs continued to shell the Great Synagogue. The communications were apparently sent before the Arabs captured Jerusalem.

The United States joined with Russia again today in a demand for forceful United Nations measures to stop the Palestine war.

Warren Austin, chief United States delegate, said he supported the Soviet resolution providing the Security Council orders the Jews and Arabs to end hostilities within thirty-six hours. The same proposal was first submitted by the United States, but defeated in the Security Council last Saturday.

Mr. Austin said he had no instructions on the American attitude toward the British demand for a four-week armistice. The British plan appeared doomed by Jewish reaction.

WEDNESDAY, JUNE 2, 1948

Both Sides Attach Conditions to Notes

Israel Asks Freedom of Access to Jerusalem; Arab Details to Follow

By the Associated Press

LAKE SUCCESS, N.Y., June 1.—Jews and Arabs accepted today the United Nations appeal for a cease-fire in Palestine.

Israel accepted the appeal for a four-week armistice in the Holy Land approximately four hours before the 11 p.m. deadline for a reply. The Arabs announced their acceptance two hours later.

Charles Malik, the Lebanese delegate, said in a press conference that the Arab League had accepted. He said a detailed reply would be sent to the Security Council later but refused to answer questions as to whether the Arab step was unconditional.

The Arab Note

The Arab note said: "The political committee of the Arab League, which met in Amman, has accepted the Security Council's request for a cease-fire for the indicated period (four weeks). The political committee will communicate its detailed reply to the Secretary General and to the President of the Security Council.

"Acceptance by the Arab governments of these proposals proves once more their genuine desire to see peace restored in the Holy Land and a just solution of the Palestine problem arrived at."

The Arab and Jewish replies to the United Nations left unanswered such questions as when the shooting would stop.

The Jews followed their acceptance by issuing a cease-fire order to their troops effective at 3 a.m. Wednesday (Israel time) on condition that the Arabs took the same step. The Arabs, in their reply, left open the actual time for the laying down of arms.

Questions Left Open

Also unanswered were diplomatic and political questions as to whether the acceptances are unconditional. The Arabs said a detailed reply would be sent to the Security Council. An Israel spokesman insisted his government's acceptance was unconditional. The Jews, however, stipulated they are making five assumptions about the plan, including one that the food supply route to Jerusalem would be opened.

Jews List Conditions

LAKE SUCCESS, N.Y., June 1 (UP).—The Jews listed the following five conditions today in their acceptance of a cease-fire proposal for Palestine:

1—That the ban on import of arms into Arab states should apply also "to deliveries of arms from stocks owned or controlled by foreign powers within those territories"—a reference to British arsenals and dumps scattered throughout the Middle East.

2—That there will be a complete military standstill the moment the cease-fire becomes effective, with neither side seeking to advance.

3—That there be free entry and exit to and from Jerusalem for "supply of food and other essentials as well as for normal civilian entry and exit."

4—That goods other than military now on their way to Israel not be interfered with in any way.

5—That Israel's "freedom to admit immigrants regardless of age will not be impaired" despite an agreement that there will be no further military recruitment.

Jews and Arabs Accept United Nations Appeal For Four-Week Truce

Arab Armor Almost Captured Jerusalem During First Week

Jews Held Virtually All Strong Points in City As British Left, But Legion Pierced Over-Extended Haganah Lines

By Kenneth Bilby

Special to the European Edition

KYRENIA, Cyprus, June 1.—One week after the Battle of Jerusalem began, Arab Legion armored units came within an inch of cracking the inner Jewish defense ring and winning all of the Holy City.

Many details of the tense forty-eight hours, beginning May 20, cannot be revealed because the battle, although stalemated, still continues. Yet those details that do not compromise military security are sufficient to depict one of modern history's most dramatic moments.

To comprehend the Jewish position when the heavy Legion thrust came, it is first necessary to recapitulate events from May 13 a day before British troops departed from Jerusalem.

On that day, all Jewish Home Guard units were mobilized. Men with three to four days' military training donned Haganah battle dress and assumed the burden of fighting for Jerusalem. Plans to use Palmach for the conquest went askew because the battle of the road around Bab El Wad continued.

The Jews had four immediate objectives—Sheikh Jarrah in northern Jerusalem, the Russian compound and the British military Zone B in the center, and military Zone A in the south. By clever infiltration, small groups of armed Jews were in each zone a day before the British left.

APRIL 20, 1946

British Right-Wing Art Girds To Save World From Picasso

By the United Press

LONDON, April 19.—The right wing of British art girded its loins today to save the world from the "immoralities" of Pablo Picasso.

In a darkly secret session the leaders of the newly-named "British League for the Rescue of Art" met during the past week to plot a campaign designed to sweep all that is Picassoesque into the world waste basket and to guide the post-war generation of art lovers into the fields of rock-ribbed tradition, which says: "You should paint things to look more or less rational."

The league, which until yesterday was known as the "British League for Sanity in Art," had a field day during the recent Picasso exhibition here. Members wrote indignant letters to "The Times" and told meetings in Bloomsbury—London's equivalent of Greenwich Village—that Picasso not only does not make sense, but that he is downright "indecent."

Picassoites replied with appropriate sneers and charged that Bloomsbury art lacked vitality and reflected the mental anemia of British painters who were alleged to subsist on tea and weak beer. Picasso and his disciples, they intimated, draw inspiration from souls lubricated with more vital liquids.

Smarting under this lash the league went "underground" and prepared for a great uprising. Frank Emmanuel, its founder and leader, reported today that his organization now has members in thirty English provincial towns and friends "throughout the world."

He said secrecy was necessary because "we don't want to give away our plans to our enemies—the people who are running this extreme modern art."

The time to strike a first blow for the cause was approaching, he said, and the league will shortly hold a public meeting in London.

SATURDAY, AUGUST 16, 1947

JULY 6, 1946

Paris Bares World's Smallest Bathing Suit And Consensus from Every Angle Is—Wow!

Garb Gets Full Coverage, Which Is More Than Can Be Said for the Wearer

Bare-Foot Boy Abroad

By John 'Tex' O'Reilly

Paris Bureau Chief

Well, the French have up an' done it again. This time they've turned out the world's smallest bathing suit. I was moseying around the rues yesterday when I fell in with a big crowd moving steadily into a place they called a piscine. It turned out to be a square swimmin' hole and they were holding a bathing beauty contest. There was a row of girls paradin' around in scanties and the judges were workin' overtime. Every one of 'em, I mean the girls, was as pretty as a spotted pup under a red wagon, but then, all of a sudden, a blonde named Micheline Bernardini, ambles out in what any dern fool could see was the smallest bathing suit in the world, including West Texas. Why folks, that suit was so small that . . . Which reminds me that back in the old days in West Texas there weren't any bathing suits. Just no excuse for 'em at all. There wasn't enough water on our ranch for the cows to drink, much less enough to swim in. That's why heaps of people were forced into drinkin' rye whiskey, especially in dry years.

Disrobement Race Seen

By William J. Humphreys

Political Correspondent

Developments shifted yesterday from the Quai d'Orsay to the Piscine Molitor where Micheline Bernardini proved that existentialism is here to stay. Miss Bernardini was certainly all here. It is understood from sources fairly close to the French government that international notes, couched in only the essential diplomatic terms but conveying worlds of meaning, are to be exchanged and there is considerable danger of a disrobement race among the big powers. Meanwhile, it was learned from other informed sources that the French are hastening to include the Bikini bathing suit in their five-year plan. In that event observers agree that this phase of the plan should take much less than five years.

EDITOR'S NOTE

For the first time in history, the entire staff of the European Edition and the foreign service of the New York Herald Tribune now in Paris insisted yesterday on covering the same assignment. Each was so determined to do the job that, for the sake of organizational morale, they were all assigned to the same story. It turned out to be an exhibition of the world's smallest bathing suit, modeled at the Piscine Molitor. Most of their stories are printed below, although some of them are still writing.

Big Four Ponder Zones

By Walter Kerr

Diplomatic Correspondent

The Foreign Ministers of Great Britain, France, the United States and Soviet Russia reached agreement on reparations on the eve of a new international complication, namely, the world's smallest bathing suit. This suit is divided into two zones, the northern zone and the southern zone. The northern zone is divided into two enclaves.

HeraldTribuneNewshawks Nudge Out Lucie Noel in Zeal to Write Fashions

Designated as the Bikini, the suit, when not worn, is carried in a blue box one and a half inches square. Experts appointed are studying the report that the suit may be passed through an ordinary finger ring. The suit has not been put on the agenda, but there is general agreement that it looked snappy on Micheline Bernardini.

Glimpses of Long Ago

By Vincent Bugeja

Compiler of 'Fifty Years Ago Today' in the European Edition

How well I remember that day in eighteen ninety-six when I saw a shapely calf protruding from under what I thought was a circus tent. It turned out to be a bathing suit of the period. Times have changed, judging from what I saw protruding from the Bikini model. As Einstein says, it's all a matter of relativity. I'm glad none of my relatives were around when I attended yesterday's display.

Perlman Plumps for Piscine

By David Perlman

Entertainment Editor

The joint was jumping yesterday out at the Piscine Molitor, where a poolful of lovelies from the Casino de Paris traipsed around in more clothes than they normally wear during a whole night's work.

A dish named Mickey Bernardini modeled the world's smallest bathing suit as a symphony orchestra swung "Oh, Promise Me." Miss Bernardini has lots of talent just where it ought to be. Among the other costumes were numbers called Revelation, which it certainly was; Tumulte, which caused plenty, and Refuge, which offered none at all if you were trying to hide behind it.

If this is what goes on normally at Molitor, night life in Paris does not hold a candle to afternoon life.

Experts Poo-Poo Test

By William Attwood

Atomic Energy Correspondent

The first showing of the Bikini suit here today started a chain reaction among the throng of sports-wear experts who penetrated the Molitor lagoon shortly after the explosive exhibition. Although most seemed stunned and incoherent, there were a few who maintained that the suit wasn't really so revolutionary.

"We'll find ways of making more spectacular suits than this one," a rival manufacturer of sports clothes asserted. "Just give us time."

Another protested that no one concern should have a monopoly of the manufacture of such suits. "We all have a right to know how so little material can conceal so much," he said.

Officials in charge of today's test declared they were satisfied with the results of the experiment. They added that the effect on the spectators was just as predicted, and vigorously denied rumors that the Bikini suit will render the so-called bathing beauty obsolete. "It will just mean that she will have to be better built," they pointed out.

By Lucie Noel

Fashion Editor

Wow!

TUESDAY, APRIL 8, 1947

FRIDAY, JUNE 25, 1948

Russians Cut Off Power To Berlin's West Zones

Population Fears Slow Starvation

Halt of Food, Coal Trains From the West Brings Biggest Post-War Crisis

By Marguerite Higgins

From the Herald Tribune Bureau

BERLIN, June 24.—Soviet economic warfare against the Western Allies and the German population of Berlin reached an unprecedented severity today, precipitating Europe's greatest post-war crisis.

Russian power cuts plunged much of western Berlin into darkness for hours, a continued Soviet blockade left the German population cut off from food and coal supplies and Russian orders even stopped deliveries of fresh milk, endangering the health of German babies.

And with only two to four weeks' food and coal reserves for the western sectors, the big question in the minds of the thoroughly alarmed population was whether the Russians would really carry through the threat of starvation implicit in their indefinite halt of food and coal trains from the west.

Starvation As Weapon

Actual starvation of the population of western Berlin is probably the only weapon that might bring success to the Russian drive to oust the Western Allies from Berlin, according to well-informed quarters.

The potentially explosive Berlin situation developed quickly tonight. During the evening 100 British and Russian troops, in full battle-dress, took up positions facing each other at a border point of their respective occupation sectors. The quarrel resulted from a Soviet attempt to seize the goods of a scrap merchant of the British sector whose yard is located near the Soviet sector. When German police got cold feet, British troops were sent along to give them moral support.

In all four sectors of the city German police were alerted.

Throughout the day, American armored cars patrolled the streets of the American-occupied sector. The Germans found them a reassuring sight.

'Never Become Communist'

German non-Communist political leaders, who have shown remarkable courage in face of Soviet threats of kidnaping and arrest, staged a highly successful rally in the French sector with the theme "Berlin will never become Communist."

Fifty thousand people jamming the athletic field on which the meeting was held sent an "emergency call to the world to help Berlin in its fight for independence."

This afternoon the British, in retaliation for the Soviet blockade of Berlin, cut off all coal and steel deliveries to the Soviet Zone as well as all other goods shipments. Whether the Soviets need Ruhr coal enough to lift their blockade remains at this point doubtful.

The excuse for the latest phase of the Soviet campaign against the Western Allies was the announcement that the west deutschmark would be introduced in the city. The American-sponsored currency will rival the new Russian-stamped mark in the east sector. The Russian mark is also in force in the Soviet Zone.

Russian Argument

The Russians argue that Berlin must be absorbed in their zone because the Western Allies by setting up a western German state have lost all right to remain in this four-power city.

Clay Holds Only Act of War Could Drive U.S. Out of Berlin

Says No Soviet Pressure Will Halt Projects of Allies in Western Zones

By Edwin Hartrich

From the Herald Tribune Bureau

FRANKFURT, June 24.—"Nothing short of an act of war can drive us out of Berlin," General Lucius D. Clay, American Military Governor, said here today, prior to boarding his plane to return to the crisis-ridden four-power occupation capital.

General Clay, who flew here from Heidelberg after conferring with his troop commanders, described the latest Soviet tactics in cutting off electricity and rail traffic into the beleaguered city as "the strongest pressure that has yet been applied to push us out of Berlin."

No Soviet pressure tactics nor any new eastern German government that might be created by the Russians will halt the American, British and French project to develop a western Germany, politically and economically, he added. Should the present Warsaw conference of Soviet leaders and Europe's ranking Communists announce the formation of a new German government, "this would not come as a surprise," General Clay said.

Asked if the Germans living in the American, British and French sectors would face starvation if all food shipments were cut off from Berlin, General Clay replied: "I don't see how it can benefit the Russians to attempt to hit at us through the Germans."

General Lucius D. Clay

SUNDAY, JUNE 27, 1948

West Sets Up Air Supply Line To Feed Its Sectors of Berlin; New Mark Cuts Currency 90%

Zones' Economy Down to Bedrock

By Edwin Hartrich

From the Herald Tribune Bureau

FRANKFURT, June 26.—At midnight tonight 90% of the monetary value of western Germany will be wiped out by a decree of the American, British and French Military Governors. Promulgation of a conversion law of one new west German deutschmark for ten old reichsmarks today, marks the first step in a drastic reformation of the whole economic structure of Germany, except for the Russian Zone.

Actually, the reorganization of the economic structure goes far beyond the 90 per cent devaluation. A far-reaching program has been launched, not only to outlaw the old reichsmarks but to prime the production pump by making the new money so scarce that Germans will have to work hard to earn it.

Churchill Supports Laborites In Decision to Stay in Berlin

Tells Conservative Party That Firm and Resolute Course Is Only Way to Ward Off Dangers; Assails Government's Policy in India

From the Herald Tribune Bureau

LONDON, June 26. — Winston Churchill told a Conservative party rally this evening that the Berlin crisis "raises issues as grave as those we now know were at stake at Munich ten years ago."

Addressing some 60,000 people at Luton, an industrial city north of London, the Conservative party leader said: "There can be no doubt that the Communist government of Russia has made up its mind to drive us and France and all the other Allies out and turn the Russian Zone of Germany into one of the satellite states under the rule of totalitarian terrorism. It is our hearts' desire that peace may be preserved, but we should all have learned by now that there is no safety in yielding to dictators, whether Nazi or Communist. The only hope of peace is to be strong."

Mr. Churchill said that Foreign Secretary Ernest Bevin would not have said Britain intends to stay in Berlin "without having made sure that the United States were equally resolved." There is no guaranty that "even a firm and resolute course will ward off dangers which now threaten us," he continued, but "such a course is not merely the best but the only chance of preventing a third war."

He pledged full Conservative party support to the stand of the Labor government on the Berlin situation.

At this point, however, Mr. Churchill departed from his support of the Labor government, and entertained his audience with one of his best oratorical harangues of "evils and humiliations almost as bad as those suffered by the defeated nations" which he said had befallen Great Britain since "one foolish afternoon" when the people voted him out of office.

Planes Will Defer Ebbing of Supplies

By Marguerite Higgins

From the Herald Tribune Bureau

BERLIN, June 26.—The British, with American support, demanded today that the Russians lift the blockade that threatens hunger for the German population in the western sectors of Berlin.

This first official Western Allied protest to the Soviet military administration came as plans were being completed for the inauguration on Monday of an unexpectedly extensive air supply service to bring food to Germans in Berlin.

The air supply armada that will tax the facilities of the air fields to the utmost is designed as an attempt to stem off the time when dwindling reserves run out. Although the air service will play an important role in gaining additional time, the air pipe line cannot possibly provide enough food and coal for 2,200,000 Germans in the western sectors. Without the air supply the reserves would start getting dangerously low in several weeks.

FRIDAY, SEPTEMBER 10, 1948

Tempelhof Terminal of the American Aerial Food Train to Berlin

Acme.

United States Air Force C47s discharge their vital food cargoes into trucks at Tempelhof Airfield, in the American sector of Berlin. The only access to the Western sectors of the city has been by air since the Russian blockade began 2 1/2 months ago.

FEBRUARY 23, 1949

Berlin Air Lift Sets Record, Flying 7,513 Tons in One Day

U.S., British Planes Land Every 1 1/2 Minutes For 24 Hours to Approach Volume Carried By Trains Before Blockade Started

By the Associated Press

BERLIN, Feb. 22.—American and British planes roared into Berlin at 1 1/2-minute intervals today to set an air-lift record.

In the twenty-four-hour period ended at noon, the sky freighters carried almost as much food and fuel to the city as it used to receive by train before the Russian blockade.

The new record was 7,513 tons, 526 tons better than the previous record set on Air Force Day, September 18.

Officials estimated that before the Russians clamped on the blockade eight months ago, freight trains used to haul about 9,000 tons a day for the supply of Berlin.

The new record was set on George Washington's birthday and on the eve of Red Army day.

Reports said the Russians planned to observe Red Army day with a ceremony tomorrow at their colossal war memorial in the Tiergarten.

The monument, guarded day and night by Soviet sentinels, lies a few hundred yards inside the British sector of the city. Angry Germans stoned it last summer, touching off the biggest street riots of the blockade.

German Air-Lift Staff To Get Free Cigarettes

BERLIN, Feb. 22 (A.P.).—German air-lift workers will get 30,000 black-market cigarettes tomorrow —for nothing.

The British announced that the cigarettes, collected in black-market raids, will be handed out to the workers at a ceremony at Gatow Airport.

THURSDAY, MAY 12, 1949

Blockade Ends After 327 Days; Traffic Roars Along Autobahn; Rail Lines Are Thrown Open

Sector Crossings Are Free in Berlin

Lights Go on in City as The Restrictions End; Reuter Hails Occasion

By Stephen White

From the Herald Tribune Bureau
Copyright New York Herald Tribune, Inc.

BERLIN, May 12 (Thursday).—The blockade of Berlin, ten months and twenty-three days old, died at 12:01 a.m. today, mourned by none.

At exactly that moment, the barriers across the highway leading from the American sector of Berlin to the British Zone swung up to the sky, and Western Allied vehicles set out under a bright moon for the Russian checkpoint, a mile away. There the Russians waved the cars forward, halting a few momentarily for perfunctory glances at their papers.

From Helmstedt, 102 miles away in the British Zone, came news of a similar scene, although there the Russians imposed a seven-minute delay for reasons of their own. A two-way race is now in progress along the highway, with military police patrolling the road to pick up the pieces.

Sector Crossing Unguarded

At the Brandenburg Gate, touchy border point where the Soviet's Unter den Linden meets the British sector's Charlottenburger Chaussee, the Soviet-sector police turned away from their vigil at the stroke of midnight. The crossing is now unguarded.

Rail lines have been thrown open. The first train, carrying correspondents and British military personnel, is scheduled to cross from Helmstedt at 2:13 a.m. and reach Berlin at 6:40. Trains carrying coal, potatoes, fruit and vegetables will follow several hours later, and return trips from Berlin will begin during the day.

For the residents of Berlin the blessing of light was the token of the blockade's end. Through the long winter Germans had to be satisfied with four hours of current at odd hours of each day. At 10 o'clock last night engineers began resetting connections at power stations, and at midnight current was available throughout Berlin at the flick of a switch.

The scene as cars rolled out of Berlin was a strange mixture of hilarity and anti-climax. Germans have neither gasoline nor the disposition for long night rides in broken-down cars. As a result, only nine cars showed up for the race to the zone all of them Western Allied. A horde of photographers, reporters and soldiers cheered them off.

Acheson Indicates Firm Stand by U.S.

Asserts Big-4 Success Hinges on Russians' Desire to Co-operate

By the Associated Press

WASHINGTON, May 11.—Secretary of State Dean Acheson indicated today that success of the approaching Big-Four conference on Germany will hinge on how far the Russians will co-operate with the Western powers on plans already laid out.

Mr. Acheson told a press conference that the United States intends to demand full guaranties of civil rights for the German people, and will not accept any proposals which do not provide for such guaranties.

Mr. Acheson declared that whether solutions can be found depends on whether the Russians will make, or consider, proposals that will not retard in any way the agreements already made by the Western powers for fitting Germany into the family of free European nations.

The Big-Four Foreign Ministers are scheduled to meet in Paris May 23.

Four-Truck British Convoy Is First to Clear Helmstedt

Gets Under Way in Movielight Glare as Germans, Reporters, Soldiers and Officials Watch

By Don Cook

Special to the Herald Tribune
Copyright New York Herald Tribune, Inc.

HELMSTEDT, Germany, May 12 (Thursday).—The blockade of Berlin ended at 12:08 a.m. today when a four-truck British military road convoy cleared the Russian autobahn checkpoint at this East-West border town.

Watched by a crowd of Germans, seventy-five newspaper and radio correspondents, British and American Army officers and enlisted men and Control Commission officials, the convoy got under way in the bright glare of movielight. It moved 100 yards down the autobahn from the British checkpoint to the Russian checkpoint gates, where big red stars and hammers and sickles had been brightly painted yesterday afternoon.

Russian officers examined the convoy papers, and the five trucks moved off down the broad wide autobahn for Berlin, eighty miles away, with the city's first land supplies from western Germany in eleven months.

Two hours later, at 2:13 a.m., the first train for Berlin since last June 24 was to clear the Helmstedt station. The train was a British-American eight-car press special, to be followed as quickly as schedules can be set up by ten coal trains, two trainloads of potatoes, and five other trains waiting with miscellaneous food and supplies.

The American Newspaper Edited and Published in Europe

European Edition

NEW YORK Herald Tribune

PRICE PER COPY:	
Austria......... 0.50 S.	Israel.......... 50 mils
Belgium... 2.50 B.Frs.	Italy.......... 30 Lire
Czechoslovakia 6 Kc.	Luxembourg2.50L.Frs
Denmark... 0.60 D.Kr.	Netherlands 0.25 Flor.
Egypt........... 3.50 P.	No Africa...... 20 Frs.
Eire........... 4 Pence	Norway... 0.60 N.Kr.
Finland...... 15 F.M.	Portugal...... 3.80 Esc.
France......... 15 Frs.	Spain........ 1.46 Pta.
Germany... 0.30 D.M.	Sweden .. 0.50 Sw.Kr.
Gt. Britain... 3 Pence	Switzerland 0.30 S.Fr.
Greece...... 1,500 Drs.	Syria, Lebanon 50S P.
Hungary.......... 1 F.	Turkey........ 25 T.P.
	U.S. Military. 5 Cents

62d Year—No. 20,709 ** PARIS, THURSDAY, AUGUST 25, 1949

THE NEW YORK HERALD ESTABLISHED IN EUROPE 1887

Hoffman, Bevin Talk Over Crisis

Eden Is Gloomy On Nation's Plight

Laborite Government's Policies Deplored by Ex-Foreign Minister

By Ned Russell

From the Herald Tribune Bureau
Copyright New York Herald Tribune Inc.

LONDON, Aug. 24. — Paul G. Hoffman, Economic Co-operation Administrator, discussed the dollar crisis of Britain and the sterling area today with Foreign Secretary Ernest Bevin, Harold Wilson, President of the Board of Trade, and other British officials.

Mr. Hoffman's discussions today began a three-day series of talks which are expected to embrace the whole problem of the ability of the United Kingdom and the sterling area to find a way of balancing their trade with the United States.

The talks are being conducted virtually on the eve of the Washington conference, beginning September 7, of the American, British and Canadian Foreign and Finance Ministers on the crucial question of attaining an equilibrium in trade between the United States and Canad...

Mickman Swims the Channel; In Water for Almost 24 Hours

Keystone.

Philip Mickman, eighteen-year-old British schoolboy, who swam the English Channel yesterday in the longest time on record—23 hours and 48 minutes.

British Schoolboy, 18, Was Carried 14 Miles by Cross-Tide, But Refused to Give Up

By the Associated Press

DOVER, England, Aug. 24.—Philip Mickman, eighteen-year-old British schoolboy, today became the youngest swimmer to conquer the...

Tito Denies Joining Plot On Albania

Asserts He Wants No Part of Territory

Rejects Albanian Protest On Frontier Violations, Jabs at the Cominform

By the Associated Press

BELGRADE, Aug. 24.—Yugoslavia officially denied tonight any part in a purported plot to carve up Albania under an agreement by which it would acquire part of the territory, with the balance going to Greece.

In a statement issued through the Ministry of Information, Marshal Tito's government said that it wanted no part of Albania's territory—that, to the contrary, it has protected Albania's interests in international affairs.

The statement was issued in response to a note of protest delivered by Albania to the Yugoslav Embassy in Tirana, complaining about supposed "provocations" by Yugoslav border patrols on Albania's northern boundary.

Denies Frontier Violations

The Yugoslav statement denied the charges about frontier violations, and charged that the border...

Cominform Is Securing Its Borders

Tightens Barriers In Anti-Tito Drive

West Allies Get Reports Of Fortifications From Baltic to the Near East

By Marguerite Higgins

From the Herald Tribune Bureau
Copyright New York Herald Tribune Inc

BERLIN, Aug. 24.—The Soviet orbit in Europe, from the Baltic Sea to the Near East, has in recent months intensified security measures, including the laying of mine fields in some sections of the east-west border and the transfer eastward of entire border villages, according to information reaching the Western Allies.

The latest effort to consolidate Communist power in Soviet Europe may, in the opinion of some Western observers, be linked to the Russian war of nerves launched this week against Yugoslavia. It is considered likely that the Soviet Union wanted to make its position as secure as possible before beginning the current diplomatic offensive against Marshal Tito and all the Yugoslavs who refuse to be unconditionally submissive to Moscow's line.

The most extensive effort to seal off eastern Europe from the west has been reported from Czechoslovakia. In the course of the summer a network of mine fields, elevated guard posts, barbed wire and other fortifications has been erected where this country borders on the American Zone of Germany.

No-Man's-Land Strips

In attempting to tighten security controls, the Czechs have in a number of areas established six-mile-wide strips as no-man's-land between their country and Germany, reliable reports state. To clear these strips, some entire villages had to be uprooted and transferred elsewhere. Recent refugees from Czechoslovakia have stated that the process of leaving the country has become extremely dangerous as compared with the risk earlier this year.

Hungary is also resorting to barbed-wire installations to protect its western borders with Austria. Western observers here point out that should these trends continue the metaphorical iron curtain of which Winston Churchill spoke may soon become a physical reality.

Mass transfers of so-called unreliable minorities have been re...

Atlantic Pact Is in Force As Truman Proclaims 12 Nations' Acceptance

Armed Services to Cut 147,000 From Pay Rolls Immediately

Reductions Will Include Some 12,000 Reserve Officers to Be Returned to an Inactive Status

From the Herald Tribune Bureau

WASHINGTON, Aug. 24.—Secretary of Defense Louis Johnson announced today that the armed services will chop 135,000 civilian employees from their pay rolls and return more than 12,000 reserve officers to an inactive status. The personnel reductions are effective immediately.

The Navy, already playing a diminishing role in the nation's defense plans, was hardest hit by the economy move. It was ordered to discharge 76,000 civilians now employed in installations in this country, Puerto Rico, Hawaii and Trinidad. The Army will drop 41,000 from its rolls and the Air Force 18,000.

The full effect of the defense cut is not expected to be felt until the next fiscal year beginning July 1, 1950. Mr. Johnson is reported to be aiming to hold defense spending in that year to $1,400,000,000-$1,500,000,000 less than proposed spending for the current fiscal year.

Fifty military installations throughout the country will be closed down, and many more will be cut sharply. The reductions were made by the individual services, Mr. Johnson said.

News of the personnel reduction brought members of Congress scurrying over to the Pentagon in angry droves to hear Mr. Johnson tell them how their home districts would be affected. He told them that the move is aimed at getting "a dollar's worth of defense for every dollar Congress gives." There is no plan, he said, to use military personnel to fill the civilian jobs.

Mr. Johnson said that the cut "goes back to my conviction not to tolerate a defense WPA."

Congressmen suggested that the armed forces ought to weed out "soft snaps, flunky positions and baby sitters" before making the announced reductions. Senator Claude Pepper, Democrat, of Florida, declared that he agreed there shouldn't be a "defense WPA," but added that he does not "want to see a WPA elsewhere." He told Mr. Johnson that it was more than a

(Continued on Page 2, Col. 6)

Foreign Diplomats Witness the Rite

President Says Stability And Peace Are Goals Of Defense Alliance

By the Associated Press

WASHINGTON, Aug. 24.—The twelve-nation Atlantic pact, binding North America and western Europe in a common defense alliance, came into force today.

The historic moment came at 11:42 a.m. when President Truman signed a proclamation declaring the treaty in effect.

High officials of participating nations witnessed the signing at a White House ceremony.

The President said: "This is a momentous occasion, not only for all signatories of the treaty, but for all peoples who share our profound desire for stability and peaceful development."

'Within UN Framework'

"By this treaty we are not only seeking to establish freedom from aggression and from use of force in the North Atlantic community, but we are also actively striving to promote and preserve peace throughout the world. In these endeavors we are acting within the framework of the United Nations Charter, which imposes on us all the most solemn obligations.

"These obligations which bind us to settle international disputes by peaceful means, to refrain from threat or use of force against the territory or independence of any country and to support the United Nations in any action it may take to preserve peace are all clearly stated in the North Atlantic treaty.

"Today, as this treaty comes into effect, it seems particularly appropriate to rededicate ourselves to carrying out the great task we have set for ourselves—the preservation of stability and peace.

'No Nation Need Fear'

"No nation need fear the results of our co-operation toward this end. On the contrary, the more closely the nations of the Atlantic community can work together for peace, the better for all people everywhere," Mr. Truman said.

TUC Council Approves Report Warning of Levies on Business

Tough Language Tells British Labor Only Harder Work Will Improve Standards

By Jack Tait

From the Herald Tribune Bureau
Copyright New York Herald Tribune Inc.

LONDON, Aug. 24.—Britain's trade union leadership approved today a special report which tells the nation's 8,000,000 organized workers in tough language that business is being taxed almost to the limit and that their only hope for an improved standard of living is to work harder.

FRIDAY, DECEMBER 9, 1949

Chiang's Regime Flees Chengtu and Sets Up Its Capital on Formosa

U.S., Britain, France Are Due To Recognize Mao Shortly

Paris Diplomatic Sources Say Such Action Is Possible Within a Matter of Weeks

Armies Under Hu Are Left Behind

2 Guerrilla Commands To Be Directed From The Capital of Sikang

---

The American Newspaper Edited and Published in Europe

European Edition

NEW YORK Herald Tribune

PRICE PER COPY:	
Austria........ 1 S.	Israel.......... 50 mils
Belgium... 2.50 B.Frs.	Italy.......... 30 Lire
Czechoslovakia 6 Kc.	Luxembourg2.50L.Frs.
Denmark... 0.60 D.Kr.	Netherlands 0.25 Flor.
Egypt........... 3.50 P.	No. Africa...... 20 Frs.
Finland........ 20 F.M.	Norway...... 0.60 N.Kr.
France......... 15 Frs.	Portugal...... 3.80 Esc.
Germany... 0.30 D.M.	Spain........ 1.30 Pta.
Gt. Britain... 3 Pence	Sweden... 0.50 Sw.Kr.
Greece....... 1.800 Drs.	Switzerland 0.30 S.Fr.
Hungary.......... 1 F.	Syria, Lebanon 50S P.
Ireland........ 4 Pence	Turkey........ 25 T.P.
	U.S. Military. 5 Cents

63d Year—No. 20,806 ** PARIS, SATURDAY, DECEMBER 17, 1949

THE NEW YORK HERALD ESTABLISHED IN EUROPE 1887

U.S. Offers Bank Plan For Europe

Would Establish A Clearing House

U.S. Is Reported to Feel Scheme Is Important As Integration Move

By Kenyon Kilbon

The United States is presenting the western European countries with a plan for establishment by April 1 of a European central bank, it was learned yesterday.

So far, the scheme is described by observers only as a working draft offered to the Europeans for discussion but it is known that considerable importance is attached to it by the Americans as a means for carrying out the "integration" asked last month by Economic Co-operation Administrator Paul G. Hoffman.

The plan was presented in detail to the Europeans at a meeting in Paris last Saturday of ECA officials and heads of member delegations to the Organization for European Economic Co-operation. Richard Bissell, assistant deputy director of ECA, is understood to have outlined the scheme. It is reported also that the details are being further presented in each country now by ECA mission chiefs.

Sort of Clearing-House

The effect of such a plan—a sort of clearing-house system—would be to push Europe much farther along the path of free trade and currency convertibility than anything now planned by the Europeans themselves, including such projects as the five-nation regional grouping of France, Italy and Benelux. It also would do away with the current use of drawing rights—credits granted bilaterally by European creditor nations to their debtors partly on the basis of dollars allotted to the creditors by the United States.

An added important feature is liberalization of trade, which has been wound into the plan on a large scale. Reportedly, one condition of membership in the pool is virtually complete elimination of import quota restrictions. The

Up in Central Park

I.N.P.

Mayor William O'Dwyer of New York and his bride-to-be, Miss Sloan Simpson, out for a stroll.

'Dry Friday' In N.Y. Seems To Be Success

No Shaving, No Bathing Edict Expected to Save

Wedding Rites For O'Dwyer in Florida Dec. 20

New York Mayor Will Marry Ex-Model; Went

Debate Set On Budget In France

Radical-Socialists Yield to Bidault

Assembly to Get Project Monday; 20-Billion Fr. Hole Must Be Filled

By William J. Humphreys

The Radical-Socialists, who had defied Premier Georges Bidault in a touch-and-go battle on the 1950 budget, yielded last night to the Premier's demand for an urgent consideration of the 2,275-billion-franc government expense sheet.

As a result of a 24-to-16 vote by the Finance Committee, the National Assembly is scheduled to start debating the record budget Monday morning. In the mean time, the committee and the Bidault Cabinet will endeavor to find means of filling a 20-billion-franc budget hole.

This was created when the Radical-Socialists, who are committed against any new taxation, refused to approve levies on industry. Former Premiers Edouard Herriot and Henri Queuille, both Radicals, then persuaded the party they would, as good republicans, have to approve .. budget.

Clear Way For Debate

Under this pressure, the Finance Committee approved the cost sheet, clearing the way for the Assembly debate. While it was in the form amended previously by the committee, its approval by the committee at least gave M. Bidault the chance to put th dispute to the Assembly as a whole.

The Socialists on the committee split forces on the vote. Among the sixteen opposition ballots, the Left-wingers found themselves keeping company with the Gaullists on the committee. There also were four abstentions, including former Premier Paul Reynaud.

In their private meeting before the committee vote, the Radical-Socialists heard Finance Minister Maurice Petche, a reception they arranged by a majority of one when the question was raised. M. Petsche reminded the Radicals that

Will Leave State Dept.

Dr. Philip C. Jessup.

Jessup to Quit State Dept. Post Early in Spring

To Start Tour of Far East As Last Mission, Will Return to Law Teaching

By Homer Bigart

From the Herald Tribune Bureau

WASHINGTON, Dec. 16.—Ambassador-at-large Philip C. Jessup, the State Department's chief trouble shooter, will resign soon after his return from a special mission to the Far East in early March, it was learned last night, in order to resume his post as professor of international law at Columbia University.

Dr. Jessup's decision, coming less than a week after the disclosure that George F. Kennan, chief policy planner of the State Department, will resign in June, means that Secretary of State Dean Acheson will lose two of his three most influential lieutenants, the third

Kostov Dies After Plea Is Rejected

Goes to Gallows In Treason Case

Presidium of Assembly Decides Not to Grant Appeal for Clemency

By the United Press

FRANKFURT, Dec. 16.—Traicho Kostov, condemned to death for treason and espionage by the Bulgarian Supreme Court Wednesday, was hanged today after his request for clemency was rejected by the Presidium of the National Assembly, the official Bulgarian agency reported as monitored here.

Text of the agency's communiqué was as follows:

"The Presidium of the National Assembly at its session of Dec. 15, 1949, considered the request for clemency of Traicho Kostov, who was condemned to death by the Supreme Court of Bulgaria for treason, espionage and sabotage, and found no reasons to attenuate the sentence pronounced against the traitor. Traicho Kostov was executed today, Friday, Dec. 16, 1949."

'Absolutely Just'

The agency also broadcast a quotation from Mr. Kostov's appeal for clemency, in which it said Mr. Kostov had stated that he "considered the verdict of the Supreme Court as absolutely just, consonant with the interests of a normal and tranquil evolution of Bulgaria, and (necessary) in its struggle against the Anglo-American imperialists and against the intrigues of their agents—Tito and his clique of traitors."

The broadcast said that Mr. Kostov had expressed "sincere sorrow" for his attitude in court, blaming it on "nervous irritation" and "the unhealthy ambition of an intellectual."

He was quoted as pledging that if the appeal were granted he would devote the rest of his life "to the expiation of his errors and in the service, ever more devoted, of his socialist country."

He was quoted as saying that he recognized that he had been guilty of the charges "and therefore I con-

Mao in Moscow, Praises 'Years' Of Soviet Help

Mao Tse-tung.

Received by Stalin Soon After Arrival

Leader of Chinese Reds Says Task Now Is to Bolster 'Peace' Front

By the Associated Press

LONDON, Dec. 16.—Mao Tse-tung, leader of the Chinese Communists, arrived in Moscow today and was almost immediately received by Premier Josef V. Stalin. A brief Moscow broadcast heard in London tonight gave no details of the meeting but said that Vyacheslav M. Molotov, Georgi Malenkov, Marshal Nikolai Bulganin and Foreign Minister Andrei Y. Vishinsky were present.

An earlier radio report said he was full of praise for Sino-Soviet friendship, and spoke warmly of Russian "aid to the cause of Chinese liberation."

It was believed to be Mao's first trip to Russia.

The chairman of the newly-formed Communist People's Republic, reached Moscow by train over the Trans-Siberian Railway.

He was met at the railway station by a group of Soviet leaders, including Mr. Molotov, Deputy Foreign Minister Andrei A. Gromyko and Marshal Bulganin, the Moscow radio said.

Speech at Station

A guard of honor lined up to welcome him at the Yaroslavl station, which was decorated with flags of the new Chinese Communist government.

In a speech at the station Mao declared: "For many years the Soviet people and the Soviet government have repeatedly given aid to the cause of the liberation of the Chinese people.

"These acts of friendship on the part of the Soviet people and the Soviet government which the Chinese people received during the days

Chinese Reds Reach Border Of Indo-China

Raise Red Flag at Village; Sikang Governor Said To Desert Nationalists

By the United Press

HONGKONG, Dec. 16.—Chinese Communist troops have reached the Indo-China border, the Peking radio announced today.

The radio said the five-star Communist flag was raised at a border village, fifty miles north of Langson, where the Kunming-Haiphong

1950–1959

Throughout the 1950s, the *Herald Tribune*'s owners were conscious of the potential for a European-based, American-edited newpaper that addressed objectively the political and economic questions of the postwar world. A series of senior business managers—Buel Weare; Ogden Reid, Jr.; Sylvan Barnet; Willet Weeks and Philip Weld—worked to develop a newspaper responsive to the needs of the new Europe. Economics and finance, advances in technology, and international political news filled the paper's columns. Americans still dominated the readership, but they were no longer confined to the cozy, semi-permanent American community of Paris. A new generation of Americans—scattered all across Western Europe—became the mainstay of the *Trib*'s audience, including corporate managers, government officials, students, travelers and military personnel.

During the first half of the decade, a special edition was published for US military servicemen stationed in Europe. This was dropped in 1955, but, after much debate, one of its elements was retained in the regular paper: the comics page. The decision to keep the page evoked memories of James Gordon Bennett, who brought American comic strips to the Paris paper as early as 1902, introducing to Europe one of the most distinctive of American popular art forms.

The 1950s also saw the arrival of the Golden Girls, a corps of newsvendors created by circulation director Paul Gendelman to hawk the paper in cafés along the Champs-Elysées and other areas of central Paris, dressed in bright yellow sweaters bearing the paper's insignia. These young women were to become internationally famous a few years later when American actress Jean Seberg played the part of a Golden Girl in Jean-Luc Godard's prize-winning film, *Breathless.*

Throughout the decade, the cold war dominated the paper's news pages. Readers became familiar with the names and faces of the Rosenbergs, Burgess and Maclean, and Senator Joe McCarthy. War in Korea and revolution in Hungary saw the same basic conflicts at work. Meanwhile, two events of the 1950s profoundly changed the United States: the 1954 Supreme Court school desegregation decision and the 1957 launching of the Soviet Sputnik. Both events triggered developments that have fundamentally transformed the way Americans live—and the way other people view them.

It was not, of course, all serious news, and the European Edition found space for the romance of the period as well. The coronation of the young Elizabeth II and the conquest of Everest by some of her subjects made headlines on the same day. And when a Hollywood movie star married a reigning European prince, the story played on the front pages for weeks.

The paper also continued to carry a variety of lively feature material drawing from American columnists as well as the European Edition's own commentators. By the end of the 1950s, Art Buchwald was being syndicated from Paris to 150 US papers.

In 1958, the Reids, whose family had controlled the *New York Tribune* since the early 1870s and the combined *Herald* and *Tribune* since 1924, sold the financially troubled *New York Herald Tribune* and its European Edition to John Hay Whitney. Heir to one of the great American fortunes, Whitney was at the time American ambassador to Great Britain. Well known as a philanthropist, he had for a long time been a leading figure in the arts, politics, education, the theater, motion pictures and horse racing. He bought the *Herald Tribune*, he said, in an effort to save it, and he poured himself and his fortune enthusiastically into that endeavor. A strong internationalist, he was fascinated by the potential of the European Edition as it expanded to serve a widening audience.

By the end of the decade, the paper was being distributed to readers in seventy-one countries, using every means that technology and imagination allowed.

Jean Seberg as the *Herald Tribune* "Golden Girl" newsvendor in the Godard film *Breathless.*

The American Newspaper Edited and Published in Europe

European Edition

NEW YORK Herald Tribune

PRICE PER COPY:	
Austria......... 1.25 S.	Italy........... 50 Lire
Belgium...... 3 B.Frs.	Luxembourg. 3 L.Frs.
Denmark... 0.60	Netherlands 0.25 Flor.
Egypt............... 5 P.	No. Africa... 25 Frs.
Finland....... 30 F.M.	Norway.. 0.60 N.Kr.
France......... 20 Frs.	Portugal.... 3.80 Esc.
Germany... 0.40 D.M.	Spain........ 1.40 Pta.
Gt. Britain. 4 Pence	Sweden.. 0.50 Sw.Kr.
Greece...... 1,800 Drs.	Switzerland 0.30 S.Fr.
Ireland....... 4 Pence	Syria.Lebanon 50 S.P.
Israel........ 50 Prut.	Turkey........ 25 T.P.
	U.S. Military. 5 Cents

63d Year—No. 20,968 ** PARIS, MONDAY, JUNE 26, 1950

THE NEW YORK HERALD ESTABLISHED IN EUROPE 1887

North Koreans Invade South Korea

Bidault Ousted In 352-230 Vote

Korean Conflict May Rally Parties

Socialist Says Situation In Far East Is More Serious Than Crisis

By William J. Humphreys

The French National Assembly, voting 352 to 230 against the government on a question of confidence, forced Premier Georges Bidault to resign Saturday.

There were no precise indications on how long the political crisis might last, but it was thought that the developments in Korea might influence the "Third Force" coalition of Radical-Socialists, Socialists and M. Bidault's Popular Republicans to patch up their quarrels.

President Vincent Auriol, who had started talks with party leaders immediately after receiving M. Bidault's resignation, continued his interviews last night. The President's constitutional duty was to find a Premier-designate with a program that could win the Assembly's confidence.

'Much More Serious'

A suggestion that the Korean incident might speed up these negotiations came from Jules Moch, former Socialist Minister of the Interior. He told newspaper men that the situation in Korea is "much more serious that our ministerial crisis."

Marcel Plaisant, a Radical-Socialist member of the Council of the Republic, was one of those leaders called to consult the President of the Republic. Afterward, he an-

Monnet Says Talks on Pool Will Continue

Nine-Day Suspension for Consultations Is Not Linked to Crisis

By Russell Hill

Jean Monnet, the chief French delegate at the six-power conference on establishment of a coal-steel pool, announced on Saturday that the negotiations would continue regardless of the French government crisis.

There will, however, be a nine-day suspension while the delegates of Germany, Italy, the Netherlands, Belgium and Luxembourg return to their capitals for consultations. This interruption is not the result of the fall of Premier Georges Bidault's government. An adjournment had already been planned because the talks have reached the stage where governmental decisions on major policy questions are necessary.

M. Bidault said Saturday morning in asking for the vote of confidence that even if it went against him—which it did—the negotiations would continue. He added, however: "Serious harm could be caused by a governmental gap."

He was apparently referring to the psychological effect on other countries of the fall of the French government at a time when it was taking the initiative in pressing so

58 Feared Lost in U.S. DC4 Crash

Airliner Is Sought In Lake Michigan

Radar-Equipped Coast Guard Vessels Search Fog-Shrouded Waters

By the Associated Press

MILWAUKEE, Wis., June 25.—Radar-equipped Coast Guard cutters searched fog-bound Lake Michigan today for a Northwest Airlines DC4 plane missing with fifty-eight persons on board.

The greatest loss of life in United States airline history was feared.

Fog immobilized search planes and most surface craft as the cutters began a systematic search of the eighty-seven-mile-wide lake with radar.

Traveling in parallel lines four miles apart, they swept the lake surface with radar beams on a path between Milwaukee, on the Wisconsin side, and Grandhaven, Mich.

It was feared that the plane plunged into the lake in a thunderstorm at midnight Friday.

Captain Leo Brissette, of a lake ore ship, told the Associated Press by radio that he had sighted a piece of wreckage "about thirty feet long" which might be part of the missing plane.

He said the wreckage, which resembled a piece of a wing, was lost to sight in the fog and he was unable to find it again.

"We saw other debris near the large object—paper cups and plates—and I saw a woman's glove," Captain Brissette said.

4 Die in British Crash

Red Troops Are 20 Miles From Seoul; Security Council Orders a Cease-Fire

Council Tells North To Retire to Border

Russia Boycotts Meeting; U.S. Denounces Attack As Illegal, Unprovoked

By the Associated Press

LAKE SUCCESS, N. Y., June 25—The United Nations Security Council tonight ordered a cease-fire in Korea.

It also demanded the return to their own territory of North Korean forces which invaded the South Korean republic.

Russia ignored the Council's special session on the Korean crisis, and is expected to hold that the order is illegal because Nationalist China participated in the Council action.

The United States sponsored a resolution demanding the end of fighting.

The vote was 9-0, with Yugoslavia abstaining.

As the Council acted in an extraordinary Sunday session, delegates pored anxiously over Washington dispatches saying the United States is sending military supplies to South Korea and that the South Koreans said they had found Russian crewmen in ten captured tanks from the North.

Core of Resolution

The Council resolution held that the invasion constitutes a breach of the peace.

Here is the core of the Council's action:

1—It called for the cessation of hostilities at once.

U.S. to Rush Arms To Aid Defenders

Diplomatic and Military Leaders Take Decision At State Dept. Meeting

By the Associated Press

WASHINGTON, June 25.—The United States intervened swiftly in the Communist invasion of South Korea today with emergency arms aid and diplomatic moves that brought President Truman speeding back to the capital from a week-end visit to Missouri.

Correspondents learned that the United States had decided to send embattled South Koreans as much arms aid as it can as fast as it can.

The decision emerged from a top level diplomatic-military meeting at the State Department.

Some military supplies were understood to be already on their way from Japan.

To Request UN Action

Another decision was to ask the United Nations Security Council—convened in an emergency session—to order a cease-fire in Korea and demand that North Korea withdraw from conquered territory.

General Omar N. Bradley, chairman of the Joint Chiefs of Staff, who has just returned from a Pacific tour, was reported to be closeted with others of the high command.

Further discussion of the Korean situation by the Joint Chiefs has been fixed for tomorrow.

General J. Lawton Collins, Army Chief of Staff, has arranged to

Truman Returns to Capital; 'Concerned But Not Alarmed'

Changes Mind on Not Letting Korea Interfere With Week End After Acheson Phones

By Carl Levin

Special to the Herald Tribune

KANSAS CITY, Mo., June 25.—President Truman, "concerned but not alarmed" at the Communist invasion of South Korea, hurriedly cut short his week end at his Independence home this afternoon to rush back to Washington.

Eben A. Ayers, assistant press secretary, announcing the sudden change of plans, said: "The President has three or four important decisions to make and he feels that he should go back to Washington right away."

Only thirty minutes earlier, at an impromptu press conference at the gate of the Truman home in Independence, Mr. Ayers had told reporters that the President had no plans to curtail his week end because of the Communist attack on the anti-Communist American-supported South Korean Republic.

The picture changed abruptly, however, when the President received a mid-day telephone call from Secretary of State Dean Acheson. It was after this call that Mr. Ayers hurried back to press headquarters in the Muehlbach Hotel here to sound the alarm for immediate departure for Washington.

Mr. Truman, who arrived yesterday afternoon to spend what he hoped would be a quiet week end with his family, arriving back in Washington about 4 p.m. Monday, received his first word of the Korean emergency in a telephone call last night from Mr. Acheson.

After last night's call, Mr. Truman also received a copy of the official cable from Korea notifying the State Department Northern

(Continued on Page 3, Col. 2)

British Foreign Office Shows Grave Concern on Korea War

Attack Is Considered Russian-Inspired; Main Fear Is That Conflict May Herald World War

50,000 Northerners In Attack at Dawn

U.S. Military Group of 500 Men Reporting on Fighting in the South

By the Associated Press

SEOUL, June 26 (Monday).—More than 50,000 North Korean Communist troops invaded the American-sponsored Republic of South Korea at dawn yesterday and by this morning had thrust to within twenty miles of the capital.

Latest reports said that at another point the Southern defenders seized a town five miles north of the border.

[Korean Ambassador to the United States John Chang told the United Nations Security Council Sunday that Ongjin Peninsula, about 100 miles northwest of Seoul, was being evacuated, the United Press said from Lake Success, N.Y.

[The Soviet-licensed news agency ADN late Sunday night distributed in Berlin a communique from the North Korean government which said the fighting started this morning with the invasion of North Korea by South Korean troops, the Associated Press reported.

[The communique, from the North Korean capital of Pyongyang, picked up by ADN from the Communist New China News Agency, asserted that South Korean troops had invaded the North Korean Republic at three border points

The American Newspaper Edited and Published in Europe

European Edition

NEW YORK Herald Tribune

PRICE PER COPY:	
Austria......... 1.25 S.	Italy........... 50 Lire
Belgium...... 3 B.Frs.	Luxembourg. 3 L.Frs.
Denmark... 0.60	Netherlands 0.25 Flor.
Egypt............... 5 P.	No. Africa... 25 Frs.
Finland....... 30 F.M.	Norway.. 0.60 N.Kr.
France......... 20 Frs.	Portugal.... 3.80 Esc.
Germany... 0.40 D.M.	Spain........ 1.40 Pta.
Gt. Britain. 4 Pence	Sweden.. 0.50 Sw.Kr.
Greece...... 1,800 Drs.	Switzerland 0.30 S.Fr.
Ireland....... 4 Pence	Syria.Lebanon 50 S.P.
Israel........ 50 Prut.	Turkey........ 25 T.P.
	U.S. Military. 5 Cents

63d Year—No. 20,970 ** PARIS, WEDNESDAY, JUNE 28, 1950

THE NEW YORK HERALD ESTABLISHED IN EUROPE 1887

Truman Orders Planes, Navy to Act In Korea, Fleet to Guard Formosa

Cabinet Try Abandoned By Queuille

Pleven Declines Auriol's Invitation to Attempt to Form a Government

By Russell Hill

Developments in the Korean crisis acted yesterday as a spur on France's political parties, which may be brought to patch up their differences over internal policy and agree on formation of a government of "public safety" embracing all groups but the Communists on the extreme Left and the Gaullists on the Right.

Assembly Deputies, with the exception of the Communists, were enthusiastic about President Truman's decision to throw American air and naval forces into the Korean battle and to step up aid to French forces fighting Communist-led irregulars in Indo-China.

The Foreign Ministry indorsed the President's announcement in cautious terms, making it clear that France approves the American decision to act on the basis of Sunday's resolution of the United Nations Security Council rather than waiting for yesterday's meeting of the Council.

The caution noticeable at the Foreign Ministry was reflected in comment from "informed sources" who said: "The intervention of the United States should be limited to pushing the Communist forces back to the 38th Parallel." This is the boundary between North and South Korea.

This seemed to indicate a fear that the conflict might spread, but many Assembly Deputies and other Frenchmen expressed the opinion that the risk was justified, since aggression must be stopped.

Queuille Gives Up

The news of Mr. Truman's announcement came after Henri Queuille, Radical-Socialist leader, had told President of the Republic Vincent Auriol that he could not take on the task of forming a

A Calculated Risk for Peace

By his bold and prompt action in ordering the United States air and sea forces "to give cover and support to the Republic of Korea forces," President Truman has taken aggressive action to preserve this world's uneasy peace. The move made by the American government carries heavy risks, including the risk of a new world war. This risk, however, was first taken by the North Korean Communists last Sunday when they launched their attack on the Republic of Korea.

Backed and guided by Moscow, the North Koreans, and the men in the Kremlin who gave the orders, decided to risk the igniting of a world war by defying the United Nations and opening Korea's civil war. To have remained silent, or, indeed, to have been merely vocal while withholding effective aid, would, once more, have indicated to the world that the democracies are impotent to act, that ruthless brute force, cannily used, can nibble away safely at the free territories of the world.

The risk of war in the action taken by the American government yesterday may perhaps be compared to the risk that the British and French would have run had they stood together in 1936 in opposition to Adolf Hitler's occupation of the Rhineland. We believe the greater risk was incurred in letting Hitler successfully carry off his occupation of the Rhineland.

The Western world does not want war. We are reluctant to believe that the Russians want war, at least today. Under the existing circumstances, the action taken by President Truman seems to us definitely a move aimed in the long run to preserve the peace. In calling upon the Chinese Nationalist government in Formosa to cease all sea and air operations against the mainland held by the Chinese Communists, the President indicates the eagerness of the American government to work out a formula for an orderly and peaceful settlement of the problems of the Far East. But, coupled with the support for the Korean Republic, the President's ordering of the 7th Fleet to prevent any attack on Formosa and the expedition of military assistance to the Philippines and Indo-China indicate equally that the American government, at last, has drawn a line against continued Communist expansion in the Far East. This should be heartening and electrifying news to free nations around the world and sobering news to Moscow.

An editorial from today's New York edition appears on Page 4

Attlee Backs U.S., Declares Attack Is 'Naked Aggression'

Warships, Planes Go Into Action

Munitions and Supplies Are 'Air, Water-Lifted'; H.Q. in Korea Forming

By the Associated Press

TOKYO, June 28 (Wednesday).—American bombers and fighter planes went into action today against the Communist invaders of South Korea, General Douglas MacArthur announced.

In a communique, General MacArthur said also that the United States Navy was taking part in combat missions off the coast of Korea and that "ammunition and supplies are being air and water-lifted to aid the South Korean forces."

The general said that a small advance echelon of American general headquarters "has been established in Korea."

[The British-sponsored Northwest German radio Tuesday night broadcast a Tass dispatch from Pyongyang claiming the "complete defeat of the South Korean forces."

[The radio quoted the Tass dispatch as saying that the South Korean government offered "unconditional surrender" to the advancing North Korean troops.]

The communiqué, which followed by only a few hours President Truman's orders to stem the Communist aggressors, gave no particulars on how many planes and naval vessels were participating in the mission. It confirmed Seoul radio broadcasts, however, that American planes were already attacking the North Korean tanks.

Invaders May Have Retreated

American intervention came after South Korean troops apparently had repelled yesterday's Communist thrust toward Seoul. Latest reports of the confused fighting below the 38th Parallel indicated last night that the North Korean troops, after approaching within nine miles of Seoul, the South Korean capital, had withdrawn northward. Some reports said they had gone back twenty miles and that the key point of Uijongbu had been recaptured by the Southerners.

Assessment of the situation by

Text of Truman Statement

Special to the Herald Tribune

WASHINGTON, June 27.—Following is the text of the announcement today by President Truman on the Korean situation:

North Korean forces have invaded the Republic of Korea and captured the capital. [Editor's note—Latest dispatches from Tokyo indicate that Seoul is still in South Korean hands.] The United Nations Security Council has called upon the invading troops to cease hostilities and withdraw to the 38th Parallel. This has not been done but, on the contrary, the invasion has been pressed forward. The Security Council has called upon all United Nations members to render every assistance in the execution of this resolution. In the circumstances, the President has ordered United States air and sea forces to give cover and support to the Republic of Korea forces.

The attack makes it amply clear that Communism has passed beyond subversion in seeking to conquer independent nations and is now resorting to armed aggression and war. It has defied the United Nations Security Council. In the circumstances, the Communist occupation of Formosa would directly threaten the security of the Pacific area and United States forces performing necessary and legitimate functions in that area.

The President has accordingly ordered the 7th Fleet, which is taking up the necessary positions, to prevent any attack on Formosa. He is also calling upon the Chinese government in Formosa to cease all sea and air operations against the mainland. The fleet will see that this is done. The future status of Formosa must await determination in connection with the restoration of Pacific security, a peace settlement with Japan, or possible UN consideration.

The President has also directed that military assistance to the Philippines be expedited and United States forces there strengthened.

The President has similarly directed that military assistance to the French and associated states' forces in Indo-China be expedited and that a United States military mission be sent to provide close working relations with those forces.

Since the return to the rule of force would have far-reaching effects, all UN members must carefully consider consequences of the latest aggression. The United States representative on the Security Council is accordingly advising it of these steps.

Security Council Considering U.S. Plea to Aid South Korea

U.S. Sends Plea To the Kremlin

Soviets Are Asked to Use Influence to Secure Withdrawal of North

By the United Press

WASHINGTON, June 27.—The State Department announced today that the United States has asked Russia to use its influence "with the North Korean authorities for the withdrawal of the invading forces and the cessation of hostilities."

The department said the American request was handed to the Soviet Foreign Office by the American Embassy but the text of the note was not disclosed here.

It was understood, however, to have informed the Russians of the measures the United States is taking to restore peace in Korea.

Issues Statement

A State Department statement said that "in reply to inquiries from the press the State Department confirms that the American Embassy at Moscow today communicated with the Soviet Foreign Office in regard to the invasion of the Republic of Korea by the North Korean armed forces.

"The embassy asked that the Soviet government use its influence with the North Korean authorities for the withdrawal of the invading forces and a cessation of hostilities."

It was learned the United States listed each action it is taking to stamp out the invasion.

Officials said the note in this respect followed the text of President Truman's statement released by the White House earlier today.

French and Viet Namese Clear Out Rebel Bases

SAIGON, June 27 (U.P.).—French and Viet Nam infantry forces, supported by artillery and fighter planes, have wiped out all Viet Minh installations in an important rebel zone southwest of Saigon, military headquarters announced

President Says U.S. Will Step Up Military Aid To Manila and Saigon

By the Associated Press

WASHINGTON, June 27.—President Truman today ordered United States planes and warships to the aid of South Korean forces.

The President directed that the United States 7th Fleet be prepared to intervene to prevent any Communist attack on the Island of Formosa, refuge of the Chinese Nationalist government.

He then asked Generalissimo Chiang Kai-shek to cease his attacks on the Chinese mainland as a contribution toward pacification of the whole area.

Mr. Truman also announced that he was stepping up military aid to the Philippines and Indo-China.

In laying down a policy of standing firm against Communist aggression in the Far Pacific, Mr. Truman said:

"The attack upon Korea makes it plain beyond all doubt that Communism has passed beyond the use of subversion to conquer independent nations and will now use armed invasion and war."

President Truman's historic decisions were reached at a high policy meeting at the White House last night, it was learned.

No Mobilization Ordered

Before announcing the decisions in a statement today, the President called both Democratic and Republican Congressional leaders to the White House to review the decisions and explain the background.

A statement of policy was handed to reporters by Presidential secretary Charles Ross while Mr. Truman was still conferring with Congressional, diplomatic, military and defense leaders.

Secretary of Defense Louis Johnson said the United States moves in the Pacific situation do not commit America to sending any land troops into action "at the moment."

As Mr. Johnson left the White

The Weather

Paris: Today's forecast: hot, fine early, becoming sultry, cloudy later. Yesterday: warm, sunny. Max. 75 (24 Cent.); min. 54 (12 Cent.).

London: Today: warm, cloudy early, fine later. Yesterday: cool, cloudy. Max. 57 (14 Cent.); min. 50 (10 Cent.).

Channel crossings: Slight.

New York: Today: warm, fair. Yesterday: warm, fair. Max. 73 (23 Cent.).

NEW YORK Herald Tribune

European Edition Published Daily in Paris

Established in Europe 1887 ** PARIS, FRIDAY, JUNE 8, 1951 Established in New York 1841

Two British Diplomats Missing Since May 25; French Police Join Hunt

Statement Is Issued At Foreign Office

One of Missing Men Was U.S. Section Head, 2d From Embassy in U.S.

By the Associated Press

LONDON, June 7.—The Foreign Office announced today that two British Foreign Office officials have been missing from their homes since May 25.

A Foreign Office spokesman said the two are Donald D. MacLean, 38, head of the American department of the Foreign Office, and Guy Francis de Moncy Burgess, 40, who returned to London on leave last month from his post as second secretary of the British Embassy in Washington.

The Foreign Office issued this statement:

"Two members of the Foreign Service have been missing from their homes since May 25. One is Mr. D. D. MacLean, the other Mr. G. F. de M. Burgess. All possible inquiries are being made. It is known that they went to France a few days ago.

"Mr. MacLean had a breakdown a year ago owing to overstrain but was believed to have fully recovered.

"Owing to their being absent without leave, both have been suspended with effect from the first of June."

Search Started

The spokesman declined to speculate on the whereabouts of the two officials, but a search by police and intelligence operatives has been started both here and in France.

The Foreign Office reported tonight that the two men have cabled their families from Paris within the last 24 hours. A spokesman added that officials are trying to confirm that the messages are genuine and not hoaxes.

"There is no reason to believe that they have taken any official papers with them," the spokesman said.

As head of the American department, Mr. MacLean would have a thorough knowledge of Anglo-American diplomatic secrets, it was believed. Mr. Burgess, having served in the British Embassy in Washington, would also have similar knowledge.

The London "Daily Herald" said MI5—Britain's secret military counter-espionage—has been called into the case.

The "Express" said all French airports and frontiers were being watched, that plain-clothes detectives were searching various Paris districts and that a check was being kept on visitors to the Soviet Embassy in London.

Other reports said the Foreign Office has alerted all British diplomatic missions in Europe, has requested friendly governments, including France, to help in the search and has alerted all Britain's secret service agents.

[In Paris, the French Ministry of the Interior said Thursday that French security police have been looking for the diplomats for the last week but have "nothing to report."

[In Bonn, Germany, a British spokesman said the search has spread throughout Western Europe. He said Western Germany was "one of several places" in which the two men are being sought.]

Mr. MacLean is the son of the late Sir Donald MacLean, a leader of Britain's Liberal party. He entered the Foreign Service in October, 1935.

He had served at diplomatic posts

(Continued on Page 2, Col. 5)

Reds Move Reserves Southward

Bolster Triangle In Central Korea

UN Units Continue Drive Within Sight of Foe's Principal Defense Lines

By the United Press

TOKYO, June 8 (Friday).—Communist reinforcements were reported moving south from Manchuria yesterday to help defend the Reds' central-front assembly area as allied troops fought to within sight of the sprawling triangular defense lines.

Four tank-led United Nations columns advanced nearer the enemy defense position, which is a triangular plateau used last month as a staging area for the Communist offensive.

The Reds counter-attacked with their biggest artillery barrages of the war in an effort to halt the relentless allied push north of the 38th Parallel.

United Nations pilots reported a "swelling tide" of Communist troop movements and convoys heading toward the area from Manchuria. The Reds were moving down both Korean coasts and funneling into the town of Pyonggang at the northern apex of the triangle.

Gain 3,000 Yards

The allies yesterday routed units of Chinese holding hill positions south and southwest of Kumhwa, southeastern anchor of the triangle, and scored gains of 3,000 yards.

UN tanks, pushing up narrow valleys, led the advance, and there seemed to be few strong ridge positions remaining to the Chinese rear guards south of Kumhwa.

On the western front, a tank and infantry task force advanced 5,000 yards ahead of the front lines below Ch... Comm... back.

On t... Korean reservo... with w... ery to... Morta... ions ... orces f... ridge...

McMahon Urges Inquiry Into Chiang's U.S. Lobby

Tells Senate Inquiry Chinese Nationalist 'Gang of Crooks Cashed In' on American Aid

By James E. Warner

From the Herald Tribune Bureau
Copyright New York Herald Tribune, Inc.

WASHINGTON, June 7.—Sen. Brien McMahon, D., Conn., today called for an investigation to determine whether Chinese Nationalists used funds provided by the United States to influence American public opinion for their cause.

He told the combined Senate Armed Services and Foreign Relations Committees that Chinese Nationalist "crooks" had "cashed in" on American aid to their cause. If any of this money "has come back into the United States to influence public opinion, this should be made known to the American taxpayers who were robbed in the first instance by this corrupt gang of crooks," he declared.

Later, in his sixth day on the witness stand—to which he returns tomorrow morning—Secretary of State Dean Acheson declared that if the so-called Nationalist China lobby has been spending money improperly to influence United States policy, the people "are entitled to know about it," but that his department is not the proper agency to investigate.

The Secretary promised to provide the group with what information the State Department has on the subject. He said he does not know its nature because he has had no time to study the material.

He declined to express any view on the truth or falsity of newspaper reports read to him by Sen. Wayne Morse, R., Ore., alleging that hundreds of millions of dollars have been spent in an attempt to influence American public opinion and Congress by the China lobby because he did not have the facts, and added:

'I should be particularly careful not to make any charges against people who could immediately respond that I was doing this because they were criticizing me. Criticism is something I have to bear as an occupation hazard and I am quite willing to bear it . . ."

President Truman, at his news conference this afternoon, declared Secretary Acheson has done an excellent job before the Senate committee and repeated that he does not intend to let Mr. Acheson leave the Cabinet. Mr. Truman said that Mr. Acheson has told the truth that has to be told, something that is seldom done these days, particularly by the opposition, according to the President.

On the House side, Rep. Clair Engle, D., Calif., issued a statement proposing a special House commit-

(Continued on Page 3, Col. 6)

Persians Bar Press From Oil Areas, Abadan

Grady Calls Reports of Soviet Reinforcements 'Part of War of Nerves'

51 Die, 47 Hurt In Train Fire at Rio de Janeiro

Suburban Train Crashes Into Gasoline Truck; Victims Locked in Cars

U.S. Hangs 7 Nazis at Landsberg

Group Is Executed For Mass Murders

War Criminals Are Last To Die in U.S. Zone; Total Numbered 275

By the Associated Press

LANDSBERG, Germany, June 7.—Seven Nazi stalwarts in Adolf Hitler's pattern of conquest died on an American gallows here early today for the mass murder of millions.

They dropped through the trap in the basement of bleak Landsberg Prison, where their Fuehrer had written "Mein Kampf."

Each used 90 seconds for a last speech on the scaffold. A source inside the closely guarded prison disclosed the substance of their last words was: "Beware of the people who say they are friends of Germany."

The doomed men referred thus to the United States, the source added.

Expected Reprieve

None of the seven faltered when called to begin the march to the gallows. All of them, believing they would win another reprieve, reportedly had dropped off to sleep last night.

At midnight the first to die was SS Col. Paul Blobel, who forsook an architect's drafting board to lead extermination squads in occupied Russia. A massacre of 60,000 at Kiev was on his record.

Then, in alphabetical order, came:

SS Col. Werner Braune, lawyer turned officer, whose troops wiped out thousands of civilians at Simferopol, in the Crimea.

SS Gen. Erich Naumann, whose ...

France For Deferring Japan Pact

Desires to Avoid Offending Russia

British Sources Report French Prefer Setup Like That in Germany

By Joseph Newman

From the Herald Tribune Bureau
Copyright New York Herald Tribune, Inc.

LONDON, June 7.—In the course of Anglo-American negotiations on a final draft peace treaty for Japan, it was learned today that France has suggested a postponement of the treaty so as not to offend the Soviet Union.

France, according to British quarters, is worried about aggressive Russian reaction to conclusion of a Japanese peace treaty unacceptable to the Soviet Union. Rather than irritate Russia further, France reportedly prefers to drop the treaty for the present and to proceed with an arrangement for Japan similar to the one being worked out for Germany.

This would be along the lines of liberalizing the occupation statute and even replacing it with an arrangement which restored a large measure of sovereignty to Japan. Individual countries would then be free to enter into direct diplomatic and economic relations with Japan.

No Formal Treaty

But there would be no formal peace treaty such as the one which is presently being drafted, and which is rejected by the Soviet Union on the ground that it is being drawn up outside the Council of Foreign Ministers. Russia says that the council alone is competent to draft the treaty and that the present procedure, which circum... ...ga. ...ussian reaction ... have been ...hat the Soviet troops in ...

...special ad...s to President ...ad of the ...ich is negotiating the final ... tonight ...conducting ... the treaty." ... the English ... reported ... and saying ... peace with ... cause of ... "that is ...

...undoubtedly ... the United ...dently was ... the faint-...

...Col. 3)

Truman Appeals to Congress To Extend Anti-Inflation Law

Wants Defense Production Act Continued After June 30 and Broadened to Cover Rents

By Raymond J. Elair

From the Herald Tribune Bureau
Copyright New York Herald Tribune, Inc.

WASHINGTON, June 7.—President Truman appealed anew to Congress today to extend and strengthen the economic-control law to "keep the heavy pressures of the next few months from becoming an unmanageable torrent of inflation."

The Defense Production act, source of the government's anti-inflation, priority and allocation powers, is due to expire June 30. Mr. Truman wants the law continued for another two years with additional authority over rents, commodity speculation, subsidies and other matters.

But Republicans in Congress are talking about a stopgap extension of 60 or 90 days to give legislators more time to study the economic picture.

Mr. Truman showed his concern over this legislative outlook by issuing at his press conference a statement urging continuance and improvement of the law.

The statement praised the New York price war as a sign the anti-inflation program is working but warned that the present price lull is "only a breathing spell." Inflationary pressures, the President warned, "will grow rapidly later this year and still more next year."

"The American people are wondering whether the programs which have started to protect them from inflation are going to be continued and strengthened to meet this growing danger," President Truman said.

"Some of the special-interest groups have come out for killing all wage and price controls. This critical issue is now before the Congress."

In an appeal aimed at the Republicans, Mr. Truman said: "The control of inflation is not a partisan issue; it is a national need."

AEC Chief Doubts Russia Got Any Post-War Atomic Data

Asserts U.S. Mass-Produces Bombs; Believes Stockpile Is Deterrent to Soviet Aggression

By the United Press

NEW YORK, June 7. — Gordon Dean, chairman of the Atomic Energy Commission, disclosed today that no spies had been discovered in the AEC, and indicated that Russia has obtained no information on post-war atomic developments.

In a major comprehensive review of America's atomic energy program, he served warning to Russia that whether the Kremlin wants to test United States atomic supremacy on military, economic or political grounds, "we mean to win."

He added his personal belief that America's stockpile of atomic weapons, now rolling out on an industrial mass production basis, is "the principal deterrent to large-scale Soviet aggression."

Eventually, he said, he was sure atomic engines for submarines and aircraft will "reduce almost to the vanishing point" naval and air force dependence on bases for fuel supply.

He added that the United States could have an atomic plant to make electric power "right now"—and will in fact have one this year—but it would not be economic.

Addresses N.Y. Chamber

Mr. Dean made his optimistic report in a speech prepared for a meeting of the New York State Chamber of Commerce.

"To our knowledge," he said, "we have never had a Fuchs or a Greenglass or a Pontecorvo or a Rosenberg in the AEC program."

The names are those of Communist spies or alleged spies in the programs associated with the AEC. Dr. Klaus Fuchs and Dr. Bruno Pontecorvo were naturalized Britons, the others Americans.

Mr. Dean emphasized that the spies succeeded only in obtaining war-time information. He made no reference to any secrets stolen in the last six years.

He said the treachery of these men had enabled Russia to gather into its possession "a considerable body of information about war-

(Continued on Page 2, Col. 2)

Four Air Chiefs Confer in Paris On Production

U.S., U.K., France and Canada Also Discuss Need for Men, Bases

By William J. Humphreys

The Air Force Chiefs of Staff of the United States, Britain, France and Canada opened a conference in Paris yesterday to discuss what French sources called the general problem of the Western reinforcement of the Western air potential for the defense of Europe."

Three principal paths of action are being considered in talks at the Ecole Superieure de Guerre, according to the French sources. They said Gen. Hoyt S. Vandenberg, of the United States; Marshal Sir John Slessor, of the United Kingdom; Gen. Charles Lecheres, of France, and Marshal W. A. Curtis, of Canada, are considering:

1—Increased plane production by the Atlantic pact nations in co-ordination with the superior output of machines and material by American aircraft factories.

2—Accelerated pilot and ground-crew training through the assistance of the large air schools in the United States and Canada.

3—Modernization of existing bases and the building of others for jet fighters and heavy bombers in the continental zones under the command of Supreme Headquarters, Allied Powers, Europe. The heavy bomber bases would be located in the Mediterranean and North African areas.

It was also reported that the four air chiefs will study the results of the recent aerial defensive exercise over northwestern Europe. In a review of this "Umbrella" exercise, Lt. Gen. Lauris Norstad, commander of Allied Air Forces, Central Europe, said fighter-field runways would have to be lengthened to accommodate jets and that overland communications would have to be improved.

Billions of Caterpillars, And Nothing to Be Done

SAULT STE. MARIE, Mich., June 7 (U.P.).—A Michigan State bug expert advised upper peninsula residents today to relax, saying the invasion by billions of caterpillars should be over in about a week.

Entomologist Ray Hudson said there wasn't much that could be done about the horde of hairy insects that humped over the area, causing thousands of dollars' damage to trees and crops.

Gimbel's Tells N.Y. Legislature Macy Advertising Is 'Nonsense'

By the United Press

NEW YORK, June 7—Gimbel's department store asked the state Legislature today to act against the "nonsense" in advertising with which, it charged, Macy's set off the city's still-booming price war.

Gimbel's vice-president, Louis Broido, turned up at a state legislative committee hearing with a girdle, bathing suit and pair of slippers which he said he bought at Macy's to prove his rival's price claims were "misleading" and "just a lot of nonsense."

The bargain field day continued and spread to food items as the legislators opened a public hearing on the price war touched off by the Supreme Court decision which invalidated state fair-trade price laws.

"The price war was due to only one thing—one large store in New York, conducted by R. H. Macy and Company—publicly proclaimed it undersells everybody at 6 per cent for cash," Mr. Broido said. "That's just a lot of nonsense. Nobody is capable of underselling everybody all of the time."

He said one of Gimbel's woman employees had gone to Macy's this morning and had purchased the feminine wearing apparel he unwrapped. He said it was bought at the same price the same articles are selling for at Gimbel's.

He asked the Legislature to outlaw advertising claims of "general underselling" to protect small merchants from the "predatory capital" of large department stores like his and Macy's.

"If we don't protect this middle class, this country will wind up with a few big monopolies and 150,000,000 proletarian workers," he said.

Macy's representatives attended the hearing, but declined an opportunity to answer Mr. Broido.

MONDAY, FEBRUARY 13, 1956

Burgess and Maclean Hold Press Conference in Moscow

Statement Discounted In London

Opinion of Eden Is Awaited Today

From the Herald Tribune Bureau
© 1956, New York Herald Tribune, Inc.

LONDON, Feb. 12.—British newspapers were unanimous today in contemptuously dismissing yesterday's assertions by Guy F. Burgess and Donald D. Maclean in Moscow that they had never been Communist agents.

Judgment here is that the two diplomats were unveiled in the Soviet capital as part of the preparations for the April visit to London of Soviet Premier Nikolai A. Bulganin and Nikita S. Khrushchev First Secretary of the Communist party.

The Foreign Office again declined any formal comment on the reappearance of its two former staff members, but it is probable that Prime Minister Sir Anthony Eden may have something to say in the House of Commons tomorrow.

Sir Anthony is due to make a statement to Commons on the results of his talks in Washington and he may include comment on the Burgess-Maclean case, since it clearly has a bearing on Anglo-American relations.

The diplomatic correspondent of the "Sunday Times" said today that many Foreign Office colleagues of Burgess and Maclean believed they had seen signs of Maclean's work in particular in recent Soviet notes to the West.

Donald D. Maclean

Guy Burgess

Petrov Again Asserts Pair Were Red Spies

By the Associated Press

CANBERRA, Australia, Feb. 12.—Vladimir Petrov, former Soviet espionage chief in Australia today challenged yesterday's statement by Guy F. Burgess and Donald D. Maclean that they were never Soviet agents while in Britain.

In a statement issued by the Australian Security Service, Petrov said: "Burgess and Maclean worked for the MGB (Soviet Ministry of State Security) and gave much secret information.

"For these reasons the MGB arranged for Burgess and Maclean to travel secretly to the Soviet Union when British security authorities discovered that they were Soviet agents."

First Statement Since '54

It was Petrov's first public statement—except for the publication of his book—since a Royal Commission investigated his defection to Australian authorities in April, 1954.

The former Soviet diplomat said he felt sure that Burgess and Maclean "made these statements at their press conference under the direction of Soviet authorities and that the statements had been issued for propaganda purposes for Russia against the Western governments.

Cites Soviet Secrecy

"If Burgess and Maclean had gone over to the Soviets with a view to achieving peace between the Soviet Union and the British and American governments, why did the Soviet authorities not reveal their whereabouts and state their alleged reasons for deserting their posts in England when much publicity was given to the matter in the press outside Russia?" he asked.

"The press in Russia had not, up to the time I left my post at the Soviet Embassy in Canberra in April, 1954, mentioned anything regarding the disappearance or the whereabouts of Burgess and Maclean.

"This is very significant to me in view of what I know about them."

Say They Were Not Red Spies

Maclean's Family Is Also in Russia

By the Associated Press

MOSCOW, Feb. 12. — Donald D. Maclean and Guy F. Burgess, two high-ranking British diplomats who disappeared into mystery five years ago, reappeared here suddenly yesterday.

They said they had been Communists since their college days, but denied they had been secret agents, as charged in a British White Paper last year.

They said they had come to the Soviet Union to work for peace and East-West understanding.

The dramatically staged development came just four days before the opening of the 20th congress of the Soviet Communist party and in the middle of a major Soviet campaign charging that the United States is sending espionage balloons over Soviet territory.

Wife, Children With Him

Maclean cleared up one additional mystery. He said his wife and children had indeed joined him here, as had long been supposed by the British.

Burgess and Maclean, who disappeared from London in May, 1951, held a news conference in the television room of the National Hotel near the Kremlin.

They did not answer questions, but handed out a statement to reporters for Reuter's news agency, "The Sunday Times," of London Tass, the Soviet news agency, and "Pravda," the Communist party newspaper. The conference lasted about five minutes.

The Moscow radio broadcast the entire statement.

It said they had come to the Soviet Union "in order to make our contribution to a policy aimed at achieving greater mutual understanding between the Soviet Union and the West, having become convinced, on the basis of official information which was at our disposal, of the fact that neither British, nor still more American, policy at that time was seriously pursuing this object."

They said they had "every possibility to know that the plans of a small but powerful" group in the West opposed a mutual understanding.

Both Reds at Cambridge

"When we were in Cambridge we both were Communists," they said, but added that the British Foreign Office had wrongfully presumed they had become Soviets agents then.

"We, neither of us, have ever been Soviet agents," they said.

...from New York, a repre-

Where in London

is the oldest market-place? The site at Billingsgate Market has been used for the sale of fish for over a thousand years.

Where in London

do they market used cars? Look under "The Automobile Market" in the Herald Tribune, Classified section. If you don't see a good buy, place an ad under "Cars Wanted."

The Weather

Paris: Today's forecast: Cloudy with scattered showers. Yesterday's temperatures: Max. 63 (17 Cent.); min. 45 (7 Cent.)

London: Today: Cool, showery, heavy at times, bright intervals. Yesterday's temperatures: Max. 59 (15 Cent.); min. 48 (9 Cent.)

Channel crossings: Rather rough.

New York: Today: Fair, milder. Yesterday's temperature: Max. 70 (21 Cent.).

NEW YORK
Herald Tribune
European Edition Published Daily in Paris

PRICE PER COPY:

Austria	4 S.	Morocco	35 Frs.
Belgium	5 B.Fr.	Netherlands	0.30 Flor.
Denmark	0.75 D.Kr.	North Africa	35 Frs.
Finland	30 F.M.	Norway	0.75 N.Kr.
France	30 Frs.	Portugal	3.80 Esc.
Germany	0.40 D.M.	Spain	4 Ptas.
Great Britain	6 Pence	Sweden	0.60 S. Kr.
Greece	4,000 Drs.	Switzerland	0.40 S.Frs.
Ireland	6 Pence	Syria, Lebanon	50 P.
Israel	125 Prut.	Turkey	60 Kurus
Italy	60 Lire	U.S. Military	10 Cents
Luxembourg	5 L.Frs.		

Established in Europe 1887 *** PARIS, TUESDAY, JUNE 2, 1953 **Established in New York 1841**

Queen Elizabeth II to Be Crowned Today; Mt. Everest Conquered by Two Climbers

Highest Peak Scaled Friday

By Gaston Coblentz

From the Herald Tribune Bureau. Copyright New York Herald Tribune, Inc.

LONDON, June 2 (Tuesday).—London was electrified last night by a report that a British expedition has conquered the long-defiant 29,002-ft. summit of Mount Everest, in the Himalayas.

A spokesman at Buckingham Palace confirmed shortly before midnight that a report of the expedition's triumph had been communicated to Queen Elizabeth II on the eve of her Coronation.

According to the report received by the palace, two men succeeded in reaching the peak: E. P. Hillary, 34, former officer of the New Zealand Air Force, who was accompanied by one of the most famous native Sherpa porters from Nepal, Tensing Bhutia.

The expedition approached Everest from its southern slopes rising out of Nepal and was led by Col. H. C. J. Hunt, of Britain.

Conquest of the peak took place Friday and the intervening three days were required to relay the news by runner to the outside world.

The British assault climaxed a long series of unsuccessful and often disastrous attempts by courageous mountain climbers from Britain and other nations.

Gift to Queen

The 1953 attempt was originally conceived and then executed with the purpose of delivering a crowning present to Queen Elizabeth II for tomorrow's historic event in Westminster Abbey.

News of the stirring achievement spread like wildfire among more than 100,000 Britons who were already sitting and sleeping on the streets of central London in order to be in choice positions for tomorrow's six-mile Coronation procession.

The report intensified the sense of pride that has been apparent in the British people as they have been preparing for the magnificent traditional Coronation proceedings.

Crowds Cheer

As the news shot through the crowd in the Mall between Trafalgar Square and Buckingham Palace, many people who had been sleeping were awakened. Sections of the crowd rose to their feet and cheered.

The first high-ranking statement on the conquest issued in London was made by S. G. Holland, Prime Minister of New Zealand, who is here for the Coronation. He said:

"Naturally, I'm extremely proud that the New Zealand member of the team has been the first Britisher to conquer the hitherto unconquerable Everest. What a grand achievement on the eve of the Coronation, and I would hope this terrific example of tenacity, the spirit of endurance and fortitude in this Coronation year might be regarded as a symbol. There are no heights or difficulties which the British people cannot overcome.

"I cannot emphasize too strongly, however, that although a New Zealander is the first to conquer Everest, this triumph has been made possible only by the combined efforts of a great many people, including the other members of the team, and the perfect organization behind them and from the lessons learned from the many previous attempts by many gallant men."

Swiss Tried Last Year

An effort to reach the summit was made by a Swiss expedition in 1952. Almost exactly a year ago, on May 28, Raymond Lambert, accompanied by the same Sherpa porter, Tensing Bhutia, set a new record by climbing to 28,215 feet. They were frustrated by fierce weather and difficulties with their oxygen equipment.

The triumph of the Hunt expedition follows 32 years of failures by one expedition after another. Before the war, from 1921 onward, Everest was repeatedly assaulted up its northern slopes from bases in Tibet.

The first seven expeditions, from 1921 to 1938, were all British. The most tragic of them was the attempt of 1924, when George L. Mallory and Andrew Irvine disappeared at 28,000 feet. Nothing more was ever seen of them.

Try Southern Approach

After World War II Nepal opened its frontiers to allow climbers to try the southern approach. Tibet fell into the hands of Chinese Communists and the northern slopes were ruled out for Westerners. The Nepalese government has permitted entry to expeditions from a total of six countries.

Hillary had taken part in an early British attempt in 1951 under the leadership of Eric Shipton. Col. Hunt's strategy this time was to make a double assault. The first was made on May 25 and is assumed to have failed.

Dulles: Mid-East Pact Is Out

By Homer Bigart

From the Herald Tribune Bureau
Copyright New York Herald Tribune, Inc.

WASHINGTON, June 1.—Secretary of State John Foster Dulles, reporting to the nation tonight on his recent trip to the Middle East and South Asia, said the dream of a Middle East defense organization against Communist aggression will have to be shelved because of the mutual hate and fear between Arab countries and Israel.

Mr. Dulles offered no immediate hope of solving the power vacuum in the Middle East. He found only "a vague desire" there for a collective security system. No such system, he said, can be imposed on the Middle East by the Western powers, and little can be done until Israel and the Arab countries settle their differences.

Calls Arabs Fearful

To help achieve Arab-Israeli peace, Mr. Dulles said, the United States should make clear that it stands firmly behind the tripartite declaration of 1950 in which this nation, Britain and France guaranteed the present frontiers and armistice lines of Israel.

This would reassure the Arab states against possible Israeli aggression, he said. The Arabs were not reassured when the declaration was announced in 1950, Mr. Dulles said, and he found them still fearful that the United States would "back the new state of Israel in aggressive expansion."

Such distrust must be eliminated, Mr. Dulles said, and the Arabs must be convinced of American impartiality.

Speaks on Radio, TV

"We cannot afford to be distrusted by millions who could be sturdy friends of freedom," he said. "They must not further swell the ranks of Communist dictators."

He claimed that Israeli leaders themselves agreed with him that United States policies should be impartial "so as to win not only the respect and regard of the Israeli but also of the Arab peoples."

Speaking on radio and television, Mr. Dulles said the Middle East paid little attention to the menace of Soviet expansion, although the northern tier of nations was more aware of the danger.

Earlier, the National Security Council, called in special session by President Eisenhower, heard Mr.

(Continued on Page 5, Col. 4)

This picture, from Eric Shipton's "The Mount Everest Reconnaissance Expedition, 1951" shows the southern route to summit (left), which was taken by Col. John C. Hunt's expedition. The route was pioneered in 1951 by the Shipton party.

J.C. Hughes Gets Draper Post

WASHINGTON, June 1 (A.P.).—President Eisenhower today nominated John C. Hughes, 61-year-old head of a New York textile firm, as the United States representative on the North Atlantic Council with the rank of ambassador.

Mr. Hughes will succeed William H. Draper jr., who resigned and returned to New York today. The NATO mission is being reorganized under a plan which Mr. Eisenhower submitted to Congress today.

Mr. Hughes also will serve as American representative on the Organization for European Economic Co-operation.

Kaufman Rejects Rosenberg Plea

NEW YORK, June 1 (U.P.).—Federal Judge Irving R. Kaufman refused today to set aside the death sentences of convicted atomic spies Julius and Ethel Rosenberg. He also refused a stay of execution pending an appeal from his ruling.

Judge Kaufman, who originally sentenced the Rosenbergs to death for transmitting atomic secrets to the Soviet Union, said the motions were "transparent and without any merit whatsoever."

Emanuel Bloch, attorney for the Rosenbergs, had argued that Judge Kaufman was without power to inflict the death penalty on the couple. He said the indictment under which they were tried was defective and called for a maximum penalty of 20 years. His motions were denied in all respects by Judge Kaufman.

VA Head Resigns

WASHINGTON, June 1 (U.P.).—President Eisenhower today accepted the resignation of Carl R Gray jr. as head of the Veterans Administration.

The White House said that Mr. Gray, a hold-over from the Truman administration, resigned because of illness. His resignation becomes effective June 30.

Eisenhower Plans New Aid Agency

By Robert J. Donovan

From the Herald Tribune Bureau
Copyright New York Herald Tribune, Inc.

WASHINGTON, June 1.—Reorganization plans, creating two new agencies under State Department policy guidance to handle, respectively, the foreign aid programs and overseas information, were sent to Congress today by President Eisenhower.

Under these proposals:

1—The Mutual Security Agency would be abolished and its functions and those of various other offices handling foreign assistance would be transferred to a new agency called the Foreign Operations Administration. Harold E. Stassen, who heads the MSA, is expected to be in charge of the new organization. In the field of policy, however, he would be subordinate to Secretary of State John Foster Dulles.

2—A new organization, known as the United States Information Agency, will be set up to absorb the sundry international information programs, including the Voice of America, which may, however, be given a new name.

A feature of this set-up will be the establishment of a particular, distinctively labeled program which will present for overseas use the official United States position on world issues. No other matter will be used on this program. Other programs will continue to carry music, entertainment and so forth, but this official program—not yet named—will strictly be the voice of the United States government.

These were the main features of four reorganization plans submitted today by the President. Two of the plans—the ones on foreign aid and overseas information—dealt with the State Department. And in accompanying statements the President made it clear that he was trying to strengthen the hand of Secretary Dulles in the conduct of foreign affairs.

"The over-all foreign affairs reorganization which I desire to achieve," he told department heads

(Continued on Page 3, Col. 2)

London's Decorations Are Finest of Century

By Gaston Coblentz

From the Herald Tribune Bureau
Copyright New York Herald Tribune, Inc.

LONDON, June 1.—Queen Elizabeth II will pass through a fairyland of color on her historic Coronation ride tomorrow.

London is more beautiful tonight than it has ever been in this century. Its fanciful and countless decorations on almost every building and street for miles on end are unprecedented in the history of recent British coronations.

They far exceed in beauty the preperations for the crowning of Queen Elizabeth's father, King George VI, in 1937. Londoners tell you that they would have given a fine show for a new King, but that they are doing something special now because they are fêting a young and beautiful new Queen.

The colors that blaze in the capital are mainly blue, red, yellow and gold. But there are other hues, among them royal purple, rose and silver.

The scene is varied from one block to the next. Each has its own pattern of stands and banners. Nowhere is there anything shabby. Some of London's drabber streets are almost unrecognizable. Even the thousands of boards put up to protect store windows from the crush of crowds in the elegant shopping streets are painted brightly.

An almost medieval air prevails in some of the famous streets. In Pall Mall, St. James' Street, the center of London's club life, stands for club members have been built three and four stories up the building fronts. Heraldic banners fly from them. There are other tented stands that recall a medieval tournament. No detail has been neglected. Even the steel tube scaffolding has been colored silver or gold.

The first sight to greet Queen Elizabeth II when she leaves Buckingham Palace on her way to Westminster Abbey will be the glittering, crowd-jammed Mall, a broad avenue half a mile long. It is adorned with high archways of blue and gold. From each archway hangs a large crown in delicate tracery.

From lampposts and scores of poles flutter rows of crimson banners bearing Queen Elizabeth II's royal cipher. At the far end of the avenue, Admiralty Arch is dressed in blue, with yellow coronets. It bears a large design of two entwin-

(Contnued on Page 2, Col. 2)

Prince Charles in Coronation Mood

From the Herald Tribune Bureau
Copyright New York Herald Tribune, Inc.

LONDON, June 1.—Prince Charles has been a problem all day long.

Confined behind the austere stone facade of Buckingham Palace, with milling thousands outside the gates, the prince is behaving just like any lively four-year-old youngster might be expected to behave on the eve of the biggest party ever.

The only outward signs are an occasional flick of a curtain on a palace window, a hasty little wave of a little arm, a bright, clean face pressed for a brief moment against a window pane.

His first quick and informal appearance was recorded shortly after 11 o'clock this morning. They were changing the guard at Buckingham Palace and thousands had gone down to see the ceremony. The curtains parted and the prince waved briefly. The curtain was suddenly pulled back into place—and the excitement was such that several women fainted in the crowd.

Then the band struck up "Teddy Bear's Picnic." Half an hour later, Prince Charles broke away from whoever was restraining him and made it to the window a second time.

Finally, after lunch, when his mother's luncheon guests were leaving the palace—the Prime Ministers of all the Commonwealth countries—he was allowed to make a proper window appearance with his sister, Princess Anne.

Baby-sitters are temporarily as short in London as they are in New York. So many parents are planning to converge on the city, starting at about 4 a.m. tomorrow, and so many baby-sitters are joining them, that very few will be left to mind the babies. Several London agencies report all their normal baby-sitting talent long since hired, so that doubling up will be the rule.

Bonfires all along the south coast of England will be a feature of Coronation Eve festivities—bonfires huge enough to be seen for 30 miles, with each to be visible from the next. Naturally, a bonfire with a 30-mile visibility takes a lot of building, and residents of Ilfracombe, in the west of England, were understandably nettled when somebody last night sneaked up and lit their pile. The first had been suitably placed on the summit of a 500-foot coastal hill, and police can find no trace of the pranksters who touched the match to it. But this morning, with a shrug, the locals went back to building another—and placing a guard around it to make sure that it stays intact until dusk tomorrow night.

Spectators Pass Night In Streets

By Don Cook

From the Herald Tribune Bureau
Copyright New York Herald Tribune, Inc.

LONDON, June 1.—London tonight, under periodic drenching from what the Weather Bureau calls "intermittent showers," was a surging, solid mass of humanity—spirits undampened and humor high in anticipation of tomorrow's Coronation pageant.

Britons—and Australians, Canadians, Pakistanis, Americans, South Africans, New Zealanders, Indians, Frenchmen, Germans and colonials—are camping out in rainy London tonight, not by the thousands or even tens of thousands but by the hundreds of thousands. They are sleeping on every square inch of ground along the Mall from Admiralty Arch to Buckingham Palace. They are parked in Hyde Park and are curled up in Trafalgar Square. They are huddled together along Piccadilly, Regent Street and Oxford Street, and bundled under canvas and blankets along Whitehall and Pall Mall.

This is a sight to swamp the statisticians and baffle the sensibilities, to tickle and delight the sense of humor. This is a good-humored crowd, laughing at the intermittent showers and at itself, and prepared by months of anticipation of tomorrow's event to see it through, come what may.

Buses Crawl

"Bet you won't be there tomorrow, Dad," a brash young man was heard calling out to an elderly wag, wearing a John Bull topper swathed in the Union Jack. He got the quick reply: "Come on, put up your money, five quid to one. What do you think your pins are for if not to stand on? I'll be here." The crowd roared its approval.

On down the Mall an ingenious sextet had strung a couple of pieces of canvas from a curb railing to the top of a reviewing stand behind and had decorated it with the sign, "Buckingham Palace Hotel, Full Up."

The buses were moving at a ten-foot crawl around Trafalgar Square and down Whitehall; damp blankets and mackintoshes were being draped over the churning radiators of the vehicles for quick drying, as bus-drivers laughingly waited to inch forward.

Crowds poured out of all the central London subway stations and headed for the Coronation route in the hope of a few inches of camping space. There was one early estimate of 400,000 camping out, but it seemed certain that the figure will be heading for the million-mark by midnight.

The expectation tomorrow is that something like 2,000,000 will be lining the route.

London buses start tomorrow morning with special runs to bring 10,300 policemen to their posts by 4 o'clock. Over 200 special "police cribs" will be operated and another 70 specials will bring 2,000 troops to their places along the route.

Atom Test Postponed

LAS VEGAS, June 1 (A.P.).—The atomic test explosion which was to have been set off near here before dawn today has been postponed until tomorrow because of adverse weather, the Atomic Energy Commission announced.

Festival Spirit Grips London

By Joseph Newman

From the Herald Tribune Bureau. Copyright New York Herald Tribune, Inc.

LONDON, June 1.—Elizabeth II, dressed in regal robes, will be crowned Queen tomorrow with all the pomp and circumstance of past centuries.

The stage has been set for the most elaborate, colorful and costly public performance of modern times.

The two gem-studded crowns which will symbolize the Queen's sovereignty over these islands and her realms in other parts of the world were moved today from the jeweler's shop which had refitted them. Together with other priceless regalia, they are being guarded in Westminster Abbey until the arrival of the Queen tomorrow.

The four-ton gilt and glass Coronation coach, having undergone final oiling and inspection, is stationed in Buckingham Palace courtyard. Tomorrow, the palace gates will be opened and the Queen, sitting beside her husband, the Duke of Edinburgh, will be drawn by eight gray horses to the Abbey.

Millions Line Streets

Several million people already have filled the streets of the procession route to the bursting point waiting to cheer and to shout "God Save the Queen!"

Never before within the memory of the oldest spectators have such multitudes from all four corners of the world been seen in the capital of the British Empire and Commonwealth. Four hundred thousand persons, unable to secure or buy any of the 200,000 seats in the government and privately-built stands, are estimated to be sleeping tonight in the streets and bordering parks so as to have a good view of the Queen tomorrow.

The Queen, after presiding at a luncheon for 11 Prime Ministers of the British Commonwealth and Empire and 80 of their associates, retired early tonight so as to be fully rested for tomorrow's strenuous day-long activities.

Trained to Diet

She will be called at 7:30 a.m. by her personal maid, Miss Margaret MacDonald, who regularly brings her tea at that hour. The Duke of Edinburgh will join her 30 minutes later for breakfast, consisting of fruit, toast and eggs.

This spare diet to which Queen Elizabeth has limited herself the last few years in the interest of her figure will have to carry her through the Coronation service until 2 p.m. She will then have lunch at the Abbey before leaving on her triumphant Coronation procession through six miles of London's leading streets on her way back to the palace.

At 9 a.m., according to the previously arranged schedule worked out to minutes and seconds, ladies-in-waiting will dress the Queen in her white satin Coronation gown weighing 30 pounds. Over this they will drape her crimson velvet robe with its long train to be carried by six noblewomen.

Due at Abbey at 11 a.m.

At 9:50 a.m., Prince Charles and Princess Anne will be brought in to see their mother in her Coronation raiment and to kiss her good by. Twenty minutes later the Queen will move down the grand staircase at the foot of which members of the palace household staff will be congregated and given the privilege of being among the first to see the Sovereign.

At 10:26 a.m., the Queen will

(Continued on Page 5, Col. 3)

Forecast Still Calls For Rain

From the Herald Tribune Bureau
Copyright New York Herald Tribune, Inc.

LONDON, June 1.—The weather outlook for Queen Elizabeth II's Coronation tomorrow worsened sharply this evening.

London's leading weather predicter, the meteorological officer of the Air Ministry, offered little comfort except to prophesy that there will be some "bright, sunny intervals" in a generally showery day.

During the Queen's processions to and from Westminster Abbey in the morning and afternoon it is also likely, he said, that the showers "will be heavy at times."

Thus, at least 2,000,000 people who will throng the procession route, may expect to get sprinkled repeatedly or even drenched. Two-hundred thousand holders of seats in mostly uncovered government and private seats run the same risk.

On-again-off-again showers began today. Sometimes the sun shone brightly, then gray clouds swept overhead and rain fell for five or ten minutes at a time.

Despite this harassment most of the thousands of early squatters at choice spots along the six-mile Coronation route clung to their positions. Some of them have been sitting and sleeping on the sidewalk along the Mall in front of Buckingham Palace since 7 p.m. yesterday and many brought raincoats and waterproof blankets. The temperature was very cool—between 50 and 55 degrees at midday.

Regardless of the weather, the Coronation will go on as scheduled in every detail. A year ago the first week of June was selected as the date for the ceremony, probably in the hope that the sun would be shining.

Maltese Ring Bells, Dance, Sing

VALETTA, June 1 (A.P.).—Church bells rang for 15 minutes throughout Malta this evening for the Coronation.

Earlier, 5,000 schoolchildren danced round a Coronation Maypole outside the Governor's Palace, then paid homage to Queen Elizabeth by joining a girls' choir in singing "God Save the Queen." Tonight a Coronation state ball is being held.

United Press.

Motor traffic and pedestrians jam street in front of Buckingham Palace on eve of today's Coronation.

FRIDAY, APRIL 6, 1951

2 Atom Spies Get Death; 3d Sentenced to 30 Years

Morton Sobell. Ethel Rosenberg. Julius Rosenberg.

Execution in May For Rosenbergs

1st U.S. Citizens Ever to Get Supreme Penalty On Charge Seem Calm

By Blaine Littell

From the Herald Tribune Bureau

Copyright New York Herald Tribune, Inc.

NEW YORK, April 5.—Julius and Ethel Rosenberg were sentenced to death today for the part they played in a Soviet espionage ring which stole atomic secrets from this country in World War II.

Morton Sobell, who was implicated to a lesser degree in the conspiracy to transmit military secrets to Russia, was sentenced to 30 years in prison, the maximum prison term provided by the espionage law.

The Rosenbergs, who heard Judge Irving R. Kaufman impose the extreme penalty at 12:08 p.m. with no outward show of emotion, are the first United States citizens in the history of American jurisprudence to be sentenced to death for espionage on behalf of a foreign power.

Judge Kaufman ordered the two spies executed in the week beginning May 21. He recommended against parole for Sobell.

OCTOBER 10, 1951

Senate Group Moves to Open Investigation on Sen. McCarthy

By Don Irwin

From the Herald Tribune Bureau

Copyright New York Herald Tribune, Inc.

WASHINGTON, Oct. 9. — The Senate elections subcommittee took the first step today toward possible action on the resolution by Sen. William Benton, D., Conn., calling for an investigation as to whether Sen. Joseph R. McCarthy, R., Wis., should be expelled from the Senate.

Sen. Guy M. Gillette, chairman, told reporters the five-member subcommittee had directed its staff to report back by Nov. 1 with "findings of fact" on the ten charges against Sen. McCarthy raised Sept. 28 by Sen. Benton. Sen. Gillette said his group would meet at that time to decide on further action.

Sen. Gillette also showed reporters a letter from Sen. McCarthy declining to appear to answer the charges. He said the subcommittee took no action on another letter from Sen. Benton urging that the inquiry be extended into the period before Sen. McCarthy's election in 1946. His original resolution asked a study of Sen. McCarthy's conduct in office.

Sen. Benton based his demand that the Senate employ its little-used expulsion machinery against Sen. McCarthy on the general charge that the Wisconsin Republican had used "calculated deceit and falsehood" both in his campaign against alleged Communists in the State Department and in other phases of his Senate career.

The general charge was supported by ten "cases" in which Sen. Benton undertook to show that Sen. McCarthy had committed "perjury" in some phases of his campaign and had deceived the Senate in others.

Sen. McCarthy's letter to Sen. Gillette, dated Oct. 4, reiterated the counter-charge of Communist ties with which he has thus far met Sen. Benton's accusations.

"Frankly, Guy," the letter said in part, "I have not and do not intend to even read, much, less answer, Sen Benton's smear attack. I am sure you realize the Benton type of material can be found in the 'Daily Worker' almost any day of the week and will continue to flow from the mouths and pens of its camp followers as long as I continue my fight against Communism."

FRIDAY, MARCH 19, 1954

Criticism of Methods Spurned by McCarthy

By Homer Bigart

Special to the Herald Tribune

Copyright New York Herald Tribune, Inc.

CHICAGO, March 18. — Sen. Joseph R. McCarthy, R., Wis., said here last night he would continue to fight Communists with his own particular methods, regardless of whether any official liked those methods or not.

"I don't give a tinker's dam how high or how low are the people in either the Republican or Democratic parties who are unhappy about our methods," Sen. McCarthy told 1,200 persons at a St. Patrick's Day dinner of the Irish Fellowship Club.

"This fight will go on as long as I am in the United States Senate," he said. Mr. McCarthy is chairman of the Senate Permanent Investigations subcommittee.

Opening a Mid-West speaking tour, Sen. McCarthy intimated that the Eisenhower administration was being taken in by the Communist line.

At an earlier press conference yesterday, Sen. McCarthy dismissed as a meaningless gesture President Eisenhower's backing of Secretary of the Army Robert T. Stevens in a test of veracity between himself and Mr. Stevens.

Presidents always support members of their official families, he said, adding, "the President reacted as he would have to do with any Cabinet member."

Sen. McCarthy said he would "back to the hilt" Roy M. Cohn, who has been charged by the Army with trying to pressure it into giving preferential treatment to Pvt. G. David Schine, former unpaid consultant to the McCarthy subcommittee. Sen. McCarthy and Mr. Cohn have charged Secretary Stevens and Army Counselor John G. Adams with trying to "blackmail" them into calling off further investigations of alleged subversion in the Army.

Greeted with cries of : "Give them hell, Joe!" and "You're in your own ballpark!" Sen. McCarthy likened his methods to those employed by St. Patrick.

"The snakes didn't like St. Patrick's methods," he said, "and the Communists don't like mine."

FRIDAY, DECEMBER 3, 1954

McCarthy Censured For Insulting Senate

By the Associated Press

WASHINGTON, Dec. 2.—The Senate today voted to condemn Sen. Joseph R. McCarthy, R., Wis., for his attacks on its special committee that recommended he be censured and for calling the extraordinary Senate session a "lynch party." The roll call was 64-23.

The vote had the effect also of wiping from the pending censure resolution one of the original counts against Sen. McCarthy—that he intemperately abused Brig. Gen. Ralph W. Zwicker.

The condemnation of Sen. McCarthy for his remarks about the special committee—he called its members "unwitting handmaidens" of the Communists—was offered and adopted as a substitute for the section relating to Gen. Zwicker. Sen. Wallace Bennett, R., Utah, offered it.

Sen. Herbert H. Lehman, D., N. Y., indicated during the debate that he might try later to get the Zwicker count put back in.

Sen. McCarthy was not present during the vote and had not been in the chamber at any time during the day's session. Aids said he had been in and out of his office.

Barring some hassle, such as an effort to revive the Zwicker count, the Senate—with approval of Sen. Bennett's amendment—was close to final action on its resolution standing as a two-point document where Sen. McCarthy is concerned.

Sen. McCarthy said last night that "I don't think the American people are at all fooled."

"They know I am being censured because I dared to do the dishonorable thing of exposing Communists in government," Sen. McCarthy said, using the word "dishonorable" in an ironic sense.

The Weather

Paris: Today's forecast: Mild, mostly fine. Yesterday's temperatures: Max. 61 (16 Cent.); min. 36 (2 Cent.).

London: Today: Milder and fair. Yesterday's temperatures: Max. 58 (14 Cent.); min. 44 (7 Cent.).

Channel crossing: Slight.

New York: Today: Mild, cloudy. Yesterday's temperature: Max. 65 (18 Cent.).

NEW YORK
Herald Tribune
European Edition Published Daily in Paris

PRICE PER COPY:

Austria	4 S.	Morocco	35 Frs.
Belgium	5 B.Fr.	Netherland	0.35 Flor.
Denmark	0.75 D.Kr.	North Africa	35 Frs.
Finland	30 F.M.	Norway	0.75 N.Kr.
France	35 Frs.	Portugal	3.80 Esc.
Germany	0.40 D.M.	Spain	5 Ptas.
Great Britain	6 Pence	Sweden	0.60 S.Kr.
Greece	4,000 Drs.	Switzerland	0.40 S.Frs.
Ireland	6 Pence	Syria, Lebanon	50 P.
Israel	175 Prut.	Turkey	60 Kurus
Italy	60 Lire	U.S. Military	10 Cents
Luxembourg	5 L.Frs.		

Established in Europe 1887 * PARIS, SATURDAY, MAY 8, 1954 Established in New York 1841

Dien Bien Phu Falls After 56-Day Siege

Soviet Bid to Enter NATO Is Rejected

By the Associated Press

LONDON, May 7.—The United States, Britain and France told Russia today the 14 Atlantic allies do not want her in their alliance.

In notes to the Kremlin, the Western three branded Russia's offer to join the North Atlantic Treaty Organization as "completely unreal." Russia as a member of NATO would be in a position "to veto every decision," the British version of the Western reply said, and added bluntly: "None of the member

Text of United States note, Page 2.

states is prepared to allow their joint defense system to be disrupted in this way."

Reply to March 31 Proposal

The Allies were answering a surprise Soviet proposal of March 31 which Red spokesman represented as a bid to restore the war time "grand alliance" that beat Hitler.

In it Russia had called for:

1—A ban on atomic weapons and a reduction of arms.

2—A Soviet-type security system for all Europe in which the United States could participate.

3—Abandonment of Allied plans to rearm West Germany within a European Defense Community.

4—Russia's own admission to NATO.

Point by point the Allies rejected the Russian arguments which accompanied these proposals—the way a schoolmaster corrects a pupil.

On disarmament, the Allies pledged to work for the success of President Eisenhower's atoms-for-peace plan and other pending United Nations negotiations.

But they warned: "If these negotiations are to succeed, a sense of security and confidence must first be established... In these (proposals) the Soviet government do not attempt to remove the actual causes of European tension. Instead, they propose a new collective security treaty which is avowedly based on the neutralization and continued division of Germany, while leaving unchanged the

Seaway Approved By Senate

By the Associated Press

WASHINGTON, May 7. — The Senate completed Congressional action on the St. Lawrence Seaway bill today, sending it to President Eisenhower for his signature.

Congressional passage represents a victory for the Eisenhower administration.

The President included the seaway bill in his 1954 legislative program.

The St. Lawrence River, which for much of its length separates the United States and Canada, will now be turned into a seaway for ships to travel between the Great Lakes and the Atlantic Ocean.

Until this year Congress always blocked the idea although every President since World War I, including President Eisenhower, was for it.

$105 Million Is U.S. Share

The work which can begin now will take six years and cost the United States about $105,000,000. It will cost Canada more. But it will be a joint task undertaken by the two countries.

It is expected to pay for itself in 50 years through tolls collected from the ships passing through. The river must be deepened in some places. Some canals and

United Press.

French Foreign Minister Georges Bidault (center) talking with Nguyen Trung Vinh (left) Viet Nam Vice-President, and Nguyen Quoc Dinh, Viet Nam Foreign Minister, after a dinner he gave for them at his villa in Geneva.

Debate Is Resumed On Korea

By Don Cook

Special to the Herald Tribune
Copyright New York Herald Tribune, Inc.

GENEVA, May 7.—General debate on the Korean peace settlement was resumed at a plenary session of the Asian conference today with speeches from the Colombian, Philippine and New Zealand delegates,

Debate on Indo-China Likely to Start Today

By the Associated Press

GENEVA, May 7. — Britain, France and the United States, in a series of unscheduled meetings tonight immediately after the announcement of the fall of Dien Bien Phu, put the final touches to their strategy for Indo-China peace talks which are expected to open tomorrow.

American Under Secretary of State Walter Bedell Smith conferred with British Foreign Secretary Anthony Eden and then saw French Foreign Minister George Bidault at the latter's lakeside villa.

A French spokesman said after the meeting that the stage was set for the Indo-China talks to open tomorrow afternoon. A definite time for the opening of the talks was to be set after a meeting with the Soviet Union later tonight or early tomorrow.

The spokesman said Russia and the West had agreed that the chairmanship of the talks should alternate between Mr. Eden and Soviet Foreign Minister Vyacheslav

30,000 Viets in Assault On 9,000 Defenders

Government Of Laniel Is Seen in Peril

Text of Laniel statement, Page 2.

By Barrett McGurn

Premier Joseph Laniel announced last night in the wake of the fall of Dien Bien Phu that France will go on fighting for a settlement protecting the liberty of its Indo-Chinese allies.

The bitter immediate reaction in French political circles raised the strong possibility, however, that M. Laniels Cabinet would be overthrown when Parliament meets again Tuesday. What sort of new government would be formed in that case and whether or not it would agree to fight on remained in doubt.

M. Laniel announced that he would call to the attention of France's allies that Indo-China is "a particularly sensitive part of Asia" and that France has been fighting alone for seven years "in the defense of the interests of all."

To Ask U.S. Aid

The words seemed to imply that France would repeat the request for fighting men which it made secretly to the United States during the past two weeks, but official sources said last night that the only thing certain is that France will appeal to the United States for still more material aid.

The fall of the main part of the Dien Bien Phu garrison is sure to cause a profound shock in France and is expected to strengthen the demands of the one-third of Parliament which is now crying for

Gen. Christian de Castries

Garrison Hailed by Eisenhower

By William J. Humphreys

'Isabelle' Still Holding Out 3 Miles South

By the United Press

HANOI, May 7.—The French Union camp of Dien Bien Phu fell at 11 a.m. today.

The shell-rocked barbed-wire fortress in northwestern Indo-China was overrun by an estimated 30,000 Communist-led Viet-Minh after a 56-day siege.

A military spokesman said "Isabelle," an isolated resistance center three miles south of the main bastion, still held out. Its 2,000 defenders were not expected to resist for long.

The fate of Brig. Gen. Christian de Castries, Dien Bien Phu commander, and his 9,000 troops was not immediately known.

There also was no news of Genevieve de Gallard-Terraube, 29, a Parisian nurse and the only woman at Dien Bien Phu.

Announcing the fall of the bastion, which marked the worst French military defeat since World War II, Gen. Henri de Navarre, commander of French Union forces in Indo-China, declared:

"Dien Bien Phu has fulfilled the mission which was assigned it by the high command."

Garrison Praised

A high French general here, tears streaming down his face, said tonight: "Dien Bien Phu is a new name to emblazon on the battle streamers of France. The garrison's resistance will never be forgotten."

Under a massive Viet Minh offensive, one after another of the resistance centers was bowled over in a night and morning of hand-

The Weather

Paris: Today's forecast: Warm and fine. Yesterday's temperatures: Max. 77 (25 Cent.); min. 45 (7 Cent.).

London: Today: Warm and cloudy, some periods. Yesterday's temperatures: Max. 75 (24 Cent.); min. 62 (17 Cent.).

Channel crossing: Slight.

New York: Today: Warm and cloudy. Yesterday's temperature: Max. 84 (29 C.).

NEW YORK
Herald Tribune
European Edition Published Daily in Paris

PRICE PER COPY:

Austria	4 S.	Morocco	35 Frs.
Belgium	5 B.Fr.	Netherlands	0.35 Flor.
Denmark	0.75 D.Kr.	North Africa	35 Frs.
Finland	30 F.M.	Norway	0.75 N.Kr.
France	35 Frs.	Portugal	3.80 Esc.
Germany	0.40 D.M.	Spain	5 Ptas.
Great Britain	6 Pence	Sweden	0.60 S.Kr.
Greece	4 Drs.	Switzerland	0.40 S.Frs.
Ireland	6 Pence	Syria, Lebanon	50 P.
Israel	175 Prut.	Turkey	60 Kurus
Italy	60 Lire	U.S. Military	10 Cents
Luxembourg	5 L.Frs.		

Established in Europe 1887 * PARIS, WEDNESDAY, JULY 21, 1954 Established in New York 1841

Lack of Unanimity'

Cohn Resigns Post As Aid of McCarthy

By the United Press

WASHINGTON, July 20.—Roy M. Cohn resigned today as chief counsel of the Senate Permanent Investigations subcommittee.

Sen. Joseph R. McCarthy, R., Wis., subcommittee chairman, released Mr. Cohn's letter of resignation which said the 27-year-old attorney was quitting because "there appears to be a lack of unanimity" about him on the subcommittee.

His letter was released shortly before the subcommittee began a closed meeting on what to do about other staff members.

A few minutes before Sen. McCarthy entered the meeting room he announced that Donald A. Surine had been transferred to his personal staff, and is no longer on the subcommittee pay roll. The subcommittee meeting had planned to consider whether Mr. Surine, an investigator, should be fired.

Flanders Pleased

Sen. Ralph E. Flanders, R., Vt., scheduled to speak in the Senate today to denounce Sen. McCarthy, said he was pleased to hear that Mr. Cohn has resigned.

"So far, so good," he said. "This, of course, does not reach the heart of the problem presented by the junior Senator from Wisconsin."

Sen. McCarthy, in a statement accompanying Mr. Cohn's letter of resignation, said: "The resignation . . . must bring great satisfaction to the Communists and fellow travelers.

"The smears and pressures to which he has been subjected make it clear that an effective anti-Communist cannot long survive on the Washington scene."

The Senator said that Mr. Cohn "rendered perhaps unrivaled service in the conviction and exposure of Communists and spies."

Refers to Cohn's Record

Sen. McCarthy said the former chief counsel prosecuted executed atomic spies Julius and Ethel Rosenberg, former Commerce Department official William Remington and top Communist party leaders.

He also credited Mr. Cohn with having "exposed Communist infiltration in the United Nations," and in the Government Printing Office, the Voice of America, Fort Monmouth, N.J., defense plants "and other key places."

Before disclosing Mr. Cohn's resignation, Sen. McCarthy said that several staff members have offered to quit because of "fantastic smear attacks."

He said that "I have been urging them not to resign," but admitted he did not know how successful the pleas to them might be.

He did not identify the staff members and did not say how

Roy M. Cohn

U.K. Offer On Suez Reported

By the Associated Press

LONDON, July 20.—Britain was reported tonight to have decided to go some way toward meeting Egyptian objections against British proposals for a settlement of the Suez Canal dispute.

The word came from diplomatic informants after a meeting of the British Cabinet and after Egyptian Ambassador Abdel Rahman Hakki conferred at the House of Commons with Minister of State Selwyn Lloyd. The nature of any possible British concession to the Egyptians was not disclosed.

Negotiations between the two

Dugdale Quits Post In Britain

By Joseph Newman

From the Herald Tribune Bureau
Copyright New York Herald Tribune, Inc.

LONDON, July 20.—Sir Thomas Dugdale resigned today as Minister of Agriculture—a casualty of the so-called battle of Crichel Down.

The battle was between the principle of private ownership of land and an insensitive mushrooming bureaucracy which defied it in the alleged interests of the state.

The feelings aroused by this battle were so intense that Prime Minister Sir Winston Churchill himself evidently was unable to save a minister for whom he and other colleagues had considerable affection.

In a valedictory speech which may mark the end of his political career, Sir Thomas announced his resignation in the Houe of Commons today. It was his 57th birthday.

Appropriated in 1937

Crichel Down is a piece of land consisting of 785 rolling acres in Dorsetshire, southwest of London. It was appropriated by the Air Ministry in 1937 for a bombing range.

After the war, when the Air Ministry no longer needed Crichel Down, it was turned over in 1949 to the Ministry of Agriculture. Instead of offering it back to its three original owners, the ministrw decided to turn it into a model farm owned by the state and leased to a tenant of the states choosing.

The storm broke when Lt. Comdr. George Marten challenged this decision and demanded the return of the greater part of Crichel Down which originally belonged to his wealthy wife, daughter of the late Lord Alington.

Eventually the government agreed to a public investigation, which was conducted by Sir Andrew Clark. This investigation disproved rumors of irregularities but accused the civil servants of the Agriculture Ministry of abuse of power.

Accepted Responsibility

Sir Thomas Dugdale, in his speech to the House of Commons admitted "mistakes and grave errors of judgment" were made by his subordinates. As minister, he said, he had to accept full responsibility.

He himself was not immediately responsible for the decision handled by the bureaucratic maze beneath him and Sir Thomas won admiration from both sides of the House for assuming the blame and warning the House of Commons against

Indo-China Cease-Fire Ready For Formal Approval at Geneva

U. S. View Clarified By Wilson

By William J. Humphreys

European Edition Bureau
Copyright New York Herald Tribune, S.A.

WASHINGTON, July 20.—Defense Secretary Charles E. Wilson told a press conference today that this country would consider defending the prospective armistice line in Indo-China if other nations joined it in "an alliance" for that purpose.

Mr. Wilson expressed this view as Washington was awaiting the final decision on Indo-China from the Geneva conference.

The Defense Secretary did not mention the Southeast Asia security arrangement proposed in April by the United States, but he gave the impression that if the project was brought into force, this government was ready to commit itself with others against further Communist aggression in the Far East.

Observing that increased American military power alone "would not improve our situation in the world," Secretary Wilson commented that two world wars had failed to establish a stable peace. "I don't think a third world war is any answer," he said.

Other Points

Other points brought out in the course of the Wilson news conference were that:

1—The United States Army, despite budget cuts calling for 225,000 fewer men by June 30, 1955, is expected to maintain 18 divisions, instead of the 17 originally foreseen. Plotted man-power reductions are to be eased.

2—The United States and Great Britain are "getting closer" to the idea of standardizing certain types of guided missiles. This "mutual defense" goal is now under discussion with Field Marshal Earl Alexander, British Defense Minister, who is now in this country.

3—Even if the strength of the United States armed forces had been double that of its present power "not a thing that has happened in the past year would have

Associated Press Wirephoto.

Viet Minh Foreign Minister Pham Van Dong (left), Jean Chauvel, French Ambassador to Switzerland (wearing glasses), and French Premier-Foreign Minister Pierre Mendès-France (right) leaving French headquarters in Geneva yesterday after discussing cease-fire in Indo-China.

Gruenther For Global Strategy

Viet Namese Calm As Armistice Nears

By the Associated Press

SAIGON, July 20.—An unusual calm settled over Indo-China

"It is not with the open hand but with a closed fist that one fights," the pro-French poster said.

Truce Line Near 17th Parallel

By Don Cook

Special to the Herald Tribune
Copyright New York Herald Tribune, Inc.

GENEVA, July 20.—A cease-fire agreement which will bring France's eight-year war in Indo-China to an end and restore an uncertain peace to Asia was virtually concluded here tonight, and awaits only the formal final approval of its negotiators.

For French Premier-Foreign Minister Pierre Mendès-France the results achieved within his self-imposed July 20 deadline represent a great personal achievement of political strength and diplomatic skill.

His prestige in French politics has been raised in the space of one short month from that of a voice in lonely opposition to that of the most powerful French Premier since Gen. Charles de Gaulle.

Results Held Good

For the anti-Communist world the bald fact is that the cease-fire involves the surrender of approximately 12,000,000 people in the rich northern Tonkin delta of Indo-China to Communist rule.

But given the crumbling military situation, the political mistakes of past French rule and the fact that France faced the future of the Indo-China war pretty much alone and unaided, the results are good if not better than should be expected. Territorially, three-quarters of Indo-China remains out of Communist hands.

For the United States the settlement is both a setback and an opportunity—a setback in its loss of territory and peoples to the Communists, but an opportunity to stabilize now on a new line in Southeast Asia behind which the economic, political and military power of the United States and the free world can be thrown to prevent any further Communist advance

Terms Outlined

TUESDAY, MAY 18, 1954

Supreme Court Voids Segregation in Schools

States Get Time to Conform

By Robert J. Donovan
From the Herald Tribune Bureau
Copyright New York Herald Tribune, Inc.

WASHINGTON, May 17.—In a historic decision portending vast social changes throughout the South and in the District of Columbia the United States Supreme Court held unanimously today that racial segregation in public schools is unconstitutional.

The decision read by Chief Justice Earl Warren to a tense courtroom declared that segregation was unlawful under the provision of the 14th Amendment to the Constitution assuring "equal protection of the laws" to all citizens.

The court, however, did not compel an immediate upheaval in the thousands of schools affected in Washington and 17 states. Instead, it granted a delay of many months—possibly a year or more—before issuing decrees enforcing its ruling.

TUESDAY, SEPTEMBER 10, 1957

Whites Bar Six Negro Pupils From North Little Rock School

Associated Press Radiophoto.
Negroes being prevented from entering North Little Rock High School yesterday by a crowd of white students and adults.

Governor Stands by Decision

Situation Is Quiet At Central High

By the Associated Press

LITTLE ROCK, Ark., Sept. 9.—White students threw back six Negro youths who tried to enter North Little Rock High School today as the first violence broke out in the Arkansas racial crisis.

North Little Rock, a separate city, is across the Arkansas River from the integration-torn city of Little Rock.

About ten white students met the six Negroes at the top of the steps leading into the school.

They grabbed the six, hustled and shoved them down the steps and across the campus almost to the street before police broke up the trouble. None of the Negroes was injured.

No Guardsmen on Duty

No National Guardsmen were on duty, but six policemen guarded the school, which opened today for the fall term.

The six Negroes tried a second time to enter when school superintendent F. B. Wright came out of the school building and gestured to them to follow him in.

But as the Negroes climbed the steps again, reinforcements, including adults, ran to the support of the white students. An estimated 1,500 persons surged around the Negroes.

Mr. Wright gave up and told four Negro adults who accompanied the Negro students to meet him at a downtown office later.

Police made no effort to escort the Negroes inside the building. Their only action was to break up the first violence.

All Quiet at Central High

All was quiet today at Central High School in Little Rock, where National Guardsmen kept watch in the week-long struggle between the state and national governments over integration.

As on the previous school days, a crowd of spectators gathered near the school, but no Negroes sought admission to the school and there were no incidents.

The North Little Rock crisis punctuated Gov. Orval E. Faubus's challenge of Federal school racial integration in what appeared the most serious state-Federal crisis since Civil War days. At Gov. Faubus's orders, National Guardsmen have kept Negroes out of Central High since school opened last Tuesday.

Today, the governor said that if the Federal government moves into Arkansas by force or in any other manner to limit his power "we will have lost our last right of local self-government."

"If blood is then shed, my conscience will be clear, but I will weep for my people," the Governor said in a speech prepared for television.

He said given the opportunity "we can accomplish an orderly and non-violent integration of our public schools in this state."

Faubus Is Defiant on TV

By Walter Lister Jr.
Special to the Herald Tribune
© 1957, New York Herald Tribune, Inc.

LITTLE ROCK, Ark., Sept. 9.—Gov. Orval E. Faubus, answering reporters' questions for the first time in more than four days, stood firm last night on his determination to maintain National Guard troops around Little Rock Central High School.

He indicated that if any backing-down were to be done, it would have to be done by the Federal government.

He said the integration stalemate here could end immediately if the Federal government would "exercise due prudence and caution."

Appearing before a national television audience, the governor was asked what could persuade him to withdraw the National Guard troops. "That's the million-dollar question," he replied.

'No Alternative'

While he said he hoped the problem would "dissipate within a week," the governor said he could see "no alternative at the moment" to some recession by the Federal government from its present stand.

"If those of Federal authority will exercise due prudence and caution and an understanding of all my inherent powers and obligations to maintain peace," Gov. Faubus said, the crisis would end quickly.

The Ozark-born governor admitted during the televised, limited access press conference that Gov. Marvin Griffin of Georgia, by addressing a White Citizens' Council meeting here two weeks ago, had "contributed to development" of the situation which, Gov. Faubus says, forced him to call out the National Guard last Monday night.

SEPTEMBER 14, 1951

Igor Stravinsky Directs Own Opera

A. P.

The Russian-born composer, left, giving last-minute instructions to Otokar Krauss, barytone, during the dress rehearsal of his opera "The Rake's Progress" which received an enthusiastic reception at its first presentation at the La Feníce theater in Venice Tuesday.

OCTOBER 12, 1951

For Services Rendered

A. P. Wirephoto.

Film star Marlene Dietrich receiving a decoration of Chevalier in the French Legion of Honor from French Ambassador Henri Bonnet at the French Embassy in Washington. She was honored for her work in France during and after World War II.

SATURDAY, JANUARY 16, 1954

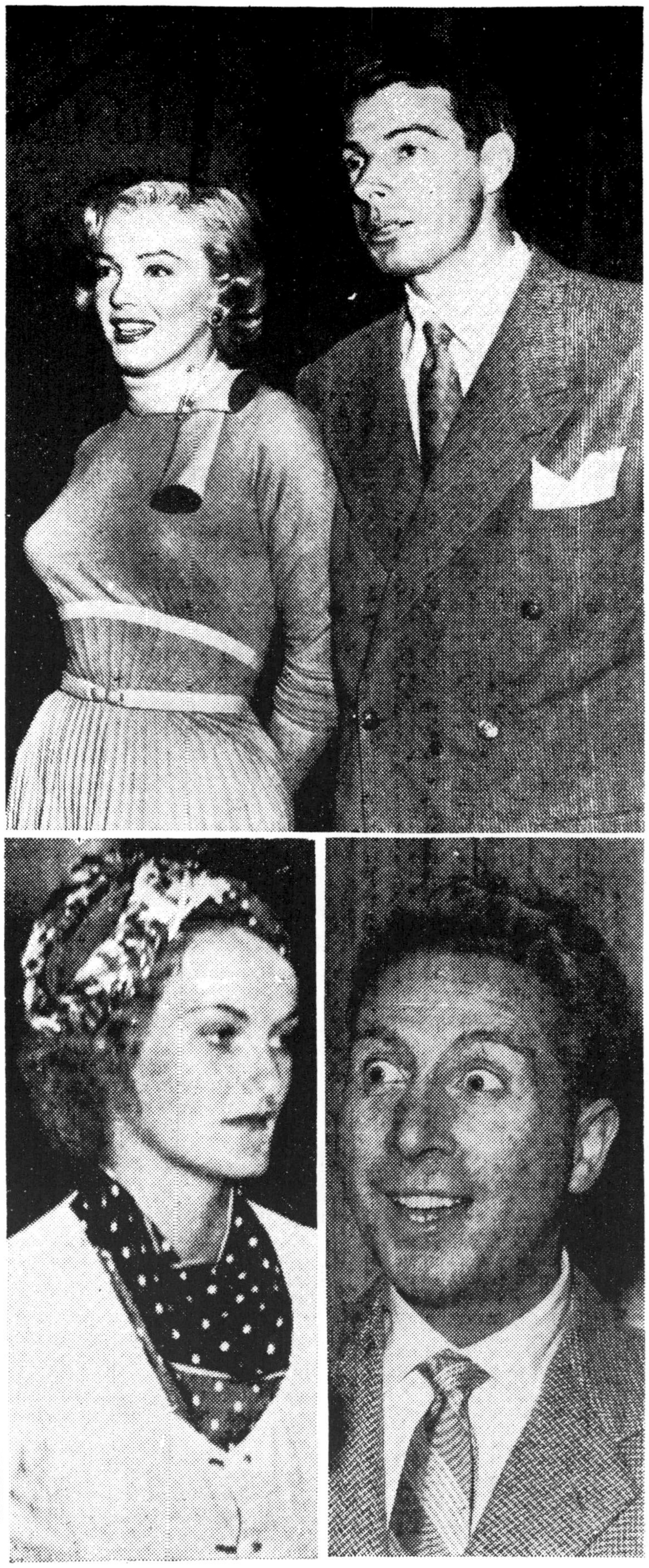

Top, blonde movie actress Marilyn Monroe and former New York Yankee baseball star Joe DiMaggia, who were married Thursday in San Francisco Municipal Court. At bottom, left, Doris Duke, American multi-millionairess, and Charles Trenet, the French singer. M. Trenet announced Thursday that he and Miss Duke will be married in the near future.

FRIDAY, MAY 25, 1951

Where are you going to-night?

ART BUCHWALD, Entertainment Editor of the European Herald Tribune, presents his brand new
• Guide to over 100 restaurants
• Guide to nightclubs, bars, etc.
• Menu dictionary in French and English
• and considerable amusing reading matter.

Buy it at book stores, kiosks, hotel desks, or in the Herald Tribune lobby, 21 R. de Berri.

PARIS after dark

Don't miss Art Buchwald in the European Herald Tribune . . . on Movies . . . on Paris After Dark . . . on Paris By Day . . . on People.

APRIL 18, 1953

Chaplin Announces in London He's Given Up U.S. Residence

By the Associated Press

LONDON, April 17. — Charlie Chaplin announced tonight he was giving up his residence in the United States because of "lies and vicious propaganda" against him.

The movie comedian said he found it "virtually impossible to continue my motion-picture work" in America under conditions which he claimed developed after World War II.

Mr. Chaplin, a British subject who spent most of his life in America, issued a statement from his suite in the smart Savoy Hotel. He penned it in long hand while sitting at a window overlooking the Thames River, and then had it typed by the hotel public relations office.

The statement was handed out, and Mr. Chaplin himself was not available for elaboration.

Mr. Chaplin flew in early this afternoon from Geneva with his wife, Oona. Mr. Chaplin refused all comment at the airport and said he would issue a statement tonight.

The statement follows: "It is not easy to uproot myself and my family from a country where I have lived for 40 years, without a feeling of sadness. But since the end of the last World War I have been the object of lies and vicious propaganda by powerful reactionary groups who, by their influence, and by the aid of America's yellow press, have created an unhealthy atmosphere, in which liberal-minded individuals can be singled out and persecuted. Under these conditions I find it virtually impossible to continue my motion-picture work and I have therefore given up my residence in the United States."

Mr. Chaplin turned in his United States re-entry permit in Geneva after driving from his Lausanne home. He offered no explanation at the time and none was asked.

Last summer the then Attorney General, James P. CcGranery, said Mr. Chaplin's name had been linked with Communism and "grave moral charges" and that the comedian would have to establish his right of re-entry through an Immigration Service examination "like any other alien." Mr. Chaplin denied in a London press interview he is or ever was a Communist party member.

FRIDAY, OCTOBER 4, 1957

Renault's Frégate with Transfluide drive.

The 1958 model of the Humber Hawk sedan.

The Jubilee Hillman De Luxe sedan.

MAY, 18, 1954

CARS FOR SALE (New)

PLAN - PLAN - PLAN

If your requirements are for a car for more than 3 weeks, there is no plan better for you (except for someone to give you one). This would be the only plan better than the Renault plan for Europe Thousands of our clients will vouch for this common sense transportation. It is simply the following: Buy the Renault for $995. Then, when you are returning, sell it to any dealer, wherever you are. Or as many people do, take it back home, for you will have fallen in love with its comfort, performance and economy. This would cost you approximately $150. If you would prefer to sell it, no PLAN could possibly guarantee to repurchase your Renault for as much as ANY dealer will pay. They just couldn't make any money this way. The reason is that the resale value is so high and the Renault so sought for by all buyers everywhere. Last but not least, remember, only French cars can be sold freely on the French market.

THAT IS OUR PLAN

RENAULT

TOURISTS

SPECIAL TAX-FREE PRICES

IMMEDIATE DELIVERY

4-door de luxe sedan **$995**

4-SEATERS - 50 M.P.G.

FREGATE $1625

6-SEATERS - 28 M.P.G.

AMSERV 52 R. de la Bienfaisance, 8e S.F.A. Building LAB. 76-40

SENSATIONAL

LOWER PRICES

which cannot be advertised here For U.S. and CANADIAN personnel

4-door de luxe sedan **$295** DOWN

FULLY EQUIPPED

FREGATE $395 DOWN

OUTSTANDING SUSPENSION

MONDAY, APRIL 16, 1956

P.S. From Monaco

Buchwald-Grimaldi Feud Still Simmers

By Art Buchwald

Special to the Herald Tribune

MONTE CARLO, April 15.—Many people, particularly members of the British press, have expressed surprise at the cool reception we personally have received at the hands of the Monegasque royal family.

"We can understand it for ourselves," they have told us, "but how can they snub somebody like you—somebody who almost got into the royal enclosure at Ascot?"

The answer is quite simple. We are being snubbed at Monaco for one simple reason. Except for a few words the present Prince exchanged with us two Christmases ago, the Buchwalds and the Grimaldis haven't spoken to each other since Jan. 8, 1297.

The reason for the feud is lost somewhere in the cobwebs of history, but it was at a time when one of our ancestors, then working for the Viking News Service, covered a battle that Rainier Grimaldi fought against the Flemish Navy. Rainier I, then an admiral, decreed that only members of the Associated, United and International Press associations could accompany him into battle, but our ancestor, disguised as a Genoese sailor, hid on board the flagship and scooped the other three news agencies by four years.

Lost Throne

In 1523, when Lucien Grimaldi, son of Lambert, and successor to his brother, Jean II, was assassinated by his nephew, Barthelemy Doria, the palace tried to hush the news up. But an alert ancestor of ours, then working for the Volga Free Press, broke the story and prevented Barthelemy from sitting on the throne.

And so it's gone down through history. There was talk that Charlotte de Grammont, daughter of Marshal de Grammont, who married the Duke of Valentinois April 28, 1659, was in love with Rudolph Buchwald, then a court reporter for "The News of the World." But we only have Rudolph's diary as evidence, and everyone in the family knows how unreliable he was.

You won't find a page in the history of Monaco where a Buchwald hasn't offended a Grimaldi or a Grimaldi hasn't offended a Buchwald. Generation after generation, the families have stayed clear of each other.

Just a couple of months ago, our Aunt Molly, of Brooklyn, was making up her guest list for our cousin Joseph's wedding to a nice girl from Flatbush. We suggested she invite Prince Rainier, who was then in the United States.

"No Grimaldis," she said, "will be allowed at Joseph's wedding."

"But, Aunt Molly," we protested, "this is the 20th century. We've got to forget ancient family feuds. Prince Rainier's a nice fellow."

"I don't care for myself," Aunt Molly said. "But you know what a long memory your Uncle Oscar has. Besides, has Prince Rainier invited Joseph to his wedding?"

No matter how much we tried to persuade Aunt Molly, she wouldn't send the Prince an invitation to Joseph's wedding. How he found out about it we'll never know, but as soon as we received this cool reception in Monaco, we knew Aunt Molly had made a mistake. The Grimaldis still had it in for the Buchwalds.

Kelly Party

We can understand Prince Rainier's attitude toward us, but we can't understand the Kelly family behaving the way they have. The Buchwalds have always liked the Kellys. Back when Mr. Kelly sr. was turned down at Henley, our father sent a telegram to the King and said: "If Jack Kelly can't row at Henley, then I won't row either."

So what happened last Saturday night? Mr. and Mrs. Kelly threw a dinner for the bridal party at the Monte Carlo Casino, and do you know where we were? We were outside in the rain holding a flashlight for a photographer from a Finnish newspaper. That's the thanks our father got for sending the telegram to the King of England.

FRIDAY, APRIL 20, 1956

Grace Kelly, Rainier Wed In Cathedral of Monaco

Associated Press Wirephoto.

Prince Rainier III and Princess Grace standing in Monaco Cathedral sanctuary during yesterday's ceremony. Below: the Prince slips the wedding ring on her finger.

Ceremony Is Solemn, Brilliant

By the Associated Press

MONTE CARLO, April 19. — Prince Rainier III of Monaco and Grace Kelly took their final vows of marriage today in the austere Monacan cathedral and sailed away into the misty blue Mediterranean on their honeymoon.

They pledged their solemn vows to support one another "for richer, for poorer, in sickness and in health." They cut the wedding cake before their brilliantly dressed guests. Barely two hours later their big American car carried them out of the castle, down the long road that hugs the rocky cliff, and to the quay.

There was anchored their white yacht, motors rolling. At 4:07 p.m. they pulled away from the dock amid a blare of whistles from yachts and visiting destroyers in the harbor.

Buchwald at Wedding As a Guest of Kellys

By Art Buchwald

Special to the Herald Tribune

MONTE CARLO, April 19.—Many people expressed surprise to see us at the Rainier-Kelly wedding after our feud with the Grimaldis, but the fact is that Jack Kelly sr., when he discovered our father had sent the first telegram to Henley protesting the fact that he could not row there, insisted we attend. And so we went as a friend of the bride.

It was obvious when we entered the cathedral that the bridegroom's family had been given the best seats. We had been given one behind a post, and when we protested to the bridegroom's family, they offered to sit us behind ex-King Farouk. We decided we could see more behind the post.

At the palace reception, after the wedding, the bridegroom's relatives an dthe bride's relatives kept separated and eyed each other suspiciously. Most of us from the Kelly side, as we ate foie gras, lobster, chicken and wedding cake, decided our Grace was too good for their Rainier, and she was a girl in a million. We decided that America had given Europe many things in the past, but nothing comparable to this beautiful princess.

In the palace courtyard, while champagne flowed, and an occasional tear dropped on the marble pavement, we toasted the royal couple. The Aga Khan, Somerset Maugham, André Maurois, Ava Gardner and countless counts and countesses, and members of the great families of France and Monaco mingled with the military and diplomatic representatives of more than 50 nations who had come to wish the prince and princess good luck, God speed and bon voyage.

The Weather

Paris: Today's forecast: Cold and cloudy early, clear periods later. Yesterday's temperatures: Max 43 (6 Cent.), min 36 (2 Cent.). Today's probable temperature: Max 39 (4 Cent.).

London: Cold, cloudy, occasional showers. Yesterday's temperatures: Max 48 (9 Cent.); min. 39 (4 Cent.).

Channel Crossing: Moderate.

New York: Cool and cloudy. Yesterday's temperature: Max 64 (18 Cent.).

NEW YORK Herald Tribune

European Edition

PRICE PER COPY:

Austria	4 S	Luxembourg	5 L.Frs.
Belgium	5 B.Fr.	Morocco	35 Frs.
Denmark	0.75 D.Kr.	Netherlands	0.25 Flor.
Egypt	6 P.	North Africa	35 Frs.
Finland	20 F.M.	Norway	0.75 N.Kr.
France	35 Frs.	Portugal	3.80 Esc.
Germany	0.40 D.M.	Spain	6 Ptas.
Great Britain	8 pence	Sweden	0.60 S.Kr.
Greece	4.50 Drs.	Switzerland	0.50 S.Frs.
Iraq	60 Fils	Syria Lebanon	50 P.
Ireland	8 pence	Turkey	70 Kurus
Israel	300 Pruta	Yugoslavia	40 dinars
Italy	60 Lire	U.S. Military	10 Cents

Established in Europe 1887 R ★ ★ PARIS, THURSDAY, NOVEMBER 1, 1956 Established in New York 1841

U.K., French Bombers Strike in Egypt; Israeli Force Racing to Cut Off Gaza Strip; Eisenhower Says U.S. Won't Be Involved

Does Not Intend To Call Congress

By the Associated Press

WASHINGTON, Oct. 31.—President Eisenhower tonight pledged there would be "no United States involvement" in the Middle East fighting.

He also told the nation and world that the decision by Britain and France to send troops to the Suez Canal zone was "taken in error."

Mr. Eisenhower has appealed urgently but in vain that the Middle East situation be left up to the United Nations.

The British and French action, the President said in his address, "can scarcely be reconciled with the principles and purposes of the United Nations, to which we have all subscribed."

"And beyond this, we are forced to doubt even if resort to war will for long serve the permanent interest of the attacking nations."

Mr. Eisenhower spoke from his White House study less than an hour after British and French planes were disclosed to be bombing military airfields in Egypt.

He said he has "no plan to call the Congress in special session."

But he promised to keep Congressional leaders of both parties abreast of developments on the new crisis.

'End the Conflict'

Mr. Eisenhower said the dedicated purpose of the United States government is "to do all in its power to localize the fighting and to end the conflict."

Mr. Eisenhower said:

"In the circumstances I have described, there will be no United States involvement in these present hostilities. I, therefore, have no plan to call the Congress in special session.

He said he is "ever more deeply convinced" that the peace-making role of the United Nations "needs further to be developed and strengthened."

"I speak particularly of increasing its ability to secure justice under international law," he said.

The President gave no hint as to concrete measures he has in mind to bolster this role of the United Nations.

To Try to Offset Veto

"At the same time it is—and will remain—the dedicated purpose of your government to do all in its power to localize the fighting and to end the conflict."

President Eisenhower promised that the government will do everything it can to get around the British and French veto in the United Nations Security Council by asking the General Assembly to as-

(Continued on Page 2, Col. 1)

Hungary's New Deal Emerging

Mindszenty Free; Coalition Seen

By Barrett McGurn

Special to the Herald Tribune

BUDAPEST, Oct. 31.—Soviet troops abandoned Budapest and Joseph Cardinal Mindszenty was freed here today in the first two victories of Hungary's week-old anti-Moscow revolution.

Negotiations began to give this decade-old satellite a democratic government.

[An angry crowd of about 2,000 demonstrated today in front of the Hungarian Parliament building demanding that the "government of murderers" resign, the Associated Press reported. The Hungarians shouted their dislike of the Communist-dominated government of new Premier Imre Nagy as Russian tanks and mechanized units retreated from the revolution-scarred capital.]

The vague outlines of five parties, Socialist and Conservative, appeared.

Telephone service with the Western world was resumed without censorship.

Newspapers of varying tendencies made their appearance and the shaken Communists, after nearly a dozen years of brutal dominance,

(Continued on Page 3, Col. 4)

Central Part of Capital A Tangle of Wreckage

By Barrett McGurn

Special to the Herald Tribune

BUDAPEST, Oct. 31.—Central Budapest is a tangle of wreckage in the wake of the past week's anti-Communist insurrection.

Wrecks of dozens of tanks, light artillery pieces and army trucks block the streets, victims of the wrath of a long-suppressed and furious population.

The military vehicles are far from the only relics of ruin. Billions of dollars worth of devastation has been visited on private homes, shops and public institutions of all sorts, some of it souvenirs of the Russian violence of the first 24 hours of the uprising, some of it the work of the insurgent population.

With Soviet troops no longer visible in central Budapest for the first time today, crowds in a mixed mood of holiday and apprehension filled the streets this morning, sightseeing among the wreckage they themselves helped create. There were incongruous scenes of many sorts: bandanna-wearing women helping one another up on tanks to peer into the ill-fated interiors, boys of less than ten playing atop a burned-out anti-tank gun for all the world the way boys slide on the polished back of the bronze lion in Brooklyn's Prospect Park.

Dozens of streetcars and buses stood with shattered windows, some of them sprawled on their sides as barricades. Occasional live grenades lay on the pavement amid mounds of glass which the neat-minded have begun to sweep up. Strollers were warned to beware of mines and of unexploded shells.

In several places power lines were down. Sheets of paper were fastened to the ends as warnings.

For whole blocks every store window was gone, but foreign witnesses agreed that the mobs which fought the tanks and the Communist party installations were remarkably "clean." Looting was rare. Some doubted it occurred at all.

"Even diamonds were left inside wrecked jewelry shop windows," one veteran of Budapest's past week reported.

The Budapest radio station, a prime propaganda organ of this

(Continued on Page 5, Col. 2)

Israeli troops advancing under cover of a smokescreen in Egyptian territory. United Press Radiophoto.

In Washington

Politicians Feel Crisis Will Sway Few Voters

By Robert J. Donovan

From the Herald Tribune Bureau. © 1956, New York Herald Tribune, Inc.

WASHINGTON, Oct. 31.—The feeling in Washington is that the Middle East crisis could not conceivably alter the outcome of the Presidential election Tuesday but that it could change votes in some areas.

Republicans believe that throughout the country as a whole President Eisenhower will, if anything, benefit politically by the fighting in Egypt.

Their reasoning is that with war clouds on the horizon, voters would have a special cause for favoring the President because of his military background. They feel that in a close state like Texas, for example, this could possibly be a rather significant factor. Republicans also point out that Adlai E. Stevenson's position on the draft and hydrogen-bomb tests is a less appealing issue in an emergency than it was, say, a week ago.

On the other hand, there is a possibility, not overlooked by the

(Continued on Page 2, Col. 3)

Stevenson Blaming Republicans

By the United Press

NEW YORK, Oct. 31.—Adlai E. Stevenson charged today that President Eisenhower and Secretary of State John Foster Dulles "bear a heavy responsibility" for the crisis in the Middle East.

The Democratic Presidential candidate accused the Eisenhower administration of "just plain deceit" in domestic policies, and added:

"The politics of misrepresentation has operated constantly in our foreign policy, too.

"Only a short time ago, my opponent assured us that there was good news from Suez. I wondered if he really didn't know how bad the situation was in the Middle East, or if he did know and decided the American people shouldn't know.

Sees 'Vaccilations'

"Unhappily, the vaccilations, the uncertainties, appeasements and provocations of the Eisenhower-Dulles policy bear a heavy responsibility for the crisis in the Middle East."

Mr. Stevenson made a whirlwind tour of Manhattan's garment district in a downpour.

In his speech he attacked the Administration's foreign policy, saying:

"Let's look where we stand today. Egypt is hostile. Israel disillusioned and evidently desperate. In a few months the Russian Communists have acquired a bridgehead in the Middle East which the Czars sought for centuries. We have split for the first time with our oldest, strongest allies—Britain and France.

Untruthfulness Alleged

"In its conduct in the Middle East, the Eisenhower-Dulles administration has been consistent in one respect only—it has not told the truth.

"To dwell on the past is instructive for the future, and it is also instructive about the decay of our foreign relations under this Administration in Washington, and I don't mean just Egypt and Israel, either—while President Eisenhower blandly assures us that never has our prestige and influence in the world been higher."

Mr. Stevenson said everyone shares the hope expressed by Mr. Eisenhower that Israel and Egypt will find a peaceful solution to their dispute and that the United

(Continued on Page 2, Col. 2)

Yugoslavia Calls For UN Assembly Talks

BULLETIN

By the Associated Press

UNITED NATIONS, N.Y., Oct. 31. The United Nations Security Council overrode British and French objection tonight and called the UN General Assembly into extraordinary session to halt the fighting in Egypt. The vote was 7-2. France and Britain voted against the measure. Belgium and Australia abstained.

By the Associated Press

UNITED NATIONS, N.Y., Oct. 31.—Yugoslavia formally proposed today that an extraordinary meeting of the United Nations General Assembly be called immediately to deal with the Middle East situation.

Joza Brilej, chief Yugoslav delegate, told the 11-nation UN Security Council that such a meeting was necessary because the vetoes of Britain and France ate last night prevented the Council from exercising its functions.

The move came after the Soviet Union demanded that the Council condemn Britain and France as aggressors and order them to withdraw their forces from Egypt. Such a move, however, would have faced certain veto.

A move to call an emergency session of the 76-nation Assembly

(Continued on Page 2, Col. 6)

Egyptians Say Fight Is Heavy

By the United Press

CAIRO, Oct. 31.—An Egyptian Army communiqué issued today said heavy fighting is still going on in the Al Auja area, near Abu Ogeila, where Israeli forces launched three successive attacks between yesterday afternoon and early this morning.

Egyptian forces, the communique said, "repulsed the attack, causing the enemy heavy losses, including four tanks."

The communiqué also said the destroyer Ibrahim Awal, after bombarding Haifa, was engaged by four Israeli ships and aircraft and the captain decided to scuttle the ship following damage received.

The communiqué said Egyptian

(Continued on Page 3, Col. 6)

Exochorda Quits Alexandria With 350 Americans Aboard

By the United Press

ALEXANDRIA, Oct. 31.—The American Export Lines passenger ship Exochorda sailed from here at dawn this morning for Naples. It carried some 350 Americans being evacuated from Egypt.

American Export Lines' two other ships in the Middle East have been taken over by the United States Navy. They are the Exermont, due in Haifa, Israel, and the Exchequer, due in Alexandria after transit through the Suez Canal.

The port of Alexandria was closed yesterday as the Exochorda was loading the luggage of the Americans. Its sailing had already been delayed to embark the families.

It left early this morning.

The 9,664-ton liner was previously due to sail at sundown last night. The Americans were sent to the

(Continued on Page 3, Col. 1)

British Commandos and their equipment are loaded aboard a ship at Valletta. United Press Radiophoto.

London Awaits Invasion News

By Gaston Coblentz

From the Herald Tribune Bureau. © 1956, New York Herald Tribune, Inc.

LONDON, Oct. 31.—Britain and France launched a military assault against Egypt late this afternoon with the declared aim of reoccupying the Suez Canal Zone.

The attack began with a bomber offensive against Egyptian military targets.

It came about 12 hours after expiration of yesterday's Anglo-French ultimatum to President Gamal Abdel Nasser of Egypt and less than two days after the invasion of Egypt by Israel.

[The Cairo radio, monitored in London by the United Press Wednesday night, said the first Anglo-French targets bombed were Cairo, Alexandria, Port Said, Ismailia and Suez.

[An earlier broadcast by the British-controlled Cyprus radio indicated the targets were airfields from which the Egyptians might launch aerial attacks against the Anglo-French invasion force.]

British officials declared "bomber aircraft are operating against military targets only and Cairo is not a military target."

British officials awaited word tonight of the expected landing of British and French troops along the Egyptian coast.

Before the air attacks began, the British government broadcast warnings to the Egyptian public to stay away from all airfields.

Shortly before 10 p.m., Foreign Secretary Selwyn Lloyd made the following statement in the House of Commons:

"Allied aircraft have commenced operations against military targets in Egypt.

"They are being limited strictly to military targets, and the civilian population were warned to keep clear before the operation started. Their aim is to obtain compliance with the cessation of hostilities by the Egyptian government.

"It is quite untrue that Cairo has been bombed."

The bombers pounding Egypt tonight are flying from Cyprus.

They are believed to be mainly British planes. However they are under the command of a joint British-French operation at Nicosia, which is styling itself "Allied Headquarters."

The first official confirmation of today's combined Anglo-French attack on Egypt did not come during British Prime Minister Sir Anthony Eden's speech to the House of Commons today but from an announcement by Allied Forces Headquarters in Cyprus.

The terse announcement only said that an "air offensive" had

(Continued on Page 3, Col. 5)

Invaders May Cut Off Gaza

Armored Force On Way to Coast

By the Associated Press

TEL AVIV, Oct. 31.—The Israeli Army claimed tonight that an armored task force has driven across Egyptian territory in an attempt to cut off the Gaza strip.

The Israelis pushed from El Ageila, south of Gaza, to try to reach El Arish, near the Mediterranean coast.

Once reached, the Egyptian-administered Gaza strip would be severed from Egypt.

Prize Airfield in Area

Along the way was a prize Egyptian airfield, a prime military target of the drive.

It was thought possible that the Israelis, after cutting off the Gaza strip, would invade it in force and occupy it.

The Israeli radio said the Gaza strip was being encircled.

Unofficial reports from the strip area said thousands of Arab refugees were fleeing in panic southward from Gaza, trying to escape Israeli encirclement.

These reports said streams of refugees were moving along the coast roads, trying to get to Egypt.

There were some 300,000 Arab inhabitants in the Gaza strip area, of which about 200,000 were Palestine refugees, who were cared for by the United Nations.

Meanwhile, the Egyptian destroyer Ibrahim el Awal, captured after

(Continued on Page 2, Col. 3)

Laborites Rap Eden For 'Reckless Folly'

BULLETIN

By the Associated Press

LONDON, Oct. 31.—Prime Minister Sir Anthony Eden tonight staked the life of his government in demanding a vote of confidence tomorrow in the House of Commons on this motion:

"That this House approves of the prompt action taken by Her Majesty's Government, designed to bring hostilities between Israel and Egypt to an end, and to safeguard vital international interest, and pledges its full support for all steps necessary to secure these ends."

From the Herald Tribune Bureau. © 1956, New York Herald Tribune, Inc.

LONDON, Oct. 31.—The British Labor party charged Prime Minister Sir Anthony Eden today with "reckless and disastrous folly" in taking military action against Egypt over the Suez Canal.

For the second consecutive day, Labor party leader Hugh Gaitskell flailed Sir Anthony and his Conservative government with strong arguments before a deeply disunited House of Commons.

Mr. Gaitskell said that millions of Britons—in his opinion a majority of the country—were profoundly shocked by the government act of military aggression in the Middle East.

Mr. Gaitskell said his party will fight relentlessly through the pressure of public opinion "to bring every pressure to bear upon the government to withdraw from the impossible situation into which they have put us."

Britain has rarely, if ever, in its modern history undertaken a military action abroad with its Parliament so profoundly split as over the current attack on Egypt. Mr. Gaitskell's speech indicated how deep and important the split is.

Here are some of the main points against Sir Anthony's decision to attack Egypt:

1—It is placing a far greater strain on Britain's alliance with the United States "than ever before."

2—It is wrecking the solidarity of the British Commonwealth.

3—It is a devastating blow to the United Nations.

4—It will expose Britain to an "almost certain" censure by two-thirds of the UN. "That is a terribly serious situation."

5—Britain has set "a terrible" example to every potential aggressor in the world.

6—"The shadow" of Russian intervention hangs over the Middle East as a result of the Anglo-French move.

7—The action against Egypt came just at the moment when events in Poland and Hungary "had given the free world its greatest hope and encouragement for ten years."

"We could legitimately feel that the ideals of democracy and liberty had just won a sensational and exciting victory," Mr. Gaitskell said. "Now this action of the government has done untold damage

(Continued on Page 2, Col. 5)

The Weather

Paris: Today's forecast: Mild and cloudy [illegible] occasional fair spells later. Yesterday's temperatures: Max. 54 (12 Cent.); min. 49 (9 Cent.). Today's probable temperature: Max. 52 (11 Cent.).

London: Cold and cloudy. Yesterday's temperatures: Max. 51 (9 Cent.); min. 49 (11 Cent.).

Channel Crossing: Moderate.

New York: Mild and fair. Yesterday's temperature: Max. 62 (17 Cent.).

NEW YORK Herald Tribune

European Edition

PRICE PER COPY:

Austria	4 S.	Luxembourg	5 L.Fm
Belgium	5 B.Fr.	Morocco	35 Fm
Denmark	0.75 D.Kr.	Netherlands	0.35 Flm
Egypt	6 P	North Africa	35 Fm
Finland	30 F.M.	Norway	0.75 N.Kr.
France	35 Frs.	Portugal	3.80 Esc.
Germany	0.40 D.M.	Spain	6 Ptas.
Great Britain	8 pence	Sweden	0.60 S.Kr.
Greece	4.50 Drs.	Switzerland	0.50 S.Fr.
Iraq	60 Fils	Syria Lebanon	50 P.
Ireland	8 pence	Turkey	70 Kurus
Israel	300 Pruta	Yugoslavia	60 dinars
Italy	60 Lire	U.S. Military	10 Cents

Established in Europe 1887 *** PARIS, MONDAY, NOVEMBER 5, 1956 Established in New York 1841

Soviet Army Crushing Hungarian Revolt; British, French Troops Embark at Cyprus

Leaflets Warn Cairo to Give In

By William J. Humphreys

Special to the Herald Tribune. © 1956, New York Herald Tribune Inc.

NICOSIA, Nov. 4.—British and French troops began embarking today on both warships and merchantmen in a Cyprus port.

Cyprus is about 14 hours away from the Suez Canal zone if the 250-mile distance is covered at the speed of the average ship.

At the same time communiques from allied headquarters on the operations and observations of Franco-British airmen over Egypt announced these developments:

1—Leaflets dropped on Cairo called on the population to accept

Communiqués—Page 6.

"the allies' proposals" for operation of the Suez Canal or run the risk of "heavy retribution."

2—Tanks and trucks moving westward "in disorder" from Ismailia on the Suez Canal to Cairo were attacked by allied aircraft with rockets and cannon fire. Coastal batteries and radar installations also were shut up.

3—The six blockade ships sunk either in the Suez Canal or its approaches by the Egyptians have resulted in "the blocking of the canal" and the trapping south of Port Said of at least seven vessels, whose nationalities were described only as "non-British."

Bridge Dropped

Late yesterday a communiqué announced that what thus far seems to be the Egyptians' only successful operation—the blocking of the canal—has been complicated by dropping the El Firdan bridge, south of Port Said, into the canal.

The second of today's communiqués said that aerial reconnaissance showed Egyptian armor was trying to seek cover amid villages.

It was said that this was being done in order to "escape attack or to bring down upon their attackers the odium of being responsible for casualties among civilians."

Today's second communiqué also pinpointed a concentration of tanks southwest of Cairo near the Giza Pyramids.

Since the canal, which appears to be at the heart of the allied police action against Egypt, lies east of Cairo there was some conjecture as to whether armor west of the Egyptian capital might mean flight.

In any event, whether the tanks were in storage, reserve or in retreat, "many of them were damaged by Royal Air Force Venoms and French Air Force Thunderstreaks (F84s) that engaged in the action.

Today's communiqué emphasized that the current aerial operations

(Continued on Page 2, Col. 6)

U.K., Paris To Reject UN Pleas

Pineau Declares Nothing Changed

By Gaston Coblentz

From the Herald Tribune Bureau © 1956, New York Herald Tribune, Inc.

LONDON, Nov. 5.—French Foreign Minister Christian Pineau said late last night after an emergency meeting with British Prime Minister Sir Anthony Eden that "nothing has changed" in the Anglo-French plan to reoccupy the Suez Canal Zone.

All indications were that the British and French governments have decided to reject the two latest United Nations pleas for an immediate cease-fire in the Middle East and to proceed with the landing of troops on the Egyptian coastline as rapidly as possible.

A large part of M. Pineau's flying trip of a few hours to the British capital was taken up with working out with the British leaders exact formulas for the Anglo-French reply to the UN demands.

Early this morning, after an interval of vacillation yesterday, the British government was reported to be again as firm as the French in its determination to go ahead with the attack on Egypt.

Stick to Conditions

The British reportedly agreed with M. Pineau that the proper way for France and Britain to reply to the UN was to stick firmly to the conditions which Britain and France laid down yesterday in answering the earlier fruitless 64-5 UN vote for a cease-fire.

The most important of the Anglo-French conditions is that Egypt must agree to the immediate occupation of the Canal Zone by Anglo-French units under all circumstances.

Now that determination to go

(Continued on Page 6, Col. 1)

United Press.

A column of Israeli troops advancing on Gaza which they later captured.

Mid-East Hope Seen By Nixon

'Stable' Political Balance Forecast

By Don Irwin

Special to the Herald Tribune © 1956 New York Herald Tribune, Inc.

CANTON, Ohio, Nov. 4. — Vice President Richard M. Nixon said last night he believes the current confused fighting in the Middle East will bring the area a "more stable" political balance, in which the Soviet Union will have no "decisive" influence.

The Vice-President indicated that he was speaking for the Administration. The speech followed up a nationally-televised talk Friday night in which he discussed the explosive Middle Eastern question with President Eisenhower's express indorsement.

Last night's appearance marked the formal end of a strenuous 40-day campaign in which staff statisticians reported he logged 33,896 miles by air, car and rail, and made an estimated 319 speeches in 36 states.

Rules Out Soviets

The talk was the sixth in a day of whistle-stopping through southeastern Ohio to support Republican Congressional candidates. He returned to Washington aboard his special train this morning.

Mr. Nixon said "almost all the world" deplores the new outbursts of violence as Israeli, British and French troops move against Egypt, but he told his audience:

"Out of the present turmoil can.

(Continued on Page 5, Col. 4)

President Said to Make His 2d-Term Plans

By the United Press

WASHINGTON, Nov. 4.—President Eisenhower is so confident of victory next Tuesday he's already making plans for his next four years in the White House, White House intimates disclosed today.

Friends who are in close touch with the Eisenhower family said the President isn't "cocky." But they said he is thinking and talking like a man who fully expects to be running the government for another term.

He already has turned the election campaign over to his lieutenants, to devote his full energies to the crisis in the Middle East and Eastern Europe.

He suffered a heavy blow today with the sudden illness of Secretary of State John Foster Dulles. He conferred with Mr. Dulles for ten minutes by telephone on plans for a new United States move in the tense diplomatic situation.

Under Secretary of State Herbert Hoover jr. took over for M. Dulles at a White House conference this morning on the Middle East and the riot-torn Soviet satellites.

The President's confidence about the election outcome reflected the belief of his personal—and political—advisers that he will be an easy victor over Democratic candidate Adlai E. Stevenson.

Friends of the President said Mr. Eisenhower makes the usual demurrers about his election chances but then goes on to talk about his future in the White House.

They said he is even talking about plans for his second inauguration.

There is active speculation in White House circles over possible Cabinet changes in a new Eisenhower administration.

The President is said to plan no wholesale clean-out of the Cabinet officers who have been under heavy fire from the Democrats this year—Mr. Dulles, Defense Secretary Charles E. Wilson and Secretary of Agriculture Ezra T. Benson.

Mr. Eisenhower considers these three men prime exponents of his

(Continued on Page 5, Col. 2)

Age Issue Raised by Stevenson

By Earl Mazo

From the Herald Tribune Bureau © 1956, New York Herald Tribune, Inc.

CHICAGO, Nov. 4.—Adlai E. Stevenson raised the health and age issues against President Eisenhower last night in the final Democratic rally of the Presidential campaign.

He charged that Mr. Eisenhower never had the inclination to work full time and now "lacks the energy" for the world's toughest job.

He also insisted "the President's age" and a Constitutional amendment that forbids his seeking a third term "make it inevitable" that Vice-President Richard M. Nixon would emerge as top man should Mr. Eisenhower win re-election.

"Do you trust Richard Nixon with decisions on the hydrogen bomb, to be chief of the armed forces, to handle th nation's dealings with foreign countries, to be fair in finding solutions for Amer-

(Continued on Page 7, Col. 5)

Israel Renews Offer Of Parley With Egypt

By Don Cook

Special to the Herald Tribune © 1956, New York Herald Tribune, Inc.

JERUSALEM (Israeli Sector), Nov. 4. — Its lightning conquest of the entire Sinai Peninsula ended, the Israeli government moved today to try to turn victory into peace—but will remain firmly in occupation of all newly conquered territory until a treaty with Egypt is signed.

Reiterating the offer to negotiate immediately with Egypt, which was made by the Israeli delegate to the United Nations General Assembly last night, Walter Eytan, Director General of the Foreign Office, issued a statement today declaring:

"For the first time in many years there is now an opportunity to make radical new decisions in the Middle East—an opportunity which if not taken now may not recur in our lifetime."

The armistice is dead, he said, and "there is no prospect of bringing it back to life."

Israel's position now is that it wants direct and immediate talks with Egypt, with no United Nations sponsorship, none of the great powers offering good offices, and nobody mediating or trying to be helpful.

It intends to stand on what it has taken until such negotiations and is confident that, once Egypt agrees to make peace, the other Arab states will follow the Egyptian lead.

As for the possibility of hostilities on the eastern frontiers with Jordan, Syria and Lebanon, it was stated categorically and unequivocally today that Israel will fight only if the Arabs launch some sort of physical attack against it.

The moving of Syrian and Iraqi troops into Jordan will not be used as excuse for an Israeli attack on the Arabs.

Meanwhile, mopping-up operations by Israeli troops went swiftly forward against the few remaining Egyptian forces in the Sinai desert.

Late Friday night, Israeli troops

(Continued on Page 6, Col. 4)

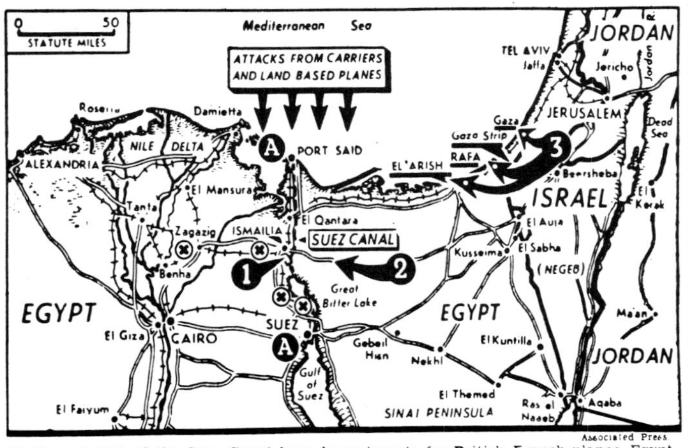

Associated Press

Both ends (A) of the Suez Canal have been targets for British-French planes. Egypt has sunk several ships to block the canal (1). Circled "X's" denote location of some of strategic Egyptian airfields raked by Anglo-French planes. Israel claimed collapse of entire Sinai Peninsula in Egypt following battle for control of key road (2) crossing wide part of the peninsula leading into Ismailia. Israeli troops captured El Arish, Rafa and Gaza City (3).

Nagy Cabinet Captured; Kadar Becomes Premier

BULLETIN

By the United Press

BERLIN, Monday, Nov. 5.—Hungarian Premier Imre Nagy has been arrested by the new Communist Hungarian revolutionary government, the East German radio announced today. It said Mr. Nagy was arrested for supporting the "counter-revolutionary forces" in Hungary.

By Robert N. Sturdevant

Special to the Herald Tribune © 1956, New York Herald Tribune, Inc.

VIENNA, Nov. 4.—The might of the Red Army appeared tonight to have snuffed out Hungary's October revolution in a dawn-to-dusk blast which silenced rebellious Budapest, captured most of the country's principal cities and sent thousands of Hungarians fleeing into Austria.

The coalition government of Premier Imre Nagy sheltering in the Parliament building on the banks of the Danube, was captured in the onrush of hundreds of Soviet tanks and supporting infantrymen which moved swiftly into all key sections of the city beginning at 4 a.m.

Janos Kadar, Communist party secretary and member of the Nagy Cabinet, was revealed in a broadcast by the Moscow radio to have turned on the revolutionary regime and established a Soviet puppet government at Szolnok, 62 miles southeast of Budapest.

Back in Moscow's Grip

Tonight, more than 20 hours after the nation-wide co-ordinated Soviet assault began, apparently reliable reports filtering through the closed border to Vienna, pointed to collapsing rebel resistance throughout the country and the rapid re-establishment of an iron Moscow grip on Hungary after its brief fling with freedom.

More than 6,000 refugees plodded through a blinding snowstorm across the Austrian border at points southeast of Vienna during the day and were given asylum by the Austrians. The Austrian government said this brought to 10,000 the number of Hungarians it has received since the revolution began Oct. 23.

Broadcasts from the Budapest radio went off the air shortly before 11 a.m. and direct contact between Budapest and Vienna by telephone ended at about the same time. Since that moment no news has been available directly from the capital city, but early this evening several radio reports were monitored from a new station calling itself the "radio of the Hungarian Army."

This radio station, heard intermittently on an unassigned wave length, said that hundreds of Soviet planes were over Budapest and that the Hungarian Army was still fighting.

Gyoer Reported Captured

The Austrian press agency however reported earlier in the day, though it gave no source, that the Russians were disarming Hungarian Army units in Budapest.

Gyoer, rebel capital in northwest Hungary, was reported to have fallen to the Russians. It lies about 40 miles inside the border.

The same fate befell Sopron a

(Continued on Page 2, Col. 3)

Dulles Has Operation On Cancerous Tissue

By the Associated Press

WASHINGTON, Nov. 4. — Preliminary laboratory tests have shown that the diseased part of the large intestine removed from Secretary of State John Foster Dulles was cancerous, the State Department announced today.

Mr. Dulles was reported to be in "good" condition at Walter Reed Army Hospital, however, with prospects he would recover.

A State Department spokesman, who reported this today, said "a thorough exploration" of Mr. Dulles's abdomen has revealed "no evidence whatsoever of extension of the lesion to any other organ."

Press officer Lincoln White said the "preliminary gross microscopical examination" of the removed tissue "shows it to be adenocarcinoma."

Informants at the Walter Reed medical center said this means "a malignant tumor."

The operation performed on Mr. Dulles yesterday consisted of snipping out the diseased section, Mr. White said, and sewing the two ends together.

Disclosed After President's Visit

He described it in these words: "Removal of the diseased tissue was accomplished with restoration of intestinal continuity."

The nature of Mr. Dulles's sudden illness was disclosed by the State Department a few hours after President Eisenhower made a bedside call on him.

At that time Maj. Gen. Leonard D. Heaton, who performed the operation, told reporters in discussing Mr. Dulles's condition: "He's doing fine."

John Foster Dulles

Reporters Safe In Budapest

WASHINGTON, Nov. 4. (U.P.).—Seven American correspondents in Budapest are safe inside the American Legation in the Hungarian capital, the State Department reported today.

Contact between the department and the legation was established in the early hours of this morning, local time, a department spokesman said.

The legation said the following American newsmen were safe:

Barrett McGurn, of the New York Herald Tribune;

John McCormack, of "The New York Times";

Henri Giniger, of "The New York Times";

Frank Bourgholtzer, of the National Broadcasting Company;

Eldon Griffith, of "Newsweek" magazine;

Ernest Leiser, of the Columbia Broadcasting System;

Russell Jones, of the United Press

The spokesman said the correspondents reached the American Legation during the night as the Russians again lowered the Iron Curtain around Hungary.

He said the department had not been in touch with the legation since "very early" this morning.

Russians Learn of Hungary

By B. J. Cutler

From the Herald Tribune Bureau © 1956, New York Herald Tribune, Inc.

MOSCOW, Nov. 4. — The Soviet Union was told today its troops have moved to crush the anti-Communist revolution in Hungary and of formation of a new pro-Soviet government in that blood-soaked nation.

Reports by the Tass news agency and Moscow radio of the new all-Communist regime implied immediate recognition and support by Russia for the "government" headed by Janos Kadar, first secretary of the Hungarian Communist party.

The ideological preparation for the new military move was contained in an editorial which covered half of "Pravda's" front page this morning denouncing Hungarian Premier Imre Nagy as "an accomplice of reactionary forces" attempting to overthrow Communist rule in the country.

In passing, the editorial mentioned the action which caused the Kremlin to view Mr. Nagy as a traitor to Communism: his repudia-

(Continued on Page 2, Col. 1)

U.S. Football

Oklahoma and Tech Win After Close Calls

By the United Press

NEW YORK, Nov. 4.—Oklahoma rallied from the brink of the season's biggest upset to beat Colorado 27-19, yesterday, and stretch its record-winning streak to 36 games.

The result was typical of the national picture as most of the country's top-ranked teams won—but only after close battles.

Georgia Tech, the nation's No. 2 team behind Oklahoma, according to the U.P. weekly poll, scored a 7-0 victory over Duke; third-ranked Tennessee downed North Carolina, 20-0; fourth-ranked Michigan State walloped Wisconsin, 32-0; sixth-ranked Ohio State shaded Northwestern, 6-2; seventh-ranked Minnesota toppled Pittsburgh, 9-6, and 13th-ranked Michigan defeated eighth-ranked Iowa, 17-14, in other games involving the highest-ranked teams.

In the "big one" at Boulder, Col., Colorado staged a spectacular first-half display of precision and solid up-front play to pile up a 19-6 lead over the favored Sooners. But Oklahoma struck back for a touchdown four minutes after the start of the second half and went ahead, 20-19, with 48 seconds left in the third period. Tommy McDonald skirted end 11 yards for th[illegible] touchdown and quarterback Jimmy Harris converted to [illegible] the Sooners ahead. They added a clinching touchdown in the fourth period on a [illegible] drive.

Georgia Tech pres[illegible] its unbeaten and untied record at Durham, N.C., when it marched 61 yards in the last ten minutes to

(Continued on Page 7, Col. 1)

Rebel Radios Heard In Calls for UN Aid

By the Associated Press

MUNICH, Nov. 4. — Desperate Hungarian rebels today called for parachute troops from the United Nations to help them in their fight against the might of the Soviet Army, Radio Free Europe reported.

RFE, American-backed private radio network, said its monitors were still picking up broadcasts from rebel radio stations as late as 2:30 p.m. Paris time.

The RFE monitors told of picking up a broadcast from Dunapentele, in south Hungary, at 1:12 p.m., in which the announcer appealed:

"We ask the United Nations to send immediate help to Hungary. We ask for parachute troops to be dropped over the Dunantul."

This would mean the Danube valley, which extends south from Budapest toward Yugoslavia.

There was no indication in the rebel broadcasts of how much strength their diminishing forces still maintained.

The 1:12 p.m. broadcast announced:

"This morning at 2:30 [illegible] Paris time), the Russian forces launched a general attack on the Hungarian people.

"We ask the United Nations to send immediate help to Hungary! We ask for parachute troops to be dropped over the Dunantul.

"We are addressing the honest millions of people in the world. Help. Help."

The station, RFE said, identified itself as the "independent Hungarian radio station." It said it would broadcast again later.

Meanwhile, in Hanover, Germany, an unknown Hungarian radio station was reported to have broadcast at 3 p.m. that "we will continue to fight for our freedom."

This was reported by a former Hungarian, now a British citizen, who said he heard the broadcast clearly over his radio, on a short-wave broadcast on the 31-meter band.

An excited announcer, the informant said, declared that "armed forces in the Retsag district are warned that Russian armored columns are approaching. Be care-

(Continued on Page 2, Col. 4)

The Weather
Paris: Cool, mostly cloudy, with occasional showers. Yesterday's temperatures: Max. 48 (9 Cent.); min. 37 (3 Cent.). Today's temperature: Max. 50 (10 Cent.).
London: Calm, fair, occasional showers. Yesterday's temperatures: Max. 50 (10 Cent.); min. 45 (7 Cent.).
Channel Crossing: Rough.
New York: Cold, possible rain. Yesterday's temperature: Max. 35 (2 Cent.).

NEW YORK Herald Tribune
European Edition

PRICE PER COPY:

Austria	4 S.	Italy	70 Lire
Belgium	5 B.Fr.	Luxembourg	6 L.Frs.
Brazil	20 Cruzeiros	Morocco	55 Frs.
Cyprus	50 Mils	Netherlands	0.40 Flor.
Denmark	1 D.Kr	North Africa	55 Frs.
Egypt	8 P.	Norway	1 N.Kr.
Finland	50 F.M.	Poland	3 Zlotys
France	45 Frs	Portugal	4.00 Esc.
Germany	0.50 D.M.	Spain	6.50 Ptas.
Great Britain	8 Pence	Sweden	0.75 S.Kr
Greece	5 Drs.	Switzerland	0.50 S.Frs.
India	1.2 Rupees	Syria, Lebanon	50 P
Iran	20 Rials	Thailand	6.00 Bahts.
Iraq	60 Fils	Turkey	2.25 T.L.
Ireland	8 Pence	Yugoslavia	40 Dinars
Israel	350 Pruta	U.S. Military	10 Cents

Established in Europe 1887 **R PARIS, FRIDAY, JANUARY 2, 1959 Established in New York 1841

Batista Flees From Country; Havana Casinos, Shops Looted

Havana's streets were filled with Cubans celebrating yesterday after they learned that President Fulgencio Batista had fled to the Dominican Republic. His departure also set off a wave of looting, as crowds sacked gambling casinos and shops. Associated Press Radiophoto

President Reaches Dominican Republic

BULLETIN

By the Associated Press

HAVANA, Jan. 1.—Rebel leader Fidel Castro's radio announced Thursday night his forces had entered the city of Santiago de Cuba, capital of Oriente Province and birthplace of the 25-month-old rebellion.

By the Associated Press

HAVANA, Jan. 1. — President Fulgencio Batista fled to the Dominican Republic today, and Cubans celebrating his departure set off an orgy of looting and fire in Havana.

The new provisional President, Carlos Piedra, took over Mr. Batista's office in the heavily fortified and sandbagged presidential palace.

Mr. Piedra sent a "cease-fire" order to the armed forces, but rebel leader Fidel Castro turned down the offer. Mr. Castro said that what had happened in Havana constituted "a coup d'état in accord with Batista," and added: "The war operations will be continued."

Rebels threatened to call momentarily a nation-wide revolutionary strike. The rebels circulated leaflets in Havana within six hours after Mr. Batista had fled.

The leaflets said the rebels wanted former Judge Manuel Urrutia to be provisional President, until general elections can be held.

The insurgents said that unless Mr. Urrutia takes over the Presidential palace, Cuba was in not only for a general strike to paralyze the nation but more bloodshed.

Mr. Castro also sent an ultimatum today to government troops defending Santiago de Cuba demanding an immediate surrender.

In a broadcast from his headquarters in the Sierra Maestra, Mr. Castro said that if the Santiago garrison failed to surrender by 6 p.m. today, the city would be stormed by rebel forces. Santiago is the second biggest city in Cuba.

Mr. Castro ordered Santiago workers to stay away from their jobs, with the exception of electric power-plant employees.

The insurgents called for a nation-wide strike until their choice for the Presidency, Manuel Urrutia, takes office. The walkout is due to start tonight.

The crowds sacked gambling casinos, looted shops and burned the plant of the newspaper "El Tiempo de Cuba," owned by a close friend of Mr. Batista, Sen. Roland Masferrer.

Mobs smashed windows and used sledgehammers against parking

(Continued on Page 2, Col. 3)

Fulgencio Batista

Downfall Explained By Batista

Guerrilla Tactics, Arms Flow Cited

By the Associated Press

CIUDAD TRUJILLO, Dominican Republic, Jan. 1.—President Fulgencio Batista of Cuba today ascribed his overthrow to rebel guerrilla warfare and their superior armament.

Mr. Batista arrived here as a self-exile this morning. The special plane that flew him from Havana also carried 40 other persons including members of his family and high government and army officials.

He said he was glad to be here but regretted the embarrassing circumstances which prompted the trip.

He said rebel leader Fidel Castro got the jump on the government by restricting his activities to guerrilla warfare against rural soldiers not trained for that type of fighting.

Hopes for Cuban Peace

By the time the rebels moved into the open in eastern Cuba, he said, they had attracted many more adherents and had superior armament to that possessed by his army.

Mr. Batista said the rebels received a continuous flow of armament, whereas the government troops could not be adequately supplied.

He said he felt satisfied he had been a good leader for Cuba, and expressed hope that Cubans will live in peace.

President-elect Andres Rivero Aguero was among the Cuban exiles who arrived shortly after Mr. Batista. He was elected in the Nov. 3 elections, but the rebels called him unacceptable.

Others here are Gen. Eleuterio Pedraza, recent Inspector General of the Army, Dr. Gonzalo Guell, Prime Minister, and Gaston Godoy Calderon, President of the Chamber of Deputies.

Cairo Said To Arrest Chief Reds

100 'Separatists' Reported Held

By Joe Alex Morris Jr.

Special to the Herald Tribune

CAIRO, Jan. 1.—Egyptian police reportedly arrested a number of key Communist leaders early today in a widespread crackdown on "separatist" elements in the United Arab Republic.

The sweep started at midnight, when many Egyptians were heralding the New Year. Three Communist-line publishing houses were shut down and reports said up to 100 key persons were arrested.

There was no official confirmation, but the move follows reported arrests of some Communists in Syria last week.

Nasser's Speech Recalled

A week ago, President Gamal Abdel Nasser, in a speech at Port Said, launched a sharp attack on Syrian Communists, accusing them of trying to destroy the union of Egypt and Syria. He promised punitive action, and Syrian region Interior Minister Abdel Hamid Serraj said later that subversive elements there would be "eradicated."

The Communist party as such has been banned for years in both Egypt and Syria.

Mr. Nasser has always made a careful distinction between local Communists and the Soviet Union. Only today he sent Soviet Premier Nikita S. Khrushchev a telegram expressing his hopes that the close relationship of the two nations "will grow steadily."

The arrests here also coincided with the ugly outbreak of street disturbances in Bagdad between Communists and Arab nationalist elements. Clashes have been reported and one Iraqi paper said there had been some 40 assassinations recently in the struggle for power within the revolutionary regime. What amounts to a press war is now taking place between Cairo and Bagdad and the recent Arab Writers Conference in Kuwait apparently just staved off breaking up in confusion when the Iraqi delegation charged other delegates were acting under imperialist orders.

There were conflicting reports on how far the anti-Communist crackdown here was going. The Egyptian party, which has always been prevented from acquiring any real strength, is split into several factions, one of which fully supports Mr. Nasser and Arab nationalism. It sharply criticizes Syrian Communist leader Khaled Bakhdash—the only open Communist ever to win a Parliamentary seat in the Arab world—for his subservience to the Soviet Union.

One report said the purge would extend into government ranks, where all pro-Communist elements would be weeded out. This reportedly included officials in the Ministry of National Guidance, Education and other branches.

Blast Kills Two In Naval Plant

INDIAN HEAD, Md., Jan. 1 (A.P.).—An explosion in a building of the Naval propellant plant here killed two employees and injured two others last night.

The explosion was followed by fire, which was declared under control after about a half-hour.

The plant, formerly known as the Naval powder factory, made gunpowder during World War II. More recently it has been working on missile propellants.

Bowl Results

BULLETIN

By United Press International

PASADENA, Calif.—At the end of one quarter of play, the University of Iowa led the Golden Bears of California, 7-0, in the Rose Bowl.

Orange
Oklahoma 21, Syracuse 6.
Sugar
LSU 7, Clemson 0.
Cotton
Air Force 0, TCU 0.

U.S. Rockets Carry Mail

NIPTON, Calif., Jan. 1 (U.P.I.).—Six thousand pieces of mail were transported over a two-mile range from Nevada to California yesterday by rockets.

The 14-foot-long, 125-pound rockets were launched from Clark County, Nev., and successfully landed at this small railroad stop in California's San Bernardino County. The rockets were powered by a zinc dust and sulphur combination fuel.

The firing of the three-inch-diameter missiles loaded with 6,000 special rocket envelopes sent in by stamp collectors marked the end of the International Geophysical Year.

California Brush Fire Still Rages

Another Curbed; 80 Homes Razed

By United Press International

LOS ANGELES, Jan. 1.—One of two wind-lashed brush fires that have blackened more than 10,000 acres and destroyed 80 homes was contained today, but the other, out of control, still burned on a 25-mile perimeter.

The New Year's Eve fires forced thousands to evacuate their homes.

The fire in Benedict Canyon that threatened the mansions of such celebrities as Doris Duke, Marion Davies, Barry Sullivan, Peter Lorre and Cameron Mitchell during the night was being mopped up today.

In the Topanga Canyon blaze, two hot spots still were plaguing fire crews as they spread toward Las Tunas Canyon on one front and edged toward Las Flores Canyon on the other. A section of Las Flores Canyon was ordered evacuated, but residents were being permitted to return to their Topanga Canyon homes.

Unseasonably warm weather, with a predicted high temperature of 80 degrees, and strong winds hampered efforts of fire crews to extinguish the flames that snaked rapidly through tinder-dry brush.

The fires were the third and fourth to ravage southern California in the last 30 days.

'59 Given Usual U.S. Greeting

300,000 Gather In Times Square

By Aaron R. Einfrank

From the Herald Tribune Bureau

NEW YORK, Jan. 1.—The year 1959 was greeted today in the traditional American manner across the country. Some people assiduously contracted hangovers, others huddled in stadiums for the annual football bowl games, and others went all out in welcoming the new year by becoming traffic and fire casualty statistics.

Last night in New York's Times square, 300,000 gathered to cheer and toot in the new year. Police Commissioner Stephen P. Kennedy assigned more than 500 patrolmen to supervise the festivities.

All over the nation special holy hour and watchnight services were held in many churches as some chose to dwell upon the more serious aspect of the passing of the old and the advent of the new.

Burn Christmas Trees

In Bangor, Maine, residents observed the occasion by burning Christmas trees in a giant bonfire. From Colorado's Pike's Peak fireworks shot up like rivals to the sputniks and the Explorer satellites. Cherryville, N.C., repeated a 150-year-old custom by firing muskets and singing an ancient German chant. Philadelphians dedicated their new Penn Center ice-skating rink with figure nines, instead of eights.

At his Gettysburg, Pa., farm, President Eisenhower spent a quiet evening with his family and friends.

Snow, freezing rain and ice covered a large section of the country as the National Safety Council announced that traffic fatalities were running ahead of advance estimates. The council had predicted that 390 would die in motor accidents over the four-day period from 6 p.m. Wednesday to midnight Sunday. On Jan. 1, 1958, 160 persons perished on the highways and **the rate so far today is accelerating at a faster pace.**

Holiday travelers stranded by airline strikes were cheered to hear of the New Year's Eve settlement of the 38-day-old strike which kept Eastern Air Lines out of operation. However, at strikebound American Airlines there was no change reported in the pilot strike, which began Dec. 20.

LSU Beats Clemson; Sooners Top Syracuse

Oklahoma Sweeps Orange Bowl, 21-6

By the Associated Press

MIAMI, Fla., Jan. 1.—Oklahoma's rangy Sooners, surely the quickest football team in the land, shocked Syracuse with three explosive, long-gaining touchdown plays today to win the Orange Bowl silver anniversary football game exactly as expected, 21-6.

A 42-yard scoring run by Prentice Gautt, first Negro ever to play for Oklahoma, and a 78-yard pass play from Brewster Hobby to Ross Coyle—the longest aerial gainer in Orange Bowl history—gave the Sooners a 14-0 lead in the first period.

These lightning thrusts failed to break the spirit of the two-touchdown underdogs from Syracuse, and it was the third quarter before Oklahoma scored again, on a 40-yard punt return by Hobby.

Syracuse Drives

Then the Syracuse players from the frigid North, who were supposed to wilt in Miami's 78-degree heat in the late stages of the game, grew stronger instead. They drove 69 yards to score on a 15-yard thrust by Mark Weber in the fourth quarter and, when the game ended, were driving in Oklahoma territory.

Despite the loss, Syracuse's brave effort did much to atone for the 61-6 beating the Orangemen took from Alabama in the Orange Bowl game of 1953—the worst humiliation any team had ever suffered in any bowl.

It was the seventh bowl victory for Oklahoma against two defeats. The Sooners now have a 6-1 bowl record under coach Bud Wilkinson, including four straight victories in the Orange Bowl.

Louisiana Wins In Sugar Bowl, 7-0

By the Associated Press

NEW ORLEANS, Jan. 1. — All-America Billy Cannon led Louisiana State to a 7-0 victory today over surprisingly tough Clemson in the Sugar Bowl.

The turning point of the game came in the third period when a fourth-down play misfired for Clemson and Duane Leopard recovered for LSU on the Clemson 11. Cannon passed ten yards to Mickey Mangham in the end zone for the touchdown. Cannon then kicked the conversion.

Clemson thrilled the crowd of 82,000 with a superb line play and hard running attack which carried to the LSU 20 just before LSU scored in the third period. At this point George Usry fumbled and Charles Strange recovered for LSU.

It was LSU's first Sugar Bowl victory in four tries.

Saved 3 Times

Three times in the first half Clemson was saved from what appeared to be certain disaster. On one occasion Durel Matherne, of LSU, fumbled on the Clemson 23 and Ray Masneri recovered for Clemson.

On another occasion, LSU punched to the Clemson 12 and then threw four incomplete passes.

Clemson's third reprieve was the closest of all. With Warren Rabb advancing and running superbly the national champions marched from their 43 to the Clemson one-yard line and J. W. Brodnax appeared to have scored a touchdown, but he fumbled at the line of scrimmage, and Doug Cline recovered for Clemson.

Rabb broke his right hand during the second period and had to leave the game—a severe blow to the offensive capabilities of LSU.

LSU had been favored to win by some two to three touchdowns, but the big, scrappy South Carolina team refused to be awed by the national champions. By the time the game was over, Clemson had managed to rub considerable luster off LSU's honors.

Business Rise Seen By Strauss

New U.S. Peaks Are Predicted

By Joseph R. Slevin

From the Herald Tribune Bureau

WASHINGTON, Jan. 1. — Secretary of Commerce Lewis L. Strauss today predicted that business activity will continue to rise in 1959.

He declared in a formal statement that the United States registered substantial gains in late 1958 and established an upward momentum that will carry the economy to new peaks this year.

"Recovery commenced in the spring," Mr. Strauss said. "Today, we start the new year from a position of increasing strength and of growing confidence." He asserted that most business barometers are rising but he cautioned that a few still lag.

Mr. Strauss put the crucial automobile industry at the head of his list of doubtful prospects. He said that automobile production "looks more hopeful," but he predicted that the automobile market will not be subjected to a thorough-going test until spring.

He singled out business plant and equipment buying and foreign purchases of United States products as other weak spots.

"The decline in business outlays for plant and equipment has been halted but there is as yet no clear-cut evidence of a renewed upswing," Mr. Strauss said. "The same generalization applies to U.S. exports of goods and services, which were reduced sharply during the recession."

Mr. Strauss reported that the job situation has improved, but he added that unemployment still is "above normal."

Fidel Castro Associated Press

U.S. Remains Neutral In Face of Cuba Strife

By David Wise

From the Herald Tribune Bureau

WASHINGTON, Jan. 1. — The United States maintained strict neutrality today in the face of the dramatic New Year's Day collapse in Cuba of Fulgencio Batista's government. Privately, top officials were hopeful that peace will now come to the strife-torn country.

But as reports arrived of increased rioting in Havana, one State Department official expressed fear that "the situation will get worse before it gets better."

The department and American Ambassador Earl E. T. Smith, in Havana, readied plans to evacuate 12,000 United States citizens in Cuba should the situation worsen.

State Department sources said it did not appear that such action would be necessary. But should the violent revolt take an anti-American turn, ships from the United States Navy bases at Guantanamo Bay, Cuba, and Key West, Fla., could be used to evacuate Americans.

Eisenhower Gets Reports

These same sources said the United States, which has maintained an official hands-off policy in the Cuba conflict, will recognize either the present government or rebel leader Fidel Castro, or any other group that can gain effective control of the country, restore order, and guarantee to meet Cuba's international obligations.

In Gettysburg, Pa., President Eisenhower was receiving intelligence reports and keeping a close watch on the fast-changing situation.

Assistant Secretary of State Roy R. Rubottom Jr., in charge of inter-American affairs, was roused from his sleep at 4:30 a.m. with news that Mr. Batista had fled to Ciudad Trujillo, Dominican Republic, with his family and aides.

(Continued on Page 2, Col. 5)

7 Dictators Out in 5 Years

By the Associated Press

NEW YORK, Jan. 1.—Seven Latin-American dictators have lost their jobs or their lives within five years. This is the list:

June 30, 1954—Pro-Communist Jacobo Arbenz Guzman, of Guatemala overthrown after a 12-day civil war.

Sept. 19, 1955—Juan D. Peron, ousted as President of Argentina.

Sept. 29, 1956—Gen. Anastasio Somoza, of Nicaragua, assassinated. His son is now President.

Dec. 12, 1956—President Paul E. Magloire of Haiti went into exile after an unsuccessful effort to perpetuate his rule.

May 10, 1957—President Gustavo Rojas Pinilla of Colombia was forced out of office by revolt.

Jan. 23, 1958—President Marcos Perez Jimenez, of Venezuela fled after resisting revolt.

Jan. 1, 1959—President Fulgencio Batista of Cuba fled at the climax of a two-year rebellion against his regime.

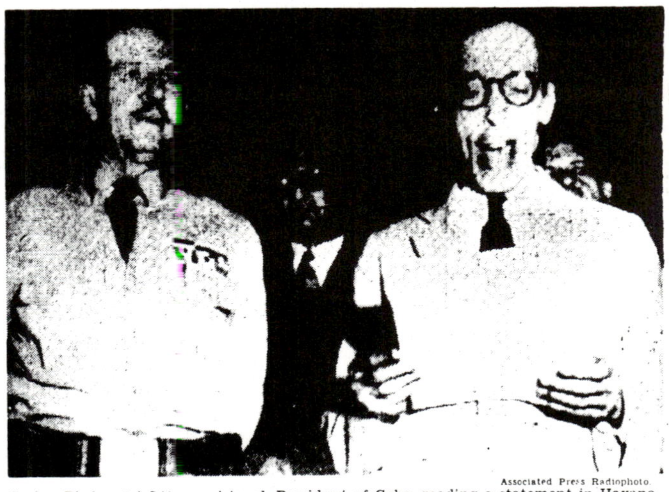

Carlos Piedra (right) provisional President of Cuba, reading a statement in Havana yesterday after President Fulgencio Batista left for the Dominican Republic and exile. With him is Maj. Gen. Eulogio Cantillo, who was head of the military junta that named Mr. Piedra President. Gen. Cantillo is now chief of the joint staff of the armed forces. Associated Press Radiophoto

The Weather

Paris: Today's forecast: Cool, foggy early, sunny later. Yesterday's temperatures: Max. 61 (16 Cent.); min. 48 (9 Cent.). Today's probable temperature: Max. 61 (16 Cent.).

London: Warm and misty early, fair later. Yesterday's temperatures: Max. 62 (17 Cent.); min. 50 (10 Cent.).

Channel Crossing: Smooth

New York: Cool, windy, occasional rain. Yesterday's temperature: Max. 60 (16 Cent.).

NEW YORK
Herald Tribune
European Edition

PRICE PER COPY:

Austria	4 S.	Italy	70 Lire
Belgium	5 B.Fr.	Luxembourg	6 L.Frs.
Brazil	12 Cruzeiros	Morocco	45 Frs.
Denmark	0.75 D.Kr.	Netherlands	0.40 Flor.
Egypt	6 P.	North Africa	45 Frs.
Finland	40 F.M.	Norway	0.90 N.Kr.
France	40 Frs.	Poland	2 Zlotys
Germany	0.50 D.M.	Portugal	4.00 Esc.
Great Britain	8 Pence	Spain	6.50 Ptas.
Greece	5 Drs.	Sweden	0.75 S.Kr.
India	1.2 Rupees	Switzerland	0.50 S.Frs.
Iran	20 Rials	Syria, Lebanon	50 P.
Iraq	60 Fils	Turkey	70 Kurus
Ireland	8 Pence	Yugoslavia	40 Dinars
Israel	350 Pruta	U.S. Military	10 Cents

Established in Europe 1887 ** PARIS, MONDAY, OCTOBER 7, 1957 Established in New York 1841

U.S. Views Satellite as Russian Victory

Fights Flare In Warsaw for Fourth Night

By William J. Humphreys
Special to the Herald Tribune

WARSAW, Oct. 6. — Clashes between riot police and civilians, touched off Thursday by university students battling for the right of free speech, tonight ranged up and down the principal thoroughfares of Warsaw for the fourth consecutive night.

At the same time, Stefan Cardinal Wyszynski, Roman Catholic Primate of Poland, told the nation's students that while he could understand their "fight," they had to remember "that our country is in a particularly difficult situation."

Those listening to the cardinal's remarks on the occasion of the university's scheduled reopening, got the impression that he was warning that hot-headed actions might push Poland into Hungary's plight of last year.

Official reports say that a total of 150 have been arrested since the riots started. Several seriously injured persons have been hospitalized. But there has been no official confirmation of any fatality, although three have been mentioned in rumors.

Tonight's main challenge to Polish government authorities was staged in front of Stalin's skyscraping architectural gift to the people of Poland—the Palace of Peace and Culture.

Hurl Bricks, Are Clubbed

There, several hundred young men, apparently from outside the student ranks as they were last night, hurled paving bricks at the riot police and received in return bruising blows from rubber truncheons.

The police, some of them appearing with rifles on their shoulders for the first time, charged and chased the demonstrators. After

Braves Nip Yanks, 7-5, In Tenth

Series Made 2-2 By 3-Run Rally

By Tommy Holmes
Special to the Herald Tribune

MILWAUKEE, Oct. 6. — Eddie Mathews, of the Braves, teed off on a pitch in the tenth inning today and the home run he hit into the rightfield bleachers climaxed a three-run rally, beat the proud Yankees of New York, 7-5, and again evened the 1957 World Series.

It also restored the famed baseball frenzy of Milwaukee, which had been chilled by the lop-sided, 12-3, victory in the third game and might have been frozen stiff if its heroes had not bounced back to win this one.

This easily was the most exciting game of the current Series and the Braves won it the hard way. The left-handed pitching of Warren Spahn anchored a 4-1 lead from

Russians Work on New One

It May Get Down With Instruments

By B. J. Cutler
From the Herald Tribune Bureau

MOSCOW, Oct. 6.—The Soviet Union is working on a new satellite designed to return to earth undamaged and with its data-laden instruments intact.

This was disclosed today by Yevgeni Fedorov, scientist in charge of Russia's upper-atmosphere research program, which already has sent history's first artificial satellite into its orbit around the earth.

The statement came as the nation's newspapers and radio stations erupted in a torrent of self-praise over Friday's successful launching of the satellite and fired taunts that the Soviet Union had "beaten" the United States and left it far behind in technical progress.

From all major newspapers, it was clear that the Kremlin was trying to convert the scientific achievement into a propaganda victory. Its purpose: to convince the world that such progress was possible only "under the wise leadership of the Communist party," as "Pravda" wrote.

Details Not Revealed

Among the hundreds of thousands of words printed about the satellite, there were almost none about its technical details. No photographs or drawings of the device have been made public. Its details are being treated almost like a military secret.

This blackout of information was even more complete about the

(Continued on Page 5, Col. 1)

Soviets Cite

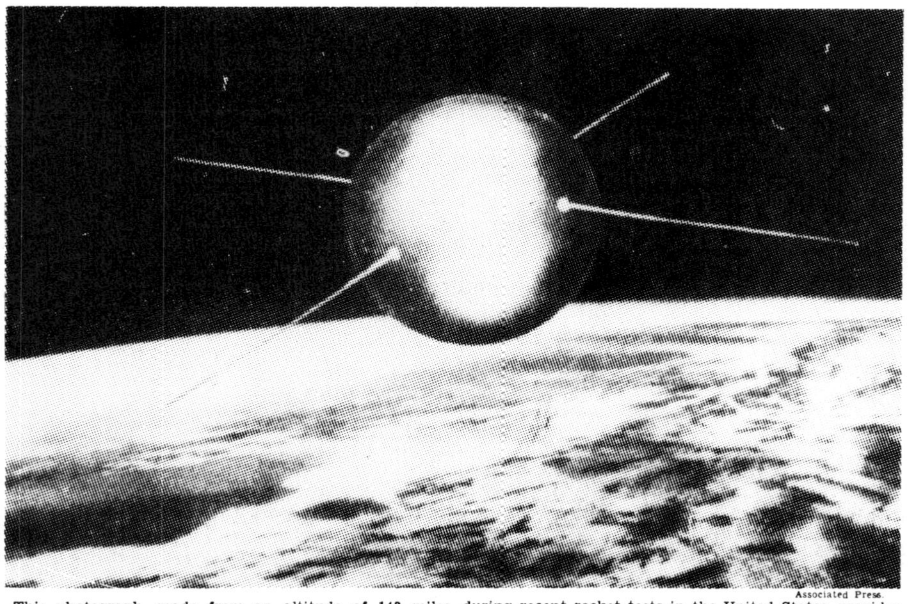

Associated Press.

This photograph, made from an altitude of 143 miles during recent rocket tests in the United States, provides background for artist's conception of the American man-made satellite in flight. Area in the background is of Southwestern United States and northern Mexico.

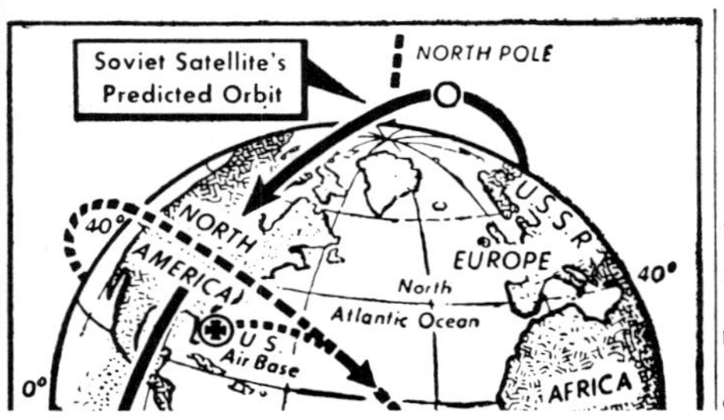

23-In. Sphere Looping World at 18,000 M.P.H.

By the Associated Press

NEW YORK, Oct. 6.—Here are pertinent facts concerning the Russian earth satellite:

LAUNCHED — Some time Friday at a secret site. Multiple-stage rockets propelled it into its orbit.

SIZE—23 inches in diameter.

WEIGHT—185 pounds, or nine times that of a similar satellite being built by the United States.

ALTITUDE—560 miles.

SPEED—18,000 miles an hour, circling the earth in 1 hour 36 min-

Coded Data

Cold-War Effect Is Assayed

Symington Calls For Investigation

Editorial—Page 4

By Robert J. Donovan
From the Herald Tribune Bureau

WASHINGTON, Oct. 6.—The rueful reaction here yesterday to news of the Soviet earth satellite was that the United States has had the daylights beat out of it in an epic contest of the 20th century.

While the Soviet projectile whizzed over this chagrined capital, the portents and consequences of Russia's new conquest of space loomed large and unencouraging. In the view of many observers here, this is what the Soviet triumph means:

1—That the Russians have scored a tremendous propaganda victory in the cold war—a victory likely to strengthen their hand diplomatically, especially in the Middle East.

Program Ahead of U.S.

2—That the Soviet rocket and missile program is far broader and more advanced than has been generally known in the United States.

3—That Soviet science is reaching into a period of possibly dazzling achievement.

4—That the Eisenhower administration may be jarred by an explosion of Congressional criticism resulting perhaps in a major Congressional investigation of American military policy. In Kansas City yesterday afternoon Sen. Stuart Symington, D., Mo., called for just such an inquiry, coupling his demand with a charge that the American people have "not been getting the truth" about missiles.

White House press secretary James C. Hagerty said that neither President Eisenhower nor other responsible American officials were taken by surprise by the Soviet announcement, even though the first word of it reached the White House

The Weather

Paris: Today's forecast: Cold and foggy early, cloudy later. Yesterday's temperatures: Max. 32 (0 Cent.); min. 28 (−2 Cent.). Today's temperature: Max. 32 (0 Cent.).

London: Cold and cloudy. Yesterday's temperatures: Max. 49 (9 Cent.); min. 41 (5 Cent.).

Channel crossing: Slight to moderate.

New York: Cold, partly cloudy. Yesterday's temperature: Max. 35 (2 Cent.).

NEW YORK
Herald Tribune
European Edition

PRICE PER COPY:

Austria	4 S.	Italy	70 Lire
Belgium	5 B.Fr.	Luxembourg	6 L.Frs.
Brazil	12 Cruzeiros	Morocco	45 Frs.
Denmark	0.90 D.Kr.	Netherlands	0.40 Flor.
Egypt	6 P.	North Africa	50 Frs.
Finland	50 F.M.	Norway	0.90 N.Kr.
France	40 Frs.	Poland	2 Zlotys
Germany	0.50 D.M.	Portugal	4.00 Esc.
Great Britain	8 Pence	Spain	6.50 Ptas.
Greece	5 Drs.	Sweden	0.75 S.Kr.
India	1.2 Rupees	Switzerland	0.50 S.Frs.
Iran	20 Rials	Syria, Lebanon	40 P.
Iraq	60 Fils	Turkey	70 Kurus
Ireland	8 Pence	Yugoslavia	40 Dinars
Israel	350 Pruta	U.S. Military	10 Cents

Established in Europe 1887 ** PARIS, MONDAY, FEBRUARY 3, 1958 Established in New York 1841

World-Looping Satellite Sending Reports

Yemenis May Join Arab State

Prince to Arrive In Cairo Today

By the Associated Press

CAIRO, Feb. 2.—Yemen is expected to announce tomorrow that it will join the new United Arab Republic.

Crown Prince Emir Seif El Islam Badr is due to arrive here tomorrow. He is Premier of the Yemen and son of the Imam Ahmad.

The United Arab Republic was proclaimed yesterday by Presidents Gamal Abdel Nasser of Egypt and Shukri Kuwatly of Syria. It united Egypt and Syria into one country. Yemen has maintained close relations with President Nasser and the Egyptian government and has readily joined military and other pacts Egypt has sponsored.

Nasser, Kuwatly Confer

Meanwhile, Presidents Nasser and Kuwatly held a three-hour meeting in Mr. Nasser's office in Kubbeh Palace. Aly Sabri, Mr. Nasser's political adviser, said they discussed speeches they will make to their respective Parliaments on Wednesday.

Opens Relations With Russia

CAIRO, Feb. 2 (U.P.). — Last week, Yemen formally opened diplomatic relations with the Soviet Union when the Soviet Ambassador to Egypt, E. Kissilev, flew to Taez, Yemen, to present his credentials as minister.

Yemen's adherence to the united Arab state would come in the midst of new allegations by Yemen that British forces based in the Aden protectorate are carrying out attacks on its southern border.

Yemeni sources here have claimed that the British attacks are motivated by Britain's desire to punish the kingdom for accepting Soviet arms. They alleged that

New Arab State Seen As Setback for Reds

By Marguerite Higgins
From the Herald Tribune Bureau

WASHINGTON, Feb. 2.—Egypt and Syria expect gradually to merge their diplomatic missions throughout the world as a result of the fusion of their two states under one flag, one Parliament and one President.

One price of the consolidation will be the loss of a United Nations seat, as it would be impossible for the new nation to keep two places.

This was reported here yesterday in diplomatic circles as Washington studied in a mood of mixed feelings the implications for the free world of the first big step toward Arab unity.

Significantly, the first reactions of concern are giving way to the view that the move may very well prove to be a setback for the Communist bloc. Washington is convinced that President Gamal Abdel Nasser of Egypt is firmly anti-Communist with regard to the domestic picture inside his country. He is viewed as far less likely to wink at attempts at subversion than the more volatile and less experienced military junta in Syria.

Despite Mr. Nasser's rapprochement with the Soviet Union in the fields of trade and aid, for example, he has dealt sternly with Communists inside Egypt, jailing those suspected of serving Russia's interests. Syria's leaders, on the other hand, have gone through the forms of outlawing the Communist party but in fact have allowed the Communists to operate openly. All this is a matter of degree, but Mr. Nasser is, from all the signs, likely to operate as a conservative force in this regard on the Syrians.

48 Dead in Collision Of C118 and Bomber

By the United Press

LOS ANGELES, Feb. 2.—A four-engined military transport with 41 persons aboard and a multi-engined Navy Neptune bomber with a crew of eight collided last night in a low-level explosion which sprayed a heavily populated area with flaming wreckage.

At least 48 persons were known dead.

The Air Force said all 41 aboard the big C118 transport bound for McGuire Air Force base, N.J., were killed. Six of the eight Navy men died in the fiery crash. Two others survived, the Los Angeles sheriff's office reported.

At least one civilian, a woman, was killed—cut in half by a large piece of the wreckage which sliced through her home in suburban Norwalk, 15 miles southeast of the center of Los Angeles.

Both Climbing on Course

The two military planes took off a minute apart from two airports separated by only five miles, and both were climbing "on course" in

Foot Issues Warning on Violence

By Joe Alex Morris Jr.
Special to the Herald Tribune

NICOSIA, Cyprus, Feb. 2.—Cyprus Gov. Sir Hugh Foot warned tonight that Cyprus faces a new wave of terror.

U.S. May Orbit 2 Other Moons

Scientist Says Satellite Works Well, May Stay in Space 'Several Months'

By Tom Lambert
From the Herald Tribune Bureau

WASHINGTON, Feb. 2.—The American space satellite Explorer wheeled high, wide and handsome on a radio-humming, looping orbit around the world today, amid indications that another Soviet and two more American man-made moons will join it within the next couple of months.

Dr. Richard W. Porter, director of American Scientific Satellite Projects for the International Geophysical Year, said the United States "bird is in good shape" and its equipment was functioning well as it swooped yesterday over Chile, Cuba, Suez, San Diego, Calif., and Savannah, Ga.

Emitting a constant "E-E-E-E-E" toned signal from its two radio transmitters, the satellite was busily relaying back to earth reports on cosmic rays in space, the density of meteorites and meteoric particles at 200 to 1,000-mile altitudes, and temperatures both within and on the exterior surface of the Explorer itself.

Complete Loop in 114 Min.

Explorer is wheeling around the world at 18,000 miles per hour on an elliptical orbit bringing it within about 200 miles of the earth at its nearest distance to the world and about 1,700 miles at its farthest. It circles the world once each 114 minutes.

Dr. William F. Pickering, of the California Institute of Technology's jet propulsion laboratory which helped develop the solid-fuel rockets which hurled Explorer into space Friday night, said the satellite's orbit was "quite satisfactorily close" to the one originally programmed.

He added, however, that the Jupiter-C rocket used to launch Explorer had generated more power than had been anticipated and thus had thrust the satellite out into space

Prestige Of U.S. Up In France

Scientific Value Of 'Moon' Noted

By Frank Kelley

The successful launching of the first American satellite had the immediate effect of restoring much of America's scientific prestige among its Western European allies, and dampened sour jokes about the American failure to get up a sputnik before the Soviets.

French commentators were quick to note that the American satellite, with an expected life-span of up to ten years, probably would yield more scientific information than did the first two Soviet satellites and could, in the end, prove of more value to the International Geophysical Year because of the instrumentation packed into a smaller space.

News of the launching came too late for French morning newspapers Saturday, but it was given smash play in the afternoon papers, with pictures of the Explorer as it took off.

PARIS, MONDAY, NOVEMBER 4, 1957

Soviets Launch Sputnik II With Dog in It

A.P. Radiophoto and Keystone.

Kudryavka (inset), now circling 936 miles above the earth in the second Soviet Sputnik launched yesterday, is the world's first satellite passenger. Another Soviet space flyer, Malyshka, is shown with her special equipment, including space suit and helmet. Three dogs, including the two shown here, have been launched in rockets recently by Soviet scientists.

Kudryavka No Amateur At Traveling in Space

By the Associated Press

LONDON, Nov. 3 — The dog riding in the new Soviet satellite was still alive, the Moscow radio reported, as the baby moon made its first whirl around the world.

Kudryavka, a husky, is riding in the new Soviet artificial earth satellite which was launched this morning.

She is the first living animal to reach outer space.

And a leading Soviet scientist gave assurances in a special bulletin over Moscow radio this afternoon that she is safe.

Prof. A. A. Blagonravov advised observers tracking Sputnik No. 2 to listen for "a hissing sound."

'Many Signals'

"This sound," he explained, "embodies a multitude of signals which tell of everything which is of interest for scientists and of how the first living being to rise to such a tremendous altitude is feeling."

Loud protests have arisen in both the United States and Britain among dog lovers protesting the cruelty to animals in sending Kudryavka on her pioneering mission.

But Prof. Blagonravov assured them she is happy.

MONDAY, JUNE 1, 1959

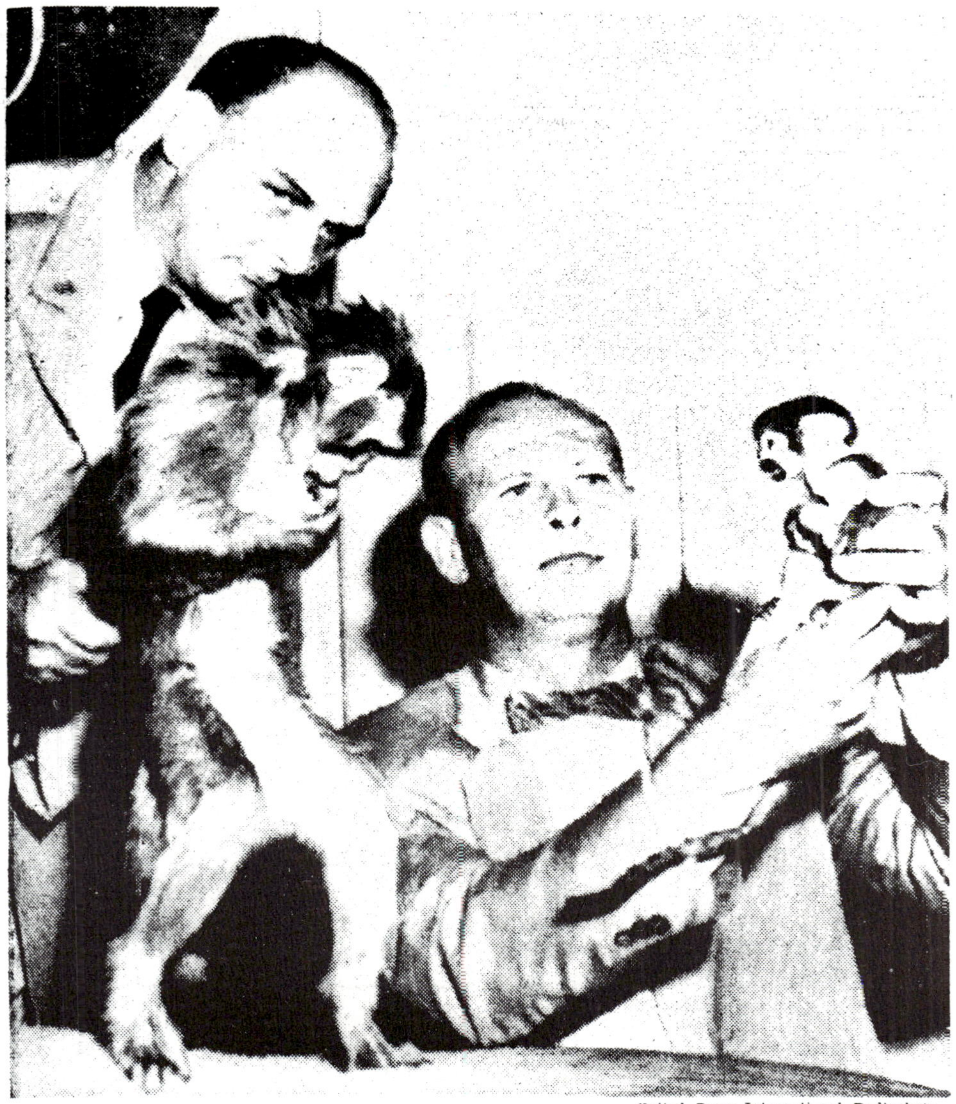

United Press International Radiophoto.

Monkeys Able (left) and Baker, recovered last week from nose cone of Jupiter rocket into space, being displayed to reporters in Washington Friday.

Two Space Monkeys Meet Press

FRIDAY, MAY 29, 1959

2 Monkeys Travel 1,500 Mi. in Nose Of Jupiter, Live

Top Speed 10,000 Mi. Per Hour

Altitude 300 Mi.; Weightless 9 Min.

By the Associated Press

CAPE CANAVERAL, Fla., May 28. —Two female monkeys returned alive today from a 1,500-mile space ride in the nose cone of an Army missile.

The Army announced that both monkeys were recovered alive from compartments of a Jupiter fired from Cape Canaveral.

The rocket had climbed to an altitude of 300 miles and flown at speeds of up to 10,000 miles per hour.

The small monkeys, named Able and Baker, are the first living creatures the United States has hurled into the farther reaches and brought back alive.

The Russians claim they brought back two dogs by parachute last August from a ride up to 281 miles altitude. In 1953, the United States Air Force recovered two monkeys after firing them some 40 miles high over New Mexico.

Today's feat represents a major breakthrough in United States effort to put a man into orbital flight.

THURSDAY, JUNE 4, 1959

4 Black Mice Sent Aloft In Discoverer III to Orbit

Recovery Is Plan of Air Force

Would Be First From a Satellite

1960-1969

Few decades have matched the 1960s in emotional extremes—political upheaval, technological progress, social unrest and rebirth. The exhilarating news with which the sixties began—the first manned space flights—deteriorated into a grim run of stories and pictures of political assassinations, civil rights clashes, antiwar protests, student riots, and continuing war in Asia and the Middle East. But brighter news also broke through: the Atom Test Ban Treaty, the landing of the first man on the moon, and progress in achieving minority rights.

For the European Edition, the news was also mixed. In 1960, the *New York Times* started publishing an International Edition in Paris, bringing the first strong English-language competition in almost thirty years. In many ways, the new competition was a spur to improved performance, as *Herald Tribune* editors and managers responded with appealing new features, including expanded business and financial coverage. But the battle for readers and advertisers was a tough, daily struggle with the outcome often in doubt.

In 1960, after forty-six years with the paper, Eric Hawkins retired with the title of editor emeritus, succeeded as editor by Bernard Cutler. André Bing was named General Manager. Roland Pinson was Bing's deputy, and later succeeded him as the paper's senior French executive. It was a difficult period for the Paris paper, a low time in Franco-American relations following the French withdrawal from NATO and the closing of US military bases in France. As the American audience shrank, the French-American management team battled to increase the paper's readership among Europeans.

Distribution became increasingly complicated. Papers had to be moved out of the narrow, crowded rue de Berri each night by truck and car, then shipped by truck, train and plane to a vast array of distant cities, where other trucks waited to carry them to local distribution points. Reaching these locations in time for the paper to be integrated into local delivery systems was the key to circulation growth, and meeting this daily challenge was the task of the new circulation director, François Desmaisons.

In May 1966, after years of competitive struggle and a back-breaking strike, the European Edition's parent paper, the *New York Herald Tribune*, was closed. Owner John Hay Whitney was determined, however, to keep the Paris paper alive and to this end he invited Katharine Graham, owner and publisher of the *Washington Post*, to join him in its ownership. The partnership was created in August, and the nameplate was changed to read, "New York Herald Tribune/Washington Post International." Immediately, the paper benefited from the availability of the joint *Los Angeles Times-Washington Post* News Service and the *Post*'s growing network of national and international correspondents.

The new partnership brought in a new publisher, Robert MacDonald, and a new editor, Murray ("Buddy") Weiss, both alumni of the *New York Herald Tribune*. Richard Morgan, who had joined the paper in 1965, was now responsible as Advertising Director for broadening the paper's revenue base.

The key to the developing commercial plan was a newly emerging audience, made up increasingly of internationally oriented business, political and professional leaders. Their native tongues were widely varied, but more and more they used English as a common international language. Their passports were of different colors, but more and more they were principally citizens of the world. Their lives—personally and professionally—were increasingly lived across national boundaries, and their need for dependable world news led them in ever greater numbers to look beyond the local and national media. To symbolize the *Herald Tribune*'s commitment to this audience, the paper's new managers decided to discontinue the famous Golden Girls and their highly visible street sales campaign on the grounds that they were too vivid an emblem of the paper's older "tourist" orientation.

Less than a year after the *Post*'s arrival, a merger agreement was concluded with the *New York Times* International Edition, and the *Times* joined the *Post* and the Whitney Communications Company in a new, three-way ownership. On May 23, 1967, the paper appeared for the first time under its new name, "International Herald Tribune," with the additional words, "Published with the New York Times and the Washington Post." The order of the names of the two parent papers was settled when Katharine Graham lost a coin-toss to *Times* publisher Arthur O. Sulzberger.

Now the vast global reporting network of the *New York Times* was also added to the Paris paper's resources. In addition, the newly named *IHT* could count on its own staffers for the special coverage that a European-based paper needed. When Paris exploded in May 1968, the *IHT* had the story of the moment in its own backyard, and everyone from finance to fashion to features rushed to cover it.

In the immediate aftermath of the merger, circulation nearly doubled, reaching 100,000 paid copies each day. But because the delivery system now covered wider areas and longer distances, the size and weight of the paper became serious matters of cost calculation. The characteristic "compactness" of the *IHT*—so popular now with busy readers—became then and still remains an editorial virtue created by economic necessity.

By 1969, continuing the tradition of innovation established by James Gordon Bennett, Jr., some seventy years before, the *IHT* was using charter flights for daily deliveries to southern and northern Europe. Circulation expanded to include nine countries in Africa and the *IHT* even went on sale in the Soviet Union, the first American non-Communist newspaper available in that country for forty years. It was obvious that something new in the history of journalism was developing out of the already well-worn rue de Berri offices. Whether the paper could now take full advantage of its unique opportunities was the question which faced the paper's new owners and managers as it entered the 1970s.

In 1966 Katharine Graham, President of the *Washington Post* Company, joined John Hay Whitney as co-owner of the European edition. The *New York Times* entered the partnership a few months later.

The Weather

PARIS: Today fair, some clouds. Temperatures 72-47 (22-8 Cent.). Tomorrow fair, with some clouds. Yesterday's temperatures 70-50 (21-10 Cent.).

LONDON: Today warm and fair. Temperatures 70-65 (21-18 Cent.). Tomorrow warm and fair. Yesterday's temperatures 63-58 (17-14 Cent.). Channel sea: Moderate.

ROME: Today clear and fair. Tomorrow hot and sunny. Yesterday's temperatures 87-70 (31-21 Cent.).

NEW YORK: Today mostly fair. Temperatures 85-60 (29-16 Cent.). Tomorrow fair. Yesterday's temperatures 85-65 (29-18 Cent.).

NEW YORK Herald Tribune

European Edition

Price Per Copy:

Algeria	0.60 N.F.	Lebanon, Syria	50 P.
Austria	4 S.	Libya	5 Piast.
Belgium	6 B Fr.	Luxembourg	6 L Frs.
Brazil	20 Cruzeiros	Morocco	65 Frs.
Canary Isl.	10 Ptas.	Netherlands	0.40 Flor.
Denmark	1 D Kr.	Norway	1 N Kr.
Egypt	9 P.T.	Poland	3 Zlotys
Finland	50 F M	Portugal	5.00 Esc.
France	0.50 N F.	South Africa	0.25 Rand
Germany	0.60 D M.	Spain	8 Ptas.
Great Britain	9 Pence	Sweden	0.75 S Kr.
Greece	5 Drs.	Switzerland	0.50 S Fr.
India	1.25 Rupees	Thailand	7.50 Baths.
Iran	20 Rials	Tunisia	0.060 Din.
Iraq, Jordan	80 Fils	Turkey	1.75 T.L.
Ireland	10 Pence	Yugoslavia	50 Dinars
Israel	55 Aguroth	U.S. Military	10 Cents
Italy	80 Lire		

74th Year in Europe - No. 24,440. ** PARIS, MONDAY, AUGUST 14, 1961 Largest circulation of any American newspaper published abroad

Reds Seal Off East Berlin to Block Refugees; Forces Threaten to Fire on Protesting Crowds

Rusk Plans Protest At Pact 'Violation'

By Fred Farris

From the Herald Tribune Bureau

WASHINGTON, Aug. 13.—Secretary of State Dean Rusk, with President Kennedy's approval, today charged that the Communist shutdown of East Berlin's border was a "flagrant violation" of Soviet-Western agreements.

The West, Mr. Rusk said, would make a "vigorous protest" against Soviet-backed restrictions on East German travel to West Berlin aimed at stemming the flood-tide of refugees headed West.

"The pretense that Communism desires only peaceful competition is exposed; the refugees, more than half of whom are less than 25 years of age, have 'voted with their feet' on whether Communism is the wave of the future," Mr. Rusk said.

United States officials were already holding urgent meetings with French and British diplomats here. The three Western military commanders in West Berlin were also conferring on what to do in the latest turn in the explosive Berlin crisis.

For days Western leaders have been apprehensive that attempts by East Germany to halt the flight to West Berlin of tens of thousands of East Germans would touch off furious rioting which in turn could lead to a spontaneous and bloody uprising or start a more general conflict.

Mr. Rusk's statement today was approved by President Kennedy week-ending in Hyannis Port, Mass.

Joseph W. Reap, State Department press officer, told reporters the Western protest would be made by the military commanders in the four-power Berlin zone, rather than on a government-to-government basis. No date was set for the protest.

Allies Unaffected

On Cape Cod, White House press secretary Pierre Salinger said Mr. Kennedy would have no immediate comment on the Berlin developments. The Chief Executive was briefed on the Berlin situation by Maj. Gen. Chester V. Clifton, his military aide, and will meet here tomorrow with Llewellyn E. Thompson jr., American envoy to Moscow.

Mr. Rusk was at his desk this morning, meeting with Assistant Secretary of State for European Affairs Foy D. Kohler, and following closely the deteriorating events in Berlin.

Mr. Rusk made clear that thus far the East German measures were aimed at East Berliners and not at the Allied position in West Berlin. There was no interference

(Continued on Page 2, Col. 7)

U.S. Studies New Plan To Disarm

By Victor Wilson

From the Herald Tribune Bureau

WASHINGTON, Aug. 13.—The United States will probably present to the United Nations this fall a far-reaching and significant disarmament proposal, John J. McCloy, President Kennedy's disarmament adviser, disclosed today.

Mr. McCloy said that he himself had had a hand in drafting the plan, that it is now under discussion in high government circles here, and that it also has been passed to the Western Allies for comment.

"It would be premature to discuss this plan now," Mr. McCloy said. But he added that this country certainly could come up with such a plan at least as "dramatic" as the one proposed by Premier Nikita S. Khrushchev at the UN session last year.

Mr. Khrushchev, before the General Assembly, suggested complete and total disarmament. He was vague, however, on inspection and controls for such a plan.

Mr. McCloy said that he would favor a disarmament plan, with proper controls, with or without an accompanying agreement on con-

(Continued on Page 2, Col. 8)

Kennedy Following Situation

Confers Today With Thompson

By David Wise

Special to the Herald Tribune

HYANNIS PORT, Aug. 13.—President Kennedy conferred with Secretary of State Dean Rusk by telephone today after being briefed on the tense East German border situation.

The President kept in touch with developments through reports from his military aide, Brig. Gen. Chester V. Clifton, who flew here this morning from Washington.

Officials for some time now have been worried about the possibility of another revolt in East Germany similar to the June, 1953, riots.

Administration quarters feel that such an uprising could force Soviet Premier Nikita S. Khrushchev to move sooner than anticipated in seeking to squeeze the Allies out of West Berlin.

Since the border closing could generate tensions leading to an explosion inside East Germany, the news was not received happily here.

Could Jeopardize Talks

The border-closing could jeopardize the East-West negotiations on Berlin which the United States and its Allies are now preparing.

Mr. Kennedy is scheduled to return to Washington tomorrow morning. He will arrive at the White House about 10:30 a.m. and is to confer at 11 a.m. with Llewellyn E. Thompson jr., United States Ambassador to the Soviet Union.

Mr. Thompson is home for consultations, but will return to the Soviet Union shortly.

When Mr. Thompson was first recalled for consultations by Mr. Kennedy shortly after Inauguration Day last January, the ambassador returned to Russia with a personal message from the Presi-

(Continued on Page 2, Col. 7)

Associated Press.

BARBED WIRE GOING UP—A group of West Berliners jeer as East German soldiers begin erecting a barbed-wire fence at the city border to block refugee flow.

Allied Routes Still Open to West Areas

By United Press International

BERLIN, Aug. 13.—The East German regime, backed by the Communist bloc, closed the East-West Berlin city border early this morning.

East German armed forces occupied East Berlin and threatened to shoot angry anti-Communists demanding reopening of their escape route to the West.

Thousands of East German soldiers, police and workers' militia with Soviet tanks in reserve stood in a city that could explode into open revolt.

The Communist East German police tonight set up machine-gun nests along the East-West border at the Brandenburg gate.

Jeering Berliners booed and fought Communist police in East Berlin and along the city dividing line this evening in the worst incidents since the 1953 East German anti-Communist uprising.

The mood along the city border became extremely tense and there appeared to be a possibility of serious trouble during the next 24 hours.

The 52,000 East Germans who have held jobs in West Berlin were ordered to give them up.

The Communists in a pre-dawn move placed West Berlin off limits in an effort to halt the mass exodus that yesterday sent a record 4.900 refugees to West Berlin.

Few Crossing Points

They enforced the ban by halting through train traffic, erecting barbed wire entanglements on the East-West city border and reducing border crossing points from 80 to 13.

The new ban said only Eastern residents with "special passes' could travel to West Berlin. That meant only persons on Communist business.

The East German action came shortly after the post-midnight release of a communiqué of the Warsaw pact nations calling on East Germany to establish "reliable supervision and control" over the West Berlin borders.

While most Berliners were asleep, East Berlin police began carrying out orders. They cut off several subway and elevated train services running between both parts of the city and set up special control points on the remainder

Check Point Unavoidable

The effect of a complicated series of changes in the subway and elevated lines was that no East Berliner could travel by train to West Berlin without passing through the East Berlin Friedrichstrasse Station with its strong control.

The Interior Ministry also said that East Germans "not working in Berlin are requested to refrain for the present from trips to Berlin."

Both the Warsaw pact communiqué and the government announcement stressed that Western Allied access routes to West Berlin from West Germany would not

(Continued on Page 2, Col. 2)

Adenauer Says West Will Act

Radio Message Beamed to East

By United Press International

BONN, Aug. 13.—West German Chancellor Konrad Adenauer tonight told his people the Western Allies will take counter measures against the closing of the border around West Berlin by the Communist East Germans.

"The West German government asks all citizens to place their confidence in these measures," the Chancellor said in a radio statement.

Dr. Adenauer did not specify what counter measures would be taken.

"It is the demand of the hour to resist the challenge from the East with determination but calmness, and not to undertake anything that could only worsen that situation and not make it better," Dr. Adenauer said.

The Chancellor recorded the statement at his home near here for RIAS, the American-controlled radio in West Berlin, to be beamed periodically this evening to East Germany.

He said the border was closed because the East German regime no longer was master of its internal difficulties.

'Condition of Weakness'

"The other East-bloc states have demanded from the (Soviet) zone government the removal of this condition of weakness and insecurity," Dr. Adenauer said.

He said the daily mass escape from East Germany to West Berlin showed the entire world the kind of pressures the people were living under and that the right of self-determination, which has been recognized throughout the world, was not granted them.

"The arbitrary action of the Pankow (East German) regime has created a serious situation," the Chancellor declared.

"Together with our allies we will take the necessary counter measures."

Foreign Minister Heinrich von Brentano will meet tomorrow morning with the Ambassadors of the United States, Britain and France.

Reprisal Ban Eyed By NATO

Allies May Bar East Germans

By Don Cook

PARIS, Aug. 13.—The North Atlantic Treaty Organization will consider this week imposing a complete NATO-wide travel ban against East Germans in retaliation for the sealing off of the Berlin sector boundary, it was learned today.

This step is one of the first in a series of possible counter-moves against the Communist bloc: It was used with some success by NATO for a brief time late in 1960. It will be discussed Wednesday at the regular meeting of the NATO Permanent Council.

It will be discussed, however, against a background of growing dissatisfaction within the alliance over the handling of Berlin diplomatic strategy by the big powers. Although Secretary of State Dean Rusk reported fairly confidently on the "state of the alliance" since his Paris visit last week, matters are less serene.

Memo by Spaak

Belgian Foreign Minister Paul-Henri Spaak has given Mr. Rusk a written memorandum on the Berlin crisis. In effect it warns that the United States is preparing for the wrong kind of a showdown with the Soviet Union. At the same time, a move is under way in NATO for a meeting of Foreign Ministers of the alliance in mid-September for a detailed examination of Western diplomatic strategy.

All of this has been engendered by Mr. Rusk's admission to the NATO Council Tuesday that the Western Big Four had not yet

(Continued on Page 2, Col. 8)

United Press International.

ON GUARD—An East German tommy-gunner guards a barbed-wire barricade set up to stop fleeing refugees.

$1 Billion U.S. Aid Accepted For Needy Latin Republics

By the Associated Press

PUNTA DEL ESTE, Uruguay, Aug. 13. — The Latin-American countries today voted to accept about $1 billion in quick American aid for the most needy of the 20 Latin-American Republics.

Only Cuba abstained in the committee vote. No country voted against the American offer. Committee action must still be confirmed by a vote in a plenary session of the Inter-American Economic and Social Conference, but this will be only a formality.

The aid is part of the $20 billion offered to Latin America over the next ten years. Yesterday the United States offered $1 billion by next March to get President Kennedy's Alliance for Progress program rolling. The offer was contained in a working document submitted to a committee studying the final declaration of the conference.

The document said that "with a view to achieving concrete results from the Alliance for Progress at the earliest possible moment," the United States will provide assistance "totaling more than $1 billion in the year ending March, 1962."

Bolivia, Chile, Uruguay and Nica-

(Continued on Page 2, Col. 6)

Eight Cézannes Are Stolen From Aix-en-Provence Show

By the Associated Press

AIX-EN-PROVENCE, Aug. 13.—Thieves broke into the Pavillon Vendôme early today and stole eight paintings by Paul Cézanne.

The pavilion has been giving an exposition of the works of Cézanne, who was born here.

Officials estimated the loss at 10 million NF (about $2 million).

It was the latest in a series of such art thefts in southern France. Last month, thieves broke into a museum at Saint-Tropez and took 57 paintings with an estimated value of $2 million.

Officials said one of the paintings taken today was Cézanne's famous "Les Joueurs de Cartes" (the card players) which had been lent to the exposition by the Louvre Museum.

Like all such famed and valued paintings, this would be extremely difficult for the thieves to dispose of to realize any money from the theft.

Others taken included "Portrait de Marie Cézanne," depicting the artist's sister, "Nature morte au gigot de mouton" (still life of a leg of lamb), "Un paysage près d'Aix, avec la Tour de César" (landscape near Aix showing Caesar's tower), "Reflets sur l'eau" (reflections on the water), "Les Crânes" (skulls), "Nature morte à la théière" (still life), and "Paysan assis" (seated peasant).

Police said the thieves got into the pavilion by cutting through a window, then opening it and a door.

They evidently acted very quietly. Two armed guards in an adjoining room, asleep or dozing, heard nothing. The pavilion's director, who lives in the same building, heard nothing either.

Talks Recessed at Met

NEW YORK, Aug. 13 (AP).—Negotiations between the Metropolitan Opera and the musicians' union were recessed late Friday for the week end with no progress reported—and prospects still dim for a 1961-62 season.

Castro to Return U.S. Plane, Will Get Patrol Vessel Back

By James E. Warner

From the Herald Tribune Bureau

WASHINGTON, Aug. 13. — The Castro government of Cuba has agreed to release an Eastern Air Lines Electra seized July 24, the State Department announced last night. For its part, the United States will return a Cuban surface patrol vessel now being held.

State Department press officer Joseph W. Reap, jr., making the announcement, asserted that the agreement "definitely is not a swap," because he said that this government would have released the $50,000 patrol boat in any case under legal procedures.

A Cuban crew will come to Key West to pick up the patrol craft Tuesday and a United States crew will fly to Havana to bring back the Electra the same day, he said.

The Cuban Foreign Ministry today hailed the agreement as "a great step forward for repression of these acts of piracy that endanger the lives of Cuban and North American citizens."

The Cuban announcement said nothing about Paris-born Albert Charles Cadon, named as the man who forced another plane to fly to Cuba last week, and now held in Havana.

The 32 passengers and five crew members of the Electra involved in the exchange were flown back to Miami the day after the seizure, although the Cuban government held the $3.200,000 airliner and the gunman, Wilfredo Roman Oquendo, a Cuban who formerly was a waiter in Miami. The Federal Bureau of Investigation wants him on charges of kidnaping, theft of the aircraft and assaulting the pilot with a deadly weapon.

On Aug. 4 Cuba had proposed a reciprocal arrangement for release of any ships or aircraft seized and brought to either country. Premier Fidel Castro gave evidence of meaning this when he promptly released not only the occupants but the plane taken over by Cadon over Mexican territory.

The State Department made no mention of it, but it was considered likely that Mr. Castro may have taken due note of belligerent demands in Congress for military action, such as sending in the Marines, if necessary, to recover planes seized and flown to Cuba.

The 40-foot patrol boat, named the SV8, was brought to Key West by three anti-Castro Cuban escapees July 29. The Coast Guard

(Continued on Page 2, Col. 5)

Carroll Given Intelligence Post

WASHINGTON, Aug. 13 (AP).—Air Force Lt. Gen. Joseph F. Carroll, 51, a former Federal Bureau of Investigation man, has been picked to head the Defense Department's joint Defense Intelligence Agency.

In recent years he has been Inspector General of the Air Force, but he was called on twice this year by Defense Secretary Robert S. McNamara to make special investigations relating to suspected security violations.

Eventually, the DIA will have a staff of about 1.500. A large proportion will be men transferred from the intelligence services of the Army, Navy and Air Force.

Associated Press Wirephoto

FREEDOM ROUTE BARRED — East German soldier, machine gun at ready, guards Berlin's Brandenburg Gate border crossing point, now closed to refugees.

Brandt Urges West to Take 'Energetic Steps' Against East

By the Associated Press

BERLIN, Aug. 13.—West Berlin Mayor Willy Brandt said today his government calls on the West to "take energetic steps" against the "illegal and inhuman" acts of East Germany in dividing the city.

Mr. Brandt said the East German regime had not only created a sort of state frontier through the center of Berlin but had also "erected the wall of a concentration camp."

Mr. Brandt appealed to East Berliners and East Germans not to revolt.

He said in a speech to the City Assembly: "Do not be provoked despite the provocation. You cannot be held in slavery forever. The barbed wire will not last forever."

The speech was broadcast over West Berlin radio stations to East Berlin and the East zone.

Interrupts Tour

The West Berlin Mayor interrupted a campaign tour to fly back for a special two-hour meeting of his government. Speaking at a news conference later, he said indignation and deep sorrow were growing among citizens in both parts of the divided city.

Mr. Brandt said the Communist actions violated the Inter-Allied agreements on Berlin. Especially mentioned was the agreement reached by the Big Four in June, 1949, to end the 11-month Soviet blockade of the city.

Instead of making conditions in East Germany bearable, he added, the regime had preferred to bar its citizens not only from West Berlin, but also from their "alleged capital" in East Berlin, he added

This was a reference to an East German communiqué that requested East Germans not working in East Berlin to stay out of the city for the time being.

Denounces Red Move

The mayor later conferred with the commanders of the three Western zones of the city.

When Mr. Brandt arrived at Tempelhof Airport early this morning, he called the Communist measures a "declaration of bankruptcy of the Communist regime."

"Instead of improving relations," he told reporters, "they want to end freedom of movement. In Berlin it is not only the freedom of movement, but the freedom to choose one's place of work that has ended."

Atlantic Air Traffic

LONDON, Aug. 13 (UPI).—Passenger traffic on North Atlantic air services increased by 4.5 per cent during the second quarter of 1961, the International Air Transport Association has announced. The figure for the April, May, June period was 500.277, compared with 478.751 for the corresponding period last year.

The Weather

PARIS: Today warm and fair. Temperatures 70-45 (21-9 Cent.). Tomorrow fair, partly cloudy. Yesterday's temperatures 64-43 (20-6 Cent.). LONDON: Today warm, cloudy, showery. Temperatures 63-57 (17-14 Cent.). Tomorrow cool, fair, showery. Yesterday's temperatures 57-53 (14-12 Cent.). Channel sea: Moderate. ROME: Today partly cloudy. Yesterday's temperatures 75-52 (24-11 Cent.). NEW YORK: Today cloudy, occasional rain. Temperatures 61-41 (16-5 Cent.). Tomorrow mostly fair. Yesterday's temperatures 61-39 (16-4 Cent.).

NEW YORK
Herald Tribune
European Edition

Price Per Copy:

Algeria	0.60 N.F.	Libya	5 Piast.
Austria	4 S	Luxembourg	6 L.Fr.
Belgium	6 B.Fr.	Morocco	65 Frs.
Brazil	20 Cruzeiros	Netherlands	0.40 Fl.
Canary Isl.	10 Ptas	Norway	1 N.Kr.
Denmark	1 D.Kr.	Poland	2 Zlotys
Egypt	9 P	Portugal	4.00 Esc.
Finland	50 F.M.	South Africa	0.25 Rand
France	0.50 N.F.	Spain	8 Ptas.
Germany	0.50 D.M.	Sweden	0.75 S.Kr.
Great Britain	9 Pence	Switzerland	0.50 S.Fr.
Greece	5 Dr.	Syria, Lebanon	50 P.
India	1.25 Rupees	Thailand	5.00 Baths
Iran	20 Rials	Tunisia	0.060 Din.
Iraq, Jordan	60 Fils	Turkey	1.75 T.
Ireland	10 Pence	Yugoslavia	50 Dinars
Israel	45 Agurot	U.S. Military	10 Cents
Italy	70 Lire		

Established in New York 1841 - in Europe 1887 R * PARIS, THURSDAY, APRIL 13, 1961 The largest circulation of any American daily newspaper published overseas

Russia Fires First Astronaut Into Space; He Lands Safely After 89 Min. in Orbit

Kennedy Calls Feat An 'Important Step'

From Cable Dispatches

WASHINGTON, April 12.—President John F. Kennedy today congratulated the Soviet Union on orbiting a man in space and returning him safely to earth.

He called the Russian achievement "an outstanding technical accomplishment."

"We congratulate the Soviet scientists and engineers who made this feat possible," Mr. Kennedy said.

"The exploration of our solar system is an ambition which we and all mankind share with the Soviet Union, and this is an important step toward that goal.

"Our own Mercury man-in-space program is directed toward that same end."

Pierre Salinger, White House press secretary, said he told Mr. Kennedy the news about the Soviet astronaut shortly after the space flight was announced by Russia this morning.

Hailed by Webb

James E. Webb, chief of the United States space agency, called the feat "obviously a splendid achievement."

He expressed hope that the Russians will share their scientific findings with the world.

Asked if he felt "demoralized" by the Russian achievement, Mr. Webb replied:

"No one likes to be beaten. They (the Russians) started earlier. We anticipated and expected that they would be first. We offer our congratulations. We are happy for them."

World Acclaim

The Soviet accomplishment was hailed around the world as one of the greatest leaps forward in the history of human progress.

Praise came from both West and East.

Communist capitals went wild with pride.

Here and there Western observers expressed fear that the exploit would give fresh weight to Soviet propaganda claims that Communism is winning its race with capitalism for global superiority.

But even these commentators conceded that, taken simply as a

(Continued on Page 2, Col. 7)

3 Astronauts Of U.S. Use Same Word

All Are 'Disappointed' At Not Orbiting First

LANGLEY AIR FORCE BASE, Va., April 12 (AP). — "Disappointed."

America's three fledling astronauts used identical expressions today to voice their feelings about a Russian beating them into orbit.

"Obviously I'm disappointed that we weren't first," said Air Force Capt. Virgil Grissom, who was here to make a routine test in a jet plane.

"Now I intend to keep on doing just what I have been doing to get on with the job—working just as hard as I can."

Comdr. Alan Shepard jr., another of the three selected as finalists for the first American manned space flight, said by telephone from Cape Canaveral, Fla.:

"For two years we have been executing specific steps of (Project) Mercury at what we feel is an appropriate speed. We shall continue to do so. I feel a deep sense of personal disappointment."

Lt. Col. John Glenn, the third member of the team, also said by phone from Cape Canaveral:

"The Russian accomplishment was a great one . . . I am naturally disappointed that we did not make the first flight to open this new era."

Germans Can't Atone, Says Israel Prosecutor

By Robert S. Bird

Special to the Herald Tribune

JERUSALEM (Israeli Sector), April 12.—The Adolf Eichmann trial erupted today with a sharp reminder from the Israeli prosecutor that German reparations to Israel are neither atonement for Nazi crimes nor help in forgetting them.

This statement was made by way of answering an argument made yesterday by Eichmann's attorney, Dr. Robert Servatius, that Eichmann could not atone for crimes of the Nazi regime but that the West German government was paying reparations to Israel for the acts of its "predecessor government."

Attorney General Gideon Hausner told the tribunal here today that the defense was saying in effect, you have received reparations—what else do you want?

"I wish to say and to emphasize that the agreement for reparations was not an atonement, nor was it a pardon, nor was it a help to forget. These crimes cannot be atoned for, cannot be pardoned and there can be no forgetting of them.

Then, in an eloquent voice, the Attorney General continued in his reference to Germany while Eichmann listened attentively as always:

"It is only possible to hope and believe that the sons will be different from the fathers, and a new generation will grow up which will not be called upon to answer for the sins of its fathers.

But for him who committed these crimes there is no pardon and no atonement. The Jewish people remembered for 2 000 years him who perhaps for the first time in history attempted to perpetrate the crime of genocide, Haman.

"The Jewish people will never forget the man who succeeded in part in carrying out this crime of genocide."

The Attorney General did not indicate to whom he was referring in this last remark—Hitler or Eichmann, but presumably to one of them.

In a session given over to the patient but legalistic effort of the government to build the structure of precedent in law for trying Eichmann here after kidnaping him from Argentina, Mr. Hausner took time out from his long recital of legal cases to denounce Eichmann as the responsible genius behind the scheme to destroy the Jews in Europe.

"For my part I should like to say at this juncture," Mr. Hausner continued, "that our argument is that Adolf Eichmann was not just an ordinary cog in the wheel. We shall attempt to prove to this court that he initiated, planned or organized and implemented the extermination of the Jews in Europe."

And he added: "This is not a

(Continued on Page 3, Col. 2)

French A-Test in December Not Full Technical Success

By Don Cook

PARIS, April 12.—The last French atomic test explosion in the Sahara Desert, on Dec. 27, 1960, was not a full technical success, it was learned today.

According to information in the hands of American atomic experts, the test device failed to perform to expectations in two major respects.

First, the explosion did not take place with the precision which was planned. This indicated that the device which was tested could not be regarded as a successful weapon prototype. Second, the yield from the explosion was less than French designers had calculated.

At the time, the test was officially described as involving "a low-yield atomic device of several kilotons." The communiqué said that radioactive fallout had been confined to an area about 60 miles long and 15 miles wide.

4th Test Expected

There were also indications at the time that this third French atomic test would complete a phase of development and that no more were planned. In the normal pattern of testing, three such blasts are generally sufficient to achieve a stage of development.

According to American information, however, it is because of the lack of full technical success in December that the French are now pressing ahead with a fourth experiment. It is rumored in Paris as possibly taking place this week end.

It is not known how the United States obtained its information. in the state of American-French atomic relations, it was scarcely volunteered by the French.

But instrumentation and air samplings can reveal a great deal about the size and nature of any atomic explosion when analyzed against the range of comparative information available to American experts.

Atomic information bears the highest secrecy classification of the French government, as it does in the United States. Very little is ever given out by the French about the progress of their atomic program.

The American analysis is of

(Continued on Page 3, Col. 4)

Space Race Began Over Decade Ago

But First Sputnik Gave It Impetus

From the Herald Tribune Bureau

NEW YORK, April 12.—The race into space has been a cold-war battle for supremacy between United States and Russian scientists for more than a decade.

It began obscurely, but burst into prominence with the launching of Russia's Sputnik I on Oct. 4, 1957. And now the Russians have demonstrated again their ability to perform the spectacular with the orbiting of the first man in space.

Little, however, is known of the early development of the Russian space program.

Hybrid Rocket

A significant day in the history of the United States program came on Feb. 24, 1949, from a flat desert valley in White Sands Proving Grounds, N.M., when a hybrid German-American rocket blasted 250 miles straight up to a point where the atmosphere is so thin that one molecule of air must travel five miles to collide with its nearest neighbor.

The rocket, dubbed Project Bumper, was a two-stage, liquid-fueled missile (the first ever to be fired successfully) constructed from one of the 100 captured German V2s brought back to this country and a 700-pound WAC-Corporal, a World War II research vehicle.

The somewhat obscure newspaper accounts of the firing indicate American officials missed the point of the venture.

Brig. Gen. Philip G. Blackmore, then commander of White Sands, said the "flight opens up new vistas for . . . exploration of the unknown regions of the atmosphere."

In Washington, Maj. Gen. Henry R. Sayler, Army Ordnance research chief, said the shot "brings nearer" the day of the "rocket satellite" but, in a reporter's words, "he would not say whether such a missile would servo a useful purpose."

First Sputnik

The rocket satellite's purpose became apparent to Americans and the world when the Russians launched their Sputnik, a 184-pound sphere circling the earth every 96 minutes with an apogee (high point) of 588 miles and a perigee (low point) of 142 miles in its orbit.

From the beginning, the United States and the Soviet Union took different tacks on their course through space.

The Russians clearly demonstrated they had the greater capability to orbit heavy payloads. At the time the 184-pound Sputnik I went into orbit, this country was planning to send up a 3.25-pound Vanguard I satellite as part of its International Geophysical Year program.

The tiny satellite made it on March 17, 1958—on the third try.

Despite disappointments with its rockets, the United States made significant progress in gathering

(Continued on Page 2, Col. 5)

Associated Press.

FIRST MAN IN SPACE — Maj. Yuri A. Gagarin.

Gagarin, 27, Was Born On a Collective Farm

From Cable Dispatches

MOSCOW, April 12. — His name means "wild duck."

It is pronounced Gah-gah-rin, with the accent on the last syllable.

Yesterday the name of Maj. Yuri Alekseivich Gagarin was unknown to the world. Today people in the streets of Moscow were hailing him as "Gaga."

Premier Nikita S. Khrushchev sent him a joyous telegram addressed to "My Dear Yuri Alekseivich."

His name has already been entered in the book of honor of the central committee of the Young Communist League.

A citation read: "For his exploit, without parallel in history, which brought eternal glory to the Soviet people, to Soviet science and technology, and represents an outstanding example of selfless service to the homeland."

Maj. Gagarin, 27, is the son of a Russian carpenter. He was born on a collective farm near Smolensk, is married and the father of two daughters, one born a month ago

He is a dedicated Communist and was admitted to party membership last year after having been a member of the Communist Youth League since 1949.

No Injury

His first words on returning to earth, according to Tass, the Soviet news agency, were:

"I ask you to tell the party, the government and Nikita Khrushchev personally that the landing was normal. I feel well. I have no bruises or injuries."

Just when the grooming of Maj. Gagarin for his pioneer journey into space began was not made clear in the biographical material released following his safe return from orbit. But it was presumed he had been a space candidate for at least a year and possibly longer.

Details of the training given the spaceman were scanty. It was officially stated that the instruction and tests he had undergone were similar to those given in the

(Continued on Page 2, Col. 3)

Space Firsts In Russia, U.S.

WASHINGTON, April 12 (UPI).—Following is a chronological summary of Soviet and United States space firsts and their launching dates:

Russia

First earth satellite, Sputnik I, Oct. 4, 1957.

First satellite with animal aboard, Sputnik II, Nov. 3, 1957

First sun satellite, Lunik I, Jan 2, 1959.

First space hit on moon, Lunik II, Sept. 12, 1959.

First photograph of far side of moon, Lunik III, Oct. 4, 1959.

First retrieval of animals from orbit, Spacecraft II, Aug. 19, 1960.

First launching from orbit, Venus Probe, Feb. 12, 1961.

First man into space, spaceship Vostok, April 12, 1961.

United States

First use of solar power cells in space, Vanguard I, March 17, 1958.

First voice from space, Project Score, Dec. 18, 1958.

First scientific exploration of interplanetary space, Pioneer V: sun satellite which transmitted information for a distance of 22.5 million miles, March 11, 1960.

First weather satellite and first cloud cover pictures from space, Tiros I, April 1, 1960.

First navigational satellite, Transit I-B, April 3, 1960.

First missile warning satellite, Midas II, May 24, 1960.

First launching of two satellites with one rocket, Transit II-A and piggyback satellite, June 22, 1960.

First passive communications satellite, Echo I, Aug. 12, 1960.

First active communications satellite, Courier 1-B, Oct. 4, 1960.

First retrieval of unoccupied spacecraft from orbit, Discoverer XIII, launched Aug. 10, and capsule recovered Aug. 11, 1960.

First surveillance satellite, Samos II, Jan. 13, 1961.

First astronomical satellite, Explorer X gamma-ray telescope, March 25, 1961.

Mercury Speed-Up Pondered

Pressure Likely For Early Effort

From the Herald Tribune Bureau

NEW YORK, April 12.—Now that the Soviets have launched a man into space, the United States program faces its most grueling test. Can the engineers and scientists of Project Mercury resist the inevitable pressure to speed things up?

Already Project Mercury has slipped at least six months. In the beginning, the National Aeronautics and Space Administration underestimated by three months the time it would take to manufacture the one-ton capsule.

It became clear that a flight of an astronaut board a Redstone rocket, originally scheduled for late fall of 1960, rescheduled for later in the year, now had been put on the books for "around the early part of 1961." Now it will be late April or early May.

This flight will only go up and down, carrying a man 100 miles up and 200 miles down range for about five minutes of weightlessness.

Eisenhower Prediction

In his budget message to Congress on Jan. 18, 1960, former President Dwight D. Eisenhower said: "It is expected that manned space flights will be attempted within the next two years."

This presumably means true orbital flight, such as the three revolutions about the earth planned for Project Mercury.

Recently Rep. Overton Brooks, D., La., chairman of the House Science and Astronautics Committee, predicted that "if all goes well" orbital launchings will get under way toward the first half of 1961.

A monkey—Ham—has already ridden the Redstone. A couple of empty capsules have been launched aboard Redstones. Several other "successful" tests have been carried out.

However, modificactions have to be carried out on the Atlas before

(Continued on Page 2, Col. 1)

U.S. Astronauts Kept Sleeping

WASHINGTON, April 12 (UPI).—Lt. Col. John Powers, press information officer for the United States astronauts, was unimpressed when a reporter woke him up today to tell him that Russia had a man in space.

"It's 3 a.m. in the morning, you jerk," Col. Powers bellowed into the telephone from Langley Air Force Base, Va.

The reporter suggested that Russia did not put a man in space every day.

"If you're wanting something from us, the answer is we are all asleep," snarled the press officer.

Is Watched on TV, Says 'I Feel Fine'

From Cable Dispatches

MOSCOW, April 12.—The Soviet Union today sent a 27-year-old airman into orbit around the earth and brought him back safely to win the man-in-space race with the United States.

Premier Nikita S. Khrushchev hailed the achievement as "an example of courage, gallantry and heroism." The streets of Moscow erupted into a demonstration of enthusiasm unparalleled since the day 16 years ago when the Nazi armies surrendered.

The man who made the first flight into space—enduring the risks of death-dealing cosmic rays and wandering meteorites—was 27-year-old Maj. Yuri Alekseivich Gagarin.

Maj. Gagarin was in the air for an hour and 48 minutes. He was returned to earth at an undisclosed spot in the Soviet Union.

200 Miles Up

The Tass news agency said it took Maj. Gagarin 89.1 minutes to orbit the earth, indicating that he had made one complete circle. It was estimated that another 20 minutes were taken in the ascent and descent.

How high Maj. Gagarin's spaceship traveled was not announced. Unofficial estimates placed the maximum height of its orbital path at about 200 miles above earth.

Maj. Gagarin's epic flight came at the end of three days of mounting excitement in the Soviet capital. Rumors that the Russians had put a man into space have filled the city since Sunday.

Some sources indicated that an attempt had in fact been made last Friday, but presumably had failed.

Mr. Khrushchev cabled his congratulations to Maj. Gagarin from the resort town of Sochi, on the Black Sea, where he is vacationing.

Radio Announcement

Foreign correspondents had been standing by their Moscow radio receivers in anticipation for the last three days.

A few minutes before 10 a.m. there was a blare of triumphant music, followed by a few bars of the simple melody of a Russian song called "How Spacious Is my Country." Then came the formal announcement:

"The world space ship Vostok (east) with a man on board was launched on April 12 in the Soviet Union on a round-the-world orbit."

The announcement said Maj. Gagarin's spaceship was launched at 9:07 a.m. Moscow time.

Soviet scientists watched on television screens as Maj. Gagarin felt himself go weightless. They maintained radio contact with the spaceship.

'I Feel Well'

"The flight is normal. I feel well," Maj. Gagarin messaged at 9:20 a.m. He was at that time over South America.

The message was repeated over loud speakers in the Soviet capital.

At 10:15 a.m. Maj. Gagarin reported from over Africa:

"The flight continues normally. I am withstanding the state of weightlessness successfully. I feel fine."

It was shortly after noon when Tass announced:

"Maj. Yuri Gagarin safely landed i nthe prearranged area of the U.S.S.R."

Talks With Khrushchev

Premier Khrushchev talked with Maj. Gagarin shortly after the landing. He asked Maj. Gagarin how he felt in flight.

"I felt good," the astronaut replied." The flight was very successful. All the apparatus of the cosmic ship functioned properly. During the flight I saw the earth from a great height. I could see the seas, the mountains, big cities, rivers and forests."

Maj. Gagarin said his wife Valentina, who had a baby a month ago, knew in advance that he was going to make the flight.

Account of Landing

The official government newspaper, "Izvestia," published an account of the landing.

"I have just seen Yuri Gagarin," said one of "Izvestia's" special correspondents in an eyewitness story. "He was getting out of the aircraft. Thick-set and smiling. Smiling as only a thoroughly happy man can."

The newspaper said Maj. Gagarin described the sky during his flight as "very, very dark, and the earth is light blue."

"Everything can be seen clearly," he told the newspaper

As Maj. Gagarin stepped out of

(Continued on Page 2, Col. 1)

Spaceman Faced Host Of Perils

Physical, Mental Strains Involved

By Earl Ubell

From the Herald Tribune Bureau

NEW YORK, April 12.—Maj. Yuri Gagarin must have run a gauntlet of terrors equal, perhaps, to those braved by Jason, the Greek mythical hero who went after the Golden Fleece.

He did not have to tame fire-breathing bulls or face a dragon, as Jason did. But he did have to ride a rocket, endure alternate weightlessness and extreme gravity and be utterly alone. The captain of the Argo might have quailed at the prospect.

Consider what the first spaceman must have experienced as a pioneer.

First, he had to take the anxiety of waiting (how long? fifteen minutes? an hour? more?) in his cabin as the great rocket beneath him was prepared with tons of explosive fuel. An accident might have blown it all to bits.

There are all sorts of escape mechanisms, of course—rockets that tear the cabin loose when, in the countdown, a dangerous situation should develop or if during the first seconds of flight the rocket should veer from course. Even so, the astronaut must think: "will they work?"

Crushing Force

When the rocket rose, the spaceman was crushed into his couch with a force equal to ten or more times his own weight. That force came from the acceleration of the rocket.

As pressure increased—it may have lasted two minutes, perhaps more—the astronaut found it difficult to breathe. His chest hurt and his cheeks and mouth drew back in an unwilling morbid grin

If you could have seen into his chest, you would have found his heart pressed against his backbone. That organ strained mightily to move blood around the body. If not enough got to the brain the astronaut would have passed out.

After about ten minutes, the cabin went into orbit. The pressure disappeared, to be replaced by no weight at all. Weightlessness occurs because the force of gravity is neutralized by the force generated

(Continued on Page 2, Col. 8)

United Press International.

OUT OF THIS WORLD—Excited Russian children peer intently at a globe outside Moscow's Planetarium as they gather to celebrate Russian man-in-space flight.

The Weather

PARIS: Today cool and cloudy early, fair later. Temperatures 48-32 (9-0 Cent.). Tomorrow mostly cloudy. Yesterday's temperatures 48-37 (9-3 Cent.).
LONDON: Today mild and cloudy. Temperatures 50-48 (10-9 Cent.). Tomorrow mild and cloudy. Yesterday's temperatures 50-47 (10-8 Cent.). Channel sea: Slight.
ROME: Today variable cloudiness. Tomorrow partly cloudy. Yesterday's temperatures 59-34 (15-1 Cent.).
NEW YORK: Today cold and fair. Temperatures 32-20 (0--7 Cent.). Tomorrow continued cold, mostly fair. Yesterday's temperatures 39-20 (4--7 Cent.).

NEW YORK
Herald Tribune
European Edition

35th Year in Europe - No. 24,603.

PARIS, WEDNESDAY, FEBRUARY 21, 1962

Largest circulation of any American newspaper published abroad

Price Per Copy:
Algeria 0.60 N.F | Austria 4 S | Belgium 6 B.Fr | Brazil 20 Cruzeiros | Canary Isl. 10 Ptas | Denmark 1 D.Kr | Egypt 9 P.T | Finland 50 F.M | France 0.50 N.F | Germany 0.60 D.M | Great Britain 9 Pence | Greece 6 Drs | India 1.25 Rupees | Iran 20 Rials | Iraq, Jordan 60 Fils | Ireland 10 Pence | Israel 70 Agoroth | Italy 80 Lire | Lebanon, Syria 50 P | Libya 5 Piast | Luxembourg 6 L.Fs | Morocco 65 Frs | Netherlands 0.40 Fl | Norway 1 N.Kr | Poland 3 Zlotys | Portugal 5.00 Esc | South Africa 0.25 Rand | Spain 8 Ptas | Sweden 0.75 S.Kr | Switzerland 0.50 S.Fr | Thailand 7.50 Baths | Tunisia 0.060 Din | Turkey 1.75 T.L | Yugoslavia 50 Dinars | U.S. Military 10 Cents

Glenn Orbits Earth Three Times, Lands Safely; Destroyer Picks Him Up in 'Excellent Condition'

'Izvestia' Discounts U.S. Probe

America Called Unreasonable

By Walter Lister jr.

From the Herald Tribune Bureau

MOSCOW, Feb. 20.—Hope for a "fruitful exchange of opinions" on Berlin between American Ambassador Llewellyn E. Thompson jr. and Soviet Foreign Minister Andrei A. Gromyko is fading fast, "Izvestia" said tonight.

The Soviet government newspaper accused the United States of being unreasonable and of slandering the "sovereignty" of East Germany.

"Izvestia" said tonight that Russia would deliver quick and destructive retaliation" to any nation that attacked East Germany.

The newspaper's article was seen as the strongest Soviet support of the East German regime since the probes began. It stated specifically that Western hopes of a softening Soviet stand on Berlin were ill-founded.

The Thompson-Gromyko Berlin soundings began Jan. 2. There have been three subsequent meetings, the most recent on Feb. 9, when Mr. Gromyko for the first time took the initiative. A fifth meeting is expected later this week or early next week.

'Useless to Discuss'

In the soundings "Izvestia" said the West has merely reiterated "two old proposals" that are "useless to discuss." It said:

1—The idea of moving the East German capital from East Berlin, which in the Western view is the Soviet Zone of Berlin, is "crazy" under existing conditions, would be comparable to instituting "foreign control over Washington," and cannot be taken seriously.

2—No less fantastic, in "Izvestia's" view, is the Western suggestion for international administration over highways and airways between West Germany and West Berlin.

The only solution that would damage no one, the newspaper said, would be the creation of a free city of West Berlin with international guarantees. But the United States, it said, does not accept this proposal.

Thus, "Izvestia" reported, "the theme of the dialogue is so narrowed that hope of fruitful exchange of opinions is fading fast."

"Izvestia" said a month and a half of discussing the Berlin situation should have taught the West that no diplomatic headway can be made with proposals "that ignore

(Continued on Page 2, Col. 7)

Associated Press.
BLAST OFF—The Atlas rocket carrying Lt. Col. Glenn into orbit leaves its launching pad at Cape Canaveral.

French Security Steps Start in Algeria, Paris

By Thomas R. Bransten

PARIS, Feb. 20.—The government today began putting massive security precautions into effect both in the main cities of Algeria and in Paris.

The measures were taken to guard against a surge of violence that the government fears may come the day that a formal cease-fire between France and the Algerian Moslem rebels is proclaimed.

According to reports from official sources, the government has ordered all security forces to be in place and on the alert by next Sunday. This is considered the earliest possible date for the announcement of a cease-fire.

[While France was preparing for the publication of the cease-fire agreement, the Algerian rebel provisional government went into session today to discuss the tentative accord. A rebel spokesman said no communiqué or statement would be issued after the meeting. The government's decision on the negotiations with France will have to be approved by the rebel assembly before the rebels will agree to sign the agreement.]

40,000-45,000 in Algiers

In Algiers, between 40,000 and 45,000 policemen and soldiers are to reinforce the present garrison of 6,000 men. A similar number would go to Oran and other reinforcements were due in the smaller cities.

Sources close to the government said that the worst trouble could

(Continued on Page 2, Col. 6)

Russians Hail Feat By Glenn

Europe Follows Flight by Radio

By United Press International

LONDON, Feb. 20.—Millions in Western Europe followed live radio broadcasts from Cape Canaveral describing the first American orbital space flight, and in Moscow a regular television program was interrupted to bring the news of Lt. Col. John H. Glenn jr.'s successful flight to the Russians.

Forgotten were the postponements that had brought criticism in much of Europe's press of America's space effort and had led the Soviet Union's pioneer spaceman, Maj. Yuri A. Gagarin, to say he was "sorry for" Col. Glenn.

Western radios broadcast the news behind the Iron Curtain. Radio Liberty, which broadcasts to Soviet Russia, and Radio Free Europe, which beams to the satellites, began their Glenn broadcasts 13 minutes after the blastoff.

George Pokrovsky, a Soviet space and ballistics expert, said he hoped that "the data from Col. Glenn's orbital flight will complete and confirm those which have been received from the flights of our first cosmonauts Gagarin and Titov."

'Satisfaction and Joy'

"I can only express the feeling of satisfaction and joy which all scientists throughout the world must have in learning of this news," he said.

In Britain, Sir Bernard Lovell, director of the Jodrell Bank radio-telescope, said: "I am delighted to hear of the successful launching." He congratulateed "all concerned on this great enterprise."

In official circles as well as on man-in-the-street levels Europeans marveled again—as they had during the Alan B. Shepard and Virgil I. Grissom sub-orbital flights—at the publicity given today's launching.

Britons, some of whom were beginning to poke fun at the repeated postponements of the Glenn

(Continued on Page 2, Col. 4)

Associated Press.
Astronaut Lt. Col. John H. Glenn jr. in his space suit.

Trip Lasts 4 Hours 56 Mins.

All Instruments Believed Intact

From Cable Dispatches

CAPE CANAVERAL, Feb. 20.—Marine Lt. Col. John H. Glenn jr. soared around the earth three times in a 4-hour 56-minute flight today and was recovered in the Atlantic in "excellent condition."

The 40-year-old steel-nerved former test pilot thus became the first American to make an orbital flight. It came ten months and ten days after Soviet cosmonaut Yuri A. Gagarin's one-orbit mission, which was followed by a 17-orbital flight by Maj. Gherman S. Titov, Aug. 6.

Col. Glenn was fired aloft from this base in his Friendship 7 capsule atop a flame-spouting Atlas rocket at 11:47 GMT. His capsule splashed into the Atlantic at 19:43 GMT, 240 miles northwest of Puerto Rico.

The landing position was only six miles from the United States destroyer Noa, one of 24 ships that had been stationed around the world for recovery of the astronaut.

The destroyer sped to the scene and lifted Col. Glenn's capsule on deck with a crane. The Noa then sent messages that the astronaut was in "excellent condition" and that all the instruments in the spacecraft were believed intact.

Triumph for Glenn

For Col. Glenn, it was a fulfillment of a longtime dream and a great personal triumph as he masterfully performed a series of exacting tasks under high gravity pressures, weightlessness and other extreme conditions of flight.

Along the way, he ate a meal of beef and vegetables from a squeeze bottle, conducted simple exercises by pulling on an elastic cord, observed breathtaking views of the earth below and made continuous instrument checks.

He did encounter some minor trouble with his space control system, but officials of the National Aeronautics and Space Administration said it was not serious.

Col. Glenn himself made the decision to complete the full three-orbit mission at a time when ground officials were considering terminating the flight after two orbits because of the difficulty.

"Affirmative. . . I'm ready to go," was Col. Glenn's quick reply when asked if he wanted to continue on his 17,530-mile-an-hour journey at altitudes ranging from 100 to 160 miles.

Due on Carrier

Plans were for Col. Glenn to be transferred to the aircraft carrier Randolph for a two-hour physical examination. Then he was to take a 90-minute plane ride to a special hospital set up on Grand Turk Island in the Bahamas.

(Continued on Page 2, Col. 1)

Minute-by-Minute Account Of U.S. Astronaut's Journey

By United Press International

CAPE CANAVERAL, Feb. 20.—A diary of Lt. Col. John H. Glenn jr.'s day (add five hours for GMT):

2:20 a.m. EST—Awakened by his personal physician for a hearty breakfast of two scrambled eggs, filet mignon, orange juice, toast, jelly and a coffee substitute.

3 a.m.—Underwent final physical examination.

4:30 a.m.—Donned his silvery, form-fitting space suit and had it pressure-checked by technicians.

5:02 a.m.—Emerged from quarters at hangar and waved three times to small crowd. Walked to a waiting transfer van where he slapped a security officer on the shoulder before ducking into the vehicle for the trip to the launching pad.

6:03 a.m.—Entered Friendship 7 space capsule after riding an elevator up the Atlas Rocket's gantry at launching pad 14.

8:25 a.m.—Gantry wheeled back, leaving gleaming white rocket standing alone. Crews started delicate job of fueling Atlas 109D.

9:36 a.m.—Report from capsule on pad: "All systems are go."

9:47 a.m.—Belching smoke and fire, the Atlas rose slowly from the pad, climbed straight up into a clear blue sky atop an orange ball of flame, and leveled off toward the east.

9:53 a.m.—More than 100 miles up, Col. Glenn reported in loud, clear voice: "I feel fine . . . The view is tremendous."

10 a.m.—Became first American launched into orbit, traveling at about 17,545 miles per hour between 100 and 160 miles above the earth.

10:25 a.m.—Tried his first food in space. Soaring over Kano, Nigeria, in a weightless condition, Col. Glenn squirted food into his mouth from a tube.

10:30 a.m.—On darkened far side of globe reported sighting "bright lights" of city of Perth, Australia. Told ground stations to "thank everybody for turning them on."

10:50 a.m.—Ground control said Col. Glenn's heartbeat and respiration were "completely normal" and the astronaut said he was "having no problems."

11:09 a.m.—Friendship 7 passed over Guaymas, Mexico, and headed back across North American continent. Col. Glenn still in voice contact with ground stations.

11:24 a.m.—Completed first orbit of earth, 97 minutes after launching.

11:28 a.m.—Col. Glenn reported "minor difficulties" with attitude-control system, which is used to keep capsule in its proper position during orbits.

11:32 a.m.—Switched to 'fly by wire" manual-control system.

11:42 a.m.—Col. Glenn made contact with the Kano, Nigeria, tracking station for second time. He told ground stations he was "a little warm" and the sun was shining through the window of his space capsule.

11:50 a.m.—Ground stations said

(Continued on Page 2, Col. 7)

Kennedy, on TV, Hails Spaceman

WASHINGTON, Feb. 20 (AP).—President Kennedy saluted spaceman John H. Glenn today, and declared that in space America must "be in a position second to none."

Speaking on television from the White House rose garden soon after Lt. Col. Glenn safely completed his three-orbit flight, Mr. Kennedy said:

"Some years ago as a Marine pilot he raced the sun across the country—and lost. Today he won.

"We have a long way to go in the space race and we started late. This is the new ocean and we must sail on it and be in a position second to none."

Mr. Kennedy appeared on television after Col. Glenn landed and said: "I know I express the great happiness of all of us that Col. Glenn has completed his trip. . . . He is the kind of American, as are the other astronauts, of whom we are proud."

Kennedy Asks Pay Raises For 1,640,000 in U.S. Jobs

By United Press International

WASHINGTON, Feb. 20.—President Kennedy asked Congress in a special message today to approve a $1 billion salary increase for 1,640,000 Federal workers. The raises were needed to bring government pay scales in line with private industry, he said.

The Federal government no longer is able to attract and keep the talented personnel it needs, the President added. Federal workers should receive pay "comparable with the salaries received by their counterparts in private life" to keep them from being lost to more lucrative jobs, he said.

"To pay more than this is to be unfair to the taxpayers—to pay less is to degrade the public service

adjustment in our top executive and professional positions to be the most vital single element of correction in this entire proposal."

Congress is expected to pass some kind of Federal pay increase this session. But a strong drive is foreseen to give most of the increase to middle and lower-income employees, rather than to the middle-to-upper brackets as Mr. Kennedy has emphasized.

Germans Fear Flood Toll of 400 or 500

By the Associated Press

HAMBURG, Feb. 20. — Flood-stricken North Germany, hit over the week end with its worst disaster since World War II, today feared the death toll might climb to 400 or 500.

The official count of bodies recovered from the flooded region rose to 277 during the day. New victims were found overnight, but they had not yet been added to the official toll.

The city government of Hamburg, busy trying to get life in order for the flood survivors, said the death count was of lesser importance now. No official would estimate the toll, but informed sources at City Hall said as many as 200 more might be added to the 253 victims already known to have died in the city.

Dead in Other Areas

The list of dead from other areas were: seven in Bremen, 11 in Lower Saxony, one in Schleswig-Holstein, and five Bundeswehr soldiers killed in rescue operations.

Hamburg city officials announced that emergency delivery of food and water to stranded citizens could be curtailed now that more regular supply routes by road and boat had been organized.

With waters receding, a plague of rats was reported in the city district of Neuenfelde. A spokesman said the rats were living on bodies of drowned animals and in trees and created a serious health problem.

Three 50-ton ferries belonging to the Bundeswehr were added to the regular Elbe River ferries in an effort to relieve traffic congestion. Long lines of cars piled up

(Continued on Page 2, Col. 5)

British to Regroup Forces; To Keep Strength in NATO

From the Herald Tribune Bureau

LONDON, Feb. 20.—The British government outlined today a major regrouping of its forces around the world.

small, highly trained army can be moved at short notice to trouble spots in British areas of commitment.

Among its main points are:

R. F. Kennedy In Rome; Will See Pope

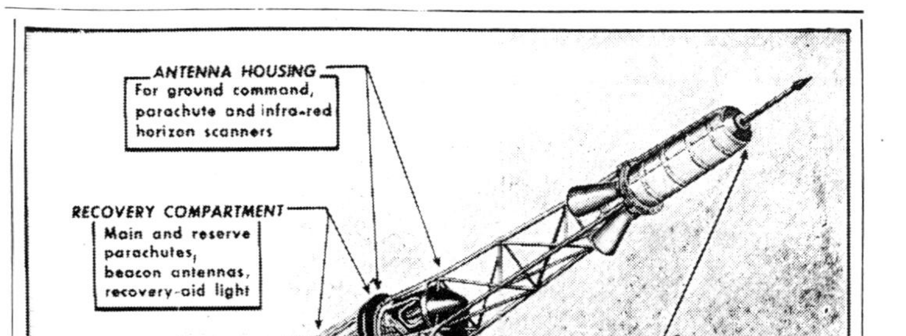

Associated Press.
A drawing of the Mercury space capsule which carried Lt. Col. Glenn into orbit.

U.S. No. 1 in Space Science, Russia Heavyweight Champ

Special to the Herald Tribune

CAPE CANAVERAL, Fla., Feb. 20.—Now that an American has gone into orbit and returned, does the space race score stand even-all between the Soviet Union and the United States?

The answer appears to be: In lifting weight, in putting a man into long orbital flight, the Russian rocketeers remain unexcelled. In launching satellites, in putting space to the use of mankind, the United States leads.

It is obvious that Maj. Gherman S. Titov's 17-orbit, 25-hour 18-minute trip far exceeded Lt. Col. John H. Glenn's flight today. Maj Titov's cabin weighed five tons; Col. Glenn's but a ton and a half.

Titov Was Sick

Back of the over-all success of Maj. Titov's flight lies a big lead in rocketry—a booster of some 800,000 pounds thrust. Our Atlas has a thrust of 360,000 pounds and it won't be until 1964 that our 1.5-million-pound thrust Saturn booster will be operational. Who knows what the Russians will have by then?

Maj. Titov's flight taught space scientists something important: weightlessness over a long period of time can make a spaceman sick. Col. Glenn's thrust into space was designed, among other things, to check this human reaction.

This biological check represents the one great scientific experiment of the United States man-in-space program. On this biological experiment the future of space travel hangs.

Presumably, Maj. Titov's nausea came from a derangement in the balance mechanism in his ears. There, three tubes of tissue at right angles to each other tell him which way is up. Each has fluid and each works like a spirit level. In the absence of the pull

(Continued on Page 2, Col. 3)

Space Ships Compared

CAPE CANAVERAL, Feb. 20 (UPI).—Here is how astronaut Lt. Col. John H. Glenn jr.'s orbital flight compares with those of Russian spacemen Maj. Yuri A. Gagarin and Maj. Gherman S. Titov:

	Glenn	Gagarin	Titov
Type of flight	Orbital	Orbital	Orbital
Numbers of orbits	3	1	17
Time in flight	4 hrs. 50 min.	108 min.	25 hrs. 18 min.
Capsule name	Friendship 7	Vostok I	Vostok II
Weight of capsule	3,000 lbs.	10,395 lbs.	10,395 lbs.
Date	Feb. 20, 1962	April 12, 1961	Aug. 6-7, 1961

More on Glenn In Inside Pages

Additional stories and photographs on Col. John H. Glenn's historic flight into orbit appear on Pages 2, 3 and 5.

The Weather

PARIS: [illegible] Yesterday's temperatures [illegible]
LONDON: Today cool and foggy [illegible] Temperatures [illegible] Cent.). Tomorrow little change. Yesterday's temperatures [illegible] Cent.). Channel sea: Smooth.
ROME: Today cloudy. Tomorrow cloudy. Yesterday's temperatures 72-52 (22-11 Cent.).
NEW YORK: Today partly cloudy, cool. Temperatures 65-45 (18-7 Cent.). Tomorrow cool. Yesterday's temperatures 64-44 (18-7 Cent.).

NEW YORK Herald Tribune
European Edition

Price Per Copy:

Algeria	0.60 N F	Italy	80 Lire
Austria	4 S	Lebanon	50 P.
Belgium	6 B.Fr	Libya	[illegible]
Brazil	20 Cruzeiros	Luxembourg	[illegible]
Canary Isl.	10 Ptas	Morocco	65 Frs.
Denmark	1 D.Kr	Netherlands	0.50 Flor.
Egypt	[illegible] P.T	Norway	[illegible] N Kr
Finland	50 F.M	Poland	[illegible] Zlotys
France	0.50 N F	Portugal	[illegible] Esc.
Germany	0.60 D M	South Africa	0.25 Rand
Great Britain	[illegible] Pence	Spain	[illegible] Ptas.
Greece	6 Drs	Sweden	1.00 S Kr.
India	1.25 Rupees	Switzerland	0.50 S Fr
Iran	20 Rials	Thailand	7.50 Baths
Iraq, Jordan	60 Fils	Tunisia	0.060 Din.
Ireland	10 Pence	Turkey	1.75 T L.
Israel	70 Aguroth	Yugoslavia	80 Dinars
		U S Military	10 Cents

[illegible]th Year in Europe - No. 24,811 ** PARIS, TUESDAY, OCTOBER 23, 1962 Largest circulation of any American newspaper published abroad

Kennedy Orders Blockade on Weapons for Cuba, Says Soviet Missile Sites There Peril Americas

Nehru Asks War Economy To Halt Red China Threat

From Cable Dispatches

NEW DELHI, Oct. 22.—[Pr]ime Minister Jawaharlal [Ne]hru today called on the [pe]ople of India to put their [ec]onomy on a war footing to [ha]lt Communist Chinese [ag]gression.

In a nationwide radio address, [th]e 72-year-old Prime Minister [tol]d Indians that Chinese attacks [ac]ross India's disputed northeast[ern] and northwestern borders [me]an "we are facing the greatest [me]nace to our freedom."

"We must change our procedure [fro]m slow-moving methods of [pe]acetime to those which produce [res]ults quickly," he said.

Urges Greater Production

"We must build up our military [stre]ngth by all means at our dis[pos]al but it is to be supported by [th]e industry of the nation and by [inc]reasing production."

It was Mr. Nehru's first call for [na]tionwide unity in the five-year [-old] border dispute.

Some opponents had criticized [hi]m in the past for failing to use [th]e border trouble as a basis for [att]empting to unify the nation.

If necessary, everything else [mu]st be sacrificed to meet the [Chi]nese threat, Mr. Nehru said. He [cal]led on workers to increase pro[duc]tion and to refrain from strik[ing].

[H]owever, he promised India's 457 [mill]ion people that economic pro[gres]s will continue. There is no [ques]tion of giving up or making [maj]or reductions in the third five-[year] plan which is now underway, [he] said.

Situation Grave

Mr. Nehru opened his talk with

United Press International

MOUNTAIN ASSAULT—Chinese troops place in position a field gun carried to its location by a helicopter.

Chinese Tank Attack, New India Front Cited

Peking Bid To Join UN Is Debated

Formosa Raps Attack on India

From Cable Dispatches

UNITED NATIONS, N.Y., Oct. 22.—Nationalist China called for rejection of the Soviet Union's annual bid to seat Communist China in the United Nations General Assembly as soon as it was made today.

Speaking to the Assembly's Political Committee, Soviet delegate Valerian A. Zorin called the issue "at the same time the most urgent and the most simple" before this year's Assembly.

He predicted that the United States will "probably cook up new tricks here this year" in an effort to block the seating of the Chinese Communists.

'Not Exempt'

Nationalist Chinese delegate Liu Chieh immediately rejoined that Communist China was unworthy of membership in the world peace body since its government "makes a virtue of aggression."

"India, the country which has tried its best to be friendly with the Chinese Communists, has not been exempt from their military adventures," Mr. Liu said.

United States delegate Adlai E. Stevenson agreed with Mr. Liu. He told the General Assembly that Communist Chinese invasions of India are but a part of the "new imperialism" practiced by the Peking regime.

Mr. Stevenson said the Communist government is not the true representative of the millions on

Associated Press.

DAY OF CRISIS—President Kennedy between meetings on the Cuba crisis at the White House yesterday.

Top Court Says Judge Can Give Voting Right

By the Associated Press

WASHINGTON, Oct. 22.—The Supreme Court agreed today that lower courts may order the registra-

only about 10 per cent of the Negro citizens, who constituted 83 per cent of the total population, were registered."

Guantanamo Base To Be Reinforced

By the Associated Press

WASHINGTON, Oct. 22.—President Kennedy declared tonight that the United States will stop and turn back any ship carrying weapons of an offensive nature to Cuba.

He announced this blockade of Cuba after stating he had "unmistakable evidence" that the Soviet Union had started to build missile sites there capable of raining nuclear destruction on the Americas.

Speaking grimly to the nation in a suddenly called radio-TV broadcast, Mr. Kennedy said the United States would wreak "a full retaliatory response upon the Soviet Union" if any nuclear missile is fired on any nation in this hemisphere.

Evidence Received

Mr. Kennedy reported that evidence received since last Tuesday has shown that—contrary to Soviet assurances—nuclear-type long-range missile sites and atomic-capable Soviet jet bombers are being established in Cuba.

He called upon Soviet Premier

Text—Page 2

Nikita S. Khrushchev to halt "this clandestine, reckless and provocative threat to world peace and to stable relations between our two nations."

Guantanamo Reinforced

He called on Mr. Khrushchev to join in "an historic effort" to end the arms race.

The President announced that he has ordered reinforcements to the United States Naval base at Guantanamo, Cuba, has evacuated dependents of military personnel from the base and placed additional units on the alert.

The outlook, he acknowledged, is risky.

"My fellow citizens," Mr. Kennedy said, "let no one doubt that this is a difficult and dangerous

Dobrynin Silent at Briefing

By Marguerite Higgins
From the Herald Tribune Bureau

WASHINGTON, Oct. 22.—Soviet Ambassador Anatoly F. Dobrynin, silent and unsmiling, was among the first foreign diplomats in Washington today to receive a thorough briefing on the new American moves in the Cuban crisis.

It was learned that instructions were sent from Washington to all its envoys in key Latin-American countries late yesterday to prepare the governments there for the blockade of Cuba.

Latin Rioting Expected

It is fully expected here that pro-Communist groups in Latin America may take to the streets in anti-Yankee rioting because of Washington's decision. So far as it is within American power, precautionary measures are being taken.

Despite precautionary measures being taken in Berlin and in this hemisphere, there has been no general North Atlantic Treaty Organization alert. For the moment

The Weather

NEW YORK Herald Tribune
European Edition

Price Per Copy:

75th Year in Europe - No. 24,816 R * PARIS, MONDAY, OCTOBER 29, 1962 Largest circulation of any American newspaper published abroad

Khrushchev Offers to Scrap Cuba Bases

Kennedy Calls 'Statesmanlike Decision' Aid to Peace

President Moves To Assure UN Role

By the Associated Press

WASHINGTON, Oct. 28.—President Kennedy today welcomed Soviet Premier Nikita S. Khrushchev's statement that he is removing offensive missiles from Cuba, and moved to see that the Soviet Union carries out its pledge.

About three hours after Mr. Khrushchev's announcement that he will dismantle his Cuban missile bases and ship their nuclear rockets back to Russia, Mr. Kennedy issued a brief statement welcoming the "statesmanlike decision" as "an important and constructive contribution to peace."

The President's reaction highlighted Washington elation—tempered with caution—over the suddenly brightened chances for peaceful resolution of the Cuban crisis on acceptable terms.

But, pending solid evidence that Mr. Khrushchev is fitting deeds to his words, there was no official acceptance of the apparent Soviet backdown. In fact, the United States military buildup continued at an unslackened pace.

The Defense Department made it clear that surveillance flights—which should give the first evidence of whether the bases are being dismantled—or being continued. And there was no relaxation in the naval blockade by which the Navy is keeping Soviet-bloc ships carrying weapons away from Cuba.

The President himself emphasized that there can be no unilateral acceptance of the Russians' statement of withdrawal.

"I welcome Chairman Khrushchev's statesmanlike decision to stop building bases in Cuba, dismantling offensive weapons and returning them to the Soviet Union under verification," he said.

In obvious reference to the United Nations role in assuring Soviet performance, Mr. Kennedy continued:

"We shall be in touch with the Secretary-General of the United Nations with respect to the reciprocal measures to assure peace in the Caribbean area."

Mr. Kennedy didn't say when the UN negotiations would start but in a letter to Mr. Khrushchev yesterday he stressed their urgency and suggested arrangements

(Continued on Page 2, Col. 7)

India Seen Set to Ask U.S. for More Weapons

From Cable Dispatches

NEW DELHI, Oct. 28.—The Indian government today was reportedly considering asking the United States for large-scale military aid following an attack by Chinese troops on a new front in the undeclared Himalaya border war.

"overwhelming numbers" in their attack on Demchok. By "overwhelming numbers" he said he meant "many times more than ours—not just two or three times as many."

The Defense Ministry released the first eyewitness account of the

U Thant To Havana Tomorrow

Sees Stevenson On Red Decision

By United Press International

UNITED NATIONS, N. Y., Oct. 28.—UN Secretary-General U Thant stood "ready for all eventualities" in the Cuban crisis tonight following Russia's agreement to dismantle its missile bases in Cuba.

The Secretary-General conferred for more than hour with United States Ambassador Adlai E. Stevenson this morning shortly after Moscow radio announced Soviet Premier Nikita S. Khrushchev's decision.

U Thant will leave for Havana Tuesday for consultations with the Cubans, a UN spokesman announced.

When Mr. Stevenson left U Thant's office this morning, it was he who said that the UN chief was "ready for all eventualities."

First eventuality was expected to be negotiation of a formal agreement to carry out Mr. Khrushchev's order to dismantle the missile bases and their weapons and ship them back to Russia.

Mr. Khrushchev agreed in his note to President Kennedy, announced by Moscow radio, that this would be done under UN observation.

Next step apparently would be appointment of a team of military observers—expected to be chosen from small-power neutrals—to go to Cuba and oversee the work of getting the bases out of the Western Hemisphere.

Cuba, however, has not yet

Associated Press Radiophoto.

ON THE SPOT—Adm. Robert Dennison, commander of the Atlantic Fleet, points to aerial photograph of the American base at Guantanamo Bay during briefing.

Pentagon: No Orders To Relax

By the Associated Press

WASHINGTON, Oct. 28.—The Defense Department said today, almost three hours after the Soviet Union's announcement that it would dismantle its missile bases

Castro Demands U.S. Leave Guantanamo

By United Press International

MIAMI, Oct. 28.—Cuban Prime Minister Fidel Castro demanded today that the United States get out of its Guantanamo naval base. His statement was broadcast over Havana radio.

In the first reference to the

Mr. Kennedy to Mr. Khrushchev that the United States would not invade Cuba and would remove its blockade if the Russian missiles were removed from the island.

Lists 'Other Measures'

Mr. Castro, in a statement to the people transmitted as an emer-

U.S. Would Renounce Cuba Attack, Blockade

From Cable Dispatches

UNITED NATIONS, N. Y., Oct. 28.—Soviet Premier Nikita S. Khrushchev announced today that he had ordered Soviet missile bases in Cuba dismantled.

He said that this withdrawal would be undertaken under United Nations verification, which would make it the first verified disarmament on an international level since the end of World War II.

Mr. Khrushchev's announcement was made in the last of a series of letters on the Cuban crisis exchanged between Mr. Khrushchev and President Kennedy over the week end.

Follows Kennedy Offer

Mr. Kennedy, for his part, had promised Mr. Khrushchev yesterday that the United States would lift its arms blockade of Cuba if the Russian rocket bases there were dismantled and removed and that there would be no United States attack or invasion of Cuba.

Mr. Khrushchev said it was his "respect and confidence" in Mr. Kennedy's assurances that led him to his decision to recall Soviet missiles from Cuba.

Mr. Kennedy welcomed the Russian decision as "statesmanlike," but there was no indication that the United States surveillance of Cuba would be eased until there was proof of the Russian withdrawal.

Elation in Washington that the United States had achieved what it had set out to do when President Kennedy imposed the blockade Wednesday was tempered by wariness and caution.

Here are the week end's rapid-sequence events:

1—The Moscow radio yesterday broadcast a message sent from Mr. Khrushchev to Mr. Kennedy Friday in which the Premier said the Soviet Union would dismantle weapons "which you call offensive" in Cuba if the United States pulled similar North Atlantic Treaty Organization missiles out of Turkey.

It was the first Soviet admission that there actually were such weapons in Cuba.

2—Mr. Kennedy replied Saturday that Russia must dismantle all missiles in Cuba before there can be any negotiations to settle the Cuban problem.

However, he said Mr. Khrush-

Premier Accepts UN Supervision

By the Associated Press

MOSCOW, Oct. 28. — Premier Nikita S. Khrushchev told President Kennedy today he had ordered Soviet rocket bases in Cuba dismantled and Russian missiles returned to the Soviet Union.

While Male Astronaut Continues to Spin

Soviet Blonde Orbiting as First Woman in Space

Says She Feels Fine; Talks to Bykovsky

By David Miller

From the Herald Tribune Bureau

MOSCOW, June 16.—A stocky blonde with a captivating smile kept a Sunday-morning date in space today as the Soviet Union successfully launched the world's first spacewoman.

Valentina Vladimirovna Tereshkova, 26, rocketed through the heavens just two days after Lt. Col. Valeri F. Bykovsky blazed the way.

"Hello Hawk, hello Hawk, this is Seagull," Valentina's high-pitched voice rang out.

"Hello Seagull, this is Hawk," Col. Bykovsky replied in the strangest boy-girl encounter in history.

Junior Lieutenant

Miss Tereshkova, a tomboyish air force junior lieutenant, spun into space in Vostok 6 (East 6) after a week of rumor and speculation that the Soviet Union was about to enter a new phase of space research.

As Col. Bykovsky, married and the father of a three-month-old son, was completing his 32d orbit in Vostok 5 and passing over the Soviet Union, the bulky capsule bearing Miss Tereshkova hurtled skyward from the secret Soviet launching station at Baikonur in central Asia.

They apparently caught sight of one another, but whether they might attempt a rendezvous was not revealed. But tonight there were rumors in Moscow that another male cosmonaut would be launched and might attempt a "docking" operation with Col. Bykovsky while Miss Tereshkova returns to earth in a day or so.

45 1/2-Hour Interval

Miss Tereshkova, a Communist party member who once worked in a tire factory and textile mill, was launched at 12:30 p.m. Moscow time (9:30 a.m. GMT), 45 1/2 hours after Col .Bykovsky went into orbit Friday.

Millions of Soviet citizens huddled around television and radio sets to follow the progress of the two flights. The first pictures of the spacewoman, flashed on Moscow television just after 2 p.m., showed the girl with a small spit-curl looped over one eye and a dimple in her chin.

Valentina—or Valya, by which she is known to her friends—seemed to wipe away the gloom of Moscow's gray skies with her smile and never-ending stream of chatter. Reception was good. She said she felt fine.

FOR FIRST WOMAN IN SPACE—Valentina Tereshkova, sober in civilian garb but smiling in cosmonaut outfit.

Civil-Rights Day in Washington

200,000 Take Part in 'March'

AP Wirephoto.

THE MARCH—Negro and white marchers carry their posters as they walk along Washington's Constitution Ave.

AP Wirephoto

A HALT IN THE MARCH—The crowd of marchers stands assembled around the Washington Monument's reflecting pool for ceremonies after the civil-rights march.

Crowd Gay And Well Behaved

Delegation Sees Capitol Leaders

From Cable Dispatches

WASHINGTON, Aug. 28.—More than 200,000 Negro and white people crowded in front of the Lincoln Memorial here today in the biggest civil-rights demonstration ever staged in the United States.

They had marched in two columns in a holiday atmosphere with songs, gaiety—and no disorder—to the foot of the memorial commemorating Abraham Lincoln.

There they heard speeches by civil-rights leaders, including the Rev. Martin Luther King, who said that the "whirlwinds of revolt" would continue to shake the foundations of the United States until Negroes received their just demands.

Leaders at Capitol

Earlier, the organizers of the march went to see Congressional leaders for "very cordial" talks on racial problems. President Kennedy arranged to see a delegation of civil-rights marchers later today.

The Weather

PARIS: Today cloudy with scattered showers. Temperatures 55-46 (13-8 Cent.). Tomorrow cloudy with occasional rain. Yesterday's temperatures 54-45 (12-7 Cent.).

LONDON: Today cool, cloudy and occasional rain. Temperatures 55-36 (13-2 Cent.). Tomorrow cool and dry. Yesterday's temperatures 55-50 (13-10 Cent.). Channel sea Moderate.

NEW YORK: Today mild and partly cloudy. Temperatures 66-50 (19-10 Cent.). Tomorrow mild, mostly cloudy. Yesterday's temperatures 65-50 (18-10 Cent.).

NEW YORK
Herald Tribune
European Edition

Price Per Copy:

Algeria	0.60 Fr	Italy	80 Lire
Austria	5 S	Lebanon	50 P
Belgium	6 B Fr.	Libya	5 Piast
Brazil	20 Cruzeiros	Luxembourg	6 L.Frs
Canary Isl.	10 Ptas	Morocco	Dh 0.70
Denmark	1 D Kr	Netherlands	0.50 Flor
Egypt	9 P T	Norway	1 N Kr
Finland	0.50 FM	Poland	3 Zlotys
France	0.50 Fr	Portugal	5.00 Esc
Germany	0.60 D M	South Africa	0.25 Rand
Great Britain	9 Pence	Spain	8 Ptas.
Greece	6 Drs	Sweden	1.00 S.Kr.
India	1.25 Rupees	Switzerland	0.50 S.Fr.
Iran	20 Rials	Thailand	7.50 Baths.
Iraq Jordan	60 Fils	Tunisia	0.060 Din.
Ireland	1/-	Turkey	1.75 T.L
Israel	70 Aguroth	Yugoslavia	80 Dinars
		U.S. Military	10 Cents

77th Year in Europe - No. 25.150 *R PARIS, SATURDAY-SUNDAY, NOVEMBER 23-24, 1963 Largest circulation of any American newspaper published abroad

KENNEDY ASSASSINATED

Is Shot Down in Car by a Hidden Sniper As He Rides Through Downtown Dallas; Johnson Quickly Sworn In as President

Shocked World Mourns Leader

PARIS, Nov. 22.—The world tonight mourned the death of President Kennedy.

Radio announcers in West Germany sobbed as they reported the news. Many ordinary people were left dumb with disbelief. Heads of state were grief-stricken.

In London, former British Prime Minister Harold Macmillan said: "I am deeply shocked and horrified." When the flash was given of the President's death, a British Broadcasting Corp. announcer said: "Sorry, we need a moment to collect ourselves."

French President Charles de Gaulle, survivor of two assassination attempts, paid a soldier's tribute in the name of France to President Kennedy.

He said: "President Kennedy died as a soldier, under fire, for his duty and in the service of his country. In the name of the French people, a friend of all times of the American people, I salute his grand example and his grand memory."

Deep Grief

In Bonn, West German Chancellor Ludwig Erhard, said: "The news fills the German people with deep grief. All those who had the lucky opportunity to make the personal acquaintance of President Kennedy, in particular the people of Berlin, are deeply grieved in this hour."

In Rome, the Pope expressed "profound grief" and went to his private chapel to pray for Mr. Kennedy. Italian President Antonio Segni said: "It is a grave loss for all humanity."

As the news spread through the streets and cafés of Rome, crowds gathered. "How did it happen? How could it happen?" were the questions.

Socialist Cries

Tears running down his cheeks, Socialist party leader Pietro Nenni said: "This is a tragedy for the whole word . . . Our affairs are small compared with this tragedy."

"Kennedy died like Lincoln," said Social Democratic leader Giuseppe Saragat. "He fell like a hero of his people and universal

(Continued on Page 3, Col. 3)

Family Informed Of News

E. M. Kennedy In Chair of Senate

From Cable Dispatches

WASHINGTON, Nov. 22.—Sen. Edward M. Kennedy, D., Mass., the President's youngest brother, was presiding over the Senate today when word came that the President had been shot. An aide informed him and he rushed from the Senate chamber.

Attorney General Robert F. Kennedy, the President's other brother and closest adviser, was having lunch at home when word of his brother's shooting reached him.

The Attorney General's personal secretary said the Attorney General was remaining at the Kennedy Hickory Hill estate in McLean, Va.

At the Justice Department, scores of workers thronged the corridor outside his fifth-floor office. The little room housing teletype machines of the two wire services was packed. Occasionally a man would rip a new report from the tickers and shout the latest developments to an anxiously listening crowd.

Parents Informed

A few assistant Attorneys General milled around Mr. Kennedy's large office, where a television set kept them up to date on developments in Dallas.

In Hyannis Port, Mass., a workman at the family home heard the news on the radio and rushed into the house to tell Mr. and Mrs. Joseph F. Kennedy, the President's parents.

Reports were that neither his father, former Ambassador Joseph P. Kennedy, nor the President's mother commented when told of the shooting.

The President's father is a semi-invalid as the result of a stroke several years ago. He was napping when the word came.

Cabinet Officers Returning to U.S.

WASHINGTON, Nov. 22 (UPI).—The military transport plane bearing Secretary of State Dean Rusk and other Cabinet ministers to a meeting in Japan turned back between Honolulu and Tokyo upon receipt of the report of the President's assassination.

On the plane with Mr. Rusk were Treasury Secretary Douglas Dillon, Commerce Secretary Luther Hodges and several other high officials.

Commodity, Stock Marts Are Closed

By the Associated Press

NEW YORK, Nov. 22.—Stock exchanges and commodity markets closed quickly today after President Kennedy was assassinated.

Price on the New York Stock Exchange had gone into a tailspin

At 2:10 p.m. the New York exchange's ticker tape flashed: "Market closed." The action was taken by a hastily assembled board of governors.

Keith Funston, president of the exchange, said the closing was ordered because of a heavy flood of orders which came to the trading floor moments after announcement of the shooting.

The American, Midwest and Pacific Coast exchanges quickly followed the Big Board's action. Also closed were the New York cotton, wool and coffee and sugar exchanges

The New York exchange's ticker tape trailed floor transactions by 20 minutes at the close

The market had opened a little higher following yesterday's sharp

(Continued on Page 7, Col. 4)

Associated Press.

MINUTES BEFORE MURDER—President Kennedy, Mrs. Kennedy and Gov. John Connally riding in the fatal motorcade.

Johnson: Apostle of New Frontier

From the Herald Tribune Bureau

WASHINGTON, Nov. 22.—Lyndon Baines Johnson, who fought John F. Kennedy bitterly for the Democratic Presidential nomination in 1960, became his foe's running mate and the chief world-wide evangelist for the New Frontier.

As the Senate majority leader from 1955 to 1960, Mr. Johnson was regarded as one of the most astute parliamentarians ever to hold the post. As the Vice-Presidential candidate he stumped the country, and especially the South for the Democratic ticket. As Vice-President he traveled around the world constantly, winning friends for the United States with his gregarious personality.

A Long Way

He has come a long way from a small farm in Texas—first as a pick-and-shovel road worker, then as a teacher, lawyer, secretary, then as a Representatives elected to six successive terms, before being elected to the Senate.

Many Senators looked upon his elevation to the Senate leadership and chairmanship of the Democratic Policy and Steering Committee with considerable misgivings. The liberal Northern Democrats considered him a conservative Southerner

Conservative Southern Democrats, on the other hand, remembered that he had been elected to the House in 1937 as a straight New Dealer "who had done too much for Negroes and Mexicans."

'Practical Progressive'

Mr. Johnson, in turn, described himself as a "practical progressive liberal without being radical; conservative without being reactionary"—a description that helped make him a leading Presidential contender in 1960

When the Democrats took control of the Senate with a hair-thin majority of one vote in January, 1955, President Eisenhower predicted a "cold war of partisan politics"

(Continued on Page 3, Col. 1)

2 Officers Also Killed; Arrest Made

Policeman Dies Chasing Suspect Who Is Caught

From Cable Dispatches

DALLAS, Nov. 22.—A Dallas policeman was shot and killed today as he chased a suspected assassin of President Kennedy through a movie theater in the Oak Cliff section of Dallas.

Police later arrested the man, Lee H. Oswald, 24. He was being interrogated to see if he had any connection with the slaying of the President.

A Secret Serviceman was also shot and killed in a separate incident shortly after the assassination.

PRESIDENTS—President Kennedy with Mr. Johnson.

Oswald was pulled screaming and yelling from the theater, after shooting the policeman, J. D. Tippet.

'All Over Now'

He brandished a pistol, which officers took away from him after a scuffle. Police officer M. N. MacDonald, who was cut across the face in the scuffle, quoted Oswald as saying after he was subdued "Well, it's all over now."

A large crowd had congregated around the theater and witnessed the arrest. Police had to hold the crowd back because many apparently connected the arrested man with the slaying of the President.

Dallas police, Secret Service agents and the Federal Bureau of Investigation are all co-operating in an all-out hunt for the President's killer.

Lt. Erich Kaminski of the Secret Service Bureau said the assassin's weapon appears to have been a "high-powered Army or Japanese rifle of about .25 caliber." The rifle had a scope on it, he said.

The entire building where the sniper was located was evacuated People were working in the building at the time of the shooting

Dallas inspector J. H. Sawyer said: "Police found the remains of fried chicken and paper on the fifth floor. Apparently the person had been there quite awhile."

Sheriff's officers took a young man into custody at the scene and questioned him behind closed doors.

Rifle Seen at Window

A Dallas television reporter said he saw a rifle being withdrawn from a window on the fifth or sixth floor of an office building shortly after the gunfire.

The Dallas Sheriff's Department said a rifle had been found on a staircase on the fifth floor of a building near the scene of the assassination.

It was a 7.65 Mauser. The German-made Army rifle had a telescopic sight with one shell left

(Continued on Page 3, Col. 2)

Gov. Connally Wounded

From Cable Dispatches

DALLAS, Texas, Nov. 22. — President John Fitzgerald Kennedy was shot to death today by an assassin armed with a high-powered rifle.

Mr. Kennedy, 46, lived about 30 minutes after a sniper cut him down from an upper-story window of a building as his open limousine passed through downtown Dallas.

Mr. Kenredy—shot in the right temple—died at Parkland Hospital, where he had been taken in a frantic but futile effort to save his life.

Lying seriously wounded at the same hospital was Gov. John Connally of Texas, who was cut down by the same fusillade—three bursts of gunfire—that killed the President.

The mantle of the Presidency automatically fell to Vice-President Lyndon B. Johnson, a native Texan who had been riding two cars behind Mr. Kennedy, the 35th President and youngest man ever elected to the post.

Mr. Johnson was officially sworn in as President at 1:38 p.m. (1938 GMT), aboard a plane at a Dallas airport preparing to fly to Washington.

Rode Together

Gov. Connally and his wife had been riding with the President and Mrs. Kennedy.

The First Lady cradled her dying husband's blood-smeared head in her arms as the Presidential limousine raced to the hospital.

"Oh, no," she kept crying.

After the shots were fired, the Secret Service driver raced away from the scene at top speed—heading for the hospital and trying to get the Presidential party out of range of further gunfire.

Secret Service agents riding with the President and in a second convertible following close behind, immediately drew pistols and automatic weapons. But they were unable to get a shot at the gunman.

Senator Heard Shots

The horror of the assassination was mirrored in an eyewitnesses account by Sen. Ralph Yarborough, D., Texas, who had been riding three cars behind Mr. Kennedy.

"You could tell something awful and tragic had happened," the Senator told newsmen. His voice breaking and his eyes red-rimmed, he said:

"I could see a Secret Service man in the President's car leaning on the car with his hands in anger, anguish and despair. I knew then something tragic had happened."

Sen. Yarborough said he counted three rifle shots as the Presidential limousine headed through a triple underpass.

One bystander said he saw a gun emerge from an upper story of a warehouse commanding an unobstructed view of the Presidential car.

4th President Assassinated

Mr. Kennedy was the first President to be assassinated since William McKinley was shot in 1901, and the fourth in United States history.

It was the first death of a President in office since Franklin D. Roosevelt succumbed to a cerebral hemorrhage at Warm Springs, Ga., in April, 1945

Shortly before Mr. Kennedy's death became known, he was administered the last rites of the Roman Catholic Church. He had been the first Roman Catholic President in American history.

Even as two clergymen hovered over the fallen President in the hospital emergency room, doctors and nurses administered blood transfusions.

Mr. Kennedy died at approximately 1 p.m., Central Standard Time (1900 GMT), according to

(Continued on Page 3, Col. 1)

The Weather

PARIS: Today cloudy early, then rain. Temperatures 52-46 (11-8 Cent.). Tomorrow cloudy with less rain. Yesterday's temperatures 55-39 (13- Cent.).

LONDON: Today cold with sunny periods and occasional showers. Temperatures 50-45 (10-7 Cent.). Tomorrow cold with sunny periods. Yesterday's temperatures 56-50 (13-10 Cent.). Channel sea: Rough.

NEW YORK: Today mostly sunny and cool. Temperatures 45-35 (7-2 Cent.). Tomorrow windy and cold. Yesterday's temperatures 46-30 (8—1 Cent.).

NEW YORK Herald Tribune

European Edition

77th Year in Europe - No. 25,151 ★ PARIS, MONDAY, NOVEMBER 25, 1963 Largest circulation of any American newspaper published abroad

Price Per Copy:

Algeria	0.60 Fr	Italy	80 Lire
Austria	5 S	Lebanon	50 P.
Belgium	6 B.Fr.	Libya	5 Piast.
Brazil	20 Cruzeiros	Luxembourg	6 L.Frs.
Canary Isl.	10 Ptas	Morocco	Dh 0.70
Denmark	1 D.Kr	Netherlands	0.50 Flor.
Egypt	9 P.T.	Norway	1 N.Kr.
Finland	0.50 FM	Poland	3 Zlotys
France	0.50 Fr	Portugal	5.00 Esc.
Germany	0.60 D.M.	South Africa	0.25 Rand
Great Britain	9 Pence	Spain	5 Ptas.
Greece	6 Drs	Sweden	1.00 S.Kr.
India	1.25 Rupees	Switzerland	0.50 S.Fr.
Iran	20 Rials	Thailand	7.50 Baths.
Iraq Jordan	60 Fils	Tunisia	0.060 Din.
Ireland	1/-	Turkey	1.75 T.L.
Israel	70 Aguroth	Yugoslavia	80 Dinars
		U.S Military	10 Cents

Oswald Is Shot Dead by Cabaret Owner Who Tells Police 'I Did It for Jacqueline;' Slain President's Body Borne to Capitol

Mrs. Kennedy And Children In Procession

From Cable Dispatches

WASHINGTON, Nov. 24.—To the muffled beat of black-draped drums, President Kennedy's body was today borne on a horse-drawn gun carriage from the White House to Capitol Hill to receive the final homage of a grieving nation. People lined the route ten and 12 deep as the solemn procession moved through the sun-swept streets, along the same route the President had taken on his inauguration less than three years ago.

Mrs. Jacqueline Kennedy, dressed in black, a veil drawn back from her pale, tired, face, rode behind the gun carriage with her children, Caroline, six on Wednesday, and John, whose third birthday is tomorrow.

Riderless Horse

In a tradition going back to ancient military ceremonial, the nation's fallen Commander in Chief was also followed by a riderless charger with boots reversed in the stirrups as a sign of mourning.

Behind a lone sailor bearing the late President's personal standard, and a pallbearer detail drawn from all branches of the services, came members of the immediate family and President Lyndon B. Johnson all traveling in a fleet of slow-moving limousines.

As the solemn procession wound slowly up to the top of Capitol Hill, an Air Force band played ruffles and flourishes, and "Hail to the Chief"—which, in life, greeted the President on his first appearance at public functions.

Same as Lincoln

The casket was carried into the rotunda of the Capitol, to lie in state on the same catafalque that bore the last remains of another assassinated President—Abraham Lincoln—nearly a century ago. It lay immediately beneath the Capitol's 180-foot-high rotunda, flanked by national and Presidential standards.

After the coffin was in place, Chief Justice Earl Warren made a powerful and moving plea for an end to "the bitterness that begets violence."

"Surely there is a lesson to be learned from this tragic event," he said.

"If we really love this country and love justice and mercy and fervently want to make the tomorrows better for those who are to follow, we can at least abjure the hatred that consumes people, the false accusations that divide us and the bitterness that begets violence," he said.

Once the Presidential wreath had been put in place, Mrs. Kennedy moved forward hand-in-hand with Caroline toward the coffin.

Touching the flag, she knelt gently and kissed it. Caroline also touched the flag and paused momentarily while her mother bowed her head. Then both stood and walked back to their places.

As the mourners stepped out of the capitol, President Johnson and

(Continued on Page 2, Col. 4)

World Leaders In Capital

Informal Summit Talks Possible

From Cable Dispatches

WASHINGTON, Nov. 24.—Monarchs, Presidents and Prime Ministers from all continents started arriving here today to join the American nation in paying their last tribute to President Kennedy.

The funeral services tomorrow will bring together perhaps the largest assemblage of national rulers in history.

From Europe there will be President Charles de Gaulle of France, King Baudouin of the Belgium, Prince Philip and Prime Minister Sir Alec Douglas-Home of Britain, Chancellor Ludwig Erhard of West Germany, 82-year-old President Eamon De Valera of Ireland, Queen Frederika of Greece and royalty or government leaders from every other country on the Continent.

Mikoyan to Attend

The Soviet Union will be represented by First Deputy Premier Anastas I. Mikoyan. No Communist Chief of State was among those planning to attend.

From the Far East there will be Crown Prince Akihito and Prime Minister Hayato Ikeda of Japan, President Diosdado Macapagal of the Philippines, Prime Minister-elect Chung Hee Park of South Korea and Prime Minister Nguyen Ngoc Tho of South Vietnam.

Diplomatic sources said an informal summit meeting between President Lyndon B. Johnson and other Western leaders may take place early in the week.

NATO Summit?

They speculated that it might lead to a more formal Atlantic Alliance summit conference in Paris in mid-December, when the North Atlantic Treaty Organization's Council of Ministers holds its annual pre-Christmas session.

Gen. de Gaulle was reportedly planning to return to Paris Tuesday afternoon. It was not known how long the other visitors would remain.

But diplomats considered it

(Continued on Page 2, Col. 3)

America to Observe Silence During Day of Mourning

From Cable Dispatches

NEW YORK, Nov. 24.—The normal life of America will stop tomorrow for periods ranging from a moment to the entire day.

Across the nation many stores, banks, schools, business firms and theaters—some for the entire day of national mourning for President Kennedy, others for the morning or during the hours of the funeral.

Many industrial firms will observe a minute of silence and others will give employees time to attend memorial services.

Theaters Shut

Even the American Telephone & Telegraph Co., whose 750,000 employees operate the nation-wide Bell Telephone System, will observe a moment of silence.

The Baltimore and Ohio Railroad will stop all its trains for one minute during the President's funeral.

In New York, the Metropolitan Opera and Broadway theaters have canceled Monday night performances, and across the nation most motion-picture houses will be closed, at least until nightfall.

All security and commodity markets, including the New York Stock Exchange, will be closed.

The big Sunday newspapers in New York and other cities carried little advertising in their main sections during one of the year's heaviest periods of advertising.

The harbors will be slowed down, with longshoremen and others who keep the ports in operation staying away from work.

Countless private affairs—dinners, debutante parties, weddings and other festive events—have been postponed or canceled.

AP Wirephoto.

END OF AN ASSASSIN—Jack Ruby, Dallas nightclub owner, aims pistol at Lee Oswald, suspected slayer of President Kennedy, at the Dallas City jail yesterday. An instant later, Ruby fired fatally wounding Lee Oswald in the stomach.

Cabinet Officers to Stay On

From Cable Dispatches

WASHINGTON, Nov. 24.—The wheels of American government, almost brought to a standstill by the tragic slaying of John F. Kennedy, have been set rolling again by a resolute President Lyndon B. Johnson.

In one of his first major acts as President, he asked the members of the Kennedy Cabinet yesterday to stay on to serve him, and got their pledge to remain as long as he wants them. From members of Congress, he received assurances of bipartisan support.

Round of Conferences

To all the ambassadors and chiefs of mission abroad he sent a message asking them to stay on the job and not submit the usual resignations.

As rain drenched the grief-stricken city, the new President drove himself through a busy day of conferences with government leaders and former Presidents spoke to the nation and made plans to address the Congress next Wednesday.

A high Administration official, in disclosing earlier that Mr. Johnson would address Congress, said: "I do not expect it to be a program speech or a partisan speech."

The address is expected to be an appeal for unity. It was noted that Harry S. Truman brought such an appeal to Congress on April 16, 1945, only four days after Franklin D. Roosevelt's death made Mr. Truman President. The nation then was engaged in World War II.

Today, among many other activities, Mr. Johnson received an intelligence briefing from John A. McCone, director of the Central Intelligence Agency, and McGeorge Bundy, Presidential Special Assistant for National Security, and discussed the situation in South Vietnam with Ambassador Henry Cabot Lodge, Secretary of State Dean Rusk and Defense Secretary Robert S. McNamara.

Attends Rites

He also attended services for the late President in St. Mark's Episcopal Church and participated in the procession bringing Mr. Kennedy's body to the Capitol.

Yesterday, he found time to call on Mrs. Jacqueline Kennedy and to attend with Mrs. Johnson a brief special service at St. John's Episcopal Church. And the 36th President issued a proclamation designating tomorrow as a national day of mourning for Mr. Kennedy.

Except for three brief visits, Mr. Johnson spent little time in the White House, where his predecessor, until this afternoon, was lying in repose in the magnificent East Room.

Mr. Johnson worked from his old suite in the Executive Office Building across the street. There, around a little table in front of the desk he has been using since he moved in as Vice-President in January, 1961, he conferred with Congressional leaders and Cabinet officials.

Ex-Presidents Call

To give what help they could as he shouldered the burdens of office, former President Dwight D. Eisenhower and Mr. Truman called on Mr. Johnson.

The two former American Presidents also visited the White House to pay their respects to Mr. Kennedy.

An aura of grief pervaded Mr. Johnson's office as the conferees shuttled in and out.

Mr. Johnson started his first full day as President at 8:45 a.m. An early morning drizzle had temporarily ended—it quickened later in the day to a steady downpour—when the wrought-iron gates of the Johnson estate in northwest Washington swung open. His black limousine rolled through, the new President seated in a corner of a back seat, looking as if he had not rested much.

Ten minutes later he was at the White House for his first official business in the oval Presidential office—a conference with Attorney General Robert F. Kennedy, brother of the slain President. The subject was not disclosed.

To 'Situation Room'

He went then to the map-bedecked "situation room," where America's security affairs are screened,

(Continued on Page 3, Col. 1)

GRIEF—Mrs. Jacqueline Kennedy watches her three-year-old son, John jr., extend an arm as the President's body is borne from the White House to the Capitol. Caroline Kennedy stands beside her brother.

Accused Assassin Killed During Prison Transfer

From Cable Dispatches

DALLAS, Nov. 24.—Lee Harvey Oswald, the accused assassin of President Kennedy, was himself shot and killed here today while being transferred under heavy guard from one prison to another. He was shot down at pointblank range by a man identified by police as 50-year-old striptease-club-owner Jack Ruby, and died two hours later.

Police said Ruby told them he shot Oswald because of a deep sense of feeling for Mrs. Jacqueline Kennedy, the President's widow. He added that he wanted to spare her the ordeal of the trial of the accused killer.

Police quoted him as saying: "I didn't want to be a hero—I did it for Jacqueline Kennedy."

Oswald was rushed to the same hospital in which President Kennedy died, but despite an emergency operation, blood transfusions and heart massage, he died at 1:07 p.m.—two days and seven minutes after the President was pronounced dead.

Fires Once

Ruby fired only one bullet. It punctured Oswald's spleen, pancreas, right kidney and liver and lodged just under the skin on the right side near the back.

Dallas Police Chief Jesse Curry said Ruby will be charged with murder.

The shooting was seen by millions of people throughout the United States. Television cameras were in the Dallas police station as Oswald was being taken, handcuffed and heavily guarded, to an armored truck for transfer to the county jail.

The jail transfer was performed publicly, Chief Curry said, because of pleas made by newsmen covering the case.

Ruby leaped ower a railling separating the public from the prisoner and police and yelled "You son of a bitch" as he shot down Oswald, who grasped his side in pain.

Eight policemen grappled Ruby to the ground and dragged him into the jail in the city hall.

May Have Spotted Killer

The black-haired accused assassin of the President had walked out of city hall and to his death handcuffed and with a tiny smile on his lips. However, he may have spotted his killer an instant before he was shot.

François Pelou, a European reporter, who watched the drama from very close by, said:

"I'm sure he saw the man. It's my feeling he knew the gun was going to fire because he jerked his hands toward his stomach in sort of reflex action even before I heard the shot."

A crowd of about 200 cheered as Oswald clutched his stomach, and fell sprawling to the ground.

"Somebody got Oswald. Hooray!" one bystander shouted.

Some of the crowd, told about the shooting as they waited for Oswald to arrive at the county jail, shouted: "They ought to give the guy (Ruby) a medal."

Oswald was rushed out in a hastily called ambulance. It arrived in two minutes and streaked for Parkland Memorial Hospital.

Writhing in pain, his left leg drawn up, his eyes closed, Oswald

(Continued on Page 2, Col. 4)

Case Against Oswald Airtight, Police Say

From Cable Dispatches

DALLAS, Nov. 24.—Police said today they had an airtight case against Lee Harvey Oswald the accused slayer of President Kennedy, before he himself was shot.

The evidence against him included a photograph of him holding what was alleged to be the 6.5 Carcano bolt-action rifle that the assassin fired at Mr. Kennedy from the fifth story of a downtown Dallas building.

The photograph also showed him holding what was alleged to be the pistol used to shoot and kill pursuing Patrolman J.D. Tippit shortly after the assassination of the President.

But even when presented with the photographs and other incriminating evidence, the 24-year-old ex-marine and self-proclaimed Marxist steadfastly maintained his innocence and denied killing either man.

Case Cinched

Despite his refusal to make a confession, homicide chief Will Fritz said: "This case is cinched."

"The man killed President Kennedy. We are convinced without any doubt he did the killing," Capt. Fritz said.

It was the shooting of Patrolman Tippitt, about four miles from where President Kennedy was shot, that gave police the break in their hunt for the President's assassin.

This was how police reconstructed Oswald's movements after the shooting.

He was spotted by his employer, R. S. Truly, superintendent of the Texas Book Depository, and a policeman searching the building from where the fatal shots were fired.

Oswald was sitting alone in the building's snack bar with a cold drink in his hand.

Mr. Tduly said: "The policeman threw a gun into Oswald's stomach and asked me if Oswald belonged there. I told him 'yes' and we both went on up the stairs for a check of other floors.

Bit Startled

"Oswald looked a bit startled—just as you or I would if someone suddenly threw a gun on you—but he didn't appear too nervous nor panicky," Mr. Truly said.

Mr. Truly said that he placed "no significance" on Oswald's presence there until later when we found him missing and I reported it."

As Oswald left the building, he was again stopped by Dallas police. Oswald told them he worked in the building and was going down to see what was going on.

Forty-five minutes later and four miles away, Patrolman J. D. Tippitt, acting on a sketchy description based on a quick glimpse of the assassin as he drew his rifle in from a fifth-floor window of the school depository, leaped out of his car in an attempt to question Oswald, who was hurrying along a street.

Shot Dead

Witnesses said Oswald whipped out a pistol and immediately shot the patrolman dead and then fled. Seconds later a passerby grabbed the microphone of the police car radio and shouted into it: "One of your men has been killed."

Police said Oswald ran into a nearby movie house.

The theater cashier phoned police to say that he looked suspicious.

Acting on the tip, Patrolman M. N. McDonald entered the theater and turned into Oswald's row.

"We were no more than a foot

(Continued on Page 2, Col. 5)

Gov. Connally Told of Death Of Kennedy

By United Press Internationa

DALLAS, Nov. 24.—Texas Gov. John Connally, out of danger and recovering satisfactorily from an assassin's bullet, learned from his wife yesterday that his personal friend, President Kennedy, is dead.

Mrs. Connally talked to the Texas Governor shortly after 7 a.m. and his first question was about the President's condition.

After hearing her answer he said: "That's what I was afraid of."

Gov. Connally, Mr. Kennedy's Navy Secretary before he resigned to run for Governor last year, was riding with Mr. Kennedy when the bullets struck.

He remained conscious after the shooting until he was put under heavy sedation. He roused slightly Friday night, but was unable to ask the question. It was his first question on waking yesterday.

President Shot First

When the shots were fired the Governor was sitting in a jump seat of the big Presidential limousine, opposite the President. His wife, Nellie, was sitting on the other jump seat, across from Mrs. Kennedy.

The President was shot first and sheriff's deputies who lined the route said there was a pause of several seconds before two more shots followed.

In that short delay, the Governor swiveled in bewilderment or horror toward the slumping President.

That movement saved his life.

"If he had not turned," said Dr. Tom Shires, chief of surgeons of the Southwest Medical Center, "the bullet would have gone through the middle of his back and probably would have punctured his heart."

As it was, the bullet tore downward from the collarbone through the right side of Gov. Connally's chest. It fragmented, smashing three ribs, and punctured his lung, then shattered his right wrist and lodged in his left leg just above the knee.

A team of three surgeons removed one of the 46-year-old Governor's ribs and repaired the lung.

Detective Saw Ruby With Gun:

'I Knew What He Would Do'

By B. H. Combest

Detective, Dallas Police Force

DALLAS, Nov. 24 (AP).—I was standing at a corner of the ramp as they led Lee Oswald out of the building, and then I saw Jack Ruby and I knew what he was going to do.

I yelled: "Jack, you son-of-a-bitch."

I tried to reach him but I couldn't get to him. He rushed right up to Oswald and put the gun just flat against his chest, and I saw a flash of fire.

I think Ruby did what he was planning on doing all this time since the President was killed. He didn't say anything as he was carried out—I think he'd already accomplished his purpose.

'Get Him Out of Here'

One of his employees had called me earlier and told me Ruby felt a sense of shame for Dallas. A lot of us knew him because of the business he was in—running a strip joint.

I helped carry Oswald to the jail basement office. Someone said: "What do you want to do with him?" and I heard someone answer: "Well, let's get him out of here fast."

I think the city jail physician said the bullet went in at a slant but did not come out the other side—that it entered his left side and you could feel it under the skin on the opposite side.

I think the gun was a .38-caliber blue steel snub-nose. Ruby pushed it right up against him.

Ruby must have climbed over the railing to get into the crowd. I didn't see him go over the railing. The first I saw was when he rushed forward.

Oswald had a powder burn about as big as a fist on his sweater.

A Day Later

Big Blackout's Effects Still Tie Up New York

From Cable Dispatches

NEW YORK, Nov. 10.—A massive trans portation snarl still gripped the Northeast today after last night's 10-hour blackout— the greatest electric power failure in history.

Millions of people stayed home from wo rk, but others tried to get into cities the best way they could as commuter trains throughout New England and New York ran hours behind schedule.

Power was virtually restored throughout the 80,000 square miles that were plunged into darkness at 5:28 p.m. yesterday. But with the lights back on, new troubles mounted.

The blackout stretched from Ontario to southern Pennsylvania, producing a cold, dark and sometimes fearful night for a sixth of the nation's population.

800,000 Stranded

In this city the power failure stranded 800,000 persons for as long as five hours below ground, many in black subway tunnels below the East river, some on the bridges overhead. Thousands of persons unable to reach suburban homes spent the night in hotel lobbies or smoky bars.

Despite New York's reputation for crime and disorder, and although the blackout came at the height of the commuter rush hour, there was no general panic and few instances of looting and vandalism.

Thousands of persons were stranded in skyscrapers, many in darkened elevators 70 and 80 stories above the street.

In all, more than 30 million persons were affected by the blackout.

Probe for Sabotage

President Johnson ordered an immediate investigation into the breakdown, which occurred in the line from the power source at Niagara Falls.

Presidential advisers reported they did not suspect sabotage, but the FBI has been put at the disposal of the Federal Power Commission all the same.

The blackout began with a dimming, then the lights flickered on again and then off again. And within minutes this great city was thrown into darkness above and below ground.

New Yorkers found themselves moving by the unfamiliar light of the moon and flashlights. The windows of skyscrapers were lit with candles

Almost 1 hours to the minute after the lights went out, power was restored in most of New York City.

The subway system, which carries 1.5 million riders during a normal morning rush hour, was practically stopped today. Only a few trains were operating. The Transit Authority explained that trains and crews scattered, that batteries had to be recharged and that power had to be converted from alternating to direct current to move the trains.

Death in Blackout

The New York Board of Education said schools for the city's one million children would open—but urged youngsters who normally use public transportation to stay home.

One death was blamed on the power failure. James A. Brown, 76, died after suffering a heart attack while fighting off an intruder who broke into his home in Chelsea, Mass., during the blackout.

Caught up in the chaos were millions of persons in New York state, Massachusetts, Connecticut, Vermont, Rhode Island, New Jersey, Pennsylvania and a large swath of Ontario province in Canada.

United Press International.

POWERLESS—New York City's blacked-out skyline silhouetted against the glow of unaffected New Jers ey cities.

Moon Lights Skyscrapers

Heart Stopped Beating In Greatest U.S. City

From Cable Dispatches

NEW YORK, Nov. 10.—For millions of New Yorkers last night there was hardly a flicker left in the American way of life.

There was no ice for highballs. The steaks in the icebox were getting soft. The television set was dead and the movies were shut.

And all because the electricity was off.

Broadway's Great White Way went inky black. The biggest transportation system in the hemisphere abruptly stopped. Elevators halted between floors. Street traffic was thrown into choas.

The great power failure that crippled the city and the northeastern corner of the United States caught millions of people by surprise in all sorts of places.

It trapped hundreds in 214 stalled elevators, high up in skyscrapers. Firemen had to hack through interior walls to bring them out.

The biggest elevator problem, of course, was at the world's tallest building, the 102-story Empire State with its 87 pasenger elevators.

High Traps

One car hung high in the heart of the building for four and a half hours. One passenger said a few of the others became ill during their long ordeal in the enclosed darkness.

Passengers stalled in the elevators of the 58-floor Pan Am Building were cheerful at first. But, as the air in the cars became stuffy, their joking died down.

In the main, however, New York's harried, moody, rushing citizenry took the blackout calmly —if not smilingly.

There were these vignettes:

—The proprietor of a midtown greeting card shop gave away 1,000 candles worth $250 when his electric-powered cash register stalled and he couldn't make change.

—A Greenwich Village tavern which specializes in a Gay Nineties atmosphere did unprecedented business; it still uses gas lights.

—A young woman was caught naked in a doctor's examining room when the lights went off.

—Scores of self-appointed deputies played policeman for a night, stepping into jammed Manhattan streets with flashlights to direct traffic.

—The Broadway opening of "The Zulu and the Zayda" was delayed 24 hours. Patrons in white ties milled around in a hotel lobby when they learned that the Metropolitan Opera performance was canceled.

A Night Aloft

—Gov. Nelson Rockefeller had to walk up 15 floors to his New York apartment because the elevator was not working. Former Sen. Kenneth Keating spent the night in his 52d floor office in the Pan Am Building. The alternative was to walk down.

—Off Broadway, one show went on by candlelight—to an audience of seven.

—At Carnegie Hall, pianist Vladimir Horowitz continued to play Chopin's "Polonaise Fantasy" when the lights went out—and never missed a note. Finally an attendant brought a flashlight.

How Did Blackout Happen?

Officials Trying To Find Answer

From Cable Dispatches

NEW YORK, Nov. 10.—How did it happen?

Why was the most populous section of the most technologically advanced nation on earth plunged into a paralyzing blackout?

At around 5:15 p.m., when wives were getting supper, there was what Consolidated Edison in New York called "an electrical disturbance" somewhere in northern New York. No one yet knows exactly what it was.

When one link in the system needs power, it draws it from another. This vast interconnection, designed to assure power in an emergency, apparently magnified a single breakdown into the biggest power failure of all time.

50,000 in New York Parade

U.S.-Wide Rallies Held Against Vietnam War

By United Press International

NEW YORK, March 27.—More than 50,000 anti-Vietnam war demonstrators paraded down Fifth Avenue all afternoon yesterday, pelted by eggs and an occasional fist, to cheer speakers at a Central Park rally.

Authorities said it was the largest pacifist demonstration ever held in the city, far surpassing the first antiwar rally held last October.

Marchers were still streaming into the park's gigantic mall, which was filled to overflowing, three hours after the parade began.

Thousands of Americans demonstrated in other cities throughout the United States.

The 50,000 New York figure was the estimate of a Parks Department official but parade organizers and veteran newsmen put the figure at between 75,000 and 100,000.

Scores of newsmen covered the unprecedented demonstration, including a ten-man news crew from the Soviet agency Tass and the Russian government newspaper "Izvestia."

Thousands of spectators, often five deep, turned out along the 22-block parade route to heckle the marchers as "Communists" and "cowards" and to show their support for the Johnson administration's policy in Vietnam.

Showing the Flag

More than 1,000 police managed to keep violence down. Only one serious case of assault was reported—against Negro demonstrators who flaunted a Viet Cong flag.

Seven arrests were made, mainly among spectators who assaulted the Negro marchers.

Two incidents preceded the parade The first was a smaller demonstration Friday night when 17 veterans of World Wars I and II made a bonfire of their discharge and separation papers in chilly Union Square to protest the war.

A crowd of about 500, mostly supporters of the veterans, watched the burnings. A few spectators hissed and heckled.

The second incident came before the parade yesterday when a Molotov cocktail was thrown at the office of one of the 70 participating organizations, the Committee for Independent Political Action.

The bottle of gasoline with a flaming rag stuck into its neck did little damage to the storefront headquarters. Earlier, members of the organizing group, the Vietnam Peace Parade Committee, said they received anonymous telephone calls warning that "if we march we can be assured we will all be dead."

The New York protest was the showpiece in a weekend of nationwide antiwar demonstrations. The marchers included veterans, clergymen, students, children and old folks. There were few beatniks

Nazis Arrested

In Washington, rival groups of pickets demonstrated near the White House. The largest group about 400, marched back and forth protesting U.S. involvement in Vietnam.

A much smaller group from George Lincoln Rockwell's American Nazi party conducted its demonstration across the street in Lafayette Park.

Two of the Nazi pickets were arrested for disorderly conduct.

San Francisco police estimated the marchers down Market Street were 7,000 strong. San Francisco was the scene of some of the worst violence in last October's demonstrations, but no outbreaks were reported in yesterday's march.

Bystanders and leather-jacketed motorcyclists heckled 1,000 marchers as they plodded along a five-mile route from Cambridge Common into Boston. Before the march started and after it got under way, six motorcyclists drove their machines in and around the group, shouting epithets.

Chicago police said they counted 2,650 marchers in a peace parade. A score of young men walked along beside the head of the procession, shouting insults. There was a brief scuffle between hecklers and marchers.

Egg-throwing hecklers disrupted an antiwar rally in the city hall plaza of Worcester, Mass. There were two arrests.

In Cleveland, Ohio, about 350 to 400 college students staged a Vietnam protest march. There were about 25 counterpickets but no incidents.

More antiwar marches took place in Miami, Gainesville, Fla., Barabo, Wis., Kenosha, Wis., Los Angeles, Philadelphia, Houston, El Paso, Denver and other cities.

Minneapolis marchers were confronted by a picket carrying a sign which read: "I'd rather fight than switch."

Three persons were arrested by police breaking up fistfights between protestors and hecklers in Detroit's Kennedy Square when 30 members of "Break Through," a Conservative group, attacked marchers.

Violence broke out at Oklahoma City, where ten sign-carrying pickets marched shoulder-to-shoulder outside the federal building.

IN NEW YORK—Demonstrators turned out in force—estimates ranged from 20,000 to 100,000—to protest for and against U.S. policy in Vietnam. In background, hecklers carry signs urging a stop to Communism "now," while in foreground antiwar demonstrators carry signs urging the return home of American fighting men.

Associated Press.

IN BOSTON—Things were rougher. David O'Brien, chairman of the Boston chapter of the Committee for Non-Violent Action, is hauled away from a sit-in in front of the Boston Army Base. Police later arrested nine others.

Associated Press.

IN TORONTO—The demonstrators were younger and poor spellers. The serious young girl at left was one of some 1,000 antiwar demonstrators who traveled to the Canadian capital of Ottawa. Apparently there wasn't room for the "m" in Vietnam.

In Europe most people who read American newspapers read the European Herald Tribune

SEPTEMBER 29, 1962

After a Lengthy Illness

Edith Piaf Sings Again on Paris Stage

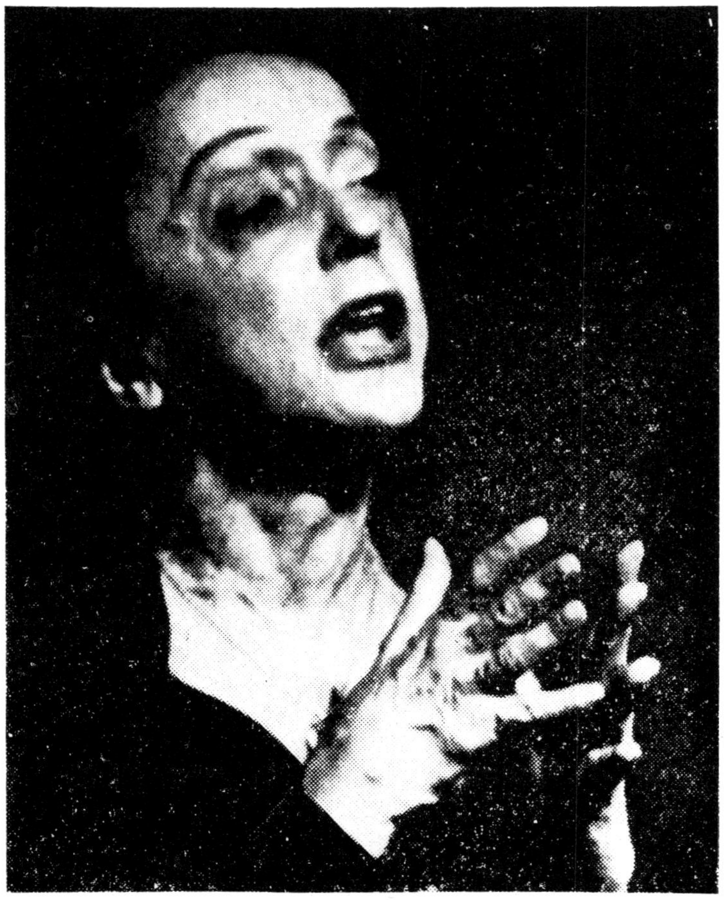

Edith Piaf.

PARIS, Sept. 28.—Edith Piaf returned to the Paris boards yesterday evening after a lengthy absence. A delirious welcome rose to greet her from the crowded auditorium of the Olympia.

The art of performance is the art of transformation. When Piaf sings, her compelling notes change the Parisian sparrow into a woodland songbird. The very physical aspects of the woman fade into her song. It is astonishing and it appears effortless, a true miracle, having nothing to do with the trickery of the show-shop.

On Thursday evening Piaf sang 12 songs, concluding with three already famous: "Non, je ne Regrette Rien," "La Foule" and "Milord." Of her new numbers: "Toi, tu n'Entends Pas," "Le Droit d'Aimer," "Emporte-Moi" (with which she opens) and "A Quoi Ça Sert l'Amour" are best, and the last—a duet by Michel Emer which she sings with Théo Sarapo—is best of all, one of the most charming and touching things she has ever done.

Théo Sarapo—whom Mlle. Piaf is to marry on Oct. 9—has a concert interlude of his own at the end of the first half of the program. A hulking, handsome youth with a beatnik coiffure, Sarapo, obviously Piaf-trained, makes a promising debut both as singer and Twister. —T. Q. C.

Wednesday, Oct. 27, 1965

Buckingham Palace Beat: 'MBE Yeah-Yeah'

Associated Press Wirephoto

FACES OF THE BRITISH EMPIRE—The Beatles proudly display their MBE medals shortly after the Buckingham Palace ceremony. They are, from left, Paul McCartney, George Harrison, John Lennon and Ringo Starr. Meanwhile, outside the palace, the rest of the empire (under 21) tries to get in place for a close look at the new heroes by bulldozing through a thin blue line of Bobbies protecting the exit.

By the Associated Press

LONDON, Oct. 26.—Queen Elizabeth smilingly honored the Beatles at Buckingham Palace today by pinning the insignia of the MBE over their youthful hearts. Outside, a crowd of Beatle fans was storming the palace gates.

"She's great," chorused the Beatles after it was all over.

Admitting they were nervous, John Lennon said: "She was so very sweet, and she put us completely at our ease."

The full name of the Beatles' honor is "The Most Excellent Order of the British Empire," but it is better known as the MBE.

Precisely at 11:45 a.m., the four of them—John Lennon, Paul McCartney, George Harrison and Ringo Starr—entered the great guilded throne room of the palace.

Bowed Mopheads

The queen, dressed in an apricot-colored silk dress, looked at the boys with a big smile.

Then, at a signal from an usher, they bowed their mopheads, took four paces forward, halted before Her Majesty and bowed again.

Alphabetically, she worked down the Beatle line, pinning on the medals and then shaking hands.

When she reached Ringo she asked: "Are you the one who started it all?"

"No, Ma'am," replied Ringo, "I was the last to join. I'm the little fellow."

Regal Smile

The queen gave them another regal smile. Aware that this was the signal to go, they walked backward four paces, turned smartly to their right and walked out of the throne room.

They gave autographs to palace servants as they came down the scarlet-carpeted grand staircase to the big hall. Palace housemaids leaned out of the windows to wave to them when they emerged to the chaos outside.

The MBE does not carry a title. However, the boys will be entitled—should they ever attend a state function—to claim precedence over the younger sons of knights and baronets.

Protest Letters

News of the award last spring touched off a flood of protest letters. Several MBE holders returned their medals in disgust.

With their personal appearances abroad and their huge foreign record sales, principally in the United States, the Beatles have won badly needed foreign currency credits which aid Britain in its balance-of-payments struggle.

While things were serene and courtly inside the palace, several thousand screaming teenagers charged into strong squads of constables guarding the great palace gates outside. The crowd was driven back.

The most violent scene occurred when the Beatles departed. Screaming hysterically, a girl in a red sweater and red jeans jumped in front of the car.

Just in Time

A police inspector dragged her back—just in time—as the car braked sharply and came to a halt.

Teenagers who had broken through the police cordons narrowly escaped the hooves of police horses.

Several hysterical girls were carried away.

Art Buchwald:

The day they stopped the carillon at the American Cathedral.

Since he did not exist, it was necessary to invent Art Buchwald. The international edition of the New York Herald Tribune accomplished his creation immediately after the war. After many years here, he went to Washington, which some people think served both of them right.

The Paris Herald (and let's knock off this nonsense about calling it the International Edition of the New York Herald Tribune and Washington Post, or you'll miss your plane) has never been much of a crusading paper when it comes to Paris, and there is a good reason why. We've always been a guest of the French government and it wouldn't be nice to tell them how to run their capital. It wouldn't be healthy either.

Art Buchwald

But there was a time once when the Paris Herald struck a blow for freedom and I happened to be involved in the incident.

It took place when I was writing a nightclub column and living just off the Avenue George-V on the Rue du Boccador, a cobblestone's throw from the beautiful American pro-Cathedral. At this moment some generous soul had decided to give the Cathedral a gift of a carillon the likes of which had not been heard in Europe since the Coronation of King Louis XIV.

The Dean of the Cathedral, a music lover, decided to share the carillon with all of the right bank of Paris, and as soon as it was installed and blessed, he proceeded to have it play on the hour, every hour, if memory serves me right, from nine o'clock in the morning until nine o'clock at night, with an added concert at noon and six o'clock.

Well as much as I loved the Cathedral, the bells were driving me nuts. I knew a plea to the Dean from a nightclub columnist would have little effect, so I decided to take the issue to the reading public of the Paris Herald.

I wrote a letter to the paper's Mailbag under a fictitious name which said:

"I am a French housewife and my husband works on the Métro all night long. He can't sleep in the daytime because your American Cathedral keeps ringing its bells. Why don't you ring them on Sundays like the Catholics do and let it go at that. *Madame Micheline Du Bois.*"

The next day I had another letter inserted in the Mailbag which said: "The Americans are trying to take over France. First they send their G.I.s then their Marshall Plan and now they blast us all day long with their carillons. Why don't you leave us French in peace? *Pierre Robespierre.*

The second letter produced real mail from many indignant Americans who didn't care about the American Cathedral as much as they did about the anti-American comments of Mr. Robespierre. There was a series of letters demanding to know where France would be without the United States. My campaign to eliminate the bells was sidetracked for a week, until I got it on the rails again with a letter which said:

"I believe the real question is not what America has done for France, but what the American Cathedral is doing to Franco-American relations. We French don't want bells ringing in our ears every hour. We don't want to be reminded what time it is. That is the big difference between Americans and Frenchmen—the bells toll for Americans to go back to work—without bells we can linger in a café as long as we want to. I say stop the bells or close the church. *Robert Dejohn.*"

The mail poured in, but we only printed the anti-bell letters.

The pro-Cathedral letters were thrown into the basket. It appeared that the people at the American Cathedral were getting nervous and at that moment one of the Deacons of the church also happened to be the General Manager of the paper. He knew vaguely I had something to do with the anti-carillon campaign and he said, "Don't you have any letters for the bells?"

I said, "Of course."

"Well, why don't we print one?" he said angrily.

I rushed to my typewriter and wrote the final letter of my campaign. It read:

"Dear Sir, I don't know what all the fuss is about the bells. They have never bothered me. *Giulio Ascerelli, Rome, Italy.*"

The General Manager gave orders that no more letters were to be printed about the bells. But lo, a few days later they stopped ringing on the hour and only rang at noon. It was a great victory for a free press, and for the next three years I slept at the Rue Boccador like a baby.

Chanel Unpins Her Mini-Enemies

By Hebe Dorsey

PARIS, July 25. — Gen. de Gaulle is *yé-yé*. Jackie Kennedy has the worst taste in the world. Françoise Hardy can't sing worth a damn and Maurice Chevalier ought to know better and retire.

Don't worry. I'm not saying all that. It's all pure Chanel, who, at 84, is as sprightly and irrepressible as ever. After shredding world personalities as if they were cole slaw, she adds triumphantly: "And go right ahead. Quote me."

Chanel can't get over that crazy, miniskirted world we're living in. "Everything is *yé-yé*," she sighs. "Even our chief of state. He's *yé-yé* general." Why does she think the general is *yé-yé*? "Because he likes Brassens songs," she says. (Brassens is a sort of singer-troubadour with a guitar.) Doesn't she like his songs? "Certainly not," she says, "they're pornographic."

Jackie Kennedy doesn't fare much better. "Her love for publicity is distasteful," Chanel says. "She's got horrible taste and she's responsible for spreading it all over America. Look at the way she was dressed when she went to London to accept the monument dedicated to her husband. Ridiculous. She's trying to look like her daughter."

Queen Is Perfect

Mrs. Kennedy was wearing Courrèges clothes, by the way.

What about the Queen of England? Doesn't Chanel think she may be wearing her skirts a wee bit on the long side? "Not at all," says Chanel. "The Queen is perfect. She has no business promoting fashions. She's an employee of the state and she does her job beautifully.

"Look how tactful she was when she came to France lately. The first few days, she wore a hat. Then when she saw that all those women"—here, another sigh—"didn't wear hats, she stopped wearing one. I am sure she's a charming woman."

Françoise Hardy gets quite a beating. "She ought to be singing in courtyards," she says. "That's about all she's good for. What's more, she's dirty. She came once to borrow some pajamas and I couldn't go anywhere near her she was so dirty. It must have been her hair. I told the *vendeuse* to ask her to have a bath and come back. She did. We lent her the pajamas."

Maurice Chevalier? He doesn't have a chance either. "He's ridiculous, singing at this age with that stupid boater," she says, lower lip forward in mimicry. "Somebody asked me to sponsor his birthday party. I wouldn't dream of it. He's plain awful—at his age he ought to retire."

Mademoiselle, as she's called around her house, still likes a few people, just the same. Her painter, for instance, American Marion Pike, who's been doing Chanel's portrait for the last five months. Miss Pike did two portraits, as a matter of fact. One is a huge, 12-by-10-foot panel showing Mademoiselle at work. The second is a more interesting, straightforward portrait.

"She's a genius and I don't know how I would have done this collection without her," Chanel says.

Just the same, every time Miss Pike isn't around, Chanel jumps on a ladder and does something to that portrait. First she changed the shoulder line, then the sleeve and finally she asked Miss Pike to make her cuffs whiter. "They look dirty," she said.

Saint Laurent is okay. "He doesn't know how to sew, mind you, poor fellow. Nobody taught him anything. But I like him." Saint Laurent is the only couturier who openly admires Chanel and doesn't mind saying so in print.

But the real bouquet is for John Fairchild ("Women's Wear Daily's" publisher), who's "the only man who knows and understands fashion."

Chanel may be hard on most everybody—but she has one saving grace. She's not too sure of herself either. As she was going back to her fittings, she said: "I have stagefright—and how! Every time, I'm terrified. I ask myself: Is it good enough or am I all wrong?"

Paris Students Battle Police 14 Hours in Latin Quarter

By James Goldsborough

PARIS, May 6.—The striking and locked-out students of Paris today transformed the Latin Quarter into what the chief of police called a "battleground."

The violence also spread into the provinces with student-police clashes reported in half a dozen cities and students reported striking in at least a dozen.

In Paris, up to 10,000 students marauded around the Left Bank and parts of the Right Bank for 14 hours, fighting large numbers of police with sticks and stones and anything movable.

The police fought back with nightsticks and tear gas grenades. A cloud of tea. gas hung over the Left Bank like thick fog. Firetrucks turned on their heavy hoses but with little effect on the charging students.

At least 40 policemen were injured, two seriously. More than 50 students were treated for injuries, including one who is in danger of losing an eye. Property damage reportedly ran into several hundreds of thousands of dollars.

Not since the days of the Algerian war have the students been on such a rampage. Parts of Paris resembled a city under siege, with parked cars shoved together to form barricades, rocks thrown from rooftops and the radio broadcasting appeals to stay out of the stricken areas.

The main Latin Quarter streets were completely closed to traffic. Only police cars and ambulances with sirens screaming were let through. Several cars were set on fire, at least two buses turned over and store windows broken.

'Brutal' Clashes

The chief of police, Maurice Grimaud, drove around from one command point to another directing the police. He described the clashes as "brutal."

Seldom has Paris seen student demonstrations to match this one in numbers, violence and organization.

The largest detachment of police ever sent to the Sorbonne was on hand at 7 a.m. today to keep the students from their announced demonstration, which the police had prohibited.

They drove the students back down to the Boulevard St. Germain from where they started on a ten-mile swing around Paris that took them down the Avenue de l'Opera, to the Palais Royal, back across to the Latin Quarter and up through Montparnasse.

STONES AWAY!—A demonstrator hurls a stone toward police lines during one of many student-riot police fights yesterday in Paris. Here students have pulled cars to block Boulevard Saint-Germain at Rue Dante.

Formal Classes at Columbia Canceled; Pickets in Clash

NEW YORK, May 6 (UPI).—Columbia University reopened classrooms for the first time in nearly two weeks today, but still striking students set up picket lines and scuffled briefly with the first undergraduates trying to enter two university buildings.

The faculty of Columbia College, largest of the university's undergraduate units, voted yesterday to cancel formal classes until the semester ends May 15.

Individual instructors were meeting with students, however, to decide how to use the remaining class time.

The student protesters, striking mainly over what they called the police brutality that ended their earlier take-over of five campus buildings, picketed in what was to be a peaceful attempt to continue to paralyze the university with a boycott of any classes. Their original complaints were over construction of a gymnasium on parkland and Columbia's defense contracts with the U.S. government.

But minor scuffles broke out in front of Butler Library and Hamilton Hall, the main Columbia College classroom buildings, when students tried to cross the picket lines to enter.

Force Renounced

Shortly after the scuffles, both groups of pickets decided to try to "discourage" people from entering the buildings but not to prevent them by force.

Mark Rudd, chairman of the university chapter of the leftist Students for a Democratic Society, which had led the student strike, said today's boycott was "80 percent effective in both the graduate and undergraduate schools."

In another development, Archibald Cox, former solicitor general of the United States, was designated chairman of a five-man fact-finding commission appointed yesterday by the university faculty's executive committee to investigate the dispute.

Prof. Cox, a 55-year-old member of the faculty of the Harvard law school, said he expected open hearings to begin Wednesday.

Unions Say 6 Million Strike

France Approaches Paralysis; De Gaulle Weighing Reshuffle

Ministers Consulted On Crisis

By Ronald Koven

PARIS, May 20.—Underlining the gravity with which he views the French labor crisis, President Charles de Gaulle today started calling in his ministers one by one to ask for their views on dealing with the current turmoil.

Their answers could determine whether they survive a sweeping cabinet shuffle, which reliable sources say Gen. de Gaulle is seriously considering.

The purpose would be to present a new, more liberal face of his regime to the strike-paralyzed country as part of a package to restore calm.

For Gen. de Gaulle, the problem wiht the reshuffle is to find a formula so that it does not appear as a surrender to the strikers. Gen. de Gaulle dislikes nothing so much as appearing to bow to outside pressure. The sources say the cabinet changes will be much broader and reach much further down inside the government than anything yet spoken of.

There is no question of replacing Prime Minister Georges Pompidou, but a number of younger figures from outside the traditional political world and known for their liberalism and competence are reportedly being actively considered for posts.

TRANSPORT—With rail service halted, army trucks brought commuters into Paris.

MAY 21, 1968

Money, Gas, Some Foods Are Scarce

By James Goldsborough

PARIS, May 20.—France approached paralysis today as the strike movement generalized to embrace several million workers. Only a few fragile links of communication remained with the outside world.

The situation deteriorated rapidly, provoking a run on stores and banks, and by the day's end there were shortages of money, gas and some foods.

On the eve of parliamentary debate on government censure, the generalization of the protest strike reached what the unions said was six million workers. The strike has touched almost every sector of the economy.

The Paris region, with 16 percent of France's population, was hardest hit. Its intricate machinery of supply, transportation and communication was badly crippled. Motor traffic, the only major form of transportation left, barely moved. It took hours to cross town. During rush hours, motorists took to the sidewalks and created jams there. Gas stations were running out of gas by noon and cars were stalled in long lines.

Taxis, the only form of public transportation left today, were to go on strike Wednesday, the day the censure motion is voted. Army trucks were brought in to help transport commuters, but stalled in traffic that often moved slower than pedestrians.

Tourists Stranded

American and British tourists clustered around their embassies for help and money to get home.

The strike, which started last week, picked up momentum today as workers returned to plants following the weekend and, in most cases, voted to strike and occupy rather than return to work.

The mining unions struck. France's main ports were strangled by longshoremen. The 22,000 workers at Michelin Tire occupied the plant in Clermont-Ferrand. Several oil refineries, including the 2,000-man Shell plant near Marseilles, closed down. International Harvester was struck, the huge Sud-Aviation plant at Rochefort was closed; all the major industries, including metallurgy, chemicals, textiles, aeronautics and automaking, were hard hit.

Associated Press

MONEY—Many Paris banks temporarily ran out of cash, cut customer transactions.

United Press International.

TRASH REMOVAL—No Paris trash collections since Saturday. This stack near Opéra.

MAY, 23, 1968

France Bars Return of Student Leader Cohn-Bendit

Move Ignites New Student Protests

PARIS, May 22.—Militant student leader Daniel Cohn-Bendit was barred from returning to France today, according to informed government sources.

The news sent more than 3,000 French students marching in protest tonight through the Latin Quarter.

"Dany the Red," who three weeks ago lit the spark that ignited French universities and brought out millions of workers to support the students, was refused re-entry into France following a brief trip to Germany and Holland.

French student leaders immediately called it an attempt by the government to "divide" the students and said they would demonstrate tonight and starting tomorrow would launch an all-out "offensive."

The first reaction to the move to bar Mr. Cohn-Bendit was one of astonishment. Student leaders said they could not understand the move coming at so delicate a time.

Informed French sources said the move was taken at the highest levels, clearly implying that it came from President Charles de Gaulle himself. They said the government was not expelling the student leader, but was simply denying him the right to re-enter France.

Daniel Cohn-Bendit haranguing a crowd in Paris.

MONDAY, MAY 27, 1968

The Young People of Paris Stand Together Against the 'System'

By James Goldsborough

PARIS, May 26.—The tear gas still hung in the Latin Quarter air yesterday as the first groups of young people gathered to discuss the previous night's fighting and plan for the night to come.

"All gathering is illegal," shouted someone listening to a transistor radio. "Pompidou says he will crush any demonstrations today."

Laughter broke out in the group of several hundred already gathered on the Place de la Sorbonne.

The young people of Paris stand together now as probably few times in their history. From the dreamiest anarchists to the "sons of bourgeois," who used to be worried only about final exams, they are united. Those not willing to fight with the mass are the minority.

Police as Symbols

They fight, they say, because the police are there and the police represent the government and the system and another generation and the mistakes of the past and everything that's got to go. They will continue to fight until the police are gone. Then they'll retreat to the classrooms they have seized and cafés to haggle about government and politics and dream of the revolution and wish the police would come back so they could get back outside again.

"But Friday night," asked someone, "the police didn't actually come into the Latin Quarter, did they? They stood there on the Pont St. Michel, didn't they, which you can hardly regard as the Latin Quarter?"

"Yes, we can," said a young man.

They started building the barricades Friday night at 8:30, just after President Charles de Gaulle's address to the nation calling for a referendum. They listened to the speech on their transistor radios and then started the barricades.

"What did he offer?" asked a boy. "All he wants is order. It is blackmail."

Ghost of Past

For the young people, Gen. de Gaulle represents the ghost of France's past. So do all politicians, even the ones against Gen. de Gaulle. When you ask the students what they think of Pierre Mendès-France or François Mitterrand, they tell you they don't think of them at all. The Communist party is no better, they say. The party is part of the system.

United Press International.

PUNCHY PUN—Fist (poing) sounds a lot like point (point) in French. The resemblance was sufficient to inspire this anti-De Gaulle poster, one of many on same subject turned out by the Ecole des Beaux Arts.

INTERNATIONAL
Herald Tribune
Published with The New York Times and The Washington Post

ADDITIONAL WEATHER — PAGE 11

No. 26.908 * R PARIS, MONDAY, JULY 21, 1969 Established 1887

MAN ON MOON

Two Astronauts Land Craft Safely, Prepare to Walk on Surface Today

By Al Rossiter Jr.

SPACE CENTER, Houston, July 20, 1969 (UPI).—Man landed on the moon today.

Two pioneers from the planet Earth, American astronauts Neil A. Armstrong and Edwin E. Aldrin, flew their fragile spacecraft to a frightening but safe touchdown at 2017:40 GMT.

Their landing realized the dreams of centuries. For the first time men actually rested on an alien world.

The lunar lander, called Eagle, balanced precariously on a jet of flame, settled with a gentle thump on the moon's Sea of Tranquillity, near the lunar equator.

It appeared to be a perfect descent—though it had never been done before

The thrusting descent engine kicked up dust as the Eagle landing craft hovered briefly before dropping the final few feet to the surface.

"Very smooth touchdown," Col. Aldrin reported with cool casualness shortly after the landing. Mr. Armstrong excused himself from further reports, saying: "We're going to be busy for a moment."

Mr. Armstrong reported man's first landing on a planet other than his own with his voice barely raised from his normal, laconic delivery.

"Contact light on. Engine off. The Eagle has landed," he said.

Thus began the culmination of centuries of man's dreams, eight years of fantastic effort and the expenditure of $24 billion.

'Quite a Lot of Rocks' at Site

Mr. Armstrong made a quick description of the touchdown scene, saying there were "quite a lot of rocks and boulders" in sight. But ground control could not restrain its enthusiasm.

"Guys, that was one beautiful job," the mission controller called.

One of the most critical measurements was the spacecraft's tilt on the surface—a greater list than 12 degrees would doom the astronauts, since the ascent stage could not properly fire.

Ground control reported an angle of just over 4 degrees—well within take-off capability—and Mr. Armstrong confirmed that measurement.

Within seconds, ground control was addressing Eagle as "tranquillity base." Mr. Armstrong found time to describe a bit of the descent.

He said the automatic guidance system was "taking us right into a football field size (area) of craters."

Mr. Armstrong said he took over control manually over the rock field "to find a reasonably smooth area."

"It looks like a collection of just about every variety of shapes, angularities, granularities, just about every variety of rocks you can find," Col. Aldrin reported.

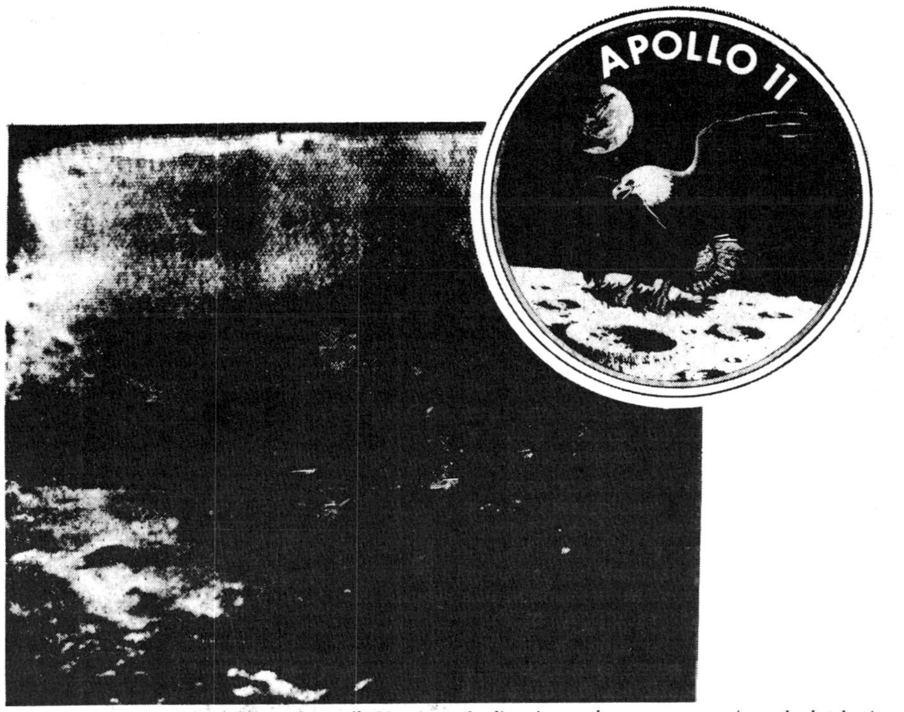

This is the Apollo-11 primary landing site on the moon as seen from the hatch of the command module and telecast back to earth. At the time the craft was about 170 miles above the Sea of Tranquillity before going into its lunar orbit.

Col. Aldrin said there didn't seem to be much color, but he said some rocks in view "look as though they will have some interesting color to them."

Later, Mr. Armstrong gave man's first description of earth as seen from the surface of the moon:

"It's big and bright and beautiful," he said.

Mr. Armstrong reported the astronauts' first reaction to moon gravity—only one-sixth of that on earth—"is just like in an airplane." He said there was no difficulty in adapting to the lower gravity. "We seem used to it already."

Both he and Col. Aldrin sounded calm and unruffled by the first manned landing on the moon.

Ground control told them: "There are lots of smiling faces in this room, all over the world." Mr. Armstrong replied: "There are two of them here."

Apollo-11 came down near the intended target in the Sea of Tranquillity. Mr. Armstrong described it as a wide level plain, its surface pitted, scattered with "literally thousands" of rocks and boulders.

During the most critical moments of the descent, Mr. Armstrong had taken control of the spacecraft to move it away from a rough, hilly, rocky area toward which the automatic system was guiding it.

The landing capped a millennium of dreams and opened the worlds of the universe to mankind.

For several long minutes the world seemed to stand still. The cool spacemen called out their final altitude figures as they dropped toward the lunar surface.

At 220 feet: "Coming down nicely."

At 75 feet: "Looking good."

At 30 feet: "Picking up some dust."

Then finally, at 2017.40 GMT: "Contact light on. Engine off. The Eagle has landed."

At the time of the landing the moon was about 238,548 miles from earth. Michael Collins, the third astronaut of the Apollo-11 team, kept the command ship Columbia orbiting the moon at an altitude of 69 miles while Mr. Armstrong and Col. Aldrin eased their way down.

Col. Collins was poised to swoop in and rescue his colleagues, had anything gone wrong. But now that they are on the lunar surface, they are beyond his reach.

"Out the window is a relatively level plain cratered with a thoroughly large number of craters of the 5-to-50-foot variety and some small 20-to-30-feet-high and literally thousands of one and two-foot craters around the area," Mr. Armstrong said.

"We see some angular blocks several hundred feet in front of us."

At her Houston home, Mrs. Aldrin stood up about two minutes before touchdown. When it came she said "I just can't believe it."

Takes Control Manually

She grabbed her father and hugged him. There was pandemonium at the Aldrin house.

Irenically—after all the controversy over whether sending men rather than machines into space was worthwhile—Mr. Armstrong indicated that the mission might have ended in disaster without a man at Eagle's controls.

He said he had to "take over manually and fly it over the rock area" toward which the guidance system was pointing the craft. The automatic system was bringing them straight down into a crater, which was surrounded "for about one or two crater diameters" with jagged boulders.

Mr. Armstrong said he flew Eagle to a "relatively good area" and brought it down in a swirl of dust.

The rock samples the astronauts will collect is one of the prime purposes of the mission. Scientists hope they will give some indication how the moon—and possibly the world—were formed, and perhaps clues to the beginning of life itself.

Mission control reported an exchange between Houston and Tranuillity Bay concerning a small fuel pressure problem in the descent engine system. The spokesman said there seemed to be some fluid trapped in a line but said: "We do not consider it a serious problem."

Mr. Armstrong's heart rate was 110 at the time the descent started, and it shot up to 156 beats per minute at touchdown. The rate quickly settled down to the 90s.

There was no immediate medical data on Col. Aldrin.

Mr. Armstrong said: "From on the surface we cannot see any stars out the window but out the overhead hatch. Buzz [Col. Aldrin] is going to give a try at looking at stars."

Columbia, the command ship, lost contact with earth

(Continued on Page 2, Col. 5)

Other News

Kennedy Faces Charge After Fatal Accident

A 29-year-old woman, a former secretary of the late Robert F. Kennedy, was killed early Sunday when a car driven by Sen. Edward M. Kennedy plunged off a bridge on Martha's Vineyard. It was reported that the senator, who was unhurt, would be charged with leaving the scene of an accident. The accident occurred shortly after midnight. Sen. Kennedy, who said he had walked around in "shock," reported it to police some eight hours later. Page 5.

AP.
Sen. Edward M. Kennedy

5 Egyptian Planes Reported Shot Down

Five Egyptian and two Israeli planes were shot down over the Suez Canal today, an Israeli spokesman reported. Day-long fighting along the canal started after an Israeli raid on an Egyptian island fortress in the Gulf of Suez. Page 6.

Nixon Plans to Outline New Welfare Policy

President Nixon will outline a "dramatic new approach" to welfare in a television broadcast Aug. 8, the White House announced. He will also discuss sharing of federal revenue with states and cities, revision of manpower training programs and reorganization of the Office of Economic Opportunity. Page 5.

Wheeler Doubts Lull Means De-Escalation

Gen. Earle G. Wheeler, chairman of the Joint Chiefs of Staff, said in Saigon that the lull in Vietnam fighting does not seem to mean de-escalation by the enemy. Before leaving Vietnam after an inspection tour, the general also denied that three North Vietnamese regiments had, as recently reported, been withdrawn across the Demilitarized Zone. Page 5.

Nixon Leads U.S. in Prayer For Astronauts' Safe Return

WASHINGTON, July 20 (UPI).—President Nixon today led the nation in prayers for a successful moon landing and safe return of the U.S. astronauts.

Mr. Nixon set up a moon watch in the White House following religious services in the east room at 11 a.m. He planned to track the mission through the day and through the early Monday morning hours when man was to set his foot on the lunar surface.

Today was Mr. Nixon's six-month anniversary in the White House, but he had to be reminded of it. He laughed when asked whether there was any connection between the anniversary and the moon landing.

The highlight of the church service was the reading by Col. Frank A. Borman, the astronaut, of the first ten verses of Genesis, the same passage read while the Apollo-8 mission he commanded circled the moon last Christmas Eve.

10 Miles Above Surface

Red Craft Enters New Orbit Nearer Moon

MOSCOW, July 20 (UPI).—The Russians announced today that their Luna-15 spacecraft went into a new orbit that sent it within 10 miles of the moon.

The orbital change increased the possibility that the Luna-15 might touch down on the moon to obtain soil samples, possibly while the Apollo-11 astronauts were carrying out their historic mission.

The Tass announcement of the change, which confirmed an earlier report from Britain's Jodrell Bank Observatory, said that the mysterious, unmanned lunar orbiter eased into the low orbit at 5:16 a.m. (1416 GMT).

The brief announcement, only the fourth communiqué issued on Luna-15 since its launching one week ago, did not provide any information on the craft's mission or the reason for the orbital change.

There have been frequent reports from unofficial but knowledgeable sources that the Luna-15 is a "moonscooper" designed to soft-land on the moon and bring soil samples back to earth.

The Tass report said that the new Luna-15 orbit carried the craft a maximum distance of 56 miles from the moon and down as low as 10 miles.

"The orbit's inclination to the plane of the lunar equator: 127 degrees; the period of revolution: one hour and 54 minutes," Tass said.

It concluded that "according to the data of the telemetric information, the systems and scientific equipment on board the station are functioning normally. The automatic station Luna-15 continues scientific exploration in near-moon outer space."

Luna-15 was launched from the Kazakhstan spaceport one week ago and entered its lunar orbit on Thursday. It held the same orbit for two days and then performed maneuvers that slightly altered its rotation path.

[In Britain a spokesman for the Jodrell Bank Observatory said that there was only an "infinitesimal chance" that it might collide with the Apollo moonship.]

Man's Advent Pollutes the Moon And Complicates Task of Analysis

By Victor Cohn

HOUSTON, July 20 (WP).—The first thing man will do to the moon is pollute it.

The lunar landing craft will dump exhaust chemicals on the lunar surface. The astronauts will exhale unmoonly gases as they walk.

These will contaminate the lunar samples the astronauts bring back, especially from the point of view of biological investigators.

This unavoidable fact about man's first lunar exploration has been dodged or minimized in most official accounts. The fact is, however, that not until later moon flights—probably not until 1970—will astronauts be able to move far enough from the lunar vehicle to collect what scientists hope will be far purer moon samples.

The fact, too, is that man has polluted the moon 19 times already. Starting with Russia's Luna-2 in 1959, 12 U.S. and seven Soviet unmanned craft have landed or crashed there.

The pollution cannot be helped if man goes to the moon. But it is an object of deep concern to biologists who want to know: "Were there once living organisms on the moon? Do any remain? Are there organic chemicals of the kind that eventually can lead to life?"

Scientists need pure moon

material, but may have to wait some time to get it.

The Apollo-11 pollution begins at its very worst—when the spidery LM makes its descent, discharging tons of fiery exhaust chemicals. Nine-tenths of these may remain in near-lunar space. Still nearly a ton could settle on the surface.

Most will be dumped near the landing site. But small amounts will settle miles away and "large amounts [illegible] more than 1,000 feet away," says one space official—this despite another official's recent statement that "out 100 feet there won't be much to worry about." One-hundred feet is probably as far as the Apollo-11 astronauts will venture. There will be at least four other possible sources of pollution:

- As much as half a ton of unburned propellant will be vented from the lunar craft's tanks just after landing. It may "freeze" in the tanks, however, because of the abrupt change in pressure.
- The astronauts' lunar tools—stowed in a folding platform on the outside of the LM—may have been contaminated by the craft's maneuvering jets.
- Some gases inside the LM cabin will be released when the hatch is opened, despite a bacterial filter system set up to minimize the contamination.
- The astronauts themselves will "outgas" from their suits as they breathe. The suits have 28 layers, but there are still leaks at the joints. "These guys will be virtually jets of gas," says one official. These gases will certainly carry earthly micro-organisms—bacteria and viruses—and organic molecules.

The scientists' problem—with these bugs or molecules and with the many exhaust chemicals and exhaust water—will be to separate what is the true moon

(Continued on Page 2, Col. 8)

Why Neil Armstrong?

By Thomas O'Toole

HOUSTON, July 20 (WP).—Why is Neil A. Armstrong the first man to walk on the moon?

Part of the reason is just plain chance. When the Apollo flights got under way last year, officials figured that it would take five or even six manned flights before they could risk a landing.

They still thought so when they were picking the crews for Apollo-10, 11 and 12. In fact, the betting at the time of Mr. Armstrong's choice was that he wouldn't make the landing—that a later crew would get the honor.

But, of course, there are more important reasons why Mr. Armstrong will be the first man on the moon. One is that he has been practicing moon landings since 1964. He has long been considered the astronaut "specialist" in moon landings.

Mr. Armstrong has also flown a strange-looking craft called the lunar landing training vehicle more often than any other astronaut. In the last year, he has flown this craft—which simulates a landing in the moon's one-sixth of earth's gravity—more than 30 times. He even crashed one last year, bailing out when the engine quit 250 feet above the ground.

Aldrin Is Factor

Another reason for Mr. Armstrong's choice lies with Col. Edwin (Buzz) Aldrin, his Apollo-11 teammate on the 70-mile descent to the lunar surface.

Col Aldrin is the astronaut expert on rendezvous in space, a specialization that will be sorely needed on this flight when the LM landing craft takes off from the moon tomorrow to rejoin the mother craft.

When Apollo officials were choosing the crew, they, of course, had Col. Aldrin's expertise in mind. Then, why did they put Mr. Armstrong and Col. Aldrin together, they asked themselves: How well do these men fit? Will they work well as a team?

It turns out that Mr. Armstrong and Col. Aldrin get on just fine. In many ways they're as alike as peas in a pod. That clinched it as far as the astronaut crew selectors went, and so Neil A. Armstrong will be mankind's first representative on the surface of the moon.

Astronauts on Moon, Prepare for First Steps

Ground control told the men on the moon that it could give a mission time check every 30 minutes if desired. They apparently were having some trouble with a time clock aboard Eagle. Earlier there had been an exchange concerning a circuit breaker in this system.

The astronauts radioed a sleepy "good morning" earlier today before racing through final preparations for the landing.

Flight Director Glynn Lunney said all systems were "operating just fine" and that the crew was about 30 minutes ahead of schedule in checking out the lunar lander.

Mr. Armstrong entered the lander in his full space suit soon after 1400 GMT and began flipping power switches. Col. Aldrin, already inside Eagle in his flight suit, returned shortly thereafter to Columbia to don his space suit.

The astronauts missed several hours sleep today because of a temporary communications problem. When ground controllers woke them one responded, "You guys sure get up early."

But Mr. Lunney said the abbreviated sleep should not affect timing of the moon walk. That still remained an open matter, to be decided on the spot.

Col. Aldrin reported shortly after awakening that he could see the entire landing area in the Sea of Tranquillity out of the moonship's window.

Yesterday, the astronauts beamed a 38-minute television show from moon orbit showing clearly the large and small craters that pepper the moon.

Col. Aldrin's scientific background showed up as he reported: "In one of the larger craters on the back side I noticed a small dark speck on the outer wall and I put the binoculars on it and I was able to see an area maybe a quarter of a mile in diameter with a fairly fresh looking dark-colored pit.

"That seemed to be in contrast to all the other little craters that you can see on the walls of the other craters. It was quite remarkable," he said.

The television camera also showed the path Eagle was to take down to its landing today.

As Apollo-11 swept over the landing site, Mr. Armstrong read out the features of the barren lunar plain.

"There's what we call Boot Hill," he said. "It occurs 20 seconds into the descent [the lander passed over that spot 20 seconds after it began its descent]."

Apollo-11 whipped around the edge of the moon and fired a six-minute rocket blast that dropped it into orbit around the moon early yesterday afternoon. It later fired the rocket a second time to set the stage for landing.

During the television show Col. Collins provided most of the commentary and a few quips.

As the spacecraft passed over the desolate Sea of Fertility, he remarked: "It doesn't look very fertile to me. But it's better for our purposes than the Sea of Crises."

The color images which appeared on TV screens closely paralleled the description provided by the astronauts. They said the first views were brownish grey and later commented that the lunar surface had a "rosier or tannish tinge."

The camera panned across craters, shadowy ridges, pancake flat stretches of moon desert.

Practicing, astronauts Edwin E. Aldrin (left) and Neil Armstrong using special tools designed for use on the moon. Col. Aldrin has a "lunar rock" in his tongs.

Col. Collins ended the telecast with the comment, "As the moon sinks slowly in the west, Apollo-11 bids good day to you."

Mr. Armstrong and Col. Aldrin gave the lunar module a two-hour inspection last night and tested the radio equipment they were to use on their descent to the moon.

"Everything looks super, we're ready to go," reported Charles Duke at the control center after engineers examined engineering data radioed from the landing ship.

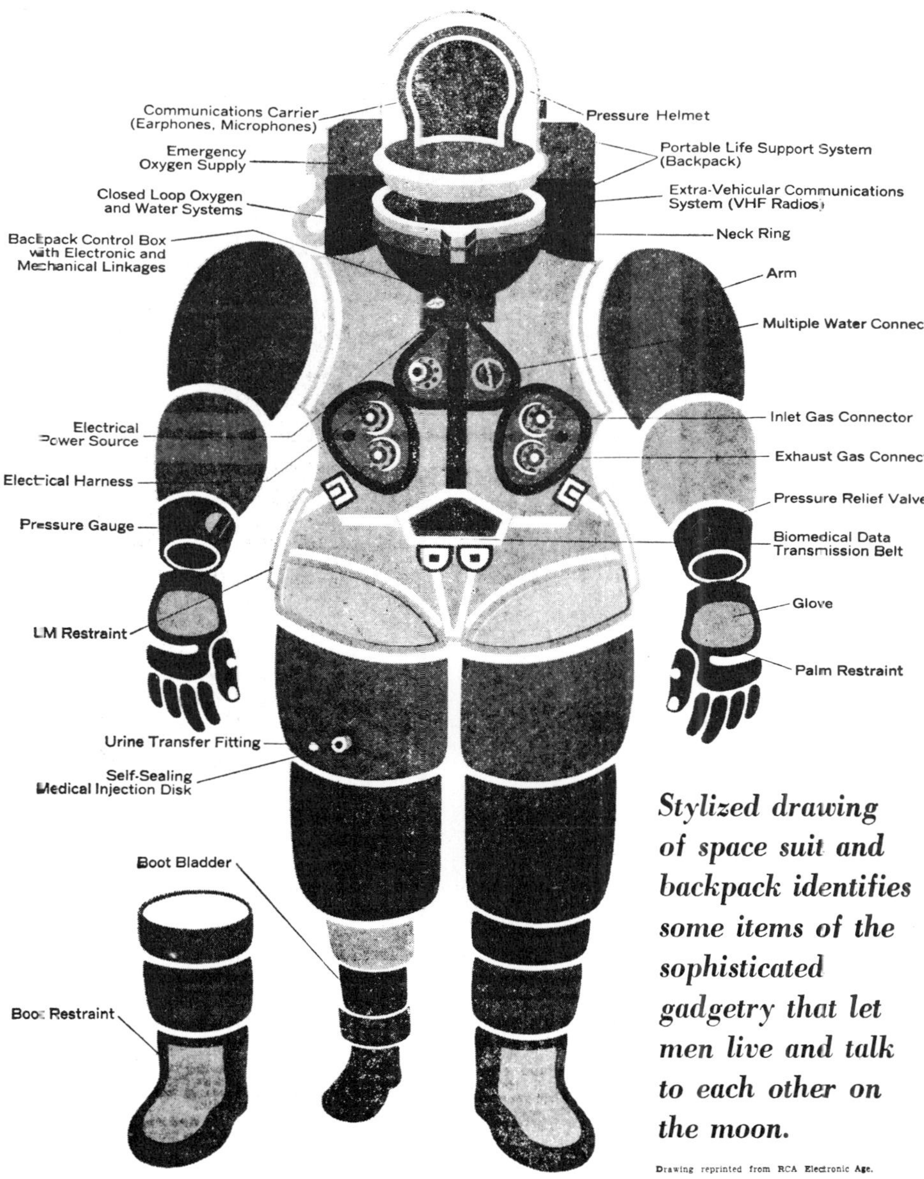

Stylized drawing of space suit and backpack identifies some items of the sophisticated gadgetry that let men live and talk to each other on the moon.

Drawing reprinted from RCA Electronic Age.

SPACE CENTER, Houston (UPI).—The bulky moonsuits Neil A. Armstrong and Edwin E. Aldrin jr. wore on the lunar surface are as protective as a spaceship but weigh a few tons less.

The garments even have their own water-cooled system to maintain body temperatures.

They are highly restrictive, however. Astronauts Armstrong and Aldrin were not able to romp in the lunar dust.

While walking on the moon, the astronauts could not shed any part of the life-sustaining suit—insulated overcoat, heavy shoes, stiff gloves or twin-visored helmets.

The suits were designed to meet a specific set of requirements, including:

- Adequate mobility on the barren, rocky moon.
- An artificial interior atmosphere of 100 percent oxygen at 3.7 pounds per square inch.
- And, up to four hours operating time on the lunar surface.

The moonsuit is composed of 16 different layers of material. Inside Apollo-11, the astronauts were cloaked in six of the layers but for survival on the plus or minus 250 degree Fahrenheit (plus 121 to minus 157 Centigrade) moon surface they also had an insulated overcoat to protect them from meteoroids.

"It's roughly equivalent to a deep sea diver's suit," explained scientist-astronaut Don L. Lind. "You're very restricted in movement of the whole body... in dexterity of the hands."

69 Pounds

The moonsuit tips the scales at 69 pounds (31.3 kilos) earth-weight, with all parts of the garment designed to protect the astronauts from meteoroid particles traveling at speeds up to 64,000 miles (103,000 kms) an hour. The two moveable visors provide protection from micrometeoroids, solar ultraviolet, infrared and visible light radiation.

The pressure glove locks into the sleeve to prevent leaks and is moulded specially for each astronaut from casts made of his hands. The "lunar overshoes" are composed of 21 different layers of insulating materials.

Inside the spacecraft, the suit can be hooked to the environmental control system by hoses. For the moonwalk the astronauts carried a 68-pound (30.8 kilo) four-hour life support backpack, plus a separate emergency supply of oxygen good for about 30 minutes.

Cool Underwear

Cooling is provided by circulation of water through a knitted undergarment with a network of plastic tubes worn next to the body. The cooled undersuit is worn only for activity outside the spacecraft.

Recently, while narrating a film showing moonwalk activities planned for the astronauts, Mr. Lind pointed to the cuff of the suit and said: "They have to notice the checklist on the cuff so they can remember the things they need to do . . . just key words to remind them of the sequence of operations."

Mr. Lind stressed the limitations of the suit in which it is not possible to bend much at the waist or lift the arms too far from the lunar surface where gravity is one sixth that on earth.

"The necessity for special surface tools is that the pressure of the suit itself tends to tip you over," Mr. Lind said. "You have a very high center of gravity and the suit wants to assume sort of a tired ape position."

But astronauts can use the suit to rest.

Mr. Lind said in earth gravity the suit holds itself up "and you can sort of relax in the suit and you slide and you sort of hold your nose on the ring dam (where the helmet connects to the suit)."

"You sort of relax in the natural position the suit assumes. It's a fairly stable position."

"If you're chinning yourself on your nose, it's not exactly relaxing, but you know, you can rest to a certain degree of success," he said.

1970-1979

By the 1970s, advances in transportation and communication were creating a community of decision makers in all parts of the world who read the same language and shared the same concerns. The *IHT* was now edited to meet the needs of this cosmopolitan audience. It was still a community newspaper, but the community it served was scattered over an ever wider terrain. Americans now made up only a minority of the paper's readership.

This changing audience posed difficult questions regarding distribution and production. It soon became obvious, for example, that the system of centralized printing in Paris could no longer provide the timely, dependable delivery that the paper's widespread audience demanded.

The answer was found in facsimile transmisssion, a new technique which allowed the same edition to be printed simultaneously at multiple sites. The *IHT* was among the first to apply this technique internationally when, in 1974, its first facsimile edition was launched in London. The completed pages were read in Paris by an electronic scanner which translated the black-and-white print into binary language. The electronic impulses were then transmitted by cable to England and decoded there so that the pages could be reconstituted for local printing just minutes after printing had begun in Paris. The new print site made it possible for the *IHT* to benefit from the air transportation and delivery facilities of both capitals, London and Paris, providing same-day delivery in an increasing number of markets.

The project worked. Circulation in the United Kingdom doubled. And in 1977, a second facsimile print site was added, in Zurich.

A second major challenge of the decade was the need to modernize the editing and typesetting processes. In 1978, under the direction of a new publisher, Robert Eckert, the *IHT* changed its address—and in the process underwent a complete technological transformation. After forty-eight years, the paper left its old home in the rue de Berri and with it the linotypes first introduced by the *Herald* to Europe in 1898, the aged typewriters, the prewar wooden desks, the massive presses—even the ink. There would be no trace of printer's ink, its particular smell, its omnipresent stain on hands, floors and walls, in the *IHT*'s new home in Neuilly, in suburban Paris. Editors would work directly on video-display terminals, processing the millions of words that rushed into the central computer each day from every corner of the world, and selecting a tiny percentage to appear in the final paper. Now complete stock market quotations from Wall Street could be set in type in Paris just a few minutes after the close of the financial markets in New York.

After the computer set the type, a much smaller production department would paste the finished columns onto page forms in just a few minutes. Finished bromide pages would then be sent to a local printer for the Paris edition (a trip that took twenty minutes or more for the motorcycle courier) or transmitted by facsimile to the London and Zurich printers—an electronic journey of four minutes per page.

As the paper became truly international—in its title, its audience, its distribution system, and its revenue base—its pages also reflected a more distinctly global outlook. In the decade's news, Mao's China opened its door a crack and the Common Market at last welcomed Great Britain. Saigon fell to the forces of Ho Chi Minh, Spain turned to democracy, Iran embraced revolution. The United States saw the first resignation of a President, and the British elected their first female Prime Minister, spotlighting the increasing presence of women at all levels of business and government.

Editor Buddy Weiss (left) checking linotype page makeup. The old linotype machines were among the traditions that disappeared when the paper modernized in 1978.

TODAY'S WEATHER—PARIS: Mostly sunny. Temp. 70-50 (21-10). Tomorrow partly cloudy. Yesterday's temp. 73-52 (23-11). LONDON: Sunny early, possible showers later. Temp. 70-54 (21-12). Tomorrow mostly sunny. Yesterday's temp. 70-55 (21-13). CHANNEL: Slight. ROME: Sunny. Temp. 66-41 (19-5). NEW YORK: Sunny. Temp. 64-50 (18-10). Yesterday's temp. 72-50 (22-10).
ADDITIONAL WEATHER—PAGE 2

INTERNATIONAL

Herald Tribune

Published with The New York Times and The Washington Post

Austria	6 S	Libya	9 Plast.
Belgium	10 B.F.	Luxembourg	10 L.Fr.
Eire (inc. tax)	1/9	Morocco	1.20 Dh.
Denmark	1.75 D.Kr.	Netherlands	0.85 Flor.
France	1.00 Fr.	Nigeria	2/6
Germany	0.90 D.M.	Norway	1.75 N.Kr.
Great Britain	1/6	Portugal	6 Esc.
Greece	8 Drs.	Spain	15 Ptas.
India	Rs. 2.25	Sweden	1.50 S.Kr.
Iran	2[illegible] Rials	Switzerland	1.00 S.Fr.
Italy	130 Lire	Turkey	2.50 T.L.
Israel	I.£1.00	U.S. Military	$0.15
Lebanon	75 P.	Yugoslavia	3.00 D

No. 27,154 * PARIS, WEDNESDAY, MAY 6, 1970 Established 1887

Associated Press.

SHOT ECHOING AROUND THE WORLD—A Kent State University student kneels screaming beside the body of a classmate killed in the melee with National Guardsmen.

Nixon Tells Congress Leaders GIs Will Exit in 6 to 8 Weeks

State Dept. Calls It A 'Hope'

By Spencer Rich

WASHINGTON, May 5 (WP).—President Nixon told members of the Senate and House Armed Services Committee today at a Cambodia war briefing that he is firmly committed to withdrawing U.S. troops from Cambodia before the monsoon rains start. The pullout was promised within six to eight weeks, the congressmen said.

[At the State Department, spokesman Robert J. McCloskey said it was "the hope" that the Cambodian action "can be terminated in six to eight weeks." It was noted that the administration's letter informing the United Nations of the incursion into Cambodia gave no time limit.]

The President also was reported to have said that the government of Cambodia had been notified of the impending thrust into Cambodia before it was undertaken, understood clearly what was planned, and did not object.

"In fact, they welcomed it," said one senator.

Sen. Henry M. Jackson, D., Wash., one of those present at the White House breakfast session, discussed the limited nature of the move of U.S. troops into Cambodia.

"What I did get was a firm commitment of the President that this was a limited thrust, with limited objectives for a limited period of time," said Sen. Jackson.

"They a
weeks—no
talked of a
Monsoon.

Sen. Jac
going to b
As I unde
pull out be
sion has
then."

Asked if
come even
achieved i
is very cle
out before

Sen. Jac
jective of t
sanctuaries
sure on th
effect was
military p

He said
change, ho
tion's stat
American
directly th
of Premier

Sen. Jac
firmed by
Senate a
present at
Flanking

(Continu

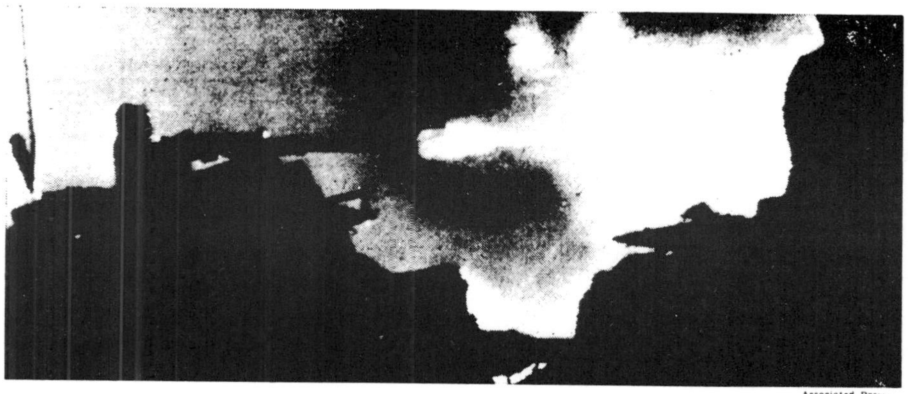

Associated Press.

BLAZING GUNS—Twin .50-caliber machine guns slash streaks of fire across the night sky as U.S. armored personnel carrier crews battle a North Vietnamese ground attack in the Memot district of Cambodia.

Airlifted U.S. and Saigon Troops Open New Cambodian Operation

By Terence Smith

SAIGON, May 5 (NYT).—United States and South Vietnamese troops were airlifted into the northeastern corner of Cambodia today in the third major allied foray across the border in six days.

A combined force of several thousand soldiers thrust into a

spokesman group of reporters at Pleiku tonight that the task force has orders not to cross into Laos. He declined to say whether those orders might be changed later.

Meanwhile, some 200 miles to the south, allied troops continued their sweeps of the enemy base camps

At least 14 Americans have been killed in the two sweeps and 54 wounded. More than 100 South Vietnamese soldiers have died and more than 400 have been wounded since the first units crossed into the Parrot's Beak last Wednesday.

The allied casualties are considered remarkably low for opera-

On April 23, Rogers Ruled Out Invasion

WASHINGTON, May 5 (UPI).—Secretary of State William P. Rogers told House members April 23 that the administration's Vietnam policy would fail 'if we escalate and we get involved in Cambodia with our ground troops."

learned yes-
the House
ittee that
id find it
ble confir-
into Cam-
with Con-
xtent pos-

f Mr. Rog-
ined after
, Md., one
n April 23,
ry's state-
smen.

expressed
. actions in
ion to send
oops along
was made
it was ap-
rs's words
d for it.

ipt

script, Mr.
ing in ans-

tive to es-
ntive is to
ize that if
involved in
und troops,
defeated."
nched into
ings on the
ongress on
isions.

nt had no
the tran-
en reports
ot entirely
n to dis-
troops into
en no pub-
as dissatis-

ldn't imag-
would have
id on April
was to be
y and that
oops would
e. He ruled
Rogers in-

When the War Came to Kent State

By Richard Harwood and Haynes Johnson

KENT, Ohio, May 5 (WP).—War came to the campus of Kent State University yesterday. When the gunfire was stilled four students were dead and at least 11 others were wounded.

It was the bloodiest confrontation of the student revolution spawned in the mid-1960s by the war in Vietnam. Two students were reported to be in critical condition with gunshot wounds. Two of the dead were young women.

This deadly encounter came not at one of the more publicized "radical" campuses of the East or West Coasts, but in the quiet countryside of "middle America."

Kent State University, with 19,000 students, sits in a rural area, well isolated from its industrial neighbors in Akron and Cleveland.

National guardsmen, drawn from farms and factories in surrounding communities, occupied the campus Friday to deal with anti-war demonstrators. Yesterday, during the noon hour, their routine occupation produced an American tragedy.

Facts Are Unknown

No one—neither students nor guardsmen nor university officials—could say precisely what happened. They all recite the same fragmentary story.

On the grassy commons behind the administration building, several hundred students massed to continue their protests against the war in Southeast Asia and against the presence of the guardsmen.

Hundreds of other students were on nearby slopes surrounding the commons. Other hundreds were leaving their classrooms, walking to lunch through the area.

Guardsmen carrying loaded rifles with bayonets fixed, were lined up facing the students on the green. They stood with their backs to the charred shell of an ROTC building destroyed by incendiaries Saturday night.

An order to disperse was given over a bullhorn. It was in keeping with an edict by Ohio's Gov. James A. Rhodes banning all outdoor demonstrations on the campus.

The order was met by shouts, obscenities and stone-throwing from the crowd.

The helmeted troopers were ordered by Brig. Gen. Robert Canterbury to move on the crowd and disperse it. The troopers [illegible] the students back, firing tear gas as they advanced. They were met with a barrage of stones and unexploded tear-gas canisters.

The guardsmen had driven the students over the crest of

(Continued on Page 2, Col. 5)

Guard Commander Feels Firing Was Not Justified

KENT, Ohio, May 5 (Reuters).—Brig. Gen. Robert Canterbury said here today he felt that National Guardsmen under his command had not been justified in firing on a crowd of demonstrators at the Kent State University campus yesterday.

Gen. Canterbury, Assistant Adjutant General of the Ohio State National Guard, told a press conference that an investigation had found that 16 of about 100 Guardsmen had discharged a total of 35 rounds at the crowd, killing four of them and wounding nine others.

Asked if he thought the Guardsmen had been correct in firing on the demonstrators, the general said: "In the light of the consequences, where four students lost their lives, it was not justified and could never be justified."

However, he stressed that the Guardsmen had fired because they feared for their lives.

"I was there, I was hit by rocks and I felt that I could have been killed," he said.

U.S. Campuses Seething, Day of Mourning Planned

By Robert Siner

WASHINGTON, May 5.—About 1,000 persons massed on the steps of the Capitol today to protest the U.S. invasion of Cambodia in a prelude to what may be the largest and most violent round of demonstrations against the Indochina war.

Anti-war groups called for rallies and vigils on Thursday, a national day of mourning Friday and a march on the White House Saturday.

The Capitol demonstrators were made up mostly of congressional aides and members of the League of Women Voters, which is holding a convention here.

Despite rejection of a demand that it consider the Cambodia question, the league recessed its convention for the day so that about 600 of its 2,200 delegates could attend the protest.

Meanwhile, with peaceful strikes and violent marches; with flower-draped crosses, black arm bands and anti-war buttons; with firebombs, window smashing and stone throwing—American college students showed their sorrow and their rage at the widening of the war and the fatal shooting of four students in Ohio.

The Senate Democratic leader Mike Mansfield of Montana, commenting on the violence at Kent State University in Ohio and other campuses said: "I hope this doesn't mean the beginning but rather the end of situations of this kind."

Sen. Frank Moss, D., Utah,

(Continued on Page 2, Col. 7)

Nix
Wil

WASHIN
ident Nix
the deaths
University
frontation
Guardsme
campus re
expressions

The
prefaced b
pathy for
victims, w
House new
He later i
is m
unfo
then
natio
stud
the
try
as s
viole
press

[T
an
shoot
lieve
demo
and
bring
curs.

M
mini
whic
"dep
prob
vesti

At
ever
actio
yest
camp
depa
camp
decli

(C

MONDAY, APRIL 26, 1971

Anti-War Rally

Below, one of the participants in the demonstration is wrapped in an American flag and holds a flower. At right, demonstrators swarm over peace monument, with protester on top waving a Viet Cong flag. In the background is the dome of the Capitol building.

Associated Press.

200,000 in Washington Anti-War March

By James M. Naughton

WASHINGTON, April 25 (NYT).—Anti-war marchers massed yesterday at a new rallying point, the Capitol, to urge Congress to assume the leadership they seek to bring the Indochina war to an immediate end.

The huge crowd, predominantly young, was peaceful as it gathered behind the White House—the focal point of other peace rallies—and strolled for three hours down Pennsylvania Avenue to the grounds of the Capitol.

The authorities estimated that the number of protesters was about 200,000—double what they had expected—and the rally's leaders set the turnout at half a million.

The crowd stood or sat on the rolling green grounds of Capitol Hill, under budding trees and amid pink and white azalea blossoms, as labor leaders, a few Congressmen and a variety of protest spokesmen exhorted Congress to stop a war that, they said, President Nixon had failed to end.

[Police today arrested 124 men and women who were participating in a Quaker peace vigil at the White House, the Associated Press reported.

[Seventy-nine women and 45 men were arrested for crossing police lines outside the presidential mansion where they had gone to voice disagreement with President Nixon's statement that he, as a Quaker, is seeking peace in Indochina.

[The charge is a minor one carrying a $25 fine.]

"We would like," one speaker said, "for the whole world to know why we are meeting here to appeal to the members of the House of Representatives and the Senate, and to say to them, 'Under the Constitution, you can end the war.'"

The theme was picked up by Rep. Bella S. Abzug of Manhattan and Rep. Herman Badillo of the Bronx, both Democrats. "You have come to the right place," Rep. Badillo said.

At the White House, the shouts and speeches could not be heard. President Nixon was at his retreat in Camp David, Md., and only the red tulips stood in massed groups outside the executive mansion.

The huge crowd at the Capitol was less electric in mood than the 70,000 to 100,000 protesters who streamed angrily to the Ellipse last May to protest the U.S. incursion into Cambodia. But it was larger.

It did not approach in numbers the 320,000 who gathered around the Washington Monument in November, 1969—the largest anti-war demonstration ever—but it seemed to be slightly more representative of adult Americans.

The National Peace Action Coalition and the People's Coalition for Peace and Justice, the two groups sponsoring today's rally, had hoped to demonstrate broad anti-war sentiment by attracting a large number of middle-aged and union members.

There were teachers and bakers and clothing workers—most from New York—among the crowd at the Capitol, eating picnic lunches on the grass and listening to the exhortations from those on the Capitol's steps.

arget

m Asuncion
er.

left their
upied Gaza
t Germany
by Israeli

ncion April
Rio de Ja-
and Iguazu
ined el-Fa-
th of his
by Israeli

al

(UPI).—A
Fatah guer-
enied any
Arabs re-
down Mrs.

t all about
these men
d. He sug-
connected
said "El-
with Para-

AP.

Jeffrey G. Miller

AP.

Allison Krause

AP.

Sandy Lee Scheuer

AP.

William K. Schroeder

Kent Coed's Epitaph: 'Flowers Are Better Than Bullets'

KENT, Ohio, May 5 (AP).—Allison Krause, a 19-year-old girl from Pittsburgh, frequently carried her pet kitten around the campus. She placed a flower in a National Guardsman's rifle barrel last Sunday and said: "Flowers are better than bullets."

Sandy Scheuer, 20, of Youngstown, Ohio, was a pretty girl with long brown hair.

William K. Schroeder, 19, of Lorain, Ohio, was psychology major, and was curious about the causes of violence on campuses.

Jeffrey G. Miller, 20, of Plainview, N.Y., was described by a home-town high school friend as "studious, not rebellious" and "quiet and intelligent."

These were the four students who died in a burst of National Guard gunfire on the sunny campus of Kent State University yesterday afternoon during an anti-war demonstration.

— INTERNATIONAL —

Herald Tribune

Published with The New York Times and The Washington Post

No. 27,882 PARIS, WEDNESDAY, SEPTEMBER 6, 1972 Established 1837

Arab Terrorists Kill 2 of Israeli Team At Olympics and Threaten 8 Hostages

Associated Press.

TALKING WITH TERRORIST—Manfred Schreiber, Munich chief of police, pointing to his watch while talking with Arab terrorist (right), outside the entrance to the Olympic Village building where Israelis were held.

Battle Is Reported at Getaway Airfield

By Jesse Abramson

MUNICH, Sept. 5 (IHT).—The Palestinian guerrillas who invaded the Israeli team quarters in the Olympic Village this morning—killing at least two team members and taking hostages—were moved from the village tonight along with their prisoners, a police spokesman said.

Buses raced to helicopters that took off with the guerrillas and hostages apparently for transfer to an airliner that would fly them out of West Germany, as demanded by the Arab terrorists.

The hostages and their captors were delivered to a military airfield, where shooting then broke out, authorities said. The guerrillas reportedly began the firing.

The airport is at Fuerstenfeldbruck, about 20 miles west of Munich.

After the hostages and guerrillas left, police stormed into the complex and a spokesman said they found three guerrillas wounded in a fight with the Israelis.

German radio said Tunisia was the country to which the guerrillas wanted to be flown.

The transfer came during a day of drama in which the Arab gunmen had insisted that Israel free 200 guerrillas held in its jails in return for the lives of the hostages.

Eight Israelis were believed being held hostage. Another Israeli was believed wounded and possibly dead. Two Israelis were definitely killed when the Arab terrorists—apparently five of them—climbed a fence around the Olympic Village before dawn and shot their way into the building quartering the Israeli team.

It was the first such violence that has ever occurred during the Olympic Games.

Although the scheduled contests in 11 sports were held through morning and afternoon sessions, Avery Brundage, winding up 20 years as president of the International Olympic Committee, suspended all competition, except games still in progress, at 4 p.m. (Story Page 14.)

A memorial service was arranged for 10 a.m. tomorrow in the 80,000-capacity Olympic Stadium. All athletes were invited to attend.

Willi Daume, president of the West German Olympic Organizing Committee, said tonight that he hoped the Games would resume tomorrow "because we feel the Olympic movement should not surrender to terrorists."

Deadline Is Given

During the long morning, the outlaws dropped a note out a window, making their demands known. Giving the West Germans a noon deadline, they demanded that helicopters be provided to take them to the airport; they wanted three planes to permit them to take the hostages to designated destinations—Arab capitals other than Amman or Beirut; the hostages were to be killed if the ultimatum was not met by noon. They described their operation as a "revolutionary and just force to give the war leaders [Israel] a hard lesson."

Associated Press.

HOODED TERRORIST—Member of Arab terrorist group that seized Israeli Olympic quarters seen yesterday on the balcony of village building where hostages are held.

Noon came and went as other deadlines were set at 1, 3, 5 and 8 p.m. There were reports that 38 police volunteers in bulletproof vests, armed with rifles and machine guns, were preparing to storm the two apartments.

The Arabs, who identified themselves as members of the Black September group, said their demands were not negotiable.

Two army tanks were brought in to the plaza fronting Building 31, where the hostages were held.

During the morning, with contests scheduled from 10 a.m. on, athletes breakfasted, then went off to their games and events. But the Olympic Village was sealed off to others. Thousands milled around outside or watched from the roof of TV studios adjacent to the village with a clear view of Building 31, which is in a corner of the housing development.

In the morning a police loudspeaker request in English that the Arabs give up had been ignored. Early in the day a call had gone through to the Israeli quarters and an Israeli answered, "It's dangerous in here. I cannot talk."

During the afternoon, Egypt's basketball team played half its match with the Philippines, then walked off the court. The entire Egyptian athletic squad later was reported to have left Munich. Other Arab states were expected to follow. (Story, Page 14.)

More than 100 Israeli tourists, shouting that Jewish blood was once again being spilled in Germany—the infamous Dachau concentration camp is nearby—marched around the village at one point. They were watched by a crowd of thousands standing on the hills built up from the rubble of wartorn Munich.

Brandt in Munich

Chancellor Willy Brandt of West Germany, expressing his horror over "this abhorrent crime violating the Olympic peace," flew here to supervise police operations and the daylong attempts at negotiations with the guerrillas.

In a TV address tonight, Mr. Brandt disclosed that ransom had been offered to the Arabs and free exit from the country, that leading politicians of the nation had offered to exchange places with the hostages, that everything had been done to rescue the Israelis. But all offers had been spurned by the terrorists, he said.

"The joy has ended for our happy games for which we planned six years," said the chancellor. "Later we will learn what has happened."

His government had a hot line open to Jerusalem, where Premier Golda Meir, after conferring with her Chief of Staff, Lt. Gen. David Elazer, spoke before the Knesset.

Thus, as one observer noted, an expert concentration of political and military brains was trying to save the lives of a small number of Israelis in a land where not so many decades ago six million Jews died.

One of the dead Israelis, left outside the apartment building with two shots in the head and one in the stomach from a submachine gun, was identified by the victim's mother, who lives in Munich, as Moshe Weinberg, a 33-year-old wrestling coach of the Israeli team. He had become a father one month ago, it was disclosed by an Israeli who said he was the victim's best friend.

Mr. Daume said Yosef Romano, 32-year-old Israeli weightlifter, had died. He gave no details.

Mrs. Meir named the hostages being held as David Berger, Yosef Gottfreund, Eliezar Halfin, Mark Slavin, Yeev Friedman, Yacov Springer, Andrei Spitzer, Kehat Shur and Amitzr Shapiro.

Other Foreigners Freed

The attackers, letting go Uruguayans and members of the Hong Kong team who also were housed in Building 31 with the Israelis, at first had 20 hostages, it was believed, but half of them escaped, including Tuvia Sokolovsky, who jumped out a window during the firing.

Mrs. Meir made a plea to all the Olympic nations "to do everything needed to rescue our citizens whose lives are in the balance."

Chancellor Brandt, wiring condolences before flying here, told Mrs. Meir, "I assure you that the federal government will do everything in its power to avert further tragedy." An emergency cabinet session was held.

The terrorists, with charcoal-blackened faces, penetrated the village, where security forces had not been able to control completely the comings and goings of 12,000 participants (including officials and administrative personnel) and some 4,000 media people, all identified by plastic badges with portraits of the holders. It was believed the Arab commandos scaled the eight-foot wire-mesh fence enclosing the village. To anyone who might have seen them they could have been athletes sneaking home after a night on the town. They carried their submachine guns in flight bags.

It was a well-planned operation.

Knock on the Door

At 4.30 a.m. in the predawn darkness, there was a knock on an apartment door. In these first Olympics being held on German soil since the Berlin games in 1936, it was a tragic reminder of (Continued on Page 2, Col. 3)

Nixon Sees 'Outrage'

World Leaders Express Horror at Munich Raid

PARIS, Sept. 5 (IHT).—Expressions of horror and condemnation of the Arab terrorists' actions at the Munich Olympics today were voiced from many parts of the world.

In San Clemente, Calif., President Nixon, through a spokesman at the Western White House, expressed a "sense of deep outrage" about the killings.

UN Secretary-General Kurt Waldheim, who called the act "dastardly," appealed to the Arabs to release the hostages. In a statement sent to the 132 UN member states, he called the incident "the more shocking for having taken place at the Olympic Games, which represent one of man's oldest and noblest efforts to foster friendship, understanding and reconciliation among the peoples of all the world."

White House spokesman Ron Ziegler said the President was following the developments closely and conferred with his chief foreign affairs aide, Henry A. Kissinger, on the incident.

Secretary of State William P. Rogers asked Israel's ambassador "to convey to the Israeli government and people our profond sorrow and sense of horror at the callous, outrageous attack this morning . . .

"With all nations and peoples around the world, we fervently hope that no further innocent lives will be sacrificed. This assault on the Israeli Olympic team is offensive to men and women of goodwill everywhere for whom the Olympic Games are a symbol of man's striving for reconciliation and peace."

Democratic presidential nominee George McGovern said he was "sickened by the outrage" and extended "deepest sympathy to the families of the victims of this shocking event.

"That a small band of terrorists could disrupt a pageant that had brought the entire world together in friendship is something that symbolizes the dangerous currents of violence loose in the world today . . .

"Until the leaders of the Mideast meet and directly negotiate an end to their war, there is the ever-present danger of more raids, more assassinations, more terrorism and more hijacking in this country and elsewhere," Sen. McGovern said in a statement.

His running mate, Sargent Shri- (Continued on Page 2, Col. 7)

Associated Press.

SPECIAL SPEECH—Israeli Premier Golda Meir addressing exceptional meeting of Knesset (parliament) yesterday regarding the Arab guerrilla attack on Israeli team. Israel was swept by anger and anxiety. Story on Page 3.

London Denies Ugandan's Charge

Amin Says British Plan to Kill Him

KAMPALA, Uganda, Sept. 5 (Reuters).—President Idi Amin today accused Britain of planning to have him assassinated before his November deadline for the expulsion of British Asians here.

In London, the Foreign and Commonwealth Office categorically denied the claim. A British spokesman said: "There is no truth in this accusation."

Gen Amin said the British plan was to cause confusion in Uganda, giving the British government time to install a leader who would agree to the Asians staying on here.

The Information Ministry here said Gen. Amin told Uganda's security council today:

"The British government, in collaboration with British Asians and Israelis and some other Western countries, is planning to assassinate me before the 90-days deadline for the departing British Asians.

"This is in order to cause confusion in the country and give them time to put in a leader who will be agreeable to Britain to keep the Asians of British citizenship in Uganda."

Gen. Amin said the British government had decided on this because it had no other way of keeping British Asians from entering Britain.

"The only way is to make the people of Uganda lose a lot of lives by fighting between themselves," he said.

According to the statement, Gen. Amin said he was directing all members of the Ugandan security forces "to be aware and watch out for any secret movements by foreign
subversive moveme
troops towards Uga
land."

Philip Berrigan Sent

HARRISBURG, Pa., Sept. 5 (Reuters).—The Rev. Father Philip Berrigan was sentenced to two year in prison today for smuggling letters in and out of his prison cell as part of an alleged plot to kidnap presidential adviser Henry A. Kissinger.

Sister Elizabeth McAlister, a min, also charged in the plot, was sentenced to one year and one day—also on the letter-smuggling charge.

Father Berrigan was sentenced to four two-year terms to be served concurrently.

The anti-war
serving a six-year
ing and pouring
files in a Selective
break-in in Maryl
He has been
months and was
courthouse here i
The government
will make no furth
secure convictions
rigan, Sister McA
six other people ori
with the more
relating to the pu
seize Mr. Kissinge

Kissinger Is Due in Moscow Sunday for 3 Days of Talks

SAN CLEMENTE, Calif., Sept. 5 (Reuters).—Presidential adviser Henry A. Kissinger will go to Moscow Sunday for three days of talks with Soviet leaders, the Western White House announced here today.

Brandt and other West German officials, including opposition leaders, before going to Moscow.

White House Press Secretary Ron Ziegler said that Mr. Kissinger and the Russian leaders would discuss matters of mutual

As Fisherman Plays 'Rule Britannia'

Icelandic Gunboat Routs Trawler

REYKJAVIK, Sept. 5 (Reuters).—A British trawler skipper today broadcast the tune "Rule Britannia" across North Atlantic waves to an Icelandic gunboat—and then found himself in the first clash of the latest "cod

sterner measures should be taken against foreign vessels fishing inside the 50-mile limit unilaterally proclaimed by Iceland on Friday. The government said the order was aimed against trawlers violating international rules by

effect on them—they only followed orders in cutting the wire."

Mr. Mollar said only one of the fishing vessel's two trawl wires was cut, so the boat could haul in its catch and its valuable equipment but could not

oat Odinn
shing boat
ntify itself
cut its wire
uled in its

st

AP).—Brit-
nd over to-

dor Niels
oned to the
eceive the

sh frigate
two heli-
to leave
rorrow for
y in north-
a will enter
ts patrol.

TUESDAY, SEPTEMBER 5, 1972

Spitz Swims to 7th Olympic Gold

100-meter butterfly—Won in a world record time of 54.3, Aug. 31.

200-meter butterfly—Won in world record time of 2:00.7, Aug. 28.

100-meter freestyle—Won in world record time of 5.12, Sept. 3.

200-meter freestyle—Won in world record time of 1:52.8, Aug. 29.

400-meter freestyle relay—Swam anchor leg on team which won in world record time of 3:26.8, Aug. 28.

400-meter medley relay—Swam third leg on team which won in world record time of 3:28.2, yesterday.

800-meter freestyle relay—Swam anchor leg on team which won in world record time of 7:35.81, Aug. 31.

MONDAY, JANUARY 29, 1973

Vietnam Cease-Fire Begins Taking Hold After Fighting Flares During First Hours

An Incident, Mistrust And a Snub Mark Signing in Paris

By James Goldsborough

PARIS, Jan. 28 (IHT).—The Vietnam peace agreement was signed here yesterday in an atmosphere as beset with uncertainty as that of Geneva 19 years ago.

As in 1954, fighting in Vietnam continued to rage at the very moment the signatories were putting pens to paper. As the champagne glasses clinked following the signing, word was coming that the Viet Cong were fighting to set up their capital in South Vietnam.

The mood here was thick with mistrust. At the last moment the Saigon delegation refused to even accept copies of the agreement which bore reference to the Provisional Revolutionary Government. And though the four delegations drank champagne together, there were no toasts.

Nor was the mood improved by a blatant French lapse that allowed a hostile crowd to chant anti-Saigon and anti-American slogans and brandish Communist flags outside the Hotel Majestic during the morning meeting, the first of two separate signing ceremonies.

French Apologize

Foreign Minister Maurice Schumann apologized to the South Vietnamese following the incident, but the South Vietnamese were clearly shaken. "It surprised and disappointed us," said a Saigon spokesman. "The French had assured us that no demonstrations would be allowed."

The Communist press had urged the turnout. But though there were no more than a thousand demonstrators present, they were noisy. Not only were the Americans and South Vietnamese booed, but the Indonesian delegate, representing his nation as a member of the International Control Commission, was greeted by a chant of "Suharto, assassin."

The two ceremonies took place in the Hotel Majestic, the site on the Avenue Kléber where the public peace talks went on for a fruitless four years and 175 sessions. It was not until Henry Kissinger and Le Duc Tho began what was to be the critical private contacts that any progress toward an agreement was made.

Hanoi Names Americans to Be Released

555 Said Tallied, 22 Dead; 1,300 Unlisted

WASHINGTON, Jan. 28 (AP).—North Vietnam has told the United States that between 500 to 600 American servicemen will be released from prisoner-of-war camps in Indochina, Pentagon sources said today. The fate of nearly 1,300 other Americans remained in doubt.

The National League of Families of American Prisoners and Missing in Southeast Asia said today that it had learned from the Pentagon that there are 555 military and 22 civilian prisoners on Hanoi's list of those to be released.

Twenty-three prisoners, including three not previously reported, have died in North Vietnamese camps, the league said. It said none of the 317 Americans believed missing or captured in Laos was accounted for on the list turned over by Hanoi.

WEDNESDAY, APRIL 30, 1975

Americans Evacuate Saigon In a Chaotic 13-Hour Airlift

Vietnamese Flee by Boat And Aircraft

From Wire Dispatches

BANGKOK, April 29.—South Vietnamese fled their homeland today in hundreds of small boats, in planes of the Saigon regime's air force and, in one case, in a charter aircraft that a jeep had prevented from taking off until 15 South Vietnamese, led by a colonel, had clambered aboard the plane.

There were reports of helicopters making unscheduled landings on U.S. Navy craft, of others ditching in the sea near the American warships, and of two small boats—carrying Americans and Vietnamese—coming under air attack until U.S. planes drove off the assailants.

There also were reports that farther along in the escape route—in the U.S. government's authorized evacuation program—there was a developing jam-up of refugees at the processing center on Guam in the Pacific.

In the unofficial exodus today, an estimated 50,000 persons were on small craft in the South China Sea, heading toward South Korean, Japanese and Taiwanese vessels that were about 10 miles off Vung Tau, a seaport 45 miles southeast of Saigon, and toward U.S. Navy ships farther out to sea.

United Press International.

COMMISSARY PLUNDERED—South Vietnamese civilians carrying away as much as they can after plundering the U.S. commissary at Newport, just north of Saigon. The commissary was closed down by the Americans as part of the evacuation process.

United Press International.

GETTING OUT—An Air America helicopter crewman helping evacuees up the ladder on top of a Saigon building, one of several evacuation sites in the downtown area from where Americans and other foreign nationals were flown to waiting ships.

Minh Regime Continues Truce Effort

SAIGON, April 29 (AP).—Dodging bullets from bitter South Vietnamese troops and fighting off desperate civilians, Americans fled Saigon today in a 13-hour airlift by an armada of 81 helicopters guarded by 800 Marines and U.S. fighter planes overhead.

Communist-led troops, meanwhile, pressed closer to Saigon and President Duong Van Minh maneuvered in search of a cease-fire.

President Ford ordered the airlift after President Minh made a radio speech ordering all Americans assigned to the U.S. defense attaché's office out of the country within 24 hours.

The helicopters landed at Tan Son Nhut Airport and on rooftops at the U.S. Embassy compound to pick up most of the remaining Americans and many Vietnamese.

In Washington, the White House said the evacuation was completed at 5:30 p.m., when the last helicopter, carrying Ambassador Graham Martin and more than 100 Americans, touched down on an American carrier in the South China Sea.

However, two hours after Washington said the operation was over, small arms fire reportedly was preventing a helicopter load of Marines from lifting off from the embassy.

The operation was originally scheduled to end at noon, but bad weather, pilot fatigue, and difficulties in helicopter rescues caused unexpected delays.

More than 400 South Vietnamese were included in the last group of evacuees. Over the 13-hour emergency airlift, 6,400 Americans and South Vietnamese were withdrawn.

America's 30-year involvement in the Indochina war was ended in tumultuous scenes, with U.S. Marines and civilians using pistol and rifle butts to smash the fingers of Vietnamese clawing at the 10-foot wall of the U.S. Embassy.

Some tried to jump the wall and landed on the barbed wire. A man and woman lay on the wire, bleeding. People held up their children, asking Americans to take them over the fence.

Both Sides Claim Gains

Israel Reports Trapping 400 Tanks at Suez Canal

From Wire Dispatches

PARIS, Oct. 7.—Fierce fighting was reported today on two fronts as Israel battled Egypt and Syria in the fourth Middle East war since 1948.

Both sides reported success in the fighting, which began yesterday at the Suez Canal and the Golan Heights. Each side accused the other of initiating battle, but United Nations observers reported that the Syrians and Egyptians had attacked—on Yom Kippur, the most solemn day of the Jewish year—without prior Israeli action.

Communiqués broadcast from Cairo and Damascus claimed at least 100 Israeli jets had been knocked out of the skies by Egyptian and Syrian fighters and anti-aircraft defenses.

The Tel Aviv military command issued no official count of Arab planes shot down, in a silence similar to the one maintained during the Israeli triumph of 1967. Egypt acknowledged 26 of its Soviet-built MiGs and "some helicopters" had been shot down by the Israelis.

A Cairo communiqué said the Egyptians had destroyed 92 Israeli tanks, 60 of them yesterday and the rest today.

A state radio broadcast said Israeli jets were raiding targets inside Egypt and Syria after dark. Warplanes also were hitting Egyptian troop concentrations and pushing Egyptian armor back toward the canal, it said.

The Cairo radio denied tonight Israeli claims that bridges across the Suez Canal had been knocked out.

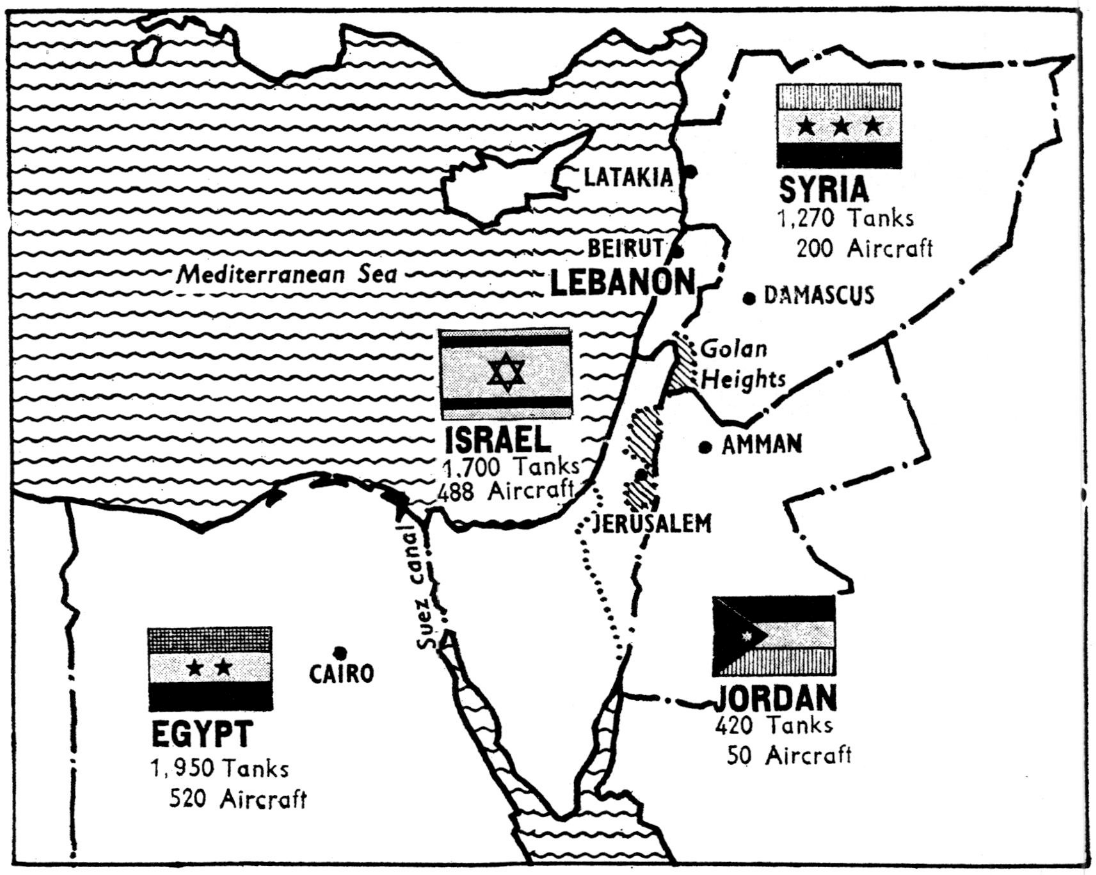

IHT.

Map shows Israel and Arab nations with comparative strength in tanks and combat aircraft. Most serious fighting was in the Golan Heights between Israel and Syria and on the Israeli-occupied east side of the Suez Canal, which Egyptian forces crossed.

United Press International.

ROLLING INTO BATTLE—An Israeli Centurion tank moves toward the Syrian border in the Golan Heights after fighting broke out. An Israeli jet flies overhead.

Cairo's Bright Lights Blacked Out

From Wire Dispatches

CAIRO, Oct. 7.—The Egyptian capital entered this second day of the new Mideast war in a calm mood, with residents and tourists milling in the streets. But at nightfall the city of six million donned the dark mantle of a capital at war.

Gone were the bright lights that had shone last night. Young boys dashed up to halted cars tonight to smear their headlights with the blue paint that is now mandatory under rules of the blackout, which was almost completely effective.

There still were no air raid sirens, but detailed instructions of what to do in an air raid —leave windows open, draw curtains and blinds, turn off gas and water, go to a shelter—were published in all papers. Cairo is only seven minutes by jet bomber from the Suez Canal.

Few people were on the streets. Those that were clustered around newsstands or sought out transistor radios to listen to government broadcasts.

Military communiqués, issued regularly over the radio yesterday and early today, dwindled as the fighting continued. At 9:30 tonight, there had been no communiqué for nearly seven hours.

Television carried a two-minute film of Egyptian tanks and troops crossing a military bridge over the Suez Canal. The soldiers were waving their guns joyfully. Other scenes in the film showed what was described as Egyptian soldiers raising their flag in the Sinai Peninsula, occupied by Israel since the June, 1967, war. Others showed a boat cruising the canal.

All of Egypt's schools, which opened only last week after the long summer vacation, were ordered by the government to close.

Motorists formed queues at service stations for gasoline following the government announcement today that it is to be rationed.

Sugar disappeared from many stores within hours of an announcement that the ration would be halved. It was a busy shopping day in this city today.

Foreign embassies, usually closed Sundays, were manned. The diplomats were following the news and checking the whereabouts of their nationals.

About 1,500 Americans, many of them in oil exploration or teaching, are in Egypt. West Germany, Britain, Italy and several other West European countries have large communities in Cairo, which has about 100 diplomatic missions.

With air and sea outlets closed, residents and visitors were forced to stay in Egypt, although many wanted to leave. The major hotels were fairly full of tourists.

Jerusalem Is Quiet— Serene on Surface

By Terence Smith

JERUSALEM, Oct. 7 (NYT).—In the midst of what will no doubt become known as the "Yom Kippur War," Jerusalem is the eye of the hurricane. Its streets are largely empty and all but a handful of its shops are closed.

Long lines of hopeful shoppers formed this morning at the supermarkets, but they were quiet—more quiet and orderly, one woman observed, than on a normal morning. All but a few of the capital's buses are gone, mobilized along with the men. Many of the taxis have been requisitioned as well, along with their drivers. It was a quiet city today, almost serene on the surface.

There is tension beneath that surface serenity, however, especially in the former Jordanian sector. The Arabs of East Jerusalem clearly have mixed feelings about the renewed fighting. They seem relieved that Jerusalem itself is not being shelled and bombed as it was in 1967, but they cannot conceal their delight at the reports of initial Arab successes on the battlefield.

In contrast to the Israeli sector, where only old men, women and children could be seen on the streets, there were hundreds of young Arab men on the sidewalks of East Jerusalem.

WEDNESDAY, JULY 24, 1974

Military Government in Greece Resigns, Calls Ex-Premier Caramanlis From Exile

Associated Press

Crowd in Athens surrounds military truck to shake hands and cheer after news that regime was resigning.

Junta Invites a Return of Civilian Rule

By Alvin Shuster

ATHENS, July 23 (NYT) —The military rulers of Greece today decided to turn over the nation to its former political leaders, ending more than seven years of dictatorship.

They promptly summoned Constantine Caramanlis, the Premier here from 1955 to 1963, to return to Greece from his self-imposed 11-year exile in Paris. It was widely believed that he would head the new government.

Greek television, in an announcement late today, said only that Mr. Caramanlis had been invited back to take part in talks with other political leaders.

[Mr. Caramanlis, 67, who has lived in Paris since 1963, flew back to Athens tonight.

[Mr. Caramanlis, a conservative politician known for his pro-Western views, said in Paris: "To repeat the words of Vice-President Truman when he was told that President Roosevelt had died I tell you this—Pray for me."

It was a day Greeks have been waiting for since a group of army colonels seized power here in April, 1967, abolished parliamentary democracy, imposed martial law and stifled all political opposition.

Today's decision, a direct result of the Cyprus crisis, was announced after the military rulers called former political leaders to a meeting and told them to take over the nation's mounting economic and political problems.

Athens Greets Cabinet's Fall With Joyous Demonstration

ATHENS, July 23 (UPI).—There was quiet in the city as the radio broadcast the news that the government had resigned. Ten minutes later, everybody was telling everybody else what had happened.

Soon a cacophony of horns, shouting and clapping erupted around the city as people tumbled out of their houses, waving Greek flags, making victory signs and chanting, "Long live the Greek Republic," "Democracy" and "He's coming."

As rumors spread that Constantine Caramanlis was returning from exile in Paris to form a government, crowds massed at the airport to welcome him.

But the center of the joy and confusion was the Parliament Building, where Greek politicians today had talks with military leaders, who decided to restore civilian rule. It was the first time since the military coup of 1967 that the leaders had consulted opposition politicians.

As the politicians emerged from the session, they were kissed and hugged, and young people clambered all over their limousines.

Later, when former government minister Evangelos Averoff left his office to walk to the Parliament Building for a second meeting, he could take no more than two steps before a young man ran up to kiss him on both cheeks, and a plump middle-aged mother blocked his path and embraced him.

As he headed towards the session, passersby applauded and pumped his hand. Two heavily built Greek matrons broke into a sprint and, holding hands, ran toward the crowd massing in Constitution Square.

As cars jammed the roads, driving around in circles and orchestrating the din with their horns, one young man did a slalom run through the traffic, bare-chested and waving his blue shirt above his head.

Such nudity violates the moral code laid down by the military regime. Police made no move to stop him, although officers with megaphones made vain efforts in Constitution Square to get the crowd to disperse.

There was no stopping the eruption of noise and movement, with even the church bells chiming in their approval.

The slogans multiplied. "Free elections," "Amnesty for all," "Down with the tyrants," Cowards, you are hidden," "Resurrection," "Prison is over," people shouted.

In a quieter expression of joy, some women walked through the streets carrying lighted candles. Everybody was smiling.

THURSDAY, AUGUST 18, 1977

Presley Dies: How Europe Took News

PARIS, Aug. 17 (NYT).—The death yesterday in Memphis of Elvis Presley has been treated as a major event in Western Europe today.

Most newspapers splashed it across their front pages, carried long obituaries, and detailed accounts of his career highlights.

Radios in Britain, France, Italy and West Germany have been playing his top hits—spanning a generation—during the last 24 hours. Television programs have carried excerpts of his films and stage performances.

In Paris, Mr. Presley's death was the top news event of the day for most of the newspapers.

French singers, who modeled their careers after his, readily acknowledged their debts to Mr. Presley.

"It was Elvis whose songs were the lullabies of our first parties," said Sylvie Vartan, a popular actress and singer.

"It's my ego that is dying," said Johnny Hallyday, one of the top French singers, and now in his mid-30s. "He remained the symbol of a whole generation of youth as Sinatra had been for the preceding one and the Beatles for the following one."

In Britain, where 16 of his records made the No. 1 spot—only one less than the Beatles—Mr. Presley was given an unusual accolade by two radio stations today which abandoned commercials and other scheduled program to play his songs.

In West Germany, where Mr. Presley spent two years with the U.S. Army, his following had been the largest on the Continent. The RCA office in Hamburg, which was Mr. Presley's main distributor in the country, reported today that its telephone switchboard was jammed with calls from record dealers ordering thousands of his records.

In Italy, radio programs portrayed the singer as a "paradoxical idol." According to one broadcast, Mr. Presley was "the kind of person hundreds of thousands of young people actually were—not just what they would like to be."

United Press International.

Elvis Presley in action.

MONDAY, JUNE 19, 1972

Attempt to 'Bug' Headquarters

Nixon Re-Election Aide Held In Break-In on Democrats

WASHINGTON, June 18 (AP). —Five men were arrested yesterday for breaking into offices of the Democratic National Committee. One a is the security coordinator for President Nixon's chief campaign committee, public records show.

Court records in the case list the man as James W. McCord jr. of 7 Winder Court, Rockville, Md. Campaign finance records filed June 10 by the Committee to Reeelct the President list James W. McCord jr. of the same address as receiving a net salary of $1,209 a month for his job as security coordinator.

Mr. McCord described himself during court proceedings as a retired agent of the Central Intelligence Agency and operator of a security consulting business.

The five men were arrested early yesterday during what the authorities described as an elaborate plot to plant lisetning devices in the offices of the Democratic party's national headquarters.

In Los Angeles, former Atty. Gen. John N. Mitchell, head of the Committee to Re-elect the President, said that Mr. McCord was "not operating either in our behalf or with our consent."

"We do not know as of this moment whether our security problems are related to the events of Saturday morning at the Democratic headquarters or not."

He did not elaborate on the nature of the security problems at his headquarters.

Wore Rhbber Gloves

According to the police after the Democratic party break-in, the five men were wearing rubber surgical gloves and had electronic equipment with them when they were surprised by plainclothes policemen who had been alerted by a security guard.

The four men arrested with Mr. McCord were listed as: Frank Sturgis, Eugenio R. Martinez, Virgillio R. Gonzalez and Bernard L. Barker.

The security guard who called the police first noticed that a door connecting a stairwell to a basemen garage had been taped so that it would not lock. The Democratic headquarters are in an office section of the Watergate hotel and apartment complex in Washington.

MONDAY, JULY 29, 1974

House Unit Votes, 27-11, to Recommend First Impeachment Article Against Nixon

Six Republicans Join Panel's 21 Democrats

By James M. Naughton

WASHINGTON, July 28 (NYT).—The House Judiciary Committee voted 27 to 11 last night to recommend the impeachment of President Nixon on a charge that he personally engaged in a "course of conduct" designed to obstruct justice in the Watergate case.

This charge is the first to be lodged against a president by a House investigating body since 1868.

Six of the committee's Republicans joined all 21 Democrats in adopting the charge which will be debated in the full House next month along with other probable articles of impeachment.

Mr. Nixon would be subjected to a trial by the Senate should a majority of the House vote to approve the article of impeachment or either of two other articles the Judiciary Committee will debate this week. Should any one of the charges be proved to the satisfaction of two-thirds of the Senate, the President would be removed from office.

Specifically, the committee voted last night to charge that the President, in violation of his constitutional oath to uphold the law, "Engaged personally and through his subordinates or agents in a course of conduct or plan designed to delay, impede and obstruct the investigation" of the burglary of the Democratic headquarters in the Watergate complex June 17, 1972.

[A number of congressmen predicted today that the full House will vote for impeachment of Mr. Nixon, AP reported. One congressman said that at least a third of the Republicans in the House would back impeachment. Another foresaw a 70-vote margin in favor of impeachment. The Senate majority whip, Robert Byrd of West Virginia, said that the votes were not yet present for a Senate conviction but added that "the possibilities for conviction, I think, are growing daily."

Ziegler Cites Anguish and Confidence

By Carroll Kilpatrick

SAN CLEMENTE, Calif., July 28 (WP).—President Nixon today returned to Washington, after two weeks in California, in "anguish" over the House Judiciary Committeee vote against him but full of "determination" to fight impeachment in the House of Representatives.

Before leaving San Clemente after 16 days at his home, the President was described by aides as confident of the outcome of the two-year Watergate crisis.

Declaring that Mr. Nixon has "a tremendous capacity of discipline," Press Secretary Ronald Ziegler said the President has "no feeling of despair" and has not allowed "anger to overtake him."

"Certainly there is anguish," Mr. Ziegler said. "Certainly there is disappointment."

But the spokesman asserted that it is incorrect to say "we have given up or that the President has given up."

FRIDAY, AUGUST 9, 1974

NIXON QUITS

'In Interest of Nation'

By Fred Farris

WASHINGTON, Aug. 8 (IHT). —President Nixon announced his resignation tonight "in the interests of the nation."

In a dramatic televised speech, he called upon the American people to unite in support of his successor, Gerald Ford, who will be sworn in at noon tomorrow as the nation's 38th President.

"America needs a fulltime President and a fulltime Congress, particularly at this time, with the problems we face at home and abroad," Mr. Nixon said.

He said he had concluded that, if he remained in office, both he and the Congress would be preoccupied with the "constitutional process" set off by the impeachment moves stemming from Watergate.

The President said, "I have never been a quitter. To leave office before my term is completed is abhorrent to every instinct in my body."

And, therefore, he said, "I shall resign effective at noon tomorrow. Vice-President Ford will be sworn in as President at that hour, in this office."

"In passing this office to the Vice-President, I do so with a profound sense of the weight that will pass to his shoulders. As he assumes that responsibility, he will deserve the help and support of all of us.

"...The first essential is to begin healing the wounds of this nation, put the bitterness and divisions of the past behind us."

Mr. Nixon, his face grim, said that he was stepping aside in the national interest. His base of support in Congress, he said, had eroded to the point where he would not have backing for the crucial decisions that confront the President.

In that situation, he said, the constitutional process that would have been served by impeachment has been fulfilled, and there is no longer a need to prolong the struggle.

"To have served in this office is to have felt a very personal sense of kinship with each and every American," he said. "In leaving it, I do so with this prayer: may God's grace be with you in all the days ahead."

With that, he ended his solemn address. The formal closing that had concluded his 36 prior speeches from the White House—the "Thank you, and good night" was omitted. There was, instead, silence, as Mr. Nixon ended almost three decades in public life as congressman, senator, Vice-President, and 37th President of the United States.

It was the first time in the 185-year chain of presidents that a chief executive resigned his office. And it was the first time that the office would be filled under the presidential succession decreed by the 25th Amendment ratified in 1967.

With Mr. Ford's choice of a new vice-president to come the country will have at its helm two men not selected in a nationwide vote.

Spaniards to Swear In King

Death of Gen. Franco at 82 Ends 36 Years of Dictatorial Regime

Juan Carlos to Preside at State Funeral Sunday

United Press International.

Prince Juan Carlos and his wife, Princess Sophia, before General Franco's coffin.

By Henry Giniger

MADRID, Nov. 20 (NYT).—With the death of Generalissimo Francisco Franco early this morning, Spain today calmly prepared for a new era under Prince Juan Carlos as its first king since 1931.

The parliament and the Council of the Realm will meet Saturday morning to hear Juan Carlos swear fidelity to the fundamental principles of a regime over which Gen. Franco prevailed for 36 years.

In a posthumous message to his people, Gen. Franco, 82, asked forgiveness from all, just as he had forgiven those who had declared themselves his enemies. He included a warning that enemies of Spain and of Christian civilization were watching. He appealed for unity.

Gen. Franco, after a tenacious five-week battle, succumbed at 4:40 this morning.

In the final medical bulletin, a medical team of 32 doctors indicated that it had continued to fight to revive him. It reported an "irreversible heart stoppage."

At 5:25 a.m., the doctors listed in the final clinical diagnosis Parkinson's disease, acute infarctus of the miocardium, acute digestive ulcers with repeated massive hemorrhaging, bacterial peritonitis, acute kidney failure, thrombophlebitis in the left thigh, bilateral bronchopneumonia, endotoxic shock and heart stoppage.

Spain today began 30 days of national mourning for Gen. Franco.

The death of the chief of state, who led rightist military forces to victory in the Spanish Civil War that ended in 1939, occurred at La Paz Hospital on the northern edge of Madrid. He had been rushed there on Nov. 7 from the Pardo Palace for surgery to stop internal bleeding.

Although Juan Carlos, 3", his designated successor, had been acting chief of state since Oct. 30, interim power passed formally to the three-member Council of the Realm, headed by Alejandro Rodriguez de Valcarcel, the speaker of the Cortes (parliament).

The panel will swear in Juan Carlos as king of Spain before a joint session of parliament and the Council of the Realm and, as king, Juan Carlos will preside over the state funeral of Gen. Franco on Sunday.

Keystone.

Gen. Francisco Franco Before His Illness

Spain's Franco: Dec. 4, 1892-Nov. 20, 1975

By Alden Whitman

NEW YORK, Nov. 20 (NYT).—One of the most durable, canny and empirical of modern dictators, Francisco Paulino Hermenegildo Teodulo Franco y Bahamonde became master of Spain in 1939 after a bloody three-year civil war, in which the scales of victory were tipped by armed assistance from Hitler and Mussolini. A second powerful factor was the worldwide support of the Roman Catholic Church.

He was also aided in winning the war by the internal weaknesses of the legitimate government, principally its inability to achieve political unity among its disparate parties and factions. Although the government put up a valiant defense, it had fatal difficulty in buying arms abroad and its armed forces, moreover, were beset by the same sort of disunity that hobbled the Cabinet.

Coming to power after victory in a civil war that had devastated Spain, Gen. Franco clinched his grip on an impoverished and backward country by systematic terror. Then, by clever diplomacy, he took Spain through World War II as a nonbelligerent while averring his attachment to the Fascist powers. Exercising patience, he waited out years of international ostracism after the war from which he was rescued by a U.S. decision in 1950 to acquire military bases in the country as a move in the cold war with the Soviet Union.

Now esteemed by the West, he was able to have his nation admitted to the UN, which had expressly barred Spain in 1946 in a resolution asserting that "in origin and nature the Franco regime is a fascist regime patterned on, and established largely as a result of aid received from, Hitler's Nazi Germany and Mussolini's Fascist Italy."

But for all the pervasiveness of his power, the Caudillo, "by the grace of God," and generalissimo of the armies of land, sea and air, and chief of state for life, was among the least majestic of modern rulers.

United Press International.

General Francisco Franco in 1936 file photo as he arrived in Salamanca to lead troops in Civil War.

Looked Gnomish

Standing but 5 feet 3 inches tall, Gen. Franco looked gnomish even in his general's gold-trimmed, olive-drab uniform with red silk sash. Unlike Hitler or Mussolini, he never stirred his people to fervor. He spoke publicly no more than three or four times a year, in a high voice that had a slight lisp.

On ceremonial occasions, he adopted an august role. Riding in his black Rolls Royce, which carried the national coat of arms in place of license plates, he was preceded by an open car filled with burly red-bereted bodyguards, and his route was flanked by policemen stationed 10 yards apart. He demanded the homage reserved for royalty, walking under a canopy, for example, at religious rites.

There seemed to be almost no rapport between him and the population. Crowds regarded him as more of an institution than a person. Among close associates he was known for his secretiveness.

Handpicked Cortes

Although Spain had a Cortes, or parliament, Gen. Franco paid it little heed. Its members were handpicked, but little legislation was ever sent to them. Gen. Franco, when he wanted to, enacted laws simply by signing and promulgating them in the Official Gazette.

He had constructed a pharaonic tomb, in which he wanted to be buried. Called the Valley of the Fallen and dedicated to the Civil War dead, it is situated close to the Escorial, near Madrid. Carved out of rock the interior is a basilica, one of the world's largest, and is surmounted by a cross 500 feet tall. Gen. Francc took a detailed interest in its construction, which covered 15 years and cost millions of pesetas.

Prince Trained for 27 Years To Take Madrid Leadership

NEW YORK, Nov. 20 (NYT).—Diffident and soft-spoken in private meetings, Juan Carlos Alfonso Victor Maria de Borbon y Borbon has been educated to be a king.

Seven years before his birth on Jan. 5, 1938, his grandfather, King Alfonso XIII, abdicated the throne of Spain. The grandson was born in Rome and, at the end of World War II, taken to Portugal.

In August, 1948, his father, Don Juan, third son of the former king, met with Spain's dictator, Generalissimo Francisco Franco, on a yacht in the Bay of Biscay. He agreed to send his son to be educated in Spain. Three months later, at age 10, the young prince entered Spain for the first time.

He attended the military, naval and air academies and was commissioned in all three branches. Helped by private tutors, he also attended Madrid University.

The 37-year-old prince, 6 feet 3 inches and 180 pounds, is a great-great-grandson of Queen Victoria of England. His height—he is a head taller than the average Spaniard—his blue eyes and his dark blond hair reflect his Nordic ancestry. He is an accomplished horseman, hunter, golfer, water skier and yachtsman.

While on an Aegean cruise in 1961, the prince met Princess Sophia of Greece. They were married in Athens in May, 1962, and are the parents of two girls, Elena and Sofia, and a son, Felipe.

Visitors say that his diffidence dwindles in face-to-face sessions, that he has a gentle, self-deprecating wit. Perhaps as a result of that nature, perhaps because of the years of preparation for his new role, the prince was able to answer with grace an interviewer who described him once as the handpicked heir of Gen. Franco.

"Yes, I'm Franco's heir," he replied. "But I'm Spain's heir as well."

WEDNESDAY, MAY 8, 1974

Crying Wolf to a 'Deaf' Correspondent

By Waverley Root

PARIS, May 7 (IHT).—Thirty-four years ago (May 9-10, 1940) the least perceptive journalist in France, or possibly in the world, was a Mutual Broadcasting System correspondent named Waverley Root. My broadcasts had been cut down to one a week, and even at that I sometimes had trouble scraping up enough news to make a good story, for the phoney war had been going on for several months, unbroken by any interesting activity except, a month earlier, the invasion of Denmark and Norway.

This was off my beat, but it struck home; it shot out from under me overnight what had become my principal job—I had been for eight years the Paris correspondent of the Copenhagen Politiken, then the largest paper in Scandinavia. The silver lining of this dark cloud was that I now seemed to have time, between weekly broadcasts, to head south and spend a few days with my wife and daughter, whom I had bundled out of Paris a few days before war was declared and who were living in Cannes.

Unfortunately, when I arrived at the Ministry of Posts each week for my broadcast, I invariably found it humming with rumors about the troops of one country or another massing on its borders, and a prospect that all hell would break out on the morrow. Each week I canceled my plans to leave Paris.

On the night of May 9, the grapevine was that the Dutch Army had mobilized along the frontier with Germany, but I had been had too often to bite this time, short of personal assurances from Queen Wilhelmina. My broadcast finished, I climbed into my 11-hp Citroën and headed south via the Place de la Concorde, which I had to cross to reach my apartment and pick up my typewriter and luggage, which included a comely young woman named Gertrude, whom I was taking along for company.

A policeman flagged me down at the entrance to the place and I reached for my papers, an automatic gesture in those days. He waved them aside. 'Be careful going through the Place de la Concorde," he said, "It's full of garbage trucks." "What in the world for?" I asked. "To keep planes from landing on it," he said. This should have been a signal to cancel my plans once more, but I ignored it. I had harkened to the cry of wolf too often. I slaloomed through the garbage trucks, which were scattered haphazardly all over the square, picked up Gertrude and the other impedimenta, and we were off.

It was a little before 4 a.m. My idea had been to make Cannes nonstop, but fatigue caught up with me at Vienne, so we stopped at a hotel on the main square and succeeded in wringing two rooms from a reluctant hotel clerk who saw no reason why a pair of normally constituted young people would want more than one.

We were not destined to get much sleep.

I was awakened by distant booming and went to the window to see what was happening. A fire engine was standing in the square across from the hotel. A small group of people beside it were staring towards Lyons. The booms in the distance meant nothing to me, for I had never heard bombs drop before.

Only later did I learn that I had been within hearing distance of the first German bombing of France outside of the zone of military operations proper—that of the Bron airdrome at Lyons.

Although I still lacked word from Queen Wilhelmina, I had now been given a rather sharp hint that something was up, but I proved incapable of translating it.

The night before, to kill time while waiting for the hour of my broadcast, I had been playing chess in the Café de Flore with Tristan Tzara, the founder of dada. He had spoken feelingly to me of a restaurant called La Mère Germaine at Châteauneuf-du-Pape. La Mère Germaine, a real person, not a trademark, covered our whole table with a colorful collection of hors d'œuvre, each more mouth-watering than the other, and I must have turned on like a light; for months Paris restaurants had been obeying the wartime restrictions that limited the number of appetizers in *hors d'œvre variés* to four.

The meal had been served outdoors, on a sort of platform overlooking miles of serried vineyards dressed in the light green of spring. The sun was bright, the day warm, and in the distance, its outlines shimmering in a heat haze, the solid tower of the Palace of the Popes rose from its rock in Avignon. Replete with the peace of good food and drink (it was then that I learned for the first time that *white* Châteauneuf-du-Pape exists), I exclaimed, "It's not possible that this country is at war!" We then drove into Avignon, where a newsboy thrust into the car a paper whose black headline shouted: "GERMANS INVADE NORTHERN FRANCE, HOLLAND, BELGIUM."

I was now "in blood stepp'd in so far that . . . returning were as tedious as go o'er," or, more prosaically, too far from my base to head back for the Ministry of Posts in Paris; there was a nearer microphone at Aix-en-Provence. I do not know the fastest speed the pre-war Citroën 11 could make, but we went faster. At one moment, roaring down a hill on one of those narrow blacktop national roads which sank so unobtrusively into the Provençal countryside, since replaced by hideous broad cement highways designed to propel you through the once lovely landscape too fast to see it (just as well, since these eyesore arteries have destroyed its beauty anyway), the two halves of the hood, torn loose by the rushing wind, rose flapping into the air like the wings of some monstrous black bird, cutting off my vision. As she felt the car slowing to a stop, Gertrude opened her eyes. I secured the hood and took off again; she quickly shut them once more and kept them shut until I had to slow down to enter Aix.

It was far too early for me to broadcast from Aix, so I telephoned from the radio station there to the ministry in Paris and asked that Nice be instructed to ready a microphone for me for a 3.15 a.m. broadcast. I also filed a cable to MBS in New York to warn them to listen for it. We took off again, not quite so fast this time, for there was now less hurry.

It was after dark when we reached the famous Esterel road which snakes its way through the forests of the Mounts of the Moors. I had driven the Esterel before, but not in a blackout with no light except that which pierced the six pinholes drilled through the black tin cups which covered the headlights, giving just enough illumination to show how dark it was. A thick fog now joined us. I remembered that there was a precipitous drop on one side of the road, so I hugged the other, as closely as I could tell where it was in the murk, thoughtlessly explaining why to Gertrude, who promptly closed her eyes again.

At 2:30 a.m. I was sitting before the mike in Nice, calling New York and getting no answer. I persevered for something like two hours, during which time nobody proved able to hear me, though at one moment I picked up Mutual's correspondent at the front talking to Mutual. I was happy to know that someone was getting through, but it was frustrating to be helplessly gagged. I again cabled New York announcing a broadcast for the following night, and the same process was repeated. I didn't dare leave my mike, dumb though it was, to start back for Paris, for fear of being caught flat-footed far off base again, so I spent five days in this futile occupation.

On the sixth, a brace of security police officers called on me at my wife's villa. Throwing my cables to New York accusingly down before me, they demanded, "Monsieur, how do you explain this?" I explained: "BROADCASTING 120315 47325" meant that I would be on the air May 12 at 3.15 a.m., using a wavelength of 473.25 meters (any radio buffs who find this last figure strange are hereby informed that I have concocted it at random, having forgotten wavelengths completely). The officers were clearly disappointed. They had flaired cipher and expected to uncover a spy, an excellent means of securing promotion.

The immediate crisis had passed, and I now dared to take the time to drive back to Paris. We covered the Esterel in daylight and I discovered with a certain feeling of shock that I had remembered its drops on the wrong side of the road; I must have been speeding over it a good deal of the time with the outer half of my offside tires resting on nothing. I did not mention this to Gertrude.

US WEATHER — PARIS: Tuesday, overcast, possible . Temp. 7-11 (45-52). Wednesday, cloudy, possible rain, cold. LONDON: Tuesday, sleet early, cloudy later. Temp. 3-7 (36- Wednesday, cloudy and cold. CHANNEL: Rough. ROME: sday, overcast. Temp. 9-17 (48-63). NEW YORK: Tuesday, Temp. 0-9 (32-48).

ADDITIONAL WEATHER — COMICS PAGE

INTERNATIONAL
Herald Tribune

Published with The New York Times and The Washington Post

Abu Dhabi	4.50 Dirh.	Greece	22 Drs.	Netherlands	1.75 Flor.
Algeria	2.75 Din.	Iceland	150 I.Kr.	Nigeria	70 K.
Austria	12 S	India	Rs. 8	Norway	3.25 N.Kr.
Bahrain	0.400 Din.	Iran	70 Rials	Oman	0.425 Rials
Belgium	23 B.Fr.	Israel	I£17.00	Portugal	25 Esc.
Cyprus	250 Mills	Italy	500 Lire	Qatar	4.00 Rials
Denmark	3.75 D.Kr.	Jordan	0.300 Fils	Saudi Arabia	3.50 Rials
Dubai	4.50 Dirh.	Kenya	Shs. 8.00	Spain	50 Ptas.
Egypt	40 P.	Kuwait	0.300 Fils	Sweden	3.00 S.Kr.
Eire	22 P.	Lebanon	£L2.75	Switzerland	1.70 S.Fr.
Finland	3.00 F.M.	Libya	Din. 0.25	Tunisia	3.25 Din
France	3 F.	Luxembourg	23 L.Fr.	Turkey	T.£. 15
Germany	1.50 D.M.	Madeira	27.5 Esc.	U.S. Mil. (Eur.)	$0.35
Great Britain	20 P.	Morocco	3.00 Dr.	Yugoslavia	20 D

No. 29.896 * PARIS, TUESDAY, MARCH 27, 1979 Established 1887

Israel and Egypt Sign Peace Treaty

United Press International

President Anwar Sadat, President Carter and Prime Minister Begin shake hands after signing yesterday.

Carter Cautions on Difficult Steps Ahead

By Fred Farris

WASHINGTON, March 26 (IHT) — President Anwar Sadat of Egypt and Prime Minister Menachem Begin of Israel today signed a peace treaty that Mr. Sadat called "a new dawn . . . emerging out of the darkness of the past."

President Carter, whose persistence in pursuit of the treaty finally paid off, signed as a happy witness.

Held on the White House lawn and televised live to Egypt and Israel, the ceremony followed 15 months of tortuous negotiations.

The Egyptian leader, whose Arab colleagues have denounced him for reaching a peace with Israel — the first Arab treaty with the Jewish state — called it "a historic turning point of great significance for all peace-loving nations."

Mr. Begin said: "Despite all the tragedies and disappointments of the past, we must never forsake that vision, that human dream [of peace]. Peace . . . is the advancement of man, the victory of a just cause, the triumph of truth . . . ."

Praised for Dedication

Mr. Carter praised the two leaders, whom he called "world statesmen," for their "dedication and determination," and proclaimed simply: "Peace has come." But Mr. Carter went on to say that it was just "the first step of peace — a first step on a long and difficult road."

"We must not minimize the obstacles that lie ahead," he said.

The president said that differences still separated Israel and Egypt "from each other and also from some of their neighbors, who fear what they have done."

"To overcome those differences, to dispel those fears," he said, "we must rededicate ourselves to the goal of a broader peace with justice for all who have lived in a state of conflict in the Middle East."

The treaty — signed in English, Hebrew and Arabic — provides for the return to Egypt of the Sinai Peninsula, captured by Israel in 1967, plus the oil fields and air-bases, which will be converted to civilian use.

In return, Israel gains recognition for the first time from an Arab nation, its most powerful and populous neighbor, with ambassadors to be exchanged early next year and cultural and trade channels opened.

Historic Table

As a throng of official guests watched and hundreds of the curious looked on from outside the White House north lawn — and Arab protesters chanted denunciations of the treaty from nearby — the three leaders walked to an oak table to put their signatures on the documents.

After the three national anthems sounded on this breezy spring day, the leaders first signed the agreed minutes recording their understandings of certain provisions of the treaty.

Then Mr. Begin and Mr. Sadat signed the three copies of the treaty — one in each language. Mr. Carter added his signature as a witness.

The three then rose, to applause, and shook hands in a three-way clasp. Mr. Carter said:

"Today we celebrate a victory — not of a bloody military campaign but of an inspiring peace campaign.

"Two leaders who will loom large in the history of nations — Anwar Sadat and Menachem Begin — have conducted this campaign with all the courage, tenacity, brilliance and inspiration of any generals who ever led men and machines onto the field of battle."

He said: "He have no illusions — we have hopes, dreams, prayers, yes — but no illusions. There now remains the rest of the Arab world, whose support and cooperation in the peace process is needed and honestly sought.

"I am convinced that other Arab people need and want peace, but some leaders are not yet willing to honor these needs and desires.

"We must now demonstrate the advantages of peace, and expand its benefits to encompass all those who have suffered in the Middle East."

The president quoted from a poem for peace, from the Koran and from the Prophet Isaiah, before saying:

"Let us now lay aside war. Let us now reward all the children of

(Continued on Page 2, Col. 7)

Associated Press

Prime Minister Begin and President Sadat at the White House yesterday.

Begin: A Study In Consistency

By William Claiborne

JERUSALEM (WP) — Shortly before his dramatic rise to prime minister almost two years ago, Menachem Begin visited the stony, inhospitable Samarian hills in the Israeli-occupied West Bank of the Jordan to celebrate the installation of a Torah scroll at the Alon Moreh Jewish settlement.

"We stand on the land of liberated Israel. There will be many, many Alon Morehs," Mr. Begin declared. Then, chiding reporters for their questions about his intentions in the West Bank, Mr. Begin said, "We don't use the word annexation. You annex foreign land, not your own country."

The shudders in Washington over Mr. Begin's ascendancy to power could be felt almost all the way to Israel, as if conservatism here were a new phenomenon. "I hope that the election of Mr. Begin will not be a step backward [from] the achievement of peace," President Carter said at the time. National security adviser Zbigniew Brzezinski, when told of Mr. Begin's election, shook his head and said, "No, no. That's wrong."

Mr. Begin emerged suddenly on the world scene dimly perceived by outsiders as a one-time Jewish underground terrorist, who carped at the established Labor government from the back benches of the

(Continued on Page 2, Col. 4)

Sadat's Journey: Hazardous Road

By Thomas Lippman

CAIRO (WP) — For Anwar Sadat, the signing of a peace treaty with Israel is the culmination of a policy that he has pursued through triumph and adversity, masterstroke and blunder, acclaim and condemnation almost from the day he took office as president of Egypt.

He publicly proclaimed his intention to seek peace almost from the beginning, but few heeded his words. Mr. Sadat, an obscure, almost clownish figure in his years as a faithful lackey of Gamal Abdel Nasser, was hardly credible as leader of Egypt, let alone as a world figure who would change the course of history.

It is not yet certain that Mr. Sadat can lead his fellow Arabs into peace as he led them into war in 1973. But, even if he falls short of that, he has irreversibly altered the life of his own country and the course of events in the Middle East.

It seems safe to say that not since Sherif Hussein of Mecca cast the Arab lot with the Allies against the Turks in World War I, ending four centuries of Ottoman dominion over the Arab world, has any Arab leader taken a leap of such historic implications.

Hussein's action had a bitter aftermath as the

(Continued on Page 2, Col. 1)

Khomeini Abolishes Revolutionary Tribunals

36 Supporters of Shah to Be Tried by Judicial Courts

From Wire Dispatches

TEHRAN, March 26 — Nine of the shah's generals and 27 supporters of his government will stand trial in the first Iranian judicial proceedings since Ayatollah Ruhollah Khomeini's revolutionaries took power last month.

Tehran radio did not say when the trial of the generals and "criminals and agents of the former regime" would begin, nor did it list the charges against them. But it asked the public to volunteer information about the accused.

Among those facing trial is Brig. Gen. Ismail Atabaki, former intelligence chief and deputy commander of army aviation. His immediate superior, Lt. Gen. Manuchehr Khosrowdad, was executed last month. Another of the accused is Maj. Gen. Jamshid Tabrizi, chief of staff of the shah's Imperial Guards.

More than 60 associates of Shah Mohammed Reza Pahlavi who were unable ... with him int... by secret rev... executed by f...

before he was fired by the shah in August, 1977.

Mr. Hoveyda, 59, is accused of waging a battle against God and his people, an offense described in the Koran as punishable by death. The revolutionary courts were suspended hours before the sentence was to be handed down. Mr. Ghotbzadeh said that the Hoveyda trial would resume in a few weeks in a judicial court.

Mr. Ghotbzadeh said that the trials and executions under the revolutionary courts were ordered by a public prosecutor who acted unchecked until he was dismissed last week.

"Khomeini thought the Revolutionary Council was in charge and he didn't want to interfere," he said. "The Revolutionary Council thought the government was in charge, and the government thought it all had Khomeini's approval.

"When the executions started in the provinces, we thought they were under the authority of the central revolutionary courts. We only realized what was really going on when we started protesting and asking who was ordering what."

Mr. Ghotbzadeh, the director of Iranian state radio and television, said that after the victory of the Islamic forces six weeks ago, the Revolutionary Council appointed by Ayatollah Khomeini named a prosecutor general to take charge of the prisoners being held at the ayatollah's headquarters.

The prosecutor proceeded on his own to create the Tehran revolu-...

Report Is Unconfirmed

Amin Says He Is Besieged At Entebbe by Tanzanians

NAIROBI, March 26 (AP) — Ugandan President Idi Amin declared today that he was being besieged by Tanzanian troops and tanks at his Entebbe residence.

Although Ugandan exiles said ...

Iraq ... To I...

GENEVA, ... Iraq today c... 24-percent i... oil at the OP... here to take... backs in Ir... Saudi Arabi... creases at th... ganization o... Countries la...

TUESDAY, NOVEMBER 22, 1977

United Press International.

Golda Meir handing President Sadat a gift for his new granddaughter.

Mrs. Meir and Sadat Share Laugh About 'Old Lady'

JERUSALEM, Nov. 21 (AP).—In a burst of warmth, Golda Meir transcended with a few grandmotherly words the history of hatred between her people and Anwar Sadat's.

"Marvelous, marvelous," the Egyptian President murmured as Mrs. Meir, 79, gave him a gift for his new granddaughter.

President Sadat's daughter, Noha, gave birth to a girl, who was named Jihan, while the Egyptian leader was praying yesterday at al-Aqsa Mosque in Jerusalem.

Mrs. Meir, who directed Israel in its 1973 war against Egypt, had turned Mr. Sadat's meeting with Israeli Labor party members into the informal kind of meeting she used to hold with her cabinet when she was prime minister.

"The beginning that you made with such courage, the hope of peace, let us continue it so that all of us can live in peace, so even an old lady like me . . ." and laughter interrupted her.

"I have always said this," interjected Mr. Sadat, recalling his contemptuous descriptions of Mrs. Meir.

"Yes, you always called me an old lady, Mr. Sadat," Mrs. Meir answered and then joined him in laughter.

The Labor party members applauded the sight, unimaginable only a week ago—Golda Meir joking with Anwar Sadat.

"We never thought that at the first meeting we would come with pens to sign a peace treaty, but we always hoped we could come together face-to-face and discuss without mediators," she told him. "No matter how faithfully, how well, the report, it's not the same with mediators. As I listened to you last night, I realized that."

Mr. Sadat later paid tribute to Mrs. Meir. "The peace process that we have started since the 1973 war was really started by Mrs. Meir when we concluded the disengagement agreement," he said.

Former Secretary of State Henry Kissinger shuttled between Jerusalem and Cairo as mediator in negotiations on the 1975 Sinai troop disengagement pact. At that point, the sides would not sit together.

After Months of Negotiation

U.S. Imprint Puts Pact Burden on Carter

By Jim Hoagland

WASHINGTON, March 26 (WP) — Egypt and Israel formally ended 30 years of war today and launched a new era of deep and direct U.S. involvement in the politics and military security of the Middle East by signing their peace treaty on the White House lawn.

The ceremony emphasized the "Made in the U.S.A." stamp now imprinted on a treaty that was to have been signed by Egypt's President Anwar Sadat and Israel's Prime Minister Menachem Begin 15 months ago on the banks of the Suez Canal in Ismailia.

The change of locale to Pennsylvania Avenue also underlines the extent to which Mr. Sadat has succeeded in shifting the Palestinian problem from his shoulders to those of President Carter who repeatedly has justified his sponsorship of the treaty by saying that it will open the way for a regional peace that will include a solution for the Palestinians.

Mr. Carter evidently has agreed to thrust the United States directly into the middle of this problem in hopes of halting a quickening erosion of U.S. influence and power in the Middle East by shoring up Mr. Sadat's rule. Ironically, Arab countries closely allied to the United States and Mr. Sadat fear that the half-finished peace ultimately will destabilize the region and doom the Egyptian leader.

The treaty documents spell out in rich detail the nature of the Egyptian-Israeli peace that has been achieved by 15 months of high-level diplomacy and interminable haggling. At the end of the three years of carefully phased steps called for by the treaty and its annexes, Mr. Sadat and Mr. Begin will have accomplished stunning gains for their countries.

Mr. Begin will have achieved a formal bilateral peace with the Arab world's largest nation and major military power, and greatly lessened the chances that the Arabs will be able to fight Israel in a conventional war.

Egypt will get back all of the Sinai Peninsula and its oil wells, an area conquered by Israel in the 1967 Six-Day War. By prolonging the negotiations after suddenly backing out of a nearly completed draft treaty in Ismailia in December, 1977, Mr. Sadat has been able to get Mr. Begin to give way on key points, including the dismantling of civilian settlements in the Sinai and early evacuation of the coastal town of El Arish.

More importantly for Mr. Sadat, the long delay has resulted in a highly visible U.S. commitment to

(Continued on Page 3, Col. 1)

Pact Sparks Bombings, Protests in Arab Capitals

...ows to 'Chop Off Hands' of 3 Treaty Signers

Beirut, predicted that President Sadat would be assassinated for signing the bilateral treaty with Israel. "We shall crush . . . the triangular alliance of Carter, Begin and Sadat under our boots," he said.

He charged that Washington had sent a "threat to create a lot of trouble for me if I didn't behave" during Mr. Carter's recent Mideast trip. "Begin also sent word that he will burn my fingers," Mr. Arafat added. "But let me tell all three of them today that I shall not only burn their fingers, but shall even chop off their hands."

Mr. Begin had said that the Palestine Liberation Organization leader would "burn his fingers" if he tried to sabotage the treaty.

Mr. Arafat's top lieutenant, Salah Khalaf, pledged that the guerrilla movement would mount attacks against U.S., British and West German interests everywhere for supporting the treaty.

After Mr. Arafat's speech, guerrillas and Lebanese leftists held protests in Beirut's Moslem sector, burning tires and firing machine guns in the air. The gunmen also insured that shopkeepers observed the strike.

Effigies Burned

Effigies of Mr. Carter, Mr. Sadat and Mr. Begin were burned at Palestinian refugee camps in Beirut and other Lebanese cities. Palestinian spokesmen said the demonstrations were peaceful.

The explosions at the U.S. Embassy in Damascus shattered windows but caused no casualties or major damage. No one claimed responsibility for the attack. Syrian witnesses said that one bomb was hurled into the embassy garden from a passing car and the other went off near the rear of the building.

The State Department had alerted U.S. missions in the Middle East to the possibility of terrorist attacks as the signing of the U.S.-spon-

(Continued on Page 2, Col. 8)

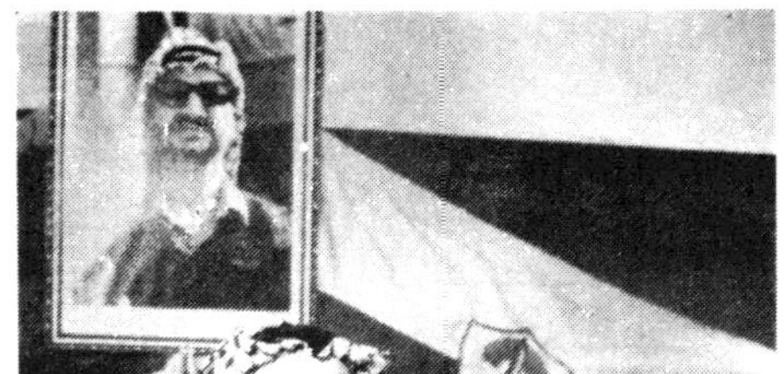

Associated Press

Yasser Arafat speaks yesterday at PLO camp outside Beirut.

THE WEATHER — PARIS: Saturday, Cloudy with sunny periods. Temp. 3-13(37-55). Sunday, Partly cloudy. LONDON: Saturday, Showers with sunny spells.Temp. 2-12(36-54). Sunday,Cloudy. CHANNEL: Slight. ROME: Saturday, Partly cloudy. Temp. 5-20(41-68). NEW YORK: Saturday, Fair. Temp. 6-16(43-61)

ADDITIONAL WEATHER — COMICS PAGE

INTERNATIONAL
Herald Tribune

Published with The New York Times and The Washington Post

Abu Dhabi ....4.50 Dirh	Greece ....22 Drs.	Netherlands ..1.75 Flor.
Algeria.........3.00 Din.	Iceland ....150 I.Kr.	Nigeria ....70 K.
Austria ....12 S.	India ....Rs. 8	Norway......3.25 N.Kr.
Bahrain ......0.400 Din	Iran ....70 Rials	Oman.......0.425 Rials
Belgium ....23 B.Fr.	Israel ....I.£17.00	Portugal.........25 Esc.
Cyprus ....250 Mills	Italy ....500 Lire	Qatar ....4.00 Rials
Denmark .....3.75 D.Kr.	Jordan ....0.300 Fils	Saudi Arabia ..3.50 Rials
Dubai ....4.50 Dirh.	Kenya ....Shs. 8.00	Spain............50 Ptas.
Egypt ....50 P.	Kuwait ....0.300 Fils	Sweden ......3.00 S.Kr.
Eire ....22 P.	Lebanon £L2.75	Switzerland ...1.70 S.Fr.
Finland........3.00 F.M.	Libya ....L.Dir 0.25	Tunisia ....3.25 Din
France ....3 F.	Luxembourg ....23 L.Fr.	Turkey ....T.£. 15
Germany ....1.50 D.M.	Madeira ......27.5 Esc.	U.S. Mil. (Eur.).....$0.35
Great Britain.......20 P.	Morocco ......3.00 Dr.	Yugoslavia........22 D.

No. 29,929 *R PARIS, SATURDAY-SUNDAY, MAY 5-6, 1979 Established 1887

United Press International

Margaret Thatcher was in a buoyant mood at Conservative headquarters on election night.

5-Year Term Appears Likely

Mrs. Thatcher Is Prime Minister With 43-Seat Commons Majority

Europeans Expecting Policy Shift

By Paul Lewis

BRUSSELS, May 4 (NYT) — The Conservative Party's victory in yesterday's British general election is likely to lead to a far-reaching although gradual shift in political relations within Western Europe that will have important implications for the United States, according to diplomatic sources here.

After nearly five years during which Britain's relations with its European partners have grown steadily more strained under the outgoing Labor administration, diplomats and officials expect that Margaret Thatcher's government will try to play a more active and constructive role in the Continent's affairs.

The Conservatives will remain as committed as Labor to securing important changes in policies of the European Economic Community that they feel are contrary to British interests. But they are likely to approach these negotiations in a more friendly spirit and end the bitter public quarreling over farm prices, fish, energy and monetary affairs which virtually paralyzed the community during Labor's last few months in office.

More significantly, many diplomats predict that an improvement in the tone of Britain's relations with Europe will in time lead a Conservative government to become the third member of the present informal French-German alliance, which effectively dominates European political affairs.

Mechanism Exists

The mechanism for creating such an informal tripartite alliance already exists through a system of regular meetings between the three leaders. "All they need is the political will to make the machinery work," a diplomat said. But it is one of the paradoxes of British politics that while the Labor party tends to be pro-American and hostile to European entangements, the Conservatives are more resentful of

(Continued on Page 2, Col. 7)

Associated Press

In British headlines, the Conservative victory was portrayed as a personal triumph for the party's leader, Margaret Thatcher.

Callaghan Resigns, Hails First Woman in Office

By R.W. Apple Jr.

LONDON, May 4 (NYT) — Margaret Thatcher, the daughter of a small-town grocer, took office today as prime minister of Britain, heiress to the tradition of Gladstone and Disraeli and Churchill, and the first woman elected to lead a European nation.

Mrs. Thatcher and the Conservative Party swept to a solid victory in yesterday's general election, piling up an overall majority of 43 seats in the House of Commons and dooming the Labor government of James Callaghan. Early this afternoon, Mr. Callaghan submitted his resignation to Queen Elizabeth II. A few minutes later, Mrs. Thatcher agreed to the queen's request that she form a government, then went directly to No. 10 Downing St. to begin work, pausing on the doorstep to recall these words of St. Francis of Assisi: "Where there is discord, may we bring harmony. Where there is error, may we bring truth. Where there is doubt, may we bring faith. Where there is despair, may we bring hope."

UPI

James Callaghan

The quotation was politically apt, because those who voted Mrs. Thatcher into office look to her to correct what they see as the errors and the excesses of socialism, and those who opposed her see her as a sower of discord. As soon as a trend was established early this morning, trade-union leaders began warning of a possible confrontation over restrictive new laws and cuts in job subsidies.

It was a day of high political drama, partly because of the novelty of a woman prime minister and partly because of her pledges to set Britain on a new course by cutting income taxes, scaling down social services and reducing the role of the state in daily life.

Although Mrs. Thatcher won a mandate solid enough to keep her in power for a full five-year term, the swing to the Tories was not large enough to suggest a national demand for immediate action, and some politicians expected her to proceed cautiously at first.

While the 53-year-old prime min-

(Continued on Page 2, Col. 7)

Champion of Individualism

The Thatcher Credo: 'Free Choice' Is All

By William Borders

LONDON, May 4 (NYT) — To Margaret Thatcher, "free choice is ultimately what life is about," and she likes to illustrate what she means in political terms with this example: "If somebody comes to me and asks, 'What are you going to do for us small businessmen?' I say, the only thing I'm going to do for you is make you freer to do things for yourselves. If you can't do it then, I'm sorry. I'll have nothing to offer you."

Judging by what she has been saying over the years, in public and in private, that is the center of Mrs. Thatcher's political philosophy — what she calls "a positive creed, to promote, not destroy, the uniqueness of the individual."

In the election campaign, Mrs. Thatcher sketched a vision of a Britain that would be rebuilt on the strong base of that kind of individualism to the economic strength it used to know, "so that once again the products stream from our factories and workshops while the customers of the world scramble over each other to buy them." She also promised a government that "would stop trying to step in and take decisions for you that you should be free to take on your own."

Now the British, having chosen the first woman to head a modern European government, will have a ...cal test ...e con... ...ffering ... coming leader of the Conservative Party and moving to the center of the national political stage, Mrs. Thatcher, a 53-year-old tax lawyer with two Oxford degrees in chemistry, has altered the party, halting what she saw as its me-too collectivism and moving it toward "the true center, the common-sense heart of British politics." A skilled handler of the people around her — mostly men — she also regularly displays an impressive grasp of facts and figures and, above all, control.

'You Didn't Complain'

Mrs. Thatcher's control, something that a lot of Britons were talking about over the few weeks of the campaign, is as renowned and as reliable as the neat appearance that she maintains even on a grueling day of handshaking. "I try to be

(Continued on Page 2, Col. 6)

The Election Returns

LONDON, May 4 (AP)—Returns from all 635 Parliamentary districts with changes in seats:

Labor	268	Gain: 11	Loss: 51
Conservative	339	Gain: 61	Loss: 6
Liberal	11	Gain: 0	Loss: 3
Scottish Nationalist	2	Gain: 0	Loss: 9
Plaid Cymru	2	Gain: 0	Loss: 1
Ind.	1	Gain: 0	Loss: 0
The Speaker	1	Gain: 0	Loss: 0
Social Democrat/Labor Party	1	Gain: 0	Loss: 0
Ulster Unionist	10	Gain: 2	Loss: 2

POPULAR VOTE

Labor	11,509,524	(36.9 Percent)
Conservatives	13,697,753	(43.9 Percent)
Liberal	4,313,931	(13.8 Percent)
Others	1,699,582	(5.4 Percent)

In the Oct. 1974 general election, final returns gave Labor 39.3 percent of the votes cast, Conservatives 35.7, Liberals 18.3, and others 6.7.

U.S. Report on Guyana Tragedy Accuses State Dept. of Lapses

By Graham Hovey

WASHINGTON, May 4 (NYT) — A government report on the Jonestown tragedy in Guyana charges the State Department with "errors and lapses" in handling and evaluating information about the People's Temple before the murders and mass suicide of last November.

The report emphasizes, however, that officials of both the State Department and the U.S. Embassy in Georgetown, Guyana, felt that they were bound by severe legal and other restraints that prevented them from probing deeply into conditions at the Jonestown settlement.

More than 900 members of the religious-political community either committed suicide or were murdered after the killing at a nearby airfield of Rep. Leo Ryan, D.-Calif., who had gone there to investigate the People's Temple, and of four persons accompanying him.

Commissioned by Secretary of State Cyrus Vance and made public yesterday, the study was carried out by two retired Foreign Service officers, John Crimmins and Stanley Carpenter.

Beginning a year ago, the report said, there were frequent examples of State Department indifference to or mishandling of information warning of impending disaster in Jonestown and a breakdown in communication within the department and betwe... ...bassy in Guyana...

Reques...

"The single m... ...stantive failure"... and the embass... scrapping of a... last June for pe... Guyanese gover... control over Jon... the alleged abus... Ambassador ... the telegram co... and telephoned... ment's desk o... asking that it b... sideration. Inste... was drafted in t... ular Affairs and... by the Bureau... Affairs, which h... tion over Guyar...

It was clear, ... the consular an... drafted the me... ambassador's re... slightest notion... the embassy's te... embassy in its... way was trying...

The report ... Burke for no... project.

The report ac... partment of "e... handling" of ... Vance last May... relatives of Jone... charged "carele... cessing and sup... of information... defector, Debo...

In the petitio... People's Templ... trying to rega... small son fro... settlement, the ... Mr. Vance, "I w... way to convince you that the situation in Jonestown is desperate."

The petition charged Mr. Jones with turning the settlement into a "concentration camp," stationing guards to prevent departures without his permission, censoring mail and threatening death to anyone proposing to leave the group.

"In the department, the petition to the secretary received very little attention," the report said. It was circulated at low levels of the department but no reply was ever sent to Mr. Stoen.

It was Mrs. Blakey who warned during an interview at the Georgetown embassy after her defection last May that Mr. Jones was conducting rehearsals for mass suicide. She signed a sworn statement to that effect before leaving Georgetown and repeated the charge in an afficavit in San Francisco and to Rep. Ryan before his departure for Guyana.

Throughout the 102-page report, the authors cite the constraints that U.S. officials in Washington and Georgetown felt in investigating Jonestown. These included the First Amendment's guarantee of religious freedom, provisions of the Privacy Act and the Freedom of Information Act, the legal presumption of innocence until guilt is proved and the fact that the Jonestown colony was subject to Guyanese, not U.S., law.

But Some Offenses 'Unpardonable'

Bazargan Says Limited Amnesty Planned

By William Branigin

TEHRAN, May 4 (WP) — Premier Mehdi Bazargan said yesterday that Iran's secretive Revolutionary Council was preparing a limited amnesty for officials and supporters of the deposed shah, but that the plan would not benefit those who committed "unpardonable crimes."

Mr. Bazargan said in an interview that it was up to the council to ... and revolutionary guards also were "necessary in the present circumstances" — that is, while police still are unable to perform their duties because of a breakdown in their ranks during the revolution.

But Mr. Bazargan, the former head of the Iranian Human Rights Committee, dodged a question about his present attitude toward the continuing revolutionary trials, which have sent at least 164 per... would be to "reduce as much as possible the number of cases tried by the revolutionary courts," limiting their jurisdiction to the unpardonable offenses yet to be defined.

It remains to be seen whether the definitions will be less vague than the fuzzy Koranic charges of "corruption of the Earth" and "warring with God and his emissaries" that already have figured in a number of death sentences.

Replying to Egypt on Sinai 'Precedent'

Israel Affirms Limits to Mideast Pullback

From Agency Dispatches

JERUSALEM, May 4 — Israel served notice to Egypt today that the Camp David accords do not obligate it to withdraw from the West Bank, the Gaza Strip and the Golan Heights, and said its army will remain in "defined security locations" there.

A Foreign Ministry spokesman was reacting to a statement by Cairo yesterday that said Israel's agreement to total withdrawal from the Sinai under the recently signed peace treaty is a precedent applicable to other occupied Arab lands.

"There is no foundation to a reported Egyptian Foreign Ministry statement to the effect that the Camp David agreements oblige Israel to evacuate Judea, Samaria [the West Bank], the Gaza district and the Golan Heights," the spokesman said.

"The opposite is the case," he said. "The negotiations on determining the border between Israel and Syria should be conducted between these two states only."

Prime Minister Menachem Begin said Wednesday that Israel would insist on retaining the Golan Heights even if Syria proposes a peace agreement, because "there is no peace without security."

The spokesman said it was agreed at the September Camp David, Md., summit that the Israeli Army would remain in the West Bank and the Gaza Strip even after the implementation of local Arab autonomy.

"While there will be a certain withdrawal of the Israeli Army from these areas, it was explicitly decided that there will be a redeployment of the army in defined security locations in Judea, Samaria and Gaza," the spokesman said.

Egypt, meanwhile, called for an Islamic summit meeting to discuss means of regaining the Arab sector of Jerusalem, which was annexed by Israel after the Six-Day War in 1967.

In a statement issued today by the Foreign Ministry, Egypt said it would attend the conference of foreign ministers of 43 Islamic countries in Morocco Tuesday on the condition that they discuss plans for a summit to deal with the Jerusalem issue.

Eight Arabs Arrested

TEL AVIV, May 4 (UPI) — Eight Israeli Arabs have been detained in the breakup of one of the biggest suspected Palestinian guerrilla networks operating within Israel, police said today.

They have been accused of conspiracy to murder and membership in the el-Fatah guerrilla organization. All are from northern Israel.

...Hits Neighboring Shores

...eny Abetting ...hnic Chinese

... to do so at the rate of about 6,000 ...

... were white and Christian, or even ... it is increasingly said here, they ... ave found acceptance in the West ... A diplomat remarked that a ship ... more than 500 Vietnamese that ... ed out of Thai waters last week ... se whereabouts have not been re... ince would have become the sub... n international search. It is pre... hat the ship was headed for Malay...

... dication of the fact that the flow ... exceeding expectations can be seen ... camp for boat people near this ... Thai town. Moved earlier this ... a larger site, its inhabitants have had to build new shanties because ... adrupling of the population to ...

... great majority of refugees from ... head for Malaysia, where nearly ... vait in badly overcrowded island ... or countries to offer them asylum. ... ho reach Thailand usually do so ... of errors in navigation or mechani... bles — or because pirates who ... hem in this direction after robbing ... d often raping the women.

... e Vietnamese grapevine (mainly fueled by letters from refugees who have made it and by foreign broadcasts), Malaysia is depicted as the best place to go. One reason is the mistaken assumption that departure for permanent asylum is quicker from Malaysia. A more justified reason is the prevalence of pirates in Thai waters.

Wristwatches are rare among the refugees here, and women's jewelry even rarer. In addition, the pirates also harvest most of the slim tablets of gold, worth about $250, that traditionally constitute Vietnamese family savings. Most of the refugee boats have been robbed more than once as they approached Thailand.

The consensus of the refugees here, who include a number of well educated and politically sophisticated people, is that the exodus will continue at a high rate and will continue to be abetted by Hanoi for Vietnamese of Chinese origin, who make up two-thirds to three-quarters of the flow. Ethnic Vietnamese will continue to make their escapes at great risk and in defiance of the government.

A highly educated refugee from southernmost Vietnam said that he had seen 12 to 15 boats under construction near his town's marketplace; the boats are generally believed to be for the transport of government-authorized refugees.

The boats are being equipped with portholes, indicating that they are meant for passengers rather than freight, said the man, who for 10 years worked with U.S.

(Continued on Page 2, Col. 5)

THURSDAY, JUNE 28, 1979

The Art Market

Ojjeh Collection Sets Records for Furniture Sales

By Souren Melikian

MONTE CARLO, Monaco, June 27 (IHT) — The sale of what Sotheby's called, with unusual lack of restraint, the "Magnifique Ensemble de Meubles et Objets d'Art Francais Collection Monsieur Akram Ojjeh," held Monday and yesterday evening at the Sporting d'Hiver, is a landmark in the history of the art market.

Expressed in financial terms, Sotheby's record is phenomenal. The net total of 54,504,000 francs — leaving only one item unsold of 1.8 percent in value of the gross total — is by far the largest ever recorded for a sale of furniture and objets d'art.

The price of 8,436,000 francs paid by the Heim Gallery in London, on behalf of an unidentified institution, for an 18th-century corner cabinet in florid Rococo style with the stamp of I. Dubois, is three times the previous record, paid in December, 1974, for a *bureau plat* with the matching cartonnier or filing box from the collection of Lady Baillie. That record was beaten a second time Monday when a magnificent commode stamped J.F. Leleu was knocked down at 4,663,000 francs to the British financier Charles Clore. This was 2½ times the highest presale estimate.

The *bureau plat* of the mid-Louis XV period, stamped BVRB for Bernard van Risenburgh, the Dutch-born cabinetmaker for the French court, was bought for 2,109,000 francs, again 2½ times the presale estimate, while a pair of Louis XV encoignures, stamped J.P. Latz, multiplied their highest estimate fourfold at 2,886,000 francs.

Enthusiasm

Such prices partly reflect the enthusiasm that top 18th-century furniture now inspires whenever its authenticity is above suspicion.

But no one could have predicted this success. The context in which the star pieces appeared was not the best. Many pieces of indifferent quality were of the kind that sells regularly at Drouot. Copies of the late 19th century were thrown in and dutifully identified in the catalog. To the suspicious, this uncomfortably suggested that possibly one or two others might have slipped by, unnoticed by the cataloger, however conscientious.

But the worst that Sotheby's had to overcome was the saga of the collection. Originally it belonged to old-master dealer Daniel Wildenstein, who had planned to sell it by auction in 1977 in London. At the 11th hour the sale was called off because Akram Ojjeh, a Syrian-born French-educated financier who is now a Saudi national, bought it in its entirety. The idea was to decorate the liner France, which he had also purchased.

Absentee Owner

Two years later, Ojjeh was selling it because, press releases said in substance, he had found out that precious furniture would deteriorate at sea, no matter what conservation measures might be taken. Dreading unfavorable comments of the kind made in the French press after the sale of the France, Sotheby's became obsessive about not having Ojjeh himself in the limelight. He was not visible anywhere. Somehow the name Wildenstein was cleverly made to hang over the collection with which he had parted.

The 8.4-million-franc cabinet.

TV networks came in force. The English dailies were heavily represented, an uncommon occurence. A popular London paper hardly notorious for any special concern for the arts ran articles before the sale, as did its French counterpart. On D-day, Sotheby's managed to have a front row of seats studded with millionaires, pitting Stavros Niarchos against Charles Clore, who outbid him for the Leleu commode.

Conversely, Niarchos won the battle against Clore when he acquired a table stamped Carlin without any pedigree for 666,000 francs. Sotheby's luck was to have such fights waged over pieces either of lesser importance or less firmly established authenticity. Niarchos, for example, paid 888,000 francs for a table with ormolu mountings, said to be by Pierre Gouthiere — plausible but not proven. It was also he who, more surprisingly, was the underbidder on a table stamped G. Jacob that raised questions in the minds of several connoisseurs, if only because the initial G. introducing Jacob's name has not been recorded, as the catalog pointed out. Without him it would have gone for less than half the whacking 1,221,000 francs it made.

High-powered dealers watched it all with their eyes popping out. "A fabulous show," said one Paris dealer. Others assured that it was all so artificial and exceptional that the event would have no bearing on the market.

This is, of course, impossible. Artificial the prices may have been, at first. But they were paid by hard-nosed financiers who cannot simply be bluffed into playing roulette at auction. This means that a new stage has now been reached, in which top furniture of the 17th and 18th centuries is in a price bracket once reserved for old masters.

THE WEATHER — PARIS: Saturday, cloudy. Temp. 13-22 (55-72). Sunday, cloudy. LONDON: Saturday, cloudy with rain at times. Temp. 13-21 (55-70). Sunday, similar. CHANNEL: Moderate. ROME: Saturday, fair. Temp. 15-25 (59-77). NEW YORK: Saturday, cloudy. Temp. 16-24 (61-75).

ADDITIONAL WEATHER — COMICS PAGE

INTERNATIONAL Herald Tribune

Published with The New York Times and The Washington Post

Austria	12 S.	Kenya	Shs. 7
Belgium	20 B.Fr.	Lebanon	£L2.25
Denmark	3.50 D.Kr.	Luxembourg	20 L.Fr.
Egypt	40 P.	Morocco	2.75 Dr.
Eire	22 P.	Netherlands	1.50Flor.
Finland	2.50 F.M.	Nigeria	70 K.
France	3.00 F.	Norway	3 N.Kr.
Germany	1.50 D.M.	Portugal	25 Esc.
Great Britain	20 P.	Spain	40 Ptas.
Greece	18 Drs.	Sweden	2.75 S.Kr.
India	Rs. 8	Switzerland	1.70S.Fr.
Iran	60 Rials	Turkey	£T. 15
Israel	I.£14.00	U.S. Military (Eur.)	$0.35
Italy	400 Lire	Yugoslavia	20 D.

No. 29,729 * PARIS, SATURDAY-SUNDAY, SEPTEMBER 9-10, 1978 Established 1887

United Press International

Israeli Prime Minister Menachem Begin and Egyptian President Anwar Sadat are shown in a photo released by the White House, each inviting the other to enter their Camp David lodge first.

Middle East Summit Gets Down To Serious Business, U.S. Says

CAMP DAVID, Md., Sept. 8 (UPI) — Detailed and serious negotiations were in progress today at the Camp David summit on the Middle East, and President Carter was playing a key role as an active participant in the talks, the White House said.

No trilateral talks were scheduled, but Mr. Carter was meeting separately with Israeli Prime Minister Menachem Begin and Egyptian President Anwar Sadat, and ministerial level discussions were under way.

U.S. officials said that the talks probably would end by the middle of next week.

[According to an Associated Press report, the Boston Herald American reported today that Mr. Begin has proposed a moratorium on future Jewish settlements as well as "new ideas" for moving toward Palestinian self-determination.

[While officials maintained the news blackout ordered by Mr. Carter, a senior Israeli adviser was quoted as saying that Mr. Begin was very flexible on his 26-point plan offered in December for limitments he will give in. One of the problems has been that these issues have not been thoroughly discussed before this summit."

[Mr. Begin's new ideas to Mr. Sadat reportedly included:

[• The Israeli Army would withdraw from its role as the police force in the West Bank and the Gaza Strip — two areas occupied since the 1967 war — into a half dozen military bases.

[• A plan providing for direct legislative elections by the 1.1 million Palestinians living in the West Bank to a parlimentary body.

[• Israel would cease construction on all future settlements in the West Bank and Gaza Strip as well

(Continued on Page 2, Col. 5)

'Would Like to Come Back'

Crawford Leaves Russia; Was Expelled, Tass Says

MOSCOW, Sept. 8 (UPI) — U.S. businessman Francis Crawford left the Soviet Union today for Frankfurt after his conviction and suspended sentence on a currency speculation charge. Tass said that he had been expelled from the country.

Crawford, who yesterday received a five-year suspended sentence... Moscow bureau of International Harvester Export Co., was summoned today to the Protocol Service Department of the Foreign Trade Ministry and told that Crawford "must immediately leave the Soviet Union."

"On the same day, U.S. citizen Crawford was expelled from the USSR," Tass said.

58 Die as Iran Clamps Martial Law on Cities

Troops Shoot Into Crowd of Demonstrators

TEHRAN, Sept. 8 (AP) — Troops fired into a crowd of several thousand anti-government demonstrators here today. The government said that 58 persons were killed and 205 wounded but unofficial reports said as many as 100 persons died.

The clash occurred just hours after the government imposed martial law in the capital and 11 other cities.

There was no immediate confirmation of reports that as many as 1,000 demonstrators, and religious and political leaders were arrested in the first day of martial law.

[Reports from other towns under the curfew order said troops surrounded the homes of prominent opposition clergy leaders and denied access to outside visitors, United Press International said.

[Political sources feared a wave of arrests throughout the country.]

Moslem Majority

Conservative religious leaders of the Shiite sect, the majority religious faction in this Moslem nation, have led a steadily growing revolt against changes in strict Moslem laws engineered by Shah Mohammed Reza Pahlavi, Iran's ruler.

The shah's program included distribution to peasants of lands owned by the clergy, gave women the right to vote and allowed them to discard their veils and attend universities.

A wide spectrum of opponents, including a radical leftists described by the shah as Islamic Marxists, have massed under the banner of the Moslem religious leaders, who are campaigning for strict adherence to Islamic law.

The martial law order, which bans gatherings by more than three persons and imposes a curfew from 9 p.m. to 5 a.m. daily, is an effort to crush the revolt that reportedly has claimed more than 1,000 lives in rioting during the last eight months.

Anti-shah demonstrators shake fists at troops who fired into air, then into crowds. United Press International

THE WEATHER — PARIS: Wednesday, cold and clear to cloudy. Temp. —5-1 (23-34). Thursday, cloudy, possible snow. LONDON: Wednesday, cloudy with rain or sleet. Temp. 2-4 (36-39). Thursday, similar. CHANNEL: Slight. ROME: Wednesday, cloudy. Temp. —5-7 (23-45). NEW YORK: Wednesday, snow. Temp. —4-3 (25-37).

ADDITIONAL WEATHER — COMICS PAGE

INTERNATIONAL Herald Tribune

Published with The New York Times and The Washington Post

Abu Dhabi	4.50 Dirh	Greece	22 Drs.	Netherlands	1.75 Flor.
Algeria	2.75 Din	Iceland	150 I.Kr.	Nigeria	70 K.
Austria	12 S.	India	Rs. 8	Norway	3.25 N.Kr.
Bahrain	0.400 Din	Iran	70 Rials	Oman	0.425 Rials
Belgium	23 B.Fr.	Israel	I.£14.00	Portugal	25 Esc.
Cyprus	250 Mills	Italy	500 Lire	Qatar	4.00 Rials
Denmark	3.75 D.Kr.	Jordan	0.300 Fils	Saudi Arabia	3.50 Rials
Dubai	4.50 Dirh	Kenya	Shs. 8.00	Spain	50 Ptas.
Egypt	40 P.	Kuwait	0.300 Fils	Sweden	3.00 S.K.
Eire	22 P.	Lebanon	£L2.75	Switzerland	1.70 S.F.
Finland	3.00 F.M.	Libya	L.Din. 0.25	Tunisia	3.25 Din
France	3 F.	Luxembourg	23 L.Fr.	Turkey	T.£. 15
Germany	1.50 D.M.	Madeira	27.5 Esc.	U.S. Mil. (Eur.)	$0.35
Great Britain	20 P.	Morocco	3.00 Dr.	Yugoslavia	20 D.

No. 29,836 ** PARIS, WEDNESDAY, JANUARY 17, 1979 Established 1887

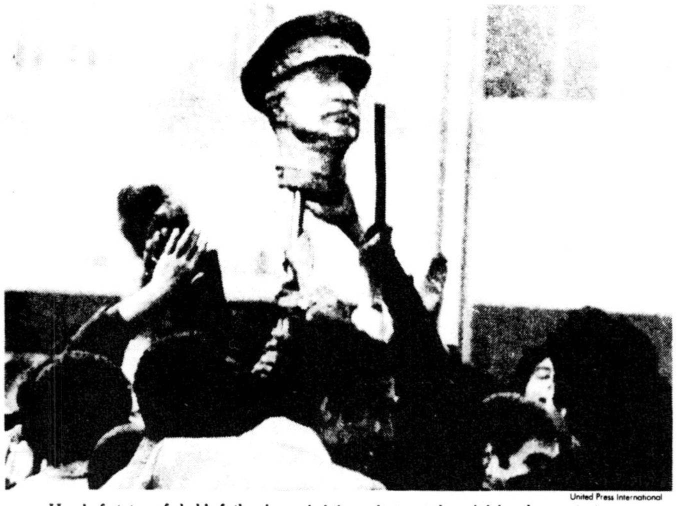

United Press International

Head of statue of shah's father is carried through streets by rejoicing demonstrators.

Heavy Action in Southwest

Cambodians Said to Oust Vietnamese From Seaport

By Henry Kamm

BANGKOK, Jan. 16 (NYT) — In their first major setback of the war, Vietnamese forces were driven out of the Cambodian port city of Kompong Som yesterday after heavy fighting, Western analysts reported yesterday.

At the same time, four Vietnamese naval patrol craft were shelling the Cambodian coast just ... of tidal flats. Supplies would have to be unloaded from freighters to lighter boats to be brought ashore, which greatly heightens the risk of such operations.

The heavy action in all of Cambodia's southwestern corner indicates strongly that the organized remnants of the forces loyal to Premier Pol Pot are determined to make this region a redoubt of ... swift drive through the country engaged each other.

Skirmishing continues around the provincial capital of Siem Reap, which raises the possibility that the celebrated temples of the old royal city of Angkor Wat are in danger. Similarly, Cambodian troops remain ensconced on the almost unassailable temple mount of Preah Vihear, another great relic of ...

Tearful Shah Leaves Iran As His Opponents Rejoice

Khomeini Tells Iran To Resist

NEAUPHLE-LE-CHATEAU, France, Jan. 16 (NYT) — Ayatollah Ruhollah Khomeini today congratulated Iranians for forcing Shah Mohammed Reza Pahlavi to leave the country, and made it clear that he aims to overthrow the government that the shah left behind in Tehran.

The shah's leading religious opponent called the shah's departure "the first step" toward ending the 50-year reign of the Pahlavi dynasty. "It is not a final victory, but the preface to our victory," he said at his headquarters in this village 20 miles from Paris.

The 78-year-old leader of Iran's Shiite Moslems, who make up 90 percent of the population, made clear that his next aim is to overthrow Premier Shahpur Bakhtiar and the regency council to which the shah has entrusted his constitutional powers during his absence abroad.

In a statement issued here this morning, which aides said was to be distributed throughout Iran in the following hours, the ayatollah reiterated a demand that the government, parliament and the regency council resign. He ordered his followers to demonstrate against them in the streets on Friday and to continue the general strike that

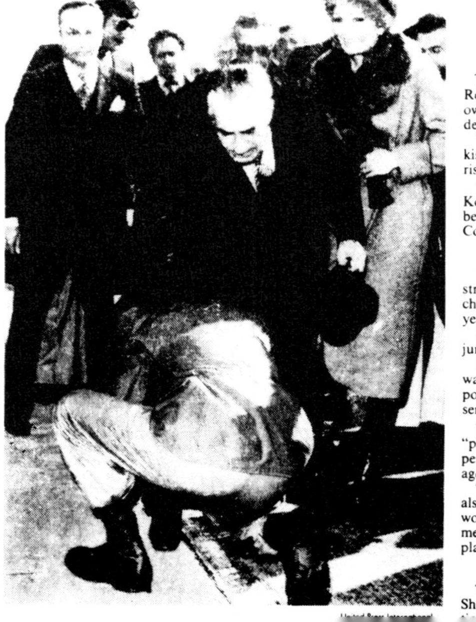

Departure of Ruler Is Seen as His Exile

TEHRAN, Jan. 16 (AP) — With tears in his eyes, Shah Mohammed Reza Pahlavi left Iran today for Egypt and the United States, piloting his own jet on a journey that many believe will end in permanent exile. His departure touched off celebrations throughout Tehran.

Two members of the shah's royal guard fell to their knees and tried to kiss the monarch's feet at Tehran's airport, but he motioned for them to rise, court sources said.

Two other officers, standing face to face, held aloft a copy of the Koran, the Moslem holy book, and the shah and Empress Farah passed beneath the impromptu arch to board the "Shah's Falcon," a Boeing 727. Court sources said that the monarch took the controls.

'Gone Forever'

"The shah is gone forever!" people chanted as millions poured into the streets of Tehran, showering each other with candies and rose water, cheering and shouting with joy at what they saw as victory in a bloody, yearlong uprising to topple the 59-year-old shah.

Motorists honked their horns and flashed their headlights. Many jumped from their cars and hugged each other.

In a statement to Iran's official Pars news agency, the shah said that he was going "on vacation because I am feeling tired." He transferred his powers to a regency council and appealed to the Iranian people to preserve the monarchy during his absence.

The shah said that the length of his stay abroad would depend on his "physical condition." But many believe that the vacation will become permanent exile and end the dynasty his soldier-father founded 54 years ago.

"I hope the government will be able to make amends for the past and also succeed in laying the foundation for the future," the shah said. "This work needs a long period of cooperation and patriotism in its utmost meaning. Our economy must start rolling again and we must have better planning for the future."

Bakhtiar Is Confirmed

The lower house of the Iranian parliament today confirmed Premier Shahpur Bakhtiar and his Cabinet by a vote of 149-43 with 13 absten-

THE WEATHER — PARIS. Friday, very cloudy, possible rain. Temp. 4-7 (3?-45). Saturday, cloudy. LONDON: Friday, cloudy and showers. Temp. 2-4 (36-39). Saturday, cloudy and colder. CHANNEL: Moderate. ROME: Friday, cloudy. Temp. 2-8 (36-46). NEW YORK: Friday, cloudy. Temp. −7—2 (19-28).

ADDITIONAL WEATHER — COMICS PAGE

INTERNATIONAL
Herald Tribune
Published with The New York Times and The Washington Post

Abu Dhabi	4.50 Dirh	Greece	22 Drs	Netherlands	1.75 Flor
Algeria	2.75 Din	Iceland	150 I Kr	Nigeria	70 K
Austria	12 S	India	Rs 8	Norway	3.25 N Kr
Bahrain	0.400 Din	Iran	70 Rials	Oman	0.425 Rials
Belgium	23 B Fr	Israel	I £14.00	Portugal	25 Esc
Cyprus	250 Mills	Italy	500 Lire	Qatar	4.00 Rials
Denmark	3.75 D Kr	Jordan	0.300 Fils	Saudi Arabia	3.50 Rials
Dubai	4.50 Dirh	Kenya	Shs 8.00	Spain	50 Ptas
Egypt	40 P	Kuwait	0.300 Fils	Sweden	3.00 S Kr
Eire	22 P	Lebanon	£L2.75	Switzerland	1.70 S Fr
Finland	3.00 F M	Libya	L Din 0.25	Tunisia	3.25 Din
France	3 F	Luxembourg	23 L Fr	Turkey	T £ 15
Germany	1.50 D M	Madeira	27.5 Esc	U.S. Mil (Eur.)	$0.35
Great Britain	20 P	Morocco	3.00 Dr	Yugoslavia	20 D

No. 29,851 — PARIS, FRIDAY, FEBRUARY 2, 1979 — Established 1887

Crowds mass alongs walls and walks at Tehran University to catch a glimpse of Ayatollah Ruhollah Khomeini yesterday.

2 Million Line Tehran Route

Khomeini Hailed in Iran, Threatens Bakhtiar Arrest

By William Claiborne

TEHRAN, Feb. 1 (WP) — Ayatollah Ruhollah Khomeini, emboldened by an enormous homecoming turnout of millions of jubilant Iranians after arriving for the first time in more than 14 years, warned that if the government refused to capitulate to his revolutionary demands and resign, he would arrest its leaders and appoint a provisional government.

Setting the stage for a critical confrontation with the beleaguered government of Premier Shahpur Bakhtiar in the next few days, Ayatollah Khomeini lashed out vituperatively at absent Shah Mohammed Reza Pahlavi, the Parliament, Mr. Bakhtiar's fragile regime and the United States — all as enemies of the people.

In an emotional, 30-minute speech at Tehran's Behesht Zahra Cemetery, where hundreds of victims of the last year's upheaval are buried, the ayatollah warned the current leaders that he would "shut their mouths" and will appoint a government "with the support of the people."

But Ayatollah Khomeini stopped short of naming a new government immediately, which moderate political leaders had feared he would do, and he made a solicitous appeal to the military to join his cause — all of which left the prospect of an imminent civil war triggered his return less certain than once feared.

However, Sadegh Ghotbzadeh, a chief Khomeini aide, said that the ayatollah will announce a provisional government in two or three days. That would be followed, he said, by a national referendum to abolish the current government, which was appointed by the shah before he left the country Jan. 16, and then an election for a constituent assembly and an Islamic republic.

Not since Lenin was sent across Germany in 1917 in a sealed train to Petrograd's Finland Station to lead the Bolsheviks against the czar has a revolutionary leader's return to his homeland seemed so full of portents as Ayatollah Khomeini's arrival in Iran this morning.

In an extraordinary display of support, Iranians from all walks of life jammed the broad thoroughfares from Mehrabad airport, where Ayatollah Khomeini arrived after a 5½-hour flight from Paris, to the cemetery 18 miles away in south Tehran, where he vowed to eliminate all vestiges of the shah's 25 years of authoritative rule.

The crowds created such immovable masses of people that the Moslem leader, 78, had to be transported the last three miles in a helicopter.

Military Role

Significantly, Ayatollah Khomeini was borne that final leg of the trip in an Iranian Army helicopter, which underscored the collaborative role that segments of the military played in the opposition leader's return.

The army, which in past months has blanketed Tehran with tanks, armored personnel carriers and trucks mounted with machine guns, was absent during the daylong welcome.

The few soldiers who were present seemed to blend into the crowds lining the motorcade route, and many of them openly participated in the jubilation. Moreover, Ayatollah Khomeini was protected at the airport by a bodyguard contingent of noncommissioned officers from the Iranian Air Force.

The throngs of Iranians who turned out, unofficially estimated at 2 million, appeared larger than the huge anti-government demonstrations of last six weeks.

As the ayatollah was driven

(Continued on Page 2, Col. 2)

Ayatollah Ruhollah Khomeini is ringed in Tehran yesterday by Moslem security marshals, who wear turbans and robes.

Says Encoding Would Hinder Verification

U.S. Warns Russia on Missile Data

By Richard Burt

WASHINGTON, Feb. 1 (NYT) — The Carter administration has warned the Soviet Union that an attempt to impede U.S. efforts to monitor a Soviet missile test on Dec. 21 has jeopardized the ability of the United States to verify Soviet compliance with the terms of a projected treaty limiting strategic arms, government officials said yesterday.

The administration, they added, has also told Moscow in recent days that if the Soviet Union, under a new treaty, tried to conceal test data in this manner, the United States would consider it a serious violation of the agreement.

The officials said that the unusual warning was prompted by a test firing of Moscow's new SS-18 missile, the largest and most lethal rocket in the Soviet arsenal. During the test, Moscow is said to have transmitted electronic messages from the missile to Soviet ground stations in code in an apparent effort to conceal the signals from U.S. listening posts on the periphery of the Soviet Union.

Since the test information, known as telemetry, is viewed by the CIA as vital to verifying Soviet compliance with a new accord, the December missile firing has complicated efforts to complete the arms negotiations. It is also seen as raising new problems for the administration in convincing the Senate that the United States could detect a Soviet effort to evade parts of the proposed agreement. So far, officials said, Moscow has not responded to the warning.

Meanwhile, the administration's handling of the telemetry issue is being debated in the U.S. government. Some aides charge that Stansfield Turner, the director of central intellience, has exaggerated the importance of the test data in verifying a new accord, thus setting back chances for a treaty with Moscow.

The officials said that in a number of conversations with President Carter, Adm. Turner had pushed for a firm U.S. position on Soviet attempts to encode test data, despite the fact that other agencies doubted the utility of such a stand.

A CIA spokesman refused to discuss the issue.

Encoding first emerged as a serious issue in the arms talks after an SS-18 test in July, when much of the missile's telemetry was sent in code.

Last fall, U.S. negotiators tried to get Moscow to accept a ban on such encoding but failed. In late December at Geneva, Secretary of State Cyrus Vance and Soviet Foreign Minister Andrei Gromyko agreed to an ambiguous provision in which Moscow was permitted to encode only missile-test data that would not hinder U.S. verification of a new accord.

However, the provision evidently does not specify what information is necessary to monitor an accord. Some officials say that this omission could allow Moscow to continue to withhold key information about new missiles. In an effort to remove this ambiguity, the administration officials said, the United States has told Moscow that the encoding of the Dec. 21 test is an example of what would be banned by

Sent Greeting To Castro

Triumphant Pope Returns From Latin American Trip

By Henry Tanner

ROME, Feb. 1 (NYT) — Pope John Paul II, tanned and happy after a triumphant but grueling seven-day trip to Latin America, was back at the window of his living quarters in the Vatican tonight, from where he waved to a cheering crowd of thousands in Saint Peter's [...]tions in Mexico and the Dominican Republic, ended his first foreign papal trip in the Protestant black Bahamas early today with a call for unity to "all other Christian brothers."

The pontiff arrived in the Bahamian capital of Nassau to the

Spain Pardons Catalan Actors In 'Insult' Case

BARCELONA, Feb. 1 (UPI) — The Spanish government has pardoned four Catalan actors sentenced to prison in a controversial court-martial for allegedly insulting the military, newspapers said today.

The Ministry of Justice informed prison authorities yesterday of the pardons for Els Joglars. They were sentenced to two years in prison last March 7.

Authorities said two other members of the troupe, who fled to France to escape trial, also would

Italy President

In Bid to Regain Power

Alleged Shah Tape: A Call for War

THE WEATHER — PARIS: Monday, wind and rain. Temp. 10-14 (50-57). LONDON: Monday, bright with showers. Temp. 7-12 (45-54). CHANNEL: Rough with gales. ROME: Monday, sunny. Temp. 10-21 (50-70). NEW YORK: Monday, sunny. Temp. 7-13 (45-55).

ADDITIONAL WEATHER — COMICS PAGE

INTERNATIONAL
Herald Tribune
Published with The New York Times and The Washington Post

Abu Dhabi	5.50 Dirh	Greece	25 Drs	Netherlands	1.75 Flor
Algeria	3.00 Din	India	Rs 9	Nigeria	70 K
Austria	12 S	Iran	95 Rials	Norway	3.25 N Kr
Bahrain	0.500 Din	Israel	I £30.00	Oman	0.540 Rial
Belgium	23 B Fr	Italy	500 Lire	Portugal	25 Esc
Cyprus	300 Mills	Jordan	310 Fils	Qatar	5.00 Rials
Denmark	3.75 D Kr	Kenya	Shs. 9.25	Saudi Arabia	4.25 Rials
Dubai	5.50 Dirh	Kuwait	350 Fils	Spain	50 Ptas
Egypt	70 P	Lebanon	£L3.00	Sweden	3.00 S Kr
Eire	30 P	Libya	L Din 0.25	Switzerland	1.70 S Fr
Finland	3.00 F M	Luxembourg	23 L Fr	Tunisia	3.25 Din
France	3 F	Madeira	27.5 Esc	Turkey	T £ 37.50
Germany	1.50 D M	Malta	22 Cents	U.S. Mil. (Eur.)	$0.35
Great Britain	25 P	Morocco	3.50 Dr	Yugoslavia	22 D

No. 30,086 — PARIS, MONDAY, NOVEMBER 5, 1979 — Established 1887

Bolivia Jets Fire To Scatter Foes Of Military Coup

By Tom Wells

LA PAZ, Nov. 4 (AP) — Two Bolivian Air Force jet fighters passed over central La Paz today with their guns firing, scattering students and workers who had gathered to protest the new military regime.

The incident followed a night of clashes between soldiers and civilians in which Red Cross and hospital officials said that at least 20 civilians were killed and 40 wounded.

A communique issued by the military administration of Col. Alberto Natusch Busch, who led a coup against the civilian government last Thursday, described last night's crackdown and the jet flights today as part of a cleanup operation.

There were no immediate reports of casualties from the plane gunfire. It appeared that the pilots sought only to intimidate the protesters and did not fire directly at them. The plaza where they had gathered also was surrounded by about 20 tanks and armored cars, and one was heard firing a cannon shot.

Civilians building barricades on city streets last night were attacked by troops who kept up gunfire barrages for about five hours.

The warplanes struck at midday about an hour after students and workers began rebuilding street barricades. The jets could be seen swooping low over the plaza and opening fire. A source who has followed closely the military situation here and was near the action said that they made a half-dozen passes and appeared to fire as they angled upward, indicating that they did not intend to shoot those in the plaza.

Earlier today, Col. Natusch declared martial law and press censorship throughout Bolivia amid speculation that dissident military units were planning a countercoup against the self-proclaimed president.

In a television address, the 47-year-old military strongman, widely known as a rightist, said that he imposed the rigid regime because "anti-democratic and anti-social sectors" were trying to "change our way of life for a totalitarian and anti-national version."

Sources said today that the police in Cochabamba had declared themselves in rebellion against the Natusch government. The report could not be confirmed.

The national labor federation called a general strike on Thursday in protest of what its leader labeled a fascist military takeover. The strike has been joined by the national businessmen's group. None of the major political parties in Bolivia has indicated support for Col. Natusch.

Another government commmunique issued today urged workers to end the general strike.

The civilian president deposed in the Natusch coup, Walter Guevara, was still in hiding with his Cabinet.

Militants Claim To Hold Bishop In El Salvador

SAN SALVADOR, Nov. 4 (AP) — Leftists holding 27 hostages in two government buildings claimed

Park Kuen Hae burns incense in front of the casket of her father, Park Chung Hee, during the state funeral Saturday.

Military's Stand Unknown

Park's Party Considers Nonpolitical President

From Agency Dispatches

SEOUL, Nov. 4 — In a plan proposed by his political heirs, the late South Korean President Park Chung Hee would be succeeded by a nonpolitical, statesman-like figure who would promise to move the country toward a gradual constitutional reform.

Kim Jong Pil and Chung Il Kwon — have been mentioned most often as his successor.

An informed source said today both are too political to be acceptable to military leaders. But the source mentioned no other possibility by name.

Demand Shah's Extradition

Students in Tehran Seize Embassy, 90 U.S. Hostages

By Sajid Rizvi

TEHRAN, Nov 4 (UPI) — Moslem students battled U.S. Marines and seized the U.S. Embassy today, taking about 90 Americans hostage to press demands that the deposed Shah Mohammed Reza Pahlavi be extradited to Iran to face Islamic justice.

About 450 Moslem youths, whose leaders said they had the tacit approval of Ayatollah Ruhollah Khomeini, stormed the embassy and fought with embassy personnel for three hours, reports said.

"We shall not give up the hostages unless the shah is given to us," a student spokesman told the few reporters allowed into the embassy compound. "So long as we are here, the embassy will remain closed," he said.

The students seized about 90 American men, women and children and 10 Iranians, the spokesman said.

U.S. Task Force

"American Marine guards armed with sophisticated weapons and tear gas resisted our advance," the spokesman said. "We were armed only with cold weapons — nobody carried any firearms."

The State Department said in Washington that there was no indication that the Americans were hurt. A special task force, headed by Assistant Secretary of State Harold Saunders, was established to handle the matter.

The shah is in Cornell Medical Center in New York recovering from gall bladder surgery. He is

Demonstrators outside U.S. Embassy in Tehran brandish a scaffold and noose bearing a poster that says "For the Shah."

Iran, the spokesman replied: "We'll come to that later. Our occupation of this building reflects popular demands. We'll respond to what our people want."

State Department spokesman George Sherman said that the head of the embassy, Charge d'Affaires Bruce Laingen, was not in the compound during the attack, and has been in constant contact with Iranian officials. "What we are trying to do, of course, is get our people released and the embassy compound vacated," Mr. Sherman said.

The student spokesman said the demonstrators discovered "very important documents related to spying," along with spying equipment, and would interrogate the hostages.

He said the takeover was planned to coincide with the anniversary of last year's university killings by the shah's troops, as well as the start of Ayatollah Khomeini's exile 16 years ago.

The attack on the U.S. Embassy was the first since leftist guerrillas raided it on Feb. 14, three days after the overthrow of the shah's regime. Ambassador William Sullivan and 70 other Americans were taken hostage inside the compound, but released within two hours.

Statue of Liberty Protest

NEW YORK, Nov. 4 (UPI) — Demonstrators handcuffed themselves to railings on the crown of the Statue of Liberty today and draped a banner from the statue demanding return of the shah to Iran for trial.

"The shah must be tried and punished," read the 20-foot banner that fluttered from the statue in a light breeze. No violence was reported. The demonstrators, who numbered six or seven, said they were Iranian students.

Message Found in Paris Apartment

Mesrine, on Tape, Says He Was Not Hero

1980-1987

Change, often sharp and dramatic, characterized the news of the 1980s, whether it came from Spain or Argentina, from Poland or the Soviet Union, from India or Egypt or the Philippines.

For the *International Herald Tribune* in its tenth decade, the pace of change also speeded up dramatically. Its publisher now was Lee Huebner, who had taken up that position in 1979. Philip Foisie served as executive editor from 1981 until his retirement in 1987, when John Vinocur took his place. René Bondy succeeded Roland Pinson as Deputy Publisher and the two Associate Publishers were Richard Morgan and Alain Lecour, the latter now overseeing the paper's unique global distribution system.

In September 1980, the *IHT* added a new dimension to its facsimile printing network by initiating an intercontinental satellite printing operation in Hong Kong, which meant that for the first time in history the same newspaper could be read on day of publication at opposite ends of the globe. The technology was much like that utilized in London and Zurich, except that the electronic signal which originated in the Paris headquarters was sent to an antenna in Brittany, from there to a satellite 23,000 miles above the Indian Ocean, and finally to a receiving dish in Hong Kong, which relayed it to the local printing plant. Again, it took just four minutes to transmit an entire page.

The Asian edition achieved a rapid success. Circulation in the area increased nearly tenfold, to 15,000 copies, in the first two years, and hit the 30,000 mark by the mid-1980s. The *IHT* also became one of the first Western papers to circulate daily in the People's Republic of China.

The success of the Hong Kong operation encouraged the paper to expand further. On October 4, 1982, the 95th anniversary of Bennett's first edition, the *IHT* inaugurated a second Asian print site, in Singapore.

Four more facsimile locations have since followed: the Hague in 1983, Marseilles in 1984, Miami in 1985, and Rome in 1987. Thus northern and southern Europe, the Middle East, South East Asia and Central and South America were all firmly brought into the *IHT*'s daily orbit. Studies were also started concerning the possibility of a printing operation in Tokyo.

Worldwide, *IHT* circulation grew at about 5 percent a year in the 1980s, to a paid daily circulation of more than 175,000 copies in 1987. As advertisers became even more interested in global marketing, the paper's advertising revenues also expanded sharply, providing the financial resources for even more growth. Although many other publications entered the field of international publishing in the 1980s, the century-old *IHT* nonetheless continued to increase its share of both advertising and circulation markets.

Journalistically, too, the paper expanded. Like so many other newspapers in the 1980s, the *IHT* devoted more attention and newsprint to business and economic news. Space for opinion and commentary was also increased, new Weekend and Travel sections were added, and a wide-ranging series of special reports was published each year. Color advertising pages began to appear, with growing frequency, for the first time since Bennett's day. The *IHT*'s own team of correspondents was substantially increased to include not only a half-dozen staff writers in Paris, but also full-time *IHT* bureaus in London, Frankfurt, Washington, New York and Singapore. And as both the *Washington Post* and the *New York Times* continued to build and improve their own news coverage, the *IHT* was the direct beneficiary of those developments as well.

Who reads the *IHT* of the 1980s? The "global village," a sociological prediction of the 1960s that became a 1970s cliché, would seem to be alive and well in the 1980s—and reading the *IHT*. Corporate directors, managers, and financiers as well as international civil servants and high-level government officials all respond to the paper's reader surveys with enthusiasm and frankness.

Different though today's paper may be from the overseas experiment launched by James Gordon Bennett, Jr., in the late nineteenth century, the traditions of that era are remembered and honored by the modern *IHT*. One of the great bronze owls that sat atop Bennett's New York headquarters building now has a place of honor in the publisher's office in Neuilly. And the Old Philadelphia Lady's famous letter to the editor still makes occasional appearances.

Although the resources and the audience have both expanded, the mission of the paper remains in one important respect similar to Bennett's of a century ago: to report interesting news with as much balance and as little bias as possible: in short, to tell what happened. Opinion is there, of course, as it was in Bennett's day, but labeled as such, and separated from the presentation of objective news.

The balance of news and commentary may not please every reader every day. But the editors of the *International Herald Tribune* take pride in the small daily miracle that is their newspaper, as it comes off presses on three continents, for distribution in more than 160 countries, bringing the world's most important news each day to the world's most important audience.

THE WEATHER -- PARIS: Tuesday, cloudy. Temp. --3-2 (?-36). LONDON: Tuesday, cloudy. Temp. 0-4 (32-39). CHANNEL: Moderate. ROME: Tuesday, partly cloudy. Temp. 4-14 (?-57). FRANKFURT: Tuesday, cloudy. Temp. —5-1 (23-34). NEW YORK: Tuesday, [illegible] Temp. 9-14 (48-57).

ADDITIONAL WEATHER DATA — PAGE 12

INTERNATIONAL Herald Tribune

Published with The New York Times and The Washington Post

Algeria	5.00 Din.	Iran	135 Rials	Nigeria	100 K
Austria	15 S	Israel	[illegible] 11.00	Norway	4.50 N.Kr.
Bahrain	0.600 Din	Italy	700 Lire	Oman	0.650 Rials
Belgium	30 B.Fr.	Jordan	400 Fils	Portugal	40 Esc.
Canada	C$1.10	Kenya	Shs. 14.00	Qatar	6.00 Rials
Cyprus	400 Mils	Kuwait	450 Fils	Saudi Arabia	5.50 Rials
Denmark	5.50 D.Kr.	Lebanon	£L3.25	Spain	70 Ptas.
Egypt	[illegible]	Libya	L.Din. 0.30	Sweden	4.50 S.Kr.
Eire	40 P	Luxembourg	30 L.Fr.	Switzerland	1.80 S.Fr.
Finland	4.50 F.M.	Madeira	45 Esc.	Tunisia	0.425 Din.
France	4.00 F	Malta	30 Cents	Turkey	T.£ 65.00
Germany	2.00 D.M.	Morocco	5.00 Dh	U.A.E.	6.50 Dirh
Great Britain	30 P	Netherlands	2.25 Flor.	U.S. Mil. (Eur.)	$0.75
Greece	40 Drs.			Yugoslavia	33 D

No. 30,487 R** PARIS, TUESDAY, FEBRUARY 24, 1981 Established 1887

Brezhnev Seeks Reagan Summit To Ease Strain

By R. W. Apple Jr.
New York Times Service

MOSCOW — Leonid I. Brezhnev Monday proposed a meeting with President Reagan as a key element in "an active dialogue" designed to halt the deterioration in relations between the United States and the Soviet Union.

"Experience shows that the crucial link here is meetings at the summit level," the Soviet leader declared in a three-hour, 40-minute speech opening the 26th congress of the Soviet Communist Party. "This was true yesterday, and it is still true today."

[Reuters reported from Washington that the Reagan administration said it was studying Mr. Brezhnev's call for summit talks with interest and would respond after consulting U.S. allies. Initial comments from European governments called for close scrutiny of Mr. Brezhnev's suggestions, Reuters reported.]

The tone of Mr. Brezhnev's remarks about East-West relations was restrained — far more moderate than recent comments in the Soviet press. He emphasized peace, not confrontation.

"Since the change of leadership in the White House, candidly bellicose calls and statements have resounded from Washington, especially designed as it were, to poison the atmosphere of relations between our two countries," Mr. Brezhnev said in a typical passage. "We would like to hope, however, that those who shape United States policy will ultimately manage to see things in a more realistic light."

The 74-year-old Soviet president and party leader spoke ambiguously about the most immediate issue facing Washington and Moscow, the strategic arms limitation treaty that the U.S. Senate has failed to ratify.

'Relevant Negotiations'

He omitted the usual Soviet demand for ratification, and he said that the Kremlin was "prepared to continue the relevant negotiations with the United States without delay, preserving all the positive elements that have so far been achieved in this area."

His language led some Western diplomats to conclude that Mr. Brezhnev was signaling Soviet willingness to begin negotiating a new treaty incorporating elements of the old one that are acceptable to Mr. Reagan and the Senate.

But Leonid M. Zamyatin, chief of the international information department of the party's Central Committee, said without amplification that this was incorrect.

Television and radio broadcasts of Mr. Brezhnev's speech, an event of the greatest importance in the Communist world, were interrupted after he had spoke for only seven minutes. An announcer then read the bulk of the long text. Just four minutes before the end of the speech, the broadcasts switched back to Mr. Brezhnev delivering his address.

The abrupt cutoff was at first interpreted as an indication that the party leader, who has been in poor

(Continued on Page 2, Col. 5)

UPI

Leonid I. Brezhnev
... at party congress Monday.

Brezhnev Says

East Bloc Registers New Fears on Poland

By John Darnton
New York Times Service

WARSAW — After six months of alternately ignoring or condemning events in Poland, the rest of Eastern Europe is beginning to show anxiety that the Polish workers' movement for democratic rights and a better standard of living will prove contagious.

Western diplomats stationed in the capitals of neighboring Communist countries say they detect a new level of concern, both in the tone of the official press and in antagonisms in the north of Eastern Europe and in the Balkans. But there have been no reports of strikes or protests in Hungary, in contrast to rumors never officially acknowledged of brief and limited incidents of worker unrest in Czechoslovakia, East Germany and Romania after the Polish strikes last summer.

The Hungarian regime of Janos Kadar, installed after the Soviet invasion of 1956, has managed to win a degree of prosperity and popular support unusual in the region, in part due to gradually eas-

Spanish Cortes Seized, Hostages Taken in Attempt at Military Coup

Calvo Sotelo, Suarez Held; King Juan Carlos 'Firmly Rejects' Action

From Agency Dispatches

MADRID — About 200 paramilitary Civil Guards, led by a rightist lieutenant colonel, seized the Cabinet and more than 300 members of the lower house of the Spanish Cortes (parliament) at gunpoint Monday and held them hostage in an attempt to overthrow the government.

King Juan Carlos quickly scheduled a speech on national television and ordered all undersecretaries of the government to remain on the job after conferring with the military chiefs of staff. An official note from the chiefs of staff said that "all necessary methods have been taken to put down this attack on the constitution and to re-establish order."

The national police surrounded the Cortes building but made no attempt to intervene. The army moved into key positions in Madrid, although army forces were not sighted near the parliament.

The attack began about 6:30 p.m. as the Congress of Deputies voted on the confirmation of Leopoldo Calvo Sotelo as the successor to Adolfo Suarez, who resigned as premier last month. Reporters said the shots were fired in the air and no one appeared to have been wounded. Mr. Calvo Sotelo and Mr. Suarez were among the hostages.

The leader of the attack, Army Lt. Col. Antonio Tejero Molina, a Francoist officer in the Civil Guard, was sentenced to seven months in prison last year by a military court for a 1978 plot to kidnap Mr. Suarez and his Cabinet.

As the siege continued Monday night, the Civil Guards separated some of the hostages. Among those moved under guard to unknown locations in the building were Mr. Suarez, Socialist leader Felipe Gonzalez, Communist leader Santiago Carrillo, Defense Minister Agustin Rodriguez Sahagun, and Lt. Gen. Manuel Gutierrez Mellado, the first deputy premier in charge of defense. Mr. Calvo Sotelo remained in the chamber.

Other reports said Mr. Suarez and Gen. Gutierrez Mellado were removed but later taken back to their seats.

King Juan Carlos, the commander in chief of the armed forces and head of state, said in a statement that he "firmly rejected the action carried out this afternoon at the parliament building." The king ordered junior ministers and officials into permanent session Monday night to guarantee democracy.

A statement released by the Interior Ministry at about 9:30 p.m. and signed by the "Government of the Nation" declared: "The situation created by an act of violence in the headquarters of the Congress of Deputies has up to now prevented the normal action of the Council of Ministers, whose members are detained in the chamber.

"In these circumstances, the secretaries of state and undersecretaries of the various ministries have constituted themselves into permanent session, on the instructions of His Majesty King Juan Carlos, to guarantee the governing of the country within civilian rules and in close contact with the council of the chiefs of staff, which is also meeting," the statement added.

A later official statement declared: "All the information received up to now by those who are by accident running the country in the name of the government agrees that the most absolute calm reigns in the whole national territory and that a rapid solution to this momentary interruption of parliamentary life is hoped for.

"Those who at this time assume in Spain full civil and military power in a temporary manner and under the leadership of His Majesty the King can guarantee to their compatriots that no act of force will destroy democratic coexistence, which the people freely desire and which is contained in the text of the constitution, which civilians and the military have sworn to protect."

The council of the chiefs of staff said all necessary steps had been taken to restore constitutional order. Their meeting was continuing late Monday night, according to another official statement.

King Juan Carlos was preparing to speak to the nation to explain the situation, said Rosa Posada, a government spokeswoman. Mrs. Posada was speaking from the Palace Hotel, opposite the occupied parliament building. Senior officials of the Civil Guard, including its commander, Maj. Gen. Jose Aramburu Topete, had just held an urgent meeting in the hotel.

200 Civil Guards

Officials said the siege began when Lt. Col. Tejero led about 200 paramilitary Civil Guards into the Congress of Deputies as votes were being cast on the confirmation of Mr. Calvo Sotelo.

Over national radio, which was covering the Cortes debate live, a reporter said "a Civil Guard officer is approaching the [speaker's] rostrum waving a pistol." Shots rang out and a voice ordered, "Hit the ground." The radio transmission then went dead, and was replaced by light music interspersed with martial music.

Lt. Col. Tejero grabbed the microphone and pointed a pistol at

Associated Press

Lt. Col. Antonio Tejero Molina speaking to Cortes deputies surrounded by armed Civil Guards.

THE WEATHER — PARIS: Wednesday, foggy early, fair later. Temp. —2-6 (28-43). LONDON: Wednesday, overcast. Temp. 2-6 (36-43). CHANNEL: Slight. ROME: Wednesday, overcast, possible rain. Temp. 3-10 (37-50). FRANKFURT: Wednesday, overcast, possible snow. Temp. —4-2 (25-36). NEW YORK: Wednesday, showers. Temp. 2-7 (36-45).

ADDITIONAL WEATHER DATA — PAGE 14

INTERNATIONAL Herald Tribune

Published with The New York Times and The Washington Post

Algeria	5.00 Din.	Iran	135 Rials	Nigeria	100 K
Austria	15 S	Israel	I.S. 11.00	Norway	4.50 N.Kr.
Bahrain	0.600 Din.	Italy	700 Lire	Oman	0.650 Rials
Belgium	30 B.Fr.	Jordan	400 Fils	Portugal	40 Esc.
Canada	C$1.10	Kenya	Shs. 14.00	Qatar	6.00 Rials
Cyprus	400 Mills	Kuwait	450 Fils	Saudi Arabia	5.50 Rials
Denmark	5.50 D.Kr.	Lebanon	£L3.25	Spain	70 Ptas
Egypt	85 P	Libya	L.Din. 0.30	Sweden	4.50 S.Kr.
Eire	40 P	Luxembourg	30 L.Fr.	Switzerland	1.80 S.Fr.
Finland	4.50 F.M.	Madeira	45 Esc.	Tunisia	0.425 Din.
France	4.00 F	Malta	30 Cents	Turkey	T.£ 65.00
Germany	2.00 D.M.	Morocco	5.00 Dh	U.A.E.	6.50 Dirh
Great Britain	30 P	Netherlands	2.25 Flor.	U.S. Mil. (Eur.)	$0.75
Greece	40 Drs.			Yugoslavia	33 D

No. 30,488 **R PARIS, WEDNESDAY, FEBRUARY 25, 1981 Established 1887

Associated Press

Prince Charles and Lady Diana Spencer met the press outside Buckingham Palace after their engagement was announced.

Charles Will Marry Lady Diana Spencer

Buckingham Palace Announces Engagement, Ending Speculation

The Associated Press

LONDON — Prince Charles, heir to the British throne, will marry 19-year-old Lady Diana Spencer, the daughter of a millionaire earl, this summer, Buckingham Palace announced Tuesday.

The brief announcement ended months of speculation that the prince, one of the world's most eligible bachelors, would marry Lady Diana, his 16th cousin once removed.

Prince Charles, 32, said in an interview that he proposed to Lady Diana over a dinner for two at his

camped outside her Knightsbridge apartment and pursued her as she drove around the city.

But the cool and composed way that Lady Diana, known to her friends as "shy Di," handled the newsmen impressed the royal family. Palace officials noted that Lady Diana was able to maintain the dignity needed by a future queen — unlike some of the prince's earlier girlfriends.

Prince Charles said in the interview that smuggling Lady Diana past reporters to his grandmother's Scottish home last year for a brief

U.S. Says 'Yes — If' On Soviet Talks Bid

By Lee Lescaze
Washington Post Service

WASHINGTON — President Reagan said Tuesday that he was "most interested" in Soviet leader Leonid I. Brezhnev's invitation to a summit meeting, but indicated that the Russians would have to meet certain conditions before he would agree to such a meeting.

Mr. Reagan said that the Soviet role in arming the insurgents in El Salvador "would be one of the things that should be straightened out" before a summit meeting could be held.

In an impromptu and brief press conference, Mr. Reagan indicated that his conditions for a summit meeting would include understandings that the two superpowers would engage in serious talks about reducing their nuclear arsenals.

[In that regard, a Soviet Embassy official, Assistant Press Counselor George Mamedov, told the International Herald Tribune on Tuesday that Moscow's position is that "we are willing immediately to reopen negotiations on limiting or — still better — reducing every kind of strategic armaments that both sides have, provided all the positive results that have been already achieved, including the SALT-2 treaty, should be safeguarded."]

Haig Response

On Monday night, Secretary of State Alexander M. Haig Jr. said that Mr. Brezhnev's proposal for a summit meeting and renewed arms limitation talks contained "new and remarkable innovations" and that the United States was very interested in examining them. "We need to study this very, very carefully," Mr. Haig said. He spoke with reporters after meeting with visiting French Foreign Minister Jean Francois-Poncet.

For his part, Mr. Francois-Poncet said that the Brezhnev proposals seemed to show a Soviet "will and spirit for dialogue that is, I

United Press International

King Juan Carlos I, left, greets Lt. Gen. Manuel Gutierrez Mellado, the first deputy premier in charge of defense, at the Royal Palace Tuesday after Gen. Gutierrez Mellado and others were released by rebellious Guards who took over the Cortes.

President Rules Out Salvador 'Vietnam'

The Associated Press

WASHINGTON — President Reagan said Tuesday that the United States had no intention of becoming involved in a Vietnam-like conflict in El Salvador.

At the same time, the president said, "We are in support of the government there against those who are attempting a violent overthrow."

He noted that the Soviet Union had denied involvement in supplying arms to the anti-government guerrillas opposing the military-ci-

that a recent lull in arms shipments through Cuba to rebels in El Salvador had diminished the possibility of swift retaliatory action by the United States against the Havana government.

Some officials speculate that Cuba and other countries have curbed arms deliveries in recent weeks out of fear that the United States may respond with military force. But others say that this may simply be a sign that the Salvadoran insurgents have enough weaponry for the time being.

Either way, acting Assistant Sec-

Madrid Coup Fails; All Hostages Freed

King Juan Carlos Key to Ending of Crisis

By Jonathan Kandell
International Herald Tribune

MADRID — Rebellious paramilitary Civil Guards, who had stormed the Spanish Cortes, surrendered Tuesday morning and released the Cabinet members and about 300 legislators whom they had held hostage for almost 18 hours.

The attempt by the approximately 150 rebels to precipitate a military coup failed when King Juan Carlos I successfully appealed to leaders of the armed forces to support the constitutional government.

There were no casualties and, aside from a brief, confusing military takeover in the Valencia region, the government continued to function normally in the rest of the country throughout the siege.

Virtually the only major national political figure not taken hostage by the rebels, King Juan Carlos played the key role in resolving the coup attempt, the latest test of Spain's fledgling democratic government.

Since Franco's death in 1975 and Spain's subsequent transition to democracy, the king has had to deal with continuing violence in the Basque region, unrest among the Civil Guard and challenges to coalition governments. Last month's resignation of Premier Adolfo Suarez — chosen by the king on July 3, 1976, to lead the government — was the latest challenge to King Juan Carlos's democratic efforts.

In a brief, laconic statement broadcast on television and radio at 1:15 a.m. Tuesday, the king said that he had met with the joint chiefs of staff and personally called upon regional military commanders "to uphold the constitutional order."

Asking the nation to remain calm, he asserted that he would "not tolerate, in any form, actions or attitudes by people who attempt to interrupt the democratic process."

The monarch, 43, appeared on television dressed in the uniform of an army general in order to emphasize his role as chief of the armed forces. Nevertheless, it still took more than 10 hours of negotiations between loyal Civil Guard commanders and the rebels to obtain a release of the legislators and the Cabinet.

Most of the legislators were released at noon on Tuesday. Police had cordoned off several blocks around the Cortes building, but a few hundred Spanish journalists were on hand to greet the legislators with applause and shouts of "Long live democracy!" and "Long live the Constitution!"

'About to Rise Up'

Virtually all the legislators, emerging very fatigued, complained about tension, particularly during the first moments of the crisis when the rebels fired machine-gun volleys at the ceiling and slapped several legislators.

"At one point, I thought that the majority of the armed forces were really about to rise up," said Oscar Alzaga, a legislator with the ruling Union of the Democratic Center.

"We have seen that the country rejects a coup," said Luis Solana, a Socialist Party legislator, "from now on, anybody who talks about a coup in this country is either a fool or a traitor."

According to several of the freed Cortes deputies, the rebel leader, Lt. Col. Antonio Tejero Molina, had told them that he expected his

Warsaw Regime Imposes Martial Law; 'Extremists,' Former Leaders Detained

From Agency Dispatches

WARSAW — Poland's Communist rulers, charging that the independent labor union Solidarity had pushed the country close to civil war, imposed martial law on Sunday and suspended a wide range of civil liberties.

A military Council of National Salvation assumed power in a nationwide operation in which about 1,000 people were reported to have been detained. Martial law authorities said they included Solidarity "extremists" and discredited former Communist leaders.

Government spokesman Jerzy Urban told reporters that Solidarity leader Lech Walesa was conferring with officials outside Warsaw and had not been arrested.

Mr. Urban said in a Sunday evening press conference that he could not provide a list of the detained unionists because "it's a continuous process.

The government said in a televised statement read by a uniformed announcer on Sunday that it had suspended activities of Solidarity, Rural Solidarity, students' organizations and journalists' associations.

"This means that the union and other organizations which have been suspended cannot conduct any activity," the statement said.

Mr. Urban insisted that the government was not outlawing Solidarity — only temporarily restricting its activities along with the activities of other trade unions.

A group of Solidarity leaders who were not arrested announced, meanwhile, that they were forming a national strike committee and said a general strike would be the appropriate reply to the government action.

"No union, no organization can allow its leaders to be repressed, and the union to be deprived of its rights," according to a communiqué issued by the group that reached Warsaw from Gdansk Sunday.

The communiqué, signed by one of Mr. Walesa's deputies, Miroslaw Krupinski, said that the proposed general strike could be called off after all detainees had been released and martial law repealed.

The Polish news agency PAP said that the council was made up of 14 generals, one admiral and five colonels. It is led by Gen. Wojciech Jaruzelski, the premier and party leader.

Gen. Jaruzelski said in an emotional broadcast early Sunday that the country had come close to the "abyss," and that the authorities acted swiftly to put the military in charge. But he added: "We do not aim at a military takeover, a military dictatorship. None of Poland's problems can be solved by force."

Troops, tanks, armored personnel vehicles and riot police took up positions in big cities and on main roads. All soldiers on patrol in Warsaw were Polish. There was no sign of Soviet troops.

Union activists in Warsaw defied martial law regulations and issued a call for an immediate general strike. Police used water cannons to disperse crowds outside the Warsaw Solidarity headquarters.

A leaflet distributed in Warsaw Sunday, signed by "Solidarity-Ursus" at the huge Ursus tractor factory, called for an "immediate general strike in the whole country" in response to the "attack on the union aimed at its liquidation."

The martial law declaration followed a decision on Saturday by the union's national leaders at a meeting in Gdansk to conduct a nationwide referendum on establishing a non-Communist government and defining Poland's military relationship with the Soviet Union. The union leaders also approved a resolution calling for an automatic general strike if the government passed a law granting itself emergency powers.

Mr. Urban declined to specify what the authorities would do if faced with a general strike, except to say that the military council had no intention of replacing workers with soldiers.

Mr. Urban said that he knew of no cases of death or injury after troops and police with riot gear and automatic weapons appeared in the streets before dawn on Sunday. Officials gave no figures for the number of arrests of Solidarity leaders and advisers early on Sunday, but knowledgeable sources said about 1,000 persons had been "interned."

Protest Strikes Reportedly Starting in Poland

Solidarity Says Troops Are Preparing to Evict Workers From Factories

By Brian Mooney
Reuters

WARSAW — Polish workers and miners were reported to have downed tools Monday in protest against martial law and the suspension of union and civilian freedoms.

The Solidarity free trade union, functioning in defiance of the military authorities, issued a list of strikebound mines and factories and said troops had surrounded a number of plants and appeared to be preparing to evict the strikers during the night curfew hours.

The Solidarity information could not be immediately confirmed in the absence of telephone and Telex services, but state radio said there were work stoppages in a number of plants.

Communications lines for all but one of the major Western news agencies in Poland were cut in Warsaw Monday night. Telephone engineers in London and Vienna said that cables used by United Press International, The Associated Press and the French news agency were cut. The British press service, Reuters, unlike the other agencies, does not run its wires through the headquarters of the news agency PAP in Warsaw.

PAP said that there were discussions in many factories, but the agency denied that there had been any interruptions in production.

Poles were told by state television Monday night that troops were used to thwart an attempted strike in a large steelworks in Katowice and that the Solidarity members who had instigated it had been rounded up.

The news agency said in a commentary that there were fears of clashes and riots if people did not comply with the requirements of martial law.

The Polish military took power on Sunday to avert what it said would be civil war and put an end to months of turmoil.

The agency said that the authorities' decision had met with the approval of Communist Party activists but said that the attitudes of Solidarity activists varied.

"Those who have definitely advocated confrontation have maintained their opinions," the agency said.

The state radio broadcast a sermon by the Polish primate, Archbishop Jozef Glemp, in which he pleaded for Poles not to resort to violence.

A Solidarity official said that the union had set up a skeleton command to direct union operations in the absence of its leaders who were rounded up during Sunday's predawn takeover.

Solidarity leader Lech Walesa was officially said to be in a government guest house. Government leaders reportedly had been conferring with Mr. Walesa in an attempt to avert a general strike.

Government spokesman Jerzy Urban told foreign reporters on Sunday that Mr. Walesa was not among those arrested. But Warsaw Radio carried no word from him Monday.

One of Solidarity's most radical leaders, Zbigniew Bujak of Warsaw, who evaded capture after the army and police detained dozens of activists and dissidents on Sunday, was arrested on Monday.

Mr. Bujak was believed to have been detained in the Warsaw suburb of Ursus, site of a huge tractor factory, the official said.

The factory was one of several surrounded by troops, according to the statement of the Solidarity's underground national commission.

Workers at the tractor factory, said on Monday evening that several thousand workers were inside. "Morale is good," an Ursus strike spokesman said.

It said that the Warsaw Fiat car factory was idle and that workers had downed tools in another major plant in the capital, the Swierczewski precision instrument works.

Witnesses said that workers at the Swierczewki factory in Warsaw blocked the main gates of their plant with a crane. The plant was one of four where workers told reporters that strikes were in progress.

It said that soldiers had entered Warsaw's national library and removed strikers earlier Monday.

The statement added that a total of 1,300 people had stopped work in Warsaw's planning office and geological institute.

Thousands in U.S., West Europe Demonstrate Against Martial Law

The Associated Press
In one of several demonstrations in Italy, youthful members of the Italian Radical Party participated in a protest march at the Polish Embassy in Rome.

The Associated Press
An honorary Solidarity member addressed a meeting at Poland's embassy in London.

Thousands of persons marched throughout Western Europe and the United States to protest the declaration of martial law in Poland. In West Berlin youths smashed windows at ticket offices of the Polish and Eastern European airlines. Tens of thousands of Americans of Polish origin organized prayer meetings and protest marches in various U.S. cities. At the same time, Western leaders discussed the move in Poland, announcing that they would observe a policy of strict nonintervention. President Reagan monitored developments in that country throughout the day and NATO declared that it was "following the situation with careful attention and great concern." Page 2.

United Press International
Americans of Polish origin demonstrated with U.S. and Polish flags in New York.

Walesa Awarded Nobel Prize

West, Church Hail Choice; Regime Silent

Compiled by Our Staff From Dispatches

GDANSK, Poland — Lech Walesa gave a shout of joy Wednesday and was tossed in the air by friends as they learned that he was the recipient of the 1983 Nobel Peace Prize.

Mr. Walesa said they heard the news on a car radio as he drove with friends on a mushroom-picking trip in woods about 50 miles (80 kilometers) from Gdansk.

On his return to his apartment in Gdansk, Mr. Walesa was greeted by a crowd of about 1,000, who chanted his name and the name of the outlawed Solidarity trade union that he headed.

Leaning from his apartment window, Mr. Walesa said he would donate the cash award of 1.5 million Swedish kronor, about $190,000 dollars, to a proposed Roman Catholic Church fund to channel aid to Poland's private farmers.

The Associated Press
Lech Walesa, winner of the 1983 Nobel Peace Prize.

Mr. Walesa said he would not seek to go to Norway himself but would ask permission from the authorities for his wife, Danuta, to go to accept the award for him.

There was no immediate official reaction from the authorities, but Andzej Konopacki, a government spokesman, said, "The award used to mean something. This depreciates the prize. It's politically motivated."

THE WEATHER — PARIS: Saturday, fair. Temp. 16-5 (61-41). Sunday, Cloudy. LONDON: Saturday, cloudy. Temp. 13-6(55-43). Sunday, cloudy. CHANNEL: Slight. ROME: Saturday, cloudy. Temp. 18-10 (64-50). FRANKFURT: Saturday, fair. Temp. 18-3 (64-36). NEW YORK: Saturday, rain. Temp. 13-6 (55-43).

ADDITIONAL WEATHER DATA — PAGE 12

INTERNATIONAL
Herald Tribune

Published with The New York Times and The Washington Post

Algeria	5.50 Din.	Israel	I.S. 22.00	Norway	5.00 N.Kr.
Austria	17 S.	Italy	1000 Lire	Oman	0.700 Rials
Bahrain	0.650 Din	Jordan	450 Fils	Portugal	45 Esc.
Belgium	33 B.Fr.	Kenya	Shs. 16.00	Qatar	6.50 Rials
Canada	C.$ 1.10	Kuwait	500 Fils	Rep. of Ireland	50 P.
Cyprus	400 Mills	Lebanon	£L3.50	Saudi Arabia	6.00 Rials
Denmark	6.00 D.Kr.	Libya	L.Din. 0.35	Spain	80 Ptas.
Egypt	90 P.	Luxembourg	33 L.Fr.	Sweden	5.00 S.Kr.
Finland	5.00 F.M.	Madeira	50 Esc.	Switzerland	1.90 S.Fr.
France	4.50 F	Malta	35 Cents	Tunisia	0.500 Din
Germany	2.00 D.M.	Morocco	5.50 Dh.	Turkey	T.£. 150.00
Great Britain	35 P.	Netherlands	2.25 Fl.	U.A.E.	6.50 Dirh
Greece	45 Drs.	Nigeria	100 K.	U.S. Mil. (Eur.)	$0.85
Iran	135 Rials			Yugoslavia	35 D.

No. 30,830 • LONDON, SATURDAY-SUNDAY, APRIL 3-4, 1982 Established 1887

Ailing After Trip, Brezhnev Reported In Moscow Hospital

By Dusko Doder
Washington Post Service

MOSCOW — President Leonid I. Brezhnev's health "deteriorated seriously" during his recent trip to Uzbekistan and he was taken on a stretcher from the airport to a hospital upon his return last week, according to well-informed Soviet sources.

The sources quoted Mr. Brezhnev's doctors as saying they expected the 75-year-old Soviet leader to recover but that he would have to remain in the hospital "for weeks." A meeting of the Communist Party Central Committee that was to have been held here this week has been postponed until May 24, the sources said.

The sources, who also said that Mr. Brezhnev suffered a mild heart attack in early February, suggested he may have had a mild stroke aboard the plane carrying him from Tashkent, the capital of Uzbekistan, to Moscow on March 25.

A spokesman for the Foreign Ministry would not comment on the report.

While reporting a "serious worsening" of his health, the sources did not suggest that Mr. Brezhnev was incapacitated.

The apparent deterioration of his condition, however, has focused new attention on Konstantin U. Chernenko, who is understood to be in charge of day-to-day affairs. Mr. Chernenko, 70, has been an associate of Mr. Brezhnev's since 1950.

In describing events leading up to Mr. Brezhnev's hospitalization, the Soviet sources said the exceptionally heavy schedule of the previous two weeks as well as climatic and other changes on the trip to Central Asia led to a general weakening of Mr. Brezhnev's condition.

During the past few years, Mr. Brezhnev has undergone periodic problems with his health. In addition to heart trouble, he is said to suffer from emphysema. People who have seen him personally in recent years have noted a slurring in his speech and hearing difficulties.

He appeared fit, however, when

(Continued on Page 2, Col. 8)

Poland Said To Release Some Troops

First of Conscripts Leave, Diplomats Say

From Agency Dispatches

WARSAW — The Polish Army appears to have begun sending home some of the draftees who had been kept in service before and after imposition of martial law in December, Western diplomatic sources said Friday.

Meanwhile, the military prosecutor's office said that authorities have sentenced 52 more persons for violations of martial law and have started investigations into the activities of another 96 persons, including a Roman Catholic priest.

The diplomatic sources said there were no signs yet of a large-scale demobilization.

The sources said that because military service was extended last year the army has about 70,000 conscripts due for release at about this time, which is twice the normal number.

If they were all sent home on time, the sources said, the army would lose about one-third of its strength. The sources added that the army's training machinery

The Associated Press

Prime Minister Margaret Thatcher of Britain leaving No. 10 Downing Street after an emergency Cabinet meeting Friday.

3 Senators Contradict Reagan on Soviet Arms

By Judith Miller
New York Times Service

WASHINGTON — President Reagan's assertion that the Soviet Union had achieved military superiority over the United States has been disputed by both proponents of a nuclear arms freeze and by one of the chief supporters of his arms policies.

At a news conference on Wednesday, President Reagan said in response to a question: "The truth of the matter is that, on balance, the Soviet Union does have a definite margin of superiority, enough so that there is what I have

Argentina Seizes Falklands; U.K. Breaks Diplomatic Ties

Reuters

LONDON — Argentine forces on Friday captured Stanley, the capital of the Falkland Islands, and British Foreign Secretary Lord Carrington announced that his country had broken diplomatic relations with Argentina.

"I must confirm that an Argentine military attack on Port Stanley in the Falkland Islands has taken place and that Port Stanley is now occupied by Argentine military forces," Lord Carrington said at a news conference.

His statement was the first official acknowledgement in London of the Argentine attack against the British colony off South America. Lord Carrington said Argentine diplomats in London were told to leave the country by Thursday.

Earlier, Argentina announced that its troops had occupied the South Atlantic islands, which lie 400 miles (640 kilometers) off its east coast and are inhabited by 1,800 English-speaking people, mainly of British descent. The islands, which are among the last of Britain's colonies, have no strategic value but there have been unconfirmed reports of offshore oil deposits.

The Falkland islanders, mainly sheep farmers, have repeatedly said they do not want to switch their allegiance to Argentina, which claims the islands as the Malvinas.

Argentina's official news agency said an invasion fleet backed by aircraft landed forces at dawn Friday at the capital, also known as Port Stanley, to capture the town, its airfield and the barracks of about 80 British Marines.

[The independent Argentine news agency DYN quoted a military source as saying that 4,000 to 5,000 Argentine troops took part in the invasion, including 800 Marines who landed on San Pedro Island, The Associated Press reported.]

A communiqué by Argentina's three-man ruling junta said the islands had been "restored to the national patrimony" by force of arms after all diplomatic efforts had failed to achieve this end. It added that any resistance to its rule would be punished.

The communiqué said that, in addition to occupying the British colonial outpost on the Falklands, Argentina had seized control of South Georgia and the South Sandwich Islands, administered by Britain as part of the Falkland Island Dependencies.

Buenos Aires named Gen. Mario Menendez as governor of the islands.

An Argentine state television channel said later that an Argentine military officer was killed and two were injured during the inva-

(Continued on Page 2, Col. 3)

The Associated Press

Cheering Argentines gather in Buenos Aires after learning of the Falklands occupation.

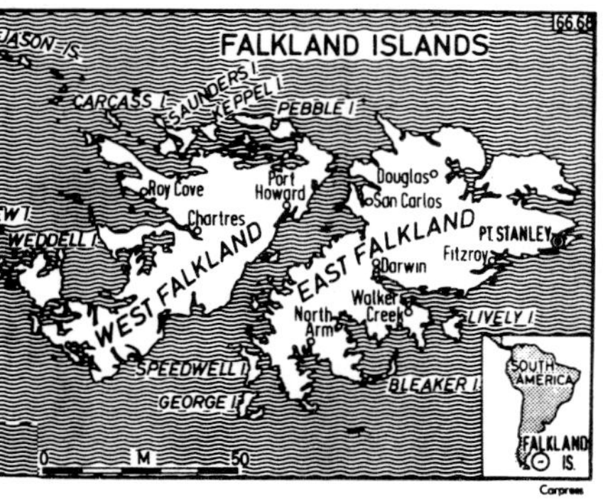

Carpress

THE GLOBAL NEWSPAPER
Edited in Paris
Printed Simultaneously in Paris, London, Zurich and Hong Kong

WEATHER DATA APPEAR ON PAGE 14

INTERNATIONAL
Herald Tribune

Published With The New York Times and The Washington Post

No. 30,891 *** PARIS, TUESDAY, JUNE 15, 1982 ESTABLISHED 1887

Argentines Report Falklands Cease-Fire

Thatcher Tells Commons 'White Flags Are Flying Over Port Stanley'

Compiled by Our Staff From Dispatches

BUENOS AIRES — The Argentine military command said Monday that a "de facto cease-fire" had halted fierce fighting between Argentine and British forces on the outskirts of the Falkland Islands' capital, Stanley, and Prime Minister Margaret Thatcher of Britain said talks were in progress on an Argentine surrender.

The command said Gen. Mario Benjamin Menéndez, the Argentine governor of the islands, met with the British field commander, Maj. Gen. Jeremy Moore, at 4 p.m. local time (1900 GMT).

Mrs. Thatcher told a jubilant House of Commons that "white flags are flying over Port Stanley." She said that "large numbers of Argentinian soldiers threw down their weapons" after British troops fought their way to the outskirts of the Falklands capital.

"Our troops have been ordered not to fire except in self-defense," she added.

Argentine Announcement

The Argentine command, referring to the besieged capital, said, "At this moment, in the zone of Puerto Argentino, there is a de facto cease-fire not concerted by either side."

Military sources in Buenos Aires said the cease-fire would last until 10 a.m. local time Tuesday, to allow Gen. Menéndez time to fly to Buenos Aires to meet with the ruling military junta.

The sources said Gen. Menéndez would tell the three-man junta the terms of his conversation with the British commander.

Mrs. Thatcher said the talks on a surrender were being conducted by Gen. Menéndez and the British deputy commander, Brigadier Charles John Waters.

Mrs. Thatcher told a jubilant House of Commons that "white flags are flying over Port Stanley."

"After successful attacks last night, Gen. Moore decided to press forward. The Argentinians retreated. Our forces reached the outskirts of Port Stanley. Large numbers of Argentinian soldiers threw down their weapons." She said British troops had been ordered not to fire except in self-defense.

"Talks are now in progress between General Menéndez and our deputy commander, Brigadier Waters, about the surrender of the Argentine forces on East and West Falkland. I will report further to the House tomorrow."

Members of Parliament greeted her announcement with loud applause.

British officers said Argentine troops were in "full retreat" Monday, fleeing a relentless British assault and pulling in from their horseshoe-shaped defense line back to Stanley.

Minutes before, the military command had reported intense fighting as British troops had moved into the outskirts of Stanley.

In Washington, Pentagon sources said that Argentine forces "are in the process of surrendering." The sources, who declined to be identified, said a cease-fire was being arranged.

Another source said a cease-fire was "getting into place," probably as a preliminary to a surrender. He said "various elements" were arranging the cease-fire, but he did not elaborate.

Surrender Not Mentioned

The account of the U.S. intelligence sources followed a British Broadcasting Corp. report that the two commanders had agreed on a cease-fire. But that report made no mention of an Argentine surrender.

The Argentine command said earlier Monday that British forces pushed within two miles (3.2 kilometers) of Stanley, reaching "key positions" of the Argentine defense.

Government sources said the Argentine president, Lt. Gen. Leopoldo Galtieri, was preparing to address the nation on television and radio later Monday.

Hills Captured

Britain said its troops stormed and captured the last two strategic hills outside Stanley in heavy fighting, precipitating a retreat of Argentine forces.

"Last night, British forces pressed forward from positions on high ground surrounding Port Stanley," Defense Secretary John Nott said in a statement.

"From their new positions, our forces can see large numbers of Argentine soldiers retreating and streaming back into Port Stanley. Our forces are moving forward to exploit their success," he said.

British troops secured key positions on Tumbledown Mountain and Mount Williams, two to three miles southwest of Stanley, as well as on Wireless Ridge to the northwest, Mr. Nott said.

The Argentine command admitted that Tumbledown Mountain and Wireless Ridge had been captured by the British.

That represented an apparently decisive consolidation of the dominant position British forces have had since taking high ground overlooking the capital early this month.

The Argentine for… from outside suppor… some deadly, effectiv… by fighter jets based … lands, apparently ha… able to mount a strong…

British Defense M… cials estimate there ar… Argentine troops man… es in and around Sta… er, some reports filed … tary censors by Brit sh… ents on the islands … strength of the Argen… at up to 10,000 men.

Britain has about … the islands.

Zone for Civi…

As many as 600 … now believed to have … up in the fighting … The British governm… there were only 250 … still in the capital, a… surprise at the large … vanced Monday by … tional Red Cross.

A Red Cross spokesman in Geneva said that Britain and Argentina had agreed to establish a neutral zone for civilians in a one-block area around the town's stone church. Most homes on the island are of frame construction but the …

… there was nothing new in an Argentine message to Pope John Paul II that included an offer of an immediate cease-fire in the Falklands followed by a mutual withdrawal of troops.

"There appears to be nothing …

British intelligence was appallingly inaccurate in making the original assessment.

Max Hastings, an Evening Standard reporter traveling with a Royal Marine unit, said in a dispatch … of shell … gentines … war. No … be doing …

… in Bue… cteristic … gains, … Mount … s Ridge, … become … nterven… ry from …

… ffensive, … e Satur… ed Sun… ies "on … t front, … terial."

… rgentine … vehicles … ng runs … at artil… results"

MONDAY, DECEMBER 12, 1983

Alfonsin Is Sworn In, Ending Rule by Military in Argentina

By Edward Schumacher
New York Times Service

BUENOS AIRES — Raúl Alfonsin was inaugurated president of Argentina over the weekend amid joyous celebrations marking the end of nearly eight years of military rule.

More than 100,000 Argentines poured into the streets Saturday to cheer the 56-year-old political moderate.

Waving flags and wearing white berets, a symbol of Mr. Alfonsin's Radical Party, the crowds rained confetti on the president as he traveled from his swearing-in before Congress to the presidential palace.

Argentines later packed the two-block Plaza de Mayo and spilled far down side streets. They chanted "Alfonsin!" as the president addressed them from a wrought-iron balcony of the Cabildo, the white-washed colonial-era city hall.

Calling himself "the most humble of Argentines," Mr. Alfonsin said: "We know that these are hard and difficult moments, but we do not have a single doubt."

"We will go forward," he said. "We will become the country that we deserve."

United Press International

President Raúl Alfonsin and former President Isabel Perón of Argentina exchanging greetings after Mr. Alfonsin was sworn in, marking a return to democracy in the nation.

Encirclement of Beirut Is Complete; Arafat Says Guerrillas Will Fight On

Compiled by Our Staff From Dispatches

BEIRUT — Israeli forces appeared Monday to have surrounded the leadership and several thousand guerrillas of the Palestine Liberation Organization in a 10-square-mile (26-square-kilometer) area of West Beirut, but Israeli leaders said they did not intend to press their attack into the city.

Israeli armored units made friendly contact with Lebanese Christian militiamen holding East Beirut, in effect sealing off the Palestinian leadership in the Moslem western part of the city. The Israelis remained poised in the … ing the defense by the guerrillas. "There is no power on earth that can force us to lay down our arms," Mr. Arafat said during a tour of guerrilla positions in Beirut.

George Habash, leader of the Popular Front for the Liberation of Palestine, vowed to turn Beirut into "a new Stalingrad," a reference to the Soviet defense of Stalingrad against Nazi armies in World War II.

By sundown the guns were virtually silent around Beirut.

Isreali Foreign Ministry officials said Palestinians guerrillas … get orders to hunt down PLO leaders at their headquarters inside the Lebanese capital and "deal them a near-mortal blow."

The Lebanese police announced Monday that almost 10,000 persons had been killed since the start of the invasion June 4. The announcement said 9,583 persons were known to have been killed and another 16,608 injured. There was no breakdown between military and civilian or between Lebanese and Palestinian casualties.

The Israeli Army refused to divulge latest its casualty figures. The last official toll put the num… caused by the Israeli invasion, bringing together for the first time since the 1975-76 civil war leaders of the major leftist and rightist political groups and representatives of the country's main religious sects.

But it was not immediately certain that all the members nominated would respond. The Shiite leader, Nabih Berri, said that the first he had heard of his appointment was on the radio, and he declined further comment.

The first meeting of the new commission was set in the presidential palace just above the hill village of Baabda, where hundreds

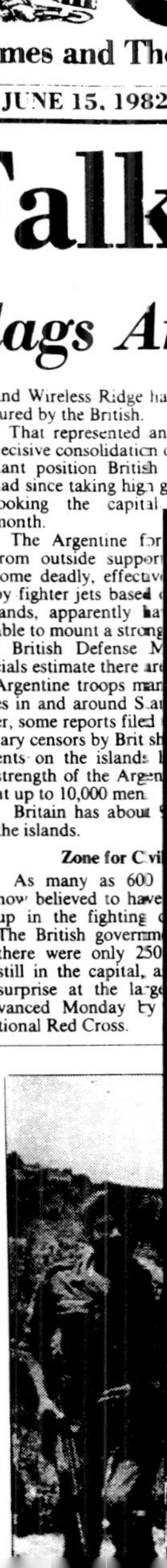

Israel Army Invades Lebanon

PLO Target Of Air, Sea, Land Assault

By Thomas L. Friedman
New York Times Service

GHANDOURRIYE, Lebanon — Israel invaded southern Lebanon by land, sea and air Sunday in a three-pronged attack aimed at destroying the main military bases of the Palestine Liberation Organization.

More than 250 Israeli tanks and armored personnel carriers, as well as thousands of infantrymen, moved past the observation posts of the United Nations peacekeeping troops in southern Lebanon at 11 a.m. and fanned out across the frontier, a UN spokesman in Beirut reported.

(In Versailles, France, President Reagan called on Israel to withdraw its troops, but Israel rejected the call, Secretary of State Alexander M. Haig Jr. reported.

(Mr. Haig told reporters that Prime Minister Menachem Begin replied Sunday to a personal message sent by Mr. Reagan as the Israeli operation began.

(Mr. Haig said, "We have sought the Israelis' withdrawal. We didn't want them to go in in the first place." Referring to the Begin message, he added, "We have not received assurances of any cessation of the Israeli operation.")

United Press International

Israeli armor moved Sunday toward the border on its way to Lebanon. The invasion was aimed at Palestinian guerrillas.

By late evening, the Israeli invasion force had taken several strategic guerrilla outposts in the craggy hills of southern Lebanon and was engaged in firefights with the Palestinians for control of scores of other strongholds along the 33-mile (53-kilometer) front, stretching from the port city of Tyre to the foothills of Mount Hermon, the UN spokesman said.

Syrian Force

By nightfall, the 30,000-man Syrian force in Lebanon, whose southernmost positions are at Jezzine, Kfar Houne, Yohmor and Rashaya, only 15 to 20 miles north of the Israeli border, had not become involved in the fighting. Lebanese government sources said, however, that the Syrians had reinforced their positions around Jezzine with both men and materiel.

[Israeli forces came into contact with Syrian troops at three points, Reuters reported, quoting a Syrian spokesman in Damascus. The Syrians had been ordered to oppose the Israelis and had been doing so since Sunday afternoon, the report said.

[But it was not clear whether the Syrians were actually fighting the Israelis or simply opposing them by holding their ground. The Syrian spokesman quoted by Reuters said the advancing Israelis had come into contact with Syrians at Jarmaq, a village only three miles east of the Palestinian stronghold of Nabatiyeh, and further east at Berghoz, as well as at a crossroads near Hasbaya.

[An Israeli Army spokesman declined to comment on reports that Syrian and Israeli forces had come into contact earlier Sunday.]

Israel Radio broadcast a statement directed at the Syrians saying that the invasion was not aimed at them and that Israeli troops would not engage Syrian units as long as they remained out of the fighting.

The Israeli Army preceded its invasion with five hours of heavy shelling and aerial bombardment of a string of suspected Palestinian guerrilla positions between the Beaufort Castle and Tyre, sending up mushroom clouds of smoke across the horizon.

The hills of south Lebanon reverberated with the sound of Israeli artillery shells hitting Palestinian redoubts nestled in the villages and caves just north of the UN peacekeeping zone, which was established to separate Israel and the Palestinians after the March, 1978, Israeli invasion.

According to UN officials in Ghandourriye and Beirut, the Israeli invasion began with armored carriers sweeping past the Dutch UN outpost at as Al-Baiyada, about three miles north of the Israeli border. The armored column then moved north along the coastal highway and engaged the Palestinian guerrillas dug in at Tyre.

Both the UN spokesman and the PLO news agency WAFA said an intense firefight raged late into the night between the Israeli armored brigade, which had driven to the outskirts of Tyre, and the Palestinian guerrillas hidden in the town's devastated buildings and Roman ruins.

The Israeli Navy reportedly blew apart the Qasimiyye Bridge spanning the Litani River north of Tyre, cutting off the Palestinians from their main supply line.

A WAFA communiqué said a joint force of Palestinians and Lebanese Moslem leftists had launched a counterattack against Israeli units ringing the city, killing 15 Israeli soldiers and knocking out 14 tanks. They did not disclose their own casualties.

The Palestinians are armed with an array of Soviet-made artillery, anti-tank guns, T-34 tanks and Kaytusha rockets of various sizes.

United Press International

A Palestinian commando in Saida, Lebanon, held the helmet Sunday of a dead Israeli helicopter pilot as the crewman's body extended from a car trunk. The Palestinians shot down the craft as Israeli forces moved into the southern part of Lebanon.

The Global Newspaper
Edited in Paris
Printed Simultaneously in Paris, London, Zurich, Hong Kong, Singapore and The Hague.

WEATHER DATA APPEAR ON PAGE 14

INTERNATIONAL Herald Tribune
Published With The New York Times and The Washington Post

No. 31,313 • PARIS, MONDAY, OCTOBER 24, 1983 ESTABLISHED 1887

More Than 150 Marines, French Paratroopers Killed in Beirut in Suicide Guerrilla Bombings

United Press International

A French paratrooper holds the hand of a soldier trapped after the bombing on Sunday at the French compound.

By William Claiborne
Washington Post Service

BEIRUT — More than 150 U.S. marines and French paratroopers were killed in two nearly simultaneous suicide guerrilla bombings Sunday morning. The bombings were the worst in Lebanon's violent history.

As rescue workers searched feverishly under floodlights Sunday evening for victims whose cries could be heard earlier from beneath the collapsed buildings, Moslem gunmen fired at the U.S. compound at Beirut International Airport, driving enraged marines into bunkers for more than two hours.

The marines listed 135 confirmed dead and 112 wounded in the blast, but the Marine spokesman, Major Robert Jordan, said Sunday night that 250 to 300 marines may have been in the building when it was blown up by a bomb estimated to weigh 2,000 pounds.

The French contingent listed 25 dead and 50 trapped under its collapsed eight-story building, with little hope left for survivors. In Paris, French officials said the known toll Sunday night was 9 dead, 14 wounded and 53 missing.

U.S. and French officials cautiously avoided pinning the blame for the attacks on any one faction or any of the factions sponsored by foreign powers.

General François Conn, commander of the French contingent, said he had "evidence" of who was responsible, but when asked if it was concrete evidence, he replied, "No, but it is more than just an idea." He would not discuss details of his suspicions.

Despite the stunning proportions of the disasters, the commanders of both the U.S. and French contingents of the multinational peacekeeping force said they were more determined than ever to stay in Beirut and bolster the Lebanese government and its army.

"These kinds of things just harden our resolve and we will continue to do what we came here to do, and that is provide assistance for a free and independent Lebanon," Colonel Timothy J. Geraghty, commander of the U.S. contingent, said at a press conference.

General Conn said in an interview that his unit was "more than ever" determined to remain in Beirut, and he said he expected a more aggressive role for his paratrioopers because of the bombings.

Major Jordan described the sporadic shooting at the marines not as sniping but "aimed firing" at the compound by machine-gun fire, automatic rifles and rocket-propelled grenades.

The Marine compound was hit repeatedly, but the rescue workers were able to resume their work after the initial volley.

The first explosion rocked the four-story Marine building adjacent to the airport terminal at about 6:20 A.M., collapsing it to less than one story as the walls caved inward to form a grotesque pile of smoldering rubble.

The eight-story French paratroopers' quarters near the sports stadium in West Beirut was reduced to a one-story pile of shattered concrete when the second bomb went off about 20 seconds later.

Major Jordan said that at the time of the impact that 150 to 300 marines were believed to be in the building. Some of them were sleeping and some were eating breakfast in a ground-floor mess hall when the bomb exploded.

Major Jordan said that moments before the explosion, the sergeant of the guard outside the building reported on his walkie-talkie that a truck had entered the parking lot of the compound and was moving at high speed across 100 yards (91 meters) toward the building. The Marine guard fired five rounds at the truck, Major Jordan said.

The truck crashed through a fence a sandbag sentry position and then through the entrance of the building's large atrium lobby before the driver detonated the explosives. He said the driver assured the maximum effect by triggering the charge just as the vehicle reached the center of the building.

The Marine compound was chaotic with rescue activity within minutes as Marine and Lebanese Army soldiers frantically tore at chunks of reinforced concrete to try to reach trapped victims.

Jeeps and trucks in an adjacent motor pool were twisted into pretzel-like masses of steel, and fires burned on top of the collapsed roof, preventing rescuers from working until an airport fire engine sprayed the rubble with foam.

Marines used improvised tools and even their hands to try to reach their trapped comrades. Other units of the multinational force sent in heavy equipment. Major Jordan explained later that the marines feared using the heavy equipment because it would shift the

(Continued on Page 2, Col. 5)

The Associated Press

The four-story building housing the U.S. Marine command center was reduced to rubble in the Beirut explosion Sunday.

No Pullout, Reagan Declares

Compiled by Our Staff From Dispatches

WASHINGTON — President Ronald Reagan, calling the suicide bomb raid that killed at least 135 U.S. Marines in Lebanon "a despicable act," said Sunday that U.S. peace-keeping forces will not be driven out of the Middle East.

In Paris, Premier Pierre Mauroy said that the 2,000-man French military contingent in Beirut would remain despite the bombing attack that killed scores of French troops.

In Rome, Prime Minister Bettino Craxi, said in a message to President Reagan: "I confirm the commitment which Italy intends to maintain in Lebanon to develop a mission of peace." Mr. Craxi sent a similar message to President François Mitterrand, his office said.

As well as contributing 2,200 troops to the four-country force, Italy has, along with Greece, also agreed in principle to send observers to monitor a ceasefire between Lebanon's warring factions.

The Greek foreign minister, Ioannis Haralambopoulos, said at a news conference, "Greece linked its agreement in principle to send observers with certain problems involved," implying the decision to send the observers still stands.

Britain's Foreign Office minister, Richard Luce, called the bombings "a gigantic atrocity," but he said that there would be no quick reaction.

He said Britain was watching the safety of its 100 troops in Beirut and had to reassess with the United States, France and Italy whether they could continue to fulfil a constructive role.

Mr. Reagan, who cut short a weekend of golfing after a gunman seized and freed two aides at a golf course in Augusta, Georgia, returned to Washington for meetings on the bombing.

The president shook his head "no" when asked if he knew who was responsible for the bombing, the largest number of U.S. military deaths since the Vietnam War. But Defense Secretary Caspar W. Weinberger suggested Iranian terrorists carried out the death mission.

"There is a lot of circumstantial evidence," Mr. Weinberger said, "but there is certainly much that

Throngs in Europe Protest U.S. Missiles

By Henry Tanner
International Herald Tribune

BONN — Hundreds of thousands of Germans, perhaps as many as a million, marched Saturday in Bonn, Hamburg, West Berlin, and between Stuttgart and Neu Ulm to protest against the stationing of U.S. Pershing-2 and cruise missiles on German soil and against the nuclear arms race in general.

Elsewhere in Europe, an antimissile demonstration in central London, said to be the largest of its kind in British history, drew hundreds of thousands of people Saturday. There were smaller demonstrations over the weekend in the center of Rome, where 350,000 people marched, and in Vienna, Paris, Stockholm, Brussels and Dublin as well as more than 140 places in the United States.

The mass marches and rallies in Germany, which concluded a 10-day campaign by the German peace movement, were good-natured and remained nonviolent. The absence of violence was viewed as a triumph for both the peace movement and the police.

Evaluations of the political impact of the protests differed. But there was a consensus that the Christian Democratic government of Chancellor Helmut Kohl would go ahead next month with its decision to permit deployment of the new Pershings.

On the other hand, leading commentators generally friendly to the government expressed the belief that the peace movement, by succeeding to remain non-violent and being able to mobilize such huge crowds, had become a lasting political force in he country and made it inevitable that Germany's role in the Western security strategy would be discussed in ever sharper terms in parliament and between the major parties.

Foreign diplomats spoke of a "collapse" of the German national consensus on European security

(Continued on Page 2, Col. 1)

U.S. Aides See No Hope for Talks With Soviet

By Bernard Gwertzman
New York Times Service

WASHINGTON — In the aftermath of the Soviet downing of a South Korean airliner, some officials in the Reagan administration say U.S. and Soviet officials may have lost their ability to hold serious discussions.

Several senior officials and Soviet affairs experts in the government said in recent interviews that they were worried that the coincidence of the attack on the plane Sept. 1 and the start of NATO's deployment of new missiles in Western Europe in December might produce the most dramatic confrontation since the Berlin and Cuban crises of the early 1960s.

However, the officials say they can only guess what the Soviet Union will do if, as expected, the negotiations in Geneva fail to produce an accord on limiting missiles and if deployment of the missiles begins on schedule.

Some senior officials, including President Ronald Reagan, seem persuaded that despite repeated

on how to respond to the airliner's downing.

On Sept. 28, a statement issued in Mr. Andropov's name said that "even if someone had any illusions as to the possible evolution for the better in the policy of the present American administration, the latest developments have finally dispelled them."

The statement is regarded by State Department officials as a tough one, indicating that the Soviet Union had decided to gear itself for what an official called "a tough winter."

Several officials said that relations between the Reagan administration and the Kremlin had never been good but that several months

meeting with Lawrence S. Eagleburger, the undersecretary of state for political affairs, that accomplished nothing, officials said. Negotiations in Geneva on arms control have been sterile, officials said.

A senior administration official said Saturday he believed that if the Reagan administration were now to propose a high-level discussion it would be rejected by Moscow.

The expectation in Washington is that if deployment of the missiles begins, the Soviet Union may deploy new missiles of its own, either in Eastern Europe, which would have limited military significance given the existing Soviet edge on missiles in Europe, or in eastern Siberia, which could threaten Alas-

Reagan Aides Seized, Freed

THE GLOBAL NEWSPAPER
Edited in Paris
Printed Simultaneously in
Paris, London, Zurich,
Hong Kong and Singapore

WEATHER DATA APPEAR ON PAGE 16

INTERNATIONAL Herald Tribune

Published With The New York Times and The Washington Post

Algeria	5.50 Din.	Israel	I.S. 32.00	Norway	5.50 N.Kr.
Austria	17 S.	Italy	1000 Lire	Oman	0.700 Rials
Bahrain	0.650 Din	Jordan	450 Fils	Portugal	50 Esc.
Belgium	33 B.Fr.	Kenya	Shs. 16.00	Qatar	6.50 Rials
Canada	C.$ 1.10	Kuwait	500 Fils	Rep. of Ireland	50 P.
Cyprus	400 Mils	Lebanon	£L4.00	Saudi Arabia	6.00 Rials
Denmark	6.50 D.Kr.	Libya	L.Din. 0.35	Spain	80 Ptas.
Egypt	90 P.	Luxembourg	33 L.Fr.	Sweden	5.50 S.Kr.
Finland	5.50 F.M.	Madeira	55 Esc.	Switzerland	1.90 S.Fr.
France	4.50 F.	Malta	35 Cents	Tunisia	0.500 Din
Germany	2.00 D.M.	Morocco	5.50 Dh.	Turkey	T.£. 150.00
Great Britain	35 P.	Netherlands	2.25 Fl.	U.A.E.	6.50 Dirh
Greece	45 Drs.	Nigeria	170 K.	U.S. Mil. (Eur.)	$0.85
Iran	135 Rials			Yugoslavia	43 D.

No. 31,020 * ZURICH, FRIDAY, NOVEMBER 12, 1982 ESTABLISHED 1887

Brezhnev, 75, Dies; Led Soviet 18 Years

Burial Set for Monday; Mourning Period Is Announced

Compiled by Our Staff From Dispatches

MOSCOW — Leonid Ilyich Brezhnev, 75, the Soviet Union's leader for 18 years, died Wednesday of a heart attack, the Soviet media announced Thursday.

Tass, quoting an official medical bulletin Thursday night, said Mr. Brezhnev died between 8 A.M. and 9 A.M. Wednesday of a heart attack caused by hardening of the arteries. The medical bulletin, signed by eight doctors, including Mr. Brezhnev's personal physician and heart specialist, Yevgeny Chazov, indicated that he had suffered several heart attacks previously.

The announcement, broadcast simultaneously over Soviet radio and by Tass, was not made until more than 24 hours after his death. At no time during the day did any official report indicate where Mr. Brezhnev had been when he died, who had been with him or what kind of medical treatment he had received when he suffered the heart attack.

There was no official word on who would assume his posts as Communist Party leader and head of state, but Yuri V. Andropov, 68, who headed the KGB until May and who has been mentioned in speculation on a successor, was named to chair the 25-member committee in charge of Mr. Brezhnev's funeral, which is scheduled for Monday.

Leonid I. Brezhnev was well-suited to the needs of an emerging superpower. Obituary, Page 4.

As the Soviet Union went into mourning for Mr. Brezhnev, only the fourth leader of the Communist Party since the 1917 revolution, Soviet leaders vowed to "ensure détente and disarmament" and to ward off the threat of nuclear war.

A statement issued by the party's Central Committee and governmental and parliamentary leaders declared, "The domestic and foreign policy of the Communist Party of the Soviet Union, formulated under the leadership of Leonid I. Brezhnev, will continue to be pursued consistently and purposefully."

The statement warned, as Mr. Brezhnev had Sunday at celebrations marking the anniversary of the revolution, that the Soviet Union "will do everything necessary for those who are fond of military ventures not to catch the land of the Soviets unawares, for the potential aggressor to know: A crushing retaliatory strike awaits him inevitably."

The leadership statement restated his contention that "aggressive circles of imperialism" were trying to undermine "peaceful co-existence" between East and West and "to push the peoples to the path of enmity and military confrontation."

The statement also sought to assure the public that Mr. Brezhnev's domestic policies would continue.

"The party will continue doing its utmost to raise the well-being of the people through intensifying production, enhancing its efficiency and quality of work and fulfilling the food program of the U.S.S.R."

A funeral announcement said Mr. Brezhnev would be buried Monday at Red Square, after his body lies in state for three days beginning Friday at the House of Soviet Trade Unions, a block from the Bolshoi Theater.

The Central Committee declared a four-day mourning period and announced that primary and secondary schools would be closed Monday. It also ordered state enterprises to stop work for five minutes at the time of the burial. Guns are to be fired in Moscow, provincial capitals and several other Soviet cities, and factories were ordered to sound their sirens for three minutes.

The state radio reported that the scheduled meeting Tuesday of the Supreme Soviet, the national parliament, would be delayed one week. Because the Central Committee traditionally holds a meeting the day before the parliament sits, that session might also have been pushed back.

The announcement of Mr. Brezhnev's death hailed him as an "ardent champion of peace and communism" and said he would "live forever in the hearts of the Soviet people and the entire progressive mankind."

Despite Mr. Brezhnev's many years in the spotlight, Muscovites showed little outward emotion after his death was announced. An employee of the state GUM department store on Red Square appeared to sum up the public reaction. "Our line will continue to be the same. There will be another person from the Politburo nominated for president," she said.

Western diplomats said they were surprised by subdued public reaction, because Mr. Brezhnev had been the object of adulation at

(Continued on Page 5, Col. 4)

Reagan's Condolences

Poland to Free Walesa,

The Global Newspaper
Edited in Paris
Printed Simultaneously
in Paris, London, Zurich,
Hong Kong, Singapore
and The Hague.

WEATHER DATA APPEAR ON PAGE 15

INTERNATIONAL Herald Tribune

Published With The New York Times and The Washington Post

Algeria	6.00 Din.	Israel	I.S. 100	Norway	6.00 N.Kr.
Austria	19 S.	Italy	1300 Lire	Oman	0.700 Rials
Bahrain	0.650 Din	Jordan	450 Fils	Portugal	80 Esc.
Belgium	40 B.Fr.	Kenya	Shs. 16.00	Qatar	6.50 Rials
Canada	C.$ 1.10	Kuwait	500 Fils	Rep. of Ireland	70 P.
Cyprus	600 Mils	Lebanon	£L4.50	Saudi Arabia	6.00 R.
Denmark	7.00 D.Kr.	Libya	L.Din. 0.35	Spain	100 Ptas.
Egypt	100 P.	Luxembourg	40 L.Fr.	Sweden	6.00 S.Kr.
Finland	6.00 F.M.	Madeira	90 Esc.	Switzerland	2.20 S.Fr.
France	5.50 F.	Malta	35 Cents	Tunisia	0.500 Din
Germany	2.30 D.M.	Morocco	5.50 Dh.	Turkey	T.£. 200.00
Great Britain	45 P.	Netherlands	2.50 Fl.	U.A.E.	6.50 Dirh
Greece	70 Dr.	Nigeria	170 K.	U.S. Mil. (Eur.)	$0.85
Iran	115 Rials			Yugoslavia	100 D.

No. 31,408 * ZURICH, SATURDAY-SUNDAY, FEBRUARY 11-12, 1984 ESTABLISHED 1887

Soviet Leader Andropov Is Dead at 69; No Official Word Is Given on Successor

U.S. Seeks Dialogue, Shultz Says

By Fred Farris
International Herald Tribune

WASHINGTON — President Ronald Reagan expressed personal condolences Friday to the Soviet leadership on the death of Yuri V. Andropov. Secretary of State George P. Shultz declared that the United States sought a "constructive dialogue" and would "work to build a more stable and more positive relationship" with the Kremlin.

Death Follows Year Of Kidney Dialysis

Compiled by Our Staff From Dispatches

MOSCOW — Yuri V. Andropov, fifth leader of the Soviet Union since the 1917 Bolshevik Revolution, died Thursday after 15 months in office, official Soviet media announced Friday. He was 69.

The radio and television broke the news to the country a day after the Communist Party general secretary and president died. A long illness had kept him out of the public for nearly six months.

An official medical report released by the Tass news agency said Mr. Andropov had undergone kid-

Brezhnev's funeral commission hours after his predecessor's death was announced. A day later, on Nov. 12, 1982, he was elected general secretary of the party.

Mr. Andropov, like Brezhnev, left no clear successor, but initial speculation focused on three members, including Mr. Chernenko.

The others are Grigori V. Romanov, 61, the hard-line former first

Yuri V. Andropov presided over repression while maintaining an image of sophistication. Page 3.

The Global Newspaper
Edited in Paris
Printed Simultaneously
in Paris, London, Zurich,
Hong Kong, Singapore,
The Hague and Marseille

WEATHER DATA APPEAR ON PAGE 22

INTERNATIONAL Herald Tribune

Published With The New York Times and The Washington Post

Algeria	6.00 Din.	Israel	I.S.750	Norway	7.00 N.Kr.
Austria	20 S.	Italy	1500 Lire	Oman	0.700 Rials
Bahrain	0.650 Din	Jordan	450 Fils	Portugal	90 Esc.
Belgium	45 B.Fr.	Kenya	Shs. 16.00	Qatar	6.50 Rials
Canada	C.$ 1.20	Kuwait	500 Fils	Rep. of Ireland	70 P.
Cyprus	C.£ 0.70	Lebanon	£L5.00	Saudi Arabia	6.00 R.
Denmark	8.00 D.Kr.	Libya	L.Din. 0.35	Spain	110 Ptas.
Egypt	100 P.	Luxembourg	45 L.Fr.	Sweden	7.00 S.Kr.
Finland	7.00 F.M.	Madeira	105 Esc	Switzerland	2.20 S.Fr
France	6.00 F.	Malta	35 Cents	Tunisia	0.500 Din
Germany	2.50 D.M.	Morocco	5.50 Dh.	Turkey	T.£. 400.00
Great Britain	50 P.	Netherlands	2.75 Fl.	U.A.E.	6.50 Dirh
Greece	80 Dr.	Nigeria	170 K.	U.S. Mil. (Eur.)	$0.85
Iran	115 Rials			Yugoslavia	170 D.

No. 31,743 * ZURICH, TUESDAY, MARCH 12, 1985 ESTABLISHED 1887

Chernenko Dies at 73 After 13 Months in Office; Gorbachov, 54, Succeeds Him as Soviet Leader

Party Choice Represents A Break With Old Guard

Compiled by Our Staff From Dispatches

MOSCOW — The choice of Mikhail S. Gorbachov as the new Soviet leader to replace Konstantin U. Chernenko indicates that the Kremlin has finally decided to break from the succession of old guard leaders who have ruled the country for decades and to turn over control to a new generation.

Mr. Gorbachov, who turned 54 on March 2, is the youngest member of the ruling Politburo. After a spectacular rise in the Communist Party hierarchy, he was elected Monday as the Communist Party's general secretary.

served during Mr. Gorbachov's trip to London in December: "This is a new style of Soviet leader — charming, with a very attractive wife, and absolutely straightforward."

Mr. Gorbachov impressed the British media and those Britons he met with his affable manner and willingness to engage in give-and-take discussion.

Prime Minister Margaret Thatcher said: "I like Mr. Gorbachov. We can do business together."

But she also noted that, while Mr. Gorbachov may be associated

Tass Reports President Was Ill 'a Long Time'

Compiled by Our Staff From Dispatches

MOSCOW — President Konstantin U. Chernenko, 73, who took power 13 months ago, died Sunday night. He was succeeded Monday as the leader of the Communist Party by Mikhail S. Gorbachov, Tass reported.

Mr. Chernenko died from complications of chronic emphysema, aggravated by a heart deficiency and cirrhosis of the liver, which the news agency said he had had "for a long time." He will be buried Wednesday in Red Square, the traditional resting place of Soviet leaders.

appointed chairman of Mr. Chernenko's funeral committee, a position that signaled he was the leading candidate for party secretary.

Tass announced the death of Mr. Chernenko almost 19 hours after he died, following a night of speculation prompted by programming changes on Soviet media, the playing of somber music on Moscow radio and the unexpected departure from the United States of a high-level Soviet delegation led by a Politburo member, Vladimir V. Shcherbitsky, as well as the departures of high-ranking delegations visiting West Germany and Yugo-

SATURDAY-SUNDAY, JUNE 15-16, 1985

Reuters

Some passengers freed from the hijacked TWA jet slid down the plane's chute and ran across the runway Friday in Beirut.

TWA Jet Hijacked to Beirut, Then Algiers

The Associated Press

ALGIERS — Hijackers demanding freedom for Shiite Moslems held by Israel seized an Athens-to-Rome TWA flight Friday with 153 persons on board and forced it to fly first to Beirut and then to Algiers. The pilot said that the hijackers had beaten passengers, threatening to kill them, and had threatened to blow up the plane.

In Beirut, the hijackers freed 17 women and two children. Two American women passengers who were freed in Beirut reported that shots were fired, and one said a man was wounded.

The hijackers, who were reportedly armed with grenades, machine guns and pistols, ordered the pilot to fly to Beirut, where the plane was refueled.

In a statement relayed by the Beirut control tower, a hijacker said that the "organization of the oppressed in the world" was responsible for the hijacking. He demanded that Lebanese Shiite Moslem guerrillas held by Israel be released to the Red Cross in Lebanon's southern port city of Sidon.

Israel is holding about 700 Lebanese, mostly Shiites, in prisons in northern Israel. Israel's Foreign Ministry said Friday that it had no comment on the hijackers' demands.

'Up to You,' Beirut Tower Tells Plane

The Associated Press

BEIRUT — *Following is a partial transcript of a conversation Friday in English between the cockpit of the hijacked Athens-to-Rome TWA plane and the Beirut International Airport control tower:*

Plane: Beirut control, TWA 847, request landing instructions.

Tower: I am unable to give you landing instructions due to the closure of the airport, sir. Advise the hijackers that. I think they understand English.

Plane: Well, yeah, they do. But they're insistent upon landing in Beirut.

Tower: You have not permission to land Beirut airport. It's up to you and to the hijackers to go on.

Plane: He has pulled a hand grenade pin and is ready to blow up the aircraft if he has to. We must, I repeat, we must land at Beirut. We must land at Beirut. No alternative.

Tower: OK. It's up to you to go on. It's up to you to go on. I can't give you permission because my responsibility doesn't give me permission for you to land. The airport is closed. Would you advise the hijacker to hold for 10 minutes? Can you hold for 10 minutes to find a solution for your problem?

Plane: TWA 847, that is a negative. We understand, we understand, but we must land at Beirut. The hijacker is insistent. Thank you.

Tower: Understand that you are landing without permission. Thank you.

Plane: Be advised we have no choice. We must land.

Tower: OK, sir. Land, land quietly. Land quietly. It's up to you, sir. As you know, the airport is not in my hands.

After two and a half hours in Beirut the plane took off for Algiers. The Algiers airport was closed to all other traffic, and the plane landed in Algiers.

[Algeria's press agency, monitored in Paris, said the hijackers had again threatened to execute hostages if their demands were not met, Reuters reported.]

[The Algerian press agency said the jet left Algiers late in the day for an unknown destination, Reuters reported. A few minutes before, an unknown number additional passengers were freed by the hijackers, the agency said.]

Initial reports said three hijackers were on the Boeing 727. But a Lebanese Transportation Ministry spokesman said that there were only two. A U.S. Embassy spokesman in Cyprus who talked to freed passengers said that they had only seen two.

In Beirut, an escape chute was lowered from the plane's front door. The freed passengers slid down to the tarmac and ran.

The hijacking was the third this week involving the Beirut airport.

One freed hostage, Irma Garza of Laredo, Texas, said the hijackers had shot a black man, apparently a passenger, in the neck. She said the man did not appear to be in serious condition, adding she did not know why he was shot.

The hijacker, speaking with a Lebanese accent, denounced what he called "American practices to control the Middle East."

■ Action by Reagan

President Ronald Reagan sent a personal message to President Chadli Benjedid asking him to allow the airliner to land at Algiers, according to sources quoted by Agence France-Presse in Washington.

MONDAY, JUNE 17, 1985

AP

Reuters

Reuters

Armed hijackers of the TWA Boeing 727 at the jet's rear stairs in Algiers, above, before it flew to Beirut on Sunday for the third time in 48 hours. At Beirut airport, top left, an official of the Amal militia, in turban, joins in negotiations with the hijackers from the control tower. A freed passenger, lower left, embraces a woman relative in Athens.

TUESDAY, OCTOBER 8, 1985

Italian Liner Carrying 440 Is Hijacked by Palestinians

Compiled by Our Staff From Dispatches

CAIRO — Palestinian guerrillas seized an Italian cruise ship carrying about 440 people Monday and threatened to blow it up if Israel did not free 50 Palestinian prisoners, Egyptian officials said.

The guerrillas boarded the 23,629-ton Achille Lauro after it left the Mediterranean port of Alexandria.

The ship was outside Egyptian territorial waters late Monday evening with about 100 passengers and 340 crew on board, according to a port official in Port Said, at the head of the Suez Canal.

Referring to radio contacts with the ship, he said the guerrillas belonged to a group called the Palestine Liberation Front.

United Press International quoted Egyptian security sources in Cairo as saying that the guerrillas were seven Palestinians who had boarded the ship as passengers.

In Rome, a statement from the office of Prime Minister Bettino Craxi said the people on board were mainly Italians. But no exact breakdown of nationalities was immediately available.

An Italian Foreign Ministry spokesman said first contacts with the Palestine Liberation Organization indicated that the organization had been unaware of the incident.

The hijacking came seven days after eight Israeli Air Force jets bombed Palestine Liberation Organization headquarters near Tunis, killing 72 persons.

Foreign Minister Giulio Andreotti was in contact with his Egyptian counterpart, Ahmed Esmat Abdel-Meguid, and with the Palestine Liberation Organization, the Italian spokesman added.

He said that the liner had left Genoa last week on a Mediterranean cruise.

The Italian news agency ANSA said that, after Alexandria, the vessel was due to call at Port Said on the Suez Canal, Limassol in Cyprus, and the Greek island of Rhodes.

It said the Achille Lauro had a crew of 350 and that 780 passengers had originally embarked on the cruise.

However, 676 passengers were not on board at the time of the hijacking because they had gone on an excursion to Cairo and were due to rejoin the vessel at Port Said.

Officials in Port Said said that the hijackers were led by a man named Omar and were threatening to blow up the ship if it were attacked.

Egyptian authorities said the ship headed into the Mediterranean to an unknown destination.

Israel said its attack on the PLO in Tunisia was in retaliation for the slaying a week earlier of three Israeli citizens on Yom Kippur, the most solemn Jewish holy day, on a yacht in Cyprus by three Palestinian gunmen. *(Reuters, UPI, AP)*

SATURDAY-SUNDAY, OCTOBER 12-13, 1985

U.S. Jets Force Hijackers to Go to Italy

By Christopher Dickey
Washington Post Service

CAIRO — "We were in the dining room ready for our dessert, when suddenly we heard gunshots and someone yelled, 'Get down on the floor'," said Viola Meskin, one of 12 Americans who were taken hostage in a two-day ordeal on the cruise ship Achille Lauro.

What followed was a violent odyssey that cost the life of a 69-year-old American invalid and often seemed to be leading nowhere.

The four Palestinian hijackers, according to American passengers at a news conference Friday, seemed uncertain about what move to make once they had started shooting.

"One minute they would try to be kind, the next minute they would do the cruelest things," Mrs. Meskin said.

At one point, Marilyn Klinghoffer, whose husband was killed, was hit with the butt of a gun when she failed to move as quickly as one of the hijackers demanded.

"The next minute," said Mrs. Meskin, "they would go get a cup if you wanted a drink of water and wash it out for you."

Mrs. Meskin said the hijackers also tried clumsily to indoctrinate the passengers. "You know, 'Reagan no good. Arafat good,' all this kind of talk," she said.

Most accounts indicated that the hijackers probably belonged to a splinter faction, the Palestine Liberation Front, rather than the Palestine Liberation Organization led by Yasser Arafat.

The Associated Press

The EgyptAir jetliner at the military airbase at Sigonella, Sicily, where it was forced to land Friday after being intercepted.

Passengers Describe Violence, Confusion

In the initial moments after bullets from the hijackers' automatic rifle hit the ceiling of the ship's dining room, Mrs. Meskin and her husband, Seymour, 71, a retired accountant from Metuchen, New Jersey, heard groans.

The hijackers had entered the dining room from the kitchen and had beaten two members of the ship's crew there, the couple said.

"They showed their power," Mrs. Meskin said. "They had hand grenades in their hands. They removed the pins and played with them."

The hijacking began Monday after the ship left the Egyptian port of Alexandria. More than 600 passengers had gone ashore for the day to visit Cairo and the pyramids and were scheduled to rejoin the vessel at Port Said.

The passengers who remained aboard but were absent at lunch were called to the dining room by the gunmen.

"We were together, I think 85 passengers," said a Belgian woman. She said the hijackers singled out the 12 Americans and the British passengers, but seemed most intent on finding Israelis.

Anna Hoerendner of Austria heard the shots at the beginning of the hijacking and ran into a cabin. She said she hid under the bed in the cabin or in the bathroom for the next 62 hours.

Hijackers herded the passengers from the dining room to an entertainment room on an upper deck and ordered them to stay there. The hostages slept intermittently on the chairs or on the floor.

Diplomats who boarded the ship Thursday said the walls of both the dining room and the show room were riddled with bullet holes, apparently from gunfire that the terrorists used to intimidate the passengers.

Reagan Says Plane Interception Is Intended to Warn Terrorists

Compiled by Our Staff From Dispatches

CATANIA, Sicily — Four U.S. Navy fighter jets intercepted an Egyptian airliner carrying the four Palestinian hijackers of an Italian liner early Friday and forced it to land in Sicily.

Italian police took the hijackers into custody, officials said. They were later charged with premeditated murder, kidnapping, hijacking of a ship and possession of arms and explosives.

In Washington, President Ronald Reagan said at a White House news conference that the operation carried the message to terrorists everywhere: "You can run but you can't hide."

U.S. officials said the action had been carried out on the president's personal orders.

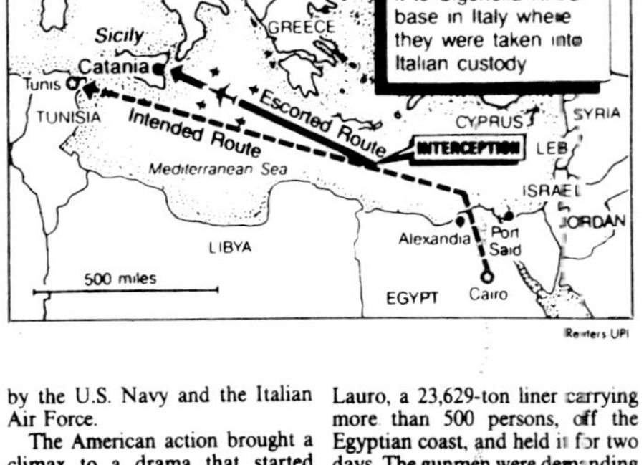

Reuters UPI

The four U.S. Navy F-14 Tomcats intercepted the EgyptAir Boeing 737 near the Greek island of Crete after it had been refused permission to land in Tunisia and Greece. The Boeing's captain agreed to follow the U.S. jets to the base of Sigonella, which is shared by the U.S. Navy and the Italian Air Force.

The American action brought a climax to a drama that started Monday when four Palestinian gunmen commandeered the Achille Lauro, a 23,629-ton liner carrying more than 500 persons, off the Egyptian coast, and held it for two days. The gunmen were demanding the release of 50 Palestinian prisoners in Israeli jails.

WEDNESDAY, JANUARY 29, 1986

U.S. Space Shuttle Explodes on Takeoff

Reuters/UPI

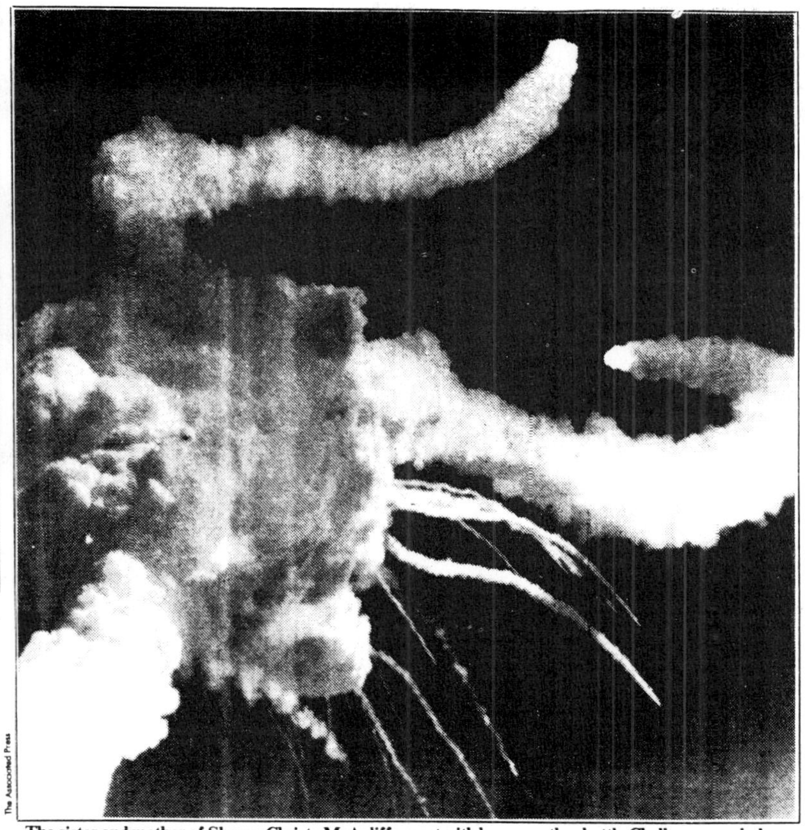

The Associated Press

The sister and mother of Sharon Christa McAuliffe react with horror as the shuttle Challenger explodes.

All 7 in Crew Are Feared Killed; Craft Disintegrates 10 Miles Up

By Howard Benedict
The Associated Press

CAPE CANAVERAL, Florida — The U.S. space shuttle Challenger exploded into a gigantic fireball 75 seconds after liftoff Tuesday, apparently killing all seven crew members aboard.

Fragments of the $1.2-billion spacecraft, one of four in NASA's shuttle fleet, fell into the Atlantic Ocean 18 miles (29 kilometers) southeast of the Kennedy Space Center launch pad.

More than two hours after the accident, officials said no announcement on the fate of the crew would be made until all search-and-rescue efforts had been exhausted. But it seemed virtually impossible that anyone could survive such an explosion.

No American astronaut ever had been killed in flight.

The cause of the accident was not immediately known.

A slow-motion replay seemed to show the initial explosion occurred in one of the ship's two rocket boosters and then the shuttle burst into a fireball above the Atlantic.

The explosion followed an apparently flawless launch, delayed for two hours as officials analyzed the danger from icicles that formed in the morning along the shuttle's new launch pad.

"There were no signs of abnormalities on the screens" as flight controllers monitored Challenger's liftoff and ascent, a source said. The source, at the Johnson Space Center in Houston, said the explosion occurred "unexpectedly and with absolutely no warning."

Mission control reported that there had been no indication of any problem with the three shuttle engines, its twin solid boosters or any other system.

The gleaming ship had risen spectacularly off the launch pad at 11:38 A.M., trailing a 700-foot (212-meter) geyser of fire when it erupted in a huge fireball and shot out of control.

The explosion occurred as Challenger was 10.35 miles high and 8 miles downrange from Cape Canaveral, speeding toward orbit at 1,977 miles per hour.

The shocking spectacle was witnessed by family and friends of the astronauts who had gathered at Cape Canaveral and by millions more around the United States and in Europe who viewed the launch on television.

Reuters-UPI

Sharon Christa McAuliffe as she went to board the spacecraft on Tuesday.

May 16, 1986

Lartigue: A Sunlit World

MARY BLUME

PARIS — An enchanting exhibition of stereoscopic photographs by Jacques-Henri Lartigue, taken from 1902 to 1928, has just opened at the Grand Palais, the repository of Lartigue's gift to the nation of 100,000 prints and 130 photograph albums. The pictures, displayed for the first time in a way that gives the proper three-dimensional effect, were taken mostly with a Spido-Gaumont camera given to Lartigue when he was 8 years old.

Now he is 92 and he sits politely at the opening, his white hair brushed forward as it was when he was a boy, his eyes as always wide with wonder, his legs coltish under lightweight cotton trousers. Lartigue and his wife, Florette, on a cold and rainy Paris day, are dressed in sunny pastels as if they were back home on the Côte d'Azur. They carry their own world with them, a world at once so ordered and enchanted that everyone feels at home with them. Strange American photographers, when they meet Lartigue, embrace him as if they had known him forever.

His photographs show a sunlit world of affection and play and discovery and comic spills where "the sun comes into the library again, the trees wave freshly on the lawn, tiny cousins collide and jump," as E.M. Forster wrote in "Marianne Thornton." They are happy memories of days we never knew and people smile when they look at the pictures and feel nostalgic. Lartigue himself is not the slightest bit nostalgic.

"Not at all, not at all," he says. He likes to repeat for emphasis. "What interests me is this moment, you must find in every day things that interest you. There is always something good."

He may be as fresh as a boy but he is not naive: he describes himself as a marathon runner who chases butterflies. To find the good one must have known its opposite — "if black did not exist there would be no white" — and to have the endurance always to find pleasure suggests discipline and taste. "It is a question of not being lazy and sometimes it is difficult." He exercises every morning, even this past winter when he was quite ill and even when he was young and came home at 6 A.M. from a night of dancing.

The Lartigues live in Opio, in the hills above the Riviera, where Florette Lartigue was born and where Lartigue spent many of the years between the wars as a fashionable portraitist and assistant to film directors: handsome, a tennis champion, a lover of fast cars and beautiful women, wearing a gardenia in the lapel of his dinner jacket so its fragrance would mingle with the perfume of his dancing partner. He was well-liked and always invited but never rich because he didn't make portraits unless it amused him.

"Mademoiselle X asks me to do her portrait (not ugly enough for me to refuse, not pretty enough for me even to remember her name)," he writes in "L'Oeil de la Memoire," his diary from the years 1932-1985 just published in Paris by Editions Carrère-Michel Lafon. When he was invited to do the official photograph of President Valéry Giscard d'Estaing, he refused because the idea didn't amuse him. Then he was persuaded to go see the president.

"He is very nice, very witty, so I said yes. Because he pleased me." His photograph of the smiling president in front of a fluttering tricolor was an engaging departure from the traditional photograph of the solemn chief of state backed by a wall of leather-bound books.

Lartigue had taken pictures all his life and pasted them in albums just as he has kept a diary. But it was not until relatively recently — in the 1960s — that his pictures were exhibited and so he remains, in the deepest sense an amateur. "Happily, I am completely amateur, I do nothing but what amuses me." Right now it amuses him to photograph gardens. He thinks he was born happy; he knows he has never been old.

Above, Lartigue's friend Sala, who died in 1929.

"I never have been and hope I never shall be. A lot of people celebrated my 90th birthday, even in Germany and England. It was all very nice, but it was they who knew I was 90. I wasn't aware of it."

The little boy who dashed to the Bois de Boulogne after school to take pictures of fashionable ladies was, he says, "just a little boy, not talkative at all. I was very sensitive, too sensitive, and I liked being alone but I was not alone because there were always people around. I don't think I've changed all that much since I was little."

When he was little, he says, he would cry in front of the windows of toy stores — not from envy but because the profusion was too great for him to appreciate and absorb. Because the only way to keep alive his sense of wonder is to be selective, his friends have on occasion thought him superficial and indifferent, while perhaps he was simply wise. In his journal, noting the queasy hysteria of the phony war period in 1940, he writes, "I am considered an ostrich to keep my joie de vivre instead of killing it in advance like everyone else."

The Global Newspaper
Edited in Paris
Printed Simultaneously
in Paris, London, Zurich,
Hong Kong, Singapore,
The Hague and Marseille

WEATHER DATA APPEAR ON PAGE 14

INTERNATIONAL
Herald Tribune
Published With The New York Times and The Washington Post

No. 32,041 09/86 * ZURICH, WEDNESDAY, FEBRUARY 26, 1986 ESTABLISHED 1887

Marcos Quits; U.S. Recognizes Aquino

The Associated Press

Corazon Aquino is sworn in; at right, Aurora Aquino, mother of her assassinated husband.

Filipinos Rejoice As Ruling Family Flees From Palace

By Michael Richardson
International Herald Tribune

MANILA — Ferdinand E. Marcos, who ruled the Philippines for 20 years, was forced out of office Tuesday night, leaving Corazon C. Aquino as the country's unchallenged president.

The United States, which diplomats said had put intense pressure on Mr. Marcos to resign, immediately recognized the government formed earlier in the day by Mrs. Aquino, who defiantly took an oath of office even before Mr. Marcos agreed to step down.

As the news of Mr. Marcos's departure spread, tens of thousands of Filipinos poured into the streets of Manila to celebrate.

They danced and sang, burned tires, set off firecrackers, honked horns and held aloft placards of Mrs. Aquino.

The Roman Catholic archbishop of Manila, Cardinal Jaime L. Sin, said in a statement, "Our long journey from the night is over and we Filipinos see a new day dawning."

U.S. officials said that Mr. Marcos was evacuated by helicopter from his palace with his wife, Imelda, other family members and close associates, including his armed forces chief of staff, General Fabian C. Ver.

They said he was taken to Clark Air Base north of Manila and from there would be flown to exile abroad. It was not clear if he had decided on a final destination.

[The White House said that Mr. Marcos would rest at the base Tuesday night, Reuters reported from Washington.

["He is in bed at Clark base and has retired for the evening," said Larry Speakes, the White House spokesman. Mr. Speakes said he did not know where Mr. Marcos would go, but he reaffirmed Washington's offer of safe haven in the United States.

[A senior Reagan administration source said that Mr. Marcos could remain at the base for a day or more.]

A television and radio station controlled by the Aquino administration said the negotiations that paved the way for the departure of the Marcoses and General Ver were handled by Juan Ponce Enrile, a former close colleague and defense minister of Mr. Marcos.

"We will provide a ring of protection around him and his family," Mr. Enrile had said in a radio interview. "We have no intention to harm him."

The defection last Saturday of Mr. Enrile and the vice chief of staff of the armed forces, Lieutenant General Fidel V. Ramos, was one of the blows that caused the collapse of the Marcos regime.

On Tuesday morning, at about the same time Mrs. Aquino was being sworn in by Claudio Teehankee, a Supreme Court justice, Mr. Marcos also took his oath of office.

In his acceptance speech, he gave no hint that he would quit. He accused his opponents of seeking, perhaps by force and intimidation, to gain power that they had failed to win in what he said was a fair election.

"This we will not allow," he said.

During the day, at least 10 persons were reported killed as rival soldiers fought in Manila's Makati financial district and around a

(Continued on Page 5, Col. 1)

The Associated Press

Mr. Marcos, with his wife, Imelda, spoke from the palace after his inauguration Tuesday.

Aquino: After Reluctance, Resolve

Husband's Murder Transformed 'Housewife' Into a Symbol

The Associated Press

MANILA — Corazon C. Aquino began her political career as a reluctant candidate, but became a determined campaigner who rallied millions of her countrymen behind a drive to end Ferdinand E. Marcos's 20 years as president.

To the surprise of many Filipinos and foreigners, the 53-year-old woman managed to channel widespread dissatisfaction with Mr. Marcos into a powerful stream of opposition that swept him from power.

She became well known only after the assassination in 1983 of her husband, Benigno S. Aquino Jr., which started the chain of events that brought down Mr. Marcos.

Mrs. Aquino is a daughter of the wealthy Cojuangco family of Tarlac province, which has sugar plantations.

Her first cousin, Eduardo Cojuangco, is a close business associate of Mr. Marcos and is believed to be one of the wealthiest men in the Philippines, controlling a coconut monopoly granted him under the Marcos administration.

After her husband was assassinated, Mrs. Aquino waged a emotionally charged campaign in the Feb. 7 presidental election and made a strong showing in balloting that was tainted by fraud, according to her supporters and to independent election observers.

She campaigned throughout the country, always smiling and always wearing yellow. The color symbolizes the yellow-ribbon homecoming that was planned for her husband when he returned from self-exile in the United States, only to be assassinated at Manila airport.

When the Marcos-controlled National Assembly completed the count Feb. 15 and announced that he had won, Mrs. Aquino refused to accept that verdict and pledged a campaign to bring down Mr. Marcos through boycotts and demonstrations.

Two military leaders of the Marcos establishment announced Saturday that they had broken with the president. They demanded that he resign and allow Mrs. Aquino to lead the nation.

By Monday, the rebels had taken over a government television station and proclaimed a provisional government headed by Mrs. Aquino. Crowds in the streets chanted her nickname, "Cory, Cory!"

Her only training in politics came from her family and through her role as the wife of a man who was considered Mr. Marcos's main political rival.

Mrs. Aquino's campaign biography listed no previous accomplishments or jobs other than that of a housewife and mother of five.

When martial law was decreed in 1972, Mr. Aquino was jailed for eight years. Mrs. Aquino has described those years as among the most traumatic in her life.

She was her husband's "eyes, ears and voice in the stifling environment of martial law," according to a biography provided by her campaign staff.

"Some people tell me I did not have any formal education in politics," she said in an interview. "But I was living with one of the best teachers in politics."

In addition, a grandfather, her father and brother were congressmen. Her other grandfather and an uncle were senators, and another uncle is in the National Assembly.

Benigno Aquino was allowed to travel to the United States for heart surgery in 1980 and spent the next three years in voluntary exile.

He decided to return to rally the opposition, and was assassinated Aug. 21, 1983, as he left the plane.

An investigation pointed to a

(Continued on Page 5, Col. 4)

Helicopters Signaled the End of an Era

By Michael Richardson
International Herald Tribune

MANILA — An eerie silence settled around the Malacanang presidential palace late Tuesday after two U.S. helicopters lifted off and vanished into darkness.

About 10 minutes later, two more helicopters clattered away.

For Josephine Antonio, 35, a government teacher who lives nearby, it was exhilarating to watch the departure into exile of Ferdinand E. Marcos, his once-powerful wife, Imelda; members of their family; the former chief of staff of the armed forces, General Fabian C. Ver, and associates.

As she stood on the road outside the palace with groups of neighbors and several journalists, she smiled and said:

"We are free again after 20 years of Marcos's rule. Most people are not sad that he has gone."

Mrs. Antonio and her husband, Jaime, realized that something unusual was happening about 8:30 P.M. Tuesday when they saw troops removing the barbed wire barricades that lined the street.

They also saw truckloads of troops and several tanks coming out of the palace grounds and driving away. In several of the trucks uniformed soldiers waved and gave peace signs.

The first two helicopters took off at 9 P.M. after Mr. Marcos, evidently realizing that he had lost his battle to stay in power, agreed in secret negotiations to yield the presidency to Corazon C. Aquino.

Later in the evening, thousands of people were reported to have invaded the palace, ransacking offices and tearing down pictures of Mr. Marcos.

'We have been living in fear of civil war. Now we can live in peace. We do not want to fight Filipino against Filipino.'

— First Lieutenant Jun Lariosa

Witnesses said that about 5,000 people swept through the ornate wrought-iron gates, pushed aside some 20 guards and forced their way into an administrative area.

The guards, marines who identified themselves as members of a reform movement within the armed forces, offered no resistance and made no attempt to stop the crowd, the witnesses said.

First Lieutenant Jun Lariosa of the Philippine Army said he was pleased that one side had surrendered in the bitter controversy over the Feb. 7 presidential election.

"We have been living in fear of civil war," he said. "Now we can live in peace. We do not want to fight Filipino against Filipino."

Crispin Valdeconto, the owner of a woodcarving business, said

(Continued on Page 5, Col. 4)

The Associated Press

After Mr. Marcos left, one of his supporters was beaten by groups who invaded the palace.

2d U.S. Cruise Missile Crashes in Canada Test

COLD LAKE, Alberta (AP) — An unarmed U.S. cruise missile crashed into the Beaufort Sea on Tuesday, moments after it was launched from a U.S. Air Force B-52 bomber for the sixth test of the low-flying missile over northwestern Canada.

U.S. to Continue Aid, Offers Haven to Marcos

By David Hoffman
Washington Post Service

WASHINGTON — The United States recognized the government of Corazon C. Aquino on Tuesday and promised to continue economic and military assistance to the Philippines.

Secretary of State George P. Shultz, in an announcement at the White House, also praised the decision of Ferdinand E. Marcos to step down peacefully.

Mr. Shultz offered "safe haven" to Mr. Marcos and his family and close associates, including the former armed forces chief of staff, General Fabian C. Ver.

Mr. Shultz said the "main fact" in the departure of Mr. Marcos was not pressure from the United States, "but what the Filipino people had to say. And it was evident in the streets of Manila."

"The new government has been produced by one of the most stirring and courageous examples of the democratic process in modern history," Mr. Shultz said.

"The United States stands ready as always to cooperate and assist the Philippines as the government of President Aquino engages the problems of economic development and national security," he said.

Mr. Shultz said the United States would continue to provide economic and military assistance to the Philippines, and "we are prepared to confer with the new government and ministers as they emerge."

Mr. Marcos was brought by a U.S. helicopter from his presidential palace to Clark Air Base, a U.S. military installation about 60 miles (97 kilometers) north of Manila.

He reportedly planned to spend the night there before traveling to his home province of Luzon. His final destination remained unclear late Tuesday.

Mr. Shultz called Mr. Marcos "a staunch friend of the United States" and said "we are gratified that his departure from office has come peacefully."

Mr. Shultz said the United States wants to see Mr. Marcos "continue on in dignity and honor, and we will do everything we can to see that that comes about."

Asked whether the United States would protect Mr. Marcos if his extradition were requested by the new Philippine government, Mr. Shultz replied that Mr. Marcos had been offered safe haven, and "that should be respected."

He also suggested that such an extradition request may not be forthcoming, because Mrs. Aquino has been calling for reconciliation in the Philippines, and "I think out of this comes this sense of the importance of nonviolence and perhaps compassion."

[A congressional source in Washington told The Associated Press that the United States had been "negotiating like mad" both with Mr. Marcos and the opposition for several days before his resignation.

["One of the main stumbling blocks was Imelda," the source said, referring to Mrs. Marcos. "Apparently, she wanted to stay and hoped to succeed him eventually."]

Iran Starts Raid in North; Iraq Sees Victory in South

Reuters

MANAMA, Bahrain — Iran said Tuesday that it had launched a successful new offensive against Iraqi forces on the northern front. Iraq, meanwhile, predicted victory on the Faw peninsula in the south.

Iran's official news agency said Iranian troops had taken strategic heights in the Kurdish mountains of northern Iraq, in an overnight attack northeast of the Kurdish provincial capital of Sulaymaniyah. Sulaymaniyah is in Iraq, about 170 miles (270 kilometers) northeast of Baghdad.

Iran said its forces had captured 25 Kurdish villages in the attack, which Prime Minister Mir Hussein Moussavi said was part of Iran's fight to lower Gulf Arab states' oil production and to raise world prices.

Iraq's official Baghdad Radio, meanwhile, said that Iran's defenses around the southern peninsula of Faw were collapsing. It made no mention of any fighting in the north.

The radio said the central column of a three-pronged Iraqi counterattack was advancing on Faw, which is at the mouth of the Shatt-al-Arab waterway. Iran overran Faw at the beginning of its southern offensive, which was begun Feb. 9.

In Tehran, Mr. Moussavi told war volunteers that the latest attack was aimed at threatening Iraq's northern oil fields and at countering the "oil conspiracy," Iran's phrase for high production by Gulf Arab states. Iran says intentional

(Continued on Page 2, Col. 1)

Gorbachev Rejects Plan By U.S. to Reduce Arms

By Andrew Rosenthal
The Associated Press

MOSCOW — Mikhail S. Gorbachev, the Soviet leader, on Tuesday rejected President Ronald Reagan's latest arms-control proposals and said that the timing of the two men's next summit meeting hinged on an "understanding" about banning nuclear tests or eliminating medium-range missiles in Europe.

Convening the 27th Communist Party Congress, Mr. Gorbachev also criticized the stagnation and corruption that marked the rule of Leonid I. Brezhnev, and he outlined plans to revive the economy.

On arms control, the Soviet leader sharply criticized Mr. Reagan's stand on space weapons, his rejection of a freeze in British and French nuclear arsenals and his call for cuts in the Soviet Union's Asian nuclear forces.

Mr. Reagan outlined those points last weekend in a letter to Mr. Gorbachev that responded to Soviet proposals made in January.

"It is hard to detect in the letter we have just received any serious preparedness . . . to get down to the business of eliminating the nuclear threat," Mr. Gorbachev said.

He said that his next meeting with Mr. Reagan, scheduled to be held in the United States this year under an agreement reached in Geneva last November, "ought to produce practical results in key areas of limiting and reducing armaments."

"There are at least two matters on which an understanding could be reached: the cessation of nuclear tests and the abolition of U.S. and Soviet intermediate-range missiles" in Europe, he said.

"If there is readiness to seek agreement, the question of the time of the meeting would be resolved of itself. We will accept any suggestion on this count," Mr. Gorbachev

(Continued on Page 5, Col. 2)

Reuters

Mr. Gorbachev addressing the party congress Tuesday.

WEDNESDAY, APRIL 30, 1986

Soviet Asks Help in 'Disaster'; A Nuclear Meltdown Is Feared

Poland Takes Steps to Fight Radiation

By Robert Gillette
Los Angeles Times Service

WARSAW — The Polish government, acknowledging that fallout from a damaged Soviet nuclear reactor poses a potential hazard to human health, said Tuesday that it would issue medication to children in affected areas to protect against radioactive iodine.

In an official statement read on the evening television news, the government said it was also temporarily restricting the sale of milk to reduce the possible intake of iodine, a hazardous but short-lived component of fission wastes.

The statement warned of the "absolute necessity" of washing all fresh vegetables carefully to remove radioactive particles.

The government spokesman, Jerzy Urban, said these precautionary steps followed daylong deliberations by a high-level government commission.

The government said its commission was in "constant and direct contact" with Soviet authorities, and was also consulting with the International Atomic Energy Agency in Vienna and with Scandinavian countries.

Wind-borne fallout from the Chernobyl reactor was first detected in a broad arc across Denmark, Sweden, Norway and Finland.

Radiation measurements made by the Polish Air Force and ground units on Tuesday showed a rising level of radioactive iodine as of 3 P.M., to levels that "could be hazardous if maintained for a longer period of time," the government statement said.

The Associated Press

Workers in a reactor room at the Chernobyl nuclear power plant in 1982.

Population Near Kiev Is Evacuated

Compiled by Our Staff From Dispatches

MOSCOW — The Soviet Union, admitting that a "disaster" had occurred at its Chernobyl nuclear power plant in the Ukraine north of Kiev, said that the population of the area had been evacuated. The government also appealed to the West for help in containing a fire at the site.

The official statement said that two persons had died.

West German and Swedish officials said it appeared that the fire, evidently in connection with a partial or total reactor core meltdown continued out of control. West German officials said that the accident was the world's worst commercial nuclear disaster.

In Washington, Mikhail Timofeev, the Soviet deputy minister of civil aviation, said that the number of injured "are in the tens, tens, tens injured in one way or another."

The official was in the United States to mark the resumption of commercial air service to the Soviet Union. He quoted "official sources" for his information and added, "The rumors are a little exaggerated. It's not a catastrophe but it is an accident."

A Kiev resident with contacts in rescue organizations who was reached by telephone by United Press International said that the death toll may have reached 2,000. Foreign journalists were barred from the region and the report could not be confirmed.

Nuclear Accidents: Where and Why

New York Times Service

NEW YORK — These incidents were among the significant accidents in the history of nucelar power:

Oct. 7, 1957 — A fire in the Windscale plutonium production reactor north of Liverpool, England, spread radioactive material throughout the countryside. In 1983, the British government said 39 people had probably died of cancer as a result.

1957 — A chemical explosion in Kasli, U.S.S.R., in tanks containing nuclear waste from a weapons program spread radioactive material over an area of about 20 square miles (about 50 square kilometers) in the Urals, forcing a major evacuation. No casualty figures were ever released.

Jan. 3, 1961 — An experimental reactor went out of control at a U.S. installation in Idaho Falls, killing three technicians, one of them impaled by a reactor control rod. Some investigators later suggested the accident was sabotage resulting from a lover's triangle.

Oct. 5, 1966 — The core of the Enrico Fermi experimental breeder reactor near Detroit partly melted when a sodium cooling system malfunctioned. No injuries occurred.

Jan. 21, 1969 — A coolant malfunction from an experimental underground reactor at Lucens Vad, Switzerland, resulted in the release of a large amount of radiation into a cavern, which was then sealed. There were no injuries.

Oct. 17, 1969 — A fuel-loading error caused a partial meltdown at a gas-cooled power reactor in Saint-Laurent, France. No injuries and a minuscule amount of radioactive material was released to the outside.

1974 — A steam-line explosion was reported in a breeder plant at Shevchenko, U.S.S.R., on the northeast shore of the Caspian Sea. Apparently no radioactive material was released.

March 22, 1975 — A technician checking for air leaks with a lighted candle caused a $100-million fire at the Browns Ferry reactor in Decatur, Alabama. The fire burned out electrical controls, lowering the cooling water to dangerous levels. No radioactive material was released.

March 28, 1979 — A series of human and equipment failures caused a significant meltdown of nuclear fuel at Three Mile Island outside Harrisburg, Pennsylvania. Official studies have said the increased health risks were minuscule. The reactor is still being decontaminated.

Aug. 7, 1979 — A release of highly enriched uranium from a top-secret nuclear fuel plant near Erwin, Tennessee, contaminated about 1,000 people with up to five times as much radiation as they would normally receive in a year.

April 25, 1981 — Officials said as many as 45 workers had been exposed to radioactivity during previous repairs of a problem-ridden plant at Tsuruga, Japan.

Sept. 23, 1983 — An accident attributed to human error at the RA-2 research reactor in Constituyentes, near Buenos Aires, claimed the life of a technician.

Jan. 6, 1986 — An overfilled cylinder of nuclear material burst after being improperly heated at a Kerr-McGee plant at Gore, Oklahoma. One worker died and 100 were injured.

MONDAY, MAY 12, 1986

11 in EC to Ban Produce From Eastern Europe

The Associated Press

BRUSSELS — All European Community countries except Italy will ban imports of fresh food from Eastern Europe because of the Chernobyl nuclear disaster, a spokesman for the EC's executive body announced Sunday.

The European Commission, fearing imports contaminated by radioactivity, had proposed the ban Wednesday.

An agreement on the ban by all 12 EC member nations was erroneously announced Saturday night by the Dutch ambassador to the EC.

But Italy informed its EC partners later that it had been misunderstood and had not agreed to the proposal, according to a spokesman for the European Commission, Michael Berendt.

Pending a unanimous agreement, Italy's 11 partners decided to individually stop importing food from seven East European countries: Bulgaria, Czechoslovakia, Hungary, Poland, Romania, the Soviet Union and Yugoslavia.

The countries are located roughly within a 620-mile (1,000-kilometer) radius of Chernobyl. The ban, which will last until May 31 in its first stage, applies to meat, cattle, pigs, poultry, game, freshwater fish, milk products, fruits, vegetables and other fresh products.

Wolfgang Rattay/Reuters

Women in Munich celebrated Mother's Day on Sunday by laying flowers at a rally to denounce West Germany's nuclear power policy after the Chernobyl disaster.

2 Black Leaders Hold Emotional Meeting

Coretta Scott King, right, the widow of Martin Luther King Jr., fought back tears at a meeting on Thursday with Winnie Mandela, the South African anti-apartheid leader, in Soweto. Page 2.

Wendy Schwegmann/Reuters

Mrs. Mandela Holds Emotional Meeting in Soweto With Mrs. King

By Serge Schmemann
New York Times Service

SOWETO, South Africa — On the last day of a trip to South Africa marked by political controversy, the widow of the Reverend Martin Luther King Jr. held an emotional one-hour meeting Thursday with Winnie Mandela, one of the most prominent black campaigners against apartheid.

Coretta Scott King, emerging from Mrs. Mandela's house in the black township of Soweto, fought back tears as she proclaimed the meeting "one of the greatest and most meaningful moments of my life."

"Mrs. Mandela is a great symbol of strength and courage and dedication for women and children and people everywhere," Mrs. King declared as Mrs. Mandela raised her fist in a salute to a cluster of black youths peering through the fence of her small yard.

Mrs. King added, "God has blessed us and I feel it is a great blessing to finally meet Winnie and to touch her."

The two black women embraced and Mrs. Mandela, the wife of Nelson Mandela, the imprisoned leader of the African National Congress, reciprocated the tributes.

Mrs. King, she said, "is a symbol of the sacrifices of our children in 1976," adding: "She is a symbol of what my people continue sacrificing for."

Mrs. Mandela's home stands within sight of the spot where police opened fire on marching blacks youths in June 1976, touching off a wave of violence that made Soweto a rallying cry for the black resistance in South Africa.

Soweto was the the scene of more turmoil earlier this month.

In South Africa, Censors Add Confusion to Rules

Reuters

JOHANNESBURG — Reporters struggled with new South African censorship regulations Friday amid confusion, delays and paradoxical rulings by the government.

Local newspapers tried to explain the extent of the new restrictions without violating them.

The mass-circulation Johannesburg Star stated in bold type across the top of its front page: "This newspaper may be censored. We are not permitted to say where, how or to what extent."

On Thursday, Pretoria imposed severe restrictions on coverage of its racial conflict and anti-government activity. The regulations also prohibit the display of bla[illegible] spaces to indicate where deletions have been made by censors.

After nearly two hours of arguing with censors Thursday night, Reuters was informed it could not quote from local editorials criticizing the regulations. The same remarks had been published throughout the world earlier Thursday.

The Star said that in complying with censorship provisions, it telexed 10 articles to the censors in Pretoria. The newspaper said that censors refused to allow the publication of six of the reports and failed to reply about the other four.

Pretoria Tightens Its Rule

Botha Cites Plan For Violence; 2 Swiss Are Held

By Alan Cowell
New York Times Service

JOHANNESBURG — The South African police said Friday that they had arrested a number of opponents of the government following Thursday's tightening of emergency rule. President Pieter W. Botha said the steps were designed to head off an impending upsurge of violence.

New South Africa restrictions prohibit journalists from transmitting dispatches on security actions, protests, detentions or "subversive statements" without clearance by censors.

The crackdown was reported to have included a cross-border raid into Swaziland that, in an unprecedented manner, led to the abduction and subsequent detention in South Africa of two Swiss nationals sympathetic to the government's black foes.

Mr. Botha said in a televised speech, "Our security forces have over the past 24 hours been compelled to conduct certain preventative security measures." He said the measures were aimed at the outlawed South African Communist Party and the African National Congress, which, he said, were "involved in the planning, coordination and execution of revolutionary violence."

Strict censorship imposed under the newest emergency regulations Thursday forbade reporters from publishing some details of the crackdown. But among those detained Friday were Zwelakhe Sisulu, editor of the church-funded New Nation newspaper, and several leaders of a campaign against white educational policy.

Mr. Sisulu, the son of the jailed nationalist Walter Sisulu, is a former Nieman Fellow at Harvard College. He was detained — and subsequently freed — earlier during South Africa's current emergency, proclaimed June 12.

There were unconfirmed reports, too, of night police raids on the homes of whites suspected of opposing the government.

The authorities announced the detention of two unidentified Swiss nationals on suspicion of working for the ANC.

Earlier, Swazi authorities said the two Swiss had been abducted from their home by men in a car with South African registration plates. The Swiss Foreign Ministry in Bern said those abducted in Swaziland were the same people as those detained in South Africa.

South Africans Celebrate — but Apart

By Alan Cowell
New York Times Service

JOHANNESBURG — In moods that varied from the subdued to the boisterous, South Africans of different races celebrated a day of contradictory anniversaries Tuesday, marking the supremacy of white power for some and, for others, the beginnings of violent attempts to overthrow it.

In Soweto, Johannesburg's sprawling black satellite, some residents lit candles in response to a call for a Christmas campaign opposed to emergency rule. In Cape Province, Andries Treurnicht, leader of a breakaway party to the right of the government, told followers at a public meeting that the anniversary "signified the right of the Afrikaners to freedom and self-determination and to defend these by means of an armed struggle if necessary."

Dec. 16 is a day filled with conflicting symbols for black and white. On that day in 1838, Afrikaner pioneers led by Andries Pretorius, trekking inland, defeated a Zulu army under Dingane at the Battle of Blood River in Natal Province after making a covenant with God that, should victory be theirs, they would hold the day holy. It has come to be viewed as a turning point in the history of the 2.8 million Afrikaners.

Also on Dec. 16, 25 years ago, black nationalist insurgents struck the first blows of a guerrilla campaign that persists to this day.

On Dec. 16, 1961, sabotage teams of the African National Congress and its now-imprisoned leader, Nelson Mandela, bombed three government offices in the Johannesburg area. It was the start of a series of more than 200 explosions over the subsequent 18 months.

While 1,000 Afrikaners gathered at their holiest shrine — the Voortrekker monument — to celebrate the Day of the Vow, however, a black campaign set to begin at the same time seemed subdued in tone, reflecting the authorities' increased readiness to silence black protest.

The main guerrilla group, the Soviet-armed African National Congress and its military wing, is outlawed, and its headquarters is in Lusaka, Zambia.

Anti-apartheid groups had urged that church bells be rung at dawn Tuesday to mark the start of a separate, 10-day "Christmas against the emergency" campaign.

Weighted under new emergency regulations outlawing virtually all residual form of black protest, however, many segregated, black townships seemed subdued. With the exception of militant areas in Soweto and Port Elizabeth, few bells rang.

South Africa has severely restricted the reporting of unrest or dissent. Correspondents may be fined or imprisoned for failing to submit to censors articles that contravene regulations.

Some reports from priests in Soweto who declined to be identified said some churches were dissuaded from ringing their bells.

Since September 1984, about 2,300 people, most of them black, have died in political violence.

Only 4,000 Persons Detained, Pretoria Says

By William Claiborne
Washington Post Service

JOHANNESBURG — The South African government said Thursday that fewer than 4,000 persons were detained in the last four months of 1986 under the country's state of emergency.

The figure represents only a fraction of the total that anti-apartheid monitoring groups say have been imprisoned without charges since emergency rule was imposed in June.

Adriaan Vlok, the minister of law and order, told Parliament that the total number held since June does not approach estimates of more than 20,000 given by opposition groups, even when taking into account detainees held for less than 30 days and not included on the list.

South Africa has severely restricted the reporting of unrest or dissent. Correspondents may be fined or imprisoned for failing to submit to censors articles that contravene regulations.

Wide discrepancies between official government figures of detainees and those issued by anti-apartheid groups have long been commonplace, but Mr. Vlok's disclosure raised serious questions about the reliability of the reporting methods either of the government or the independent monitoring groups.

There was confusion about the total numbers detained since, in September, the government gave Parliament a list of more than 9,000 persons held for more than 30 days. Mr. Vlok's aides said the new list was not an addition, but represented the number detained for more than 30 days between Sept. 12 and Jan. 1.

Mr. Vlok said that among the 3,857 detainees on his list are 281 children under the age of 15, including three under the age of 12 and 18 who are just 12.

Helen Suzman, a member of Parliament from the liberal opposition Progressive Federal Party, said Thursday that "many thousands" of detainees who were held for less than 30 days and not included in the official statistics would account for part of the gap.